Contemporary Authors®

NEW REVISION SERIES

ISSN 0275-7176

Contemporary Authors®

**A Bio-Bibliographical Guide to
Current Writers in Fiction, General Nonfiction,
Poetry, Journalism, Drama, Motion Pictures,
Television, and Other Fields**

JAMES G. LESNIAK
Editor

NEW REVISION SERIES
volume 31

Gale Research Inc. • *DETROIT* • *NEW YORK* • *LONDON*

STAFF

James G. Lesniak, *Editor, New Revision Series*

Marilyn K. Basel, Kevin S. Hile, Sharon Malinowski, Michael E. Mueller, Kenneth R. Shepherd,
Diane Telgen, and Thomas Wiloch, *Associate Editors*

Marian Gonsior, Margaret Mazurkiewicz, Jani Prescott,
and Michaela Swart Wilson, *Assistant Editors*

Jean W. Ross and Walter W. Ross, *Interviewers*

Cheryl Gottler, W. Kenneth Holditch, Anne Janette Johnson, and Susan Salter, *Contributing Editors*

Hal May, *Senior Editor, Contemporary Authors*

Mary Rose Bonk, *Research Supervisor*

Jane Cousins, Andrew Guy Malonis, and Norma Sawaya, *Editorial Associates*

Mike Avolio, Reginald A. Carlton, Catherine A. Coulson, Shirley Gates,
Steve Germic, Sharon McGilvray, Renee L. Naud, Diane Linda Sevigny,
and Tracey Head Turbett, *Editorial Assistants*

The paper used in this publication meets the minimum requirements
of American National Standard for Information Sciences—Permanence
Paper for Printed Library Materials, ANSI Z39.48-1984.

Printed in the United States of America.

Published simultaneously in the United Kingdom
by Gale Research International Limited
(An affiliated company of Gale Research Inc.)

Contents

Indexing note: All *Contemporary Authors New Revision Series* entries are indexed in the *Contemporary Authors* cumulative index, which is published separately and distributed with even-numbered *Contemporary Authors* original volumes.

Authors and Media People
Featured in This Volume

Alan Ayckbourn (British playwright)—Sometimes called the "British Neil Simon," Ayckbourn is one of England's most successful living playwrights. His comedies, most of which have had long runs on London's West End, explore the mundane lives of middle-class Englishmen, and sometimes use the techniques of the Experimental Theatre.

Marion Zimmer Bradley (American science fiction and fantasy author)—Bradley is the author of one of the best-loved series in science fiction/fantasy; her "Darkover" novels are so popular that they have inspired their own fan clubs, magazines, and story collections. In addition, Bradley has written the mainstream bestseller *The Mists of Avalon,* which presents the Arthurian legend from the point of view of the major female characters.

Jimmy Breslin (American novelist and free-lance journalist)—Literary voice for New York City's Irish-American working class and exponent of the New Journalism, Breslin is best known for news commentary that defends the ordinary man against bureaucracy. He received a Pulitzer prize in 1986 for his collected newspaper columns.

E. E. Cummings (American poet who died in 1962)—Cummings was both a popular and an avant-garde poet whose distinctive language and use of lower-case letters are immediately recognizable. Jenny Penberthy, writing in the *Dictionary of Literary Biography,* said Cummings was "among the most innovative of twentieth-century poets."

Peter Dickinson (Zambian-born British author of mysteries and children's fiction)—With a reputation for imaginative plots and characterization, Dickinson is noted for the quality of his juvenile fiction and his avant-garde mysteries. His award-winning books include the mystery novels *The Glass-Sided Ant's Nest* and *The Old English Peep Show,* and the young adult novel *Tulku.*

Rainer Werner Fassbinder (German screenwriter, film director, and producer who died in 1982)—One of Germany's most important modern film directors, Fassbinder was considered the filmmaker primarily responsible for the revitalization of the German cinema in the 1970s. His work, including "Katzelmacher," "Ali: Fear Eats the Soul," and "Why Does Herr R. Run Amok?," has received awards from West German film organizations and from the Cannes Film Festival.

Marilyn French (American novelist, educator, and literary scholar)—French, whose goal is to change the Western social and economic structure, is perhaps best known for the cogent, feminist aspects of her work. Her explosive and provocative first novel, *The Women's Room,* has become a major novel of the women's movement. (Entry contains interview.)

Martin Gilbert (British historian)—As the official biographer of Winston S. Churchill, Gilbert has authored the longest biography in publishing history, according to the *Guinness Book of World Records.* He is also known for *The Holocaust: A History of the Jews of Europe during the Second World War* and other works on Jewish history.

George J. W. Goodman (American journalist, novelist, and author of nonfiction)—Using the pseudonym Adam Smith, Goodman has clarified economic theory for television audiences on his PBS program "Adam Smith's Money World." He has also written about Wall Street and high finance in *The Money Game, Supermoney,* and *Paper Money.* (Entry contains interview.)

Shere Hite (American cultural historian)—Hite is known for her best-selling studies of human sexuality, *The Hite Report: A Nationwide Study of Female Sexuality, The Hite Report on Male Sexuality,* and *Women and Love: A Cultural Revolution in Progress.* Though some critics find the three volumes significant because they allow women and men to speak for themselves, others take issue with Hite's research methodology and her feminist approach.

Maureen Howard (American author and literary critic)—Although Howard is well known for her literary criticism, her talents as a novelist have also been highly praised. Reviewers enjoy Howard's books for their clarity, linguistic precision, and character development. Her autobiography *Facts of Life* won a National Book Critics Circle Award in 1980, and her novels *Grace Abounding* and *Expensive Habits* have both won the PEN/Faulkner Award for fiction. (Entry contains interview.)

David Ignatow (American poet)—The recipient of numerous awards, Brooklyn-born Ignatow is celebrated for confronting the physical realities of life in his writing. His direct-statement poetry, including the collections *The Gentle Weight Lifter, Rescue the Dead,* and *Facing the Tree,* is appreciated for its relentless authenticity.

Stanley Karnow (American journalist)—Karnow, a veteran correspondent in Asia, is noted for his thorough yet entertaining books on Asian history. In such works as his Pulitzer Prize-winning *In Our Image: America's Empire in the Philippines,* he explores the entire histories of Asian countries, not just their relationships with the United States.

William Kennedy (American journalist and novelist)—Best known for his cycle of novels set in his hometown of Albany, New York, Kennedy is celebrated for both his journalism and fiction. In works such as *Billy Phelan's Greatest Game* and *O Albany!,* he recreates the dazzle and despair of Albany's underside. His novel *Ironweed,* a portrait of an indigent baseball player during the Depression, won a Pulitzer Prize. (Entry contains interview.)

William X. Kienzle (American mystery writer)—Kienzle, a former Roman Catholic priest who left the priesthood after twenty years of service, is known for his series of mystery novels featuring Father Robert Koesler, a liberal priest whose knowledge of Catholicism and church law assists him in solving crimes. Kienzle's mysteries, including *The Rosary Murders, Deadline for a Critic,* and *Eminence,* are noted for addressing serious issues as well as providing clever solutions. (Entry contains interview)

William Manchester (American journalist and historian)—Manchester's massive, exhaustively researched biographies and popular histories, such as *The Death of a President, The Glory and the Dream: A Narrative History of America,* and *American Caesar: Douglas MacArthur, 1880-1964,* have received both popular and critical acclaim. Manchester became a reluctant figurehead for journalistic freedom in 1967, when he was almost sued by Jackie Kennedy over the text of *The Death of a President.* His more recent work includes a multivolume popular biography of Winston Churchill.

Bobbie Ann Mason (American short-story writer and novelist)—Although her two novels, *In Country* and *Spence + Lila,* have proved successful, Mason is better known as a writer of prize-winning short fiction. Her stories about western Kentucky working-class and farm people dealing with rapid change are noted for their vivid re-creation of the geographical and spiritual milieu. (Entry contains interview)

James M. McPherson (American historian)—McPherson's *Battle Cry of Freedom,* a one-volume history of the American Civil War, earned a 1989 Pulitzer Prize. His other history titles include *The Struggle for Equality: Abolitionists and the Negro in the Civil War and Reconstruction* and *Ordeal by Fire: The Civil War and Reconstruction.* (Sketch includes interview.)

Bill Moyers (American broadcast journalist)—Winner of nine Emmy Awards and four Peabody Awards for his television work, Moyers is best known for hosting such Public Broadcasting System programs as "Creativity," "A Walk Through the Twentieth Century" and "Joseph Campbell and the Power of Myth."

John O'Hara (American novelist and short story writer who died in 1970)—A prolific and popular author who originated the "typical" *New Yorker* magazine story, O'Hara won a New York Drama Critics Circle Award and a Donaldson Award for his musical "Pal Joey" and a National Book Award for the novel *Ten North Frederick.*

Jean Piaget (Swiss psychologist who died in 1980)—Called "one of the two towering figures of twentieth-century psychology" by Jerome S. Bruner in the *New York Times Book Review,* Piaget studied the psychological development of children and adolescents. His books include *The Language and Thought of the Child, The Child's Conception of the World,* and *The Origin of Intelligence in the Child.*

V. S. Pritchett (British story writer and literary critic)—Called "an eminent man of letters" by Harry S. Marks in the *Dictionary of Literary Biography,* Pritchett writes fiction about the British lower middle-class in a low-key, conversational style. His essays appear in *The Myth-Makers* and *The Tale Bearers,* while his fiction is collected in *The Saint and Other Stories, Blind Love and Other Stories,* and *Collected Stories.*

Georges Remi (Belgian cartoonist who died in 1983)—Better known under his pseudonym Herge, Remi was the creator of the phenomenally popular comic strip character Tintin, an intrepid boy reporter whose assignments took him around the world. The comic strip was noted for its lively humor, detailed artwork, and eccentric characters. Some 300 million people are said to have read Tintin's adventures in 33 languages.

Stephen Spender (British poet)—Spender is one of the most influential members of the "Auden Generation," a group of British poets of the 1930s who wrote of everyday life, rejecting traditional "poetic" subjects. His poem "The Pylons" is often cited as representative of the school. His books include *Collected Poems, 1928-1985,* as well as *World within a World: An Autobiography of Stephen Spender* and *The Journals of Stephen Spender, 1939-1983.*

Jesse Stuart (American regionalist writer who died in 1984)—Named Poet Laureate of Kentucky in 1954, Stuart wrote of his native Appalachia, particularly Greenup County, Kentucky, in fiction, nonfiction, and poetry. Ruel E. Foster claimed the author "created a *place* and wedged it everlastingly in the imagination of America."

Garry Trudeau (American cartoonist and playwright)—Trudeau is the creator of the popular comic strip "Doonesbury," which is syndicated to some eight hundred newspapers. Often more political than humorous, the Pulitzer Prize-winning strip is sometimes printed on the editorial rather than the comics page of the newspaper and has been adapted as a musical.

Louis Untermeyer (American poet, editor, and translator who died in 1977)—The author, editor, and translator of more than one hundred books, Untermeyer is credited with having introduced a vast reading audience to the contemporary poets of America and England. In 1956, he was awarded a Poetry Society of America Award for his services to poetry.

Tennessee Williams (American playwright who died in 1983)—One of the major American playwrights of the twentieth century, Williams wrote explosive dramas marked by poetic dialogue and tragic, lonely characters. A winner of four New York Drama Critics Circle Awards and two Pulitzer Prizes, Williams is best known for his plays "The Glass Menagerie," "A Streetcar Named Desire," "Cat on a Hot Tin Roof," and "Night of the Iguana."

Bob Woodward (American journalist)—Famous for his role in breaking the Watergate scandal in the early 1970s, Woodward won a Pulitzer Prize for *All the President's Men,* his account of that story. His continuing investigative work for the *Washington Post* has led him to probes of the Supreme Court, Congress, and the CIA, as well as the life of actor John Belushi, whom he profiles in the bestseller *Wired.*

Paul Zindel (American dramatist and novelist)—Zindel is the author of the well-known play "The Effect of Gamma Rays on Man-in-the-Moon Marigolds," winner of a Pulitzer Prize and an Obie Award. His young adult novels, including *The Pigman,* feature sympathetic misfits or outsiders faced with overwhelming problems.

Preface

The *Contemporary Authors New Revision Series* provides completely updated information on authors listed in earlier volumes of *Contemporary Authors (CA)*. Entries for active individual authors from *any* volume of *CA* may be included in a volume of the *New Revision Series*. The sketches appearing in *New Revision Series* Volume 31, for example, were selected from more than twenty previously published *CA* volumes.

As always, the most recent *Contemporary Authors* cumulative index continues to be the user's guide to the location of an individual author's listing.

Compilation Methods

The editors make every effort to secure information directly from the authors. Copies of all sketches in selected *CA* volumes published several years ago are routinely sent to the listees at their last-known addresses. Authors mark material to be deleted or changed and insert any new personal data, new affiliations, new writings, new work in progress, new sidelights, and new biographical/critical sources. All returns are assessed, more comprehensive research is done, if necessary, and those sketches requiring significant change are completely updated and published in the *New Revision Series*.

If, however, authors fail to reply or are now deceased, biographical dictionaries are checked for new information (a task made easier through the use of Gale's *Biography and Genealogy Master Index* and other Gale biographical indexes), as are bibliographical sources such as *Cumulative Book Index* and *The National Union Catalog*. Using data from such sources, revision editors select and revise nonrespondents' entries that need substantial updating. Sketches not personally reviewed by the biographees are marked with an asterisk (*) to indicate that these listings have been revised from secondary sources believed to be reliable, but they have not been personally reviewed for this edition by the authors sketched.

In addition, reviews and articles in major periodicals, lists of prestigious awards, and, particularly, requests from *CA* users are monitored so that writers on whom new information is in demand can be identified and revised listings prepared promptly.

Format

CA entries provide biographical and bibliographical information in an easy-to-use format. For example, individual paragraphs featuring such rubrics as "Addresses," "Career," and "Awards, Honors" ensure that a reader seeking specific information can quickly focus on the pertinent portion of an entry. In sketch sections headed "Writings," the title of each book, play, and other published or unpublished work appears on a separate line, clearly distinguishing one title from another. This same convenient bibliographical presentation is also featured in the "Biographical/Critical Sources" sections of sketches where individual book and periodical titles are listed on separate lines. *CA* readers can therefore quickly scan these often-lengthy bibliographies to find the titles they need.

Comprehensive Revision

All listings in this volume have been revised and/or augmented in various ways, though the amount and type of change vary with the author. In many instances, sketches are totally rewritten, and the resulting *New Revision Series* entries are often considerably longer than the authors' previous listings. Revised entries include additions of or changes in such information as degrees, mailing addresses, literary agents, career items, career-related and civic activities, memberships, awards, work in progress, and biographical/critical sources. They may also include extensive bibliographical additions and informative new sidelights.

Writers of Special Interest

CA's editors make every effort to include in each *New Revision Series* volume a substantial number of revised entries on active authors and media people of special interest to *CA*'s readers. Since the *New Revision Series* also includes sketches on noteworthy deceased writers, a significant amount of work on the part of *CA*'s editors goes into the revision of entries on important deceased authors. Some of the prominent writers, both living and deceased, whose sketches are contained in this volume are noted in the list on pages vii-viii headed Authors and Media People Featured in This Volume.

Exclusive Interviews

CA provides exclusive, primary information on certain authors in the form of interviews. Prepared specifically for *CA,* the never-before-published conversations presented in the section of the sketch headed "*CA* Interview" give users the opportunity to learn the authors' thoughts, in depth, about their craft. Subjects chosen for interviews are, the editors feel, authors who hold special interest for *CA*'s readers.

Authors and journalists in this volume whose sketches contain exclusive interviews are Ravi Batra, Marilyn French, George J. W. Goodman, Larry Heinemann, Maureen Howard, William Kennedy, William X. Kienzle, Bobbie Ann Mason, and James M. McPherson.

Contemporary Authors Autobiography Series

Designed to complement the information in *CA* original and revision volumes, the *Contemporary Authors Autobiography Series* provides autobiographical essays written by important current authors. Each volume contains from twenty to thirty specially commissioned autobiographies and is illustrated with numerous personal photographs supplied by the authors. Common topics of discussion for these authors include their motivations for writing, the people and experiences that shaped their careers, the rewards they derive from their work, and their impressions of the current literary scene.

Autobiographies included in the series can be located through both the *CA* cumulative index and the *Contemporary Authors Autobiography Series* cumulative index, which lists not only personal names but also titles of works, geographical names, subjects, and schools of writing.

Contemporary Authors Bibliographical Series

The *Contemporary Authors Bibliographical Series* is a comprehensive survey of writings by and about the most important authors since World War II in the United States and abroad. Each volume concentrates on a specific genre and nationality and features approximately ten major writers. Series entries, which complement the information in other *CA* volumes, consist of three parts: a primary bibliography that lists works written by the author, a secondary bibliography that lists works about the author, and a bibliographical essay that thoroughly analyzes the merits and deficiencies of major critical and scholarly works.

These bibliographies can be located through both the *CA* cumulative index and the *Contemporary Authors Bibliographical Series* cumulative author index. A cumulative critic index, citing critics discussed in the bibliographical essays, also appears in each *Bibliographical Series* volume.

CA Numbering System

Occasionally questions arise about the *CA* numbering system. Despite numbers like "97-100" and "130," the entire *CA* series consists of only 103 physical volumes with the publication of *CA New Revision Series* Volume 31. The following information notes changes in the numbering system, as well as in cover design, to help users better understand the organization of the entire *CA* series.

CA First Revisions	• 1-4R through 41-44R (11 books) *Cover:* Brown with black and gold trim. There will be no further *First Revisions* because revised entries are now being handled exclusively through the more efficient *New Revision Series* mentioned below.
CA Original Volumes	• 45-48 through 97-100 (14 books) *Cover:* Brown with black and gold trim. • 101 through 130 (30 books) *Cover:* Blue and black with orange bands. The same as previous *CA* original volumes but with a new, simplified numbering system and new cover design.
CA New Revision Series	• *CANR*-1 through *CANR*-31 (31 books) *Cover:* Blue and black with green bands. Includes only sketches requiring extensive change; **sketches are taken from any previously published *CA* volume.**

CA **Permanent Series**	• *CAP*-1 and *CAP*-2 (2 books) *Cover:* Brown with red and gold trim. There will be no further *Permanent Series* volumes because revised entries are now being handled exclusively through the more efficient *New Revision Series* mentioned above.
CA **Autobiography Series**	• *CAAS*-1 through *CAAS*-12 (12 books) *Cover:* Blue and black with pink and purple bands. Presents specially commissioned autobiographies by leading contemporary writers to complement the information in *CA* original and revision volumes.
CA **Bibliographical Series**	• *CABS*-1 through *CABS*-3 (3 books) *Cover:* Blue and black with blue bands. Provides comprehensive bibliographical information on published works by and about major modern authors.

Retaining *CA* Volumes

As new volumes in the series are published, users often ask which *CA* volumes, if any, can be discarded. The Volume Update Chart on page xiii is designed to assist users in keeping their collections as complete as possible. All volumes in the left column of the chart should be retained to have the most complete, up-to-date coverage possible; volumes in the right column can be discarded if the appropriate replacements are held.

Cumulative Index Should Always Be Consulted

The key to locating an individual author's listing is the *CA* cumulative index, which is published separately and distributed with even-numbered original volumes. Since the *CA* cumulative index provides access to *all* entries in the *CA* series, the latest cumulative index should always be consulted to find the specific volume containing a listee's original or most recently revised sketch.

Those authors whose entries appear in the *New Revision Series* are listed in the *CA* cumulative index with the designation **CANR-** in front of the specific volume number. For the convenience of those who do not have *New Revision Series* volumes, the cumulative index also notes the specific earlier volumes of *CA* in which the sketch appeared. Below is a sample index citation for an author whose revised entry appears in a *New Revision Series* volume.

> Clavell, James (duMaresq) 1925- CANR-26
> Earlier sketch in CA 25-28R
> See also CLC 6, 25

For the most recent *CA* information on Clavell, users should refer to Volume 26 of the *New Revision Series,* as designated by "CANR-26"; if that volume is unavailable, refer to *CA* 25-28 First Revision, as indicated by "Earlier sketch in CA 25-28R," for his 1977 listing. (And if *CA* 25-28 First Revision is unavailable, refer to *CA* 25-28, published in 1971, for Clavell's original listing.)

Sketches not eligible for inclusion in a *New Revision Series* volume because the biographee or a revision editor has verified that no significant change is required will, of course, be available in previously published *CA* volumes. Users should always consult the most recent *CA* cumulative index to determine the location of these authors' entries.

For the convenience of *CA* users, the *CA* cumulative index also includes references to all entries in these related Gale literary series: *Authors and Artists for Young Adults, Authors in the News, Bestsellers, Black Writers, Children's Literature Review, Concise Dictionary of American Literary Biography, Contemporary Literary Criticism, Dictionary of Literary Biography, Short Story Criticism, Something About the Author, Something About the Author Autobiography Series, Twentieth-Century Literary Criticism,* and *Yesterday's Authors of Books For Children.*

Acknowledgments

The editors wish to thank Nancy D. Taylor for her assistance with copyediting.

Suggestions Are Welcome

The editors welcome comments and suggestions from users on any aspect of the *CA* series. If readers would like to suggest authors whose *CA* entries should appear in future volumes of the *New Revision Series,* they are cordially invited to write: The Editors, *Contemporary Authors New Revision Series,* 835 Penobscot Bldg., Detroit, MI 48226-4094; or, call toll-free at 1-800-347-GALE.

Volume Update Chart

IF YOU HAVE:	YOU MAY DISCARD:
1-4 First Revision (1967)	1 (1962) 2 (1963) 3 (1963) 4 (1963)
5-8 First Revision (1969)	5-6 (1963) 7-8 (1963)

Both 9-12 First Revision (1974)
  AND *Contemporary Authors Permanent Series,*
  Volume 1 (1975)
	9-10 (1964)
	11-12 (1965)

Both 13-16 First Revision (1975)
  AND *Contemporary Authors Permanent Series,*
  Volumes 1 and 2 (1975, 1978)
	13-14 (1965)
	15-16 (1966)

Both 17-20 First Revision (1976)
  AND *Contemporary Authors Permanent Series,*
  Volumes 1 and 2 (1975, 1978)
	17-18 (1967)
	19-20 (1968)

Both 21-24 First Revision (1977)
  AND *Contemporary Authors Permanent Series,*
  Volumes 1 and 2 (1975, 1978)
	21-22 (1969)
	23-24 (1970)

Both 25-28 First Revision (1977)
  AND *Contemporary Authors Permanent Series,*
  Volume 2 (1978)
	25-28 (1971)

Both 29-32 First Revision (1978)
  AND *Contemporary Authors Permanent Series,*
  Volume 2 (1978)
	29-32 (1972)

Both 33-36 First Revision (1978)
  AND *Contemporary Authors Permanent Series,*
  Volume 2 (1978)
	33-36 (1973)

37-40 First Revision (1979)	37-40 (1973)
41-44 First Revision (1979)	41-44 (1974)
45-48 (1974) 49-52 (1975) ↓ ↓ 130 (1990)	NONE: These volumes will not be superseded by corresponding revised volumes. Individual entries from these and all other volumes appearing in the left column of this chart will be revised and included in the *New Revision Series.*
Volumes in the *Contemporary Authors New Revision Series*	NONE: The *New Revision Series* does not replace any single volume of *CA.* All volumes appearing in the left column of this chart must be retained to have information on all authors in the series.

Contemporary Authors ®

NEW REVISION SERIES

* Indicates that a listing has been revised from secondary sources believed to be reliable but has not been personally reviewed for this edition by the author sketched.

AAKER, David A(llen) 1938-

PERSONAL: Born February 11, 1938, in Fargo, N.D.; married; children: two. *Education:* Massachusetts Institute of Technology, B.S., 1960; Stanford University, M.S., 1967, Ph.D., 1969.

ADDRESSES: Home—18 Eastwood Dr., Orinda, Calif. 94563. *Office*—School of Business Administration, University of California, Berkeley, Calif. 94720.

CAREER: Texas Instruments, Inc., Houston, Tex., cost engineer, 1960-61, sales engineer, 1961-63, product sales manager, 1963-65; Stanford University, Stanford, Calif., instructor in statistics, 1967; University of California, Berkeley, acting assistant professor, 1968-69, assistant professor, 1969-72, associate professor, 1972-76, professor of marketing statistics, 1976—, J. Gary Shansby Professor of Marketing Strategy, 1982—.

MEMBER: American Marketing Association, American Statistical Association, Institute of Management Sciences, Tau Beta Pi.

AWARDS, HONORS: Special merit award from Thompson Gold Medal Competition, 1972; received award from *Journal of Marketing,* 1985.

WRITINGS:

(Editor and contributor) *Multivariate Analysis in Marketing: Theory and Application,* Wadsworth, 1971, 2nd edition, 1979.
(Editor with George S. Day) *Consumerism: Search for the Consumer Interest,* Free Press, 1971, 4th edition, 1982.
(With John G. Meyers) *Advertising Management: An Analytical Approach,* Prentice-Hall, 1975, 3rd edition, 1987.
(With Day) *Marketing Research: Private and Public Sector Decisions,* Wiley, 1980, 3rd edition, 1986.
Developing Business Strategies, Wiley, 1984, 2nd edition, 1988.
Strategic Market Management, Wiley, 1984.

Contributor of about twenty articles and reviews to business journals, including *Management Science, Harvard Business Review, Journal of Advertising Research, Journal of Marketing Research,* and *Journal of Marketing.* Member of editorial board of *Journal of Marketing Research,* 1969— and *Journal of Business Research,* 1973—; associate editor of *Management Science,* 1971—.*

ABSALOM, Roger Neil Lewis 1929-

PERSONAL: Born October 28, 1929, in Bebington, England. *Education:* Christ Church, Oxford, B.A. (with honors), 1952; Institute of Linguists, F.I.L., 1960.

ADDRESSES: Office—Department of Historical and Critical Studies, Sheffield City Polytechnic, Psalter Ln., Sheffield, England.

CAREER: English teacher at British schools in Pescara and Milan, Italy, 1956-60; Cambridgeshire College of Arts and Technology, Cambridge, England, lecturer, 1960-66, senior lecturer, 1966-70, principal lecturer in Italian, 1970-73; Sheffield City Polytechnic, Sheffield, England, lecturer in Italian history and language and head of department of modern languages, 1973-86, reader in modern languages, 1986-89, honorary research fellow in Italian history, 1989—. Visiting scholar, Woodrow Wilson Institute, Washington, D.C., 1982. Visiting lecturer and consultant.

MEMBER: Society for Italian Studies, Royal Institute of International Affairs, Institute of Linguists, Association for the Study of Modern Italy, Society for the Study of Labour History.

AWARDS, HONORS: Co-recipient of Premio Prato from City of Prato Council, 1980, for article (in Italian) on the role of the Allies in Florence, Italy, 1944-45; grants from British Academy, 1983, Gladys Krieble-Delmas Foundation, 1984, and Australian War Memorial, 1988.

WRITINGS:

"A" Level French, National Extension College (NEC), 1966.
Passages for Translation from Italian, Cambridge University Press, 1967.
"A" Level Italian, NEC, 1968.
Mussolini and the Rise of Italian Fascism, Methuen, 1969.
(Editor) *The May Events: France, 1968,* Longman, 1970, published as *France: The May Events, 1968,* 1971.
(Editor with Sandra Potesta) *Advanced Italian,* Cambridge University Press, 1970.
Comprehension of Spoken Italian, Cambridge University Press, 1978.
(With others) *French: Advanced Level* (six volumes), NEC, 1980.
Leo S. Olschki, editor, *Gli Alleati e la ricostruzione in Toscana (1944-1945): Documenti anglo-americani,* Volume 1, Ac-

1

cademia Toscana di Scienze e Lettere la Colombaria (Florence), 1988.

Italy (textbook), Longman, 1990.

Also author of *A Strange Alliance: Aspects of Escape and Survival in Italy, 1943-45.*

CONTRIBUTOR

Ian Greenlees, editor, *Italia e Gran Bretagna nella lotta di liberazione* (title means "Italy and Great Britain in the Fight for Freedom"), La Nuova Italia, 1977.

Eric Cahm and Vladimir Fisera, editors, *Socialism and Nationalism,* Volumes 1 and 3, Spokesman Books, 1979.

Ettore Rotelli, editor, *La ricostruzione in Toscana dal CLN ai partiti* (title means "Reconstruction in Tuscany from the National Liberation Committee to the Restoration of Party Rule"), Volume 1, Il Mulino (Bologna), 1980.

G. Rochat and others, editors, *Linea Gotica,* [Milan], 1986.

Moving in Measure, Hull University Press, 1989.

Fernand Braudel, editor, *Prato storia di una citta. 4. Il modello pratese (1943-a oggi),* Le Monnier/Comune di Prato (Florence), 1989.

Also contributor to scholarly journals, including *Italian Studies, Oral History Journal,* and *Journal of Institutional Management in Higher Education.*

SIDELIGHTS: Roger Neil Lewis Absalom once wrote *CA:* "I have moved steadily from languages and linguistics to contemporary history over the last thirty years. I now regard myself as a (somewhat eccentric) historian of mentalities. The seed of this was sown during the four years I lived in Italy (from 1956 to 1960), when I became obsessed with trying to understand the historical roots of current Italian political behaviors and culture.

"These seemed (and still seem) to have little to do with the Risorgimento and 'The Making of Italy' as described in the textbooks. What fascinates the close observer in Italy is the unique blend—in its material and cultural life—of the archaic and the ultramodern. Italians, moreover, are Europe's greatest experts in the art of eluding the encroachments of the State: even Fascist dictatorship scarcely scratched the surface of this profoundly-rooted culture of individual survival and the preservation of identity.

"Exploring the remoter parts of the central Apennines in the 1950s (before they were touched by the 'economic miracle'), I came to realize the central role of the Italian hill-peasants and their values in maintaining the vitality of this culture. When they migrated en masse to the towns they took these values—this cultural armor—with them. They are, paradoxically, entrepreneurial and egalitarian at one and the same time: the two major parties in Italy have, in their own ways, learned to benefit politically from this contradiction and, consequently, are in no hurry to resolve it. Both, in practice, want to limit 'modernization' in order to continue their informal power-sharing. The Church has always known how to play this game; the Italian Communists have learned it better than any others. The matter is important because Italy's post-1945 developmental path may help us to understand the workings of 'cities of peasants' elsewhere in the world, and the kind of political arrangements that may prevent them from exploding."

*   *   *

ACKERMAN, Diane   1948-

PERSONAL: Born October 7, 1948, in Waukegan, Ill.; daughter of Sam (a restaurant owner) and Marcia (Tischler) Fink. *Educa-*

tion: Attended Boston University, 1966-67; Pennsylvania State University, B.A., 1970; Cornell University, M.F.A., 1973, M.A., 1976, Ph.D., 1978.

ADDRESSES: Home—126 Texas Lane, Ithaca, N.Y. 14850.

CAREER: Writer. Social worker in New York City, 1967; government researcher at Pennsylvania State University, 1968; Cornell University, Ithaca, N.Y., teaching assistant, 1971-78, lecturer, 1978-79; University of Pittsburgh, Pittsburgh, Pa., assistant professor of English, 1980-83; Washington University, St. Louis, Mo., director of writers' program and writer in residence, 1984-86; *New Yorker,* New York City, staff writer, 1988—. Writer in residence, William and Mary College, 1983, Ohio University, 1983; visiting writer, Columbia University, 1986, New York University, 1986, Cornell University, 1987. Member of literature panel, New York State Council on the Arts, 1980-83; member of advisory board, Planetary Society, 1980—; member of literature panels. Has participated in readings, residencies, and workshops.

AWARDS, HONORS: Academy of American Poets Poetry Prize, Cornell University, 1972; Corson Bishop French Prize, Cornell University, 1972; Abbie Copps Prize, Olivet College, 1974; Rockefeller graduate fellowship, 1974-76; Heermans-McCalmon Playwriting Prize, Cornell University, 1976; creative writing fellowships, National Endowment for the Arts, 1976, and Creative Artists Public Service Program, 1980; Corson Bishop Poetry Prize, Cornell University, 1977; poetry prize, *Black Warrior Review,* 1981; Pushcart Prize VIII, 1984; Peter I. B. Lavan Younger Poet Award, Academy of American Poets, 1985; fellowship, National Endowment for the Arts, 1986; semifinalist, Journalist-in-Space Project.

WRITINGS:

(With Jody Bolz and Nancy Steele) *Poems: Ackerman, Bolz, and Steele* (chapbook), Stone Marrow Press, 1973.

"Ideas into the Universe" (series of nine radio programs), Canadian Broadcasting Corp. (Toronto), 1975.

(Contributor) Carl Sagan, *Other Worlds,* Bantam, 1975.

The Planets: A Cosmic Pastoral (poems), Morrow, 1976.

Wife of Light (poems), Morrow, 1978.

Twilight of the Tenderfoot: A Western Memoir, Morrow, 1980.

Lady Faustus (poems), Morrow, 1985.

On Extended Wings: An Adventure in Flight (memoir), Atheneum, 1985.

Reverse Thunder (play), Lumen, 1988.

A Natural History of the Senses (nonfiction), Random House, 1990.

Jaguar of Sweet Laughter: New and Selected Poems, Random House, 1990.

Where the Sun Dines, and Other Adventures in Natural History (nonfiction), Random House, in press.

Contributor to anthologies, including *The Morrow Anthology of Younger Poets,* edited by Dave Smith and David Bottoms, Morrow, 1985; *Norton Introduction to Literature,* edited by Jerome Beaty and J. Paul Hunter, 4th edition, Norton, 1986; *Norton Introduction to Poetry,* edited by Hunter, 3rd edition, Norton, 1986; *The Paris Review Anthology,* edited by George Plimpton, Norton, 1989; and numerous other poetry and prose anthologies. Contributor of poems and nonfiction to literary journals, periodicals, and newspapers, including *New Yorker, Poetry, Life, Omni, Kenyon Review, American Poetry Review, Parnassus: Poetry in Review, Michigan Quarterly Review, Paris Review,* and *New York Times;* contributor of reviews to *New York Times Book Review.*

WORK IN PROGRESS: The Metaphysical Mind: Studies in a Comprehensive Muse, critical study.

SIDELIGHTS: Diane Ackerman once said in *Contemporary Poets:* "People sometimes ask me about all of the Science in my poetry, thinking it odd that I should wish to combine Science and Art, and assuming that I must have some inner pledge or outer maxim I follow. But the hardest job for me is trying to keep Science out of my poetry. We live in a world where amino acids, viruses, airfoils, and such are common ingredients in our daily sense of Nature. Not to write about Nature in its widest sense, because quasars or corpuscles are not 'the proper realm of poetry,' as a critic once said to me, is not only irresponsible and philistine, it bankrupts the experience of living, it ignores much of life's fascination and variety. I'm a great fan of the Universe, which I take literally: as one. All of it interests me, and it interests me in detail. . . .

"I try to give myself passionately, totally, to whatever I'm observing, with as much affectionate curiosity as I can muster, as a means to understanding a little better what being human is, and what it was like to have once been alive on the planet, how it felt in one's senses, passions and contemplations. I appear to have a lot of science in my work, I suppose, but I think of myself as a Nature poet, if what we mean by Nature is, as I've said, the full sum of Creation."

MEDIA ADAPTATIONS: On Extended Wings: An Adventure in Flight was adapted for the stage in 1987 by Norma Jean Giffin.

AVOCATIONAL INTERESTS: Astronomy, skin diving, horseback riding, flying planes.

BIOGRAPHICAL/CRITICAL SOURCES:

BOOKS

Contemporary Poets, St. James, 1985.

PERIODICALS

Los Angeles Times, October 20, 1985.
New Republic, November 20, 1976.
Newsweek, September 22, 1986.
New York Times, April 26, 1987.
New York Times Book Review, June 29, 1980, December 22, 1985.
Washington Post, June 10, 1980.

*   *   *

ACKROYD, Peter R(unham) 1917-

PERSONAL: Born September 15, 1917, in Derby, England; son of Jabez Robert and Winifred (Brown) Ackroyd; married Evelyn A. Nutt (a justice of the peace), July 25, 1940; children: Jane, William, Simon, Jennifer, Sarah. *Education:* Cambridge University, B.A., 1938, M.A., 1942, Ph.D., 1945; New College, London, B.D. (honors), 1940, M.Th., 1942.

ADDRESSES: Home—Lavender Cottage, Middleton, Saxmundham, Suffolk 1P17 3NQ, England.

CAREER: Congregational minister in Essex, England, 1943-47, and London, England, 1947-48; University of Leeds, Leeds, England, lecturer in Old Testament and biblical Hebrew, 1948-52; Cambridge University, Cambridge, England, university lecturer in divinity, 1952-61, Hulsean lecturer, 1960-62; University of London, King's College, London, Samuel Davidson Professor of Old Testament Studies, 1961-82, fellow, 1969—, dean of faculty of theology, 1968-69. Ordained deacon in Church of England,

1957, priest, 1958. Visiting professor at Lutheran School of Theology, Chicago, Ill., 1967, 1976, University of Toronto, 1972, University of Notre Dame, 1983, and Emory University, 1985. Selwyn Lecturer in New Zealand, 1970. Lecturer and/or examiner in Jordan and Israel, 1961, 1966, Nigeria and Ghana, 1963-64, and Sweden and Finland, 1968; lecturer in New Zealand, Australia, India, Ceylon, 1970, and Japan, 1983. Select preacher at Cambridge University, 1955, and Oxford University, 1962; honorary curate of Holy Trinity Church, Cambridge University, 1957-61; member of Commission on Religious Education in Schools, 1967-70.

MEMBER: Society for Old Testament Study (president, 1972; foreign secretary, 1985-89), Palestine Exploration Fund (honorary secretary, 1963-70; chairman, 1987—).

AWARDS, HONORS: D.D. from St. Andrews University, 1970.

WRITINGS:

Freedom in Action, Independent Press, 1951.
The People of the Old Testament, Chatto & Windus, 1959.
Continuity: A Contribution to the Study of the Old Testament Religious Tradition (inaugural lecture), Basil Blackwell, 1962.
The Old Testament Tradition, National Society (London), 1963.
(Contributor) D. W. Thomas, editor, *Archaeology and Old Testament Study,* Oxford University Press, 1967.
Exile and Restoration: A Study of Hebrew Thought of the Sixth Century, B.C., Westminster, 1968.
Israel under Babylon and Persia, Oxford University Press, 1970.
Chronicles I and II: Ezra, Nehemiah, Ruth, Jonah, I and II Maccabees, Mowbray, 1970.
(Contributor) *Interpreter's One Volume Commentary on the Bible,* Abingdon, 1971.
First Book of Samuel, Cambridge University Press, 1971.
Second Book of Samuel, Cambridge University Press, 1977.
(Contributor) *Israel's Prophetic Tradition,* edited by Richard Coggins, Anthony Phillips, and Michael Knibb, Cambridge University Press, 1982.
Doors of Perception: Guide to Reading the Psalms, S.C.M. Press, 1983.
The Major Prophets: A Commentary on Isaiah, Jeremiah, Lamentations, Ezekiel, Daniel, edited by Charles M. Laymon, Abingdon, 1983.
Studies in the Religious Tradition of the Old Testament, S.C.M. Press, 1987.

TRANSLATOR INTO ENGLISH

L. Koehler, *Hebrew Man,* Harper, 1956.
E. Wuerthwein, *The Text of the Old Testament,* Basil Blackwell, 1957.
(And reviser) M. Noth, *History of Israel,* A. & C. Black, 1960.
O. Eissfeldt, *The Old Testament: An Introduction,* Harper, 1965.

EDITOR

Bible Key Words, five volumes, A. & C. Black, 1961-64.
(With Barnabas Lindars) *Words and Meanings* (essays), Cambridge University Press, 1968.
(With others) *Cambridge History of the Bible: From the Beginnings to Jerome,* Cambridge University Press, 1970.
(With others) *Studies in Biblical Theology,* S.C.M. Press, 1971.
Bible Bibliography, 1967-1973, Old Testament: The Book Lists of the Society for Old Testament Study, 1967-1973, Basil Blackwell, 1974.

Also editor, with others, of "Cambridge Bible Commentary" series, Cambridge University Press, 1961—, "Oxford Bible" series, Oxford University Press, 1983—, and "Cambridge Commentaries on Writings of the Jewish and Christian World, 200 B.C. to A.D. 200" series, Cambridge University Press, 1984—.

OTHER

Contributor to *Chamber's Encyclopaedia* and *Hastings Dictionary of the Bible.* Also contributor of articles and reviews to theological and other learned journals in England and abroad, including *Journal of Near Eastern Studies, Theology, Zeitschrift fuer die alttestamentliche Wissenschaft, Svensk Exegetish Aarsbok, Vetus Testamentum.* Editor, *Palestine Exploration Quarterly,* 1971-86; book list editor, Society for Old Testament Study, 1967-73.

*   *   *

ADORJAN, Carol (Madden) 1934-
(Kate Kenyon, a house pseudonym)

PERSONAL: Surname is pronounced A-*dor*-ian; born August 17, 1934, in Chicago, Ill.; daughter of Roland Aloysius (a salesman) and Marie (Toomey) Madden; married William W. Adorjan (an industrial representative), August 17, 1957; children: Elizabeth Marie, John Martin and Katherine Therese (twins), Matthew Christian. *Education:* Mundelein College, B.A. (magna cum laude), 1956.

ADDRESSES: Home—1667 Winnetka Rd., Glenview, Ill. 60025.

CAREER: Writer. High school English teacher, St. Scholastica High School, Chicago, Ill., 1956-59. Writer in residence, National Radio Theatre, 1980, and Illinois Arts Council, 1981-82. Corresponding secretary, Off Campus Writers' Workshop, 1967-69.

AWARDS, HONORS: Josephine Lusk Prize, Mundelein College, 1956, for short story, "Coin of Decision"; first prize, *Earplay 1972,* University of Wisconsin, for "The Telephone"; Midwest Professional Playwrights fellowship, 1977; Illinois Arts Council completion grant, 1977-78; first prize, Dubuque Fine Arts Society's National One-Act Playwriting Contest, 1978; Ohio State Award, 1981, for adaptation of *The Sea Wolf.*

WRITINGS:

JUVENILES

Someone I Know, Random House, 1968.
Jonathan Bloom's Room, J. Philip O'Hara, 1972.
(Contributor) N. Gretchen Greiner, editor, *Like It Is,* Broadman, 1972.
The Cat Sitter Mystery, J. Philip O'Hara, 1976.
Pig Party, Children's Press, 1981.
The Electric Man, Children's Press, 1981.
(Adaptor) *The Sea Wolf,* National Radio Theatre, 1981.
(Under house pseudonym Kate Kenyon) *The Eighth Grade to the Rescue,* Scholastic, Inc., 1987.
(Under house pseudonym Kate Kenyon) *Those Crazy Class Pictures,* Scholastic, Inc., 1987.
(Under house pseudonym Kate Kenyon) *The Big Date,* Scholastic, Inc., 1988.
(Under house pseudonym Kate Kenyon) *The Revolt of the Eighth Grade,* Scholastic, Inc., 1988.
(With Yuri Rasovsky) *WKID: Easy Radio Plays,* Albert Whitman, 1988.
The Copy Cat Mystery, Avon, 1990.

That's What Friends Are For, Scholastic, Inc., 1990.

OTHER

Also author of radio plays, including "The Telephone," "Friends," "A Safe Place," "The Outcasts of Poker Flat," and "Portions Mechanically Reproduced." Contributor of short stories and articles to national magazines, including *Today, Woman's Day, North American Review, American Girl, Ingenue,* and *Redbook,* and to newspapers.

WORK IN PROGRESS: A novel; a screenplay.

SIDELIGHTS: Carol Adorjan told *CA:* "I have been writing for as long as I can remember. It was only about fifteen years ago, however, that I began to think of myself as 'a writer' rather than as 'someone who wrote.' Once I realized that writing defined who I am and not merely what I do, commitment followed. Now I perceive writing as both art and business, and I spend time and energy on both aspects." The author continued: "I am interested in reality and illusion as they affect our individual lives and our relationships with others. My themes grow out of this concern. My continuing goal is to treat my material with compassion and humor."

AVOCATIONAL INTERESTS: Photography.

*   *   *

AINSBURY, Ray
See PAINE, Lauran (Bosworth)

*   *   *

AINSBURY, Roy
See PAINE, Lauran (Bosworth)

*   *   *

AINSWORTH, Ray
See PAINE, Lauran (Bosworth)

*   *   *

AINSWORTH, Roy
See PAINE, Lauran (Bosworth)

*   *   *

AINSWORTHY, Roy
See PAINE, Lauran (Bosworth)

*   *   *

ALLEN, Clay
See PAINE, Lauran (Bosworth)

*   *   *

ALLEN, Edward D(avid) 1923-

PERSONAL: Born January 29, 1923, in Perth Amboy, N.J.; married Virginia Garibaldi, 1946; children: two sons. *Education:* Montclair State College, B.A., 1943; University of Wisconsin, M.A., 1948; University of Grenoble, French Diploma, 1950; Ohio State University, Ph.D., 1954; additional study, Mexico City College, six summers.

ADDRESSES: Home—165 West Schreyer Pl., Columbus, Ohio 43214. *Office*—College of Education, Ohio State University, 1945 North High St., Columbus, Ohio 43210.

CAREER: Belleville High School, Belleville, N.J., teacher of French, 1943-45; Ohio State University, Columbus, instructor of Spanish and French, 1945-55, assistant professor, 1955-58, associate professor, 1958-62, professor of foreign language education, 1962-80, director of summer language institute at Lyon, France, beginning 1965. Visiting lecturer, Ohio Wesleyan University, 1955-56.

MEMBER: American Association of Teachers of French, American Association of Teachers of Spanish and Portuguese, Modern Language Association of America, American Council on the Teaching of Foreign Languages, Association for Supervision and Curriculum Development, Ohio Modern Language Teachers Association (secretary-treasurer, 1956-59).

WRITINGS:

(With Frank Otto and Leona Glenn) *The Changing Curriculum: Modern Foreign Languages,* Association for Supervision and Curriculum Development, 1968.
(With Rebecca M. Valette) *Modern Language Classroom Techniques: A Handbook,* Harcourt, 1972, revised and expanded edition published as *Classroom Techniques: Foreign Languages and English as a Second Language,* 1977.
(Editor with Renate A. Schulz, Reid A. Baker, and Alice Omaggio) *Teaching for Communication in the Foreign Language Classroom: A Guide for Building the Curriculum,* National Textbook Co., 1976.
(With Lynn A. Sandstedt and Brenda Wegmann) *Habla Espanol? An Introductory Course,* Holt, 1976, 3rd edition, 1985, abridged edition published as *Habla Espanol? Essentials,* 1978, 3rd edition, 1986.

Contributor to *Encyclopedia of Education, Encyclopedia Americana,* and to professional journals.*

*   *   *

ALLEN, Jordan
    See DUMKE, Glenn S.

*   *   *

ALLEN, Roland
    See AYCKBOURN, Alan

*   *   *

ALMONTE, Rosa
    See PAINE, Lauran (Bosworth)

*   *   *

ALTER, Judith (MacBain) 1938-
    (Judy Alter)

PERSONAL: Born July 22, 1938, in Chicago, Ill.; daughter of Richard Norman (a physician) and Alice (Peterman) MacBain; married Joel Alter (a physician), May 16, 1964 (divorced August, 1982); children: Colin, Megan, Jamie, Jordan. *Education:* University of Chicago, B.A., 1961; Northeast Missouri State University, M.A., 1964; Texas Christian University, Ph.D., 1970.

ADDRESSES: Home—Fort Worth, Tex. *Office*—Texas Christian University Press, Box 20783, Fort Worth, Tex. 76129. *Agent*—Ray Peekner Literary Agency, 3210 South Seventh St., Milwaukee, Wis. 53215.

CAREER: Chicago Osteopathic Center, Chicago, Ill., typist and secretary, 1954-61; Kirksville College of Osteopathic Medicine,

Kirksville, Mo., writer and editor in public relations, 1962-64; Fort Worth Osteopathic Hospital, Fort Worth, Tex., secretary, 1965-66, editor of employee publication, 1965-73, public relations consultant, 1971-73; Texas College of Osteopathic Medicine, Fort Worth, director of publications, 1972; free-lance writer, 1973-75; Texas Christian University, Fort Worth, instructor in English as a second language, 1975-76; Texas College of Osteopathic Medicine, acting director of public information, 1977-78, associate director of news and information, 1978-80; Texas Christian University, Texas Christian University Press, editor, 1982-87, director, 1987—.

MEMBER: Western Writers of America (member of board of directors, 1976-77; president, 1985-86), Authors Guild, Texas Institute of Letters.

AWARDS, HONORS: Texas Institute of Letters Award, 1985, for *Luke and the Van Zandt County War.*

WRITINGS:

UNDER NAME JUDY ALTER

(With Phil Russell) *The Quack Doctor,* Branch-Smith, 1974.
Stewart Edward White (pamphlet), Boise State University, 1975.
Dorothy Johnson (pamphlet), Boise State University, 1975.
After Pa Was Shot (juvenile), Morrow, 1978.
(With Sam Pearson) *Single Again,* Branch-Smith, 1978.
The Texas ABC Book, Branch-Smith, 1981.
(With Joyce Roach) *Texas and Christmas,* Texas Christian University Press, 1983.
Luke and the Van Zandt County War, Texas Christian University Press, 1984.
Mattie (novel), Doubleday, 1988.
Growing up in the Old West, F. Watts, 1989.
Women of the Old West, F. Watts, 1989.
Maggie and a Horse Named Devildust, Ellen Temple, 1989.
Maggie and the Search for Devildust, Ellen Temple, 1989.
Maggie and Devildust—Ridin' High!, Ellen Temple, 1990.

Also author of *So Far from Paradise,* a novel serialized in the *Ft. Worth Star Telegram,* 1986. Author of book reviews and a column, "Along Publishers Row," for *Roundup,* and "Women's Lit.," a review column in the *Fort Worth Star Telegram,* 1974-75.

WORK IN PROGRESS: A juvenile novel; continuing research on Texana.

SIDELIGHTS: Judy Alter comments: "I always wanted to write—I feel as if publication has come after years of paying dues. I am very interested in Texas history as a viable subject for juvenile and adult fiction. I am most grateful to contacts made through Western Writers of America. I see discouragement for the new writer with no contacts, and wish the system could be changed.

"My interest in Western literature grew out of American literature studies in graduate school but gradually I have become more interested in popular literature rather than academic studies. But my writing began as strictly non-fiction, and it was a long, slow transition. For a long time, I thought I simply couldn't write fiction, and lots of short story manuscripts buried in my files seem to support that idea."

She adds: "Now I see myself, both as editor and author, as more and more interested in the undeveloped potential of regional fiction for young adult readers. Both my juvenile novels are rooted in Texas, growing out of actual historical events."

AVOCATIONAL INTERESTS: Cooking, gardening, reading.

BIOGRAPHICAL/CRITICAL SOURCES:

PERIODICALS

Fort Worth Star Telegram, May 9, 1978.

*   *   *

ALTER, Judy
   See ALTER, Judith (MacBain)

*   *   *

AMOR, Anne Clark 1933-
   (Anne Clark)

PERSONAL: Born February 4, 1933, in London, England; daughter of John (an engineer) and Violetta (Bird) Ryan; married Norman Victor Clark (a telephone engineer), July 14, 1956 (divorced January, 1981); married Abdallah Amor (a gymnasium proprietor), February 23, 1982; children: (first marriage) Peter Norman, Miranda Anne. *Education:* Birkbeck College, London, B.A. (with honors), 1968.

ADDRESSES: Home—16 Parkfields Ave., London NW9 7PE, England. *Agent*—A.M. Heath, 79 St. Martin's Ln., London WC2N 4AA, England.

CAREER: Greater London Council, London, England, administrative officer for Department of Housing, 1951-81; writer, 1975—.

MEMBER: Lewis Carroll Society, William Morris Society, Beatrix Potter Society.

WRITINGS:

UNDER NAME ANNE CLARK

Beasts and Bawdy (a study of medieval animal lore), Taplinger, 1975.
Lewis Carroll: A Biography, Shocken, 1979.
The Real Alice: Lewis Carroll's Dream Child (biography), Stein & Day, 1981.

UNDER NAME ANNE CLARK AMOR

Mrs. Oscar Wilde: A Woman of Some Importance (biography), Sidgwick & Jackson, 1983.
William Holman Hunt: The True Pre-Raphaelite (biography), Constable & Co., 1989.
(Editor and author of introduction) *The Letters of Archdeacon Charles Dodgson to His Son Skeffington,* Lewis Carroll Society, 1989.

OTHER

Contributor of book reviews to periodicals, including *Literary Review* and *Books and Bookmen.* Editor of *Jabberwocky* (journal of the Lewis Carroll Society), 1969-75.

WORK IN PROGRESS: An Elizabethan biography; a novel.

SIDELIGHTS: Anne Clark's 1979 biography, *Lewis Carroll,* traces the life of the Reverend Charles Lutwidge Dodgson, best known under the Carroll pseudonym as the author of *Alice's Adventures in Wonderland* and *Through the Looking-Glass.* In the *Times Literary Supplement* Humphrey Carpenter observes that of the "endless stream" of biographies of Lewis Carroll, "Miss Clark's book is not only the most readily available at the moment, but also one of the best." Carpenter further notes that the work offers fresh information unknown to earlier biographers and that it is "particularly enlightening on the relationship between Dodgson/Carroll and Alice Liddell" (the little girl for whom *Wonderland* was written). While Clark's biography makes no judgment concerning the nature of their relationship, Carpenter believes that some of Clark's findings "would seem to support those who believe that [thirty-year-old Carroll] was really 'in love' with [ten-year-old] Alice . . . and perhaps even hoped to marry her one day."

Washington Post Book World reviewer Elizabeth Sewell considers two other areas of the book noteworthy. She mentions the discussion of Carroll's photography and the "expanded account given here of his connections with that other great Victorian photographer, Julia Cameron, of their personalities and work." In addition, Sewell commends Clark's attention to Carroll's religious views, particularly "his unwillingness to proceed from the diaconate to the priesthood, backing this up with careful and detailed work on his clerical father and the relations between father and son; also Carroll's strict segregation of religion and laughter."

Clark's *The Real Alice* follows Alice Liddell from her childhood meeting with Carroll through her marriage and the births of her three sons to her death in 1934 at the age of eighty-two. In a *Washington Post Book World* review, Reid Beddow comments that *The Real Alice* "paints a charming portrait of Victorian family life." Carpenter, in the *Times Literary Supplement,* lauds Clark's tracing of "a family tree that would surely have delighted Dodgson, showing as it does that Alice Liddell was almost a royal 'Queen Alice' " because of her distant relationship with the present royal family.

Mrs. Oscar Wilde: A Woman of Some Importance, the author's third biography, written as Anne Clark Amor, details the life of Constance Wilde, wife of the Irish poet, playwright, and humorist. According to *Times Literary Supplement* critic John Stokes, the very reticent Constance Wilde "eludes even a novelist's imagination." Amor's biography, Stokes notes, "endeavors to release another woman from the imprisoning male view." In a London *Times* review Bevis Hillier observes, "The more one reads, the more one's admiration for [Constance] grows." Hillier further states that Amor's portrayal of Constance explodes "convincingly the canard that she was stupid" and conveys "her beauty, charm and tenderness, her wonderful loyalty and courage in a situation which few women in history have to face" (the disgrace ensuing from the discovery of her husband's homosexuality and his resulting subsequent imprisonment). Hillier's review also credits Amor for maintaining the focus on "Constance Wilde's life, not Oscar's: He is only allowed on scene when his life impinges on hers." William French in the Toronto *Globe & Mail* sums up Amor's achievement with this book: "In this poignant biography . . . Amor restores Constance Wilde to her rightful place with an enthusiasm and reverence that stops just short of elevating her to sainthood. The respect seems deserved."

Anne Clark Amor describes for *CA* her fourth biography: "*William Holman Hunt: The True Pre-Raphaelite* traces Hunt's childhood and early struggle against parental opposition to become an artist, his founding of the Pre-Raphaelite Brotherhood with Millais and Rossetti, the hostility of the Royal Academy, and his success in the face of adverse criticism. The second part of the book concentrates on his adventures in Syria, the death of his wife after a year of marriage, and his struggle to bring up his infant son. His second marriage, to his deceased wife's sister, was illegal in England until the law was changed in 1907."

About her writing background, Amor told *CA:* "Although I knew from the age of eight that I had a vocation for writing, I was hustled into the first steady job that presented itself, and found myself trapped by economic necessity. When my compulsion to write re-asserted itself, I turned, not to the detective fiction that had been the focus of my childish imagining, but to a serious study of mediaeval animal lore. I strayed accidentally into the field of biography at the suggestion of my publisher and found it greatly to my liking. Now, after four successful biographies, I find myself turning in the direction of the novel."

Mrs. Oscar Wilde has been published in French.

BIOGRAPHICAL/CRITICAL SOURCES:

PERIODICALS

Globe & Mail (Toronto), May 12, 1984.
Times (London), July 14, 1983.
Times Literary Supplement, November 13, 1981, June 24, 1983.
Washington Post Book World, December 23, 1979, October 10, 1982.

* * *

ANDERSEN, Christopher P(eter) 1949-

PERSONAL: Born May 26, 1949, in Pensacola, Fla.; son of Edward Francis (a commander in the U.S. Navy) and Jeanette (Peterson) Andersen; married Valerie Jean Hess (a banker), February 3, 1972; children: Katherine. *Education:* University of California, Berkeley, B.A. (political science), 1971.

ADDRESSES: Home—38 Hesseky Meadow, Woodbury, Conn. 06798. *Office*—200 East 66th St., New York, N.Y. 10021. *Agent*—Ellen Levine, 432 Park Ave., Suite 1205, New York, N.Y. 10016.

CAREER: Time, New York City, correspondent in San Francisco, Calif., 1969-71, staff writer in New York City, 1971-72, and in Montreal, Quebec, 1972-74; *People,* New York City, assistant editor, 1974-75, associate editor, 1975-80, senior editor, 1980-86.

MEMBER: Players Club.

WRITINGS:

The Name Game, Simon & Schuster, 1977.
A Star Is a Star Is a Star!: The Life and Loves of Susan Hayward, Doubleday, 1980.
The Book of People, Putnam, 1981.
Father, the Figure and the Force, Warner, 1983.
(With Albert M. Myers) *Success over Sixty,* Summit, 1984.
The New Book of People, Putnam, 1986.
The Po-Po Principle, Pan Productions, 1986.
The Baby Boomer's Name Game, Putnam, 1987.
The Serpent's Tooth, Harper & Row, 1987.
Young Kate, Holt, 1988.
(With John Marion) *The Best of Everything: The Definitive Insider's Guide to Collecting—For Love and Money,* Simon & Schuster, 1989.
Citizen Jane: The Turbulent Life of Jane Fonda, Holt, 1990.

Contributor of articles to periodicals, including *New York Times, Reader's Digest, Ladies' Home Journal,* and *Life.*

SIDELIGHTS: Christopher P. Andersen once told *CA:* "As a professional journalist since the age of seventeen, I have done stories on thousands of personalities, from presidents to axe murderers to movie stars. Hence my books have all dealt with people—some famous, most not—and what motivates them. In short, how and why we all do what we do. It is a daunting pursuit, but it is hard to think of a more rewarding one."

BIOGRAPHICAL/CRITICAL SOURCES:

PERIODICALS

Chicago Tribune, July 14, 1985, July 15, 1985, July 16, 1985.
New York Times, October 6, 1986.
New York Times Book Review, September 13, 1987, August 7, 1988.
People, August 17, 1987.
Washington Post Book World, October 30, 1977, July 19, 1987, August 7, 1988.

* * *

ANDERSON, (Helen) Jean 1931-

PERSONAL: Born October 12, 1931, in Raleigh, N.C.; daughter of Donald Benton (a university vice-president) and Marian (Johnson) Anderson. *Education:* Attended Miami University, Oxford, Ohio, 1947-49; Cornell University, B.S., 1951; Columbia University, M.S., 1957. *Politics:* Independent.

ADDRESSES: Home—1 Lexington Ave., New York, N.Y. 10010. *Agent*—The Karpfinger Agency, Suite 2800, 500 Fifth Ave., New York, N.Y. 10010.

CAREER: Iredell County, N.C., assistant home demonstration agent, 1951-52; North Carolina Agricultural Extension Service, Raleigh, woman's editor, 1952-55; *Raleigh Times,* Raleigh, N.C., woman's editor, 1955-56; *Ladies' Home Journal,* New York, N.Y., assistant editor, 1957-61, editorial associate, 1961-62, copy editor, 1962, managing editor, 1963; *Venture* (magazine), senior editor, 1964-68, contributing editor, 1968-71; free-lance writer, 1968—.

MEMBER: American Home Economics Association, Home Economists in Business, Les Dames D'Escoffier, New York Women's Culinary Alliance, New York Travel Writers, New York Culinary Historians, Gamma Phi Beta, Phi Kappa Phi, Omicron Nu.

AWARDS, HONORS: Pulitzer traveling scholarship, 1957; Southern Women's Achievement Award, 1962; George Hedman Memorial Award, 1971; R. T. French Tastemaker Award for best basic cookbook of the year and best overall cookbook of the year, 1975, for *The Doubleday Cookbook;* R. T. French Tastemaker Award for best specialty cookbook of the year, 1980, for *Half a Can of Tomato Paste and Other Culinary Dilemmas;* Seagram Award for best international cookbook of the year, International Association of Cooking Professionals, 1986, for *The Food of Portugal.*

WRITINGS:

Henry the Navigator: Prince of Portugal, Westminster, 1969.
The Haunting of America: Ghost Stories from Our Past, Houghton, 1973.

COOKBOOKS

(With Yeffe Kimball) *The Art of American Indian Cooking,* Doubleday, 1965.
Food Is More than Cooking: A Basic Guide for Young Cooks, Westminster, 1968.
(Editor) *Family Circle Illustrated Library of Cooking: Your Ready Reference for a Lifetime of Good Eating,* twelve volumes, Rockville House, 1972.
The Family Circle Cookbook, Quadrangle, 1974.
(With Elaine Hanna) *The Doubleday Cookbook,* Doubleday, 1975, revised edition published as *The New Doubleday Cookbook,* 1985.
Recipes from America's Restored Villages, Doubleday, 1975.

The Green Thumb Preserving Guide: The Best and Safest Way to Can and Freeze, Dry and Store, Pickle, Preserve and Relish Home-Grown Vegetables and Fruits, Morrow, 1976.
The Grass Roots Cookbook, Quadrangle, 1977.
(With Ruth Buchan) *Half a Can of Tomato Paste and Other Culinary Dilemmas,* Harper, 1980.
Jean Anderson Cooks, Morrow, 1982.
Unforbidden Sweets, Arbor House, 1982.
Jean Anderson's New Processor Cooking, Morrow, 1983.
Jean Anderson's New Green Thumb Preserving Guide, Morrow, 1985.
The Food of Portugal, Morrow, 1986.
(With Hanna) *Micro Ways* (Literary Guild selection), Doubleday, 1990.

Contributor of articles to periodicals, including *Family Circle, Bon Appetit, Gourmet, Food and Wine, Ladies Home Journal, Better Homes and Gardens, Connoisseur, New York Times Magazine,* and *Travel and Leisure.* Columnist for *Newsday* and *Los Angeles Times* syndicate.

WORK IN PROGRESS: A book on low cholesterol desserts for Doubleday.

SIDELIGHTS: Jean Anderson's cookbooks have "sensible comments on just about everything gastronomic," reports *Time* reviewer Michael Demarest. For instance, *The Food of Portugal,* Anderson's recent examination of a relatively unknown cuisine, goes into some detail about Portugese specialties and local ingredients. Minnie Bernardino, writing in the *Los Angeles Times,* explains that "Anderson's style of thoroughness in recipes from her past cookbooks is carried through in this new book."

BIOGRAPHICAL/CRITICAL SOURCES:

PERIODICALS

Los Angeles Times, December 21, 1986.
Time, November 22, 1982.

*   *   *

ANDREWS, A. A.
  See PAINE, Lauran (Bosworth)

*   *   *

APPLEBEE, Arthur N(oble) 1946-

PERSONAL: Born June 20, 1946, in Sherbrooke, Quebec, Canada; born a U.S. citizen; son of Roger K. (a university dean) and Margaret (Aitken) Applebee; married Marcia Lynn Hull (a teacher), June 15, 1968 (divorced); married Judith A. Langer (a university professor), May 23, 1982. *Education:* Yale University, B.A. (cum laude), 1968; Harvard University, M.A.T., 1970; University of London, Ph.D., 1973.

ADDRESSES: Home—Vly Creek Farm, R.D. 1, Box 311, Voorheesville, N.Y. 12186. *Office*—School of Education, University of Albany, State University of New York, 1400 Washington Ave., Albany, N.Y. 12222.

CAREER: National Council of Teachers of English, Urbana, Ill., part-time staff assistant, 1964-69; Massachusetts General Hospital, Child Development Laboratory, Boston, research assistant and psychologist, 1969-71; University of Lancaster, Lancaster, England, research associate at International Microteaching Unit, 1973-74; Tarleton High School, Tarleton, England, English and drama teacher, 1974-76; National Council of Teachers

of English, staff associate, 1976-80, and associate director of ERIC Clearinghouse on Reading and Communication Skills, 1978-80; Stanford University, School of Education, Stanford, Calif., associate professor, 1980-86, professor of education, 1987; State University of New York-Albany, professor, 1987—, director of Center for the Learning and Teaching of Literature, 1987—. Visiting lecturer, University of California, Berkeley, summer, 1978.

MEMBER: International Reading Association, National Conference on Research in English (president, 1986), American Educational Research Association, National Council of Teachers of English, National Association of Teachers of English (England).

AWARDS, HONORS: Columbia University Teachers College Book Prize, 1967, for "outstanding constructive interest in educational issues"; Promising Researcher Award from National Council of Teachers of English, 1974; Outstanding Young Men of America Award, 1978; National Conference on Research in English fellow, 1984; Richard A. Meade Award for research in English education, 1989, for *How Writing Shapes Thinking;* recipient of grants from National Institute of Education and National Council of Teachers of English.

WRITINGS:

Tradition and Reform in the Teaching of English: A History, National Council of Teachers of English, 1974.
The Child's Concept of Story: Ages Two to Seventeen, University of Chicago Press, 1978.
A Survey of Teaching Conditions in English, 1977, National Council of Teachers of English, 1978.
Writing in the Secondary School: Current Practice in English and the Content Areas, National Council of Teachers of English, 1981.
(With others) *Reading, Thinking and Writing: Results from the 1979-80 National Assessment of Reading and Literature,* Education Commission of the States, 1981.
Contexts for Learning to Write: Studies of Secondary School Instruction, Ablex Publishing, 1984.
(Co-author) *How Writing Shapes Thinking: A Study of Teaching and Learning,* National Council of Teachers of English, 1987.

WITH J. LANGER AND I. MULLIS

The Reading Report Card: Progress toward Excellence in Our Schools; Trends in Reading over Four National Assessments, 1971-1984, National Assessment of Educational Progress, 1985.
Writing: Trends across the Decade, 1974-1984, National Assessment of Educational Progress, 1986.
The Writing Report Card; Writing Achievement in American Schools, National Assessment of Educational Progress, 1986.
Literature and U.S. History: The Instructional Experiences and Factual Knowledge of High School Juniors, National Assessment of Educational Progress, 1987.
Learning to Be Literate in America: Reading, Writing, and Reasoning, National Assessment of Educational Progress, 1987.
Spelling, Punctuation, and Grammar: The Conventions of Writing Used by 9-, 13-, and 17-Year-Olds, National Assessment of Educational Progress, 1987.
Who Reads Best? Factors Related to Reading Achievement, National Assessment of Educational Progress, 1988.

Understanding Direct Writing Assessment: Reflections on a South Carolina Writing Study, National Assessment of Educational Progress, 1989.

(And with L. Jenkins) *The Writing Report Card, 1984-88: Findings from the Nation's Report Card,* National Assessment of Educational Progress, 1990.

Crossroads in American Education: A Summary of Findings, National Assessment of Educational Progress, 1990.

CONTRIBUTOR

Language As a Way of Knowing, Ontario Institute for Studies in Education, 1977.

Leon F. Williams, *Workload Starter Kit for Secondary English Teachers,* National Council of Teachers of English, 1980.

Martin Nystrand, editor, *What Writers Know: The Language, Process, and Structure of Written Discourse,* Academic Press, 1982.

Charles R. Cooper, editor, *Researching Response to Literature and the Teaching of Literature,* Ablex Publishing, 1985.

Martin Lightfoot and Nancy Martin, *The Word for Teaching is Learning,* Heinemann, 1988.

Also contributor to *Informal Reasoning in Education, Vital Signs: Bringing Together Reading and Writing, Handbook of Curriculum Research,* and *Literacy and Diversity.*

OTHER

Contributor to *Encyclopedia of Educational Research,* Macmillan, 1982, and *Developing Basic Skills Programs in Secondary Schools,* 1982. Contributor to psychology and education journals in England and the United States. Editor, *Research in the Teaching of English,* 1984—.

SIDELIGHTS: Arthur N. Applebee told *CA:* "Early involvement in various projects and activities of the National Council of Teachers of English led to a continuing concern with educational issues and a specific interest in language and language learning. This interest has had diverse manifestations, leading to studies in educational psychology, learning disabilities, educational history, curriculum evaluation, and most recently the teaching of literature. Various studies that I have directed have provided a not particularly encouraging portrait of students' experiences in American schools. My work has sought to understand why conditions are so bleak, and to propose some viable alternatives. Writing about learning is itself a learning process; it is never clear exactly what the recommendations will look like until we begin to write them up to share outside of our research group."

*   *   *

ARCHER, Dennis
    See PAINE, Lauran (Bosworth)

*   *   *

ARDEN, John   1930-

PERSONAL: Born October 26, 1930, in Barnsley, Yorkshire, England; son of Charles Alwyn (a manager of a glass works) and Annie Elizabeth (Layland) Arden; married Margaretta Ruth D'Arcy (a playwright), 1957; children: Francis Gwalchmei (deceased), Finn, Adam, Jacob, Neuss. *Education:* King's College, Cambridge, B.A., 1953; Edinburgh College of Architecture, diploma, 1955.

ADDRESSES: Agent—Margaret Ramsay Ltd., 14a Goodwin Court, London WC2N 4LL, England.

CAREER: Architectural assistant in London, England, 1955-57; playwright, 1957—. Fellow in playwriting, University of Bristol, Bristol, England, 1959-60; visiting lecturer in politics and drama, New York University, 1967; Regents' lecturer, University of California, Davis, 1973; writer in residence, University of New England, Australia, 1975. Co-founder of Corrandulla Arts and Entertainment Club, Corrandulla, Ireland, 1971, and Galway Theatre Workshop, 1975. *Military service:* British Army, Intelligence Corps, 1949-50.

AWARDS, HONORS: British Broadcasting Corp. Northern Region prize for "The Life of Man"; *Encyclopaedia Britannica* prize, 1959, and Vernon Rice award, 1966, both for *Serjeant Musgrave's Dance: An Unhistorical Parable;* Bristol University fellowship in playwriting, 1959-60; *Evening Standard* (London) "most promising playwright" award, 1960; Trieste Festival prize, 1961, for "Soldier, Soldier"; Arts Council Award, 1973; recipient with husband John Arden, award from Arts Council, 1974, for *The Ballygombeen Bequest* and *The Island of the Mighty: A Play on a Traditional British Theme in Three Parts; The Old Man Sleeps Alone* included in *Best Radio Plays of 1982; Silence among the Weapons: Some Events at the Time of the Failure of a Republic* considered for Booker McConnell prize for fiction, 1982.

WRITINGS:

PLAYS

"All Fall Down," produced in Edinburgh, Scotland, 1955.

"The Waters of Babylon" (also see below), first produced in London at Royal Court Theatre, October 20, 1957; produced in New York City, 1958, and in Washington, D.C., at Washington Theatre Club, 1967.

"When Is a Door Not a Door?" (also see below), first produced in London at Central School of Speech and Drama, 1958.

"Live Like Pigs" (also see below), first produced in London at Royal Court Theatre, September 30, 1958; produced Off-Broadway at Actor's Playhouse, June 7, 1965.

Serjeant Musgrave's Dance: An Unhistorical Parable (also see below; first produced in London at Royal Court Theatre, October 22, 1959; produced Off-Broadway at Theatre de Lys, March 8, 1966; revised version with John McGrath produced on tour as "Serjeant Musgrave Dances On," 1972), Methuen, 1960, Grove, 1962, with notes and commentary by R. W. Ewart, Longman, 1982, with notes and commentary by Glenda Leeming, Methuen, 1982, revised 1966 script, Studio Duplicating Service, 1986.

The Workhouse Donkey: A Vulgar Melodrama (also see below; first produced in Sussex, England, at Chichester Festival Theatre, July 8, 1963), Methuen, 1964, Grove, 1967.

Ironhand (adaptation of Goethe's *Goetz von Berlichingen;* first produced in Bristol, England, at Bristol Old Vic Theatre, November 12, 1963), Methuen, 1965, Grove, 1967.

"Woyzeck" (adaptation of Alban Berg's opera "Wozzeck") first produced in London, 1964.

Armstrong's Last Goodnight: An Exercise in Diplomacy (also see below; first produced in Glasgow, Scotland, at Glasgow Citizens' Theatre, May 5, 1964; produced in Boston, 1966), Methuen, 1965, Grove, 1976.

"Fidelio" (adaptation of libretto by Joseph Sonnleithner and Friedrich Treitschke of opera by Beethoven), first produced in London, 1965.

"Play without Words," first produced in Glasgow, 1965.

Left-Handed Liberty: A Play about Magna Carta (commissioned by the City of London to celebrate the 750th anniversary of the sealing of the Magna Carta; first produced in London at Mermaid Theatre, June 14, 1965), Methuen, 1965, Grove, 1966.

"The Soldier's Tale" (adaptation of opera by Igor Stravinsky; libretto by Charles Ramuz), first produced in Bath, England, 1968.

"The True History of Squire Jonathan and His Unfortunate Treasure" (also see below), first produced in London at Ambiance Lunch Hour Theatre, June 17, 1968.

PLAYS; WITH WIFE, MARGARETTA D'ARCY

"The Happy Haven" (two-act; also see below), first produced in Bristol at Bristol University, 1960; produced in London at Royal Court Theatre, September 14, 1960; produced in New York City, 1967.

The Business of Good Government: A Christmas Play (one-act; first produced as "A Christmas Play," in Somerset, England, at Brent Knoll Church of St. Michael, December, 1960; produced in New York City, 1970), Methuen, 1963, reprinted, 1983, Grove, 1967.

Ars Longa, Vita Brevis (one-act; first produced on the West End at Aldwych Theatre by the Royal Shakespeare Co., 1964), Cassell, 1965.

"Friday's Hiding" (one-act; also see below), first produced in London, 1965; produced in Edinburgh at the Lyceum Theatre, 1966.

The Royal Pardon; or, The Soldier Who Became an Actor (first produced in Devon, England, at Beaford Arts Centre, September 1, 1966; produced in London at Arts Theatre, 1967), Methuen, 1967.

(And with Cartoon Archetypical Slogan Theatre) "Harold Muggins Is a Martyr," first produced in London at Unity Theatre Club, June, 1968.

The Hero Rises Up: A Romantic Melodrama (two-act; first produced in London at Round House Theatre, November 6, 1968), Methuen, 1969.

(And with Muswell Hill Street Theatre) "Granny Welfare and the Wolf," first produced in London at Ducketts Common, Turnpike Lane, March, 1971.

(And with Muswell Hill Street Theatre) "My Old Man's a Tory" (one-act), first produced in London at Wood Green, March, 1971.

(And with Socialist Labour League) "Two Hundred Years of Labour History" (two-act), first produced in London at Alexandra Palace, April, 1971.

(And with Writers Against Repression) "Rudi Dutschke Must Stay," first produced in London at British Museum, spring, 1971.

The Ballygombeen Bequest (first produced in Belfast, Northern Ireland, at St. Mary and St. Joseph's College Drama Society, May, 1972; produced in London at Bush Theatre, September 11, 1972), Scripts, 1972.

The Island of the Mighty: A Play on a Traditional British Theme in Three Parts (first produced on the West End at Aldwych Theatre, December 5, 1972), with illustrations by authors, Eyre Methuen, 1974.

(And with Corrandulla Arts Entertainment Club) "The Devil and the Parish Pump" (one-act), first produced in County Galway, Ireland, at Gort Roe, Corrandulla Arts Centre, April, 1974.

The Non-Stop Connolly Show: A Dramatic Cycle of Continuous Struggle in Six Parts (first produced in Dublin at Liberty Hall, March 29, 1975, produced in London at Ambiance Lunch Hour Theatre, May 17, 1976), Pluto, Parts 1 and 2: *Boyhood 1868-1889* [and] *Apprenticeship, 1889-1896,* 1977, Part 3: *Professional, 1896-1903,* Part 4: *The New World,*

1903-1910, Part 5: *The Great Lockout, 1910-1914,* and Part 6: *World War and the Rising, 1914-1916,* 1978.

(And with Galway Theatre Workshop) "The Crown Strike Play" (one-act), first produced in Galway at Eyre Square, December, 1975.

(And with Galway Theatre Workshop) "Sean O'Scrudu," first produced in Galway at Coachman Hotel, February, 1976.

(And with Galway Theatre Workshop) "The Mongrel Fox" (one-act), first produced in Galway at Regional Technical College, October, 1976.

(And with Galway Theatre Workshop) "No Room at the Inn" (one-act), first produced in Galway at Coachman Hotel, December, 1976.

(And with Galway Theatre Workshop) "Silence," first produced in Galway at Eyre Square, April, 1977.

(And with Galway Theatre Workshop) "Mary's Name" (one-act), first produced in Galway at University College, May, 1977.

(And with Galway Theatre Workshop) "Blow-In Chorus for Liam Cosgrave," first produced in Galway at Eyre Square, June, 1977.

Vandaleur's Folly: An Anglo-Irish Melodrama; The Hazard of Experiment in an Irish Co-operative, Ralahine, 1831 (two-act; first produced at Lancaster University, 1978), Eyre Methuen, 1981.

The Little Gray Home in the West: An Anglo-Irish Melodrama, Pluto, 1982.

RADIO/TELEVISION PRODUCTIONS

"Soldier, Soldier: A Comic Song for Television" (also see below), BBC, 1960.

"Wet Fish: A Professional Reminiscence for Television" (also see below), BBC, 1961.

"The Bagman; or, The Impromptu of Muswell Hill" (radio play; also see below), British Broadcasting Corp. (BBC-Radio), 1970.

(With D'Arcy) "Keep Those People Moving" (radio play), BBC-Radio, 1972.

(With D'Arcy) "Portrait of a Rebel" (television documentary about Sean O'Casey), Radio-Telefis Eireann (Dublin), 1973.

"To Put It Frankly" (radio play), BBC-Radio, 1979.

Pearl: A Play about a Play within a Play (radio play), Eyre Methuen, 1979.

The Adventures of the Ingenious Gentlemen (two-part adaptation of Cervantes' *Don Quixote*), BBC-Radio, 1980.

"Garland for a Hoar Head" (radio play), BBC-Radio, 1982.

"The Old Man Sleeps Alone" (radio play), BBC-Radio, 1982.

(With D'Arcy) *Whose Is the Kingdom?* (radio play broadcast in nine parts by BBC-Radio, 1988), Methuen, 1988.

COLLECTIONS

Three Plays (contains "The Waters of Babylon," "Live Like Pigs," and "The Happy Haven"), introduction by John Russell Taylor, Penguin, 1964, reprinted, 1984, Penguin (Baltimore), 1965.

Soldier, Soldier, and Other Plays (contains "Soldier, Soldier: A Comic Song for Television," "Wet Fish: A Professional Reminiscence for Television," "When Is a Door Not a Door?" and "Friday's Hiding"), Methuen, 1967.

Two Autobiographical Plays (contains "The True History of Squire Jonathan and His Unfortunate Treasure" and "The Bagman; or, The Impromtu of Muswell Hill"), Methuen, 1971.

Plays (includes "Serjeant Musgrave's Dance: An Unhistorical Parable," "The Workhouse Donkey: A Vulgar Melodrama," and "Armstrong's Last Goodnight: An Exercise in Diplomacy"), Methuen, 1977, Grove, 1978.

OTHER

(With D'Arcy) *To Present the Pretence: Essays on the Theatre and Its Public,* Eyre Methuen, 1977, Holmes & Meier, 1979.
Vox Pop: The Last Days of the Roman Republic (novel), Harcourt, 1982 (published in England as *Silence among the Weapons: Some Events at the Time of the Failure of a Republic,* Methuen, 1982).
Books of Bale (novel), Methuen, 1988.
(With D'Arcy) *Awkward Corners* (essays), Methuen, 1988.

Also author of "The Life of Man," 1956. Contributor to anthologies, including *New English Dramatists,* Penguin, Volume 3, 1961, Volume 4, 1962, and *Scripts 9,* 1972.

SIDELIGHTS: British playwright John Arden may not be as well-known outside his native land as are some of his contemporaries of the radical writers school that emerged during the 1950s and 1960s. But like John Osborne, author of "Look Back in Anger," and David Edgar, whose many agitprop dramas rocked the stage, Arden takes a hard look at English life, examining the conflicts behind the traditions. As Stanley Lourdeaux describes it in a *Dictionary of Literary Biography* article, when the fledgling playwright Arden began his professional career in 1957, "critics hastily placed him with other 'angry young men' of the period. Recent critics have labeled Arden the British [Bertolt] Brecht because of his generally Marxist politics in his recent social drama. But neither his present politics nor the 'angry' nonconformity of his protagonists tells the story of why he gradually rejected the appearance of 1950s social realism for that of improvisation."

Arden's early theatrical efforts "scrutinized the basic social tension between aggressive survivors and the institutions meant to pacify them," continues Lourdeaux, who points to "The Waters of Babylon," a 1957 production, as an illustration. It is the story of Sigismanfred Krankiewicz—Krank for short—a Pole who emigrates to London as an architectural assistant (the playwright's original career). When Krank runs up against local authorities for harboring too many boarders, many of them prostitutes, at his private boardinghouse, the immigrant rebels by becoming involved in a corrupt local lottery. Krank's schemes are contrasted against his friend Paul's, who is an amateur anarchist given to building bombs in the name of Polish patriotism. But Polish patriotism "makes little sense to Krank in a world gone mad, as he explains when Paul almost shoots him after learning that he was a soldier in the German army at Buchenwald," notes Lourdeaux. Eventually, Paul does shoot Krank and kills him, though accidentally, and "the random results of the entire scene undermines Krank's clever individualism as well as social justice," Lourdeaux writes.

In his book *Anger and After: A Guide to the New British Drama,* John Russell Taylor remarks that "behind Arden's work there seems to be brooding one basic principle: not exactly the obvious one that today there are no causes—that would be altogether too facile, and in any case just not true—but that there are too many." In the opinion of Simon Trussler, in his published study *John Arden,* "The Waters of Babylon" is "extravagantly plotted, generously peopled—a scenically-shuttling kaleidoscope of down-at-heel London life in the early 1950s. Coincidence functions here not with the shyly intruding excuses of the well-made play but as a fine art in itself, a satisfaction of improbable expectations. And the characters, a racial mixture of Poles, English,

Irish, and West Indians, embody in this comedy of contemporary humours many of the mythic archetypes of urban life, caught from an unexpected angle."

Another Arden work to satirically examine the conflict between the classes is "Live Like Pigs." Like "The Waters of Babylon," this play "contains earthy and zestful language and depends greatly on performance," according to Lourdeaux. "Arden presents the chaos of the gypsylike Sawney family who are forced out of their broken run-down tramcar and made to live in the local housing project. The Sawneys quickly manage to insult their new neighbors, the Jacksons, who eventually incite a vigilante group to run the unappreciative vulgar family out of the project."

"Live Like Pigs" looks "superficially naturalistic, but one has only to consider the sturdy-beggarly tongue in which the Sawneys speak to realize that Arden is here employing a device which was to become more familiar in his historical plays for distinguishing a way of life through its language," says Trussler. "The ballads which introduce the scenes, and the occasional snatches of song within them, underline the danger of approaching the play naturalistically." The purpose of song in this work, the critic continues, "is in marked contrast to the deliberately interruptive purpose it usually serves in Brecht's: balladry is best regarded as another of Arden's invented languages, the problems it poses dramatic rather than musical."

Called by the Irish dramatist Sean O'Casey "far and away the finest play of the present day," "Serjeant Musgrave's Dance: An Unhistorical Parable," a 1958 Arden drama, centers on a fanatical officer of the nineteenth-century British army who exacts a bizarre revenge on the life of a soldier killed by a sniper. He in fact wants no fewer than five men to die to avenge the young private; then calls for more murders to mark another soldier's death, although that one was accidental. "Serjeant Musgrave's Dance," in M. W. Steinberg's view, "is largely an exploration of the place of violence in society and our varying responses to it." The *Dalhousie Review* writer adds that "the moral-political question is given sharpest focus and most acute and challenging dramatic expression through Serjeant Musgrave, a zealot so convinced of the absolute rightness of his cause that he is willing to adopt horrifying means to achieve his goal, and so unswerving and single-minded in his devotion to his avowed purpose that he refuses to be distracted by any consideration not immediately relevant."

"[It] would make for easier acceptance of *Serjeant Musgrave's Dance* if the fanatical sergeant were to be either wholly condemned or wholly approved of," states G. W. Brandt, the author of *Contemporary Theatre.* "But is it not disturbing to see a morally sensitive man trying to start a public massacre? It is. Does his fanaticism invalidate his moral protest as such? It does not. The contradiction between laudable indignation and reprehensible conclusions drawn from it may either alienate the spectators out of all sympathy with the play (as happened to some critics), or else it may jolt them into stirring moral speculation (as was the experience of some other critics)."

That "Serjeant Musgrave's Dance" evoked a divided, if emotional, reaction in critics proved a point of discussion to Malcolm Page: "Clearly there are grounds for uncertainty about the import of the play; difficulties in comprehension arose mainly because neither method nor subject was what the critics expected," he writes in *Drama Survey.* The play "suggests that pacifists are not sure enough about what they are trying to do, and have not understood the complexities of the world," Page says. And "there are several other ideas in the play, perhaps too many. Musgrave and his followers are obsessed with guilt at the evil in which they joined, raising the issue of how to expiate it. . . . Musgrave touches, too, on the question of what principle is: where and how can one begin to apply principles in an imperfect world; does the quest of absolute principle lead to madness?"

In another *Drama Survey* article, John Mills reacts both to "Serjeant Musgrave's Dance" and to Page's assessment of it. To Page's opinion that the work asks "why pacifist ideas have not had more influence," Mills responds that "though I agree with much of [Page's] commentary, I think that the play is a little more hopeful than he indicates. For one thing, it seems to me that *Musgrave* is less about pacifism than it is about anarchism, a doctrine [with] which the play tentatively (as Arden himself might put it) agrees."

The playwright does not lack for personal anger, "but he is the dramatist par excellence who translates that anger into situations of a strictly impersonal nature," in the words of Arnold P. Hinchcliffe in his book *British Theatre 1950-70.* "Arden's characters are primarily used as representatives, and his plots bring about conflicts between social groups. His characters, of course, exist as very colourful individuals, but their personality is shaped at all times to suggest what they stand for . . . and add to the picture of the community as a whole. Thus, isolated town or national politics reflected in local government is observed with an accurate social eye and a strong historical sense which combine to 'translate the concrete life of today into terms of poetry that shall at the one time illustrate that life and set it within the historical and legendary tradition of our culture,' " he says, quoting Arden.

To Lourdeaux, Arden "began his career in theater as a trained architect who was guided by the basic foundation of social drama only to turn more and more explicitly political material. Though at first interested in epic figures like Hitler and King Arthur, Arden tempered his taste to the smaller stature of men like Sigismanfred Krankiewicz and Serjeant Musgrave whose vivid speech and improvised actions supplanted the significance of seemingly realistic plots. With other fierce survivors like the Sawneys in *Live Like Pigs,* [the playwright] seemed to have settled on contemporary social realism."

Arden's career took another turn, though, when he began collaborating on plays with his wife, the Irish actress and playwright Margaretta D'Arcy. The professional partnership was a natural move, as Arden explains in a *Contemporary Authors Autobiography Series* article. "She was closely involved with the most progressive aspects of the theatre of that time, aspects of which I knew nothing, with my limited Shakespearean provincial orientation and my academic (and indeed pompous) attitude towards the stage. She gave me a copy of Brecht—a writer I had only heard of: she introduced me to the works of Beckett, Strindberg, Toller, Behan," he writes. "Her name now appears, sometimes first, sometimes second, together with mine, upon a great deal of published work which nonetheless the male critics, managements, publishers, and broadcasters, will insist upon referring to as 'Arden's.' Or, worse, 'the Ardens'.' It also appears on work of her own, but this did not appear until after the collaborative pieces."

The Non-Stop Connolly Show: A Dramatic Cycle of Continuous Struggle in Six Parts is a marathon collaboration between Arden and D'Arcy; a six-part cycle lasting nearly 24 hours, with a huge cast of historical characters, the production traces the life of Irish socialist leader James Connolly from boyhood through the Easter Uprising in 1916, an important and inspiring event in the history of Irish nationalism. Writing of the two traditions in Ireland, "vicious, merciless violence" and pacifism, Desmond

Hogan points out in *New Statesmen* that Connolly exemplified neither, but "ultimately opted for a bloody revolution on a minor scale not so much to break from Britain but to let out his own protest against Britain's centuries of manhandling Ireland." Although Lourdeaux considers the play "too long and the characters too numerous for viewers to focus exclusively on any one character or action in this complex political tapestry," Hogan suggests that "one feels one is in the presence of great drama and that the drama was made from a cold eye, an eye which like Yeats's, penetrated lies, phobias, images which dressed other images, and came up with—even if only for moments at a stretch—a mind-boggling authenticity."

Concluding an essay on Arden in *Modern Drama,* Joan Tindale Blindheim declares the playwright "a conscious and imaginative explorer of visual effects and stage resources. His knowledge of stage history and his trained eye add dimensions to his work that are often absent from that of more 'literary' writers. There are aspects that must not be ignored when [Arden's] contribution to the drama is considered, and it is through them that he is likely to make a lasting contribution to the theatre too, in helping to break down theatre conventions and in striving towards a richer and more active relationship between actors and audience."

BIOGRAPHICAL/CRITICAL SOURCES:

BOOKS

Anderson, Michael, *Anger and Detachment: A Study of Arden, Osborne and Pinter,* Pitman, 1976.

Armstrong, William A., general editor, *Experimental Drama,* G. Bell & Sons, 1963.

Brandt, G. W., *Contemporary Theatre,* Stratford-Upon-Avon Studies 4, Edward Arnold, 1962.

Contemporary Authors Autobiography Series, Volume 4, Gale, 1986.

Contemporary Literary Criticism, Gale, Volume 6, 1976, Volume 13, 1980, Volume 15, 1980.

Dictionary of Literary Biography, Volume 13: *British Dramatists since World War II,* Gale, 1982.

Gilman, Richard, *Common and Uncommon Masks: Writings on Theatre, 1961-1970,* Random House, 1971.

Hayman, Ronald, *John Arden,* Heinemann Educational Books, 1968.

Hinchcliffe, Arnold P., *British Theatre 1950-1970,* Rowman & Littlefield, 1974.

Hunt, Albert, *Arden: A Study of His Plays,* Eyre Methuen, 1974.

Kennedy, Andrew K., *Six Dramatists in Search of a Language: Studies in Dramatic Language,* Cambridge University Press, 1975.

Leeming, Glenda, *John Arden,* edited by Ian Scott-Kilvert, Longman, 1974.

Lowenfels, Walter, editor, *The Playwrights Speak,* Delacorte, 1967.

Lumley, Frederick, *New Trends in 20th Century Drama: A Survey since Ibsen and Shaw,* Oxford University Press, 1967.

Marowitz, Charles, *The Encore Reader: A Chronicle of New Drama,* Methuen & Co., 1965.

Roy, Emil, *British Drama since Shaw,* Southern Illinois University Press, 1972.

Taylor, John Russell, *Anger and After: A Guide to the New British Drama,* Methuen, 1962.

Trussler, Simon, *John Arden,* Columbia University Press, 1973.

Tschudin, Marcus, *A Writer's Theatre: George Devine and the English Stage Company at the Royal Court, 1956-1965,* Lang, 1972.

Wellworth, George, *The Theatre of Protest and Paradox,* New York University Press, 1964.

Williams, Raymond, *Drama from Ibsen to Brecht,* Oxford University Press, 1969.

PERIODICALS

Dalhousie Review, autumn, 1977.
Drama Survey, summer, 1967, winter, 1968.
Hibbert Journal, autumn, 1966.
Modern Drama, December, 1968, March, 1978.
New Statesman, April 11, 1980.
Times Literary Supplement, January 7, 1965, March 3, 1978, August 27, 1982.

—*Sketch by Susan Salter*

*   *   *

ARMOUR, John
    See PAINE, Lauran (Bosworth)

*   *   *

ARMS, Johnson
    See HALLIWELL, David (William)

*   *   *

ARMSTRONG, D(avid) M(alet)   1926-

PERSONAL: Born July 8, 1926, in Melbourne, Victoria, Australia; son of John Malet (a commodore in the Royal Australian Navy) and Philippa Suzanne (Marett) Armstrong; married Madeleine Annette Haydon (a librarian and drama critic), March 3, 1950; married Jennifer Mary De B. Clark (a social worker), December 31, 1982. *Education:* University of Sydney, B.A., 1950; Exeter College, Oxford, B.Phil., 1954; University of Melbourne, Ph.D., 1960. *Politics:* "Liberal/Democratic, anti-Communist." *Religion:* Atheist.

ADDRESSES: Home—206 Glebe Point Rd., Glebe, Sydney, New South Wales 2037, Australia. *Office*—Philosophy Department, University of Sydney, Sydney, New South Wales 2006, Australia.

CAREER: University of London, Birkbeck College, London, England, assistant lecturer in philosophy, 1954-55; University of Melbourne, Melbourne, Victoria, Australia, 1956-63, began as lecturer, became senior lecturer in philosophy; University of Sydney, Sydney, New South Wales, Australia, Challis Professor of Philosophy, 1964—. Visiting assistant professor, Yale University, 1962; visiting professor, Stanford University, 1965, 1968, University of Texas at Austin, 1980, 1989, and University of Wisconsin at Madison, 1985. *Military service:* Royal Australian Navy, 1945-46.

WRITINGS:

Berkeley's Theory of Vision, Melbourne University Press, 1960.
Perception and the Physical World, Humanities, 1961.
Bodily Sensations, Humanities, 1962.
(Editor) George Berkeley, *Berkeley's Philosophical Writings,* Macmillan, 1965.
A Materialist Theory of the Mind, Humanities, 1968.
Belief, Truth and Knowledge, Cambridge University Press, 1973.
Universals and Scientific Realism, Volume 1: *Nominalism and Realism,* Volume 2: *A Theory of Universals,* Cambridge University Press, 1978.
The Nature of Mind, and Other Essays, Cornwell University Press, 1981.

What Is a Law of Nature?, Cambridge University Press, 1983.
(With Norman Malcolm) *Consciousness and Causality,* Blackwell, 1984.
Universals: An Opinionated Introduction, Westview, 1989.
A Combinatorial Theory of Possibility, Cambridge University Press, 1989.

Contributor to professional journals.

BIOGRAPHICAL/CRITICAL SOURCES:

BOOKS

Bogdan, Radu J., editor, *Profiles, D. M. Armstrong,* Reidel Publishing, 1984.

PERIODICALS

Times Literary Supplement, August 24, 1973, October 19, 1984, January 11, 1985.

*   *   *

ARNOLD, Eve   1913-

PERSONAL: Born in 1913; married. *Education:* Studied medicine; attended New School for Social Research, 1947-48 (studied photography with Alexey Brodovitch).

ADDRESSES: Home—26 Mount St., Flat 3, London W.1, England. *Agent*—Magnum Photos, 72 Spring St., New York, N.Y. 10012.

CAREER: Photojournalist. Magnum Photos (cooperative photography agency), New York and Paris, free-lance photographer for advertising agencies and periodicals, including *Life, Stern, Match, Vogue,* and the London *Times,* 1951—. Filmmaker; films include "Beyond the Veil," 1973. Exhibitions of photographs include "In China," Brooklyn Museum, 1980, United States tour, 1980-82, and a showing of her photographs of Marilyn Monroe at London's Knoedler Gallery, 1987.

AWARDS, HONORS: American Library Association selected *In China* as a notable book of 1980.

WRITINGS:

WITH OWN PHOTOS

The Unretouched Woman, Knopf/Random House, 1976.
Flashback!: The 50's, Knopf, 1978.
In China (Book-of-the-Month Club selection), Knopf, 1980.
In America, Knopf, 1983.
Marilyn Monroe: An Appreciation (Book-of-the-Month Club selection), Borzoi/Knopf, 1987.
All in a Day's Work, Bantam Books/ Hamish Hamilton, 1989.

PHOTOGRAPHER

(With others) *For God's Sake, Care,* introduction by David Frost, foreword by General Frederick Coutts, Constable, 1967.
The Opening Ceremony of Cullinan Hall, October 10, 1958, Houston, Texas (photographic essay), text by Hugo V. Neuhaus, Jr., [Houston], 1972.
(With others) *The 1974 Marilyn Monroe Datebook,* commentary by Norman Mailer, Alskog/Simon & Schuster, 1973.
Private View: Inside Baryshnikov's American Ballet Theatre (Book-of-the-Month Club selection), text by John Fraser, Bantam, 1988.

OTHER

Contributor of articles to *Le Nouveau Photocinema* and *Camera 35.*

WORK IN PROGRESS: A book of photos from the U.S.S.R. as a companion to *In China* and *In America,* and a retrospective of her life's work, both for Knopf.

SIDELIGHTS: While Eve Arnold was studying to become a doctor in the 1940s, her boyfriend presented her with a Rolleicord camera. She enrolled in Alexey Brodovitch's photography class at the New School for Social Research in New York City and with one of her first assignments—a fashion show—determined the tenor of her future photographic works. Instead of snapping glossy, high-fashion pictures, Arnold sought to convey the vitality of local shows in Harlem. Brodovitch liked the project so much that he encouraged his student to pursue it for a year and a half; the study eventually culminated in a major article for London's *Picture Post.*

Arnold stopped studying medicine and joined the prestigous Magnum photography agency in 1951, becoming its first woman member. During the 1950s she often photographed stories that dealt with minority groups—women, the aged, the poor, blacks—for popular magazines. She treated her subjects kindly, candidly, attempting to capture honestly the common flow of life. In the 1960s and '70s Arnold's photographs concentrated on the more political subjects of the black civil-rights struggle and the women's movement, yet her photos still retained an emphasis on individuals.

In *Flashback!: The 50's,* Arnold presents a portfolio of her photographs, with personal commentary, from the 1950s—a decade that Douglas Davis described in *Newsweek* as "the golden age of American postwar photojournalism" in "its last and sweetest phase." Picture magazines like *Life* and *Look* were most popular and photographers were encouraged to use extreme measures to capture powerful, memorable images. The life of the fifties photojournalist, Arnold recalled in her book, was "free and adventurous."

Because of her affiliation with the powerful Magnum agency, Arnold photographed numerous celebrities and prominent figures, including Dwight D. Eisenhower, Joseph McCarthy, Marilyn Monroe, and Joan Crawford. She also covered political stories, religious gatherings, fads, and fashions. According to Davis, the fifties was the last decade to be defined by photojournalism before television assumed the role, and *Flashback!* is "a superb collection of some of the decade's most sharp-eyed pictures." He also maintained that "Eve Arnold's prints are so bound up with the 50's, so faithful to the pace and rhythm of the decade, that they exert an irresistible nostalgic attraction." A critic in the *New Republic* expressed a similar sentiment: "[This] is sharp-eyed, unpretentious photojournalism at its best. Arnold's pictures of the decade of Ike, falsies, McCarthy, Marilyn and Little Rock (touchstone words she cites in her graceful account of her work) literally tell the stories. . . . The impact of such pictures is not easy or ephemeral: they stick." *Village Voice* reviewer Eliot Fremont-Smith deemed all the photos in the book "revealing" and some, "deeply affecting." He concluded, "This is one of the more rewarding photo books of the year."

In 1973 Arnold made a film, "Behind the Veil," about the harems in Arabia, and more particularly about the position of women in Muslim society. In 1976 she expanded on that theme for her second collection, *The Unretouched Woman.* In this collection she examined the humor, incongruities, and pathos of the lives of women around the world. "I am a woman and I wanted to know about women," Arnold stated. "I realize now that through my work . . . I have been searching for myself, my time, and the world I live in." Taken over a span of nearly twenty-five years, the pictures range from peasants performing backbreaking daily tasks with great dignity to Joan Crawford putting on makeup and Marilyn Monroe touring. In *Ms.,* Annie Gottlieb deemed *The Unretouched Woman* an "eloquent, poignant feast of images." The reviewer added, "Arnold's photographs are formally and technically superb. In the manner of the best art, they move the heart through the balance of the eye. . . . Reality is enhanced by light but never censored or romanticized." *Newsweek* book critic Walter Clemons found the collection "expert photojournalism" with a text as "forthright" as its photos.

In 1979 Arnold made two trips to China—the first to the more familiar places; the second to far-flung areas not normally visited by foreigners. The result was *In China,* a collection of 179 photographs with text, under the four headings "Landscape," "People," "Work," and "Living." Fremont-Smith acknowledged that the volume was one of "the year's best book 'portraits' of 'faraway lands'" but wondered if the photos were truly representative. "The celebrative factor . . . seems generically to preclude ugliness, poverty, boring routine, anger and landscapes and artifacts that are less than quaintly or arrestingly photogenic," he observed. Beverly Beyette of the *Los Angeles Times Book Review* disagreed, however, noting that Arnold "does not take picture post-cards. She photographs laundry drying on the balconies of a modern apartment house, a dormitory for women oil-field workers, a demonstration by people out of work in Shanghai." A *New York Times Book Review* critic determined that *In China* was "surely one of the handsomest picture books of the year," showing "the most appealing faces since Steichen's Family of Man exhibit."

Arnold followed *In China* with *In America,* a photographic look at her native country. *Newsweek*'s Mark Stevens judged it "an enjoyable melting pot of the many styles and races and characters that make up modern America." Her highest achievement in the collection, he said, was "not a single image, but the composite portrait carried away of a vigorous and varied nation."

Arnold's work spans a wide range of subjects. She has traveled the world and photographed people and scenes in more than thirty countries, including Jamaica, Cuba, Haiti, Malta, Tunisia, Austria, the U.S.S.R., Egypt, South Africa, and Portugal. *All in a Day's Work,* an all-color volume, collects photos from Arnold's thirty-five year career, with sample photos from many of the countries she has visited. Some of her books have been printed in several languages. *Marilyn Monroe: An Appreciation,* for example, has been published in France, Spain, Italy, Japan, Germany, Canada, and Britain. Arnold told *CA* that Mary Blume, writing in the *International Herald Tribune* in 1985, said, "In a distinguished career Eve Arnold has photographed Everyone with a capital 'e' and also everyone. Robert Capa once said that metaphorically speaking her work falls between Marlene Dietrich's legs and the bitter lives of migrant potato pickers."

BIOGRAPHICAL/CRITICAL SOURCES:

BOOKS

Harbutt, Charles and Lee Jones, editors, *America in Crisis: Photographs for Magnum,* Holt, 1969.

PERIODICALS

Chicago Tribune Book World, December 7, 1980.
Los Angeles Times Book Review, November 30, 1980.
Ms., June, 1977.
New Republic, December 16, 1978.
Newsweek, December 13, 1976, September 25, 1978, December 12, 1983.

New York Times Book Review, November 23, 1980, December 4, 1983.
Publishers Weekly, September 19, 1980.
Times (London), September 4, 1987.
Times Literary Supplement, November 14, 1980.
Village Voice, December 13, 1976, September 18, 1978, December 10, 1980.
Washington Post Book World, November 30, 1980.
You and Your Camera, May 10, 1979.

* * *

ASHBROOK, James B(arbour) 1925-

PERSONAL: Born November 1, 1925, in Adrian, Mich.; son of Milan Forest (a minister) and Elizabeth (Barbour) Ashbrook; married Patricia Cober (a social worker), August 14, 1948; children: Peter, Susan, Martha, Karen. *Education:* Denison University, B.A. (with honors), 1947; Colgate Rochester Divinity School, B.D., 1950; Union Theological Seminary and William White Institute of Psychiatry, graduate fellow, 1954-55; Ohio State University, M.A., 1962, Ph.D., 1964. *Politics:* Democrat.

ADDRESSES: Home—1205 Wesley Ave., Evanston, Ill. 60202. *Office*—Garrett-Evangelical Theological Seminary, Northwestern University, 2121 Sheridan Rd., Evanston, Ill. 60201.

CAREER: Clergyman of American Baptist Church; pastor in Rochester, N.Y., 1950-54, and Granville, Ohio, 1955-60; Colgate Rochester Divinity School, Rochester, N.Y., associate professor, 1960-65, professor of pastoral theology, 1965-69, professor of psychology and theology, 1969-81; Northwestern University, Garrett-Evangelical Theological Seminary, Evanston, Ill., professor of religion and personality and advisory member of graduate faculty, 1982. Teaching fellow, Graduate Theological Union, 1987—; adjunct professor, Northern Baptist Theological Seminary, 1984—. Visiting lecturer at Denison University, 1958-60, and Princeton Theological Seminary, 1970-71. Summer clinical pastoral training at Rochester State Hospital, 1949, Bellevue General Hospital, 1950, and Illinois State Training School for Boys, 1951. Consultant and supervisor, Counseling Center, University of Rochester, 1969-75, and Genesee Ecumenical Pastoral Counseling Center, 1975-81; consultant to Chief of U.S. Air Force Chaplains, 1969, to Rochester Board of Education, 1969-73, to Family Court of Monroe County (N.Y.), 1972-74, and to St. Ann's Home for the Elderly, 1972-85.

MEMBER: American Association of Pastoral Counselors (diplomate; chairman of centers and teaching committee, 1970-71), American Academy of Religion, Society for the Scientific Study of Religion, American Psychological Association (clinical), American Board of Professional Psychology, Phi Beta Kappa.

AWARDS, HONORS: Faculty fellowship, American Association of Theology Schools, 1963-64, 1971-72; postdoctoral fellowship, University of Rochester Center for Community Studies, 1971-73; alumni citation, Denison University, 1972; LL.D., Denison University, 1976; designated "a pioneer in pastoral psychotherapy," American Association of Pastoral Counselors/ Institutes of Religion and Health, 1987.

WRITINGS:

(Contributor) Simon Doniger, editor, *The Minister's Consultation Clinic,* Channel Press, 1955.
(Contributor) Hans Hoffman, editor, *Religion and Mental Health,* Harper, 1961.
(Contributor) David Belgum, editor, *Religion and Medicine,* Iowa State University Press, 1967.

(Contributor) William Bier, editor, *Psychological Testing for Ministerial Selection,* Fordham University Press, 1970.
Be/Come Community, Judson, 1971.
In Human Presence: Hope, Judson, 1971.
Humanitas: Human Becoming and Being Human, Abingdon, 1973.
The Old Me and a New i: An Exploration of Personal Identity, Judson, 1974.
Responding to Human Pain, Judson, 1975.
(With Paul W. Walaskay) *Christianity for Pious Skeptics,* Abingdon, 1977.
The Human Mind and the Mind of God: Theological Promise in Brain Research, University Press of America, 1984.
The Brain and Belief: Faith in Light of Brain Research, Wyndham Hall Press, 1988.
(Editor with John E. Hukle, Jr.) *At the Point of Need—Living Human Experience: Essays in Honor of Carroll A. Wise,* University Press of America, 1988.
Paul Tillich in Conversation, Wyndham Hall Press, 1988.
Faith and Ministry in Light of the Double Brain, Wyndham Hall Press, 1989.
Brain, Culture, and the Human Spirit: Foundational Essays, Wyndham Hall Press, 1990.

Member of editorial board, "Ministry Monograph" series, 1965-70. Contributor to psychology and religion journals. Associate editor, *Review of Religious Research,* 1982-89; member of editorial advisory board, *Journal of Pastoral Care,* 1965—; consulting editor, *Journal of Counseling Psychology,* 1968-74.

* * *

ASHBY, Carter
See PAINE, Lauran (Bosworth)

* * *

ASHE, Geoffrey (Thomas) 1923-

PERSONAL: Born March 29, 1923, in London, England; son of Arthur William (a travel agency general manager) and Thelma (Hoodless) Ashe; married Dorothy Irene Train (a teacher), May 3, 1946; children: Thomas, John, Michael, Sheila, Brendan. *Education:* University of British Columbia, B.A. (first class honors), 1943; Trinity College, Cambridge University, B.A. (first in English Tripos), 1948. *Religion:* Catholic.

ADDRESSES: Home—Chalice Orchard, Well House Lane, Glastonbury, Somerset BA6 8BJ England. *Agent*—Candida Donadio & Associates, Inc., 231 West 22nd St., New York, N.Y. 10011.

CAREER: Writer. Polish University College, London, England, lecturer in English, 1948-50; Newman Neame (publishers), London, industrial research assistant, 1949-51; Ford Motor Co. of Canada, Windsor, Ontario, administrative assistant, 1952-54; Post Office Department, Toronto, Ontario, technical officer, 1954-55; Polytechnic, London, lecturer in management studies, 1956-67. Visiting professor of English, University of Southern Mississippi, 1982, University of Alabama at Birmingham, 1984, Wilfred Laurier University, Canada, 1985, and University of Minnesota, Duluth, 1986; Thomas Lamont Visiting Professor, Union College, Schenectady, N.Y., 1984; lecturer and contributor to television programs.

MEMBER: International Arthurian Society, Royal Society of Literature (fellow).

WRITINGS:

The Tale of the Tub: A Survey of the Art of Bathing through the Ages, Newman Neame, 1950.
King Arthur's Avalon: The Story of Glastonbury, Collins, 1957.
From Caesar to Arthur, Collins, 1960.
Land to the West: St. Brendan's Voyage to America, Collins, 1962.
The Land and the Book, Collins, 1965.
The Carmelite Order, Carmelite Press, 1965.
Gandhi: A Study in Revolution, Stein & Day, 1968.
(Editor and contributor) *The Quest for Arthur's Britain,* Pall Mall, 1968.
All About King Arthur (juvenile), W. H. Allen, 1969, published in the United States as *King Arthur in Fact and Legend,* T. Nelson, 1971.
Camelot and the Vision of Albion, Heinemann, 1971.
(With others) *The Quest for America,* Pall Mall, 1971.
The Art of Writing Made Simple, W. H. Allen, 1972.
The Finger and the Moon (novel), Heinemann, 1973.
Do What You Will: A History of Anti-morality, W. H. Allen, 1974.
The Virgin, Routledge & Kegan Paul, 1976.
The Ancient Wisdom, Macmillan, 1977.
Miracles, Routledge & Kegan Paul, 1978.
A Guidebook to Arthurian Britain, Longman, 1980.
Kings and Queens of Early Britain, Methuen, 1982.
Avalonian Quest, Methuen, 1982.
The Discovery of King Arthur, Doubleday, 1985.
The Landscape of King Arthur, Webb & Bower, 1987.
(With Norris J. Lacy) *The Arthurian Handbook,* Garland, 1988.

Author of play, "The Glass Island," 1964. Columnist in *Resurgence* magazine, 1973-78. Contributor to numerous periodicals, including *Speculum.* Associate editor of *The Arthurian Encyclopedia,* Garland Press, 1986.

WORK IN PROGRESS: British Myths, "an attempt to do for Britain" what Robert Graves did in *Greek Myths* and *Hebrew Myths; The Dawn behind the Dawn,* "a more serious development of *The Ancient Wisdom* in the light of recent new ideas about the prehistory of Europe and Asia."

SIDELIGHTS: The writings of Geoffrey Ashe represent an eclectic selection of religious, historical, and mythological topics. He has written extensively on the historical and literary aspects of Arthurian legend and has been involved with archaeological excavations in search of Camelot, but the scope of his works remains essentially diverse. "Geoffrey Ashe has written the best biography of Gandhi that I know," writes Henrietta Buckmaster in the *Christian Science Monitor. Gandhi: A Study in Revolution* is "a model of fairness, proportion and restraint," according to Martin E. Marty in the *New York Times Book Review.* "In a time when Gandhi usually receives ideological or tractarian treatment, it is refreshing to have a simple narrative, a straight biography of a very human being." Marty makes reference to one of the central difficulties confronting the Gandhi biographer: overcoming the cult of personality and mythology surrounding the religious and political leader to reveal the "very human" man beneath. Describing the success with which Ashe copes with this problem, Francis Watson says in the *Spectator* that "Mr. Ashe has sunk his shafts in the immense material to convince us of what Einstein suggested we might one day scarcely believe, 'that such a one as this ever in flesh and blood walked upon this earth.' While the tribute is quoted, its suggestion of the superhuman is satisfactorily avoided."

Another formidable task for the biographer of Gandhi is the task of making a balanced and coherent presentation of the different periods in the Indian leader's life, while sifting through an enormous mass of detail. Philip Altbach, reviewing *Gandhi* in *Commonweal,* believes that the focus of the book is uneven: "Like most of Gandhi's other biographers, [Ashe] spends too much time on the South African experience and does not go into enough detail about India." Marty, however, disagrees: "The plot line of Gandhi's life in Britain, South Africa, and India is necessarily complex, [but] the reader will not be lost in detail. [Ashe's] quotations from Gandhi are pithy and pointed; the anecdotes are spare but illuminating." In a *Punch* article on the book, Honoria J. Scannard asserts that Ashe's "greatest achievement is to present this eminently spiritual leader as a man who was also ruthlessly practical and passionately human."

Ashe has also written about the cult of the Virgin Mary, the search for Camelot, and other inter-related topics of religion, philosophy, and mythology. Writing in the *New Statesman,* Jonathan Raban calls *Camelot and the Vision of Albion* "an enterprising foray into [the] rich seam of indigenous English mythology." The volume proposes the idea that Arthurian legend, in all of its many manifestations, reflects an innate desire in mankind for a golden age as embodied in a paradisiacal setting such as Camelot. According to Raban, Ashe's "real interest lies in the notion of a submerged 'British spirit,' personified by an Arthur/Albion figure" traced through figures such as Shelley and Gandhi, and a hero of Arthurian dimensions who is yet to come.

Ashe's focus on the legendary king continues in a number of books published in the eighties. In *The Discovery of King Arthur,* Ashe proposes to locate the historical monarch. A likely candidate, he maintains, is a military leader famous for his exploits in the Gallic campaign of 469-470 A.D. During this time, "there was indeed military action among the pro-Roman Burgundians who were aided by their British cousins," James P. Carley comments in the *Globe and Mail.* "[Ashe] also notes that the subsequent retreat led them near the Burgundian town of Avallon," writes Carley, who calls Ashe's arguments "persuasive." Carley suggests that this discovery is not celebrated more because, in his words, "the real Arthur is the *legend,* not the *fact*—a conclusion Ashe himself would probably accept."

BIOGRAPHICAL/CRITICAL SOURCES:

PERIODICALS

Booklist, May 15, 1972.
Christian Science Monitor, July 18, 1968.
Commonweal, March 13, 1970.
Globe and Mail (Toronto), April 13, 1985.
New Statesman, January 15, 1971.
New York Review of Books, November 11, 1976.
New York Times Book Review, July 21, 1968, August 29, 1977.
Punch, May 8, 1968.
Spectator, March 22, 1968.
Times Literary Supplement, October 16, 1969.

*   *   *

AVERY, Richard
   See COOPER, Edmund

*   *   *

AVIRGAN, Anthony Lance 1944-
   (Tony Avirgan)

PERSONAL: Born November 30, 1944, in Philadelphia, Pa.; son of Jerome and Francis (Nelson) Avirgan; married Martha Spencer Honey (a journalist), September 25, 1971; children: Shanti Hue, Jody Troi. *Education:* Attended Pennsylvania State University, 1959-61. *Religion:* Atheist.

ADDRESSES: Home and office—Apartado 518, Centro Colon 1007, San Jose, Costa Rica.

CAREER: Worked as a professional motorcycle racer, 1961-65; market research consultant, 1965-68; antiwar organizer, 1968-73; newspaper, television, and radio reporter in Africa, 1973-83, in Central America, 1983—.

WRITINGS:

ALL UNDER NAME TONY AVIRGAN; ALL WITH WIFE MARTHA S. HONEY

War in Uganda: The Legacy of Idi Amin, Lawrence Hill, 1982.
La penca: Reporte de una investigacion, Editorial Porvenir, 1985, translation published as *La Penca on Trial in Costa Rica,* 1987.
John Hull: El finguero de la CIA, Varitec, 1989.

SIDELIGHTS: Tony Avirgan told *CA:* "I lived ten years in Africa writing for newspapers, reporting for radio, and making television news films, and am currently doing the same in Central America. I feel it is important to give the Third World a voice in the media of the industrialized world."

*   *   *

AVIRGAN, Tony
  See AVIRGAN, Anthony Lance

*   *   *

AYCKBOURN, Alan   1939-
(Roland Allen)

PERSONAL: Surname is pronounced Ache-born; born April 12, 1939, in Hampstead, London, England; son of Horace (a concert musician) and Irene (Worley) Ayckbourn; married Christine Roland, May 9, 1959; children: Steven Paul, Philip Nicholas. *Education:* Attended Haileybury and Imperial Service College, Hertfordshire, England, 1952-57.

ADDRESSES: Office—Stephen Joseph Theatre-in-the-Round, Valley Bridge Parade, Scarborough YO11 2PL, England. *Agent*—Margaret Ramsay Ltd., 14 A, Goodwin's Ct., St. Martin's Lane, London WC2N 4LL, England.

CAREER: Stephen Joseph Theatre-in-the-Round Company, Scarborough, England, stage manager and actor, 1957-59, writer and director, 1959-61; Victoria Theatre, Stoke-on-Trent, England, actor, writer, and director, 1961-64; British Broadcasting Corporation (BBC), Leeds, Yorkshire, England, drama producer, 1965-70; Stephen Joseph Theatre-in-the-Round Company, writer and artistic director, 1970—. Visiting playwright and director, National Theatre, London, England, 1977, 1980, 1986-88. Also acted with several British repertory companies.

AWARDS, HONORS: London Evening Standard best comedy award, 1973, for *Absurd Person Singular,* best play awards, 1974, for *The Norman Conquests,* 1977, for *Just Between Ourselves,* and 1987, for *A Small Family Business; Plays and Players* best new play awards, 1974, for *The Norman Conquests,* and 1985, for *A Chorus of Disapproval;* named "playwright of the year" by Variety Club of Great Britain, 1974; D.Litt, University of Hull, 1981, University of Keele, 1987, and University of Leeds, 1987; *London Evening Standard* Award, Olivier Award, and *Drama*

Award, all 1985, all for *A Chorus of Disapproval;* named Commander of the British Empire, 1987; Director of the Year Award, *Plays and Players,* 1987, for production of Arthur Miller's *A View from the Bridge.*

WRITINGS:

PLAYS

(Under pseudonym Roland Allen) "The Square Cat," first produced in Scarborough at Library Theatre, June, 1959.
(Under pseudonym Roland Allen) "Love after All," first produced in Scarborough at Library Theatre, December, 1959.
(Under pseudonym Roland Allen) "Dad's Tale," first produced in Scarborough at Library Theatre, December 19, 1960.
(Under pseudonym Roland Allen) "Standing Room Only," first produced in Scarborough at Library Theatre, July 13, 1961.
"Xmas v. Mastermind," first produced in Stoke-on-Trent, England at Victoria Theatre, December 26, 1962.
"Mr. Whatnot," first produced in Stoke-on-Trent at Victoria Theatre, November 12, 1963, revised version produced in London at Arts Theatre, August 6, 1964.
"The Sparrow," first produced in Scarborough at the Library Theatre, July 13, 1967.
Relatively Speaking (first produced as "Meet My Father" in Scarborough at Library Theatre, July 8, 1965, produced on the West End at Duke of York's Theatre, March 29, 1967), Samuel French, 1968.
We Who Are About To . . . (one-act; includes "Countdown"; first produced in London at Hampstead Theatre Club, February 6, 1969; also see below), published in *Mixed Doubles: An Entertainment on Marriage,* Methuen, 1970.
Mixed Doubles: An Entertainment on Marriage (includes "Countdown," and *We Who Are About to . . .;* first produced on the West End at Comedy Theatre, April 9, 1969), Methuen, 1970.
How the Other Half Loves (first produced in Scarborough at Library Theatre, July 31, 1969, produced on the West End at Lyric Theatre, August 5, 1970), Samuel French, 1971.
"The Story So Far," produced in Scarborough at Library Theatre, August 20, 1970, revised version as "Me Times Me Times Me," produced on tour March 13, 1972, second revised version as "Family Circles," produced in Richmond, England at Orange Tree Theatre, November 17, 1978.
Ernie's Incredible Illucinations (first produced in London, 1971), Samuel French, 1969.
Time and Time Again (first produced in Scarborough at Library Theatre, July 8, 1971, produced on the West End at Comedy Theatre, August 16, 1972), Samuel French, 1973.
Absurd Person Singular (first produced in Scarborough at Library Theatre, June 26, 1972, produced on the West End at Criterion Theatre, July 4, 1973), Samuel French, 1974.
Mother Figure (one-act; first produced in Horsham, Sussex, England at Capitol Theatre, 1973, produced on the West End at Apollo Theatre, May 19, 1976; also see below), published in *Confusions,* Samuel French, 1977.
The Norman Conquests (trilogy; composed of *Table Manners, Living Together,* and *Round and Round the Garden;* first produced in Scarborough at Library Theatre June, 1973, produced on the West End at Globe Theatre, August 1, 1974), Samuel French, 1975.
Absent Friends (first produced in Scarborough at Library Theatre, June 17, 1974, produced on the West End at Garrick Theatre, July 23, 1975), Samuel French, 1975.
"Service Not Included" (television script), produced by British Broadcasting Corporation (BBC), 1974.

Confusions (one-acts; includes *Mother Figure, Drinking Companion, Between Mouthfuls, Gosforth's Fete,* and *A Talk in the Park;* first produced in Scarborough at Library Theatre, September 30, 1974, produced on the West End at Apollo Theatre, May 19, 1976), Samuel French, 1977.

(Author of book and lyrics) "Jeeves" (musical; adapted from stories by P. G. Wodehouse), music by Andrew Lloyd Webber, first produced on the West End at Her Majesty's Theatre, April 22, 1975.

Bedroom Farce (first produced in Scarborough at the Library Theatre, June 16, 1975, produced on the West End at Prince of Wales's Theatre, November 7, 1978, produced on Broadway at Brooks Atkinson Theatre, 1979; also see below), Samuel French, 1977.

Just Between Ourselves (first produced in Scarborough at Library Theatre, January 28, 1976, produced on the West End at Queen's Theatre, April 22, 1977; also see below), Samuel French, 1978.

Ten Times Table (first produced in Scarborough at Stephen Joseph Theatre-in-the-Round, January 18, 1977, produced on the West End at Globe Theatre, April 5, 1978; also see below), Samuel French, 1979.

Joking Apart (first produced in Scarborough at Stephen Joseph Theatre-in-the-Round, January 11, 1978, produced on the West End at Globe Theatre, March 7, 1979), Samuel French, 1979.

(Author of book and lyrics) "Men on Women on Men" (musical), music by Paul Todd, first produced in Scarborough at Stephen Joseph Theatre-in-the-Round, June 17, 1978.

Sisterly Feelings (first produced in Scarborough at Stephen Joseph Theatre-in-the-Round, January 10, 1979, produced on the West End at Olivier Theatre, June 3, 1980; also see below), Samuel French, 1981.

Taking Steps (first produced in Scarborough at Stephen Joseph Theatre-in-the-Round, September 27, 1979, produced on the West End at Lyric Theatre, September 2, 1980), Samuel French, 1981.

(Author of book and lyrics) *Suburban Strains* (musical; first produced in Scarborough at Stephen Joseph Theatre-in-the-Round, January 20, 1980, produced in London at Round House Theatre, February 2, 1981), music by Todd, Samuel French, 1981.

Season's Greetings (first produced in Scarborough at Stephen Joseph Theatre-in-the-Round, September 24, 1980, revised version first produced in Greenwich, England at Greenwich Theatre, January 27, 1982, produced on the West End at Apollo Theatre, March 29, 1982), Samuel French, 1982.

(Author of book and lyrics) "Me, Myself, and I" (musical), music by Todd, first produced in Scarborough at Stephen Joseph Theatre-in-the-Round, June, 1981.

Way Upstream (first produced in Scarborough at Stephen Joseph Theatre-in-the-Round, October, 1981, produced in London at National Theatre, October 4, 1982), Samuel French, 1983.

(Author of book and lyrics) "Making Tracks" (musical), music by Todd, first produced in Scarborough at Stephen Joseph Theatre-in-the-Round, December 16, 1981.

Intimate Exchanges (first produced in Scarborough at Stephen Joseph Theatre-in-the-Round, June 3, 1982, produced on the West End at the Ambassadors Theatre, August 14, 1984), Samuel French, 1985.

"It Could Be Any One of Us," first produced in Scarborough at Stephen Joseph Theatre-in-the-Round, October 9, 1983.

A Chorus of Disapproval (first produced in Scarborough at Stephen Joseph Theatre-in-the-Round, May 3, 1984, produced on the West End at the Lyric Theatre, June 11, 1986), Samuel French, 1985, screenplay adaptation by Ayckbourn and Michael Winner, Southgate Entertainment, 1989.

Woman in Mind (first produced in Scarborough at Stephen Joseph Theatre-in-the-Round, June 3, 1985, produced on the West End at Vaudeville Theatre, September 3, 1986), Faber, 1986, Samuel French, 1987.

"The Westwoods," first produced in Scarborough at Stephen Joseph Theatre-in-the-Round, May 1984, produced in London at Etcetera Theatre, May 31, 1987.

A Small Family Business (first produced on the West End at Olivier Theatre, June 5, 1987), Faber, 1987, Samuel French, 1988.

Henceforward . . . (first produced in Scarborough at Stephen Joseph Theatre-in-the-Round, July 30, 1987, produced on the West End at Vaudeville Theatre, November 21, 1988), Faber, 1989.

"Man of the Moment," first produced in Scarborough at Stephen Joseph Theatre-in-the-Round, August 10, 1988.

Mr. A's Amazing Maze Plays (first produced in Scarborough at Stephen Joseph Theatre-in-the-Round, November 30, 1988), Faber, 1989.

"The Revenger's Comedies," first produced in Scarborough at Stephen Joseph Theatre-in-the-Round, June 13, 1989.

OMNIBUS VOLUMES

Three Plays (contains *Absurd Person Singular, Absent Friends,* and *Bedroom Farce*), Grove, 1979.

Joking Apart and Other Plays (includes *Joking Apart, Just Between Ourselves,* and *Ten Times Table*), Chatto & Windus, 1979.

Sisterly Feelings and Taking Steps, Chatto & Windus, 1981.

SIDELIGHTS: Alan Ayckbourn is generally considered Great Britain's most successful living playwright. For well over two decades Ayckbourn comedies have been appearing regularly in London's West End theatres, earning the author handsome royalties as well as an international reputation. London *Times* reviewer Anthony Masters observes that Ayckbourn's work since the mid-1960s "is rich in major and minor masterpieces that will certainly live and are now overdue for revival." A prolific writer who often crafts his dramas just shortly before they are due to be staged, Ayckbourn extracts wry and disenchanted humor from the dull rituals of English middle-class life. To quote *Nation* contributor Harold Clurman, the dramatist is "a master hand at turning the bitter apathy, the stale absurdity which most English playwrights now find characteristic of Britain's lower-middle-class existence into hilarious comedy." *Dictionary of Literary Biography* essayist Albert E. Kalson describes a typical Ayckbourn play as an "intricately staged domestic comedy with a half-dozen intertwined characters who reflect the audience's own unattainable dreams and disappointments while moving them to laughter with at least a suggestion of a tear." In the London *Times,* Andrew Hislop comments that the plays, translated into two dozen languages, "are probably watched by more people in the world than those of any other living dramatist."

Kalson suggests that Ayckbourn's work "is rooted in the Home Counties, his characters' speech patterns reflecting his upbringing." Indeed, although Ayckbourn was born in London, he was raised in a succession of small Sussex towns by his mother and her second husband, a provincial bank manager. Ayckbourn told the *New York Times* that his childhood was not comfortable or cheery. "I was surrounded by relationships that weren't altogether stable, the air was often blue, and things were sometimes flying across the kitchen," he said. *New York Times* contributor

Benedict Nightingale finds this youthful insecurity reflected in Ayckbourn's writings, since the characters "often come close to destroying each other, though more commonly through insensitivity than obvious malice." At seventeen Ayckbourn determined that he wanted to be an actor. After several years with small repertory companies, during which he learned stage managing as well as acting techniques, he took a position with the Stephen Joseph Company in Scarborough. According to Kalson, his continuing association with that group "eventually turned a minor actor into a major playwright." Nightingale is philosophical about Ayckbourn's creative development. "If he had been a happier man," the critic writes, ". . . he wouldn't have wanted to write plays. If he had been a more successful actor, he would have had no need to do so. If he'd known happier people in his early life, his plays wouldn't be so interesting. And if he had not been an actor at all, it would have taken him much longer to learn how to construct his plots, prepare his effects and time his jokes."

Ayckbourn began his tenure at Scarborough as an actor and stage manager. He has described the company as "the first of the fringe theatres," with interests in experimental theatre-in-the-round work and other so-called underground techniques. As he gained experience, Ayckbourn began to agitate for larger roles. The group leader, Stephen Joseph, had other ideas, however. In *Drama,* Ayckbourn reminisced about his earliest attempts at playwrighting. Joseph told him, "If you want a better part, you'd better write one for yourself. You write a play, I'll do it. If it's any good. . . . Write yourself a main part." Ayckbourn appreciated the latter advice especially, calling it "a very shrewd remark, because presumably, if the play had not worked at all, there was no way I as an actor was going to risk my neck in it." Ayckbourn actually wrote several plays that were staged at Scarborough in the early 1960s—pseudonymous works such as "The Square Cat," "Love after All," "Dad's Tale," and "Standing Room Only." According to Ian Watson in *Drama,* these "belong to Ayckbourn's workshop period, and today he is careful to ensure that nobody reads them, and certainly nobody produces them."

Eventually Ayckbourn gave up acting when he discovered his particular muse—the fears and foibles of Britain's middle classes. As he began to experience success outside of Scarborough, however, he continued to craft his work specifically for that company and its small theatre-in-the-round. A large majority of his plays have debuted there, despite the lure of the West End. "My plays are what one would expect from someone who runs a small theater in a community such as Scarborough," Ayckbourn told the *Chicago Tribune.* "That means the cost for the play is about the budget for one production in the company's season, and the subject matter offers the audience a chance to see something they know, to laugh at jokes they've heard before." Kalson likewise notes that the playwright "bears in mind the requirements of the Scarborough audience, many of them his neighbors, upon whom he depends for the testing of his work. He will neither insult nor shock them, respecting their desire to be entertained. He provides them with plays about the life he observes around him, sometimes even his own." *Los Angeles Times* correspondent Sylvie Drake writes: "Alan Ayckbourn is a blithe spirit. He has been writing plays for actors he knows in a theater in Scarborough, England, without much concern for the rest of the world. Since that 'rest of world' admires nothing more than someone with the audacity to pay it no attention, it promptly embraced his idiosyncratic comedies and totally personal style."

Ayckbourn's early plays "succeeded in resuscitating that most comatose of genres, the 'farcical comedy,' " according to Nightingale in *New Statesman.* In *Modern Drama,* Malcolm Page similarly characterizes the early works as "the lightest and purest of comedies, giving [Ayckbourn] the reputation of being the most undemanding of entertainers." Plays such as *Relatively Speaking, How the Other Half Loves,* and *Absurd Person Singular* "abound with the basic element of theatrical humor, that is incongruity, the association of unassociable elements," to quote Guido Almansi in *Encounter.* Typically revolving around extramarital affairs or class conflicts, the comedies begin with a peculiar situation that grows inexorably out of control, with mistaken identities, unclarified misunderstandings, and overlooked clues. *New York Times* commentator Walter Goodman writes: "How Mr. Ayckbourn contrives to get his people into such states and persuade us to believe that they are reasonable is a secret of his comic flair." With the enthusiastic reception for *Relatively Speaking,* concludes Oleg Kerensky in *The New British Drama: Fourteen Playwrights since Osborne and Pinter,* Ayckbourn established himself "as a writer of ingenious farcical comedy, with an ear for dialogue and with a penchant for complex situations . . . and ingenious plots." That reputation led some critics to question Ayckbourn's lasting contribution to the theatre, but subsequent plays have clarified the author's more serious intentions. Kalson concludes: "Beyond the easy jokes, the mistaken identities, the intricate staging, Ayckbourn was learning a craft that would enable him, always within the framework of bourgeois comedy, to illuminate the tedium, the pain, even the horror of daily life recognizable not only in England's Home Counties, . . . or in gruffer, heartier northern England, . . . but all over the world."

Throughout his years of playwrighting, Ayckbourn has taken risks not easily reconciled with popular comedy. Some American critics have labeled him "the British Neil Simon," but in fact his characters often must contend with an undercurrent of humiliation, mediocrity, and embarrassment that Simon does not address. In the *Chicago Tribune,* Howard Reich writes: "The best of Ayckbourn's work . . . is funny not only for what its characters say but because of what they don't. Between the wisecracks and rejoinders, there breathe characters who are crumbling beneath the strictures of British society." Ayckbourn may pillory the manners and social conventions of the middle classes, but he also concerns himself with the defeats that define ordinary, often hopeless, lives. According to Alan Brien in *Plays and Players,* the author "shows . . . that what is funny to the audience can be tragic to the characters, and that there is no lump in the throat to equal a swallowed laugh which turns sour." *New York* magazine contributor John Simon suggests that Ayckbourn "extends the range of farce, without cheating, to cover situations that are not farcical—the fibrillations of the heart under the feverish laughter. And he keeps his characters characters, not walking stacks of interchangeable jokebooks." As Guido Almansi notes in *Encounter,* the playwright "knows how to operate dramatically on what seems to be utterly banal: which is certainly more difficult than the exploitation of the sublime."

A favorite Ayckbourn theme is the pitfalls of marriage, an institution in which the playwright finds little joy. *New Yorker* correspondent Brendan Gill contends that the author "regards human relationships in general and the marriage relationship in particular as little more than a pailful of cozily hissing snakes." Richard Eder elaborates in the *New York Times:* "His characters are simply people for whom the shortest distance between two emotional points is a tangle; and who are too beset by doubts, timidities and chronic self-complication to have time for anything as straightforward as sex." Harold Hobson also observes in *Drama* that behind Ayckbourn's foolery "he has this sad conviction that marriage is a thing that will not endure. Men and women may get instant satisfaction from life, but it is not a satisfaction that will last long. . . . It is when Ayckbourn sees the tears of life, its underlying, ineradicable sadness, that he is at his superb best." *Bedroom Farce* and *Absurd Person Singular* both tackle the thorny side of marriage; the two plays are among Ayckbourn's most successful. In *New Statesman,* Nightingale concludes that in both works Ayckbourn "allows his people to have feelings, that these feelings can be hurt, and that this is cause for regret. . . . There are few sadder things than the slow destruction of youthful optimism, not to mention love, trust and other tender shoots: Mr. Ayckbourn makes sure we realise it."

Throughout his career Ayckbourn has demonstrated a reluctance to be limited by conventional staging techniques. This tendency, born in the Scarborough theatre-in-the-round atmosphere, has become an abiding factor in the playwright's work. "Alan Ayckbourn's comedies have become such money-spinners and he himself has won such general critical acclaim that it is difficult to think of him as an experimental dramatist," writes Shorter. "He has however probably done as much as any other living playwright to use the stage with an original sense of its scope—to stretch its scenic and dramatic possibilities." Some Ayckbourn plays juxtapose several floors of a house—or several different houses—in one set; others offer alternative scenes decided at random by the actors or by a flip of a coin. According to J. W. Lambert in *Drama,* Ayckbourn's "ingenuity in thus constructing the plays positively makes the head spin if dwelt upon; but of course it should not be dwelt upon, for however valuable the challenge may have been to his inventive powers, it is to us only an incidental pleasure. The value of the work lies elsewhere—in its knife-sharp insights into the long littleness of life and in its unflagging comic exhilaration." Page likewise insists that while his staging skills "are frequently dazzling, Ayckbourn claims our attention for his insights about people: he prompts us to laugh, then to care about the character and to make a connection with ourselves, our own behavior, and possibly beyond to the world in which we live."

The Norman Conquests, first produced in 1973, combines Ayckbourn's theme of the frailty of relationships with an experimental structure. The piece is actually a trilogy of plays, any one of which can be seen on its own for an understanding of the story. Together, however, the three parts cover completely several hours in the day of an unscrupulous character named Norman, whose "conquests" are generally restricted to the seduction of women. In the *Chicago Tribune,* Richard Christiansen suggests that the three plays "fit together like Chinese boxes. Each comedy has the same cast of characters, the same time frame and the same house as a setting; but what the audience sees on stage in the dining room in one play may happen off stage in the living room in another, and vice versa. Though each play can be enjoyed on its own, much of the fun relies on the audience knowing what is going on in the other two plays." Almansi writes: "As we view the second and then the third play of the trilogy, our awareness of what is going on in the rest of the house and likewise the satisfaction of our curiosity grow concurrently. We enjoy guessing what preceded or what will follow the entrance or the exit of the actor from the garden to the lounge, or from the latter to the kitchen, and we slowly build up a complete picture of the proceedings, as if we were Big Brother enjoying a panoptic and all-embracing vision. I dare surmise that this innovation will count in the future development of theatrical technique." Gill comments that despite its length, the farce "is likely

to make you laugh far more often than it is likely to make you look at your watch."

Page, among others, sees a gradual darkening of Ayckbourn's vision over the years. The author's plays, writes Page, "challenge an accepted rule of contemporary comedy: that the audience does not take home the sorrows of the characters after the show. This convention—a matter of both the dramatist's style and the audience's expectations—verges on breakdown when Ayckbourn shifts from farce to real people in real trouble." London *Times* reviewer Bryan Appleyard similarly contends that in recent Ayckbourn dramas "the signs are all there. Encroaching middle age and visionary pessimism are beginning to mark [his] work." This is not to suggest that the author's plays are no longer funny; they simply address such themes as loneliness, adultery, family quarrels, and the twists of fate with candor and sincerity. "Up to now, we have thought of Ayckbourn as the purveyor of amusing plays about suburban bumblers," writes Dan Sullivan in a *Los Angeles Times* review of Ayckbourn's futuristic comedy *Henceforward.* "Here we see him as a thoughtful and painfully honest reporter of the crooked human heart—more crooked every year, it seems." Appleyard observes that Ayckbourn "appears to be entering a visionary middle age and the long-term effect on his plays is liable to be stronger polarization. Villains will really be villains . . . and heroes may well at last begin to be heroes." Indeed, Ayckbourn seems to have become interested in the acceleration of moral decay in his country; plays such as *Way Upstream, A Chorus of Disapproval,* and *A Small Family Business* explore small communities where extreme selfishness holds sway. In the *Chicago Tribune,* for instance, Matthew Wolf calls *A Small Family Business* "a strong study of one man's seduction into a milieu of moral filth." Christiansen concludes that the cumulative effect of these plays puts Ayckbourn "into his rightful place as an agile and insightful playwright in the front ranks of contemporary theatre."

Drama essayist Anthony Curtis declares that Ayckbourn's career "is shining proof that the well-made play is alive and well." Now entering his fourth decade as a playwright, Ayckbourn continues to craft at least one full-length work a year; he also directs his own and others' works in Scarborough and at London's National Theatre. In *Drama,* Michael Leech writes: "There are those who compare [Ayckbourn] to a latterday Moliere, those who say he is a mere play factory, others who might opine that he veers violently between the two extremes. Certainly he is one of our most prolific and gifted writers of comedy, with characters pinned to the page with the finesse and exactness of a collector of unusual butterflies. . . . And he can look back on a body of work that for most writers would be a life-time's effort." London *Times* commentator Andrew Hislop finds Ayckbourn "at the summit of his career. . . . The security of his Scarborough nest has enabled him to continue his work remarkably unaffected by those who have overpraised him, comparing him to Shakespeare, and those who have unjustly reviled him, regarding him as a vacuous, right-wing boulevardier." Certainly Ayckbourn has more champions than critics, both in England and abroad. Hobson, for one, concludes that the public responds to Ayckbourn's work "because he is both a highly comic writer and, dramatically speaking, a first-class conjuror. The tricks he plays in some of his work are stupendous. They are miracles of human ingenuity." Shorter also observes that as a playwright, Ayckbourn is "homely," "comforting," "immediately accessible," and "easily enjoyed." The critic adds: "Witness the crowded audiences of laughing shirt-sleeved holiday-makers. . . . They are never made to frown or allowed to yawn. . . . They are too busy . . . recognizing themselves, or at any rate each other. They are in fact what Mr. Ayckbourn calls his 'source material,' and he means to stick close to it, despite his popular success and the wealth it has brought him."

Ayckbourn told the *Los Angeles Times* that his ambition is to write "totally effortless, totally truthful, unforced comedy shaped like a flawless diamond in which one can see a million reflections, both one's own and other people's." He also commented in the London *Times* that the best part of his work "is not the clapping, it's the feeling at the end of the evening, that you have given the most wonderful party and those five hundred strangers who came in are feeling better. . . . I don't know, but they are sort of unified into a whole and that is marvelous. That's really like shutting the door on a good party and thinking—that went well!"

MEDIA ADAPTATIONS: A Chorus of Disapproval was produced as a feature film in Great Britain in 1989.

BIOGRAPHICAL/CRITICAL SOURCES:

BOOKS

Contemporary Literary Criticism, Gale, Volume 5, 1976, Volume 8, 1978, Volume 18, 1981, Volume 33, 1985.
Dictionary of Literary Biography, Volume 13: *British Dramatists since World War II,* Gale, 1982.
Elsom, John, *Post-War British Theatre,* Routledge & Kegan Paul, 1976.
Hayman, Ronald, *British Theatre since 1955: A Reassessment,* Oxford University Press, 1979.
Joseph, Stephen, *Theatre in the Round,* Barrie & Rockcliff, 1967.
Kerensky, Oleg, *The New British Drama: Fourteen Playwrights since Osborne and Pinter,* Hamish Hamilton, 1977.
Taylor, John Russell, *The Second Wave: British Drama for the Seventies,* Methuen, 1971.
Taylor, John Russell, *Contemporary English Drama,* Holmes & Meier, 1981.
Watson, Ian, *Alan Ayckbourn: Bibliography, Biography, Playography, Theatre Checklist, No. 21,* T.Q. Publications, 1980.
Watson, Ian, *Conversations with Ayckbourn,* Macmillan (London), 1981.
White, Sidney Howard, *Alan Ayckbourn,* Twayne, 1985.

PERIODICALS

Chicago Tribune, July 17, 1982, July 15, 1983, August 2, 1987.
Drama, autumn, 1974, summer, 1978, spring, 1979, summer, 1979, January, 1980, October, 1980, first quarter, 1981, second quarter, 1981, autumn, 1981, spring, 1982, summer, 1982, winter, 1982, Volume 162, 1986.
Encounter, December, 1974, April, 1978.
Guardian, August 7, 1970, August 14, 1974.
Listener, May 23, 1974.
Los Angeles Times, January 20, 1983, March 6, 1984, March 30, 1987, October 28, 1987.
Modern Drama, March, 1983.
Nation, March 8, 1975, December 27, 1975, April 21, 1979.
New Republic, November 9, 1974.
New Statesman, May 31, 1974, July 5, 1974, December 1, 1978, June 13, 1980.
Newsweek, October 21, 1974.
New York, October 28, 1974, December 22, 1975, April 16, 1979, April 2, 1984.
New Yorker, October 21, 1974, December 22, 1975, April 9, 1979.
New York Times, October 20, 1974, February 16, 1977, April 4, 1977, March 25, 1979, March 30, 1979, March 31, 1979, May 1, 1979, October 16, 1981, May 29, 1986, June 15, 1986, June 25, 1986, October 3, 1986, October 29, 1986, November 26, 1986, July 20, 1987, April 15, 1988, June 5, 1988.
Plays and Players, September, 1972, September, 1975, January, 1983, May, 1983, April, 1987.
Observer, February 13, 1977, March 4, 1979.
Sunday Times (London), June 3, 1973, June 8, 1980.
Sunday Times Magazine, February 20, 1977.
Time, May 9, 1979, August 13, 1984.
Times (London), January 5, 1976, January 19, 1980, February 4, 1981, February 2, 1982, June 7, 1982, August 18, 1982, October 6, 1982, October 10, 1983, May 4, 1984, June 4, 1985, April 9, 1986, September 5, 1986, November 5, 1986, December 15, 1986, June 1, 1987, June 8, 1987, June 27, 1987, February 10, 1988, November 23, 1988.
Tribune, February 13, 1981.
Washington Post, July 10, 1977.

—*Sketch by Anne Janette Johnson*

B

BAGWELL, William Francis, Jr. 1923-

PERSONAL: Born January 19, 1923, in Donalds, S.C.; son of William Francis and Eula (Dodson) Bagwell; married Maude Ellis Magill. *Education:* Attended Carnegie Institute of Technology, 1943-44, St. Andrews University, 1945, and Union Theological Seminary, 1947; Furman University, B.A., 1947; Columbia University, M.S., 1950; Emory University, graduate study, 1951-52; New York University, Ph.D., 1968. *Religion:* Society of Friends.

ADDRESSES: Home—P.O. Box 285, Donalds, S.C. 29638.

CAREER: Church World Service, New York City, news bureau director, 1947-49; George Washington University, Washington, D.C., special writer and public relations representative, 1952-55; Furman University, Greenville, S.C., director of news service and editor of alumni magazine, 1955-58; American Friends Service Committee, High Point, N.C., community relations regional director, 1958-65; Quaker Program at the United Nations, New York City, program associate, 1965-67; Cheyney State University, Cheyney, Pa., professor of social science and director of college-community services, 1967-83. Visiting professor of sociology, University of Maryland, European Division in Germany, 1975; program consultant in continuing education, University of North Carolina at Greensboro, 1978; visiting lecturer in sociology, Lander College, 1981-82. Founder and first president, Human Relations Council, Greenville, S.C., 1956-58; member, North Carolina Advisory Committee to the U.S. Civil Rights Commission, 1959-62. *Military service:* U.S. Army, Medical Corps, 1943-46.

MEMBER: United Nations Association (board member of Manhattan chapter, 1966-67), American Civil Liberties Union, N.A.A.C.P., National Urban Education Association, American Friends Service Committee (member of the board, Southern Region, 1986—), Adult Education Association, National Association of Human Rights Workers, Fellowship of Reconciliation, Carolinians Historical Society, Sigma Delta Chi.

AWARDS, HONORS: Quaker Leadership grant, 1960; Mary Campbell Memorial grant for research in human relations, 1965; Kappa Delta Pi human relations award, 1965, New York University Founders Day Award, 1969.

WRITINGS:

(Contributing editor) *Equal Protection of the Laws in North Carolina,* North Carolina Advisory Committee to the U.S. Civil Rights Commission, 1962.

(Contributing editor) *A Guide for Improving Teacher Education in Human Rights,* University of Oklahoma, 1971, revised edition, 1973.

School Desegregation in the Carolinas, University of South Carolina Press, 1972.

Her First Hundred Years: The Life and Times of Dora Martin Dodson, 1878-1980, Beebe Press, 1980.

The Martin Family of Old Abbeville District, South Carolina: The Story of a Family and a Region, Beebe Press, 1981, revised edition, 1988.

The Days of a Man: Poems of a Lifetime, Beebe Press, 1983.

From Royalty to Slavery to Freedom: The Story of One Carolina Black Family's Heritage, Beebe Press, 1988.

(Contributing editor) *The Dodson Family of North Farnham Parish, Virginia: A History and Geneology of Their Descendents,* Southern Historical Press, 1989.

Contributor of poems, book reviews, and articles on human rights and human relations to *Quaker Life, Friends Journal, Christian Century, Town and Country Church, Commission, World Call, Highroad, American Bard* and *Cheyney Faculty Journal.*

WORK IN PROGRESS: Research in human relations, black studies, and social history of the South.

SIDELIGHTS: William Francis Bagwell, Jr., told *CA:* "I was encouraged and challenged by several teachers in high school and college to develop my writing skills. One of these mentors I remember especially—she also challenged us students to 'think big,' to 'think long-range' and to set our life goals 'a little higher than you really think you can achieve so that you will never lack for motivation.' I took her advice literally and in an informal journal which I kept during my late teens, I listed the two major goals: to try to do something toward helping to develop a peaceful world, and to do all I could to bring about changes in the unjust racial scene which existed, especially in the South where I had grown up. I have learned that these goals were considerably higher than I could hope to accomplish alone, but they have led me into a most exciting, challenging, and often frustrating but satisfying career, or series of careers! From being a conscientious objector in the Army Medical Corps in World War II, to losing a job for refusing to sign one of those atrocious 'loyalty oaths' during the McCarthy era of the 1950s, to becoming deeply involved in the Civil Rights Movement for several years in the 1950s-60s, to working as a human relations consultant with U.N. staff and delegates and U.S. peace groups during the late 1960s to providing consultation to various groups and agencies and institutions on 'racism,' 'sexism,' 'ageism,' and other human rights/human relations issues while teaching at Cheyney State and other colleges from 1967 to recent years—my adult years have been busy enough that I have had little time to lie on the beach and daydream about utopia. I haven't reached those youthful goals, but I have learned to understand and appreciate myself and others much more and I have come to know from experience the complexities of social problems and social change and that the kind of goals which I chose years ago must be sought for and fought for by every generation as long as we humans inhabit this planet (and universe)."

Bagwell is currently "spending full time restoring [his] ancestral farm/homestead and doing research and writing, and lecturing."

* * *

BAILEY, Sydney D(awson) 1916-

PERSONAL: Born September 1, 1916, in Hull, England; son of Frank Burgess (a grain broker) and Elsie (a teacher; maiden name, May) Bailey; married Jennie Elena Brenda Friedrich (a social worker), April 26, 1945; children: Martin Dawson, Marion Elizabeth. *Education:* Attended secondary school in Worksop, Nottinghamshire, England. *Religion:* Society of Friends (Quakers).

ADDRESSES: Home and office—19 Deansway, East Finchley, London N2 0NG, England.

CAREER: National Newsletter, London, England, editor, 1946-48; Hansard Society for Parliamentary Government, London, secretary, 1948-54; Society of Friends (Quakers), New York City, representative to United Nations, 1954-58; Carnegie Endowment for International Peace, New York City, research fellow, 1958-60; writer, 1960—. Former chairman of Division of International Affairs, British Council of Churches; Council on Christian Approaches to Defence and Disarmament, founding member, former chairman, currently vice-president. Member of advisory committees of British Foreign Office. *Wartime service:* Society of Friends, attached to ambulance unit, 1940-46; served in China-Burma-India Theatre.

MEMBER: International Institute for Strategic Studies, Royal Institute of International Affairs, American Society for International Law.

AWARDS, HONORS: Rufus Jones Award, World Academy of Art and Science, 1984, for contribution to world peace; Doctor of Civil Law, Oxford University, 1985.

WRITINGS:

(Editor) *Aspects of American Government,* Hansard Society for Parliamentary Government, 1950.
Constitutions of British Colonies (pamphlet), Hansard Society for Parliamentary Government, 1950.
(Editor) *Parliamentary Government in the Commonwealth,* Philosophical Library, 1951.
Lords and Commons (pamphlet), H.M.S.O., 1951.
(Contributor) Norman J. Padelford, editor, *Contemporary International Relations Readings, 1950-1951,* Harvard University Press, 1951.

Parliamentary Government (pamphlet), British Council, 1952, 2nd edition, 1958.
Ceylon, Hutchinson, 1952.
(Editor) *The British Party System,* Praeger, 1952, 2nd edition, 1953.
Naissance du nouvelles democraties (title means "The Birth of New Democracies"), Armand Colin, 1953.
Parliamentary Government in Southern Asia, Institute of Pacific Relations, 1953.
(Editor) *Problems of Parliamentary Government in Colonies,* Hansard Society for Parliamentary Government, 1953.
(Editor) *The Future of the House of Lords,* Praeger, 1954.
British Parliamentary Democracy, Houghton, 1958, 3rd edition, 1970.
The General Assembly of the United Nations, Praeger, 1960, 2nd edition, 1964, reprinted, Greenwood Press, 1978.
The Secretariat of the United Nations, Praeger, 1962, 2nd edition, 1964, reprinted, Greenwood Press, 1978.
The Troika and the Future of the United Nations (pamphlet), Carnegie Endowment for International Peace, 1962.
(Contributor) Saul H. Medlovitz, editor, *Legal and Political Problems of World Order,* World Law Fund, 1962.
A Short Political Guide to the United Nations, Praeger, 1963.
(Contributor) Evan Luard, editor, *The Evolution of International Organization,* Thames and Hudson, 1966.
(Contributor) *Peace Is Still the Prize,* S.C.M. Press, 1966.
(Contributor) Richard A. Falk and Mendlovitz, editors, *The Strategy of World Order,* World Law Fund, 1966.
(Contributor) Robert W. Gregg and Michael Barkun, editors, *The United Nations System and Its Functions,* Van Nostrand, 1968.
The Veto in the Security Council (pamphlet), Carnegie Endowment for International Peace, 1968.
Voting in the Security Council, Indiana University Press, 1970.
Chinese Representation in the Security Council and General Assembly of the United Nations, Institute for the Study of International Organization, 1970.
(Contributor) George Cunningham, editor, *Britain and the World in the Seventies,* Weidenfeld & Nicolson, 1970.
The Peaceful Settlement of International Disputes, United Nations Institute for Training Research, 1970, 3rd edition, 1971.
Prohibitions and Restraints in War, Oxford University Press, 1972.
The Procedure of the United Nations Security Council, Clarendon Press, 1975, 2nd edition, 1988.
(Contributor) K. Venkata Raman, editor, *Dispute Settlement through the United Nations,* Oceana, 1977.
Christian Perspectives on Nuclear Weapons, British Council of Churches, 1981.
(Contributor) Davidson Nicol, editor, *Paths to Peace,* Pergamon, 1981.
How Wars End: The United Nations and the Termination of Armed Conflict, 1946-1964, two volumes, Clarendon Press, 1982.
(Contributor) Paul Albrecht and Ninan Koshy, editors, *Before It's Too Late: The Challenge of Nuclear Disarmament,* World Council of Churches, 1983.
The Making of Resolution 242, Nijhoff, 1985.
(Contributor) *New Dictionary of Christian Ethics,* S.C.M. Press, 1986.
(Contributor) *United Nations—Still Humanity's Best Hope,* UNA, 1986.
War and Conscience in the Nuclear Age, Macmillan, 1987.

Human Rights and Responsibilities in Britain and Ireland: A Christian Perspective, Macmillan, 1988.

Contributor of several hundred articles to periodicals, including *Economist, Spectator, Review of Politics, World Today, Survival, Theology, International Affairs,* and *American Journal of International Law.* Editor of *Parliamentary Affairs,* 1948-54.

WORK IN PROGRESS: A study of the Arab-Israeli wars of 1947-49, 1956, 1967, and 1973, and the different peace processes after each; a study of the negotiation and implementation of the armistice in Korea.

SIDELIGHTS: In a *New Society* review of Sydney D. Bailey's *How Wars End: The United Nations and the Termination of Armed Conflict, 1946-64,* critic Adam Roberts notes that "there is a vast literature on how wars are fought; there is at least a respectable body of literature on how they begin; but much less is known about how they end." Bailey's book is an attempt to deal with this subject, which Roberts calls "both interesting and important, not least because, in this grossly over-warmed world in which we live, stopping wars before they get out of hand is an obvious prerequisite for survival."

In his extensive research for *How Wars End,* Bailey read many hundreds of books and documents and found that since 1945 there have been about 150 "small wars" throughout the world. "Many of them," says Roberts, "ended without the direct involvement of the United Nations," but Bailey limits his study to seven well-documented cases in which the UN played a leading role. *Guardian* reviewer David Ennals notes that the UN "usually becomes involved [in conflicts] at the eleventh hour when the situation is already critical or when the fighting has actually begun. And if it fails to achieve a ceasefire it is listed as another UN failure." Bailey concentrates on UN successes, analyzing the means by which peaceful settlements are achieved, and, more importantly, writes Ennals, suggesting "the enormously wide range of methods by which the services of the UN can be brought into play. . . . The simple message of this far from simple book is that the United Nations must be used to far greater effect than has so far been the case." In Bailey's words, the UN ought to "be engaged far more in prophylactic diplomacy." Furthermore, notes *Jewish Chronicle* reviewer Jon Kimche, "Bailey's name will be blessed by every student, politician and diplomat for years to come for providing this invaluable information in such a compact, well-organised and accessible manner."

This recommendation concurs with the observations of other critics who find Bailey's books to be consistently perceptive and objective on the subject of international politics. In a *Middle East International* review, Harold Beeley states, "Sydney Bailey's writings . . . have earned him a unique reputation for the meticulous and dispassionate analysis of the work of the United Nations." In *The Making of Resolution 242,* for example, says Beeley, "He is too modest to push his argument beyond the limits of the unquestionable evidence; but within those limits he leaves nothing unremarked, and no student of the subject can afford to ignore his work." Writing about *War and Conscience in the Nuclear Age* in a *Times Literary Supplement* review, Geoffrey Best suggests, "What [Bailey] is perhaps uniquely good at is presenting international humanitarian law (as he prefers to call it) in terms which the serious-minded common man can understand, and pinpointing the parts which most invite conscientious scrutiny."

Sydney Bailey told *CA* that he began writing while recuperating in a Calcutta hospital during World War II: "I had been in China with a Quaker ambulance unit, and as we were constantly on the move and had no access to Western newspapers or radios, we knew almost nothing about what was happening in the outside world. After Japanese forces had occupied Burma, there were no land routes out of unoccupied China, so when I became seriously ill, the U.S. Air Force flew me over the Hump (the Himalayas) to India. I had a long spell in hospital, and after I'd read the few books in English in the hospital library, I began to occupy my time by writing a weekly newsletter on world affairs for my erstwhile colleagues in the Chinese interior.

"When I got back to London in 1944, I ran into George Orwell, who was then literary editor of the *Tribune.* Orwell asked me to review some books about China, and I soon graduated to writing short weekly pieces on Asian politics. Orwell undoubtedly influenced my style: he once told me that economy and simplicity of language are essential if we are to resist tyranny.

"Although I remain unrepentantly British, I have traveled widely and spent seven happy years in the United States. I seem to be drawn to trouble spots like Northern Ireland and the Middle East. I have been fortunate, because I have found friendship wherever I have traveled, and I have never felt threatened. Although my formal education ended when I was fifteen, I have tried to write as a scholar, but for practitioners rather than for other scholars. All my books deal with some aspect or other of building a more just and peaceful world, including seven volumes about the political functions of the United Nations. I know the UN has many defects, but it's the only UN we have. It is easy to criticise it, but the challenge is to improve it.

"I work at a cluttered desk overlooking a cheerful garden. I usually draft in my head first, often while driving, and then write in manuscript. When the material has been typed, I revise and abridge ruthlessly, as early in the day as possible, when my mind is still reasonably sharp. I find that editors and publishers are more cooperative with authors who submit intelligible typescripts. I have only one piece of advice to aspiring writers of nonfiction: Don't put everything you know into your first book."

AVOCATIONAL INTERESTS: Music, photography, people.

BIOGRAPHICAL/CRITICAL SOURCES:

PERIODICALS

American Journal of International Law, Volume 78, 1984.
Guardian (Manchester), November 11, 1982.
Jewish Chronicle, May 27, 1983, June 12, 1987.
Journal of International Affairs, winter, 1984.
Middle East, January, 1983.
Middle East International, November 22, 1985.
New Society, December 2, 1982.
Times Literary Supplement, July 15, 1988.

*   *   *

BALDWIN, Christina 1946-

PERSONAL: Born April 16, 1946, in Great Falls, Mont.; daughter of Leo E. Baldwin (a social service administrator) and Connie McGregor (a real estate agent; maiden name, Anderson). *Education:* Macalester College, B.A. (cum laude), 1968; Columbia Pacific University, M.A., 1986. *Politics:* "Feminist." *Religion:* "Yes."

ADDRESSES: Home—Golden Valley, Minn. *Office*—c/o The Lazear Agency, 430 First Ave. N., Minneapolis, Minn. 55401. *Agent*—The Lazear Agency, 430 First Ave. N., Minneapolis, Minn. 55401.

CAREER: American Friends Service Committee, San Francisco, Calif., peace intern, 1968-69, Philadelphia, Pa., coordinator of youth affairs, 1970-71; American Bicentennial Commission, St. Paul, Minn., director of community relations, 1975; Chrysalis Center for Women, Minneapolis, Minn., counselor, 1976; Community Programs in Arts and Sciences, St. Paul, writer-in-residence and teacher, 1977—; A Writer for Writers (consulting service), Minneapolis, proprietor, 1983—. Teacher of writing classes, University of Minnesota Continuing Education in the Arts. Partner in Educare Psychotherapy (private clinical practice), 1978-86. Lecturer and conductor of seminars.

MEMBER: National Organization for Women, Authors Guild, Authors League of America, Writers' Union.

WRITINGS:

One to One: Self-Understanding through Journal Writing, M. Evans, 1977.
Words in Our Pockets: The Feminist Writers Guild Handbook, Booklegger Press, 1984.
(With Lynne Burmyn) *Kid Signs: An Astrological Guide for Parents,* St. Martin's, 1985, new edition, Fawcett, 1988.
(With Judith N. Brown) *A Second Start: A Widow's Guide to Financial Survival at a Time of Emotional Crisis,* Simon & Schuster, 1986.
Life's Companion: Journal Writing as a Spiritual Quest, Bantam, 1990.

WORK IN PROGRESS: "Yes."

AVOCATIONAL INTERESTS: Local social activism ("think globally; act locally"), hiking, beachcombing, reading, good conversation, walking her dog.

* * *

BALL, Nicole (Janice) 1948-

PERSONAL: Born February 29, 1948, in Utica, N.Y.; daughter of Ira Milton (a lawyer) and Jeanne Catherine (Wantz) Ball. *Education:* Attended University of Geneva, 1968-69; University of Pennsylvania, B.A., 1970; University of Sussex, M.A., 1971.

ADDRESSES: Home—Gaithersburg, Md. *Office*—National Security Archive, Washington, D.C.

CAREER: University of Sussex, Brighton, England, research fellow at Institute for the Study of International Organisation, 1971-76; independent researcher, 1976-79; Swedish Institute of International Affairs, Stockholm, visiting research associate, 1980-86; National Security Archive, Washington, D.C., director of analysis, 1987—.

AWARDS, HONORS: World Hunger was named an outstanding academic book of 1981-82 by *Choice.*

WRITINGS:

Regional Conflicts and the International System: A Case Study of Bangladesh (monograph), Institute for the Study of International Organisation, University of Sussex, 1975.
Hunger and International Development: A Bibliography, Center for the Study of Armament and Disarmament, California State University, Los Angeles, 1978.
World Hunger: A Guide to the Economic and Political Dimensions, American Bibliographical Center-Clio Press, 1981.
Militaer och politik i tredje vaerlden (title means "The Military and Politics in the Third World"), Swedish Institute of International Affairs, 1981.
The Military in the Development Process: A Guide to Issues, Regina Press & Publishing, 1982.

(Editor with Milton Leitenberg) *The Structure of the Defence Industry: An International Study,* Croom Helm, 1983.
Third-World Security Expenditure: A Statistical Compendium, National Defense Research Institute (Stockholm), 1984.
Security and Economy in the Third World, Princeton University Press, 1988.
(Translator) Catherine Clement, *The Weary Sons of Freud,* Verso/Methuen, 1988.

CONTRIBUTOR

Stephanie G. Neuman and Robert E. Harkavy, editors, *Arms Transfers in the Modern World,* Praeger, 1979.
Asbjoern Eide and Marek Thee, editors, *Problems of Contemporary Militarism,* Croom Helm, 1980.
Helena Tuomi and Raimo Vaeyrynen, editors, *Militarization and Arms Production,* Croom Helm, 1983.
William Page, editor, *The Future of Politics,* Francis Pinter, 1983.
Bo Huldt, editor, *Militarization of Politics and Politization of the Military,* Swedish Institute of International Affairs, 1983.
In Pursuit of Disarmament: Conversion from Military to Civil Production in Sweden; Report by the Special Expert Inga Thorsson, Volume II, Liber, 1985.
Thomas Ohlson, editor, *Arms Transfer Limitations and Third World Security,* Oxford University Press, 1988.

OTHER

Contributor of approximately thirty articles and reviews to international studies journals.

* * *

BANKSON, Douglas (Henneck) 1920-

PERSONAL: Born May 13, 1920, in Valley, Wash.; son of Russell Arden (an author, editor, and journalist) and Ella (Henneck) Bankson; married Beverly Olga Carlson, June 12, 1943; children: Jon Douglas, Daniel Duke, Barbro Sloan. *Education:* University of Washington, B.A., 1943, M.A., 1948, Ph.D., 1954.

ADDRESSES: Home—3892 West 15th Ave., Vancouver, British Columbia, Canada V6R 2Z9.

CAREER: Seattle Star, Seattle, Wash., reporter and columnist, 1942-43, 1945-46; Beatty Stevens Agency (advertising firm), Seattle, head copywriter and account executive, 1946-50; Frye Art Museum, Seattle, research director, 1951-52; free-lance advertising account executive, 1952-54; University of Idaho, Moscow, instructor in English, 1955-57; University of Montana, Missoula, assistant professor of English, 1957-59, associate professor of drama, 1959-65, associate director of University of Montana Theare and resident playwright, 1959-65; University of British Columbia, Vancouver, professor of creative writing, 1965-85, chairman of department, 1977-82, professor emeritus, 1985—. Member of Faculty Association, University of British Columbia. Director, Masquer Summer Theatre, 1961-65; co-founder and director, New Play Centre, 1970-72, president, 1972-83; vice president, Green Thumb Players, 1978-82. *Military service:* U.S. Navy, 1943-46; became lieutenant junior grade.

MEMBER: Canadian Association of University Teachers, Playwrights Union of Canada.

WRITINGS:

PLAYS

"Shellgame" (two-act), first produced in Missoula, Mont., at University of Montana Theatre, October, 1960, revised version first produced Off-Off-Broadway at Playbox Theatre, July, 1968.

"The Ball" (one-act), first produced at University of Montana Theatre, March, 1961.

"Nature in the Raw Is Seldom" (one-act), first produced at University of Montana Theatre, March, 1962.

"Fallout" (two-act), first produced at University of Montana Theatre, February, 1963.

"Shootup" (one-act), first produced at University of Montana Theatre, March, 1963.

"Resthome" (two-act), first produced at University of Montana Theatre, March, 1965.

"The Ants Go Marching" (two-act), first produced in Bellingham, Wash., at Western Washington State College Theatre, May, 1966.

"Stonehenge" (two-act), first produced in Halifax, Nova Scotia, at Neptune Theatre, May, 1972.

"Lenore Nevermore" (two-act; also see below), first produced in Vancouver, B.C., at Troupe Theatre, May, 1972.

"The Schweinhuef Quartet" (one-act), first produced in Vancouver at Tamahnous Theatre, June, 1978.

"Felicity" (two-act), frist produced in Vancouver, B.C., at the Kitsilano Theatre, May, 1982.

"Dying Echoes: For Edgar Allan Poe" (two-act), first produced in Richmond, B.C., at the Gateway Theatre, November, 1984, revised version first appeared as "Mr. Poe" (two-act) in Calgary, Alberta, at the International Theatre Symposium, June, 1985.

BALLETS

"The Waterwitch" (one-act), music by Dolas Bakos, first produced at University of Montana Theatre, May, 1960.

"Magoo" (one-act), music by Bakos, first produced at University of Montana Theatre, May, 1960.

RADIO PLAYS

"Signore Lizard," Canadian Broadcasting Corp. (CBC-Radio), 1975.

"Lenore Nevermore" (adapted from own play), CBC-Radio, 1976.

"Whistle," CBC-Radio, 1977.

"Ella," CBC-Radio, 1981.

OTHER

Also author of *Cave-in,* a novel, with Wallace Graves, 1955, "The Waterfinder," a film script commisioned by CBC-TV, 1966, "Poe," a two-act opera libretto with music by S. M. Clark, 1983, and "Cherry Tree," a film screenplay, with Jacob Zilber, 1974. Contributor of stories to *Carolina Quarterly;* contributor of book reviews, news and feature stories, and articles to newspapers and magazines.

*   *   *

BARNETTE, Henlee H(ulix) 1911-

PERSONAL: Born August 14, 1911, in Taylorsville, N.C.; son of William Alexander and Winnie Helen Barnette; married Charlotte Ford (died July, 1953); married Helen Poarch (a teacher), June 9, 1956; children: (first marriage) John, Wayne; (second marriage) Martha, James. *Education:* Wake Forest University, B.A., 1940; Southern Baptist Seminary, Th.M., 1943, Th.D., 1948, Ph.D., 1975.

ADDRESSES: Home—2909 Meadowlark Ave., Louisville, Ky. 40206. *Office*—Norton Psychiatric Clinic, 200 East Chestnut St., Louisville, Ky. 40402.

CAREER: Ordained to ministry, 1935; served as pastor for churches in North Carolina and Kentucky, and as superintendent of Central Baptist Mission in Louisville, Ky. Samford University, Birmingham, Ala., assistant professor of sociology, 1946-47; Stetson University, De Land, Fla., professor of sociology, 1947-51; Southern Baptist Seminary, Louisville, professor of Christian ethics, 1951-77; University of Louisville, School of Medicine, Louisville, clinical professor of psychiatry and behavioral sciences, 1977—.

MEMBER: Baptist World Alliance (member of study commission on ethics), American Society of Christian Ethics (member of board of directors, 1962-66), American Association for the Advancement of Science, Ethics, Society, and Life Sciences.

AWARDS, HONORS: Carnegie Foundation research grant, 1949-50; faculty fellowship from American Association of Theological Schools, Harvard University, 1959-60; distinguished alumnus award from Wake Forest University, 1970; distinguished service award from Christian Life Commission of Southern Baptist Convention, 1971; distinguished citizens award from city of Louisville.

WRITINGS:

Introducing Christian Ethics, Broadman, 1961.
An Introduction to Communism, Baker Book, 1964.
The New Theology and Morality, Westminster, 1967.
Crucial Problems in Christian Perspective, Westminster, 1970.
The Drug Crisis and the Church, Westminster, 1971.
The Church and the Ecological Crisis, Eerdmans, 1972.
Exploring Medical Ethics, Mercer University Press, 1982.
Your Freedom to Be Whole, Westminster Press, 1984.

WORK IN PROGRESS: Research on bioethics.

*   *   *

BARROWS, Anita 1947-

PERSONAL: Born January 13, 1947, in Brooklyn, N.Y.; daughter of Joseph (a pharmaceutical consultant) and Sylvia (Kanfer) Barrows; married Richard Friedman (a computer scientist), October 31, 1972. *Education:* San Francisco State College (now University), B.A., 1969; Boston University, M.A., 1970; attended Camberwell School of Arts and Crafts, 1973; University of California, Berkeley, Ph.D. candidate, 1975—.

ADDRESSES: Home and office—546 The Alameda, Berkeley, Calif. 94707. *Agent*—Jonathan Clowes, 22 Prince Albert Rd., London NW1 7ST, England.

CAREER: Poet and translator. Private tutor; University of California Extension, Berkeley, instructor in English, 1972, 1974. Teacher and administrative assistant, California "Poetry in the Schools" program, 1972, 1974.

AWARDS, HONORS: Award from *Atlantic,* 1964, for poem entered in high school writing contest; award from *New Magazine,* 1971, for "Upon a Time," a sequence of poems.

WRITINGS:

Emigration (poems), Spindrift Press, 1972.
No More Masks, Doubleday, 1973.
The Limits, Black Mesa, 1982.

TRANSLATOR

Didier Coste, *Sink Your Teeth in the Moon,* Calder & Boyars, 1974.
Julia Kristeva, *About Chinese Women,* Urizen, 1977.
Felix Milani, *The Convict,* St. Martin's, 1978.

Marguerite Duras, *Whole Days in the Trees,* Calder & Boyars, 1984.
Simone Benmussa, *Benmussa Directs: Portrait of Dora by Helene Cixous and the Singular Life of Albert Nobbs by Simone Benmussa,* Riverrun Press, 1985.

OTHER

Poetry editor for KPFA-Radio, Berkeley, Calif., 1970-72.

WORK IN PROGRESS: Two translations for Calder & Boyars, Roland Dubillard's "The Beet Garden," a play, and Rene De Obaldia's *Innocentines;* a book of children's poetry; two children's books; additional translations; poetry.

SIDELIGHTS: "Feel I am undergoing a long apprenticeship, annexing various voices, experiences, teachings, to my own voice," Anita Barrows wrote *CA.* "Hopefully the apprenticeship will last all my life, in which sense I consider all of my work to be one piece. Am fluent in French and Italian, do translations for the discipline of it and the love of working as a craftsman with language."*

*   *   *

BARTLETT, Kathleen
    See PAINE, Lauran (Bosworth)

*   *   *

BASS, William M(arvin III)   1928-

PERSONAL: Born August 30, 1928, in Staunton, Va.; married Mary Anna Owen (a nutritionist), August 8, 1953; children: Charles E., William Marvin IV, James O. *Education:* University of Virginia, B.A., 1951; University of Kentucky, M.S., 1956; University of Pennsylvania, Ph.D., 1961.

ADDRESSES: Home—8201 Bennington Dr., Knoxville, Tenn. 37919. *Office*—Department of Anthropology, 252 South Stadium Hall, University of Tennessee, Knoxville, Tenn. 37916.

CAREER: University of Kentucky, Lexington, administrative assistant in counseling office, 1954-55, acting director of counseling office, 1955-56; University of Pennsylvania, School of Medicine, Philadelphia, instructor in physical anthropology, 1960; University of Nebraska, Lincoln, instructor in anthropology, 1960; University of Kansas, Lawrence, instructor, 1960-61, assistant professor, 1961-64, associate professor, 1964-67, professor of anthropology, 1967-71; University of Tennessee, Knoxville, professor of anthropology and head of department, 1971—. Physical anthropologist on river basin surveys, Smithsonian Institution, summers, 1956-62, 1964-70. *Military service:* U.S. Army, 1951-53.

MEMBER: American Association of Physical Anthropologists (fellow), American Anthropological Association (fellow), Current Anthropology (associate), Society of American Archaeology, Plains Conference for Anthropology, Missouri Archaeological Society, Kansas Academy of Science, Anthropological Society of Washington, D.C., Sigma Xi.

AWARDS, HONORS: National Science Foundation grants, 1962, 1963, 1965, 1967, and 1969; National Park Service grants, 1963 and 1966; Wenner-Gren Foundation (for travel to Iran), 1964; H. Bernard Fink Award for excellence in teaching, 1965; National Geographic Society grant, 1968; University of Tennessee Alumni Public Distinguished Professor Award, 1978.

WRITINGS:

(Contributor) R. F. G. Spier, *Field Handbook of the Human Skeleton,* Missouri Archaeological Society, 1962.
(With David R. Evans, Richard L. Jantz, and Douglas H. Ubelaker) *The Leavenworth Site Cemetery: Archaeology and Physical Anthropology,* University of Kansas Publications in Anthropology, 1971.
Human Osteology, Missouri Archaeological Society, 1971, 2nd edition published as *Human Osteology: A Laboratory and Field Manual of the Human Skeleton,* edited by Evans, 1971.
A Review of Human Origins, University of Tennessee Press, 1972.
(Contributor) *Fay Tolton and the Initial Middle Missouri Variant,* Missouri Archaeological Society, 1976.
(With Larry Miller and Ramona Miller) *Human Evidence in Criminal Justice,* Pilgrimage, 1983.
(Contributor) Ted A. Rathbun and Jane E. Buikstra, *Human Identification: Case Studies in Forensic Anthropology,* C. C Thomas, 1984.

Writer of course materials in anthropology for University of Kansas; author or co-author of about seventy reports and articles based on archaeological and anthropological investigations, including series published by Smithsonian Institution, 1969. Contributor of about fifteen reviews to professional journals.*

*   *   *

BATCHELOR, Reg
    See PAINE, Lauran (Bosworth)

*   *   *

BATRA, Raveendra N(ath)   1943-
    (Ravi Batra)

PERSONAL: Born June 27, 1943, in Punjab, India; immigrated to the United States, 1966; naturalized U.S. citizen, 1976; son of Harish C. (a professor of Sanskrit) and Kusum (Thakur) Batra; married Diane J. Spiegel (in business), February 21, 1970 (divorced, 1981); married wife, Sunitra, 1986; children: (first marriage) Marlo Sheila. *Education:* Punjab University, B.A., 1963; Delhi School of Economics, M.A., 1965; Southern Illinois University, Carbondale, Ph.D., 1969.

ADDRESSES: Office—Department of Economics, Southern Methodist University, Dallas, Tex. 75275.

CAREER: Hindu College, Delhi, India, assistant lecturer in economics, 1965-66; Southern Illinois University, Carbondale, assistant professor of economics, 1969-70; University of Western Ontario, London, assistant professor of economics, 1970-72; Southern Methodist University, Dallas, Tex., associate professor, 1972-73, professor of economics and head of department, 1973—.

MEMBER: American Economic Association.

AWARDS, HONORS: Canada Council fellowship, 1971-72.

WRITINGS:

UNDER NAME RAVI BATRA

Studies in the Pure Theory of International Trade, St. Martin's, 1973.
The Pure Theory of International Trade under Uncertainty, Wiley, 1975.

The Downfall of Capitalism and Communism: A New Study of History, Humanities, 1979, 2nd revised edition, Taylor Publishing (Dallas, Tex.), 1990.

Muslim Civilization and the Crisis in Iran, Ananda Marga Publications, 1980.

Prout: The Alternative to Capitalism and Marxism, Ananda Marga Publications, 1980.

Regular Cycles of Money, Inflation, Regulation and Depression, Venus Books, 1985, reprinted as *Regular Economic Cycles: Money, Inflation, Regulation and Depression,* St. Martin's, 1989.

The Great Depression of 1990: Why It's Got to Happen—How to Protect Yourself, Venus Books, 1985.

Surviving the Great Depression of 1990: Protect Your Assets and Investments—And Come Out on Top, Simon & Schuster, 1988.

Prout and Economic Reform in the Third World, Ananda Marga Publications, 1989.

Contributor of numerous articles to economic journals.

SIDELIGHTS: In what *Los Angeles Times Book Review* critic Paul Erdman calls "an unusual mixture of Far Eastern philosophical/historical thoughts on the phenomenon of cyclicality in our society based on the theories of an Indian by the name of P. R. Sarkar," Ravi Batra's book *The Great Depression of 1990: Why It's Got to Happen—How to Protect Yourself* has caused much debate among critics. Although Batra, who became a full professor of economics at Southern Methodist University at the young age of thirty, has outstanding academic credentials and has made accurate predictions about the Iran-Iraq war, the European recession, and the incredible rise in the Dow-Jones industrial average, many economists doubt his theories when they learn they are based on the teachings of the Indian guru, Prabhat Ranjan Sarkar.

Sarkar, the leader of India's Ananda Marga (Path of Bliss) sect, teaches in his *Human Society* that "societies are successively characterized by four groups—laborers, warriors, intellectuals and acquisitors," reports a *People* article by Eric Levin and Anne Maier. "The poor laborers never get to run things, but the other three dominate in turn until the acquisitors rule the roost to the detriment of everybody else." Batra picks up this theory and applies it to U.S. history, which he says is ruled by acquisitors, or capitalists. Because the American government is structured to aid the wealthy, its laws have made it possible for one percent of the population to own over a third of the nation's wealth. When the disparity between the upper and lower classes becomes great enough, the economic structure of the country collapses and a depression occurs. According to Batra, such collapses happen in thirty or sixty year cycles, the last one being the Great Depression of the 1930s.

Because Sarkar was once imprisoned for murder, basing an economic theory on the guru's philosophy has seriously undermined Batra's credibility in the eyes of his fellow economists, even though Sarkar was later acquitted on appeal. Other critics, however, have been more objective in finding flaws in Batra's theories. Economist William N. Parker, for one, notes in the *New York Times Book Review* that Batra's cycle theory ignores "the serious depression of the mid-1890's." *New York Times*'s Christopher Lehmann-Haupt also points out that while "it may be true that those who forget the past are condemned to repeat it, it's also true that when the past does repeat itself it rarely appears the same."

Nevertheless, some authorities like author and former investment banker Michael M. Thomas advise us not to disregard Batra's ideas. Of the economist's book *Surviving the Great Depression of 1990: Protect Your Assets and Investments—And Come Out on Top,* Thomas asserts in the *New York Times Book Review:* "Hogwash it is not, although gospel it certainly isn't either. Mr. Batra's findings and views on the effects on the American economy of wealth concentration deserve airing and serious debate. His conclusion that Armageddon will take the form of a precipitous collapse of the dollar abroad and . . . at home seems as realistic as any other that I've seen put forward." And Parker remarks that although the economist's theory is not perfect, "Mr. Batra may be on to something" in his analysis of Sarkar's teachings.

To survive the coming depression, Batra suggests people liquidate their assets and keep their money in sound banks for safe keeping. But in order to prevent the predicted crisis and avoid more depressions in the future, the author believes that a new form of government policy will be needed. He discusses this possibility in *Prout: The Alternative to Capitalism and Marxism* and in the second edition of *The Downfall of Capitalism and Marxism.* Prout was originally developed by Sarkar and is an acronym for Progressive Utilization Theory. A system similar to capitalism, Prout would allow free enterprise, but would levy a progressive property tax on the wealthiest segments of the population. More bank regulations and a wealth tax would also be part of Prout. Batra recognizes, however, that such proposals would not be popular in Washington, D.C., or on Wall Street, but he predicts that the 1990 depression could make them necessary. "It all sounds very far out," acknowledges Lehmann-Haupt. "Which is what makes you worry that he may be right."

AVOCATIONAL INTERESTS: Meditation, tennis, studying yoga, philosophy, and religion.

CA INTERVIEW

CA interviewed Raveendra N. Batra by telephone on September 6, 1989, at his office at Southern Methodist University in Dallas, Texas.

CA: According to an article in Dallas Life Magazine, your father, who was a professor in India, wanted you to become a police chief or a magistrate.

BATRA: Yes, something like that!

CA: Was he disappointed when you didn't follow his plan?

BATRA: He was initially, sort of. But when I got a scholarship to come to the United States, he was very happy.

CA: Why did you want to come to the United States?

BATRA: I wanted to do my Ph.D. in economics, and the U.S. has more advanced studies in economics than India. I went to Southern Illinois University, which offered me a scholarship.

CA: At first you planned to get your degree and return to India, but you stayed on and became a citizen of the United States. How did that come about?

BATRA: I got married to an American girl, and that was my main reason for staying on. She wouldn't have liked it in India.

CA: How do you feel about India now? Do you miss it in some way?

BATRA: I wish I could do something about their economic development. There is so much corruption and bureaucracy in the country that I sometimes wish I could do something to destroy the corruption and help them develop faster. I don't go back to India frequently, but I did go in February of 1988.

CA: Could you act as a financial consultant to the Indian government?

BATRA: No. The theories that I offer are so unorthodox that even my fellow Indians don't want to take them on—especially when I condemn corruption; then they don't want anything to do with me.

CA: The religion you practice is somewhat different from the religion practiced by many Americans today. Isn't that something you might miss about India?

BATRA: I really don't miss that, because religion in India is practiced in your own home. A certain technique of meditation is taught, and you can stay at home and practice it. You don't have to go to a church or a temple.

CA: You meditate each day, I believe. What kind of schedule do you follow for that?

BATRA: In the past I used to meditate many hours each day, sometimes up to ten hours. But now I'm so busy that it's whenever I can find time, usually one or two hours.

CA: Your economic theory is based largely on that of your mentor, P. R. Sarkar. You attended a lecture of his about twenty-five years ago that seems to have changed your life.

BATRA: Yes. I was looking for a teacher at that time, a genuine teacher who could supply some solutions to India's economic problems and India's corruption. He said that the only way was to have an all-round development of your personality. He said that if you want to work for society, first you have to build yourself, because social work is not really a job. People can quite often reject your suggestions, and you have to fight injustices and bureaucracies. So you have to build yourself first, and then, after you've acquired great strength of mind, you plunge into social work. I asked him, "How do you build yourself?" and he said, "The only way is to do a lot of meditation, to let your weaknesses come to the surface of your mind and then come out. Meditation does that." That whole approach impressed me a lot. He also taught me a way of meditation which was another eye-opener to me. After that I followed his teachings.

CA: You incorporated a lot of his thought into you own economic theory, didn't you?

BATRA: Yes. What was so amazing to me also about him was that he wasn't just a religious man, but also a great scholar of history and economics and many other disciplines and social sciences. I was still a student at the time I met him; I looked at his theories and did not understand them then. But later on, after I did my Ph.D. and studied other philosophers and economists, I could appreciate the beauty of his thought, and how original and different it was. Then I could easily incorporate his ideas into current economic theory.

CA: That was in the mid-1970s?

BATRA: That's right. I think it was in 1976 when I just got fed up with all the things I was doing in modern economic theory. Every economist was writing articles full of mathematics, ab-

stract models that had nothing to do with reality. Everybody wanted to make his own writing look like a scholarly work by making it as difficult and esoteric as possible without reaching any in-depth conclusions. That's when I decided to switch and try something else. The first thing I went to was Sarkar's theories.

CA: A lot of your economic theory is based on economic cycles. Were you influenced at all in this regard by such people as Toynbee and Spengler?

BATRA: Very much so. I studied Toynbee and Spengler, and also the objections of their critics. I studied St. Augustine's philosophy of history. I studied many people who believe in cycles, and I incorporated their work into Sarkar's philosophy.

CA: You made the remarkable predictions of the fall of the Shah of Iran in the late 1970s, the coming of the Ayatollah Khomeini, and the long war between Iran and Iraq. Do you feel you have a gift of prophecy?

BATRA: I don't know about a gift of prophecy. I just applied Sarkar's theories and the idea of cycles, and I felt that the only way to popularize the ideas I believed in and also to destroy the useless economic theories of today would be to make correct predictions. That's what I wanted to do. I did not make predictions lightly: I studied every aspect of society and the economy and then came to certain conclusions which led to my predictions.

CA: You made many of your well-known predictions in a lecture you gave at the University of Oklahoma in 1978. Besides the ones I've just mentioned, you predicted that communism would fall. That's quite interesting, because just recently we see communism falling in Poland and a great deal of change and also ethnic unrest in Russia.

BATRA: Yes. When I made that forecast, I said that communism would fall by the year 2010. I think the beginning of the fall has already started. I do look upon the changes in Poland as a first step. But I never mentioned China in my prediction. I said that the Russian idea of communism would fall. China will go on for several more decades the way it is.

CA: Most of your predictions I've read have come true or are coming true. Have you made any predictions that have really missed?

BATRA: I have modified some predictions in the past, when I discovered new data. For instance, in 1979 I thought oil prices would keep rising, as everybody else did at that time. But in 1980 or 1981, I looked at new data I found in American economic history and changed my mind. Then I said that oil prices would fall sharply in the eighties. That was one prediction I modified to some extent. But I haven't really changed my mind on any of my predictions.

CA: What's uppermost in people's minds when they read your latest books, The Great Depression of 1990 *and* Surviving the Great Depression of 1990, *is your prediction that we're going to have a depression in 1989 or 1990. When we saw the stock market crash in October 1987, did you see that as a first step in the predicted depression?*

BATRA: In my first book on this subject, I wrote that the stock market would keep rising until 1989, would reach its peak in that year, and would then crash. But the crash occurred in '87, although the peak has just come this month. It's now possible that the crash has already occurred, but that stocks will begin a long-term decline in the next two or three months. There may not be another crash, but stocks will decline over the long term and a depression will occur anyway. My prediction of the depression still stands. Whether it will be preceded by a crash or a long-term decline really doesn't matter much to me; what's more important is whether we're going to have a depression or not. I think the depression will start in 1990. It won't look like a depression in 1990, because that will just be a starting point. But by 1991 or 1992, definitely we will know that we are in a deep depression.

CA: In a lot of your predictions, you pinpoint the time of an event with amazing accuracy. You've been saying for quite a while that the depression would come in 1990. What you've said just now, that a depression could begin in 1990, seems more understandable to me.

BATRA: When historians look at the past, they will say that the depression began in 1990, although in that year itself it won't be called a depression. In the case of the 1930s, the depression was called the depression of 1929, even though in 1930 itself there was no depression. The coming one will begin in 1990.

CA: You've got very good credentials, including a position at a leading university and the publication of books and specialized articles in your field. Are there other economists of your stature who are predicting a full-scale depression, as you are?

BATRA: I don't know of any. After the stock market crash, many people jumped on the bandwagon. Now that things appear to be going well, they have jumped off. But I haven't changed my opinion.

CA: Nobel Prize-winning economist Milton Friedman has said that, because of safeguards installed after the 1929 crash, we're depression-proof. How do you respond to that?

BATRA: All I can say is, look at the forecasting record. He has elegant and eloquent theories, but what's the use of such eloquence if your forecasts are consistently wrong? Friedman has made many wrong forecasts, especially for the eighties: all the forecasts he made for the eighties have been wrong. His forecast for the late eighties was right, but that was only one. Lately, all that he has said has never occurred.

CA: Do other leading economists look upon your ideas as rather far-out?

BATRA: They consider them very far-out; they think of me as a nut. When you ask them why their forecasts are always wrong, they say, "You're lucky." I say, "Fine. Why don't you stay with a lucky guy, then?"

CA: Do you still foresee the depression as lasting six or seven years?

BATRA: Yes.

CA: You've warned readers against buying real estate. Does that advice still hold?

BATRA: Yes. That's the worst thing you could get into at this time.

CA: You said in your two books about the depression that there's some possibility we could avert a depression. Do you still consider that to be true?

BATRA: There is some possibility, I think, that the depression may not come in 1990. It may come in 1992. After all, this is a six-decade cycle. But I don't think depression can be avoided.

CA: We're all inclined to shrug caution off to some extent in the good times and worry when we're certain the wolf is at the door. Depression or not, are there personal economic guidelines you feel we should live by more or less consistently?

BATRA: Rather than answer this question in a short interview, I will direct your attention to the advice given in my *Surviving the Great Depression of 1990.* Since I wrote this book in 1988, most international events have followed my expectations.

CA: Are you still advising people to set aside a certain amount of money to keep at home and in safety-deposit boxes?

BATRA: No. In *Surviving the Great Depression of 1990* I shied away from that idea. Instead I went for good banks, of which I gave a list. Some banks will survive the depression, and money in those banks will be better placed than money kept at home or in a safety-deposit box.

CA: Back in 1987 you started a grass-roots movement called SAD, for Stop Another Depression. How is that going?

BATRA: I've gotten a lot of response to that. We get several hundred letters every week, even now. I have one volunteer working with me, and he answers the letters.

CA: You were very disappointed with Reaganomics. Do you think President Bush is an improvement in any way over his predecessor?

BATRA: No. It's the same thing. In fact, Bush is even somewhat worse. He's advocating a reduction in the capital-gains tax, a step which would add further to the concentration of wealth. There is no difference, really.

CA: Teaching seems to be a very important part of your life. Do you find good students and maybe even some future economists in your classes at SMU?

BATRA: Yes, there are a few.

CA: What's planned for the future that you can talk about?

BATRA: I will go on teaching at SMU. Most likely the depression will start soon. If my health permits, I will become active in trying to keep it as short as possible.

BIOGRAPHICAL/CRITICAL SOURCES:

PERIODICALS

Dallas Life Magazine, July 26, 1987.
Globe and Mail (Toronto), August 15, 1987.
Los Angeles Times, August 27, 1987.
Los Angeles Times Book Review, August 16, 1987.
New York Times, June 18, 1987, August 30, 1987.
New York Times Book Review, July 12, 1987, October 23, 1988, October 29, 1989.
People, October 12, 1987.
Washington Post, August 17, 1987.

—*Interview by Walter W. Ross*

BATRA, Ravi
   See BATRA, Raveendra N(ash)

*   *   *

BECK, Harry
   See PAINE, Lauran (Bosworth)

*   *   *

BECKET, Henry S. A.
   See GOULDEN, Joseph C. (Jr.)

*   *   *

BEDFORD, Kenneth
   See PAINE, Lauran (Bosworth)

*   *   *

BEER, Samuel Hutchison   1911-

PERSONAL: Born July 28, 1911, in Bucyrus, Ohio; son of William Cameron and Jesse Blanche (Hutchison) Beer; married Roberta Frances Reed, June 22, 1935; children: Katherine, Frances, William Reed. *Education:* University of Michigan, A.B., 1932; Oxford University, B.A., 1935; Harvard University, Ph.D., 1943. *Politics:* Democrat. *Religion:* Presbyterian.

ADDRESSES: Home—87 Lakeview Ave., Cambridge, Mass. 02138. *Office*—Department of Government, Harvard University, Cambridge, Mass. 02138.

CAREER: Democratic National Committee, Washington, D.C., staff member, 1935-36; *New York Post,* New York City, reporter, 1936-37; *Fortune,* New York City, writer and researcher, 1937-38; Harvard University, Cambridge, Mass., instructor, 1938-42, assistant professor, 1946-48, associate professor, 1948-53, professor of government, 1953-71, Eaton Professor of Science of Government, 1971—, chairman of department, 1954-58. Messenger Lecturer, Cornell University, 1969. *Military service:* U.S. Army, 1942-45; became captain; received Bronze Star.

MEMBER: American Political Science Association, Americans for Democratic Action (chairman of Massachusetts chapter, 1955-57; national chairman, 1959-62), Phi Beta Kappa.

AWARDS, HONORS: Rhodes Scholar, 1932-35; Fulbright and Guggenheim fellow, 1953-54; Woodrow Wilson Foundation Award, 1966, for *British Politics in the Collectivist Age.*

WRITINGS:

The City of Reason, Harvard University Press, 1949, reprinted, Greenwood Press, 1968.
(Editor) Karl Marx and Friedrich Engels, *The Communist Manifesto,* Harlan Davidson, 1955, reprinted, 1987.
Treasury Control: The Coordination of Financial and Economic Policy in Great Britain, Clarendon Press, 1956, 2nd edition, 1957, reprinted, Greenwood Press, 1982.
(Editor with Adam B. Ulam, and author of Parts I and II) *Patterns of Government: The Major Political Systems of Europe,* five parts, Random House, 1958, 3rd edition (also see below), 1973.
(Contributor) William N. Chambers and Robert H. Salisbury, editors, *Democracy in the Mid-Twentieth Century: Problems and Prospects,* Washington University Press, 1960.
Modern British Politics: A Study of Parties and Pressure Groups, Faber, 1965, 3rd edition, Norton, 1980.

(Contributor) Robert A. Goldwin, editor, *Liberalism and Conservatism,* Public Affairs Conference Center, University of Chicago, 1965.
British Politics in the Collectivist Age, Knopf, 1965, revised edition published as *Modern British Politics: Parties and Pressure Groups in the Collectivist Age,* Norton, 1982.
(Editor with Richard E. Barringer) *The State and the Poor,* Winthrop Publishers, 1970.
Modern Political Development (Part I of *Patterns of Government,* 3rd edition), Random House, 1974.
The British Political System (Part II of *Patterns of Government,* 3rd edition), Random House, 1974.
(Contributor) Anthony King, editor, *The New American Political System,* American Enterprise Institute for Public Policy Research, 1978.
(With others) *Federalism: Making the System Work,* Center for National Policy, 1982.
Britain Against Itself: The Political Contradictions of Collectivism, Norton, 1982.

Contributor to scholarly journals. Associate editor, *American Political Science Review.**

*   *   *

BEER, William Reed   1943-

PERSONAL: Born July 13, 1943, in Charlotte, Mich.; son of Samuel Hutchison (a professor) and Roberta Frances (Reed) Beer; married Rose Salisbury (a professor), July 10, 1975; children: Nicole, Joshua. *Education:* Harvard University, B.A. (cum laude), 1965; Fondation Nationale des Sciences Politiques, Certificat d'Etudes Politiques, 1966; New School for Social Research, Ph.D., 1974.

ADDRESSES: Office—Department of Sociology, Brooklyn College of the City University of New York, Bedford Ave. & Avenue H, Brooklyn, N.Y. 11210.

CAREER: Brooklyn College of the City University of New York, Brooklyn, N.Y., instructor, 1969, lecturer, 1969-74, assistant professor, 1974-79, associate professor, 1979-84, professor of sociology, 1984—. Fulbright lecturer at University of Strasbourg, 1974-75; visiting professor, New York University, 1979—. Resident director, New York/Paris Exchange Program, 1982-83. South Huntington Public Library, vice-president, 1979, president, 1980, and member of board of trustees. Elder, Presbyterian Church of Sweet Hollow, Melville, Long Island, 1983—.

MEMBER: American Sociological Association, Tocqueville Society, Fulbright Alumni Association, Association des Professeurs Francais en Amerique, Appalachian Mountain Club, New York Road Runners Club.

AWARDS, HONORS: Fulbright grants, 1965-66, 1974-75, 1983.

WRITINGS:

(Translator) Marc Bloch, *Slavery and Serfdom in the Middle Ages,* University of California Press, 1975.
(Contributor) Milton Esman, editor, *Ethnic Conflict in the Western World,* Cornell University Press, 1977.
(Contributor) Raymond Hall, editor, *Separatism: A Comparative Approach,* Pergamon, 1979.
The Unexpected Rebellion: Ethnic Activism in Contemporary France, New York University Press, 1980.
(Translator) Michel Crozier, *Strategies for Change: The Future of French Society,* MIT Press, 1982.
Househusbands: Men and Housework in American Families, J. F. Bergin, 1983.

(Editor) *Language and National Unity: A Study in Bilingual and Polylingual Nations,* Rowman & Allanheld, 1984.

(Translator) Pascal Bruckner, *The Tears of the White Man: Compassion as Contempt,* Free Press, 1986.

(Editor) *Relative Strangers: Studies of Stepfamily Processes,* Rowman & Littlefield, 1988.

Strangers in the House: The World of Stepsiblings and Half-siblings, Transaction Books, 1989.

Contributor to *Historical Dictionary of the French Third Republic.* Contributor to scholarly journals.

WORK IN PROGRESS: A book about American stepfamilies, for publication in 1990.

SIDELIGHTS: William Reed Beer told *CA:* "I am an equal-time househusband, and I make excellent chili. I have done thirty parachute jumps and have climbed all forty-seven of the four-thousand-foot peaks of the White Mountains in New Hampshire. I have been to Africa twice on speaking tours for the United States Information Agency, and I speak Spanish and Hebrew. I teach sociology, English, and French. My writing includes fiction, nonfiction, and translations. I have run three marathons, and have recently completed a major triathlon (swimming, running, and bicycling). All this means that I am either trying to be a Renaissance man or part of me is still seventeen years old."

*   *   *

BEICHMAN, Arnold 1913-

PERSONAL: Born May 17, 1913, in New York, N.Y.; son of Solomon and Mary (Maltman) Beichman; married Doris Modry, 1936 (divorced, 1946); married Carroll Aikins (a teacher), 1950; children: (first marriage) Anthony, Janine (Mrs. Takeo Yamamoto); (second marriage) Charles, John. *Education:* Columbia University, B.A., 1934, M.A., 1967, Ph.D., 1973. *Politics:* Independent. *Religion:* None.

ADDRESSES: Home—Box 37, Naramata, British Columbia, Canada. *Office*—Hoover Institution, Stanford University, Stanford, Calif. 94305-6010.

CAREER: Newsday, Hempstead, N.Y., reporter, feature-writer, 1939-41; *PM,* New York City, city editor and assistant managing editor, 1944-46; *Electrical Union World,* New York City, editor, 1949-65; International Confederation of Free Trade Unions, Brussels, Belgium, press officer, 1951-62; University of Massachusetts, Boston, lecturer, 1970-73, associate professor of politics, 1973-80; Okanagan College, Penticton, British Columbia, staff member, 1980-82; Stanford University, Hoover Institution, Stanford, Calif., visiting scholar, 1982-86, research fellow, 1987—. Visiting professor, University of British Columbia and University of Calgary. Lecturer for Canadian Institute of International Affairs, 1965, 1966, and for U.S. Information Service, 1973; lecturer at Canisius College, 1973, 1974, National Humanities Faculty, 1973, and Georgetown University, 1973, 1974.

MEMBER: American Political Science Association, Consortium for the Study of Intelligence (founding member).

WRITINGS:

(Contributor) Donald Robinson, editor, *The Dirty Wars: Guerrilla Actions and Other Forms of Unconventional Warfare,* Delacorte, 1968.

The "Other" State Department: The U.S. Mission to the U.N.—Its Role in the Making of Foreign Policy, Basic Books, 1968.

Nine Lies about America, Library Press, 1972.

(With J. F. Otero and B. J. Widick) *Alternative Perspectives on Labor's Foreign Policy,* International Labor Program, Georgetown University, 1974.

(With Mikhail S. Bernstam) *Andropov: New Challenge to the West,* Stein & Day, 1983.

Herman Wouk: The Novelist as Social Historian, Transaction Books, 1984.

Contributor of articles and reviews to *Christian Science Monitor, Chronicles, National Review, New Leader, Newsweek, New York, New York Herald Tribune, New York Times Magazine,* and other periodicals. Columnist, Washington (D.C.) *Times;* former editor, *Columbia Spectator.*

WORK IN PROGRESS: The Long Pretense: Soviet Treaty Diplomacy from 1945.

*   *   *

BELLOWS, Thomas J(ohn) 1935-

PERSONAL: Born August 15, 1935, in Chicago, Ill.; son of Charles Everett (a railroad employee) and Dorothy (Morrison) Bellows; married Marilyn Denise Corbell; children: (previous marriage) Roderick Alan, Adrienne Marie, Jeannine Louise, Derek John, Marshall Everett; (present marriage) Scott Anthony, Justin Thomas, Trevor Cullen, Ethan Forrest. *Education:* Attended American University, 1956, and University of California, Los Angeles, 1956-57; Augustana College, Rock Island, Ill., B.A., 1957; University of Florida, M.A., 1958; Yale University, M.A., 1960, Ph.D., 1968. *Religion:* Methodist.

ADDRESSES: Office—Division of Social and Policy Sciences, University of Texas, San Antonio, Tex. 78285.

CAREER: West Georgia College, Carrollton, assistant professor of political science, 1962-64, 1966; Nanyang University, Singapore, visiting professor, 1965; University of Arkansas, Fayetteville, 1967-81, began as assistant professor, became associate professor of political science, chairman of department, 1971-78; University of Texas, San Antonio, director of social and policy sciences division, 1981-88, professor of political science, 1988—. Visiting professor, National Chengchi University, Taiwan, 1979. President, University of Arkansas Foundation for International Exchange of Students, 1971-73.

MEMBER: American Political Science Association, Association for Asian Studies, British Association of Malaysia and Singapore, Southwest Conference on Asian Studies (member of board of directors, 1972-75), Phi Beta Kappa, Phi Alpha Theta, Phi Kappa Phi.

WRITINGS:

The People's Action Party of Singapore: Emergence of a Dominant Party System, Southeast Asia Studies, Yale University, 1970.

(With Stanley Erikson and Herbert R. Winter) *Political Science: Introductory Essays and Readings,* Duxbury, 1971.

(With Winter) *People and Politics: An Introduction to Political Science* (textbook; includes teacher's manual), Wiley, 1977, 3rd edition, Macmillan, 1985.

Contributor to professional journals, including *Asian Affairs, Asian Survey, Wilson Quarterly, Transaction/SOCIETY, Asian Journal of Public Administration, Air University Review, World Affairs,* and *Journal of Thought.*

WORK IN PROGRESS: A book on the security situation in Pacific Asia; (with Winter) *Conflict and Compromise: An Introduction to Politics* for Scott, Foresman.

BENNETT, Gordon C. 1935-

PERSONAL: Born September 1, 1935, in Philadelphia, Pa.; son of Harold Walter and Agnes (Raff) Bennett; married Ruth Packer, June 8, 1957; children: Brad Alan, Cherry Lynn. *Education:* Dickinson College, A.B., 1957; Berkeley Baptist Divinity School, M.Div., 1960; Temple University, M.A., 1967.

ADDRESSES: Home—1743 Russell Rd., Paoli, Pa. 19301. *Office*—Department of Communication Arts, Eastern College, St. Davids, Pa. 19087.

CAREER: Clergyman of American Baptist Convention; minister of churches in Fredericktown, Ohio, 1960-65, and Narberth, Pa., 1965-68; Eastern College, St. Davids, Pa., instructor, 1968-70, assistant professor, 1970-79, associate professor of speech and drama, 1979—. Actor in and director of church and campus plays; co-founder of King's Players, chancel drama team playing in the Philadelphia area.

MEMBER: Religious Speech Communication Association (chairman of religious drama committee), Speech Association of the Eastern States, Fellowship of Reconciliation.

AWARDS, HONORS: Book award, Religious Communication Association, 1976, for *Happy Tales, Fables, and Plays.*

WRITINGS:

(With William D. Thompson) *Dialogue Preaching: The Shared Sermon,* Judson, 1969.
God Is My Fuehrer: A Dramatic Interpretation of the Life of Martin Niemoeller, Friendship, 1970.
Readers Theatre Comes to Church, John Knox, 1972, revised edition, Meriwether Publishing, 1985.
From Nineveh to Now, Bethany Press, 1973.
Happy Tales, Fables, and Plays, John Knox, 1975.
S Is for Sloane, Performance Publishing, 1978.
Solomon Grundy, Theatre World Publishing, 1978.
Acting out Faith: Christian Theatre Today, CBP Press, 1986.
The New Abolitionists: The Story of Nuclear Free Zones, Brethren Press, 1987.

Also author of a drama for the Biennial Convention of the American Baptist Churches, 1981, and, with Hugh Pease, of "HMS SinNoMore." Contributor to religion publications.

SIDELIGHTS: Gordon C. Bennett told *CA:* "Sometimes I write plays simply to satisfy the muse that's in me, to let an idea find form for its own sake or simply to entertain with a good story, without attempting to incarnate any profound idea. Other times I make my craft subject to Christ, using drama as a ministry to spark Christian growth, and to awaken the human conscience in terms of promoting peace and social justice. The idolatry of militarism and nuclearism and the importance of peacemaking are common themes in my plays. The real crunch comes with the struggle to avoid writing drama that is too propositional: one has to avoid sermonizing and let the action of the play be the message, as much as possible. Sometimes religious drama makes it as art and sometimes it doesn't, but to me theatre at its best is a temple in which divine truth finds embodiment; thus, both the human spirit and the divine are served. Thornton Wilder's plays are perhaps the best example of this; his major works are a happy combination of excellent workmanship and profound spiritual insight."

The author later added: "Since 1980 I have written more passionately and prolifically on nuclear weapons issues—leaving my playwriting interests aside for the present—since I am convinced that if we cannot prevent a nuclear holocaust nothing else mat-

ters. I found it fruitful and exciting to examine the Nuclear Free Zone movement in *The New Abolitionists.* This was the first work I had done which required extensive interviewing. I found great inspiration in recording the comments and actions of individuals around the nation who are engaging in Nuclear Free Zone advocacy—indeed, a lifesaving, planet-protecting and respecting action on behalf of God's created world."

AVOCATIONAL INTERESTS: Playing tennis, bicycling, camping, writing, amateur acting, gardening, peace movement work.

*   *   *

BENTON, Peggie 1906-
(Shifty Burke)

PERSONAL: Born October 19, 1906, in Valetta, Malta; daughter of Charles Edward (an army officer) and Winifred (Jay) Pollock; married Hubert Steel Lambert, February 11, 1926 (divorced March 20, 1931); married Kenneth Carter Benton (a writer), March 2, 1938; children: (first marriage) Alexander Pollock, Charles Mark; (second marriage) Timothy John. *Education:* Ecole Professionelle, Neuchatel, diploma, 1925; attended Madrid University. *Politics:* "Liberal with a small 'l'." *Religion:* Church of England.

ADDRESSES: Home—2 Jubilee Terrace, Chichester PO19 1XL, England.

CAREER: Writer. British Foreign Service, 1936-48, personal assistant and press reader, British Legation, Vienna, Austria, 1936-38, personal assistant, British Consulate, Riga, Latvia, 1939-40, research assistant, British Embassy, Madrid, Spain, 1941-43, research assistant, British Embassy, Rome, Italy, 1944-48.

MEMBER: Institute of Linguists (fellow), Society of Authors, National Book League.

AWARDS, HONORS: Darmstadt Gastronomic Fair Bronze Medal, 1964, for *Meat at Any Price;* Frankfurt Book Fair Bronze Medal, 1966, for *Fish for All Seasons.*

WRITINGS:

COOKBOOKS

(Translator) Edouard Alexandre Pozerski (under pseudonym Edouard de Pomiane), *Cooking in Ten Minutes,* Bruno Cassirer, 1948, 3rd edition, Faber, 1967.
(Self-illustrated) *Finnish Food for Your Table,* Bruno Cassirer, 1960.
(Editor and translator) Pozerski (under psuedonym Edouard de Pomiane), *Cooking with Pomiane,* Bruno Cassirer, 1962, Roy, 1963.
(With Lyon) *Chicken & Game,* Faber, 1964.
(With Lyon) *Fish for All Seasons,* Faber, 1966.
(With Lyon) *Eggs, Cheese & Milk,* Faber, 1971.

OTHER

(Under pseudonym Shifty Burke) *Peterman,* Arthur Barker, 1966.
One Man Against the Drylands: Fight for the Drylands, Collins-Harvill, 1972.
Fight for the Drylands, Collins, 1977.
Baltic Countdown, Centaur Press, 1984.

Also author of *Brick as an Element in Design* and *Forum World Features.*

SIDELIGHTS: Peggie Benton speaks French, German, Italian, Portuguese, Spanish.

* * *

BENTON, Will
See PAINE, Lauran (Bosworth)

* * *

BERLYE, Milton K. 1915-

PERSONAL: Born November 2, 1915, in Gloversville, N.Y.; son of Zanwell and Celia (Klauser) Berlye; married Ruth Gold, January 25, 1942; children: Jay Lynn, Sharon Kay. *Education:* State University of New York College at Oswego, B.S., 1940; New York University, M.A., 1947.

CAREER: Monticello Central School, Monticello, N.Y., teacher and administrator, beginning 1942.

MEMBER: National Education Association, American Industrial Arts Association, American Vocational Association, New York State Teachers Association, Monticello Teachers Association.

WRITINGS:

The Encyclopedia of Working with Glass, Oceana, 1968, revised edition, Dodd, 1983.
Selling Your Art Work: A Marketing Guide for Fine and Commercial Artists, A. S. Barnes, 1973, 2nd edition published as *How to Sell Your Artwork: A Complete Guide for Commercial and Fine Artists,* Prentice-Hall, 1978.
Your Career in the World of Work, Bobbs-Merrill, 1975.
(With Hobart H. Conover and Sanford D. Gordon) *Business Dynamics,* Bobbs-Merrill, 1982.

Also author of fifteen radio stories produced on shows such as "Grand Central Station," "Stars Over Hollywood," and "Telephone Hour," as well as material for daytime dramas and stories for television movies. Contributor to *New York State Education, School Shop, Industrial Arts and Vocational Education,* and *Camp Tips.*

SIDELIGHTS: Milton K. Berlye has U.S. patents on a bookbinding machine and a transporting truck.*

* * *

BERMANT, Chaim (Icyk) 1929-

PERSONAL: Born February 26, 1929, in Breslev, Poland; son of Azriel (a rabbi) and Feiga Tzirl (Daets) Bermant; married Judith Weil, December 17, 1962; children: Alisa, Eve, Azriel, Daniel. *Education:* Attended Rabbinical College, Glasgow, Scotland, 1948-50; University of Glasgow, M.A., 1955, M.Litt., 1960; London School of Economics and Political Science, M.Sc., 1957. *Politics:* Liberal conservative. *Religion:* Jewish.

ADDRESSES: Home—18 Hill Rise, London NW11 6NA, England. *Agent*—Aitken & Stone, 29 Fernshaw Rd., London SW10 0TG, England.

CAREER: Teacher in London, England, 1955-56; economist in London, 1956-58; television writer in Glasgow, Scotland, 1958-59, and in London, 1959-61; *London Jewish Chronicle,* London, features editor, 1961-66; free-lance writer, 1966—.

WRITINGS:

FICTION

Jericho Sleep Alone, Holt, 1963.
Berl Make Tea, Holt, 1964.
Ben Preserve Us, Holt, 1964.
Diary of an Old Man, Holt, 1966.
Swinging in the Rain, Hodder & Stoughton, 1967.
Here Endeth the Lesson, Eyre & Spottiswoode, 1969.
Now Dowager, Eyre & Spottiswoode, 1971.
Roses Are Blooming in Picardy, Eyre & Spottiswoode, 1972.
The Last Supper, St. Martin's, 1973.
The Second Mrs. Whitberg, Allen & Unwin, 1976, St. Martin's, 1977.
The Squire of Bor Shachor, Allen & Unwin, 1977.
Now Newman Was Old, Allen & Unwin, 1978, St. Martin's, 1979.
Belshazzar: A Cat's Story for Humans (juvenile), Allen & Unwin, 1979.
The Patriarch: A Jewish Family Saga, St. Martin's, 1981.
On the Other Hand, Robson Books, 1982.
House of Women, St. Martin's, 1983.
Dancing Bear, Weidenfeld & Nicolson, 1984, St. Martin's, 1985.
Titch, St. Martin's, 1987.
The Companion, Robson Books, 1987, St. Martin's, 1988.

OTHER

Israel, Walker & Co., 1967.
(Editor with Murray Mindlin) *Explorations: An Annual on Jewish Themes,* Barrie & Rockliff, 1967.
Troubled Eden: The Anatomy of Anglo-Jewry, Basic Books, 1969.
The Cousinhood: The Anglo-Jewish Gentry, Macmillan, 1971.
The Walled Garden: The Saga of Jewish Family Life and Tradition, Macmillan, 1975.
Point of Arrival: A Study of London's East End, Macmillan, 1975.
Coming Home, Allen & Unwin, 1976.
The Jews, New York Times Co., 1977.
(With others) *My LSE,* edited and introduced by Joan Abse, Robson Books, 1977.
(With M. Weitzman) *Ebla: An Archeological Enigma,* New York Times Co., 1979.
What's the Joke?: A Study of Jewish Humour, Weidenfeld & Nicolson, 1986.

SIDELIGHTS: "If you haven't run into Chaim Bermant before, you are in for a treat," asserts Martin Levin of the *New York Times Book Review.* "His field of specialization concerns middle-class Orthodox Jews, habitat Glasgow. But you don't have to be Jewish to enjoy his wry humor," explains the critic, for the author "excels at creating a social climate rich in ethnic commonalities and personal differences. Both are instantly recognizable." For example, Bermant's first novel *Jericho Sleep Alone* presents "a fresh landscape in which some familiar figures are animated with a wit often subtle and oblique," notes Levin. Jericho Broch is a young Jewish Scotsman who cannot overcome his own indecisiveness and lack of specific ambition, and subsequently drifts through school and relationships. "The story, though, is not a great deal," comments *New Statesman* contributor Stephen Hugh-Jones; "what is, is the sense of place, of age, the particularities of word and feeling." The critic adds that *Jericho Sleep Alone* "is told with (and in no way diminished by) a very lively and unsubtly funny wit."

Bermant moves his subject from the uncertain tumult of youth to the staunch passivity of the elderly in *The Diary of an Old Man;* nevertheless, notes Robert Taubman in the *New States-*

man, the narrative "has the same colloquial style, scepticism and liveliness as the 60-years-younger lot—and less sentimentality." Covering a month in diarist Cyril's life, the novel relates his reaction to the deaths of his last two friends—"and it's a relief to read a novel so much about death that doesn't do it for black jokes," remarks Taubman. Nicholas Samstag presents a similar assessment, stating in the *Saturday Review:* "That [the passing of time until death] is [the elderly's] chief preoccupation is made clear, without sentimentality but with great skill and a wry precision." "The special quality of Chaim Bermant's most unusual novel can only be conveyed in the expressions [of the characters]," states Aileen Pippett in the *New York Times Book Review.* The critic elaborates, remarking that Bermant "reproduces [the characters] with exactitude, never striking a false note, giving unforgettable glimpses into the tragicomic life of lonely old age in Britain's welfare state today. Each character is firmly realized."

A *Times Literary Supplement* reviewer believes that it is Cyril's character in particular which enhances the work: "[This] is a book which clearly might have been depressing, or trivial, or sentimental. . . . But Mr. Bermant manages to avoid the dangers, mainly because he achieves an extraordinary completeness of identification with his diarist." Cyril, continues the critic, makes *The Diary of an Old Man* "into something which is often richly funny, occasionally touching, and always true to the facts." As Samstag similarly comments, the novel is "a little masterpiece . . . because Mr. Bermant has written here a superb fantasy disguised as a realistic novel. Into his dreary tapestry he has managed to work threads of gold, crimson, and lettuce green, expressing gallantry, gusto, gaiety, and a human goodness that I wish I believed in." Concludes the critic: "For a little while, experiencing that suspension of disbelief which only the most artful of fantasists can create, I was convinced."

These accurate portrayals have led some critics to observe an anthropological tendency in Bermant's work. In *The Patriarch: A Jewish Family Saga,* for example, Bermant "writes about Jews with a curious blend of intimacy and objectivity, like an affectionate anthropologist," asserts Annie Gottlieb in the *New York Times Book Review;* "he captures the specialness without the shame." And *Spectator* contributor Nick Totton observes that in *The Second Mrs. Whitberg,* "like any self-respecting anthropologist, Mr. Bermant's formal role is not to judge but to describe. However, as with the most interesting anthropology," the critic adds, "scientific objectivity is tempered with enough pure affection to leave the reader gently wondering if civilisation is worth so much after all." Totton concludes: "Information, wit, invention, style, conviction—what more can one ask from an anthropological whodunnit?"

Although he has had success in "providing an entirely new perspective on that tough old recidivist, the Jewish Family Novel," as the *Los Angeles Times*'s Elaine Kendall describes it, Bermant departs from type in his recent novel *The Companion.* Relating the relationship of stingy widow Martha Crystal and her "lady's companion," Phyllis, through a series of difficulties, *The Companion* is a "funny, original and surprisingly poignant novel," maintains Kendall. The critic adds that while the relatively simple characters "may seem unprepossessing ingredients for a comic novel, Bermant does wonders with them." Told through the voice of fifty-five-year-old Phyllis, the novel's "successes are the moments at which humor and pathos, riding in tandem, emerge from behind the calculated sparsity of Phyllis's account," comments Penelope Lively in the *New York Times Book Review.* While Lively finds Phyllis's first-person chronicle inconsistent at times, *Washington Post Book World* contributor Linda Barrett Osborne believes that "Bermant's narrative is perfectly,

irreverently sustained: a devastating series of one-liners highlighting the symbiotic relationship of his eccentric protagonists." "By taking a fundamentally bleak and static situation, inventing two remarkably complementary characters supported by assorted figures of fun," concludes Kendall, in *The Companion* "Bermant has created and ironic and altogether memorable novel, as delicately calibrated as a jeweler's scale."

Bermant told *CA:* "I suppose I was driven to write by a sort of hedonism, for it gave me a pleasure offered by no other occupation and, unlike other activities which I need not name, it still does. Yet, I did not think it could offer a livelihood, and I dabbled at many things before taking my life in my hands in 1966 and throwing up a secure and fairly lucrative post to devote myself to full time writing and, somehow, I have survived. I used to be in television and journalism before taking up full-time authorship, and I still turn to both between books because they get me out of the house and keep me in touch with people and events, and because I value them—journalism especially—as a discipline. Writing books can be a form of self-indulgence because one has almost all the time and space in the world, whereas journalism with its deadlines and space limitations concentrates the mind wonderfully.

"As I have a fairly large family and live in a fairly spacious house, I am compelled to approach my work in a thoroughly professional manner and am at my typewriter daily from 9:30 to 1:30, whether I have anything to write or not (for I don't know whether I have until I start). In the afternoon I answer letters, fend off creditors, etc., and return to my desk again after dinner. On most working days I do not rise from my labors 'til about 10 P.M. I sometimes shudder at the torrents of words I produce—on average about five thousand a day. I begin my working day by re-reading my previous day's output, and if it yields a thousand usable words I feel I have done well."

BIOGRAPHICAL/CRITICAL SOURCES:

BOOKS

Contemporary Literary Criticism, Volume 40, Gale, 1986.

PERIODICALS

Los Angeles Times, February 21, 1985, December 22, 1987, October 28, 1988.
New Statesman, April 3, 1964, March 12, 1965, October 1, 1965, June 24, 1966.
New Yorker, February 18, 1974, January 25, 1988.
New York Times Book Review, June 12, 1966, May 21, 1967, January 13, 1974, October 3, 1976, August 2, 1981, January 31, 1988, October 23, 1988.
Saturday Review, May 13, 1967.
Spectator, April 7, 1973, August 28, 1976.
Times Literary Supplement, April 9, 1964, March 11, 1965, September 23, 1965, June 23, 1966, March 31, 1972, April 20, 1973.
Washington Post Book World, September 4, 1988.

—*Sketch by Diane Telgen*

*   *   *

BERNADETTE
  See WATTS, (Anna) Bernadette

*   *   *

BETANCOURT, Jeanne 1941-

PERSONAL: Born October 2, 1941, in Burlington, Vt; daughter of Henry (a certified public accountant) and Beatrice (Mario)

Granger; married Jeffrey Betancourt (a city planner), July 1, 1967; children: Nicole. *Education:* New York University, B.A. and M.A.

ADDRESSES: Home—New York, N.Y.

CAREER: Junior and senior high school teacher of English and film studies in Vermont and New York, N.Y., 1963—. Member of faculty of New School for Social Research. Member of preview committee for first International Film Festival, 1972; member of reviewing committee of film division at Brooklyn Public Library. Member of advisory board for Media Center for Children. Has developed workshops for librarians and educators on film programming for adolescents.

MEMBER: New York Women in Film (president).

WRITINGS:

Women in Focus, Pflaum, 1974.
SMILE! How to Cope with Braces, Knopf, 1982.
Am I Normal? (adaptation of film of same title), Avon, 1983.
Dear Diary (adaptation of film of same title), Avon, 1983.
The Rainbow Kid (novel), Avon, 1983.
The Edge, Scholastic, 1985.
Turtle Time, Avon, 1985.
Puppy Love, Avon, 1986.
Between Us, Scholastic, 1986.
Sweet Sixteen and Never . . ., Bantam, 1987.
Home Sweet Home, Bantam, 1988.

Contributor to *Women In Film.* Contributing editor, *Channel.*

WORK IN PROGRESS: A book on her years as a nun.

SIDELIGHTS: Jeanne Betancourt served as a Catholic nun for six years.*

* * *

BHATT, Jagdish J(eyshanker) 1939-

PERSONAL: Born February 17, 1939; came to the United States, 1961, naturalized citizen, 1976; son of Jeyshanker Mancharam and Kamala (Jeyshanker) Bhatt; married January 22, 1970; wife's name, Meena; children: Amar Jagdish, Anita Jagdish. *Education:* University of Baroda, B.Sc. (with honors), 1961; University of Wisconsin—Madison, M.S., 1963; further graduate study at University of New Mexico, 1966-67, University of California, Santa Barbara, 1968-69, and Stanford University, 1971-72; University of Wales, Ph.D., 1972.

ADDRESSES: Home—11 Midlands Dr., East Greenwich, R.I. 02818. *Office*—Department of Physics (Geology-Oceanography), Community College of Rhode Island, 400 East Ave., Warwick, R.I. 02886.

CAREER: Jackson Community College, Jackson, Mich., instructor in physics and chemistry, 1964-65; Oklahoma Panhandle State College (now University), Goodwill, instructor in geology and physical sciences, 1965-66; University of Northern Iowa, Cedar Falls, instructor in geology, summer, 1967; Stanford University, Stanford, Calif., research scholar and scientist in geology, 1971-72; State University of New York at Buffalo, assistant professor of oceanography, geology, and environmental sciences, 1972-74; Community College of Rhode Island, Warwick, assistant professor, 1974-79, associate professor, 1979-84, professor of geology and oceanography, 1984—. Member of Rhode Island Ocean Technology Task Force Committee, 1975-76. Developed courses in oceanography and programs in ocean training and off-shore technology. U.S. Representative,

Scientific Advisory Committee, International Oceanographic Conference, Tokyo, Japan, 1990. Geo-resources and environmental consultant, 1972-75.

MEMBER: International Oceanographic Foundation, Geological Society of America, Oceanic Society.

AWARDS, HONORS: Wolfson doctoral fellowship at University of Wales, 1970-71; nominee, Chancellor's Award for Excellence in Teaching, State University of New York at Buffalo, 1973; Jefferson Award, 1983, and Distinguished Teacher Award, 1984, Community College of Rhode Island Foundation; honored as "Contemporary Author" by Archives of Bowling Green State University, 1983; Instructor Excellence Award, from Phi Theta Kappa (Pi Omicron chapter), National Honor Society, Community College of Rhode Island, 1989.

WRITINGS:

Laboratory Manual on Physical Geology, Guymon, 1966.
Laboratory Manual on Physical Sciences, Guymon, 1966.
Cretaceous History of Himalayan Geosyncline, Guymon, 1966.
(Contributor) J. G. C. Anderson, A. P. Macmillan, and John Platt, editors, *Mineral Exploitation and Economic Geology,* University of Wales, 1971.
Environmentology: Earth's Environment and Energy Resources, Modern Press, 1975.
Geochemistry and Petrology of South Wales Main Limestone (Mississippian), Modern Press, 1976.
Geologic Exploration of Earth (manual), Modern Press, 1976.
Oceanography: Exploring the Planet Ocean, with instructor's manual, Van Nostrand, 1978, 2nd edition, Celecom, 1983.
Applied Oceanography: Mining, Energy, and Management, University Microfilms, 1979.
(Coordinator) *Applied Oceanography Manuals,* Volume 1: *Mineral Resources and Geologic Processes,* Volume 2: *Marine Fisheries,* Volume 3: *Sea-Farming,* Volume 4: *Ocean Energy,* Volume 5: *Sea Mammals,* Volume 6: *Marine Pollution,* Volume 7: *Underwater Habitat by Man,* Community College of Rhode Island Press, 1983.
Oceanography Year 2000 and Beyond, Celecom, 1989.
Oceanography Textbook, Macmillan, in press.
Geolab Studies, Celecom, in press.

Contributor to marine/earth science journals in England and the United States.

WORK IN PROGRESS: Exploring the Earth's History: Laboratory Manual; Ocean Enterprise; Odyssey of the Damned, a science fiction novel; *Odyssey of Perception: Selected Poems.*

SIDELIGHTS: Jagdish J. Bhatt writes that his contributions to the study of geology and oceanography include a demonstration of the role of bacteria in the formation of nodular cherts in marine limestones, explanation of the true geochemical and geological nature of South Wales marine limestones, and development of educational curricula on marine technology. He feels that his books provide a comprehensive treatment of contemporary issues of environmental pollution, energy resources, population, food technology, and global management of earth's resources, and a most comprehensive treatment of theoretical and practical ocean-related matters.

Bhatt told *CA:* "As a writer I have always been driven by the philosophy of local to global cooperation as the best way to fulfill the challenge of freeing ourselves from the earthly drudgeries of energy and food shortages, population and pollution dilemma, and from the rising entropy of stress per capita particularly during the present century.

"I consider that the art of organized-thoughts expression is the main business of writing. Therefore, it is a *sine qua non* that writers aim this art not for their ego-pivoting instrument of fame but use it as a powerful means of circumventing human shortcomings, including eradication of intellectual provincialism. By the same token, the art of creative communication (regardless of the writer's background as a scientist, poet, or philosopher) should consistently be affirmed as a fire of imagination ready to erode the darkness of our superfluous values, artificial barriers, wars, racism, colonialism and various other unproductive madness permanently from the face of the planet before mankind embraces the fascinating virgin terrain of the twenty-first century. At the near end of the present century, I cannot resist the temptation of envisioning mankind's unified gift of a world society relatively free of the above-mentioned scars and dilemmas. Perhaps writers, through the power of constructive expression, could significantly contribute in their own significant way. The joy of such a gift remains in the fact that we may redeem all the historic blunders we have ever made since we came to be known as *Homo sapien,* that is, man the wise, with a single mighty stroke of progress!

"Another immediate challenge writers of the world at present are facing is the issue of human rights. Although this issue transcends the planetary spatio-temporal complex of geography and history, let us not ignore equally vital issues of human responsibilities and human obligations. Writers of diversified backgrounds must keep the flame of the above-mentioned trinity in the limelight, particularly in light of the fact that it is a prerequisite for our gift to the younger generations of the next century.

"Finally, writers must make a concerted local to global effort to guard the indispensable values, including the fabric of our society—family unity—against the juggernaut technology. Although technology yields constructive fruits of communication, transportation and myriads of materialistic comforts and pleasures, its latent power of dehumanization must not be taken for granted.

"I have quickly flashed some of these reflections in the hope that readers of *CA* will become aware of the responsibility and challenge of writing in coming years. The art of writing demands martinet discipline of mind and dedication to one's mission in life, and unfortunately during the process of creative writing beloved ones often suffer a great deal. In the final analysis, it is worth the commitment if the quality of one's work is effective in erasing a fraction of our contemporary shadows."

*　　　*　　　*

BIBO, Bobette
See GUGLIOTTA, Bobette

*　　　*　　　*

BIEN, Joseph Julius 1936-

PERSONAL: Born May 22, 1936, in Cincinnati, Ohio; son of Joseph Julius and Mary (Adams) Bien; married Francoise Neve (a professor), April, 1965. *Education:* Xavier University, B.S., 1957, M.A., 1958; University of Paris, Ph.D., 1968.

ADDRESSES: Home—Columbia, Mo. *Office*—Department of Philosophy, University of Missouri, Columbia, Mo. 65211.

CAREER: University of Texas at Austin, assistant professor of philosophy, 1968-73; University of Missouri—Columbia, associate professor, 1973-79, professor of philosophy, 1979—, chair-

man of department, 1976-80, 1981—. Visiting professor of philosophy, Texas A & M University, 1980; honor lecturer, Mid-American State Universities, 1985-86. Member of international board of advisors, Center for Advanced Research in Phenomenology, 1982—.

MEMBER: International Phenomenological Association, American Philosophical Association, Society for Phenomenology and Existential Philosophy, Society for Political and Social Philosophy (president, 1979-80, 1986-87), Central States Philosophical Association (president, 1978-79), Central States Slavic Conference (secretary/treasurer, 1977, 1984), Southern Society for Philosophy and Psychology, Southwestern Philosophical Society.

WRITINGS:

(Translator) Maurice Merleau-Ponty, *Adventures of the Dialectic,* Northwestern University Press, 1973.
(Contributor) Garth Gillan, editor, *Horizons of the Flesh: Critical Reinterpretations of Merleau-Ponty's Thought,* Southern Illinois University Press, 1973.
(Editor with David Stewart) *Political and Social Essays by Paul Ricoeur,* Ohio University Press, 1974.
(Contributor) C. Wellman, editor, *Equality and Freedom: Past, Present and Future,* Franz Steiner, 1977.
(Contributor) Richard Zaner and Donald Idhe, editors, *Interdisciplinary Phenomenology,* Nijhoff, 1978.
History, Revolution and Human Nature: Marx's Philosophical Anthropology, John Benjamins, 1984.
(Editor with O. A. Robinson) *Leviathan,* Klare, 1985.
(Contributor) R. Gorman, editor, *Biographical Dictionary of Neo-Marxism,* Greenwood Press, 1985.

Contributor to journals, including *Southwestern Journal of Philosophy, Man and World, Review of Metaphysics, Philosophy Today, Cahiers d'Action Litteraire, Dialogue, Journal of Social Philosophy, Marx Centeuno, Human Studies, Kulturni Radnik, Philosophy and Phenomenological Research,* and *Studia Filozofizne.* Associate editor, "Philosophical Currents" series, B. R. Gruner, 1973—; associate editor, *Marx Centeuno,* 1985—.

WORK IN PROGRESS: A book concerning the political concept of legitimacy; a book in French about Hungarian philosopher Gyorgy Lukacs.

*　　　*　　　*

BISHOP, Martin
See PAINE, Lauran (Bosworth)

*　　　*　　　*

BITTER, Gary G(len) 1940-

PERSONAL: Born February 2, 1940, in Hoisington, Kan.; son of Solomon and Alvera Bitter; married Kay Burgat (a writer), August 19, 1962; children: Steve, Mike, Matthew. *Education:* Kansas State University, B.S., 1962; Kansas State Teachers College (now Emporia State University), M.A., 1965; attended University of Michigan, 1965-66; University of Denver, Ph.D., 1970.

ADDRESSES: Home—8531 East Osborn, Scottsdale, Ariz. 85251. *Office*—College of Education, Arizona State University, Tempe, Ariz. 85287-0111.

CAREER: Teacher of mathematics and science at public high schools in Derby, Kan., 1962-65, and of mathematics in public schools in Ann Arbor, Mich., 1965-66; Washburn University,

Topeka, Kan., instructor in mathematics education, 1966-67; Colorado College, Colorado Springs, instructor in mathematics and computer education, 1968-70; Arizona State University, Tempe, assistant professor, 1970-72, associate professor, 1973-77, professor of education, 1977—. Lecturer at University of Colorado, 1968-70; professor of mathematics education at University of Northern Colorado, summer, 1973, Montana State University, summer, 1975, Temple University, summer, 1980, and Boston University, summer, 1980. National Science Foundation, reviewer of science education proposals, 1977, 1981, 1983, 1986-88, principal investigator of grants, 1981-82, 1985-57, 1989-91. Consulting mathematics editor, General Cassette Corp., 1970-75; consultant to Kaman Nuclear Co., and to numerous school systems, government organizations, and corporations.

MEMBER: International Society for Technology in Education (board of directors, 1986-88; president-elect, 1989-90; president, 1990-91), American Association of University Professors, American Education Research Association, Association of Educational Data Processing (board of directors, 1974-75), Mathematical Association of America, National Council of Teachers of Mathematics, School Science and Mathematics, Association for Computing Machinery, Arizona Association of Educational Data Systems (president, 1972-74; board of directors, 1974-75), Arizona Association of Elementary-Kindergarten-Nursery Education, Arizona Association of Teachers of Mathematics (board of directors, 1972-75), California Mathematics Association, Phi Delta Kappa.

AWARDS, HONORS: National Science Foundation fellowships, summers, 1963-68, 1970; Outstanding Children's Book Awards, National Science Teachers Association, 1975, 1979, 1981; National Migrant Educator of the Month Award, *Migrant Education News,* 1976; Outstanding Educator, International Society for Technology in Education, 1988.

WRITINGS:

(With Lyle Mauland) *Limits: Computer Extended Calculus,* University of Denver Press, 1970.
(With Mauland) *Functions: Computer Extended Calculus,* Denver University Press, 1970.
(With Wilson Y. Gateley) *BASIC for Beginners,* McGraw, 1970, 2nd edition, 1978.
(With W. S. Dorn and D. L. Hector) *Computer Applications for Calculus,* Prindle, 1972.
(With Jon Knaupp) *Mathematics Activity Manual,* Addison-Wesley, 1972.
(With Gateley) *Basic Fibel,* R. V. Deckers, 1973, 2nd edition, 1980.
(Contributor) N. K. Silvaroli and Lynn Searfoss, editors, *Communications, Reading, and Mathematics,* D. A. Lewis Associates, 1975.
(With Charles Geer) *Materials for Metric Instruction,* ERIC, 1975.
(With K. Maurdeff and Jerald Mikesell) *Investigating Metric Measure,* McGraw, 1975.
(With Mikesell) *Discovering Metric Measure,* McGraw, 1975.
(With Tom Metos) *Exploring with Metrics,* Messner, 1975.
(With Maurdeff and Mikesell) *Multiplication and Division Games and Ideas,* McGraw, 1976.
(With Maurdeff and Mikesell) *Activities Handbook for Teaching the Metric System,* Allyn & Bacon, 1976.
(With Maurdeff and Mikesell) *Addition and Subtraction Games and Ideas,* McGraw, 1976.

(Contributor) *Measurement in School Mathematics Yearbook,* National Council of Teachers of Mathematics, 1976.
Calculator Power (six workbooks), EMC Corp., 1977.
(With Metos) *Exploring with Pocket Calculators,* Messner, 1977.
(With Mikesell) *Teachers Handbook of Metric Activities,* Allyn & Bacon, 1977.
(With J. Engelhardt and J. Wiebe) *Math H.E.L.P.,* EMC Corp., 1977.
(With Engelhardt and Wiebe) *One Step a Time,* EMC Corp., 1977.
Exploring with Solar Energy, Messner, 1978.
Activities Handbook for Teaching with the Hand-Held Calculator, Allyn & Bacon, 1980.
(With wife, Kay Bitter, and A. Kopplin) *Hand Calculator Games,* McGraw, 1981.
Microcomputers in Education, Arizona State University, 1982.
Emerging Technology and Strategies for Marketing Educational Technology Innovation, U.S. Department of Education, 1982.
Microcomputer Applications for Calculus, Prindle, 1983.
Computers in Today's World, Wiley, 1983.
Exploring with Computers, revised edition, Messner, 1983.
(With Ruth Camuse) *Using a Microcomputer in the Classroom,* Reston, 1983, 2nd edition, Prentice-Hall, 1988.
(With Nancy R. Watson) *The Apple LOGO Primer,* Reston, 1983.
(With Watson) *The Commodore 64 LOGO Primer,* Reston, 1984.
(With Watson) *The IBM-PC LOGO Primer,* Reston, 1984.
Addison-Wesley Computer Literacy, Addison-Wesley, 1986.
(With Paul M. Cook) *IBM BASIC for Business,* Prentice-Hall, 1986.
(With Roger Goodberlet) *Macintosh BASIC for Business,* Prentice-Hall, 1987.
(With others) *Mathematics Methods for the Elementary and Middle School: A Comprehensive Approach,* Allyn & Bacon, 1988.
Microcomputers in Education Today, McGraw, 1989.
Appleworks in the Classroom Today, McGraw, 1989.
(With Mikesell) *Using the Math Explorer Calculator: A Sourcebook for Teachers,* Addison-Wesley, 1990.

Contributor to *Encyclopedia of Computer Science,* 1983. Author of columns published in *Teacher,* 1980-81, *Educational Computer,* 1981-83, and *Electronic Learning,* 1982-83. Also contributor to mathematics and education journals. *School Science and Mathematics,* associate editor, 1980-81, editor, 1981-88. *Two Year Mathematics Journal,* member of editorial board, 1970, editor of section, "The Computer Corner," 1973-79; member of advisory board, *Teacher,* 1977-79; member of editorial boards, *Journal of Computers in Science and Mathematics Teaching,* 1981-90, and *Electronic Publishing,* 1981-83.

* * *

BITTLINGER, Arnold (Georg) 1928-

PERSONAL: Born June 13, 1928, in Edenkoben, Germany; son of Georg Friedrich (a parson) and Wilhelmine Margarete (Jung) Bittlinger; married Ilse Baumann, November 17, 1953; children: Sulamith, Andreas, Clemens, Stephan. *Education:* University of Mainz-Heidelberg, 1952; passed theological examination (B.D. equivalent), 1952; University of Geneva, Diploma Sc.Oec. (M.S.T. equivalent in theological ecumenical sciences), 1972; University of Birmingham, Ph.D., 1977.

ADDRESSES: Office—World Council of Churches, 150 Route de Terney, CH-1211 Geneva 20, Switzerland.

CAREER: Lutheran clergyman, 1952—; general secretary of German Inter-School Christian Fellowship, 1952-55; pastor in Ludwigshafen am Rhine, 1956-59; national director of evangelism for Lutheran Church, Klingenmuenster/Pfalz, Germany, 1959-68; director of Ecumenical Academy Schloss Craheim, Wetzhausen, Germany, 1968-77; World Council of Churches, Geneva, Switzerland, consultant on charismatic renewal, 1978—. Member of faculty of St. John's University, 1971—; member of core team in dialogue between Vatican and Charismatic Movement, 1972-76. Member of board of directors of Student Mission in Germany, 1952-59, SCM-Postgraduate Fellowship, 1955-67, and Marburger Kreis (Oxford Group), 1959-73; director of Studiengemeinschaft fuer Seelsorge, Bibelkunde und Teamarbeit.

MEMBER: Verband Deutscher Schriftsteller, Institute for Ecumenical and Cultural Research (fellow), Lions Club.

AWARDS, HONORS: Fellow in residence at Institute for Ecumenical and Cultural Research, 1971-72.

WRITINGS:

Die Ordnung der Dienste im Neuen Testament, privately printed, 1966.
Gnadengaben, R. F. Edel, 1966, translation by Herbert Klassen published as *Gifts and Graces: A Commentary on I Corinthians 12-14,* Hodder & Stoughton, 1967, Eerdmans, 1968.
Glossolalia: Wert und Problematik des Sprachenredens, Kuehne, 1967, 3rd edition, 1969.
Treuhaender Gottes, privately printed, 1967, translation by Clara K. Dyck published as *Gifts and Ministries,* Eerdmans, 1973.
(Editor) Carl Schneider, *Praktische Bibelkunde,* Die Rufer, 1968.
Im Kraftfeld des Heiligen Geistes, R. F. Edel, 1968, 4th edition, 1972.
Das Abendmahl im Neuen Testament und in der fruehen Kirche, Kuehne, 1969.
Ratschlaege fuer eine Gemeinde: Der Brief des Paulus an die Philipper, Kuehne, 1970, translation by Susan Wiesman published as *A Letter of Joy,* Bethany Fellowship, 1974.
(With Killian McDonnell) *The Baptism in the Holy Spirit as an Ecumenical Problem,* Charismatic Renewal Services, Inc., 1972.
Biblische Seelsorge, Oekumenischer Schriftendienst, 1973.
(Contributor) Claus Heitmann and Heribert Muehlen, editors, *Erfahrung und Theologie des Heiligen Geistes,* Koesel-Verlag, 1974.
(Contributor) J. Elmo Agrimson, editor, *Gifts of the Spirit and the Body of Christ: Perspectives on the Charismatic Movement,* Augsburg, 1974.
Papst und Pfingstler: Der romisch osatholisch, Peter Lang, 1978.
(Editor) *The Church Is Charismatic,* World Council of Churches, 1981.

Also author of booklets and devotional books. Contributor to *Lexikon zur Bibel* and to *Studia Liturgica* and other journals, occasionally under a pseudonym.

SIDELIGHTS: Arnold Bittlinger traveled throughout the United States in 1962, sponsored by the Lutheran World Federation, to study evangelism, stewardship, and congregational life. That trip and his 1971-72 stay at the Institute for Ecumenical and Cultural Research in Collegeville have been factors in his writings on the Charismatic Movement. Besides German, he also speaks English and French, and reads Spanish, Portuguese, Dutch, Italian, Latin, Greek, and Hebrew.

BIOGRAPHICAL/CRITICAL SOURCES:

BOOKS

Hollenweger, Walter, *Pentecostals: The Charismatic Movement in the Churches,* Augusburg, 1972.

* * *

BITTON, Davis 1930-

PERSONAL: Born February 22, 1930, in Blackfoot, Idaho; son of Ronald Wayne and Lola (Davis) Bitton; married Peggy Carnell, June 1, 1955 (divorced, 1981); married JoAn Borg Morris, October 18, 1985; children: (first marriage) Ronald, Kelly, Timothy, Tera, Stephanie. *Education:* Brigham Young University, B.A., 1956; Princeton University, M.A., 1958, Ph.D., 1961. *Religion:* Church of Jesus Christ of Latter-day Saints (Mormon).

ADDRESSES: Home—119 B St., Salt Lake City, Utah 84103. *Office*—Department of History, University of Utah, Salt Lake City, Utah 84112.

CAREER: University of Texas at Austin, instructor, 1959-62, assistant professor of history, 1962-64; University of California, Santa Barbara, assistant professor of history, 1964-66; University of Utah, Salt Lake City, associate professor, 1966-71, professor of history, 1971—. *Military service:* U.S. Army, 1953-55.

MEMBER: Mormon History Association (president, 1970-71), Sixteenth Century Studies Council, Utah State Historical Society.

WRITINGS:

The French Nobility in Crisis, 1560-1640, Stanford University Press, 1969.
(Editor) *The Reminiscences and Civil War Letters of Levi Lamoni Wight: Life in a Mormon Splinter Colony on the Texas Frontier,* University of Utah Press, 1970.
Guide to Mormon Diaries and Autobiographies, Brigham Young University Press, 1977.
(With Leonard J. Arrington) *The Mormon Experience: A History of the Latter-day Saints,* Knopf, 1979.
(With Gary L. Bunker) *Mormon Graphic Image, 1834-1914,* University of Utah Press, 1983.
(With Maureen Beecher) *New Views of Mormon History,* University of Utah Press, 1987.
(With Arrington) *Mormons and Their Histories,* University of Utah Press, 1988.
Les Mormons, Cerf, 1989.

WORK IN PROGRESS: Early modern historiography; Biblical exegesis.

BIOGRAPHICAL/CRITICAL SOURCES:

PERIODICALS

New York Times Book Review, August 10, 1980.

* * *

BLACK, Stanley Warren III 1939-

PERSONAL: Born July 8, 1939, in Charlotte, N.C.; son of Stanley Warren, Jr. (a banker) and Julia (Wilkes) Black; married Roberta Burr Callison, June 26, 1965; children: Stanley Wilkes, Sarah Constance. *Education:* University of North Carolina, A.B., 1961; Yale University, M.A., 1963, Ph.D., 1965.

ADDRESSES: Home—6608 Jocelyn Hollow Rd., Nashville, Tenn. 37205. *Office*—Department of Economics, Vanderbilt University, Box 6106, Station B, Nashville, Tenn. 37240.

CAREER: Council of Economic Advisers, Washington, D.C., staff economist, 1965-66; Princeton University, Princeton, N.J., assistant professor of economics, 1966-71, research associate in international finance, 1969-71; Federal Reserve, Board of Governors, Washington, D.C., visiting professor of economics, 1971-72; Vanderbilt University, Nashville, Tenn., associate professor, 1972-76, professor of economics, 1977—; Institute of International Economic Studies, Stockholm, Sweden, research fellow, 1975-76. Visiting professor, Rutgers University, 1970-71, and Yale University, 1980-81. Consultant, Federal Reserve Bank of New York, 1969; special assistant to Undersecretary of State for Economic Affairs, 1977-78.

MEMBER: American Economic Association, Economet Society.

AWARDS, HONORS: Ford Foundation research grant in international economic order, 1979-81.

WRITINGS:

International Money Markets and Flexible Exchange Rates, Princeton University Press, 1973.
Floating Exchange Rates and National Economic Policy, Yale University Press, 1977.
(Contributor) R. Lambra and W. Witte, editors, The Political Economy of Domestic and International Monetary Relations, Iowa State University Press, 1981.
The Banking System: A Preface to Public Interest Analysis, Public Interest Economics Foundation, c. 1985.
(With others) Foundations of Financial Management: First Canadian Edition, Irwin, 1987.

Contributor to journals, including Yale Economic Essays, Review of Economics and Statistics, Econometrica, Industrial and Labor Relations Review, Journal of Finance, and Review of Economic Studies. Member of editorial board, Southern Economic Journal, 1980-83.*

*   *   *

BLACKLIN, Malcolm
See CHAMBERS, Aidan

*   *   *

BLAKE, Robert W(illiam)   1930-

PERSONAL: Born January 25, 1930, in Springfield, Vt.; son of Kenneth D. (a salesman) and Erma Rhoda (Curtis) Blake; married Carol Ann Clark (a teacher), October 30, 1953; children: David, Brett, Robert W. Education: American International College, A.B., 1952; Boston University, A.M., 1954; University of Rochester, Ed.D., 1964. Politics: Republican. Religion: Episcopalian.

ADDRESSES: Home—61 College St., Brockport, N.Y. 14420. Office—Department of Education and Human Development, State University of New York College at Brockport, Brockport, N.Y. 14420.

CAREER: Worked as an English teacher in Massachusetts, 1957-58; Canandaigua Academy, Canandaigua, N.Y., English teacher, 1959-61, chairman of department of English, 1960-61, vice-principal, 1961-62; State University of New York College at Brockport, associate professor, 1963, professor of education, 1963—, chairman of department of curriculum and instruction, 1970—, coordinator of Teaching English to Speakers of Other Languages (TESOL), coordinator of English education. Vestry-

man, lay reader, and usher, Episcopalian Church. Military service: U.S. Army, 1955-56.

MEMBER: National Council of Teachers of English, National Teachers of English to Speakers of Other Languages, National Association for Supervision and Curriculum Development, New York State English Council (president, 1971-72; fellow, 1972), New York State Teachers of English to Speakers of Other Languages.

AWARDS, HONORS: Fellow Award, New York State English Council, 1974; award for excellence in college teaching, New York State English Council, 1978.

WRITINGS:

(With Paul McKee, Arno Jewett, and Corinne Watson) English for Meaning 7, Houghton, 1966.
The Effect of Special Instruction on the Ability of Seventh and Eighth Graders, U.S. Office of Education, 1966.
Language for Meaning 7, Houghton, 1978.
Language for Meaning 9, Houghton, 1981.
Reading, Writing and Interpreting Literature: Pedagogy, Positions, and Research, New York State English Council, 1989.
Whole Language: Explorations and Applications, New York State English Council, 1989.

Contributor to monographs and periodicals, including English Record, English Journal, Connecticut English Journal, Arizona English Bulletin, Indiana English Journal, English Education, Kansas English, Elementary English, Record, Midwest Educational Review, and Clearinghouse. Editor, English Record, 1967-70; editor, The Daily Sailor, 1979-81; editor, New York State English Council Monographs, 1987—.

WORK IN PROGRESS: Literature as a Way of Knowing: Critical Thinking and Moral Reasoning through Literature.

SIDELIGHTS: Robert W. Blake told CA: "I am currently working on a research monograph, Literature as a Way of Knowing, in which I maintain that although the prevailing model for critical thinking in our culture is 'scientific' and 'logical-mathematical,' literary knowing is, in many significant, qualitative ways, superior to scientific knowing. The plan of the book is to describe the current models of critical thinking—with their advantages and disadvantages—describe the elements of literary knowing, show how worthwhile literary pieces—through analysis and discussion—train individuals to read in special ways, to learn about themselves and about others, and to internalize through the study of literature the enduring values of a culture."

*   *   *

BLEGVAD, Lenore   1926-

PERSONAL: Born May 8, 1926, in New York, N.Y.; daughter of Julius C. (a mechanical engineer) and Ruth (a teacher; maiden name, Huebschman) Hochman; married Erik Blegvad (an illustrator), September 12, 1950; children: Peter, Kristoffer. Education: Vassar College, B.A., 1947; studied art in New York, N.Y. and Paris, France.

ADDRESSES: Home—Mountain Spring Farm, Wardsboro, Vt. 05355.

CAREER: Painter and writer. Exhibited abstract paper mache sculpture in London, 1975.

WRITINGS:

JUVENILES; ILLUSTRATED BY HUSBAND, ERIK BLEGVAD

Mr. Jensen and Cat, Harcourt, 1965.

One Is for the Sun, Harcourt, 1968.
The Great Hamster Hunt, Harcourt, 1969.
Moon-Watch Summer, Harcourt, 1972.
(Editor) *Mittens for Kittens and Other Rhymes about Cats,* Atheneum, 1974.
(Editor) *Hark! Hark! the Dogs Do Bark: And Other Rhymes about Dogs,* Atheneum, 1975.
(Editor) *This Little Pig-a-wig and Other Rhymes about Pigs,* Atheneum, 1978.
(Editor) *The Parrot in the Garret and Other Rhymes about Dwellings,* Atheneum, 1982.
Anna Banana and Me, Atheneum, 1985.
This Is Me, Random House, 1986.
Rainy Day Kate, Macmillan, 1987.

SIDELIGHTS: Lenore Blegvad told *CA:* "I divide my time between writing and painting, and which one I do at any given moment is dictated by various things: mood, inspiration, location (we live part of each year in Vermont, London and the south of France). I find the creative effort for each equally exciting, arduous, and absorbing. The change from one occupation to the other brings new insights every time and somehow suits me to perfection."

Blegvad has studied under Moses Sayer, Andre Lhote, Fernand Leger, and other artists.

BIOGRAPHICAL/CRITICAL SOURCES:

PERIODICALS

Book World, November 3, 1968, August 31, 1969.

* * *

BLISS, (John) Michael 1941-

PERSONAL: Born January 18, 1941, in Canada; son of Quartus (a physician) and Anne (Crow) Bliss; married Elizabeth Haslam (a teacher), June 29, 1963; children: James, Laura, Sara. *Education:* University of Toronto, B.A., 1962, M.A., 1966, Ph.D., 1972.

ADDRESSES: Home—314 Bessborough Dr., Toronto, Ontario, Canada M4G 2L1. *Office*—Department of History, University of Toronto, Toronto, Ontario, Canada M5S 1A1.

CAREER: University of Toronto, Ontario, lecturer, 1968-72, assistant professor, 1972-74, associate professor, 1974-78, professor of history, 1978—, member of governing council, 1976-78. Member of board of directors, Women's College Hospital.

MEMBER: Royal Society of Canada (fellow), Canadian Historical Association, American Association for the History of Medicine.

AWARDS, HONORS: City of Toronto Book Awards, 1978, for *A Canadian Millionaire: The Life and Business Times of Sir Joseph Flavelle, Bart., 1858-1939,* and 1982, for *The Discovery of Insulin;* Sir John A. Macdonald Prize, Canadian Historical Association, 1978, University of British Columbia Medal for Canadian Biography, 1978, Award of Merit, Toronto Historical Board, 1979, and F-X. Garneau Medal for the most outstanding contribution to Canadian history in the period 1978-1982, Canadian Historical Association, 1985, all for *A Canadian Millionaire;* National Magazine Awards, Canada, for business writing, 1981, and for political writing, 1982; Jason A. Hannah Medal for Medical History, Royal Society of Canada, 1983, and William H. Welch Medal, American Association for the History of Medicine, 1984, both for *The Discovery of Insulin;* National Business

Book Award, 1987, for *Northern Enterprise: Five Centuries of Canadian Business;* B. Tyrrell Medal, Royal Society of Canada, 1988.

WRITINGS:

Canadian History in Documents, 1763-1966, McGraw, 1966.
A Living Profit: Studies in the Social History of Canadian Business, 1883-1911, McClelland & Stewart (Toronto), 1974.
Confederation, 1867, F. Watts, 1975.
A Canadian Millionaire: The Life and Business Times of Sir Joseph Flavelle, Bart., 1858-1939, Macmillan, 1978.
The Discovery of Insulin, McClelland & Stewart (Toronto), 1982, University of Chicago Press, 1984.
Banting: A Biography, McClelland & Stewart, 1984.
Northern Enterprise: Five Centuries of Canadian Business, McClelland & Stewart, 1987.

Contributor of numerous scholarly articles and chapters to anthologies. Columnist, *Report on Business Magazine.* Contributor of articles and reviews to Canadian magazines.

SIDELIGHTS: Michael Bliss is a Canadian historian who specializes in the history of business, economics, and modern medicine. He has won a number of awards for his writing in all these areas, but he told *CA* that, among all his books, "*The Discovery of Insulin* is the book I wish to be remembered for." A professor of history at the University of Toronto, where insulin was discovered by Fred Banting and a team of researchers in 1922, Bliss's account of how this effective drug for diabetes was refined "has moments of pure genius," according to *Washington Post Book World* critic Peter H. Desmond. "Thoroughly researched and well written, *The Discovery of Insulin* deserved a place on the bookshelf alongside such eye-openers as James Watson's *The Double Helix* and Nicholas Wade's *The Nobel Duel.*"

BIOGRAPHICAL/CRITICAL SOURCES:

PERIODICALS

Globe and Mail (Toronto), March 24, 1984, March 9, 1985, July 18, 1987.
New York Times, September 14, 1982.
Times Literary Supplement, March 16, 1984.
Washington Post Book World, January 4, 1983.

* * *

BLOCK, Allan (Forrest) 1923-

PERSONAL: Born October 6, 1923, in Oshkosh, Wis.; son of Isadore Myron (a salvager) and Valeria (Greenblatt) Block; married Jean Keller, December 23, 1947 (divorced, 1963); married Fleur Bullock (a photographer and painter), August 23, 1965 (divorced June, 1974); children: (first marriage) Mona F. Young, Aurora, Paul. *Education:* Attended University of Wisconsin, 1939-41, and Columbia University, 1945-46.

ADDRESSES: Home—R.F.D. Bible Hill Rd., Francestown, N.H. 03043.

CAREER: Owner of sandal and leather-craft store in New York, N.Y., 1950-69, and in Francestown, N.H., 1969—. *Wartime service:* American Field Service, ambulance driver, 1941-43; served in Burma.

MEMBER: New England Poetry Club.

AWARDS, HONORS: Second prize for poetry, *Yankee,* 1970; Borestone Mountain poetry award, 1971, for "Through Old Farmhouse Windows."

WRITINGS:

POETRY

The Swelling under the Waves, Tiger's Eye Publishing, 1948.
Twenty Poems, Flatiron, 1961.
Beside Myself, Flatiron, 1962.
Living Around It, Flatiron, 1964.
In Noah's Wake, William Bauhan, 1972, 2nd edition, 1973.

Contributor to anthologies, including *Best Poems of 1970: Borestone Mountain Poetry Awards,* edited by Lionel Stevenson, Pacific Books, 1971; *Flowering after Frost,* edited by Michael McMahon, Branden Press, 1975; *Traveling America with Today's Poets,* edited by David Kherdian, Macmillan, 1977; and *I Sing the Song of Myself,* edited by Kherdian, Morrow, 1978. Contributor of poetry to journals.

WORK IN PROGRESS: Another book of poems.

*   *   *

BOND, Lewis H.
   See PAINE, Lauran (Bosworth)

*   *   *

BOND, Ruskin 1934-

PERSONAL: Born May 19, 1934, in Kasauli, India; son of Aubrey Alexander (in Royal Air Force) and Edith (Clerke) Bond. *Education:* Attended Bishop Cotton School, Simla, India, 1943-50.

ADDRESSES: Home—Ivy Cottage, Landoor, Mussoorie, Uttar Pradesh, India.

CAREER: Full-time writer, 1956—.

AWARDS, HONORS: John Llewellyn Rhys Memorial Prize for the most memorable work of 1957 by a writer under thirty, for *The Room on the Roof.*

WRITINGS:

The Room on the Roof (novel), Deutsch, 1956, Coward, 1957, reprinted, Penguin (India), 1988.
Grandfather's Private Zoo, India Book House, 1967.
Panther's Moon, Random House, 1969.
Angry River, Hamish Hamilton, 1972.
The Blue Umbrella, Hamish Hamilton, 1974.
The Cherry Tree, Hamish Hamilton, 1980.
A Flight of Pigeons, India Book House, 1980.
The Young Vagrants, India Book House, 1980.
The Road to the Bazaar, Julia MacRae (London), 1981.
Flames in the Forest, Julia MacRae, 1982.
Tales and Legends from India, Julia MacRae, 1983.
Earthquake, Julia MacRae, 1984.
Tigers Forever, Julia MacRae, 1984.
Getting Granny's Glasses, Julia MacRae, 1985.
Cricket for the Crocodile, Julia MacRae, 1986.
Adventures of Rama & Sita, Julia MacRae, 1987.
The Night Train at Deoli and Other Stories, Penguin, 1988.
The Eyes of the Eagle, Julia MacRae, 1988.
Time Stops at Shamli and Other Stories, Penguin, 1989.
Ghost Trouble, Julia MacRae, 1989.
Snake Trouble, Julia MacRae, 1990.
Dust on the Mountain, Julia MacRae, 1990.

Also contributor to anthologies. Contributor of short stories and articles to periodicals, including *Short Story International, Read-*

er's Digest, Christian Science Monitor, School, Cricket, New Renaissance, and *Blackwood's.*

WORK IN PROGRESS: Short stories; children's books; *Himalayan Flowers* (nonfiction).

SIDELIGHTS: Ruskin Bond's books deal with life in his native India. Bond told *CA:* "My interests (children, mountains, folklore, nature) are embodied in [my books]. . . . Once you have lived in the mountains, you belong to them and must come back again and again. There is no escape." He adds that *Dust on the Mountain* "strongly expresses" his concern for the degradation of the environment in the Himalayas.

Some of Bond's books have been translated into French, German, Dutch, Danish, and Spanish.

MEDIA ADAPTATIONS: A Flight of Pigeons was filmed as "Junoon" in Hindi.

AVOCATIONAL INTERESTS: Old songs (favorite singer, Nelson Eddy).

*   *   *

BONNER, Jack
   See PAINE, Lauran (Bosworth)

*   *   *

BOSWORTH, Frank
   See PAINE, Lauran (Bosworth)

*   *   *

BOVEE, Ruth
   See PAINE, Lauran (Bosworth)

*   *   *

BOYLE, Mark
   See Kienzle, William X(avier)

*   *   *

BRADFORD, Will
   See PAINE, Lauran (Bosworth)

*   *   *

BRADLEY, Concho
   See PAINE, Lauran (Bosworth)

*   *   *

BRADLEY, Marion Zimmer 1930-
   (Elfrida Rivers)

PERSONAL: Born June 3, 1930, in Albany, N.Y.; daughter of Leslie (a carpenter) and Evelyn (a historian; maiden name, Conklin) Zimmer; married Robert A. Bradley, October, 1949 (divorced, 1963); married Walter Henry Breen (a numismatist), February, 1964; children: (first marriage) David Robert; (second marriage) Patrick Russell, Moira Evelyn Dorothy. *Education:* Attended New York State College for Teachers (now State University of New York at Albany), 1946-48; Hardin-Simmons College, B.A., 1964; additional study at University of California, Berkeley. *Politics:* None.

ADDRESSES: Home—Berkeley, Calif. *Office*—P.O. Box 245-A, Berkeley, Calif. 94701. *Agent*—Scott Meredith Literary Agency, Inc., 845 Third Ave., New York, N.Y. 10022.

CAREER: Writer and musician; editor, "Marion Zimmer Bradley's Fantasy Magazine."

MEMBER: Authors Guild, Science Fiction Writers of America, Mystery Writers of America, Horror Writers of America, Gay Academic Union, Alpha Chi.

AWARDS, HONORS: Invisible Little Man Award, 1977; Leigh Brackett Memorial Sense of Wonder Award, 1978, for *The Forbidden Tower;* Locus Award for best fantasy novel, 1984, for *The Mists of Avalon.*

WRITINGS:

SCIENCE FICTION/FANTASY

The Door through Space [bound with *Rendezvous on Lost Planet* by A. Bertram Chandler], Ace Books, 1961, reprinted, Arrow, 1979.
Seven from the Stars [bound with *Worlds of the Imperium* by Keith Laumer], Ace Books, 1962.
The Colors of Space, Monarch, 1963, revised edition, Donning, 1988.
Falcons of Narabedla [and] *The Dark Intruder and Other Stories,* Ace Books, 1964.
The Brass Dragon [bound with *Ipomoea* by John Rackham], Ace Books, 1969.
Hunters of the Red Moon, DAW Books, 1973.
The Parting of Arwen (short story), T-K Graphics, 1974.
The Endless Voyage, Ace Books, 1975, expanded edition published as *Endless Universe,* 1979.
The Ruins of Isis, Donning, 1978.
(With brother, Paul Edwin Zimmer) *The Survivors,* DAW Books, 1979.
The House between the Worlds, Doubleday, 1980, revised edition, Del Rey, 1981.
Survey Ship, Ace Books, 1980.
Web of Light (also see below), Donning, 1982.
The Mists of Avalon, Knopf, 1983.
(Editor and contributor) *Greyhaven: An Anthology of Fantasy,* DAW Books, 1983.
Web of Darkness (also see below), Donning, 1983.
The Inheritor, Tor Books, 1984.
(Editor) *Sword and Sorceress* (annual anthology), Volumes 1-5, DAW Books, 1984-88.
Night's Daughter, Ballantine, 1985.
(With Vonda McIntyre) *Lythande* (anthology), DAW Books, 1986.
The Fall of Atlantis (contains *Web of Light* and *Web of Darkness*), Baen Books, 1987.
The Firebrand, Simon & Schuster, 1987.
Warrior Woman, DAW Books, 1988.

"DARKOVER" SCIENCE FICTION SERIES

The Sword of Aldones [and] *The Planet Savers,* Ace Books, 1962, reprinted as *Planet Savers: The Sword of Aldones,* 1984.
The Bloody Sun, Ace Books, 1964, revised edition, 1979.
Star of Danger, Ace Books, 1965, reprinted, 1988.
The Winds of Darkover [bound with *The Anything Tree* by Rackham], Ace Books, 1970, reprinted, 1985.
The World Wreckers, Ace Books, 1971, reprinted, 1988.
Darkover Landfall, DAW Books, 1972.

The Spell Sword, DAW Books, 1974.
The Heritage of Hastur (also see below), DAW Books, 1975.
The Shattered Chain (also see below), DAW Books, 1976.
The Forbidden Tower, DAW Books, 1977.
Stormqueen!, DAW Books, 1978.
(Editor and contributor) *Legends of Hastur and Cassilda,* Thendara House Publications, 1979.
(Editor and contributor) *Tales of the Free Amazons,* Thendara House Publications, 1980.
Two to Conquer, DAW Books, 1980.
(Editor and contributor) *The Keeper's Price and Other Stories,* DAW Books, 1980.
Sharra's Exile (also see below), DAW Books, 1981.
(Editor and contributor) *Sword of Chaos,* DAW Books, 1981.
Children of Hastur (includes *The Heritage of Hastur* and *Sharra's Exile*), Doubleday, 1981.
Hawkmistress!, DAW Books, 1982.
Thendara House (also see below), DAW Books, 1983.
Oath of the Renunciates (includes *The Shattered Chain* and *Thendara House*), Doubleday, 1983.
City of Sorcery, DAW Books, 1984.
(Editor and contributor) *Free Amazons of Darkover,* DAW Books, 1985.
(With the Friends of Darkover) *Red Sun of Darkover,* DAW Books, 1987.
(With the Friends of Darkover) *The Other Side of the Mirror and Other Darkover Stories,* DAW Books, 1987.
(Editor and contributor) *Four Moons of Darkover,* DAW Books, 1988.

OTHER

Songs from Rivendell, privately printed, 1959.
A Complete, Cumulative Checklist of Lesbian, Variant, and Homosexual Fiction, privately printed, 1960.
Castle Terror (novel), Lancer, 1965.
Souvenir of Monique (novel), Ace Books, 1967.
Bluebeard's Daughter (novel), Lancer, 1968.
(Translator) Lope de Vega, *El Villano en su Rincon,* privately printed, 1971.
Dark Satanic (novel), Berkley Publishing, 1972, reprinted, Tor Books, 1988.
In the Steps of the Master (teleplay novelization), Tempo Books, 1973.
Men, Halflings, and Hero Worship (criticism), T-K Graphics, 1973.
The Necessity for Beauty: Robert W. Chamber and the Romantic Tradition (criticism), T-K Graphics, 1974.
The Jewel of Arwen (criticism), T-K Graphics, 1974.
Can Ellen Be Saved? (teleplay novelization), Tempo Books, 1975.
(With Alfred Bester and Norman Spinrad) *Experiment Perilous: Three Essays in Science Fiction,* Algol Press, 1976.
(Contributor) Darrell Schweitzer, editor, *Essays Lovecraftian,* T-K Graphics, 1976.
Drums of Darkness (novel), Ballantine, 1976.
The Catch Trap, Ballantine, 1979.

Also author of novels under undisclosed pseudonyms. Contributor, sometimes under Elfrida Rivers and other pseudonyms, to anthologies and periodicals, including *Magazine of Fantasy and Science Fiction, Amazing Stories,* and *Venture.*

WORK IN PROGRESS: The Forest House, a novel about Eilan, the Druid princess who falsified omens; *The Black Trillium,* a novel, with fellow fantasy writers Andre Norton and Julian May.

SIDELIGHTS: Marion Zimmer Bradley is author of one of the best-loved series in science fiction and fantasy; her "Darkover" novels have not only inspired their own fan magazines, or "fanzines," but also a series of story collections in which other authors set their tales in Bradley's universe. A lost colony rediscovered after centuries of neglect by Earth's "Terran Empire," Darkover has developed its own society and technology, both of which produce internal and external conflicts. Darkover fascinates so many readers because it is a world of many contradictions; not only do the psychic abilities of the natives contrast with the traditional technologies of the empire, but a basically repressive patriarchal society coexists (however uneasily) with groups such as an order of female Renunciates, the "Free Amazons." Consisting of over twenty books and spanning many years of the world's history, "the Darkover novels test various attitudes about the importance of technology, and more important, they study the very nature of human intimacy," claims Rosemarie Arbur in *Twentieth-Century Science Fiction Writers.* The critic explains that "by postulating a Terran Empire the main features of which are advanced technology and bureaucracy, and a Darkover that seems technologically backward and is fiercely individualistic, Bradley sets up a conflict to which there is no 'correct' resolution." The permutations of this basic conflict have provided Bradley with numerous opportunities to explore several themes in various ways.

For example, Susan M. Shwartz observes in *The Feminine Eye: Science Fiction and the Women Who Write It* that one theme in particular provides a foundation for the Darkover novels: "For every gain, there is a risk; choice involves a testing of will and courage." Unlike some fantasy worlds where struggles are easily decided, "on Darkover any attempt at change or progress carries with it the need for pain-filled choice," Shwartz comments. While Bradley provides her characters with ample avenues of action, "in the Darkover books, alternatives are predicated upon two things," the critic outlines: "sincere choice and a willingness to pay the price choice demands." *The Shattered Chain,* for example, "in terms of its structure, plot, characterization, and context within the series, is about all the choices of all women on Darkover and, through them, of all people, male and female, Darkovan and Terran."

The Shattered Chain is one of Bradley's most renowned Darkover novels and, as Arbur describes it in her study *Marion Zimmer Bradley,* "is one of the most thorough and sensitive science-fiction explorations of the variety of options available to a self-actualizing woman; not only does it present us with four strong and different feminine characters who make crucial decisions about their lives but its depth of characterizations permits us to examine in detail the consequences of these decisions." The novel begins as a traditional quest when Lady Rohana, a noblewoman of the ruling class, enlists the aid of a tribe of Free Amazons to rescue a kidnapped kinswoman from a settlement where women are chained to show that they are possessions. But while the rescue is eventually successful, it is only the beginning of a series of conflicts; Rohana's experiences force her to reevaluate her life, and both the daughter of the woman she rescued and a Terran agent who studies the Amazons find themselves examining the limits of their own situations. "As we see in *The Shattered Chain,*" Shwartz concludes, "the payment for taking an oath is the payment for all such choices: pain, with a potential for achievement. In Bradley's other books, too, the price of choice is of great importance."

In coming to this conclusion about the price of choice, Bradley emphasizes two other themes, as Laura Murphy states in the *Dictionary of Literary Biography:* "The first is the reconciliation of conflicting or opposing forces—whether such forces are represented by different cultures or by different facets of a single personality. The second," the critic continues, "closely related to the first, is alienation or exile from a dominant group." While these ideas are featured in Bradley's Darkover series, they also appear in the author's first big mainstream best seller, *The Mists of Avalon.* "Colorfully detailed as a medieval tapestry, *The Mists of Avalon . . .* is probably the most ambitious retelling of the Arthurian legend in the twentieth century," Charlotte Spivack maintains in *Merlin's Daughters: Contemporary Women Writers of Fantasy.* The critic adds that this novel "is much more than a retelling. . . . [It] is a profound revisioning. Imaginatively conceived, intricately structured, and richly peopled, it offers a brilliant reinterpretation of the traditional material from the point of view of the major female characters," such as Arthur's mother Igraine, the Lady of the Lake, Viviane, Arthur's half-sister, the enchantress Morgaine, and Arthur's wife, Gwenhwyfar.

In addition, Bradley presents the eventual downfall of Arthur's reign as the result of broken promises to the religious leaders of Avalon; while Arthur gained his crown with the aid of Viviane and the Goddess she represents, the influence of Christian priests and Gwenhwyfar lead him to forsake his oath. Thus not only does Bradley present Arthur's story from a different viewpoint, she roots it "in the religious struggle between matriarchal worship of the goddess and the patriarchal institution of Christianity, between what [the author] calls 'the cauldron and the cross,' " describes Spivack. In presenting this conflict, Bradley "memorably depicts the inevitable passing of times and religions by her use of the imagery of different simultaneous worlds, which move out of consciousness as their day ebbs," remarks Maude McDaniel in the *Washington Post.* "Bradley also compares head-on the pre-Christian Druidism of Britain and the Christianity that supplants it, a refreshing change from some modern writers who tend to take refuge at awkward moments in cryptic metaphysics."

Despite this praise for Bradley's fresh approach, McDaniel finds *The Mists of Avalon* too motionless in its treatment of the Arthurian legend: "It all seems strangely static," the critic writes, "set pieces the reader watches rather than enters. Aside from a couple of lackluster jousts, everything is intrigue, jealousy and personal relationships, so that finally we are left with more bawling than brawling." *Science Fiction Review* contributor Darrell Schweitzer concurs, for while he finds *The Mists of Avalon* "certainly an original and quite well-thought-out version," he faults the novel for changes which are "all in the direction of the mundane, the ordinary." The critic explains: "Most of the interesting parts happen offstage. Alas, for whatever reason the women, Morgaine in particular, just aren't that central to the whole story. They aren't present at the crucial moments."

Maureen Quilligan, however, believes that Bradley's emphasis on Morgaine and the other female characters is both effective and appropriate; as she writes in the *New York Times Book Review,* by "looking at the Arthurian legend from the other side, as in one of Morgaine's magic weavings, we see all the interconnecting threads, not merely the artful pattern. . . . 'The Mists of Avalon' rewrites Arthur's story so that we realize it has always also been the story of his sister, the Fairy Queen." By presenting another side, the critic adds, "this, the untold Arthurian story, is no less tragic, but it has gained a mythic coherence; reading it is a deeply moving and at times uncanny experience." "In short," concludes Beverly Deweese in another *Science Fiction Review* article, "Bradley's Arthurian world is intriguingly different. Undoubtedly, the brisk pace, the careful research and the provocative concept will attract and please many readers. . . . [But] overall, *Mists of Avalon* is one of the best and most ambitious of the Arthurian novels, and it should not be missed."

Bradley uses similar themes and approaches in reworking another classic tale: *The Firebrand,* the story of the fall of Troy and of Kassandra, royal daughter of Troy and onetime priestess and Amazon. As the author remarked in an interview with *Publishers Weekly*'s Lisa See, in the story of Troy she saw another instance of male culture overtaking and obscuring female contributions: "During the Dorian invasion, when iron won out over bronze, the female cult died," Bradley explained. "The Minoan and Mycenaean cultures were dead overnight. But you could also look at [that period of history] and say, here were two cultures that should have been ruled by female twins—Helen and Klytemnestra. And what do you know? When they married Menelaus and Agamemnon, the men took over their cities. I just want to look at what history was really like before the women-haters got hold of it. I want to look at these people like any other people, as though no one had ever written about them before." The result of Bradley's reconstruction, as *New York Times Book Review* contributor Mary Lefkowitz describes it, is that Kassandra "becomes active, even aggressive; she determines the course of history, despite the efforts of her father, her brothers and other brutal male warriors to keep her in her place." "The dust of the war fairly rises off the page," notes a *Publishers Weekly* reviewer, "as Bradley animates this rich history and vivifies the conflicts between a culture that reveres the strength of women and one that makes them mere consorts of powerful men."

Despite this emphasis on female viewpoints in *The Firebrand* and her other fiction, Bradley is not a "feminist" writer. "Though her interest in women's rights is strong," elaborates Murphy, "her works do not reduce to mere polemic." Arbur similarly states that the author "refuses to allow her works to wander into politics unless true concerns of realistic characters bring them there. Her emphasis is on character, not political themes." "Bradley's writing openly with increasing sureness of the human psyche and the human being rendered whole prompted Theodore Sturgeon to call the former [science fiction] fan 'one of the Big ones' currently writing science fiction," Arbur relates in *Twentieth-Century Science Fiction Writers.* "That she has extended her range" beyond science fiction and into "mainstream" fiction, the critic concludes, "suggests that Sturgeon's phrase applies no longer only to the science-fiction writer Marion Zimmer Bradley continues to be, for she has transcended categories."

AVOCATIONAL INTERESTS: "Currently very active in feminist and gay rights," supports Merola, an opera apprentice program.

BIOGRAPHICAL/CRITICAL SOURCES:

BOOKS

Alpers, H. J., editor, *Marion Zimmer Bradley's Darkover,* Corian, 1983.
Arbur, Rosemarie, *Leigh Brackett, Marion Zimmer Bradley, Anne McCaffrey: A Primary and Secondary Bibliography,* G. K. Hall, 1982.
Arbur, Rosemarie, *Marion Zimmer Bradley,* Starmont House, 1985.
Breen, Walter, *The Gemini Problem: A Study of Darkover,* T-K Graphics, 1975.
Breen, Walter, *The Darkover Concordance: A Reader's Guide,* Pennyfarthing Press, 1979.

The Darkover Cookbook, Friends of Darkover, 1977, revised edition, 1979.
Dictionary of Literary Biography, Volume 8: *Twentieth-Century American Science Fiction Writers,* Gale, 1981.
Lane, Daryl, editor, *The Sound of Wonder, Volume 2,* Oryx, 1985.
Magill, Frank, editor, *Survey of Science Fiction Literature,* Volume 1, Salem Press, 1979.
Magill, Frank, editor, *Survey of Modern Fantasy Literature,* Volume 1, Salem Press, 1983.
Paxson, Diana, *Costume and Clothing as a Cultural Index on Darkover,* Friends of Darkover, 1977, revised edition, 1981.
Spivack, Charlotte, *Merlin's Daughters: Contemporary Women of Fantasy,* Greenwood Press, 1987.
Staicar, Tom, editor, *The Feminine Eye: Science Fiction and the Women Who Write It,* Ungar, 1982.
Twentieth-Century Science Fiction Writers, St. James Press, 1986.
Wise, S., *The Darkover Dilemma: Problems of the Darkover Series,* T-K Graphics, 1976.

PERIODICALS

Algol, winter, 1977/1978.
Fantasy Review of Fantasy and Science Fiction, April, 1984.
Los Angeles Times Book Review, February 3, 1983.
Mythlore, spring, 1984.
New York Times Book Review, January 30, 1983, November 29, 1987.
Publishers Weekly, September 11, 1987, October 30, 1987.
San Francisco Examiner, February 27, 1983.
Science Fiction Review, summer, 1983.
Washington Post, January 28, 1983.
West Coast Review of Books, Number 5, 1986.

—*Sketch by Diane Telgen*

*   *   *

BRADSHAW, Buck
See PAINE, Lauran (Bosworth)

*   *   *

BRADY, Nicholas
See LEVINSON, Leonard

*   *   *

BRAZELL, Karen   1938-

PERSONAL: Born April 25, 1938, in Buffalo, N.Y.; daughter of Charles Cary Woodard (an electrician) and Josephine Mary (Bordonoro) Woodard Watson Gay; married James Reid Brazell (a professor), August 27, 1961 (divorced March, 1978); children: Katherine Ann Rivera, Stephen Reid. *Education:* Attended College of Wooster, 1956-58, and International Christian University, 1958-60; University of Michigan, B.A., 1961, M.A., 1962; Columbia University, Ph.D., 1969. *Politics:* Democrat.

ADDRESSES: Home—311 Roat St., Ithaca, N.Y. 14850. *Office*—Department of Asian Studies, 378 Rockefeller Hall, Cornell University, Ithaca, N.Y. 14853.

CAREER: Princeton University, Princeton, N.J., assistant professor of Japanese literature, 1969-74; Cornell University, Ithaca, N.Y., associate professor, 1974-79, professor of Japanese literature, 1979—, chairperson of department of Asian studies,

1977-82, director of East Asia program, 1987—. Visiting professor, University of California, Berkeley, 1984. Member, Social Science Research Council-American Council of Learned Societies joint committee on Japan, 1973-78, and Council for International Exchange of Scholars advisory screening committee in Japanese studies, 1974-77. Member of board of trustees, Cornell University, 1979-83.

MEMBER: Association for Asian Studies (member of Northeast Asia council, 1974-77), Association of Teachers of Japanese (member of executive committee, 1981-83, member of board of directors, 1989—), Phi Beta Kappa (senator-at-large, 1976-82; member of board of trustees, 1977-82).

AWARDS, HONORS: Fulbright-Hayes fellowship and Social Science Research Council-American Council of Learned Societies joint committee on Japan grant for research in Kyoto, Japan, both 1972-73; National Book Award Translation Prize, 1974, for *The Confessions of Lady Nijo;* National Endowment for the Humanities fellowship, 1974; Cornell University Society for the Humanities fellowship, 1976-77; Japan Foundation fellowship for research in Kyoto, 1978, 1985; National Institute of Japanese Literature Research fellowship in Tokyo, 1988-89.

WRITINGS:

(Contributor of translation) Donald Keene, editor, *Twenty Plays of the Noh Theater,* Columbia University Press, 1970.
(Translator) *The Confessions of Lady Nijo,* Doubleday, 1973.
(With Monica Bethe) *Noh as Performance: An Analysis of the Kuse Scene of "Yamamba"* (monograph), China-Japan Program, Cornell University, 1978.
(With Bethe) *Dance in the Noh Theater,* Volume 1: *Dance Analysis,* Volume 2: *Plays and Scores,* Volume 3: *Dance Patterns,* Cornell East Asia Program, 1982.
(Editor) *Twelve Plays of the Noh and Kyogen Theaters,* Cornell East Asia Program, 1988.

Contributor of articles and reviews to *Harvard Journal of Asiatic Studies, Monumenta Nipponica, Journal of Japanese Studies, Journal of the Association of Teachers of Japanese, World Literature Today, Parabola, Literature East and West, Par Rapport,* and *Journal of Asian Studies.* Assistant editor, *Journal of Asian Studies,* 1975-78; associate editor, *Journal of Japanese Studies,* 1978-81.

*   *   *

BRENDON, Piers (George Rundle) 1940-

PERSONAL: Born December 21, 1940, in Cornwall, England; son of George (a writer) and Frances (a journalist; maiden name, Cook) Brendon; married Vyvyen Davis (a teacher), 1968; children: George, Oliver. *Education:* Magdalene College, Cambridge, M.A., 1965, Ph.D., 1970. *Politics:* Labour.

ADDRESSES: Home—4B Millington Rd., Cambridge, England. *Agent*—Curtis Brown Ltd., 162-168 Regent St., London W1R 5TA, England.

CAREER: Cambridgeshire College of Arts and Technology, Cambridge, England, lecturer in history, 1966-79, head of department, 1977-79; writer, 1979—. Occasional lecturer and broadcaster.

WRITINGS:

(Editor with William Shaw) *Reading They've Liked,* Macmillan, 1967.
(Editor with Shaw) *Reading Matters,* Macmillan, 1969.
(Editor with Shaw) *By What Authority?,* Macmillan, 1972.

Hurrell Froude and the Oxford Movement, Merrimack Books Service, 1974.
Hawker of Morwenstow: Portrait of a Victorian Eccentric, J. Cape, 1975.
Eminent Edwardians, Secker & Warburg, 1979, Houghton, 1980.
(With Rex Bloomstein) "Auschwitz and the Allies" (documentary), British Broadcasting Corp. (BBC-TV), 1981.
The Life and Death of the Press Barons, Secker & Warburg, 1982, Atheneum, 1983.
Winston Churchill: A Biography, Harper, 1984 (published in England as *Winston Churchill: A Brief Life,* Secker & Warburg, 1984).
(With Bloomstein) "Human Rights" (documentary), Thames TV, 1984.
Ike: His Life and Times, Harper, 1986 (published in England as *Ike: The Life and Times of Dwight D. Eisenhower,* Secker & Warburg, 1986).
Our Own Dear Queen, Secker & Warburg, 1986, David & Charles, 1987.
Thomas Cook: 150 Years of Popular Tourism, Secker & Warburg, in press.

Co-author of other television documentary scripts. Contributor of reviews to numerous periodicals and newspapers, including the London *Times, New York Times, Observer, Mail on Sunday,* and *Columbia Journalism Review.*

WORK IN PROGRESS: Research on a history of the 1930s.

SIDELIGHTS: With *The Life and Death of the Press Barons,* "Piers Brendon has revived, with elegance and distinction, the discipline of digestible history which gave writers like Barbara Tuchman their early success: a 'tissue of innumerable biographies,' only lightly drawn together with generalizations, strongly spiced by anecdote, and written in a style that combines bravura with allusiveness," states Roy Foster in the *Times Literary Supplement.* "This is a more substantial achievement than it may sound; the subjects for such an approach need to be carefully selected, the terrain well mapped, and the material produced with a sustained flourish," the critic continues. "His new book succeeds on these levels." *The Life and Death of the Press Barons* is a "witty study of the press lords of England and America," summarizes *Washington Post Book World* contributor Bernard A. Weisberger, containing "some 250 of the funniest and shrewdest pages of business and cultural history that you are likely to find between covers in any given year." Tracing the careers and idiosyncracies of executives such as Joseph Pulitzer, Horace Greeley, William Randolph Hearst, and James Gordon Bennett, the author "offers routine cautions on the growth of conglomerates and other sober matters," observes the *New York Times*'s Walter Goodman, "but the main pleasures of his book lie in the portraits of the men who made the papers." Although these anecdotes constitute a major portion of the book, "the range of sources behind *The Life and Death of the Press Barons* is eclectic and interesting, and some of the best material . . . comes from unpublished sources," Foster concludes. "What emerges is on one level a gallery of eccentrics, and on another a series of studies in the tactics of power."

Brendon narrows his focus to a single individual in *Winston Churchill: A Biography;* because many in-depth studies of the British Prime Minister have been written, "Brendon has wisely settled for a 'brief life,' which is in effect a brilliant sketch for a portrait," remarks *Times Literary Supplement* contributor C. M. Woodhouse. Despite its brevity, "*Winston Churchill* is nonetheless a brilliant *tour de force*," asserts Joe Mysak in the *National*

Review, "even if it is not quite Winston Churchill. Recounting ninety years at breakneck speed, especially ninety years as densely packed as Churchill's, inevitably produces distortion." The critic explains that while the author "is not seduced by the minutiae of experience, and he is not tedious," nevertheless "he is better at telling what his subject did than what he was like."

London *Times* contributor Woodrow Wyatt, however, claims that "small blemishes apart, a reader who does not want to know too much about Churchill can safely begin here." By using a variety of anecdotes, "Brendon builds a convincing picture of the great man," Woodhouse notes. "His judgment is good and his style succinct. His view of Churchill is entirely without hagiography . . . [exposing] the warts and all." "Most important of all," concludes Mysak, "Mr. Brendon demonstrates that Churchill was one of those relics, those dinosaurs, who fought all his life for duty, honor, and country." That the author "does so within the boundaries he has set for himself, in a Churchillian 'reconnaissance in force,' proves a stylish mastery that the flaws of this book cannot vitiate."

The author's aim in *Ike: His Life and Times,* "as with his previously acclaimed study of Winston Churchill, was to write a succinct and readable biography and this he has achieved admirably," Edward Hamilton observes in the *Spectator.* Brendon's study of former president Dwight D. Eisenhower "is fluently written, witty and never loses sight of the subject," the critic adds. "If sometimes the judgments are too sweeping, the tone too flippant in the desire for the memorable phrase, all can be forgiven. This is a tour-de-force and should confirm Brendon as one of the best writers of history at work today." *New York Times Book Review* contributor Townsend Hoopes similarly calls *Ike* a "witty [and] perceptive" analysis that is "new and arresting in . . . the author's moral penetration and his concentration on gathering evidence to show Eisenhower's chronic vacillation and remarkably opaque moral standards." While the critic also faults Brendon for the occasional oversimplification, "nevertheless, this is a telling analysis that is bound to have an impact on the current debate over Eisenhower's proper place in history."

"Rich with insight and good humor, taking Eisenhower from boyhood through his two presidential terms," as Guy Halverson describes it in the *Christian Science Monitor,* Brendon's biography "is especially useful . . . [in] demythologiz[ing] the Eisenhower-as-instant-hero viewpoint that has arisen in recent years." Fred Greenstein explains in a *Washington Post Book World* article that "there are two quite separable kinds of Eisenhower revisionism" that have improved the former president's rating over previous assessments. "Brendon has read [this] new scholarship on Eisenhower and delved into the archives," the critic elaborates. "He is familiar with the seeming contradictions" of Eisenhower's presidential career, and his challenges to the new theories "lead him to raise important questions." Greenstein adds that "although Brendon is unable to do full justice to his subject or his own commendable aims, he provides an original account of an historical actor about whom much more remains to be said." "As the author convincingly demonstrates," writes Hamilton, "Eisenhower was a highly complex man whom it was all too easy to take at his own apparent estimation. . . . Brendon calls him 'one of the most enigmatic characters ever to occupy the White House' and admits there will never be a last word on him," the critic concludes. "Meanwhile however, Piers Brendon's book will do just fine."

Brendon told *CA:* "Were I to fill in this section properly, it would consist of a paean of nihilistic hatred and Swiftian vituperation directed at almost every aspect of public life I can think of, from Mrs. Thatcher to dumping nuclear waste in the seas, from racialism to killing whales, from sports and sportspersons to the drivel excreted by the media. In short, the only optimistic features on my horizon are private ones—family, friends, and work."

BIOGRAPHICAL/CRITICAL SOURCES:

PERIODICALS

Christian Science Monitor, June 24, 1983, October 3, 1986.
National Review, November 2, 1984.
New York Times, April 7, 1983.
New York Times Book Review, April 20, 1980, November 30, 1986.
Spectator, January 10, 1987.
Times (London), April 5, 1984, November 13, 1986.
Times Literary Supplement, February 18, 1983, April 13, 1984.
Washington Post Book World, April 24, 1983, September 7, 1986.

—*Sketch by Diane Telgen*

*   *   *

BRENNAN, Will
     See PAINE, Lauran (Bosworth)

*   *   *

BRENNER, Barbara (Johnes)   1925-

PERSONAL: Born June 26, 1925, in Brooklyn, N.Y.; daughter of Robert Lawrence (a real estate broker) and Marguerite (Furboter) Johnes; married Fred Brenner (an illustrator), March 16, 1947; children: Mark, Carl. *Education:* Attended Seton Hall College (now University), 1942-43, Rutgers University, 1944-46, New York University, 1953-54, and New School for Social Research, 1960-62. *Politics:* Independent.

ADDRESSES: Home—Box 1826, Hemlock Farms, Hawley, Pa. 18428.

CAREER: Prudential Insurance Co., copywriter, 1942-46; free-lance artist's agent, 1946-52; free-lance writer, 1957—. County chairman, Committee for a Sane Nuclear Policy, 1960-61.

MEMBER: Authors Guild, Authors League of America.

AWARDS, HONORS: New York Herald Tribune Children's Spring Book Festival honor book award, 1961, for *Barto Takes the Subway; Washington Post Book World* Spring Book Festival honor book award, 1970, and American Library Association notable book citation, both for *A Snake-Lover's Diary;* National Science Teachers Association and Children's Book Council award, 1974, for *Lizard Tails and Cactus Spines,* 1977, for *On the Frontier with Mr. Audubon,* 1979, for *Beware! These Animals Are Poison,* and 1980, for *Have You Heard of a Kangeroo Bird?: Fascinating Facts about Unusual Birds;* American Library Association notable book citation, 1978, for *Wagon Wheels;* Best of the Best Award from *School Library Journal,* 1982, for *On the Frontier with Mr. Audubon.*

WRITINGS:

JUVENILES

Somebody's Slippers, Somebody's Shoes, W. R. Scott, 1957.
Barto Takes the Subway, Knopf, 1961.
A Bird in the Family (Junior Literary Guild selection), W. R. Scott, 1962.
Amy's Doll, Knopf, 1963.
The Five Pennies, Knopf, 1963.
Beef Stew, Knopf, 1965.

The Flying Patchwork Quilt, illustrated by husband Fred Brenner, Knopf, 1965.

Mr. Tall and Mr. Small, W. R. Scott, 1966.

Nicky's Sister, Knopf, 1966.

Summer of the Houseboat, Knopf, 1968.

Faces, illustrated with photographs by George Ancona, Dutton, 1970.

A Snake-Lover's Diary, W. R. Scott, 1970.

A Year in the Life of Rosie Bernard, Harper, 1971, revised edition, Avon, 1983.

Is It Bigger Than a Sparrow?: A Box for Young Bird Watchers, Knopf, 1972.

Walt Disney's "Three Little Pigs," Random House, 1972.

Bodies, illustrated with photographs by Ancona, Dutton, 1973.

If You Were an Ant, Harper, 1973.

Walt Disney's "The Penguin That Hated the Cold," Random House, 1973.

Hemi: A Mule, Harper, 1973.

Baltimore Orioles, illustrated by J. Winslow Higginbottom, Harper, 1974.

Cunningham's Rooster, illustrated by Anne Rockwell, Parents' Magazine Press, 1975.

Lizard Tails and Cactus Spines, illustrated with photographs by Merrit S. Keasey III, Harper, 1975.

Little One Inch, illustrated by F. Brenner, Coward, 1977.

On the Frontier with Mr. Audubon, Coward, 1977.

We're Off to See the Lizard, illustrated by Shelley Dietreichs, Raintree Editions, 1977.

Wagon Wheels, illustrated by Don Bolognese, Harper, 1978.

Our Class Presents Ostrich Feathers: A Play in Two Acts (first produced Off-Broadway, 1965), illustrated by Vera B. Williams, Parents' Magazine Press, 1978.

Beware! These Animals Are Poison, illustrated by Jim Spanfeller, Coward, 1979.

(With May Garelick) *The Tremendous Tree Book,* Four Winds Press, 1979.

Have You Ever Heard of a Kangeroo Bird?: Fascinating Facts about Unusual Birds, illustrated by Irene Brady, Coward, 1980.

The Prince and the Pink Blanket, illustrated by Nola Langner, Four Winds Press, 1980.

A Killing Season, Four Winds Press, 1981.

Mystery of the Plumed Serpent, Knopf, 1981.

Mystery of the Disappearing Dogs, Knopf, 1982.

A Dog I Know, Harper, 1983.

The Gorilla Signs Love, Lothrop, 1984.

The Snow Parade, Crown, 1984.

Saving the President, Messner, 1987.

The Falcon Sting, Bradbury, 1988.

(With Garelick) *Two Orphan Cubs,* Walker, 1989.

OTHER

Careers and Opportunities in Fashion (young adult), Dutton, 1964.

(Editor) Edward Turner and Clive Turner, *Frogs and Toads,* Raintree, 1976.

(Editor) Ralph Whitlock, *Spiders,* Raintree, 1976.

Love and Discipline (adult), Ballantine, 1983.

Bank Street's Family Guide to Home Computers (adult), Ballantine, 1984.

(With Joanne Oppenheim and Betty Boeghold) *Choosing Books for Kids* (adult), Ballantine, 1986.

Contributor of articles to periodicals. Editor of "Talkabout Program" for Adult Resource Books.

SIDELIGHTS: Barbara Brenner is a respected, award-winning author specializing in works of both fiction and nonfiction for young people that deal with animals, nature, and ecology. Reviewers praise Brenner for writing interesting and appealing books that are at the same time informative and educational.

One example of Brenner's talent is her book on the life of the great ornithologist, John James Audubon. In a review of *On the Frontier with Mr. Audubon,* Paul Showers writes in the *New York Times Book Review* that "Brenner again demonstrates her gift for invention and respect for facts. This is a combination of fiction and fact that works so well it might almost be the thing it imitates." Showers goes on to explain that this book is "written in the polite but colloquial language of the frontier sketching in Audubon's biographical background and recording events of the journey as they might have been observed by a serious, very perceptive 13-year-old."

Barbara Brenner discussed with *CA* some of her thoughts on being a writer: "All the circumstances of my life conspired to make me a writer—just lucky, I guess. I grew up in Brooklyn, which supplied the color, and my mother had died when I was a year old, which supplied the sensitivity. We were poor, which gave me the social outlook and my father was ambitious for me, which developed the intellectual curiosity. Not to carry this any further, here I am, loving what I do and still surrounded by extraordinary stimuli. My husband is an artist, and we work together on books whenever we can. Our sons are both grown; one is a biologist, to whom I owe my interest in reptiles, and the other one is a musician, with whom I share an interest in music which has crept into at least one of my books. The wild animals here in rural Pennsylvania are rich sources of inspiration for my work."

AVOCATIONAL INTERESTS: Gardening, yoga, travel, birdwatching.

BIOGRAPHICAL/CRITICAL SOURCES:

PERIODICALS

New York Times Book Review, March 27, 1977.

*　　*　　*

BRENNI, Vito J(oseph) 1923-

PERSONAL: Born March 15, 1923, in Highland, N.Y.; son of John and Marietta (Fabrizio) Brenni. *Education:* State University of New York at Albany, A.B., 1947; Columbia University, M.A., 1949, M.S., 1952; State University of New York College at New Paltz, M.A., 1970; Michigan State University, Ph.D., 1978.

CAREER: West Virginia University, Morgantown, reference librarian, 1951-57; New York Public Library, Economics Division, part-time reference librarian, 1958-59; Villanova University, Villanova, Pa., chief reference librarian, 1960-62; Duquesne University, Pittsburgh, Pa., assistant professor of library science, 1962-65; State University of New York at Albany, assistant professor of library science, 1965-66; State University of New York College at Plattsburgh, bibliographer, 1966-68; College of Librarianship, Aberystwyth, Wales, visiting professor of library science, 1968-69; Sienna Heights College, Adrian, Mich., director of libraries, 1971-74. *Military service:* U.S. Army, Field Artillery, 1943-46; served in Germany.

MEMBER: American Library Association, Catholic Library Association.

WRITINGS:

(Editor) *West Virginia Authors: A Bibliography,* West Virginia Library Association, 1957.

(Editor) *American English: A Bibliography,* University of Pennsylvania Press, 1964, reprinted, Greenwood Press, 1981.

(Editor) *Edith Wharton: A Bibliography,* West Virginia University Library, 1966.

(Editor) *William Dean Howells: A Bibliography,* Scarecrow, 1973.

(Editor) *Essays on Bibliography,* Scarecrow, 1975.

The Bibliographic Control of American Literature: 1920-1975, Scarecrow, 1979.

(Compiler) *Book Illustration and Decoration: A Guide to Research,* Greenwood Press, 1980.

(Compiler) *Book Binding: A Guide to the Literature,* Greenwood Press, 1982.

Book Printing in Britain and America, Greenwood Press, 1983.

(Editor) *The Art and History of Book Printing: A Topical Bibliography,* Greenwood Press, 1984.

Contributor to *Bulletin of Bibliography* and *Catholic Library World.*

AVOCATIONAL INTERESTS: International travel, art, music, philosophy, religion.*

*   *   *

BRESLIN, James 1930-
(Jimmy Breslin)

PERSONAL: Born October 17, 1930, in Jamaica, N.Y.; son of James Earl and Frances (a high school teacher and social worker; maiden name, Curtin) Breslin; married Rosemary Dattolico, December 26, 1954 (died June, 1981); married Ronnie Eldridge (an executive), 1982; children: (first marriage) James and Kevin (twins), Rosemary, Patrick, Kelly, Christopher; (stepchildren) Daniel, Emily, Lucy. *Education:* Attended Long Island University, 1948-50.

ADDRESSES: Agent—Sterling Lord Agency, 660 Madison Ave., New York, N.Y. 10021.

CAREER: Worked as a copyboy at the *Long Island Press,* 1948; sportswriter for several newspapers, including the *New York Journal-American,* all in New York City, 1950-63; *New York Herald Tribune* (later *New York World Journal Tribune*), New York City, began as sportswriter, became columnist, 1963-67; *New York Post,* New York City, columnist, 1968-69; author and free-lance journalist in New York City, 1969—; *New York Daily News,* New York City, columnist, 1978-88; *Newsday,* Long Island, N.Y., columnist, 1988—. Contributing editor and initiating writer, *New York* magazine, 1968-71, *New Times* magazine, 1973. Commentator, WABC-TV, 1968-69, WNBC-TV, 1973. Host of "Jimmy Breslin's People," ABC-TV, 1987. Actor in television programs, commercials, and feature film "If Ever I See You Again." Democratic primary candidate for president of New York City council, 1969; delegate to Democratic National Convention, 1972.

MEMBER: Writers Guild of America, Screen Actors Guild, American Federation of Television and Radio Artists, New York Boxing Writers Association.

AWARDS, HONORS: Best Sports Stories Award, E. P. Dutton & Co., 1961, for magazine piece "Racing's Angriest Young Man"; award for general reporting from Sigma Delta Chi and Meyer Barger Award from Columbia University, both 1964, both for article on the death of President John F. Kennedy; New York Reporters Association Award, 1964; Pulitzer Prize and George Polk Award, both 1986, both for collected newspaper columns; American Society of Newspaper Editors award, 1988, for commentary-column writing.

WRITINGS:

UNDER NAME JIMMY BRESLIN

Sunny Jim: The Life of America's Most Beloved Horseman, James Fitzsimmons (nonfiction), Doubleday, 1962.

Can't Anybody Here Play This Game? (nonfiction), edited by Dick Schapp, Viking, 1963, reprinted, Penguin, 1982.

The World of Jimmy Breslin (collected articles), annotated by James G. Bellows and Richard C. Wald, Viking, 1967.

The Gang That Couldn't Shoot Straight (novel), Viking, 1969, reprinted, Penguin, 1987.

(With Norman Mailer, Peter Maas, Gloria Steinem, and others) *Running against the Machine: The Mailer-Breslin Campaign* (collected speeches, policy statements, interviews, etc.), edited by Peter Manso, Doubleday, 1970.

World without End, Amen (novel; Book-of-the-Month Club alternate selection) Viking, 1973.

How the Good Guys Finally Won: Notes from an Impeachment Summer (nonfiction), Viking, 1975.

(With Schaap) *.44* (novel), Viking, 1978.

Forsaking All Others (novel), Simon & Schuster, 1982.

The World According to Breslin (collected columns), annotated by Michael J. O'Neill and William Brink, Ticknor & Fields, 1984.

Table Money (novel; Literary Guild selection), Ticknor & Fields, 1986.

He Got Hungry and Forgot His Manners (novel), Ticknor & Fields, 1987.

Contributor to numerous newspapers and magazines, including *Penthouse, Sports Illustrated, Saturday Evening Post, Time,* and *New York.*

SIDELIGHTS: For more than two decades, James ("Jimmy") Breslin has provided the literary voice for a group that for many years had had none—that of New York City's Irish-American working class from the Queens neighborhoods in which Breslin himself grew up. As novelist and columnist for various New York newspapers, Breslin encompasses the "New Journalism" ideals that originated in the 1970s, wherein the writer, far from distancing himself from his subject, instead becomes passionately and personally involved in the story. And so Breslin wrote about politics by throwing himself into the political arena in 1969 by running (unsuccessfully) for president of the New York City council under mayoral candidate Norman Mailer. Their platform: Make New York City America's 51st state. However, in 1977, Breslin became another type of celebrity when accused "Son of Sam" serial murderer David Berkowitz made the columnist the sole recipient of letters sent periodically while officials were combing the city for Berkowitz.

A former sportswriter, Breslin uses the native poetry of the street to make his points. His columns often defend the ordinary man against the bureaucracies of government and industry. Breslin "seems to play by different rules than most reporters, which is probably why it took the Pulitzer committee so long to honor him," notes Jonathan Alter in a 1986 *Newsweek* article published just after the Pulitzer Prize panel finally honored the writer. "For years Breslin's fabled ear for dialogue has struck some colleagues as a bit *too* good, too epigrammatic for the way people really speak between quotation marks," Alter continues. To this charge Breslin responds in the *Newsweek* piece that other reporters "take a cop on the beat and make him sound like he's the under secretary of state. *They're* the ones who make up quotes."

Still, Breslin's dramatic columns once caused a wag to remark, on hearing that the reporter was publishing his first novel, "So what? He's been writing fiction for years." *The Gang That Couldn't Shoot Straight,* the book that marked Breslin's move into fiction, disappointed some critics with what they saw as stereotypical portrayals of comic hoodlums on the make. Thomas Meehan of the *New York Times,* for example, while noting that the book "may be the best first novel written all year by a defeated candidate for President of the City Council," finds the story's humor comes mostly from "mayhem—funny, perhaps, to those capable of getting a laugh out of someone being blown up, garroted, or pitched headfirst off a bridge." Though *New York Times Book Review* critic Christopher Lehmann-Haupt was similarly unimpressed overall with *The Gang That Couldn't Shoot Straight,* he shares Meehan's view that Breslin does touch the book with sharply satirical jabs at New York City. "Indeed, the best parts of the novel (and Breslin addicts should agree) are such throwaway details [as Breslin provides]," adds Meehan, "again, the sort of thing this author does so well in his magazine and newspaper pieces."

Breslin took account of his own background for his next novel, *World without End, Amen,* the tale of a New York cop of Irish background whose racist views and weary existence are challenged when he takes a trip to his mother country and witnesses "The Troubles" ongoing between Catholic and Protestant Irish. "Because [protagonist Dermot Davey's] life is coming apart, the reader might well expect that his visit to the land of his forebears will open up new vistas, not only of social conscience but of meaning, and that the ruined cop will somehow find himself quixotically in the cause of the Irish Republic," writes *Washington Post Book World* reviewer Richard Brown. "This is not the author's intent, however, and except for a moving encounter between father and son in a bar in Derry, . . . the found father is of little significance, and the idea of Ireland as homeland is of even less." In the opinion of *Commentary* critic Dorothy Rabinowitz, "There is no hope for the Dermots and their families, Breslin wishes to teach us—not because they are poor or uncultured or incurious (for so are their kin in Ulster), but because they are political reactionaries. That so much of life's worth should be thought to depend on a certain politics might be thought extraordinary in another time than ours. Yet this is a cornerstone of belief for Breslin, as it is for the sensibility he represents."

Harvey Gardner, writing in the *New York Times Book Review,* finds a split in the quality of *World without End, Amen.* "In a skillful Breslin style the first third of the book draws the picture of Dermot and the cop world he knows. There is a great deal of grim humor, and where humor fails, one sees a satisfaction in showing succinctly the causes of human inadequacy." However, says Gardner, when the action moves to Northern Ireland, the "New York idiom" that Breslin employs "often seems inappropriate. That is something one does not like to say of a writer so much to be valued for his rightness about things on his own turf." A *Times Literary Supplement* reviewer offers a different point of view when he states: "If the story were merely a moral tale of a victor humanized by being made a victim, it would have little to offer but the pleasure afforded by a just come-uppance. Beyond that, though, *World without End, Amen* is memorable for being an account of Northern Ireland by a thuggish but not wholly unfeeling character who cannot work out whether he is a foreigner, or a stranger, or both, or neither. It is a confusion probably shared by half the people in Britain."

The critical success of *World without End, Amen* has helped make Breslin a force to be reckoned with in fictional circles. Two further novels, *Forsaking All Others* and *Table Money,* have caught considerable attention. The former is a reworking of the *Romeo and Juliet* theme involving young lovers trapped by crime and poverty. "Another depiction of an underdog-eat-underdog world," as *Time's* R. Z. Sheppard puts it, *Forsaking All Others* presents a Puerto Rican lawyer, raised in the slums, who falls for the pampered daughter of a local Mafioso. "Breslin knows the sorry streets of the Bronx. He knows the fear and the quick violence and the hunger that line the curb like children at a parade," states James F. Vesely in a *Detroit News* article. "He understands how people doing small, everyday things can suddenly be in the middle of horrible events." The author "attaches a long and sultry fuse to the plot's ethnic charge," says Sheppard. The critic continues that Breslin "has been accused of many things, though never of wearying his readers. Some, however, may be dissatisfied with the loose connections [among the main characters]. Both story lines meander and end abruptly as if Breslin had run out of anecdotes. But he is a brilliant descriptive journalist and compensates on nearly every page with energetic, often humorous scenes." "This is good, solid work," concludes Vesely. "Not since Piri Thomas' *These Mean Streets* has the plight of the Puerto Rican poor been described so harshly and so well. And for Breslin, this one puts him back on those mean streets where his best writing dwells."

Table Money, a 1986 publication, drew cheers as an insightful look at the lives of working-class "sandhogs," the men who dig the vast tunnels that bring water to New York City. Breslin traces the generations of one family of sandhogs, the Morrisons, back to the first immigrant from Ireland in the nineteenth century. But by 1970, when the novel takes place, the latest Morrison man, Owney, newly returned from Vietnam with a Medal of Honor, becomes plagued by self-doubt when his wife Dolores decides to better their station in life by attending medical school. One writer, George James in the *New York Times Book Review,* expresses surprise that "the blue-collar bard of the Borough of Queens [would write] a strongly feminist novel!" But Breslin's depiction of the strong-willed Dolores, who forges ahead while her husband slips into obscurity, does not surprise her creator. As Breslin tells James, *Table Money* was written during a time in his life when "my wife contracted an illness and I wound up for some time taking care of the house [and six children] and getting closer to a woman than I ever had been before—unfortunately so, in illness. I came out of it with a lot of wreckage in my hands, but I learned from it."

In a *New York Times Book Review* piece on *Table Money,* James Carroll says that "this hero's story, like that of many all-too-American males, becomes the painful story of an alcoholic." The author, Carroll continues, "tells it with an unsparing, almost cruel detachment—sheer truthfulness—that leaves the reader wincing each time Morrison veers into yet another friendly neighborhood bar. But at the same time, in one of this novel's achievements, [Breslin describes] the experience of alcoholism as if from inside it, and the reader is left in the grip of an infinite sorrow." Other critics share Carroll's view that what makes *Table Money* a valuable work is its sense of place and character detail. Breslin "knows how the borough works, how the pride of the people reacts aggressively against condescending Manhattan snobberies, how the stresses of modern life are affecting young people in the strictly old church community of which he writes," as *New York Times* reviewer Richard F. Shepard sees it. And

Newsweek's Peter S. Prescott applauds the book's "energy, its muscularity, its thickly textured portrait of a world and a way of life that most people who read books know little of."

Breslin followed *Table Money* with another novel, *He Got Hungry and Forgot His Manners,* but the latter did not receive as much attention, partly because the "deep, bitter, almost Kafkaesque satire," as Lehmann-Haupt calls it in a *New York Times* review, cannot appeal to as wide an audience. *He Got Hungry and Forgot His Manners* is a tall tale involving events surrounding the controversial racial attacks that occurred at Howard Beach, Queens, in 1986. D'Arcy Cosgrove, a priest dispatched by order of the Vatican to the borough following the attacks, believes the incident was sexually motivated. Described in the novel as "a man bristling with celibacy," Cosgrove arrives in Queens accompanied by a seven-foot-tall African cannibal, whose idiosyncratic eating habits accounts for the novel's title. To *Time*'s R. Z. Sheppard, "Cosgrove and his giant sidekick are farcical figures meant to illustrate the failures of both church and state when dealing with morality and poverty. . . . The kinks in New York's welfare bureaucracy are authentic and darkly humorous, but the black characters are not developed beyond their jive. Father D'Arcy's mission is unfocused, his misadventures are a blur, and his conversion from guardian of orthodoxy to radical activist unbelievable, even for farce." Lehmann-Haupt also finds faults in Breslin's style, but adds that "it is easiest to get through such [rough] patches by thinking of the novel as a high-speed animated cartoon."

In his nonwriting life, Breslin has enjoyed a longtime reputation as an iconoclast. Most notably, he has a unique, and personal, style of giving notice to quit: He puts out ads in the *New York Times* and posts signs on his front lawn. For instance, when in 1986 his talk show, "Jimmy Breslin's People," was juggled around the late-night schedule by its network, ABC, then unceremoniously deposited in the undesirable time-slot of 1:30 a.m., Breslin paid for a front-page *Times* ad stating, "ABC Television Network, your services, such as they are, will no longer be required as of 12/20/86," which was the end of his 13-week contract. The *Times* ad was a device Breslin had used before, when he informed the *New York Post,* in 1969, that he intended to give up his column, telling his editor: "Robert J. Allen: You are on your own."

"I'm very rude in the course of business because I got no time," Breslin admits in Alter's *Newsweek* piece, adding, "bombast never hurt anybody." And in the wake of a Pulitzer Prize and other professional kudos, Breslin has developed, in the words of *People* reporter Ken Gross, "a new kind of arrogance, . . . now that the committees and critics agree with what he has been saying for years, namely that he's the best in the business." As Breslin tells Gross, "I waited long enough. Where were they?"

MEDIA ADAPTATIONS: The Gang That Couldn't Shoot Straight was adapted into a feature film.

BIOGRAPHICAL/CRITICAL SOURCES:

BOOKS

Authors in the News, Volume 1, Gale, 1976.
Breslin, Jimmy, *He Got Hungry and Forgot His Manners,* Ticknor & Fields, 1987.
Breslin, Jimmy, *Running against the Machine: The Mailer-Breslin Campaign,* edited by Peter Manso, Doubleday, 1969.
Breslin, Jimmy, *The World According to Breslin,* annotated by Michael J. O'Neill and William Brink, Ticknor & Fields, 1984.

Contemporary Literary Criticism, Gale, Volume 4, 1975, Volume 43, 1987.
Graauer, Neil A., *Wits & Sages,* Johns Hopkins University Press, 1984.

PERIODICALS

Chicago Tribune Book World, October 5, 1986.
Commentary, December, 1975.
Commonweal, August 29, 1975.
Detroit News, August 1, 1982.
Los Angeles Times Book Review, July 25, 1982, May 18, 1986.
New Republic, July 19, 1982.
Newsweek, August 9, 1982, May 12, 1986, May 26, 1986.
New York Times, November 21, 1969, May 19, 1975, May 23, 1978, June 16, 1982, October 26, 1984, May 8, 1986, May 5, 1987, January 11, 1988.
New York Times Book Review, November 30, 1969, August 26, 1973, May 11, 1975, June 20, 1982, May 18, 1986.
People, June 16, 1986, December 15, 1986.
Time, June 12, 1975, June 14, 1982, May 5, 1986, January 4, 1988.
Times Literary Supplement, May 14, 1970, May 3, 1974.
Washington Post Book World, August 12, 1973, July 4, 1982, June 1, 1986.*

—*Sketch by Susan Salter*

*   *   *

BRESLIN, Jimmy
   See BRESLIN, James

*   *   *

BREYER, N(orman) L(ane)   1942-

PERSONAL: Born June 9, 1942, in Brooklyn, N.Y.; son of Sidney and Helen (Winters) Breyer; married Elaine Schwartz, July 10, 1965; children: Geniffer Michele, Joshua Aaron. *Education:* Fairleigh Dickinson University, B.A., 1964; Miami University, Oxford, Ohio, M.S., 1966; Florida State University, Ph.D., 1969. *Religion:* Jewish.

CAREER: University of Connecticut, Storrs, assistant professor of educational psychology, beginning 1969. Consultant on behavior modification to groups and organizations.

MEMBER: American Psychological Association, American Educational Research Association, Association for the Advancement of Behavior Therapy, Devereux Institute for Research and Training (fellow), Phi Delta Kappa.

AWARDS, HONORS: National Institute for Mental Health fellowship, 1966-68.

WRITINGS:

(Editor) *Behavior Modification in the Classroom,* MSS Educational Publishing, 1970.
Staff Development and Evaluation, Crofts, 1971.
(Editor with S. Axelrod and others) *An Annotated Bibliography of Selected Behavior Modification Studies,* H & H Enterprises, 1972, revised edition (with Axelrod) published as *Behavior Modification: An Annotated Bibliography of Selected Behavior Modification Studies,* 1973.
(With Axelrod) *Managing Behavior,* H & H Enterprises, 1973.
(With Axelrod) *Summaries of Selected Behavior Modification Studies,* H & H Enterprises, 1973.
An Integrated Approach to Psychological Services, H & H Enterprises, 1975.

Contributor to numerous professional journals, including *Journal of School Psychology* and *Psychological Reports.* *

*   *   *

BRINDEL, June (Rachuy) 1919-

PERSONAL: Born June 5, 1919, on a farm near Little Rock, Iowa; daughter of Otto (a farmer) and Mina (Balster) Rachuy; married Bernard Brindel (a composer and teacher of music), 1939; children: Sylvia Mina, Paul, Jill. *Education:* University of Chicago, B.A., 1945, M.A., 1958. *Politics:* "Radical reform." *Religion:* Humanist.

ADDRESSES: Home—2740 Lincoln Lane, Wilmette, Ill. 60091.

CAREER: Early work ranged from dime store clerk to secretary to a poet laureate, and included factory and office jobs and freelance writing; Chicago City College, Wright Campus, Chicago, Ill., professor of English, 1958-81. Teacher of creative drama and children's theater at National Music Camp, Interlochen, Mich., summers, 1958-67. Lecturer at numerous universities, including Stanford University, University of Southern California, Graduate Theological Seminary at Berkeley, Wright State College, Northwestern University, Trinity College, and Massachusetts Institute of Technology. Has conducted extended writers' workshops at Wichita State University and University of California at Santa Cruz.

MEMBER: Author's Guild, Poets and Writers, PEN, Feminist Writers Guild, Society of Midland Authors, Phi Beta Kappa.

AWARDS, HONORS: Chicago Poets and Writers prize, 1965; Wilmette Children's Theatre prize, 1970; first prize from Wilmette Children's Theatre, 1971, for "Automaton, King of Machines"; C. S. Lewis Prize, 1973; Pulitzer Prize nomination, 1980, for *Ariadne;* Illinois Arts Council, fellowship, 1984, 1985; literary award for short sotry, 1985; PEN Syndicated Fiction Project winner, 1986.

WRITINGS:

"Automaton, King of Machines" (play for children), first produced in Interlochen, Michigan, at National Music Camp in 1967.
Luap (Junior Literary Guild selection), Bobbs-Merrill, 1971.
Ariadne (novel), St. Martin's, 1980.
Nobody Is Ever Missing, Story Press, 1984.
Phaedra: A Novel of Ancient Athens, St. Martin's, 1985.

Collaborator with husband, Bernard Brindel, on songs and a recording for children. Contributor of poems and stories to numerous periodicals, including *Carolina Quarterly, Perspective, Iowa Review, Kansas Quarterly, Sing Heavenly Muse, Muse's Brew, Beloit Poetry Journal, Other Voices, Cimmaron Review, Discourse,* and *Spoon River Quarterly;* also contributor of book reviews and literary essays to *Chicago Tribune, Fiction International, Story Quarterly, Chicago Defender, Xenia Daily Gazette,* and *Mad River Weekly.*

WORK IN PROGRESS: A novel, *Clytemnestra;* short stories.

SIDELIGHTS: June Brindel writes *CA:* "During recent years I have been studying the ancient myths which have most influenced Western civilization for the purpose of discovering the truths they will yield if reimagined in the light of contemporary archaeological research and through a woman's viewpoint. Astonishing results so far: Monsters turn into women of unfashionable faiths; heroes turn into invaders. It is an archetypal revolution—enormously helpful in providing insight into the persis-

tence of destructive, irrational mind-sets. Much work remains to be done. All the old stories must be rewritten. All the silenced must be given voice."

*   *   *

BROOKS, H(arold) Allen 1925-

PERSONAL: Born November 6, 1925, in New Haven, Conn.; son of Harold A. and Mildred (McNeill) Brooks. *Education:* Dartmouth College, B.A., 1950; Yale University, M.A., 1955; Northwestern University, Ph.D., 1957. *Religion:* Protestant.

ADDRESSES: Home—9 River Ridge Rd., Hanover, N.H. 03755.

CAREER: W. J. Megin Construction Co., Naugatuck, Conn., apprentice, 1950-52; University of Illinois at Urbana-Champaign, assistant professor of architecture, 1957-58; University of Toronto, Toronto, Ontario, lecturer, 1958-61, assistant professor, 1961-64, associate professor, 1964-71, professor of fine art, 1971-86, professor emeritus, 1986—. Mellon Professor at Vassar College, 1970-71. Visiting professor at Dartmouth College, 1969, and Architectural Association School of Architecture, London, England, annually, 1972-82; guest lecturer at universities in the United States, Canada, England, France, Germany, Scotland, the Netherlands, and Switzerland; fellow of Victoria University.

MEMBER: International Committee on Monuments and Sites, Society for the Study of Architecture in Canada, Canadian Association for American Studies, Society of Architectural Historians (president, 1964-66; former member of board of directors), Society of Architectural Historians of Great Britain.

AWARDS, HONORS: Canada Council fellowships, 1962-63, 1975-76, 1977-79; Guggenheim fellowship, 1973; Alice Davis Hitchcock Book Award from Society of Architectural Historians, 1973, for *The Prairie School: Frank Lloyd Wright and His Midwest Contemporaries;* D. Eng., Technical University of Nova Scotia, 1984.

WRITINGS:

(Contributor) *Studies in Western Art: Acts of the Twentieth International Conference of the History of Art,* Volume 4, Princeton University Press, 1963.
(Contributor) H.D. Bullock and Terry B. Norton, editors, *The Pope-Leighey House,* National Trust for Historic Preservation, 1970.
The Prairie School: Frank Lloyd Wright and His Midwest Contemporaries, University of Toronto Press, 1972, 2nd edition, 1975, Norton, 1976.
(Editor) *Prairie School Architecture: Studies from the "Western Architect,"* University of Toronto Press, 1975.
(Contributor) Paul E. Sprague, *Guide to Frank Lloyd Wright and Prairie School Architecture in Oak Park,* privately printed, 1976.
(Editor and contributor) *Writings on Wright: Selected Comment on Frank Lloyd Wright,* MIT Press, 1981.
(Contributor) Helen Searing, editor, *In Search of Modern Architecture,* MIT Press, 1982.
Frank Lloyd Wright and the Prairies School, Braziller, 1984.
(Editor and contributor) *Le Corbusier,* Princeton University Press, 1987.

General editor and contributor, *The Le Corbusier Archive,* thirty-two volumes, Garland Publishing, 1982-84. Contributor to

Encyclopedia of World Art. Contributor of articles and reviews to art and architecture journals.

WORK IN PROGRESS: Le Corbusier's Formative Years: Charles-Edouard Jeanneret at La Chaux-de-Fonds, a biography/architectural history of life and work of Le Corbusier till the age of 33 in 1920.

SIDELIGHTS: H. Allen Brooks wrote: "I am especially interested in the psychological importance of architecture as it affects our mental health and well-being. Too many people take architecture for granted and fail to comprehend what a significant impact it has upon us.

"As for the manner in which I write, my answer to such a question is inevitably 'with an eraser' since I rewrite and edit my longhand manuscript so often (perhaps on the order of fifteen times) while trying to obtain the most precise meaning, devoid of ambiguity, and to create a rhythm of words that flow almost like poetry."

*   *   *

BROXHOLME, John Franklin 1930-
(Duncan Kyle, James Meldrum)

PERSONAL: Born June 11, 1930, in Bradford, England; son of Norman F. (a valuer) and Margaret (Smith) Broxholme; married Alison Millar Hair (a teacher), September 22, 1956; children: Helen, Christopher, Lindsay. *Education:* Educated in Bradford, England.

ADDRESSES: Home and office—Oak Lodge, Valley Farm Rd., Newton, Sudbury, Suffolk, England. *Agent*—Rupert Crew Ltd., 1A King's Mews, Gray's Inn Rd., London WC1N 2JA, England.

CAREER: Telegraph & Argus (newspaper), Bradford, England, reporter, 1946-48, 1950-53; *Leicester-Mercury,* Leeds, England, sub-editor, 1953-56; *Yorkshire Post,* Leeds, member of staff in features department, 1956-57; Odhams Press Ltd., London, England, assistant editor of *Today—The New John Bull* (magazine), 1957-64, editor of *TV World* (magazine), 1964-68, editorial director of Odhams Magazines, 1968-69; full-time writer, 1969—. *Military service:* British Army Intelligence Corps, 1948-50.

MEMBER: Crime Writers' Association (chairman, 1976-77).

WRITINGS:

UNDER PSEUDONYM DUNCAN KYLE

A Cage of Ice, St. Martin's, 1970.
Flight into Fear, St. Martin's, 1972.
A Raft of Swords, St. Martin's, 1973.
The Suvarov Adventure, St. Martin's, 1974.
Terror's Cradle, St. Martin's, 1975.
White-out, St. Martin's, 1976.
In Deep, St. Martin's, 1976.
Black Camelot, St. Martin's, 1978.
Green River High, St. Martin's, 1979.
Stalking Point, St. Martin's, 1981.
The King's Commissar, St. Martin's, 1984.
The Dancing Men, Holt, 1985.
The Honey Ant, Collins, 1988.

OTHER

(Contributor under name John Franklin Broxholme) John Dodge, editor, *The Practice of Journalism,* Heineman, 1968.

(Under pseudonym James Meldrum) *The Semonov Impulse,* Weidenfeld & Nicolson, 1975.

WORK IN PROGRESS: Another book.

SIDELIGHTS: Under the pseudonym Duncan Kyle, John Franklin Broxholme "writes thinking man's thrillers," says a *Time* critic, "that invariably become best-sellers in Britain, and for good reason: they combine all too human characters, masterly plotting, and impeccable research." Reviewing *A Cage of Ice* in the *New York Times,* Thomas Lask finds the book thoroughly convincing: "Most of the action takes place in the middle of bare Arctic wastes with nothing but ice, snow, wind and water of polar cold to mark the landscape. Duncan Kyle . . . knows this white emptiness like his right hand; there is nothing bookish about his telling what it means to live in these subzero temperatures, what the merest exposure can do to human flesh, what safeguards have to be taken and how vehicles and other machines have to be coaxed to perform their functions." Lask calls the work "a good tight thriller that provides first-rate armchair excitement with a tension that doesn't let up until the last page."

BIOGRAPHICAL/CRITICAL SOURCES:

PERIODICALS

New York Times, August 20, 1971, January 2, 1977, August 22, 1986.
Time, October 3 1978.

*   *   *

BURKE, Shifty
See BENTON, Peggie

*   *   *

BURNHAM, Charles
See PAINE, Lauran (Bosworth)

*   *   *

BUXTON, (Edward) John (Mawby) 1912-

PERSONAL: Born December 16, 1912, in Bramhall, Cheshire, England; son of Alfred Mellor and Ethel Marion (Mawby) Buxton; married Marjorie Lockley, April 12, 1939 (died July 1, 1977). *Education:* Attended Malvern College, 1926-31; New College, Oxford, B.A., 1935, M.A., 1938. *Politics:* Conservative. *Religion:* Church of England.

ADDRESSES: Home—The Grove, East Tytherton, Chippenham, Wiltshire SN15 4LX, England.

CAREER: Oxford University, New College, Oxford, England, lecturer in English literature, 1946-48, fellow, 1949-79, emeritus fellow, 1979—, university lecturer, 1967-72, reader in English literature, 1972-79, reader emeritus, 1979—. Warton Lecturer, British Academy, 1970. *Military service:* British Army, 1939-46; prisoner of war, 1940-45; became lieutenant.

MEMBER: Society of Antiquaries (fellow), Keats-Shelley Memorial Association (member of committee), Malone Society (member of council).

AWARDS, HONORS: Atlantic Award in English Literature from Rockefeller Foundation, 1946; Leverhulme grant, 1951.

WRITINGS:

Westward, J. Cape, 1942.
Such Liberty (poems), Macmillan, 1944.

Atropos and Other Poems, Macmillan, 1946.

A Marriage Song for the Princess Elizabeth, Macmillan, 1947.

The Redstart, Collins, 1950, De Graff, 1953.

(With R. M. Lockley) *Island of Skomer: A Preliminary Survey of the Natural History of Skomer Island, Pembrokeshire,* Staples, 1950.

(Editor and author of introduction) Michael Drayton, *Poems,* two volumes, Harvard University Press, 1953.

Sir Philip Sidney and the English Renaissance, St. Martin's, 1954, 3rd edition, 1986.

(Editor and author of introduction) Charles Cotton, *Poems,* Harvard University Press, 1958.

(Contributor) H. E. Bell and R. L. Ollard, editors, *Historical Essays, 1600-1750,* A. & C. Black, 1963.

Elizabethan Taste, Macmillan, 1963, St, Martin's, 1964, reprinted, Humanities, 1983.

A Tradition of Poetry, St. Martin's, 1967.

Byron and Shelley: The History of a Friendship, Harcourt, 1968.

(Contributor) W. W. Robson, editor, *Essays and Poems Presented to Lord David Cecil,* Constable, 1970.

(Contributor) *The Warden's Meeting,* Oxford University Society of Bibliophiles, 1977.

The Grecian Taste, Macmillan, 1978.

(Editor with P. Williams) *New College, Oxford, 1379-1979,* New College, Oxford University Press, 1979.

(Editor) *The Birds of Wiltshire,* Wiltshire Library and Museum Service, 1981.

(Editor and author of forward) *The Compleat Angler,* Oxford University Press, 1982.

(Contributor) Andrew Swarbrick, editor, *The Art of Oliver Goldsmith,* Barnes and Noble, 1984.

(Contributor) P. Vassallo, editor, *Byron and the Mediterranean,* University of Malta, 1986.

(Contributor) Van Dorsten, Baker-Smith, and Kinney, editors, *Sir Philip Sidney: 1586 and the Creation of a Legend,* Leiden University Press, 1986.

General editor, "Oxford Paperback English Texts" series. Also general editor with Norman Davis, *Oxford History of English Literature,* Oxford University Press, 1973—. Poetry included in numerous anthologies, including *The Terrible Rain: The War Pots, 1934-45,* Methuen, 1966, and *Poems of the Second World War,* Everyman's Press, 1985. Contributor to "English Renaissance Studies" series, 1980. Contributor to *Cambridge Bibliography of English Literature, Encyclopaedia Britannica, Collier's Encyclopedia,* and to *Modern Language Review, Review of English Studies, Times Literary Supplement, English Literary Renaissance, Apollo, Keats-Shelley Memorial Association Bulletin,* and other journals and periodicals.

WORK IN PROGRESS: An edition of poems of Samuel Daniel.

SIDELIGHTS: John Buxton spent the years from 1935-36 in Palestine, on archaeological work. He has also traveled in the United States, West Indies, the Himalayas, and most countries of western Europe.

AVOCATIONAL INTERESTS: Ornithology and gardening.

C

CALLEO, David P(atrick) 1934-

PERSONAL: Born July 19, 1934, in Binghamton, N.Y.; son of Patrick and Gertrude (Crowe) Calleo; married Avis Thayer Bohlen. *Education:* Yale University, B.A. (magna cum laude), 1955, M.A., 1957, Ph.D., 1959.

ADDRESSES: Home—626 A St. N.E., Washington, D.C. 20002. *Office*—1619 Massachusetts Ave. N.W., Washington, D.C. 20036.

CAREER: Brown University, Providence, R.I., instructor in political science, 1959-60; Yale University, New Haven, Conn., 1961-67, began as instructor, became assistant professor of political science; U.S. Department of State, consultant to undersecretary for political affairs, 1967-68; Johns Hopkins University, School of Advanced International Studies, Washington, D.C., professor and director of European Studies Program, 1968—, Dean Acheson chair, 1988—, Washington Center of Foreign Policy Research, research associate, 1968-79, director, 1974-75. Research fellow, Nuffield College, Oxford University, 1966-67; senior Fulbright lecturer in Germany, 1975; associate fellow, John Edwards College, Yale University. Project director, Twentieth Century Fund, 1981-85. Trustee, Jonathan Edwards Trust, Yale University. Vice-president and member of board of trustees, Lehrman Institute. President and trustee, Washington Foundation for European Studies. *Military service:* U.S. Army Reserve, 1956-65; became captain.

MEMBER: International Political Science Association, International Institute for Strategic Studies, Council on Foreign Relations, American Political Science Association, Council on Foreign Relations, Century Association, Metropolitan Club of Washington, D.C., Brook's (London).

AWARDS, HONORS: Gladys M. Kammerer Award for best book analyzing American national policy, American Political Science Association, 1973, for *American and the World Political Economy;* fellowships from Rockefeller Foundation, Guggenheim Foundation, and Social Science Research Council; Fulbright fellowship, 1982; NATO fellowship, 1983.

WRITINGS:

Europe's Future: The Grand Alternatives, Horizon, 1965.
Coleridge and the Idea of the Modern State, Yale University Press, 1966.
Europe's Future, Hodder & Stoughton, 1967.

Britain's Future, Horizon, 1968.
The Atlantic Fantasy, Johns Hopkins Press, 1970.
(Contributor) Robert Osgood, editor, *Retreat from Empire?: The First Nixon Administration,* John Hopkins Press, 1973.
(With Benjamin M. Rowland) *America and the World Political Economy,* 1973.
(With Rowland) *American and the World Political Economy,* Indiana University Press, 1974.
(Contributor) Wolfram F. Hanrieder, editor, *The United States and Western Europe: The Political, Economic, and Strategic Perspectives,* Winthrop, 1974.
(Editor with Cleveland, Kindleberger, and Lehrman, and contributor) *Money and the Coming World Order,* New York University Press, 1976.
(Contributor) Rowland, editor, *Balance of Power or Hegemony: The Interwar Monetary System,* New York University Press, 1976.
(Contributor) Ernst-Otto Czempiel and Dankwart A. Rustow, editors, *The Euro-American System: Economic and Political Relations between North America and Western Europe,* Westview, 1976.
(Contributor) James Chace and Earl Ravenal, editors, *Atlantis Lost: U.S.-European Relations after the Cold War,* New York University Press, 1976.
(Contributor) Robert S. Skidelsky, editor, *The End of the Keynesian Era: Essays on the Disintegration of the Keynesian Political Economy,* Holmes & Meier, 1977.
The German Problem Reconsidered: Germany in the World Order, 1870 to the Present, Cambridge University Press, 1978.
(Contributor) Hanrieder, editor, *West German Foreign Policy: 1949-1979,* Westview, 1979.
The Imperious Economy, Harvard University Press, 1982.
Beyond American Hegemony: The Future of the Western Alliance, Basic Books, 1987.
(Editor with Robert W. Tucker, George Liska, and Osgood) *SDI AND U.S. Foreign Policy,* Westview, 1987.
(Contributor) Carol L. Holtfrerich, editor, *Economic and Strategic Issues in U.S. Foreign Policy,* Walter de Gruyter, 1988.

Contributor of articles to periodicals, including *Social Research, Political Science Quarterly, Foreign Affairs,* and *Foreign Policy.*

SIDELIGHTS: David P. Calleo's *The Imperious Economy* "presents a major challenge to conventional economic thinking about the causes of virulent inflation," states Grant D. Aldonas in the *Los Angeles Times Book Review.* In *The Imperious Economy,* Calleo charges that the devaluation of the American dollar during the past two decades is a result not of deficit spending during the Vietnam War, as is commonly assumed, but rather of older problems that stem from the United States' historic inability to reconcile domestic and foreign objectives. Calleo "unfolds a subtle analysis of how inflation became embedded in the national fabric," Daniel Yergin writes in *Washington Post Book World.* The importance of *The Imperious Economy,* comments Aldonas, is that it "challenges assumptions and forces us to confront the complex interdependence of decisions at home with stature abroad."

Calleo argues in *The Imperious Economy* that the United States' chronic monetary inflation began during the Kennedy era when the government pushed for full employment as a panacea for domestic social unrest while at the same time spent large amounts of capital to maintain its global economic hegemony and military superiority. In order to achieve both full employment and world dominance, Calleo maintains, the United States began a policy of deficit spending in both good times and bad, thus increasing the flow of American currency without any corresponding real growth.

Richard J. Barnett comments in the *New York Times Book Review* that *The Imperious Economy* "is really an essay on the paradoxes of American Power." Calleo's argument is that in its pursuit of greater economic and military power the United States contradicts its goal of restoring post-World War II Europe and Japan to economic stability and independence and deriving a more equitable world economic balance. "Calleo has long been a student of U.S.-European relations," writes Aldonas. "He is at his best bringing out essential elements of our alliance and explaining why our security and economic interests sometimes differ. . . . This book is a must for those who hope to join the international economic debate."

BIOGRAPHICAL/CRITICAL SOURCES:

PERIODICALS

Los Angeles Times Book Review, July 4, 1982.
New York Times Book Review, July 18, 1982.
Washington Post Book World, November 5, 1978, August 29, 1982.

*   *   *

CALLISON, Brian (Richard)   1934-

PERSONAL: Born July 13, 1934, in Manchester, England; son of Thomas T. and Kathleen Alice (Pounder) Callison; married Phyllis Joyce Jobson, May 12, 1958; children: Richard, Mark. *Education:* Attended Dundee College of Art, 1954-56.

ADDRESSES: Home—West Bankhead, Kellas, Angus, Scotland. *Office*—c/o Collins, 8 Grafton St., London W1X 3LA, England.

CAREER: British Merchant Navy, deck officer, 1951-54; managing director of a construction company, 1956-63; general manager of an entertainment center, 1963-67; full-time writer, 1967—. *Military service:* Royal Naval Auxiliary Service, 1965—; section officer.

MEMBER: Society of Authors, Royal Institute of Navigation, Association of Nautical Institutes.

WRITINGS:

A Flock of Ships, Putnam, 1970.

A Plague of Sailors, Putnam, 1971.
The Dawn Attack, Putnam, 1972.
A Web of Salvage, Putnam, 1973.
Trapp's War, Dutton, 1974.
A Ship Is Dying, Dutton, 1975.
A Frenzy of Merchantmen, Collins, 1977.
An Act of War, Dutton, 1977.
The Judas Ship, Dutton, 1978.
Trapp's Peace, Collins, 1979, Dutton, 1980.
The Auriga Madness, Collins, 1980.
The Sextant, Collins, 1981.
Spearfish, Collins, 1983.
The Bone Collectors, Collins, 1984.
A Thunder of Crude, Collins, 1986.
Trapp and World War III, Collins, 1988.
The Trojan Hearse, Collins, 1990.

SIDELIGHTS: Brian Callison's work has been published in England, Germany, Iceland, Japan, Finland, Poland, and seven other countries of Europe.

BIOGRAPHICAL/CRITICAL SOURCES:

PERIODICALS

Best Sellers, June 1, 1970.
New York Times Book Review, June 14, 1970, April 8, 1973, February 6, 1977.

*   *   *

CALTER, Paul (William)   1934-

PERSONAL: Born June 18, 1934, in New York, N.Y.; son of Arthur and Frances Calter; married Margaret Carey, May 13, 1959; children: Amy, Michael. *Education:* Cooper Union, B.S., 1962; Columbia University, M.S., 1966.

ADDRESSES: Home—33 South Pleasant St., Randolph, Vt. 05060. *Office*—Department of Mathematics, Vermont Technical College, Randolph, Vt. 05061.

CAREER: Columbia University, New York, N.Y., senior research assistant at Heat and Mass Flow Analyzer Laboratory, 1952-57, 1959-60; Kollsman Instrument Corp., Elmhurst, N.Y., development engineer, 1960-65; Intertype Co., Brooklyn, N.Y., senior project engineer, 1965-68; Vermont Technical College, Randolph, began as assistant professor, became professor of mathematics, 1968-89, Director of Summer Mathematics Institutes, 1989—. *Military service:* U.S. Army, 1957-59; served in Medical Corps.

MEMBER: International Sculpture Society, Volunteers for International Technical Assistance, Optical Society of America, American Society of Mechanical Engineers, Society for Technical Communication, Mathematical Association of America, American Mathematical Association of Two-Year Colleges, Authors Guild, University Club.

AWARDS, HONORS: Faculty Fellow Award, Vermont State Colleges, 1987.

WRITINGS:

Problem Solving with Computers, McGraw, 1973.
Graphical and Numerical Solution of Differential Equations, Educational Development Center, 1977.
Magic Squares (mystery novel), Thomas Nelson, 1977.
Schaum's Outline of Technical Mathematics, McGraw, 1978.
Fundamentos di Matematica, McGraw, 1980.
Technical Mathematics, Prentice-Hall, 1983, 2nd edition, 1990.

Practical Math Handbook for the Building Trades, Prentice-Hall, 1983.

Technical Mathematics with Calculus, Prentice-Hall, 1984, 2nd edition, 1990.

Math for Electricity and Electronics, McGraw, 1984.

Math for Computer Technology, Prentice-Hall, 1986.

Technical Calculus, Prentice-Hall, 1988.

Also author of a learning module, "Graphical and Mechanical Solution of Differential Equations," Educational Development Center, 1977. Contributor to *Review of Scientific Instruments* and *Journal of Engineering Graphics.*

WORK IN PROGRESS: Introduction to Technical Mathematics, for Prentice-Hall.

AVOCATIONAL INTERESTS: Painting, sculpture, mountaineering.

*   *   *

CARGOE, Richard
  See PAYNE, (Pierre Stephen) Robert

*   *   *

CARR, Pat M(oore)   1932-
  (Pat M. Esslinger)

PERSONAL: Born March 13, 1932, in Grass Creek, Wyo.; daughter of Stanley (an oil camp supervisor) and Bea (Parker) Moore; married Jack H. Esslinger, June 4, 1955 (divorced July, 1970); married Duane Carr (a professor and writer), March 26, 1971; children: Stephanie, Shelley, Sean, Jennifer. *Education:* Rice University, B.A., 1954, M.A., 1955; Tulane University, Ph.D., 1960.

ADDRESSES: Home—HCR 61, Box 583, Elkins, Ark. 72727.

CAREER: Texas Southern University, Houston, Tex., instructor in English, 1956-58; Dillard University, New Orleans, La., assistant professor of English, 1960-61; Louisiana State University in New Orleans (now University of New Orleans), assistant professor of English, 1961-62, 1965-69; University of Texas at El Paso, assistant professor, 1969-72, associate professor, 1972-78, professor of English, 1978-79; University of New Orleans, assistant professor of English, 1987-88; Western Kentucky University, Bowling Green, Ky., assistant professor, 1988—.

MEMBER: International Women's Writing Guild, Poets and Writers, Phi Beta Kappa, Phi Kappa Phi.

AWARDS, HONORS: Short fiction award, *South and West,* 1969; Mark IV Award, Library of Congress, 1970, for *Beneath the Hill of the Three Crosses;* National Endowment for the Humanities grant, 1973; short fiction award, Iowa School of Letters, 1977, for *The Women in the Mirror;* short story award, Texas Institute of Letters, 1978, for "Indian Burial"; Arkansas Endowment for the Humanities grant, 1985; Green Mountain Fiction Award, 1987.

WRITINGS:

(Under name Pat M. Esslinger) *Beneath the Hill of the Three Crosses* (stories), South & West, 1970.

The Grass Creek Chronicle (novel), Endeavors in Humanity, 1976.

Bernard Shaw, Ungar, 1976.

The Women in the Mirror, University of Iowa Press, 1977.

Mimbres Mythology, Texas Western Press, 1979, new edition, 1989.

In Fine Spirits (Civil War letters), Washington County Historical Society, 1986.

Night of the Luminarias (stories), Slough, 1986.

Sonahchi (myth-tales), Cinco Puntos Press, 1988.

Also contributor to *Best American Short Stories;* also contributor to *Encyclopedia of World Literature* and *Guide to American Women Writers.* Contributor of articles and stories (before 1971, under name Pat M. Esslinger) to periodicals, including *Southern Review, Yale Review, Arizona Quarterly, Modern Fiction Studies, Kansas Quarterly, Seattle Review,* and *Western Humanities Review.*

WORK IN PROGRESS: A Perfectly Splendid Time, a novel set in Civil War Arkansas; a collection of modern stories; a collection of stories set during the Civil War.

SIDELIGHTS: Pat M. Carr told *CA:* "Every place I've lived has marked my work, but probably my Wyoming childhood and my years in South America, Texas, and New Orleans have provided my favorite settings. I've been exceedingly fortunate in that my generation has been able to experience a wide range of conflicts and emotions from the most silent to the most articulate and has possibly come to Matthew Arnold's conclusion that 'Ah, love, let us be true to one another.' All of my own themes, at least, lead there."

*   *   *

CARREL, Mark
  See PAINE, Lauran (Bosworth)

*   *   *

CARTER, Nevada
  See PAINE, Lauran (Bosworth)

*   *   *

CASE, Fred E.   1918-

PERSONAL: Born March 20, 1918, in Logansport, Ind.; son of Fred W. Case; married Lola Austin, 1947. *Education:* Indiana University, B.S., 1942, M.B.A., 1948, D.B.A., 1951.

ADDRESSES: Home—P.O. Box 767, Pacific Palisades, Calif. 90272. *Office*—Graduate School of Business Administration, University of California, 405 Hilgard Ave., Los Angeles, Calif. 90024.

CAREER: Indiana University at Bloomington, School of Business, assistant dean, 1946-50; University of Florida, School of Business, Gainesville, assistant professor, 1950-51; University of California, Los Angeles, Graduate School of Business Administration, assistant dean and professor, 1951—. Commissioner, Building and Safety Division, City of Los Angeles. *Military service:* U.S. Army, 1942-46; became major; received Bronze Star, Medal of War, and, for Italian campaign, Italy-Corona d'Italia and three campaign stars.

MEMBER: Society of Real Estate Appraisers, American Institute of Real Estate Appraisers, American Real Estate and Urban Economics Association, Regional Science Association, Western Regional Science Association (president), Lambda Alpha.

AWARDS, HONORS: George L. Schmutz memorial award, 1962; Ford faculty research fellowship, 1963; first place manuscript award, Society of Real Estate Appraisers, 1980.

WRITINGS:

Modern Real Estate Practice, Allyn & Bacon, 1957.
Los Angeles Real Estate, University of California Press, 1961.
Real Estate, Allyn & Bacon, 1962.
(With others) *Financial Institutions,* Simmons-Boardman, 1963.
(With Sanders A. Kahn and Schimmel) *Real Estate Appraisal and Investment,* Ronald, 1963, 2nd edition, 1978.
Real Estate Brokerage, Prentice-Hall, 1965, 2nd edition published as *Real Estate Brokerage: A Systems Approach,* 1983.
(Contributor) *Essays in Honor of Leo Grebler,* Real Estate Research Program, 1965.
Black Capitalism: Problems in Development, Praeger, 1972.
Inner City Housing and Private Enterprise, Praeger, 1972.
Real Estate Economics: A Systematic Introduction, California Association of Realtors, 1974.
(With John M. Clapp) *Real Estate Financing,* Ronald, 1978.
Investment Guide to Home and Land Purchase, Prentice-Hall, 1978.
Investing in Real Estate, Prentice-Hall, 1978, 2nd revised edition, 1988.
Real Estate Brokerage: An Analysis, Federal Trade Commission, 1980.
(With Jeffrey Gale) *Environmental Impact Review and Housing: Process Lessons from the California Experience,* Praeger, 1982.
Professional Real Estate Investing: How to Evaluate Complex Investment Alternatives, Prentice-Hall, 1983.
(With Norman Strunk) *Where Deregulation Went Wrong: A Look at the Causes behind Savings and Loan Failures in the 1980s,* United States League of Savings Institutions, 1988.

WORK IN PROGRESS: Economics of Greed and the Uses of Avarice: California Housing, 1950-2000; Real Estate Asset Management.

SIDELIGHTS: Fred E. Case told *CA:* "My writings flow primarily from my research interests. I will see what I think is a problem that needs solving (usually in housing or city problems), will seek research funding, and [will] chew away at the problem. Usually articles, monographs, and speeches follow as I seek a way to make sense of the problem I have been studying. Clippings, notes, and typed drafts accumulate until they become so numerous I have to write and get rid of them. Unfortunately, when I finish a book I think of all the things I should have written, and that starts a new writing process."

The bulk of Case's work has been research- and nonfiction-oriented. He contemplates a move toward other literary genres, as he notes that "my files are beginning to bulge with materials that could go into fiction. I have things to say about the real estate industry, builders, public officials, and their power plays. I also see the university as needing some exposure in terms of academic politics, a most dangerous activity."

*   *   *

CASSADY, Claude
  See PAINE, Lauran (Bosworth)

*   *   *

CAWS, Mary Ann   1933-

PERSONAL: Born September 10, 1933, in Wilmington, N.C.; daughter of Harmon Chadbourn and Margaret Devereux (Lippitt) Rorison; married Peter James Caws (a professor of philoso-

phy), June 2, 1956 (divorced, 1987); children: Hilary Brooke, Matthew Rorison. *Education:* Bryn Mawr College, B.A. (cum laude), 1954; Yale University, M.A., 1956; University of Kansas, Ph.D., 1962. *Politics:* Democrat. *Religion:* Anglican.

ADDRESSES: Home—140 East 81st St., New York, N.Y. 10028. *Office*—Graduate School and University Center, City University of New York, 33 West 42nd St., New York, N.Y. 10036.

CAREER: Barnard College, New York City, lecturer in French, 1962-63; City University of New York, New York City, Hunter College, lecturer, 1964-65, assistant professor of French, 1966-67, Hunter College and Graduate School and University Center, associate professor, 1970-74, professor of Romance languages and comparative literature, 1974—, distinguished professor of French and comparative literature, 1983—, distinguished professor of French, English, and comparative literature, 1987—. Visiting assistant professor of French, University of Kansas, fall, 1963; member of French faculty, Sarah Lawrence College, 1965, comparative literature faculty, Princeton University, 1978, and faculty in criticism, Dartmouth College School of Theory and Criticism, 1988; member, Columbia Theory of Literature Seminar, 1973—; director, National Endowment for the Humanities Summer Seminar for College Teachers, 1980, 1986.

MEMBER: Modern Language Association of America (member of executive council, 1973-77; second vice-president, 1981-82; first vice-president, 1982-83; president, 1983-84), American Association of Teachers of French, French Institute, American Association of University Professors, Academy of Literary Studies (president, 1985), American Comparative Literature Association (board, 1978—; vice-president, 1987; president, 1989-91), Association for the Study of Dada and Surrealism (treasurer, 1967-69; president, 1970-72).

AWARDS, HONORS: Guggenheim fellowship, 1972; Fulbright fellowship, 1972; National Endowment for the Humanities grant, summer, 1974, fellowship, 1978; named Officier des Palmes Academiques, 1983; D.H.L., Union College, 1983.

WRITINGS:

Surrealism and the Literary Imagination: A Study of Gaston Bachelard and Andre Breton, Mouton, 1966.
The Poetry of Dada and Surrealism: Aragon, Breton, Tzara, Eluard, Desnos, Princeton University Press, 1970.
The Inner Theatre of Recent French Poetry: Cendrars, Tzara, Peret, Artaud, Bonnefoy, Princeton University Press, 1972.
Andre Breton, Twayne, 1973.
(Translator and editor) Tristan Tzara, *Approximate Man and Other Writings,* Wayne State University Press, 1973.
(Editor) *About French Poetry: From Dada to "Tel Quel," Text and Theory,* Wayne State University Press, 1974.
The Presence of Rene Char, Princeton University Press, 1976.
(Translator and annotator with Jonathan Griffin) Rene Char, *Poems,* Princeton University Press, 1976.
Rene Char, Twayne, 1977.
The Surrealist Voice of Robert Desnos, University of Massachusetts Press, 1979.
The Eye in the Text: Essays on Perception, Mannerist to Modern, Princeton University Press, 1981.
A Metapoetics of the Passage: Architextures in Surrealism and After, University Press of New England, 1981.
(Editor and translator with Jean-Pierre Cauvin) *The Poems of Andre Breton: A Bilingual Anthology,* University of Texas Press, 1981.

(Editor and translator with Patricia Terry) *Roof Slates and Other Poems of Pierre Reverdy,* Northeastern University Press, 1982.

(Editor and author of introduction) Stephane Mallarme, *Selected Poetry and Prose,* New Directions, 1982.

(Editor) Saint-John Perse, *Selected Poems,* New Directions, 1982.

(Editor with Hermine Riffaterre) *The Prose Poem in France: Theory and Practice,* Columbia University Press, 1983.

(Editor) *Writing in a Modern Temper: Essays on French Literature and Thought, in Honor of Henri Peyre,* Stanford University Press, 1983.

(Translator) Tzara, *Cinema Calendrier du Coeur Abstrait Maisons,* Thomas Press, 1983.

Yves Bonnefoy, Twayne, 1984.

(Editor) *Textual Analysis: Some Readers Reading,* Modern Language Association, 1985.

Reading Frames in Modern Fiction, Princeton University Press, 1985.

(Editor and translator) Andre Breton, *Mad Love,* University of Nebraska Press, 1987.

(Contributor) Susan Suleiman, editor, *The Female Body in Western Perspective,* Harvard University Press, 1987.

(Contributor) Nancy Miller, editor, *The Poetics of Gender,* Columbia University Press, 1987.

Edmond Jabes, Editions Rodopi, 1988.

(Editor) *Perspectives on Perception: Art, Philosophy, and Literature,* Peter Lang, 1989.

(Translator) Breton, *The Communicating Vessels,* University of Nebraska Press, 1989.

The Art of Interferences: Stressed Readings in Verbal and Visual Texts, Polity Press and Princeton University Press, 1989.

Women of Bloomsbury: Virginia, Vanessa, and Carringtons, Routledge, 1990.

(Editor) *Reading the City,* Gordon & Breach, 1990.

(Translator) Marcelin Pleynet, *Robert Motherwell,* Rizzoli International, 1990.

(Translator) Jacques Derrida and Paule Thevenin, *Antonin Artaud: Portraits and Drawings,* Abbeville Press, 1990.

Director, *Le Siecle eclate: Dada, surrealisme et avant-gardes,* 1974—. Contributor of articles, notes, and reviews to *Novel, Contemporary Literature, Romanic Review, Cahiers Dada Surrealisme, L'Esprit Createur, Books Abroad, French Review, Diacritics, Twentieth Century Literature,* and several language journals. *Dada/Surrealism,* co-director, 1972—, editor, 1973—; editorial consultant, *Diacritics,* 1975—; member of editorial boards, *New York Literary Forum, Studies on Twentieth Century Literature, Poesis, Comparative Literature Review,* and *PMLA* (1978-80).

SIDELIGHTS: Mary Ann Caws is well known for her studies of surrealism, particularly the writings of Andre Breton. In a *New York Review of Books* article about her critical work *Andre Breton,* Roger Shattuck observes that although Caws "is so attentive to Breton's ideas and images that she seriously neglects the fluctuating tonalities of his style," he admires the "compactness and sensitivity" of the book. In fact, the critic adds, "the two chapters on Breton's adventure journals and on his poetry offer the best criticism in English of his literary achievement." Regarding *The Poems of Andre Breton,* which Caws co-edited and translated, *Los Angeles Times Book Review* critic Robert Atwan comments that the "editors could have offered a smaller sample of later poetry," but ultimately finds "the flaws in this admirably introduced and annotated bilingual edition are minimal. *The Poems of Andre Breton* will surely appeal to anyone undaunted

by an art that so dazzlingly resists American expectations." Roger Cardinal similarly concludes in the *Times Literary Supplement* that "this anthology supersedes previous selections in its generous sweep across the whole body of Breton's verse."

In *The Eye in the Text: Essays on Perception, Mannerist to Modern,* Caws examines the way the literary eye perceives visual and verbal art. "Broadly informed by classical and contemporary artists and commentators, Caws makes a strong case for the intertextuality of art and poetry," summarizes a *Choice* reviewer. "This is an extraordinarily profound book that is destined to become a major text in esthetic theory," B. F. Dick likewise declares in *World Literature Today.* "Even now it is an invaluable guide to creative perception."

BIOGRAPHICAL/CRITICAL SOURCES:

PERIODICALS

Choice, January, 1982.
Los Angeles Times Book Review, January 23, 1983.
New York Review of Books, June 1, 1972.
Times Literary Supplement, October 7, 1977, April 27, 1984, September 27, 1985.
Washington Post Book World, June 27, 1982.
World Literature Today, winter, 1978, summer, 1982.

*   *   *

CHACKO, David   1942-

PERSONAL: Born January 3, 1942, in Pittsburgh, Pa.; son of Joseph W. and Evelyn (Paterline) Chacko; married Susan Myers (a systems programmer), November, 1968. *Education:* Wright State University, B.A.; University of Connecticut, M.A.

ADDRESSES: Home—52 Shawnee Dr., Trumbull, Conn. 06611.

CAREER: University of Bridgeport, Bridgeport, Conn., assistant professor of English, beginning 1971; writer. *Military service:* U.S. Air Force, 1962-66.

MEMBER: Modern Language Association of America, American Association of University Professors, Authors Guild, Authors League of America.

AWARDS, HONORS: Creative writing fellowship, Book-of-the-Month Club, 1968.

WRITINGS:

Price (novel), St. Martin's, 1973.
Gage (novel), St. Martin's, 1974.
(Editor with Dick Allen) *Detective Fiction: Crime and Compromise* (text), Harcourt, 1974.
Brick Alley, Delacorte, 1981.
The Black Chamber (novel), St. Martin's, 1988.
White Gamma, St. Martin's, 1988.

WORK IN PROGRESS: Emme's Book of Miracles, a novel.

SIDELIGHTS: "In the ranks of espionage literature," a *Newsweek* reviewer says of David Chacko's novel *Gage,* "this fast-paced tale of intrigue is noteworthy, above all, for its stylistic virtuosity." Chacko's novels are known for their tight and complex plots, but "aside from the strenuous action, the big plus in 'Gage' is Chacko's sophisticated writing style," *New York Times Book Review* critic Newgate Callendar details. "He uses the language with virtuoso precision." As the *Newsweek* writer concludes, "Chacko's performance in this, his second novel, is impressive."

AVOCATIONAL INTERESTS: Travel.

BIOGRAPHICAL/CRITICAL SOURCES:

PERIODICALS

Newsweek, November 11, 1974.
New York Times Book Review, July 21, 1974.*

*   *   *

CHAMBERS, Aidan   1934-
(Malcolm Blacklin)

PERSONAL: Born December 27, 1934, in Chester-le-Street, County Durham, England; son of George Kenneth Blacklin (a funeral director) and Margaret (Hancock) Chambers; married Nancy Harris Lockwood (former editor of *Children's Book News*), March 30, 1968. *Education:* Attended Borough Road College, London, England, 1955-57.

ADDRESSES: Home and office—"Lockwood," Station Rd., Woodchester, Stroud, Gloucestershire GL5 5EQ, England. *Agent*—Pat White, Rogers, Coleridge & White, Ltd., 20 Powis Mews, London W11 1JN, England.

CAREER: Teacher of English and drama at various schools in England, 1957-68; full-time writer, 1968—. Co-founder and editorial publisher, Turton & Chambers, 1989—; publisher and proprietor, Thimble Press; publisher, *Signal: Approaches to Children's Books,* and *Young Drama: The Magazine about Child and Youth Drama.* Tutor, Further Professional Studies Department, University of Bristol, 1970-82; visiting lecturer, Westminster College, Oxford, 1982—. Has produced children's plays for stage and written and presented several radio and television programs, including "Bookbox," Radio Bristol, 1973-75, and "Children and Books," BBC Radio, 1976. *Military service:* Royal Navy, 1953-55.

MEMBER: Society of Authors.

WRITINGS:

FOR YOUNG PEOPLE

Johnny Salter (play; produced in Stroud, Gloucestershire, 1965), Heinemann Educational, 1966.
The Car (play; produced in Stroud, 1966), Heinemann Educational, 1967.
Cycle Smash (novel), Heinemann, 1967.
The Chicken Run (play; produced in Stroud, 1967), Heinemann Educational, 1968.
Marle (novel), Heinemann, 1968.
Mac and Lugs, Macmillan, 1971.
Haunted Houses, Pan Books, 1971.
Don't Forget Charlie and the Vase, Macmillan, 1971.
Ghosts 2 (short stories), Macmillan, 1972.
More Haunted Houses, Pan Books, 1973.
Great British Ghosts, Pan Books, 1974.
Great Ghosts of the World, Pan Books, 1974.
Snake River, Almqvist och Wiksell (Stockholm), 1975, Macmillan, 1977.
Book of Flyers and Flying, Kestrel Books, 1976.
Ghost Carnival: Stories of Ghosts in Their Haunts, Heinemann, 1977.
Breaktime (novel), Bodley Head, 1978, Harper, 1979.
Fox Tricks (short stories), Heinemann, 1980.
Seal Secret (novel), Bodley Head, 1980, Harper, 1981.
The Dream Cage: A Comic Drama in Nine Dreams (play; produced in Stroud, 1981), Heinemann, 1982.
Dance on My Grave (novel), Bodley Head, 1982, Harper, 1983.

The Present Takers (novel), Bodley Head, 1983, Harper, 1984.
Nik: Now I Know (novel), Harper, 1987 (published in England as *Now I Know,* Bodley Head, 1987).

EDITOR OF BOOKS FOR YOUNG PEOPLE

(With wife, Nancy Chambers) *Ghosts,* Macmillan, 1969.
(With N. Chambers) *World Zero Minus: An SF Anthology,* Macmillan, 1971.
I Want to Get Out: Stories and Poems by Young Writers, Macmillan, 1971.
(With N. Chambers) *Hi-Ran-Ho: A Picture Book of Verse,* Longman, 1971.
Book of Ghosts and Hauntings, Kestrel Books, 1973.
(With N. Chambers) *In Time to Come: An SF Anthology,* Macmillan, 1973.
Fighters in the Sky, Macmillan, 1976.
Funny Folk: A Book of Comic Tales, Heinemann, 1976.
Book of Cops and Robbers, Kestrel Books, 1977.
Men at War, Macmillan, 1977.
Escapers, Macmillan, 1978.
War at Sea, Macmillan, 1978.
(Under pseudonym Malcolm Blacklin) *Ghosts 4,* Macmillan, 1978.
Animal Fair, Heinemann, 1979.
Ghosts That Haunt You, Kestrel Books, 1980.
Loving You Loving Me, Macmillan, 1980.
Ghost after Ghost, Kestrel Books, 1982.
Plays for Young People to Read and Perform, Thimble Press, 1982.
Out of Time: Stories of the Future, Bodley Head, 1984.
Shades of Dark, P. Hardy, 1984.
(With Jill Bennett) *Poetry for Children: A "Signal" Bookguide,* Thimble Press, 1984.
A Sporting Chance: Stories of Winning and Losing, Bodley Head, 1985.
A Quiver of Ghosts, Bodley Head, 1987.
(And contributor) *A Haunt of Ghosts,* Harper, 1987.
Love All, Bodley Head, 1988.
On the Edge, Macmillan, 1990.

OTHER

"Everyman's Everybody" (play), produced in London, 1957.
The Reluctant Reader, Pergamon, 1969.
Introducing Books to Children, Heinemann Educational, 1973, revised edition, Horn Book, 1983.
(Editor) *The Tenth* [and Eleventh] *Ghost Book,* Barrie & Jenkins, two volumes, 1975-76, published in one volume as *The Bumper Book of Ghost Stories,* Pan Books, 1976.
Booktalk: Occasional Writing on Children and Literature, Bodley Head, 1985, Harper, 1986.
The Reading Environment, Thimble Press, 1990.

Also author of television series "Ghosts," 1980, and "Long, Short and Tall Stories," 1980-81. Contributor to *Winter Tales for Children 4,* Macmillan. General editor, Macmillan "Topliners" series, books designed for adolescents reluctant to read the usual fiction found in publishers' lists. Author of column, "Letter from England," *Horn Book.* Contributor to *Books and Bookmen, Times Educational Supplement, Teachers' World,* and *Books for Your Children.* Reviewer for *Children's Book News.*

WORK IN PROGRESS: Criticism of current children's fiction; novels and stories.

SIDELIGHTS: "Aidan Chambers is one of the most articulate and important voices speaking about children's literature today," asserts John Cech in the *Christian Science Monitor.* A long-time advocate of encouraging children to read for pleasure from an early age, Chambers "is convinced that literature . . . is central to living and that children cannot discover the full breadth and depth of this experience for themselves," notes a *Times Literary Supplement* critic about *Introducing Books to Children.* "Out of the fullness of his conviction and with the fire of his zeal he has written a thoroughly practical and useful book." Chambers also believes that children should not be limited to works designed for a young audience; juvenile and even adult fiction can help expand the young reader's world. "Chambers's overriding concern," summarizes Lachlan Mackinnon in the *Times Literary Supplement,* "is that children should be presented with literature that is imaginatively challenging and which reflects formally the complexity of the world in which they are growing up."

In *Booktalk: Occasional Writing on Children and Literature,* for example, Chambers investigates various ways in which children and literature interact, and "brings to his writing a good deal of adult critical sophistication," remarks Mackinnon. Nevertheless, the critic faults some of the book's essays as "clotted with theory." Cech, however, says *Booktalk* "is chock-full of good ideas, . . . insightful, patient, funny, moving, and always aware of the authors and readers who are taking part in the dialogue of its pages. At a time when leading critics of adult literature are saying that contemporary literary criticism and scholarship have lost touch with people," the critic concludes, "Chambers has kept both his touch and his clear voice."

In keeping with his promotion of complex and realistic fiction for adolescents, Chambers has written several young adult novels which incorporate literary devices and serious issues into their stories. *Breaktime,* for instance, reflects the construction of James Joyce's *Ulysses* in its account of a young man's holiday in the English countryside. The novel intersperses traditional narrative with excerpts from the youth's diary, and includes pictures, letters, and other graphic effects. But *Breaktime* "is not only a linguistic *tour de force,* filled with typographical experiments," comments Geraldine DeLuca in *Lion and the Unicorn;* the novel "is also finally an involving story of a young man's . . . intellectual growth."

Other critics, however, believe that Chambers's stylistic devices obscure the story; *New York Times Book Review* contributor Richard Yates, for example, avers that the verbal tricks come "close to swamping the novel. And you can tell that the author doesn't need his affectations: Whenever he puts them aside he writes well." "Initially the book's idiosyncrasies are irritating," DeLuca admits, but adds that "once one gets used to the work, there is pleasure to be found in it. . . . [Chambers] is attempting to write a Joycean novel as an adolescent would, with all the energy and none of the moderation of age." *Breaktime,* the critic states, "is a gift, and the genre, if one can claim this work as a contribution, is richer for it." "With humour and wit, with ingenuity and candour," Margery Fisher of *Growing Point* similarly concludes, "the author has offered one piece of one kind of truth in a spirit of technical and emotional investigation."

Chambers's subsequent novels have similarly treated serious issues with an intricate style; *Dance on My Grave* follows a stormy homosexual relationship between two adolescent boys, while *Nik: Now I Know* deals with a young man's exploration of Christianity and his own beliefs. While the latter novel highlights religion as one of its themes, it "contains no evangelism, nor any evangelical characters," writes Colin Greenland in the *Times Literary Supplement.* Chambers "avoids pre-empting his readers' responses by means of a variety of alienation effects," includ-

ing excerpts from notes and tapes by the characters and literary quotations. "In this ambience of overt artifice, readers are invited to participate in the parallel enquiries, intellectual, spiritual and forensic, as components of the reading process," the critic continues. "They are required to accept two or three palpable manipulations of plot . . . , but never an assertion of values, let alone truth," Greenland concludes, noting that the novel's "zeal is for integrity, not salvation."

Dance on My Grave likewise has some "extremely well done" portions, comments David Rees in the *Times Literary Supplement.* "The intensity and passion of Hal's feelings for and commitment to Barry are vivid and real, and equally convincing is Hal's rage and sense of let-down when he realizes . . . that his lover wants something more casual than he can offer." "This is a serious book, not just the study of a single experience but an attempt to define personality, to encapsulate a stage in growing up, even in an undictatorial way to make a statement of philosophy," observes Fisher. *Dance on My Grave* "is a book that makes its point through raucous humour and implied feeling, through the sharp observation of a boy and his blundering apprehensions of the way others observe him. If teenage novels are to justify their existence," the critic maintains, "it will be by this kind of honest, particularised, personal writing."

BIOGRAPHICAL/CRITICAL SOURCES:

BOOKS

Contemporary Literary Criticism, Volume 35, Gale, 1985.

PERIODICALS

Christian Science Monitor, June 6, 1986.
Drama, winter, 1968.
Growing Point, November, 1978, July, 1982.
Lion and the Unicorn, winter, 1979-80.
New York Times Book Review, April 29, 1979.
Times Literary Supplement, October 16, 1969, November 23, 1973, December 1, 1978, July 18, 1980, July 23, 1982, November 26, 1982, September 30, 1983, August 16, 1985, April 3, 1987.

—*Sketch by Diane Telgen*

*   *   *

CHANG, Lee
   See LEVINSON, Leonard

*   *   *

CHARD, Judy 1916-
(Lyndon Chase, Doreen Gordon)

PERSONAL: Born May 8, 1916, in Gloucester, England; daughter of Thomas (an army officer) and Dorothy Isabel (Juan) Gordon; married Maurice Noel Chard (a field manager), July 26, 1941. *Education:* Educated in England. *Religion:* Church of England.

ADDRESSES: Home—Morley Farm, Highweek, Newton Abbey, Devon TQ12 6NA, England.

CAREER: Writer. David & Charles (publishers), Newton Abbot, England, director of studies for Writers' College, 1988—. Has worked as a typist and personal secretary in Birmingham, London, and Wolverhampton, England. Tutor in creative writing, Workers Educational Association and Devon County Council, both Devon, England. Broadcaster for British Broadcasting Corp. (BBC); lecturer throughout England.

MEMBER: Crime Writers Association.

WRITINGS:

NOVELS; ALL PUBLISHED BY R. HALE

Through the Green Woods, 1974.
The Weeping and the Laughter, 1975.
Encounter in Berlin, 1976.
The Uncertain Heart, 1976.
The Other Side of Sorrow, 1977.
In the Heart of Love, 1978.
Out of the Shadows, 1978.
All Passion Spent, 1979.
Seven Lonely Years, 1980.
The Darkening Skies, 1981.
Haunted by the Past, 1982.
When the Journey's Over, 1983.
Where the Dream Begins, 1983.
Hold Me in Your Heart, 1983.
Rendezvous with Love, 1984.
To Live with Fear, 1984.
Wings of the Morning, 1985.
A Time to Love, 1986.
Person Unknown, 1987.
Enchantment, 1989.

Also author of *Murder Casebook;* also author, under pseudonym Lyndon Chase, of *Tormentil.* Also author of nonfiction for Obelisk Publications, *Tales of the Unexplained, Haunted Happenings,* and *Burgh Island;* also author of nonfiction works *Along the Lemon, Along the Dart, Along the Teign, Devon Mysteries, The South Hams, About Widecombe,* and *My Devon Life;* also author of several radio broadcasts based on her nonfiction. Contributor of short stories, sometimes under pseudonym Doreen Gordon, to periodicals, including *Argosy, Woman's Realm, My Weekly, Story World, London Mystery Magazine, Edgar Wallace Mystery Magazine,* and *Lady. Devon Life,* columnist, 1972—, editor, 1983-87.

WORK IN PROGRESS: Two serials for Thomson; a sequel to *Devon Mysteries;* a correspondence course for David & Charles.

SIDELIGHTS: Judy Chard told *CA:* "It may be of interest to note that I started to write when I was fifty, and into the last ten years I have crammed a lifetime of work and living, meeting new people, and, in fact, my whole life has changed as a result. Most important of all has been my teaching role for the Workers Educational Association, which has opened up a whole new world of helping people who are deeply interested in writing, giving them, too, a new interest."

Chard later explained to *CA:* "Since this [last] entry I have been the editor of a county glossie magazine, written about six more novels, gone on with my teaching and giving talks all over the country on writing, the occult, legends, etc., and done extensive broadcasting for the BBC. At the age of 73 I applied for and got the job as Director of Studies for the Writer's College run by the well-known publishers David & Charles of Newton Abbot for whom, in addition to controlling ten tutors in various subjects, I assign students to courses and am myself preparing a course for the more mature student to record their memories which will run into twelve assignments of approximately 7000 words each, so don't let anyone tell me any age is too old to work. The years don't count; it's how you feel inside, and I intend to go on until at least 100!"

CHARLIER, Roger H(enri) 1921-
(Marco, Henri Rochard, Scott, Roger Wallace)

PERSONAL: Born November 10, 1921, in Antwerp, Belgium; naturalized U.S. citizen; son of Armand A. J. (chief of Legal Affairs Division of the City of Antwerp) and Pauline B. (a teacher; maiden name, Uyterhoeven) Charlier; married Patricia Mary Simonet (an associate professor of education and psychology), June 17, 1958; children: Constance Cecelia-Paula, Jean-Armand Leonard. *Education:* Royal Athenaeum of Antwerp, A.A. (summa cum laude), 1939; Free University of Brussels, M.Pol.Sc., 1941, M.S., 1945; State University of Liege, B.S. (geography; cum laude), 1942, B.S. (geology), 1943; University of Erlangen, Ph.D. (magna cum laude), 1947; Industrial College of the Armed Forces, Diploma, 1952; University of Paris, Litt.D. (magna cum laude), 1957, Sc.D. (summa cum laude), 1958.

ADDRESSES: Home—4055 North Keystone Ave., Chicago, Ill. 60641.

CAREER: Teacher at secondary school in Belgium, 1941-42; deputy director of various assembly centers in Germany for United Nations Relief and Rehabilitation Administration, 1946-48; Polycultural University, Washington, D.C., associate professor of geography and chairman of department, 1950-52; Finch College, New York, N.Y., professor of physical sciences, chairman of department, and professor of mathematics, 1952-55; Hofstra University, Hempstead, N.Y., professor of geology and geography and chairman of department, 1955-58; University of Paris, Faculty of Sciences, Paris, France, adjunct professor of geology, 1958-59; University of Minnesota, Minneapolis, visiting professor of education, 1959-60; Parsons College, Fairfield, Iowa, professor of earth sciences, 1960-61; Northeastern Illinois University, Chicago, professor of geology, geography, and oceanography, 1961-86, coordinator of earth sciences, 1961-65, research scholar, 1962-64.

Professional lecturer on travel and foreign affairs, 1949—; lecturer, U.S. Information Service, 1971—. Teacher, Berlitz School, Newark, N.J., 1951-52; visiting professor or lecturer at universities in the United States and Europe, including DePaul University, 1965-67, University of Bordeaux, 1970-73 and 1983-84, Free University of Brussels, 1971-88, and University of Maryland; exchange senior scientist, Academy of Romania, 1968 and 1978-79, and Academy of Sciences of Bulgaria, 1979; professor emeritus, University of Brussels, 1989—. Travel project director for various agencies, 1948-71, and director of Division of Educational Travel, University Travel, Inc., Chicago, 1963-67. Newspaper correspondent in Europe, 1945-50; staff member, Lovania Publishers, Belgium, 1988—. Affiliated with several international institutes and commissions, including the European Economic Commission, 1986—. *Military service:* Belgian Army, 1940-44; became major; joined underground after King Leopold's surrender and was imprisoned by Germans for work with Allies.

MEMBER: Centre International d'Histoire de l'Oceanographie, Geological Society of America (fellow), American Association for the Quaternary, Association of American Geographers, American Association for the Advancement of Science, National Education Association, American Association of University Professors, Academie Nationale des Sciences, Arts, et Belles-Lettres, Societe Belge d'Etudes Geographiques, Societe Royale Belge de Geographie, Societe Royale de Zoologie d'Anvers, Societe Belge de Geologie, Hydrologie et Paleontologie, New Jersey Academy of Science (fellow; president, 1954-57), Chi Beta Phi.

AWARDS, HONORS: Carnegie Corporation fellow, 1953; special fellow, French Government, 1958; Chevalier, Ordre des Palmes Academiques (France), 1969; Medaille du Merite Touristique (Belgium), 1969; Cravate et Medaille de Vermeil des Arts, Sciences et Lettres (France), 1971; Knight of the Order of Leopold (Belgium), 1973; Medaille d'Or de l'Avancement du Progres, 1973; Grande Medaille de l'Universite de Bordeaux, 1974; Grande Medaille d'Or des Arts, Sciences et Lettres, 1979. Recipient of grants from the governments of South Africa, Zambia, and Rhodesia, 1968, Israel, 1969, Romania, 1970, and Belgium, 1976 and 1978, and from the National Science Foundation, International Research and Exchange Committee, North Atlantic Treaty Organization, International Oceanography Commission, and other organizations.

WRITINGS:

Cours d'analyse infinitesimale, five volumes, G. Schreiber (Brussels), 1940.
(Under pseudonym Henri Rochard) *I Was a Male War Bride* (novel), Montgrove Press, 1947.
The Gifted: A National Resource, Bureau of Educational Research, University of Minnesota, 1960.
Introductory Earth Science, Burgess, 1960.
(Under pseudonym Henri Rochard) *Pensees* (poetry), Montgrove Press, 1962.
(Under pseudonym Henri Rochard) *For the Love of Kate* (novel), Exposition Press, 1963.
Introduction to Oceanography, Maplegrove & Montgrove, 1964.
(With others) *Discovering Hawaii: A Series of Seminars,* Western New Mexico University, 1965.
The Physical Environment: A Brief Outline, W. C. Brown, 1966.
(Editor) *Geography of the USSR,* Northeastern Illinois State College, 1967.
Harnessing the Energies of the Ocean (booklet), Marine Technology Society (Washington, D.C.) and Northeastern Illinois State College, 1970.
(Editor with wife, Patricia S. Charlier, and John J. Karpeck) *The World around Us: A Book of Readings,* MSS Educational Publishing, 1970.
(Editor) *A Digest of Master's Theses in Geography at Northeastern Illinois University,* Northeastern Illinois University, 1972.
(Contributor) B. L. Gordon, editor, *Marine Resources,* Book & Tackle, 1972.
Esquisse d'un cours d'oceanographie regionale, Institut de Geologie du Bassin d'Aquitaine (Bordeaux), 1973.
(Contributor) J. B. Ray, editor, *The Oceans and Man,* Kendall/Hunt, 1975.
Economic Oceanography, Flemish Free University (Brussels), 1977.
(Contributor) Gordon, editor, *Energy from the Sea,* Book & Tackle, 1977.
Ocean Resources: An Introduction to Economic Oceanography, University Press of America, 1978.
(Contributor) N. Ginsburg and E. M. Bergese, editors, *Ocean Yearbook,* University of Chicago Press, Volume 1, 1978, Volume 4, 1984, Volume 9, 1989.
Marine Science and Technology: An Introduction to Oceanography, University Press of America, 1980.
Tidal Energy, Van Nostrand, 1982.
(Contributor) J. Olson, editor, *Small Energy Resources,* UNITAR, 1987.
(With John R. Justus) *Ocean Energy,* Elsevier, 1990.

Also author of *The Study of Rocks,* 1971, *The Study of Oceans,* 1971, *Our Physical Environment,* 1980, and *Marine Geology,*

1980. Contributor, sometimes under pseudonyms Roger Wallace, Scott, and Marco, of about six hundred articles to periodicals, newspapers, and scientific and other scholarly journals in the United States and abroad. Translation editor, *Newsletter of International Geographic Union,* 1954-56; contributing editor, *Oceanic Index,* 1955-88; consulting editor, *Foreign Language Quarterly,* 1956-61, and *Hexagon,* 1961-63.

WORK IN PROGRESS: A book with Alexandre M. Thys, *Economic Oceanography of Mineral Resources.*

SIDELIGHTS: In addition to his native French and English, Roger H. Charlier is fluent in German, Italian, Flemish, Dutch, and Swahili; he has a working knowledge of several other languages, including Spanish, Afrikaans, and the Scandinavian languages. He and his wife visit Europe, South America, and Central America annually and have also made numerous trips to Asia, Africa, and the Pacific area.

MEDIA ADAPTATIONS: *I Was a Male War Bride* was made into a film starring Cary Grant by Twentieth Century-Fox in 1949.

*   *   *

CHASE, Glen
    See LEVINSON, Leonard

*   *   *

CHASE, Lyndon
    See CHARD, Judy

*   *   *

CHEW, Ruth 1920-
    (Ruth Silver)

PERSONAL: Born April 8, 1920, in Minneapolis, Minn.; daughter of Arthur Percy (a writer) and Pauline (Foucar) Chew; married Aaron B. Z. Silver (a lawyer), April 18, 1948; children: David, Eve (Mrs. Hugh Hamilton Sprunt, Jr.), George, Anne (Mrs. Mark Gloekler), Helen. *Education:* Attended Corcoran School of Art, 1936-40, and Art Students League of New York, 1973—. *Religion:* None.

ADDRESSES: *Home*—305 East Fifth St., Brooklyn, N.Y. 11218.

CAREER: Writer and illustrator. Artist for *Washington Post,* Washington, D.C., 1942-43, Grey Advertising Agency, New York, N.Y., 1944-46, and Kresge-Newark Department Store, Newark, N.J., 1946-48.

AWARDS, HONORS: Four Leaf Clover Award for Author of the Year, Lucky Book Club, 1976-77; Colorado Children's Book Award nomination, for *Witch in the House;* Arizona Young Readers' Award nomination, for *The Witch's Buttons.*

WRITINGS:

BOOKS FOR CHILDREN; SELF-ILLUSTRATED

The Wednesday Witch, Scholastic Book Services, 1969.
Baked Beans for Breakfast, Scholastic Book Services, 1970, published as *The Secret Summer,* 1974.
No Such Thing as a Witch, Scholastic Book Services, 1971.
Magic in the Park, Scholastic Book Services, 1972.
What the Witch Left, Scholastic Book Services, 1973.
The Hidden Cave, Scholastic Book Services, 1973, published as *The Magic Cave,* Hastings House, 1978.

The Witch's Buttons, Scholastic Book Services, 1974.
The Secret Tree House, Scholastic Book Services, 1974.
Witch in the House, Scholastic Book Services, 1975.
The Would-Be Witch, Scholastic Book Services, 1976.
The Trouble with Magic, Scholastic Book Services, 1976.
Summer Magic, Scholastic Book Services, 1977.
Witch's Broom, Dodd, 1977.
The Witch's Garden, Scholastic Book Services, 1978.
Earthstar Magic, Scholastic Book Services, 1979.
The Wishing Tree, Hastings House, 1980.
Secondhand Magic, Holiday House, 1981.
Mostly Magic, Holiday House, 1982.
The Magic Coin, Scholastic, Inc., 1983.
The Witch at the Window, Scholastic, Inc., 1984.
Trapped in Time, Scholastic, Inc., 1986.
Do It Yourself Magic, Scholastic, Inc., 1987.
The Witch and the Ring, Scholastic, Inc., 1989.
Magic of the Black Mirror, Scholastic, Inc., 1990.

ILLUSTRATOR

Carol Morse, *Three Cheers for Polly,* Doubleday, 1967.
E. W. Hildick, *The Questers,* Hawthorn, 1970.
Val Abbott, *The Mystery of the Ghost Bell,* Dodd, 1971.
Ann McGovern, *Shark Lady,* Scholastic Book Services, 1978.

SIDELIGHTS: Ruth Chew told *CA* that "before I entered first grade, I started telling myself stories. I drew pictures about the stories on any piece of paper that was blank." She continued writing and drawing throughout her childhood and even completed a children's book while in art school; it wasn't until after her children were grown, however, that she "decided to illustrate children's books and trudged around with samples for five years before I got an assignment," Chew continued. Now the author and illustrator of over twenty-five children's books, Chew says: "I think I'm the luckiest person alive!"

AVOCATIONAL INTERESTS: Travel (especially to England and France).

BIOGRAPHICAL/CRITICAL SOURCES:

PERIODICALS

Flatbush Life, May 30, 1977.
New York Times, May 22, 1977.

* * *

CHILDS, David (Haslam) 1933-

PERSONAL: Born September 25, 1933, in Bolton, England; son of John Arthur (an industrial worker; mayor of Bolton) and Ellen (Haslam) Childs; married Monir Pishdad, June, 1964; children: Martin, Julian. *Education:* London School of Economics and Political Science, B.Sc., 1956, Ph.D., 1962; University of Hamburg, graduate study, 1956-57.

ADDRESSES: *Office*—Department of Politics, University of Nottingham, Nottingham NG7 2RD, England.

CAREER: School teacher in London, England, until 1961; television scriptwriter on documentary films, 1961-64; school teacher and teacher in further education courses, 1964-66; University of Nottingham, Nottingham, England, began as lecturer, became senior lecturer, 1966-76, reader in politics, 1976—, professor of German politics, 1989—, founder and director of Institute of German, Austrian, and Swiss Affairs, 1987—. Candidate for Parliament, 1964.

MEMBER: Association of University Teachers, Association for Study of German Politics (chairman, 1981—), University Asso-

ciation for Contemporary European Studies, European Movement (chairman, 1981-86; secretary, 1986-88), Anglo-German Association (member of executive committee, 1987—).

WRITINGS:

From Schumacher to Brandt: The Story of German Socialism, 1945-1964, Pergamon, 1966.
East Germany, Praeger, 1969.
Germany since 1918, Harper, 1971.
Marx and the Marxists: An Outline of Practice and Theory, Benn, 1973.
(Contributor) Roger Tilford, editor, *The Ostpolitik and Political Change in Germany,* Lexington Books, 1975.
Britain since 1945, Benn, 1979, 2nd edition, 1988.
(Editor) *The Changing Face of Western Communism,* Croom Helm, 1980.
(Contributor) James Riordan, editor, *Sport under Communism: The U.S.S.R., Czechoslovakia, the G.D.R., China, Cuba,* Hurst & Co., 1981.
(With Jeffrey Johnson) *West Germany: Politics and Society,* Croom Helm, 1981.
The G.D.R.: Moscow's German Ally, Allen & Unwin, 1983, 2nd edition, 1988.
(Editor) *Honecker's Germany,* Allen & Unwin, 1985.
(Editor with T.A. Baylis and M. Rueschemeyer) *East Germany in Comparative Perspective,* Routledge & Kegan Paul, 1989.
(Editor with Janet Wharton) *Children in War,* University of Nottingham, 1989.
(Contributor) Karl Koch, editor, *West Germany Today,* Routledge & Kegan Paul, 1989.

Also contributor to *Collier's Encyclopedia.* Contributor to periodicals, including *Times Literary Supplement, Times Higher Educational Supplement, Current History, Guardian, Contemporary Review,* and *World Today.* Founder and senior editor of *Politics and Society in Germany, Austria and Switzerland* (*PASGAS*), 1988—.

SIDELIGHTS: The *Times Literary Supplement* describes David Childs as "an acknowledge expert" on East Germany. In a *Times Literary Supplement* review of *The G.D.R.: Moscow's German Ally,* critic Timothy Garton Ash states, "It is an extremely comprehensive, fast-packed short survey, drawing on a wide range of sources for illustration."

BIOGRAPHICAL/CRITICAL SOURCES:

PERIODICALS

Times Literary Supplement, January 10, 1971, June 8, 1984.

* * *

CHIU, Hungdah 1936-

PERSONAL: Born March 23, 1936, in Shanghai, China; son of Han-ping (a lawyer) and Min-non (Yang) Chiu; married Yuan-yuan Hsieh, May 14, 1966; children: Wei-hsueh (son). *Education:* National Taiwan University, LL.B., 1958; Long Island University, M.A. (with honors), 1962; Harvard University, LL.M., 1962, S.J.D., 1965.

ADDRESSES: *Home*—6168 Devon Dr., Columbia, Md. 21044. *Office*—21029 University of Maryland Law School, 500 West Baltimore St., Baltimore, Md. 21201.

CAREER: National Taiwan University, Taipei, Taiwan, Republic of China, associate professor of international law, 1965-66; Harvard University, School of Law, Cambridge, Mass., research associate in law, 1966-70; National Chengchi University, Taipei, professor of law, 1970-72; Harvard University, School of Law, research associate in law, 1972-74; University of Maryland, School of Law, Baltimore, associate professor, 1974-77, professor of law, 1977—. Research fellow, Institute of International Relations, Mucha, Taipei, 1967-73; International Law Association delegate to United Nations conference on law of the sea, 1976-82. *Military service:* Chinese Army (Republic of China), 1958-60; became second lieutenant; public defender in Judge-Advocate Office, 1959-60.

MEMBER: International Law Association (Taiwan branch), British Institute of International and Comparative Law, Chinese Society of American Law (member of executive council), American Society of International Law (member of Panel on China and International Order, 1969-73; chairperson of Interest Group of Law of Pacific Region, 1987—), Association for Asian Studies, American Association for Chinese Studies (vice-president, 1982-84; president, 1985-87), Association of Chinese Social Scientists in North America (president, 1984-86), Association of American Law Schools (chairperson of section of international legal exchange, 1986-88).

WRITINGS:

IN ENGLISH

The Capacity of International Organizations to Conclude Treaties, Nijhoff (The Hague), 1966.
(With D. M. Johnston) *Agreements of the People's Republic of China, 1949-67: A Calendar,* Harvard University Press, 1968.
The People's Republic of China and the Law of Treaties, Harvard University Press, 1972.
(With C. S. Leng) *Law in Chinese Foreign Policy,* Oceana, 1972.
(Editor and contributor) *China and the Question of Taiwan: Document and Analysis,* Praeger, 1973.
(Co-author) *People's China and International Law: A Documentary Study,* two volumes, Princeton University Press, 1974.
(Co-editor) *Legal Aspects of U.S.-Republic of China Trade and Investment,* School of Law, University of Maryland, 1977.
(Editor and contributor) *Normalizing Relations with the People's Republic of China: Problems, Analysis, and Documents,* School of Law, University of Maryland, 1978.
(Editor and contributor) *China and the Taiwan Issue,* Praeger, 1979.
Agreements of the People's Republic of China: A Calendar of Events 1966-80, Praeger, 1981.
(Co-editor and contributor) *Multi-System Nations and International Law: The International Status of Germany, Korea, and China,* School of Law, University of Maryland, 1981.
(Editor and contributor) *Chinese Yearbook of International Law and Affairs,* Occasional Papers, Volume I, 1981, Volume II, 1982, Volume III, 1983, Volume IV, 1984, Volume V, 1985, Volume VI, 1986, Volume VII, 1987.
(Co-editor and contributor) *China: Seventy Years after the 1911 Hsin-hai Revolution,* University Press of Virginia, 1984.
(Co-author) *Criminal Justice in Post-Mao China,* State University Press of New York, 1985.
(Editor and contributor) *Survey of Recent Developments in China (Mainland and Taiwan), 1985-1986,* Occasional Papers, 1987.
(Co-editor and contributor) *The Future of Hong Kong,* Greenwood Press, 1987.
(Editor and contributor) *The Draft Basic Law of Hong Kong: Analysis and Documents,* Occasional Papers, 1988.

IN CHINESE

Hsien-tai Kuo-chi fa wen-t'i (title means "Selected Problems of Modern International Law"), New Century Publishing Co. (Taipei), 1966.
Chung-Kuo Kuo-chi-fa wen-t'i O lun-chi (title means "Essays on Chinese International Law Problems"), Taiwan Commercial Press (Taipei), 1968.
(Editor) *Hsien-tai Kuo-chi fa (ts'an-k'ao wen-chien)* (title means "Modern International Law, Reference Documents"), San-Min Book Co. (Taipei), 1972.
(Editor) *Hsien-tai Kuo-chi fa* (title means "Modern International Law"), San-Min Book Co., 1973.
Kuan-yu Chung-kuo ling-tu ti kuo-chi wen-t'i lun chi (title means "Collected Essays on International Law Problems Concerning Chinese Territory"), Taiwan Commercial Press, 1975.
(Co-editor and contributor) *Chung-kuo t'ung-i yu Kuo-kung ho-t'an wen-t'i yen-chiu lun-wen-chi* (title means "Essays on the Question of Reunification of China and Nationalist-Communist Negotiation"), World Journal, 1981.
Chung-mei kuan-hsi lun-chi (title means "Essays on Sino-American Relations"), Time Cultural Publishing, 1979.
Hsien-tai kuo-chi-fa chi-pen wen-chien (title means "Basic Documents of International Law"), San-Min Book Co., 1984.
(Co-editor and contributor) *K'ang-chan sheng-li te tai-chia* (title means "The Price of Winning the War against Japan"), Lien-ching Publishing Co., 1986.
(Editor and contributor) *Chung-kuo kuo-chi-fa yu kuo-chi shih-wu nien-pao* (title means "Chinese Yearbook of International Law and International Affairs"), Taiwan Commercial Press, Volume I, 1985, Volume II, 1986, Volume III, 1987.
(Co-editor and contributor) *Chung-kung t'an-p'an ts'e-lueh yen-chiu* (title means "A Study of the Negotiation Strategy of the Chinese Communists"), Lien-ching Publishing Co., 1987.
(Co-editor and contributor) *Chung-hua Min-kuo tang-ch'ien Ke-hsing K'e-t'i* (title means "Current Problem of Reform Confronting the Republic of China"), Time Cultural Publishing Co., 1988.

OTHER

Contributor to professional journals, including *International Lawyer, American Journal of International Law, Harvard Journal of International Law, Ocean Development and International Law, Asian Survey, Journal of Asian Studies,* and *China Quarterly.*

WORK IN PROGRESS: The International Law of the Sea: Cases, Documents, and Readings, with Gary Knight.

*   *   *

CIPLIJAUSKAITE, Birute 1929-

PERSONAL: Born April 11, 1929, in Kaunas, Lithuania; daughter of Juozas (a professor of medicine) and Elena (Stelmokaite) Ciplijauskas. *Education:* Lycee Lithuanien (Tuebingen), diploma of maturity, 1948; University of Montreal, M.A., 1956; Bryn Mawr College, Ph.D., 1960.

ADDRESSES: Office—Department of Spanish, University of Wisconsin, Madison, Wis. 53706.

CAREER: University of Wisconsin—Madison, instructor, 1960-61, assistant professor, 1961-64, associate professor, 1964-68, professor of Spanish literature, 1968-73, John Bascom Professor of Spanish literature, 1973—. Visiting professor, State

University of New York at Stony Brook, 1978, Siegen University, 1983, and Harvard University, 1988. Member, Institute for Research in the Humanities, 1974—.

MEMBER: Association for Advancement of Baltic Studies (vice-president, 1982-84).

AWARDS, HONORS: Guggenheim fellow, 1967-68; Institute for Research in the Humanities (Madison, Wis.), fellow, 1971-72; Camargo Foundation fellow, 1985.

WRITINGS:

La soledad y la poesia espanola contemporanea, Insula (Madrid), 1962.

El poeta y la poesia: Del romanticismo a la poesia social, Insula, 1966.

(Editor) Luis de Gongora, *Sonetos completos,* Castalia (Madrid), 1968.

Deber de plenitud: La poesia de Jorge Guillen, SepSetenas (Mexico), 1972.

Baroja: Un estilo, Insula, 1973.

(Editor) *Jorge Guillen,* Taurus, 1976.

Los noventayochistas y las historia, Porrua Turanzas (Madrid), 1981.

(Editor) de Gongora, *Sonetos,* Hispanic Seminary of Medieval Studies (Madison, Wis.), 1981.

(Translator) Juan Ramon Jimenez, *Sidabrinukas ir as,* [Madison], 1982.

La mujer insatisfecha, Edhasa (Barcelona), 1984.

La femina contemporanea (1970-1985), Anthropos (Barcelona), 1988.

(Translator) Maria Victoria Atencia, *Svenciausios Karalienes Ekstazes,* Malaga, 1989.

(Editor with C. Maurer) *La voluntad de humanismo: Homenaje a Juan Marichal,* Anthropos, 1990.

WORK IN PROGRESS: Editing *Novisiomos, postnovisiomos, clasicos: la poesia de los anos 80 en Espana* for Origenes (Madrid).

BIOGRAPHICAL/CRITICAL SOURCES:

PERIODICALS

Books Abroad, winter, 1970.

*   *   *

CLAIBORNE, Robert (Watson, Jr.) 1919-

PERSONAL: Born May 15, 1919, in High Wycombe, Buckinghamshire, England; son of Robert W. (an attorney) and Virginia (McKenney) Claiborne; married Adrienne Aaron, August 26, 1945 (divorced, 1965); married Sybil Resnik Nukanen (a writer), April 24, 1965; children: (first marriage) Amanda Susan, Samuel McKenney; (second marriage) Jan Stacy (stepson). *Education:* Attended Massachusetts Institute of Technology, 1936-37, and Antioch College, 1937-39; New York University, A.B. (magna cum laude), 1942.

ADDRESSES: Agent—Smith-Skolnik, 23 East Tenth St. #712, New York, N.Y. 10003.

CAREER: Lathe operator and union official in New Jersey and New York, 1942-45; folksinger and music teacher in New York City, 1946-57; *Scientific American,* New York City, associate editor, 1957-60; *Medical World News,* New York City, associate, news, and managing editor, 1960-64; *Life Science Library,* New York City, editor, 1964-65; writer. Lecturer on ecology, New School for Social Research, 1971-72.

MEMBER: National Association of Science Writers, National Writers Union, Authors Guild, Authors League of America.

WRITINGS:

(With Samuel Goudsmit) *Time,* Time, Inc., 1966.

(With Walter Modell and Al Lansing) *Drugs,* Time, Inc., 1968.

Climate, Man and History, Norton, 1970.

On Every Side the Sea, American Heritage Press, 1971.

The First Americans, Time-Life, 1973.

(Editor with Victor McKusick) *Medical Genetics,* HP Publishing, 1973.

God or Beast: Evolution and Human Nature, Norton, 1974.

The Birth of Writing, Time-Life, 1974.

The Summer Stargazer: Astronomy for Absolute Beginners, Coward, 1975, revised edition, Penguin, 1981.

(Editor with Gerald Weissman) *Cell Membranes: Biochemistry, Cell Biology and Pathology,* HP Publishing, 1975.

(With Lionel Casson and Bryan M. Fagen) *Mysteries of the Past,* American Heritage Press, 1977.

Our Marvelous Native Tongue: The Life and Times of the English Language, Times Books, 1983.

Saying What You Mean: A Commonsense Guide to American Usage, Norton, 1986.

Loose Cannons and Red Herrings: A Book of Lost Metaphors, Norton, 1988.

The Roots of English: A Reader's Handbook of Word Origins, Times Books, 1989.

(Editor with McKusick) *Medical Genetics II,* Norton, 1989.

Contributor of articles and reviews to *Harper's, Nation, New York Times, Village Voice, Science Digest, Smithsonian,* and other periodicals. Part-time senior editor, *Hospital Practice,* 1966-88.

WORK IN PROGRESS: Who Decides?: The Politics of Technology, for Dutton; *With No Apologies: Memoirs of an Unreconstructed Rebel.*

SIDELIGHTS: Robert Claiborne's study *Our Marvelous Native Tongue: The Life and Times of the English Language* traces English back to its roots in several other languages, such as the Indo-European dialects and the Italic vocabulary. The inspiration for the work, as the author writes in the preface of the book, began "when I was ten and studying French with my mother. To help me remember the meaning of French *siege* (seat) she pointed out that it was obviously related to English 'siege,' in which an army *sits* down around a town and waits for it to surrender. This incident, and doubtless many similar ones now forgotten, began my lifelong fascination with words: where they came from, why they mean what they do and how different words are related." Claiborne has since parlayed his interest in words into three more books: *Saying What You Mean* (on usage), *Loose Cannons and Red Herrings* (on what he calls "lost metaphors"), and *The Roots of English* (on word origins).

"Basically, I tend to think of myself as a teacher whose medium happens to be print rather than the classroom," Claiborne told *CA.* "But since (unlike most teachers) I don't have a captive audience, I also try to be a storyteller, though my stories are of course fact, not fiction. Because I believe in playing fair with the reader, I try to present not just conclusions but the facts and reasoning that underlie the conclusions. I have an abiding hatred of writers (names on request) who justify nonsensical propositions by distorting facts or simply inventing them—and try to show them up when I get the chance."

AVOCATIONAL INTERESTS: Aikido, body-surfing, gardening, photography, poker, travel, writing letters to the editor, the National Writers Union.

BIOGRAPHICAL/CRITICAL SOURCES:

BOOKS

Claiborne, Robert, *Our Marvelous Native Tongue: The Life and Times of the English Language,* Times Books, 1983.

PERIODICALS

Best Sellers, June 1, 1970.
New Yorker, June 6, 1983.
New York Times Book Review, September 18, 1983.
Tribune Books (Chicago), May 3, 1987.
Washington Post, December 3, 1974.

* * *

CLARK, Anne
See AMOR, Anne Clark

* * *

CLARK, Badger
See PAINE, Lauran (Bosworth)

* * *

CLARK, Wesley James 1950-

PERSONAL: Born December 25, 1950, in Toronto, Ontario, Canada; son of Wesley John (an accountant) and Dorothy (a bookkeeper; maiden name, Hatton) Clark; married Sandra Lee Williams (a computer systems analyst), April 17, 1976; children: Trevor William, Ehren Robert. *Education:* University of Waterloo, B.Sc., 1975, M.Sc., 1977. *Religion:* Anglican.

ADDRESSES: Home—991 Buckskin Way, Orleans, Ontario, Canada K1C 2Y7. *Office*—Ringette Canada, 1600 James Naismith Dr., Gloucester, Ontario, Canada K1L 5N4.

CAREER: Kitchener Rangers Hockey Club, Kitchener, Ontario, athletic therapist, 1975-77; Ringette Canada, Gloucester, Ontario, national coaching chairman, 1978-82, executive director, 1982—. Technical director of Ontario Ringette Association, 1978-82; member of Canadian Standards Association committee for certification of hockey and lacrosse equipment; member of Committee on Consultation, Government of Canada—Fitness and Amateur Sport.

MEMBER: Senior (Sport) Managers Council.

WRITINGS:

(With B.D. McPherson, Ronald Martenuk, and others) *An Analysis of the System of Age Group Swimming in Ontario,* Canadian Amateur Swimming Association, 1977.
(Editor) *Ringette Level I Coach's Manual,* National Sport and Recreation Centre (Ottawa, Ontario), 1979.
Ringette in Your School: A Teacher's Guide, Ontario Ringette Association, 1980.
(Editor with Patrick Doherty) *Ringette Fundamentals: For the Instructor, Teacher, and Coach,* Ontario Ringette Association, 1981.
(With Edmund Vaz) *The Professionalization of Young Hockey Players,* University of Nebraska Press, 1982.
(Editor) *Ringette Level II Coach's Manual,* National Sport and Recreation Centre, 1983.

(With others) *Sport Development Perspective,* Ringette Canada, 1989.

FILMSCRIPTS

(Co-author) "This Is Ringette," released by Al Stewart Enterprises, 1980.
(Co-author and producer) "Equipment for Ringette," released by National Sport and Recreation Centre and Ringette Canada, 1981.
"Goaltending Skills: Ringette Skills Series," released by National Sport and Recreation Centre, 1981.
"Ringette Skills: Ringette Skills Series," released by National Sport and Recreation Centre, 1981.
"Skating: Ringette Skills Series," released by National Sport and Recreation Centre, 1981.
"Ringette for Life," released by Ringette Canada, 1989.

OTHER

Contributor to sports magazines. Editor of numerous publications.

WORK IN PROGRESS: A History of Ringette in Canada.

SIDELIGHTS: Wesley James Clark told *CA:* "My past and present jobs allow me to continue writing. The diversity of their requirements has created interesting experiences. Since graduating in kinesiology in 1977 I have been working for the sport of ringette—first at the provincial, then at the national levels. Ringette is a winter team sport, played on ice by females. Similar to floor hockey, players skate, pass, shoot, and score using a stick similar to a bladeless hockey stick and a round, pneumatic rubber ring. Invented in Canada, the game is spreading to the northern United States, Europe, and other countries.

"My involvement in this new but growing sport has allowed me to continue my interest in writing through the publication of materials about the sport. Unfortunately, my writing work is limited by a lack of creative time and the need for continued development of ringette materials. Work in other areas is therefore restricted. Nevertheless, I would like to compile a history of the sport of ringette from existing materials and from interviews with persons who have been involved with the sport from its beginning."

Clark adds: "I have recently become involved in the area of determining an effective consultation mechanism for the Government of Canada—Fitness and Amateur Sport, along with a committee of high profile government and sport representatives. We hope to reach new levels in cooperation between government and client organizations. Writing a perspective on this area is extremely interesting and rewarding.

"Because of recent trends in hockey and the high degree of visibility of the sport, especially in Canada, there are many influences a young player must deal with when pursuing hockey as a pastime or a future career. Violence in the National Hockey League, aggressive behavior in junior hockey, and values persistent in the sport influence the development and values of young hockey players. The major problem seems to be the enforcement or lack of enforcement of existing rules in the sport. In certain instances 'good' penalties are encouraged, thus creating a permissiveness in breaking the rules in advantageous situations. On other occasions rule infractions are ignored if they have no great effect on the game or if a foul can be made behind the back of the referee. Such values infiltrate minor hockey to give players the impression and belief that breaking the rules is okay if you can get away with it. Skating and other skills are sacrificed in favor of these professionalized values, and the purpose of sport is lost."

He concludes: "I think that every person should have an opportunity to participate in sport and/or recreation at their own level of ability. Whether it be recreational or competitive, the opportunity to be involved should be facilitated by sport and recreation organizers and government. Too many people are forced out of sport at an early age because of the lack of opportunity and the concentration on competitive sport. While competitive sport has its place, recreational activity must be opened to the masses and promoted on a wide scale. Sport must get back to basics and the concept of 'sport for all.' "

AVOCATIONAL INTERESTS: Travel (including Canada, the United States, and Europe), home remodelling and decorating, coaching and administrating sports on a volunteer basis (including hockey and lacrosse).

*   *   *

CLARKE, Richard
See PAINE, Lauran (Bosworth)

*   *   *

CLARKE, Robert
See PAINE, Lauran (Bosworth)

*   *   *

CLODFELTER, Micheal D. 1946-

PERSONAL: Born December 6, 1946, in Winfield, Kan.; son of Lutie D. (a truck driver) and Betty (a clerk; maiden name, Hotchkin) Clodfelter; married Rena Katherine Dyce (a library professional), August 1, 1967; children: Thomas Debs. *Education:* Fort Hays Kansas State College, A.B., 1971. *Politics:* Democratic Socialist. *Religion:* None.

ADDRESSES: Home—1515 Maryland, Lawrence, Kan. 66044.

CAREER: Has worked as a dishwasher, farmhand, janitor, painter, and night watchman; writer, 1967—. *Military service:* U.S. Army, 1965-67; served in Vietnam; became sergeant; received 6 medals including Purple Heart.

WRITINGS:

The Pawns of Dishonor, Branden Press, 1976.
(Contributor) *The Vietnam Experience* (anthology), Volumes V and VI, Boston Publishing, 1983.
(Contributor) John Pratt, editor, *Vietnam Perspectives* (anthology), Viking, 1983.
(With John Musgrave) *The Vietnam Years: 1,000 Questions and Answers,* Quinlan Press, 1986.
Mad Minutes and Vietnam Months: A Soldier's Memoir, McFarland & Co., 1988.
Military History Magazine's Trivia Quiz Book II, Empire Press, 1989.
A Statistical History of the Korean War, Merriam Press, 1990.
A Statistical History of the Vietnam War, Merriam Press, 1990.

Also contributor to anthologies, including Cranston Knight, editor, *Vietnam: An Anthology of Voices,* 1983, and *Tour of Duty,* 1986; also contributor to student underground newspapers. Contributor of articles, stories, and poetry to periodicals, including *Vietnam Journal, Military History Journal, Weapons and Warfare Monthly, Perimeter, Tellus, Samisdat,* and *Vietnam Heroes.*

WORK IN PROGRESS: Dakota Campaigns: The Sibley and Sully Expeditions against the Sioux, 1863-65.

SIDELIGHTS: Micheal D. Clodfelter told *CA:* "My first published work . . . concerns my months of service in the Vietnam War. My current literary efforts continue to be focused on military history and upon the effects of war upon the human condition. I hope that my research and writing may in some small way help to illuminate the experience of war in both a personal and historical sense."

*   *   *

COBB, James Charles 1947-

PERSONAL: Born April 13, 1947, in Anderson, S.C.; son of Joel Edward (a farmer) and Modena (Vickery) Cobb; married Lyra McMichael (an editor), June 8, 1969; children: Benjamin C. *Education:* University of Georgia, A.B., 1969, M.A., 1972, Ph.D., 1975.

ADDRESSES: Home—5116 Buckhead Trail, Knoxville, Tenn. 37919. *Office*—Department of History, University of Tennessee, Knoxville, Tenn. 37996.

CAREER: University of Maryland at College Park, visiting assistant professor of history, 1975-77; University of Northern Iowa, Cedar Falls, assistant professor, 1977-80, associate professor of history, 1980-81; University of Mississippi, University, professor of history and Southern studies and director of Southern studies program, 1981-87; University of Alabama, Tuscaloosa, professor of history and director of University Honors Program, 1987-89; University of Tennessee, Knoxville, Bernadotte E. Schmitt Chair of Excellence, 1989—.

MEMBER: Organization of American Historians, Southern Historical Association.

WRITINGS:

The Selling of the South, Louisiana State University Press, 1982.
Industrialization and Southern Society, 1877-1984, University Press of Kentucky, 1984.
The Last South: Society, Politics and Culture in the Mississippi Delta from the Antebellum Era to the Present, Oxford University Press, 1990.

Contributor to history, urban studies, and literary journals.

WORK IN PROGRESS: Continuing research on the impact of economic development on society and culture in the South.

*   *   *

COCCIOLI, Carlo 1920-

PERSONAL: Born May 15, 1920, in Leghorn, Italy; son of Attilio and Anna (Duranti) Coccioli. *Education:* University of Naples and University of Rome, D.Sc. *Religion:* Roman Catholic.

ADDRESSES: Home—Apartado Postal 27.529, Mexico City 06760 D.F., Mexico.

CAREER: Author, 1946—. *Military service:* Italian Army, officer; employed by Allied Forces in Psychological Warfare Branch, 1944-45; received Medaglia d'Argento al V.M. (star medal) for activities in anti-fascist Resistance.

AWARDS, HONORS: Charles Veillon Prize, 1950, for *Il Giuoco;* Selezione Campiello Prize and Basilicata Prize, both 1976, both for *Memoires du Roi David;* Scanno Prize, 1978, for *Fabrizio Lupo;* Grand Prix du Rayonnement de la Langue Francaise, 1982; Ordre des Arts et des Lettres, 1989.

WRITINGS:

Il Migliore e l'Ultimo (novel), Vallecchi, 1946.

La difficile speranza (novel), La Voce, 1947.
La Piccola Valle di Dio (novel), Vallecchi, 1948, translation by Campbell Nairne published as *The Little Valley of God,* Heineman, 1956, Simon & Schuster, 1957.
Il cielo e la terra (novel), Vallecchi, 1950, reprinted, Rusconi, 1977, translation by Frances Frenaye published as *Heaven and Earth,* Prentice-Hall, 1952.
Il Giuoco (novel), Garzanti, 1950.
Le bal des egares (novel), Flammarion, 1951.
Fabrizio Lupo (novel), Table Ronde (Paris), 1952, reprinted, Rusconi, 1978, translation by Bernard Frechtman published as *The Eye and the Heart,* Heinemann, 1960, published as *Fabrizio's Book,* Shorecrest, 1966.
La Ville et le sang (novel), Flammarion, 1955.
L'immagine e le stagioni (novel), Plon, 1956, translation by Hans Koningberger published as *Manuel the Mexican,* Simon & Schuster, 1958.
Journal, Table Ronde, 1957.
Le caillou blanc (novel), Plon, 1958, translation by Elizabeth Sutherland and Vera Bleuer published as *The White Stone,* Simon & Schuster, 1960.
Un suicide (novel), Flammarion, 1959.
Ambroise (novel), Flammarion, 1961.
Soleil (novel), Plon, 1961.
Omeyotl: diario messicano, Vallecchi, 1962.
L'Aigle Azteque est tombe (novel), Plon, 1964.
L'erede di Montezuma, Vallecchi, 1964.
Le corde dell'arpa (novel), Longanesi, 1967.
Documento 127, Club degli Autori, 1970.
Le tourment de Dieu, Fayard, 1971.
Hommes en fuite: la grande aventure des Alcooliques Anonymes, Fayard, 1972.
Uomini in fuga, Rizzoli, 1973, reprinted, Jaca Book, 1989.
Memoires du Roi David, Table Ronde, 1976.
Requiem per un cane, Rusconi, 1977.
Le case del lago (novel), Rusconi, 1980.
La casa di Tacubaya, Editoriale Nuova, 1982.
Los sexenios felices, Diana S.A., 1985.
Rapato a zero, Vallecchi, 1986.
Piccolo Karma, Mondadori, 1987.
Yo Cuauhtemoc, SEP Setentas, 1988.
La sentencia del Ayatola, Diana S.A., 1989.
Budda e il suo glorioso mondo, Rusconi, 1990.

Also author of plays "Los fanaticos," "La colline de la lune," and "El esperado." Author of column for *Excelsior* (Mexico City). Regular contributor to Italian periodicals. Coccioli's books have been translated into German, Swedish, Norwegian, Polish, Portuguese, Spanish, Dutch, Czech, and other languages.

*   *   *

COLE, E(ugene) R(oger) 1930-
(Peter E. Locre)

PERSONAL: Born November 14, 1930, in Cleveland, Ohio; son of Bernard James (an electrical engineer) and Mary Louise (Rogers) Cole. *Education:* Sulpician Seminary of the Northwest, B.A., 1954, M.Div., 1958; Central Washington State College (now Central Washington University), A.B., 1960; Harvard University, independent research, 1969-70: Seattle University, M.A., 1970. *Politics:* Independent. *Religion:* "Christotheism."

ADDRESSES: Home—9810 Cove Dr., North Royalton, Ohio 44133. *Office*—P.O. Box 91277, Cleveland, Ohio 44101.

CAREER: Ordained Roman Catholic priest, 1958; Central Washington State College (now Central Washington Univer-

sity), Ellensburg, Newman moderator, 1958-59; high school English teacher, director of drama, and chairman of department in parochial schools in Yakima, Wash., 1959-69; free-lance writer, editor, and researcher, 1969—. Business manager, Experiment Press, 1959-60; chaplain, St. Elizabeth Hospital, 1959-61; poetry critic, National Writers Club, 1969-72; poet-in-service, Poets & Writers, Inc., 1974—; member of election board, Lake County, Ind., 1974-79; contract bridge instructor, 1975—; adult education instructor, 1977-79; Christian counsellor and instructor, 1980—; founder, Godspeople, Inc., 1985—; editorial consultant, Bellflower Press, 1988—.

MEMBER: International Platform Association, International Poetry Society, World-Wide Academy of Scholars, Western World Haiku Society, Authors Guild, Authors League of America, Poetry Society of America (judge, 1970), National Writers Club, Academy of American Poets, Society of Scholarly Publishing, American Contract Bridge League, Sir Thomas Beecham Society, Society for the Study of Midwestern Literature, Poetry Society (London), Eighteen Nineties Society (London), Poets' League of Greater Cleveland, Friends of Cleveland Public Library, Friends of the Lilly Library, Chicago Symphony Orchestra Association, Kappa Delta Pi.

AWARDS, HONORS: Poetry Broadcast Award, 1968; Musical Expertise Award, 1970; Annual Mentor Poetry Award, 1974; Dragonfly Award, 1974; Danae International Poetry award, 1974; Pro Mundi Beneficio Award, Academia Brasileira de Ciencias Humanas, 1975; Readers Union Award, 1976; Diploma di Merito, Universita delle Arti, 1982; World University, Litt.D., 1983; Cleveland Orchestra Marathon Award, 1983; International Cultural Diploma of Honor, 1989.

WRITINGS:

The Great "O" Antiphons: An Original Translation, Harvester Press, 1956.
What Did St. Luke Mean by "Kecharitomene"? (monograph), Catholic University of America Press, 1958.
Experiment in Poetry (promopoem), Windy House, 1959.
Which End, the Empyrean? (one-act play), Alan Swallow/ Experiment Press, 1959.
Spring as Ballet: A Dalhousie In-plano, Review Publishing, 1961.
(Editor and author of foreword) *Experiment,* Alan Swallow/ Experiment Press, 1961.
Three Cycle Poems of Yeats (monograph), School of Philosophy, University of Southern California, 1965.
Mrs. H and What Have You, Concordia Press, 1966.
Woman, You: Illustrapoem, Our Times Press, 1967, revised, 1969.
April Is the Cruelest Month (Poet Lore drama), Literary Publications Foundation, Inc., 1970.
(Editor with James Edwards, and author of foreword) *Grand Slam: 13 Great Short Stories about Bridge,* Putnam, 1975 (published in England as *Grand Slam: Thirteen Great Bridge Stories* (Readers Union Book Club selection), Bodley Head, 1975).
(Editor with others) *In the Beginning,* Confrontation Books, 1978.
Falling Up: Haiku and Senryu, Kamazu Press, 1979.
Act & Potency: Poems, Apeiron Press, 1980.
Ding an sich: Anapoems, Wainwright, 1985.
Uneasy Camber: Early Poems and Diversions, 1943-1950 (limited edition), Greystone Press, 1986.
A Key to "Ding an sich: Anapoems," Wainwright, 1986.
Godspeople: Not a Church but a People, Pilgrims Press, 1987.

(Under pseudonym Peter E. Locre) *Songpoems/Poemsongs: New Lyrics,* Weyburne Publications, 1988.

(Editor and author of foreword) *Litany: Cynewulf to Vachel Lindsay,* GreenSpan Press, 1989,

(With Marjorie Zeyen) *Earthly Existence,* Collegium Associates, 1991.

CONTRIBUTOR

Loren Phillips, editor, *Autumn Leaves,* Blue River Poetry Press, 1957.

C. E. Harper, editor, *Experiment Theatre,* Alan Swallow/Experiment Press, 1959.

Melville Cane and others, editors, *The Golden Year: The Poetry Society of America Anthology 1910-1960,* Fine Editions Press, 1960, reprinted, Books for Libraries Press, 1969.

Jacques Cardonnet, editor, *La Poesie contemporaine aux Etats-Unis* (title means "Contemporary Poetry in the United States"), Editions de la Revue Moderne, 1962.

Jon Edgar Webb, editor, *The Outsider of the Year,* Loujon Press, 1963.

David Ross, editor, *Best Broadcast Poetry,* Young Publications, 1969.

Virginia R. Mollenkott, editor, *Adam among the Television Trees: An Anthology of Verse by Contemporary Christian Poets,* Word Books, 1971.

Charles Angoff and others, editors, *The Diamond Anthology,* A. S. Barnes, 1971.

Noel Gardner, editor, *Nor All Your Wit,* New Dawn Publications, 1973.

Robert Novak, editor, *The Windless Orchard Calendar,* Orchard Press, 1978.

Evelyn Petry, editor, *The Clover Collection of Verse,* Clover Publishing, 1974.

John Westburg, editor, *Down to Earth Poems: Eleven Years of Award-Winning Poems, 1964-1974,* Westburg Associates, 1979.

Alfred Dorn, editor, *Poetry and Science,* Poetry Society, 1981.

Dorothy K. Bestor, *Aside from Teaching, What in the World Can You Do?,* University of Washington Press, 1982.

Robert Conrad, editor, *Glinka, Glinka, Little Tsar,* Cleveland Orchestra/WCLV Press, 1983.

Robert Wallace, editor, *Light Year '86: The Annual of Light Verse and Funny Poems,* Bits Press, 1985.

Judson Jerome, editor, *Poet's Market,* Writer's Digest Books, 1988, 1989, 1990.

Leatrice Lifshitz, editor, *Only Morning in Her Shoes,* University Press, 1990.

OTHER

Author of musical composition "Werther: Tone Poem for Piano," first aired on WERE-Cleveland, 1948, lyrics for male production of "Finian's Rainbow," first performed in Seattle, May, 1958, hymns "Lord Who Said," "Warned by the Precepts," and "O Holy Lord," written on Bach melodies and included in *Hymns at Mass,* 1958, and "Chronicle for Tape," a dramatic monologue with music of Hindemith, recorded in 1960. Also author of two one-act plays, "The Death of Mad Tasso" and "The Lottery," both unpublished and unproduced. Contributor, sometimes under pseudonyms, to newspapers, and to more than seventy literary journals, and popular magazines, including *Saturday Review, Dalhousie Review, Northwest Review, Southern Humanities Review, Beloit Poetry Journal,* and *La Voix des poetes.* Associate editor, *Harvester,* 1955; guest editor, *Experiment: An International Review,* 1961; editorial participant, *This Is My Best,* 1970.

WORK IN PROGRESS: Saki's Cup: The Wit and Wisdom of H. H. Munro; I, Jesus; The Best Two-Liners from Martial; The Eruption of Vesuvius Eye-Witnessed by Pliny; Dryden's The Hind and the Panther, edited for easy reading; *Praeterita,* a book of poems; *The Annotated "Act"; Grand Slam Redoubled,* a third collection of bridge stories.

SIDELIGHTS: E. R. Cole told *CA:* "At the top of a business card of mine are the words: ACTUM NE AGAS (Terence). Freely translated, the phrase means 'Don't do what's already been done.' I think that pretty well describes the animating spirit of my work—whether it be poetry, drama, fiction, essay, and whether it be authored or edited by me. Whenever an idea really excites me, it's usually because of its freshness—its 'not-having-been-done-before-ness.' While reading Ring Lardner's 'Contract' many years ago, it suddenly occurred to me that a collection of such stories (bridge) would not only be welcome to lovers of good fiction and bridge, but would make a unique contribution to the world of anthologies. It was this latter consideration that became the driving force behind *Grand Slam: Thirteen Great Short Stories about Bridge,* which quickly found publishers both here and in Great Britain, and was a book club selection there.

"As another side to this, I have found myself trying to turn some of the most difficult, abstract and often prosaic ideas from the past—philosophical and theological ideas which I believe to be still valid today—into drama and poetry of dazzling modernity. In *Which End, the Empyrean?,* I have Francesca and Paolo playing God to each other in the afterlife, thus eternizing their earthly choice. *April Is the Cruelest Month* pits the Aristotelian view of 'the most important thing' (full self-realization) against an excessively 'divine' one. My efforts to contemporize ancient—and especially metaphysical—thought have resulted in several books of poetry: *Falling Up,* a Heraclitean sequence of 'ith'—ideotypographic haiku and senryu; *Act and Potency,* the first book of poems to be directly inspired by the work of Aristotle, principally his *Metaphysics; Ding an sich,* in which I introduce a new poetry—the 'anapoem'—that I like to think is the perfect wedding (in content and form) of philosophy and poetry. The book is a 'parallel sequence' showing both Buberian and Aristotelian influences."

AVOCATIONAL INTERESTS: Book collecting (first editions), piano, classical discology, concertgoing, ballet, art history, Latin, Greek, French, philosophy, logistics, patrology, bridge, chess, backgammon, deltiology, Mexican archeology, Egyptology, Assyriology.

BIOGRAPHICAL/CRITICAL SOURCES:

BOOKS

Mollenkott, Virginia R., editor, *Adam among the Television Trees: An Anthology of Verse by Contemporary Christian Poets,* Word Books, 1971.

Sachen, William, *Bridge: A Reference Guide,* Garland Publishing, 1984.

Slavitt, Michael S., *E. R. Cole: A Bibliography,* Research Publishers, 1989.

Truscott, Alan F., editor, *The Official Encyclopedia of Bridge,* Crown, 1984.

PERIODICALS

Booklist, September 1, 1975.
Boston Globe, May 18, 1975.
Guardian (Manchester), January 11, 1976.
Kirkus Reviews, April 15, 1975.

Minneapolis Tribune, August 3, 1975.
National Observer, August 2, 1975, October 25, 1975.
Ohioana Quarterly, winter, 1983, spring, 1987, summer 1988, autumn, 1988.
Publishers Weekly, April 21, 9175.
Sports Illustrated, June 30, 1975.
St. Louis Post-Dispatch, December 9, 1975.
Trade, fall, 1978.
Washington Star, June 14, 1975.
Word Ways, May, 1987, August, 1987.

*   *   *

COLETTA, Paolo Enrico 1916-

PERSONAL: Born February 3, 1916, in Plainfield, N.J.; son of Alberto Sisto (a tailor) and Maria (Rappoli) Coletta; married Alicevelyn Warner, January 15, 1940 (died, 1967); married Maria Bellina Boyer, September 5, 1967; children: (first marriage) Dana Maria (Mrs. Lawrence Murphy); (stepchildren) Bernarr Boyer, Paula Maria. *Education:* Junior College of Connecticut, A.A., 1936; University of Missouri, B.S., 1938, M.A., 1939, Ph.D., 1942.

ADDRESSES: Home—1519 Riverdale Dr., Winchester-on-Severn, Annapolis, Md. 21401.

CAREER: University of Missouri—Columbia, instructor in history, 1940-42; Stephens College, Columbia, Mo., instructor in social science, 1942-43; South Dakota State College (now University), Brookings, instructor in history, 1946; University of Louisville, Louisville, Ky., instructor in social science, 1946; U.S. Naval Academy, Annapolis, Md., 1958-83, associate professor, 1958-63, professor of history, beginning 1963, and lecturer in sea power and national policy, beginning 1971, became Distinguished Meritorious Professor. Visiting professor, University of Maryland Extension, 1959-62; Fulbright lecturer, University of Genoa, 1971; visiting summer professor at University of Nebraska, 1949, 1952, 1953, and at Colorado College, 1963. *Military service:* U.S. Navy, 1943-46. U.S. Naval Reserve, 1951-73; retired as captain.

MEMBER: American Historical Association, U.S. Naval Institute, American Military Institute, Society of Historians for Foreign Relations, Organization of American Historians, National Geographic Society, Naval Reserve Association, Pacific Historical Society, Southern Historical Association, Nebraska State Historical Society, Phi Delta Kappa.

WRITINGS:

(Contributor) W. W. Jeffries, editor, *Geography and National Power,* U.S. Naval Institute, 1953, 4th edition, 1968.
(With Gerald E. Wheeler) *An Outline of World Naval History,* Annapolis Academy Press, 1956.
(Contributor) H. Wayne Morgan, editor, *The Gilded Age,* Syracuse University Press, 1963.
William Jennings Bryan, University of Nebraska Press, Volume I: *Political Evangelist, 1860-1908,* 1964, Volume II: *Progressive Politician and Moral Statesman, 1909-1915,* 1969, Volume III: *Political Puritan, 1915-1925,* 1969.
(Contributing editor) *Threshold to American Internationalism: The Foreign Policies of William McKinley,* Exposition Press, 1970.
(Contributor) Arthur M. Schlesinger, Jr., editor, *History of Presidential Elections,* Chelsea House, 1971.
(Contributor) Schlesinger, editor, *History of U.S. Political Parties,* Chelsea House, 1972.
William Howard Taft, University Press of Kansas, 1973.

(Contributor) Alexander DeConde, editor, *Encyclopedia of American Foreign Policies,* Scribner, 1978.
The U.S. Navy and Defense Unification, 1947-1953, University of Delaware Press, 1979.
Admiral Bradley A. Fiske and the American Navy, Regents Press of Kansas, 1979.
Bowman Hendry McCalla: A Fighting Sailor, University Press of America, 1979.
French Ensor Chadwick: Scholarly Warrior, University Press of America, 1980.
(Contributing editor) *American Secretaries of the Navy,* Naval Institute Press, 1980.
(Contributor) Gerald K. Haines and J. Samuel Walter, editors, *American Foreign Relations: A Historiographical Review,* Greenwood Press, 1981.
A Bibliography of American Naval History, Naval Institute Press, 1981.
(Editor-in-chief) *U.S. Navy and Marine Corps Bases,* two volumes, Greenwood Press, 1985.
An Annotated Bibliography of U.S. Marine Corps History, University Press of America, 1985.
A Survey of U.S. Naval Affairs, 1865-1917, University Press of America, 1985.
Patrick N. L. Bellinger and U.S. Naval Aviation, University Press of America, 1987.
William Howard Taft: A Bibliography, Meckler Corp., 1989.
Naval Power in World War I: The Atlantic and Mediterranean, University Press of America, 1989.

Also contributor to encyclopedias. Contributor of more than seventy-five articles and reviews to history journals.

*   *   *

COLLINS, John M(artin) 1921-

PERSONAL: Born May 14, 1921, in Kansas City, Mo.; son of John M. (a newspaper editor) and Jessie F. (Wagner) Collins; married Gloria O. Demers, November 11, 1950; children: Sean K. *Education:* University of Kansas City, B.A., 1949; Clark University, Worcester, Mass., M.A., 1951; attended Industrial College of the Armed Forces, 1967, and National War College, 1969.

ADDRESSES: Home—1001 Priscilla Lane, Alexandria, Va. 22308. *Office*—Congressional Research Service, Library of Congress, Washington, D.C. 20540.

CAREER: U.S. Army, career officer, 1942-72; retired as colonel; Library of Congress, Congressional Research Service, Washington, D.C., senior specialist in national defense, 1972—.

WRITINGS:

Grand Strategy: Principles and Practices, U.S. Naval Institute, 1973.
Imbalance of Power: Shifting U.S.-Soviet Military Strengths, Presidio Press, 1978.
American and Soviet Military Trends since the Cuban Missile Crisis, Center for Strategic Studies and International Studies, Georgetown University, 1978.
U.S.-Soviet Military Balance: Concepts and Capability, 1960-1980, Aviation Week (New York), 1980.
U.S. Defense Planning: A Critique, Westview, 1982.
U.S.-Soviet Military Balance, 1980-1985, Pergamon, 1985.
Green Berets, Seals, and Spetsnaz: U.S. and Soviet Special Military Operations, Pergamon, 1987.
Military Space Forces: The Next Fifty Years, Pergamon, 1989.

Also author of more than twenty major studies for the Congressional Research Service. Contributor to numerous professional publications.

*   *   *

CONANT, Ralph W(endell) 1926-

PERSONAL: Born September 7, 1926, in Hope, Me.; son of Earle Raymond (a business executive) and Margaret (Long) Conant; married Audrey Karl (a teacher), August 27, 1950; children: Beverlie Elaine, Lisa Audrey, Jonathan Arnold. *Education:* University of Vermont, B.A., 1949; University of Chicago, M.A., 1954, Ph.D., 1959. *Politics:* Democrat. *Religion:* Unitarian.

ADDRESSES: Home—Box 2200, North Vassalboro, Me. 04962.

CAREER: Staff associate, National Municipal League, 1957-59; director, Citizens for Michigan, 1959-60; University of Denver, Denver, Colo., assistant professor, 1960-62; Massachusetts Institute of Technology and Harvard University, Joint Center for Urban Studies, Cambridge, Mass., assistant to the director, 1962-66; Brandeis University, Lemberg Center for the Study of Violence, Waltham, Mass., associate director, 1967-69; University of Houston, Houston, Tex., professor of political science and director of Institute for Urban Studies, 1969-75; Rice University, Houston, professor of urban studies and president of Southwest Center for Urban Research, 1969-75; Shimer College, Mt. Carroll, Ill., president, 1975-78; Unity College, Unity, Me., president, 1978-81; president of Public Research, Inc., 1981—; Mercy College, Dobbs Ferry, N.Y., acting dean for admissions, 1987-89. Member of Regional Health Advisory Committee, U.S. Department of Health, Education and Welfare. *Military service:* U.S. Army, 1943-45, 1951-53. U.S. Army Reserves, 1945-68; became major.

MEMBER: American Political Science Association.

WRITINGS:

(Editor) Milton Greenburg and Sherrill Cleland, *State Constitutional Revision in Michigan,* [Detroit], 1960.
Politics of Regional Planning in Greater Hartford, Greater Hartford Chamber of Commerce, 1964.
(Editor) *The Public Library and the City,* MIT Press, 1965.
The Politics of Community Health, Public Affairs Press, 1968.
Civil Disobedience, Rioting and Insurrection, Lincoln Filene Center for Citizenship and Public Affairs, 1968.
(Editor with Molly Apple Levin) *Problems in Research on Community Violence,* Praeger, 1969.
The Prospects for Revolution: A Study of Riots, Civil Disobedience and Insurrection in Contemporary America, Harper's Magazine Press, 1971.
The Metropolitan Library, MIT Press, 1972.
(With Alan Shank) *Urban Perspectives: Politics and Policies,* Holbrook, 1975.
The Conant Report: A Study of the Education of Librarians, MIT Press, 1980.
(With T. Easton) *Using Consultants: A Consumer's Guide for Managers,* Probus, 1985.
(With Easton) *Cutting Loose: Making the Transition from Employee to Entrepreneur,* Probus, 1985.
(With B. Carroll and Easton) *Private Means—Public Ends,* Praeger, in press.

Contributor to *American Scholar, Urban Affairs Quarterly, Library Journal, Wilson Library Bulletin, A.L.A. Bulletin, International Journal of Health Education, American Behavioral Scientist,* and other journals.

AVOCATIONAL INTERESTS: Mountain climbing, golfing, skiing, European travel.

BIOGRAPHICAL/CRITICAL SOURCES:

PERIODICALS

Nation, June 14, 1971.

*   *   *

CONN, Jan E(velyn) 1952-

PERSONAL: Born July 8, 1952, in Asbestos, Quebec, Canada; daughter of Herbert Murray Keith (a mining engineer) and Florence Elliot (a registered nurse; maiden name, Cole) Conn. *Education:* Concordia University, Montreal, Quebec, B.Sc., 1977; Simon Fraser University, M.Sc., 1981, Ph.D., 1987.

ADDRESSES: Home—25 Sword St., Toronto, Ontario, Canada M5A 3N3. *Office*—Universid Central de Venezuela, Instituto de Zoologia Tropical, Apartado 47058, Caracas 1041-A, Venezuela.

CAREER: Macdonald College, Ste. Anne de Bellevue, Quebec, museum technician at Lyman Museum of Entomology, 1977-78; Simon Fraser University, Burnaby, British Columbia, research technician, 1981-82; University of Venezuela, Caracas, postdoctoral researcher, 1988-90. Part-time writer, 1982—.

MEMBER: League of Canadian Poets, Writers Union of Canada, Entomological Society of Canada; Entomological Society of America, Society of the Study of Evolution, American Mosquito Control Association.

AWARDS, HONORS: Canada Council grant for Japan, 1982, for Brazil, 1987.

WRITINGS:

Red Shoes in the Rain (poems), Fiddlehead Poetry Books, 1984.
The Fabulous Disguise of Ourselves, Vehicle Press (Montreal), 1986.
South of Tudo Bem Cafe, Vehicle Press, 1989.

Work represented in anthologies, including *Anything Is Possible,* edited by Mary di Michele, Mosaic Press, 1984. Contributor of poems to periodicals, including *Event, Fiddlehead, Germination, Poetry Canada Review, Poetry Nippon, Prism International, Room of One's Own, Sepia, This Magazine, Toronto Life, Catalyst, Malahat Review, Quarry, Les Cahiers de la Femme,* and *Moosehead Review.*

WORK IN PROGRESS: An untitled manuscript of poems primarily set in Venezuela.

SIDELIGHTS: Jan Conn once told *CA* that several reasons prompted her to choose Japan for her Canada Council grant in 1982: "I knew the roads were good (essential for a ten-speed bike), I felt I would be safe traveling alone, the country is small enough for me to see a great deal of it (in fact, I cycled more than four thousand kilometers in two months), and I wanted to see what had happened since World War II. Three places in particular had a strong impact on my writing: Sado Island, Oki Islands, and Kyushu. I stayed in a Buddhist temple on Sado for ten days. I saw tiny, quiet fishing villages, green jewels of rice fields, old temples, the public baths. Oki Islands are a string of small islands off northwestern Honshu. Oki-Dozen National Park, on the west coast of Dozen Island, was compelling and the landscape reminded me of Wales—high green meadows, pastures for cows, sea fog, and the lonely cries of birds. The road across Kyushu (especially from Mt. Aso to Oita) was the only place in Japan I had a sense of limitless space. There was little traffic and the highway went up and down like a roller-coaster with fields of cabbages, rows of young Cryptomeria, and blue mountains going off endlessly. The silence seemed intensified by my knowledge of the recent floods in Nagasaki, which I narrowly missed.

"Guatemala (where I did my doctoral research on black flies which vector the nematode which causes onchocerciasis, or river blindness) was a whole other story.

"The main theme of my work has been using landscape as metaphor, but that is changing to poems that allow a more emotional/personal voice to surface. I'd rather read my work at readings or have people read my books than talk a lot about form and content. I'm happiest when I'm writing, but need the discipline and balance of my scientific research."

*   *   *

COOPER, David E(dward)   1942-

PERSONAL: Born October 1, 1942, in England; son of Edward (a businessman) and Lilian (Turner) Cooper. *Education:* Oxford University, B.A. (first class honors), 1964, B.Phil., 1966, M.A., 1969.

ADDRESSES: Home—Heathside, Links Green Way, Cobham, Surrey, England. *Office*—Department of Philosophy, University of Surrey, Guildford, Surrey GU2 5XH, England.

CAREER: Oxford University, Oxford, England, lecturer in philosophy, 1966-69; University of Miami, Coral Gables, Fla., visiting professor of philosophy, 1969-72; University of London, London, England, lecturer in philosophy, 1972-74; University of Surrey, Guildford, Surrey, England, reader in philosophy, 1974—.

MEMBER: Royal Institute of Philosophy, Royal Anthropological Society, Aristotelian Society, Mind Association, American Philosophical Association.

WRITINGS:

Philosophy and the Nature of Language, Longmans, Green, 1973.
Presupposition, Mouton & Co., 1974.
(Editor) *The Manson Murders: A Philosophical Inquiry,* Schenkman, 1974.
Knowledge of Language, Prism, 1975.
Illusions of Equality, Routledge & Kegan Paul, 1980.
Authenticity and Learning: Nietzsche's Educational Philosophy, Routledge & Kegan Paul, 1983.
(Editor) *Education, Values, and Mind: Essays for R. S. Peter,* Routledge & Kegan Paul, 1986.
Metaphor, Basil Blackwell, 1986.

Contributor to professional journals.*

*   *   *

COOPER, Edmund   1926-1982
(Richard Avery)

PERSONAL: Born April 30, 1926, in Marple, Cheshire, England; died March 11, 1982; son of Joseph (a shopkeeper) and Harriet (Fletcher) Cooper; married Joyce Plant (a teacher), April 13, 1946 (divorced, 1963); married Valerie Makin, October

19, 1963; married Dawn Freeman Baker, September 1, 1980; children: (first marriage) Glynis (Mrs. David Reeve), Daryl, Troy, Guy; (second marriage) Shaun, Justine, Regan, Jason. *Education:* Educated at Manchester Grammar School, 1937-41; Didsbury Teacher's Training College, teacher's certificate, 1948. *Religion:* Agnostic.

ADDRESSES: Home and office—"Stammers," Madehurst, near Arundel, Sussex, England.

CAREER: After leaving school, worked as warehouse laborer, then as a British civil servant; teacher in various English schools, 1948-50; free-lance writer and critic, 1950-60; journalist with British Iron and Steel Research Association, London, England, 1960-61, and Federation of British Industries, London, 1962; Esso Petroleum, Ltd., London, staff writer, 1961-66; full-time writer, 1966-82. Lecturer in creative writing, Chichester College, 1975-76. *Military service:* British Merchant Navy, 1944-46; served as radio officer; received Normandy Star, Africa Star, and Atlantic Star.

MEMBER: PEN.

WRITINGS:

SCIENCE FICTION

Deadly Image (novel), Ballantine, 1958 (published in England as *The Uncertain Midnight,* Hutchinson, 1958, reprinted, Coronet, 1974).
Tomorrow's Gift (short stories), Ballantine, 1958.
Seed of Light (novel), Ballantine, 1959.
Voices in the Dark (short stories), Digit Books, 1960.
Tomorrow Came (short stories), Panther Books, 1963.
Transit (novel), Lancer Books, 1964.
All Fools' Day (novel), Walker & Co., 1966.
A Far Sunset (novel), Walker & Co., 1967.
News from Elsewhere (short stories), Mayflower Books, 1968, Berkley Publishing, 1969.
Five to Twelve (novel), Hodder & Stoughton, 1968, Putnam, 1969.
The Last Continent (novel), Dell, 1969.
Sea-Horse in the Sky (novel), Hodder & Stoughton, 1969, Putnam, 1970.
The Square Root of Tomorrow (short stories), R. Hale, 1970.
Son of Kronk (novel), Hodder & Stoughton, 1970, published as *Kronk,* Putnam, 1971.
Unborn Tomorrow (short stories), R. Hale, 1971.
(With Roger L. Green) *Double Phoenix,* Ballantine, 1971.
The Overman Culture (novel), Hodder & Stoughton, 1971, Putnam, 1972.
Gender Genocide (novel), Ace Books, 1972 (published in England as *Who Needs Men?,* Hodder & Stoughton, 1972).
The Cloud Walker (novel), Ballantine, 1973.
The Tenth Planet (novel), Putnam, 1973.
The Slaves of Heaven (novel), Putnam, 1974.
Prisoner of Fire (novel), Hodder & Stoughton, 1974, Walker & Co., 1976.
Merry Christmas, Ms. Minerva (novel), R. Hale, 1978.
Jupiter Laughs, and Other Stories, Hodder & Stoughton, 1979.
A World of Difference (short stories), R. Hale, 1980.

"THE EXPENDABLES" SERIES; UNDER PSEUDONYM RICHARD AVERY

The Deathworms of Kratos, Fawcett, 1975.
The Rings of Tantalus, Fawcett, 1975.
The Wargames of Zelos, Fawcett, 1975.
The Venom of Argus, Fawcett, 1976.

OTHER

Wish Goes to Slumber Land (for children), Hutchinson, 1960.

Also author of unpublished novels *The Hollow Man, A Conflict of Woman,* and *The Albatross Syndrome;* author of unpublished poetry collections *The Long Way Home* and *Memories of a Blue-eyed Computer.* Science fiction book reviewer, *Sunday Times* (London), beginning 1967. Contributor of short stories to numerous magazines in various countries, including *American Mercury, B.B.C., Courier, Everybody's, John Bull, London Mystery Magazine, Mirror Pocket Book,* and *Saturday Evening Post.*

Cooper's books have been translated into several languages, including French, Italian, German, Portuguese, Japanese, and Dutch. The University of Wyoming holds a collection of his manuscripts.

WORK IN PROGRESS: A collection of fantasy stories, tentatively titled *The Infinite Worlds of Maybe;* a novella, "The Gold Bug."

SIDELIGHTS: Science fiction writer Edmund Cooper's style has been described as "one part Edgar Rice Burroughs, two parts Sir James Frazer, and three parts of his own science fantasy," as a *Books and Bookmen* reviewer commented. When his work first appeared in the late 1950s, "Cooper quickly established himself as an urbane stylist whose sometimes almost intuitive grasp of science fiction's key themes and images could distinguish his best fiction and almost redeem his lesser works," Gary K. Wolfe summarized in *Twentieth-Century Science Fiction Writers.* While the plots of his novels were frequently conventional—many times dealing with the results of a nuclear holocaust—nevertheless "at best, [Cooper] was a writer capable of witty and literate variations on familiar themes," concluded Wolfe, "and one who for all his faults managed to establish a clear identity despite his use of such themes."

Cooper once told *CA* that he had "recently become very disillusioned with technology and politics. No civilization is immortal . . . Western civilization will disintegrate in the early 21st century." He added that he has "not lost faith in humanity but believes that there will be a new dark age before another and possibly more viable civilization emerges."

MEDIA ADAPTATIONS: The 1957 M-G-M film "The Invisible Boy" was based on a Cooper story; *The Uncertain Midnight* was made into a ten-part serial and shown on television in Switzerland and other countries in the 1960s; film rights to *Transit* have been sold to Twentieth Century-Fox.

AVOCATIONAL INTERESTS: Chess, music, "trying to discover what people are really like."

BIOGRAPHICAL/CRITICAL SOURCES:

BOOKS

Twentieth-Century Science Fiction Writers, St. James Press, 1986.

PERIODICALS

Books and Bookmen, September, 1967, May, 1968, November, 1973.
New Statesman, July 14, 1967.
Observer, January 10, 1971, September 3, 1972, December 23, 1973.
Times Literary Supplement, February 15, 1974.

OBITUARIES:

PERIODICALS

Locus, May, 1982.*

*   *   *

CORBIN, Charles B.   1940-

PERSONAL: Born October 20, 1940, in Toledo, Ohio; son of Don E. (a school principal) and D'Esta June (Wolford) Corbin; married Mary Catherine Milligan, June 12, 1964; children: Charles, Jr., John David, William Robert. *Education:* University of New Mexico, B.S., 1960, Ph.D., 1965; University of Illinois, M.S., 1962. *Religion:* Protestant.

ADDRESSES: Home—3402 East Cherokee St., Phoenix, Ariz. 85044. *Office*—Department of Health and Physical Education, Arizona State University, Tempe, Ariz. 85287.

CAREER: Public school teacher in Albuquerque, N.M., 1960-61; College of Santa Fe, Santa Fe, N.M., assistant professor of health and physical education 1964-65; assistant professor, University of Toledo, Toledo, Ohio, 1965-67; Texas A & M University, College Station, associate professor, 1967-71, director of health and physical education research laboratory; Kansas State University, Manhattan, professor of physical education, 1971-82, head of department, 1971-75, director of motor development research lab, 1975—; Arizona State University, Tempe, professor of physical education and exercise science, 1982—.

MEMBER: North American Society for Psychology of Sport and Physical Activity, American Alliance for Health, Physical Education and Recreation, American College of Sports Medicine, American Academy of Physical Education (fellow), National College Physical Education Association, Phi Epsilon Kappa, Phi Delta Kappa.

WRITINGS:

(With Linus Dowell and Carl Landiss) *Concepts and Experiments in Physical Education,* Kendall/Hunt, 1968.
Becoming Physically Educated in the Elementary School, Lea & Febiger, 1969, 2nd edition, 1976.
(With Dowell, Homer Tolson, and Ruth Lindsey) *Concepts of Physical Education,* W. C. Brown, 1970, 7th edition (with Lindsey) published as *Concepts of Physical Fitness,* 1990.
Inexpensive Games Equipment, W. C. Brown, 1973.
A Textbook of Motor Development, W. C. Brown, 1974, 2nd edition, 1980.
The Athletic Snowball, Human Kinetics, 1977.
(With Lindsey) *Fitness for Life,* 2nd edition, Scott, Foresman, 1983, 3rd edition, 1990.
(Coauthor) *Choosing Good Health,* Scott, Foresman, 1983.
The Ultimate Fitness Book, Leisure Press, 1984.
Health for Life, Scott, Foresman, 1990.

Creator of record albums in physical education for Education Activities, Inc. Contributor to professional journals and magazines. Editor of *Quest;* member of editorial board, Journal of *Sport Psychology.*

SIDELIGHTS: Charles B. Corbin once told *CA:* "Physical fitness is too often perceived as being something for those with good physical skills: the athletes of the world. A major goal of my writing is to convince people that exercise is for everyone. No matter who you are you can enjoy the benefit of exercise and good physical fitness. It is never too late to begin. Regardless of age, sex or ability there is some form of activity that can be done to help you look your best, enjoy life, and benefit your health."

CORTEZ, Jayne 1936-

PERSONAL: Born May 10, 1936, in Arizona; children: Denardo Coleman.

ADDRESSES: Box 96, Village Station, New York, N.Y. 10014.

CAREER: Poet. Has lectured and read her poetry alone and with musical accompaniment throughout the United States, Europe, Africa, Latin America, and the Caribbean.

AWARDS, HONORS: Creative Artists Program Service poetry award, New York State Council on the Arts, 1973, 1981; National Endowment for the Arts fellowship in creative writing, 1979-86; New York Foundation for the Arts award, 1987.

WRITINGS:

POETRY

Pissstained Stairs and the Monkey Man's Wares, Phrase Text, 1969.
Festivals and Funerals, Bola Press, 1971.
Scarifications, Bola Press, 1973.
Mouth on Paper, Bola Press, 1977.
Firespitter, Bola Press, 1982.
Coagulations: New and Selected Poems, Thunder's Mouth Press, 1982.

OTHER

Celebrations and Solitudes: The Poetry of Jayne Cortez (sound recording), Strata-East Records, 1975.
Unsubmissive Blues (sound recording), Bola Press, 1980.
There It Is (sound recording), Bola Press, 1982.
"War on War" (screenplay), UNESCO (Paris), 1982.
"Poetry in Motion" (screenplay), Sphinx Productions (Toronto, Canada), 1983.
Maintain Control (sound recording), Bola Press, 1986.

Contributor to anthologies, including *We Speak as Liberators,* edited by Orde Coombs, Dodd, 1970; *The Poetry of Black America,* edited by Arnold Adoff, Harper, 1972; *New Black Voices,* edited by Abraham Chapman, New American Library, 1972; *A Rock against the Wind: Black Love Poems,* edited by Lindsay Patterson, Dodd, 1973; *Giant Talk,* edited by Quincy Troupe and Rainer Schulte, Random House, 1975; *Homage a Leon Gontran Damas,* Presence Africaine, 1979; *Black Sister,* edited by Erlene Stedson, Indiana University Press, 1981; *Powers of Desire,* edited by Ann Snitow, Christing Stansell, and Sharon Thompson, Monthly Review Press, 1983; *Confirmation,* edited by Amina and Amiri Baraka, Quill, 1983; *Early Ripening: American Women's Poetry Now,* edited by Marge Piercy, Chapman & Hall, 1987; and *Women on War,* edited by Daniela Gioseffi, Simon & Schuster, 1988. Contributor to numerous periodicals, including *Free Spirits, Mother Jones, UNESCO Courier, Black Scholar, Heresies,* and *Mundus Artium.*

SIDELIGHTS: In a review of Jayne Cortez's *Pissstained Stairs and the Monkey Man's Wares, Negro Digest* critic Nikki Giovanni remarks: "We haven't had many jazz poets who got inside the music and the people who created it. We poet about them, but not of them. And this is Cortez's strength. She can wail from Theodore Navarro and Leadbelly to Ornette and never lose a beat and never make a mistake. She's a genius and all lovers of jazz will need this book—lovers of poetry will want it." About Cortez's *Unsubmissive Blues,* Warren Woessner asserts in *Small Press Review* that the record "is the most accomplished collaboration between a poet and jazz group that I've listened to in recent years." He continues: "*Unsubmissive Blues* is an unqualified

success. The sum of this collaboration is always greater than its individual pieces."

But although the influence of music is readily evident in Cortez's work, the poet also seeks to convey a message in her work. Barbara T. Christian states in *Callaloo* that "it is eminently clear from her selected edition [*Coagulations: New and Selected Poems*] that Jayne Cortez is a blatantly political poet—that her work intends to help us identify those who control our lives and the devastating effects such control has on our lives, and she rouses us to do something about it. . . . Like the poets and warrior whose words and actions it celebrates, Jayne Cortez's *Coagulations* is a work of resistance."

BIOGRAPHICAL/CRITICAL SOURCES:

PERIODICALS

Callaloo, Volume 9, number 1, 1986.
Negro Digest, December, 1969.
Small Press Review, March, 1981.

*   *   *

COSTIGAN, Daniel M.   1929-

PERSONAL: Born February 13, 1929, in Orangeburg, N.Y.; son of John E. (an artist) and Ida (Blessin) Costigan; married Dorothy Knopczyk, September 15, 1956; children: Drew Keith, Christopher John. *Education:* R.C.A. Institutes, graduate, 1950; New York University, B.S., 1964. *Religion:* Protestant.

ADDRESSES: Home—8 Wyndmoor Way, Edison, N.J. 08820. *Office—Rahway News-Record/Clark Patriot,* P.O. Box 1061, Rahway, N.J. 07065. *Agent*—Patricia Lewis 133 West 72nd St., Room 601, New York, N.Y. 10023.

CAREER: Worked as a radio technician, 1948-61; free-lance writer, 1955—; Bell Laboratories, Holmdel, N.J., engineer in micrographic and electronic information systems development, beginning 1961; Bellcore, Piscataway, N.J., engineer in micrographic and electronic information systems development; currently editor and columnist, *Rahway News-Record/Clark Patriot,* Rahway, N.J.; editorial writer and associate editor, *Atom Tabloid,* Rahway. Chairman of publications committee, National Micrographics Association (now Association for Information and Image Management), 1978-80. *Military service:* U.S. Army, 1951-53.

MEMBER: National Writers Club, Theatre Historical Society, Telephone Pioneers of America, Kappa Tau Alpha.

AWARDS, HONORS: Fellow, Association for Information and Image Management.

WRITINGS:

(Contributor) Charles Preston, editor, *The Jokeswagen Book,* Random House, 1966.
FAX: The Principles and Practice of Facsimile Communication, Chilton, 1971.
Micrographic Systems, National Micrographics Association, 1975, 2nd edition, 1980.
Electronic Delivery of Documents and Graphics, Van Nostrand, 1978.
(Contributor) Janet Field, editor, *Graphic Arts Manual,* Arno/Musarts, 1980.
Encore for a Worthy Performer, Rahway Landmarks, 1984.

Contributor to numerous periodicals, including *Radio Electronics, Popular Electronics, Medical Times, Journal of Micrographics, World Car Guide,* and *Road & Track.*

WORK IN PROGRESS: Trials and Triumphs of an American Artist, a book-length biography of John E. Costigan; *Never Trust a Columnist Who Uses a Pen Name,* a collection of original anecdotes.

SIDELIGHTS: Daniel M. Costigan told *CA:* "As an aspiring writer of both fiction and fact, my principal idol had been the late Nevil Shute, the noted British romantic engineer/novelist. Though I have not exactly followed his formidable example, his achievement has convinced me that the engineer's clinical mentality need not necessarily deter him from a literary career."

AVOCATIONAL INTERESTS: Amateur stereo photography, music, electronics, historic preservation.

*   *   *

CRABB, Lawrence J(ames), Jr. 1944-

PERSONAL: Born July 13, 1944, in Evanston, Ill.; son of Lawrence J. (in sales) and Isabel (an occupational therapist; maiden name, Craigmile) Crabb; married Rachel Lankford, June 18, 1966; children: Keplen, Kenton. *Education:* Ursinus College, B.A., 1965; University of Illinois, M.A., 1969, Ph.D., 1970. *Religion:* "Conservative Evangelical Protestant."

ADDRESSES: Office—Institute of Biblical Counseling, 16075 West Belleview Ave., Morrison, Colo. 80465.

CAREER: University of Illinois at Urbana-Champaign, assistant professor of psychology and staff psychologist at Psychological Counseling Center, 1970-71; Florida Atlantic University, Boca Raton, director of Psychological Counseling Center, 1971-73; private practice of clinical psychology in Boca Raton, 1973-82; Grace Theological Seminary, Winona Lake, Ind., chairman of department of Biblical counseling, 1982-89; Colorado Christian University, Denver, chairman of department of Biblical counseling, 1989—.

MEMBER: American Psychological Association.

WRITINGS:

Basic Principles of Biblical Counseling, Zondervan, 1975.
Effective Biblical Counseling: A Model for Helping Caring Christians Become Capable Counselors, Zondervan, 1977.
(With father, Lawrence J. Crabb, Sr.) *The Adventures of Captain Al Scabbard No. 1,* Moody, 1981.
(With L. J. Crabb, Sr.) *The Adventures of Captain Al Scabbard No. 2,* Moody, 1981.
The Marriage Builder: A Blueprint for Couples and Counselors, Zondervan, 1982.
Encouragement: The Key to Caring, Zondervan, 1984.
Understanding People, Zondervan, 1987.
Inside, Out, NAV Press, 1988.

Contributor of articles and reviews to religious magazines and psychology journals.

SIDELIGHTS: Lawrence J. Crabb, Jr., wrote *CA:* "Motivated by a desire to see a clear and thorough Biblical view of counseling developed, I have written and intend to continue writing books which integrate conservative evangelical Christianity with psychological concern and to think through the role of the local church in meeting the needs of the people. I am committed to a theistic world view in which an infinite personal God is the Supreme Being and has revealed Himself in Scripture and in His Son, Jesus Christ. To the best of my awareness, I endeavor to . . . reflect this world view in my writings."

CRONIN, Joseph M(arr) 1935-

PERSONAL: Born August 30, 1935, in Boston, Mass.; son of Joseph Michael (an administrator) and Mary (Marr) Cronin; married Marie Whalen, June 21, 1958; children: Maureen, Kathleen, Elizabeth, Anne, Joseph, Timothy, Patricia. *Education:* Harvard University, A.B. (magna cum laude), 1956, M.A.T., 1957; Stanford University, Ed.D., 1965. *Religion:* Roman Catholic.

ADDRESSES: Office—330 Stuart St., Boston, Mass. 02116.

CAREER: Hollis Junior High School, Braintree, Mass., teacher, 1951-58; Cubberly Senior High School, Palo Alto, Calif., teacher and department chair, 1958-61; E. W. Broome Jr. High School, Rockville, Md., principal, 1961-64; Stanford University, Stanford, Calif., instructor and assistant director of school board studies research for Great Cities Project, 1964-65; Harvard University, Graduate School of Education, Cambridge, Mass., assistant professor, 1965-68, associate professor of education, 1968-71, associate dean, 1971-72; Commonwealth of Massachusetts, Executive Office of Educational Affairs, Boston, secretary of educational affairs, 1972-75; Illinois Board of Education, Springfield, state superintendent of education, 1975-80; Massachusetts Higher Education Assistance Corp., Boston, president, beginning 1980; currently affiliated with department of educational administration, Boston University, Boston. *Military service:* U.S. Army Reserve, 1957-63; became staff sergeant.

MEMBER: American Association of School Administration, American Arbitration Association, American Educational Research Association (vice-president, 1972-74), Phi Delta Kappa.

AWARDS, HONORS: Named secondary school principal of the year, Crofts Educational Service, 1963; outstanding magazine editorial award, Education Press Writers of America, 1969.

WRITINGS:

(With Herold C. Hunt and Howard Stevenson) *The Educational Research Council of America: An Evaluation, 1959-69,* Harvard University Graduate School of Education, 1969.
(With others) *Organizing and Governing Public Education in New York,* [Cambridge, Mass.], 1971.
The Control of Urban Schools: Perspective on the Power of Educational Reformers, Free Press, 1973.
(With Richard M. Hailer) *Organizing an Urban School System for Diversity: A Report on the Boston Public School Department,* Heath, 1973.
Preschool Learning Activities for the Physically Disabled: A Guide for Parents, Illinois Office of Education, c. 1976.
(Editor with Sylvia Q. Simmons) *Student Loans: Risks and Realities,* Auburn House, 1987.

Contributor to *Phi Delta Kappan, Daedelus,* and *American School Board Journal.*

*   *   *

CULBERT, David H(olbrook) 1943-

PERSONAL: Born July 7, 1943, in San Antonio, Tex.; son of Robert William (a lawyer) and Dorothy Fairfax (Kift) Culbert; married Lubna Aranki, May 26, 1979. *Education:* Studied at Mozarteum, Salzburg, Austria, 1963-64; Oberlin College, B.A. (magna cum laude) and B.Mus., both 1966; Northwestern University, Ph.D., 1970.

ADDRESSES: Home—1464 Silliman Dr., Baton Rouge, La. 70808. *Office*—Department of History, Louisiana State University, Baton Rouge, La. 70803.

CAREER: Arms Control and Disarmament Agency, Washington, D.C., summer intern, 1962-63; Yale University, New Haven, Conn., assistant professor of history, 1970-71; Louisiana State University, Baton Rouge, assistant professor, 1971-76, associate professor, 1976-83, professor of history, 1983. Organist and choirmaster at Episcopal church. Co-producer with Peter Rollins of film "Television's Vietnam: The Impact of Visual Images," Humanitas Films, 1982, revised version broadcast on Public Broadcasting Service Television (PBS-TV), 1986; director of historical research and associate producer of film "Huey Long," broadcast on PBS-TV. Fellow at Woodrow Wilson International Center for Scholars, Smithsonian Institution, 1976-77, guest scholar, 1978; fellow at National Humanities Institute, Yale University, 1977-78; member of American Film Institute's advisory council on the use of film in education; judge at Connecticut Film Festival, 1977, and American Film Festival, 1978; public speaker in the United States and abroad, including television appearances.

MEMBER: International Association for Audio-Visual Media in Historical Research and Education (vice president, 1983; president, 1987-89), American Historical Association, Organization of American Historians (chairman of Erik Barnouw Prize committee and committee on radio, television, and film media), American Studies Association, Society of American Archivists, Popular Culture Association, Society of Historians of American Foreign Relations, Society for Cinema Studies, Modern Language Association of America, Phi Beta Kappa, Pi Kappa Lambda.

AWARDS, HONORS: Grant from Newberry Library's Institute in Quantitative Family and Community History, 1975; grants from Rockefeller Foundation, 1979, 1981, Lyndon Johnson Foundation, 1979, National Endowment for the Humanities, 1980-81, Earhart Foundation, 1980, American Council of Learned Societies, 1982, British Academy, 1982, and Province of Bologna, 1983; fellow of W. K. Kellogg Foundation, 1981-1983; Erik Barnouw Award, Association of American Historians, 1986, for film "Huey Long."

WRITINGS:

News for Everyman: Radio and Foreign Affairs in Thirties America, Greenwood Press, 1976.
Mission to Moscow: The Feature Film as Official Propaganda (annotated film script), University of Wisconsin Press, 1980.
Triumph of the Will: A Documentary History, University Publications of America, 1986.
Information Control and Propaganda: Records of the Office of War Information, University Publications of America, Part 1: *The Director's Central Files,* 1987, Part 2: *Office of Policy Coordination, Series A: Propaganda and Policy Directives for Overseas Programs, 1942-1945,* 1987.

CONTRIBUTOR

David E. Kyvig, editor, *FDR's America,* Forum Press, 1976.
William Adams and Fay Schreibman, editors, *Television Network News: Issues in Content Research,* George Washington University Press, 1978.
John E. O'Connor and Martin A. Jackson, editors, *American History/American Film: Interpreting the Hollywood Image,* Ungar, 1979.
Bonnie G. Rowan, editor, *Scholars' Guide to Washington D.C. Film and Video Collections,* Smithsonian Institution Press, 1980.
Peter Rollins, editor, *Hollywood as Historian,* University Press of Kentucky, 1983.

O'Connor, editor, *American History/American Television,* Ungar, 1983, 2nd edition, 1988.
K. R. M. Short, editor, *Film and Radio Propaganda in World War II,* Croom Helm, 1983.
Nicholas Pronay and Keith Wilson, editors, *The Political Reeducation of Germany and Her Allies after World War II,* Croom Helm, 1985.
Robert A. Divine, editor, *Exploring the Johnson Years,* University of Kansas Press, 1987.

Editor in chief, *Film and Propaganda in America: A Documentary History,* five volumes, Greenwood Press. Contributor of numerous articles to history, film, and popular culture journals. Member of editorial board of *Historical Journal of Film, Radio, and Television.*

WORK IN PROGRESS: With Martin Loiperdinger, *Nazi Cinema Propaganda and the Riefenstahl Myth,* for Cambridge University Press.

SIDELIGHTS: David Culbert told *CA:* "In part I have been fascinated by visual and aural images precisely because I never had a single teacher right through my doctoral adviser who placed any emphasis on visual materials or believed that such things would enhance one's learning. In fact, field trips were banned after the fourth grade on the grounds that it could not be proved that they were more educational than sitting in the classroom. I suppose I must want to prove my many wonderful teachers wrong though they have armed me with an immense amount of skepticism about inflated claims for the impact of media and the amazing results that may accrue from using media. My particular obsession is to gauge the impact of aural and visual media on political decision-making, the area that we know the least about in comparison with such things as whether people learn from media or the impact of media on children.

"In retrospect, the reason I found the subject so fascinating has to do with music. In playing the organ, the duration of sound—the distance between sounds—is as important to musical understanding as the sound. I think I liked Edward Murrow's radio broadcasts because, as I argued in my first book, he was essentially a musician of the spoken word, understanding how the distance between words can enhance meaning. My continuing fascination with music explains my interest in nonverbal forms of communication. And the interest in film and television allows my background in music some obvious scope in terms of soundtrack research.

"I feel the presumed impact of television is greatly exaggerated. If the students I teach are part of a video generation, they are utterly unable to express in words what they see. I must stress the visual part of any film they see because they cannot express in words what they see. Students never look at photographs in textbooks because they assume 'it won't be on the exam.' Just relaxing and watching television is not the same as being able to explain what one has seen.

"Historians are very reluctant to use nonprint materials in their research. Bringing aural and visual materials into historical explanation is one of the major changes that may occur in my lifetime (if I live long enough).

"I suppose I love propaganda because of the game involved in the efforts of one person to trick another. The subject is fascinating, but the implicit chicanery is what makes the subject so appealing. There is little real difference between advertising, education, and propaganda. Many Americans continue to believe that propaganda is something to be associated with Goebbels; they certainly don't associate it as a potent force in their own lives.

Nobody is exposed to more propaganda than we Americans with our round-the-clock advertising culture."

BIOGRAPHICAL/CRITICAL SOURCES:

PERIODICALS

Air University Review, July-August, 1983.
American Quarterly, fall, 1979.
Journal of Contemporary History, July, 1983.
Times Literary Supplement, May 15, 1981.

*   *   *

CULBERTSON, Judi 1941-

PERSONAL: Born March 1, 1941, in Norfolk, Va.; daughter of Hubert Roe (an engineer and U.S. Coast Guard captain) and Charlotte (Hess) Chaffee; married Paul Culbertson, June 21, 1962 (marriage ended, 1970); married Thomas Randall (a social worker), June 22, 1974; children: (first marriage) Andrew William. *Education:* Wheaton College, Wheaton, Ill., B.A., 1962.

ADDRESSES: Home—211 Hawthorne St., Port Jefferson, N.Y. 11777. *Office*—Suffolk County Department of Social Services, Hauppauge, N.Y. 11788. *Agent*—Heide Lange, Sanford J. Greenburger Associates, Inc., 825 Third Ave., New York, N.Y. 10022.

CAREER: Eternity (magazine), Philadelphia, Pa., editorial assistant, 1962-64; Middle Country School District II, Centereach, N.Y., substitute teacher, 1966-70; Suffolk County Department of Social Services, Hauppauge, N.Y., social worker, 1970—.

WRITINGS:

(With Patti Bard) *Games Christians Play,* Harper, 1967.
(With Bard) *The Little White Book on Race,* Lippincott, 1970.
(With husband, Tom Randall) *Permanent Parisians: A Guide to the Cemeteries of Paris,* Chelsea Green, 1986.
(With Randall) *Permanent New Yorkers: A Biographical Guide to Cemeteries of New York,* Chelsea Green, 1987.
(With Randall) *Permanent Californians: A Biographical Guide to the Cemeteries of California,* Chelsea Green, 1989.

Contributor to magazines, including *Glamour, Cosmopolitan, Working Mother, Chevron USA,* and to newspapers, including *New York Times, Washington Post, Boston Globe,* and *Cleveland Plain Dealer.*

WORK IN PROGRESS: Permanent Londoners.

SIDELIGHTS: Judi Culbertson told *CA:* "My writing is now focused on travel stories, humorous home essays and behavioral articles based on a social work background. . . . But serious or satirical, all center around a fascination with human behavior and are written with the hope of further identifying or illuminating it." In *Permanent Parisians: A Guide to the Cemeteries of Paris,* for example, Culbertson and co-author Tom Randall describe the various tombs and vaults of Paris; in addition, they relate stories of the cemeteries' inhabitants. The result, writes Harriet Choice in the *Chicago Tribune,* "is an unusual delight." *Permanent Parisians* also contains lists of walking tours, maps, and photos, the critic notes, concluding that "students of necrology and armchair travelers will find it equally enjoyable."

AVOCATIONAL INTERESTS: Travel, reading, dancing.

BIOGRAPHICAL/CRITICAL SOURCES:

PERIODICALS

Chicago Tribune, May 25, 1986.
Los Angeles Times, December 4, 1988.

Washington Post Book World, October 11, 1987.

*   *   *

CUMMINGS, E(dward) E(stlin) 1894-1962

PERSONAL: Born October 14, 1894, in Cambridge, Mass.; died September 3, 1962, in North Conway, N.H.; buried in Forest Hills Cemetery, Boston, Mass.; son of Edward (a professor of sociology and political science and a Unitarian minister) and Rebecca Haswell (Clarke) Cummings; married Elaine Orr Thayer, March 19, 1924 (divorced, 1925); married Anne Minnerly Barton, May 1, 1929 (divorced, 1932); married (common law) Marion Morehouse, 1934; children: (first marriage) Nancy. *Education:* Harvard University, A.B. (magna cum laude), 1915, M.A., 1916.

CAREER: Poet, painter, novelist, and playwright. Charles Eliot Norton Professor of Poetry, Harvard University, 1952-53. One-man exhibitions at American British Art Centre, 1949, and Rochester Memorial Gallery, 1959. *Wartime service:* Served as an ambulance driver with the Norton-Harjes Ambulance Service in France, 1917; detained on suspicion of treason and held in a French internment camp, 1917; U.S. Army, private, 1918-1919.

MEMBER: National Academy of Arts and Letters.

AWARDS, HONORS: Dial (magazine) Award, 1925, for distinguished service to American letters; Guggenheim fellowship, 1933 and 1951; Levinson Prize, *Poetry* (magazine), 1939; Shelley Memorial Award, Poetry Society of America, 1945; Academy of American Poets fellowship, 1950; Harriet Monroe Poetry Award, 1950; Eunice Teitjens Memorial Prize, *Poetry,* 1952; National Book Award special citation, 1955, for *Poems, 1923-1954;* Festival Poet, Boston Arts Festival, 1957; Bollingen Prize in Poetry, Yale University, 1958; Oscar Blumenthal Prize, *Poetry,* 1962.

WRITINGS:

POEMS

(Contributor) *Eight Harvard Poets,* L. J. Gomme, 1917.
Tulips and Chimneys (also see below), T. Seltzer, 1923, enlarged edition, Golden Eagle Press, 1937.
Puella Mia, Golden Eagle Press, 1923.
XLI Poems, Dial, 1925.
& (also see below), privately printed, 1925.
is 5, Boni & Liveright, 1926, reprinted, Liveright, 1985.
Christmas Tree, American Book Bindery, 1928.
W(ViVa), Liveright, 1931, reprinted, 1979.
(Contributor) Peter Neagoe, editor, *Americans Abroad: An Anthology,* Servire, 1932.
No Thanks, Golden Eagle Press, 1935, reprinted, Liveright, 1978.
1/20, Roger Roughton, 1936.
Collected Poems, Harcourt, 1938.
50 Poems, Duell, Sloan & Pearce, 1940.
1 x 1, Holt, 1944.
Xaipe: Seventy-One Poems, Oxford University Press, 1950, reprinted, Liveright, 1979.
Poems, 1923-1954, Harcourt, 1954.
95 Poems, Harcourt, 1958.
100 Selected Poems, Grove, 1958.
Selected Poems, 1923-1958, Faber, 1960.
73 Poems, Harcourt, 1963.
A Selection of Poems, Harcourt, 1965.
Complete Poems, 1923-1962, two volumes, MacGibbon & Kee, 1968, revised edition published in one volume as *Complete Poems, 1913-1962,* Harcourt, 1972.

Poems, 1905-1962, edited by Firmage, Marchim Press, 1973.

Tulips & Chimneys: The Original 1922 Manuscript with the 35 Additional Poems from &, edited by Firmage, Liveright, 1976.

(Contributor) Nancy Cummings De Forzet, *Charon's Daughter: A Passion of Identity,* Liveright, 1977.

Love Is Most Mad and Moonly, Addison-Wesley, 1978.

(Chaire), Liveright, 1979.

Complete Poems, 1910-1962, Granada, 1982.

Hist Whist and Other Poems for Children, edited by Firmage, Liveright, 1983.

Etcetera: The Unpublished Poems of E. E. Cummings, edited by Firmage and Richard S. Kennedy, Liveright, 1984.

In Just-Spring, Little, Brown, 1988.

Hist Whist, illustrated by Deborah Kogan Ray, Crown, 1989.

OTHER

The Enormous Room, Boni & Liveright, 1922, revised edition, Liveright, 1978.

Him (three-act play; first produced in New York at the Provincetown Playhouse, April 18, 1928), Boni & Liveright, 1927, new edition, Liveright, 1970.

[No title] (collection of stories), Covici Friede, 1930.

CIOPW (artwork), Covici Friede, 1931.

Eimi (travel diary), Covici Friede, 1933, 4th edition, Grove, 1958.

(Translator) Louis Aragon, *The Red Front,* Contempo, 1933.

Tom (ballet based on *Uncle Tom's Cabin* by Harriet Beecher Stowe), Arrow Editions, 1935.

Anthropos: The Future of Art, Golden Eagle Press, 1944, reprinted, Norwood, 1978.

Santa Claus: A Morality (play), Holt, 1946.

i: six nonlectures, Harvard University Press, 1953.

E. E. Cummings: A Miscellany, Argophile Press, 1958, revised edition edited by George Firmage, October Press, 1965.

(With wife, Marion Morehouse) *Adventures in Value,* Harcourt, 1962.

Fairy Tales, Harcourt, 1965.

Three Plays and a Ballet, edited by Firmage, October House, 1967.

Selected Letters of E. E. Cummings, edited by F. W. Dupee and George Stade, Harcourt, 1969.

"E. E. Cummings Reads His Collected Poetry, 1943-1958" (recording), Caedmon, 1977.

Little Tree (juvenile), Crown, 1987.

SIDELIGHTS: "Among the most innovative of twentieth-century poets," according to Jenny Penberthy in the *Dictionary of Literary Biography,* E. E. Cummings experimented with poetic form and language to create a distinct personal style. A Cummings poem is spare and precise, employing a few key words eccentrically placed on the page. Some of these words were invented by Cummings, often by combining two common words into a new synthesis. He also revised grammatical and linguistic rules to suit his own purposes, using such words as "if," "am," and "because" as nouns, for example, or assigning his own private meanings to words. Despite their nontraditional form, Cummings' poems came to be popular with many readers. "No one else," Randall Jarrell claimed in his *The Third Book of Criticism,* "has ever made avant-garde, experimental poems so attractive to the general and the special reader." By the time of his death in 1962 Cummings held a prominent position in twentieth-century poetry. John Logan in *Modern American Poetry: Essays in Criticism* called him "one of the greatest lyric poets in our language." Stanley Edgar Hyman wrote in *Standards: A Chronicle of Books for Our Time:* "Cummings has written at least a dozen

poems that seem to me matchless. Three are among the great love poems of our time or any time." Malcolm Cowley admitted in the *Yale Review* that Cummings "suffers from comparison with those [poets] who built on a larger scale—Eliot, Aiken, Crane, Auden among others—but still he is unsurpassed in his special field, one of the masters."

Cummings decided to become a poet when he was still a child. Between the ages of eight and twenty-two, he wrote a poem a day, exploring many traditional poetic forms. By the time he was in Harvard in 1916, modern poetry had caught his interest. He began to write avant-garde poems in which conventional punctuation and syntax were ignored in favor of a dynamic use of language. Cummings also experimented with poems as visual objects on the page. These early efforts were included in *Eight Harvard Poets,* a collection of poems by members of the Harvard Poetry Society.

After graduating from Harvard, Cummings spent a month working for a mail order book dealer. He left the job because of the tedium. In April of 1917, with the First World War raging in Europe and the United States not yet involved, he volunteered for the Norton-Harjes Ambulance Service in France. Ambulance work was a popular choice with those who, like Cummings, considered themselves to be pacifists. He was soon stationed on the French-German border with fellow American William Slater Brown, and the two young men became fast friends. To relieve the boredom of their assignment, they inserted veiled and provocative comments into their letters back home, trying to outwit and baffle the French censors. They also befriended soldiers in nearby units. Such activities led in September of 1917 to their being held on suspicion of treason and sent to an internment camp in Normandy for questioning. Cummings and Brown were housed in a large, one-room holding area along with other suspicious foreigners. Only outraged protests from his father finally secured Cummings' release in December of 1917; Brown was not released until April of the following year. In July of 1918, with the United States entering the war, Cummings was drafted into the U.S. Army and spent some six months at a training camp in Massachusetts.

Upon leaving the army in January of 1919, Cummings resumed his affair with Elaine Thayer, the wife of his friend Schofield Thayer. Thayer knew and approved of the relationship. In December of 1919 Elaine gave birth to Cummings' daughter, Nancy, and Thayer gave the child his name. Cummings was not to marry Elaine until 1924, after she and Thayer divorced. He adopted Nancy at this time; she was not to know that Cummings was her real father until 1948. This first marriage did not last long. Two months after their wedding, Elaine left for Europe to settle her late sister's estate. She met another man during the Atlantic crossing and fell in love with him. She divorced Cummings in 1925.

The early twenties were an extremely productive time for Cummings. In 1922 he published his first book, *The Enormous Room,* a fictionalized account of his French captivity. Critical reaction was overwhelmingly positive, although Cummings' account of his imprisonment was oddly cheerful in tone and freewheeling in style. He depicted his internment camp stay as a period of inner growth. As David E. Smith wrote in *Twentieth Century Literature, The Enormous Room*'s emphasis "is upon what the initiate has learned from his journey. In this instance, the maimed hero can never again regard the outer world (i.e., 'civilization') without irony. But the spiritual lesson he learned from his sojourn with a community of brothers will be repeated in his subsequent writings both as an ironical dismissal of the values of his contemporary world, and as a sensitive, almost mystical celebration of the quality of Christian love." John Dos Passos, in a review of the book for *Dial,* claimed that "in a style infinitely swift and crisply flexible, an individual not ashamed of his loves and hates, great or trivial, has expressed a bit of the underside of History with indelible vividness." Writing of the book in 1938, John Peale Bishop claimed in the *Southern Review:* "The *Enormous Room* has the effect of making all but a very few comparable books that came out of the War look shoddy and worn."

Cummings' first collection of poems, *Tulips and Chimneys,* appeared in 1923. His eccentric use of grammar and punctuation are evident in the volume, though many of the poems are written in conventional language. "The language of *Tulips and Chimneys,* . . . like the imagery, the verse forms, the subject matter, and the thought, is sometimes good, sometimes bad," wrote Robert E. Maurer in the *Bucknell Review.* "But the book is so obviously the work of a talented young man who is striking off in new directions, groping for original and yet precise expression, experimenting in public, that it seems uncharitable to dwell too long on its shortcomings."

The original manuscript for *Tulips and Chimneys* was cut down by the publisher. These deleted poems were published in 1925 as *&,* so titled because Cummings wanted the original book to be titled *Tulips & Chimneys* but was overruled. Another collection quickly followed: *XLI Poems,* also in 1925. In a review of *XLI Poems* for *Nation,* Mark Van Doren defined Cummings as a poet with "a richly sensuous mind; his verse is distinguished by fluidity and weight; he is equipped to range lustily and long among the major passions." At the end of 1925 *Dial* magazine chose Cummings for their annual award of $2,000, a sum equalling a full year's income for the writer. The following year a new collection, *Is 5,* was published, for which Cummings wrote an introduction meant to explain his approach to poetry. In the introduction he argued forcefully for poetry as a "process" rather than a "product."

It was with these collections of the 1920s that Cummings established his reputation as an avant-garde poet conducting daring experiments with language. Speaking of these language experiments, M. L. Rosenthal wrote in *The Modern Poets: A Critical Introduction:* "The chief effect of Cummings' jugglery with syntax, grammar, and diction was to blow open otherwise trite and bathetic motifs through a dynamic rediscovery of the energies sealed up in conventional usage. . . . He succeeded masterfully in splitting the atom of the cute commonplace." "Cummings," Richard P. Blackmur wrote in *The Double Agent: Essays in Craft and Elucidation,* "has a fine talent for using familiar, even almost dead words, in such a context as to make them suddenly impervious to every ordinary sense; they become unable to speak, but with a great air of being bursting with something very important and precise to say." Bethany K. Dumas wrote in her *E. E. Cummings: A Remembrance of Miracles* that "more important than the specific devices used by Cummings is the use to which he puts the devices. That is a complex matter; irregular spacing . . . allows both amplification and retardation. Further, spacing of key words allows puns which would otherwise be impossible. Some devices, such as the use of lowercase letters at the beginnings of lines . . . allow a kind of distortion that often reenforces that of the syntax. . . . All these devices have the effect of jarring the reader, of forcing him to examine experience with fresh eyes." S. I. Hayakawa also remarked on this quality in Cummings' poetry. "No modern poet to my knowledge," Hayakawa wrote in *Poetry,* "has such a clear, childlike perception as E. E. Cummings—a way of coming smack against things with unaffected delight and wonder. This candor . . . results in

breath-takingly clean vision." Norman Friedman explained in his *E. E. Cummings: The Growth of a Writer* that Cummings' innovations "are best understood as various ways of stripping the film of familiarity from language in order to strip the film of familiarity from the world. Transform the word, he seems to have felt, and you are on the way to transforming the world."

Other critics focused on the subjects of Cummings' poetry. Though his poetic language was uniquely his own, Cummings' poems were unusual because they unabashedly focused on such traditional and somewhat passe poetic themes as love, childhood, and flowers. What Cummings did with such subjects, according to Stephen E. Whicher in *Twelve American Poets,* was, "by verbal ingenuity, without the irony with which another modern poet would treat such a topic, create a sophisticated modern facsimile of the 'naive' lyricism of Campion or Blake." This resulted in what Whicher termed "the renewal of the cliche." Penberthy detected in Cummings a "nineteenth-century romantic reverence for natural order over man-made order, for intuition and imagination over routine-grounded perception. His exalted vision of life and love is served well by his linguistic agility. He was an unabashed lyricist, a modern cavalier love poet. But alongside his lyrical celebrations of nature, love, and the imagination are his satirical denouncements of tawdry, defiling, flat-footed, urban and political life—open terrain for invective and verbal inventiveness."

This satirical aspect to Cummings' work drew both praise and criticism. His attacks on the mass mind, conventional patterns of thought, and society's restrictions on free expression, were born of his strong commitment to the individual. In the "nonlectures" he delivered at Harvard University Cummings explained his position: "So far as I am concerned, poetry and every other art was, is, and forever will be strictly and distinctly a question of individuality." As Penberthy noted, Cummings' consistent attitude in all of his work was "condemning mankind while idealizing the individual." "Cummings' lifelong belief," Bernard Dekle stated in *Profiles of Modern American Authors,* "was a simple faith in the miracle of man's individuality. Much of his literary effort was directed against what he considered the principal enemies of this individuality—mass thought, group conformity, and commercialism." For this reason, Cummings satirized what he called "mostpeople," that is, the herd mentality found in modern society. "At heart," Logan explained, "the quarrels of Cummings are a resistance to the small minds of every kind, political, scientific, philosophical, and literary, who insist on limiting the real and the true to what they think they know or can respond to. As a preventive to this kind of limitation, Cummings is directly opposed to letting us rest in what we believe we know; and this is the key to the rhetorical function of his famous language."

Cummings was also ranked among the best love poets of his time. "Love always was . . . Cummings' chief subject of interest," Friedman wrote in his *E. E. Cummings: The Art of His Poetry.* "The traditional lyric situation, representing the lover speaking of love to his lady, has been given in our time a special flavor and emphasis by Cummings. Not only the lover and his lady, but love itself—its quality, its value, its feel, its meaning—is a subject of continuing concern to our speaker." Love was, in Cummings' poems, equated to such other concepts as joy and growth, a relationship which "had its source," wrote Robert E. Wegner in *The Poetry and Prose of E. E. Cummings,* "in Cummings' experience as a child; he grew up in an aura of love. . . . Love is the propelling force behind a great body of his poetry." Friedman noted that Cummings was "in the habit of associating love, as a subject, with the landscape, the seasons, the times of day, and with time and death—as poets have always done in the past."

Cummings' early love poems were frankly erotic and were meant to shock the Puritanical sensibilities of the 1920s. Penberthy noted that the poet's first wife, Elaine, inspired "scores of Cummings's best erotic poems." But, as Wegner wrote, "In time he came to see love and the dignity of the human being as inseparable." Maurer also commented on this change in Cummings' outlook; there was, Maurer wrote, a "fundamental change of attitude which manifested itself in his growing reverence and dedication to lasting love." Hyatt H. Waggoner, writing in *American Poets from the Puritans to the Present,* noted that "the love poems are generally, after the 1920s, religious in tone and implication, and the religious poems very often take off from the clue provided by a pair of lovers, so that often the two subjects are hardly, if at all, separable." Rushworth M. Kidder also noted this development in the love poems, and he traced the evolution of Cummings' thoughts on the subject. Writing in his *E. E. Cummings: An Introduction to the Poetry,* Kidder reported that in the early poems, love is depicted as "an echo of popularly romantic notions, and it grows in early volumes to a sometimes amorphous phenomenon seasoned by a not entirely unselfish lust. By [his] last poems, however, it has come to be a purified and radiant idea, unentangled with flesh and worlds, the agent of the highest transcendence. It is not far, as poem after poem has hinted, from the Christian conception of love as God." Waggoner concluded that Cummings "wrote some of the finest celebrations of sexual love and of the religious experience of awe and natural piety produced in our century, precisely at a time when it was most unfashionable to write such poems."

In addition to his poetry, Cummings was also known for his play, *Him,* and for the travel diary, *Eimi. Him* consisted of a sequence of skits drawing from burlesque, the circus, and the avant-garde, and jumping quickly from tragedy to grotesque comedy. The male character is named Him; the female character is Me. "The play begins," Harold Clurman wrote in *Nation,* "as a series of feverish images of a girl undergoing anaesthesia during an abortion. She is 'me,' who thinks of her lover as 'him.' " In the program to the play, staged at the Provincetown Playhouse, Cummings provided a warning to the audience: "Relax and give the play a chance to strut its stuff—relax, stop wondering what it's all 'about'—like many strange and familiar things, Life included, this Play isn't 'about,' it simply is. Don't try to enjoy it, let it try to enjoy you. DON'T TRY TO UNDERSTAND IT, LET IT TRY TO UNDERSTAND YOU." Clurman believed that "the play's purest element is contained in duos of love. They are the most sensitive and touching in American playwriting. Their intimacy and passion, conveyed in an odd exquisiteness of writing, are implied rather than declared. We realize that no matter how much 'him' wishes to express his closeness to 'me,' he is frustrated not only by the fullness of his feeling but by his inability to credit his emotion in a world as obscenely chaotic as the one in which he is lost."

In 1931 Cummings traveled to the Soviet Union. Like many other writers and artists of the time, he was hopeful that the communist revolution had created a better society. After a short time in the country, however, it became clear to Cummings that the Soviet Union was a dictatorship in which the individual was severely regimented by the state. His diary of the visit, in which he bitterly attacked the Soviet regime for its dehumanizing policies, was published in 1933 as *Eimi,* the Greek word for "I am." In it, he described the Soviet Union as an "uncircus of noncreatures." Lenin's tomb, in which the late dictator's preserved body is on display, especially revolted Cummings and inspired him to

create the most impassioned writing in the book. "The style which Cummings began in poetry," Bishop wrote, "reaches its most complete development in the prose of *Eimi.* Indeed, one might almost say that, without knowing it, Cummings had been acquiring a certain skill over the years, in order that, when occasion arose, he might set down in words the full horror of Lenin's tomb." In tracing the course of his thirty-five day trip through the Soviet Union, Cummings made frequent allusion to Dante's *Inferno* and its story of a descent into Hell, equating the two journeys. It is only after crossing back into Europe at book's end that "it is once more possible for [Cummings] to assume the full responsibility of being a man . . . ," Bishop wrote. "Now he knows there is but one freedom . . . , the freedom of the will, responsive and responsible, and that from it all other freedoms take their course." Kidder called *Eimi* "a report of the grim inhumanities of the Soviet system, of repression, apathy, priggishness, kitsch, and enervating suspicion." For some time after publication of *Eimi,* Kidder reported, Cummings had a difficult time getting his poetry published. The overwhelmingly left-wing publishers of the time refused to accept his work. Cummings had to resort to self-publishing several volumes of his work during the later 1930s.

In 1952, Cummings was invited to give the Charles Eliot Norton lectures in poetry at Harvard University. His lectures, later published as *i: six nonlectures,* were highly personal accounts of his life and work, "autobiographical rambles," as Penberthy described them. The first two lectures reminisce about his childhood and parents; the third lecture tells of his schooldays at Harvard, his years in New York, and his stay in Paris during the 1920s. The last three lectures present his own ideas about writing. In his conclusion to the lecture series Cummings summed up his thoughts with these words, quoting his own poetry where appropriate: "I am someone who proudly and humbly affirms that love is the mystery-of-mysteries, and that nothing measurable matters 'a very good God damn'; that 'an artist, a man, a failure' is no mere whenfully accreting mechanism, but a givingly eternal complexity—neither some soulless and heartless ultrapredatory infra-animal nor any understandingly knowing and believing and thinking automaton, but a naturally and miraculously whole human being—a feelingly illimitable individual; whose only happiness is to transcend himself, whose every agony is to grow."

Critics of Cummings' work were divided into two camps as to the importance of his career. His detractors called his failure to develop as a writer a major weakness; Cummings' work changed little from the 1920s to the 1950s. Others saw him as merely clever but with little lasting value beyond a few technical innovations. Still others questioned the ideas in his poetry, or seeming lack of them. George Stade in the *New York Times Book Review* claimed that "intellectually speaking, Cummings was a case of arrested development. He was a brilliant 20-year-old, but he remained merely precocious to the end of his life. That may be one source of his appeal." James G. Southworth, writing in *Some Modern American Poets,* argued that Cummings "is too much out of the stream of life for his work to have significance." Southworth went on to say that "the reader must not mistake Mr. Cummings for an intellectual poet."

But Cummings' supporters acclaimed his achievement. In a 1959 essay reprinted in his collection *Babel to Byzantium,* James Dickey proclaimed: "I think that Cummings is a daringly original poet, with more vitality and more sheer, uncompromising talent than any other living American writer." Although admitting that Cummings' work was not faultless, Dickey stated that he felt "ashamed and even a little guilty in picking out flaws" in the poems, a process he likened to calling attention to "the aesthetic defects in a rose. It is better to say what must finally be said about Cummings: that he has helped to give life to the language." In similar terms, Rosenthal explained that "Cummings's great forte is the manipulation of traditional forms and attitudes in an original way. In his best work he has the swift sureness of ear and idiom of a Catullus, and the same way of bringing together a racy colloquialism and the richer tones of high poetic style." Maurer believed that Cummings' best work exhibited "a new and delightful sense of linguistic invention, precise and vigorous." Penberthy concluded that "Cummings's achievement deserves acclaim. He established the poem as a visual object . . .; he revealed, by his x-ray probings, the faceted possibilities of the single word; and like such prose writers as Vladimir Nabokov and Tom Stoppard, he promoted sheer playfulness with language. Despite a growing abundance of second-rate imitations, his poems continue to amuse, delight, and provoke."

BIOGRAPHICAL/CRITICAL SOURCES:

BOOKS

Baum, S. V., editor, *EETI: E. E. Cummings and the Critics,* Michigan State University Press, 1962.

Blackmur, Richard P., *The Double Agent: Essays in Craft and Elucidation,* Arrow Editions, 1935.

Contemporary Literary Criticism, Gale, Volume 1, 1973, Volume 3, 1975, Volume 8, 1978, Volume 12, 1980, Volume 15, 1980.

Cummings, E. E., *The Enormous Room,* Boni & Liveright, 1922, revised edition, Liveright, 1978.

Cummings, E. E., *Is 5,* Boni & Liveright, 1926, reprinted, Liveright, 1985.

Cummings, E. E., *Eimi,* Covici Friede, 1933, 4th edition, Grove, 1958.

Cummings, E. E., *i: six nonlectures,* Harvard University Press, 1953.

Cummings, E. E., *Selected Letters of E. E. Cummings,* edited by F. W. Dupee and George Stade, Harcourt, 1969.

Dekle, Bernard, *Profiles of Modern American Authors,* Tuttle, 1969.

Deutsch, Babette, *Poetry in Our Time,* Doubleday, 1963.

Dickey, James, *Babel to Byzantium,* Farrar, 1968.

Dictionary of Literary Biography, Gale, Volume 4: *American Writers in Paris, 1920-1939,* 1980, Volume 48: *American Poets, 1880-1945,* second series, 1986.

Dumas, Bethany K., *E. E. Cummings: A Remembrance of Miracles,* Barnes & Noble, 1974.

Fairley, Irene, *E. E. Cummings & Ungrammar: A Study of Syntactic Deviance in His Poems,* Windmill Press, 1975.

Firmage, George J., *E. E. Cummings: A Bibliography,* Wesleyan University Press, 1960.

Friedman, Norman, *E. E. Cummings: The Art of His Poetry,* Johns Hopkins University Press, 1960.

Friedman, Norman, *E. E. Cummings: The Growth of a Writer,* Southern Illinois University Press, 1964.

Friedman, Norman, *E. E. Cummings: A Collection of Critical Essays,* Prentice-Hall, 1972.

Hoffman, Frederick J., *The Twenties: American Writing in the Postwar Decade,* revised edition, Collier, 1962.

Hyman, Stanley Edgar, *Standards: A Chronicle of Books for Our Time,* Horizon, 1966.

Jarrell, Randall, *The Third Book of Criticism,* Farrar, 1969.

Kennedy, Richard S., *Dreams in the Mirror: A Biography of E. E. Cummings,* Liveright, 1980.

Kidder, Rushworth M., *E. E. Cummings: An Introduction to the Poetry,* Columbia University Press, 1979.

Marks, Barry, *E. E. Cummings,* Twayne, 1963.

Mazzaro, Jerome, editor, *Modern American Poetry: Essays in Criticism,* McKay, 1970.

Norman, Charles, *E. E. Cummings: The Magic-Maker,* revised edition, Duell, Sloan & Pearce, 1964.

Rosenthal, M. L., *The Modern Poets: A Critical Introduction,* Oxford University Press, 1960.

Rotella, Guy L., *E. E. Cummings: A Reference Guide,* G. K. Hall, 1979.

Southworth, James G., *Some Modern American Poets,* Basil Blackwell, 1950.

Triem, Eve, *E. E. Cummings,* University of Minnesota Press, 1969.

Waggoner, Hyatt H., *American Poets from the Puritans to the Present,* Houghton, 1968.

Wegner, Robert E., *The Poetry and Prose of E. E. Cummings,* Harcourt, 1965.

Whicher, Stephen E. and Lars Ahnebrink, editors, *Twelve American Poets,* Almquist & Wiksell, 1959.

PERIODICALS

Bucknell Review, May, 1955.

Contemporary Literature, autumn, 1976.

Dial, July, 1922.

Georgia Review, summer, 1978.

Journal of Modern Literature, April, 1979 (special Cummings issue).

Nation, July 8, 1925, May 11, 1974.

New York Times Book Review, July 22, 1973.

Poetry, August, 1933, August, 1938.

Southern Review, summer, 1938, summer, 1941.

Twentieth Century Literature, July, 1965.

Wake, spring, 1976 (special Cummings issue).

Yale Review, spring, 1973.

OBITUARIES:

PERIODICALS

New York Times, September 4, 1962.*

—*Sketch by Thomas Wiloch*

*   *   *

CUMMINGS, Ray(mond King) 1887-1957

PERSONAL: Born August 30, 1887, in New York, N.Y.; died of a stroke, January 23, 1957, in Mount Vernon, N.Y.; married first wife, Janet Matheson (divorced); married second wife, Gabrielle Wilson; children: (first marriage) Harry Matheson; (second marriage) Elizabeth Starr (Mrs. Russell Gibson Hill). *Education:* Attended Princeton University.

CAREER: Writer, 1919-57. Early occupations included gold prospecting, working on oil fields and orange plantations; worked as an editor for Thomas Alva Edison, 1914-19.

WRITINGS:

SCIENCE FICTION NOVELS

The Girl in the Golden Atom, Methuen, 1922, Harper, 1923.
The Man Who Mastered Time, McClurg, 1929.
The Sea Girl, McClurg, 1930.
Tarrano the Conqueror, McClurg, 1930.
Brigands of the Moon, McClurg, 1931.
Into the Fourth Dimension, Swan, 1943.
The Shadow Girl, Swan, 1946, Ace, 1962.
The Princess of the Atom, Avon, 1950.
The Man on the Meteor, Swan, 1952.

Beyond the Vanishing Point, Ace, 1958.
Wandl, the Invader, Ace, 1961.
Beyond the Stars, Ace, 1963.
A Brand New World, Ace, 1964.
The Exile of Time, Avalon, 1964.
Explorers into Infinity, Avalon, 1965.
Tama of the Light Country, Ace, 1965.
Tama, Princess of Mercury, Ace, 1966.
The Insect Invasion, Avalon, 1967.

OTHER

Contributor of over seven hundred and fifty short stories under various pseudonyms to numerous periodicals.

SIDELIGHTS: Ray Cummings was a popular author of science fiction, detective and horror stories whose work is little known today except among collectors of pulp magazines. His first and most successful novel, *The Girl in the Golden Atom,* is about a man who discovers a drug which allows him to change size and have incredible adventures on a world that exists on an atom of gold. A number of Cummings novels after the publication of *The Girl in the Golden Atom,* such as *Explorers into Infinity, The Princess of the Atom,* and *Beyond the Vanishing Point,* were based on this concept of a size-altering drug. The best Cummings novels, noted Erich S. Rupprecht in the *Dictionary of Literary Biography,* are his earlier works, which are "often clear, spare, and straightforward." After publishing numerous books based on variations of his first idea, the author's writing became repetitious, careless, and cliched, according to Rupprecht. But al-though the critic points out that "it would be easy to sneer at Cumming's work today," he also recognizes that "had it not been for pioneers like Cummings writing in the early decades of the century and helping to popularize this new genre, it is doubtful whether science fiction would have achieved the success it now enjoys."

BIOGRAPHICAL/CRITICAL SOURCES:

BOOKS

Dictionary of Literary Biography, Volume 8: *Twentieth-Century American Science Fiction Writers,* Gale, 1981.

[sketch reviewed by daughter, Elizabeth Starr Hill]

*   *   *

CURTIN, Patricia Romero
   See ROMERO, Patricia W.

*   *   *

CURTIS, Richard Hale
   See LEVINSON, Leonard

*   *   *

CUSTER, Clint
   See PAINE, Lauran (Bosworth)

D

DAHLBERG, Edward   1900-1977

PERSONAL: Born July 22, 1900, in Boston, Mass.; died February 27, 1977, in Santa Barbara, Calif.; son of Saul Gottdank (a barber) and Elizabeth Dahlberg (a hairdresser); married Fanya Fass, 1926 (divorced); married Winifred Sheehan Moore, 1942; married Rlene LaFleur Howell, 1950; married Julia Lawlor, June 13, 1967; children: (second marriage) Geoffrey, Joel. *Education:* Attended University of California, Berkeley, 1921-23; Columbia University, B.S., 1925.

CAREER: Writer. Teacher at James Madison High School and Thomas Jefferson High School, New York City, 1925-26; New York University, New York City, visiting lecturer in Graduate School, 1950, 1961, lecturer in School of General Education, 1961-62; University of Missouri at Kansas City, Carolyn Benton Cockefair Professor, 1964-65, professor of language and literature, beginning 1966. Visiting professor at Columbia University, 1968. *Military service:* U.S. Army, private.

MEMBER: National Institute of Arts and Letters.

AWARDS, HONORS: Attended McDowell Colony, 1930; National Institute of Arts and Letters grant, 1961; Rockefeller Foundation grant, 1965, 1966; Ariadne Foundation grant, 1970; Cultural Council Foundation award, 1971; National Foundation on Arts and Humanities award; Longview Foundation grant; CAPS grant; National Endowment for the Arts grant.

WRITINGS:

Bottom Dogs (also see below; novel), with introduction by D. H. Lawrence, Putnam (London), 1929, Simon & Schuster, 1930, reprinted, AMS Press, 1976.
From Flushing to Calvary (also see below; novel), Harcourt, 1932.
Kentucky Blue Grass Henry Smith (prose poem), White Horse Press (Cleveland), 1932.
Those Who Perish (also see below; novel), John Day, 1934, reprinted, AMS Press, 1977.
(Author of introduction) Kenneth Fearing, *Poems,* Dynamo (New York), 1936.
Do These Bones Live (criticism), Harcourt, 1941, revised edition published in England as *Sing O Barren,* Routledge, 1947, 2nd revised edition published as *Can These Bones Live,* New Directions, 1960.
The Flea of Sodom (essays), New Directions, 1950.

The Sorrows of Priapus (also see below; philosophy), New Directions, 1957.
Moby Dick: An Hamitic Dream, Fairleigh Dickinson University, 1960.
(With Herbert Read) *Truth Is More Sacred* (critical exchange on modern literature), Horizon, 1961.
Alms for Oblivion (essays), University of Minnesota Press, 1964.
Because I Was Flesh (autobiography), New Directions, 1964.
Reasons of the Heart (aphorisms), Horizon, 1965.
Cipango's Hinder Door (poems), University of Texas Press, 1966.
The Leafless American, and Other Writings, edited by Harold Billings, Roger Beacham, 1967.
The Edward Dahlberg Reader, edited by Paul Carroll, New Directions, 1967.
Epitaphs of Our Times: The Letters of Edward Dahlberg, edited by Edwin Seaver, Braziller, 1967.
The Carnal Myth: A Look into Classical Sensuality (also see below), Weybright, 1968.
The Confessions of Edward Dahlberg, Braziller, 1971.
(Compiler and contributor) *The Gold of Ophir: Travels, Myths and Legends in the New World,* Dutton, 1972.
The Sorrows of Priapus: Consisting of The Sorrows of Priapus and The Carnal Myth, Harcourt, 1973.
The Olive of Minerva; or, The Comedy of a Cuckold, Crowell, 1976.
Bottom Dogs, From Flushing to Calvary, Those Who Perish, and Hitherto Unpublished and Uncollected Works, Crowell, 1976.

CONTRIBUTOR

Henry Hart, editor, *American Writers' Congress,* International Publishers, 1935.
Martha Foley and David Burnett, editors, *Best American Short Stories, 1961-1962,* Houghton, 1962.
Stanley Burnshaw, editor, *Varieties of Literary Experience,* New York University Press, 1962.
Louis Filler, editor, *The Anxious Years,* Putnam, 1963.

Also contributor to volumes of *New Directions in Prose and Poetry,* edited by James Laughlin, New Directions.

OTHER

Contributor of short stories, reviews, essays, and articles to *Nation, New Republic, New York Times, Holiday, Poetry, This Quarter, Twentieth Century, Massachusetts Review, New York*

Review of Books, New York Times Book Review, and other publications.

WORK IN PROGRESS: At the time of his death in 1977 Dahlberg was reported to have been working on two books: *Rightness Is All* and *Jesus, Man or Apocrypha.*

SIDELIGHTS: Throughout his long and varied literary career, Edward Dahlberg was a puzzle to many American critics. His distinctive, eccentric, and often archaic style caused the literary establishment to either dismiss his work or to praise him as a genius. As Edmund White explained in the *New Republic,* "Dahlberg continues to be one of the most unaccountable forces in American letters, a phenomenon that every critic seeks, in one way or another, either to justify or dismiss." Why Dahlberg chose to write in such a singular manner was also a puzzle to critics. "Even critics who are theoretically quite opposed to examining a man's work as a pendant to his life find themselves worrying over how Dahlberg *got to be this way,*" as White wrote. Dahlberg was also adept at shedding labels that confined his talents. His early books earned him the title of "proletarian novelist," but he later gained critical recognition for his poetry, which was rich in allusion, while his work as an essayist, philosopher and literary critic earned him yet further accolades. Perhaps his most widely respected work is an autobiography, *Because I Was Flesh.* X. J. Kennedy, writing in the *New York Times Book Review,* called Dahlberg "a rare figure among American writers: a man of letters in the European sense, a versatile performer in more than one genre."

Perhaps the overriding feature of Dahlberg's work, particularly during the 1960s, was his stance as a sophisticated outsider who berated the culture of his day, as a curmudgeon who hurled invective at those whom he thought his inferiors. This attitude did not endear him to many readers. He "is not," Robert M. Adams admitted in the *New York Review of Books,* "an easy writer to like. . . . He is given to vociferous protests about his own genuineness and authenticity; and to make it the more exemplary, he vigorously denigrates almost all his contemporaries and most of his predecessors." Arno Karlen of the *New York Times Book Review* compared Dahlberg to the poet John Donne, "the poet-preacher whose bitterness and warmth were also those of a sensual man alive to regret, whose life's lessons were also burned into his bones, making him somber and sardonic, witty and kind with sensual pessimism. Sometimes Dahlberg sours into misogynous rant, which is ungenerous and thus unbecoming; just as his diction may become labored, so his pessimism may become a truculent pose."

To fashion the raw experience of life into art, Dahlberg employed myth, "which, in his best work, functions as a way of giving depth, perspective, and perhaps order" to life, according to Adams. Raymond Rosenthal, writing in the *Nation,* called Dahlberg "a lone searcher for the true myths of human destiny in our violent, barren, raddled land." Dahlberg himself explained his use of myth in these words: "Until he is connected with the fens, the ravines, the stars, [man] is more solitary than any beast. Man is a god, and kin to men, when he is a river, a mountain, a horse, a moon. . . . The American legend is the mesa and the bison; it is the myth of a tragic terrain stalked by banished men." In his article for the *Dictionary of Literary Biography,* Larry R. Smith quoted Dahlberg as saying: "As for myself, I'm a medievalist, a horse and buggy American, a barbarian, anything, that can bring me back to the communal song of labor, sky, star, field, love."

Much of Dahlberg's fiction was drawn from his troubled childhood. Dahlberg was born illegitimately at a charity hospital in Boston in 1900. His mother was Elizabeth Dahlberg, married and the mother of three other children, and his father was Elizabeth's lover, a Jewish barber named Saul Gottdank. Following Dahlberg's birth, the couple took him and moved to Dallas, Texas. Once there, Gottdank stole Elizabeth's money, left town, and abandoned her. Later reconciliations in Memphis and New Orleans ended with similar betrayals. Elizabeth wandered about the South and Midwest for several years before settling in Kansas City, where she opened a hair salon. But the family's troubles continued. Despite the successful business, Elizabeth was to lose her money to a string of opportunistic men. One of these men suggested that she send Edward to an orphanage so he would not be exposed to the immorality of the Kansas City streets. She did so in 1912, and Edward entered the Jewish Orphan Asylum in Cleveland. With his admission to the orphanage, Smith remarked, "life turned from harsh to grim" for the young boy. Children at the orphanage were called by their numbers instead of their names; the windows in the building were barred; and the boredom and brutality of the place caused Dahlberg to suppress his emotions.

Upon reaching legal age in 1917, Dahlberg left the orphanage and served a brief stint as a Western Union messenger in Cleveland before making his way back to Kansas City and his mother. In the next few years Dahlberg was to work in the stockyards as a drover and serve in the U.S. Army as a private. He also wandered about the American West as a hobo, working as a dishwasher, cook, and day laborer to pay his way. In 1919 he made his home at the Los Angeles YMCA. It was there he met Max Lewis, an older, self-educated man who taught Dahlberg to appreciate such writers as Friedrich Nietzsche, Samuel Butler, and Ralph Waldo Emerson. Dahlberg developed an interest in learning, and Lewis encouraged him to attend college. In 1921 Dahlberg enrolled at the University of California at Berkeley, where he majored in philosophy and anthropology. He transferred to Columbia University in 1923 to finish his degree. Upon graduation in 1925, Dahlberg taught at James Madison and Thomas Jefferson high schools in New York City.

After marrying Fanya Fass, the daughter of a Cleveland industrialist, in 1926, Dahlberg and his new wife moved to Europe. The couple divorced soon after arriving. For a time Dahlberg was a part of the expatriate group of American writers living in Paris. He became friends with Hart Crane, Robert McAlmon, and Richard Aldington. While living in Brussels in 1928, he completed his first novel, *Bottom Dogs,* based on his childhood experiences at the orphanage and as a hobo traveling in the American West. The novel was marked by Dahlberg's use of coarse slang and his often graphic descriptions of down-and-out workers, farmers, and wanderers. It was published in England in 1929 and in the United States in 1930.

In his introduction to *Bottom Dogs,* D. H. Lawrence praised Dahlberg as a naturalist writer who successfully recreated the psychological mind-set of society's underclass. The novel's style, Lawrence wrote, "seems to me excellent, fitting the matter. It is sheer bottom-dog style, the bottom-dog mind expressing itself direct, almost as if it barked. That directness, that unsentimental and non-dramatised thoroughness of setting down the under-dog mind surpasses anything I know. I don't want to read any more books like this. But I am glad to have read this one, just to know what is the last word in repulsive consciousness, consciousness in a state of repulsion."

Several critics agreed with Lawrence, finding that *Bottom Dogs* accurately reflected the language and life of the lowest levels of society. Herbert Leibowitz of the *American Scholar* judged the novel's language to be "bare of mythical adornments, a flat morose voice moving over the terrain of memory, never straying from its tone of inert defeat, as the hero, Lorry Lewis, wanders across America. There is no connection among characters, just a drab amnesia, the stylistic counterpart of the Great Depression." Walter Allen, writing in his *The Modern Novel,* maintained that *Bottom Dogs* "communicates hopelessness, the hopelessness of the . . . lives of the bottom dogs, men and women who can sink no lower in the social and economic system."

For writing of society's underclass in the language of the streets, Dahlberg became immensely influential. Other writers adopted the approach, which came to be known during the 1930s as social realism or proletarian writing. In his book *Proletarian Writers of the Thirties,* Jules Chametsky described Dahlberg as a pioneer of proletarian writing: "Dahlberg's language of disgust, his imagery of rot and decay—and most importantly—his pioneering exploration of the bottom-dog milieux of flophouses, hobo jungles, and freight cars certainly places him in the vanguard of that school." J. D. O'Hara in the *New York Times Book Review* credited Dahlberg with having spawned the proleterian school of writing, but "those writers who had seized on his 'Bottom Dogs' style worked it to death in the service of Communism."

In his next two novels, *From Flushing to Calvary* and *Those Who Perish,* Dahlberg continued to write of his early life, garnering a reputation as one of the decade's leading proletarian novelists. Writing in the *Massachusetts Review,* Frank MacShane called these early books "socially committed. . . . More deeply, they were fed by [Dahlberg's] own anger at injustice. They were written in a colloquial style suited, as was thought, to the proletariat." Dahlberg's political inclinations moved him to work with other leftist writers of the 1930s. He helped to organize the communist-dominated American Writers' Congress of 1935, where he delivered a paper entitled "Fascism and Writers." By the late 1930s, however, his novels, although critically accepted, "showed no artistic growth, so Dahlberg, who meanwhile had fallen out with the Communists and who had genuine literary ambitions, ceased writing and began to read," according to MacShane. Dahlberg later repudiated his early novels as "mediocre manipulations of his childhood and young manhood, disfigured by self-pity," as Leibowitz explained. He also referred to the books as "dunghill fiction."

For many years Dahlberg wrote no new fiction, instead devoting his time to an intense study of literature. In this study he rejected most of the authors and books of the twentieth century, preferring such earlier writers as Shakespeare, Cervantes, Melville, Poe, Dickinson, and especially Thoreau. His readings of their works resulted in a writing style drastically different from his proletarian approach of the 1930s. He left behind the "linguistic void and gibbering of robots that he says marked much of the fiction and discourse of the thirties," Leibowitz stated.

Dahlberg's new style, first presented in the essay collection *Do These Bones Live* (later published as *Can These Bones Live*), is rich in biblical cadence, allusions, and aphoristic pronouncements. It is, White maintained, "a new language, an amalgam of 17th-century prose, moralizing in the style of La Rochefoucauld and queer classical learning. The effect of this language is in turn unintelligible, beautiful and ludicrous." Brom Weber in the *Saturday Review* claimed that "Dahlberg's baroque exuberance marks a return to the florid style of Melville and, beyond him in time, of Puritans Cotton Mather and Nathaniel Ward, whose fervid prose, like that of Dahlberg, is rich in rare and archaic diction, allusions to and quotations from more ancient savants, paradoxes, contradictions, factual errors, misinterpreta-

tions, impatience with contemporaries, and powerful self-assertiveness."

Do These Bones Live, "a brilliant and profound survey of American literature," as Allen Tate called it in the *Sewanee Review,* also introduced Dahlberg's support for a mythical kind of writing meant to endow ordinary life with greater significance. As John Wain wrote in the *New York Review of Books,* Dahlberg's later work "was largely concerned to transmogrify experience into myth: to give to everyday episodes that range of implication which animates the great anonymous world-explaining stories of mankind." Accordingly, Dahlberg criticized such earlier American writers as Whitman and Poe, citing the limitations of their work in comparison to such writers as Dante, who had used myth more effectively. He also condemned modernist writing, especially the works of Eliot and Pound. *Do These Bones Live,* Weber explained, "is the literary and cultural criticism of an impassioned lyric poet."

During the 1940s and 1950s, Dahlberg published little new work. Then, beginning in the early 1960s, he entered a period of production that was surprising for a middle-aged writer, publishing an average of one new book every year. Perhaps the most important of these later works was the autobiography *Because I Was Flesh,* a book in which Dahlberg came to terms with the circumstances of his early life and, in particular, with his mixed feelings about his mother. Adams described *Because I Was Flesh* as "Dahlberg's extended tribute to his mother" as well as the author's "one sustained achievement."

Critics praised Dahlberg for successfully transforming the story of his life into a form of myth. *Because I Was Flesh,* according to Wain, "succeeds in the tremendous undertaking of mythologizing modern America, as thoroughly as Joyce mythologized Dublin." Smith explained that "the book is a synthesis of Dahlberg's pithy epigrams, his concise realistic detail, and his passages of philosophical reverie. It fuses myth and reality in a flowing style that encompasses emotion, thought, and humor." MacShane noted that in *Because I Was Flesh* the "bare narrative was given substance by the rich prose in which it was written—a prose that incorporated literary, historical and mythical references so as to give the story greater resonance than was possible when accepting the limitations of colloquial English. The danger of the method is that it can be artificially literary and therefore pretentious; but *Because I Was Flesh* is grounded in observed reality." Leibowitz concluded: "*Because I Was Flesh* is a masterpiece of Oedipal obsession, a poetic memoir of primal sunderings and rages."

Although he had been writing poetry for many years, it was only during the 1960s that Dahlberg published his work in book form. *Cipango's Hinder Door* and *The Leafless American, and Other Writings* present thirty of his poems, most of them mythologizing American history as well as Dahlberg's own personal past. Cipango is the name of the mythical Asian land which Columbus believed he had discovered when he landed in the New World, Kennedy explained in his review of *Cipango's Hinder Door.* Thus, "Dahlberg's theme is the discovery of a new world—the rediscovery, to be exact [and] the rediscovery of America is another name for a discovery of himself," Kennedy concluded. "Dahlberg's poetry," Smith observed, "can be described as epigrammatic, lyric, densely mythical in reference . . ., rhythmic, intense, and progressing in associative or lyrical leaps." Donald W. Baker of *Poetry* claimed that "the best of his work, alive with incantatory rhythms and a prophetic tone, generates the power of psalm and prayer."

Much of Dahlberg's later reputation was colored by his often acrid commentary on contemporary literature and society. O'Hara labeled these comments as being "consistently hostile, vituperative, personally insulting and wrong." Several critics compared Dahlberg to biblical figures like Ishmael and Jeremiah who spoke out against the sinful ways of their time. Benjamin T. Spencer, in an article for *Twentieth Century Literature,* credited Dahlberg with "the stance of an Old Testament prophet" and a "self-appointed mission to cleanse the Augean stables of literature." Saul Maloff remarked in *Commonweal* that "the jeremiad is his characteristic tone. . . . Dahlberg is a crank in a peculiarly American grain, a solitary who sets himself intransigently against all contemporary literary conventions and traditions, and rails against the mainstream and all its tributaries as they churn unheeding past."

His controversial criticism focused on what Dahlberg saw as contemporary literature's lack of morals, and on the limitations of a rational and scientific worldview. White summarized Dahlberg's "moral analysis" as a belief "that sexuality is permanently at war with man's higher aspirations and must be disciplined; that human companionship is a great good, though difficult to find and keep; that instinct is often more trustworthy than reason; that accumulating wisdom, however, is honorable, if vain practice; that each person's character is so inflexible it cannot be significantly improved; that the machine age is an abomination; and that life is tragic." Rosenthal explained that Dahlberg's "cause, his importance, lie in his ingrained suspicion of the rationalistic, scientific heritage which has imprisoned intellect in our time. He knows, instinctively . . . that above reason and the soul or spirit stands . . . the good of the intellect, the light of wisdom which is a perpetual source of interpretation and transformation. Dahlberg instinctively knows that the method of this form of intellect is the explanation of myths, the presentation of symbols, the search for ancient wisdom."

Because of the singular nature of his vision and the sometimes scathing words he had for his contemporaries, Dahlberg's literary standing is still undecided. Dahlberg, Tate believed, "like Thoreau whom he admires more than any other nineteenth-century American, eludes his contemporaries; he may have to wait for understanding until the historians of ideas of the next generation can place him historically. For we have at present neither literary nor historical standards which can guide us into Mr. Dahlberg's books written since *Bottom Dogs.*" Smith called him "a rare American poet of mythography as well as lyric personal verse. His extraordinary prose style is at times of erudite obscurism, and at [other times] personal and poetic. . . . In Edward Dahlberg the writing is the man, and there is much in the experience of that life to make his work tragically, comically, even beautifully unique." August Derleth described Dahlberg as being "as much a genius as anyone of whom I can think, past or present." He credited Dahlberg's sheer talent as the cause of critical resistance to his work: "The world is seldom ready to extend genius a helping hand, but only to salute genius when he who possessed it is safely underground." Writing in the *New York Times Book Review* about his career as a writer, Dahlberg once claimed: "I never put together a shoal of vowels and consonants for mammon or for that other whore, fame. I propose to go along as I always have done, sowing dragon's teeth when necessary, and seeding affections in the souls of my unknown readers if I can."

BIOGRAPHICAL/CRITICAL SOURCES:

BOOKS

Allen, Walter, *The Modern Novel,* Dutton, 1964.

Billings, Harold, editor, *Edward Dahlberg: American Ishmael of Letters,* Roger Beacham, 1968.
Billings, Harold, *A Bibliography of Edward Dahlberg,* University of Texas Press, 1971.
Contemporary Literary Criticism, Gale, Volume 1, 1973, Volume 7, 1977, Volume 14, 1980.
Dahlberg, Edward, *Bottom Dogs,* Putnam, 1929, Simon & Schuster, 1930.
Dahlberg, Edward, *Because I Was Flesh,* New Directions, 1964.
Dahlberg, Edward, *Confessions of Edward Dahlberg,* Braziller, 1971.
DeFanti, Charles, *The Wages of Expectation: A Biography of Edward Dahlberg,* New York University Press, 1978.
Dictionary of Literary Biography, Volume 48: *American Poets, 1880-1945, Second Series,* Gale, 1986.
Madden, Donald, editor, *Proletarian Writers of the Thirties,* Southern Illinois University Press, 1968.
Moramarco, Fred, *Edward Dahlberg,* Twayne, 1972.
Williams, Jonathan, editor, *Edward Dahlberg: A Tribute,* David Lewis, 1971.
Wilson, Edmund, *The Shores of Light,* Farrar, Straus, 1952.

PERIODICALS

American Scholar, summer, 1975.
Atlantic, March, 1971.
Book World, June 2, 1968, July 21, 1968, February 16, 1969.
Christian Science Monitor, April 13, 1967.
Commonweal, February 19, 1971.
Contemporary Literature, spring, 1977.
Massachusetts Review, spring, 1964, spring, 1978.
Nation, November 11, 1968.
National Review, September 19, 1967.
New Republic, August 3, 1968, February 6, 1971.
Newsweek, January 23, 1967.
New York Review of Books, August 24, 1967, January 2, 1969.
New York Times Book Review, December 19, 1965, June 19, 1966, January 15, 1967, March 5, 1967, August 18, 1968, April 18, 1976.
Poetry, March, 1967.
Saturday Review, March 6, 1971.
Sewanee Review, spring, 1961.
Southern Review, spring, 1965, summer, 1967.
Twentieth Century Literature, December, 1975.
Western Humanities Review, summer, 1966.

OBITUARIES:

PERIODICALS

New York Times, February 28, 1977.
Publishers Weekly, March 21, 1977.
Time, March 14, 1977.
Washington Post, March 2, 1977.*

—*Sketch by Thomas Wiloch*

*　　　*　　　*

DANA, Amber
See PAINE, Lauran (Bosworth)

*　　　*　　　*

DANA, Richard
See PAINE, Lauran (Bosworth)

DANIELOU, Alain 1907-

PERSONAL: Born October 4, 1907, in Neuilly-sur-Seine, France; son of Charles (a writer and politician) and Madeleine (an educator and founder of religious order; maiden name, Clamorgan) Danielou. *Education:* Educated in France, India, and the United States; attended St. John's College. *Religion:* Hindu.

ADDRESSES: Home—Colle Labirinto, Zagarolo, 00039 Rome, Italy.

CAREER: Hindu University, Benares, India, research professor of Sanskrit literature on music, 1949-54; International Institute for Comparative Music Studies, Venice, Italy, and Berlin, Germany, director, 1962-79. Has also worked as a singer, dancer, and painter.

MEMBER: French Institute of Indology, Ecole Francaise d'Extreme-Orient.

AWARDS, HONORS: Chevalier Legion d'honneur, 1967; Commandeur Arts et Lettres, 1970; Officier Merite National, 1975.

WRITINGS:

Visages de l'Inde Medievale, photographs by Raymond Burnier, Hermann (Paris), 1950, reprinted, 1985.

Le Betail des dieux: et autres contes gangetiques (also see below; title means "The Cattle of the Gods"; contains *Le Betail des dieux* and *Les Fous de dieu*), Buchet/Chastel (Paris), 1962, reprinted, 1983.

Hindu Polytheism, Princeton University Press, 1964, published as *The Gods of India: Hindu Polytheism,* Inner Traditions International (New York), 1985.

(Translator) *Ilango Adigal, Shilappadikaram: The Ankle Bracelet,* New Directions, 1965.

Inde du nord: Collection "Les Traditions Musicales" (title means "Musical Traditions of Northern India"), Buchet/Chastel, 1966, published as *La musique de l'Inde du nord,* 1985.

Semantique musicale: essai de psycho-physiologie auditive (title means "Musical Semantics"), Hermann, 1967, new edition with preface by Fritz Winckel and introduction by Francoise Escal, 1978, translation published as *Musical Semantics,* Inner Traditions, 1991.

The Ragas of Northern Indian Music, Barrie & Rockliff, 1968.

Histoire de l'Inde (title means "History of India"), Fayard, 1971, revised edition, 1983.

(With Jacques Brunet) *La Situation de la musique et des musiciens dans les pays d'orient,* Olschki, 1971, translation by John Evarts published as *The Situation of Music and Musicians in the Countries of the Orient,* 1971.

Yoga: Methode de reintegration, L'Arche, 1973, revised edition, 1982, translation by the author published as *Yoga: The Method of Reintegration,* University Books, 1973, new edition, Inner Traditions International, 1991.

La Sculpture erotique hindoue (title means "Erotic Hindu Sculpture"), Buchet/Chastel, 1973.

Les fous de Dieu: Contes gangetiques (also see below; title means "God's Madmen"), Buchet/Chastel, 1976, revised edition, 1984.

Les Quatre Sens de la vie: La Structure sociale de l'Inde traditionnelle (title means "The Four Aims of Life: Social Structures of Traditional India"), Buchet/Chastel, 1976, revised edition, 1984, translation published as *Four Aims of Life,* Inner Traditions, 1988.

(Translator and adaptor) *Trois pieces de theatre de Harsha* (title means "The Plays of Harsha"), Buchet/Chastel, 1977.

Le Temple hindou (title means "The Hindu Temple"), Buchet/Chastel, 1977. *Shiva et Dionysos: Mythes et rites d'une religion pre-aryenne,* Fayard, 1979, translation by K. F. Hurry published as *Shiva and Dionysus: The Religion of Nature and Eros,* East-West Publications, 1982, reprinted, Inner Traditions, 1984.

(Author of introduction) Jorge Luis Borges, *Le Congres du monde,* F. M. Ricci (Milan), 1979, published as *The Congress of the World,* introduction translated by John Shepley, translation by Alberto Manguel, 1981.

(Author of introduction) *L'Epopee fantastique des dieux hindous dans le theatre d'ombre javanais,* Editions Trismegiste, 1982.

Le chemin du labyrinthe: souvenirs d'Orient et d'Occident (autobiography), Laffont, 1982, translation by Marie-Claire Cournand published as *The Way to the Labyrinth: Memories of East and West,* New Directions, 1987.

(Translator with T. V. Gopala Iyer) Shattan, *Manimekhalai ou le scandale de la Vertue,* Flammarion (Paris), 1987, translation published as *Manimekhalai: The Dancer with the Magic Bowl,* New Directions, 1987.

La Fantaisie des Dieux et L'aventure Humaine, Edition du Rocher (Paris/Monaco), 1985, translation published as *While the Gods Play: Shaiva Oracles and Predictions on the Cycles of History and the Destiny of Mankind,* translation by Barbara Bailey, Michael Baker, and Deborah Lawlor, Inner Traditions International, 1987.

Fools of God (selections from *Fous de Dieu*), translation by David Rattray, Hanuman Books, 1988.

Hierarchy and Social Order: Traditional India's Social Structures, Inner Traditions International, 1991.

Introduction to the Study of Musical Scales, South Asia Books, 1979, reprinted, Fine Line Books (Oxford, England), 1991.

Also author of *Bharata Natyam: danse classique de L'Inde,* 1970, and *La Musique dans la societe et la vie de l'Inde.* Translator of *Le Shiva Svarodaya-Ancien traite de presages et premonitions d'apres le Souffle Vital.* Editor of UNESCO collection of Oriental and traditional music recordings.

SIDELIGHTS: Alain Danielou, whom *Interview* contributor Andrew Harvey calls "the foremost living interpreter of Hinduism," spent his adolescence in Paris during the 1920s, where he befriended Cocteau and Stravinsky. The father of the king of Afghanistan (another boyhood friend) invited Danielou to visit the East. During this time he travelled to India, where he spent fifteen years; three of his books, *Shivan and Dionysus, The Four Aims of Life,* and *While the Gods Play* originated from his experiences there. The books, writes Harvey, are "remarkable for their clarity, scholarship, and uninhibited celebration of erotic and mystical ecstasy."

Danielou told *CA* that his "main interest is explaining Hindu traditional civilization, religion and culture to the outside world." He continued: "Hinduism especially in its oldest, Shivaite form, never destroyed its past. It is the sum of human experience from the earliest times. Nondogmatic, it allows every one to find his own way. Ultimate reality being beyond man's understanding, the most contradictory theories or beliefs may be equally inadequate approaches to reality. Ecological (as we would say today), it sees man as part of a whole where trees, animals, men and spirits should live in harmony and mutual respect, and it asks everyone to cooperate and not endanger the artwork of the creator. It therefore opposes the destruction of nature, of species, the bastardisation of races, the tendency of each one to do what he was not born for. It leaves every one free to find his own way of realization human and spiritual be it ascetic or erotic or both. It does not separate intellect and body, mind and matter, but sees the Universe as a living continuum. I believe any sensible man is unknowingly a Hindu and that the only hope for man lies in the abolition of the erratic, dogmatic, unphilosophical creeds people today call religions."

Danielou told Harvey that he wants to stress "the fundamental unity of human endeavors to understand the nature of the world and to re-create a love and admiration for what I would call 'the divinity of presence.' " He continued, "All the effort of Indian wisdom has been toward understanding things. The problem of the West is that it wants to change the world without understanding it."

AVOCATIONAL INTERESTS: Painting, playing Western and Indian music.

BIOGRAPHICAL/CRITICAL SOURCES:

PERIODICALS

Interview, January, 1989.

*   *   *

D'ARCY, Margaretta (Ruth) 1934-

PERSONAL: Born in 1934; married John Arden (a playwright), 1957; children: Francis Gwalchmei (deceased), Finn, Adam, Jacob, Neuss.

ADDRESSES: Agent—Margaret Ramsay Ltd., 14a Goodwin's Court, London WC2N 4LL, England.

CAREER: Playwright. Associated with Noman Productions, 1963; co-founder of Corrandulla Arts and Entertainment Club, Corrandulla, Ireland, 1971, artistic director 1973-74; associated with Galway Theatre Workshop, 1975-77; co-founder of Galway Women's Entertainment, 1982, and Women's Sceal Radio, 1986. Member, H-Block/Armagh Action Group, 1980-81.

MEMBER: Writers' Guild of Great Britain, Society of Irish Playwrights, Irish Council of Civil Liberties, Haringey Irish Society, Irish Writers' Union, Aosdana, Irish Nicaragua Solidarity, Anti-Apartheid.

AWARDS, HONORS: Recipient with husband John Arden, award from Arts Council, 1974, for *The Ballygombeen Bequest* and *The Island of the Mighty: A Play on a Traditional British Theme.*

WRITINGS:

PLAYS

(Co-author) "Vietnam War Game" (thirteen-hour marathon), first produced in New York City at New York University, 1967.
(Co-author) "Little Red Riding Hood" (one-act), first produced in London at Haringey, 1971.
(Co-author) "The Henry Dubb Show" (eight-hour marathon), first produced at University of California, Los Angeles, 1973.
"A Pinprick of History" (one-act), first produced in London at the Almost Free Theatre, 1977.
"Irish Women's Voices" (one-act), first produced in London at Women's Space, 1978.
"The Trial and Imprisonment of Countess Markievicz" (one-act), first produced in London at Caxton House, 1979.

PLAYS; WITH HUSBAND, JOHN ARDEN

"The Happy Haven" (two-act; also see below), first produced in Bristol at Bristol University, 1960; produced in London at Royal Court Theatre, September 14, 1960; produced in New York City, 1967.
The Business of Good Government: A Christmas Play (one-act; first produced as "A Christmas Play," in Somerset, England, at Brent Knoll Church of St. Michael, December, 1960; produced in New York City, 1970), Methuen, 1963, reprinted, 1983, Grove, 1967.
Ars Longa, Vita Brevis (one-act; first produced on the West End at Aldwych Theatre by the Royal Shakespeare Co., 1964), Cassell, 1965.
"Friday's Hiding" (one-act; also see below), first produced in London, 1965; produced in Edinburgh at the Lyceum Theatre, 1966.
The Royal Pardon; or, The Soldier Who Became an Actor (first produced in Devon, England, at Beaford Arts Centre, September 1, 1966; produced in London at Arts Theatre, 1967), Methuen, 1967.
(And with Cartoon Archetypical Slogan Theatre) "Harold Muggins Is a Martyr," first produced in London at Unity Theatre Club, June, 1968.
The Hero Rises Up: A Romantic Melodrama (two-act; first produced in London at Round House Theatre, November 6, 1968), Methuen, 1969.
(And with Muswell Hill Street Theatre) "Granny Welfare and the Wolf," first produced in London at Ducketts Common, Turnpike Lane, March, 1971.
(And with Muswell Hill Street Theatre) "My Old Man's a Tory" (one-act), first produced in London at Wood Green, March, 1971.
(And with Socialist Labour League) "Two Hundred Years of Labour History" (two-act), first produced in London at Alexandra Palace, April, 1971.
(And with Writers Against Repression) "Rudi Dutschke Must Stay," first produced in London at British Museum, spring, 1971.
The Ballygombeen Bequest (first produced in Belfast, Northern Ireland, at St. Mary and St. Joseph's College Drama Society, May, 1972; produced in London at Bush Theatre, September 11, 1972), Scripts, 1972.
The Island of the Mighty: A Play on a Traditional British Theme in Three Parts (first produced on the West End at Aldwych Theatre, December 5, 1972), with illustrations by authors, Eyre Methuen, 1974.
(And with Corrandulla Arts Entertainment Club) "The Devil and the Parish Pump" (one-act), first produced in County Galway, Ireland, at Gort Roe, Corrandulla Arts Centre, April, 1974.
The Non-Stop Connolly Show: A Dramatic Cycle of Continuous Struggle in Six Parts (first produced in Dublin at Liberty Hall, March 29, 1975, produced in London at Ambiance Lunch Hour Theatre, May 17, 1976), Pluto, Parts 1 and 2: *Boyhood 1868-1889* [and] *Apprenticeship, 1889-1896,* 1977, Part 3: *Professional, 1896-1903,* Part 4: *The New World, 1903-1910,* Part 5: *The Great Lockout, 1910-1914,* and Part 6: *World War and the Rising, 1914-1916,* 1978.
(And with Galway Theatre Workshop) "The Crown Strike Play" (one-act), first produced in Galway at Eyre Square, December, 1975.
(And with Galway Theatre Workshop) "Sean O'Scrudu," first produced in Galway at Coachman Hotel, February, 1976.
(And with Galway Theatre Workshop) "The Mongrel Fox" (one-act), first produced in Galway at Regional Technical College, October, 1976.

(And with Galway Theatre Workshop) "No Room at the Inn" (one-act), first produced in Galway at Coachman Hotel, December, 1976.

(And with Galway Theatre Workshop) "Silence," first produced in Galway at Eyre Square, April, 1977.

(And with Galway Theatre Workshop) "Mary's Name" (one-act), first produced in Galway at University College, May, 1977.

(And with Galway Theatre Workshop) "Blow-In Chorus for Liam Cosgrave," first produced in Galway at Eyre Square, June, 1977.

Vandaleur's Folly: An Anglo-Irish Melodrama; The Hazard of Experiment in an Irish Co-operative, Ralahine, 1831 (two-act; first produced at Lancaster University, 1978), Eyre Methuen, 1981.

The Little Gray Home in the West: An Anglo-Irish Melodrama, Pluto, 1982.

RADIO/TELEVISION/FILM PRODUCTIONS

(With Arden) "Keep Those People Moving" (radio play), British Broadcasting Corp. (BBC-Radio), 1972.

(With Arden) "Portrait of a Rebel" (television documentary about Sean O'Casey), Radio-Telefis Eireann (Dublin), 1973.

(With Arden) *Whose Is the Kingdom?* (radio play broadcast in nine parts by BBC-Radio, 1988), Methuen, 1988.

Also author of video film "Circus Expose of the New Cultural Church," screened at the Celtic Film Festival, 1987, and of television scripts "When Irish Eyes Are . . . " and "Petrifaction."

OTHER

Three Plays (contains "The Waters of Babylon," "Live Like Pigs," and "The Happy Haven"), introduction by John Russell Taylor, Penguin, 1964, reprinted, 1984, Penguin (Baltimore), 1965.

(With Arden) *To Present the Pretence: Essays on the Theatre and Its Public,* Eyre Methuen, 1977, Holmes & Meier, 1979.

Tell Them Everything: A Sojourn in the Prison of Her Majesty Queen Elizabeth II at Ard Macha (Armagh), Pluto, 1981.

(With Arden) *Awkward Corners* (essays), Methuen, 1988.

Contributor to journals, including *New Statesman* and *Dialog.*

SIDELIGHTS: In the 1950s, Irish actress and playwright Margaretta D'Arcy formed a professional partnership with husband and playwright John Arden, who writes in a *Contemporary Authors Autobiography Series* article: "She was closely involved with the most progressive aspects of the theatre of that time, aspects of which I knew nothing, with my limited Shakespearean provincial orientation and my academic (and indeed pompous) attitude towards the stage. . . . Her name now appears, sometimes first, sometimes second, together with mine, upon a great deal of published work which nonetheless the male critics, managements, publishers, and broadcasters, will insist upon referring to as 'Arden's.' Or, worse, 'the Ardens.' It also appears on work of her own, but this did not appear until after the collaborative pieces."

"Together they moulded the finest interpretation of Irish history ever achieved dramatically," according to Desmond Hogan in a *New Statesman* review of one of their most notable collaborations, *The Non-Stop Connolly Show: A Dramatic Cycle of Continuous Struggle in Six Parts.* A cycle lasting nearly 24 hours, with a huge cast of historical characters, the production traces the life of Irish socialist leader James Connolly from boyhood through the Easter Uprising in 1916, an important and inspiring event in the history of Irish nationalism. Writing of the two traditions in Ireland, "vicious, merciless violence" and pacifism, Desmond Hogan points out in *New Statesmen* that Connolly exemplified neither, but "ultimately opted for a bloody revolution on a minor scale not so much to break from Britain but to let out his own protest against Britain's centuries of manhandling Ireland." The play premiered on the stage of Dublin's Liberty Hall on the evening of March 29, 1975, and, writes Hogan: "Many people attended this vigil, not just socialists and Republicans but young people who had long tired trying to make something out of their history. . . . It finished appropriately about seven in the morning . . . amid a swish of flags, orange and green." Although in a *Dictionary of Literary Biography* essay, Stanley Lourdeaux considers the play "too long and the characters too numerous for viewers to focus exclusively on any one character or action in this complex political tapestry," Hogan suggests that "one feels one is in the presence of great drama and that the drama was made from a cold eye, an eye which like Yeats's, penetrated lies, phobias, images which dressed other images, and came up with—even if only for moments at a stretch—a mind-boggling authenticity."

D'Arcy once told *CA:* "My creative spark is largely derived from my experience of British imperialism in Ireland, and the suffering and bitterness that it causes. I have been twice in jail in Northern Ireland for speaking out against injustices there. I am against state repression, and all other repressions that impede human development and civil liberties, but I express my feeling chiefly through comedy and satire."

BIOGRAPHICAL/CRITICAL SOURCES:

BOOKS

Arden, John, and Margarette D'Arcy, *To Present the Pretence: Essays on the Theatre and Its Public,* Eyre Methuen, 1977.

Contemporary Authors Autobiography Series, Volume 4, Gale, 1986.

Dictionary of Literary Biography, Volume 13: *British Dramatists since World War II,* Gale, 1982.

Itzen, Catherine, *Stages of the Revolution,* Eyre Methuen, 1980.

PERIODICALS

Listener, November 14, 1968.
New Society, January 18, 1979.
New Statesman, April 11, 1980.
Other Stages, spring/summer, 1980.

*　　*　　*

DASH, Joan 1925-

PERSONAL: Born July 18, 1925, in Brooklyn, N.Y.; daughter of Samuel (a lawyer) and Louise (Sachs) Zeiger; married Jay Gregory Dash (a professor of physics), June 23, 1945; children: Michael, Elizabeth, Anthony. *Education:* Barnard College, B.A. (with honors), 1946. *Religion:* Jewish.

ADDRESSES: Home—4542 52nd St. N.E., Seattle, Wash. 98105. *Agent*—Charlotte Gordon, 235 East 22nd St., New York, N.Y. 10010.

CAREER: Writer.

MEMBER: Hadassah, Seattle Free-Lancers, Phi Beta Kappa.

WRITINGS:

A Life of One's Own: Three Gifted Women and the Men They Married, Harper, 1973, published as *A Life of One's Own:*

Margaret Sanger, Edna St. Vincent Millay, Maria Goeppert-Mayer, Paragon House, 1988.

Summoned to Jerusalem: The Life of Henrietta Szold, Harper, 1979.

Contributor of stories and articles to journals.

WORK IN PROGRESS: A nonfiction book for children, for Messner.

BIOGRAPHICAL/CRITICAL SOURCES:

PERIODICALS

Los Angeles Times, February 29, 1980.
New York Times, September 22, 1979.
New York Times Book Review, October 14, 1979.

*　　*　　*

DAVIES, P. C. W.
See DAVIES, Paul (Charles William)

*　　*　　*

DAVIES, Paul (Charles William) 1946-
(P. C. W. Davies)

PERSONAL: Born April 22, 1946, in London, England; son of Hugh and Pearl (Birrel) Davies; married Susan Woodcock, July 27, 1972; children: Caroline, Victoria, Annabel, Charles. *Education:* University College, London, B.Sc. (with first class honors), 1967, Ph.D., 1970.

ADDRESSES: Office—Department of Physics, University of Adelaide, Adelaide, South Australia 5001, Australia.

CAREER: Cambridge University, Cambridge, England, Fellow of the Institute of Theoretical Astronomy, 1970-72; University of London, King's College, London, England, lecturer in mathematics, 1972-80; University of Newcastle-upon-Tyne, Newcastle-upon-Tyne, England, professor of theoretical physics, 1980-90; University of Adelaide, Adelaide, Australia, professor of mathematical physics, 1990—.

MEMBER: Institute of Physics (London; fellow).

WRITINGS:

The Runaway Universe, Harper, 1978 (published in England as *Stardom: A Scientific Account of the Beginning and End of the Universe,* Fontana, 1979.
Other Worlds, Dent, 1980, published as *Other Worlds: A Portrait of Nature in Rebellion, Space, Superspace, and the Quantum Universe,* Simon & Schuster, 1980, published as *Other Worlds: Space, Superspace, and the Quantum Universe,* Simon & Schuster, 1981.
The Edge of Infinity: Beyond Black Holes to the End of the Universe, Dent, 1981, published as *The Edge of Infinity: Where the Universe Came From and How It Will End,* Simon & Schuster, 1982.
God and the New Physics, Simon & Schuster, 1983.
Superforce: The Search for a Grand Unified Theory of Nature, Simon & Schuster, 1984.
Quantum Mechanics, Routledge & Kegan Paul, 1984.
Fireball, Heinemann, 1987.
The Cosmic Blueprint: New Discoveries in Nature's Creative Ability to Order the Universe, Simon & Schuster, 1987.

UNDER NAME P. C. W. DAVIES

The Physics of Time Asymmetry, Universe of California Press, 1974, 2nd edition, 1977.

Space and Time in the Modern Universe, Cambridge University Press, 1977.
The Forces of Nature, Cambridge University Press, 1979, 2nd revised edition, 1986.
The Search for Gravity Waves, Cambridge University Press, 1980.
(With N. D. Birrell) *Quantum Fields in Curved Space,* Cambridge University Press, 1982.
The Accidental Universe, Cambridge University Press, 1982.
(With Julian Brown) *The Ghost in the Atom,* Cambridge University Press, 1986.
(With Brown) *Superstrings: A Theory of Everything?,* Cambridge University Press, 1988.
(Editor) *The New Physics,* Cambridge University Press, 1989.

WORK IN PROGRESS: What Is Man?, to be published by Simon & Schuster.

SIDELIGHTS: Paul Davies has sought in his books to bring the realms of space, time, and physics to the public. As Davies once told *CA,* "In my books I try to communicate to the layperson the sense of excitement and awe which I myself feel when confronted by the challenge of modern physics. Though I may entertain, startle, provoke and perhaps baffle the reader, my primary aim is to share with them some glimpses of nature's dazzling secrets revealed by the power of scientific analysis." In *The Runaway Universe* the author examines cosmology—the science of the universe as a whole—and explores how the universe, space, time, and existence came into being. He introduces the reader to some basic scientific ideas, including relativity and the concept of entropy, and contemplates the fate of an ever-expanding, energy-losing universe. Calling this book "one of the most readable surveys to date," Malcolm Browne of the *New York Times* notes that Davies "suggests some ingenious and mind-boggling ways in which man might prolong his existence a billion billion years after most of the universe has become cold and dead." Davies proposes, for example, that future man might be able to control the energy in black holes, releasing it when other sources of energy have been depleted. "This is a book whose horizons are as distant as man can imagine," Browne claims.

Although Browne commends Davies for introducing his readers to "both the proven and the speculative aspects of the subject," Gerald Jonas of the *New York Times Book Review* objects to "the impression that certain issues have been settled to everyone's satisfaction." The reviewer remains unconvinced that the calculations underlying current scientific cosmology are firmly based and expresses skepticism when calling to mind those existing mysteries of space and physics that cannot be explained by current theories. Jonas writes: "[Davies] is at pains to distinguish fact from speculation. . . . By the very nature of his exposition, however, he cannot do justice to the possibility that current scientific cosmology may be, like the cosmologies of the past, a conceptual house of cards. . . . There is still room for doubt, and humility, in our confrontation with the universe."

In *Other Worlds* Davies describes the revolution in physics and philosophy precipitated by the quantum theory and the theories of relativity. As Richard Dyott notes in his review for the *Chicago Tribune,* these theories subverted the Newtonian concept of man as a cog in a clockwork universe, subject to the same laws of cause and effect that govern all other natural objects. Quantum theory in particular disputes this viewpoint, he explains, because it asserts that the laws of chance control all events. In philosophical terms, the theory returns man to the center of things and suggests that reality is a perception of the human mind, as are past, present, and future. Walter Sullivan observes in the *New York Times* that *Other Worlds* was "almost as much philosophy as science. Like any treatment of subjects so alien to our daily experiences, it is not easy to read, but it opens the mind to vistas normally reserved to those who lean on arcane mathematics to formulate their ideas." And Dyott holds that Davies "manages to cope lucidly with such concepts as super space, the beginning of the world, and black holes—all without mathematical formula. . . . This is surely a book to be read not only for information's sake, but also for the sense of achievement of man's attempts to understand the universe."

Continuing his efforts to explain the complexities of the universe to the lay reader, Davies's sixth book, *Superforce: The Search for the Grand Unified Theory of Nature,* discusses science's endeavors to tie together the laws of physics "with a clarity and imagination that come from a true understanding of the material," according to *New York Times Book Review* contributor David N. Schramm. Colin A. Ronan remarks in the *Times Literary Supplement* that "in spite of some minor historical slips, *Superforce* is a magnificent exposition of modern particle physics and its hunt for the unity of nature." But as in *Other Worlds,* Davies does not restrict himself solely to physics, says Ronan, who notes that "the author is not afraid to raise, in a provocative last chapter, the question of whether, perhaps, some vast cosmic plan underpins the whole of creation."

Davies goes into more detail about his philosophy in *God and the New Physics* and *The Cosmic Blueprint: New Discoveries in Nature's Creative Ability to Order the Universe.* Asserting in *God and the New Physics* that "science offers a surer path to God than religion," Davies "tries to cover all possible sources of faith in God's existence in light of the 'new physics' of [Albert] Einstein, [Niels] Bohr, and [Stephen] Hawkings and others trying to assemble a 'unified' theory of the universe," says *Washington Post Book World* critic John Tirman. However, Tirman concludes, "Davies' effort is bound to fail, despite [the author's] eloquence, knowledge and winsome faith in science. The 'new physics' simply does not answer the basic puzzles of existence." Other critics like *New York Times Book Review* writer Timothy Ferris reproach Davies because his "insights into religion seldom plumb very deep." Because Davies's background is more firmly rooted in science than religion, Brian Pippard also avers in the *Times Literary Supplement* that in *God and the New Physics* the author "might have done better to stick more closely to physics since neither theology nor popular religion has much in common with the sort of arguments he deploys."

In *The Cosmic Blueprint* Davies argues that there exist as yet undiscovered laws of physics which will ultimately explain that the universe is actually self-organizing, and that these laws can explain the processes of evolution. "What makes his approach worthy of consideration," writes *Los Angeles Times*'s Lee Dembart, "is that even though it rejects chance as the ultimate explanatory principle of the universe, it does not rely on a creator to explain all that we see around us." *Washington Post Book World* contributor Don Colburn comments: "It's an intriguing theory, provocatively argued, and of course one that cannot be proved or disproved. What is most impressive is that the evidence Davies marshals in its support is scientific, not theological." It is for this knowledge of physics and his ability to lucidly convey the ideas behind scientific theories that many critics have praised Davies's books. "When Mr. Davies settles down to the business of explaining physics," concludes Ferris, "he proves to be one of the most adept science writers on either side of the Atlantic."

BIOGRAPHICAL/CRITICAL SOURCES:

PERIODICALS

Chicago Tribune, June 19, 1980.
Los Angeles Times, March 18, 1988.
Los Angeles Times Book Review, October 6, 1985.
Newsweek, November 12, 1984.
New York Times, January 9, 1979, April 7, 1981.
New York Times Book Review, November 26, 1978, May 3, 1981, April 25, 1982, June 26, 1983, November 20, 1983, December 9, 1984, December 23, 1984, October 20, 1985.
Times Literary Supplement, July 29, 1983, June 21, 1985.
Voice Literary Supplement, April, 1982.
Washington Post Book World, January 3, 1984, May 8, 1988.

*   *   *

DAVIS, Audrey
    See PAINE, Lauran (Bosworth)

*   *   *

DAVIS, Fitzroy   1912-1980

PERSONAL: Born February 27, 1912, in Evanston, Ill.; died of cancer September 30, 1980, in Putnam, Conn.; son of Frank Parker (a patent lawyer) and Edith Amanda (Kelly) Davis. *Education:* Williams College, A.B., 1933; Columbia University, M.A., 1961; studied singing with Carolyn Reilly, 1938-47, Helen Foots Calhoun, 1956-58, and Mina Haker, 1959; studied acting with Lee Strasberg, 1939-41, and Wendell Phillips, 1944-45; studied drawing and painting at Academy of Fine Arts and Art Institute of Chicago. *Politics:* Independent. *Religion:* Protestant.

ADDRESSES: Home—R.F.D. 2, Putnam, Conn. 06260.

CAREER: Actor, 1935-62; writer, beginning 1942; singer, 1962-70; painter. Writer for Metro-Goldwyn-Mayer, Columbia Pictures, and United Artists; actor for Coronet and Britannica studios, and in television specials; appeared at Lincoln Center; host of fifteen-minute interview program, "Backstage with Fitzroy Davis," WBKB Chicago, 1946-47. Worked as stage manager, director, and professional lecturer. Displayed water-colors in one-man shows, 1936, 1940, 1941, 1944. Instructor in speech at St. John's University, 1961-62. Other jobs included importer of maple syrup, salesman, and billing clerk.

MEMBER: Institute for Advanced Studies in the Theatre Arts, American Federation of Television and Radio Artists, Authors League of America, American National Theatre and Academy, American Educational Theatre Association, Midland Authors Society (secretary, 1952-54), Phi Beta Kappa, Arts Club (Chicago), Williams Club (New York City).

WRITINGS:

Quicksilver (novel), Harcourt, 1942, reprinted, Curtiss, 1972.
(Scriptwriter) "Song of Russia," Metro-Goldwyn-Mayer, 1943.
(Scriptwriter with George S. George and Fred Schiller) "The Heat's On," Columbia, 1943.
Through the Doors of Brass, Dodd, 1974.

Also author of a travel book about Egypt and a biography, *Conrad Veidt and the Third Reich;* author of unproduced plays "Little Coquette," "Comrade Baby," with Eugenie Leontovitch, "Curtain Going Up," adapted from a play by Chester Erskine, "Crossfire," and "Silver Fire." Book reviewer on stage, screen, and television for *Chicago Tribune* Sunday book section,

1949-55. Contributor to magazines and newspapers, including *New York Times, Christian Science Monitor, New Yorker,* and *Theatre Arts.*

WORK IN PROGRESS: A sequel to *Through the Doors of Brass;* an autobiography from 1912-1927; a travel book on Argentina.

SIDELIGHTS: Actor, writer, and concert baritone Fitzroy Davis once wrote *CA:* "[I] am not a household name, and tend to avoid the spotlight, eschew paying a press agent and enjoy coming to New York on visits to see shows and hear music and going around totally anonymously, as just Joe Bloke, whereas once I was dying to keep my name in the public eye all the time. At my home in Connecticut, I live very quietly, with my dog, alone, doing all the manual work around the place except the snow plowing."

AVOCATIONAL INTERESTS: Travel, stamp collecting, water color painting.*

*   *   *

DAVIS, Gordon
   See LEVINSON, Leonard

*   *   *

DAWSON, Clay
   See LEVINSON, Leonard

*   *   *

DEAN, Malcolm   1948-

PERSONAL: Born April 29, 1948, in Newcastle, England; son of Thomas Craig and Mildred Catharine (Hoggard) Dean. *Education:* Sheridan College, Oakville, Ontario, Canada, graduate.

ADDRESSES: Office—P.O. Box 6299, Toronto, Ontario, Canada M5W 1P7.

CAREER: Publisher, writer, office automation consultant, composer, poet, and filmmaker, 1967—. Canadian Broadcasting Corp. (CBC), Toronto, Ontario, junior news editor for National Radio News Service, 1975; Canadian Press, Toronto, news editor for "Broadcast News," 1975-76; CBC-Radio, Toronto, freelance documentarist, 1977-79; Laidler Radio Productions, Toronto, executive producer, 1979-80; Hudsmith & Dean Productions, Toronto, partner, 1980—; Infodyne Corporation, Toronto, president, 1984—.

AWARDS, HONORS: Creativity award, North York Board of Education, 1967, for "Concerto for Tuba."

WRITINGS:

"Helen" (film), North York Board of Education, 1967.
"Christopher's Movie Matinee" (film), National Film Board, 1968.
"The Pyramids" (radio documentary), Canadian Broadcasting Corp. (CBC-FM Radio), 1978.
"The Book of the Dead" (radio documentary), CBC-FM Radio, 1978.
"Ancient Egypt" (three-part record album), CBC-FM Radio, 1978
"Astrology: The Cosmic Conspiracy" (five-part record album), CBC-FM Radio, 1979.
"Astrocartography" (audio documentary), Astro-Carto-Graphy, 1980.
(Editor) James Neely and Eric Tarkington, *Ephemeris of Chiron, 1890-2000* (monograph series), Phenomena Publications, 1980, 2nd edition, 1982.

The Astrology Game, Beaufort Books, 1980.
Censored!: Only in Canada, Virgo Press, 1981.
Diet Strategy, Bantam, 1982.
Word Processing Systems, BISI (Toronto), 1985.
Electronic Typewriters, BISI, 1985.

Also author, with Philip Hudsmith, of screenplays "The Reluctant Matador," 1985, and "Blitz in Europe." Contributor to *Rights and Freedoms.* Editor, *Phenomena: The Newsjournal of Cosmic Influence Research,* 1977-79.

WORK IN PROGRESS: Several films and books.

SIDELIGHTS: Malcolm Dean once told *CA:* "All creatures seek to end their suffering. The status quo is neither necessary nor desirable. Therefore, I explore areas of forbidden, suppressed, or denied knowledge in order to shed light on the nature of the universe. Too few stones have been turned over; people are tripping over boulders all the time without realizing they have stubbed their toes.

"*The Astrology Game* contains the only published and complete bibliography of thirty years of statistical evidence accumulated in favor of planetary influences by the French psychologists Michel and Francoise Gauquelin. *Censored!: Only in Canada* is the first fully documented history of Canadian film censorship; it includes capsule histories of U.S. and British film censorship as well."

BIOGRAPHICAL/CRITICAL SOURCES:

Globe and Mail (Toronto), November 22, 1980.

Jersey Journal, May 4, 1981.

NOW, October 29, 1981.

Toronto Star, November 23, 1980, March 15, 1981.

Vancouver Province, January 4, 1981.

Vancouver Sun, February 6, 1981.*

*   *   *

de BRISSAC, Malcolm
   See DICKINSON, Peter (Malcolm)

*   *   *

DEBUS, Allen G(eorge)   1926-

PERSONAL: Born August 16, 1926, in Chicago, Ill.; son of George Walter William (a manufacturer) and Edna Pauline (Schwenneke) Debus; married Brunilda Lopez-Rodriguez, August 25, 1951; children: Allen Anthony George, Richard William, Karl Edward. *Education:* Northwestern University, B.S., 1947; Indiana University, A.M., 1949, additional study, 1950-51; University College, London, graduate study, 1959-60; Harvard University, Ph.D., 1961.

ADDRESSES: Home—Deerfield, Ill. *Office*—Social Sciences 209, University of Chicago, 1126 East 59th St., Chicago, Ill. 60637.

CAREER: Abbott Laboratories, North Chicago, Ill., research and development chemist, 1951-56; University of Chicago, Chicago, Ill., assistant professor, 1961-65, associate professor, 1965-68, professor of the history of science, 1968-78, Morris Fishbein Professor of the History of Science and Medicine, 1978—, director of Morris Fishbein Center for the Study of the History of Science and Medicine, 1971-77. Visiting distinguished professor, Arizona Center for Medieval and Renaissance Studies, 1984. Member of Institute for Advanced Study, Princeton, 1972-73. Member of international advisory, Institute for the History of Science and Ideas, Tel-Aviv University, and Center for the History of Science and Philosophy, Hebrew University of Jerusalem. Holder of chemical patents.

MEMBER: Internationale Paracelsus Gesellschaft, Academie Internationale d'Histoire des Sciences (corresponding member), Societe Internationale d'Histoire de la Medicine, History of Science Society (member of council, 1962-65, 1987-89; program chairman, 1972), American Institute of the History of Pharmacy, American Chemical Society (associate; member of executive committee, History of Chemistry Division, 1969-72), American Association for the Advancement of Science (fellow; chairman of electorate nominating committee, Section L, 1974), American Association for the History of Medicine, British Society for the History of Science, Society for the Study of Alchemy and Early Chemistry (member of council, 1967—), Midwest Junto for the History of Science (president, 1983-84), Society of Medical History of Chicago (member of council, 1969-77; secretary-treasurer, 1971-72; vice-president, 1972-74; president, 1974-76).

AWARDS, HONORS: Research grants from American Philosophical Society, 1961-62, National Science Foundation, 1961-63, 1971-74, National Institutes of Health, 1962-70, and American Council of Learned Societies, 1966, 1974-75, 1977-78; Social Science Research Council and Fulbright fellow in England, 1959-60; Guggenheim fellow, 1966-67; overseas fellow, Churchill College, Cambridge University, 1966-67, 1969; National Endowment for the Humanities fellow at Newberry Library, 1975-76, fellow at Folger Shakespeare Library, 1987; Edward Kremers Award, American Institute of the History of Pharmacy, 1978; Pfizer Book Award, History of Science Society, 1978, for *The Chemical Philosophy;* fellow, Institute for Research in the Humanities, University of Wisconsin—Madison, 1981-82; honorary D.Sc., Catholic University of Louvain, 1985; Dexter Award, Division of the History of Chemistry, American Chemical Society, 1987.

WRITINGS:

The English Paracelsians, Oldbourne, 1965, F. Watts, 1966.
(With Robert P. Multhauf) *Alchemy and Chemistry in the Seventeenth Century,* William Andrews Clark Memorial Library, 1966.
(Author of introduction) Elias Ashmole, *Theatrum Chemicum Britannicum,* Johnson Reprint, 1967.
The Chemical Dream of the Renaissance (lecture at Churchill College, Cambridge University), Heffer, 1968, Bobbs-Merrill, 1972.
(Editor) *World Who's Who in Science from Antiquity to the Present,* Marquis, 1968.
Science and Education in the Seventeenth Century: The Webster-Ward Debate, American Elsevier, 1970.
(Editor and contributor) *Science, Medicine and Society in the Renaissance: Essays in Honor of Walter Pagel,* two volumes, Neale Watson, 1972.
(With Brian A. L. Rust) *The Complete Entertainment Discography, 1898-1942,* Arlington House, 1973, revised edition, Da Capo Press, 1989.
(Editor and contributor) *Medicine in Seventeenth-Century England,* University of California Press, 1974.
(Author of introduction) John Dee, *The Mathematicall Praeface to the Elements of Geometrie of Euclid of Megara,* Science History Publications, 1975.

The Chemical Philosophy: Paracelsian Science and Medicine in the Sixteenth and Seventeenth Centuries, two volumes, Science History Publications, 1977.
Man and Nature in the Renaissance, Cambridge University Press, 1978.
Robert Fludd and His Philosophical Key, Science History Publications, 1979.
Science and History: A Chemist's Appraisal, University of Coimbra, 1984.
Chemistry, Alchemy and the New Philosophy, 1550-1700, Variorum, 1987.
(Editor with Ingrid Merkel, and contributor) *Hermeticism and the Renaissance: Intellectual History and the Occult in Early Modern Europe,* Folger Books, 1988.

Editor, "History of Science and Medicine" series, University of Chicago Press. Annotator of three-record set, "Music of Victor Herbert," Smithsonian Institution, 1979. Contributor of about one hundred articles to professional journals.

WORK IN PROGRESS: The French Paracelsians: The Chemical Challenge to Medical and Scientific Tradition in Early Modern France, for Cambridge University Press.

SIDELIGHTS: Man and Nature in the Renaissance has been translated into Italian, Spanish, Japanese, and Chinese.

*   *   *

DELANEY, Franey
   See O'HARA, John (Henry)

*   *   *

De MILLE, Nelson
   See LEVINSON, Leonard

*   *   *

DENKER, Henry 1912-

PERSONAL: Born November 25, 1912, in New York, N.Y.; son of Max (a fur manufacturer) and Jennie (Geller) Denker; married Edith Rose Heckman, December 5, 1942. *Education:* New York University, LL.B., 1934. *Politics:* Liberal Democrat. *Religion:* Jewish.

ADDRESSES: Home—241 Central Park West, New York, N.Y. 10024. *Agent*—Mitch Douglas, International Creative Management, 40 West 57th St., New York, N.Y. 10019.

CAREER: Admitted to the Bar of New York State, 1935; practiced law in New York City, 1935-58; Research Institute of America, New York City, executive, 1938-40; Standard Statistics, New York City, tax consultant, 1940-42; novelist and writer for radio, television, stage and screen, 1947—. Drama instructor, American Theatre Wing, 1961-63, College of the Desert, 1970.

MEMBER: Dramatists Guild (member of council, 1967-70), Authors Guild, Authors League of America (member of council), Academy of Television Arts and Sciences (member of council, 1967-70), Writers Guild East.

AWARDS, HONORS: Peabody Award, Christopher Award, *Variety* Showmanship Award, and Brotherhood Award of National Conference of Christians and Jews, all for radio series "The Greatest Story Ever Told"; Ohio State Award.

WRITINGS:

I'll Be Right Home, Ma, Crowell, 1949.

My Son, the Lawyer, Crowell, 1950.

Salome, Princess of Galilee, Crowell, 1952.

That First Easter, illustrations by Ezra Jack Keats, Crowell, 1959.

The Director, R. W. Baron, 1970.

The Kingmaker, McKay, 1972.

A Place for the Mighty: A Novel about the Superlawyers, McKay, 1973.

The Physicians: A Novel of Malpractice, Simon & Schuster, 1974.

The Experiment, Simon & Schuster, 1975.

The Starmaker, Simon & Schuster, 1977.

The Scofield Diagnosis, Simon & Schuster, 1977.

The Actress, Simon & Schuster, 1978.

Error of Judgment, Simon & Schuster, 1979.

Horowitz and Mrs. Washington (also see below), Putnam, 1979.

The Warfield Syndrome, Putnam, 1980.

Outrage (also see below), Morrow, 1982.

The Healers, Morrow, 1983.

Kincaid, Morrow, 1984.

Robert, My Son, Morrow, 1985.

Judge Spencer Dissents, Morrow, 1986.

The Choice, Morrow, 1987.

The Retreat, Morrow, 1988.

A Gift of Life, Morrow, 1989.

Payment in Full, Morrow, 1990.

PLAYS

(With Ralph Berkey) *Time Limit* (first produced on Broadway at Booth Theatre, January 24, 1956; also see below), French, 1956, typescript entitled *Valour Will Weep,* [New York], 1956.

"Olive Oglivie," first produced on West End at Aldwych Theatre, March 12, 1957.

A Far Country (three-act; first produced on Broadway at Music Box Theatre, April 4, 1961), Random House, 1961.

"Venus at Large," first produced on Broadway at Morosco Theatre, April 12, 1962.

A Case of Libel (three act; based on *My Life in Court* by Louis Nizer; first produced on Broadway at Longacre Theatre, October 10, 1963), Random House, 1964.

"A Sound of Distant Thunder," first produced in Paramus, N.J., at Paramus Playhouse, 1967.

What Did We Do Wrong? (two-act comedy; first produced on Broadway at Helen Hayes Theatre, October 22, 1967), French, 1967.

"The Headhunters," first produced in New Hope, Pennsylvania, at Bucks County Playhouse, September, 1971.

The Second Time Around (three-act comedy; first produced on Broadway at Morosco Theatre, 1976), S. French, 1977.

Horowitz and Mrs. Washington (two-act comedy based on his novel; produced on Broadway at Golden Theatre, 1980), S. French, 1980.

"Outrage" (based on his novel), produced in Washington, D.C., at The Kennedy Center, 1983.

Also author of plays "Judge Spencer Dissents" and "Tea with Madame Bernhardt."

SCREENPLAYS

"Time Limit!" (based on his play), United Artists, 1957.

"The Hook" (based on a novel by Vahe Katcha), Metro-Goldwyn-Mayer, 1962.

"Twilight of Honor" (based on a novel by Al Dewlen), Metro-Goldwyn-Mayer, 1963.

TELEVISION AND RADIO SCRIPTS

"Laughter for the Leader" (radio play), broadcast on "Columbia Workshop," Columbia Broadcasting System (CBS), 1940.

"Me? I Drive a Hack" (radio play), broadcast on "Columbia Workshop," CBS, 1941.

"Radio Reader's Digest," CBS, 1943-46.

(And producer/director) "The Greatest Story Ever Told" (radio plays), American Broadcasting Co. (ABC), 1947-57.

The Wound Within (three-act television play broadcast on "U.S. Steel Hour," CBS, September 10, 1958), Batten, Barton, Durstine & Osborn, Inc., 1958.

"*Give Us Barabbas.*" (television play broadcast on "Hallmark Hall of Fame," National Broadcasting Corp. [NBC], March, 1961), Compass Productions, 1961.

"A Case of Libel" (television play based on his play), ABC, February, 1969.

"The Choice" (television play), broadcast on "Prudential On-stage," NBC, March, 1969.

"The Man Who Wanted to Live Forever," broadcast on "Movie of the Week," ABC, December, 1969.

"First Easter," broadcast on "Hallmark Hall of Fame," NBC, March, 1970.

"The Heart Farm," broadcast on "Movie of the Week," ABC, March, 1971.

"The Court Martial of Lieutenant Calley" (television play), ABC, 1975.

"A Time for Miracles" (television play), ABC, 1980.

WORK IN PROGRESS: "HeadMistress," a screenplay; and "Follow My Lead," a television play.

SIDELIGHTS: Novelist and playwright Henry Denker once told *CA* that he "found two areas of early education of enormous value in later writing. Early religious education with a view toward becoming a rabbi turned out to be of enormous importance in working on 'The Greatest Story Ever Told' and the other religious books and TV specials I have done. Also legal training and experience turned out to be of great help in doing *A Case of Libel,* 'Twilight of Honor,' and *The Adversaries.* In each instance, the work concerned a trial and much highly technical legal knowledge was required. For the rest, reading of periodicals provides a varied source of ideas. And research on a topic once selected seems to provide information for yet other subjects."

In recent years, Denker has addressed the issues of race relations in "Horowitz and Mrs. Washington," and the criminal justice system in "Outrage." Both stories began as novels, then were adapted for the stage. In "Horowitz and Mrs. Washington," Horowitz, an elderly Jewish man who has been mugged and suffered a stroke, forms an uneasy alliance with his black nurse, Mrs. Washington. As the author explains in a *Los Angeles Times* article, the idea for the play came from his years observing in New York's Central Park "the same sight: an elderly Jewish man either with a walker or in a chair and a black woman taking care of him. Having witnessed that scene for so many years, I thought, 'There must be a story beyond that hour that they spend in the park.' So this is about the relationship of two people, totally mismatched." Denker drew on his years as a practicing lawyer for "Outrage," the story of a man's quest for justice. After his daughter has been raped and killed, and the convicted criminal released on a technicality, the protagonist, Dennis Riordan, tracks down and kills the rapist/murderer. After Riordan turns himself in to the police, he finds himself at the center of a heated trial of his own. Though not based on a real case, the legal proceedings involved in "Outrage" are totally accurate, according to the author in a *Washington Post* interview with Megan Rosenfeld. "I've been concerned about what I call an unfair administration of justice for several years," Denker tells Rosenfeld. "It's great for legal scholars to sit around and debate the issues, but I'm worried about the people. Something has to be done before it's too late for the courts to reform themselves." Denker added that "writing is a hobby as well as a profession and one is never at ease when not engaged in writing on some work. As a result the tendency is to work seven days a week when engaged in a long project such as a novel or a play. Days of the week lose their relevance and it is actually a struggle to interrupt the work for any save the gravest of reasons."

AVOCATIONAL INTERESTS: Travel and tennis.

BIOGRAPHICAL/CRITICAL SOURCES:

PERIODICALS

Los Angeles Times, March 6, 1988.
Washington Post, December 12, 1982.

*   *   *

DENTON, Jeremiah A(ndrew), Jr. 1924-

PERSONAL: Born July 15, 1924, in Mobile, Ala.; son of Jeremiah Andrew (a businessman) and Irene Claudia (Steele) Denton; married Kathryn Jane Maury, June 6, 1946; children: Jeremiah Andrew III, Donald, James, William, Madeleine, Michael, Mary Elizabeth. *Education:* Attended Spring Hill College, 1942-43; U.S. Naval Academy, B.S., 1947; attended Armed Forces Staff College, 1958-59, and Naval War College, 1963; George Washington University, M.A., 1964. *Religion:* Roman Catholic.

ADDRESSES: Home—Route 1, Box 305, Theodore, Ala. 36582.

CAREER: U.S. Navy, career officer, 1946-77, retired as rear admiral, officer on U.S.S. *Valley Forge,* 1946-47, involved in the testing, evaluation, and flying of airships, 1948-52, and airborne early warning aircraft, 1952-56, attack carrier air wing operations officer, prospective commanding officer, and attack aircraft pilot on U.S.S. *Independence,* 1964-65, prisoner of war in North Vietnam, 1965-73, commandant of Armed Forces Staff College, Norfolk, Va., 1974-77; Spring Hill College, Mobile, Ala., executive assistant to the president, 1977-80; U.S. Senator from Alabama, 1981-87. Sol Feinstone Lecturer, U.S. Military Academy, 1975; consultant, Christian Broadcasting Network, 1978-80. Member of board of regents, Spring Hill College.

MEMBER: National Forum Foundation (founder; formerly Coalition for Decency), Reserve Officers Association (honorary life member), Veterans of Foreign Wars, Catholic War Veterans, Ends of the Earth Society, Knights of Columbus, Knights of Malta, Rotary International.

AWARDS, HONORS: Military—Navy Cross, Navy Commendation Medal, Distinguished Service Medal, three Silver Stars, Distinguished Flying Cross, five Bronze Stars, two Air Medals, two Purple Hearts. Civilian—D.H.L., Spring Hill College, 1973; John Paul Jones Award, Navy League, 1973; Court of Honor Award, Alabama National Exchange Club, 1973; honored by a resolution of the State Legislature of Alabama, 1973; Silver Medal from Pope Paul VI in private audience, 1974; Valley Forge Freedoms Foundation awards, 1974 and 1976; Armed Forces Award, Veterans of Foreign Wars, 1974; For God and Country Award, Capitol Hill First Friday Club, 1974; Celtic Cross Award, Catholic War Veterans, 1974; Cross of Military Service, United Daughters of the Confederacy, 1975; Douglas MacArthur Meritorious Service Award, Norfolk chapter, Association of the U.S. Army, 1977; H.H.D., St. Leo's College; LL.D., Troy State University.

WRITINGS:

(With Ed Brandt) *When Hell Was in Session,* Readers Digest Press, 1976.
(With others) *Great Issues 81: A Forum on Important Questions Facing the American Public,* Troy State University, 1981.

Contributor to *Columbia* (magazine).

WORK IN PROGRESS: A book, proposed title either *Thy Kingdom Come* or *One Nation under God.*

SIDELIGHTS: In February of 1973, Jeremiah A. Denton, Jr., disembarked from a plane at Clark Air Force Base in the Philippines, becoming the first American prisoner of war released by the North Vietnamese. His seven-and-one-half year term as a P.O.W., recounted in his memoir *When Hell Was in Session,* included torture and solitary confinement; nevertheless Denton, the ranking officer at his prison compound, was able to develop a program of organized resistance for the prisoners to follow. "I tried to put out involved orders saying that you should die before giving the enemy classified information," Denton told the *New York Times.* The prisoners forced the North Vietnamese "to be brutal to us. And this policy was successful in that the consequent exposure to their brutality ultimately caused United States public and official pressure to bear so heavily on our captors that treatment was eventually improved and meanwhile our honor was preserved." In addition, the Navy captain was able to outwit his captors during a forced confession: blinking his eyes during the videotaping, Denton sent the message "torture" in Morse code. "The story of one man's deep, personal investment in an impersonal war," describes *West Coast Review of Books* contributor Laurence D. Wilson, *When Hell Was in Session* "removes the reader from the abstract and often impersonal strategies of . . . [other war] books, and forces us to look at the substance of casualty, injury, and prisoner of war lists."

Denton found a very different moral atmosphere in the United States after his return, and upon retiring from the Navy he founded the Coalition for Decency (now the National Forum Foundation), a group designed to promote family values and good citizenship, especially among adolescents. As Denton once told *CA,* further books of his will deal with "progress of the United States toward material and social greatness," which he defines as "free enterprise moderated by love of God and neighbor. Both progress and survival are now at risk because in having difficulty coping with an unprecedented national affluence, we are forgetting and abandoning the values by which we have survived and achieved affluence." In 1980, however, Denton decided he could advance his views more effectively as a legislator rather than as an author, and ran for office. His election as Senator from Alabama made him the first Republican to hold that post since the Reconstruction, and he lost no time in expressing his opinion "that America is being destroyed by sexual immorality and Soviet-sponsored political 'disinformation,'" as *Time* writer William A. Henry III describes it. The senator's campaign against what he sees as subversive influences has led to criticism of his anti-Soviet views as "McCarthy-like" and naive. But, Denton told Henry, "I'm going to stand up and take it. By the time I'm finished, the press will take the lead rather than question my McCarthyite characteristics."

MEDIA ADAPTATIONS: When Hell Was in Session was made into a NBC television movie starring Hal Holbrook.

BIOGRAPHICAL/CRITICAL SOURCES:

BOOKS

Denton, Jeremiah A., Jr. and Ed Brandt, *When Hell Was in Session,* Readers Digest Press, 1976.

PERIODICALS

New York Times, February 13, 1973, March 31, 1973, April 30, 1973, April 25, 1981.
Publishers Weekly, September 20, 1976.
Time, June 8, 1981.
Washington Post, December 7, 1980, April 24, 1981.
West Coast Review of Books, January, 1977.*

*   *   *

DeSIANO, Francis P(atrick) 1945-

PERSONAL: Born May 7, 1945, in New York, N.Y.; son of Frank P. and Angelina (Florio) DeSiano. *Education:* St. Paul's College, Washington, D.C., B.A., 1968, M.A., 1972; Boston University, D.Min., 1990.

ADDRESSES: Home—3015 Fourth St. N.E., Washington, D.C. 20017.

CAREER: Entered Congregation of St. Paul (Paulists), ordained Roman Catholic priest, 1972; associate pastor of Roman Catholic church in Portland, Ore., 1972-75; vocation director of Paulist Fathers in New York City, 1975-78; St. Paul the Apostle Church, New York City, pastor, 1978-87. Director, Parish Based Evangelism, 1989—.

AWARDS, HONORS: Honorary diploma from Power Memorial Academy, 1983.

WRITINGS:

Searching for Sense: The Logic of Catholic Belief, Paulist Press, 1975.
Presenting the Catholic Faith, Paulist Press, 1986.

Contributor to periodicals, including *Thomist, Pastoral Life, American Benedictine Review,* and *Catholic World.*

WORK IN PROGRESS: Collecting meditations on the Sunday readings of the Mass, for Paulist Press.

SIDELIGHTS: Francis P. DeSiano commented: "As a Catholic priest working in American society, I consider religion to be a vital subject for modern life. Americans have come to think of religion as a secret, private exercise that has little voice in the public arena of our life. Such a construction not only makes religious practice tend toward the arcane, but also deprives American life of important intellectual and human dialogue.

"No task is more important for a religious writer than to express the reality of the human spirit in deep, cogent and intelligible terms.

"My interests in conversion have grown over the years. The changes that all of us go through in our lives, the deepening of our commitments and insights, provide access to the modern discovery of God and the conversion (and re-conversion) of modern people to God. How such changes happen in our lives, what meanings they betoken, and what possibilities they open for us all fascinate me as a person, a believer and a clergyman.

"My writing has gotten somewhat lighter and cleaner, thanks, I think, to years of pastoral work in New York. My searching for the dominant images of my experience help me grapple with the images of God as God is present in all our experience. So, more than looking for words, I look for images, parables, signs that show rather than words that contain data.

"My current work, evangelization, challenges me to develop what is richest in the Catholic intellectual and religious tradition into new forms of public religious discourse, hopefully free of the abuses often attributed to evangelists in American life (the *Elmer Gantry* syndrome). Such a challenge makes no sense if the evangelists just 'talk to others.' The talking must be two-way. The evangelists must not only preach but also, in great humility, listen."

*   *   *

de TOLEDANO, Ralph
See TOLEDANO, Ralph de

*   *   *

DEVON, John Anthony
See PAYNE, (Pierre Stephen) Robert

*   *   *

DICKINSON, Peter (Malcolm) 1927-
(Malcolm de Brissac)

PERSONAL: Born December 16, 1927, in Livingstone, Northern Rhodesia (now Zambia); son of Richard Sebastian Willoughby (a colonial civil servant) and May Southey (a tomb restorer; maiden name, Lovemore) Dickinson; married Mary Rose Barnard (an artist), April 20, 1953; children: Philippa Lucy Anne, Dorothy Louise, John Geoffrey Hyett, James Christopher Meade. *Education:* Attended Eton College, five years; King's College, Cambridge, B.A., 1951. *Politics:* "Leftish." *Religion:* "Lapsed Anglican."

ADDRESSES: Home—Bramdean Lodge, Bramdean, Alresford, Hants SO24 0JN, England. *Agent*—A. P. Watt, Ltd., 20 John St., London WC1N 2DL, England.

CAREER: Writer of mystery novels and juvenile books. *Punch,* London, England, assistant editor, 1952-69. *Military service:* British Army, 1946-48 ("chaotic period as a conscript").

MEMBER: Crime Writers Association.

AWARDS, HONORS: Crime Writers Association Award for best mystery of the year, 1968, for *The Glass-sided Ants' Nest,* and 1969, for *The Old English Peep Show;* American Library Association Notable Book Award, 1971, for *Emma Tupper's Diary; Guardian* Award, 1977, for *The Blue Hawk; Boston Globe-Horn Book* Award for nonfiction, 1977; Whitbread Award and Library Association Carnegie Medal, both 1979, both for *Tulku; The Flight of Dragons* and *Tulku* were named to the American Library Association's "Best Books for Young Adults 1979" list; Library Association Carnegie Medal, 1982, for "City of Gold"; *Horn Book* nonfiction award for *Chance, Luck, and Destiny.*

WRITINGS:

ADULT MYSTERY NOVELS

The Glass-sided Ants' Nest, Harper, 1968 (published in England as *Skin Deep,* Hodder & Stoughton, 1968).
The Old English Peep Show, Harper, 1969 (published in England as *A Pride of Heroes,* Hodder & Stoughton, 1969, new edition, Mysterious Press, 1988).
The Sinful Stones, Harper, 1970 (published in England as *The Seals,* Hodder & Stoughton, 1970).

Sleep and His Brother, Harper, 1971, reprinted, Pantheon, 1986.
The Lizard in the Cup, Harper, 1972.
The Green Gene, Pantheon, 1973.
The Poison Oracle, Pantheon, 1974.
The Lively Dead, Pantheon, 1975.
King and Joker, Pantheon, 1976.
Walking Dead, Hodder & Stoughton, 1977, Pantheon, 1978.
One Foot in the Grave, Hodder & Stoughton, 1979, Pantheon, 1980.
The Last House-Party, Pantheon, 1982.
Hindsight, Pantheon, 1983.
Death of a Unicorn, Pantheon, 1984.
Skeleton-in-Waiting, Pantheon, 1989.

FOR CHILDREN

The Weathermonger (first novel in trilogy; also see below), Gollancz, 1968, Little, Brown, 1969, reprinted, Delacorte, 1986.
Heartsease (second novel in trilogy; also see below), illustrated by Robert Hales, Little, Brown, 1969, reprinted, Delacorte, 1986.
The Devil's Children (third novel in trilogy; also see below), illustrated by Robert Hales, Little, Brown, 1970, reprinted, Delacorte, 1986.
Emma Tupper's Diary (Junior Literary Guild selection), Little, Brown, 1971, reprinted, Dell, 1988.
The Dancing Bear, illustrated by David Smee, Gollancz, 1972, Little, Brown, 1973, reprinted, Dell, 1988.
The Iron Lion, illustrated by Marc Brown, Little, Brown, 1972.
The Gift, illustrated by Gareth Floyd, Gollancz, 1973, Little, Brown, 1974.
The Changes: A Trilogy (contains *The Weathermonger, Heartsease,* and *The Devil's Children*), Gollancz, 1975.
(Editor) *Presto! Humorous Bits and Pieces,* Hutchinson, 1975.
Chance, Luck and Destiny (miscellany), illustrated by Smee and Victor Ambrus, Gollancz, 1975, Little, Brown, 1976.
The Blue Hawk, illustrated by Smee, Little, Brown, 1976.
Annerton Pit, Little, Brown, 1977.
Tulku, Dutton, 1979.
Hepzibah, illustrated by Sue Porter, Eel Pie (Twickenham, England), 1978, Godine, 1980.
City of Gold and Other Stories from the Old Testament, illustrated by Michael Foreman, Pantheon, 1980.
The Seventh Raven, Dutton, 1981.
Giant Cold, illustrated by Alan E. Cober, Dutton, 1981.
Healer, Gollancz, 1983, Delacorte, 1985.
Mole Hole, Peter Bedrick, 1987.
Merlin Dreams, illustrated by Alan Lee, Chivers Press, 1987, Delacorte, 1988.
A Box of Nothing, illustrated by Ian Newsham, Delacorte, 1988.
Eva, Delacorte, 1989.

OTHER

Mandog (television script), British Broadcasting Co. (BBC-TV), 1972.
The Flight of Dragons, illustrated by Wayne Anderson, Harper, 1979.
A Summer in the Twenties (novel), Pantheon, 1981.
Tefuga: A Novel of Suspense, Bodley Head, 1985, Pantheon, 1986.
Perfect Gallows: A Novel of Suspense, Pantheon, 1987.

SIDELIGHTS: "The only thing we may predict about Peter Dickinson is that his next book will always be unpredictable," concludes a *Junior Bookshelf* reviewer about the Zambian-born English author. Although the article refers to Dickinson's books

for children, the same statement is true about his adult novels. Dickinson's imaginative children's tales and unconventional adult novels have both been praised by critics for their original plots. "Peter Dickinson," says Michael Dirda in the *Washington Post Book World,* "possesses the enviable talent of being able to write all kinds of books equally well. His mystery novels—such as *The Glass-Sided Ants' Nest* and *The Poison Oracle*—have won England's equivalent of the Edgar; his novel, *Tefuga,* earned acclaim for its depiction of whites and blacks in Africa; and his children's fiction has been set, with easy mastery, in both the distant past and near future." Discussing what his writing means to him personally, the author tells *New York Times* contributor Eden Ross Lipson: "I believe the crucial thing for a writer is the ability to make up coherent worlds. I'm like a beachcomber walking along the shores of invention. . . . The imagination is like the sea, full of things you can't see but can possibly harvest and use."

Dickinson's writings encompass many subjects, from Buddhism in Tibet and life in sixth-century Byzantium in his children's books, to the powers of hypnosis and animal/human communication in his mystery novels. Whatever background material does not come readily to hand from present-day facts or history, he creates himself. For example, Dickinson's first stories for children, which are contained in *The Changes: A Trilogy,* depict a modern England in which the Arthurian wizard Merlin has been revived. Under the drugged control of a chemist, Merlin instills an antipathy in the English populace for all technology, thrusting Britain back into the fifth century. *Times Literary Supplement* critic Allen J. Hubin calls the first book in the trilogy, *The Weathermonger,* "surely one of the most original of first novels."

Dickinson's success in creating such imaginative situations is grounded in his ability to add realistic details. "The reader accepts the huge improbabilities," says another *Times Literary Supplement* article, "because they are placed in a setting which is consistent and convincing." Some reviewers like Joanna Hutchinson, however, feel that "the weakness of the trilogy lies in the cause of the Changes" occurring in England. In *Children's Literature in Education,* Hutchinson remarks that *Heartsease* and *The Devil's Children,* the second and third books of the trilogy, "simply ask one to accept the Changes without explanation, and are more successful [than *The Weathermonger*] because of it." Another strength of the later books in the trilogy, according to some critics, is their greater emphasis on characterization. In *The Devil's Children,* Margery Fisher of *Growing Point* observes that in "using the Changes to illustrate the growing-up of a girl, the author has given them an emotional dimension deeper than that of the earlier books."

Besides this unique creation of an atavistic England, Dickinson has also written such original situations for his young audiences as a strange unhistorical Egypt in *The Blue Hawk,* a girl with remarkable healing powers in *The Healer,* a bizarre world called "the Dump," where universes are created out of primordial nothingness in *A Box of Nothing,* and, more recently in *Eva,* a tale in which a girl's personality is transferred into a chimpanzee's mind. Many of the author's works, however, are based on historical fact mixed in with a touch of fancy. The Whitbread Award-winning *Tulku,* for example, is set in China during the Boxer Rebellion. The story traces the adventure of a boy named Theodore, who escapes the destruction of his missionary father's settlement. While fleeing the settlement, he joins an English woman, Mrs. Jones, and her lover, a Chinese poet, who are seeking exotic plants. The travellers then meet a lama who declares that either Theodore or Mrs. Jones's unborn child is the reincarnation of the holy Tulku. Together, Theodore and Mrs. Jones's experiences lead them on widely different physical and spiritual journeys.

"*Tulku* is an exciting, beautifully written adventure story which intelligently illuminates . . . a number of different spiritual perspectives and mystical ideologies," praises Winifred Rosen in the *Washington Post Book World*. Rosen adds that Dickinson's knowledge of the art, architecture, and religion of Tibet help add realism to the story; but it is the fact that "his characters never lose their integrity because each one is affected by what happens in the monastery according to his or her level of spiritual development" which is the most important factor in giving *Tulku* "its ring of truth."

Character is also emphasized in *Healer*, where the protagonist is a sixteen-year-old boy named Barry, who has another id-like personality within him which he calls "Bear." One day he fixes the glasses of a pudgy, precociously serious girl named Pinkie, who is able to cure his migraines just by holding his hands. The tension starts when Pinkie's stepfather cloisters her in the "Foundation of Harmony," a cult which he founded to investigate nonmedical healing, and charges people exorbitant fees for Pinkie's curative powers. In order to save Pinkie, Barry needs to get in touch with his feelings ("Bear"), so that he can confirm his true motivations for rescuing a girl six years younger than himself. Caroline Moorehead believes that "*Healer* works because its characters work." The reviewer continues in her London *Times* article that Pinkie and Barry are more understandable than the adult characters "whose behavior is never wholly explained—but then, in a child's eye, is adult behavior ever wholly explicable? It is precisely this twist which makes *Healer* such a clever book."

Other extraordinary powers play a part in Dickinson's *The Gift*. In this case, young Davy Price has inherited his Welsh ancestors' gift of clairvoyance. Because of this ability, he is able to stop a robbery. But in so doing, he becomes flooded by the demented thoughts of Wolf, "a half-wit out to destroy the Prices," as Jane Abramson describes him in *School Library Journal*. The question for Davy then becomes whether his powers are a gift or a curse. *Gift*, writes Hutchison, "is a story of suspense, mystery and excitement and also one in which character is drawn with great sympathy and understanding. . . . Much of this insight into other people is shown through [Davy's sister] Penny, whose sensitivity to others is a gift too, a gift which the book suggests is of greater value and more reliable than Davy's."

Dickinson often uses similarly extraordinary elements in his mystery novels, such as *Sleep and His Brother* and *One Foot in the Grave*. The former deals with children who suffer from a sleeping sickness which makes them telepathic, and the latter uses the power of hypnosis in its resolution. These two books, along with four others, feature Dickinson's only series character, Inspector James Pibble. Pibble is a middle-aged, self-deprecating, unglamorous detective from New Scotland Yard, whose first appearance in *The Glass-sided Ants' Nest* "established Dickinson as a mystery writer," according to Earl F. Bargainnier in *The Armchair Detective*. The author relates that the creation of such an unheroic detective was due to his desire to create "a detective who was not at all James Bondish, was unsexy, easily browbeaten, intelligent, fallible," quotes Bargainnier. This approach to the detective story has made the Pibble mysteries popular with readers and critics alike. Some reviewers, like *New York Times Book Review* contributor Newgate Callendar, have come to expect that "any book in which James Pibble appears is *ipso facto*, going to be a good book."

One of the main characteristics of Dickinson's mystery novels, remarks Bargainnier, is that they are "playful"; not because of Pibble alone, but rather because "his introspective nature is used as a contrast to his odd cases." In *The Glass-sided Ants' Nest*, for example, Pibble must solve a case involving a New Guinean tribe that has been brought to England by an anthropologist. "Needless to say," notes Bargainnier, "the cultural differences provide a test for Pibble—and many possibilities for Dickinsonian play." *The Old English Peep Show* takes place at a country estate complete with lions that wander around freely and an operable scaffold; and *The Sinful Stones* concerns a cult in the Hebrides from which Pibble must escape with, as Bargainnier describes, "a ninety-year-old winner of the Nobel prize, who is only lucid at four-hour intervals; a drunken nurse; and a teenaged schizophrenic."

Dickinson's last Pibble novel, after which he abandoned the character, is an even more unconventional mystery novel. In *One Foot in the Grave*, the reader meets Pibble, now a retired convalescent home resident, as he is trying to kill himself to avoid encroaching senility. Before committing the act, however, he stumbles upon a murder, and the rest of the novel depicts Pibble as he struggles with his weakening ratiocinative powers to solve the case. Nick B. Williams describes this last Pibble book in the *Los Angeles Times Book Review* as "just possibly a masterpiece of its genre and caviar for the mystery zealot."

For his original use of characterization in the Pibble mysteries, Dickinson has become known to critics as a mystery novelist who is willing to break the mold of ordinary plot devices, a reputation he maintains in his later detective books. "Most crime writers use the detective form as a guideline . . .," states *Voice Literary Supplement* reviewer Geoffrey O'Brien, "Peter Dickinson works his variations on the frame itself." As in his children's stories, this sometimes means creating imaginary backgrounds for his plots. Dickinson's *Green Gene*, for instance, depicts a world in which people of Celtic ancestry have inherited a gene which turns their skin green. The result is that the white population segregates the Celts and revokes their voting rights. Trouble begins when the Celts organize a terrorist group. In *King and Joker*, the author creates a fictive English royal family that descends from Queen Victoria's grandson, The Duke of Clarence. Also present in Dickinson's mysteries, as with his juvenile books, is his capacity to add convincing and relevant detail, as he does in *The Poison Oracle*. For this book, the author has developed an entire society of marsh people whose language and culture Dickinson has worked out in detail. "Dickinson's skill in this area should turn many sf writers green with envy and admiration," opines Richard E. Geis of *Alien Critic*.

Despite their diversity, Dickinson's crime novels maintain several common denominators, Bargainnier believes. "First and foremost," the critic writes, "is that . . . Dickinson is scrupulous in supplying clues and relating *all* apparently unrelated event. Second, . . . [they] combine the comic to some degree with mystification, without ever degenerating into the silly. Third, as with Pibble, Dickinson elaborately delineates the psychology of his protagonists, all of whom are unlikely detectives." The combination of these elements into what *New York Times* reviewer Anatole Broyard calls "avant-garde suspense writing," inspires *Washington Post Book World* contributor Robin W. Winks to label Dickinson as "one of the most interesting—some would say outrageous—talents working over the broad terrain between the 'straight novel' and the murder mystery." Winks continues: "Reviewers invariably pronounce his books highly original, beautifully written, and rightly so."

More recently, the novelist has been gaining recognition for writing period pieces which fall under neither the mystery nor the juvenile literature category. *Tefuga: A Novel of Suspense* is set in both modern times and in 1920s Nigeria, and addresses the issue of British colonization in Africa. Another novel which takes place in the 1920s is *A Summer in the Twenties,* which is centered around a general strike in England. Because of the great range of subjects which the author has chosen for his books and his skill in presenting them, critics like *New York Times Book Review* contributor Georgess McHargue feel that Dickinson is a writer who, "disdaining repetition, . . . has chosen to dazzle and delight his readers of all ages with a rainbow of skills and a carnival of characters from the high serious to the low comic. . . . [With] Peter Dickinson, there are only exceptions and no rule."

BIOGRAPHICAL/CRITICAL SOURCES:

BOOKS

Contemporary Literary Criticism, Gale, Volume 12, 1980, Volume 35, 1985.
Townsend, John Rowe, *Writing for Children: An Outline of English-Language Children's Literature,* revised edition, Lippincott, 1974.
Townsend, John Rowe, *A Sounding of Story-tellers,* Viking Kestrel, 1979.

PERIODICALS

Alien Critic, November, 1974.
Armchair Detective, summer, 1980.
Chicago Tribune Book World, July 19, 1970, January 3, 1988.
Children's Literature in Education, summer, 1975.
Growing Point, July, 1970, March, 1979.
Junior Bookshelf, October, 1983.
Los Angeles Times, November 9, 1983, January 8, 1984, November 23, 1984, June 18, 1988.
Los Angeles Times Book Review, May 18, 1980, May 4, 1986.
New York Times, June 1, 1976, February 15, 1980, October 14, 1983.
New York Times Book Review, May 14, 1972, January 29, 1978, September 16, 1979, April 20, 1980, August 9, 1981, May 6, 1984, May 18, 1984, August 18, 1985, April 20, 1986, January 10, 1988, May 8, 1988.
School Library Journal, October, 1974.
Spectator, May 9, 1981.
Times (London), August 25, 1983.
Times Literary Supplement, March 14, 1968, June 26, 1969, April 28, 1972, April 12, 1976, April 30, 1976, March 25, 1977, November 21, 1980, May 1, 1981, July 24, 1981, June 4, 1982, May 27, 1983, September 30, 1983, May 16, 1986, November 25, 1988.
Voice Literary Supplement, February 23, 1984.
Washington Post, February 9, 1980, June 9, 1986.
Washington Post Book World, May 13, 1979, July 27, 1981, December 18, 1983, May 12, 1985, July 20, 1986, February 21, 1988, February 12, 1989.

—*Sketch by Kevin S. Hile*

*   *   *

DILLARD, J(oey) L(ee) 1924-

PERSONAL: Born June 26, 1924, in Grand Saline, Tex.; son of Marvin L. (a wholsesaler of produce) and Thelma (Aly) Dillard; married Jane Reed Montgomery, December 28, 1958 (divorced, 1961); married Margie Ivey (an editor), December 22, 1972 (died June 7, 1981); married Mary Lord Beasley, April 27, 1985; children: (first marriage) Kenneth Joseph. *Education:* Southern Methodist University, B.A. (with highest honors), 1949, M.A., 1951; University of Texas, Ph.D., 1956. *Politics:* Liberal Democrat. *Religion:* Episcopalian.

ADDRESSES: Home—1637 Jackson Ave., Portsmouth, Ohio 45662.

CAREER: Southern Methodist University, Dallas, Tex., lecturer and instructor in English, 1949-51; Texas College of Arts and Industries (now Texas A & I University), Kingsville, associate professor of English, 1955-59; Inter-American University, San German, Puerto Rico, Teacher of English to Speakers of Other Languages (TESOL) program, director, 1959-60; U.S. Agency for International Development, Yaounde, Cameroon, descriptive linguist, 1963-64; Lamar State College of Technology (now Lamar University), Beaumont, Tex., associate professor of English, 1965-66; Trinity College, Washington, D.C., lecturer in dialectology, 1966-67; Universite Officielle de Bujumbura, Burundi, Fulbright lecturer in TESOL program, 1967-68; Yeshiva University, Ferkauf Graduate School of Humanities and Social Sciences, New York, N.Y., visiting lecturer in linguistics, 1968-71; Northwestern State University of Louisiana, Natchitoches, 1975-89, began as assistant professor, became professor of English. Visiting professor of sociolinguistics, Georgetown University, 1967; visiting professor of English, State University of New York College at Potsdam, summer, 1968; visiting professor of linguistics, University of Southern California, summer, 1969, and Linguistics Institute, University of North Carolina, summer, 1972. Fulbright lecturer, Universidad Central del Ecuador, Quito, Ecuador, 1959-60. Director of urban language study for District of Columbia, 1966-67. *Military service:* U.S. Navy, 1943-45.

MEMBER: American Name Society, Linguistic Society of America, Phi Beta Kappa.

AWARDS, HONORS: American Council of Learned Societies grant, University of Texas, summer, 1960; American Philosophical Society grant, 1987.

WRITINGS:

(With W. P. Lehmann) *The Alliterations of the Edda,* Department of Germanic Languages, University of Texas, 1954.
Afro-American Vehicle and Other Names, Institute of Caribbean Studies, 1965.
(Contributor) E. B. Atwood and A. A. Hill, editors, *Language, Literature, and Culture of the Middle Ages and Later,* University of Texas at Austin, 1969.
(Contributor) John Swed and Norman Whitten, editors, *Afro-American Anthropology: Current Perspectives,* Free Press, 1970.
(Contributor) Dell Hymes, editor, *Pidginization and Creolization of Language,* Cambridge University Press, 1971.
Black English: Its History and Usage in the United States, Random House, 1972.
All-American English, Random House, 1975.
(Editor) *Perspectives on American English,* Mouton, 1980.
American Talk: Where Our Words Came From, Random House, 1976.
Lexicon of Black English, Seabury, 1977.
(Editor) *Perspectives on American English,* Mouton, 1980.
(With Albert Marckwardt) *American English,* Oxford University Press, 1981.
Toward a Social History of American English, De Gruyter, 1985.
(With others) *How to Score with English,* Kendall/Hunt, 1985.

Contributor to *Linguistic-Cultural Differences and American Education,* 1969. Contributor of about thirty articles and reviews to academic journals, including *Language Learning, American Speech, Caribbean Studies, Names,* and *Nueva Revista.*

WORK IN PROGRESS: Research on maritime contact languages, history of American English, for Longman, Ltd., and research on Afro-American language and culture.

* * *

DOBSON, Christopher (Joseph Edward) 1927-

PERSONAL: Born January 14, 1927, in London, England; son of Christopher John (a businessman) and Rose (Payne) Dobson; married Shirley Dear (a golfer); children: Lesley Anne, Christopher, Nicholas, Geraldine. *Education:* Attended Selwyn College, Cambridge. *Politics:* Conservative. *Religion:* Church of England.

ADDRESSES: Home—Edgewood House, Watermill Lane, Bexhill, Sussex, England. *Agent*—Curtis Brown Ltd., 162-168 Regent St., London W1R 5TA, England.

CAREER: Journalist and writer, 1949—. Foreign correspondent in London, England, for *London Daily Mail, London Sunday Telegraph,* and *London Daily Express. Military service:* Royal Air Force and British Army, 1945-48; became lieutenant.

MEMBER: Institute of Journalists.

AWARDS, HONORS: International Journalist of the Year award, 1967.

WRITINGS:

Black September: Its Short, Violent History, Macmillan, 1974.
(With Ronald Payne) *The Carlos Complex: A Study in Terror,* Putnam, 1977, revised edition, Coronet, 1978.
(With Payne) *The Terrorists: Their Weapons, Leaders, and Tactics,* Facts on File, 1979, revised and updated edition, 1982.
(With others) *The Cruelest Night,* Little, Brown, 1980.
(With Payne) *Counterattack: The West's Battle against the Terrorists,* Facts on File, 1982.
(With Payne) *Who's Who in Espionage,* St. Martin's, 1985.
The Day They Almost Bombed Moscow: The Allied War in Russia, 1918-1920, Atheneum, 1986.
(With Payne) *The Never-Ending War: Terrorism in the 80s,* Facts on File, 1987.

Also author of *The Human Jungle* and, with Mohammed Hassenein Heikal, *The Cairo Documents.*

SIDELIGHTS: Christopher Dobson once told *CA:* "I have specialized in covering wars and terrorism, and have become recognized as an authority on terrorism, broadcasting and televising regularly on this subject. But I would rather go fishing."

BIOGRAPHICAL/CRITICAL SOURCES:

PERIODICALS

Los Angeles Times, July 15, 1979.
Los Angeles Times Book Review, August 11, 1985.
Saturday Review, March 15, 1980.
Spectator, December 27, 1975, April 2, 1977.
Times Literary Supplement, October 12, 1984.*

* * *

DODD, Edward
See DODD, Edward Howard, Jr.

DODD, Edward Howard, Jr. 1905-1988
(Edward Dodd; W. M. Hill, a pseudonym)

PERSONAL: Born June 25, 1905, in New York, N.Y.; died of prostate cancer, December 19, 1988, in Putney, Vt.; son of Edward Howard (a publisher) and Mary Elizabeth (Leggett) Dodd; married Roxana Foote Scoville, August 6, 1932 (divorced, 1950); married Camille Oberweiser Gilpatric, October, 1952; children: (first marriage) Louise Armstrong (Mrs. Desmond V. Nicholson), Roxana Foote (Mrs. Ledlie Laughlin), Edward Howard III. *Education:* Yale University, B.A. (cum laude), 1928. *Politics:* Democratic. *Religion:* None.

ADDRESSES: Home—Windmill Hill, Putney, Vt. 05346. *Office*—Dodd, Mead & Co., 79 Madison Ave., New York, N.Y. 10016.

CAREER: After graduation sailed across the Pacific on a small schooner with four Yale classmates, 1928-29; Dodd, Mead & Co., New York, N.Y., worked in shipping room, 1929, book salesman, 1930-35, member of editorial department, 1935-37, head of editorial department, beginning 1937, member of board of directors, beginning 1938, vice-president, 1941, president, 1953-57, chairman of editorial board, 1957-82, chairman of board of directors, 1966-75; retired to write full-time and travel to Polynesia. Trustee, Marlboro School of Music and Putney Grammar School. *Wartime service:* Office of Strategic Services, 1942-45; editor for Research and Analysis Branch, later Mediterranean theater officer. Also served for three years in the New York National Guard, Squadron A, 101st Cavalry.

MEMBER: Elihu Society, Alpha Delta Phi, Century Association and Yale Club (both New York).

WRITINGS:

Great Dipper to Southern Cross: The Cruise of the Schooner "Chance" through the South Seas, Dodd, 1930.
The First Hundred Years: A History of Dodd, Mead & Co., Dodd, 1939.
Of Nature, Time and Teale, Dodd, 1960.
(Under pseudonym W. M. Hill) *Tales of Maui,* Dodd, 1964.
(Under name Edward Dodd) *The Ring of Fire,* Dodd, Volume 1: *Polynesian Art,* 1967, Volume 2: *Polynesian Seafaring,* 1972, Volume 3: *Polynesia's Sacred Isle,* 1976, Volume 4: *The Rape of Tahiti,* 1983.
(Editor under name Edward Dodd) *The Polynesian Journal of Henry Byam Martin,* Peabody Museum of Salem, 1981.
(Under name Edward Dodd) *The Island World of Polynesia: A Survey of the Many Varied Cultures of the Ancient Race,* edited by Dorrit Merton, Windmill Hill, in press.

Contributor to periodicals, including *Publishers Weekly.*

SIDELIGHTS: After graduating from Yale, Edward Howard Dodd, Jr. sailed across the Pacific with several schoolmates. The trip began a life-long fascination with the Pacific—particularly Polynesia—and led Dodd to write several works on Polynesian life and culture. His most renowned was the four-part *The Ring of Fire,* whose volumes combined research with an entertaining narrative; in *Polynesian Art,* for instance, despite "an informal literary style, Dodd makes a serious attempt to improve the art history of this area," remarked *Natural History* contributor Philip Gifford. The result, commented E. S. Dodge in the *New York Times Book Review,* was "not only a good book but the best written book in the primitive-art field yet to appear." Alexander Laing similarly wrote in a *Nation* review of *Polynesian Seafaring* that despite some disorganization, Dodd's work was "probably the most comprehensive source in print of illustrative evidence on the structure of traditional deep-sea craft built in the islands." The critic concluded that "neither as disciplined nor as dull as most of the [works] in this field," *Polynesian Seafaring* was "an exercise in love and imagination."

AVOCATIONAL INTERESTS: Wildflowers, gardening, woodwork.

BIOGRAPHICAL/CRITICAL SOURCES:

PERIODICALS

Nation, September 4, 1972.
Natural History, January, 1968.
New York Times Book Review, October 29, 1967.
Washington Post Book World, August 14, 1983.

OBITUARIES:

PERIODICALS

Los Angeles Times, December 22, 1988.
New York Times, December 21, 1988.*

*   *   *

DOUTY, Norman F(ranklin) 1899-

PERSONAL: Surname is pronounced *Doubt*-y; born January 14, 1899, in Rebersburg, Pa.; son of Robert Ambrose (a lumberman) and Ida A. (Beck) Douty; married Susan L. Colman, March 24, 1947 (died, 1955); married Isabel M. Gray, April 2, 1956. *Education:* Attended Philadelphia School of the Bible, 1919-20; Northern Baptist Theological Seminary, Th.B., 1923.

ADDRESSES: Home—Swengel, Pa. 17880.

CAREER: Ordained minister of the Baptist Church, 1922; pastor in Gilman, Ill., 1921-23, Philadelphia, Pa., 1923-25, and East Lansing, Mich., 1956-57; Grand Rapids Baptist Theological Seminary, Grand Rapids, Mich., president, 1944-45.

WRITINGS:

Has Christ's Return Two Stages?, Pageant, 1956, revised edition published as *The Geat Tribulation Debate,* Gibbs, 1976.
Another Look at Seventh Day Adventism, with Special Reference, Questions on Doctrine, Baker Book, 1962.
The Case of D. M. Canright: Seventh Day Adventist Charges Examined, Baker Book, 1964.
The Douty-Smith and Beck-Price Families, privately printed, 1974.
The Death of Christ: A Treatise Which Answers the Question "Did Christ Die Only for the Elect?," Reiner Publications, 1973, revised edition, Williams & Watrous, 1978.
The Abrahamic Covenant: The Heir of the World, Gibbs, 1984.
Good Reason for Believing, privately printed, 1984.

Also author of pamphlet, *Loving Kindness of the Sovereign God.*

*   *   *

DREXLER, J. F.
See PAINE, Lauran (Bosworth)

*   *   *

DRUCKER, Malka 1945-

PERSONAL: Born March 14, 1945, in Tucson, Ariz.; daughter of William Treiber (a clothing manufacturer) and Francine (a writer; maiden name, Epstein) Chermak; married Steven

Drucker (a certified public accountant), August 20, 1966 (divorced, 1987); children: Ivan, Max. *Education:* University of California, Los Angeles, B.A., 1967; University of Southern California, teaching credential, 1968.

ADDRESSES: Home—1726 Kelton Ave., Los Angeles, Calif. 90024. *Agent*—Andrea Brown, 301 West 53rd St., New York, N.Y. 10019.

CAREER: Writer, 1975—. Teacher at University of Judaism, University of Southern California, and Idyllwild School of Music and Art. Member of board, Idyllwild School of Music and Art.

MEMBER: Society of Children's Book Writers, Association of Jewish Librarians, P.E.N., Beyond Baroque (member of board), California Council on Literature for Children and Young People, Southern California Children's Bookseller's Association.

AWARDS, HONORS: Jewish Book Award nominations, 1982, for *Passover: A Season of Freedom,* and 1984, for *Shabbat: A Peaceful Island;* award for excellence in a series, Southern California Council on Literature for Children and Young People, 1982, for "Jewish Holidays" series; Janusz Korczak Prize in Children's Literature, Anti-Defamation League, 1988, for *Eliezer Ben-Yehuda: The Father of Modern Hebrew.*

WRITINGS:

(With Tom Seaver) *Tom Seaver: Portrait of a Pitcher* (juvenile; a *Sports Illustrated* Book-of-the-Month Club alternate selection), Holiday House, 1978.
The George Foster Story (juvenile), Holiday House, 1979.
(With Elizabeth James) *Series TV: How a Television Show Is Made,* Clarion, 1983.

"JEWISH HOLIDAYS" SERIES

Hanukkah: Eight Nights, Eight Lights, Holiday House, 1980.
Passover: A Season of Freedom, Holiday House, 1981.
Rosh Hashanah and Yom Kippur, Holiday House, 1981.
Sukkot: A Time to Rejoice, Holiday House, 1982.
Shabbat: A Peaceful Island, Holiday House, 1983.
Celebrating Life: Jewish Rites of Passage, Holiday House, 1984.
Frida Kahlo: Her Life and Art, Bantam, 1991.
Jewish Holidays ABC, Harcourt, in press.

OTHER

Also author of *Eliezer Ben-Yehuda: The Father of Modern Hebrew,* Dutton.

SIDELIGHTS: Malka Drucker told *CA* that *Tom Seaver: Portrait of a Pitcher* "was not to be a book about baseball; it was to be about a man who happened to play the game and what the game meant to him." The biography received mixed reviews. While a critic for the *New York Times Book Review* criticized the book as a "fairly flat portrait," the same reviewer also praised it for providing the reader with insights into Seaver's home life and the adjustments required in the lives of the family of a major-league baseball player. A *Booklist* writer described the book as an "exciting sports biography," in which "most of the author's fictionalization is realistic enough not to threaten the book's credibility."

About her writing career, Malka Drucker told *CA:* "When I was fourteen, my pet parakeet died, and I was miserable. I picked up my old diary, long abandoned, and wrote of my grief. The words healed me, and I developed a new respect for the power I possessed with words. Also, both my parents are writers. Can anyone influence me more strongly?

"I like to write about those things that have interested me since childhood; going to baseball games and celebrating Jewish holidays are both vivid, sweet memories for me. When you're a Jewish kid in New York, baseball and religious ceremonies are the most important things in your life, so why not write about them?"

She adds: "I sympathize with the struggle every child has in making sense of the world. I remember my own, and it serves as my creative mine."

BIOGRAPHICAL/CRITICAL SOURCES:

PERIODICALS

Best Sellers, June, 1978.
Booklist, July 1, 1978.
Kirkus Reviews, June 1, 1978.
New York Times Book Review, April 30, 1978.

* * *

DUCHESNE, Antoinette
    See PAINE, Lauran (Bosworth)

* * *

DULIEU, Jean
    See van OORT, Jan

* * *

DUMKE, Glenn S. 1917-1989
    (Jordan Allen, Glenn Pierce)

PERSONAL: Born May 5, 1917, in Green Bay, Wis.; died June 30, 1989; son of William Frederick (a purchasing agent) and Marjorie (Schroeder) Dumke; married Dorothy D. Robison, February 3, 1945. *Education:* Occidental College, B.A., 1938, M.A., 1939; University of California, Los Angeles, Ph.D., 1942.

ADDRESSES: Home—16332 Meadow Ridge Rd., Encino, Calif. 91436.

CAREER: Occidental College, Los Angeles, Calif., instructor, 1940-43, assistant professor, 1943-46, associate professor, 1946-50, professor of history, 1950-51, Norman Bridge Professor of Hispanic American History, 1951-57, dean of faculty, 1950-57; San Francisco State College (now University), San Francisco, Calif., president, 1957-61; California State University System, chancellor, 1962-82, chancellor emeritus, beginning 1982; Institute for Contemporary Studies, San Francisco, president, 1982-86; president, Foundation for the 21st Century, 1986-89. Commissioner of National Commission on Accrediting, 1959-65, 1970-74; chairman of California Council for Economic Education, 1968; chairman of West Interstate Commission for Higher Education, 1976-77; director of Los Angeles World Affairs Council; vice-chancellor for academic affairs of California State Colleges, 1961-62; member of board of trustees of Joint Council on Economic Education and Industry Education Council of California; member of board of trustees of University of Redlands, 1970-79; member of board of directors of American Council on Education, 1967-68; member of executive committee of California Council for the Humanities in Public Policy, 1974-77; member of executive committee of American Friends of Wilton Park; member of founding board of U.S. Air Academy Foundation's Civilian/Military Institute; member of U.S. Department of Education national advisory committee on accreditation and institutional eligibility; member of West Coast advisory board of Institute of International Education.

Past chairman of board of governors of Economic Literacy Council of California; past member of executive committee of Council on Postsecondary Accreditation; past member of board of trustees of KCET-TV; past member of board of directors of Barclay's Bank of California, Olga Co., Farmer's Insurance Group, and Trust Services of America, Inc.; past director of California Chamber of Commerce and of Los Angeles Area Chamber of Commerce, 1974-79.

MEMBER: American Management Association (past member of board of trustees), American Association of State Colleges and Universities, Newcomen Society in North America, California Historical Society, Bohemian Club, California Club, Town Hall Club, Commonwealth Club, Regency Club.

AWARDS, HONORS: Grant from Rockefeller Foundation, 1945; honorary degrees include LL.D. from Occidental College, 1960, University of Bridgeport, 1963, Transylvania College, 1968, Pepperdine College (now University), 1969, Our Lady of the Lake University, 1977, Dickinson State College, 1978, and California State University, 1982, and D.H.L. from University of Redlands, 1962, Hebrew Union College, 1968, and Windham College, 1969; West German Order of Merit, 1965; named educator of the year by Southern California Industry-Education Council, 1967; Officer of British Order of St. John, 1978; Commander of Swedish Royal Order of the North Star, 1979; Medal of Culture from Taiwan's minister of education, 1980; distinguished service award from American Association of State Colleges and Universities, 1982; Bill of Rights Commemoration Committee, 1982; award for individual excellence in education from Freedoms Foundation, 1982; George Washington Medal, 1982.

WRITINGS:

The Boom of the Eighties in Southern California, Huntington Library, 1944.
Mexican Gold Trail: The Journal of a Forty-Niner, Huntington Library, 1945.
(With Osgood Hardy) *A History of the Pacific Area in Modern Times,* Houghton, 1949.
(Editor of revision) Robert G. Cleland, *From Wilderness to Empire: A History of California,* Knopf, 1959.

UNDER PSEUDONYM JORDAN ALLEN

The Condor (novel), Tower, 1980.
Texas Fever (novel), Zebra Books, 1980.
Cavern of Silver (novel), Walker & Co., 1982.

UNDER PSEUDONYM GLENN PIERCE

Tyrant of Bagdad (novel), Little, Brown, 1955.
King's Ransom (novel), Medallion Books, 1986.

OTHER

Contributor of articles and reviews to magazines, including *U.S. News and World Report, Saturday Review, New Generation,* and *Westways.**

* * *

DUNNAHOO, Terry 1927-
    (Margaret Terry)

PERSONAL: Born December 8, 1927, in Fall River, Mass,; daughter of Joseph Alfred (a mill worker) and Emma (a mill worker; maiden name, Dolbec) Janson; married Thomas William Dunnahoo (a cinematographer), September 18, 1954; children: Kim, Sean, Kelly. *Education:* Attended parochial schools in Massachusetts. *Politics:* "I vote for the man—or the woman." *Religion:* Roman Catholic.

ADDRESSES: Home—4061 Tropico Way, Los Angeles, Calif. 90065.

CAREER: Writer. Has worked as a teacher of creative writing in the gifted program, Los Angeles Public Schools, and as an instructor in creative writing and a mentor on the Teacher Advisory Board, UCLA Extension. Lecturer to private groups, writer's conferences, and seminars, colleges, and schools. Consultant to Disney Educational Media Company, Asselin Television Productions, and California Arts Commission.

MEMBER: International PEN (president, Los Angeles Center, 1975-77; member of board of directors), Authors Guild, Authors League of America, Society of Children's Book Writers, California Writer's Club (member of board of directors), Southern California Council on Literature for Children and Young People (member of board of directors), Friends of Children and Libraries (member of board of directors), Women in Film.

AWARDS, HONORS: Southern California Council on Literature for Children and Young People's nonfiction award, 1975, for *Before the Supreme Court: The Story of Belva Ann Lockwood;* Teacher of the Year, UCLA Extension, 1985; Dorothy C. McKenzie Award, 1988, for distinguished contribution to the field of children's literature.

WRITINGS:

Emily Dunning, Reilly & Lee, 1970.
Nellie Bly: A Portrait, Reilly & Lee, 1970.
Annie Sullivan: A Portrait, Reilly & Lee, 1970.
Before the Supreme Court: The Story of Belva Ann Lockwood, Houghton, 1974.
Who Cares about Espie Sanchez?, Dutton, 1976.
This Is Espie Sanchez, Dutton, 1976.
Who Needs Espie Sanchez?, Dutton, 1977.
(Under pseudonym Margaret Terry) *The Last of April,* Bouregy, 1981.
(Under pseudonym Margaret Terry) *Bridge to Tomorrow,* Bouregy, 1983.
Break Dancing, F. Watts, 1985.
How to Write Children's Books, Janson, 1985.
Alaska, F. Watts, 1987.
U.S. Territories, F. Watts, 1988.
How to Win a School Election, F. Watts, 1989.
The Lost Parrots of America, Crestwood, 1989.
The Truth about Pearl Harbor, F. Watts, 1991.

Contributor of reviews to *Los Angeles Herald-Examiner* and *West Coast Review of Books.* Editor, *West Coast Review of Books.*

SIDELIGHTS: Terry Dunnahoo told CA: "When I speak to groups of hopeful writers, whether they are children or adults, I'm asked what my favorite book was when I was a child. I tell them I didn't have a favorite book. My family was so poor we had no books and there was no library where I could get any. The only books I knew or heard about while I was in elementary school were my French, religious books. Then, when I got to high school, I had to work three jobs at the same time to stay in school and had no time to read. One of the jobs was in a sweat shop sewing parts of dresses. I was paid for each seam I sewed and if I didn't work at top speed I couldn't earn enough money to stay in school. Actually, if I didn't work at top speed I would have been fired, and then I definitely couldn't have stayed in school. Still, I felt slaving in a sweat shop was one step above

slaving in a mill, which is where my parents worked. I was the first person in my family to graduate from high school. After that I worked my way through business school and, eventually, worked for an attorney in Fall River and as a civilian for the U.S. Navy on Guam. When I reached the point where I had no more classes and only one job to take up my time, I started reading several books a month. I still don't have a favorite book. I read anything that interests me.

"The other question I often get from children and adults is what and who influenced me to write. No particular incident influenced me. No teacher encouraged me. But when my daughter was thirteen, although she read fiction, she seldom read nonfiction. So I decided to write a biography she would read. That biography was *Nellie Bly.* The book sold to the first editor I sent it to and I was a writer. And, for a while, I couldn't imagine doing anything else. However, now I've branched out in different areas related to writing. I speak at writers' conferences throughout the United States, I teach creative writing, I review books, I do manuscript analysis, and I've become active in writer's organizations.

"Each gives me a feeling of helping others. But none gives me more satisfaction than meeting my audience during lecture tours, especially the young people who take Espie Sanchez, one of my fictional characters, so seriously that they believe she's a real person. One of those people was able to escape from the gang she belonged to, graduate from high school and get a job. My books have influenced other readers in different ways. One became a doctor because she read my book *Emily Dunning.* But the former gang member, who now lives a happy and productive life because of my books about Espie Sanchez, is the perfect example of how strongly writers can change people's lives."

*   *   *

DURHAM, John
   See PAINE, Lauran (Bosworth)

*   *   *

DUTOURD, Jean (Hubert) 1920-

PERSONAL: Born January 14, 1920, in Paris, France; son of Francois and Andree (Haas) Dutourd; married Camille Lemercier, May 22, 1942; children: Frederic, Clara. *Education:* Sorbonne, University of Paris, Ph.D., 1940.

ADDRESSES: Home—c/o Flammarion, 106 rue Petit le Roy, F-94 Chevilly-Larue, BP 403, F-94512 Rungis Cedex, France.

CAREER: Journalist for the daily newspapers, *Liberation, Franc-Tireur,* and *L'Aurore,* all in Paris, France, 1944-47; British Broadcasting Corp. (BBC), London, England, program assistant, 1947-50; Editions Gallimard (publishing house), Paris, editor, 1950-66; film critic for *Carrefour* (weekly film and theatre review), 1954-62; columnist for *La Tribune de Geneve* (daily newspaper), 1955-65; *Candide* (weekly newspaper), television critic, 1962-63, columnist, 1966-67; *France-Soir* (daily newspaper), drama critic, 1963-70, columnist, 1970—. *Military service:* French Army, 1940; fought with French Resistance, 1940-44; twice captured by the Germans and escaped both times; received commander of Merite, Legion d'honneur.

MEMBER: French Writers Union (president, 1958-59), Academie Francaise.

AWARDS, HONORS: Prix Stendahl, 1946, for *Le Complexe de Cesar;* Prix Courteline, 1951, for *Une Tete de chien;* Prix Interallie, 1952, for *Au Bon Beurre;* Prix de Monaco, 1961, for body of work.

WRITINGS:

Le Complexe de Cesar (essays), Laffont, 1945, 10th edition, 1946.

Le Dejeuner du lundi (novel), Laffont, 1947.

L'Arbre, piece en trois journees (three-act play; first produced in Paris at Marigny Theatre, 1956), Gallimard, 1948.

Une Tete de chien (novel; also see below), Gallimard, 1950, translation by Robin Chancellor published as *A Dog's Head,* Lehmann, 1951, Simon & Schuster, 1953.

Le petit Don Juan: Traite de la seduction (essays), Laffont, 1950.

Au Bon Beurre; ou, Scenes de la vie sous l'occupation (novel; also see below), Gallimard, 1952, translation by Chancellor published as *The Best Butter,* Simon & Schuster, 1955 (published in England as *The Milky Way,* Museum Press, 1955).

Doucin, confession (novel; also see below), Gallimard, 1955, translation by Chancellor published as *Five A.M.,* Simon & Schuster, 1956.

Les Taxis de la Marne (autobiographical essays), Gallimard, 1956, translation by Harold King published as *The Taxis of the Marne,* Simon & Schuster, 1957.

Le Fond et la forme: Essai alphabetique sur le morale et sur le style (essays), three volumes, Gallimard, 1958-65.

L'Ame sensible (criticism), Gallimard, 1959, translation by Chancellor published as *The Man of Sensibility,* Simon & Schuster, 1961.

Les Dupes (short stories; includes "Definition de la dupe," "Baba; ou, L' Existence," "Ludwig Schnorr; ou La Marche de l'histoire," "Emtle Tronche; ou, Le Diable et l'athee," and "Andre Breton; ou, L'Anatheme"), Gallimard, 1959.

Les Horreurs de l'amour (novel), Gallimard, 1963, translation by Chancellor published as *The Horrors of Love,* Doubleday, 1967.

La Fin des Peaux-Rouges (stories), Gallimard, 1964, translation by Grace T. Mayes published as *The Last of the Redskins,* Doubleday, 1965.

Le Demi-Solde (memoirs), Gallimard, 1965, reprinted, 1983.

Pluche; ou, l'amour de l'art (novel; also see below), Flammarion, 1967, translation by Chancellor published as *Pluche; or, the Love of Art,* Doubleday, 1970.

Petit journal, 1965-1966 (diary), Julliard, 1969.

L'Ecole des jocrisses (essays), Flammarion, 1970.

Le Paradoxe du critique (critical essay), Flammarion, 1971.

Le Crepuscule des loups (short stories), Flammarion, 1971.

Le Printemps de la vie (novel; also see below), Flammarion, 1972, translation by Denver and Helen Lindley published as *The Springtime of Life,* Doubleday, 1974.

Sept saisons (critical essays; includes "Le Paradoxe du critique" and "Impressions de theatre"), Flammarion, 1972.

Carnet d'un emigre (essays), Flammarion, 1973.

2024 (novel), Gallimard, 1975.

Cinq ans chez les sauvages (novel), Flammarion, 1977.

Mascareigne; ou, la Schema (novel; also see below), Julliard, 1977.

Les Choses comme elles sont: Entretiens avec Jacques Paugam (interviews), Stock, 1978.

Les Matinees de Chaillot, Societe de Production Litteraire, 1978.

Oeuvres romanesques (novel collection; contains *Une Tete de chien, Au Bon Beurre; ou, Scenes de la vie sous l'occupation, Doucin, confession, Pluche; ou, l'amour de l'art, Le Printemps de la vie, Mascareigne; ou, la Schema,* and *Moralites*), Flammarion, 1979.

(With Maurice Schumann) *Discours de reception de M. Jean Dutourd a l'Academie Francaise et reponse de M. Maurice Schumann,* Flammarion, 1980.

Le Bonheur et autres idees, Flammarion, 1980.

Memoires de Mary Watson (novel), Flammarion, 1980.

Un Ami qui vous du bien: Petit manuel a l'usage des auteurs de lettres anonymes (anecdotes and satires), Flammarion, 1981.

De la France consideree comme une maladie (article collection), Flammarion, 1982.

Henri; ou, l'education nationale (novel), Flammarion, 1983.

Le Socialisme a tete de Linotte (essays and lectures), Flammarion, 1983.

Le Septennat des vaches maigres, Flammarion, 1984.

Le Mauvais esprit (interviews), Olivier Orban (Paris), 1985.

La Gauche, la plus bete du monde (political satire), Flammarion, 1985.

Le Spectre de la rose (political satire), Flammarion, 1986.

Le Seminaire de Bordeaux (novel), Flammarion, 1987.

Ca bouge dans le pret a porter, Flammarion, 1989.

EDITOR

Stendahl, Hachette, 1961.

Marie Henri Beyle, *Les plus belles lettres,* Calmann-Levy, 1962.

Antoine Rivarol, *Rivarol,* Mercure de France, 1963.

OTHER

Also author of privately printed critical essays, *La Mort du Chasseur, Hemingway,* 1961, *"Papa" Hemingway,* 1961, and of a pamphlet, *Rivarol, un oracle pour notre epoque,* 1961. Author of columns, "La Tribune de Jean Dutourd," in *La Tribune de Geneve,* 1955-65; "Le Petit Journal de Jean Dutourd," in *Candide,* 1966-67; and "Le Semaine de Jean Dutourd," in *France-Soir,* 1970—. Contributor to numerous French and foreign newspapers, journals, and magazines.

SIDELIGHTS: In the tradition of Voltaire and Honore de Balzac, Jean Dutourd is a French critic, novelist, and satirist who disguises his concerns about society under a cloak of wit and ribald comedy. A decorated soldier who fought with the French Resistance during World War II, Dutourd first gained wide recognition with the satirical novels *A Dog's Head* and *The Best Butter. The Best Butter,* set in post-war France, is a risque account of a family's involvement with the black market in an effort to succeed in the dairy business. While this is a realistic work, *A Dog's Head* is a fantasy about a middle-class Frenchman who is born with the head of a dog. Beneath this story's humorous situation, however, lies "a ferocious commentary on the conduct of the human race," reveals Charles J. Rolo in the *New York Times.* Although the fierceness of Dutourd's fantasy has startled some critics, others like *New York Herald Tribune* contributor P. L. Travers have called *A Dog's Head* "a tiny masterpiece in the French classical tradition."

To some literary reviewers, such as Henry Peyre, *A Dog's Head* and *The Best Butter* represent the author's best work. Nevertheless, Peyre writes in a *Saturday Review* article that a longer Dutourd novel like *The Horrors of Love* still "sparkles with intelligence." The theme of *The Horrors of Love,* Peyre explains, "is the banality and dreariness of adultery." But this story about a politician who has an affair with his secretary is also juxtaposed by a fictional conversation between Dutourd and his friend after the affair has led to murder. Their discussion not only addresses this tragic story, but also touches upon several concerns about society in general. "The commentary of Dutourd and his friend is witty and caustic," writes *New York Times* critic Thomas

Lask, while the story of the two lovers "is dark colored and pathetic." In Lask's opinion, this "is a combination that does not quite go." But a *New Yorker* reviewer feels that *The Horrors of Love* "is a brilliant and provocative excursion through the frontier country between the territories of criticism and fiction."

Other novels by Dutourd, such as *Pluche; or, the Love of Art,* also combine story narrative with insights about the state of contemporary society. In *Pluche* the narrator, who is the title character, is an artist who transfers his energies into writing a diary during a dry spell in his aritistic creativity. Between his commentary about art, money, public tastes, and other subjects, Pluche tells about his conflict with his brother-in-law, whom he feels has sold his artistic soul to paint profitable, artless works that appeal to the masses. "In hands less dexterous than those of Jean Dutourd," asserts a *Time* critic, ". . . Pluche could easily have turned into a one-dimensional poseur, both dated and familiar. Instead, Pluche and his rhetorical posturing melt smoothly into Dutourd's richly perceived Parisian setting and fluent, entertaining narrative."

Dutourd's sense of humor is also evident in his nonfiction works, such as his memoir, *The Taxis of the Marne,* and *The Man of Sensibility,* a book of criticism. "Both in fiction . . . and in nonfiction . . .," avers one *Time* reviewer, Dutourd "has shown himself an accomplished satirical duelist and a sardonic chronicler of French middle-class life." He is, notes Peyre, "one of the few contemporary French writers who . . . still insists upon laughing at life, at others, and even at themselves."

AVOCATIONAL INTERESTS: Painting, fencing (former champion of Paris).

BIOGRAPHICAL/CRITICAL SOURCES:

PERIODICALS

Best Sellers, June 15, 1967, May 1, 1970.
Library Journal, March 1, 1970.
New Yorker, October 14, 1967.
New York Herald Tribune, March 1, 1953.
New York Times, February 15, 1953, October 14, 1967.
New York Times Book Review, May 24, 1970.
Saturday Review, May 27, 1967.
Time, June 9, 1967, April 27, 1970.
Times Literary Supplement, May 14, 1971.

*   *   *

DUTTON, Paul 1943-

PERSONAL: Born December 29, 1943, in Toronto, Ontario, Canada; son of Cuthbert J. (an accountant) and Eileen (Danaher) Dutton. *Education:* Attended University of Western Ontario, 1961-65. *Politics:* None. *Religion:* None.

ADDRESSES: Home—68 Kendal Ave., Apt. 1, Toronto, Ontario, Canada M5R 1L9.

CAREER: Poet; substitute teacher at public schools in Toronto, Ontario, 1967-69; Prentice-Hall of Canada, Toronto, production editor, 1969-71; McClelland & Stewart Ltd., Toronto, copywriter, 1971-78; Holt, Rinehart & Winston of Canada Ltd., Toronto, promotion manager, 1978-82; John Wiley & Sons Canada Ltd., Toronto, marketing manager, 1982-86; full-time writer, musician, and performer, 1986—. Has given poetry readings and performances throughout Canada, Europe, and the United States. Book reviewer for Metro Focus/Rogers Cable Television, 1982-83.

MEMBER: League of Canadian Poets.

WRITINGS:

(With Rafael Barreto-Rivera, Steve McCaffery, and bpNichol; as The Four Horsemen) *Horse d'Oeuvres* (poetry), General Publishing, 1975.
So'Nets (poetry), Ganglia Press, 1976.
The Book of Numbers (poetry and prose), Coach House Press, 1979.
(With Barreto-Rivera, McCaffery, and Nichol; as The Four Horsemen) *A Little Nastiness* (poetry), grOnk, 1980.
(With Barreto-Rivera, McCaffery, and Nichol; as The Four Horsemen) *Schedule for Another Place* (poetry), Booksl-inger, 1981.
(With Barreto-Rivera, McCaffery, and Nichol; as The Four Horsemen) *The Prose Tattoo: Selected Performance Scores,* Membrane Press, 1983.
(With Sandra Braman) *spokesheards* (poetry), Longspoon Press, 1983.
Additives, Imprimerie Dromadaire, 1988.

CONTRIBUTOR TO ANTHOLOGIES

Steve McCaffery and bpNichol, editors, *The Story So Four,* Coach House Press, 1976.
John Robert Colombo, editor, *The Poets of Canada,* Hurtig, 1978.
McCaffery and Nichol, editors, *Sound Poetry: A Catalogue,* Underwhich Editions, 1978.
Dennis Lee, editor, *The New Canadian Poets, 1970-1985,* McClelland & Stewart, 1985.
M. Cochrane and Lee, editors, *Into the Night Life,* Nightwood Editions, 1986.

OTHER

Also author/composer of cassette, "Fugitive Forms," Membrane Press/New Fire Tapes, 1987; also author/composer, with The Four Horsemen, of record albums, including "Canadada," Griffin House, 1973, "Live in the West," Starborne Productions, 1977, and "Blues, Roots, Legends, Shouts and Hollers," Starborne Productions, 1980; also author/composer, with The Four Horsemen, of cassette, "2 Nights/4 Horsemen," Underwhich Editions, 1988. Contributor of poetry, fiction, and essays to periodicals, including *Canadian Forum, Descant, Gryphon, Musicworks, Capilano Review, Open Letter,* and *Rune.*

WORK IN PROGRESS: Visionary Portraits, a serial poem; *Several Women Dancing,* a novel, "ostensibly about a man obsessed with a stripper, but focused on themes of memory, sexual identity, relationships and their psychological components, and the difference between obsession and love"; *Imp's Roves,* an "ongoing sequence of improvised sound patterns"; "Plus One," a cassette of duets with various musicians; *Oblique Motion,* a novel about an idiosyncratic musician who inhabits the various worlds of classical. jazz, rock, and avant-garde musics.

SIDELIGHTS: Paul Dutton told *CA:* "The primary motivation for my writing has been the impulse to create beauty with language and to explore its potential for emotional communication and discovery. I remain fascinated with the richness and ambiguity of words, the secrets of the unconscious that they can reveal, and their ability to lead one to truth. In all of this, sound and rhythm in language are of critical importance to me. I remain constantly aware of the fact that speech is a bodily function, and this has led me to the composition of abstract vocal pieces, such as can be heard on 'Blues, Roots, Legends, Shouts and Hollers,' 'Fugitive Forms,' and in my work with The Four Horsemen. When you consider the vast range of sounds that the human organism is capable of emitting and that the English language avails itself of only forty-five of them, you can understand the impetus to construct nonverbal 'voice poems.' The energizing factor (for performer and audience) adds further appeal to this means of visceral communication.

"A key circumstance in my career has been my work with The Four Horseman [comprising Dutton, Rafael Barreto-Rivera, Steve McCaffery, and bpNichol], which provides an ongoing framework for development of language performance and of more traditional literary expression. My poetry and prose have benefited inestimably from the workshop character of the group's interaction. The Four Horsemen formed in Toronto in 1970 after Barreto-Rivera attended a sound poetry performance by Nichol and McCaffery and expressed a desire 'to jam' with them. I was invited along by Nichol and our first, unrehearsed performance drew an enthusiastic response from the audience and ourselves. Over the years we built a repertoire of poetry performance pieces consisting of or blending abstract vocal expression, chant, verbal and nonverbal voice elements, tonality, atonality, rhythmic and/or arrhythmic structures or nonstructures, and movement, all variously scored or improvised as suited our inclination or inspiration. This work found favor—and often disfavor—with literary, musical, and theatre audiences. At its best it is visceral, dynamic, profound, and entertaining. Its flavor and effect cannot be satisfactorily described or transcribed: it is a poetry of the body and the voice that must be heard and seen to be experienced. The tragically early passing of bpNichol in 1988 means that The Four Horsemen are no more, but the three of us who remain are continuing to perform as 'The Horsemen.'

"Music has always been a powerful force in my life, and it is the musicality of language that remains a persistent preoccupation, both in poetry and prose. If I have learned nothing else from writing, it is that (for me) an unwavering fidelity to the musicality of language leads to clarity of thought, precision of diction, and constantly surprising revelations about self and reality. In addition to my verbal compositions for the printed page, my love of music has contributed to my lasting involvement in the creation of sound poetry (or 'voice poetry,' as I prefer to term my works in the genre). My work in this genre has led to collaborations with individuals in a broad range of art forms: improvisational musicians, composers, dancers, mimes, actors, and—of course—other sound poets. Since 1986 I have undertaken increasing collaborations with musicians, both in duet settings and with established combos and in jazz and free improvisational contexts.

"The art of performance is a major part of my literary career. My readings combine all the elements of my literary foci, comprising poems, prose, and sound pieces (exclusively acoustic, as electronic voice composition currently holds no interest for me). I see none of these as ascendant over another and devote equal energy to them all, both in composition and performance. I read in public regularly and widely. Because I am not a traveler by temperament, my expeditions have always been reading expeditions, and I have toured extensively throughout Canada and the United States for solo readings and performances with The Four Horsemen. The more venturesome of such expeditions have been a tour of England and Wales in the spring of 1984, in conjunction with an appearance at the International Sound Poetry Festival in London, performances in Paris and Amsterdam with The Four Horsemen in 1985, in Amsterdam with the Four Horsemen in 1986, and in Tarascon, France, with The Horsemen in 1988 at the AGRIPPA Fifth International Festival of Contemporary Poetry.

"All art has two primary functions: to explore and manifest the unconscious and to entertain. I have always concurred with Isaac Bashevis Singer's contention that 'the artist is an entertainer, in the highest sense of the word.' While entertainment may appear to be at odds with the exploration and manifestation of the unconscious, it is nonetheless my perception that the successful artist achieves this fusion, whatever the medium worked in and whatever the mood or emotion worked with (and, by the way, however much or not the artist may be conscious of doing so). I believe that this element lifts any artist's work beyond the realm of politics, factions, schools, trends, and fashions, because the work will then touch a common human chord that transcends those ephemeral elements, no matter how much the artist may be personally involved in them."

*　　*　　*

DVORETSKY, Edward 1930-

PERSONAL: Born December 29, 1930, in Houston, Tex.; son of Max (a salesman) and Anna Lea (Greenfield) Dvoretsky; married Charlotte Silversteen, August 1, 1953; children: Toban. *Education:* Rice University, B.A., 1953; Harvard University, M.A., 1954, Ph.D., 1959.

ADDRESSES: Home—2035 Ridgeway Dr., Iowa City, Iowa 52245. *Office*—Department of German, University of Iowa, Iowa City, Iowa 52242.

CAREER: Rice University, Houston, Tex., instructor, 1956-59, assistant professor, 1959-64, associate professor of German, 1964-67; University of Iowa, Iowa City, professor of German, 1967—, chairman of department, 1969-79.

MEMBER: Modern Language Association of America, American Association of Teachers of German, Lessing Society, American Goethe Society, PEN, Midwest Modern Language Association (chairman of German section, 1970-71), Authorenkreis Plesse, Phi Beta Kappa, Delta Phi Alpha.

AWARDS, HONORS: Fulbright fellowship in Germany, 1953, 1958; Old Gold research fellowship, 1968.

WRITINGS:

(Translator and author of introduction) Gotthold Ephriam Lessing, *Emilia Galotti,* Ungar, 1962, Mary S. Rosenberg, 1979.
The Enigma of "Emilia Galotti," Nijhoff, 1963.
The Eighteenth-Century English Translations of "Emilia Galotti," Rice University Press, 1966.
Lessing: Dokumente zur Wirkungsgeschichte, 1755-1968, Kuemmerle, Volume 1, 1971, Volume 2, 1972.
(Translator and author of introduction) Lessing, *Philotas,* Akademischer Verlag, 1981.
Lessing Heute—Beitrage zur Wirkungesgeschichte, Akademischer Verlag, 1981.
Der Teufel und sein Advokat—Gedichte und Prosa, Stoedtner Verlag, 1981.
Tief im Herbstwald, Graphikum, 1983.
(Co-author) *Windfusse—The Feet of the Wind,* Im Verlag Zum Halben Bogen, 1984.
(Co-author) *Im Osten wie im Westen/Both East and West,* Graphikum, 1987.
(Co-author) *Fische, Huehnerschlachtlieder und die Laidenschaften,* Graphikum, 1989.

CONTRIBUTOR

Al'Leu, editor, *Lyrik 82/83,* Edition Leu, 1984.

K. Ruediger, editor, *Jahrbuch deutscher Dichtung,* Der Karlsruher Bote, 1984.

Ruediger, editor, *Der Karlsruher Bote,* Der Karlsruher Bote, 1984.

Joachim Kuehne, *Stumme Zeichen,* Boesche Verlag, 1986.

Werner Manheim, editor, *Carl Heinz Kurz,* Graphikum, 1986.

Friedheim Pichlmaier, *Weit ueber dem Land,* Graphikum, 1987.

C. H. Kurz, *Das grosse Buch der Renga-Dichtung,* Graphikum, 1987.

Margaret Buerschaper, editor, *Traenen im Schweigen,* Graphikum, 1988.

Kurz, editor, *Das dritte Buch der Renga-Dichtung/The Third Book of Renga Poetry,* Graphikum, 1989.

Grete Wassertheuer, *Spuren der Zeit,* Weber, 1989.

Ed Haymes, editor, *Crossings/Kreuzungen,* Camden House, 1990.

Contributor of poetry and translations to anthologies. Contributor of articles, poems, translations, and reviews to language and other journals.

E

EBEL, Suzanne
  See GOODWIN, Suzanne

*   *   *

EBERSOLE, A(lva) V(ernon), Jr. 1919-

PERSONAL: Born June 27, 1919, in Liberal, Kan.; son of Alva V. (a civil servant) and E. Lucia (Cash) Ebersole; married Carmen Iranzo (a writer), September 24, 1949. *Education:* Mexico City College, B.A., 1949, M.A., 1951; University of Kansas, Ph.D., 1957.

ADDRESSES: Home—Calle America, 3, Real de Montroy, Valencia, Spain. *Office*—Department of Romance Languages, University of North Carolina, Chapel Hill, N.C. 27514.

CAREER: Pacific School of Languages, San Diego, Calif., instructor in Spanish, 1951-52; University of Illinois, Urbana, instructor in Spanish, 1957-59; University of Massachusetts—Amherst, assistant professor, 1959-61, associate professor of Spanish, 1961-62; Adelphi University, Garden City, N.Y., professor of Spanish and chairman of department, 1962-68; University of North Carolina at Chapel Hill, professor of Spanish, 1968-85, director of UNC-at-Seville Program, 1973-85, professor emeritus, 1985—. *Military service:* U.S. Marine Corps, 1937-41. U.S. Naval Reserve, 1944-45.

MEMBER: American Association of Teachers of Spanish and Portuguese, Modern Language Association of America, Association Internacional de Hispanistas, American Association of University Professors, Sigma Delta Pi, Pi Delta Phi.

WRITINGS:

El ambiente espanol visto por Juan Ruiz de Alarcon, Castalia, 1959.
(Editor) Calderon de la Barca, *La desdicha de la voz,* Castalia, 1963.
(Editor) Juan Ruiz de Alarcon, *Obras completas,* Castalia, 1966.
(Editor) Guillen de Castro, *El narciso en su opinion,* Taurus, 1968.
Cinco cuentistas contemporaneos, Prentice-Hall, 1969.
Seleccion de comedias del Siglo de Oro espanol, Castalia, 1974.
(Editor) Ruiz de Alarcon, *La verdad sospechosa,* Catedra, 1976.
Disquisiciones sobre el burlador de Seville, Almar, 1978.
Perspectivas de la comedia, II, Albatros, 1980.
Perspectivas de la novela, Albatros, 1981.

Santos Diaz Gonzalez, censor, Albatros, 1983.
Los sainetes de Ramon de la Cruz: Nuevo examen, Albatros, 1983.
La obra teatral de Luciano Francisco Comella, Albatros, 1985.
Dos documentos de 1627 sobre la economia de Espana, Albatros, 1986.
(Editor) Juan Timoneda, *El patranuelo,* Clasicas Albatros, 1987.
(Editor) Francisco de Quevedo, *Sentencias filosoficas,* Clasicos Albatros, 1988.
Sobre arquetipos, simbolos y metateatro, Albatros, 1988.

Contributor to journals. Founder and editor, *Hispanofila,* 1957-87; editor, *Estudios de hispanofila* and *Coleccion Siglo de Oro.*

WORK IN PROGRESS: A revised edition of Juan Ruiz de Alarcon's *Obras completas.*

AVOCATIONAL INTERESTS: Music (presents concerts, with wife, specializing in Spain's Golden Age).

*   *   *

ECKARDT, A(rthur) Roy 1918-

PERSONAL: Born August 8, 1918, in Brooklyn, N.Y.; son of Frederick William (an electrician) and Anna (Fitts) Eckardt; married Alice Lyons (a writer and professor), September 2, 1944; children: Paula Jean, Stephen Robert. *Education:* Brooklyn College (now Brooklyn College of the City University of New York), B.A., 1942; Yale University, M.Div., 1944; Columbia University, Ph.D., 1947. *Politics:* Democrat.

ADDRESSES: Home—Beverly Hill Rd., Box 619A, Coopersburg, Pa. 18036. *Office*—Department of Religion Studies, Maginnes Hall, Lehigh University, Bethlehem, Pa. 18015.

CAREER: Clergyman of United Methodist Church; Hamline University, St. Paul, Minn., assistant professor of philosophy and religion, 1946-47; Lawrence College, Appleton, Wis., assistant professor of religion, 1947-50; Duke University, Durham, N.C., assistant professor of religion, 1950-51; Lehigh University, Bethlehem, Pa., associate professor, 1951-56, professor of religion, beginning 1956, head of department, 1951-80, professor emeritus, 1980—. Visiting professor of Jewish studies, City University of New York, 1973; visiting scholar at the Oxford centre for post-graduate Hebrew studies, 1982-83. Member of board of directors, National Committee on American Foreign Policy; member of international committee, Institute for Contemporary Jewry, Hebrew University of Jerusalem. Special advisor, United States Holocaust Memorial Commission.

MEMBER: American Academy of Religion (president, 1956), Phi Beta Kappa, Pi Gamma Mu.

AWARDS, HONORS: Ford Foundation fellow, Harvard University, 1955-56; Distinguished Alumnus Award, Brooklyn College, 1963; Lilly Foundation fellow, Cambridge University, 1963-64; National Foundation for Jewish Culture fellow, 1968-69; L.H.D., Hebrew Union College—Jewish Institute of Religion, 1969; Rockefeller fellow, University of Tuebingen, 1975-76; Jabotinsky Centennial Medal, 1980; Maxwell Fellow, Centre for Hebrew Studies, Oxford University, 1989-90. Recipient with wife, Alice L. Eckardt: Human Relations Award, American Jewish Committee of Philadelphia, 1971; Myrtle Wreath Achievement Award, Allentown chapter of Hadassah, 1971; Achievement Award, Eastern Pennsylvania Hadassah, 1975.

WRITINGS:

Christianity and the Children of Israel, Kings Crown Press, 1948.
The Surge of Piety in America, Association Press, 1958.
Elder and Younger Brothers: The Encounter of Jews and Christians, Scribner, 1967.
(Editor) *The Theologian at Work,* Harper, 1968.
(With wife, Alice L. Eckardt) *Encounter with Israel: A Challenge to Conscience,* Association Press, 1970.
(Editor) *Christianity in Israel* (booklet), American Academic Association for Peace in the Middle East, 1971.
Your People, My People, Quadrangle, 1974.
(With A. L. Eckardt) *Long Night's Journey into Day,* Wayne State University Press, 1982, revised edition, 1988.
Jews and Christians, Indiana University Press, 1986.
For Righteousness' Sake, Indiana University Press, 1987.
Black-Woman-Jew, Indiana University Press, 1989.

CONTRIBUTOR

Harold E. Fey and Margaret Frakes, editors, *The Christian Century Reader,* Association Press, 1962.
Gregory Baum, editor, *Ecumenical Theology Today,* Paulist Press, 1964.
George A. F. Knight, editor, *Jews and Christians,* Westminster, 1965.
Gerald H. Anderson, editor, *Christian Mission in Theological Perspective,* Abingdon, 1967.
The Anatomy of Peace in the Middle East, American Academic Association for Peace in the Middle East, 1969.
James E. Wood, Jr., editor, *Jewish-Christian Relations in Today's World,* Baylor University Press, 1971.
Harold Hart, editor, *Punishment,* Hart Publishing, 1972.
Alvin H. Rosenfeld and Irving Greenberg, editors, *Confronting the Holocaust,* Indiana University Press, 1978.
Norma H. Thompson and Bruce K. Cole, editors, *The Future of Jewish-Christian Relations,* Character Research, 1982.
Richard W. Rousseau, editor, *Christianity and Judaism,* Ridge Row Press, 1983.

OTHER

Also contributor, with A. L. Eckardt, to *Annals* of the American Academy of Political and Social Science, 1981. Contributor to more than fifteen scholarly journals. Editor, *Journal of American Academy of Religion,* 1961-69.

WORK IN PROGRESS: Christology: Restoring the Jesus of History; Sitting in the Earth and Laughing: The Sense and Nonsense of Humor.

SIDELIGHTS: A. Roy Eckardt told *CA:* "Reinhold Niebuhr has had a profound influence on my thought and theological viewpoint. He brought together an understanding of human nature in the individual and society with a keen perception of how political and social institutions must be devised to protect and foster both."

BIOGRAPHICAL/CRITICAL SOURCES:

BOOKS

Davies, Alan, *Anti-Semitism and the Christian Mind,* Herder & Herder, 1964.
Talmage, Frank E., *Disputation and Dialogue,* Ktav, 1975.

PERIODICALS

Christian Century, April 24, 1968, March 10, 1971.
Commentary, June, 1968.
New York Times Book Review, April 7, 1968.
Western Humanities Review, summer, 1968.

* * *

EDWARDS, Josh
See LEVINSON, Leonard

* * *

EFIRD, James M(ichael) 1932-

PERSONAL: Born May 30, 1932, in Kannapolis, N.C.; son of James R. (in textiles) and I. Z. (Christy) Efird; married Joan Shelf, June 30, 1951 (divorced November, 1971); married Vivian Poythress, March 7, 1975; children: (first marriage) Whitney Michelle. *Education:* Davidson College, A.B., 1954; Louisville Presbyterian Seminary, B.D., 1958; Duke University, Ph.D., 1962. *Religion:* Presbyterian.

Home—2609 Heather Glen Rd., Durham, N.C. 27712. *Office*—Duke University Divinity School, Durham, N.C. 27706.

CAREER: Ordained minister of Presbyterian Church, 1958; Duke University Divinity School, Durham, N.C., assistant professor, 1962-68, associate professor, 1968-85, professor of Biblical interpretation, 1985—, director of academic affairs, 1971-75.

MEMBER: Society of Biblical Literature and Exegesis, Phi Beta Kappa.

WRITINGS:

(Editor and contributor) *The Use of the Old Testament in the New and Other Essays,* Duke University Press, 1972.
These Things Are Written: An Introduction to the Religious Ideas of the Bible, John Knox, 1978.
Daniel and Revelation: A Study of Two Extraordinary Visions, Judson, 1978.
Jeremiah: Prophet under Siege, Judson, 1979.
The New Testament Writings: History, Literature, and Interpretation, John Knox, 1980.
Christ, the Church, and the End: Studies in Colossians and Ephesians, Judson, 1980.
The Old Testament Writings: History, Literature, and Interpretation, John Knox, 1982.
The Old Testament Prophets Then and Now, Judson, 1982.
Biblical Books of Wisdom, Judson, 1983.
How to Interpret the Bible, John Knox, 1984.

Marriage and Divorce, Abingdon Press, 1985.

End-Times, Abingdon Press, 1986.

Revelation for Today, Abingdon Press, 1989.

A Grammar for New Testament Greek, Abingdon Press, 1900.

Contributor of articles to *Harper's Bible Dictionary,* 1986.

WORK IN PROGRESS: Four Portraits of Jesus: A Study of the Gospels; New Testament Teaching about the Return of Jesus; Introduction to Paul; Introduction to a Study of the Bible.

*   *   *

ELLENS, J(ay) Harold 1932-

PERSONAL: Born July 16, 1932, in McBain, Mich.; son of John S. (a mechanic) and Grace (Kortmann) Ellens; married Mary Jo Lewis (a clinical social worker), September 7, 1954; children: Deborah, Jacqueline, Daniel, Rebecca, Harold, Brenda. *Education:* Calvin College, B.A., 1953; Calvin Seminary, M.Div., 1956; Princeton Theological Seminary, Th.M., 1965; Wayne State University, Ph.D., 1970; attended Cranbrook Institute for Advanced Pastoral Studies, 1965, and Educational Sciences Institute of Oakland Community College, 1972; also attended Command and General Staff College, 1969, Industrial College of the Armed Forces, 1970, Special Warfare School, 1971, U.S. Army War College, 1977, and National Defense University, 1979. *Politics:* Independent.

ADDRESSES: Home and office—26705 Farmington Rd., Farmington Hills, Mich. 48018.

CAREER: Ordained Christian Reformed minister, 1956; Newton Christian Reformed Church, Newton, N.J., pastor, 1961-65; University Hills Christian Center, Farmington, Mich., pastor, 1965-69, director, 1969-79; United Presbyterian Church in the United States of America, Presbytery of Detroit, Detroit, Mich., pastor/psychologist in special ministries, 1980—; Westminster Church of Detroit, Detroit, interim senior pastor, 1984-85. Private practice of psychotherapy, 1965—. Certified social worker, 1984; national certified counselor, 1984.

Resource leader, National Defense University, 1980, 1981; liaison officer, U.S. Military Academy of West Point, 1982-85. Member of faculty at U.S. Army Staff College, 1964-70, 1973; part-time instructor at Calvin Seminary, 1967-70; part-time associate professor at Oakland Community College, 1970-76; lecturer at Wayne County Community College, 1968-72, and Wayne State University, 1972-76; professor of communications psychology at Oakland University, 1973-79; distinguished lecturer in communication, Wheaton University, 1977, 1978, 1979; teaching fellow, Princeton Theological Seminary, 1978-79; Finch Lecturer, Fuller Theological Seminary, January, 1981. Staff therapist and member of board of directors of Midwest Mental Health Clinic; member of board of directors of Farmington Community Arts Council. Appeared on WXYZ-TV, WJBK-TV, and WWJ-TV (three national network affiliates in Detroit) and their radio counterparts, including hosting one-hour show sponsored by Christian Communications Council, Detroit Council of Churches, 1968-75. Has conducted research and lectured in Europe, the Near East and Far East, South America, Africa, China, and Japan, 1957-87. *Military service:* U.S. Army, chaplain, 1956-61. U.S. Army Reserve, chaplain, 1955-56, 1961—; present rank, colonel.

MEMBER: International Christian Studies Association (member of board of directors), International Council of Psychologists (life member), Christian Association for Psychological Studies, International (life member; executive director, 1974—), Eirene

Internationale, Institute for Antiquity and Christianity (member of board of directors and national advisory board), American Academy of Religion, American Institute for Archaeology, Society for the Scientific Study of Religion, Speech Communication Association of America, American Association for Counseling and Development, Association for Clinical Pastoral Education, American Association of Pastoral Counselors, Association for Reformed Communication, Process Psychology Institute, Paul Tillich Society, Institute for Religion and Wholeness (member of national advisory board), University Professors for Academic Order (member of board of directors), Military Chaplains Association (life member; member of board of directors), Reserve Officers Association (life member; national chaplain, 1978-79, 1982-83), Association of the United States Army, Military Order of the World Wars.

AWARDS, HONORS: Awarded Maltese Cross as Knight of Grace in the Knights of Malta by Queen Juliana of the Netherlands, 1974, for lecture series on the ethics of international power.

WRITINGS:

Format Development in Religious TV, Wayne State University, 1970.

Models of Religious Broadcasting, Eerdmans, 1974.

(Contributor) *Research in Mental Health and Religious Behavior,* PSI Press, 1976.

Chaplain (Major General) Gerhardt W. Hyatt: An Oral History, U.S. Army War College, 1977.

(Author of foreword) Henry Stob, *Ethical Reflections,* Eerdmans, 1978.

The International Directory, Christian Association for Psychological Studies, Volume II, 1979, Volume III, 1982, Volume IV, 1984.

Eternal Vigilance, Reserve Officers Association of the United States, 1980.

God's Grace and Human Health, Abingdon, 1982.

(Editor, and author of foreword) John S. Ellens, *Life and Laughter,* Catalogues Plus, 1983.

(Editor, and author of preface) *The Beauty of Holiness: Symbolism in Westminster Church of Detroit,* 2nd edition, Bookcrafters, 1985.

Stress Management: Self and Ministry, Academy of Health Sciences, 1985.

What Is the Role of the Chaplain in the Face of Man's Inhumanity to Man?, Academy of Health Sciences, 1985.

(Contributor) David G. Benner, editor, *Baker Encyclopedia of Psychology,* Baker Book, 1985.

(Contributor) Edgar W. Smith, Jr., editor, *International Standard Bible Encyclopedia,* Eerdmans, 1985.

Psychotheology: Key Issues, UNISA Press (Johannesburg), 1986.

Spiritual Vigilance, SADFSHG Information Systems (Johannesburg), 1986.

(With William L. Hiemstra and Richard Houskamp) *God's Grace in Free Verse,* Christian Association for Psychological Studies, 1986.

(Editor with LeRoy Aden) *The Church and Pastoral Care,* Baker Book, 1987.

(Editor with Aden) *Hiltner and Pastoral Care,* Westminster, 1987.

(Contributor) Benner, editor, *Christian Counseling and Psychotherapy,* Baker Book, 1987.

(Contributor) H. Newton Maloney, editor, *Psychology and Religion,* Baker Book, 1987.

(Contributor) Benner, editor, *Psychotherapy and Christian Faith,* Baker Book, 1987.

(Editor with Aden) *Life Span Growth and Development,* Baker Book, 1987.
(Contributor) Rodney Hunter and others, editors, *Dictionary of Pastoral Care,* Abingdon, 1987.
Psychology in Worship, Harper/Christian Association for Psychological Studies, 1987.
(Editor with Aden) *Psychospiritual Health and Pathology,* Baker Book, 1988.
(Contributor) Benner, editor, *Personality and Biblical Anthropology,* Baker Book, 1988.

Also author of book on psychology and theology; also author of tape series on psychology, theology, liturgy, and the confessional in Catholic and Protestant practice. Contributor of over one hundred articles to periodicals, including *Reformed Journal, Journal of Psychology and Theology,* and *Banner.* Editor-in-chief, *Journal of Psychology and Christianity,* 1975—, and *Bulletin* of Christian Association for Psychological Studies, 1976-81.

WORK IN PROGRESS: Americanism and Christ; People, Purpose, and Providence; Readings in Psychology and Theology, with H. Newton Maloney.

SIDELIGHTS: J. Harold Ellens told *CA:* "My childhood in the Depression impressed me indelibly with the scope of human need and suffering. My training in a German pietist family oriented me on the spiritual/psychological dimension of human need as well as [in] the physical/social dimensions. My father's patient and theological/philosophical orientation in thought and behavior, particularly in terms of a dynamic and congenial notion of divine providence, indued me with a durable strength and sense of the inherent hopefulness of things. My experience as a military officer clarified for me that change can be achieved with the appropriate method and strategy, if the objective is clarified. Opportunities for pastoral ministry and psychotherapeutic care of people channelled the above and structured the arena in which I invested my energies as an author.

"I began to write by publishing articles in popular journals and rewriting for publication the essence of my Ph.D. dissertation. I was ambitious to do so because it seemed to me I had generated key information and conceptualized insights that could be genuinely helpful to the potential readers and professional scholars especially in the helping professions.

"Through my books I hope to achieve an increased appreciation in the mind of the technical professional and of the thoughtful general reader for the significant relationship between the insights of historic Judeo-Christian theological thought and practice on the one hand and [the] contemporary message of the psycho-social sciences. This relationship is particularly crucial in the matters of anthropology or an understanding of the nature of persons. It has definitive potential impact upon the shaping of human self-understanding and world views. Such an appreciation of the significant relationship will enhance scholarship universally and will provide improved satisfying perceptions for the unquenchable human quest for meaning.

"I have only moderate appreciation of most of the work that is being done today in literature, theology, social science, and ethics. We seem to be living in a growing vacuum of creative skill, genuine innovation of conceptual models, and stimulating address to the cosmic issues and images which have driven the great writers of the past. A paucity of vision and courage for reaching across the boundaries and frontiers of thought prevails. The great prophets of our century are virtually all dead. We seem now, for the most part, to be living off the scraps snatched rather superficially from the thought, method, images, and issues of the

past prophets. I am anxiously looking for the possibility that the onset of the new century will see a breakthrough for a new age of prophetic thinkers. That will probably require the reduction of the large amount of energy currently expended in dealing with the anxiety of the present thermonuclear age and its contest of forces. Only a freeing of the psychological energies of our culture and some significant breakthroughs in the horizons of our cultural and technological world will sufficiently stimulate the human community and inspire it with the hopeful worthwhileness of things to make great ideas and great writing likely. Until then there is likely to continue to be a general preoccupation with the sordid, violent, depressive, and cynical in life."

Some of Ellens's work has been published in Spanish and Portuguese.

AVOCATIONAL INTERESTS: Studying the development of human linguistics, archaeology, art history, general history, and philosophy.

*　　*　　*

ELTING, John R(obert) 1911-

PERSONAL: Born February 15, 1911, in Spokane, Wash.; son of Robert C. (a business manager) and Myrtle (Welborn) Elting; married Ann M. Clancy, November 6, 1935. *Education:* Stanford University, B.S., 1932; Colorado State College of Education, M.A., 1948. *Religion:* Deist.

ADDRESSES: Home and office—28 Stillman, Cornwall-on-Hudson, N.Y. 12520.

CAREER: Billings High School, Billings, Mont., teacher of general science and biology, 1936-40 and 1947-48. Served in U.S. Army, 1933-36 and 1940-48, career officer, 1950-68, serving as a teacher at Armed Forces Information School, 1948-51, and at United States Military Academy, 1951-54 and 1957-65; retired as colonel, 1968. Military historian and consultant, 1968—.

MEMBER: Company of Military Historians (member of board of governors).

AWARDS, HONORS: Military—Legion of Merit, Bronze Star, Purple Heart, Army Commendation Ribbon with two Oak Leaf clusters.

WRITINGS:

(Associate editor) *West Point Atlas of American Wars,* Praeger, 1959.
(With Vincent Joseph Esposito) *A Military History and Atlas of the Napoleonic Wars,* Praeger, 1964.
(Editor) *Military Uniforms in America,* Presidio Press, Volume 1: *The Era of the American Revolution, 1755-1795,* 1974, Volume 2: *Years of Growth, 1796-1851,* 1977, Volume 3 (with Michael J. McAfee): *Long Endure: The Civil War Period, 1852-1867,* 1982, Volume 4 (with McAfee): *The Modern Era,* 1988.
The Battle of Bunker's Hill, Philip Freneau, 1975.
The Battles of Saratoga, Philip Freneau, 1977.
Battles for Scandinavia, Time-Life, 1981.
American Army Life, Scribner, 1982.
(With Dan Cragg and Ernest Deal) *A Dictionary of Soldier Talk,* Scribner, 1984.
The Superstrategists, Scribner, 1985.
(Contributor) Donald D. Horward, editor, *Napoleonic Military History: A Bibliography,* Garland Publishing, 1986.
(Contributor) David D. Chandler, editor, *Napoleon's Marshals,* Macmillan, 1987.

Swords around a Throne: Napoleon's Grande Armee, Free Press, 1988.
The War of 1812, Algonquin Press, 1990.

Consultant to Time-Life Books on "World War II," "The Civil War," and "The Third Reich" series. Contributor to *Encyclopedia Americana* and *Random House Dictionary;* contributor to magazines, including *Military Collector* and *Historian.*

SIDELIGHTS: In *Swords around a Throne: Napoleon's Grande Armee,* which *Washington Post Book World* contributor Douglas Porch calls a "thorough and immensely entertaining book," Napoleonic historian John R. Elting "explains how Napoleon managed to meld 1.35 million French conscripts, . . . numerous French volunteers and legions of foreigners into a force that, between 1800 and 1815, deprived European diplomacy of much of its creativity." In detailing the numerous operations of Napoleon's forces, "almost no aspect of the life of the Grande Armee escapes Elting's attentions," the critic remarks; William Jackson explains in the London *Times* that in this "exceptional" book "Elting creates a fascinating picture of the people, their motives and their methods. . . . He exposes to our gaze all the inner workings of that incredibly complex human organism." As Porch concludes: "What is certain is that, as a social history of the men who made the Napoleonic era such a dynamic one, *Swords around a Throne* is unlikely to be surpassed."

Elting told *CA:* "Military history and military intelligence are similar, and fascinating, disciplines. The military historian collects bits of information, sometimes conflicting, and must sift through them and put together a picture of events that makes sense. It's worse than any jigsaw puzzle, because many of those bits will prove false and must be discarded. After you at last get the job done, there may be additional frustrations—higher headquarters may ignore or flinch from acting on your intelligence estimate or the publisher may refuse your book.

"Sifting through military reports and serving, however briefly, in Bill Mauldin's fraternity of 'them as gets shot at' can give you a cynical outlook on our military past. My writing of *The Battle of Bunker's Hill* and *The Battles of Saratoga* was much inspired by a vast mistrust of the accepted versions of both and wonder as to what actually happened. As usual, once I had dug down, the facts were much more interesting than the fables. I've written some books—*Battles for Scandinavia, American Army Life, Superstrategists*—because a publisher wanted them, and I concluded that I had a few useful ideas on the subjects.

"The longer I work at military history, the more impressed I am with how much I still have to learn. To merely scratch the surface, a military historian needs to know the weapons on the period he proposes to cover—their range, rate of fire, accuracy, reliability; he needs to know the means of transportation available for supply and the roads, rivers, seas, and canals by which supplies can be moved; and he needs to know the clothing and equipment of the individual soldier, the means of transmitting orders and information, the medical problems, weather, and terrain."

AVOCATIONAL INTERESTS: Travel (Scotland, Western Europe).

BIOGRAPHICAL/CRITICAL SOURCES:

PERIODICALS

Times (London), May 27, 1989.
Washington Post Book World, November 13, 1988.

EMPSON, William 1906-1984

PERSONAL: Born September 27, 1906, in Yokefleet, Howden, East Yorkshire, England; died April 15, 1984, in London, England; son of A. R. and Laura (Micklethwait) Empson; married Hester Henrietta Crouse, 1941; children: William Hendrick Mogador, Jacobus Arthur Calais. *Education:* Winchester College, 1920-25; Magdalen College, Cambridge, B.A., 1929, M.A., 1935.

ADDRESSES: Home—Studio House, 1 Hampstead Hill Gardens, London N.W. 3, England.

CAREER: Bunrika Daigaku, Tokyo, Japan, chair of English literature, 1931-34; Peking National University (then part of South-Western Combined Universities), Peking, China, professor of English literature, 1937-39; British Broadcasting Co., London, England, editor in monitoring department, 1940-41, Chinese editor, 1941-46; Peking National University, Peking, China, professor of English, 1947-52; Sheffield University, Sheffield, England, professor of English literature, 1953-1971, became professor emeritus. Visiting fellow, Kenyon College, Gambier, Ohio, summers, 1948, 1950, and 1954; visiting professor, University of Toronto, 1973-74, and Pennsylvania State University, University Park, 1974-75.

AWARDS, HONORS: Ingram Merrill Foundation Award for Literature, 1968; D.Litt., from University of East Anglia, Norwich, 1968, University of Bristol, 1971, and University of Sheffield, 1974; knighted, 1979.

WRITINGS:

Letter IV (poems), privately printed, 1929.
Seven Types of Ambiguity: A Study of its Effects on English Verse (criticism), Chatto & Windus, 1930, revised edition, 1947, Meridan, 1957.
Poems, privately printed, 1934, Chatto & Windus, 1935.
Some Versions of Pastoral, Chatto & Windus, 1935, New Directions, 1950, published as *English Pastoral Poetry,* Norton, 1938, reprinted, Books for Libraries, 1972.
(Editor and translator from technical into basic English) John Haldane, *Outlook of Science,* Routledge & Kegan Paul, 1935.
(Editor and translator from technical into basic English) Haldane, *Science and Well-Being,* Routledge & Kegan Paul, 1935.
(With George Garrett) *Shakespeare Survey,* Brendin Publishing Co., 1937.
The Gathering Storm (poems), Faber, 1940.
Collected Poems of William Empson, Harcourt, 1949, enlarged edition, 1961.
The Structure of Complex Words, New Directions, 1951, 3rd edition, Rowman, 1979.
(Contributor) Derek Hudson, *English Critical Essays: Twentieth Century, Second Series,* Oxford University Press, 1958.
Milton's God, Chatto & Windus, 1961, New Directions, 1962, enlarged edition, Cambridge University Press, 1981.
(Author of introduction) John R. Harrison, *The Reactionaries: Yeats, Lewis, Pound, Eliot, Lawrence,* Schocken, 1967.
(Editor) *Shakespeare's Poems,* New American Library, 1969.
(Editor with David Pirie) *Coleridge's Verse: A Selection,* Faber, 1972, Schocken, 1973.
Using Biography (criticism), Harvard University Press, 1984.
Essays on William Shakespeare, edited by Pirie, Cambridge University Press, 1986.
The Royal Beasts and Other Works, edited by John Haffenden, Chatto & Windus, 1986.

Argufying, edited by Haffenden, Chatto & Windus, 1988.
Faustus and the Censor, edited by John Henry Jones, 1988.

SIDELIGHTS: Sir William Empson, professor of English literature at Sheffield University for nearly twenty years, "revolutionized our ways of reading a poem," notes a London *Times* writer. The school of literary criticism known as New Criticism gained important support from Empson's *Seven Types of Ambiguity: A Study of Its Effects on English Verse.* This work, together with his other published essays, has become "part of the furniture of any good English or American critic's mind," G. S. Fraser remarks in *Great Writers of the English Language: Poets.* Empson will also be remembered for "the peculiar, utterly original and startling tenor of his works," says the *Times* writer. Radically different from the romantic poetry produced by Dylan Thomas and Empson's other peers, Empson's poetry employed a more objective, nonsentimental language that reflected his competence as a mathematician and his reverence for science. The *Times* article relates that his first collection, *Poems,* "made an immediate deserved and explosive impact such as the literary scene in Britain knows only two or three times in a century."

John Gross of the *New York Times Book Review* relates, "An essentially positive critic, [Empson] had the gift of being able to show you qualities in a work you would never have seen without him, and the even more important gift of enlarging your imagination, encouraging you to go on looking for yourself." This new approach to poetry appreciation centered on the reader's close attention to the properties of poetic language opened up a new field of literary criticism—a remarkable accomplishment, considering that Empson did so without proposing to alter previous methods of criticism; neither did he revise the standards by which literature is traditionally judged, nor did he invent new ways to reclassify well-known works of literature, Hugh Kenner points out in *Gnomon: Essays on Contemporary Literature.* Empson's explanations of how meaning is carried in poetic language have made poetry accessible to hundreds of readers, Kenner observes.

Perhaps most helpful to erstwhile readers of poetry is Empson's first book-length work of criticism, *Seven Types of Ambiguity.* In general usage, a word or reference is deemed ambiguous if it has more than one possible meaning. In *Seven Types,* Empson wrote, "I propose to use the word in an extended sense, and shall think relevant to my subject any verbal nuance, however slight, which gives room for alternative reactions to the same piece of language." Empson's seven types are briefly defined in the table of contents: "First-type ambiguities arise when a detail is effective in several ways at once. . . . In second-type ambiguities two or more alternative meanings are fully resolved into one. . . . The condition for the third type ambiguity is that two apparently unconnected meanings are given simultaneously. . . . In the fourth type the alternative meanings combine to make clear a complicated state of mind in the author. . . . The fifth type is a fortunate confusion, as when the author is discovering his idea in the act of writing . . . or not holding it in mind all at once. . . . In the sixth type what is said is contradictory or irrelevant and the reader is forced to invent interpretations. . . . The seventh type is that of full contradiction, marking a division in the author's mind."

Ambiguity impedes communication when it results from the writer's indecision, Empson wrote in *Seven Types:* "It is not to be respected in so far as it is due to weakness or thinness of thought, obscures the matter at hand unnecessarily . . . or when the interest of the passage is not focussed upon it, so that it is merely an opportunism in the handling of the material, if the reader will not understand the ideas which are being shuffled, and will be given a general impression of incoherence." However, the protean properties of words—their ability to carry multiple meanings in a variety of ways—are a major component of poetic language, and being aware of how this facet of language operates is one of the pleasures of poetry, said Empson. "*Seven Types* is primarily an exercise intended to help the reader who has already felt the pleasure understand the nature of his response," a *Contemporary Literary Critics* contributor suggests.

"Some of Empson's early critics felt that he had simply written himself a license to search for multiple meanings with no awareness of the controlling context in which the local ambiguity appears," reports the same contributor. On the contrary, Empson guides critics to consider "purpose, context and person" in addition to "the critical principles of the author and of the public he is writing for" when explicating meaning. *Hudson Review* contributor Roger Sale believes that the book has been too harshly judged in many reviews. He writes, "Most discussions have picked on its least interesting aspects, its use of the word 'ambiguity' and its ranging of the 'types' along a scale of 'advancing logical disorder.' But these matters are really minor. . . . The book, [Empson] says, is not philosophical but literary, and its aim is to examine lines Empson finds beautiful and haunting. . . . But in at least fifteen places Empson shows that the aim of analysis is not so much understanding lines as uncovering whole tracts of the mind, and the book is studded with the right things said about a poet or an historical period." In fact, concludes Robert M. Adams in the *New York Review of Books,* "Already certain passages of Empsonian exegesis . . . have attained classic status, so that the text can't be intelligently considered without them. . . . I think he had, though in lesser measure, Dr. Johnson's extraordinary gift for laying his finger on crucial literary moments; and that alone is likely to ensure him a measure of permanence."

Some Versions of Pastoral addresses the modern propensity to express nostalgia for idyllic world views that belong to the past. According to Empson, pastoral literature implied "a beautiful relation between rich and poor [and made] . . . simple people express strong feelings . . . in learned and fashionable language (so that you wrote about the best subject in the best way)." Empson maintains that contemporary expressions of the pastoral are for the most part pretenses: "in pastoral you take a limited life and pretend it is the full and normal one." Writing in *Modern Heroism: Essays on D. H. Lawrence, William Empson, and J. R. R. Tolkien,* Sale contends that by examining a series of leader/heroes from the sixteenth century forward, Empson means to say that the moieties that used to bind leaders to their people no longer exist—in Sales's words, "the people have become a mob and the hero painfully alienated"—and that, therefore, the role of hero or Christ-figure is not attainable.

Sale believes that *Some Versions of Pastoral* is Empson's best book, although it too has been misjudged as a literary work and misused as a critical tool. Sale notes that "in [this book] he can move from the work at hand to his vision with almost no shoving of the evidence, so even though his prose and organization may seem difficult on first reading, he turns with almost indescribable grace from the smallest particular to the largest generalization and then back to various middle grounds. When one becomes used to the book and begins to hear the massive chords of its orchestrations supporting even the most irrelevant aside, the effect is one only the greatest books can produce—it envelopes and controls such large areas of the imagination that for a while one is willing to admit it is the only book ever written. As a modern work of persuasion it is unrivaled."

Milton's God is "a diatribe against Christianity which Empson feels has had a monopoly on torture-worship, sexual repression and hypocrisy," the *Contemporary Literary Critics* essayist relates. Milton's God, Empson maintains, seems to want to set aside the cruelty of his absolute rule, and "has cut out of Christianity both the torture-horror and the sex-horror, and after that the monster seems almost decent." Questioning Milton's orthodoxy on these grounds, Empson presents Milton as a humanist—a view that raised a "furor" among the "entrenched Miltonic establishment," says Adams. It was, he says, the eccentric professor's "last raid on the academic chicken coop" before his retirement from the University of Sheffield in 1971.

Empson's own humanism accounts in part for his open-minded approach to the topic of meaning in literature. Kenner notes: " 'The object of life, after all,' [Empson] tells us late in *Ambiguity*, 'is not to understand things, but to maintain one's defenses and equilibrium and live as well as one can; it is not only maiden aunts who are placed like this.' " In *Milton's God*, he declared his agreement with philosopher Jeremy Bentham "that the satisfaction of any impulse is in itself an elementary good, and that the practical ethical question is how to satisfy the greatest number." Empson's poetry and criticism are the natural extensions of his views. Empson offers "not a theory of literature or a single method of analysis but a model of how to read with pleasure and knowledge," notes *New Statesman* reviewer Jon Cook. In *Using Biography*, for example, he demonstrates how familiarity with an author's life helps the critic to empathize with the author, allowing the critic to apply corresponding personal experiences to see into an author's intentions. The resulting insights on Andrew Marvell and W. B. Yeats, says James Fenton in the London *Times*, owe more to Empson's speculations and free associations than to systematic analysis of biographical detail. According to Cook, Empson makes it clear that it is far worse to succumb to "the critical habit of pressing literary works into the service of authoritarian and repressive ideologies, all this, of course, under the comforting guise that to receive authority in this way does us good."

Although Empson is best known for his criticism, *Preliminary Essays* author John Wain writes: "It may well be that criticism will be read and remembered while poetry is forgotten, for criticism breeds fresh criticism more easily than poetry breeds fresh poetry; but in Empson's case it would be a pity if he were known simply as the 'ambiguity' man, and not as a poet." A. Alvarez writes in *Stewards of Excellence*, "The poetry of William Empson has been more used [as a model] than that of any other English poet of our time." As the upheavals of World War II threatened to render romanticism and pastoralism obsolete, poets were challenged to find language and forms equal to the age. "Empson's verse was read with an overwhelming sense of relief after the brash and embarrassed incoherence of wartime and post-war poetry," notes Alvarez, who elaborates, "there is something in his work which encourages other writers to use it for their own ends. It has, I think, an *essential* objectivity. . . . In the later poems what goes in as strong personal feeling comes out as something more general; whilst in the earlier work all the personal energy goes into a particularly impersonal business."

In addition, Empson's best verses "have a quality of mystery and incantation which runs quite counter to his professed rationalism," notes Robert Nye in the London *Times*. The poems, says a writer for the London *Times*, were perceived by some critics to be like "exercises: ingenious, resembling staggeringly clever crossword puzzles, abstruse, riddling—in a word, over-intellectual. But as Edwin Muir and other shrewder readers noted, their real keynote was passion. They represent, as Emp-

son put it in one of the most famous of them, a style learned from a despair. The subject matter of the great ones . . . is the nature of sexual passion and the nature of political passion." Writers found in Empson's verse the balance between intense emotion and detachment that seemed appropriate to describe life in the contemporary world.

Alvarez believes that Empson's poetry depends on his control over a large range of ideas: "[Empson] is less interested in saying his own say than in the agility and skill and variety with which he juggles his ideas. So it is a personal poem only at a remove: the subject is impersonal; the involvement is all his effort to make as much as he can out of the subject, and in the accomplishment with which he relates his manifold themes so elegantly together. Empson's, in short, is a poetry of wit in the most traditional sense. . . . And, like most wit, the pleasure it gives is largely in the immaculate performance, which is a rare pleasure but a limited one."

In tracing the development of Empson's poetry, Alvarez says of the early poems: "In his sardonic way, Empson made his polish and inventiveness seem like a personal claim for sanity, as though he saw everything in a fourth and horrifying dimension but was too well-mannered to say so. Hence the wry despair and vigorous stylishness seemed not at all contradictory." He notes that "It is as a stylist of poetry and ideas that, I think, Empson is most important. He took over all [T. S.] Eliot's hints about what was most significant in the English tradition, and he put them into practice without any of the techniques Eliot had derived from the French and Italians. And so his poetry shows powerfully and with great purity the perennial vitality of the English tradition; and in showing this it also expresses the vitality and excitement of the extraordinarily creative moment when Empson began writing."

BIOGRAPHICAL/CRITICAL SOURCES:

BOOKS

Alvarez, A., *Stewards of Excellence*, Scribner, 1958.
Contemporary Literary Criticism, Gale, Volume 3, 1975, Volume 8, 1981, Volume 19, 1981, Volume 33, 1985, Volume 34, 1985.
Contemporary Literary Critics, St. James, 1977.
Crane, R. S., *Critics and Critics: Ancient and Modern*, University of Chicago Press, 1952.
Dictionary of Literary Biography, Volume 20: *British Poets, 1914-1945*, Gale, 1983.
Gill, Roma, editor, *William Empson: The Man and His Work*, Routledge & Kegan Paul, 1974.
Hamilton, Ian, editor, *The Modern Poet: Essays from "The Review"*, MacDonald, 1968.
Hyman, Stanley Edgar, *The Armed Vision: A Study in the Methods of Modern Literary Criticism*, Knopf, 1948, revised edition, 1955.
Kenner, Hugh, *Gnomon: Essays in Contemporary Literature*, McDowell, 1958.
Makers of Modern Culture, Facts on File, 1981.
Norris, Christopher, *William Empson and the Philosophy of Literary Criticism*, Athlone Press, 1978.
Sale, Roger, *Modern Heroism: Essays on D. H. Lawrence, William Empson, and J. R. R. Tolkien*, University of California Press, 1973.
Untermeyer, Louis, *Lives of the Poets*, Simon & Schuster, 1959.
Vinson, James, editor, *Great Writers of the English Language: Poets*, St. Martins, 1979.
Wain, John, *Preliminary Essays*, Macmillan (London), 1957.

William Empson: The Man and His Work, Routledge & Kegan Paul, 1974.
Wills, J. H., *William Empson,* Columbia University Press, 1969.

PERIODICALS

Criticism, fall, 1966.
Hudson Review, spring, 1952, autumn, 1966.
Nation, June 16, 1962.
New Statesman, October 12, 1984.
New York Review of Books, April 11, 1985.
New York Times Book Review, May 20, 1984.
Observer, September 30, 1984.
Scrutiny, Volume 2, number 3, December, 1933.
Southern Review, autumn, 1938.
Time, April 18, 1949, August 10, 1962.
Times (London), October 25, 1984, February 8, 1985, November 13, 1986.
Times Literary Supplement, November 14, 1986, January 1, 1988, February 26, 1988.
Washington Post Book World, May 19, 1985.
Yale Review, June, 1962.

OBITUARIES:

PERIODICALS

Chicago Tribune, April 18, 1984.
Times (London), April 16, 1984, February 28, 1985.
Times Literary Supplement, November 14, 1986, January 1, 1988, February 26, 1988.
Washington Post, April 17, 1984.
Washington Post Book World, May 19, 1985.*

—*Sketch by Marilyn K. Basel*

*   *   *

ENGEL, (Aaron) Lehman   1910-1982

PERSONAL: Born September 14, 1910, in Jackson, Miss.; died of cancer August 29, 1982, in New York, N.Y.; son of Ellis (a clothing and shoe salesman) and Juliette (a part-time book-keeper; maiden name, Lehman) Engel. *Education:* Attended Cincinnati Conservatory of Music, 1926-27, Cincinnati College of Music, 1927-29, and University of Cincinnati; graduate of Juilliard School, 1934; studied composition with Roger Sessions, 1935. *Politics:* None. *Religion:* None.

ADDRESSES: Home—350 East 54th St., New York, N.Y. 10022.

CAREER: Composer of concert works for various solo instruments, orchestra, and voice; composer of incidental music for plays; composer for choreogrpher Martha Graham, beginning 1932; composer and conductor of musical works for theater, television, films, and radio, including "Murder in the Cathedral," "Streetcar Named Desire," and "Li'l Abner." Conductor, Madrigal Singers, 1935-39; conductor at Lewisohn Stadium, New York City, 1951, and for New Friends of Music at Town Hall, New York City, 1952; guest conductor for St. Louis Municipal Opera, 1968—, and Turkish State Opera, 1968; conductor of more than sixty recordings for RCA-Victor, Columbia, Decca, Brunswick, and Atlantic; conducted concerts at Carnegie Hall, and Kennedy Center for the Performing Arts. Musical director, Dallas State Fair Musicals, Dallas, Tex., 1949-52, and for many works on Broadway. Lecturer, Salzburg Seminar in American Studies, 1968; guest lecturer at numerous universities and organizations throughout the United States, including Yale University, University of Southern California, Columbia University,

New York University, and Smithsonian Institution; instructor, Neighborhood Playhouse School. Director of music department, American Musical and Dramatic Theater Academy, 1962—; director of workshops for composers and lyricists for Broadcast Music, Inc.; director of musical theater development for Columbia Pictures-Screen Gems. Stage director; executive director, Development Musical Theatre Properties, Columbia Pictures; producer. President, Arrow Music Press, Inc.; member of advisory board, Henry Street Settlement's Music School; member of board of directors, Everyman Associates, Inc., and Foundation of the Theatre and Music Collection, Museum of the City of New York; member of advisory board, New York High School of Performing Arts. Consultant. *Military service:* U.S. Navy, 1942-46; became lieutenant; initially conductor, then chief composer for film division.

MEMBER: Authors Guild, Authors League of America, Broadcast Music Inc., Concert Artists Guild (former president), American Guild of Composers, League of Composers (member of composer's committee), Players Club, Century Associations, Sigma Alpha Mu.

AWARDS, HONORS: D.Mus., Boguslawski College of Music (Chicago), 1944, Cincinnati Conservatory College of Music, 1971; Society for the Publication of American Music award, 1946; Antoinette Perry Awards ("Tonys") for musical direction of "The Consul," 1950, and for conducting "Wonderful Town" and Gilbert and Sullivan operettas, both 1953; Henry Bellamann Foundation Memorial Award, 1964; award of merit from Cultural Division of Republic of Austria, and Scroll from Consular Law Society, for Outstanding Achievement in the Theatre, both 1968; D.H.L. from Millsaps College, citation for outstanding contribution to musical theater from Hartford Conservatory, and honorary doctorate of music from University of Cincinnati, all 1971; Deems Taylor Award from American Society of Composers, Authors, and Publishers, for *Words with Music: The Broadway Musical Libretto,* and Special Citation for Contribution to Quality of Life through Music, the International Language, from Jackson Chamber of Commerce, both 1973; Light Opera of Manhattan Award, 1974; Grammy Hall of Fame award, 1976, for "Porgy and Bess" recording; special award, New England Theatre Conference, 1977; Spirit of the City Award, Hammond Museum, and Distinguished Alumni Award, University of Cincinnati College-Conservatory, both 1978; Certificate of Appreciation, Smithsonian Institution, 1979; National Endowment for the Humanities grant for oral history of the making of the American musical theater (1940-65).

WRITINGS:

Renaissance to Baroque (seven volumes), Flammer, 1931.
Music for the Classical Tragedy, Flammer, 1953.
Planning and Producing the Musical Show, Crown, 1957, revised edition, 1966. *The American Musical Theatre: A Consideration* (Literary Guild selection), Macmillan, 1968, revised edition, 1975.
Words with Music: The Broadway Musical Libretto, Macmillan, 1972.
Getting Started in the Theater, Macmillan, 1973.
This Bright Day (autobiography), Macmillan, 1973.
Their Words Are Music, Crown, 1975.
The Critics, Macmillan, 1976.
The Making of a Musical, Macmillan, 1977.
Getting the Show On, Macmillan, 1983.

Author of two-volume *The Musical Theater Workshop* (includes twenty-four tapes), Norton, *Poor Wayfaring Stranger,* Mercury, and *Folk Songs* (anthology), Theodore Presser. Contributor to

World Book Encyclopedia, 1973. Contributor to periodicals, including *New York Times Magazine, New York Times, Chicago Tribune, Theatre Arts,* and *Woman's Home Companion.*

WORK IN PROGRESS: Oral History of the Contemporary American Musical Theatre.

SIDELIGHTS: Lehman Engel "probably knew more about musical comedy and its musical technique than anybody else," fellow-composer Harold Rome told Josh Barbanel for the *New York Times. Words with Music: The Broadway Musical Libretto* details Engel's theories on the construction of a successful musical. In a review of the book, Eudora Welty wrote in the *New York Times Book Review* that *Words with Music* "is the Compleat Musical Manual, in which everything [Engel's] young writers and composers need to know is set forth. What works and what doesn't work and why is made specific." Welty continued: "The same virtues that will make it of lasting importance to [writers and composers] are what make it of interest to the general reader, who can take pleasure in the company of an expert writing with penetration on the subject he knows best. In doing so he conveys a world, and we are struck by his force of feeling for the theater itself." A *New Yorker* reviewer commented: "Nearly everyone interested in the theatre can learn something from this book. It is comprehensive in its scope and penetrating in matters of detail."

Engel's autobiography, *This Bright Day,* records his more than forty years in American musical theatre. The book includes anecdotes on various shows and describes relationships with performers who ranged from dancer/choreographer Martha Graham to singing cowboy Gene Autry. Another *New Yorker* contributor wrote: "The memoirs of this warmhearted man and gifted musician are both personal and artistic history. . . . [Either] good nature or artistry . . . would suffice to make an absorbing book; together they make an irresistible one."

AVOCATIONAL INTERESTS: Theater, gourmet restaurants, world travel.

BIOGRAPHICAL/CRITICAL SOURCES:

PERIODICALS

New Yorker, June 3, 1972, April 29, 1974.
New York Times Book Review, May 28, 1972.

OBITUARIES:

PERIODICALS

Newsweek, September 13, 1982.
New York Times, August 30, 1982.*

*   *   *

ESFANDIARY, F M
    See FM-2030

*   *   *

ESMEIN, Jean   1923-

PERSONAL: Surname is pronounced Es-*meh;* born December 1, 1923, in Poitiers, France; son of Paul (a law professor and author) and Marcelle (Roux) Esmein; married Suzanne Esteve (a museum librarian), August 4, 1945; children: Pierre, Bernard. *Education:* Ecole Nationale des Langues Orientales Vivantes, diplome, 1956; Ecole Pratique des Hautes Etudes, titulaire, 1958; Tokyo University, graduate study, 1971.

ADDRESSES: Home—30 rue Saint Come, Luzarches, France 95270. *Office*—University of Technology of Compiegne, BP 649, 60206 Compiegne, France.

CAREER: Marine Nationale (French Navy), career officer, 1942-58, became commander; Compagnie des Machines Bull (computers), Paris, France, manager of scientific computing center, 1959-65; French Embassy, Peking, China, press attache, 1965-68; Credit Lyonnais (bank), Tokyo, Japan, representative for the Far East, beginning 1969; INSEAD (European Business Administration Institute), Euro-Asia Centre, Fontainebleau, France, secretary general, 1979-82; Credit Lyonnais, Bombay, India, general representative for South Asia, 1982-84; CESTA, Paris, associate professor, 1985-88; University of Technology of Compiegne, Compiegne, France, associate professor, 1989—.

MEMBER: Association for Computing Machinery, Computers Art Society, Strategic Management Society, Association du Pacte d'Amitie Kyoto-Paris (assistant secretary general, 1958—).

AWARDS, HONORS: Prix Jean Mermoz, 1979, for body of literary work. Military: Croix du Combattant, Croix de Guerre, Officier de la Legion d'Honneur.

WRITINGS:

La Revolution culturelle chinoise, Le Seuil, 1970, translation by W. J. F. Jenner published as *The Chinese Cultural Revolution,* Doubleday, 1973.
(Contributor) *Melanges offerts a M. Charles Haguenauer,* Asiatheque, 1980.
1/2, un demi plus, Fondation pour les Etudes de Defense Nationale, 1983.
L'Evolution des Systemes Japonais, Documentation Francaise, 1986.
Les Bases de la Puissance du Japan, College de France, Documentation Francaise, 1988.
(Contributor) *Histoire du Japan,* Hozvath, 1990.

Contributor to *Larousse Encyclopedique.*

WORK IN PROGRESS: Translating Ooka Shohei's *Leyte Senki* ("Chroniques de la bataille de Leyte").

BIOGRAPHICAL/CRITICAL SOURCES:

PERIODICALS

Times Literary Supplement, May 28, 1970, May 21, 1976.

*   *   *

ESSLINGER, Pat M.
    See CARR, Pat M(oore)

*   *   *

EVANS, David Allan   1940-

PERSONAL: Born April 11, 1940, in Sioux City, Iowa; son of Arthur Clarence (an editor) and Ruth (Benson) Evans; married Janice Kaye (a secretary), July 4, 1958; children: Shelly, David, Karlin. *Education:* Attended Augustana College, Sioux Falls, S.D., 1958-60; Morningside College, B.A., 1962; University of Iowa, M.A., 1964; University of Arkansas, M.F.A., 1971. *Politics:* Democrat.

ADDRESSES: Home—1222 Third St., Brookings, S.D. 57006. *Office*—English Department, Box 2275A, South Dakota State University, Brookings, S.D. 57007.

CAREER: Marshalltown Community College, Marshalltown, Iowa, instructor in English, 1964-65; Adams State College, Alamosa, Colo., assistant professor of English, 1966-68; South Dakota State University, Brookings, assistant professor, 1968-75, associate professor, 1975-78, professor of English, 1978—. Writer in residence, South Dakota Arts Council, 1973—, and Iowa Arts Council, 1975; writer and scholar in residence, Wayne State College, Wayne, Neb., 1980.

MEMBER: Poetry Society of America, Association of Writers Programs, Sports Literature Association.

AWARDS, HONORS: Borestone Poetry Award, 1969; National Endowment for the Arts grant, 1974; writing grant, South Dakota Arts Council, 1988; South Dakota Centennial Poet, 1989.

WRITINGS:

(Editor with Tom Kakonis) *From Language to Idea,* Holt, 1971.
(Editor with Kakonis) *Statement and Craft,* Prentice-Hall, 1972.
Among Athletes (poems), Folder Editions, 1972.
(Editor) *New Voices in American Poetry,* Winthrop, 1973.
Train Windows, Ohio University Press, 1976.
(Contributor) *A Book of Readings,* Best Cellar Press, 1979.
(Editor) *The Poetry of Sport/The Sport of Poetry,* South Dakota State University Foundation, 1979.
(General editor and contributor) *What the Tallgrass Says,* Center for Western Studies, 1982.
Real and False Alarms, BkMk Press, 1985.
Remembering the Soos, Plains Press, 1986.

WORK IN PROGRESS: The Carnival, poems; *The Maze,* a novel.

SIDELIGHTS: David Allan Evans once told *CA:* "To me, writing poems has always meant finding the right, i.e. best-for-me, relationship between experience and words. Those experiences have been, for the most part, physical ones, hence my many poems on sports, athletes. I am a slow, usually patient writer. I take revision seriously."

*   *   *

EVERETT, Peter 1931-

PERSONAL: Born June 1, 1931, in Hull, Yorkshire, England.

ADDRESSES: Home—9 Laitwood Rd., London S.W. 12, England.

CAREER: Has been employed as a gardener, foundry man, and furniture salesman; writer, 1962—.

AWARDS, HONORS: Independent Television award for drama, 1962; Maugham award, 1965; Arts Council of Great Britain grant, 1970.

WRITINGS:

"Day at Izzard's Wharf " (play; first broadcast on radio, 1959), first produced in Canterbury, England, 1962.
A Day of Dwarfs (novel), Neville Spearman, 1962.
The Instrument (novel), Hutchinson, 1962.
"The Daguerreotypes" (play), first produced in London, 1963.
Negatives (novel; also see below), J. Cape, 1964, Simon & Schuster, 1965.
The Fetch (novel), J. Cape, 1966, Simon & Schuster, 1967.
(With Roger Lowry) *Negatives* (screenplay adaptation of Everett's novel), Continental, 1968.
Visions of Heydritch (novel), W. H. Allen, 1979.
A Death in Ireland (novel), Little, Brown, 1981.
You'll Never Be Sixteen Again: An Illustrated History of the British Teenager, introduction by John Peel, BBC Publications, 1986.

Also author of radio plays "Night of the March Hare," 1959, "Private View," 1966, "The Cookham Resurrection," 1975, "Buffo," 1976, "Me and Mr. Blake," 1977, "Harmonium," 1978, "Martyr of the Hive," 1980, and "Over the Rainbow," 1980; author of television plays "The Girl Who Loved Robots," 1965, "Hurt Hawks," 1974, "Hoodwink," 1975, and "Freedom of the Dig," 1978; author of screenplay "The Last of the Long-haired Boys," 1971. Contributor of poems to *Botteghe Oscure.*

AVOCATIONAL INTERESTS: Jigsaw puzzles, games of all sorts.

BIOGRAPHICAL/CRITICAL SOURCES:

PERIODICALS

New York Times Book Review, May 16, 1965.
Saturday Review, June 5, 1965.
Spectator, March 25, 1966.
Times Literary Supplement, March 31, 1966.*

F

FAGAN, Brian M(urray) 1936-

PERSONAL: Born August 1, 1936, in Birmingham, England; naturalized U.S. citizen; son of Brian Walter and Margaret (Moir) Fagan; married Lesley Ann Newhart, March 16, 1985; children: Lindsay, Anastasia. *Education:* Pembroke College, Cambridge, B.A. (with honors), 1959, M.A., 1962, Ph.D., 1963.

ADDRESSES: Home—170 Hot Springs Rd., Santa Barbara, Calif. 93108. *Office*—Department of Anthropology, University of California, Santa Barbara, Calif. 93106.

CAREER: Livingstone Museum, Livingstone, Northern Rhodesia (now Zambia), keeper of prehistory, 1959-65; British Institute of History and Archaeology in East Africa, Nairobi, Kenya, director of Bantu studies project, 1965-66; University of Illinois at Urbana-Champaign, visiting associate professor of anthropology, 1966-67; University of California, Santa Barbara, associate professor, 1967-68, professor of anthropology, 1969—, director of Center for the Study of Developing Nations, 1969-70, associate dean of research and graduate affairs, 1970-72, associate dean of College of Letters and Science, 1972-73, dean of instructional development, 1973-76. University of Capetown, lecturer, 1960, visiting professor, 1982; Munro Lecturer, University of Edinburgh, 1967; Richard M. Nixon Visiting Scholar and Lecturer, Whittier College, 1976; lecturer in African history at campuses throughout United States. Zambia Monuments Commission, member, 1960-65, secretary, 1960-62; director of Kalomo/Choma Iron Age project, 1960-63, of Lochinvar research project, 1963-64, and of Bantu studies project in Kenya, Uganda, and Tanzania; conducted archaeological research in Zambia and Northern Nigeria, 1969-70. Has presented papers to numerous conferences in the United States, Africa, England, and Europe. Consultant on innovative instruction, New Mexico State University, 1973; consultant to administrator and head of mission, Evaluation of International Audio-Visual Resource Service, United Nations Fund for Popular Activities, 1976. *Military service:* Royal Navy, 1954-56.

MEMBER: Royal Geographical Society (fellow), Royal Anthropological Institute (fellow), Society for American Archaeology, South African Archaeological Society, Prehistoric Society, Current Anthropology (associate), New York Academy of Sciences (fellow), Santa Barbara Yacht Club.

AWARDS, HONORS: Grants from Wenner Gren Foundation, 1967, 1968, and National Science Foundation, 1968-70, 1970-71; Guggenheim fellow, 1972-73; Commonwealth Club Gold Medal for nonfiction, 1975, for *The Rape of the Nile;* Hanson Cup from Cruising Association, 1975, for a cruise to Scandinavia.

WRITINGS:

(Editor) *Victoria Falls: A Handbook to the Victoria Falls, the Batoka Gorge and Part of the Upper Zambesi River,* 2nd edition, Commission for the Preservation of Natural and Historic Monuments and Relics, Northern Rhodesia, 1964.

(With G. C. R. Clay) *The Life and Work of David Livingstone: A Brief Guide to the Livingstone Collections in the Livingstone Museum,* revised edition, National Museums of Zambia, 1965.

Southern Africa during the Iron Age, Praeger, 1965.

(Editor) *A Short History of Zambia, from the Earliest Times until A.D. 1900,* Oxford University Press, 1966.

Iron Age Cultures in Zambia, Humanities, Volume 1: *Kalomo and Kangila,* 1967, Volume 2 (with S. G. H. Daniels and D. W. Phillipson): *Dambwa, Ingombe Ilede, and the Tonga,* 1969.

(Editor) *Introductory Readings in Archaeology,* Little, Brown, 1970.

(Author of introduction and editorial note) Randall MacIver, *Medieval Rhodesia,* Cass & Co., 1971.

(With Francis L. van Noten) *The Hunter-Gatherers of Gwisho,* Musee Royal de l'Afrique Centrale, 1971.

(Editor) Louis S. B. Leakey, *The Stone Age Cultures of Kenya Colony,* Cass & Co., 1971.

In the Beginning: An Introduction to Archaeology, Little, Brown, 1972, 7th edition, 1991.

Men of the Earth: An Introduction to World Prehistory, Little, Brown, 1974, 2nd edition published as *People of the Earth: An Introduction to World Prehistory,* 1977, 6th edition, 1989.

(Editor) *Corridors in Time: A Reader in Introductory Archaeology,* Little, Brown, 1974.

(With John Talbot Robinson) *Human and Cultural Development,* Indiana Historical Society, 1974.

(With Robinson) *The Rape of the Nile: Tomb Robbers, Tourists, and Archaeologists in Egypt,* Scribner, 1975.

(With Roland Oliver) *Africa in the Iron Age, c. 500 B.C. to A.D. 1400,* Cambridge University Press, 1975.

(Author of introductions) *Avenues to Antiquity: Readings from Scientific American,* W. H. Freeman, 1976.

Elusive Treasure: The Story of Early Archaeologists in the Americas, Scribner, 1977.

Quest for the Past: Great Discoveries in Archaeology, Addison-Wesley, 1977.

(Editor and author of introduction) *Civilization: Readings from Scientific American,* W. H. Freeman, 1978.

Archaeology: A Brief Introduction, Little, Brown, 1978, 4th edition, 1991.

World Prehistory: A Brief Introduction, Little, Brown, 1979.

Return to Babylon: Travelers, Archaeologists, and Monuments in Mesopotamia, Little, Brown, 1979.

California Coastal Passages: From San Francisco to Ensenada, Capra, 1981.

Prehistoric Times, W. H. Freeman, 1983.

A Cruising Guide to California Channel Islands, photographs by Graham Pomeroy, Western Marine, 1983, 3rd edition, 1989.

The Aztecs, W. H. Freeman, 1984.

Clash of Cultures, W. H. Freeman, 1984.

Bareboating, International Marine Publishing, 1985.

Anchoring, International Marine Publishing, 1985.

The Adventure of Archaeology, National Geographic Society, 1985.

The Great Journey: The Peopling of Ancient America, Thames & Hudson, 1987.

CONTRIBUTOR

W. W. Bishop and J. D. Clark, editors, *Background to Evolution in Africa,* University of Chicago Press, 1967.

Roland Oliver, editor, *The Middle Age of African History,* Oxford University Press, 1968.

Leonard M. Thompson, editor, *African Societies in Southern Africa,* Praeger, 1969.

Oliver and J. D. Fage, editors, *Papers in African Prehistory,* Cambridge University Press, 1970.

J. R. Gray and David Birmingham, editors, *Pre-Colonial African Trade,* Oxford University Press, 1970.

P. L. Shinnie, editor, *The African Iron Age,* Oxford University Press, 1971.

Also contributor to *UNESCO History of Africa,* Volume 2, 1984. Contributor of over one hundred articles and reviews to professional journals and newspapers.

WORK IN PROGRESS: A major account of North American archaeology.

SIDELIGHTS: Brian Fagan told *CA:* "I became interested in popular writing about archaeology while working in Zambia, where national history had to be created from excavations rather than written records. There I was involved in radio and TV as well as in guidebooks and newspaper writing and scientific articles and monographs. Since coming to the U.S. in 1966, I have been involved in the teaching of large introductory archaeology courses and in much popular lecturing, occupations which led me into textbook writing and then into trade books.

"My trade career began with a chance letter from Scribners about an article I wrote for *Archaeology* on tomb robbers, a letter that led to *The Rape of the Nile* and a whole new vista of writing opportunity. I have continued to write about archaeology for the general public ever since, for the subject is becoming increasingly specialized as it grows. There is a real danger that undisturbed archaeological sites will vanish in North America in the next generation unless the public realizes the immorality of collecting artifacts from Indian sites for personal gain. Such sites are, after all, the archives of American Indian history. I told some of the story of the destruction of American Indian history in my *Elusive Treasure.*

"A lifetime interest has been cruising under sail. We have spent the last three summers sailing in Europe on our 41-foot cutter, *Catticus Rex,* and won the Cruising Association's Hanson Trophy for a cruise to Finland in 1975. I . . . plan to do more writing about sailing in the future.

"I speak French, and [am] deeply involved in the use of media for undergraduate teaching, have an abhorrence for bureaucrats developed when I served as an academic dean, and love cats. Two of them dominate our lives, indeed did everything they could to prevent this paragraph being written by sitting on my pen."

*　　*　　*

FANG, Irving E. 1929-

PERSONAL: Born May 4, 1929, in New York, N.Y.; son of Isidor (a garment worker) and Kate (Grosin) Fang; married Shirley Campbell, September 11, 1954 (divorced December, 1972); married Junko Kobayashi, June 14, 1978; children: (first marriage) Rachel, Daisy. *Education:* University of California, Los Angeles, B.A., 1951, M.S., 1960, Ph.D., 1966.

ADDRESSES: Home—2297 Folwell St., St. Paul, Minn. 55108. *Office*—School of Journalism and Mass Communication, University of Minnesota, Minneapolis, Minn. 55455.

CAREER: North Platte Telegraph-Bulletin, North Platte, Neb., reporter, 1952; *Florence Morning News,* Florence, S.C., reporter, 1952-53; *Montgomery Advertiser,* Montgomery, Ala., reporter, 1953-54; Reuters (news service), rewrite editor in London, England, 1954-55; *Daily Times,* Lagos, Nigeria, editorial adviser, 1955; *San Gabriel Valley Tribune,* Covina, Calif., wire editor, 1955-57; *Pasadena Independent* and *Star-News,* Pasadena, Calif., editorial writer, 1957-59; KABC-Television News, Los Angeles, Calif., writer, 1960-66; American Broadcasting Co. News, New York, N.Y., and Los Angeles, Calif., member of election unit, 1966, writer, 1966-67, assistant manager of political unit, 1967-69, consultant to political unit, 1969—; University of Minnesota, Minneapolis, associate professor, 1969-73, professor of journalism and mass communication, 1973—. Lecturer at California State College (now University), Long Beach, 1965-66. *Military service:* U.S. Army, 1947-48.

MEMBER: Association for Education in Journalism, Radio-Television News Directors Association, Northwest Broadcast News Association.

AWARDS, HONORS: Freedoms Foundation Medal, 1959, for editorial writing; International Business Machines fellowship, 1965, for use of a computer in humanities research; Broadcast Preceptor Award, 1978, for *Those Radio Commentators!*

WRITINGS:

Polls Apart (booklet), American Broadcast Co. News, 1967.

Television News: Writing, Editing, Filming, Broadcasting, Hastings House, 1968, 3rd edition published as *Television News, Radio News,* Rada, 1980, 4th edition, 1985.

Television/Radio News Workbook, Hastings House, 1974.

Those Radio Commentators!, foreword by Lowell Thomas, Iowa State University Press, 1977.

(With Dennis Feltgen) *Smile When the Dewpoint Drops,* Rada, 1981.

The Computer Story, Rada, 1987.

Contributor to periodicals and academic journals, including *Journal of Broadcasting, Saturday Review, Journalism Quarterly, Quill, Journal of Behavioral Science,* and *Research Libraries.*

SIDELIGHTS: Irving E. Fang is a respected and seasoned journalist who shares his experience and knowledge with the students attending his classes at the University of Minnesota as well as with the readers of his books and workbook on journalism and mass communication. Fang's book, *Television News: Writing, Editing, Filming, Broadcasting,* according to S. W. Little of *Saturday Review,* is "a thoroughgoing text on the whole process of television news coverage. . . . It covers everything from how news assignments are made to the number of syllables per sentence a news script can safely carry." M. B. Cassata states in the *Library Journal* that "this book's message is remarkably explicit; the reader is given a rigorous behind-and-at-the-scenes look at what it takes to bring the news to the viewer." And Laurence Goldstein states in *Nation* that Fang's *Television News* "is a lucid, accurate document of the place to which television news has evolved in the late 1960s. It clearly shows the potential television journalist the wide range of skills he must master and it offers useful advice in mastering each skill."

BIOGRAPHICAL/CRITICAL SOURCES:

PERIODICALS

Library Journal, January 15, 1969.
Nation, April 14, 1969.
Saturday Review, November 9, 1968.

*   *   *

FANNING, Robbie 1947-

PERSONAL: Born January 30, 1947, in West Lafayette, Ind.; daughter of James Edwin (a sociologist) and Roberta (a home economist; maiden name, Edwards) Losey; married Anthony David John Fanning (a writer and computer analyst), May, 1969; children: Kali Koala. *Education:* Attended Knox College, 1964-66; University of the State of New York Regents External Degree Program, B.S., 1978; California State University, Dominguez Hills, M.A. candidate.

ADDRESSES: Home—Menlo Park, Calif. *Office*—P.O. Box 2634, Menlo Park, Calif. 94026. *Agent*—McIntosh & Otis, 475 Fifth Ave., New York, N.Y. 10017.

CAREER: Lecturer and teacher at short-term workshops on a variety of topics at several locations in United States, beginning 1974; San Jose State University, San Jose, Calif., instructor in writing, 1980-88; Open Chain Publishing, Menlo Park, Calif., publisher, 1987—.

MEMBER: Authors League of America, Authors Guild, Committee of Small Magazine Editors and Publishers, Publishers Marketing Association, Small Magazine Publishers Association, National Standards Council, American Sewing Guild, Center for the History of American Needlework (member of advisory council), California Writers, Peninsula Stitchery Guild (chairwoman, 1974).

AWARDS, HONORS: Medical Self-Care Award, Better Homes and Gardens Book Club, 1980, for *Get It All Done and Still Be Human.*

WRITINGS:

Decorative Machine Stitchery, Butterick, 1976.
(With husband, Tony Fanning) *Here and Now Stitchery* (on ethnic embroidery), Butterick, 1978.
(With T. Fanning) *Keep Running,* Simon & Schuster, 1978.

Open Chain's Selected Annotated Bibliography of Self-Publishing, Fibar Designs, 1978.
Open Chain's Selected Annotated Bibliography of Self-Study in the Needlearts, Fibar Designs, 1978.
100 Butterflies (juvenile novel), Westminster, 1979.
(With T. Fanning) *Get It All Done and Still Be Human,* Chilton, 1980, revised edition, Open Chain, 1990.
The Complete Book of Machine Quilting, Chilton, 1980.
The Complete Book of Machine Embroidery, Chilton, 1986.
(With Nancy Zieman) *Busy Woman's Sewing Book,* Open Chain, 1988.
(With Zieman) *Busy Woman's Fitting Book,* Open Chain, 1989.

Editor, "Creative Machine Arts Series," Chilton, 1986—. Contributor to national magazines and newspapers, including *Better Homes and Gardens, Good Housekeeping Needlecraft, California Living,* and *Whole Earth Software Catalog.* Editor and publisher, *Open Chain,* 1975-84; contributing editor, *Threads.*

WORK IN PROGRESS: Another juvenile novel; a small business guide; a writing textbook; a book based on her columns.

SIDELIGHTS: Robbie Fanning told *CA:* "As a writer, I love to communicate clearly and simply my personal enthusiasms, to act as a catalyst between people and ideas, and then to listen and watch the rest of the world. To aspiring writers of any age I offer two words: 'Namaste' (Buddhist for 'I salute the light within you') and 'Persist' (probably more important than talent)."

*   *   *

FANTEL, Hans 1922-

PERSONAL: Born March 1, 1922, in Vienna, Austria; married Shea Smith (a magazine editor), 1968. *Education:* Tarkio College, B.S., 1945; also attended University of Missouri and New School for Social Research.

ADDRESSES: Home—187 East Broadway, New York, N.Y. 10002. *Agent*—Theron Raines, Raines & Raines, 71 Park Ave., Suite 4A, New York, N.Y. 10016.

CAREER: U.S. Air Force Research and Development Center, Dayton, Ohio, technical translator and editor, 1948-52; Associated Science Translators, Inc., Newark, N.J., president, 1952-54; free-lance translator in London, England, 1954-56; *Stereo Review* (magazine), New York, N.Y., associate editor, 1956-62; writer, 1962—.

MEMBER: National Association of Science Writers.

AWARDS, HONORS: D.H.L., Tarkio College, 1973.

WRITINGS:

(With Renatus Hartogs) *Four-Letter Word Games,* M. Evans, 1967.
(With Hope Buyukmici) *Unexpected Treasure,* M. Evans, 1968.
Johann Strauss: Father and Son, and Their Era, David & Charles, 1971, published as *The Waltz Kings: Johann Strauss, Father and Son, and Their Era,* Morrow, 1972.
The True Sound of Music: A Practical Guide to Sound Equipment for the Home, Dutton, 1973.
William Penn: Apostle of Dissent, Morrow, 1974.
ABC'S of Hi-Fi and Stereo, 3rd edition, H. W. Sams, 1974.
Durable Pleasures: A Practical Guide to Better Tape Recording, Dutton, 1976.
Better Listening: A Practical Guide to Buying and Enjoying Stereo Equipment for the Home, Scribner, 1981.

(Translator from the German) Tom Bottomore and William Outhwaite, editors, *Max Weber and Karl Marx,* Allen Unwin, 1982.

(With Ivan Berger) *The New Sound of Stereo: The Complete Buying Guide to Buying and Using the Latest Hi-Fi Equipment,* New American Library, 1986.

Author of syndicated column published in the *New York Times.* Contributor to numerous magazines, including *New York Times Magazine, Opera News,* and *Rolling Stone.*

*   *   *

FARKAS, Philip (Francis) 1914-

PERSONAL: Born March 5, 1914, in Chicago, Ill.; son of Emil Nelson (an advertising executive) and Anna (Cassady) Farkas; married Margaret Groves, May 11, 1939; children: Carol (Mrs. Stephen Mumma), Lynn (Mrs. Roy Weddle), Jean (Mrs. John Van Minnen), Margaret Frances (Mrs. Terry Radke). *Education:* Educated in Chicago, Ill.; studied with Louis Dufrasne and at training school for Chicago Symphony Orchestra. *Politics:* "Fluctuates." *Religion:* Christian Science.

ADDRESSES: Home—2232 East Cape Cod Dr., Bloomington, Ind. 47401. *Office*—School of Music, Indiana University, Bloomington, Ind. 47405.

CAREER: Solo French horn with Kansas City Philharmonic, 1933-36, with Chicago Symphony Orchestra, 1936-41, 1947-60, with Cleveland Orchestra, 1941-45, 1946-47, and with Boston Symphony Orchestra, 1945-46. Teacher of French horn at Kansas City Conservatory, 1933-36, Chicago Musical College, 1937-40, Cleveland Institute of Music, 1946-47, Roosevelt University, 1948-56, DePaul University, 1948-56, and Northwestern University, 1952-60; Indiana University at Bloomington, distinguished professor of music, 1960-84, distinguished professor emeritus, 1984—. Member of Chicago Symphony Woodwind Quintet, 1937-60, and American Woodwind Quintet, 1960-82. Performer and teacher at Aspen Music Festival, 1960-76, gives lecture-performances at colleges and music conventions.

MEMBER: International Horn Society, American Federation of Musicians, American Navion Society, Aircraft Owners and Pilots Association, Phi Mu Alpha Sinfornia.

AWARDS, HONORS: Honorary Mus.D. from Eastern Michigan University, 1978.

WRITINGS:

The Art of French Horn Playing, Summy-Birchard, 1956.
(Editor) *French Horn Passages from Contemporary French Music,* Elkan-Vogel, 1956.
The Art of Brass Playing, Wind Music, 1962.
(Editor with Milan Yancich) *Complete First Horn Parts to Tchaikowsky's Major Orchestral Works,* Wind Music, 1969.
A Photographic Study of Forty Virtuoso Horn Players' Embouchures, Wind Music, 1971.
The Art of Musicianship, Musical Publications, 1976.

SIDELIGHTS: Until recently, Philip Farkas flew his own Navion plane to most of his lecture engagements.

*   *   *

FASSBINDER, Rainer Werner 1946-1982

PERSONAL: Born May 31, 1946, in Bad Woerishofen, Germany (now West Germany); died June 10, 1982, in Munich,

West Germany, of an overdose of cocaine and sleeping pills; son of Helmut (a physician) and Liselotte Pempeit (a translator and actress; maiden name, Eder) Fassbinder; married Ingrid Caven (an actress), 1970 (divorced). *Education:* Attended Fridi-Leophard Studio, c. 1966.

ADDRESSES: Home—Munich, West Germany. *Office*—c/o New Yorker Films, 16 West 61st St., New York, N.Y. 10023.

CAREER: Writer, director, and producer of plays and films; actor. Actor in Munich Action Theatre, 1967-68, and in motion pictures, including "Tonys Freunde," 1967, "Baal," 1969, "Katzelmacher," 1969, "Warnung vor einer heiligen Nutte," 1971, "Faustrecht der Freiheit," 1975, and others. Director of Theatre am Turm in Frankfurt, West Germany, 1974-75. Founder of Antitheatre, 1968; co-founder of Film-Verlag der Autoren, 1970.

MEMBER: PEN.

AWARDS, HONORS: West German Film Critics Prize and Federal Film Prize, both 1969, both for "Katzelmacher"; Federal Film Prize, 1970, for "Warum laeuft Herr R. amok?"; Critics Award, Cannes Film Festival, 1974, for "Angst isst die Seele auf"; Berlin Film Festival first prize, 1979, for "Die Ehe der Maria Braun"; Golden Bear prize, Berlin Film Festival, 1982, for "Die Sehnsucht der Veronika Voss"; German Academy of Producing Arts television award; Patron award (Gerhard-Hauptmann prize); and other film awards.

WRITINGS:

SELF-DIRECTED PLAYS

"Iphigenie auf Taurus" (adapted from the play by Johann Wolfgang von Goethe), first produced at Antiteater (Munich, West Germany), 1968.
"Pioniere in Ingolstadt" (adapted from the play by Marie-Louise Fleisser), first produced at Antiteater, 1968.
"Ajax" (adapted from the writings of Sophocles), first produced at Antiteater, 1968.
"Orgie Ubu" (adapted from the play "Ubu Roi," by Alfred Jarry), first produced at Antiteater, 1968.
"Anarchie in Bayern," first produced at Antiteater, 1969.
"Werwolf," first produced at Antiteater, 1969.
Katzelmacher (also see below; first produced at Antiteater), Verlag der Autoren, 1969.
(With John Gay) *Die Bettleroper* (also see below; first produced at Antiteater), Verlag der Autoren, 1970.
Das brennende Dorf (adapted from the writings of Lope de Vega; also see below; first produced at Antiteater), Verlag der Autoren, 1970.
Blut am Hals der Katze (also see below; first produced at Antiteater), Verlag der Autoren, 1970.
Bremer Freiheit [and] *Ein buergerliches Trauerspiel* (also see below; first produced at Antiteater), Verlag der Autoren, 1971.
Die bitteren Traenen der Petra von Kant (also see below; first produced at Antiteater), Verlag der Autoren, 1973.
(With Hans Guenther Pflaum) *Das bisschen Realitaet, das ich brauche* (first produced at Antiteater), Hanser, 1976.

SELF-DIRECTED SCREENPLAYS

"Der Stadtstreicher" (short film; released in the United States as "The City Bums"), Roser-Film, 1965.
"Das kleine Chaos" (short film; released in the United States as "The Small Chaos"), Roser-Film, 1966.
"Liebe ist kaelter als Tod" (released in the United States as "Love Is Colder Than Death"), Antiteater-X-Film, 1969.
"Katzelmacher" (also see below), Antiteater-X-Film, 1969.

"Goetter der Pest" (released in the United States as "Gods of the Plague"), Antiteater, 1969.

(With Michael Fengler) "Warum laeuft Herr R. amok?" (released in the United States as "Why Does Herr R. Run Amok?"), Antiteater and Mara-Film, 1969.

"Der amerikanische Soldat" (released in the United States as "The American Soldier"), Antiteater, 1970.

(With Fengler) "Die niklashauser Fahrt" (released in the United States as "The Niklashauser Drive"), Janus Film und Fernsehen, 1970.

"Rio das Mortes," Janus Film und Fernsehen/Antiteater-X-Film, 1970.

"Whity," Atlantis Film/Antiteater-X-Film, 1970.

"Warnung vor einer heiligen Nutte" (released in the United States as "Beware of a Holy Whore"), Antiteater-X-Film/Nova International, 1970.

"Haendler der vier Jahreszeiten" (released in the United States as "The Merchant of Four Seasons"), Tango Film, 1971.

"Die bitteren Traenen der Petra von Kant" (also see below), Tango Film, 1972.

"Effi Briest" (adapted from the novel by Theodore Fontane), Tango Film, 1974.

(With Christian Hohoff) "Faustrecht der Freiheit" (released in the United States as "Fox and His Friends" and as "Survival of the Fittest"; also released as "First-Right of Freedom"), Tango Film, 1975.

(With Kurt Raab) "Mutter Kuesters faehrt zum Himmel" (released in the United States as "Mother Kuesters Goes to Heaven"), Tango Film, 1975.

"Satansbraten" (released in the United States as "Satan's Brew"), Albatros Productions, 1976.

"Chinesisches Roulette" (released in the United States as "Chinese Roulette"), Albatros-Film/Les Films du Losange, 1977.

"Die dritte Generation" (released in the United States as "The Third Generation"), Tango Film/Project Filmproduktion im Filmverlag der Autoren, 1978.

"Die Ehe der Maria Braun" (released in the United States as "The Marriage of Maria Braun"), Albatros-Film, 1978.

"In einem Jahr mit 13 Monden" (released in the United States as "In a Year with 13 Moons"), [West Germany], 1978.

(With Peter Marthesheimer and Pea Frohlich) "Lola," United Artists Classics, 1982.

SELF-DIRECTED TELEVISION SCRIPTS

"Pioniere in Ingolstadt" (released in the United States as "Recruits in Ingolstadt"; adapted from the writings of Marie-Louise Fleisser), Janus Film und Fernsehen/Antiteater, 1971.

"Acht Stunden sind kein Tag" (released in the United States as "Eight Hours Don't Make a Day"; contains "Jochen und Marion," "Oma und Gregor," "Franz und Ernst," "Harald und Monika," and "Irmgard und Rolf"), WDR-TV, 1972-73.

"Wildwechsel" (released in the United States as "Game Pass"; adapted from the play by Franz Xaver Kroetz), Intertel, 1973.

(With Fritz Mueller-Scherz) "Welt am Draht" (released in the United States as "World on a Wire"; adapted from the novel by Daniel F. Galouye), WDR-TV, 1973.

"Angst isst die Seele auf " (released in the United States as "Ali: Fear Eats the Soul"), Tango Film, 1974.

"Martha," WDR-TV, 1974.

"Ich will doch nur, dass ihr mich liebt" (released in the United States as "I Only Want You to Love Me"), [West Germany], 1976.

"Berlin Alexanderplatz" (based on the novel by Alfred Doeblin; first produced for West German television), Teleculture Films, 1980.

"Querelle" (based on the novel, *Querelle de Brest,* by Jean Genet), [West Germany], 1982, Triumph Films, 1983.

"Bolwieser" (released in the United States as "The Stationmaster's Wife"; adapted from the book by Oskar Maria Graf), Bavaria Atelier, 1983.

OTHER

Antiteater (plays; contains "Katzelmacher," "Preparadise sorry now," and "Die Bettleroper"), Suhrkamp, 1970.

Antiteater 2 (plays; contains "Bremer Freiheit," "Blut am Hals der Katze," and "Das Kaffeehaus," the last adapted from the play by Carlo Goldoni), Suhrkamp, 1972.

Stuecke 3 (plays; contains "Die bitteren Traenen der Petra von Kant," "Das brennende Dorf," and "Der Muell, die Stadt und der Tod"; also see below), Suhrkamp, 1976.

(With Daniel Schmid) "Schatten der Engel" (screenplay; released in the United States as "Shadows of Angels"; adapted from "Der Muell, die Stadt und der Tod"), [West Germany], 1976.

SIDELIGHTS: Although Rainer Werner Fassbinder was the most prolific filmmaker of the German "new wave," his popularity was considerably less than peers Werner Herzog and Wim Wenders. This was due, in part, to Fassbinder's synthesis of style and content in a manner that American audiences found flashy, yet detached. His pessimistic intertwining of politics and love was especially evident in "Ali: Fear Eats the Soul," in which the love affair between a Moroccan immigrant and an elderly German woman is undermined by racism in their community, and "Fox and His Friends," where the homosexual community is a metaphor for class struggle. Some critics intimated that "Fox and His Friends" was a painfully autobiographical film, for Fassbinder himself played Fox, a poor homosexual who finds himself surrounded by potential lovers after winning a lottery. When Fox finally exhausts his funds, he once again finds himself unattended.

Fassbinder's films were a testimony of "someone who has come to the realization that life is a series of dirty tricks and the world a place where the system of rewards and punishments is nothing if not arbitrary," remarked *New York Times* critic Vincent Canby. This philosophy suffused the themes of love and politics present in his films. Fassbinder's productions, wrote John O'Kane in the *International Directory of Films and Filmmakers,* explored "the forms of melodrama and the family romance as a way to place social issues within the frame of sexual politics." This was evident in such productions as "The Bitter Tears of Petra von Kant," "Martha," and "Frauen in New York."

The director's political beliefs were similarly pessimistic, as evidenced in "Mother Kusters Goes to Heaven," the story of a widow attempting to redeem her husband's reputation after his murder-suicide. Because her husband was a factory worker, Mother Kusters is approached by a bourgeois Communist couple trying to convince her that her husband was a martyr; they next try to involve her in a political campaign. Mother Kusters's dealings with anarchists and other Communists also prove exploitive. "As a social critic," wrote Canby in another *New York Times* review, "Mr. Fassbinder is equally skeptical of all prefabricated solutions. His sympathies are with the left, but he doubts everything except the will to survive. All other impulses . . . can be co-opted and exploited by the Establishment."

Fassbinder's nihilism also covered rebellion. In films such as "Love Is Colder Than Death" and "The American Soldier," he depicted the hopelessness and boredom that comes from living apart from society. He was especially fond of portraying the rebel as a Humphrey Bogart-like gangster. In "The American Soldier," a Vietnam veteran-turned-killer is psychologically undermined by the isolation of his occupation; and in "The Gods of the Plague," the gangster dies unceremoniously in a supermarket. For Fassbinder, the rebel, especially one who took his cues from the cinema, was doomed to failure.

In later films, Fassbinder's condemnation of resistance was usurped by one of participation. His despair for cooperation was obvious in "Why Does Herr R. Run Amok?," in which the boredom of Herr R.'s lower-middle-class existence sparks a moment of insanity, resulting in Herr R. killing his family and himself. Herr. R.'s behavior equals that of the husband in "Mother Kusters Goes to Heaven." In the end of that film, Fassbinder depicted Mother Kusters's decision to join society as hopeless. As Canby noted, Fassbinder saw "a gradual, peaceful accommodation to outrageous circumstance as the worst surrender of all."

Some critics suggested that Fassbinder's cinematic style worked detrimentally with his screenplays. Following the work of the Danish Hollywood director Douglas Sirk, who filmed such movies as "The Tarnished Angels" and "Imitation of Life," Fassbinder relied heavily on mirrors, enclosures, and exaggerated angles to emphasize the melodrama. But Sirk's films tended to be glamourized soap operas, and his direction brought both humor and irony to the films. Fassbinder, however, only confused reviewers by favoring Sirk's techniques over realist ones. *New Republic* contributor Stanley Kaufmann believed that "there's a sense of real ability with greased fingers—the form of the work keeps slipping through them." Kaufmann claimed that Fassbinder envied "Sirk his American phase . . ., and, out of a different base, . . . tried to emulate it. But the result [was] neither sound high art nor sound pop art—just one more display of talent in an unfilled work." Other reviewers insisted that Fassbinder's Sirkian style obliviated the content. Gilliat wrote, "The extreme formalism of his best later work tends to hide their warmth."

One of the director's last efforts, "Berlin Alexanderplatz," which first appeared as a fifteen-and-a-half hour television series in West Germany before playing in American cinemas, is generally considered today to be the best of Fassbinder's last few films. It is based on the important two-volume, serio-comic novel by Alfred Doeblin, which Fassbinder had reread many times. For some critics, like *New York Times* contributor James M. Markham, the director's interest in the related themes of love, life, and power culminated in "Alexanderplatz." "The Wunderkind of the postwar German film was mesmerized by the figure of Franz Biberkopf, the proletarian protagonist" in Doeblin's novel, declared Markham. He added that Fassbinder often insisted: "I am Biberkopf." The story, set in late-1920s Berlin, is, according to Fassbinder, whom Kevin Thomas of the *Los Angeles Times* quoted, "The story of two men whose little lives on this earth are destroyed because they never get the opportunity to muster up the courage even to recognize, much less be able to admit to themselves, that they desire each other in an unusual way."

Compared to other 1980s films by Fassbinder, such as "Querelle" and "Lola," "Berlin Alexanderplatz" received the highest critical praise. Indeed, Canby asserted, "Its importance goes far beyond the Fassbinder career, though we must now reevaluate

that career in light of 'Berlin Alexanderplatz,' a 1980 work that has the effect of being the coda we did not see in Fassbinder's final film, the lamentable 'Querelle.' " Successes like "Alexanderplatz" redeemed Fassbinder for his less acclaimed works; and some critics claimed that it was his prolificity which was responsible for such triumphs. "Like many prodigal artists," declared Gilliat, "he seems to correct any mistake he finds in a film by immersing himself in the next picture." *Village Voice* critic Andrew Sarris opined: "I think that artists should be measured by quantity as well as by quality. . . . Too many contemporary artists futz around by meditating on the one Great Work that shall redeem them. More often . . . great works emerge not in splendid isolation, but in fruitful communion with many lesser works."

"Neither Mr. Fassbinder's admirers nor his detractors ever ceased marveling at his astonishing productivity," wrote *New York Times* reviewer Janet Maslin. Producing three or four films a year, Fassbinder pushed himself for financial reasons, Maslin explained. But Maslin also quoted the director as once saying: "it also depends on my psyche. I must constantly be working." He later added, continued Maslin: "I cannot work in a more subtle way than I am working already. Even if I had more time, my films wouldn't have been any different." Although the list of his movie credits was cut short, Fassbinder remains one of the most important German directors of modern times. He was, asserted Maslin, the "film maker most responsible for the resurgence of German cinema in the 1970's." Canby eulogizes Fassbinder as "a master of movies, a cinema artist who also worked well on the stage and in television, the most gifted, most original film-making talent since Jean-Luc Godard."

BIOGRAPHICAL/CRITICAL SOURCES:

BOOKS

Contemporary Literary Criticism, Volume 20, Gale, 1982.
International Directory of Films and Filmmakers, Volume 2, St. James, 1984.
Rayns, Tony, editor, *Fassbinder,* British Film Institute, 1976.

PERIODICALS

Chicago Tribune, January 16, 1981.
Film Quarterly, summer, 1975, winter, 1976-77, fall, 1979, spring, 1980.
Horizon, September, 1977.
Los Angeles Times, March 2, 1983, April 14, 1983, July 31, 1983.
New Republic, September 29, 1979.
New Yorker, June 14, 1976, May 30, 1977.
New York Post, March 7, 1977.
New York Times, October 8, 1979, October 26, 1979, September 9, 1980, February 16, 1981, June 20, 1982, April 29, 1983, June 24, 1983, July 10, 1983, August 7, 1983, August 10, 1983, November 5, 1985, March 17, 1986.
Time, March 20, 1978.
Times Literary Supplement, September 19, 1980.
Washington Post, December 19, 1976, February 1, 1980, November 23, 1982.
Village Voice, July 11, 1977, August 29, 1977.

OBITUARIES:

PERIODICALS

Chicago Tribune, June 11, 1982.
Detroit Free Press, June 11, 1982.
Los Angeles Times, June 11, 1982.
Newsweek, June 21, 1982.
New York Times, June 11, 1982, June 19, 1982.

Time, June 21, 1982.
Times (London), June 11, 1982.
Washington Post, June 11, 1982.*

* * *

FAY, Stephen (Francis John) 1938-

PERSONAL: Born August 14, 1938, in Littleborough, England; son of Gerard (a journalist) and Alice Mary (Bentley) Fay; married Prudence Butcher, August 29, 1964; children: Matthew, Susanna. *Education:* University of New Brunswick, B.A., 1958, M.A., 1959; London School of Economics and Political Science, graduate study, 1959-60.

ADDRESSES: Home—17 College Cross, London N.1, England.

CAREER: Canadian Atlantic Provinces Office (diplomatic and trade representatives), London, England, economist, 1959-61; *Glasgow Herald,* Glasgow, Scotland, leader writer and industrial correspondent in Glasgow and London, 1961-64; *Sunday Times,* London, various editorial posts, 1964-84; *Business Magazine,* London, editor, 1986-89; associate editor, *Independent on Sunday,* 1989—.

WRITINGS:

(With Lewis Chester and Hugo Young) *The Zinoviev Letter,* Heinemann, 1967, Lippincott, 1968.
Measure for Measure: Reforming the Unions, Chatto & Windus, 1970.
(With Chester and Magnus Linklater) *Hoax: The Inside Story of the Clifford Irving-Howard Hughes Affair,* Viking, 1972.
(With Phillip Knightley) *The Death of Venice,* Praeger, 1976.
Beyond Greed: The Hunts and Their Silver Bubble, Viking, 1982 (published in England as *The Great Silver Bubble,* Hodder & Stoughton, 1982).
(With Roger Wood) *The Ring: Anatomy of an Opera,* Secker & Warburg, 1984, Longwood, 1985.
Portrait of an Old Lady: Turmoil at the Bank of England, Viking, 1987.

WORK IN PROGRESS: Peter Hall, a biography.

SIDELIGHTS: In 1979 and 1980, a small group of investors, led by the Hunt brothers of Texas, attempted to control the silver market by buying large quantities of the metal and driving up prices. "The tale of how the Hunts and their shadowy international consorts moved toward the peak of the silver mountain and how they were toppled on the verge has been mined with great skill by Stephen Fay, a British journalist with an engaging manner, a respect for the line between fact and surmise, and an ability to convey his own fascination with the commodities market and its denizens," summarizes Walter Goodman in the *New York Times Book Review.* In *Beyond Greed: The Hunts and Their Silver Bubble,* Fay "provides essential explanations of how the market is supposed to work and how it really works, the difference between bullion and bull. . . . He hops about the globe, offering sharp sketches of rascals and respectables, though it is not always easy to tell them apart." In addition, notes economist John Kenneth Galbraith in the *Atlantic,* "Fay writes with a justifiable awe of the large sums—always in the tens and often in the hundreds of millions—that were involved in the silver caper . . . [and] also with a pleasant absence of indignation." "Mr. Fay has made it all seem . . . simple and straightforward," observes the *New York Times*'s Christopher Lehmann-Haupt. "And this is quite remarkable when you consider the numbers involved."

Times Literary Supplement contributor Richard Lambert similarly states that Fay's account "makes gripping reading when it deals with matters of public record," in addition to giving "a very clear and comprehensive explanation of the extremely complicated way in which the commodity markets operate." Nevertheless, the critic faults Fay for being "occasionally driven to flights of fancy and to rather irritating *Dallas*-style writing" in relating the history of the Hunts and their collaborators. In contrast, Lehmann-Haupt believes that "what with the secrecy of the Hunt brothers—or perhaps one should say, what with their selective lapses of memory when they were finally investigated . . . —it is impressive how much Mr. Fay has managed to dig up. Only once does he resort to pure speculation," continues the critic, "and this involves only a relatively minor passage of events." *Beyond Greed* "is well written and admirably researched," remarks Galbraith, "some minor errors notwithstanding. Mr. Fay is an Englishman, an exponent of the modern British art form that consists in taking some subject of current interest, not necessarily one involving criminal intent, tracking down all details and ramifications, and presenting the results in wholly literate fashion," the critic concludes. "This he has done with the Hunts and the silver bubble."

BIOGRAPHICAL/CRITICAL SOURCES:

PERIODICALS

Atlantic, May, 1982.
New York Times, May 15, 1972, December 21, 1982.
New York Times Book Review, June 25, 1972, November 21, 1976, April 18, 1982.
Spectator, June 19, 1982.
Times (London), August 23, 1984.
Times Literary Supplement, August 4, 1972, December 17, 1976, August 6, 1982.
Washington Post, May 21, 1982.

* * *

FEINGOLD, Henry L(eo) 1931-

PERSONAL: Born February 6, 1931, in Ludwigshafen am Rhein, Germany (now West Germany); son of Marcus M. (a merchant) and Frieda (Singer) Feingold; married Vera Schiff (an artist), February 7, 1954; children: Margo Rachel, Judith Eva. *Education:* Brooklyn College (now Brooklyn College of the City University of New York), B.A., 1953, M.A., 1954: New York University, Ph.D., 1966. *Religion:* Jewish.

ADDRESSES: Home—280 Ninth Ave., New York, N.Y. 10001. *Office*—Department of History, Bernard M. Baruch College of the City University of New York, 17 Lexington Ave., New York, N.Y. 10010.

CAREER: Bernard M. Baruch College of the City University of New York, New York, N.Y., 1968—, began as assistant professor, professor of history, 1976—. *Military service:* U.S. Army, Intelligence, 1954-57, 1961.

MEMBER: American Jewish Historical Society (former chairman of academic council), Association of Jewish Studies (member of executive committee), Jewish Historical Society of New York (member of executive committee), Leo Baeck Institute (fellow).

AWARDS, HONORS: Presidential Award for Excellence in Scholarship, Bernard M. Baruch College of the City University of New York, 1986; Leon Jolson Award for *The Politics of Rescue: The Roosevelt Administration and the Holocaust, 1938-44.*

WRITINGS:

The Politics of Rescue: The Roosevelt Administration and the Holocaust, 1938-44 (*Commentary* Book Club selection), Rutgers University Press, 1970, expanded and updated edition, Schocken, 1980.

Zion in America: The Jewish Experience from Colonial Times to the Present (*Commentary* Book Club selection), Twayne, 1975, revised edition, Hippocrene, 1981.

A Midrash on American Jewish History, State University of New York Press, 1982.

Contributor to professional journals. Editor, *American Jewish History,* 1978-83; member of editorial board, *YIVO Annual, Shoah,* and *Reconstructionist.*

WORK IN PROGRESS: Entering the Main Stream: American Jewry, 1920-1945.

SIDELIGHTS: Historian Henry L. Feingold's *The Politics of Rescue: The Roosevelt Administration, 1938-44* investigates the reasons why both United States government agencies and American Jewish organizations refused to provide proper aid to help persecuted Jews during World War II.

BIOGRAPHICAL/CRITICAL SOURCES:

PERIODICALS

National Review, December 15, 1970.
Time, March 2, 1981.

*   *   *

FEINSTEIN, Elaine   1930-

PERSONAL: Born October 24, 1930, in Bootle, England; daughter of Isidore and Fay (Compton) Cooklin; married Arnold Feinstein (an immunologist), July 22, 1957; children: Adam, Martin, Joel. *Education:* Cambridge University, B.A., 1952, M.A., 1955.

ADDRESSES: Agent—Gill Coleridge, Anthony Sheil Associates, Ltd., 2-3 Morwell St., London WC1B 3AR, England.

CAREER: Cambridge University Press, London, England, editorial staff member, 1960-62; Bishop's Stortford Training College, Hertfordshire, England, lecturer in English, 1963-66; University of Essex, Wivenhoe, England, assistant lecturer in literature, 1967-70; full-time writer, 1971—. Has also worked as a journalist.

MEMBER: Poetry Society, Eastern Arts Association.

AWARDS, HONORS: Arts Council grants, 1970, 1977; Daisy Miller Award, 1971, for fiction; F.R.S.L.

WRITINGS:

POETRY

In a Green Eye, Goliard Press, 1966.
The Magic Apple Tree, Hutchinson, 1971.
At the Edge, Sceptre Press, 1972.
The Celebrants and Other Poems, Hutchinson, 1973.
Some Unease and Angels, Green River Press, 1977, 2nd edition, Hutchinson, 1982.
The Feast of Euridice, Faber, 1981.
Badlands, Hutchinson, 1986.

FICTION

The Circle (novel), Hutchinson, 1970.
The Amberstone Exit (novel), Hutchinson, 1972.
Matters of Chance (short stories), Covent Garden Press, 1972.

The Glass Alembic (novel), Hutchinson, 1973, published as *The Crystal Garden* (novel), Dutton, 1974.
The Children of the Rose (novel), Hutchinson, 1974.
The Ecstasy of Dr. Miriam Garner (novel), Hutchinson, 1976.
The Shadow Master (novel), Hutchinson, 1977, Simon & Schuster, 1978.
The Silent Areas (short stories), Hutchinson, 1980.
The Survivors (novel), Hutchinson, 1982.
The Border (novel), Hutchinson, 1984.
Mother's Girl (novel), Dutton, 1988.
All You Need (novel), Hutchinson, 1989.

OTHER

(Editor) *Selected Poems of John Clare,* University Tutorial Press, 1968.
The Selected Poems of Marina Tsvetayeva, Oxford University Press, 1971, reprinted, Dutton, 1987.
"Breath" (teleplay), British Broadcasting Corporation (BBC), 1975.
(Translator) *Three Russian Poets: Margarita Aliger, Yunna Moritz & Bella Akhmadulina,* Carcanet Press, 1979.
(Editor with Fay Weldon) *New Stories,* Arts Council of Great Britain, 1979.
"Echoes" (radio play), 1980.
"Lunch" (teleplay), 1981.
"Lear's Daughters" (play), first produced in London at Battersea Arts Centre, September 27, 1982.
"The Diary of a Country Gentlewoman" (teleplay; twelve-part series), ITV, 1984.
Bessie Smith (biography; Lives of Modern Women Series), Viking, 1986.
A Captive Lion: The Life of Marina Tsvetayeva, Dutton, 1987.
(Translator with Antonina W. Bouis) Nika Turbina, *First Draft,* Marion Boyars, 1988.

Also author of essays and reviews for periodicals, including *Times Literary Supplement.*

SIDELIGHTS: Elaine Feinstein is an English writer whose works include poetry, fiction, plays, and translations of several well-known Russian poets. Such diversity of interest and talent is relatively rare, but according to Michael Schmidt in the *Times Literary Supplement,* all of Feinstein's disparate writings "are very much one voice." The granddaughter of Jews who fled persecution in Tsarist Russia, Feinstein retains a strong preoccupation with her background and upbringing; this fascination with her Eastern European origins informs both her poetry and most of her novels. *Dictionary of Literary Biography* contributor Peter Conradi calls Feinstein "a writer who has made fragmentation and deracination her special topics" and adds that she "has developed a language of formidable efficiency for evoking each, and for searching for authentication in the teeth of each. If her earliest books defamiliarized the ordinary world and the domestic self, her later books appropriately domesticated the exotic." *New Yorker* essayist George Steiner likewise notes that a "pulse of narrative and of dramatic voice is vivid in [Feinstein's] verse," and in the *New Statesman,* Peter Buckman calls the author "a discovery, a writer of limitless simplicity and mistress of a musical prose that can apparently find rhythm anywhere."

Feinstein was born in Bootle, Lancashire and brought up in the industrial town of Leicester in the English Midlands. Her father owned a factory, but his success with it fluctuated wildly. Although her family was never destitute, Feinstein did know some genteel poverty in her childhood. An only child, she was raised to respect religion, but it was only after the Second World War that she came to realize just what being Jewish meant. Feinstein told the *Contemporary Authors Autobiography Series* that her childhood sense of security "was exploded, once and for all, at the war's end, when I read what exactly had been done to so many children, as young as I was, in the hell of Hitler's camps. You could say that in that year I became Jewish for the first time. That is not something I regret. But no doubt the knowledge of human cruelty damaged me. For a very long time afterwards, I could feel no ordinary human emotion without testing it against that imagined experience, and either suspecting it or dismissing it." Conradi puts it another way. After the war, he writes, Feinstein came "to an understanding of the degree to which being Jewish could mean to suffer and live in danger."

Feinstein was educated with a grant provided by the Butler Education Act of 1944, receiving both her Bachelor's and Master's degrees from Cambridge University. In 1957, two years after leaving Cambridge, she married Arnold Feinstein, an immunologist. For several years thereafter she devoted herself to rearing three sons, but she was also able to work as an editor for Cambridge University Press and as a part-time English lecturer at several colleges. Her first volume of poetry, *In a Green Eye,* was published in 1966. According to Deborah Mitchell in the *Dictionary of Literary Biography,* the book "already shows an unassuming sureness of diction and imagery. . . . The poems are simple and generously affectionate—she is always anxious to do justice to whomever she is 'portraying' as well as to express her own relationship with the individual. There is also an unsentimental recognition that, in human relationships, people are tied to one another, pushing and pulling toward and away from one another in mutual dependency."

For a time in the late 1960s Feinstein joined a poetry group in an effort to gain more contact with her poetic voice. The group helped her to do that, primarily because she came to disagree with its insistence on "Englishness" as a motivating characteristic. Conradi suggests that members of the group "wished to de-Europeanize themselves, to make a cult of and to explore the history of their particular Englishness. This helped [Feinstein] define herself against any such cult, as a person who had never definitely 'settled' in England, and whose roots, if she had them and was not nomadic, were certainly not to be discovered in a nationalist version of 'Little England.'" Thereafter Feinstein's work began to explore her ancestry and heritage as well as the horrors inflicted on modern Jews. Her poetry was especially influenced by the verse of Marina Tsvetayeva, a Russian author of the early twentieth century.

Feinstein told *CA:* "I began to write poetry in the '60's very *consciously* influenced by American poets; at a time when the use of line, and spacing, to indicate the movement of poetry, was much less fashionable than it is now among young British poets. It was my translations from the Russian of Marina Tsvetayeva, however, that gave me my true voice, or at least made me attend to a strength and forward push, *against* and *within* a formal structure, that I could have only learnt from Tsvetayeva herself. In the wholeness of her self exposure, she opened a whole world of experience. Without her, I should never have written novels, still less plays."

Feinstein's early novels "came out of domestic and personal experience whose woes and wonders they to some degree make lyrical," to quote Conradi. A favorite early theme with Feinstein is a woman's search for identity within and outside of familial relationships. In the *Times Literary Supplement,* D. M. Thomas observes that Feinstein wants to show "that women's dreams are common and commonplace, because of their depressed lives." Both *The Circle* and *The Amberstone Exit* feature young women

so mired in domestic or family responsibilities that they cannot fully explore themselves. Mitchell contends that Feinstein's early work, "concerned with the world of personal emotion and relationships and with the domestic environment, is remarkable for its economy, its stringent emotional honesty, and tough ironic humor, as well as an intensity and richness of metaphor unusual with this sort of subject matter." Most critics agree, however, that the death of Feinstein's parents in 1973 marks the author's movement into new thematic territory. Conradi states: "It was about this time that [Feinstein] began to enquire into Jewish history more systematically and enlarge her reading. A wish to make her characters more securely substantial also entered into this investigation; the result was not merely more substantial characterization, but also more satisfying mythmaking." To quote *Times Literary Supplement* correspondent Susannah Clapp, Feinstein's characters began to be "not just incidentally irritated or pleased by their dreams and memories, but changed and controlled by them. . . . Some of [her] most persuasive writing . . . describes people in the grip of flashback or nightmare."

Mitchell writes: "In a complex process Feinstein has combined traditional myths with myths she has created out of themes that arose originally from direct reactions to her personal experience and that have been gradually clarified and set into a broader historical perspective." In works such as *The Shadow Master, The Ecstasy of Dr. Miriam Garner,* and *The Border,* Feinstein leaves not only the boundaries of England but the constraints of realism; characters confront the drama of Jewish history, and one way or another it begins to control their lives. Lorna Sage describes Feinstein's intentions in the *Times Literary Supplement:* "Elaine Feinstein has long been obsessed with the persistence of the past in her characters' lives," Sage declares. "The last war, the holocaust, the webs of violence, fanaticism, exile and betrayal that make up recent history (especially Jewish history) reach out to reclaim her cosmopolitan, clever, 'free' people again and again." Conradi observes that in many of Feinstein's novels "someone falls dangerously ill, sick beyond the reach even of modern pharmacy, and it is often the past which can be said figuratively to have sickened them, and which has returned to get them." In *New Statesman,* Clapp contends that this obsession with the past is represented by ghostly visitations. "Now the spectres have been unleashed," Clapp concludes, "and, though it's not easy to give whole-hearted assent to their original necessity, the open acknowledgment of their presence brings remarkable release."

One of Feinstein's best known novels is *The Survivors,* a multi-generational story of two Jewish families who flee Odessa for turn-of-the-century Liverpool. In the *Times Literary Supplement,* Peter Lewis describes the families: "The Gordons are extremely well-to-do and middle-class, and have been assimilated to a considerable extent into English social life. The Katz family is working class, belongs to the Liverpool equivalent of a ghetto (within a slum area), and is orthodox in religion." The tale revolves around a marriage between the Gordon and Katz families, and the subsequent offspring of that union. Lewis notes a good probability that Feinstein "has transmuted her family and personal history into fiction in *The Survivors,* which is full of insights into the changing patterns of Jewish life during this century." *Listener* contributor John Mellors finds more to praise than just the novel's story, however. "It is the poet's precision and verbal fastidiousness which make *The Survivors* far more than just another family chronicle," Mellors writes. Neil Philip offers a similar opinion in *British Book News. The Survivors,* concludes Philip, "is an exceptional novel: intimate, engrossing, economical, yet covering sixty years, two world wars and immense social change. It is Elaine Feinstein's remarkably sure grip on her material which enables her to treat such large themes, to encompass three generations, to manage such a large cast, without losing sight of the personal, the individual, the sense of the minute as well as the year. . . . Fiction as rich and rewarding as this is rare."

Her novels and short stories may attract a wider readership, but Feinstein is also respected in British literary circles for her poetry. In *Spectator,* Emma Tennant calls the author "a powerful poet, whose power lies in the disarming combination of openness and sibylline cunning, a fearless and honest eye on the modern world, the smallest domestic detail, the nerve-bare feelings of people lashed together in marriage, parental and filial relationships—and then, suddenly, like a buried sketch emerging from under an accepted picture and proving to be of a totally different subject, terrifying, uneasy, evoking the old spells that push us this way and that in our lives of resisted superstitions." Tennant adds that the works "have lives of their own, they are very delicately observed. And, in poems which can seem at first spare and slight, there is a powerful undertow of sane love." Mitchell expresses a similar opinion. "The poems come from a familiar world but there is nothing cozy or reassuringly safe about Feinstein's domesticity," Mitchell writes. ". . . [Feinstein's] poems are faithful to the actual experience described . . . but she is less interested, finally, in realism for its own sake than in the 'making strange' of familiar experience to enable the reader to recognize its importance once more." Schmidt discusses Feinstein's style, noting that her language "evokes a memory, thought or perception in just the way it came to consciousness—brokenly, or in a pondered fashion, or suddenly in a flash. This is not language miming experience, but miming rather the process by which experience is registered and understood. Thus the freshness of her writing, the occasional obscurities, and the sense that despite the apparent self-consciousness of style, she is paradoxically the least artificial, the least *literary* of writers. The poems are composed . . . not to *be* poems but to witness accurately to how she experiences."

Feinstein's interest in the poet Tsvetayeva, who she calls "my teacher of courage," has continued for more than twenty years. Feinstein has not only translated Tsvetayeva's poetry, she has also written a biography entitled *A Captive Lion: The Life of Marina Tsvetayeva.* In a *Spectator* review, Peter Levi contends that the work "as it now stands is like the ultimate Tsvetayeva poem, a painful extension of the painful life, with its final focus on a nail used for tethering horses from which she hung herself. It is not the kind of truth one enjoys hearing." Most critics have praised Feinstein's translations from the Russian—a difficult undertaking given the disparities between the two languages. Levi observes that some of the resultant works "are magnificent poems that do not look like translations at all, they are so good." *Spectator* correspondent Emma Fisher writes: "The thought, the feeling, even the wit, [Feinstein] transfers into plain but intense English, sometimes using rhyme, assonance and regular metres, but often preferring to let the words make their own awkward, blatant shapes on the page." According to Ellendea Proffer in the *New York Times Book Review,* readers "can only be grateful for her work in bringing this difficult poet [Tsvetayeva] into English, and certainly it can be said that these are the best translations available."

Conradi feels that Feinstein's "impressive progress as a novelist can be seen . . . as an emancipation of prose from a provincial sense of its limits," a discovery the author gleaned from her work on Tsvetayeva. Conradi adds that Feinstein "wants to write novels which *move* her readers, as the great novels of the past have done, and to involve them in the fate of her characters so that they will care about what happens to them." Addressing herself to Feinstein's poetic contributions, Mitchell writes: "The mature achievement of her verse has been recognized by a small number of diverse critics, [although] . . . the very individuality which is so refreshing in her work, as well as its diversity, has puzzled a sometimes parochial English reading public." Nevertheless, concludes Mitchell, Feinstein is "something of a rarity among writers—equally at home in verse and fiction, being too well aware of the distinct qualities of each form to make one an adjunct of the other. The cross-fertilization between narrative and lyric means that she is continually developing new and enriching approaches to writing poetry." Schmidt declares that as she enters her third decade as a professional writer, Feinstein has become the creator of "a richly *moral* art" that "eschews facile effect, focuses on its subject, not its audience." In Peter Lewis's opinion, Feinstein "is well on the way to being a writer of infinite variety."

BIOGRAPHICAL/CRITICAL SOURCES:

BOOKS

Contemporary Authors Autobiography Series, Volume 1, Gale, 1984.
Contemporary Literary Criticism, Volume 36, Gale, 1986.
Dictionary of Literary Biography, Gale, Volume 14: *British Novelists since 1960,* 1983, Volume 40: *Poets of Great Britain and Ireland since 1960,* 1985.
Schmidt, Michael and Grevel Lindop, editors, *British Poetry since 1960,* Carcanet Press, 1972.
Schmidt, Michael and Peter Jones, editors, *British Poetry since 1970,* Carcanet Press, 1980.

PERIODICALS

Books, October, 1970.
British Book News, July, 1982.
Chicago Tribune Book World, December 29, 1985.
Contemporary Review, January, 1979.
Encounter, September-October, 1984.
Globe and Mail (Toronto), March 15, 1986.
Harper's, June, 1974.
Listener, August 20, 1970, November 28, 1974, September 28, 1978, March 11, 1982.
Literary Review, April, 1982.
London Review of Books, July 5-19, 1984.
Los Angeles Times, June 6, 1985.
Los Angeles Times Book Review, December 11, 1988.
Nation, June 25, 1988.
New Statesman, August 21, 1970, May 7, 1971, August 4, 1972, April 11, 1975, June 4, 1976.
New Yorker, June 3, 1974, April 29, 1985.
New York Review of Books, October 8, 1987.
New York Times, February 25, 1974, August 21, 1987.
New York Times Book Review, May 19, 1974, November 4, 1979, September 27, 1987.
Observer, August 16, 1970, August 20, 1972, May 27, 1973, April 20, 1975.
Spectator, June 5, 1976, September 24, 1977, September 23, 1978, June 16, 1979, February 9, 1980, March 7, 1987.
Times (London), November 9, 1985, April 2, 1987, January 21, 1988.
Times Literary Supplement, August 28, 1970, August 11, 1972, June 29, 1973, December 7, 1973, April 25, 1975, June 4, 1976, February 3, 1978, October 6, 1978, January 18, 1980,

February 22, 1980, February 26, 1982, June 8, 1984, July 17, 1987, July 31, 1987, January 22, 1988.
Village Voice, May 27, 1986.

—*Sketch by Anne Janette Johnson*

* * *

FELDMAN, Ruth 1911-

PERSONAL: Born May 21, 1911, in East Liverpool, Ohio; daughter of Mendel (in business) and May (a musician; maiden name, Rosenthal) Wasby; married Moses D. Feldman (a lawyer), May 3, 1934 (died March 4, 1963). *Education:* Attended Western Reserve University (now Case Western Reserve University), 1927-29; Wellesley College, B.A., 1931.

ADDRESSES: Home and office—221 Mount Auburn St. Apt. 307, Cambridge, Mass. 02138.

CAREER: Painter; work exhibited in shows. Poet, translator and editor. Has lectured at numerous universities and institutions in the United States and Italy, including Harvard University, Cornell University, Brandeis University, Boston University, University of Bologna, University of Urbino, and Center for American Studies in Rome.

MEMBER: PEN, American Literary Translators Association, Poetry Society of America, New England Poetry Club.

AWARDS, HONORS: Devil's Advocate award, Poetry Society of America, 1971, for "Delos"; John Florio Award, Translators Association (England), 1976, for translating *Shema: Collected Poems of Primo Levi;* Members' Prize, New England Poetry Club, 1977; Sotheby's International Poetry Competition Prize, 1982; International Translator's Prize, Circe Sabaudia (Italy), 1984; literary translators fellowship, National Endowment for the Arts, 1988.

WRITINGS:

POEMS

The Ambition of Ghosts, Green River Press, 1979.
Poesie di Ruth Feldman, La Giuntina, 1981.
To Whom It May Concern, William Bauhan, 1986.
Perdere la strada nel tempo, Edizioni del Leone (Venice), 1990.

EDITOR AND TRANSLATOR; WITH BRIAN SWANN

Lucio Piccolo, *Collected Poems of Lucio Piccolo,* Princeton University Press, 1972.
Andrea Zanzotto, *Selected Poetry of Andrea Zanzotto,* Princeton University Press, 1975.
Primo Levi, *Shema: Collected Poems of Primo Levi,* Menard, 1976.
Italian Poetry Today, New Rivers Press, 1979.
Rocco Scotellaro, *The Dawn Is Always New: Selected Poetry of Rocco Scotellaro,* Princeton University Press, 1980.
Vittorio Bodini, *The Hands of the South: Selected Poetry of Vittorio Bodini,* Charioteer, 1981.
Bartolo Cattafi, *The Dry Air of The Fire: Selected Poetry of Bartolo Cattafi,* Ardis, 1982.
Primo Levi, *The Collected Poems of Primo Levi,* Faber, 1988.

OTHER

(Translator) Primo Levi, *Moments of Reprieve,* Summit Books, 1986.
(Translator) Margherita Guidacci, *Liber Fulguralis: Poems of Margherita Guidacci,* University of Messina Press, 1986.
(Translator) Margherita Guidacci, *A Book of Sibyls,* Rowan Tree, 1989.

Contributor to anthologies, including *Penguin Book of Women Poets,* Penguin, 1978; *A Book of Women Poets,* Schocken, 1980; *Anthology of Magazine Verse,* Monitor, 1981; *Literary Olympians II,* Crosscurrents, 1987; *Editor's Choice II,* Spirit That Moves Us, 1987; *Women at War,* Simon & Schuster, 1988; *Affinities I,* Latitudes Press; *Border Crossings,* Latitudes Press; *New York Times Book of Verse.* Contributor of poems and translations to numerous magazines and newspapers, including *Nation, Southern Review, AGN 1, Sewanee Review, Nimrod, Yankee, Malahat Review, Yale Review, New York Times,* and *Prairie Schooner.* Co-editor, *Modern Poetry in Translation,* 1975.

WORK IN PROGRESS: Landscape with Ruins, selected poetry of Margherita Guidacci.

SIDELIGHTS: Ruth Feldman once told *CA:* "I have loved Italy since my first trip there in 1936. I have worked with and visited many of Italy's leading poets. I find translating a constant and fascinating challenge. It is too often poorly done. My original motivation remains the same: to make things I like and admire accessible to people who do not know Italian, while preserving the language's spirit and style. I started writing my own poetry when my husband died."

Many of Feldman's poems have been translated into Italian and published in Italian magazines.

* * *

FESTINGER, Leon 1919-1989

PERSONAL: Born May 8, 1919, in New York, N.Y.; died of liver cancer, February 11, 1989, in New York, N.Y.; son of Alex and Sarah (Solomon) Festinger; married Mary Ballou, October 23, 1943; married Trudy Bradley, September 7, 1968; children: (first marriage) Catherine, Richard, Kurt; (second marriage) one daughter. *Education:* City College of New York (now City College of the City University of New York), B.S., 1939; Iowa State University, M.A., 1940, Ph.D., 1942.

ADDRESSES: Home—37 West 12th St., New York, N.Y. 10011. *Office*—Department of Psychology, New School of Social Research, 66 West 12th St., New York, N.Y. 10011.

CAREER: University of Rochester, Rochester, N.Y., instructor, 1943-45; Massachusetts Institute of Technology, Cambridge, associate professor of psychology, 1945-48; University of Michigan, Ann Arbor, associate professor and program director of Research Center for Group Dynamics, 1948-51; Stanford University, Stanford, Calif., professor of psychology, 1955-68; New School for Social Research, New York, N.Y., Else and Hans Staudinger Professor of Psychology, 1968—.

MEMBER: American Psychological Association (fellow; president of division 8, 1963), American Academy of Arts and Sciences (fellow).

AWARDS, HONORS: Distinguished Scientist Award, American Psychological Association, 1959.

WRITINGS:

(Co-author) *Theory and Experiment in Social Communication,* University of Michigan Research Center for Group Dynamics, 1950.
(With Stanley Schacter and Kurt Back) *Social Pressures in Informal Groups: A Study of Human Factors in Housing,* Harper, 1950.
(With Harold H. Kelley) *Changing Attitudes through Social Contact,* University of Michigan Research Center for Group Dynamics, 1951.

(Editor with Daniel Katz) *Research Methods in the Behavioral Sciences,* Dryden Press, 1953.
(With Henry W. Riecken and Schacter) *When Prophecy Fails: A Social and Psychological Study of a Modern Group That Predicted the Destruction of the World,* University of Minnesota Press, 1956.
A Theory of Cognitive Dissonance, Row, Peterson, 1957.
(With H. Lawrence) *Deterrents and Reinforcement: The Psychology of Insufficient Reward,* Stanford University Press, 1962.
(With Vernon Allen and others) *Conflict, Decision, and Dissonance,* Stanford University Press, 1964.
(Editor) *Retrospections on Social Psychology,* Oxford University Press, 1980.
The Human Legacy, Columbia University Press, 1983.

Contributor to professional journals.*

* * *

FICKERT, Kurt J(on) 1920-

PERSONAL: Born December 19, 1920, in Pausa, Germany; son of Kurt Alfred (a mechanic) and Martha (Saerchinger) Fickert; married Lynn B. Janda, August 6, 1946; children: Linda (Mrs. Matthew Mosbacher), Jon, Chris. *Education:* Hofstra College (now University), A.B., 1941; New York University, M.A., 1947, Ph.D., 1952. *Politics:* Independent. *Religion:* Lutheran.

ADDRESSES: Home—33 South Kensington Pl., Springfield, Ohio 45504. *Office*—Department of Languages, Wittenberg University, Springfield, Ohio 45501.

CAREER: Hofstra College (now University), Hempstead, N.Y., instructor, 1947-52, assistant professor of German, 1952-53; Florida State University, Tallahassee, instructor in German, 1953-54; Fort Hays Kansas State College, Hays, assistant professor, 1956-60, associate professor, 1960-67, professor of German, 1967-86, professor emeritus, 1966—, adjunct professor, 1966-68, chairman of department of languages, 1969-75. *Military service:* U.S. Army Air Forces, 1942-45; served in Pacific theater.

MEMBER: American Association of Teachers of German, German Studies Association, Ohio Poetry Day Association (president, 1971-75), Phi Eta Sigma, Phi Beta Kappa.

AWARDS, HONORS: Fulbright grant for teachers of German, Germany, 1957; Stephen Vincent Benet Narrative Poem Award, 1968, for "Struggle with Loneliness," from *Poet Lore;* citation for meritorious achievement, Society for German-American Studies, 1973; New England Prize, *Lyric* (magazine), 1976; second prize, Poets and Patrons, 1978; first prize, Yukuhara Haiku Society of Japan, 1978; first prize, Ohio Poetry Society, 1979; second prize, World Order of Narrative Poets, 1980, 1984; National Endowment for the Humanities grant, 1982; Panola Prize, *Lyric,* 1983; Poetry Prize, *Writer's Digest,* 1985; Broadside Series Winner, *The Red Pagoda,* 1987; First Prize, Orbis Rhyme Revival Award; Third Prize, Erasmus Darwin Award, World Order of Narrative Poets, 1988.

WRITINGS:

To Heaven and Back: The New Morality in the Plays of Friedrich Duerrenmatt, University Press of Kentucky, 1972.
Herman Hesse's Quest, York, 1978.
Kafka's Doubles, Peter Lang, 1979.
Signs and Portents: Myth in the Work of Wolfgang Borchert, York, 1980.
Franz Kafka: Life, Work, and Criticism, York, 1984.
Neither Left nor Right: The Politics of Individualism in Uwe Johnson's Work, Peter Lang, 1987.

CONTRIBUTOR

Anthology of German Poetry, Anchor Books, 1960.
(Author of introduction) Otto Dix, *Der Krieg,* Garland, 1972.
(Author of introduction) Ferdinand Avenarius, *Das Bild als Narr,* Garland, 1972.
Living in the Present, Acheron Press, 1982.
Nachrichten aus den Staaten: Deutsche Literatur in den USA, Olms, 1983.
Manfred Jurgensen, *Johnson: Ansichten, Einsichten, Aussichten,* Francke, 1989.

Contributor of articles to *German Quarterly, Monatshefte, Germanic Notes, Contemporary Literature, Explicator,* and *Modern Drama,* of stories to *Beacon Review* and *Home Planet News,* of poems to *Lyrica Germanica, German-American Studies, Poet Lore, Bitterroot, Poetry Venture, Speak Out, Lunatic Fringe, Change, Southern Humanities Review, Lyric, Blue Unicorn Thirteen* and *Z-Miscellaneous.* Contributor of a translation of a story from German in *Dimension,* and of Emily Dickinson poems into German in *Higginson Journal of Poetry.*

WORK IN PROGRESS: Fantastic Truth: Truth in Fiction.

SIDELIGHTS: Kurt J. Fickert wrote to *CA,* "The eye sees upside down, / but the mind knows the sky from the ground. / Clothed in a body of some mass / spun on a globe like a glass / tumbling through infinity, / the mind invented gravity. / In a world of barren sound / intelligence sought and found / words—a symbolic code / and gave us a name and abode. / To solve its own mystery, / the mind engages in poetry."

* * *

FISHER, Margot
See PAINE, Lauran (Bosworth)

* * *

FitzGERALD, Barbara
See NEWMAN, Mona Alice Jean

* * *

FLECK, Betty
See PAINE, Lauran (Bosworth)

* * *

FLYNN, George
See PAINE, Lauran (Bosworth)

* * *

FM-2030
(F M Esfandiary)

PERSONAL: Name legally changed, 1988; born in Brussels, Belgium; son of A. H. Sadigh (a diplomat) and Mohtaram Esfandiary. *Education:* Attended schools in the Middle East, Europe, and the United States.

ADDRESSES: Office—P.O. Box 24421, Los Angeles, Calif. 90024. *Agent*—Curtis Brown Ltd., Ten Astor Pl., New York, N.Y. 10003.

CAREER: Member of Conciliation Commission for Palestine, United Nations, 1952-54; writer, 1954—. Researcher on social problems in Iran, 1961-62. Worked at various times as counselor in camps for children in New York and California. Lecturer in futurist philosophy at New School for Social Research, Smithsonian Institution, University of California, Los Angeles, Extension Division, and elsewhere.

AWARDS, HONORS: Farfield Foundation grant, 1965; Rockefeller Foundation grant, 1966; Bread Loaf Writers Conference fellowship, 1966.

WRITINGS:

UNDER NAME F M ESFANDIARY

Day of Sacrifice (novel), Obolensky, 1959.
The Beggar (novel), Obolensky, 1965.
Identity Card (novel), Grove, 1966.
(Contributor) William Moynihan, editor, *Essays Today,* Harcourt, 1968.
(Contributor) *Extending Horizons,* Random House, 1969.
Optimism One (nonfiction), Norton, 1970.
Up-Wingers (nonfiction), John Day, 1973.
(Contributor) Maxwell Norman, editor, *Dimensions of the Future,* Holt, 1974.
(Contributor) Maggie Tripp, editor, *Woman Year 2000,* Arbor House, 1974.
(Contributor) *The Future of the Family,* Prentice-Hall, 1977.
Telespheres (nonfiction), Fawcett, 1977.

OTHER

Are You a Transhuman? (nonfiction), Warner Books, 1989.

Contributor, sometimes under name F M Esfandiary, to *Nation, New York Times Magazine, Science Digest, New York Times,* and other periodicals.

WORK IN PROGRESS: Countdown to Immortality; other nonfiction books.

SIDELIGHTS: "Most books are too long, too wordy, too slow [for our times]," told FM-2030, who changed his name from F M Esfandiary to symbolize his belief in the future, to *Futurist* interviewer Mico Delianova. Believing that "modern readers do not have the patience to slush through a mass of verbiage," FM-2030 contends that "any book over 100 or 150 pages is not worth reading. The author has not crystallized the ideas effectively," he explains. That is why the author's nonfiction books are concise publications that read, in Delianova's words, "like rapid printouts." A futurist who maintains that "we are now moving beyond the age of print," FM-2030 tries to "approximate the rhythms of electronics" in his prose. Nor is that the most radical feature of his writing. According to critics, the content of FM-2030's books is even more controversial than his style; *Los Angeles Times* contributor William Overend, for instance, observes that FM-2030 "sees a world where there will be no schools, national governments, conventional family units or traditional parent-child relationships. And that's just for openers."

FM-2030 has detailed his ideas in books such as *Optimism One, Up-Wingers,* and *Telespheres,* which together, he told Delianova, "constitute the synthesis of a triumphant new philosophy of the future." Unlike doomsayers and cynics who see mankind heading into an era of shrinking resources and spiraling costs, FM-2030 foresees a prosperous future for humanity. "We are at the beginning of an age of limitless abundance," he remarked in a *New York Times* interview, adding that "there is no scarcity; there is only the psychology of scarcity. People brought up in the puritan old world of sacrifice and privation believe they don't re-

ally deserve abundance, leisure and pleasure; and yet that's exactly what we're moving toward."

FM-2030 also postulates the advent of "total body prostheses" and "memory transfers" which will help individuals achieve immortality, citing developments such as joint implants and hearing aids as current developments demonstrating the potential for human-machine combinations. As *New York Times* writer Leslie Bennetts reports, FM-2030 believes that this transformation will come about "through the gradual evolution of these 'gawky, fragile animal bodies' into more durable, even eternal alternatives. Malfunctioning parts will be replaced with 'durable, versatile components'; nonflesh implants will be substituted for original parts. The result will be what [the futurist] calls 'telebodies,' comprising many micro-electronic parts."

FM-2030 believes social structures will also be transformed. Schools will be abolished and replaced by teleducation; centralized cities, which are already "obsolete," will become museums, and people will move from one instant community (called telecommunities) to another; globalism and space colonies will supersede nations and people will abandon their national identities to become "Universal." Institutions such as the nuclear family and marriage itself will also disappear. As part of his effort to promote futuristic thinking, FM-2030 has published *Are You a Transhuman,* a series of self-monitors that analyze people's attitudes toward technological and social change. "This book is intended to help the reader monitor his or her rate of personal growth in a world that I see changing rapidly," he told Connie Koenenn of the *Los Angeles Times.* "By regularly measuring our ability to change, we can better come to grips with how we are doing. Are we falling behind? Are we keeping up with the times?"

While some have praised FM-2030 for pushing people to think in unconventional ways, he also has his critics. He receives the heaviest opposition for his suggestion that the family unit be abolished and for his description of motherhood as a source of escape for women fearing involvement with the world. ("Parenthood," he told *CA,* "is the ultimate chauvinism.") To his adversaries, FM-2030 offers the reassurance that in time his theories will seem acceptable, even normal: "Please keep in mind that 20 years ago computers were scary to us," he told *Los Angeles Times* writer Marilyn Elias. "In five or seven years, things that may be scary [today] will be . . . routine. We'll have absorbed and accepted them. We'll even be eager for them, as we're eager to use our personal computers now." Besides which, he told the *New York Times,* "the thrust of history and evolution is . . . irreversible, and no government [or anti-future forces] can stop or even slow down the cumulative [thrust] of change."

AVOCATIONAL INTERESTS: World affairs, the United Nations, global planning, normative philosophy, the post-industrial world, space, physical immortality, the future.

BIOGRAPHICAL/CRITICAL SOURCES:

PERIODICALS

Detroit News, March 22, 1978.
Futurist, June, 1978.
Los Angeles Times, March 20, 1978, April 26, 1985, January 11, 1989.
New Yorker, September 12, 1959.
New York Herald Tribune Book Review, August 30, 1959.
New York Times, July 24, 1966, August 31, 1966, November 8, 1966, July 11, 1979.
New York Times Book Review, November 14, 1965.
Time, December 24, 1965.

Washington Post, December 30, 1973, January 27, 1978.

* * *

FONTENOT, Mary Alice 1910-

PERSONAL: Surname is pronounced *Fon*-te-no; born April 16, 1910, in Eunice, La.; daughter of Elias Valrie and Kate (King) Barras; married Sidney J. Fontenot, September 6, 1925 (died, 1963); married Vincent L. Riehl, Sr., November 14, 1966; children: (first marriage) Edith (Mrs. Burton Ziegler), R. D. (deceased), Julie (Mrs. Michael Landry). *Education:* Attended school in Eunice, La. *Religion:* Roman Catholic.

ADDRESSES: Home—431 Holden Ave., Lafayette, La. 70506. *Office*—Crowley Post-Signal, Crowley, La. 70526.

CAREER: New Era, Eunice, La., reporter, columnist, and women's news writer, 1946-50; *Eunice News,* Eunice, La., editor, 1950-53; *Daily World,* Opelousas, La., columnist, 1953-71; *Daily Advertiser,* Lafayette, La., women's news reporter, 1958-60; *Rayne Tribune,* Rayne, La., editor, 1960-62; area editor, 1962-69, columnist, 1969-71, for *Daily World; Crowley Post-Signal,* Crowley, La., columnist and feature writer, 1977—.

MEMBER: League of American Pen Women, Louisiana Press Women.

AWARDS, HONORS: First prize from National Press Women, 1966; Louisiana Literary Award, Louisiana Library Association, 1976, for *Acadia Parish, La.,* Volume 1: *A History to 1900.*

WRITINGS:

The Ghost of Bayou Tigre (juvenile), Claitors, 1964.
(Editor) *Quelque Chose Douce* (cookbook), Claitors, 1964.
(Editor) *Quelque Chose Piquante* (cookbook), Claitors, 1966.
(With husband, Vincent L. Riehl, Sr.) *The Cat and St. Landry* (biography), Claitors, 1972.
(Editor with Mercedes Vidrine) *Beaucoup Bon* (cookbook), Claitors, 1973.
Acadia Parish, La., Claitors, Volume 1: (with Paul B. Freedland) *A History to 1900,* 1976, Volume 2: *A History to 1920,* 1979.
(With daughter, Julie Landry) *The Louisiana Experience: An Introduction to the Culture of the Bayou State,* Claitors, 1983.
The Star Seed: A Story of the First Christmas, Pelican, 1985.
(With daughter, Edith Ziegler) *The Tensas Story,* Claitors, 1987.

Regular contributor to *Acadiana Profile* magazine.

"CLOVIS CRAWFISH" JUVENILE SERIES

Clovis Crawfish and His Friends, Claitors, 1962, revised edition, Pelican, 1985.
. . . *and the Big Betail,* Claitors, 1963, reprinted, Pelican, 1988.
. . . *and the Singing Cigales,* Claitors, 1964, reprinted, Pelican, 1981.
. . . *and Petit Papillon,* Claitors, 1966, reprinted, Pelican, 1985.
. . . *and the Spinning Spider,* Claitors, 1968, reprinted, Pelican, 1987.
. . . *and the Curious Craupaud,* Claitors, 1970, reprinted, Pelican, 1986.
. . . *and Michelle Mantis,* Claitors, 1976.
. . . *and Etienne Escargot,* Pelican, 1979.
. . . *and the Orphan Zo-Zo,* Pelican, 1983.
. . . *and Simeon Suce-Fleur,* Pelican, 1990.

FOSTER, Harry
See PAINE, Lauran (Bosworth)

* * *

FOWLER, William Morgan, Jr. 1944-

PERSONAL: Born July 25, 1944, in Clearwater, Fla.; son of William Morgan (a U.S. post office employee) and Eleanor (Brennan) Fowler; married Marilyn Louise Noble (an elementary school teacher), August 11, 1968; children: Alison Louise, Nathaniel Morgan. *Education:* Northeastern University, B.A. (magna cum laude), 1967; University of Notre Dame, M.A., 1969, Ph.D., 1971. *Politics:* Democrat. *Religion:* Roman Catholic.

ADDRESSES: Home—323 Franklin St., Reading, Mass. 01867. *Office*—Department of History, Northeastern University, Boston, Mass. 02115.

CAREER: Northeastern University, Boston, Mass., assistant professor, 1971-77, associate professor, 1977-80, professor of history, 1980—, acting associate dean of college of arts and sciences, 1977. Lecturer at universities and museums. Consultant to historical societies and other organizations. *Military service:* U.S. Army Reserve, 1970-84; became captain.

MEMBER: North American Society of Oceanic Historians, Organization of American Historians, U.S. Naval Institute, Naval Historical Foundation, Pilgrim Society (fellow), Paul Revere Memorial Association, New England Historic and Genealogical Society, Colonial Society of Massachusetts, Massachusetts Historical Commission, Rhode Island Historical Society, Newport Historical Society, Reading Antiquarian Society (member of board of directors), Boston Marine Society (honorary member).

AWARDS, HONORS: National Endowment for the Humanities fellow, 1975; American Philosophical Society grant, 1976; Phi Alpha Theta Prize, *Choice* magazine best history book list, and Winship Award nomination, *Globe* Book Fair, all 1976, all for *Rebels under Sail: The American Navy during the Revolution;* named one of Boston's ten best teachers, *Real Paper,* 1977.

WRITINGS:

William Ellery: A Rhode Island Politico and Lord of Admiralty, Scarecrow, 1973.
Rebels under Sail: The American Navy during the Revolution, Scribner, 1976.
(Editor with Wallace Coyle) *The American Revolution: Changing Perspectives,* Northeastern University Press, 1979.
The Baron of Beacon Hill: A Biography of John Hancock, Houghton, 1980.
Jack Tars and Commodores: The American Navy 1783-1815, Houghton, 1984.
(Contributor) James C. Bradford, editor, *Command under Sail: Makers of Naval Tradition,* Naval Institute Press, 1985.

Contributor to *World Book Encyclopedia* and *Dictionary of American Military Biography;* contributor to professional journals, including *American Neptune, Rhode Island History, New York Historical Society Quarterly,* and *Harvard Magazine.* Managing editor, *New England Quarterly,* 1981—.

SIDELIGHTS: A professor of history at Northeastern University, William Morgan Fowler, Jr. has written several books about the early United States, including two works that trace the history of the U.S. Navy. "But it seems unfair to call this author a professor, or his book a lesson," novelist Tom Clancy states in his *Washington Post* review of *Jack Tars and Commodores: The American Navy, 1783-1815.* "Fowler does not write like many academics. His book is a lively mixture of hard facts and fluent prose, and he has the wit to alternate between the military and political arenas at a pace sufficiently brisk to maintain the reader's interest." In his account of the founding of the new nation's navy, Fowler "deals with the politics, sometimes schematically," notes the *Los Angeles Times*'s Richard Eder; "but his real pleasure, and ours, is his account of shipbuilding, battles and the quirks and quarrels of the early captains and commodores. His writing tends to yo-ho-ho," the critic continues; nevertheless, "if [Fowler] is a mite touched by hemp and pitch it is an attractive excess, giving the book descriptive and narrative vigor." Clancy similarly observes that "the general reader could hardly ask for more, and this entertaining and informative volume could well have lasted longer. Fowler is easily a good enough writer to retain interest longer than a mere 264 pages." He concludes that *Jack Tars and Commodores* "is an uncommonly concise portrait of another age both different from and similar to our own."

BIOGRAPHICAL/CRITICAL SOURCES:

PERIODICALS

Christian Science Monitor, January 7, 1977.
Los Angeles Times, June 11, 1984.
Newsweek, January 14, 1980.
Washington Post, August 1, 1984.

*   *   *

FOX, Levi 1914-

PERSONAL: Born August 28, 1914, in Leicestershire, England; son of John William and Julia (Stinson) Fox; married Jane Richards; children: Roger James, Elizabeth Jane, Patricia Mary. *Education:* Oriel College, Oxford, B.A. (with first-class honors), 1936, M.A., 1938; University of Manchester, M.A., 1938.

ADDRESSES: Home—27 Welcombe Rd., Stratford-upon-Avon, England. *Office*—Shakespeare Centre, Stratford-upon-Avon, England.

CAREER: Shakespeare Centre, Stratford-upon-Avon, England, director of Shakespeare Birthplace Trust, 1945-89. *Military service:* British Army, 1940-43.

MEMBER: International Shakespeare Association (deputy chairman), Royal Society of Literature (fellow), Royal Historical Society (fellow), Society of Antiquaries of London (fellow).

AWARDS, HONORS: Honorary doctorate, George Washington University, 1964; New York University medal, 1964; named officer of the Order of the British Empire, 1964; named deputy lieutenant of County of Warwick, 1967; D. Litt., Birmingham University, 1986; elected life trustee of Shakespeare's birthplace, 1989.

WRITINGS:

Leicester Abbey, City of Leicester Publicity Department, 1938.
The Administration of the Honor of Leicester in the Fourteenth Century, E. Backus, 1940.
The History of Coventry's Textile Industry, privately printed, 1944.
Leicester Castle (pamphlet), Leicester Publicity and Development Department, 1944.
Coventry's Heritage: An Introduction to the History of the City, Coventry Evening Telegraph, 1947, 2nd edition, 1957.
(With Percy Russell) *Leicester Forest,* E. Backus, 1948.

Shakespeare's Town, Stratford-upon-Avon: A Pictorial Record with Historical Introduction and Descriptions, H. & J. Busst, 1949.
Stratford-upon-Avon, Garland Publishing, 1949.
(Author of introduction and notes) Gerald Gardiner, *Oxford: A Book of Drawings,* Garland Publishing, 1951.
Stratford-upon-Avon: An Appreciation, Jarrolds, 1952.
The Borough Town of Stratford-upon-Avon, privately printed, 1953.
(Editor) *English Historical Scholarship in the Sixteenth and Seventeenth Centuries,* Oxford University Press, 1956.
Stratford-upon-Avon: Official Guide, privately printed, 1958.
William Shakespeare: A Concise Life (pamphlet), Jarrolds, 1959.
Shakespeare's Town and Country, Cotman House, 1959.
Shakespeare's Stratford-upon-Avon: A Souvenir in Colour with Historical Descriptions, J. Salmon, 1962.
Shakespeare's Birthplace: A History and Description, Jarrolds, 1963.
(Editor) William Shakespeare, *Sonnets,* Cotman House, 1963.
Stratford-upon-Avon in Colour: A New Pictorial Guide, Jarrolds, 1963.
The Shakespearian Properties, Jarrolds, 1964, new edition, 1981.
The Shakespeare Anniversary Book, Jarrolds, 1964.
(Editor) *Correspondence of the Reverend Joseph Greene: Parson, Schoolmaster, and Antiquary, 1712-1790,* H.M.S.O., 1965.
Celebrating Shakespeare: A Pictorial Record of the Celebrations Held at Stratford-upon-Avon during 1964 to Mark the Four-Hundredth Anniversary of the Birth of William Shakespeare, privately printed, 1965.
New Place: Shakespeare's Home (pamphlet), Jarrolds, 1966.
(Editor) *A Shakespeare Treasury,* Cotman House, 1966.
A Country Grammar School: A History of Ashby-de-la-Zouch Grammar School through Four Centuries, 1567 to 1967, Oxford University Press, 1967.
(Editor) *The Stratford Shakespeare Anthology,* Cotman House, 1968.
The Shakespeare Book, Jarrolds, 1969, new edition, 1972.
Shakespeare's England, Putnam, 1972.
In Honour of Shakespeare: The History and Collections of the Shakespeare Birthplace Trust, Jarrolds, 1972.
A Splendid Occasion: The Stratford Jubilee of 1769 (pamphlet), V. Ridler, 1973.
Stratford Past and Present: A Pictorial Record of the Ancient Town of Stratford, Oxford Illustrated Press, 1975.
Stratford-upon-Avon and the Shakespeare Country, Jarrolds, 1975.
Shakespeare's Flowers, Jarrolds, 1978.
Shakespeare's Birds, Jarrolds, 1978.
The Shakespeare Centre, Stratford-upon-Avon, Jarrolds, 1982.
The Early History of King Edward VI School, Stratford-upon-Avon, Dugdale Society, 1984.
Stratford-upon-Avon, Shakespeare's Town, Jarrolds, 1986.
Historic Stratford-upon-Avon, Jarrolds, 1986.
Mary Arden's House and the Shakespeare Countryside Museum, Jarrolds, 1989.

General editor of the publications of the Dugdale Society of Warwickshire. Contributor to Shakespeare studies and history journals.

WORK IN PROGRESS: Research on historical records of Stratford-upon-Avon and Warwickshire.

FRANCOEUR, Robert T(homas) 1931-

PERSONAL: Born October 18, 1931, in Detroit, Mich.; son of George Antoine (a steel consultant) and Julia Ann (Russell) Francoeur: married Anna Kotlarchyk (an accountant), September 24, 1966; children: Nicole Lynn, Danielle Ann. *Education:* Sacred Heart College, B.A., 1953; St Vincent College, M.A., 1958; University of Detroit, M.S., 1961; University of Delaware, Ph.D., 1966; also attended Fordham University and Johns Hopkins University. *Politics:* Democrat. *Religion:* Roman Catholic.

ADDRESSES: Home—2 Circle Dr., Rockaway, N.J. 07866. *Office*—Department of Biology, Farleigh Dickinson University, Madison, N.J. 07940.

CAREER: Former Catholic priest; Fairleigh Dickinson University, Department of Biological and Allied Health Sciences, Madison, N.J., instructor, 1965-66, assistant professor, 1966-70, associate professor, 1970-75, professor of human embryology, sexuality, and biomedical ethics, 1975—, former chairman of biological sciences. Visiting professor at twenty-two universities and medical schools; frequent lecturer at colleges, universities, and professional conferences; has appeared on national and local television and radio programs. Has completed documentary programs for Public Broadcasting Authority of New Jersey and Canadian Broadcasting Corp. (CBC). Participant in study of ethical, legal, and social implications of advances in biomedical and behavioral research and technology mandated by the U.S. Congress. Consultant to the United Nations, the American Medical Association, and the New York Bar.

MEMBER: World Future Society, Society for the Scientific Study of Sex (fellow, 1987; president, eastern region, 1988-90), American Association of Sex Educators, Counselors, and Therapists, American College of Sexologists (charter member).

AWARDS, HONORS: Annual award of the Educational Foundation for Human Sexuality, 1978.

WRITINGS:

Evolving World, Converging Man, Holt, 1970.
Utopian Motherhood: New Trends in Human Reproduction, Doubleday, 1970, revised edition, A. S. Barnes, 1972.
(Author of introduction) Beatrice Bruteau, *Worthy is the World: The Hindu Philosophy of Sri Aurobindo,* Fairleigh Dickinson University Press, 1971.
(Contributor) Kenneth Vaux, editor, *To Create a Different Future: Religious Hope and Technological Planning,* Friendship, 1972.
(Contributor) Seymour Farber and Joseph Alioto, editors, *Teilhard de Chardin: In Quest of the Perfection of Man,* Fairleigh Dickinson University Press, 1972.
Eve's New Rib: Twenty Faces of Sex, Marriage and Family, Harcourt, 1972.
(With wife, Anna K. Francoeur) *Hot and Cool Sex: Cultures in Conflict,* Harcourt, 1974.
(Editor with A. K. Francoeur) *The Future of Sexual Relations,* Prentice-Hall, 1974.
Becoming a Sexual Person, Wiley, 1982, abridged edition published as *Becoming a Sexual Person: A Brief Edition,* 1984, 2nd edition of original, Macmillan, 1990.
Biomedical Ethics: A Guide to Decisions, Wiley, 1983.
(Contributor) Eleanor Macklin and Roger Rubin, editors, *Contemporary Families and Alternative Lifestyles, A Handbook of Research and Theory,* Sage Publications, 1983.
(Contributor) Lester Kirkendall and Arthur Gravatt, editors, *Marriage and the Family in the Year 2020,* Prometheus, 1984.

(Contributor) Jeannine Gramick and Pat Furey, editors, *The Vatican and Homosexuality,* Crossroads, 1988.
(Contributor) W. Eicher and G. Kockott, editors, *Sexology,* Springer-Verlag, 1988.
(Contributor) Jose Leyson, editor, *Sexual Rehabilitation of the Spinal-Cord-Injured Patient,* Humana Press, 1989.
(Editor) *Taking Sides: Clashing Views on Controversies in Human Sexuality,* Dushkin Publishing Group, 1987, 2nd edition, 1989.
(Contributor) Ed Doerr and James W. Prescott, editors, *Abortion Rights and Fetal "Personhood,"* Centerline Press, 1989.
(Editor-in-chief) Norman A. Scherzer and Timothy Perper, co-authors, *A Descriptive Dictionary and Atlas of Sexuality,* Greenwood Press, 1990.
(Contributor) Robert H. Iles, editor, *The Gospel Imperative in the Midst of AIDS: Towards a Prophetic Theology,* Morehouse Publishing Co., 1990.
(Contributor) Michael Perry, editor, *Handbook of Sexology, Volume 7: Childhood and Adolescent Sexology,* Elsevier Scientific Publishers, 1990.

Contributor of articles to scientific and popular magazines, including *Forum, Journal of Sex Research, Medical Aspects of Human Sexuality, Journal of Allied Health, Journal of Bioethics,* and *The Truth Seeker.* Contributing editor, *Forum.*

SIDELIGHTS: Robert T. Francoeur told *CA* that his readers have always found it hard to label him or fit him into a comfortable pigeonhole. "I started off in college majoring in philosophy and English," he continued, "and graduated tied for last place in my class because I refused to fit into 'the mold.' Then I shifted gears, pursued Master's degrees in theology and biology. After working for three years as a Catholic priest, my interest in evolution, Teilhard de Chardin, and theology led me into a doctorate in experimental embryology and teaching in a large private secular university. In the past twenty years, I've worn many hats as a 'bioanthropologist,' a theologian, a sexologist, a medical ethicist, a specialist in alternative life-styles, textbook writer, and expert on the social implications of reproductive technologies. My problem is I'm always looking for the whole picture. Using artificial insemination or embryo transplants to save endangered animal species is interesting in itself, but I'm also interested in the transfer of such technologies to humans and their impact on our values and lifestyles. The challenge of the whole picture leads me into many unusual situations but I really enjoy working and learning with people with different perspectives and professional interests."

BIOGRAPHICAL/CRITICAL SOURCES:

PERIODICALS

Baltimore Sun, February 7, 1971.
Medical World News, November 27, 1970.
Newsweek, November 23, 1970.

*   *   *

FREIBERG, Stanley K(enneth) 1923-

PERSONAL: Surname is pronounced *Fry*-berg; born August 26, 1923, in Merrill, Wis.; son of Arthur (a laborer) and Ann Freiberg; married Marjorie Ellen Speckhand, June 29, 1947 (deceased); children: Timothy, Teresa. *Education:* University of Wisconsin—Madison, B.A., 1948, M.A., 1949, Ph.D., 1957. *Religion:* "All are one."

ADDRESSES: Home—1523 York Place, Victoria, British Columbia, Canada V8R 5X1.

CAREER: Teacher of English at Lutheran high school in Houston, Tex., 1952-54; Cottey College, Nevada, Mo., assistant professor of English literature, 1954-58, head of department, 1956-58; University of Redlands, Redlands, Calif., assistant professor of English literature, 1958-63; University of Nevada, Reno, assistant professor, 1963-64, associate professor of English literature, 1965-66; University of Baghdad, Baghdad, Iraq, professor of English literature and director of foreign language studies, both 1964-65; University of Calgary, Calgary, Alberta, professor of English literature, 1966-79; writer, 1979—. Teacher of writing and drama at University of Ottawa; teacher of literature at University of Victoria and University of Calgary. *Military service:* U.S. Army, Infantry, 1943-46; served as combat rifleman in European and Pacific theaters; became staff sergeant.

AWARDS, HONORS: Canada Council arts grant, 1980.

WRITINGS:

The Baskets of Baghdad: Poems of the Middle East, Crest, 1968.
Plumes of the Serpent: Poems of Mexico, Crest, 1973.
The Caplin-Crowded Seas: Poems of Newfoundland, Crest, 1975.
Nightmare Tales (short stories of Nova Scotia), Borealis Press, 1980.
Mad Blake at Felpham (dramatic monologue; first performed under title "Blake on a Bed of Dreams," at Open Space Gallery, Vancouver, British Columbia, May 6, 1989), Newport Bay Publishing, 1987.
The Hidden City: A Poem of Peru, Newport Bay Publishing, 1988.

Contributor to *Queen's Quarterly, Ariel,* and *Dalhousie Review.*

WORK IN PROGRESS: "Sverre, King of Norway," a historical dream play of the 12th century based on the *Saga of Sverre,* partially dictated by Sverre himself; and "Dream Fugue," an attempt to dramatize the parallel achievements of Blake and Beethoven in their respective arts—both pillars of Romanticism, both dead in 1827.

SIDELIGHTS: Stanley K. Freiberg told *CA:* "Professors Helen White and Ruth Wallerstein, of the University of Wisconsin, were my finest teachers, conveying through their knowledge and emotion the importance of art. William Blake and Samuel Taylor Coleridge have been the most noticeable literary sources influencing my work: Blake in his commitment to religion and art as indivisible, and Coleridge on matters of technique and aesthetics. Travel has been a dominant factor in my understanding of humanity's underlying unity and in the appreciation of its variety in that unity.

"The fundamental intention of my work is, as it was for George Eliot, to extend human sympathy. That intention has not altered through the years; however, the presentational modes of my work have become more and more varied. Many of my poems tend to be pictorial, employing the artifacts and scenery of a particular place well known to me; but, even as is evident in my short stories (wherein realistic events are eventually transformed to the level of Coleridgian nightmare), the poems, characteristically, are dramatically heightened beyond simple realism.

"My recently published Inca poem, 'The Hidden City,' provided subject matter ideally suited to the above-mentioned approach; for I was able to dramatize the Empire of the Incas 'from founding myth to echo' through the use of both literal depictions and imaginative episodes woven into an already existing framework of history and rich mythology. This work, written some years ago, contains four laments in the form of soliloquies which,

doubtless, exerted a great deal of influence upon the composition of *Mad Blake at Felpham,* a two-act dramatic monologue.

"The Blake drama, however, was prompted mainly by my personal belief that William Blake's insights into present day society are so pertinent and profound that the man and his works must be kept continually in mind. Rona Murray, a critic of the drama, which was performed in 1989 under the title 'Blake on a Bed of Dreams,' noted her own discouraging realization that 'those aspects of life that grieved the poet most . . . are with us today to a degree quite as great as when Blake was writing.'

"Yet, Blake never ceased to believe that through the arts moral progress and human harmony are possible. I don't believe there can be a better reason for anyone trying to write."

BIOGRAPHICAL/CRITICAL SOURCES:

BOOKS

Moss, John, *A Reader's Guide to the Canadian Novel,* McClelland & Stewart, 1981.

*   *   *

FRENCH, Marilyn 1929-
(Mara Solwoska)

PERSONAL: Born November 21, 1929, in New York, N.Y.; daughter of E. Charles and Isabel (Hazz) Edwards; married Robert M. French, Jr. (a lawyer), June 4, 1950 (divorced, 1967); children: Jamie, Robert M. III. *Education:* Hofstra College (now University), B.A., 1951, M.A., 1964; Harvard University, Ph.D., 1972.

ADDRESSES: Home—New York, N.Y. *Agent*—Charlotte Sheedy Literary Agency, 145 West 86th St., New York, N.Y. 10024.

CAREER: Writer and lecturer. Hofstra University, Hempstead, N.Y., instructor in English, 1964-68; College of the Holy Cross, Worcester, Mass., assistant professor of English, 1972-76; Harvard University, Cambridge, Mass., Mellon fellow in English, 1976-77. Artist-in-residence at Aspen Institute for Humanistic Study, 1972.

MEMBER: Modern Language Association of America, Society for Values in Higher Education, Virginia Woolf Society, James Joyce Society, Phi Beta Kappa.

WRITINGS:

The Book as World: James Joyce's "Ulysses," Harvard University Press, 1976.
The Women's Room (novel), Summit Books, 1977.
The Bleeding Heart (novel; Book-of-the-Month Club alternate selection), Summit Books, 1980.
Shakespeare's Division of Experience, Summit Books, 1981.
(Author of introduction) Edith Wharton, *House of Mirth,* Jove Books, 1981.
(Author of introduction) Wharton, *Summer,* Jove Books, 1981.
Beyond Power: On Women, Men, and Morals (essays), Summit Books, 1986.
Her Mother's Daughter (novel), Summit Books, 1987.

Also author of two unpublished novels. Contributor of articles and stories, sometimes under pseudonym Mara Solwoska, to journals, including *Soundings* and *Ohio Review.*

SIDELIGHTS: Novelist, educator, and literary scholar Marilyn French is perhaps best known for the cogent, feminist aspect of her work. "My goal in life," she asserts in an *Inside Books* interview with Ray Bennett, "is to change the entire social and economic structure of western civilization, to make it a feminist world." Noting that "feminism isn't a question of what kind of genitals you possess," she explains: "It's a kind of moral view. It's what you think with your head and feel with your heart." French, whose own feminism has been heightened by her life experience, was married with children before she read Simone de Beauvoir's *The Second Sex,* a book thematically concerned with the importance of women not living through men. Considered by many to be the first text of the current feminist movement, the book greatly impressed and influenced her, especially "the sections on women writers who kept postponing doing their literary work," French told *CA.* Soon thereafter she began to write short stories that expressed her own feelings and frustrations. Divorced in 1967, she earned a doctorate from Harvard through fellowships, and then launched an impressive academic career marked by the publication of her thesis, *The Book as World: James Joyce's "Ulysses."* In 1977, her explosive and provocative first novel, *The Women's Room,* not only granted her the financial freedom to pursue writing full-time but has, itself, become a major novel of the women's movement. And although critics respond to her work by frequently focusing on its polemics—praising in the nonfiction what they challenge in the fiction—her many readers indentify with and admire what French has to say.

"I wanted to tell the story of what it is like to be a woman in our country in the middle of the twentieth century," French explained to a *New York Times* interviewer about *The Women's Room.* Calling it "a collective biography of a large group of American citizens," Anne Tyler describes the novel's characters in the *New York Times Book Review:* "Expectant in the 40's, submissive in the 50's, enraged in the 60's, they have arrived in the 70's independent but somehow unstrung, not yet fully composed after all they've been through." The novel is about Mira, a submissive and repressed young woman whose conventional childhood prepares her for a traditional marriage, which ends suddenly in divorce and leaves her liberated but alone. "The tone of the book is rather turgid, but exalted, almost religious," says Anne Duchene in the *Times Literary Supplement,* "a huge jeremiad for a new kind of Fall, a whole new experience of pain and loss."

Writing about *The Women's Room* in the *Washington Post Book Review,* Brigitte Weeks contends that "the novel's basic thesis—that there is little or no foreseeable future for coexistence between men and women—is powerfully stated, but still invokes a lonely chaos repellent to most readers." Uncomfortable with what she perceives as the woman-as-victim perspective in *The Women's Room,* Sara Sanborn elaborates in *Ms.,* "My main objection is not that French writes about the sufferings of women; so have the best women writers. But the women of, say, George Eliot or Virginia Woolf, hampered as they are, live in the world of choice and consequence. They are implicated in their own fates, which gives them both interest and stature. The characters in this book glory in the condition which some men have ascribed to women: they are not responsible." In her interview with *People* magazine's Gail Jennes, French states: "Books, movies, TV teach us false images of ourselves. We learn to expect fairy-tale lives. Ordinary women's daily lives—unlike men's—have not been the stuff of literature. I wanted to legitimate it and I purposely chose the most ordinary lives [for the characters in the novel]—not the worst cases. . . . I wanted to break the mold of conventional women's novels." However, in the *New York Times Book Review,* Rosellen Brown notes that the novel "declared the independence of one victimized wife after another."

"French wonders not only if male-female love is *possible,* but whether it's *ethical* in the contemporary context," writes Lindsy Van Gelder in a *Ms.* review of French's second novel, *The Bleeding Heart.* "How, in other words, does one reconcile one's hard-won feminist insights about the way the System works with one's longing to open one's heart completely to a man who, at the very least, benefits from an oppressive System buttressed, in part, by women's emotional vulnerability?" *The Bleeding Heart* centers on Dolores, a liberated professor of Renaissance literature on leave researching a new book at Oxford, when she meets Victor, an unhappily married father of four in England on business. Compromising her feminist principles by engaging in an impassioned but frustratingly combative affair with him, Dolores ultimately realizes that she cannot live with him without descending into predictably prescribed roles. Commenting in *Newsweek* that "French makes her point and touches lots of raw contemporary nerves," Jean Strouse queries, "What happens when nobody wants to be the wife?" According to Brown, *The Bleeding Heart* represents "an admirably honest admission of the human complications that arise after a few years of lonely integrity: What now? Must one wait for love until the world of power changes hands? Is there a difference between accommodation and compromise among lovers? Accommodation and surrender? How to spell out the terms of a partial affirmation?"

In the *Village Voice,* Laurie Stone observes that the political thesis of *The Bleeding Heart* is: "Although a feminist may love a man, she will ultimately have to reject him, since men axiomatically live by values inimical to women." Describing it as "a novel of love and despair in the seeming ruins of post-'60s angst and the ill-defined emotional territory of the '70s," Thomas Sanchez suggests in the *Los Angeles Times Book Review,* however, that "this is less a novel of people and their fierce concerns for survival than a melodrama of symbols clothed in philosophical and political garb." Furthermore, Sanchez calls the novel "maddening" in the sense that "French has mistaken politics for prose." But according to R. Z. Sheppard in *Time,* French softens the militancy in this novel: "Her soul on ice, Marilyn French sounded like a feminist Eldridge Cleaver [in *The Women's Room*]. *The Bleeding Heart* suggests a slight thaw. Its core is a seemingly endless and inconclusive dialogue—SALT talks in the gender wars." And *Nation* contributor Andrea Freud Loewenstein suggests that although *The Bleeding Heart* is "a depressed and depressing book," it is "not a destructive one." In the words of Alice Hoffman in the *New York Times Book Review,* "French continues to write about the inner lives of women with insight and intimacy. What she's given us this time is a page-turner with a heart."

A criticism frequently leveled at French is that "her novels suffer from a knee-jerk feminist stereotype in which all men are at worst, brutal and, at best, insensitive," notes Susan Wood in the *Washington Post Book World.* Astonished at the bitterness and anger that French expresses in *The Women's Room* and *The Bleeding Heart,* critics often object to the anti-male stance in her fiction. For example, Libby Purves writes in the London *Times* that *The Women's Room* is "a prolonged—largely autobiographical—yell of fury at the perversity of the male sex. . . . The men in the novel are drawn as malevolent stick figures, at best appallingly dull and at worst monsters." And referring in the *Chicago Tribune Book World* to a "persistently belligerent anti-male bias" in *The Bleeding Heart,* Alice Adams feels this one-sided characterization only serves to disenfranchise many readers who might otherwise read and learn from French's literature. Richard Phillips writes in the *Chicago Tribune* that "to read one of her novels . . . means wincing through hundreds of pages of professed revulsion over the male species of human kind. Man means power, control, rage. Even the nice guys finish last. Men are bastards. Women suffer. It is a message written with all the subtlety of a sledgehammer, but one that, French argues, is only a mirror reflection of what men themselves are taught from birth: Contempt for women." But, as French explains to Phillips: "Contempt for women is not an accident, it is not a by-product of our culture. It is the heart. The culture is founded on it. It is the essential central core; without it, the culture would fall apart."

"Just as feminists have identified and denounced misogyny in books written by men, it behooves us all to arraign those books which exude a destructive hatred of men," opines Suzanne Fields in the *Detroit News.* "Such feelings can infect and calcify in dangerous ways. To intersperse torrid sex scenes with tirades against men for the imagined crime of being men merely allows villains and victims to exchange places. The rules of the game, weighted as they are to create those villains and victims, go unchallenged." However, to those critics who charge that French portrays male characters as "stick figures," "empty men," and "cardboard villains," and to readers who do not realize her purpose in creating one-sided male characters, French responds in the *New York Times:* "That infuriates me. Every time I see that I see orange. The men are there as the women see them and feel them— impediments in women's lives. That's the focus. . . . Aristotle managed to build a whole society without mentioning women once. Did anyone ever say: 'Are there women in (Joseph Conrad's) Nigger of the Narcissus?'"

Praising French's skill in eliciting response from her readers, Weeks declares that "as a polemic [*The Women's Room*] is brilliant, forcing the reader to accept the reactions of the women as the only possible ones." Noting that "the reader, a willing victim, becomes enmeshed in mixed feelings," Weeks observes that the novel "forces confrontations on the reader mercilessly." Although Weeks acknowledges the novel's flaws, she concludes, "*The Women's Room* is a wonderful novel, full of life and passions that ring true as crystal. Its fierceness, its relentless refusal to compromise are as stirring as a marching song." Yet, as Van Gelder points out in *Ms.,* despite the fact that it "is a book whose message is 'the lesson all women learn: men are the ultimate enemy,'" men do not seem to be "especially threatened by the book"; those who choose to read it probably have some degree of commitment to feminism in the first place. "The best compliment I can pay it is that I kept forgetting that it was fiction," remarks the *New York Times'* Christopher Lehmann-Haupt. "It seized me by my preconceptions and I kept struggling and arguing with its premises. Men can't be that bad, I kept wanting to shout at the narrator. There must be room for accommodation between the sexes that you've somehow overlooked. And the damnable thing is, she's right."

"Many women will recognize the world French has given us," remarks Wood. If not explicitly autobiographical, French's fiction seems at least validated by her own life experience. And when asked why she continues "to deal with men, especially if her own novels are not autobiographical, as she insists" French told Phillips that "whatever my inclinations were, and however I lead my life, I would still be writing about women and men, because women and men live on this Earth. And I assume that the Earth is going to go on being peopled." Despite mixed critical reviews, reader response to her work has been tremendous. Countless women readers have written to French to say that what she wrote in *The Women's Room,* for example, is their truth; and as French relates to Jennes, "There is nothing in [*The Women's Room*] I've not felt." Noting that the novel "speaks

from the heart to women everywhere," a *Publishers Weekly* reviewer writes: "It is as if French had been taking notes for twenty years. Her dialogue, her characterizations, her knowledge of the changing relationships, sexual and otherwise, between men and women in a complex world of shifting values, are all extraordinary. It is, French says, women who best support women in crisis times." According to *Publishers Weekly*'s Barbara Bannon, it is this "genuine sympathy for other women caught in life situations, trivial or deadly serious, for which they were never prepared that made Marilyn French's first novel, *The Women's Room,* such a breakthrough bestseller in hardcover and paperback."

Suggesting still another reason for French's popularity, Bannon observes that "in both of French's novels women's commitment to raising children as one of the most important elements in their lives is clearly recognized and accepted as fact, and it is her understanding of this, her refusal to look down on such a traditional women's role, that makes her novels accessible to many women who might not relate to a more formalized 'feminist' position." As she tells Angela Brooks in the London *Times,* "I don't care whether it's a popular message or not. You can't have it all." In an interview for the *Chicago Tribune,* French relates to Beth Austin: "Women of my generation risked everything. We left our husbands, which meant that we had no money. And we had the kids, and we didn't have jobs. We were facing, and many of us entered, poverty. Some of us are still in that poverty, some of us are not." In the *New York Times,* French remarks to Nan Robertson: "Men believe men are central to women's lives and they're not even when they become economically central, even psychologically, when we have to please them. Children are the center of a woman's life. Work is always central. When you have children, they become your work, your opus."

In *Her Mother's Daughter,* a forgiving look at motherhood, French writes about the maternal legacy bequeathed to daughters by examining four generations of an immigrant family through the experiences of its women. Anastasia, the narrator, attempts to overcome several generations of wrongs by living like a man, sexually free and artistically and commercially successful. Her success, however, is juxtaposed with the hardships and sufferings endured by the women before her, and her emancipation, according to Anne Summers in the *Times Literary Supplement,* "is shown to be more illusory than real; despite every conceivable change in outward forms, it is the older women's experience which imprints itself on her inner life." Reviewing the novel in *Tribune Books,* Beverly Fields indicates that the novel "elaborates a theme that runs more or less quietly through her first two books: the ways in which female submission to male society, with its accompanying suppression of rage, is passed like contagion from mother to daughter." Marie Olesen Urbanski observes in the *Los Angeles Times Book Review* that "the more educated or liberated the mother is, the more pervasive is her sense of a guilt from which there is no absolution. . . . 'Her Mother's Daughter' celebrates mothers. It depicts the high price mothers pay for children who say they do not want, but who must have their sacrifices. . . . Has Mother's Day come at last?"

French's nonfiction seeks the origins of male dominance in society. In *Shakespeare's Division of Experience,* for example, she posits that the female's capacity to bear children has historically aligned her with nature and, consequently, under man's compulsion to exercise power over it. In the *New York Times Book Review,* Geoffrey H. Hartman describes the subject of the book as "the relationship between political power and the 'division' of experience according to gender principles. It is a division that has proved disastrous for both sexes, she writes: To the male is attributed the ability to kill; to the female the ability to give birth; and around these extremes there cluster 'masculine' and 'feminine' qualities, embodied in types or roles that reinforce a schizoid culture and produce all sorts of fatal contradictions." Calling it "the finest piece of feminist criticism we have yet had," Laurence Lerner notes in the *Times Literary Supplement* that "her concern is not merely with Shakespeare." Recognizing that "she believes the identification of moral qualities with genders impoverishes and endangers our society," Lerner adds that French thinks "every human experience should be reintegrated." Lerner continues that "whereas for Shakespeare the greatest threat may have lain in nature, it now lies in control; she therefore confesses an animus against 'the almost total dedication to masculine values that characterizes our culture.' "

Remarking that "French is intelligent, nothing if not ingenious, and obviously sincere," Anne Barton suggests in the *New York Review of Books* about *Shakespeare's Division of Experience* that "there is something very limiting, however, about the assumption upon which all her arguments are based." For example, Barton continues, "Although she does grudgingly admit from time to time that rationality, self-control, individualism, and 'permanencies' may have some little value, she is distrustful of 'civilization,' and of the life of the mind. She also leaves a major contradiction in her position unexplored. On the one hand, she indignantly denies that women are any 'closer to nature' than men. . . . On the other hand, it is not clear that the qualities she values, and according to which she would like to see live lived by both sexes, are all—in her terms—feminine." According to S. Schoenbaum in the *Washington Post Book World,* "She accepts what is after all common knowledge: that the gender principles aren't gender-specific—biological males can accommodate feminine values, and females aren't exempt from masculine power struggles. And, along with overlap, there exists the possibility for synthesis."

Beyond Power: On Women, Men, and Morals, writes Lawrence Stone in the *New York Times Book Review,* "is a passionate polemic about the way men have treated women over the past several millenniums." And according to Paul Robinson in the *Washington Post Book World,* "Nothing in her previous books, however, prepares one for the intellectual range and scholarly energy of *Beyond Power,* which is nothing less than a history of the world (from the cavewomen to the Sandinistas) seen through the critical prism of contemporary feminism." Mary Warnock explains in the *Times Literary Supplement* that French's "general thesis is that men, who have hitherto governed the world, have always sought power above all else, and, in the interests of power, have invented the system of patriarchy which dominates all Western art, philosophy, religion and education. Above all it now dominates industry and politics."

Recognizing the veracity of French's claims in the book, Stone states: "The history of the treatment of women by men in the last 2,500 years of Western civilization is truly awful. One therefore has to sympathize with her passionate indignation and admire the singleminded zeal with which she has pursued her theory through the millenniums." Nevertheless, Stone finds the book flawed. For instance, pointing to the "relentless cruelty and selfishness" that anthropologists have discovered in some of the primitive peoples that French has perceived as utopian, Stone comments: "French's attempt to resuscitate the noble savage in feminist drag is not convincing. Moreover, worship of a female does not do much to affect the lot of women one way or the other." Observing that "she is a formidable woman to argue with," Purves wonders whether the patriarchal system, whether "strife, competition, rivalry, the concentration of power and

even war itself," is not responsible for even a few benefits to the world; but French responds by explaining, "We are always told this. That commercial links and inventions and knowledge of other nations come from war; but who is to say that these things wouldn't have happened anyway? There is no way we can know how the world would have been without men's domination." Calling it "a brilliant study of power and control showing how those two related systems have affected the lives of men and women throughout human history," though, Richard Rhodes concludes in the *Chicago Tribune Book World* that "it ranks high among the most important books of the decade."

Because of the types of books French writes as well as the reaction that they frequently generate, many "people think I cause divorces because women are reading my books," French tells Phillips. "A lot of men like to think that it's all me, that it is all my doing. They don't understand where women are coming from-because they don't listen to women, ever." Pointing out that the sex war is still raging, French adds: "Of course, it's disguised. We love each other. We go to bed with each other. We flirt with each other. But underneath all this is the ancient history of male supremacy over females." Phillips observes, though, that "French seems neither concerned nor likely to moderate her vilification of men simply to heal the wounds of ostracism. Mankind is the enemy, after all, and French cannot give up an inch in her crusade against male supremacy. Never."

Suggesting that whatever hope there is for the future rests with those "young men who are different [from their fathers], who take responsibility for their children," French indicates to Austin that "the cultural myth for men is, first of all, that if they are real men they are alone. They are not bound into the female sphere, which is the sphere of the domestic." French sympathizes with the male, though, and believes that they, too, suffer from a patriarchal society. "You see most men are living a lie," French tells Purves. "Any human being is living a lie who pretends to be in control, even of themselves. I find it ironic that the sex which cannot control its sex organ is the one that considers itself fit to control the world. Most women who do gain power now only fall prey to the same delusion." French adds that "women who have totally accepted the male world" suffer the same "alienation, loneliness, sterility." And as she declares in an interview with Grace Glueck in the *New York Times Book Review,* "I don't want women to be like men. Women still are full of the old, traditional female virtues. . . . They create the felicities of life. These things are important, *essential,* and I don't want women to give them up. I want men to learn them. I want to feminize the world."

AVOCATIONAL INTERESTS: Amateur musician; parties, cooking, travel.

MEDIA ADAPTATIONS: The Women's Room was produced a television movie in 1980.

CA INTERVIEW

CA interviewed Marilyn French by telephone on May 15, 1989, at her home in New York, New York.

CA: The Women's Room *became a feminist classic novel in much the same way Betty Friedan's* The Feminine Mystique *had become a sort of bible for the liberation movement that started to take off in the 1960s. What new kind of audience and reception does your first novel find today?*

FRENCH: Unfortunately the audience is exactly the same; it's women who didn't read it the first time around. There's always a new generation of women, and many young women write me these days. The situation hasn't really changed. We like to think it has because feminism has accomplished so much in getting women access to graduate schools, to the workplace, to credit. But the problem is never going to end until we decide on a way to raise children that shares the responsibility for them not just with men but with society at large. Society needs children; children are the most important thing we produce. But you'd never know it to look at our national budget.

CA: Your 1987 novel, Her Mother's Daughter, *speaks to that problem exceptionally well. It shows that mothering is learned by example, and that society should bear part of the blame that's heaped on mothers. But it also demonstrates that simply placing the child-rearing burden on men doesn't work either. Where do we go from there?*

FRENCH: The situation in *Her Mother's Daughter* doesn't work because someone is being exploited; it doesn't matter whether it's the man or the woman. And I'm not saying that government should bear the whole burden. I'm a little bit appalled at some of the things that we expect government to do for us. Though I'm not a conservative by any means, sometimes I think we hold government responsible for things that are our own responsibility. But it is the responsibility of the social organism as a whole to enable people to give birth to children and raise them at the same time. None of our workplaces are set up to help in this. If you work in an office, you know damned well that you don't want a screaming kid in the next room.

CA: Some businesses now do have their own day-care centers so that mothers can bring their children along and have lunch with them.

FRENCH: Yes; that's a step.

CA: How would you assess the feminist movement today overall? What do you consider its successes and failures?

FRENCH: You catch me at a time of enormous positive feeling. I think what's going on right now is extraordinary. I am presently writing a history of women, so I'm immersed in tracing back things like law codes, and I'm very aware of how women's rights over their own bodies were taken away by law as far back as 3000 B.C., and how every time women started to get back some of these rights (because, say, of loose governmental structure), new laws would immediately be passed putting them back in their place. In other words, for five thousand years men have had the right to beat women, to use them sexually, to sell them, buy them, to abuse them in any way they wanted.

Suddenly—I would say in the last two years—the newspapers are being flooded by cases of wife abuse, child sexual abuse, rape. And for the first time in five thousand years, these things are being declared wrong. I think that's because of feminism. You get a girl when she's six months old—a baby—and you start buggering her, which is what the huge sex case in Cleveland, England, was all about. Or you wait until she's ten or thirteen. You also beat her up if she doesn't like it. You have a trained person. By the time she's an adult woman, she knows her place; she's not going to make waves. She knows who's boss. And you have created a population of intimidated people. If that is declared wrong, if that has to stop and we have to find social mechanisms to make it stop, we're going to see a whole different generation of people.

CA: Did the women's history you're writing grow out of the enormous work you did on Beyond Power: Women, Men, and Morals?

FRENCH: Yes, it did. Chapter 3 of *Beyond Power* was on the history of women. It was a long chapter but it was only a brief study, given the enormous history of women. My agent had the idea that it could be televised, so we made a deal with Thames Television in England to produce it, and I agreed to write a book from which the television show would be drawn, which would be broader than the chapter in *Beyond Power*. Then that branch of the company was affected by Thatcher's new revisions for television in England. So here I am, stuck writing this book with no television at the other end. But I'm learning an enormous amount in writing it; it's quite a discipline for me.

CA: You were, I've read, an accomplished pianist by the age of fourteen. Was music ever a career possibility for you?

FRENCH: Yes. I used to write music, and until I was about twelve, I thought I was going to be a composer. Then a piano teacher of mine gave me *Etude* magazine as a Christmas present, and I read it from cover to cover, whether I understood it or not; it was so wonderful to me. And I realized that there was only one woman composer, Cecile Chaminade. Oh, there were others, but very few, even if you include Clara Schumann and other people that we know now. And none of them ever composed major works, because they were always involved in raising children. If you have eight children, as Clara Schumann did, you don't have much time for this sort of thing. So it came to me that it was not going to be a possibility for me. But I think that I would have gone back to writing even if that hadn't been the case. A writer was the first thing I thought I'd be, when I was very little.

CA: You were inspired to write on a schedule, you told the Chicago Tribune, *by something you read in Simone de Beauvoir's* The Second Sex. *By the time you were divorced and teaching at Harvard, you had the discipline to write* The Book as World: James Joyce's "Ulysses" *and* The Women's Room. *When did you begin to feel confirmed as a writer, recognized?*

FRENCH: I had written long before those books were published. I started to write in 1957; I wrote every day and I sent my stuff out. But what I didn't realize was that I was a feminist when there wasn't any feminism. There was no language of feminism, no understanding of feminist perspective. I would get these strange letters back saying that I wrote well but there was something a little off. So I didn't get published. I wrote for twenty years without getting published, except for a few short stories. It wasn't a question of discipline; it was a question of an audience. I felt as though I'd been walking around the world with my hand held out for twenty years and no one had taken it until the Joyce book. That book made me feel good, and of course *The Women's Room* was an overwhelming experience. I always thought I was going to be a Virginia Woolf. I never thought anything that I had to say would reach a popular audience.

CA: Many positive changes had already taken place for women when The Women's Room *was published. Was there a tremendous affirmation of the book from its first readers?*

FRENCH: From readers, yes, it was instantaneous. Not from critics—they were very upset by it. The reviews I got were what you'd call mixed.

CA: Her Mother's Daughter, *you've said, is a tribute to your own mother and grandmother. Were there inspirations beyond the autobiographical?*

FRENCH: Oh yes. I felt that motherhood itself was a neglected topic. It's the oldest profession, notwithstanding what they say about the second oldest. It is enormously significant. It changes your life in a way that nothing else does; your life is never, ever the same again once you've had children. Because childbearing seemed to be and in fact was involuntary for most women over most of time, no one ever paid attention to what women actually felt as mothers. There began in the eighteenth century to be a prescriptive literature telling them what they *should* feel and what they *should* be doing, but no one ever cared about what they really felt.

There have been an awful lot of books in the last decade about motherhood from the perspective of the children, from which mothers look bad. Mothers fail. If you look at just the mother and the child, the child is right. It's a little kid; it doesn't have any power; the mother has it all. A child can see what the mother is doing wrong in a way that she can't. But no one ever put in perspective what that woman was going through at the same time, and that she had once been a little girl also, and that she had had an experience of motherhood from the child's point of view. We know from animal experiments that mothering is learned; it doesn't come with the genes. If you don't learn to be a mother from your mother, you don't know how to be one.

I wanted to put motherhood itself at the center of the stage. That story was my grandmother's life and my mother's life. And it was my life at least as far as Anastasia's childhood was concerned; once she reached adolescence, it was fictional. But I wanted to show the complexity and the inevitability of some parts of the experience of motherhood, and the terrible drain that it is on women. It's a source of richness; I don't mean that it isn't. But I don't think very poor women trying to support two or three children feel it to be a source of richness. And yet they do not abandon their children. Another thing that I'm finding as I write my history book is that when things get really tough, men just leave. Women, on the whole, don't. They take the responsibility for the children, and they starve with them or die with them.

CA: Are there aspects of your fiction that you feel have been overlooked or undervalued?

FRENCH: No one seems to realize that I don't write with my uterus. My novels take me as long as they do, and they are as hard as they are, because I think through the style and structure so completely and I revise so carefully. I work towards a style that seems very light and conversational and easy, like a woman talking to another woman across the coffee table; I work to create no sense of superiority in the narrator over the reader. That's something not many writers do, certainly not most male writers. One of the marks of literature is that the narrator knows more than the reader and is telling the reader what he needs to know. I try very hard to avoid that, and to make whatever poetry is in the work arise out of the mundane. My works are very carefully structured, the voice is very carefully chosen, and I think most people are not aware of that.

CA: I think your novels are unusual also in that they're many stories brought together. Do they start out even bigger and get pared down?

FRENCH: Probably, yes. But my politics is my style. I think literature should deal with communal experience, and you have a number of choices if you're doing that. Shakespearean comedies deal with communal experience. You have a main character who is female, but you also have a whole lot of other characters, each with their own eccentricities and problems, and each with a voice; the comedies are not dominated by one character the way

the tragedies are. The ending of a Shakespearean comedy is the community coming together, usually in a marriage ceremony, leaving out perhaps only the most disruptive element—you may not let Malvolio be in the final scene, for example. In *The Women's Room,* I wanted each story to be told, because each of them was a little different. None of the stories that I told in the book was the most terrible I know. I took the most typical. But in the novels since then I've tried simply to weave the stories in as part of the texture, so that there's a sense of community without breaking the focus to look at a lot of other people.

CA: In Beyond Power *you wrote, "Because the highest value of feminism is pleasure, not power, feminists, female and male, perform a service by living their own lives with an eye to integration, fullness of experience, and pleasure." Then you say that the last word has been degraded by patriarchal thinking. How would you define the kind of pleasure you prescribe?*

FRENCH: It's satisfaction on the deepest level. I don't know that we have a language to describe it, but we all know what it feels like. It's like having mashed potatoes at dinner, one of these forbidden things that no sophisticated New Yorker would ever do. Let's say you spent an afternoon with your mother, and that afternoon she was there for you and she loved you and she let you know it. Or you spent an afternoon with some friends, and everyone got along and everyone was supporting each another and something nice was happening around you. It's that kind of very deep satisfaction—which comes also with work, and it comes from being with your children if you get along with your children. It always involves the deepest parts of the self. And it's fragile: it can't be held onto. Maybe you've spent a wonderful afternoon with your friends, you've been out on a picnic, say. The children were behaving, you all loved each other, you were doing a little flirting and the flirting felt good. You try to perpetuate it. You say, "Oh, let's all come back to my house for dinner." And you all do, and it falls apart. You can't hold onto it. And what I see as masculine in the world is the effort to take these fragile experiences and make them permanent through institutions like marriage, or Society as opposed to community. It doesn't work. It simply creates oppression.

CA: Do you see no hope for marriage as a useful and even positive institution?

FRENCH: People are always going to be attracted to each other sexually, to want the companionship of another. Whether you call it marriage or something else, I don't care; I'm not interested in it. What I'm interested in is the children. Sexual attraction doesn't last, it's the most fleeting of emotions, and the children get pushed around. I'm absolutely in favor of divorce. I don't believe people who don't like each other should stay together, and I don't think it's good for the children. But what happens to the children? It's this responsibility for the major task of any society that bothers me. Women get stuck with it. The result is that women are in the lowest fifth of the poverty level in this country. They can't work and raise the kids at the same time. If they go to work and leave the kids, then the kids get wild. Husbands do not take responsibility for children when they leave their wives, even financial responsibility.

CA: I do see couples in which the fathers are taking more responsibility for the day-to-day care of the children.

FRENCH: I see a little change: a little more interest on the part of the father, a little more attention. But that doesn't change what happens in the case of divorce; I don't see any major change there. It's going to have to be a structural change, a change in the nature of work.

CA: What role do you feel fiction writers have played in the victories of the feminist movement?

FRENCH: I believe that fiction is a moral enterprise, if I can use that exalted term. I know that's an unfashionable view, but I believe it. I agree with Horace that the purpose of art is to teach and to delight. And I think that writers, no matter what their politics are, stretch the moral sense by thinking about things and examining them and writing out the possibilities—stretching conventions, offering alternative ways of looking and feeling. I think that's the function of fiction.

CA: Do you think there are any male writers whose work has played a part in promoting saner male-female relationships?

FRENCH: I hate to say no off the top of my head, because there may be someone I'm not thinking of. I don't think men are capable now of dealing with male-female relations, but I think they can redefine what it is to be a man, and some are doing that. The definition of maleness has always been control, in the Western world. I think what we are seeing now is a lot of male fiction writers who are writing about the loss of or lack of control. In that sense they're helping, because they're redefining a role that has been very rigidly perceived.

CA: You've noted in Beyond Power *and elsewhere that the feminist movement has no major, all-encompassing organization. Do you think it can best be carried on from here as an individual struggle with just a few organized groups representing specific political and social concerns?*

FRENCH: I think it's best the way it is. Feminism is a shared perspective. It's a language, a point of view, a way of feeling and thinking that is shared among millions of women now who are working in grass-roots ways on hundreds of different projects in their own towns, their own communities, their own universities. I do a lot of speaking, so I go out across the country quite a bit and I see them. Maybe what they're trying to do is just get rid of the doctor on campus because he's a butcher and he doesn't like girls. Or maybe they're trying to get women more of a voice in a professional association. But whatever they're doing, they're doing what interests them, what they get pleasure from. That's the most satisfying kind of work to do, and it's also the kind that gets the most results. I think it has to be like that. If anyone tried to take it over and declare an ideology, it would be hideous. That's exactly what we're opposed to.

CA: Women's studies has become a respected and useful academic discipline. Do you envision a time when it will effect changes in the older formal disciplines?

FRENCH: It's already happening. It's happening in history, where women are actually making their way into history books. Granted it's very, very slow. It has not happened in political science. It is happening in psychology. I'm very much in touch with these things now because of this book I'm writing.

CA: As a critic by virtue of your books on Joyce and Shakespeare as well as shorter writings, what do you feel feminist criticism has contributed to literary criticism at large?

FRENCH: Feminism has made us aware of what we were generally unconscious of. The status quo that lies behind works of literature of the past or works of political thought or whatever has suddenly been pointed up as an ideology. We didn't realize it before. This realization isn't due just to feminism, but sometimes you have to have two or three go-overs before you realize something. For instance, Nietzsche pointed out long ago, in the nineteenth century, that philosophy deals with man as if man had no body and no emotions. Now feminist criticism is saying this over and over again, that the whole way the human is approached is as if he never got up and shaved in the morning, never had a kid come down with measles, and certainly never fell in love with someone who was hard to take. But if philosophy is about the theory of how to live well, as I think it should be, then you need to go all the way. Man is not just a brain.

I remember being very moved by and putting in one of my early novels (which didn't get published) a passage from Ernst Cassirer in which he said that the rational man is unmoved by his circumstances. I don't know what I was thinking—this was long ago, when I was in my thirties—I just know that it hit me with a special force. I guess now that I was asking, What about if man is woman, and she gets pregnant: how can she be above her circumstances? Or how can someone whose life circumstances place him in a concentration camp rise above these circumstances? But at the time I was seeing Cassirer as a kind of god, as you tend to when you're young and you read these exalted thinkers. It wasn't that I was saying he was wrong, it was just that it bothered me. I think feminism puts all of that in perspective. It gives you a handle.

CA: How do you feel about the work of feminist women in publishing?

FRENCH: I think it's absolutely magnificent. I said earlier that I was feeling very positive, and one reason was that the slime under the rug, as I call this stuff that goes on in the home, is being held up and looked at and declared wrong. The other ground for my positive thinking is that the most brilliant, interesting, stimulating stuff is coming out of feminist work in sociology, in history, in psychology, and in philosophy. I'm just waiting for it to come out in political science. There have been a couple of books in that field that have been worthwhile, but we need to go further there. This stuff, which is what all students will be reading in the next twenty or thirty years, is going to be the groundwork for the next world.

CA: It strikes me that you've been fortunate (that good fortune having been helped along by hard work) in being able to express your ideas in both fiction and nonfiction. That must have been very satisfying to you.

FRENCH: It has. Writing novels is very hard. It draws from a part of you that it's hard for me to get at. And when I finish a novel, I couldn't possibly start another one right away. I have to regear and remulch. Being able to move to a different kind of difficulty, which writing nonfiction is, being able to move between the two, is like letting two crops grow on the same patch of soil, each of which refurbishes it for the other.

BIOGRAPHICAL/CRITICAL SOURCES:

BOOKS

Contemporary Literary Criticism, Gale, Volume 10, 1979, Volume 18, 1981.

PERIODICALS

Chicago Tribune, May 4, 1980, February 7, 1988.
Chicago Tribune Book World, March 9, 1980, June 23, 1985.

Detroit News, April 20, 1980.

Library Journal, November 15, 1977.

Los Angeles Times Book Review, May 4, 1980, April 19, 1981, August 25, 1985, October 18, 1987.

Ms., January, 1978, April, 1979, May, 1980.

Nation, January 30, 1988.

Newsweek, March 17, 1980.

New York Review of Books, June 11, 1981.

New York Times, October 27, 1977, March 10, 1980, March 16, 1981.

New York Times Book Review, October 16, 1977, November 11, 1977, March 16, 1980, March 22, 1981, June 12, 1983, June 23, 1985, October 25, 1987.

People, February 20, 1978.

Publishers Weekly, August 29, 1977, August 21, 1978, March 7, 1980.

Time, March 17, 1980, July 29, 1985.

Times (London), March 18, 1982, January 22, 1986, October 15, 1987, October 19, 1987.

Times Literary Supplement, February 18, 1977, April 21, 1978, May 9, 1980, June 4, 1982, January 24, 1986, October 23, 1987.

Tribune Books, October 11, 1987.

Village Voice, March 24, 1980.

Virginia Quarterly Review, Volume 54, number 2, 1978.

Washington Post, May 7, 1980.

Washington Post Book World, October 9, 1977, March 9, 1980, March 8, 1981, June 2, 1985, October 18, 1987.

—Sketch by Sharon Malinowski

—Interview by Jean W. Ross

*   *   *

FROST, David (Paradine) 1939-

PERSONAL: Born April 7, 1939, in Tenterden, Kent, England; son of Wilfrid John Paradine (a Methodist minister) and Mona Eveline (Aldrich) Frost; married Lynn Frederick, January, 1981 (divorced, 1982); married Carina Fitzalan Howard, March, 1983; children: (second marriage) Miles. *Education:* Gonville and Caius College, Cambridge, B.A. and M.A.

ADDRESSES: Home—46 Egerton Crescent, London SW3, England.

CAREER: Worked as a performer in nightclubs and as a trainee with Rediffusion Ltd. (a commercial television contracting firm), London, England; performer and writer of television variety shows "That Was the Week That Was," for British Broadcasting Corp. (BBC-TV), 1962-63, and for National Broadcasting Co. (NBC), 1963-64, "Not So Much a Programme, More a Way of Life," BBC-TV, 1964-65, and "Frost Report," BBC-TV, 1965-67; host of television interview show "Frost Programme" for Independent Television (ITV) and concurrently as a disc jockey on BBC-Radio, 1966-68; host of three television shows for Rediffusion Ltd., "Frost on Friday" (discussion), "Frost on Saturday" (interview), and "Frost on Sunday" (variety), 1968-69; host of "David Frost Show" for Westinghouse Broadcasting Co., 1969-72; also appeared in television shows "David Frost at the Phonograph," 1966, "David Frost's Night out in London," 1966-67, "Frost over England," 1967, "The Nixon Interviews," 1977, "Headliners with David Frost," 1978, and "The Next President," 1987. Founder and chief executive of David Paradine Productions; joint founder, London Weekend Television, 1967; founding director, TV-AM, 1983. Performer of one-man stage act, "An Evening with David Frost," at Edinburgh Festi-

val, 1966; producer of movie "The Rise and Fall of Michael Rimmer," 1970.

AWARDS, HONORS: Golden Rose award at the International Television Festival, Montreux, Richard Dimbleby award, Royal Television Society's Silver Medal, and Television Personality of the Year award from the Guild of Television Producers and Directors, all 1967, all for "Frost over England,"; Emmy Awards, National Academy of Television Arts and Sciences, 1970 and 1971; Order of the British Empire, and Religious Heritage of America Award, both 1970; Albert Einstein Award in communication arts, 1971; LL.D., Emerson College.

WRITINGS:

(Editor with Ned Sherrin) *That Was the Week That Was,* W. H. Allen, 1963.

(With Christopher Booker and others) *How to Live under Labour; or, At Least, Have as Much Chance as Anybody Else,* Heinemann, 1964.

(With Anthony Jay) *To England with Love,* Hodder & Stoughton, 1967, revised edition published as *The English,* Avon, 1968.

The Presidential Debate, 1968: David Frost Talks with Vice-President Hubert H. Humphrey and Others, Stein & Day, 1968.

The Americans, Stein & Day, 1970.

Billy Graham Talks with David Frost, A. J. Holman, 1971.

"I Gave Them a Sword": Behind the Scenes of the Nixon Interviews, photos by John Bryson, Morrow, 1978.

(With Michael Deakin) *The Book of the World's Worst Decisions,* illustrated by Arnie Levin, Crown, 1983 (published in England as *I Could Have Kicked Myself: David Frost's Book of the World's Worst Decisions,* Futura, 1983).

(With Deakin) *Who Wants to Be a Millionaire?,* illustrated by William Rushton, Deutsch, 1983, published as *David Frost's Book of Millionaires, Multimillionaires, and Really Rich People,* Crown, 1984.

(With Deakin) *If You'll Believe That You'll Believe Anything,* illustrated by Rushton, Methuen, 1986.

AUTHOR OF INTRODUCTION; "THE BLUFFER'S GUIDE" SERIES

Bluff Your Way in Opera, Crown, 1971.

. . . *in Music,* Crown, 1971.

. . . *in Cinema,* Crown, 1971.

. . . *in Wine,* Crown, 1971.

. . . *in Art,* Crown, 1971.

. . . *in Literature,* Crown, 1971.

. . . *in Antiques,* Crown, 1972.

. . . *in Football,* Crown, 1972.

. . . *in Interior Decorating,* 1972.

. . . *in Gourmet Food,* 1972.

. . . *in Theatre,* 1972.

. . . *in Travel,* 1972.

OTHER

Former columnist for London *Observer;* contributor of dramatic criticism to *Spectator,* and of humorous articles to *Punch.*

SIDELIGHTS: Many Americans who have followed David Frost's career as a television interviewer and journalist realize that the Briton first rose to fame in his native country as a nightclub performer and comedian whose shows "That Was the Week That Was" and "Not So Much a Programme, More a Way of Life" took a satiric look at society and current events. In fact, the latter series was terminated by the BBC in its second year for airing a biting sketch of the Duke of Windsor on the night his sister died. For Frost, who once turned down an offer to play professional soccer, the shows served as a stepping stone to a lucrative career in the United States.

Frost's greatest challenge as an interviewer occurred in eleven weeks between 1976 and early 1977. During that time, he spent twenty-nine hours interviewing former President Richard Nixon for a series of shows that eventually were edited down to four ninety-minute sessions. The segments dealt with Watergate, Nixon's foreign policy, the Vietnam War abroad and at home, and the president's final days. Special versions of the series were also prepared for Britain, France, Italy, and Australia. While some critics dismissed the interviews as a "pseudo-event," most agreed with *Newsweek*'s assessment that they were "a rare combination of journalism, history and live television." Frost went on to document the making of the series in his book *"I Gave Them a Sword": Behind the Scenes of the Nixon Interviews.*

Critical reaction to this work focuses on the interviewer's dedication and tenacity in getting his elusive subject to talk. "Indeed," notes J. Anthony Lewis in a *New York Times Book Review* piece, "[the book] is most compelling in its picture of the way Mr. Frost puts together a blockbuster like this one—shuttling back and forth between earnest conferences with his journalists, tough negotiations with Mr. Nixon's agents, wheeling and dealing with packagers, hard sells to advertisers, leaking material to television critics or magazines. . . . Not surprisingly, [Frost] sometimes loses track of where journalism ends and commerce begins." Charles Wheeler, writing in the *Times Literary Supplement,* has mixed feelings about Frost's personal remembrances: The "account of how he secured the interviews, found sponsors, swotted for the great encounter and finally persuaded Nixon to confess that he had let down the American people is a less valuable contribution to the Nixon record than a transcript of the conversations would have been. His inclusion of the Thoughts of Frost . . . is a needless, muddling embellishment. Nevertheless, he proved to be a superbly briefed, tough, persistent questioner and, by getting Nixon on the record under the pressure of cross-examination, may have made it much more difficult for the ex-President to rewrite history in his own memoirs."

Most of Frost's other books take a lighter look at life. In *Who Wants to be a Millionaire?,* for instance, the author packs the volume "with amusing stories of how the very rich get their money, spend their money, lose their money, or hoard their money," according to a *Spectator* critic, who adds that such a lighthearted volume "has no pretensions to explore beyond the unattested anecdote, and will provide many a good joke for an after-dinner speaker."

BIOGRAPHICAL/CRITICAL SOURCES:

BOOKS

Frischauer, Willi, *Will You Welcome Now . . . David Frost,* Hawthorn, 1971.
Frost, David, *"I Gave Them a Sword": Behind the Scenes at the Nixon Interviews,* Morrow, 1978.
Rayburn, Wallace, *Frost: Anatomy of a Success,* Macdonald, 1968.

PERIODICALS

Life, March 22, 1968.
Los Angeles Times, April 3, 1987, November 28, 1987.
Newsweek, May 9, 1977.
New York Times, February 7, 1978.

New York Times Book Review, February 25, 1968, February 26, 1978.
Saturday Review, July 13, 1968.
Spectator, June 4, 1983.
Times Literary Supplement, April 21, 1978.
Village Voice, March 13, 1978.
Washington Post Book World, March 12, 1978.*

*   *   *

FROST, Joni
    See PAINE, Lauran (Bosworth)

*   *   *

FRY, C(harles) George 1936-

PERSONAL: Born August 15, 1936, in Piqua, Ohio; son of Sylvan Jack and Lena Freda Marie (Ehle) Fry; married Brigitte Gertrud Langer, December 28, 1961 (divorced October 2, 1970); married Christel Heischmann, November 24, 1971 (divorced, 1980). *Education:* Capital University, B.A. (with honors), 1958; Ohio State University, M.A., 1961, Ph.D., 1965; Evangelical Lutheran Theological Seminary, B.D. (with honors), 1962, M.Div., 1977; Winebrenner Theological Seminary, D.Min., 1978. *Politics:* Independent.

ADDRESSES: Home—158 West Union St., Circleville, Ohio. *Office*—Office of the Protestant Chaplain, St. Francis College, Fort Wayne, Ind. 46808.

CAREER: Clergyman of Lutheran Church, vicar in Columbus, Ohio, 1961-62; Wittenberg University, Springfield, Ohio, instructor in history, 1962-63; pastor in Columbus, 1963-66; Capital University, Columbus, instructor, 1963-65, assistant professor, 1966-71, associate professor of religion and history, 1971-75; Concordia Theological Seminary, Fort Wayne, Ind., associate professor of historical theology and director of missions education, 1975-84; St. Francis College, Fort Wayne, protestant chaplain, 1982—. Interim minister, Arbor Grove Congregational Church, Jackson, Mich., 1980, First Presbyterian Church, Huntington, Ind., 1988-89, and St. Luke's Lutheran Church, Fort Wayne, 1989-90.

Visiting professor, Damavand College, 1973-74, Concordia Lutheran Seminary, 1978, 1982, Indiana University, 1982—, Purdue University, 1982—, Graduate School of Christian Ministries, Huntington College, 1986—, and Graduate School of Missions, Wheaton College, 1987, 1988; visiting lecturer, Wittenberg University, 1971, Northern England Institute for Christian Education, University of Durham, 1984; visiting theologian at churches in Columbus, 1971-72, National Presbyterian Church of Mexico, 1977, 1979, conference of the Lutheran churches in Venezuela, 1981, and the Lutheran church in Nigeria, 1983. Instructor, John F. Kennedy Special Warfare Center, Fort Bragg, N.C., 1983; Joseph J. Malone post-doctoral fellow, Egypt, 1986. Member of North American executive committee, Fellowship of Faith for the Muslims, 1970-80; member of North American Conference on Muslim Evangelization, 1977-78; member of Lutheran-Baptist dialogue team, Lutheran Council/United States of America, 1978-81. Member of board, Damavand College, 1976—, Samuel Zwemer Institute, 1977-82, Fort Wayne International Affairs, 1982—, Lutheran Liturgical Renewal, 1983—, Greater Fort Wayne Campus Ministry, 1983—, and Indiana Churches United for Ministry in Higher Education, 1984—. Participant in Indiana Professors Study Tour, Persian Gulf, 1987.

MEMBER: American Historical Association, American Academy of Religion, Conference on Faith and History, Foundation for Reformation Research (Ohio representative), American Association of University Professors, Organization of American Historians, National Association of College and University Chaplains, American Association for Counseling and Development, Association for Religious and Values Issues in Counseling, British Interplanetary Society (fellow), Ohio Historical Society, Ohio Academy of History, Phi Alpha Theta, Kappa Alpha Pi.

AWARDS, HONORS: Research grant for study in Turkey, Regional Council for International Education, 1969; Praestantia Award, Capital University, 1970.

WRITINGS:

The Supper Guest, Ohio State University Printing, 1971.
(With James R. King) *The Middle East: Crossroads of Civilization,* C. E. Merrill, 1973.
The Christian Ministry to Muslims Today, Fellowship of Faith for Muslims (Toronto), 1977.
A Guide to the Study of the World of Islam, Fellowship of Faith for Muslims, 1977.
(With King) *Islam: A Survey of the Muslim Faith,* Baker Book, 1980, 2nd edition, 1982.
(With Duane W. H. Arnold) *The Way, the Truth, and the Life: An Introduction to Lutheran Christianity,* Baker Book, 1982.
(With King) *Great Asian Religions,* Baker Book, 1984.
(With Arnold) *Francis: A Call to Conversion,* Zondervan, 1988.
(With Jon Paul Fry) *Congregationalists and Evolution: Asa Gray and Louis Agassiz,* University Press of America, 1989.
(With J. P. Fry) *Pioneering a Theology of Evolution: Washington Gladden and Pierre Teilhard de Chardin,* University Press of America, 1989.
(With Raymond J. Graves) *America and the Soviet Union, 1948-1988,* Westwood Community Press, 1989.
(With Graves) *America and the Third World,* Westwood Community Press, 1989.
(With J. P. Fry) *Avicenna's Philosophy of Education: An Introduction,* Three Continents, 1989.

PUBLISHED BY CONCORDIA THEOLOGICAL SEMINARY PRESS

Ten Contemporary Theologians, 1976.
Islam: An Evangelical Perspective, 1976.
(With Harold H. Zietlow) *Christian Missions: History,* 1976.
(With Zietlow) *Christian Missions: Strategy,* 1976.
(Editor) *European Theology, 1648-1914,* 1976.
(Editor) *Protestant Theology, 1914-1975,* 1977.
(With John M. Drickamer) *Lutheranism in America,* 1979.
(With Drickamer) *The Age of Lutheran Orthodoxy, 1530-1648,* 1979.
(With Arnold) *A Lutheran Reader,* 1982.
Raymond Lull: Apostle to the Muslims, 1983.
Iran and Japan: Two Models of Modernization, 1983, 2nd edition, Westwood Community Press, 1989.

EDITOR

(With Donald E. Bensch, and contributor) *The Middle East in Transition,* Capital University Press, 1970.
(With James L. Burke, and contributor) *The Past in Perspective,* MSS Educational Publishing, 1971.

(With Burke, and contributor) *The Emergence of the Modern World, 1300-1815,* MSS Educational Publishing, 1971.
(With Burke, and contributor) *The Search for a New Europe, 1919-1971,* MSS Educational Publishing, 1971.
(With King) *An Anthology of Middle Eastern Literature from the Twentieth Century,* Wittenberg University, 1974.

OTHER

Also contributor to *The New Schaff-Herzog Encyclopedia of Religious Knowledge,* Baker Book, *Dictionary of Christianity in America,* Inter-Varsity Press, *Great Lives from History,* Salem Press, and *Evangelical Dictionary of Theology,* Baker Book.

WORK IN PROGRESS: With Jon Paul Fry, *Pioneers of Science Fiction: Jules Verne and H. G. Wells; Washington Gladden as a Preacher.*

AVOCATIONAL INTERESTS: Hiking, painting, science fiction.

*   *   *

FURMAN, Gertrude Lerner Kerman 1909-
(Gertrude Kerman)

PERSONAL: Born August 29, 1909, in Quebec City, Quebec, Canada; daughter of Leon and Deborah (Ortenberg) Lerner; married first husband, Joseph Kerman, May 29, 1936; children: (first marriage) Patricia Clare, Julie Beth. *Education:* McGill University, B.A. (summa cum laude), 1929; additional study at New School for Social Research, Columbia University, and New York University.

ADDRESSES: Home—21 Chapel Pl., Great Neck, N.Y. 10211.

CAREER: Former Broadway actress; associated with producers Leland Hayward and Gilbert Miller; instructor-playwright, Off-Broadway Adelphi College, Children's Center for Creative Arts, Garden City, N.Y.; director, Children's Theater. Instructor in dramatic writing, adult program of Great Neck (N.Y.) Schools; director, Great Neck School of Drama; executive producer, director, Great Neck Community Theatre.

MEMBER: Authors League of America, American Educational Theatre Association, Delta Phi Epsilon.

WRITINGS:

(Under name Gertrude Kerman) *Plays and Creative Ways with Children,* Harvey, 1961.
(Under name Gertrude Kerman) *Shakespeare for Young Players: From Tens to Teens,* Harvey, 1964.
(Under name Gertrude Kerman) *Cabeza de Vaca, Defender of the Indians,* Harvey, 1974.

Also author of radio plays and magazine articles on the theater.

WORK IN PROGRESS: A book tentatively entitled *Contemporary Dramatic Impersonations for Young People.*

BIOGRAPHICAL/CRITICAL SOURCES:

PERIODICALS

Montreal Gazette, July 5, 1962.
Montreal Star, July 5, 1962.*

G

GADO, Frank 1936-

PERSONAL: Born November 15, 1936, in Fairview, N.J.; son of Beniamino Eugenio (a provisions salesman) and Teresa (Grimaldi) Gado; married Gunilla Stenman, October 22, 1967; children: Anna Teresa, Tobias Eugenio, Carin Johanna. *Education:* Dartmouth College, A.B., 1958; Harvard University, law study, 1958; Duke University, M.A., 1960, Ph.D., 1968.

ADDRESSES: Home—1131 Adams Rd., Schenectady, N.Y. 12308. *Office*—Department of English, Union College, Union St., Schenectady, N.Y. 12308.

CAREER: Union College, Schenectady, N.Y., instructor, 1963-68, assistant professor, 1968-70, associate professor, 1970-81, professor of English, 1981—, chairman of department, 1974. Fulbright-Hays lecturer in American literature, University of Uppsala, 1966-67, 1969-70.

AWARDS, HONORS: National Endowment for the Humanities fellow, 1975-76.

WRITINGS:

First Person: Conversations with Novelists on Writers and Writing, Union College Press, 1973.
(Contributor) Joseph P. Strelka, editor, *Literary Criticism and Philosophy,* Pennsylvania State University Press, 1982.
(Author of introduction) Sherwood Anderson, *The Teller's Tales: Short Stories,* Union College Press, 1983.
The Passion of Ingmar Bergman, Duke University Press, 1986.

Contributor of book reviews to *New Republic, Studies in Short Fiction, American Literature,* and *Studia Neophilologica.* Editor, Union College Press, 1982—.

WORK IN PROGRESS: Research in autobiography as a genre.

SIDELIGHTS: Frank Gado is competent in Swedish, Italian, and Piedmontese (a dialect of Italy).

*   *   *

GALLAGHER, Richard
See LEVINSON, Leonard

GAMMOND, Peter 1925-

PERSONAL: Born September 30, 1925, in Northwich, Cheshire, England; son of John Thomas (a clerk) and Dorothy (Heald) Gammond; married Elizabeth Ann Hodgson (a teacher), July 31, 1954; children: John Julian, Stephen. *Education:* Attended Wadham College, Oxford, 1943, 1947-50. *Politics:* Socialist. *Religion:* Church of England.

ADDRESSES: Home and office—Craven Cottage, Dunboe Pl., Shepperton, Middlesex, England.

CAREER: Decca Record Co., London, England, editor, 1953-60; free-lance writer, 1960—. Composer and broadcaster. *Military service:* British Army, Royal Armoured Corps, 1943-47; became sergeant.

MEMBER: Rotary International.

WRITINGS:

(Editor and contributor) *The Decca Book of Jazz* (a Jazz Book Club selection), Muller, 1958.
(Editor and contributor) *Duke Ellington: His Life and Music* (a Jazz Book Club selection), Roy, 1958.
101 Things, Elek, 1960.
(With Peter Clayton) *A Guide to Popular Music,* Phoenix House, 1960, Philosophical Library, 1961.
Terms Used in Music, Phoenix House, 1960.
(With Charles Fox, Alexis Korner, and Alun Morgan) *Jazz on Record,* Hutchinson, 1960, Greenwood Press, 1978.
(With Burnett James) *Music on Record: A Critical Guide,* Hutchinson, Volume I, 1962, Volume II, 1962, Volume III, 1963, Volume IV, 1963, Greenwood Press, 1978.
(With Clayton) *Fourteen Miles on a Clear Night: An Irreverent, Sceptical and Affectionate Book about Jazz Records* (a Jazz Book Club selection), P. Owen, 1966.
Bluff Your Way into Music, Wolfe Publishing, 1966, revised edition, 1984.
The Meaning and Magic of Music, Hamlyn, 1968, Golden Books, 1970.
Your Own, Your Very Own (music hall scrapbook), Allan, Shepperton, 1971.
One Man's Music, Wolfe Publishing, 1971.
(Editor) *Best Music Hall and Variety Songs,* Wolfe Publishing, 1972.
Scott Joplin and the Ragtime Era, St. Martin's, 1975.

(Editor) *Music Hall Songbook,* David & Charles, 1975.
Musical Instruments in Colour, Blandford, 1975, published as *Musical Instruments in Colour,* Macmillan, 1976.
(Contributor) *The Dictionary of Composers,* Book Club Associates, 1977.
The Illustrated Encyclopedia of Recorded Opera, Salamander, 1979.
The Magic Flute, Barrie & Jenkins, 1979.
The Music Goes Round and Round, Quartet Books, 1980.
(Editor with Raymond Horricks) *Music on Record: Brass Bands,* Stephens, 1980.
(Editor) *The Good Old Days Songbook,* British Broadcasting Corp. Publications/EMI, 1980.
Offenbach: His Life and Times, Midas, 1980, Paganiniana, 1981.
An Illustrated Guide to Composers of Opera, Salamander, 1980.
An Illustrated Guide to Composers of Classical Music, Salamander, 1980.
(Editor with Horricks) *Music on Record: The Big Bands,* Stephens, 1981.
Schubert, Eyre Methuen, 1981.
(Contributor) *The New Oxford Companion to Music,* Oxford University Press, 1983.
Bluff Your Way in Golf, Ravette, 1986.
Opera on Compact Disc, Salamander, 1986.
(With Clayton) *The Guinness Jazz A-Z,* Guinness, 1986.
Bluff Your Way in Class, Ravette, 1987.
Duke Ellington, Apollo, 1987.
(With Clayton) *Bluff Your Way in Jazz,* Ravette, 1987.
(Editor) *The Illustrated Encyclopedia of Classical Music,* Salamander, 1988.
The Bluffer's Guide to Bluffing, Ravette, 1988.
The Guinness Jazz Companion, Guinness, 1989.
Bluff Your Way in Opera, Ravette, 1989.

Also author of numerous record jacket notes. Also contributor to "The Great Composers and Their Music" series, Marshall Cavendish. Reviewer for *Which Compact Disc?,* 1987—. Contributor to recording industry journals and newspapers. Editor, *Audio Record Review,* 1966-70; music editor, *Hi-Fi News and Record Review,* 1970-80.

WORK IN PROGRESS: The Oxford Companion to Popular Music; books on Jelly Roll Morton and John Betjeman.

SIDELIGHTS: Peter Gammond told *CA:* "My ambition to be a creative writer was sidetracked, after a period with Decca Record Co., into writing about music and records. It is sometimes frustrating to be typecast, but at least it is a source of constant commissions. I have always attempted to write about music in understandable terms and have become increasingly interested in the field of popular music. I am also trying to give more time to writing music, and some fictional work is now under way."

AVOCATIONAL INTERESTS: Tennis, golf, book-collecting.

* * *

GANN, L(ewis) H(enry) 1924-

PERSONAL: Name originally Ludwig Hermann Ganz; born January 28, 1924, in Mainz, Germany (now West Germany); son of Hermann Friedrich (a merchant) and Charlotte (Fromberg) Ganz; married Rita Herta Niesler, September 6, 1950; children: Margarita Herta Charlotte, Thomas Michael. *Education:* Oxford University, B.A., 1950, M.A., 1954, M.Litt., 1955, D.Phil., 1964.

ADDRESSES: Office—Hoover Institution, Stanford University, Stanford, Calif. 94305.

CAREER: Rhodes-Livingstone Institute, Lusaka, Northern Rhodesia (now Zambia), historian, 1951-52; University of Manchester, Manchester, England, assistant lecturer, 1952-54; National Archives of Rhodesia and Nyasaland, Salisbury, Rhodesia, archivist and editor, 1954-63; Stanford University, Hoover Institution, Stanford, Calif., 1964—, began as research associate, became deputy curator of African collection, currently senior fellow. Resident scholar, Historische Kommission zu Berlin, 1980; member, Institute for Advanced Study, Princeton University, 1990; senior research associate, St. Antony's College, Oxford. *Military service:* British Army, Royal Fusiliers, 1944-47; became sergeant.

MEMBER: African Studies Association (Great Britain and United States), Royal Historical Society (fellow), American Historical Association, Conference on British Studies, Leo Baeck Institute.

WRITINGS:

The Birth of a Plural Society: The Development of Northern Rhodesia under the British South Africa Company, 1894-1914, University of Manchester Press, 1958, reprinted, Greenwood Press, 1982.
(Contributor) V. W. Brelsford, editor, *Handbook to the Federation of Rhodesia and Nyasaland,* Cassell, 1960.
(With Peter Duignan) *White Settlers in Tropical Africa,* Penguin, 1962, reprinted, Greenwood Press, 1977.
A History of Northern Rhodesia: Early Days to 1953, Chatto & Windus, 1964.
(With Michael Gelfand) *Huggins of Rhodesia: The Man and His Country,* Allen & Unwin, 1964.
A History of Southern Rhodesia: Early Days to 1934, Chatto & Windus, 1965.
(With Duignan) *Burden of Empire: An Appraisal of Western Colonialism in Africa South of the Sahara,* Praeger, 1967.
(Editor with Duignan and contributor) *Colonialism in Africa, 1870-1960,* Cambridge University Press, Volume 1: *The History and Politics of Colonialism, 1870-1914,* 1969, Volume 2: *The History and Politics of Colonialism, 1914-1960,* 1970, Volume 3, 1971, Volume 5: *A Bibliographic Guide to Colonialism in Sub-Saharan Africa,* 1974, Volume 4: *The Economics of Colonialism,* 1975.
Central Africa: The Former British States, Prentice-Hall, 1971.
Guerrillas in History, Hoover Institution, 1971.
(With Duignan) *Africa and the World at Large: An Introduction to the History of Sub-Saharan Africa from Antiquity to 1840,* Chandler Publishing, 1972.
(With Duignan) *The Rulers of German Africa, 1884-1914,* Stanford University Press, 1977.
(With Duignan) *The Rulers of British Africa, 1870-1914,* Stanford University Press, 1978.
(Editor and contributor with Duignan) *African Proconsuls: European Governors in Africa,* Free Press, 1978.
(With Duignan) *The Rulers of Belgian Africa, 1884-1914,* Princeton University Press, 1979.
(With Duignan) *South Africa: War, Revolution, or Peace?,* Hoover Institution, 1979.
(With Duignan) *Why South Africa Will Survive,* St. Martin's, 1980.
(With Duignan) *Africa South of the Sahara: The Challenge to Western Security,* Hoover Institution, 1981.
(With Duignan) *The Middle East and North Africa: The Challenge to Western Security,* Hoover Institution, 1981.
(With Thomas H. Henriksen) *The Struggle for Zimbabwe: Battle in the Bush,* Praeger, 1981.
Africa between East and West, Tafelberg (Cape Town), 1983.

(Contributor) Ramon H. Myers and Mark R. Peattie, editors, *The Japanese Colonial Empire, 1895-1945,* Princeton University Press, 1983.

Dictionary of National Biography: Supplement, 1971-1980, Oxford University Press, 1983.

(With Duignan) *The United States and Africa: A History,* Cambridge University Press, 1984.

(With Duignan) *The Hispanics in the United States: A History,* Westview, 1986.

(Contributor) Duignan and Robert Jackson, editors, *Politics and Government in African States, 1960-1985,* Croom Helm, 1986.

(Editor) *The Defense of Western Europe,* Auburn House, 1987.

(Editor and contributor with Arthur J. Knoll) *Germans in the Tropics,* Greenwood Press, 1987.

(Contributor) Stig Forster, Wolfgang J. Mommsen, and Ronald Robinson, editors, *Bismarck, Europe and Africa: The Berlin Conference 1884-1885, and the Onset of Partition,* Oxford University Press, 1988.

Contributor of articles to newspapers, magazines, and journals. Member of editorial board, *Intercollegiate Review.*

WORK IN PROGRESS: A book with Duignan, tentative title *The Making of the Atlantic Community, 1945-1958,* for Basil Blackwell, publication scheduled for 1990 or 1991.

*   *   *

GANSS, George Edward   1905-

PERSONAL: Born September 18, 1905, in St. Louis, Mo.; son of Edward Adam and Adelaide J. (Wessels) Ganss. *Education:* St. Louis University, A.B., 1930, A.M., 1931, Ph.D., 1934; St. Mary's College, St. Marys, Kan., L.S.T., 1938.

ADDRESSES: Home and office—Institute of Jesuit Sources, Fusz Memorial, 3700 West Pine, St. Louis, Mo. 63108.

CAREER: Entered Society of Jesus (Jesuits), 1924; ordained Roman Catholic priest, 1937; Marquette University, Milwaukee, Wis., instructor, 1939-40, assistant professor, 1940-48, associate professor, 1948-53, professor of classics and theology, 1953-62; St. Louis University, School of Divinity, St. Louis, Mo., professor of theology and classics, 1962-74, emeritus professor, 1974—, director of Institute of Jesuit Sources, 1962—. Delegate to General Congregation of Society of Jesus in Rome, 1965-66. *Wartime service:* Auxiliary chaplain to servicemen attending Marquette University, 1942-46.

MEMBER: American Assistancy Seminar on Jesuit Spirituality (chairman, 1968—).

AWARDS, HONORS: L.H.D., Loyola University of Chicago, 1977.

WRITINGS:

(Translator) *St. Peter Chrysologus: Selected Sermons,* Fathers of the Church, 1953.

(Contributor) *The Fathers of the Church,* Catholic University of America, 1953.

St. Ignatius' Idea of a Jesuit University, Marquette University Press, 1954, 2nd edition, 1956.

The Jesuit Educational Tradition and St. Louis University: Some Bearings for the University's Sesquicentennial, 1818-1968, St. Louis University Press, 1969.

(Translator from the Spanish and author of introduction and commentary) *St. Ignatius of Loyola: The Constitutions of the Society of Jesus,* Institute of Jesuit Sources, 1970.

(Editor) Ignacio Iparraguirre, *Contemporary Trends in Studies on the Constitutions of the Society of Jesus: Annotated Bibliographical Orientations,* Institute of Jesuit Sources, 1974.

(Editor) William V. Bangert, *A Bibliographical Essay on the History of the Society of Jesus,* Institute of Jesuit Sources, 1976.

(Editor) Thomas H. Clancy, *An Introduction to Jesuit Life: The Constitutions and History through 435 Years,* Institute of Jesuit Sources, 1976.

(Editor) *Jesuit Religious Life Today: The Principal Features of Its Spirit, in Excerpts from Papal Documents, St. Ignatius' Constitutions, the 31st and 32nd General Congregations, and Letters of Father General Pedro Arrupe,* Institute of Jesuit Sources, 1977.

(Author of foreword) Clancy, *The Conversational Word of God: A Commentary on the Doctrine of St. Ignatius of Loyola Concerning Spiritual Conversation, with Four Early Jesuit Texts,* Institute of Jesuit Sources, 1978.

(Author of foreword) Eduoard Pousset, *Life in Faith and Freedom: An Essay Presenting Gaston Fessard's Analysis of the Dialectic of the Spiritual Exercises of St. Ignatius,* Institute of Jesuit Sources, 1980.

(Editor) Gladys W. Gruenberg, *Labor Peacemaker: The Life and Works of Father Leo C. Brown,* Institute of Jesuit Sources, 1981.

(Editor) Jules J. Toner, *A Commentary on Saint Ignatius' Rules for the Discernment of Spirits: A Guide to the Principles and Practice,* Institute of Jesuit Sources, 1982.

(Translator with others) Pedro Arrupe, *In Him Alone Is Our Hope: Texts on the Heart of Christ, 1966-1983,* Institute of Jesuit Sources, 1984.

(Editor with P. C. Fischer) Josef F. Schutte, *Valignano's Mission Principles for Japan,* Volume 1: *The Solution 1580 to 1582,* Institute of Jesuit Sources, 1985.

(Author of foreword) Candido de Dalmases, *Ignatius of Loyola, Founder of the Jesuits: His Life and Work,* Institute of Jesuit Sources, 1985.

(Editor) Bangert, *A History of the Society of Jesus,* 2nd revised edition, Institute of Jesuit Sources, 1986.

(Editor) David M. Stanley, *I Encountered God!: The Spiritual Exercises with the Gospel of St. John,* Institute of Jesuit Sources, 1986.

(Author of foreword) Stanley, *A Modern Scriptural Approach to the Scriptural Exercises,* Institute of Jesuit Sources, 1986.

Contributor to *Archivum Historicum Societatis Iesu, Jesuit Educational Quarterly, Thought,* and *Review for Religious.* Editor, *Studies in the Spirituality of Jesuits,* 1969—.

WORK IN PROGRESS: Research in Jesuit spirituality.

SIDELIGHTS: George Edward Ganss has travelled extensively in Western Europe, South America, and India.*

*   *   *

GARNER, Hugh   1913-1979
(Jarvis Warwick)

PERSONAL: Born February 22, 1913, in Batley, Yorkshire, England; brought to Canada in 1919; died June 30, 1979; son of Matthew and Annie (Fozard) Garner; married Marie Alice Gallant, July 5, 1941; children: Barbara Ann, Hugh, Jr. *Education:* Attended technical high school in Toronto, Ontario.

ADDRESSES: Home—33 Erskine Ave., Toronto, Ontario, Canada, M4P 1Y6.

CAREER: Novelist, short story writer, and journalist. Public relations director for J. K. Cooke Enterprises, 1951. *Military ser-*

vice: Machine gunner in International Brigade, 1937; served in Spain. Canadian Army, 1939-40. Royal Canadian Navy, 1940-45; served in Africa and Atlantic theater.

MEMBER: Association of Canadian Television and Radio Artists, Saint George Society.

AWARDS, HONORS: Shared *Northern Review* prize, 1951, for "The Conversion of Willie Heaps," which was included in *Best American Short Stories* for 1952; Canadian Governor General's Award for Fiction, 1963, for *Hugh Garner's Best Stories;* the Hugh Garner Co-operative, a housing development in Toronto's Cabbagetown was dedicated in his honor, 1982. Recipient of three Canada Council senior arts fellowships.

WRITINGS:

Storm Below (novel), Collins, 1949, Simon & Schuster, 1970.
Cabbagetown, Collins, 1950, revised edition, Ryerson, 1968.
(Under pseudonym Jarvis Warwick) *Waste No Tears,* Export, 1950.
Present Reckoning, Collins, 1951.
The Yellow Sweater, and Other Stories, Collins, 1952.
The Silence on the Shore, McClelland and Stewart, 1962.
Best Stories, Ryerson, 1963, published as *Hugh Garner's Best Stories,* Ryerson, 1968, reprinted, 1987.
Author, Author! (humorous essays), Ryerson, 1964.
Men and Women: Stories, Ryerson, 1966.
"A Trip for Mrs. Taylor" (one-act play; also see below), first produced in Brockville, Ontario, at the Brockville Theatre Guild, November 4, 1966.
(Author of foreword) Alice Munro, *Dance of the Happy Shades,* Ryerson, 1968.
The Sin Sniper (detective novel), Simon & Schuster of Canada, 1970, published as *Stone Cold Dead,* Paperjacks, 1978.
A Nice Place to Visit (detective novel), Ryerson, 1971.
Violation of the Virgins, and Other Stories, McGraw-Hill Ryerson, 1971.
Three Women: A Trilogy of One-Act Plays (contains "Some Are So Lucky," "The Magnet," and "A Trip for Mrs. Taylor"), Simon and Pierre, 1973.
One Damn Thing after Another (memoirs), McGraw-Hill Ryerson, 1973.
Death in Don Mills: A Murder Mystery, McGraw-Hill Ryerson, 1975.
The Intruders (novel), McGraw-Hill Ryerson, 1976.
The Legs of the Lame, and Other Stories, Borealis Press, 1976.
Murder Has Your Number: An Inspector DuMont Mystery, McGraw-Hill Ryerson, 1978.
A Hugh Garner Omnibus, McGraw-Hill Ryerson, 1978.

Also author of television dramas aired in Canada, England, and Australia. Writer of daily column in *Toronto Telegram,* 1966. Contributor of about five hundred articles and stories to magazines. Associate editor of *Saturday Night,* 1952-54; editor of *Liberty,* 1963. Garner's work has been translated into several languages, including Afrikaans and Rumanian, and is represented in more than seventy anthologies. His papers are collected at the Douglas Library at Queen's University in Canada.

SIDELIGHTS: In a career that spanned thirty years, novelist, short story writer, and journalist Hugh Garner authored seventeen books, more than four hundred pieces of journalism, numerous short stories, and several radio and television scripts. Born in England and brought to Toronto at the age of six by his parents, Garner developed an early empathy with the working-class poor after his mother was deserted by his father. During the Depression, he road the rails throughout the United States and Can-

ada prior to volunteering in the Mackenzie-Papineau brigade of the Loyalist cause in the Spanish civil war. After a brief stint in the army, Garner enlisted in the navy, to which he ascribed the origins of his lifelong battle with liquor dependency. Referring to Garner's heavy-smoking, hard-drinking lifestyle, Barbara Amiel remarked in *Maclean's* that "it was a moot point whether it was the alcohol or coal tar that had finally stopped him," for at the time of his death, Garner "had already passed into literary legend." Describing him as a "maverick in his life and in his fiction," J. M. Zezulka noted in a *Dictionary of Literary Biography* essay: "His vision, in his novels and in the short stories which are his most memorable work, was formed by his multifarious experiences during the Depression, the Spanish civil war, North Atlantic convoy duty, and by his sympathy for what he called the bottom half of humanity."

In a *Canadian Literature* review of Garner's memoirs, *One Damn Thing after Another,* George Woodcock described the author as "dedicated and obsessed." And although in *Saturday Night,* Doug Fetherling referred to Garner as "just an intellectual misanthrope," he felt that this also made him "fresh and rather appealing." Characterizing Garner as a "comfortable writer," Sandra Martin stated in a *Books in Canada* review of his last collection of stories, *The Legs of the Lame:* "Invariably he tells a story that has both a beginning and an end and he uses a style that, while colourful, is devoid of artifice and pretentiousness." Pointing out that "Garner avoided pretension as assiduously as he shunned literary coteries or fashions," Zezulka added that Garner "loved telling stories, and he had tremendous respect for his craft."

Drawing upon his experiences in the navy, Garner's first novel, *Storm Below,* focuses on the death of a sailor at sea; however, "the novel's real interest lies in Garner's handling of the crew's superstitious reactions to the presence of a dead body aboard ship and in his exploration of their private thoughts and lives," wrote Zezulka. And Claude T. Bissell found "many shining virtues" in what he described in the *University of Toronto Quarterly* in 1950 as "the best Canadian novel based upon war experience" thus far. While his fiction is described by Desmond Pacey in a *Contemporary Novelists* essay as "honest and workmanlike," he is especially praised for his skillful characterizations. Garner created characters who "who live in all dimensions," said Nancy Kavanaugh, adding in a *Canadian Author and Bookman* review of *Men and Women,* a collection of short stories, that although his characters are "uncomfortable to read about," his stories are "fascinating, perhaps because we recognize some aspects of our own lives or personalities here portrayed." Describing Garner's general fictional world as "filled with little people," Martin elaborated, however, that "whether bartenders, clerks, mechanics, prostitutes, drunks, or murders, the characters are diminished by the sordid pettiness of their lives; they respond physically, often brutally."

It was Garner's second novel, however, that provided the author with a bestseller and critical plaudits as well; and according to Fetherling in *Saturday Night,* the novel has "dominated his reputation." *Cabbagetown,* named after the Toronto slum of Garner's own youth, chronicles the struggles of several families to survive the Depression. Garner returned to Cabbagetown in other volumes, including *Waste No Tears,* a story about the poor and what they must do to survive slum life, *The Silence on the Shore,* about the complex interrelationships among tenants in a rundown boarding house, and finally *The Intruders,* a novel in which he focused "on the disillusioned suburbanites who have infiltrated Cabbagetown in search of community involvement," wrote Zezulka. "What these middle-class professional families discover, however, is that consciousness is difficult to overcome. In the end they relinquish the neighborhood to those who have always been there, the punks and the drunks and the working poor."

In the opinion of Val Clery, in *Books in Canada,* Garner is "unique amongst Canadian writers in being able to catch authentically the North American furies that haunt the lonely and the rootless and the poor." Noting that "Garner has often been praised for his good heart when it is really his good ear and sharp eye that deserve our admiration," Miriam Waddington added in *Canadian Literature* that the author's "concern with truth places his work in the realm of social realism." Suggesting, however, that Garner comes very close "to the ideals of American naturalism," J. R. MacGillivray explained in the *University of Toronto Quarterly* that "he concentrates on the plight of the little man in an industrialized and war-minded society; he accumulates details that render the ugliness and monotony of the urban background."

While some critics have responded negatively to what they detect as a certain repetitive and cliched quality to Garner's work, other critics find this sentiment irrelevant. For instance, in a *Tamarack Review* piece about *Silence on the Shore,* Michael Hornyanski indicated that despite the fact that "Garner's writing is often bad—repetitious, cliched, ponderous, insistent on labouring the obvious," the author effectively re-created "just the basic bedrock reality which we all start from." And according to John Moss in *Patterns of Isolation,* "Garner has successfully wedded document and melodramatic sentiment into a steadfastly singular and ironic vision of reality."

Although a writer of realism who championed the cause of the down-and-out, he had no "doctrinaire political or social remedies to preach," wrote Pacey. Garner's deep novelistic insight represents "the depth of experience, of actuality, rather than of philosophy or moral vision," suggested Moss. And according to Amiel, "He was something of a cracker-barrel philosopher and it was his populist message that made his novels more than just a good read." In Pacey's estimation, "Garner has earned a special niche in Canadian literary history by the way in which he has persevered in the realistic treatment of urban life," adding in a *Contemporary Novelists* essay that Garner "remained consistently true to social realism and . . . eschewed experiments with symbolism, surrealism, or stream of consciousness." Calling him the "true journeyman of Canadian writing," Clery maintained that Garner "deserves (and is too infrequently given) the attention and the respect of the writers in his wake."

BIOGRAPHICAL/CRITICAL SOURCES:

BOOKS

Contemporary Literary Criticism, Volume 13, Gale, 1980.
Contemporary Novelists, St. James/St. Martin's, 1976.
Dictionary of Literary Biography, Volume 68: *Canadian Writers, 1920-1959, First Series,* Gale, 1988.
Fetherling, Doug, *Hugh Garner,* Forum House, 1972.
Garner, Hugh, *One Damn Thing after Another* (memoirs), McGraw-Hill Ryerson, 1973.
Moss, John, *Patterns of Isolation,* McClelland and Stewart, 1974.
Stuewe, Paul, *Hugh Garner and His Works,* ECW, 1984.

PERIODICALS

Books in Canada, November, 1971, March, 1977.
Canadian Author and Bookman, autumn, 1966.
Canadian Literature, autumn, 1971, winter, 1974.
Journal of Canadian Fiction, spring, 1972.

Maclean's, July 16, 1979.
Saturday Night, November, 1968, November, 1973, July-August, 1976.
Tamarack Review, winter, 1963, fall, 1969.
University of Toronto Quarterly, April, 1950, April, 1952.*

—*Sketch by Sharon Malinowski*

* * *

GARRISON, Karl C(laudius) 1900-1980

PERSONAL: Born August 14, 1900, in Gaston County, N.C.; died July, 1980; son of Rufus J. (a farm owner) and Susie (Mauney) Garrison; married Ruby Heafner, 1924 (divorced, 1942); married Linnea Malmborg, 1943; children: (first marriage) Karl Claudius, Jr. *Education:* Attended Lenoir Rhyne College, 1917-18, 1919-21; George Peabody College for Teachers of Vanderbilt University, B.S., 1922, Ph.D., 1927; University of North Carolina, M.S., 1926. *Politics:* Independent Democrat. *Religion:* Lutheran.

ADDRESSES: Office—Department of Educational Psychology, University of Georgia, Athens, Ga. 30601.

CAREER: George Peabody College for Teachers of Vanderbilt University, Nashville, Tenn., instructor in educational psychology, 1927-28; North Carolina State College (now North Carolina State University at Raleigh), Raleigh, professor of psychology and chairman of department, 1928-40; Central Connecticut State College, New Britain, professor of education and psychology, 1941-46; Georgia State College for Women (now Georgia College), Atlanta, professor of psychology, 1946-47; Frostburg State College, Frostburg, Md., dean of instruction, 1947-48; University of Georgia, Athens, professor of education and chairman of department of educational psychology, 1948-65, professor emeritus, 1965-80. Visiting professor of education, Old Dominion College, beginning 1965.

MEMBER: American Psychological Association (fellow), Council for Exceptional Children, American Education Association, Southeastern Psychological Association, Southern Society for Philosophy and Psychology, Phi Delta Kappa, Phi Kappa Phi, Kappa Delta Pi, Kappa Phi Kappa, Psi Chi, Pi Gamma Mu.

AWARDS, HONORS: Lenoir Rhyne College distinguished alumni award, 1962.

WRITINGS:

(With brother, Sidney C. Garrison) *The Psychology of the Elementary School Subjects,* Johnson Publishing (Richmond), 1929.
Psychology of Adolescence, Prentice-Hall, 1934, 7th edition (with son, Karl Claudius Garrison, Jr.), 1975.
(With S. C. Garrison) *Fundamentals of Psychology in Secondary Education,* Prentice-Hall, 1936.
The Psychology of Exceptional Children, Ronald, 1940, 4th edition (with Dewey G. Force), 1965.
Growth and Development, Longmans, Green, 1950, revised edition, 1959.
(Contributor) J. Stanley Gray, editor, *Psychology in Use,* 2nd edition, American Book Co., 1951.
(Contributor) Gray, *Psychology in Industry,* McGraw, 1952.
(With Gray) *Educational Psychology: An Integration of Psychology and Educational Practices,* Appleton, 1955, 3rd edition (with Robert A. Magoon), 1972.
(Editor with Magoon) *Special Education for the Exceptional,* Sargent, 1955.

(Contributor) A. A. Roback, editor, *Present-Day Psychology,* Philosophical Library, 1956.

(With Albert J. Kingston and Harold Bernard) *The Psychology of Childhood,* Scribner, 1966.

(With Franklin R. Jones) *Psychology of Human Development,* World Publishing, 1969, 2nd edition, 1985.

Contributor of about seventy articles to education and psychology journals.

WORK IN PROGRESS: With Gilbert Ragland, 5th edition of *The Psychology of Exceptional Children.**

*   *   *

GAT, Dimitri V(sevolod) 1936-

PERSONAL: Born October 5, 1936, in Pittsburgh, Pa.; son of John Dimitri and Anne (a librarian; maiden name, Prunte) Gat; married Margaret Ann Moses, June 24, 1967; children: Christine, Alexandra. *Education:* Attended Carnegie Institute of Technology (now Carnegie-Mellon University), 1954-57; University of Pittsburgh, B.A., 1960, M.A. (library science), 1963. *Politics:* "Indifferent." *Religion:* None.

ADDRESSES: Office—Institute for Government Services, Middlesex House, University of Massachusetts, Amherst, Mass. 01002. *Agent*—Curtis Brown, Ltd., 30 Astor Pl., New York, N.Y. 10003.

CAREER: Hagan Chemicals and Controls, Pittsburgh, Pa., advertising assistant, 1960-62; Harvard University, Cambridge, Mass., cataloger and administrator in Harvard Library, 1963-66, assistant librarian in Graduate School of Education Library, 1967-69; Mount Holyoke College, South Hadley, Mass., assistant librarian, 1969-71; University of Massachusetts, Amherst, assistant professor of English and technical communication, 1971-76, editorial associate, Institute for Governmental Services, 1976—.

MEMBER: Science Fiction Writers of America.

AWARDS, HONORS: Atlantic short story contest for college students, honorable mention, 1959, for "Queen's Gambit Declined," and fourth prize, 1960, for "Nancynancynancynancy."

WRITINGS:

The Shepherd Is My Lord, Doubleday, 1971.

(With Bill Heward) *Some Are Called Clowns: A Season with the Last of the Great Barnstorming Baseball Teams,* Crowell, 1974.

(With Arthur Eve) *Municipal Grants: How to Get and Administer Them,* Institute for Governmental Services, University of Massachusetts, 1977.

(Editor) *Teachers in Transition: New Directions, New Meanings: The Proceedings of the Leadership Institute for Home Economics Teachers, May 5-8, 1977,* compiled by Rima Miller, Institute for Governmental Services, University of Massachusetts, 1977.

(With Eve) *Municipal Grants: Acquisition and Management,* Institute for Governmental Services, University of Massachusetts, 1979.

Nevsky's Return (novel), Avon, 1982.

Editor, *Harvard Librarian,* 1966-67.

SIDELIGHTS: Dimitri V. Gat once told *CA:* "I've discovered years of writing fiction with little success is good training for non-fiction. Now I do both—and well, too. . . . George Plimp-

ton said about *Some Are Called Clowns*—'one of the best sports books in the last ten years. . . .' "

AVOCATIONAL INTERESTS: Music, golf, squash racquets, vegetable gardening, film, poker.

BIOGRAPHICAL/CRITICAL SOURCES:

PERIODICALS

New York Times Book Review, October 10, 1982.*

*   *   *

GAUQUELIN, Michel (Roland) 1928-

PERSONAL: Born November 13, 1928, in Paris, France; son of Roland (a dental surgeon) and Madeleine (Lenoir) Gauquelin; married Marie-Catherine Cadilhac, May 10, 1986. *Education:* Sorbonne, University of Paris, Ph.D., 1954.

ADDRESSES: Home—8 rue Amyot, Paris, France 75005. *Office*—Bibliotheque RETZ, 114 Champs Elysees, Paris, France 75008. *Agent*—Georges Borchardt, 136 East 57th St., New York, N.Y.

CAREER: Psychologist and writer in Paris, France, 1956-66; Bibliotheque RETZ (publishers), Paris, editor of psychology book series, 1967—; Laboratoire d'Etudes des Relations entre Rythmes Cosmiques et Psychophysiologiques, Paris, founder and director, 1969—. *Military service:* French Military Reserve, 1953-54; became lieutenant.

MEMBER: International Society of Chronobiology, International Society of Sport Psychology, International Society of Biometeorology, International Society of Characterology, International Committee for the Study of Ambient Factors (member of board of directors).

AWARDS, HONORS: Medal for psychological writings from 16th Congress of Health, Ferrara, Italy, 1969.

WRITINGS:

L'Influence des astres: Etude critique et experimentale (title means "The Influence of Stars: A Critical and Experimental Study"), Le Dauphin, 1955.

(With M. F. Gauquelin) *Methodes pour etudier la repartition des astres dans le mouvement diurne* (title means "Methods for the Study of the Stars' Distribution in the Diurnal Movement"), privately printed, 1957.

Les Hommes et les astres (title means "Men and Stars"), Denoel, 1960.

L'Astrologie devant la science, Planete, 1965, translation by James Hughes published as *The Scientific Basis of Astrology: Myth of Reality?,* Stein & Day, 1969 (published in England as *Astrology and Science,* P. Davies, 1970).

(With M. F. Gauquelin and Francois Richaudeau) *Methode de lecture rapide* (title means "Method of Speed Reading"), Centre d'Etude et de Promotion de la Lecture, 1966.

L'Heredite planetaire, Planete, 1966, revised edition published as *Planetary Heredity,* ACS, 1988.

The Cosmic Clocks: From Astrology to a Modern Science, Regnery, 1967, revised edition, ACS, 1982.

Le Sante et les conditions atmospheriques, Hatchette, 1967, translation by Joyce E. Clemow published as *How Atmospheric Conditions Affect Your Health,* Stein & Day, 1971, revised edition, Aurora Press, 1984.

Songes et mensonges de l'astrologie, Hachette, 1969, translation by Richard Leigh published as *Dreams and Illusions of Astrology,* Prometheus Books, 1979.

Connaitre les autres (title means "To Know the Others"), Centre d'Etude et de Promotion de la Lecture, 1970.

(Editor) *La Psychologie moderne de A a Z* (title means "Modern Psychology from A to Z"), Centre d'Etude et de Promotion de la Lecture, 1971.

(With Jacques Sadoul) *L'Astrologie* (title means "Astrology"), Denoel, 1972.

(With M. F. Gauquelin) *20 tests pour se connaitre* (title means "Twenty Tests to Know Oneself"), Denoel, 1972.

Cosmic Influences on Human Behavior, Stein & Day, 1973, revised edition, Aurora Press, 1984.

Rythmes biologiques, rythmes cosmiques (title means "Biological Rythms, Cosmic Rythms"), Gerard, 1973.

La Cosmo-Psychology (title means "Cosmo-Psychology"), Retz, 1975.

The Spheres of Destiny, Dent, 1980.

Your Personality and the Planets, Stein & Day, 1981.

(With M. F. Gauquelin) *The Gauquelin Book of American Charts,* ACS, 1982.

The Truth about Astrology, translation by Sarah Matthews, Basil Blackwell, 1983.

Birthtimes: A Scientific Investigation of Astrology, translation by Matthews, Hill & Wang, 1983.

Written in the Stars: The Best of Michel Gauquelin, Sterling Publications, 1988.

Neo-Astrology: A Copernician Revolution, Penguin Books/Arkana, 1990.

Also writer of television programs on psychology and cosmic influences. Contributor to over thirty publications of Laboratoire d'Etudes des Relations entre Rythmes Cosmiques et Psychophysiologiques. Contributor to *Psychology Today, Figaro Litteraire,* and other periodicals. Scientific editor, *Psychologie* (Paris), 1970—; psychology publications editor, Centre d'Etude et de Promotion de la Lecture (Paris), 1972—.

SIDELIGHTS: Michel Gauquelin once told *CA:* "Until the beginning of this century, science believed that man was in isolation on earth, separated from the rest of the universe. Now we know that the biological clocks of our brain and our body are attuned to the movement of the cosmic forces. . . . This new conception should have not only scientific but also philosophical and even poetical implications for modern thought."

AVOCATIONAL INTERESTS: Tennis.

BIOGRAPHICAL/CRITICAL SOURCES:

PERIODICALS

Human Behavior, November, 1976.
Los Angeles Times Book Review, December 25, 1983.
New Behavior, May 29, 1975.
Newsweek, August 29, 1981.
Observer Review, January 3, 1971.
Times Literary Supplement, September 18, 1970.
Washington Post Book World, April 6, 1969.

*   *   *

GAYA-NUNO, Juan Antonio   1913-1975

PERSONAL: Born in 1913, in Soria, Spain; died in 1975. *Education:* University of Madrid, Ph.D., 1934.

ADDRESSES: Home—Calle Ibiza 23, 7o A, Madrid 9, Spain.

CAREER: Writer. Member of Coimbra Institute.

AWARDS, HONORS: Lazaro Galdiano Art Critics' Prize, 1974.

MEMBER: Spanish Art Critics Association (vice-president), Art Critics Academy, Hispanic Society of America.

WRITINGS:

Madrid, Editorial Aries, 1944, 2nd edition, 1950.
El romanico en la provincia de Soria, Instituto Diego Velazquez, 1946.
Historia del arte espanol (title means "History of Spanish Art," Editorial Plus-Ultra, 1946, 5th edition, 1973.
El Escorial, Editorial Plus-Ultra, 1947.
Zurbaran, Ediciones Aedos, 1948.
Burgos, Editorial Aries, 1949.
El arte espanol en sus estilos y en sus formas, Ediciones Omega, 1949.
Autorretratos de artistas espanoles, Argos, 1950.
La pintura espanola en el medio siglo, Ediciones Omega, 1952.
El santero de San Saturio, Castalia, 1953, 2nd edition, 1965.
Velazquez y su siglo, Espasa-Calpe, 1953.
Historia y guia de los museos de Espana (title means "History and Guide of the Museums of Spain"), Espasa-Calpe, 1955, 2nd edition, 1968.
La pintura, Ediciones Pegaso, 1955.
Escultura espanola contemporanea (title means "Contemporary Spanish Sculpture"), Ediciones Guadarrama, 1957.
El arte en su intimidad, Aguilar, 1957.
La pintura espanola fuera de Espana: Historia y catalogo, Espasa-Calpe, 1958.
Entendimiento del arte, Taurus, 1959.
Un conflicto: Literatura y arte, Taurus, 1960.
La pittura italiana al Prado, Sansoni, 1961.
La arquitectura espanola en sus monumentos desaparecidos, Espasa-Calpe, 1961.
Francisco Arias, Direccion General de Bellas Artes, 1961.
Teoria del romanico, Publicaciones Espanolas, 1962.
20 anos de pintura espanola, Editora Nacional, 1962.
Tratado de mendicidad, Taurus, 1962.
La pintura y la lirica de Cristobal, Ponce de Leon, 1963.
Bibliografia critica y antologica de Velazquez, Fundacion Lazaro Galdiano, 1963.
Escultura Iberica (title means "Iberian Sculpture"), Aguilar, 1964.
Pequenas teorias de arte, Taurus, 1964.
La pintura espanola en los museos provinciales (title means "Spanish Painting in Provincial Museums"), Aguilar, 1964.
Pintura europea perdida por Espana, de Van Eyck a Tiepolo, Espasa-Calpe, 1964.
El arte europea en peligro, y otros ensayos, Editora y Distribuidora Hispano Americana, 1964.
Sentido de la filosofia contemporanea, Universidad Central de Venezuela, 1965.
Museo del Louvre (title means "The Louvre Museum"), Aguilar, 1965.
La espeluznante historia de la calavera de Goya, Edizioni dell'Elefante, 1966.
Historia del cautivo: Episodios nacionales, Mexico, 1966.
Arte del siglo decimonono (title means "Nineteenth Century Art"), Editorial Plus-Ultra, 1966.
Bibliografia critica y antologica de Picasso, Universidad de Puerto Rico, 1966.
(Contributor) Javier Rubio, *Formas de la escultura contemporanea,* Aguado, 1966.
(With Jose Pijoan y Soteras) *Arte europeo de los siglos XIX y XX* (title means "European Art of the Nineteenth and Twentieth Centuries"), Espasa-Calpe, 1967.
Los gatos salvajes y otras historias, Taurus, 1968.

Historia del Museo del Prado (1819-1969), Editorial Everest, 1969.

Velazquez: Biografia ilustrada, Ediciones Destino, 1970.

La Espana de los museos, Direccion General de Promocion del Turismo, 1970.

(With Jose Caso Gonzalez and Joaquin Arce) *Los conceptos de rococo, neoclasicismo y prerromanticismo en la literatura espanola del siglo XVIII* (title means "The Concepts of Rococo, Neoclassicism, and Pre-Romanticism in Eighteenth Century Spanish Literature"), Universidad de Oviedo, 1970.

Museos de Madrid (title means "Museums of Madrid"), Editorial Everest, 1970.

El Museo del Prado, Editorial Everest, 1970.

La pintura espanola del siglo XX (title means "Twentieth Century Spanish Painting"), Iberico Europea de Ediciones, 1970, 2nd edition, 1972.

Sartre, *Ediciones de la Biblioteca,* Universidad Central de Venezuela, 1971.

(With Concha de Marco) *Soria,* Editorial Everest, 1971.

La superacion de la filosofia y otros ensayos, Universidad Central de Venezuela, Ediciones de la Biblioteca, 1972.

Dibujos de Vela Zanetti, Iberica Europea de Ediciones, 1972.

Francisco Gutierrez Cossio: Vida y obra, Iberico Europea de Ediciones, 1973.

Diego Velazquez, Publicaciones Espanolas, 1974.

Juan Gris, Ediciones Poligrafa, 1974, translation by Kenneth Lyons published under same title, New York Graphic Society, 1975.

Historia del arte universal (title means "History of World Art"), Editorial Everest, 1974.

Historia de la critica de arte en Espana (title means "History of Art Criticism in Spain"), Iberico Europea de Ediciones, 1975.

L'Opera complete di Murillo, Rizzoli, 1978.

Author of monographs and booklets, *Alonso Berruguete en Toledo,* 1944, *El Romanico en la provincia de Vizeaya,* 1944, *Eugenio Lucas,* 1948, *Picasso,* 1950, *Salvadore Dali,* 1950, 2nd edition, 1954, *Zurbaran en Guadalupe,* 1951, *Francisco Cossio,* 1951, *Ramon Rogent,* 1951, *Pancho Cossio: Estudio,* 1954, *La Pintura romanica en Castilla,* 1954, *Claudio Coello,* 1957, *Francisco Mateos,* 1957, *Ataraxia y desasosiego en el arte,* 1958, *La Fase austera de Cesar Manrique,* 1958, *Fernando Gallego,* 1958, *La Joven pintura figurativa en la Espana actual,* 1959, *Luis de Morales,* 1961, *Maximo,* 1961, *Juan de Echevarria,* 1965, *Alvara Delgado,* 1965, *Los Monstruos prestigiosos,* 1971, *Vida de Acisclo Antonio Palomino,* 1981, and *Madrid Monumental,* Editorial Plus-Ultra.*

*   *   *

GETHERS, Peter 1953-

PERSONAL: Born April 10, 1953, in New York, N.Y.; son of Steven and Judith Gethers. *Education:* Attended University of California, Berkeley, 1970-72, University of London, 1972-73, and University of California, Los Angeles, 1973-74.

ADDRESSES: Home—74 5th Ave. #6A, New York, N.Y. 10011. *Office*—Villard Books/Random House, 201 East 50th St., New York, N.Y. 10022. *Agent*—International Creative Management, 40 West 57th St., New York, N.Y. 10019.

CAREER: Bantam Books, Inc., New York City, executive editor, 1975-80; Random House, Inc., New York City, editor, 1980-83; Villard Books, New York City, vice president and editorial director, 1983—.

MEMBER: National Academy of Television Arts and Sciences, Writers Guild of America (East), Authors League of America.

WRITINGS:

The Dandy (novel), Dutton, 1978.
(Co-author) *Rotisserie League Baseball* (nonfiction annual), Bantam, 1985, 1987, 1989, 1990.
Getting Blue (novel), Delacorte, 1987.

Also author (with Roman Polanski) of film "The Master and Marguerita"; author of several television scripts for the series "Kate and Allie." Contributor to *Esquire, Our Times,* and *New York Daily News Sunday Magazine.*

WORK IN PROGRESS: Flame, a novel; *The Cat Who Went to Paris,* a nonfiction book.

SIDELIGHTS: The Dandy, Peter Gether's first novel, describes what Joseph McLellan in a *Washington Post* review calls the "monster of the '70s". The protagonist of the novel is a 30-year-old man named Eugene Toddmann who deals with life by detaching himself from it emotionally. Thus, the only reaction he allows himself whenever tragedy strikes is curiosity. He becomes asocial, an attitude that leads him to kill the closest thing he has to a best friend in a dual over a woman he does not even care about. "Clearly, we are dealing here with a monster," writes McLellan, "a walking abstraction, but I suspect it is a monster that looms as a sort of ideal for more than one young man of our era." "It is no small undertaking to center a book on a nearly abstract character and yet hold the reader's interest for over 200 pages," McLellan later notes, "but Gethers has done it with a virtuoso flourish."

In another *Washington Post* article, Tom Miller praises the characters and writing in Gether's *Getting Blue,* a novel about one athlete's rise to the top of professional baseball. "Often Gether's personality sketches jump off the page and demand rereading in admiration of their precision," Miller attests. The reviewer also admires the author's accurate depiction of the earlier years of baseball: "His observations about black-white relations in 1950s minor-league baseball are sensitively—and, I suspect, accurately—portrayed." But despite the book's strengths, Miller concludes that "the three or four story lines don't end concurrently, and we're left with a book whose parts are far greater than their sum."

BIOGRAPHICAL/CRITICAL SOURCES:

PERIODICALS

Washington Post, August 24, 1978, April 7, 1987.

*   *   *

GILBERT, Martin (John) 1936-

PERSONAL: Born October 25, 1936, in London, England; son of Peter (a manufacturing jeweler) and Miriam (Green) Gilbert; married Helen Robinson (a potter), July 29, 1963; married Susie Sacher (a historian), June 12, 1974; children: (first marriage) Natalie; (second marriage) two sons. *Education:* Magdalen College, Oxford, B.A. (first class honors), 1960; St. Anthony's College, Oxford, graduate research, 1960; Merton College, Oxford, M.A., 1964. *Politics:* "Skeptic."

ADDRESSES: Home—Seven Lansdowne Crescent, London W. 11, England. *Office*—Merton College, Oxford OX1 4JD, England.

CAREER: Merton College, Oxford, England, fellow and member of governing body, 1962—, official biographer of the late Sir Winston Churchill, 1968-88. Research assistant to Randolph S. Churchill on official life of Winston Churchill, 1962-67. Nongovernmental representative, U.N. Commission on Human Rights, 43rd Session, Geneva, 1987. Visiting professor at University of South Carolina, Columbia, 1965, University of Tel Aviv, 1979-80, and University of Jerusalem, 1980; governor, Hebrew University of Jerusalem, 1980—; visiting lecturer at universities in America, South Africa, and the Soviet Union. Consultant on modern history to newspapers and television. *Military service:* British Army, student at Joint Service School for Linguists, 1955-57.

MEMBER: Royal Society of Literature (fellow), Athenaeum Club.

AWARDS, HONORS: Academy Award for best documentary film, 1981, for "Genocide"; D.Litt., Westminster College, Fulton, Mo., 1981.

WRITINGS:

(With Richard Gott) *The Appeasers,* Houghton, 1963, 2nd edition, Weidenfeld & Nicolson, 1967.

The European Powers, 1900-1945, Weidenfeld & Nicolson, 1965, New American Library, 1966.

Recent History Atlas, 1870 to the Present Day, Weidenfeld & Nicolson, 1966, Macmillan, 1968, 3rd edition published as *Recent History Atlas, 1860-1960,* Weidenfeld & Nicolson, 1977.

The Roots of Appeasement, Weidenfeld & Nicolson, 1966, New American Library, 1967.

Winston Churchill (Clarendon biography for grades 6-9), Oxford University Press (London), 1966, Dial, 1967, 2nd edition, Oxford University Press, 1970.

British History Atlas, Weidenfeld & Nicolson, 1968, Macmillan, 1969.

American History Atlas, Weidenfeld & Nicolson, 1968, Macmillan, 1969, revised edition, Weidenfeld & Nicolson, 1985.

Jewish History Atlas, Macmillan, 1969, 3rd edition, 1985.

Atlas of World War I, Macmillan, 1970, (published in England as *First World War Atlas,* Weidenfeld & Nicolson, 1970, reprinted as *First World War History Atlas,* 1971).

The Second World War, Chatto & Windus, 1970.

Winston S. Churchill (official biography; also see below), Houghton, Volume 3 (with Randolph S. Churchill): *The Challenge of War, 1914-1916,* 1971, Volume 4: *The Stricken World, 1917-1922,* 1974, Volume 5: *The Prophet of Truth, 1923-1939,* 1976, Volume 6: *Finest Hour, 1939-1941,* 1983, Volume 7: *Road to Victory, 1941-1945,* 1986, Volume 8: *Never Despair, 1945-1965,* 1988.

Russian History Atlas, Macmillan, 1972, published as *Imperial Russian History Atlas,* Routledge & Kegan Paul, 1978.

Sir Horace Rumbold: Portrait of a Diplomat, 1869-1941, Heinemann, 1973.

The Arab-Israeli Conflict: Its History in Maps, Weidenfeld & Nicolson, 1974, 4th edition, 1984, published as *Atlas of the Arab-Israeli Conflict,* Macmillan, 1975.

Churchill: A Photographic Portrait, Houghton, 1974.

The Jews of Russia: Their History in Maps and Photographs, National Council for Soviet Jewry of the United Kingdom and Ireland, 1976.

The Jews of Arab Lands: Their History in Maps, World Organization of Jews from Arab Countries/Board of Deputies of British Jews, 1976.

Jerusalem History Atlas, Macmillan, 1977, (published in England as *Jerusalem Illustrated History Atlas,* Board of Deputies of British Jews, 1979).

Exile and Return: The Struggle for a Jewish Homeland, Lippincott, 1978, (published in England as *Exile and Return: The Emergence of Jewish Statehood,* Weidenfeld & Nicolson, 1978).

The Holocaust: A Record of the Destruction of Jewish Life in Europe during the Dark Years of Nazi Rule, Board of Directors of British Jews, 1978, Hill & Wang, 1979.

Final Journey: The Fate of the Jews in Nazi Europe, Allen & Unwin, 1978, Mayflower Books, 1979.

The Children's Illustrated Bible Atlas, W. H. Allen, 1979.

Soviet History Atlas, Routledge & Kegan Paul, 1979.

Churchill, Doubleday, 1980.

Auschwitz and the Allies, Holt, 1981.

Churchill's Political Philosophy, Oxford University Press for the British Academy, 1981.

The Macmillan Atlas of the Holocaust, Macmillan, 1982, (published in England as *Atlas of the Holocaust,* M. Joseph, 1982).

Winston Churchill: The Wilderness Years, Houghton, 1982.

The Jews of Hope, Macmillan, 1984, Viking, 1985.

Jerusalem: Rebirth of a City, Viking, 1985.

The Holocaust: The Jewish Tragedy, Collins, 1986.

The Holocaust: A History of the Jews of Europe during the Second World War, Holt, 1986.

Shcharansky, Hero of Our Time, Viking, 1986.

The Second World War: A Complete History, Holt, 1989.

EDITOR

Britain and Germany between the Wars, Longmans, Green, 1964, Barnes & Noble, 1966.

Plough My Own Furrow: The Life of Lord Allen of Hurtwood, Longmans, Green, 1965.

Sir James Robert Dunlop Smith, *Servants of India: A Study of Imperial Rule from 1905 to 1910* (as told through Smith's correspondence and diaries), Longmans, Green, 1966.

A Century of Conflict, 1850-1950: Essays for A. J. P. Taylor, Hamish Hamilton, 1966, Atheneum, 1967.

Churchill ("Great Lives" series), Prentice-Hall, 1967.

Lloyd George, Prentice-Hall, 1968.

Winston Churchill, 1874-1965, Grossman, 1969, (published in England as *Winston Churchill: A Collection of Contemporary Documents,* J. Cape, 1969).

(With R. S. Churchill) *Winston S. Churchill: Companion Volume 2* (companion volume to R. S. Churchill's *Winston S. Churchill: Young Statesman, 1919-1914,* Houghton, 1968), Part 1: *1901-1907,* Part 2: *1907-1911,* Part 3: *1911-1914,* Houghton, 1969.

(Sole editor) *Winston S. Churchill* (companion volumes of edited documents to accompany official biography), Houghton, *Companion Volume 3: 1914-1916,* 1972; *Companion Volume 4* Part 1: *January 1917-June 1919,* Part 2: *July 1919-March 1921,* Part 3: *April 1921-November 1922,* 1975; *Companion Volume 5,* Part 1: *The Exchequer Years, 1922-1929,* 1976, Part 2: *The Wilderness Years, 1929-1935,* Part 3: *The Coming of War, 1936-1939,* 1982.

OTHER

(Compiler) *The Coming of War, 1939,* Jackdaw Publications, 1973.

(With Marvin Hier) "Genocide" (film script), narrated by Elizabeth Taylor, Arnold Schwartzman/Simon Wiesenthal Center, 1981.

Contributor of articles and reviews to *History, Sunday Telegraph, Times* (London), *Guardian, Sunday Times* (London), *Evening Standard, Jewish Chronicle* (London), *Jerusalem Post* (Jerusalem), *Spiegel* (Hamburg), and *Tworczosz* (Warsaw).

SIDELIGHTS: "If Martin Gilbert had written nothing but the authorized biography of Winston Churchill on which he has been toiling since 1968," says Joseph Lelyveld in the *New York Times,* "he would have to be regarded as one of the most prolific of British historians." Gilbert inherited the project from Winston's son Randolph, designated the official Churchill biographer by his father. He served as one of Randolph's chief researchers from 1963 until Randolph's death in 1968, when the biography's British publishers asked the 32-year-old historian to take over the project. Over the next twenty years, Gilbert completed six volumes of biography containing some eight and a half million words, based on fifteen tons of Churchill material. The complete biography contains about fifteen thousand pages of text—an accomplishment that the 1986 *Guinness Book of World Records* ranks as the longest biography in publishing history.

One of the factors contributing to the length of the biography lies in Gilbert's extensive use of primary source material: original letters, memoranda, and other documents relating to Churchill's career, all arranged in chronological order. Several of the biography's volumes are accompanied by companion texts of these documents. Gilbert traces his tendency to focus on primary sources back to his association at Oxford University with the controversial modern historian Alan J. P. Taylor. He told *Publishers Weekly* interviewer Michele Field, "I suppose I belong to his 'school.' He set up a school without intending to: a school of skepticism. In my case it has been refined to a belief in the constant return to the primary material." "The rule," he continues, "is that you can debate the primary material but you don't enter into debate with the secondary material or with other historians. I think that's what Alan Taylor taught, and the glory is that it leads to a very different kind of history."

Reviewers differ in their opinions of the effectiveness of Gilbert's presentation. While appreciating the immense scale of Gilbert's task, many of them feel that, especially in the last volumes, the historian has emphasized primary sources at the expense of historical interpretation. Michael Howard, writing in the *Spectator* about volume eight of the biography, *Never Despair,* notes that Gilbert "lays out the raw materials from which the biographer must select so as to present a balanced, lively and insightful portrait of his subject: materials inert until they are brought to life by a critical and creative historical imagination." Howard feels that Gilbert needs to set Churchill's final years in the wider perspective of the post-war world. Although *Times Literary Supplement* contributor Alistair Horne, writing about the seventh volume, *Road to Victory,* declares that "there is virtually no analysis of decisions taken, no criticism of errors, no imposition of the author's own opinions," he also adds that "Gilbert allows the facts, day by day, to speak for themselves; and very effectively they do so."

Although Gilbert is best known for the Churchill biography, his interests have led him in many other directions as well. Of Jewish heritage himself—his grandparents emigrated from Eastern Europe to Great Britain around the turn of the century—the historian has explored many different aspects of modern Jewish history, ranging from a look at nineteenth-century Jerusalem to an extensive history of the Holocaust to the plight of Jews unable to leave the Soviet Union: the "refuseniks." He has also corresponded extensively with Jews in the Soviet Union, written a biography of the Jewish Soviet activist Anatoly Shcharansky, and

dedicated several volumes of the Churchill biography to Jewish friends denied permission to leave Russia.

In *The Holocaust: A History of the Jews of Europe during the Second World War,* Gilbert uses many of the same procedures as he did in the Churchill biography, employing many primary sources and keeping his personal intervention to a minimum. The author, states Elie Wiesel in the *Chicago Tribune Book World,* "offers us a fascinating work that overwhelms us with its truth. Statistics, documents, memoirs, journals, reflections and analyses; he uses everything at his disposal to describe the inhuman power of evil, the humanity of the victims and the indifference of the spectators." In this book Gilbert tells "the story of what actually happened, rather than . . . why it happened or what might have happened instead," declares John Gross in the *New York Times.* "As far as possible," Gross continues, "he has attempted to let the victims speak for themselves, drawing on an enormous amount of documentary research (much of it into sources that have only become available in recent years), and talking to numerous survivors. He has also used his professional skills as a historian . . . to sort out and appraise his material, to strike a balance between different aspects of the story, and (not least) to weave the scattered and often fragmentary evidence into a seamless narrative." The result, claims A. J. Sherman in the *New York Times Book Review,* is an "impressive achievement," which serves "to remind us of ordinary human beings living and suffering behind the mass anonymity of statistics."

BIOGRAPHICAL/CRITICAL SOURCES:

BOOKS

Guinness Book of World Records, 1986 edition, Bantam, 1986.

PERIODICALS

Chicago Tribune, June 25, 1986, February 3, 1987.
Chicago Tribune Book World, February 16, 1986.
Globe and Mail (Toronto), August 30, 1986, January 17, 1987, September 2, 1989.
Los Angeles Times Book Review, February 2, 1986, July 6, 1986, March 22, 1987.
New Republic, January 3-10, 1976, May 21, 1977, February 16, 1987.
New Statesman, June 6, 1975.
New York Review of Books, April 10, 1986, September 25, 1986, May 7, 1987.
New York Times, April 28, 1984, August 20, 1985, February 4, 1986, May 10, 1986, October 19, 1986, November 25, 1986.
New York Times Book Review, January 13, 1985, February 9, 1986, May 25, 1986, December 14, 1986, October 23, 1988.
Publishers Weekly, November 14, 1986.
Spectator, October 30, 1971, June 7, 1975, October 30, 1976, February 8, 1986, April 26, 1986, September 27, 1986, June 4, 1988.
Time, October 31, 1988.
Times (London), January 13, 1982, September 24, 1986, September 25, 1986, August 17, 1989.
Times Literary Supplement, June 5, 1975, June 21, 1985, May 23, 1986, February 13, 1987, May 27-June 2, 1988, September 1-7, 1989.
Tribune Books (Chicago), September 18, 1988.
Washington Post Book World, June 1, 1986, December 21, 1987, October 16, 1988.*

—*Sketch by Kenneth R. Shepherd*

GILHOOLEY, Jack
See GILHOOLEY, John

*   *   *

GILHOOLEY, John 1940-
(Jack Gilhooley)

PERSONAL: Born June 26, 1940, in Philadelphia, Pa.; son of John Charles (an insurance executive) and Margaret (Cotter) Gilhooley. *Education:* Syracuse University, B.A., 1962; Villanova University, M.A. (theatre), 1964; University of Pennsylvania, M.A. (American civilization), 1966.

ADDRESSES: Home—639 West End Ave., New York, N.Y. 10025.

CAREER: Western Connecticut State College, Danbury, assistant professor of theatre, 1965-68; Jersey City State College, Jersey City, N.J., assistant professor of theatre and American literature, 1969-78; full-time writer, 1978—. Guest artist and lecturer at University of Kansas, Vassar College, University of New Hampshire, Syracuse University, Williams College, Rutgers University, and University of Colorado.

MEMBER: American Federation of Teachers, Screen Actors Guild, Dramatists Guild, Authors League of America, New Dramatists (Alumni), Actors Equity Association, National Theatre Workshop of the Handicapped (member of board of directors).

AWARDS, HONORS: Shubert Playwriting Award, 1972; Mac-Dowell Colony fellowship, 1976; guest playwright at Eugene O'Neill Memorial Foundation, 1977; National Endowment for the Arts grant, 1978; guest playwright, Edward Albee Foundation, 1978, at Millay Colony, 1979, at Dorset Colony, 1980, 1981, 1982, and 1984, at Yaddo, 1983, at Sundance Institute Playwrights Conference, 1983, at Aspen Playwrights Conference, 1984, and Tyrone Guthrie Institute (Ireland), 1984; commissions from Actors Theatre of Louisville and National Public Broadcasting System.

WRITINGS:

PLAYS; UNDER NAME JACK GILHOOLEY

"The Last Act" (one-act), first produced Off-Off-Broadway at 13th Street Theatre, 1971.
"The Entrepreneurs of Avenue B" (one-act), first produced 13th Street Theatre, 1971.
"Homefront Blues" (two-act), first produced in New York City at Manhattan Theatre Club, 1973.
"The Comeback" (one-act), first produced in New York City at Theatre for the New City, 1973.
"The Last Christians" (two-act), first produced in New York City at The Open Space in Soho, 1975.
"The Time Trial" (also see below; two-act), first produced at the New York Shakespeare Festival, 1975.
"The Competitors" (one-act), first produced Off-Broadway at E.T.C. Co., 1976.
"Mummer's End" (two-act), first produced in Washington, D.C., at the Folger Theatre, 1977.
"The Elusive Angel" (two-act), first produced in Waterford, Conn., at the O'Neill Foundation, 1977, produced Off-Broadway at the Phoenix Theatre, 1977.
"Afternoons in Vegas" (also see below; two-act), first produced in Portsmouth, N.H., at Theatre by the Sea, 1977.
The Brixton Recovery (also see below; two-act; first produced in Indianapolis, Ind., at Indiana Repertory Theatre, 1977,

produced in New York City at Westside Mainstage, 1981), Samuel French, 1982.
"Dancin' to Calliope" (one-hour radio play), first produced by Earplay, 1980.
"Descendants" (two-act), first produced at Indiana Repertory Theatre, 1980.
"Shirley Basin" (two-act), first produced in Evanston, Ill., at North Light Repertory Theatre, January 6, 1982, produced Off-Off-Broadway at South Street Theatre Company, January 18, 1982.

OTHER

Also author of stage plays "Bankers Hours," 1979, "Relations," 1980, "The Man in the Water" (also known as "Winterfire"), 1982, "The Kiss," 1984, "The Checkered Flag," 1984, and "Flin Flon," 1984. Author of television script "The Brothers," 1977, and of radio script "Earplay," 1980. Also author of screenplays "Afternoons in Vegas," "The Time Trial," and "The Brixton Recovery," all based on his plays.

WORK IN PROGRESS: "Inishmore," "Cookie's Dream," and "Spunk, the Stealer," two-act plays; an untitled musical about the Irish Civil War.

SIDELIGHTS: "I certainly don't know *how* I became a playwright, although, on occasion, I wonder *why*," Jack Gilhooley once told *CA.* "There's nothing in my background that would have warranted such a pursuit. . . . I tend to write about subcultures and/or families. I don't know why and I wasn't aware of it until I looked back after my first couple of years of writing. I don't know if this will change and I don't know, at this point, if it should. I tend to stay as far away as possible from autobiographical inclusions. Intially, for me it is too painful. Secondly, for the audience it is too commonplace."

Gilhooley has found success as the author of such plays as "Mummer's End," "The Elusive Angel," and "The Brixton Recovery." In "Mummer's End," Gilhooley uses the annual Mummer's Day parade held in Philadelphia to point up the divisions in one family and, by extension, the conflicts in American society as a whole. The *New York Times*'s Richard Eder praised Gilhooley for ingenuously "joining the reality of his engaging characters with the warring strands of American tradition that they represent." In "The Elusive Angel," which the *New York Post*'s Clive Barnes refers to as "a domestic drama as sentimental as an O. Henry short story [with] all the merits of its craftsmanship to commend it," Gilhooley explores the plight of an impoverished couple who are ruthlessly exploited when they try to adopt a baby. And in "The Brixton Recovery," an Irish-American prizefighter falls in love with a Jamaican barmaid in the racially mixed Brixton section of London. Praising the play in his *New York Times* column, Mel Gussow continues: "It is [Gilhooley's] achievement that with only two characters and in two hours' playing time he can convey an almost movielike canvas of a section of London today and of a self-defeating profession, the seedy, international world of club fighters." And though Gussow notes that the story "stops short of an emotional payoff; it ends not with a knockout punch but a question mark," the critic ultimately finds "The Brixton Recovery" has "a precise sense of character, atmosphere and imagery."

BIOGRAPHICAL/CRITICAL SOURCES:

PERIODICALS

New York Post, December 27, 1977, January 30, 1982.
New York Times, February 7, 1977, May 26, 1977, December 28, 1977, January 17, 1981, January 27, 1982.*

GILLESPIE, John T(homas) 1928-

PERSONAL: Born September 25, 1928, in Fort William, Ontario, Canada; came to the United States in 1955, naturalized U.S. citizen in 1963; son of William and Jean (Barr) Gillespie. *Education:* University of British Columbia, B.A., 1948; Columbia University, M.A., 1957; New York University, Ph.D., 1970.

ADDRESSES: Home and office—360 East 72nd St., New York, N.Y. 10021.

CAREER: Elementary school teacher in British Columbia, 1950-55; school librarian in Hicksville, N.Y., 1956-57, and Roslyn, N.Y., 1957-63; Long Island University, C. W. Post Center, Greenvale, N.Y., associate professor, 1963-71, professor of library science, 1971-86, dean of Palmer Graduate Library School, 1971-76, 1980-82, vice-president for academic affairs, 1982-85. Adjunct assistant professor at Long Island University, 1960-63. Circulation librarian at Hunter College of the City University of New York, 1959-61.

MEMBER: American Library Association, Association of American Library Schools, Association for Educational Communication and Technology, National Education Association, New York Library Association (member of board of directors; president, 1962), New York Library Club, Nassau-Suffolk School Library Association (president, 1960), Phi Delta Kappa, Kappa Delta Pi.

WRITINGS:

(With Diana L. Lembo) *Junior Plots,* Bowker, 1966.
The Secondary School Library as an Instructional Materials Center, New York State Department of Education, 1969.
(With Lembo and Ralph J. Folcarelli) *Library Learning Laboratory,* Fordham Publishing, 1969.
(With Lembo) *Introducing Books,* Bowker, 1970.
(With Diana L. Spirt) *The Young Phenomenon: Paperbacks in Our Schools,* American Library Association, 1971.
Paperback Books for Young People, American Library Association, 1971, 2nd edition, 1977.
(With Spirt) *Creating a School Media Program,* Bowker, 1973.
More Junior Plots, Bowker, 1977.
A Model School District Media Program, American Library Association, 1977.
(With Christine Gilbert) *Best Books for Children,* Bowker, 1978, 4th edition, 1990.
Home and School Reading and Study Guides, New Book of Knowledge, 1980.
(With Spirt) *Administering the School Library Media Center,* Bowker, 1983.
The Elementary School Paperback Collection, American Library Association, 1984.
The Junior High School Paperback Collection, American Library Association, 1984.
The Senior High School Paperback Collection, American Library Association, 1986.
Junior Plots 3, Bowker, 1987.
Senior Plots, Bowker, 1989.

SIDELIGHTS: John T. Gillespie told *CA:* "The basic principles of learning have remained the same throughout the years: children learn as individuals, children learn at various rates, children learn according to different styles and patterns, and education is a continuous process. In an attempt to translate these principles into practice, educators have realized that a unified media program involving all forms and types of educational materials and equipment is a necessity. There has been increased support of the library media center concept from many agencies, organi-zations, and professional personnel because those who are involved in education now realize that a sound media program is a prerequisite for high quality education."

*   *   *

GLENDENNING, Donn
See PAINE, Lauran (Bosworth)

*   *   *

GLENN, James
See PAINE, Lauran (Bosworth)

*   *   *

GLOVACH, Linda 1947-

PERSONAL: Surname is pronounced *Glo-*vack; born June 24, 1947, in Rockville Centre, N.Y.; daughter of John Maurice (a maintenance engineer) and Elvira (Martone) Glovach. *Education:* Attended Farmingdale University, 1965-66, Art Students League of New York, 1966-68, and California Art Center College of Design, 1969. *Politics:* Liberal.

ADDRESSES: Home and office—237 8th Ave. Sea Cliff, Long Island, N.Y. 11579.

CAREER: Free-lance artist. Has worked as a secretary and a hostess at Disneyland, Anaheim, Calif. Speaker in grade schools in Brentwood, N.Y., and local Long Island libraries and schools.

MEMBER: Defenders of Wildlife, Society for Animal Rights, Catholic Society for Welfare of Animals, Library Club of Bayshore.

AWARDS, HONORS: Art Students League of New York award for book illustration, 1970.

WRITINGS:

CHILDREN'S BOOKS; ALL SELF-ILLUSTRATED

Hey, Wait for Me! I'm Amelia, Prentice-Hall, 1971.
The Cat and the Collector, Prentice-Hall, 1972.
The Little Witch's Black Magic Cookbook, Prentice-Hall, 1972.
The Little Witch's Black Magic Book of Disguises (Junior Literary Guild selection), Prentice-Hall, 1973.
The Rabbit and the Rainmaker, Prentice-Hall, 1974.
The Little Witch's Black Magic Book of Games, Prentice-Hall, 1974.
The Little Witch's Christmas Book, Prentice-Hall, 1974.
The Little Witch's Halloween Book, Prentice-Hall, 1975.
The Little Witch's Thanksgiving Book, Prentice-Hall, 1976.
(With Charles Keller) *The Little Witch Presents a Monster Joke Book,* Prentice-Hall, 1976.
The Little Witch's Book of Yoga, Prentice-Hall, 1979.
The Little Witch's Birthday Book, Prentice-Hall, 1981.
The Little Witch's Carnival Book, Prentice-Hall, 1982.
The Little Witch's Spring Holiday Book, Prentice-Hall, 1983.
The Little Witch's Valentine Book, Prentice-Hall, 1984.
The Little Witch's Cat Book, Prentice-Hall, 1985.
The Little Witch's Summertime Book, Prentice-Hall, 1986.
The Little Witch's Book of Toys, Prentice-Hall, 1986.

Also author of *The Little Witch's Dinosaur Book.*

WORK IN PROGRESS: Two novels for teenagers, *Laura's Story* and *The Sugar-Coated Kid;* a picture book, *Beebo and His*

Friends; another "Little Witch" book; research on San Juan Capistrano mission in California, for a picture book for children.

SIDELIGHTS: Linda Glovach has lived a year in Haiti and the Virgin Islands.

AVOCATIONAL INTERESTS: Biking, running, traveling, gardening, and raising cats and Afghan hounds.

* * *

GLUCK, Herb 1925-

PERSONAL: Born August 11, 1925, in Brooklyn, N.Y.; son of Otto (a merchant) and Gussie Ellen Gluck; married Mary Neal Robison (a surgical nurse), August 7, 1947; children: Robert, Marcy, Abbey. *Education:* Educated in public schools in Brooklyn, N.Y. *Politics:* Democrat. *Religion:* Jewish.

ADDRESSES: Home—250 Hidden Lane, Otis, Mass. 01253. *Agent*—Scott Meredith Literary Agency, Inc., 845 Third Ave., New York, N.Y. 10022.

CAREER: Pyramid Publications, Inc., New York, N.Y., managing editor, beginning 1972; writer. Editor, Associated Press, 1973. *Military service:* U.S. Navy, 1943-46.

MEMBER: Professional Football Writers Association.

WRITINGS:

Pro Football '73, Pyramid Publications, 1973.
Pro Football '74, Pyramid Publications, 1974.
Baseball's Great Moments, Random House, 1974.
While the Gettin's Good, Bobbs-Merrill, 1975.
(With Alex Karras) *Even Big Guys Cry,* Holt, 1977.
(With Jerry Lewis) *Jerry Lewis in Person,* Atheneum, 1982.
(With Mickey Mantle) *The Mick,* Doubleday, 1985.

Editor of *Sports Today, Gridiron, Sports Forum,* and *Pro Football Guide.*

AVOCATIONAL INTERESTS: Photography, art research.

* * *

GOODHART, A. L.
See GOODHART, Arthur Lehman

* * *

GOODHART, Arthur Lehman 1891-1978
(A. L. Goodhart)

PERSONAL: Born March 1, 1891, in New York, N.Y.; died November 10, 1978, in London, England; son of Philip J. and Martha (Lehman) Goodhart; married Cecily M. Carter, July 2, 1924; children: Philip, William Howard, Charles Albert Eric. *Education:* Yale University, A.B., 1912, M.A., 1914; Cambridge University, B.A. and LL.B., 1914, M.A., 1918, LL.M., 1926, LL.D., 1931.

ADDRESSES: Home—London, England.

CAREER: Admitted to the bar in United States, 1915; served as assistant corporation counsel of New York City, 1915-17; American Mission to Poland, counsel, 1919; called to the Bar, London, England; Inner Temple, England, barrister at Law, 1919; Cambridge University, Corpus Christi College, Cambridge, England, teacher and fellow, 1919-31, secretary to vice chancellor, 1921; University College, Oxford University, Oxford, England,

professor of jurisprudence and fellow, 1931-53, chairman of faculty, beginning 1937, master 1951-63. Lincoln's Inn, Honorable Bencher, 1938, King's Counsel, 1943. Yale University, visiting professor, 1929, associate fellow of Jonathan Edwards College, 1933. Visiting professor, Harvard Law School, 1964, University of Virginia Law School, 1965, McGill University Law School, 1966. Fellow, Nuffield College, Oxford University, 1944. Curator, Bodleian Library, 1947. Chairman, Southern Region Price Regulation Committee, 1940-48. Member, Lord Chancellor's Law Revision Committee, 1937, Alternative Remedies Committee, 1945, Supreme Court Committee, 1947, Monopolies Commission, 1954-57, Royal Commission on the Police, 1960, Scottish Constitution Committee, 1969. *Military service:* U.S. Army, served in World War I; became captain.

MEMBER: International Law Association (chairman), Societe International de Philosophie du Droit (vice president), International Association of University Professors (president, 1948), American Law Institute, New York City Bar Association (scholar in residence, 1966-67), Society of Public Teachers of Law (president, 1950), Pedestrians Association (president, 1950), Yale Club, City Club (New York), Athenaeum Club, Oxford and Cambridge Club, Queen's Savile, University Club, Century Club, Phi Beta Kappa, Alpha Delta Phi.

AWARDS, HONORS: Honorary degrees from many institutions, including Cambridge University, Dartmouth College, Harvard University, and Princeton University; Officier d'Academie of France, 1920; honorary fellow, Corpus Christi College, Cambridge, 1942, British Academy, 1952, Trinity College, 1955, Trinity Hall, 1960; decorations from foreign governments, including Knight Commander of Order of the British Empire, 1948.

WRITINGS:

Poland and the Minority Races, Brentano's, 1920, reprinted, Arno, 1971.
Essays in Jurisprudence and the Common Law (collection of previously published essays), Cambridge University Press, 1931.
The British Constitution (revision of article first published in *Outpost*), British Information Service (New York, N.Y.), 1946.
We of the Turning Tide, F. W. Preece, 1947.
Five Jewish Lawyers of the Common Law, Oxford University Press, 1949, enlarged edition, Books for Libraries Press, 1949.
The History of the 2/7 Australian Field Regiment, Rigby, 1952.
Nature and Purpose of a University, Birkbeck College, 1952.
English Law and Moral Law, Stevens, 1953.
(Editor) Frederick Pollock, *Jurisprudence and Legal Essays,* Macmillan, 1961, reprinted, Greenwood Press, 1978.
Law of the Land, University Press of Virginia, 1966.
Lord Wright, 1869-1964, Oxford University Press, 1967.
Israel, the United Nations and Aggression, Anglo-Israel Association, 1968.

Also author of *Sir William Searle Holdsworth, 1871-1944,* Selden Society, *What Acts of War Are Justifiable,* 1941, and *English Contributions to the Philosophy of Law,* 1949; author of foreword to *The Definition of Law,* by Hermann U. Kantobowicz, 1958. General editor, with H. G. Hanbury, of "A History of English Law" series, by William Searle, Methuen. Author of booklets on law. Editor, *Cambridge Law Journal,* 1921, and *Law Quarterly Review,* 1926-75.

UNDER NAME A. L. GOODHART

The Legality of the General Strike in England (first published in *Yale Law Journal*, February, 1927), W. Heffer & Sons, 1927.

(Contributor) *Problems of War and Peace*, Grotius Society (London), 1927.

Precedent in English and Continental Law: An Inaugural Lecture Delivered Before the University of Oxford, Stevens & Sons, 1934.

(Author of foreword) *The Function of a University in a Modern Community*, Basil Blackwell, 1943.

SIDELIGHTS: While maintaining his United States citizenship, Arthur Lehman Goodhart became a prominent member of the British Bar and well-known figure at Oxford University. He was one of the few Americans to achieve the status of Queen's counselor. At Oxford University, he was the first American to chair the law faculty and to direct one of the colleges.

OBITUARIES:

PERIODICALS

New York Times, November 11, 1978.*

*   *   *

GOODMAN, George J(erome) W(aldo) 1930-
(Adam Smith)

PERSONAL: Born August 10, 1930, in St. Louis, Mo.; son of Alexander Mark and Viona (Cremer) Goodman; married Sallie Cullen Brophy, October 6, 1961; children: Alexander Mark, Susannah Blake. *Education:* Harvard University, B.A. (magna cum laude), 1952; attended Oxford University (Rhodes scholar), 1952-54.

ADDRESSES: Office—Adam Smith's Money World, 45 West 45th St., New York, N.Y. 10036.

CAREER: Reporter for *Collier's*, 1956, and *Barron's*, 1957; *Time* and *Fortune*, New York City, associate editor, 1958-60; Lincoln Fund, New York City, portfolio manager and vice president, 1960-62; screenwriter in Los Angeles, Calif., 1962-65; *New York Magazine*, New York City, co-founder, 1967, contributing editor and vice president, 1967—; *Institutional Investor* (magazine), New York City, charter editor, 1967-72; editorial chairman, *N.J. Monthly*, 1976-79; *New York Times*, New York City, member of editorial board, 1977; *Esquire*, New York City, executive editor, 1978-81; chairman, Continental Fidelity Group, 1980—. Director, Hyatt Hotels, 1977-81, USAIR, Inc., and Cambrex, Inc. Host and editor-in-chief of "Adam Smith's Money World," broadcast on public television nationwide, 1984—. Trustee, C. J. Jung Foundation, and Urban Institute, Washington, D.C., 1986—. Glassboro State College, Glassboro, N.J., trustee, 1967-71, co-chairman of presidential selection committee, 1968. Executive vice president and director, Institutional Investor Systems, 1969-72. Member of advisory council, economics department, Princeton University, 1970-89. Harvard University, member of representative committee on shareholder responsibility, 1971-74, member of visiting committee, psychology and social relations department, 1974-80, occasional lecturer. Member of visiting committee, Middle East Institute. Member of advisory committee (publications), U.S. Tennis Association, 1978-83. *Military service:* U.S. Army, 1954-56.

MEMBER: Writer's Guild of America (West), Authors Guild, Authors League of America (director), Association of Harvard Alumni (director, 1972-75), Harvard Club (New York City), Century Association (New York City).

AWARDS, HONORS: G. M. Loeb Award for Distinguished Achievement in Writing about Business and Finance, University of Connecticut, 1969; media award for economic understanding, Amos Tuck School, Dartmouth College, 1978, for television documentary, "The Forty-Five Billion Dollar Connection"; Emmy Award for outstanding interviewer nomination, 1985, for "Adam Smith's Money World"; Emmy awards for news and public affairs broadcasting, 1986, 1987, and 1988, for "Adam Smith's Money World."

WRITINGS:

NOVELS

The Bubble Makers, Viking, 1955.
A Time for Paris, Doubleday, 1957.
(With Winthrop Knowlton) *A Killing in the Market*, Doubleday, 1958.
The Wheeler Dealers (also see below), Doubleday, 1959.

SCREENPLAYS

"The Wheeler Dealers," Metro-Goldwyn-Mayer (MGM), 1963.
"The Americanization of Emily," MGM, 1964.

NONFICTION; UNDER PSEUDONYM ADAM SMITH

The Money Game (Literary Guild alternate selection), Random House, 1968.
Supermoney (Literary Guild selection), Random House, 1972.
Powers of Mind (Book-of-the-Month Club selection), Random House, 1975.
Paper Money (Book-of-the-Month Club selection), Summit Books, 1981.
The Roaring Eighties (Literary Guild alternate selection), Summit Books, 1988.

OTHER

Bascombe, the Fastest Hound Alive (juvenile), with pictures by Paul Galdone, Morrow, 1958.

Occasional columnist, *Newsweek*, 1973; author of column, "Unconventional Wisdom," *Esquire*, 1979-88. Contributor to *Readings in Economics*, edited by Paul Samuelson, and many other anthologies. Contributor of articles to periodicals. Goodman's papers are housed in Special Collections, Mugar Library, at Boston University.

SIDELIGHTS: In addition to his career as a journalist, writer and editor, George J. W. Goodman, formerly affiliated with magazines such as *Time, Fortune* and *Esquire*, has enjoyed a two-stage career as an author. During the first stage he wrote fiction and a children's book published under his own name; in the second stage, he wrote a string of bestselling nonfiction books on money, published under the name "Adam Smith." Goodman the journalist is "a thorough and conscientious reporter"; Goodman the novelist "is clever, urbane, good-humored, [and] eloquent," comments Jeff Riggenbach of the *Los Angeles Times*. And his "Adam Smith" books on the inner workings of contemporary American economics are well-known around the world.

In the 1950s and early '60s, Goodman was a reporter for *Collier's* and *Barron's*. During this time he also published several well-received satires on upper-class life. *The Bubble Makers*, which follows the conflict between a Harvard student and his wealthy grandfather, is an "original and entertaining first novel," says Dan Wickenden in the *New York Herald Tribune Book Review*. Wickenden also appreciates the author's "uncommonly sound style" and "a notable ability to create character." *A Time for Paris* looks in on two American graduates who fall in love on a cruise ship headed for Europe. *New York Times* contributor Judith Quehl commends Goodman for his skillfully combined "lunatic escapades, a handful of warm and witty characters and an undeniable gift for a clever turn of phrase."

A Killing in the Market, written with Winthrop Knowlton, combines information on the stock market with international intrigue. A broker's assistant sets out to rescue the boss's daughter after she has been kidnapped by a mysterious European investor in an aerospace firm. *San Francisco Chronicle* critic L. G. Offord describes this battle between rich Americans and Russian agents as "both exciting and funny." James Sandoe of the *New York Herald Tribune Book Review* comments, "The authors, working with such highly topical stuff as guided missiles, seem to have had as much fun with this as they provide for us."

Goodman's fourth generally well-received novel also displays his gift for comedy and his fine ear for sassy dialogue. *The Wheeler Dealers,* a story about the pyrotechnics that develop when a Texas oil baron meets a lady broker, is "a skillful blend of sophisticated repartee, belly laughs, and satirical observation, topped with an invaluable lesson on how to push up the price of a stock," Jerry Cowle notes in the *Chicago Sunday Tribune.* A children's book Goodman wrote in 1958, however, has been read perhaps more often than his novels. *Bascombe, the Fastest Hound Alive* has been extremely popular among young readers for nearly twenty years. "I wish my other books had so long a life," he tells *New York Times* writer Edwin McDowell.

During the sixties, Goodman left his position as associate editor for *Time* and *Fortune* magazines to become vice president of the Lincoln Fund. Then he spent a few years in Los Angeles, California, writing a screenplay for a film based on *The Wheeler Dealers.* Though the comedy was a success, he returned to New York to be the editor of *Institutional Investor* magazine. Goodman identifies himself as a person who follows a variety of interests. He tells Frances Lear in a *Lear's* interview, "I think I'm a person who likes to learn things. I do the things I do because I like learning about them. The only reason I know anything about Wall Street is that I was curious to know why some people make money and others don't."

Goodman's writing about money management in the early sixties brought him a new identity and fame. He was contributing articles on Wall Street to *New York* magazine, a *New York Herald Tribune* supplement, when he inadvertently became the namesake of an eighteenth-century American economist. Back at Oxford, where Goodman was a Rhodes scholar, he had noticed that Governors of the Bank of England signed their articles with names from Roman history; he followed suit, and signed the name "Procrustes" to an article about securities analysts, so that he could write freely without losing his welcome among his sources. The article appeared, however, with the byline "Adam Smith." Incensed, Goodman demanded to know which editor had given him that name, but no one confessed until some time after he became a bestselling writer.

The Money Game, Goodman's first venture into book-length nonfiction, was a bestseller a week after its release in 1968 and remained so for a year. Its overnight success established the reputation of "Adam Smith." Eric Berne of the *New York Times Book Review* relates that *The Money Game* benefits from the author's wide range of expertise. "Smith II has tried everything, knows everything and everybody, and has read everything, that a man in the marketplace should. He knows about games, and intuition, and anxiety, and identity, and he knows that a person-

ality profile can be inferred from a stock portfolio. . . . And he knows that the stock market behaves like a woman, although it is run by men." However, Berne attributes the book's phenomenal success, for the most part, to its author's sense of humor. Previously, the topic of money had been handled with intimidating language spoken in serious tones. "But now comes Smith II laughing not only all the way to the bank, but also inside the bank, which takes as much courage as laughing at a funeral or in church, since for most people solemnity is the essence of money, and it is believed that if you laugh, Mammon will get sulky and bounce your check," Berne states. Because it demystifies the hallowed halls of high finance, *The Money Game,* he feels, is "the best book there is about the stock market and all that goes with it."

"It could be argued that [the author's] particular perspective gives excessive emphasis to [Wall] Street's jazzier phenomena," notes C. J. Rolo in *Book World.* For this reason, *The Money Game* may be more appealing to adventuring neophytes than to conventional investors, states Rolo. But he deems it required reading for anyone who seeks insight into the human elements of Wall Street activity. The human factors of investing seldom turn out according to expectations, Goodman relates. "Of course, people who make a lot of money frequently don't think about money. They only think about the game they're playing," he told Lear. "Even people on Wall Street are playing a game: They're concerned about what they make, what the other guy makes, but the money *as* money doesn't mean anything." Furthermore, he says in his book, some players will consistently set themselves up to lose, or spend small gains instead of using them to build wealth.

The gap between people who have wealth and those who do not is widening, and the possession of "supercurrency" makes the difference, Goodman says in the first section of *Supermoney,* his next best seller. Business owners who can sell, merge, or go public with their companies at a rate based on a multiple of their earnings have "supercurrency," he explains. "Compounding net worth, not just increasing income or finding new tax-shelters, is the name of this particular game, and it is what has made the recently really rich really rich," Eliot Fremont-Smith writes in *Saturday Review.* "The same zesty style" makes *Supermoney* as readable as prior books, says the reviewer, yet "nervousness licks at the edges of its charm. The message of *Supermoney* is not simply that nobody really knows how to play the game, but that the game may be ending." Later sections of *Supermoney* explain that sudden major losses such as were sustained in 1970 threaten the whole economy; that some "sure thing" investments can and do go wrong; and that several attitudes fundamental to business are changing. Defer gratification, and you may lose it altogether, many people feel; business itself supports this attitude through advertising. The expectation that work leads to certain rewards is also no longer to be taken for granted.

Reviewers note that much of what Goodman relates in *Paper Money* is bad news as well. In it, Goodman explains "the international monetary system and . . . the largest transfer of wealth in history, which is taking place between the oil-importing and exporting nations," McDowell writes. Goodman takes us through a series of disasters to explain how each has contributed to the perilous condition of the American dollar. A reviewer for the *Economist* maintains that *Paper Money* "is just as racy, just as good a mixture of anecdote and research [as *The Money Game*], but it is much harder to laugh this time. . . . The money game has got crazier in a disturbing way; the rulebook has been discarded and nobody knows how to rewrite it." The realities which economics must describe and predict are less stable than in the past; there seems to be no consensus regarding our actual position in the world economy and how to make the most of it. In the midst of this, comments Leonard Silk in the *New York Times Book Review,* Goodman "strives for sanity," balancing the bad news with the possibility of a better future. "Along the way, we've seen money lose its value, banking catastrophes, mass unemployment, the poisoning of once healthy societies, the collapse of the international economic system and the breeding of monstrous wars in the swamps of rotting economies. History tells us that there is plenty to be scared about, but also that we might get through, if we are not too selfish or stupid," Silk summarizes. Writing in the *Washington Post Book World,* Robert Lekachman offers the consolation that "Goodman's bad news is delivered in prose it is a pleasure to read."

In *The Roaring Eighties,* Goodman tackles the aftershocks of the spending and debt that characterized the decade. After speaking to people at all levels of economic power, he relates their often disconcerting experiences, responding with pertinent questions about the future. Fortunes are being made—and lost—in new and surprising ways, and the changed economic climate is not an improvement on the past, Goodman maintains. *Newsweek* reviewer Bill Powell and others comment that *The Roaring Eighties* is not the "analysis of these remarkable times" they had expected. Many of the issues described may be familiar due to greater coverage of business news in the media, so that the book does not have the flavor of inside information that enhances the other books, Powell suggests. Susan Lee of the *New York Times Book Review,* however, defends the author's treatment of the times: "We could not ask for a more genial, knowledgeable companion for a tour of the national financial landscape. . . . He is able to describe events in a common-sense way that makes them accessible and that puts him way ahead of most financial commentators."

Goodman's style also animates *Powers of Mind,* a book that relates his personal quest for relaxation techniques to share with his colleagues in the marketplace, says Elsa First in the *New York Times Book Review.* Goodman "writes with enough pizzazz, jump-cutting, and Woody Allen one-liners to keep even the weariest commodities trader alert," she notes. His tour through the realm of psychic experience, transcendental meditation, Esalen, and Zen highlights its humorous aspects. Martin Gardner, a *New York Review of Books* contributor, cites the author's interview with EST (Erhard Seminars Training) proponent Jack Rosenberg, now known as Erhard. Erhard told Goodman that what you get from a seminar is the assurance that whatever already exists is perfect as it is, and beyond that, there is no greater idea to "get." "You lose, of course, your $250 initiation fee, that's what EST gets," Gardner quips, rephrasing Goodman's punchline. Though the author's quick tour leaves some relevant ground uncovered, in the end Goodman expresses some valuable connections between the mysteries of subatomic particle physics, poetry, and religion, *Time* reviewer R. Z. Sheppard notes. Sheppard comments, "Given his subject matter, the author could have settled for far less. Instead he provides a bestseller with a considerable educational function as well as high entertainment"—a comment which sums up the appeal of nearly all of Goodman's books.

"*Powers of Mind* is further evidence that [Goodman's] publishing instincts are like those of a surfer who knows just when to catch the curl of the wave," Sheppard notes. Even Goodman's lesser acclaimed works of "participatory journalism," as Sheppard calls them, have reached millions of appreciative readers. And *The Money Game,* now published in seventeen languages, is read around the world.

CA INTERVIEW

CA interviewed George J. W. Goodman (Adam Smith) by telephone on May 16, 1989, at his office in New York, New York.

CA: You've been widely known as a financial writer since the publication of your 1968 book The Money Game *and have most recently written* The Roaring Eighties, *but you began as a fiction writer, with the publication in 1955 of* The Bubble Makers. *Was the money man there all along, waiting for the right time to emerge?*

GOODMAN: No, not at all. When I began to write, I thought of myself as a very traditional writer. I was going to write magazine articles, nonfiction books, novels, plays, screenplays, and so on. In fact, in my twenties I did write three novels and a mystery and a children's book. But the income wasn't very great, even though they had good reviews. I was interested in the stock market anyway, so I set out to learn about it as what I thought would be a supplement to my regular activity of writing chiefly fiction. It was a kind of accident that the Adam Smith stuff started. And of course the Adam Smith pieces which appeared in *New York Magazine* and were the genesis of *The Money Game* had novelistic techniques in them, such as a lot of dialogue and the use of metaphor.

CA: The accident you refer to was having acquired your nom de plume by the pen stroke of an editor for a piece you'd written?

GOODMAN: That's right. And even when I did that piece, I did not intend to keep it up. I looked at my two activities as separate, the stock market writing enabling me to live, and the other writing being what I was all about. I hadn't thought of crossing them, but when I began to do it, it worked very well.

CA: When was your cover finally blown?

GOODMAN: The first Adam Smith piece appeared in the fall of 1966, and *The Money Game* came out in May, 1968. My identity became known at the end of the summer of 1968, when the book was a number-one bestseller, or a little after that. There was a lot of curiosity. A *New York Times* reporter named Henry Raymont came to my house for the weekend and I was telling a lot of stories about it, but I never thought he would write it up.

CA: One of the appealing qualities of The Money Game *is its humor, which I think also set a tone for the later books about money. How did you come to approach the usually solemn topic of making money with something less than reverence?*

GOODMAN: I was doing it under a pseudonym, which was a big help. I think if I had used my own name, I would probably have been as grave as was traditional. One of the novels that I wrote, *The Wheeler Dealers,* had a setting on Wall Street, and it was literally a comedy. It was made into a 1963 movie that was very much the genre comedy of the time, with Lee Remick and James Garner.

CA: I'm curious about the juvenile book you referred to earlier, which was called Bascombe, the Fastest Hound Alive. *You told the* New York Times Book Review *that* Bascombe *was still prompting fan letters from second graders.*

GOODMAN: That's true; they came for twenty years.

CA: How did the juvenile book come about? Is there a story behind it?

GOODMAN: There is. I was writing a novel called *A Time for Paris,* and there was a scene in the book that was set in England and involved a character who was going beagling. My brother, who was going to the University of Missouri, had a basset hound, a very characteristic one—dependent, stubborn, and all the things basset hounds are. He had some good stories about the dog, and I stopped at one point in writing *A Time for Paris,* dropped the point of view down to about one foot, and wrote this story about a basset hound. My agent sent it to a juvenile book publisher and they took it right away, after some funny exchanges. It had a nice artist, and it stayed in print for twenty-five years. I bought a basset hound five years later. Nature imitated art.

CA: Did you finally leave fiction writing without a backward look? Have you missed it?

GOODMAN: It's a different frame of mind. I do a weekly television program, and I have done until recently a monthly column called "Unconventional Wisdom." I'm very much involved in what happened today and public policy and all that kind of thing. My experience with writing fiction, which is now some time ago, is that you have to be quiet. You have to let your unconscious take over to some extent, and you have to have a time and place every day where you do it. It's as much a habit as getting into shape, running or rowing a scull or anything else—you have to do it in a very disciplined way. I couldn't do it in my current life. I don't know how the people who do it, like Bill Buckley, manage it. I can't, because my mind is just not on it. I may not have given it up forever, but I can't do it now.

CA: As everybody knows, there are enough how-to-make-money books to fill a museum, and they keep coming. Is there any solid financial advice you can give that's good for all weathers?

GOODMAN: It would be very aphoristic. What's said in *The Money Game* is still true. It focuses on people. "The stock doesn't know you own it" is still very good advice. And "if you don't know who you are, this is a lousy place to find out." That kind of stuff is good for all weathers.

CA: Where should the small investor with no professional connection to the financial world turn for advice on how to grow and prosper?

GOODMAN: I think the first thing you have to do is want to do it. Many people don't; they want to grow and prosper, but they don't want to put in the effort. On the other hand, if you like it, it becomes far more than a way to grow and prosper. It is daily theater, and it's a way of looking at the world and following the world. I enjoy that very much because there's always something happening, always change—and you can turn change to your advantage. There are all kinds of books, from ordinary primers on. Peter Lynch wrote a very good book this year called *One Up on Wall Street;* I have an endorsement on the cover. Different things come along at different times.

CA: You just mentioned wanting to work at becoming prosperous, and "Do you really want to be rich?" is one of your persistent questions to readers. Is the example of Michael Phillips, the deliberately not rich ex-banker you wrote about in The Roaring Eighties, *likely to become a model for the future?*

GOODMAN: There are already many people who have other standards than wealth by which they measure life; I know many

of them. There are musicians who want to make music and lawyers who practice pro bono law and teachers who really enjoy teaching. They make a decent living, but they don't want to spend all of their time thinking about material things.

CA: In an interview for Lear's, *you noted that people who've had an athletic background do well in the money businesses because of the competitive spirit nurtured in sports. Traditionally, men have the athletic background. Do you feel women are quickly acquiring that spirit of competition that they haven't come by in the same way men have?*

GOODMAN: Absolutely. In the past, except in certain prescribed sports—field hockey, for example—the things that women did were not directly competitive. I suppose there was always horsemanship, and of course there was always a level of competition in other sports. There are a lot of women now in the financial world because they have found it easier actually to become analysts and things like that on Wall Street than perhaps to be in some of the older manufacturing and processing industries. I see a lot of them.

CA: As you said in The Roaring Eighties, *"The creative juices of the Elizabethans may have gone into sonnets; the creative juices of the '80s went into thinking up new securities," and later, "The four-letter word of the 1980s is debt." What should we do in the immediate future, both individually and as a nation, to right ourselves in that regard?*

GOODMAN: You can call attention to these things, but I don't think you can rule against them. It sort of plays itself out after a while. I certainly notice when there's an article that says CEOs now pay themselves fifty-three times what the shop foreman gets, and that's up from forty-six times. In *The Roaring Eighties* there are a lot of comparisons between certain industries and the kind of industries that serve those people that are making all the money. You can be making five million dollars a year, but if you get sick, you're still tended in the hospital by a nurse who's making twenty thousand dollars a year, and your children are guarded when they cross the street by a policeman making twenty-four-thousand dollars a year, and so on. That's part of life, and it's very much a part of our standard of living. A bank account, after all, doesn't make a standard of living.

CA: In The Roaring Eighties *you also talk about the views of University of Chicago professor Allan Bloom, who lamented in* The Closing of the American Mind *the cultural emptiness of education today. In an ideal education, what kind of economics-related reading would you like to see?*

GOODMAN: I think you have to start with the kind of education Dr. Bloom was talking about. I do believe that the daily and weekly reporting of economic matters has gotten much better, but it would be hard to think of classics in the field that everybody should read in the way you might read *Middletown* in sociology or *Catch-22* in World War II irony. I'm hard put to think of money and financial classics. If I had to draw up a list, I probably could do it, but none of the titles would have the same ring as classics in the humanities or the sciences.

CA: You often refer in your writing to Carl Jung, and you've served as a trustee of the C. J. Jung Foundation. How do you feel his work might have influenced your own?

GOODMAN: I don't think there's a direct influence, but Carl Jung looked at the myths that societies held sacred, and he looked at ways of behavior that were sort of tribal in nature. I haven't reread him—and I certainly didn't read all of him—but after you absorb a little of that, you tend to look at everyday activities from his point of view, and it continues to come back. That happened just this morning, when I was looking at a presentation somebody made on a topic that is right in the headlines, and one we've done a segment of our television show about: the American effort to stay ahead of the Japanese technologically. Part of the problem in this area is that Wall Street has no patience for long-range investing, and the author of this particular work was saying that the herd all grazes off in the same direction. Without getting into Dr. Jung's elaborate psychological hierarchy, I can certainly see a lot of it in the world around me.

CA: In "A Literary Illusion" [Esquire, February, 1989] you spoke of the intimacy between writer and reader as one of the reasons to keep writing. What are the special satisfactions of your PBS television show, "Adam Smith's Money World"?

GOODMAN: It's an unusual opportunity in that it is a kind of weekly personal essay. It's not right on the news and it isn't network, so it isn't fragmented and it isn't aimed to commandeer the lowest-common-denominator audience. You have the ability to talk in a personal tone on a topic, and the one that I mentioned is one that we just did. You get the opportunity to learn about something, to explain it first to yourself and then to other people, and to come to some sort of conclusion about where we are in relation to it. The satisfaction is very much the same satisfaction that you get in writing, but in another medium that has different characteristics. It's more immediate and has a broader reach, but it also vanishes into the air and cannot be passed from hand to hand.

CA: You somehow keep a lively sense of humor through all your writing, television appearances, and the other things you do. How do you manage it? It must get pretty hectic at times.

GOODMAN: It gets very hectic, but then you build up a fear that it won't be. You can get used to anything, but I think a period of quiet would be very difficult.

CA: Any thoughts you'd like to add about the success of Adam Smith?

GOODMAN: Adam Smith, as it developed, was very much a part of *New York Magazine* when it began, in the sixties. There was a small group of people who were all about the same age and who were writing in a different manner from their elders. Tom Wolfe, Jimmy Breslin, Gloria Steinem, and I were all in that group; in fact, we used to be called the Varsity. What characterized us was that we put ourselves into situations in which we could describe what it was like to be in those situations as well as writing about them from the outside. That was Tom's description of the New Journalism, and he castigated the Old Journalism as being the *New Yorker* and what he called "the literary gentlemen in the grandstand." That did have a big influence. What has happened since is that everybody has gone off in his or her own way. Tom has stayed with writing and done the most masterful job in *The Bonfire of the Vanities.* I sent him a note saying that *The Roaring Eighties* was just the sketches for *The Bonfire of the Vanities;* his book is the real satiric and intellectual masterpiece of this generation. Gloria went off and took up her causes. Breslin has done his own thing as a daily journalist. You always think of the other path, about what it would have been like to have stayed with

writing fiction. But you can't do it all. Times change and perceptions change.

CA: Perhaps you'll be able to get back to writing fiction someday, if that's still a thing you'd like to do.

GOODMAN: Well, I might. But even there the world has changed from what I learned. I was very lucky; I had a very good education in writing. I went to Harvard College at a time when its writing courses and English courses were very strong, and I took something like three or three-and-a-half years of writing courses with people like Archibald MacLeish and Theodore Morrison. I often thought that, getting a liberal arts degree in a place like Harvard, you didn't learn anything that was useful; but in later years I realized that I had actually learned how to write, as much as you can learn how to write by the age of twenty or twenty-one.

But the world I was growing up into and the world now are terribly different. It's far more fragmented now; it's very difficult. The problem is not writing the novel, it's getting someone to read it. That essay you were quoting about the intimacy between the writer and the reader starts out with a rather harsh comment on the times and economics of the book business itself. It's dominated by a couple of chains, and now they say it's getting like the movies, where you have two weekends to make it and then if you don't, you're out. It's a different way of life. Many things do get exposed: you can write TV, you can write movies. But it's relatively rare to write a novel and have it widely read. It's not a part of our common culture the way it was before mass media went into homes—before television, and possibly before radio.

I remember reading a description of H. G. Wells and John Galsworthy and other English writers around the turn of the century. They were the movie stars of the time; they were world-famous at a time when English was the language being read everywhere. There were no competing images, so the images that they presented to the world were the ones that were paid attention to and absorbed. Now there's nothing more commanding than the image on the screen. Tolstoy could write Anna Karenina today, but it would have a hard time getting the worldwide audience that "Dallas" has. The questions about who shot J. R. Ewing and what's happening next are more universal than what happened to Anna Karenina.

CA: And that means, among other things, that young people are missing a lot.

GOODMAN: Yes. Once, talking with my college-age children, I referred to a woman as a real Becky Sharp. They looked blank and I said, "Now I guess you're going to tell me you don't know who Anna Karenina is." They said, "Name three heavy-metal bands." I couldn't, but I can now.

BIOGRAPHICAL/CRITICAL SOURCES:

PERIODICALS

Book World, June 2, 1968.
Chicago Sunday Tribune, September 6, 1959.
Commonweal, November 29, 1968, March 17, 1973.
Economist, March 28, 1981.
Esquire, February, 1989.
Lear's, September, 1989.
Life, December 20, 1968.
Los Angeles Times, April 10, 1981, March 24, 1985.
National Observer, June 10, 1968.
New Statesman, March 16, 1973.
Newsweek, June 17, 1968, December 5, 1988.

New York, April 7, 1969, August 18, 1969.
New York Herald Tribune Book Review, August 28, 1955, November 17, 1957, May 11, 1958.
New York Review of Books, December 11, 1975.
New York Times, August 28, 1955, December 8, 1957, May 4, 1958, March 9, 1981.
New York Times Book Review, September 27, 1959, May 26, 1968, July 14, 1968, October 15, 1972, November 2, 1975, March 22, 1981, March 29, 1981, November 27, 1988.
Publishers Weekly, January 15, 1979.
San Francisco Chronicle, June 22, 1958, January 11, 1969.
Saturday Review, June 21, 1968, September 9, 1972, October 21, 1972, February, 1981.
Time, November 27, 1972, October 27, 1975.
Times Literary Supplement, October 24, 1968, August 3, 1973.
Virginia Quarterly Review, winter, 1969.
Washington Post Book World, February 22, 1981.

—Sketch by Marilyn K. Basel

—Interview by Jean W. Ross

*　　*　　*

GOODRICH, Lloyd   1897-1987

PERSONAL: Born July 10, 1897, in Nutley, N.J.; died of cancer, March 27, 1987, in New York, N.Y.; son of Henry Wickes and Madeleine (Lloyd) Goodrich; married Edith Havens, January 12, 1924; children: David Lloyd, Madeleine Lloyd Noble. *Education:* Attended Art Students League and National Academy of Design.

ADDRESSES: Office—Whitney Museum of American Art, 945 Madison Ave., New York, N.Y. 10021.

CAREER: Employed by Macmillan Publishing Co., Inc., New York City, 1923-25; *Arts* (magazine), associate editor, 1925-27, European editor, 1927-28, associate editor, 1928-29, contributing editor, 1929-31; Whitney Museum of American Art, New York City, research curator, 1935-47, associate curator, 1947-48, associate director, 1948-58, director, 1958-68, advertising director, 1968-71, became director emeritus, also member of board of trustees. Member of New York regional committee for Public Works Art Project, 1933-34; Archives of American Art, member of New York regional board, and chairman of committee on government and art, beginning 1948; member of Sara Roby Foundation, beginning 1956; member of advisory committee, Art for the White House, 1960-63. Member of advisory board, Carnegie Study of American Art; member of Smithsonian Art Commission; co-chairman of Joint Artists-Museums Committee; member of council of Cornell University's College of Architecture.

MEMBER: International Art Critics Association, American Academy of Arts and Sciences (fellow), Association of Art Museum Directors, Drawing Society, American Institute of Interior Designers (honorary member), American Federation of the Arts (director; trustee; honorary vice-president), National Council on Arts and Government (vice-chairman, beginning 1962), American Friends of Tate Gallery, Edward MacDowell Association (member of board of directors).

AWARDS, HONORS: Awards from *Art in America,* 1959, and National Art Materials Trade Association, 1964; D.F.A., Cornell College (Mount Vernon, Iowa), 1963, and Colby College, 1964; award of merit, Philadelphia Museum College of Art, 1964; Creative Arts award, Brandeis University, 1970; award for excellence in art history, Art Dealers Association of America, 1977; citation for distinguished service to the arts, American Academy and Institute of Arts and Letters, 1979; citation for distinguished contribution to American art history, Archives of American Art, 1979; Governor's Award, Skowhegan School of Painting and Sculpture, 1981; Alfred Harcourt Award in biography and memoirs, 1984, for *Thomas Eakins.*

WRITINGS:

Kenneth Hayes Miller, Arts Publishing Corp., 1930.
H. E. Schnakenberg, Whitney Museum of American Art, 1931.
Thomas Eakins: His Life and Work, Whitney Museum of American Art, 1933, reprinted, AMS Press, 1970.
Winslow Homer, Macmillan, 1944, reprinted, Whitney Museum of American Art, 1973.
American Watercolor and Winslow Homer (monograph), Walker Art Center (Minneapolis, Minn.), 1945.
Albert P. Ryder Centenary Exhibition, Whitney Museum of American Art, 1947.
Yasuo Kuniyoshi: Retrospective Exhibition, Whitney Museum of American Art, 1948.
Max Weber, Macmillan, 1949.
Edward Hopper, Penguin, 1949.
John Sloan, Macmillan, 1952.
(With Atsuo Imaizumi) *Kuniyoshi: Catalogue of Kuniyoshi's Posthumous Exhibition,* Bajutou Shuppan-sha, 1954.
(Editor) *The Museum and the Artist,* American Federation of the Arts, 1958.
Four American Expressionists: Doris Caesar, Chaim Gross, Karl Knaths, Abraham Rattner, Praeger, 1959.
Albert P. Ryder, Braziller, 1959.
Winslow Homer, Braziller, 1959.
Young America, 1960, Praeger, 1960.
(With John I. H. Baur) *American Art of Our Century,* Praeger, 1961 (published in England as *American Art of the Twentieth Century,* Thames & Hudson, 1962).
(With Edward Bryant) *Forty American Artists under Forty, from the Collection of the Whitney Museum of American Art,* Praeger, 1962.
The Drawings of Edwin Dickinson, Yale University Press, 1963.
(Author of preface) Andrew Wyeth, *The Four Seasons: Paintings and Drawings,* Art in America, 1963.
Pioneers of Modern Art in America: The Decade of the Armory Show, 1910-1920, Praeger, 1963.
Edward Hopper: Exhibition and Catalogue, Whitney Museum of American Art, 1964.
(Author of foreword) Baur, editor, *Between the Fairs: Twenty-five Years of American Art, 1939-1964,* Praeger, 1964.
Edwin Dickinson, Whitney Museum of American Art, 1965.
Young America, 1965: Thirty American Artists under Thirty-five, Whitney Museum of American Art, 1965.
Art of the United States, 1670-1966, Whitney Museum of American Art, 1966.
Three Centuries of American Art, Praeger, 1966.
Raphael Soyer, Praeger, 1967, reprinted, 1987.
Sao Paulo Nine: United States of America, Smithsonian Institution Press, 1967.
The Graphic Art of Winslow Homer, New York Museum of Graphic Art, 1968.
(With Patricia FitzGerald Mandel) *John Heliker,* Praeger, 1968.
Winslow Homer's America, Tudor, 1969.
Five Paintings from Thomas Nast's Grand Caricature, Swann Collection of Caricature and Cartoon, 1970.
(With Doris Bry) *Georgia O'Keeffe,* Praeger, 1970.
Edward Hopper, Abrams, 1971, new edition, 1976.

(Editor) *Realism and Surrealism in American Art: From the Sara Roby Foundation Collection,* American Federation of Arts, 1971.

Americans: Individualists at Work, American Federation of Arts, 1972.

Reginald Marsh, Abrams, 1972.

The White House Gardens, Great American Editions, 1973.

Winslow Homer, New York Graphic Society, 1973.

Thomas Eakins, two volumes, Harvard University Press, 1983.

Author of *Fifty Years of Painting by Max Weber,* 1969, and *Harold Sterner,* 1971; also author of text for many museum catalogues. Contributor to *New Art in America,* 1957. Assistant art critic for *New York Times,* 1929. Chairman of editorial board, *Magazine of Art,* 1942-50; member of editorial boards, *Art Bulletin* and *Art in America,* beginning 1946; member of international scientific council, *Enciclopedia dell'Arte.*

SIDELIGHTS: A former director of New York's Whitney Museum of American Art, Lloyd Goodrich devoted his long career to cataloging and defining the history of art in this country. As a writer, Goodrich specialized in showing the man behind the artist. This is most evident in his final work, *Thomas Eakins,* the story of one of America's greatest realists, published when the author was well into his eighties. Goodrich had produced a previous volume on the painter—in 1933—but many critics agreed that the revised version opened up new perspective on the subject. The new book, noted *New Republic* critic John Canaday, "supersedes his own earlier one and gives the coup de grace to any recent contenders for the title of definitive work." Canaday also called *Thomas Eakins* "an instant classic," echoing the view of John Wilmerding. In a *New York Times Book Review* piece, Wilmerding saw the two-volume biography as "a crowning achievement of the author's long and productive career. . . . It is both factual and fitting that this particular biographer should remind us that 'Eakins loved old age, the marks of years and experience, the essential character,'" Wilmerding concluded. "How satisfying that Mr. Goodrich's long and distinguished life of scholarship should deal with an artist who painted the triumphant vitality of old age."

BIOGRAPHICAL/CRITICAL SOURCES:

BOOKS

Goodrich, Lloyd, *Thomas Eakins,* two volumes, Harvard University Press, 1983.

PERIODICALS

New Republic, November 29, 1982.
New York Times Book Review, January 2, 1983.

OBITUARIES:

PERIODICALS

Detroit Free Press, March 30, 1987.
New York Times, March 28, 1987.
Washington Post, March 29, 1987.*

*   *   *

GOODWIN, Suzanne
(Suzanne Ebel; Cecily Shelbourne, a pseudonym)

PERSONAL: Born in London, England; daughter of Clement (a director) and Charlotte (a musician; maiden name, Collins) Ebel; married John Goodwin (publicity director for National Theatre), October, 1948; children: Marigold Goodwin Sebastian,

James, Timothy. *Education:* Educated at Roman Catholic convent schools in England and Belgium.

ADDRESSES: *Home*—52-A Digby Mansions, Hammersmith Bridge Rd., London W6 9DF, England. *Agent*—Curtis Brown Ltd., 162-168 Regent St., London W1R 5TB, England.

CAREER: Former journalist for London *Times;* Young & Rubicam, New York, N.Y., public relations director in London office, 1950-72; full-time writer, 1972—.

AWARDS, HONORS: Romantic Novel of the Year Award, Romantic Novelists Association, 1964, for *Journey from Yesterday;* best tourist guide award, 1985, for *London's Riverside.*

WRITINGS:

NOVELS

The Winter Spring, Bodley Head, 1978.
The Winter Sisters, Bodley Head, 1980.
Emerald, Magnum Publications, 1980.
Julia's Sister, Severn House Publishers, 1981.
Floodtide, Sphere Books, 1983.
(With Jill Bennett) *Godfrey, a Special Time Remembered,* Hodder & Stoughton, 1983.
Sisters, St. Martin's, 1984.
Cousins, St. Martin's, 1985.
Daughters, St. Martin's, 1987.
Lovers, St. Martin's, 1988.
To Love a Hero, M. Joseph, 1989.

UNDER NAME SUZANNE EBEL; ROMANTIC NOVELS

Journey from Yesterday, Collins, 1964.
The Half Enchanted, Collins, 1965.
The Love Campaign, Collins, 1966.
A Perfect Stranger, Collins, 1967.
Name in Lights, Collins, 1967.
A Most Auspicious Star, Collins, 1968.
Somersault, Collins, 1969.
Portrait of Jill, Collins, 1970.
Dear Kate, Collins, 1970.
To Seek a Star, Collins, 1971.
The Family Feeling, Collins, 1972.
Girl by the Sea, Collins, 1973.
Music in Winter, Collins, 1974.
A Grove of Olives, Collins, 1975.
River Voices, Collins, 1976.
The Double Rainbow, Collins, 1977.
A Rose in the Heather, Collins, 1978.

OTHER

(Under name Suzanne Ebel) *Guide to the Cotswolds* (nonfiction), Ward, Lock, 1973.
"Chords and Dischords" (radio play), British Broadcasting Corp., 1975.
(Under name Suzanne Ebel) *London's Riverside* (nonfiction), Luscombe, 1976.
(Under pseudonym Cecily Shelbourne) *Stage of Love,* Putnam, 1977.
London's Riverside (guide book), Constable, 1985.

Contributor of stories to magazines.

WORK IN PROGRESS: A novel, set in England—partly in London and mainly in Stratford-upon-Avon, Warwickshire—during 1947-49.

SIDELIGHTS: Suzanne Goodwin writes: "I have written since I was a teenager. I write regularly every day, sometimes for as long as nine hours. I feel that writing has something strongly in common with painting: it catches the mood, the character, the flavour of life. We own a flat in the south of France, I speak fluent French, and the French influence of art and nature has an effect on my writing, as the English atmosphere does."

BIOGRAPHICAL/CRITICAL SOURCES:

PERIODICALS

Times (London), February 25, 1983.

*   *   *

GORDON, Angela
See PAINE, Lauran (Bosworth)

*   *   *

GORDON, Donald Ramsay 1929-

PERSONAL: Born September 14, 1929, in Toronto, Ontario, Canada; son of Donald and Maisie Gordon; married wife, Helen Elizabeth (an anesthetist), December 21, 1953; children: Donald John, Bruce, Keith. *Education:* Queen's University, B.A. (with honors), 1953; University of Toronto. M.A., 1955; London School of Economics and Political Science, additional study, 1956-63.

ADDRESSES: Home—134 Iroquois Pl., Waterloo, Ontario, Canada N2L 2S5.

CAREER: Canadian Press, Toronto, Ontario, writer and filing editor, 1949-55; *Financial Post,* Toronto, assistant editor, 1955-56; affiliated with Clyde Brothers Circus, Oklahoma City, Okla., 1956; Canadian Broadcasting Corp., London, England, European correspondent, 1957-63; University of Calgary, Calgary, Alberta, assistant professor, 1963-65, associate professor of political science, 1965-66; University of Waterloo, Waterloo, Ontario, assistant professor, 1966-67, associate professor of political science, 1967-69, associate professor in Faculty of Arts, part-time, 1969-70; Earthrise, Inc., Ottawa, Ontario, director and project coordinator, 1970; University of Waterloo, associate professor of political science, part-time, 1970-71, associate professor in Arts 100 Project, 1971-72, associate professor of Arts 100 communications, 1972-75; consultant, 1975-79; Canadian Radio-Television and Telecommunications Commission, Ottawa, research and policy consultant, 1981-83; Image Corp., Waterloo, chief writer, 1981—.

Member, Royal Commission on the Status of Women in Canada, 1967. Co-host of "20,000 Questions," CBC Television, 1966-67; presenter of arctic film, "The Edge of Evolution," 1978. Research consultant to Senate Committee on the Mass Media in Canada, 1969-70, and to Royal Commission on Violence in the Communications Industry, 1976-77.

MEMBER: Association of Canadian Radio and Television Artists, University Film Association, Kropotkin Institute (director, 1960—), Canadian Authors Association, Canadian Society of Children's Authors, Illustrators and Performers.

AWARDS, HONORS: Communications fellowship, Ford Foundation, 1954; travel and research award, International Institute of Education, 1962-63; research award, Canada Council, 1969; Kropotkin Institute prize, 1981.

WRITINGS:

Language, Logic, and the Mass Media, Holt, 1966.
(Contributor) J. King Gordon, editor, *Canada as a Middle Power,* Canadian Institute of International Affairs, 1966.

The New Literacy, University of Toronto Press, 1971.
The Rock Candy Bandits (juvenile), McBain, 1984.
Fineswine, McBain, 1984.

S.P.E.E.D., McBain, 1985.
The Sex Shoppe, Lugus Publications, 1989.
The Choice, Lugus Publications, 1989.

Also author of pamphlets and reports, including "Mass Media and the Rule of Law in Canada," report for Task Force on Government Information, 1969. Also contributor to television in Canada, the United States, and England. Contributor to periodicals, including *Canadian Commentator, MacLean's, Toronto Globe and Mail, Times, Spectator, New Statesman,* and *Financial Post.*

WORK IN PROGRESS: "Novels on baseball and (blush) the meaning of life, as yet untitled."

SIDELIGHTS: Donald Ramsay Gordon told *CA:* "Coming to humility late in life has meant more than the usual amount of squirming over past follies of pride and arrogance. Fortunately the affectations of surviving maidens have persisted just enough to ward off deep gloom or despair. There is still much to do in terms of revenge on editors, lies to children. nasty notes to politicians, and canoe-based conversations with loons."

*   *   *

GORDON, Doreen
See CHARD, Judy

*   *   *

GORDON, Ruth 1896-1985

PERSONAL: Original name Ruth Jones; born October 30, 1896, in the Mt. Wollaston section of Quincy, Mass.; died August 28, 1985, in Edgartown, Martha's Vineyard, Mass., of a stroke; cremated; daughter of Clinton (a factory foreman and retired seaman) and Annie Tapley (Ziegler) Jones; married Gregory Kelly (an actor), 1918 (died, 1927); married Garson Kanin (a director and playwright), December 4, 1942; children: Jones Harris Kanin (son). *Education:* Attended American Academy of Dramatic Arts, 1914-15; studied singing with Keith Davis.

CAREER: Actress and writer. Began acting career as an extra in silent films, Fort Lee, N. J., 1915; made her Broadway debut as Nibs in "Peter Pan" at the Empire Theatre, 1915; co-owner with first husband, Gregory Kelly, of a repertory theatre in Indianapolis, Ind., during the 1920s. Stage appearances included: "Seventeen," 1917, "Clarence," 1920, "Tweedles," 1923, "Holding Helen," 1925, "Saturday's Children," 1928, "Serena Blandish," 1929, "Ethan Frome," 1935, "The Country Wife," 1936, "A Doll's House," 1937, "The Three Sisters," 1942, "Over Twenty-One," 1943-45, and "The Matchmaker," 1954-57. Film appearances included: "Abe Lincoln in Illinois," 1940, "Dr. Ehrlich's Magic Bullet," 1940, "Information, Please," 1940, "Two-Faced Woman," 1941, "Action in the North Atlantic," 1942, "Edge of Darkness," 1943, "Inside Daisy Clover," 1966, "Rosemary's Baby," 1967, "Whatever Happened to Aunt Alice?," 1968, "Where's Poppa?," 1970, "Harold and Maude," 1971, "Every Which Way but Loose," 1978, and "Any Which Way You Can," 1980. Television movie appearances included: "Rosemary's Baby II," 1976, "The Great Houdini," 1976, "The Perfect Gentleman," 1977, "Don't Go to Sleep," 1982, and "The Secret World of the Very Young," 1985. Television series appearances included: "The Flip Wilson Show," "Love Boat," "The Bob Newhart Show," "Rhoda," and "Taxi."

MEMBER: Dramatists Guild, Actors' Equity Association, Authors League of America.

AWARDS, HONORS: Academy Award nomination, Writers Guild award nomination, and Box Office Ribbon Award, all 1949, all for screenplay "Adam's Rib"; Academy Award nomination and Golden Globe Award for best supporting actress, both 1966, both for "Inside Daisy Clover"; Academy Award for best supporting actress, 1968, for "Rosemary's Baby"; Emmy Award, 1979, for guest appearance on "Taxi" television series; Holland Society gold medal, 1980; her hometown of Quincy, Mass., held a Ruth Gordon Day and dedicated the Ruth Gordon Center for the Performing Arts in November of 1984; Emmy Award nomination, 1985, for "The Secret World of the Very Young"; named member of Theatre Hall of Fame.

WRITINGS:

Myself among Others, Atheneum, 1971.
My Side: The Autobiography of Ruth Gordon, Harper, 1976.
Ruth Gordon: An Open Book, Doubleday, 1980.
Shady Lady (novel), Arbor House, 1981.

PLAYS

Over Twenty-One (first produced on Broadway at the Music Box Theatre in 1943), Random House, 1944.
Years Ago (first produced in New York City at the Mansfield Theatre in 1947; also see below), Viking, 1947, acting edition, Dramatists Play Service, 1974.
"The Leading Lady," first produced in New York City at the National Theatre in 1948.
(Adaptor) "A Very Rich Woman" (based on Philippe Heriat's play "Les Joies de Famille"), first produced on Broadway at the Belasco Theatre, 1965.
"Ho, Ho, Ho" (two-act), first produced in Stockbridge, Mass., at the Berkshire Theatre Festival, 1976.

Contributor of play to anthology *Best Plays of 1943-44,* 1944.

SCREENPLAYS

(With husband, Garson Kanin) "A Double Life," Universal, 1947.
(With Kanin) "Adam's Rib," Metro-Goldwyn-Mayer, 1950.
(With Kanin) "The Marrying Kind," Columbia, 1952.
(With Kanin) "Pat and Mike," Metro-Goldwyn-Mayer, 1952.
"The Actress" (based on her play *Years Ago*), Metro-Goldwyn-Mayer, 1953.

Also author of "Hardhat and Legs," 1978.

SIDELIGHTS: Ruth Gordon's career spanned seven decades and ranged from films to television to the Broadway stage. One of the grand ladies of the American theatre, Gordon played such memorable roles as Mattie Silver in "Ethan Frome," Mrs. Pinchwife in "The Country Wife," and Mrs. Levi in "The Matchmaker," later remade as "Hello, Dolly!" Her film work included roles in "Abe Lincoln in Illinois," 1940, "Action in the North Atlantic," 1942, "Edge of Darkness," 1943, and "Where's Poppa?," 1970. For her role as a Satanist neighbor in 1967's "Rosemary's Baby," Gordon won an Academy Award, while her role in the offbeat "Harold and Maude" won her a cult following on the nation's college campuses. In addition, she and her husband Garson Kanin wrote several successful screenplays, including the Katharine Hepburn-Spencer Tracy vehicles "Adam's Rib" and "Pat and Mike."

"I didn't get organized until I was four," Gordon jokingly claimed in her autobiography *Ruth Gordon: An Open Book.* That is when she first realized that with determination and perseverance, she could do anything she wanted. "Never be helpless" was one of Gordon's favorite expressions. But the fierce determination that brought her many successes in a long career was often matched by failure. She admitted in a speech in 1984, at the dedication of the Ruth Gordon Center for the Performing Arts: "I never face the facts. I never listen to good advice. I'm a slow starter, but I get there."

At fifteen Gordon decided to become an actress after seeing Hazel Dawn in the musical "The Pink Lady." Her father disapproved; he wanted her to be a physical education teacher. "I wanted to do something a little more sexy than that," Gordon later explained, and so in 1914 she left Quincy, Massachusetts, for the American Academy of Dramatic Arts in New York with $50 pinned to her corset. Her father, a retired seaman, reluctantly agreed to the move, but gave her his old spyglass. "He told me I could hock it if I needed money," Samuel G. Freedman quoted Gordon explaining in the *New York Times.* "He said, 'If you're going to be an actress, you'll be in and out of hock shops all your life.'" Gordon admitted later that in her early years as an actress she had on occasion been forced to visit hock shops, but she always kept her father's spyglass.

By her junior year at drama school, Gordon had failed as an actress. Her performance in the annual review was so poor that the school's president personally told her she had no talent and must leave. But she was determined to succeed, reasoning that if others could learn the craft of acting, so could she. By 1915 Gordon was working as an extra in silent films. She played a taxi dancer in Irene and Vernon Castle's first film, for which she received $1.25 a day and two ham sandwiches. Later that year she made her Broadway debut in the role of Nibs, one of the Lost Boys, in "Peter Pan." But her first starring role, in "Seventeen" by Booth Tarkington, was a critical fiasco. Heywood Broun in the *New York Tribune* claimed, "Anyone who looks like that and acts like that must get off the stage." But the play enabled Gordon to meet the actor Gregory Kelly, and they were married in 1918. During the 1920s the couple ran a repertory theatre in Indianapolis, and Gordon played in such hits as "Clarence" and "Holding Helen." She later claimed that Kelly had taught her how to act. He died of heart trouble in 1927.

During the late 1920s and 1930s Gordon became one of the American theatre's most respected actresses. Her roles in such plays as "Saturday's Children," in which she starred with Humphrey Bogart, and "Serena Blandish" brought her critical acclaim. But "she burst into stardom," according to Freedman, with her role as Mattie Silver in 1936's "Ethan Frome." The following year she starred as Mrs. Pinchwife in the Restoration comedy "The Country Wife," proving to the London audience that an American actress could handle the British comedy role. It marked the first time an American actress had performed at the prestigious Old Vic Theatre. In his review of the play for the *New York Times,* Alexander Woollcott called Gordon's work "the most richly comic performance [he had] ever seen given by any actress in any country at any time in any play." Later that same year, Gordon played Nora Helmer in Ibsen's "A Doll's House" to yet further acclaim. By the 1940s, Richard Pearson reported in the *Washington Post,* "critics were comparing her to Helen Hayes, one critic writing that while Miss Hayes was the deeper actress, Miss Gordon was the wittier." At the height of her stage success Gordon gave birth to her only child, Jones Harris, the son of her lover Jed Harris, the Broadway producer. Because Harris was a married man, the child was kept a secret from all but close family members.

In 1940 Gordon turned to films, taking the role of Mary Todd in "Abe Lincoln in Illinois." Some critics thought she stole that film. Other screen appearances quickly followed, including roles in "Information, Please," "Edge of Darkness," "Action in the North Atlantic," and "Two-Faced Woman," the last Greta Garbo film. Meanwhile, Gordon appeared in such Broadway productions as "The Three Sisters" and in her own play, "Over Twenty-One," which ran for 221 performances. In 1942 she married Garson Kanin, a playwright some sixteen years her junior. The couple collaborated on several screenplays together, including the successful "A Double Life," in 1948, and "The Marrying Kind," in 1952. Their two scripts for Katharine Hepburn and Spencer Tracy, "Adam's Rib" and "Pat and Mike," established the acting pair's legendary "battle of the sexes" screen relationship, and earned Gordon a reputation as a keen writer of witty dialogue.

Gordon's stature as an actress was such that writers like Thornton Wilder and Booth Tarkington wrote plays specifically for her. Tarkington created several roles for her, including the lead in 1923's "Tweedles." Wilder's 1938 play "The Merchant of Yonkers" was also meant for Gordon. She turned it down at the time and the play quickly folded. Sixteen years later it was revised and successfully produced as "The Matchmaker," with Gordon playing the lead role of Dolly. The play enjoyed a 486-performance run on Broadway and was later adapted as the musical "Hello, Dolly!," with such leading ladies as Carol Channing, Pearl Bailey, and Barbra Streisand following in Gordon's footsteps.

After a break from the screen of some 24 years Gordon returned to film acting in 1966 with "Inside Daisy Clover." She played the Dealer, a role that earned her a Golden Globe Award and an Academy Award nomination. Her return to films at the age of seventy, according to a writer for the London *Times,* "started virtually a new career in which she created a memorable gallery of eccentric and sinister characters." Among her most famous film characters was Mia Farrow's Satanist neighbor in 1967's "Rosemary's Baby." The part won Gordon her only Academy Award. Upon accepting the award from the Academy, Gordon caustically remarked: "I can't tell you how encouraging a thing like this is." Also memorable was her appearance as a funeral-loving eccentric in 1971's "Harold and Maude." The film bombed at the box office but became a cult favorite on college campuses. It did not make a profit until 1983. When Gordon finally received her check for $50,000 that year, she nearly threw it away. "I thought it was one of those sweepstakes from Reader's Digest," Karen Wada reported her saying in the *Los Angeles Times.* She also appeared as Clint Eastwood's mother in the popular comedies "Every Which Way but Loose" and "Any Which Way You Can." Gordon's television work during the 1970s and 1980s included guest spots on "The Flip Wilson Show," "Love Boat," "The Bob Newhart Show," and as Carlton's mother on "Rhoda." For her appearance on "Taxi," playing a wealthy woman who tries to buy Alex Reiger's friendship, Gordon received an Emmy Award.

During the many years she worked on stage, in films, and on television, Gordon was a friend to many prominent people in the arts and entertainment, including Humphrey Bogart, Roman Polanski, Edith Wharton, J. D. Salinger, and Louis B. Mayer. She also was a member of the so-called Algonquin Round Table, a group of writers who met for lunch at New York's Algonquin Hotel during the 1920s. The group included Dorothy Parker, Al-exander Woollcott, Heywood Broun, Robert Benchley, and Edna Ferber. In the 1930s and 1940s, she dined at the White House with Franklin and Eleanor Roosevelt.

Gordon's "roguish heart and enduring grace lighted the world's stages and motion picture screens for seven decades," Wada remarked. At the time of Gordon's death in 1985, Helen Hayes was quoted by Freedman as saying, "She was a total original. There was no one else like her, and no one had the courage to try to imitate her." Always working, Gordon had four movies waiting for release at the time of her death. She had also been nominated for an Emmy Award for her role in the television movie "The Secret World of the Very Young."

"I wanted to be an actress in 1912," Gordon wrote in *Ruth Gordon: An Open Book.* "I want to be an actress today. That walk from the darkness backstage through the door or opening in the scenery where I make an entrance into the bright lights with that big dim mass out beyond, which bursts into applause, then the first terrifying sound that comes out of my throat, which they describe as a voice, but that first instant it is the siren of terror and intention and faith and hope and trust and vanity and security and insecurity and blood-curdling courage which is acting." Shortly before her death Gordon spoke to Valerie Wells, who was writing a book on death and dying. Her thoughts on the subject were later published in the *Chicago Tribune:* "I don't want to be buried anywhere," Gordon said. "I'm wild about the bright lights—my life is made up of bright lights—so I want to be cremated and just go right into the bright lights and that's it."

BIOGRAPHICAL/CRITICAL SOURCES:

BOOKS

Author Speaks, Bowker, 1977.
Gordon, Ruth, *Myself among Others,* Atheneum, 1971.
Gordon, Ruth, *My Side: The Autobiography of Ruth Gordon,* Harper, 1976.
Gordon, Ruth, *Ruth Gordon: An Open Book,* Doubleday, 1980.

PERIODICALS

Chicago Tribune, September 2, 1985.
Cinema, Number 35, 1976.
Life, January 6, 1947.
Newsweek, March 22, 1982.
New York Post, May 8, 1971.
New York Times, October 21, 1974, August 8, 1976, January 26, 1977, September 8, 1985.
New York Times Book Review, August 15, 1971, October 10, 1976.
New York Times Magazine, January 12, 1947, October 5, 1969.
Pageant, March, 1949.
Publishers Weekly, May 31, 1971.
Saturday Review, May 22, 1971, June 12, 1971.
Theatre Arts, December, 1946.
Tribune Books (Chicago), November 21, 1982.

OBITUARIES:

PERIODICALS

Boston Herald, August 29, 1985.
Detroit Free Press, August 29, 1985.
Los Angeles Times, August 29, 1985.
Newsweek, September, 9, 1985.
New York Times, August 29, 1985.
Times (London), August 30, 1985.
Washington Post, August 29, 1985.*

—*Sketch by Thomas Wiloch*

GORMAN, Beth
See PAINE, Lauran (Bosworth)

*   *   *

GOULDEN, Joseph C. (Jr.) 1934-
(Henry S. A. Becket)

PERSONAL: Surname is pronounced "Golden"; born May 23, 1934, in Marshall, Tex.; son of Joseph C. (a book dealer) and Lecta Mahon (Everett) Goulden; married Emily Jo Corns, July 15, 1961; married Leslie Cantrell Smith, June 21, 1979; children: (first marriage) Joseph III, James Craig. *Education:* Attended University of Texas, 1952-56.

ADDRESSES: Home—1534 29th St. N.W., Washington, D.C. 20007. *Agent*—Carl D. Brandt, Brandt & Brandt Literary Agents, Inc., Paramount Bldg., 1501 Broadway, New York, N.Y. 10036.

CAREER: Free-lance writer. Molybdenum miner in Colorado, 1953; *Marshall News-Messenger,* Marshall, Tex., reporter, 1956; *Dallas News,* Dallas, Tex., reporter, 1958-61; *Philadelphia Inquirer,* Philadelphia, Pa., 1961-68, began as reporter, became Washington bureau chief; Accuracy in Media, Inc. (AIM), Washington, D.C., media critic, 1989—. *Military service:* U.S. Army, 1956-58.

AWARDS, HONORS: Recipient of numerous journalistic awards, including reporting awards from State Bar of Texas, 1960, and Pennsylvania and Philadelphia Press Associations, 1964; National Magazine Award, Columbia Graduate School of Journalism, 1969, for *Nation* issue on the Law Enforcement Assistance Administration; Carr P. Collins Award, Texas Institute of Letters, 1972, for *The Superlawyers: The Small and Powerful World of the Great Washington Law Firms;* Francis Parkman Prize, University of Texas, 1976, for *The Best Years: 1945-50.*

WRITINGS:

NONFICTION

The Curtis Caper, Putnam, 1965.
Monopoly, Putnam, 1968.
Truth Is the First Casualty: The Gulf of Tonkin Affair—Illusion and Reality, Rand McNally, 1969.
The Money Givers, Random, 1971.
Meany: The Unchallenged Strong Man of American Labor, Atheneum, 1972.
The Superlawyers: The Small and Powerful World of the Great Washington Law Firms (Literary Guild selection), Weybright & Talley, 1972.
The Benchwarmers: The Small and Powerful World of the Great Federal Judges (Literary Guild selection), Weybright & Talley, 1974.
The Best Years: 1945-1950 (Book-of-the-Month Club selection), Atheneum, 1976.
(Editor) *Mencken's Last Campaign,* New Republic Books, 1976.
The Million Dollar Lawyers (Literary Guild selection), Putnam, 1978.
Korea: The Untold Story of the War (Book-of-the-Month Club alternate), Times Books, 1982.
Jerry Wurf: Labor's Last Angry Man, Atheneum, 1982.
(With Paul Dickson) *There Are Alligators in Our Sewers, and Other American Credos,* Delacorte, 1983.
(With Alexander W. Raffio) *The Death Merchant: The Rise and Fall of Edwin P. Wilson* (Literary Guild selection), Simon & Schuster, 1984.

(Under pseudonym Henry S. A. Becket) *Dictionary of Espionage: Spookspeak into English,* Stein & Day, 1986.
Fit to Print: A. M. Rosenthal and His Times, Lyle Stuart, 1988.

Contributor to periodicals, including *Harper's, National Review, Nation, Penthouse, Texas Monthly,* and *Texas Observer.*

WORK IN PROGRESS: A book about Woodrow Wilson.

SIDELIGHTS: "One of the countries best investigative reporters," according to a *Nation* critic, Joseph C. Goulden's years of experience as a staff member for several newspapers, in addition to his free-lance writing, have resulted in a growing collection of respected analyses. He has published books covering a wide variety of topics, ranging from biographies to his revealing histories of the Korean and Vietnam conflicts. Of these books, Goulden told *CA* that he considers *The Best Years: 1945-1950* to be a pivotal work "because it marked my transition from journalist to attempted serious writer of history, even if in the popular sense."

The Best Years is a heavily-researched effort on Goulden's part to provide his audience with certain insights into the post-war era that are untainted by nostalgia. Because of this approach, the book illustrates that these years in American history, while not without their good points, should not be idealized. Indeed, the author shows that in some ways the post-war boom years had as many social and political problems as today's world. "Goulden's catalogue of post-war problems," observes *New York Times Book Review* contributor Martin F. Nolan, "seems astonishingly contemporary: inflation, housing, veterans affairs, censorship, Congressional deadlock and even talk of spirituality and Presidential campaigning." Anne Chamberlin adds in the *Washington Post Book World* that because of his balanced perspective Goulden "never bogs down in rage, no tender memories mist his eye. He just opens the lens and lets the good times roll."

Shedding new light on the years immediately following those covered in *The Best Years,* Goulden turns his investigative expertise to the much-forgotten Korean conflict in his book entitled *Korea: The Untold Story of the War.* "How the United States was drawn into the war as centerpiece of the United Nations, to battle North Korea and then Communist China to a stalemate, is explored in depressing detail in an enthralling account by Joseph Goulden: few heroes emerge," remarks Sam Hall Kaplan in the *Los Angeles Times.* According to Kaplan, Goulden also leaves few stones unturned in this account which took five years to research and write. Critics stress the fact that many new classified documents were made available to Goulden as a result of the Freedom of Information Act. Accordingly, Robert A. Divine explains in the *New Republic* that Goulden reviewed sources ranging from "CIA intelligence reports to a series of high level memoranda and cables between the Joint Chiefs of Staff and MacArthur's headquarters in Tokyo. He also uses . . . material in the Truman Library . . . to throw a great deal of light on decisionmaking in Washington."

However, even with these previously undisclosed documents at hand, some reviewers feel Goulden has failed to unearth anything vitally new in his study. It is Divine's opinion that "most of what Goulden covers is familiar. . . . He neglects many important and still unexplored aspects of the war. There is virtually nothing on the home front except for MacArthur's triumphal reception after his dismissal. In vain the reader searches for an analysis of public attitudes, a consideration of the economic impact of the war, or a connection between Korea and McCarthyism. . . . The greatest service of Goulden's book is to remind us of this forgotten war and force us to confront its troublesome strategic issues." In the *New York Times Book Review,* however,

John Curtis Perry commends Goulden's endeavor by noting that "we already have narrative histories of that war . . . , though none recent enough to have exploited the rich lode of hitherto highly classified American documents now available under the Freedom of Information Act. From these new sources Mr. Goulden has much to relate. He has an eye for the vivid anecdote and persuades his reader to turn the page."

Truth Is the First Casualty is Goulden's comprehensive study of the Gulf of Tonkin incidents which sparked the Vietnam War. The author's balanced treatment of this controversial subject is praised by such differing editorial voices as the *Armed Forces Journal* and the *New York Review of Books.* According to *New York Review of Books* contributor Peter Dale Scott, for instance, Goulden has written a "fascinating book . . . . [He] has made good use of his years of experience in Washington. . . . His method is to stick closely to the official documents (above all the neglected Fulbright Committee Hearing of 1968) and first-hand interviews with witnesses the Committee failed to call. . . . The result is devastating. It is now even more clear that the Tonkin Gulf Resolution (in his words) 'contains the fatal taint of deception.' The [Johnson] Administration had withheld much vital information in formulating the simple story of 'unprovoked attack' by which that resolution was pushed through Congress." *Nation* critic Richard J. Walton likewise maintains that Goulden's study is "of the first importance. . . . This book poses [deeply serious questions] about the American system of government in the postwar years." Goulden "has given us vital facts about one of the crucial events, or nonevents, in American history," continues Walton; "future historians will be grateful."

BIOGRAPHICAL/CRITICAL SOURCES:

PERIODICALS

Boston Globe, February 27, 1983.
Globe and Mail (Toronto), April 1, 1989.
Los Angeles Times, August 29, 1982, March 10, 1983, September 12, 1984.
Los Angeles Times Book Review, August 29, 1982, November 13, 1988.
Nation, November 17, 1969, June 26, 1972, November 6, 1972.
New Republic, February 17, 1982, November 22, 1982.
Newsweek, August 20, 1984.
New York Review of Books, January 29, 1970, May 4, 1972.
New York Times, July 27, 1976, February 17, 1983, August 25, 1984.
New York Times Book Review, May 28, 1972, June 20, 1976, June 27, 1976, April 11, 1982, September 12, 1982, September 9, 1984, October 16, 1988.
Saturday Review, November 1, 1969.
Time, August 13, 1984, October 17, 1988.
Times Literary Supplement, July 19, 1985.
Washington Post, September 13, 1988.
Washington Post Book World, August 8, 1976, September 14, 1978, February 21, 1982, August 1, 1982, October 9, 1988.

* * *

GRACE, John Patrick 1942-
(Patrick E. O'Keefe)

PERSONAL: Birth-given name, Patrick Early O'Keefe; name legally changed in 1979; born September 6, 1942, in Chicago, Ill.; son of Fred L. (a high school football coach) and Berenice E. (an elementary school teacher; maiden name, Walsh) O'Keefe; married Jo Spitzer, July 17, 1965 (divorced December 23, 1975);

married Jennifer Lynne Mock (a junior high school French teacher), September 29, 1979; children: (first marriage) Paul Bennet, Bruce Patrick, Sean Vincent, Joy Marie; (second marriage) Gabrielle-Marie. *Education:* Loyola University of Chicago, B.A., 1964; Columbia University, M.S., 1965; University of North Carolina at Chapel Hill, M.A., 1980, Ph.D., 1988. *Politics:* Independent. *Religion:* Roman Catholic.

ADDRESSES: Home—Residence Aurelia, 76, rue d'Etigny, 64000 Pau, France. *Office*—University of Pau, 64000 Pau, France.

CAREER: Associated Press, reporter in Chicago, Ill., 1965-67, editor at foreign desk in New York City, 1967-68; correspondent in Rome, Italy, 1968-72; free-lance writer in Rome, 1972-73; *Greensboro Record,* Greensboro, N.C., health and religion writer, 1973-75; free-lance writer, 1975-78; University of North Carolina at Chapel Hill, teaching assistant in Italian and English, and instructor in continuing education, 1978-86; University of Pau, Pau, France, teacher of Italian, 1986—. Taught journalism at Pro Deo International University, Rome, 1972, and at University of North Carolina at Chapel Hill, 1974-75; radio stringer in Rome for Columbia Broadcasting System (CBS), National Broadcasting Co. (NBC), and Voice of America, 1969-73; reporter for WPIX-TV, New York City, 1973; coordinator of Yokefellow Prison Ministry at Orange County Prison Camp, 1983-86. Guest host of talk show for WGHP-TV, Highpoint, N.C., 1975. Consultant to Institute for Southern Studies, Durham, N.C., 1977. *Military service:* U.S. Army Reserve, 1965-68. U.S. Air Force Reserve, 1968-72.

AWARDS, HONORS: First place award for feature writing from North Carolina Press Association, 1974, for a humorous profile of the massage parlor subculture; Landmark Newspaper Group award, 1975, for sustained excellence in reporting.

WRITINGS:

(Under name Patrick E. O'Keefe) *Jerusalem Lives!,* photographs by Jeff Wayman, Donning, 1976.
(Under name Patrick E. O'Keefe) *Greensboro: A Pictorial History,* photographs by Wayman, Donning, 1977.
Hearing His Voice, Ave Maria Press, 1979.
(With Kim Kollins) *It's Only the Beginning,* Highland Books, 1989.

Contributor to periodicals, including *Atlantic Monthly, Time, Newsweek, PMLA,* and *Bulletin de Litterature Ecclesiastique.*

WORK IN PROGRESS: Two projects.

SIDELIGHTS: John Patrick Grace told *CA:* "A cardinal event in my life was receiving the baptism of the Holy Spirit in May, 1975, and becoming immersed in the charismatic movement, first among Catholics, then more interdenominationally. My own experiences of perceiving God speaking to me through an interior voice and meeting scores of other Christians who claimed similar experiences led me to write *Hearing His Voice.*

"I am interested in cross-cultural fertilizations, especially in the realm of religion. I have participated in many interdenominational gatherings, as well as some within single denominations, and I am intellectually and emotionally caught up in what I consider a move by the Holy Spirit to reunite Christendom.

"*Greensboro: A Pictorial History* and *Jerusalem Lives!* were both projects of special joy because I had to work in tandem with photographer Jeff Wayman, whose own insights into the subjects enriched the text. I highly recommend new writers tackling a pictorial project with a good photographer. The amount of text needed is usually not overwhelming, and you get involved with the visual effect of each page, blending pictures and type."

It's Only the Beginning tells the story of Kim Kollins, American evangelist transplanted to Europe. The book has appeared in French and is scheduled for a German edition as well.

AVOCATIONAL INTERESTS: Travel (including the Mediterranean, the Middle East, and the Orient).

*   *   *

GRAFF, Gerald (Edward) 1937-

PERSONAL: Born June 28, 1937, in Chicago, Ill.; son of David R. and Mollie (Newman) Graff. *Education:* University of Chicago, A.B., 1959; Stanford University, Ph.D., 1963. *Politics:* Left-radical. *Religion:* Jewish.

ADDRESSES: Office—Department of English, Northwestern University, Evanston, Ill. 60201.

CAREER: University of New Mexico, Albuquerque, assistant professor of English, 1963-66; Northwestern University, Evanston, Ill., assistant professor, 1966-70, associate professor, 1970-78, professor of English, 1978—, chairman of department, 1977—.

WRITINGS:

Poetic Statement and Critical Dogma, Northwestern University Press, 1970.
(Editor with Barbara Heldt Monter) W. B. Scott, *Chicago Letter and Other Parodies,* Ardis, 1978.
Literature against Itself: Literary Ideas in Modern Society, University of Chicago Press, 1979.
(Editor with Reginald Gibbons) *Criticism in the University,* Northwestern University Press, 1985.
(Editor with Monter) Scott, *Parodies, Etc. and So Forth,* Northwestern University Press, 1985.
Professing Literature: An Institutional History, University of Chicago Press, 1987.
(Editor with Michael Warner) *The Origins of Literary Studies in America: A Documentary Anthology,* Routledge, Chapman & Hall, 1988.

Contributor to literary journals.

SIDELIGHTS: A professor of English at Northwestern University, Gerald Graff has written about the development of different trends in literary studies. In *Literature against Itself: Literary Ideas in Modern Society,* for instance, Graff argues "that recent critical thought has been undermining belief in the power of language to connect us with the world," Harry Levin summarizes in the *New York Times Book Review.* In his analysis of recent literary criticism, Graff "offers a body of commentary the shrewdness and cogency of which are constantly arresting," notes *Virginia Quarterly Review* contributor N. A. Scott. While Graff's thesis that current critics have trivialized the literature they examine is occasionally "encumbered" by ideology, Scott concludes that *Literature against Itself* "does, nevertheless, in what it principally sets out to do, conduct a wonderfully trenchant and illuminating inquiry."

Similarly, with *Professing Literature: An Institutional History* "Graff attempts to undermine the present organization of the English department by a historical treatment of the institutionalized teaching of literature," observes Stacey D'Erasmo in the *Village Voice.* The author, whom *Times Literary Supplement* contributor Chris Baldick calls "among the most perceptive ob-

servers of modern literary criticism," suggests that "institutional pressures and inertias . . . have generated the complex pattern of hostilities now entrenched between professors of literature," thus fragmenting literary scholarship into fields such as "women's" and "Afro-American" studies. *Professing Literature* "is a solidly researched and convincingly argued work," the critic continues, and while Graff "ventures too infrequently outside the campus, his fascinating account of the literary academy in the United States from the 1840s to the present day avoids inconsequential gossip and keeps its most pressing arguments continuously before the reader's attention." "Graff wants to move these struggles [between literary schools of thought] out of the convention and into the classroom," D'Erasmo notes. *Professing Literature* contains some "lively academic and cultural arguments," Kermit Vanderbilt concludes in *American Literature.* Graff "has given us a stimulating critique of our institutional literary research, criticism, theory, and pedagogy."

BIOGRAPHICAL/CRITICAL SOURCES:

PERIODICALS

American Literature, March, 1988.
New York Times Book Review, August 5, 1979.
Times Literary Supplement, November 6-12, 1987.
Village Voice, May 3, 1988.
Virginia Quarterly Review, autumn, 1979.*

*   *   *

GRAFTON, Sue 1940-

PERSONAL: Born April 24, 1940, in Louisville, Ky.; daughter of Chip W. (an attorney and writer) and Vivian (a high school chemistry teacher; maiden name, Harnsberger) Grafton; married third husband Steven F. Humphrey (a professor of philosophy), October 1, 1978; children: (first marriage) Lee Flood Filges; (second marriage) Jay Schmidt, Jamie Schmidt. *Education:* University of Louisville, B.A., 1961.

ADDRESSES: Home—1084 Garcia Rd., Santa Barbara, Calif. 93103. *Agent*—Molly Friedrich, Aaron Priest Agency, 122 East 42nd St., New York, N.Y. 10168.

CAREER: Screenwriter and author.

AWARDS, HONORS: Christopher Award, 1979, for teleplay "Walking through the Fire"; Mysterious Stranger Award, Cloak and Clue Society, 1982-83, for *"A" Is for Alibi;* Shamus Award for best hardcover private eye novel, Private Eye Writers of America, and Anthony Award for best hardcover mystery, Mystery Readers of America, both 1985, both for *"B" Is for Burglar;* Macavity Award for best short story, and Anthony Award, both 1986, both for "The Parker Shotgun"; Edgar Award nomination, Mystery Writers of America, 1986, for teleplay "Love on the Run"; Anthony Award, 1987, for *"C" Is for Corpse.*

WRITINGS:

Keziah Dane, Macmillan, 1967.
The Lolly-Madonna War (also see below), P. Owen, 1969.
"A" Is For Alibi (Mystery Guild main selection), Holt, 1982.
"B" Is for Burglar (Mystery Guild main selection), Holt, 1985.
"C" Is for Corpse (Mystery Guild main selection), Holt, 1986.
"D" Is for Deadbeat, Holt, 1987.
"E" Is for Evidence, Holt, 1988.
"F" Is for Fugitive, Holt, 1989.
"G" Is for Gumshoe, in press.

SCREENPLAYS

(With Rodney Carr-Smith) "Lolly-Madonna XXX" (motion picture screenplay adapted from her novel, *The Lolly-Madonna War*), Metro-Goldwyn-Mayer, 1973.

"Walking through the Fire" (adapted from the novel by Laurel Lee), Columbia Broadcasting Corp. (CBS-TV), April, 1979.

"Sex and the Single Parent" (adapted from the book by Jane Adams), CBS-TV, October, 1979.

"Nurse" (adapted from the book by Peggy Anderson), CBS-TV, April, 1980.

"Mark, I Love You" (adapted from the book by Hal Painter), CBS-TV, December, 1980.

(With husband, Steven F. Humphrey) "A Caribbean Mystery" (adapted from the novel by Agatha Christie), CBS-TV, March, 1983.

(With Humphrey and Robert Aller) "A Killer in the Family," American Broadcasting Co. (ABC-TV), October, 1983.

(With Humphrey and Robert Malcolm Young) "Sparkling Cyanide" (adapted from the novel by Agatha Christie), CBS-TV, November, 1983.

(With Humphrey) "Love on the Run," National Broadcasting Co. (NBC-TV), October, 1985.

(With Humphrey) "Tonight's the Night," ABC-TV, February, 1987.

OTHER

(Contributor) *Mean Streets* (includes "The Parker Shotgun"), Mysterious Press, 1986.

Also author, with Humphrey, of pilot for CBS television series, "Seven Brides for Seven Brothers," first broadcast September, 1982. Contributor of scripts to television series, including "Rhoda," 1975.

SIDELIGHTS: Sue Grafton, say Andrea Chambers and David Hutchings in *People* magazine, "is perhaps the best of the new breed of female mystery writers, who are considered the hottest segment of the market." In her mystery stories featuring California private investigator Kinsey Millhone, Grafton has chosen to feature a heroine, rather than the traditional male hero. Nonetheless, as Deirdre Donahue observes in *USA Today,* "Grafton draws on elements of the classic private-eye genre." In Kinsey Millhone, David Lehman of *Newsweek* tells prospective readers, "you'll find a thoroughly up-to-date, feminine version of Philip Marlowe, Raymond Chandler's hard-boiled hero."

The hard-boiled detective story traditionally features a male protagonist and a lot of action—gunplay, bloodshed, and general mayhem. Heroes such as Dashiell Hammett's Sam Spade (in *The Maltese Falcon*), Raymond Chandler's Marlowe (in *The Big Sleep*), and Ross MacDonald's Lew Archer (in *The Moving Target*) defined masculinity for a generation of readers, with their "loner" mentalities, and their sensitivity to the profound difference between the city streets and the normal world. Yet Grafton's Kinsey Millhone is as popular as any of her precursors, male or female. *New York Times Book Review* contributor Vincent Patrick suggests that the reason behind her popularity is that she is, in fact, a traditional hero: "Chandler's concept of a detective hero was that 'he must be the best man in his world, and a good enough man for any world.' Gender aside, Kinsey fills that prescription perfectly."

Other than establishing a heroine in a traditionally male role, critics suggest that Grafton has left the framework of the hard-boiled detective story intact. Ed Weiner writes in the *New York Times Book Review* that neither Grafton nor any of her peers "have gone so far as to redefine the genre. They play it fairly safe and conventional. But in their work there is thankfully little of the macho posturing and luggish rogue beefcake found so often in the male versions, no Hemingwayesque mine-is-bigger-than-yours competitive literary swaggering." Instead, Weiner explains, "she has successfully replaced the raw, masculine-fantasy brutality and gore of the [Robert] Parkers and [Jonathan] Valins and [Elmore] Leonards with heart-pounding, totally mesmerizing suspense."

"When I decided to do mysteries," Grafton explains to Bruce Taylor in an interview in the *Armchair Detective,* "I chose the classic private eye genre because I like playing hardball with the boys. I despise gender-segregated events of any kind." Part of Kinsey's appeal lies in Grafton's concept of her character, whom she sees as "a stripped-down version of me," she tells Taylor. "She's the person I would have been had I not married young and had children. She'll always be thinner and younger and braver, the lucky so-and-so. Her biography is different, but our sensibilities are identical. At the core, we're the same. . . . Because of Kinsey, I get to lead two lives—hers and mine. Sometimes I'm not sure which I prefer."

BIOGRAPHICAL/CRITICAL SOURCES:

PERIODICALS

Armchair Detective, winter, 1989.
Globe and Mail (Toronto), June 20, 1987, May 21, 1988.
Newsweek, June 7, 1982, June 9, 1986.
New York Times Book Review, May 23, 1982, May 1, 1988, May 21, 1989.
People, July 10, 1989.
USA Today, July 27, 1989.
Washington Post Book World, May 18, 1986, June 21, 1987.

* * *

GRAYSON, Richard (A.) 1951-

PERSONAL: Born June 4, 1951, in Brooklyn, N.Y.; son of Daniel (a businessman) and Marilyn (a nutritionist; maiden name, Sarrett) Grayson. *Education:* Brooklyn College of the City University of New York, B.A., 1973, M.F.A., 1976; Richmond College of the City University of New York, M.A., 1975.

ADDRESSES: Home—2001 Southwest 98 Ter., Ft. Lauderdale, Fla. 33324. *Office*—350 West 85th St. #44, New York, N.Y. 10024.

CAREER: Fiction Collective, Brooklyn, N.Y., editorial assistant, 1975-77; Long Island University, Brooklyn, lecturer in English, 1975-78; City University of New York, lecturer in English at Kingsborough Community College, Brooklyn, 1978-81, Brooklyn College, Brooklyn, 1979-81, John Jay College of Criminal Justice, 1984-86, and Baruch College, 1986-87; Broward Community College, Fort Lauderdale, Fla., instructor in English, 1981-83; Florida International College, Miami, instructor in computer education, 1986—; Compu Learn Systems, Ft. Lauderdale, Fla., director of training, 1986—. Writer in residence, Rockland Center for the Arts, West Nyack, N.Y., 1988-89.

MEMBER: PEN, Association of Computer Educators, Authors Guild, Authors League of America, Associated Writing Programs, Mensa, Brooklyn College Alumni Association (member of board of directors, 1973-81), Phi Beta Kappa.

AWARDS, HONORS: Ottillie Grebanier Drama Award, Brooklyn College, 1973; scholarships from National Arts Club, 1977, to study at Bread Loaf Writer's Conference, and from Santa Cruz Writing Conference, 1978; fellowships from Virginia Center for the Creative Arts, 1979 and 1981, MacDowell Colony, 1980 and 1987, Florida Arts Council, 1982 and 1988, and Millay Colony for the Arts, 1984; fellowship in residence, Center for Mark Twain Studies, Elmira College, 1990.

WRITINGS:

Disjointed Fictions, X Archives, 1978.
With Hitler in New York and Other Stories, Taplinger, 1979.
Lincoln's Doctor's Dog and Other Stories, White Ewe, 1982.
Eating at Arby's: The South Florida Stories (pamphlet), Grinning Idiot Press, 1982.
I Brake for Delmore Schwartz, Zephyr Press, 1983.
The Greatest Short Story That Absolutely Ever Was, Lowlands, 1989.
Narcissism and Me, Mule & Mule, 1990.

Contributor of short stories to more than 165 periodicals, including *Epoch, Texas Quarterly, Confrontation, Shenandoah, Carleton Miscellany,* and *Transatlantic Review;* contributor of nonfiction to *People, Miami News, Palm Beach Post, New York Post,* and many other periodicals. Humor columnist, *Hollywood Sun-Tattler,* Hollywood, Fla., 1986-87.

WORK IN PROGRESS: A collection of related short stories.

SIDELIGHTS: Unconventional, imaginative, and possessed of an offbeat sense of humor, Richard Grayson is the author of several collections of short stories that examine life from a perspective many critics find refreshingly different. Originally published in a variety of small magazines, his stories "are full of insanity, nutty therapists, cancerous relatives, broken homes, fiction workshops, youthful theatricals at Catskill bungalow colonies and the morbid wizardry of telephone-answering machines," notes Ivan Gold in the *New York Times Book Review.* Some also feature such unlikely "characters" as the voice of the cold that "assassinated" President William Henry Harrison in 1841 and Sparky, Abraham Lincoln's doctor's puppy, who grows up to become a successful politician and lecturer (the latter story was inspired by an article Grayson once read that stated most recent best-sellers have dealt with presidents, diseases, or animals—hence, "Lincoln's Doctor's Dog"). As Mark Bernheim observes in *Israel Today,* "Grayson is able to create a full range of masks from behind which the artist peers out to make his criticisms of artificial modern life."

Commenting in *Best Sellers,* Nicholas J. Loprete, Jr., also asserts that Grayson's stories "display a versatility which commands attention. [The author] can parody human excess and human frailty, parent-child relationships, and recreate a 1960's scene with poignancy. He is serious and comic, charming, given to outrageous puns, and a sharp-eyed observer of and participant in Life's absurdities."

In short, declares Lynne Gagnon in the *Ventura County News,* "Richard Grayson gets the prize for making us laugh about the ridiculous insaneness surrounding our lives. But the award is two-fold; he also forces us to examine people and what they do to us. And more importantly what we do to them."

Richard Grayson himself once told *CA:* "Writing has been the primary way I've defined myself; at first it was therapy, but now, I hope, it has become something more. I see the writer's first job as giving the lowdown on himself, and through himself, on humanity. As I reluctantly leave the longest adolescence in history, I find myself happily becoming less self-conscious, more patient. I would like to avoid becoming pompous, but I'm afraid statements like these are among the mine fields on the road to absurd

self-importance. I have a lot to learn about writing (and other things)."

BIOGRAPHICAL/CRITICAL SOURCES:

BOOKS

Contemporary Literary Criticism, Volume 38, Gale, 1986.

PERIODICALS

Aspect, Number 72/73, 1979.
Athens Daily News, July 18, 1983.
Best Sellers, May, 1982.
Des Moines Register, October 21, 1983.
Israel Today, May 8, 1983.
Kings Courier, August, 1978.
Los Angeles Times, July 17, 1979.
Miami News, April 13, 1984.
New York Times Book Review, August 14, 1983.
Orlando Sentinel, April 18, 1982, January 14, 1984.
USA Today, October 15, 1983.
Ventura County News, February 4, 1980.

*   *   *

GREGER, Debora 1949-

PERSONAL: Born August 16, 1949, in Walsenberg, Colo. *Education:* Attended Whitman College, 1967-68; University of Washington, Seattle, B.A., 1971; University of Iowa, M.F.A., 1974.

CAREER: George Mason University, Fairfax, Va., assistant professor of English, 1977-78; California State University, Chico, assistant professor of English, 1978-80; University of Florida, Gainesville, associate professor of English, 1985—; writer. Distinguished poet in residence at Wichita State University, 1983; visiting assistant professor, Department of English, Ohio University, 1988. In residence at MacDowell Colony, 1976, 1977, and 1978, Millay Colony for the Arts, 1976, and Yaddo, 1976 and 1977.

AWARDS, HONORS: Poetry fellowship from Fine Arts Work Center (Provincetown, Mass.), 1975-77; Grolier Poetry Award, 1976; award from *Nation,* 1977; grant from National Endowment for the Arts, 1978; fellowship from Mary Ingraham Bunting Institute at Radcliffe College, 1980-81; grant from Ingram Merrill Foundation, 1981; Amy Lowell Traveling Poetry Scholar fellowship, 1982-83; grant from National Endowment for the Arts, 1985; grant from Guggenheim Foundation, 1987; Peter I. B. Lavan Younger Poets Award, 1987.

WRITINGS:

Provisional Landscapes (prints), Penumbra Press, 1974.
Movable Islands (poetry), Princeton University Press, 1980.
Cartography (poetry), Penumbra Press, 1980.
Normal Street (poetry chapbook), Sea Pen Press, 1983.
Blank Country (poetry chapbook), Meadow Press, 1985.
And (poetry), Princeton University Press, 1986.
The 1,002nd Night (poetry), Princeton University Press, 1990.

Contributor of poems to periodicals, including *New Yorker, Yale Review,* and *Southwest Review.*

WORK IN PROGRESS: A new book of poems.

BIOGRAPHICAL/CRITICAL SOURCES:

PERIODICALS

American Poetry Review, January/February, 1982.
New York Times Book Review, September 28, 1986.

Virginia Quarterly Review, autumn, 1980.

* * *

GRIFFITHS, Michael C(ompton) 1928-

PERSONAL: Born April 7, 1928, in Cardiff, Wales; son of Charles Idris Ewart and Myfanwy (Jones) Griffiths; married Valerie Kipping (a theological teacher), July 21, 1956; children: John Anderson, Elizabeth Bronwen, Nigel Timothy, Stephen Glyndwr. *Education:* Peterhouse College, Cambridge, B.A., 1952; Ridley Hall, Cambridge, M.A., 1954. *Religion:* Christian.

ADDRESSES: Home—8, Ellis Ave., Onslow Village, Guildford, Surrey GU2 5SR, England.

CAREER: Traveling secretary, Inter-Varsity Fellowship, 1954-57; Overseas Missionary Fellowship, missionary in Japan, 1958-68, general director in Singapore, 1969-80; London Bible College, Middlesex, England, principal, 1980-89. *Military service:* Royal Army Medical Corps, 1947-49; became corporal.

AWARDS, HONORS: D.D., Wheaton College, 1974.

WRITINGS:

Consistent Christianity, Inter-Varsity Press, 1960.
Christian Assurance, Inter-Varsity Press, 1962.
Take My Life, Inter-Varsity Press, 1967.
Give up Small Ambitions, Inter-Varsity Press, 1970.
Three Men Filled with Spirit, Overseas Missionary Fellowship, 1970.
Take off Your Shoes, Overseas Missionary Fellowship, 1971.
Cinderella with Amnesia, Inter-Varsity Press, 1975.
Changing Asia, Lion Publishing, 1977.
Cinderella's Betrothal Gifts, Overseas Missionary Fellowship, 1978.
Shaking the Sleeping Beauty, Inter-Varsity Press, 1980.
What on Earth Are You Doing?, Inter-Varsity Press, 1983.
The Example of Jesus, Hodder & Stoughton, 1985.
Saving Grace, MARC, 1986.
God Is Great, God Is Good, Navpress, 1987.
Get Your Act Together, Cinderella, Inter-Varsity Press, 1989.

Contributor to journals and newspapers.

WORK IN PROGRESS: Several books.

SIDELIGHTS: Michael C. Griffiths has travelled widely in the Far East, Europe, Australia, New Zealand, South Africa, and North America. He speaks Japanese fairly well and knows some German. His books have been translated into German, Chinese, Japanese, Indonesian, Vietnamese, Urdu, French, Portuguese, Dutch, Swedish, Hungarian, and Korean.

AVOCATIONAL INTERESTS: Mountains, fishing, growing alpine plants and tropical orchids.

* * *

GRIPARI, Pierre 1925-

PERSONAL: Born January 7, 1925, in Paris, France. *Politics:* Neo-fascist. *Religion:* Epicurism.

CAREER: Writer. Has worked as a farm hand, dance hall pianist, and at clerical jobs.

WRITINGS:

Lieutenant Tenant (three-act comedy; based on Youri Tynianov's short story, "Sous Lieutenant Kije"), [Paris], 1962.
Pierrot la lune, La Table Ronde, 1963.

L'Incroyable equipee de Phosphore Noloc et de ses compagnons (novel), La Table Ronde, 1964.
Diable, Dieu et autres contes de menterie, La Table Ronde, 1965.
Contes de la rue Broca (juvenile), La Table Ronde, 1967, translation in part by Doriane Grutman published as *Tales of the Rue Broca,* Bobbs-Merrill, 1969.
La Vie, la mort et la resurrection de Socrate-Marie Gripotard (novel), La Table Ronde, 1968.
L'arriere monde (short stories), Editions Robert Morel, 1972.
Gueule d'Aminche, Editions Robert Morel, 1973.
Le Solilesse (poems), L'Age d'homme, 1975.
Frere Gaucher ou le voyage en Chine (novel), L'Age d'homme, 1975.
Reveries d'un Martien en exil (short stories), L'Age d'homme, 1976.
Pedigree du vampire, L'Age d'homme, 1977.
Pieces enfantines, L'Age d'homme, 1977.
Nanasse et Gigantet: Conte en forme d'echelle, Grasset, 1977.
Vies paralleles de Roman Branchu, L'Age d'homme, 1978.
Cafe-theatre, L'Age d'homme, 1979.
Texas Jim, ou, Le coboye triste, Ecole des Loisirs, 1980.
Le marchand de fessees, Grasset, 1980.
L'Evangile du rien, L'Age d'homme, 1980.
Critique et autocritique, L'Age d'homme, 1981.
Enter de poche, L'Age d'homme, 1981.
Paraboles et fariboles, L'Age d'homme, 1981.
Pieces mystiques, L'Age d'homme, 1982.
Pieces poetiques, L'Age d'homme, 1982.
Petrouille du conte, L'Age d'homme, 1983.
Les contes de la Folie Metricourt, Grasset, 1983.
Du rire et de L'horreur, Julliard, 1984.
Gueule d'Aminche, L'Age d'homme, 1984.
Jean-Yves a qui rien n'arrive, Grasset-Jeunesse, 1985.
Gripari, mode d'emploi, L'Age d'homme, 1985.
Adaptations theatales, L'Age d'homme, 1985.
Le septieme lot, L'Age d'homme, 1986.*

* * *

GROSS, Joel 1951-

PERSONAL: Born March 22, 1951, in New York, N.Y.; son of David Charles (an editor) and Esther (Pearl) Gross; married Linda Sanders, May, 1983. *Education:* Queens College of the City University of New York, B.A. (with high honors in English), 1971; Columbia University, M.A. (with high honors), 1973. *Politics:* Liberal Democrat. *Religion:* Jewish.

ADDRESSES: Home—165 East 66th St., New York, N.Y. 10021.

CAREER: Writer.

WRITINGS:

Bubble's Shadow (novel), Crown, 1970.
The Young Man Who Wrote Soap Operas (novel), Scribner, 1975.
1407 Broadway (novel), Seaview, 1978.
The Books of Rachel (novel), Seaview, 1979.
Maura's Dream (novel), Seaview, 1981.
Home of the Brave (novel), Seaview, 1982.
This Year in Jerusalem (novel), Putnam, 1983.
The Lives of Rachel (novel; Book-of-the-Month Club alternate), New American Library, 1984.
"Clean Sweep" (play), first produced Off-Broadway at the Perry Street Theatre in New York City, February 10, 1984.
"Haven" (play), first produced Off-Broadway at South Street Theater, 1985.
Spirit in the Flesh (novel), New American Library, 1986.

Sarah (novel), Morrow, 1987.
"Mesmer" (play), first produced at Williamstown Theatre Festival, 1988.

SIDELIGHTS: Joel Gross began writing when he was nineteen. More than three million copies of his bestselling paperback novels are in print.

*   *   *

GUGLIOTTA, Bobette   1918-
(Bobette Bibo)

PERSONAL: Surname is pronounced Gu-*lyot*-ta; born November 8, 1918, in Chicago, Ill.; daughter of Irving M. (a music composer) and Aline (Waite) Bibo; married Guy Frank Gugliotta (a naval officer and marine engineer), June 2, 1940; children: Guy Bibo. *Education:* Attended Stanford University, University of Southern California, and University of California, Los Angeles.

ADDRESSES: Home—1204 Sharon Heights Dr., Menlo Park, Calif. 94025.

CAREER: Foothill International League, Los Altos Hills, Calif., founder and first chairman, 1962-65; Young Women's Christian Association (YWCA), Honolulu, Hawaii, master of ceremonies on beach club radio program, 1965-66; Recording for the Blind, Palo Alto, Calif., reader and auxiliary member, 1969—. Founded University of Hawaii foreign student program, 1965-66.

MEMBER: Authors Guild, Authors League of America.

WRITINGS:

Nolle Smith: Cowboy, Engineer, Statesman, Dodd, 1971.
Katzimo, Mysterious Mesa, Dodd, 1974.
(Contributor under name Bobette Bibo) *Mickey Mouse: Fifty Happy Years,* Crown, 1977.
Pigboat 39: An American Sub Goes to War, University Press of Kentucky, 1984.
Women of Mexico: The Consecrated and the Commoners, Floricanto Press, 1989.

(Contributor) *Houghton Mifflin Literary Readers, Book Five,* Houghton, 1989.

Contributor to *Storyboard.*

WORK IN PROGRESS: Smears of Blood: The Ordeal of Dr. Albert Abrams, a seminal biography of a maligned genius of medicine.

SIDELIGHTS: Bobette Gugliotta told *CA:* "I wrote my first story (about Mickey Mouse) at age eleven for Walt Disney. Upon return from three years residence in Ecuador, I ran across a volume entitled *Mickey Mouse: Fifty Happy Years.* My work, 'The Story of Mickey Mouse,' was reprinted under my maiden name Bobette Bibo. It was a pleasure to know I'd gone on writing and that a ten year publication drought had broken with [my] current book, *Pigboat 39.* But it is worth the stamina and effort when you might be doing other fascinating things with live people? When you're young, you're sure it's worth any amount of toil. As you get older, you begin to wonder. But by then—you're hooked."

More recently, she added, "The growing power of publishers over writers, and their indifference to the plight of writers, is cause for concern. Magazines used to pay upon acceptance. Now, most of them pay upon publication. They hold your manuscript as long as they choose. They make interest on your money while you wait and wait. And if you sell a book, once it's in print, you have to suspend writing to contact bookstores, TV shows, newspapers, etc.—that is, if you want people to buy your book. The publisher won't do it except for the ten best sellers. Time and tunnel-vision are of the utmost importance to an author's project. How can you hawk your wares and do serious writing at the same time?"

BIOGRAPHICAL/CRITICAL SOURCES:

PERIODICALS

Los Altos Town Crier, December 29, 1971.
Palo Alto Times, January 11, 1972.

H

HADLEY, Charles D(avid), Jr. 1942-

PERSONAL: Born June 5, 1942, in Springfield, Mass.; son of Charles David (a handgun repair expert) and Caroline (Filip) Hadley; divorced; children: Nathaniel. *Education:* University of Massachusetts, B.A., 1964, M.A., 1967; University of Connecticut, Ph.D., 1971.

ADDRESSES: Home—3117 Constance St., New Orleans, La. 70115. *Office*—Department of Political Science, University of New Orleans, New Orleans, La. 70148.

CAREER: University of New Orleans, New Orleans, La., instructor, 1970-71, assistant professor, 1971-74, associate professor, 1974-86, professor of political science, 1986—, assistant to chairman of Department of Political Science, 1971-75, coordinator of graduate studies, 1975-76, assistant dean of College of Liberal Arts, 1976-79, director of internship program, 1982—, campus coordinator of University of New Orleans-City Hall internship program, 1982-88, university internship coordinator and liaison for Washington Center, 1988—. University of Connecticut, Institute for Social Inquiry, research fellow, summer, 1972, visiting assistant professor, 1973-74. Visiting professor, Institut fuer Politikwissenschaft, Universitaet Innsbruck, Austria, 1987. Member of Textbook Adoption Committee, Department of Education for State of Louisiana, 1985. Consultant.

MEMBER: American Political Science Association (special representative, 1982-85), Southern Political Science Association (member of executive council, 1978-81, vice president, 1989-90), Louisiana Political Science Association, Committee for Party Renewal (member of executive committee, 1984—), Irish Channel Neighborhood Association (member of board of directors, 1976-78, 1981, vice president, 1978, 1982, president, 1983-85), Preservation Resource Center (member of neighborhood council, 1981—), Children's Community, Inc. (member of board of directors, 1989—), Council for International Visitors of Greater New Orleans (member, 1988—, member of board of directors, 1989—), Pi Sigma Alpha, Omicron Delta Kappa (faculty adviser of University of New Orleans Circle).

AWARDS, HONORS: Younger Humanist Fellowship, National Endowment for the Humanities, 1973.

WRITINGS:

(With Everett C. Ladd, Jr.) *Political Parties and Political Issues: Patterns in Differentiation since the New Deal,* Sage Publications, 1973.

(With Ladd) *Transformations of the American Party System: Political Coalitions from the New Deal to the 1970s,* Norton, 1975, 2nd edition, 1978.

(Contributor) Richard G. Braungart, editor, *Society and Politics,* Prentice-Hall, 1976.

(Contributor) Robert P. Steed, Laurence W. Moreland, and Tod A. Baker, editors, *Party Politics in the South,* Praeger, 1980.

(Contributor) Edward V. Heck and Alan T. Leonhard, editors, *Political Ideas and Institutions,* Kendall/Hunt, 1983.

(Contributor) Steed, Moreland, and Baker, editors, *The 1984 Presidential Election in the South,* Praeger, 1986.

(Contributor) Moreland, Baker, and Steed, editors, *Blacks in Southern Politics,* 1987.

(With Harold W. Stanley) *The Southern Presidential Primary: The Democratic Path to the Presidency?* (monograph), University of Rochester, 1987.

(With Stanley) *Super Tuesday 1988: Regional Results, National Implications* (monograph), University of Rochester, 1989.

(Contributor) Moreland, Baker, and Steed, editors, *The 1988 Presidential Election in the South,* Praeger, 1990.

(Editor with Baker, Moreland, and Steed; contributor with Stanley) *Political Parties in the Southern States: Party Activists and Partisan Coalitions,* Praeger, 1990.

Works have appeared in anthologies, including *Society and Politics,* 1976, *Political Opinion and Behavior,* 1976, and *National Government and Policy in the United States,* 1977. Contributor to *Dictionary of American History.* Contributor of articles and reviews to political science and sociology journals, including *Journal of Political Science, American Politics Quarterly,* and *Dialogue. Journal of Politics,* news and notes editor, 1974-78, member of editorial board, 1977-78.

WORK IN PROGRESS: Louisiana Government and Politics: Development, Structure, and Policy, with Joseph G. Tregle and Ralph E. Thayer, for University of Nebraska Press; "The Impact of Party ID and Election System in Presidential Primaries," with Stanley; "Super Tuesday Surveys: Insights and Hindsights," with Stanley; and "The Continued Capture of the Presidential Selection Process: Lessons of National Party Rules and Political Participation."

SIDELIGHTS: Charles D. Hadley, Jr., once told *CA:* "My research and writing is in the broader context of political change and its impact on the political system demographic, partisan, and attitudinal. It explores the question of future political party dominance at both the national and regional (especially the South and Louisiana) levels. Having lived in the South and Louisiana since 1970, I continue to be more interested in the impact of social and attitudinal change on the politics of those areas, especially the gradual evolution of an eventually competitive Republican Party in what was once the Solid South (Democratic) and of an increasingly liberal Democratic Party. Moreover, Louisiana significantly weakened its political party system with the implementation of an open elections system which negates the use of political party labels on the ballot and in campaigning for office; the law runs counter to the national trend to strengthen political parties.

"The research is a natural outgrowth of my belief in a strong two-party system and of political party involvement in my youth. Election to the Westfield (Massachusetts) Republican City Committee, which I represented in two Massachusetts Republican Conventions, has also had an impact on my research as has a change in partisan affiliation and participation in a recent Louisiana Democratic Convention. An invitation to be on the advisory committee and eventually become part of the inner circle (reelection campaign Steering Committee) of Louisiana State Representative Mary Landrieu led to my active involvement in Louisiana Democratic politics."

Hadley later added: "My continued active involvement in Louisiana politics gives me a better understanding of political change, a perspective which improves my writing."

*   *   *

HAINES, Gail Kay 1943-

PERSONAL: Born March 15, 1943, in Mt. Vernon, Ill.; daughter of Samuel Glen and Audrey (Goin) Beekman; married Michael Philip Haines (an oral surgeon), May 8, 1964; children: David Michael, Cindy Lynn. *Education:* Washington University, St. Louis, Mo., A.B., 1965.

ADDRESSES: Home—4145 Lorna Ct. S.E., Olympia, Wash. 98503.

CAREER: Mallinckrodt Chemical Works, St. Louis, Mo., analytical chemist, 1965-66; writer, 1969—.

AWARDS, HONORS: Science Writing Award, American Institute of Physics, and Governor's Writers Award, Washington State, both 1989, both for *Micromysteries: Stories of Scientific Investigation.*

WRITINGS:

JUVENILES

The Elements, F. Watts, 1972.
Fire, Morrow, 1975.
Explosives, Morrow, 1976.
Supercold/Superhot, F. Watts, 1976.
What Makes A Lemon Sour?, Morrow, 1977.
Brainpower, F. Watts, 1978.
Natural and Synthetic Poisons, Morrow, 1979.
Cancer, F. Watts, 1980.
Baking in a Box, Cooking on a Can, Morrow, 1981.
Test Tube Mysteries, Putnam, 1982.
The Great Nuclear Power Debate, Putnam, 1985.
Which Way Is Up?, Atheneum, 1986.
Micromysteries: Stories of Scientific Investigation, Putnam, 1988.

SIDELIGHTS: Gail Kay Haines told *CA:* "I have always been fascinated by science, especially reading and writing about it. Chemistry is my favorite, because it is the science I know the most about, but writing books keeps me learning all kinds of things from up-to-minute research to ancient history. I think children want more than just the basic science information they get in school—they want to know what is going on today and what the future holds, and that is what other juvenile nonfiction writers and I try to explore."

*   *   *

HALL, Elizabeth 1929-

PERSONAL: Born September 17, 1929, in Bakersfield, Calif.; daughter of Edward Earl (an accountant) and Ethel Mae (Butner) Hall; married Freddie Roy Mason, 1946 (divorced, 1966); married Scott O'Dell, 1967 (died, 1989); children: Susan Elizabeth Anderson, David Frederic Mason. *Education:* Bakersfield College, A.A., 1947; Fresno State College (now California State University, Fresno), B A., 1964.

ADDRESSES: Home—Waccabuc, N.Y. *Agent*—McIntosh & Otis, Inc., 310 Madison Ave., New York, N.Y. 10017.

CAREER: Shafter Branch Library, Shafter, Calif., librarian, 1958-66; University of California, Irvine, librarian, 1966-67; *Psychology Today,* Del Mar, Calif., associate editor, 1967-68, assistant managing editor, 1968-72, managing editor, 1972—75, managing editor in New York City, 1975-76; Harcourt Brace Jovanovich, Inc., New York City, editor of *Human Nature* (magazine), 1976-79; writer and behavioral science journalist, 1979—.

MEMBER: International Society on Infant Studies, American Association for the Advancement of Science, Society for Research in Child Development, Gerontological Society, Textbook Author's Association, Authors Guild.

AWARDS, HONORS: National Media Award honorable mention from American Psychological Foundation, 1974, for *Why We Do What We Do,* and 1976, for *From Pigeons to People.*

WRITINGS:

Voltaire's Micromegas, Golden Gate, 1967.
Phoebe Snow, Houghton, 1968.
Stand Up, Lucy!, Houghton, 1971.
Why We Do What We Do: A Look at Psychology, Houghton, 1973.
From Pigeons to People: A Look at Behavior Shaping, Houghton, 1975.
(Editor) *Developmental Psychology Today,* 2nd edition (Hall was not associated with earlier edition), CRM Books, 1975, 3rd edition (with Robert E. Schell), 1979, 5th edition (with Lois Hoffman and Scott Paris), Random House, 1988.
Possible Impossibilities: A Look at Parapsychology, Houghton, 1977.
(With Michael Lamb and Marion Perlmutter) *Child Psychology Today,* Random House, 1982, 2nd edition, 1986.
(Editor) *Psychology Today: An Introduction,* 5th edition (Hall was not associated with earlier editions), Random House, 1982, 7th edition, 1990.
(With Ray Rosen) *Sexuality,* Random House, 1984.
(With Perlmutter) *Adult Development and Aging,* Wiley, 1985, 2nd edition, 1990.
(Contributor) Carol Tavris, editor, *Everywoman's Emotional Wellbeing,* Doubleday, 1986.
(Editor) *Principles of Psychology Today,* Random House, 1987.
(With John Kotre) *Seasons of Life,* Little, Brown, 1990.

FILMS WITH PETER DRUCKER

(And John Humble) "The Manager as Entrepreneur," Bureau of National Affairs Films, 1971.

(And Vermont Royster) "Tomorrow's Customs," Bureau of National Affairs Films, 1971.

(And Charles De Carlo) "The Future of Technology," Bureau of National Affairs Films, 1971.

(And De Carlo) "Coping with Technological Change," Bureau of National Affairs Films, 1971.

(And Jerry Wurf) "Who's Gonna Collect the Garbage?," Bureau of National Affairs Films, 1971.

(And Robert Hansberger) "Social Needs as Business Opportunities," Bureau of National Affairs Films, 1971.

(And Hansberger) "Pollution Control-The Hard Decision," Bureau of National Affairs Films, 1971.

(And Dan Seymour) "The Multinational Corporation," Bureau of National Affairs Films, 1971.

(And Humble) "The Innovative Organization," Bureau of National Affairs Films, 1971.

FILMS WITH B. F. SKINNER

"A Conversation with B. F. Skinner," CRM Films, 1972.
"Token Economy: Behaviorism Applied," CRM Films, 1972.
"Business, Behaviorism and the Bottom Line," CRM Films, 1972.

WORK IN PROGRESS: Thunder Rolling in the Mountain, in collaboration with late husband Scott O'Dell.

* * *

HALL, N(orman) John 1933-

PERSONAL: Born January 1, 1933, in Orange, N.J.; son of Norman C. and Lucille (Hertlein) Hall; married Marianne E. Gsell, October 13, 1968; children: Jonathan. *Education:* Seton Hall University, A.B., 1955, M.A., 1967; New York University, Ph.D., 1970.

ADDRESSES: Home—44 West 10th St., New York, N.Y. 10011. *Office*—Department of English, Bronx Community College of the City University of New York, Bronx, N.Y. 10453.

CAREER: New York University, New York City, part-time lecturer in English, 1967-70; Bronx Community College of the City University of New York, Bronx, N.Y., assistant professor, 1970-75, associate professor, 1975-78, professor of English, 1978—; Graduate School and University Center of the City University of New York, New York City, professor, 1980—; City University of New York, New York City, distinguished professor, 1983—. Part-time lecturer in English, New School for Social Research, 1970-74.

MEMBER: Modern Language Association of America.

AWARDS, HONORS: Research awards from American Council of Learned Societies, 1973, and City University of New York; fellowships from National Endowment for the Humanities, 1974, Guggenheim Foundation, 1977 and 1984, and American Council of Learned Societies, 1980.

WRITINGS:

(Editor) Anthony Trollope, *The New Zealander,* Clarendon Press, 1972.
Salmagundi: Byron, Allegra, and the Trollope Family, Beta Phi Mu, 1975.
Trollope and His Illustrators, Macmillan (London), 1980.
(Editor) *The Trollope Critics,* Macmillan (London), 1981.

(General editor) *Selected Works of Anthony Trollope,* 62 volumes, Arno Press, 1981.
(Editor) *The Letters of Anthony Trollope,* Volume 1: *1835-1870,* Volume 2: *1871-1882,* Stanford University Press, 1983.
(Editor) Max Beerbohm, *The Illustrated Zuleika Dobson,* Yale University Press, 1985.
(Editor) Beerbohm, *Rossetti and His Circle,* new and enlarged edition, Yale University Press, 1987.

Contributor to literature journals.

WORK IN PROGRESS: Trollope: A Biography, for Clarendon.

* * *

HALLIWELL, David (William) 1936-
(Johnson Arms)

PERSONAL: Born July 31, 1936, in Brighouse, Yorkshire, England; son of Herbert (a managing director of a textile firm) and Ethel (Spencer) Halliwell. *Education:* Attended Huddersfield College of Art, 1953-59; Royal Academy of Dramatic Art, diploma, 1961. *Politics:* Libertarian Socialist.

ADDRESSES: Home—8 Crawborough Villas, Charlbury, Oxford OX7 3TS, England. *Agent*—Vernon Conway, 19 London St., London W2 1HL, England.

CAREER: Actor in Nottingham, England, 1962, Stoke-on-Trent, England, 1962-63, and London, England, 1963-67; Quipu Productions, London, co-founder and director, 1966-76; director of plays in London at New Arts Theatre, 1966-67, Little Theatre, 1971-73, Bankside Globe Theatre, 1974, and New End Theatre, 1975; director for productions of other managements, in Edinburgh, Scotland, at Traverse Theatre, 1971, in London for National Theatre at Young Vic Theatre, 1975, Royal Court, 1976-77, Kingston Overground Theatre, 1978, and in Sheffield, England, at Sheffield Crucible, 1978; director at Old Red Lion, 1982. Visiting fellow at University of Reading, 1970; resident dramatist at Royal Court, 1976-77, and Hampstead Theatre, 1978-79. Interviewer for Thames Television "Question '68" show, 1968.

MEMBER: Equity, Writers Guild of Great Britain (member of radio committee, 1982-83; chair of radio committee, 1983-84; chair of theatre committee, 1984-86; member of executive council, 1983-86), Theatre Writers Union (member of negotiating team, 1976-82), Dramatists Club, Alibi Club.

AWARDS, HONORS: Named most promising playwright by *Evening Standard,* 1966, for *Little Malcolm and His Struggle against the Eunuchs;* John Whiting Award, 1978, for "Prejudice" (later retitled "Creatures of Another Kind").

WRITINGS:

PLAYS

Hail Scrawdyke (produced in New York, 1966), Grove, 1966 (published in England as *Little Malcolm and His Struggle against the Eunuchs* [first produced in London at Unity Theatre, March 30, 1965], Samuel French, 1966).
K. D. Dufford Hears K. D. Dufford Ask K. D. Dufford How K. D. Dufford'll Make K. D. Dufford (first produced in London at Lambda Theatre, 1969; later retitled "K. D. Dufford"), Faber, 1970.
A Discussion, Faber, 1971.
Muck from Three Angles, Faber, 1971.
A Who's Who of Flapland and Other Plays, Faber, 1971.

"An Amour, and a Feast" (first produced in London at Little Theatre, January, 1972), published in *Fun Art Bus Book,* Methuen, 1971.

"Meriel the Ghost Girl" (first produced as a television play, 1976; produced at Old Red Lion, 1982), published in *The Mind Beyond* (anthology), Penguin, 1976.

The House, Methuen, 1979.

UNPUBLISHED PLAYS

(With David Calderisi) "The Experiment," first produced in London at New Arts Theatre, January 16, 1967.

"The Girl Who Didn't Like Answers," first produced in London at Mercury Theatre, June 29, 1971.

"A Last Belch for the Great Auk," first produced in London at Mercury Theatre, 1971.

"Bleats from a Brighouse Pleasureground," first produced in London at Little Theatre, 1972.

"Janitress Thrilled by Prehensile Penis," first produced in London at Little Theatre, 1972.

"An Altercation," first produced in London at the Covent Garden Street Festival, 1973.

"The Freckled Bum" (first play of quartet), first produced in London at Bankside Globe Theatre, 1974.

"Minyip" (second play of quartet), first produced in London at Bankside Globe Theatre, 1974.

"Progs" (third play of quartet), first produced at British Drama League, 1975.

"A Process of Elimination" (final play of quartet), first produced at Howff, 1975.

"Prejudice" (later retitled "Creatures of Another Kind"), first produced in Sheffield at Sheffield Crucible, 1978.

"A Rite Kwik Metal Tata," first produced in Sheffield at Sheffield Crucible, 1979.

"Was It Her?," first produced at Old Red Lion, 1982.

"A Tomato Who Grew into a Mushroom," first produced by Oxfordshire Touring Theatre Co., 1987.

OTHER

Also author, under pseudonym Johnson Arms, of *They Travelled by Tube* (biographies of notable people who moved by means of London's Underground subway system), Butterworth. Also author of unpublished plays, "Wychways along the Evenlode," 1986, and "The Cutteslowe Walls," 1987. Also author of television plays, including "A Plastic Mac in Winter," 1963, "Cock, Hen and Courting Pit," 1966, "Triptych of Bathroom Users," 1972, "Blur and Blank via Checkheaton," 1972, "Triple Exposure," 1972, "Steps Back," 1972, "Daft Mam Blues," 1976, "Pigmented Patter," 1976, "Treewomen of Jagden Crag," 1976, "Speculating about Orwell," 1983, and "There's a Car Park in Witherton"; also author of radio plays, "Spongehenge," 1982, "Grandad's House," 1984, "Shares of the Pudding," 1985, "Do It Yourself," 1986, "Bedsprings," 1988, and "In Solitary," 1988, all for British Broadcasting Corp.

WORK IN PROGRESS: Three stageplays: "Franklin and Wilkins" (working title), about the two scientists who did not discover the double helix, for Hampstead Theatre, "Demonstrations" (working title), for actor Michael White, and "Bonds" (working title), for National Theatre; a television play, "One Said This Then the Other Said That" (working title), for actor John Cleese; a filmscript, "Pulling On"; a radio play, "Crossed Lines."

SIDELIGHTS: David Halliwell told *CA:* "A very basic motivating factor in my career has been a compulsion to surpass other people in some way (accompanied by a compulsion to be inferior

to them). When I was an art student, I realised I had no chance of surpassing other students as a graphic artist, and so I turned to the theatre, writing and acting in revue sketches. I work out the overall framework of a play in my head before I write a single word. This often takes longer than the writing. Then I write numerous drafts, each one a development on its predecessor, until I have a producible text. I revise this text during rehearsal.

"I like to direct my own plays in the theatre, and I believe that the writing and directing of a play are both parts of the same task, given that the playwright is an experienced director. The opinion that a playwright is incapable of . . . directing his or her own work is a prejudice, an artificial separation not found in any other medium. In addition to directing my own plays, I have directed plays by Pinter, Shaw, Tony Connor, and Brian Friel, amongst others. I perform in my own plays and those of other playwrights.

"My advice to aspiring dramatists is: listen to people talking wherever you are. My own main interest as a playwright is the psychology underlying behavior. For the whole of my writing career I have been seeking the means to understand psychodynamics and express them in dramatic form. Between February and April, 1988, I managed to consummate this endeavor in a radio play called In Solitary. Although this is a minor work I intend to continue the approach in major works in all media but particularly in the theatre."

Halliwell adds, "I have been influenced by many people—by other writers, including Sean O'Casey, D. H. Lawrence, George Orwell, James Joyce, Norman Mailer, Samuel Beckett, Harold Pinter, and Sigmund Freud, but more by artists in other disciplines, including Charles Chaplin, George Burns, Bix Beiderbeck, Tommy Ladnier, Charles Parker, and Charles Mingus."

MEDIA ADAPTATIONS: Hail Scrawdyke was used as the basis for the film "Little Malcolm," 1973.

BIOGRAPHICAL/CRITICAL SOURCES:

PERIODICALS

City Limits, November, 1981.
Event, November, 1981.
New Statesman, September 26, 1969.
Plays and Players, October, 1970.
Time Out, November, 1981.
Witney Gazette, January, 1987.

* * *

HARCOURT, Palma
(John Penn, a joint pseudonym)

PERSONAL: Born in Jersey, Channel Islands; married Jack H. Trotman. *Education:* Attended Jersey Ladies College; M.A., St. Anne's College, Oxford.

ADDRESSES: 7, Elizabeth Ave., St. Brelade, Jersey, Channel Islands. *Agent*—Murray Pollinger, 4 Garrick St., London W.C.2, England.

CAREER: Writer.

MEMBER: Crime Writers' Association, Army and Navy Club (London).

WRITINGS:

Climate for Conspiracy, Collins, 1974.
A Fair Exchange, Collins, 1975, McKay, 1976.
Dance for Diplomats, Collins, 1976.

At High Risk, Collins, 1977.
Agents of Influence, Collins, 1978.
A Sleep of Spies, Collins, 1979.
Tomorrow's Treason, Collins, 1980, Scribner, 1981.
The Twisted Tree, Collins, 1982.
Shadows of Doubt, Collins, 1983.
(Contributor) *Winter's Crimes 14* (anthology), Macmillan, 1983.
The Distant Stranger, Beaufort Book Co., 1984.
A Cloud of Doves, Collins, 1985.
A Matter of Conscience, Collins, 1986.
Limited Options, Collins, 1987.
Clash of Loyalties, Collins, 1988.
Cover for a Traitor, Collins, 1989.
Double Deceit, Collins, 1990.
The Reluctant Defector, Collins, 1991.

UNDER JOINT PSEUDONYM JOHN PENN, WITH HUSBAND JACK H. TROTMAN

Notice of Death, Collins, 1982.
An Ad for Murder, Scribner, 1983.
Deceitful Death, Collins, 1983.
A Will to Kill, Collins, 1983.
Stag-Dinner Death, Scribner, 1984.
Mortal Term, Scribner, 1984.
A Deadly Sickness, Collins, 1985.
Unto the Grave, Collins, 1986.
Barren Revenge, Collins, 1986.
Accident Prone, Collins, 1987.
Outrageous Exposures, Collins, 1988.
A Killing to Hide, Collins, 1990.
Stone Sharpens Knife, Collins, 1991.

OTHER

Also contributor of short stories, under name Palma Harcourt, to *John Creasey Anthology,* 1984.

SIDELIGHTS: Many of Palma Harcourt's books have been translated into numerous languages and have appeared in large print and audio versions.

MEDIA ADAPTATIONS: Many of Palma Harcourt's books have been dramatized by British Broadcasting Corp. (BBC).

BIOGRAPHICAL/CRITICAL SOURCES:

PERIODICALS

Times (London), February 7, 1985.

*   *   *

HARE, R(ichard) M(ervyn) 1919-

PERSONAL: Born March 21, 1919, in Backwell, near Bristol, England; son of Charles Francis Aubone (a paint manufacturer) and Louise Kathleen (Simonds) Hare; married Catherine Verney, December 7, 1947; children: John Edmund, Bridget Rachel, Amy Louise, Ellin Catherine. *Education:* Balliol College, Oxford, B.A., M.A., 1947. *Religion:* Church of England.

ADDRESSES: Home—Saffron House, Ewelme, Oxford OX9 6HP, England. *Office*—Department of Philosophy, University of Florida at Gainesville, Gainesville, Fla. 32611.

CAREER: Oxford University, Oxford, England, fellow and tutor in philosophy at Balliol College, 1947-66, university lecturer in philosophy, 1951-66, Wilde Lecturer in Natural and Comparative Religion, 1963-66, White's Professor of Moral Philosophy and fellow of Corpus Christi College, 1966-83; University of

Florida at Gainesville, graduate research professor of philosophy, 1983—. Visiting fellow, Princeton University, 1957, Australian National University, 1966, Center for Advanced Study in Behavioral Sciences, Stanford University, 1980; visiting professor, University of Michigan, 1968, University of Delaware, 1974. Member of committees on medical practices, Church of England Board for Social Responsibility, 1962-79; member, National Road Safety Advisory Council, 1966-69. *Military service:* British Army, Royal Artillery, 1939-45; became lieutenant; served with Indian Mountain Artillery; prisoner of war in Singapore and Siam, 1942-45.

MEMBER: British Academy (fellow), Aristotelian Society (president, 1972-73), American Academy of Arts and Sciences (honorary foreign member).

AWARDS, HONORS: Honorary fellow, Balliol College, 1974, Corpus Christi College, 1983; Tanner Award, 1979.

WRITINGS:

Oxford's Traffic: A Practical Remedy, privately printed, 1948.
The Language of Morals, Oxford University Press, 1952.
Freedom and Reason, Oxford University Press, 1963.
Practical Inferences, Macmillan (London), 1971.
Essays on Philosophical Method, Macmillan, 1971.
Essays on the Moral Concepts, Macmillan, 1972.
Applications of Moral Philosophy, Macmillan, 1972.
(Contributor) Sterling M. McMurrin, editor, *The Tanner Lectures on Human Values,* Volume 1: *1980,* University of Utah Press, 1980.
Moral Thinking, Oxford University Press, 1981.
Plato, Oxford University Press, 1982.
Hare and Critics: Essays on Moral Thinking, edited by Douglas Seanor and N. Fotion, Oxford University Press, 1988.
Essays in Ethical Theory, Oxford University Press, 1989.
Essays on Political Morality, Oxford University Press, 1989.

Contributor to volumes of essays and to professional journals.

AVOCATIONAL INTERESTS: Music, gardening.

BIOGRAPHICAL/CRITICAL SOURCES:

PERIODICALS

Times (London), January 7, 1982.
Times Literary Supplement, January 19, 1973, July 2, 1982, March 11, 1983.

*   *   *

HARRER, Heinrich 1912-

PERSONAL: Born July 6, 1912, in Carinthia, Austria; son of Joseph (a postal officer) and Johanna (Penker) Harrer; married Charlotte Wegener, 1938 (divorced, 1942); married Margaretta Truxa, 1953 (divorced, 1958); married Katharina Haarhaus (in public relations), August 10, 1962; children: (first marriage) Peter. *Education:* University of Graz, graduated in geography, 1938. *Religion:* Protestant.

ADDRESSES: Home—Neudorf 577, 9493-Mauren, Liechtenstein.

CAREER: Explorer, 1938—. Interned in India, 1939-44, and Tibet, 1944-51. Member of expedition in first ascent of north wall of Eiger, Switzerland, 1938, and of expeditions to the Himalayas, 1939, 1951, to the Andes, 1953, to Alaska, 1955, to Ruwenzori, Africa, 1957, to West New Guinea, 1961-62, to Nepal, 1965, to Surinam, 1966, to Sudan, 1970, to North Borneo, 1971,

1972, to Alaknanda (Valley of Flowers), 1974, to Andaman Islands, 1975, to Zangkar-Ladakh, 1976, and to Brazil. Has made 35 films of his expeditions; has made several television appearances.

MEMBER: National Geographic Society (United States), Himalayan Club, Austrian Alpine Club, Kitzbuehl Golf Club, Austrian Golf Association (honorary president, 1964), Explorers Club (New York; honorary member), Royal and Ancient Golf Club of St. Andrew's.

AWARDS, HONORS: World Champion of students downhill skiing, 1937; Austrian National Amateur Golf Champion, 1958; awarded title of Professor by the president of the Republic of Austria, 1964; Austrian National Seniors Golf Champion, 1970; honorary citizen of Huettenberg, 1983; best documentary book prize, Donauland, 1982; 70th birthday Orders from Germany, Austria, Carinthia, and Styria, 1982; Gold Medal, Humboldt Society, 1985.

WRITINGS:

Sieben Jahre in Tibet, Ullstein, 1952, translation by Richard Graves published as *Seven Years in Tibet,* Hart-Davis, 1953, Dutton, 1954, reprinted, J. P. Tarcher, 1982.
Meine Tibet Bilder (title means "My Tibet Pictures"), Heering, 1953.
Die weisse Spinne: die Geschichte der Eiger-Nordwand, Ullstein, 1958, translation by Hugh Merrick published as *The White Spider: History of the North Face of the Eiger,* Dutton, 1960, 2nd revised edition, Hart-Davis, 1976.
(With Thubten Jigme Norbu) *Tibet, verlorene Heimat* (biography), Ullstein, 1960, translation by Edward Fitzgerald published as *Tibet Is My Country: Biography of Thubten Jigme Norbu,* Hart-Davis, 1960, Dutton, 1961.
(Author of foreword) *Die Leiden eines Volkes* (title means "The Suffering of a People"), Veritas, 1961, 3rd revised edition, Tibethilfe, 1962.
Ich komme aus der Steinzeit, Ullstein, 1963, translation by Fitzgerald published as *I Come from the Stone Age,* Hart-Davis, 1964, Dutton, 1965.
(Compiler) *Tibetausstellung* (title means "Exhibition of Tibet"), Giestel, 1966.
(Editor) Sven Anders Hedin, *Reisen mit Sven Hedin* (title means "Travels with Sven Hedin"), F. A. Brockhaus, 1967.
Huka-Huka, Ullstein, 1968.
Die Goetter sollen siegen (title means "The Gods Should Conquer"), Ullstein, 1968.
(Compiler with Heinrich Pleticha) *Entdeckungsgeschichte aus erster Hand* (title means "First-Hand Story of Discovery"), Arena, 1968.
Geister und Daemonen (title means "Ghosts and Demons"), Ullstein, 1969.
Unter Papuas: Mensch und Kultur seit ihrer Steinzeit (title means "Among the Papuans: Man and Culture since Their Stone Age"), Umschau, 1976.
Die letzten Fuenfhundert: Expedition zu der Zwergvoelkern auf den Andamanen (title means "The Last Five Hundred: An Expedition to the Dwarves of the Andamans"), Ullstein, 1977.
Ladakh: Goetter und Menschen hinterm Himalaya, Umschau, 1978, translation published as *Ladakh: Gods and Mortals behind the Himalayas,* Ungar, 1981.
Geheimnis Afrika (title means "Secret Africa"), Umschau, 1979.
(With Axel Thorer and K. R. Walddorf) *Unterwegs: Handbuch fuer Reisende* (title means "Underway: A Handbook for Travellers"), Brockhaus, 1980.

Der Himalaya blueht (title means "The Himalayas Flourish"), Umschau, 1980.
Rinpotsche von Ladakh, Umschau, 1981.
Wiedersehn mit Tibet, Ulverscroft, 1983, translation by Ewald Osers published as *Return to Tibet,* Schocken, 1984.

Also author of *The Last Caravan,* 1980, and *Meine Forschungsreisen. Seven Years in Tibet* has been translated into forty languages.

MEDIA ADAPTATIONS: Seven Years in Tibet was made into a motion picture shown at international film festivals at Cannes and Edinburgh.

BIOGRAPHICAL/CRITICAL SOURCES:

PERIODICALS

New York Times Book Review, February 28, 1965.
Times Literary Supplement, June 22, 1984.

*   *   *

HARRIS, Julian (Earle) 1896-1988

PERSONAL: Born September 3, 1896, in Henderson, N.C.; died October 20, 1988; son of Samuel Rogers and Rosalie (Hicks) Harris; married Elizabeth Marshall, 1928; children: Ann (Mrs. Mitsuru Yasuhara). *Education:* University of North Carolina, B.A., 1917; Columbia University, M.A., 1920, Ph.D., 1923; L'Ecole des Hautes Etudes, Paris, Eleve Titulaire, 1923.

ADDRESSES: Home—1309 Edgehill Dr., Madison, Wis. 53705.

CAREER: Virginia Episcopal School, Lynchburg, master in English and French, 1917-18; Columbia University, New York, N.Y., instructor, 1919-22; University of Wisconsin—Madison, 1924-88, began as instructor, became professor, department chair, 1942-58, humanities division chair, 1952-55. *Military service:* U.S. Army, World War I; served in France; became sergeant first class.

MEMBER: American Association of Teachers of French (president, 1950-54), American Association of Teachers of Italian, American Association of University Professors, Modern Language Association of America, Sinfonia, Madison Literary Club (president, 1956), Language and Literature Club (University of Wisconsin), University Club (Madison), Phi Beta Kappa, Phi Delta Theta.

AWARDS, HONORS: Chevalier de la Legion d'Honneur, 1949; Officier de la Legion d'Honneur, 1959; Officier, Palmes Academiques, 1967.

WRITINGS:

(With Andre Leveque) *Conversational French for Beginners,* Holt, 1946, revised edition published as *French Reader for Colleges,* 1949, abridged edition with photographs by Peter Buckley published with teachers' manual as *Basic French Reader,* 1956, 5th edition published as *Basic Conversational French,* 1973, 8th edition, 1987.
(Editor) *The Humanities: An Appraisal,* University of Wisconsin Press, 1950.
The American Way of Life (pamphlet series), University of Wisconsin Press, 1952-55.
(With Helene Monod-Cassidy) *Petites Conversations* (with teachers' guide), illustrations by Bill Armstrong, University of Wisconsin Press, 1956, children's edition, 1958.
(With Leveque) *Intermediate Conversational French,* Holt, 1960, 3rd edition, 1972.

(With Monod-Cassidy) *Nouvelles Conversations: Aventures de Jean-Pierre et Francoise,* Heath, 1961.
(With Leveque and Monod-Cassidy) *Conversations d'aujourd'hui,* Heath, 1962.
(Author of introduction and notes) Crestien de Troyes, *Yvain, ou, Le chevalier au lion,* modern French translation by Andre Mary, Dell, 1963.

Contributor to journals and papers. Editor, *French Review,* 1955-62.

SIDELIGHTS: When the Army Specialized Training Program and the Civil Affairs Training Program were set up in preparation for the invasion of Europe during World War II, several universities, including the University of Wisconsin, were given the job of teaching European languages to large numbers of soldiers. Julian Harris and Andre Leveque knew of no textbook that could hope to accomplish the task in the limited time available to them so they set out to formulate their own lessons. Harris told *CA* that they "wrote a simple little dialog in French to be taught to the students in uniform in the first hour of the first day of the course. The students were literally thrilled to be able to understand and say a few things in French before the end of the first hour." Harris and Leveque "promptly decided that instead of having students memorize lists of words, idioms, and the rest, [they] would teach them to use entire French phrases in familiar contexts." They introduced a new dialog each day, reviewed the phrases already learned, and gradually introduced the elements of grammar. The method was such a success that civilian students demanded to be taught that way. Harris and Leveque published the course in 1946 as *Basic Conversational French.*

[Death date provided by Julian E. Harris Estate]

*   *   *

HARRISON, Fred
   See PAINE, Lauran (Bosworth)

*   *   *

HART, Francis
   See PAINE, Lauran (Bosworth)

*   *   *

HARTLEY, Travis
   See PAINE, Lauran (Bosworth)

*   *   *

HASBROUCK, Kenneth E(dward), Sr.   1916-

PERSONAL: Born June 30, 1916, in Gardiner, N.Y.; son of Josiah LeFevre (a farmer) and Agnes (Riley) Hasbrouck; married Alice M. Jackson, July 10, 1948; children: Kenneth E., Jr., Charles Jackson. *Education:* Teachers College at New Paltz (now State University of New York College at New Paltz), B.E., 1946; New York University, M.A., 1948, further graduate courses.

ADDRESSES: Home—401 Route 208, New Paltz, N.Y. 12561. *Office*—Huguenot Historical Society, Box 339, New Paltz, N.Y. 12561; and Young-Morse Historic Site, 370 South Rd., Poughkeepsie, N.Y. 12601.

CAREER: Teacher of social studies, 1941-42, 1946-72; Huguenot Historical Society (maintains, among other projects, Hugue-

not St. as a national historic site), New Paltz, N.Y., president, 1960—, director, 1972—; Young-Morse Historic Site, Poughkeepsie, N.Y., president, 1979—. County historian, Ulster County, N.Y., 1960—. *Military service:* U.S. Army Air Forces, 1941-46; became sergeant major.

MEMBER: Huguenot Society of America, Sons of the American Revolution, St. Nicholas Society, New England Genealogical Society, New York Genealogical and Biographical Society, Holland Society of New York, Huguento Historical Society (New Paltz, N.Y.), Hasbrouck Family Association (president, 1957-71).

WRITINGS:

(With Ruth P. Heidgerd) *The Deyo (Deyoe) Family,* Stillwagon Press, 1951, reprinted, Huguenot Historical Society, 1980.
Street of the Huguenots, Tuttle, 1952.
History of Gardiner, N.Y., Stillwagon Press, 1955.
The Hasbrouck Family in America, Volumes 1-2, Smith Publishing, 1961, reprinted, Huguenot Historical Society, 1986, Volume 3, Huguenot Historical Society, 1974, Volume 4, Huguenot Historical Society, 1984, Volume 5, Huguenot Historical Society, 1987.
The Bevier Family in America, Huguenot Historical Society, 1970.
Three Hundred Years of the VerNooy Family in America, Smith Publishing, 1971.
The Crispell Family in America, Huguenot Historical Society, Volume 1, 1976, Volume 2, 1984, Volume 3, 1989.
The Giraud-Gerow Family in America: First Four Generations in America, Gerow Family Association, Huguenot Historical Society, Volume 1, 1981, Volume 2, 1982, Volume 3, 1986.

Contributor to newspapers and magazines, including *Daily Freeman, Kingston, De Halve Maen, New Paltz Independent.*

*   *   *

HASSLER, Donald M. (II)   1937-

PERSONAL: Born January 3, 1937, in Akron, Ohio; son of Donald M. (a businessman) and Fran (Parsons) Hassler; married Diana Cain, October 8, 1960 (died September 19, 1976); married Sue Smith, September 13, 1977; children: (first marriage) Donald M. III, David. *Education:* Williams College, B.A., 1959; Columbia University, M.A., 1960, Ph.D., 1967. *Religion:* Presbyterian.

ADDRESSES: Home—1226 Woodhill, Kent, Ohio 44240. *Office*—Department of English, Kent State University, Kent, Ohio 44240.

CAREER: University of Montreal, Montreal, Quebec, instructor in English, 1961-65; Kent State University, Kent, Ohio, assistant professor, 1967-71, associate professor, 1971-77, professor of English, 1977—, director of experimental college, 1973-83, chair of undergraduate studies and director of writing certificate program in English, 1987—.

MEMBER: Modern Language Association of America, American Society for Eighteenth-Century Studies, Keats-Shelley Association, American Association of University Professors, Science Fiction Research Association, Ohio Poets Association, Phi Beta Kappa.

AWARDS, HONORS: Woodrow Wilson fellow, 1959.

WRITINGS:

The Comedian as the Letter D: Erasmus Darwin's Comic Materialism, Nijhoff, 1973.

On Weighing a Pound of Flesh (poetry), Defiance College Publications, 1973.

Erasmus Darwin, Twayne, 1974.

(Contributor) Theodore Besterman, editor, *Studies on Voltaire and the Eighteenth Century,* Voltaire Foundation, 1976.

(Contributor) Joseph Olander and Martin Greenberg, editors, *Isaac Asimov,* Taplinger, 1977.

Comic Tones in Science Fiction, Greenwood Press, 1982.

Hal Clement, Starmont House, 1982.

Patterns of the Fantastic, Starmont House, Volume 1, 1983, Volume 2, 1984.

(Co-editor) *Death and the Serpent,* Greenwood Press, 1985.

Isaac Asimov, Starmont House, 1989.

Work appears in annual anthologies of Ohio Poets Association, 1969—. Contributor to *Hiram Poetry Review, Canadian Poetry, Fiddlehead, Descant, Canadian Forum,* and other periodicals. *Extrapolation* (science fiction journal), co-editor, 1987-89, editor, 1990—.

WORK IN PROGRESS: A collection of poems; a collection of essays on the relation of modern science fiction to the eighteenth century.

*   *   *

HASTINGS, March
See LEVINSON, Leonard

*   *   *

HAWKINS, Hugh (Dodge) 1929-

PERSONAL: Born September 3, 1929, in Topeka, Kan.; son of James Adam and Rena (Eddy) Hawkins. *Education:* DePauw University, A.B., 1950; Johns Hopkins University, Ph.D., 1954.

ADDRESSES: Home—RFD 2, Amherst, Mass. 01002. *Office*—Department of History, Amherst College, Amherst, Mass. 01002.

CAREER: University of North Carolina at Chapel Hill, instructor, 1956-57; Amherst College, Amherst, Mass., instructor, 1957-59, assistant professor, 1959-64, associate professor, 1964-69, professor of history, 1969-75, Anson D. Morse Professor of History and American Studies, 1975—. Fulbright lecturer in West Germany, 1973-74; visiting associate, Center for Studies in Higher Education, University of California, Berkeley, 1978-79, 1982-83.

MEMBER: American Historical Association, Organization of American Historians, American Studies Association, American Association of University Professors, History of Education Society, Conference on Peace Research in History, Southern Historical Association.

AWARDS, HONORS: Moses Coit Tyler Award, American Historical Association, 1959, for *Pioneer: A History of the Johns Hopkins University, 1874-1889;* Guggenheim fellow, 1961-62; M.A., Amherst College, 1969; National Endowment for the Humanities fellow, 1982-83.

WRITINGS:

Pioneer: A History of the Johns Hopkins University, 1874-1889, Cornell University Press, 1960.

(Editor and author of introduction) *Booker T. Washington and His Critics: The Problem of Negro Leadership,* Heath, 1962,

2nd edition published as *Booker T. Washington and His Critics: Black Leadership in Crisis,* 1974.

The Abolitionists: Immediatism and the Question of Means, Heath, 1964, 2nd edition published as *The Abolitionists: Means, Ends, and Motivations,* 1972.

(Editor and author of introduction) *The Emerging University and Industrial America,* Heath, 1970, enlarged edition, R. E. Krieger, 1985.

Between Harvard and America: The Educational Leadership of Charles W. Eliot, Oxford University Press, 1972.

WORK IN PROGRESS: A book on the associational impulse in American higher education.

*   *   *

HAYDEN, Jay
See PAINE, Lauran (Bosworth)

*   *   *

HAYES, Steven C(harles) 1948-

PERSONAL: Born August 13, 1948, in Philadelphia, Pa.; son of Charles Aloysius, Jr. (a sales manager) and Ruth Esther (Dryer) Hayes; married Angela Fe Butcher, June, 1972 (divorced, 1979); married Linda J. Parrott, September, 1987; children: Camille Rose, Charles Frederick. *Education:* Loyola Marymount University, B.A. (cum laude), 1970; attended San Diego State University, 1971-72; West Virginia University, M.A., 1973, Ph.D., 1977. *Politics:* Democrat.

ADDRESSES: Home—Box 6501, Incline Village, Nev. 89450. *Office*—Department of Psychology, University of Nevada, Reno, Reno, Nev. 89557-0062.

CAREER: West Virginia University, Morgantown, instructor in psychology, 1973-74, lecturer, 1974; psychology trainee at Veterans Administration Hospital, Salem, Va., 1973, and at Robert F. Kennedy Youth Center, Morgantown, 1973-74; Brown University, Providence, R.I., intern in psychology, 1975-76; University of North Carolina, Greensboro, instructor, 1976-77, assistant professor, 1977-82, associate professor of psychology, 1982-86; University of Nevada, Reno, professor of psychology and director of clinical training, 1986—.

MEMBER: American Association for the Advancement of Science, American Psychological Society (secretary-treasurer, 1988-89), American Psychological Association for Behavior Analysis, Association for the Advancement of Behavior Therapy (chairperson of film program, 1977-78; coordinator of student affairs, 1978; assistant program chair, 1980; chairperson of Task Force on Student Involvement, 1980-81), Society for the Experimental Analysis of Behavior (member of board of directors, 1983-89).

AWARDS, HONORS: Grant from National Institute of Mental Health, 1976-77; American Psychological Association fellow, 1985; American Psychological Society, 1989.

WRITINGS:

(Editor) *Research in Opportunities in Clinical Psychology Internships,* American Psychological Association, 1979.

Abnormal Psychology, University of North Carolina, 1979.

(With John D. Cone) *Environmental Problems/Behavioral Solutions,* Brooks/Cole, 1980.

(With David H. Barlow and Rosemary O. Nelson) *The Scientist-Practitioner: Research and Accountability in Clinical and Educational Settings,* Pergamon, 1983.

(Contributor with A. J. Brownstein) S. Modgil and C. Modgil, editors, *B. F. Skinner: Consensus and Controversy,* Falmer, 1986.

(Contributor) N. Jacobson, editor, *Psychotherapists in Clinical Practice: Cognitive and Behavioral Perspectives,* Guilford, 1987.

(Editor with Nelson, and contributor) *The Conceptual Foundations of Behavioral Assessment,* Guilford Press, 1987.

(Contributor) E. R. Rahdert and J. Grabowski, editors, *Adolescent Drug Abuse: Analyses of Treatment Research,* National Institute on Drug Abuse, 1988.

Rule-Governed Behavior, Cognition, Contingencies, and Instructional Control, Plenum, 1989.

(Contributor with S. M. Melancon) M. Ascher, editor, *Paradox in Psychotherapy,* Guilford, 1989.

(Contributor with J. R. Haas) M. Thase and others, editors, *Handbook of Outpatient Treatment of Adults,* Plenum, 1989.

(Editor with L. J. Hayes) *Verbal Relations: Proceedings of the Second International Institute of Verbal Relations,* Mexico City, in press.

Also contributor to a dozen other books on clinical psychology, behavior modification, and reasearch. Contributor of about eighty articles to psychology journals. Editor of *Student Recorder,* 1974-75; *Journal of Applied Behavior Analysis,* member of board of editors, 1978-80, associate editor, 1980-83; *Behavioral Assessment,* assistant editor, 1980-82, guest associate editor, 1983, member of board of editors, 1983—; member of board of editors of *Behavior Modification,* 1979-83, *Journal of Consulting and Clinical Psychology,* 1979-85, *Behavior Analyst,* 1982—, *Behaviorists for Social Action Journal,* 1982—, *Behaviorism,* 1983—, *Journal of the Experimental Analysis of Behavior,* 1985-88, and *Behavioral Residential Treatment,* 1983—.

SIDELIGHTS: Steven C. Hayes once told *CA:* "My interest is in applying B. F. Skinner's radical behaviorism to complex problems of human functioning, such as feelings, thoughts, and language. Radical behaviorism, in my opinion, represents this century's greatest intellectual achievement in the behavioral sciences. It has been widely misunderstood, however. In everyday language, 'behavior' is distinguished from emotions, thoughts, expectations, and so on. People then believe that 'radical behaviorism' must exclude all these other human activities from consideration. While some early forms of behaviorism did so, radical behaviorism views *all* human action (including totally private actions, such as thinking) to be behavior. Unlike methodological behaviorism, this approach does not believe that scientifically valid phenomena must be publicly observable. Rather, observations are scientifically valid if their sources of control are the phenomena itself and not other events, such as the norms in the culture. Thus, an observation of a feeling is not, on the face of it, any more or less valid than an observation of an overt behavior. In this way, distinctions such as subjective/objective and inside the skin/outside the skin become theoretically meaningless.

"In a sense, radical behaviorism is to behavioral science as Zen Buddhism is to religion. All behavior, including the observations of the scientist himself, are analyzed in terms of the dynamic relationship between this event and concrete events in space and time that proceed and follow it. What is rejected by this view is dualism, mentalism (not in the sense of private behavior, but in the sense of nonphysical events), and a cautious view toward scientific terms that are not based directly in experience, but are simply 'logical.'

"I'm attracted to such a view because it allows us to approach complex phenomena without getting completely lost in our mainstream cultural views of them. We have a hard time looking at human action without processing our experience of it through a powerful cultural meatgrinder of dualistic attitudes, expectations, beliefs, and so on. Radical behaviorism, in a sense, blows the mind of psychology, so that we can begin to see behavior (even the behavior called 'beliefs about behavior') as we actually experience it to be."

*   *   *

HAYS, H(offmann) R(eynolds) 1904-1980

PERSONAL: Born March 25, 1904, in New York, N.Y.; died of a heart attack, October 10, 1980, in Southampton, N.Y.; son of Hoffmann Reynolds and Martha (Stark) Hays; married Juliette Levine (an interior designer), 1934; children: Daniel, Henry, Penelope, Martha. *Education:* Cornell University, B.A., 1925; Columbia University, M.A., 1928; attended University of Liege, 1930-31. *Politics:* "Left—Liberal." *Religion:* Atheist.

ADDRESSES: Home—P.O. Box 22, Baiting Hollow Road, East Hampton, N.Y. 11937. *Agent*—Oliver Swan, Collier Associates, 875 Avenue of the Americas, Suite 1003, New York, N.Y. 10001.

CAREER: Poet, novelist, critic, playwright, translator, and educator. City College (now of the City University of New York), New York, N.Y., instructor in English, 1928-29; University of Minnesota, Minneapolis, instructor in English, 1929-33; Wagner College, Staten Island, N.Y., teacher of drama and playwriting for New York Writers Conference, 1950-55; Fairleigh Dickinson University, Rutherford, N.J., associate professor of English, 1955-59, acting head of drama department, 1960-63; Southampton College, Long Island University, Southampton, N.Y., coordinator of drama program, 1965-69. Director of American Historical Theatre, Federal Theatre Project, until 1938. Organizer of poetry readings and chairman of literary committee, East Hampton's Guild Hall, 1975-77.

MEMBER: International PEN, Writers Guild (East).

AWARDS, HONORS: Putnam Award, 1963, for *In the Beginnings: Early Man and His Gods.*

WRITINGS:

POETRY

Strange City, Four Seas (Boston), 1929.
Selected Poems, 1933-1967, Kayak Books, 1968.
Inside My Own Skin, Kayak Books, 1975.
Portraits in Mixed Media, Survivors' Manual (Oceanside, N.Y.), 1978.

Also author of numerous uncollected poems. Poetry also appeared in several anthologies, 1926-80.

NOVELS

Stranger on the Highway, Little, Brown, 1943.
Lie Down in Darkness (Crime Book Club selection), Reynal & Hitchcock, 1944.
The Takers of the City, Reynal & Hitchcock, 1946.
The Envoys, Crown, 1955.

NONFICTION

From Ape to Angel: An Informal History of Social Anthropology (Hudson Book Club and Midcentury Book Club selection), illustrations by Sue Allen, Knopf, 1958, reprinted, 1981.

In the Beginnings: Early Man and His Gods (Hudson Book Club selection), Putnam, 1963.

The Dangerous Sex: The Myth of Feminine Evil (Hudson Book Club selection), Putnam, 1964.

Explorers of Man: Five Pioneers in Anthropology (juvenile), Macmillan, 1971.

Birds and Beasts and Men: A Humanist History of Zoology (Saturday Review Book Club selection), Putnam, 1972.

Children of the Raven: The Seven Indian Nations of the Northwest Coast, McGraw, 1975.

TRANSLATOR

Bertolt Brecht, *The Trial of Lucullus: A Play for Radio,* New Directions, 1943.

(And editor) *Twelve Spanish American Poets* (parallel text in Spanish and English), Yale University Press, 1943, reprinted, Beacon Press, 1972.

(And author of biographical and bibliographical notes) Dudley Fitts, editor, *Anthology of Contemporary Latin-American Poetry* (parallel text in Spanish, Portuguese, or French, and English), New Directions, 1947, reprinted, Greenwood Press, 1976.

(And editor and author of introduction) Brecht, *Selected Poems,* (parallel text in German and English), Reynal, 1947, reprinted, Harcourt, 1987.

Jose Revueltas, *The Stone Knife* (novel), Reynal, 1947.

Brecht, *The Rise of Arturo Ui,* [New York], 1957.

Juan Ramon Jimenez, *Selected Writings,* Farrar, Straus, 1957.

(And editor) *Selected Poems of Jorge Carrera Andrade,* State University of New York Press, 1972.

(And contributor of essay) Cesar Vallejo, *Selected Poems,* edited with an introduction by Louis Hammer, Sachem Press, 1981.

Also translator of Brecht's *Mother Courage,* 1941.

OTHER

(With Oscar Saul) "Medicine Show" (musical), first produced on Broadway, 1940.

The Kingdom of Hawaii (juvenile), New York Graphic Society, 1964.

(With Daniel Hays) *Charley Sang a Song* (juvenile), illustrations by Uri Shulevitz, Harper, 1964.

Crisis, illustrations by Gerson Lieber, Ox Head Press (Menomonie, Wis.), 1969.

Women: The Dangerous Sex (sound recording; lecture), Everett/Edwards (DeLand, Fla.), 1976.

Author of other plays, including "Ballad of Davy Crockett," 1936, restaged with music by Kurt Weill as "One Man from Tennessee," 1938. Also author of about twenty-five teleplays produced on "Television Playhouse," "Pulitzer Prize Theatre", and "Studio One," 1950-55. Author of television adaptation of Henry James' *The Marriages.* Hays' biography of Vincent Van Gogh was published in *The Best Television Plays of 1950-1951.*

WORK IN PROGRESS: A biography of anthropologist Franz Boas, for Prentice-Hall; poems.

SIDELIGHTS: Educator, poet, translator, anthropologist, critic, and author, H. R. Hays began his career as a playwright. His best known play, "The Ballad of Davy Crockett," was later restaged with music by Kurt Weill as "One Man from Tennessee." Involved with the Federal Theatre Project during the 1930s, serving as director of the American Historical Theatre in New York City, Hays was especially influenced by the socially conscious literature produced during the Great Depression and

his work reflects a profound regard for social justice. At the end of the decade, he spent a summer in Mexico and became interested in Spanish American literature. He taught himself Spanish, translating such Latin American poets as Pablo Neruda and Cesar Vallejo, and was especially recognized for his highly acclaimed anthology, *Twelve Spanish American Poets.* While he became the major American translator of Bertolt Brecht, his appreciation for Latin American culture continued and was manifested in his novels, as well. *Stranger on the Highway* takes place in sixteenth-century Mexico, and *The Envoys* depicts the revolutionary hopes of the people of Peru.

Hays' diverse interests spanned areas from anthropology to zoology and were expressed in several genres. His study of social anthropology resulted in *From Ape to Angel: An Informal History of Social Anthropology, In the Beginnings: Early Man and His Gods* and *The Dangerous Sex: The Myth of Feminine Evil,* which was praised by feminists during the 1960s. Author of numerous plays, many of which were produced during the early days of live television, Hays also continued to write poetry throughout his life. Although he published four volumes of work, which is stylistically derived from the imagist work of William Carlos Williams and Ezra Pound as well as Latin American and French surrealism, most of his work remains uncollected.

MEDIA ADAPTATIONS: Stranger on the Highway was purchased by Twentieth Century Film Co.; *Lie Down in Darkness* was purchased by Charles Feldman Film Co.

BIOGRAPHICAL/CRITICAL SOURCES:

PERIODICALS

Street, Volume 2, number 3, 1978.
Voyages, winter, 1969 (Hays issue).

OBITUARIES:

BOOKS

Annual Obituary 1980, St. Martin's, 1981.

PERIODICALS

New York Times, October 18, 1980.*

*   *   *

HAZARD, John N(ewbold)   1909-

PERSONAL: Born January 5, 1909, in Syracuse, N.Y.; son of John Gibson and Ada (DeKalb) Hazard; married Susan Lawrence, 1941; children: John Gibson, William Lawrence, Nancy, Barbara Peace. *Education:* Yale University, B.A., 1930; Harvard University, LL.B., 1934; Moscow Juridicial Institute, certificate, 1937; University of Chicago, J.S.D., 1939.

ADDRESSES: Home—20 East 94th St., New York, N.Y. *Office*—Columbia University, 435 West 116th St., New York, N.Y.

CAREER: Admitted to Bar of New York, 1935; Institute of Current World Affairs, New York City, fellow, 1934-39; Baldwin, Todd & Young, New York City, associate, 1939-41; United States Government, Foreign Economics Administration, Washington, D.C., deputy director of Soviet branch, 1941-46; Columbia University, New York City, professor of public law, 1946-77, Nash Professor Emeritus of Law, 1977—.

MEMBER: International Academy of Comparative Law (titular), American Society of International Law (honorary vice president, 1973—), American Association for the Advancement of

Slavic Studies (treasurer, 1960—), Century Club (New York), University Club (Washington), Authors Club (London).

AWARDS, HONORS: LL.D. from University of Freiburg, 1969, Lehigh University, 1970, University of Leiden, 1975, and University of Paris, 1977. Presidential Certificate of Merit.

WRITINGS:

Soviet Housing Law, Yale University Press, 1939.

(Editor) *Soviet Legal Philosophy,* Harvard University Press, 1951.

Law and Social Change in the U.S.S.R., Stevens, 1953, reprinted, Hyperion Press, 1986.

The Soviet System of Government, University of Chicago Press, 1957, 5th edition, 1980.

Settling Disputes in Soviet Society: The Formative Years of Legal Institutions, Columbia University Press, 1960, reprinted, Octagon Books, 1985.

(With Isaac Shapiro) *The Soviet Legal System; Post-Stalin Documentation and Historical Commentary,* Oceana, 1962.

(Editor) *Papers on Communist Law,* Columbia University Law School, 1963.

(With Stanley Lubman, Isaac Shapiro, and Jacqueline Shapiro) *Soviet Law and Western Legal Systems: A Manual for Comparison,* Parker School of Foreign and Comparative Law, Columbia University, 1963, revised edition with Peter B. Maggs published as *The Soviet Legal System: Contemporary Documentation and Historical Commentary,* 1969, reprinted, Oceana, 1986.

Communists and Their Law: A Search for the Common Core of the Legal Systems of the Marxist Socialist States, University of Chicago Press, 1969.

(Editor with Wenceslas J. Wagner) *Legal Thought in the United States of America under Contemporary Pressures,* Emile Bruylant (Brussels), 1970.

(Editor with Wagner) *Law in the United States of America in Social and Technological Revolution: Reports from the United States of America on Topics of Major Concern,* Emile Bruylant, 1974.

(Editor with Wagner) *Law in the U.S.A. in the Bicentennial Era: Reports from the United States of America on Topics of Major Concern,* American Association for the Comparative Study of Law, 1978.

(Editor with Wagner) *Law in the U.S.A. for the 1980's: Reports from the United States of America on Topics of Major Concern,* American Association for the Comparative Study of Law, 1982.

Managing Change in the U.S.S.R.: The Politico-Legal Role of the Soviet Jurist, Cambridge University Press, 1983.

Recollections of a Pioneering Sovietologist, Oceana, 1984.

New Materials and the Soviet Legal System: Law in the Eighties, Oceana, 1984.

Managing editor, *American Slavic and East European Review,* 1951-59; member of board of editors, *American Journal of International Law* and *American Journal of Comparative Law.*

WORK IN PROGRESS: Law in the Communist World for University of Chicago Press.

BIOGRAPHICAL/CRITICAL SOURCES:

PERIODICALS

Times Literary Supplement, January 13, 1984.*

HAZO, Samuel (John) 1928-

PERSONAL: Born July 19, 1928, in Pittsburgh, Pa.; son of Sam and Lottie (Abdou) Hazo; married Mary Anne Sarkis (a legal secretary), June 11, 1955. *Education:* University of Notre Dame, B.A. (magna cum laude), 1948; Duquesne University, M.A., 1955; University of Pittsburgh, Ph.D., 1957. *Politics:* Independent. *Religion:* Roman Catholic.

ADDRESSES: Home—785 Somerville Dr., Pittsburgh, Pa. *Office*—Department of English, Duquesne University, Pittsburgh, Pa.

CAREER: Pittsburgh Post Gazette, Pittsburgh, Pa., assistant financial editor, 1949; Shady Side Academy, Pittsburgh, teacher of Latin, 1953; Duquesne University, Pittsburgh, instructor, 1955-58, assistant professor, 1958-60, associate professor, 1960-61, professor of English, 1964 associate dean of college, 1961-66. Director, International Poetry Forum, Pittsburgh. Lecturer and poetry reader at more than two hundred colleges and universities. Commentator on weekly broadcast, "Boolznark," for KDKA, 1960. *Military service:* U.S. Marine Corps, 1950-53; became captain.

AWARDS, HONORS: James V. Mitchell Memorial Award for Playwriting, 1948, for a one-act play; nominated for Pulitzer Prize and National Book Award, 1962, both for *The Quiet Wars;* D.Litt., Seton Hill College, 1965; National Book Award nomination, 1973, for *Once for the Last Bandit;* D.H.L., Thiel College, 1981, and Wilkes College, 1987; Governor's Award for excellence in the arts, Pennsylvania, 1986.

WRITINGS:

POETRY

Discovery and Other Poems, Sheed, 1959.

The Quiet Wars, Sheed, 1962.

Listen with the Eye, photographs by James P. Blair, University of Pittsburgh Press, 1964.

My Sons in God: Selected and New Poems, University of Pittsburgh Press, 1965.

Blood Rights, University of Pittsburgh Press, 1968.

(Translator) Adonis (Ali Ahmed Said) *The Blood of Adonis,* University of Pittsburgh Press, 1971, new edition published as *Transformations of the Lover,* International Poetry Forum, 1982.

(With George Mama) *Twelve Poems,* Byblos Press, 1972.

Seascript: A Mediterranean Logbook, Byblos Press, 1972.

Once for the Last Bandit, University of Pittsburgh Press, 1972.

Quartered, University of Pittsburgh Press, 1974.

Inscripts, Ohio University Press, 1975.

To Paris, New Directions, 1981.

Thank a Bored Angel: Selected Poems, New Directions, 1983.

The Color of Reluctance, Dooryard Press, 1986.

Nightwords, Sheep Meadow, 1987.

Silence Spoken Here, Marlboro Press, 1988.

Stills, Macmillan, 1989.

OTHER

Hart Crane: An Introduction and Interpretation, Barnes & Noble, 1963, revised edition published as *Smithereened Apart: A Critique of Hart Crane,* Ohio University Press, 1978.

(Editor) *The Christian Intellectual: Studies in the Relation of Catholicism to the Human Sciences,* Duquesne University Press, 1963.

(Editor) *A Selection of Contemporary Religious Poetry,* Paulist Press, 1963. (Translator with Beth Luey) Denis de Rougement, *The Growl of Deep Waters,* University of Pittsburgh Press, 1976.

The Very Fall of the Sun, (novel), Popular Library, 1978.

The Wanton Summer Air, North Point, 1982.

SIDELIGHTS: Samuel Hazo, director of the International Poetry Forum, has received critical acclaim for his poetry and for his translations of the work of Adonis (Ali Ahmed Said), who wrote in Arabic. Hazo is sometimes referred to as co-author of *The Blood of Adonis,* since his translations "were bold and ingenious reworkings, particularly brilliant at illuminating the fine nuances and cross-hatchings of the short lyrics," Michael Beard observes in *World Literature Today.*

Suffering, aging, and death are recurring themes in Hazo's own poetry, and many reviewers suggest that his sincerity and honesty in dealing with these subjects are what attract readers to his work. A critic for *Virginia Quarterly Review* notes that *Blood Rights,* one of Hazo's more popular collections, establishes him "as one of the most honest and gifted of modern poets. Hazo's poems are . . . the poems of a deeply religious man facing up to the hard realities of . . . the suffering of a fallen world." Many reviewers conclude that Hazo's seemingly natural ability to deal with issues in a honest, open way stems from the fact that he often draws from his own experiences to write his poetry. "What emerges is a portrait of a reflective, somewhat self-centered man who writes candidly about his experiences," explains Elizabeth Knies in *Commonweal.*

A number of reviewers, however, interpret Hazo's soul-searching manner as self-indulgent. J. C. Sorensen notes in *Library Journal* that Hazo "has a tendency to identify with legendary and emblematic images." And a writer for *Choice* believes that some of Hazo's poetry "suffers from self-conscious refinement. Post-romantic poets are acutely aware of themselves in the creative process and often tell us how they write in their poems. For Hazo, this 'poet-in-process' is the major motif throughout the poems." However, this same reviewer praises works like *Once for the Last Bandit* because it "contains enough good poems to make it worthwhile." A *Kliatt* reviewer comments more favorably, "*Thank A Bored Angel: Selected Poems* contains the kind of generous, accumulated wisdom one associates with fine teaching. . . . For Hazo is a confirmed student of life and these poems reflect that constant effort at learning all one can before death."

While the themes of Hazo's poetry have remained the same, the form of his poetry has changed over the years. His earlier poems were noted for their highly technical mastery and traditional style. With the publication of *Listen with the Eye,* Hazo began composing poetry in iambic free verse. Still considered a master of the technical aspects of poetry by many of his fans, Hazo no longer writes in the structured, rhythmic style of his earlier collections *Discovery* and *The Quiet Wars.* The intensely personal poems Hazo chose from eight of his previous books for *Thank A Bored Angel* show his versatility as a craftsman, writes William B. Hill in a *Best Sellers* review. The effect of Hazo's experiments in verse, Hill feels, "is freedom and continuity disciplined by form. . . . Generally, . . . these poems, which must have cost tremendous toil, have an air of spontaneity that is given by a rich imagination."

Some critics feel that the changes of technique in Hazo's poetry represent an important development, while others view them as problematic. Karl Malkoff of *Commonweal* sums up both views. "Hazo's earlier poems are more technically proficient than his later work," he states, explaining that "the handling of formal elements is more evident, easier to judge, intellectual structures are tighter, there is often a sharp neo-metaphysical wit working, the frequent sense of tour de force. But these rules are arbitrary," the reviewer concedes. "The later poems have a power of their own; and it seems obvious that in them Hazo has managed to master the form that most accurately expresses his vision of reality." Thelma Scott Kiser, who appreciates Hazo's "originality and freshness," offers this assessment of *Thank a Bored Angel* in the *Sunday Independent:* "All who respond to good poetry will be glad for his gift and will likely often remark . . . 'I wish I'd written that.' "

AVOCATIONAL INTERESTS: Tennis.

BIOGRAPHICAL/CRITICAL SOURCES:

PERIODICALS

Best Sellers, January, 1983, September, 1983.
Choice, December, 1972, March, 1975.
Commonweal, January 5, 1973, July 4, 1975.
Kliatt, fall, 1983.
Library Journal, March 15, 1972, October 15, 1974.
Minnesota Review, May/July, 1965.
New York Times Book Review, November 21, 1965.
Poetry, June, 1973, July, 1975.
Saturday Review, October 9, 1965.
Sunday Independent (Kentucky), June 26, 1983.
Virginia Quarterly Review, winter, 1969.
World Literature Today, autumn, 1983.

* * *

HEADY, Eleanor B(utler) 1917-1979

PERSONAL: Born March 13, 1917, in Bliss, Idaho; died 1979; daughter of Arthur Harrison and Effie (Carrico) Butler; married Harold F. Heady (a professor of ecology), June 12, 1940; children: Carol Marie De Maria, Kent Arthur. *Education:* University of Idaho, B.A., 1939. *Politics:* Liberal Republican. *Religion:* Congregationalist.

ADDRESSES: Home and office—1864 Capistrano Ave., Berkeley, Calif. 94707. *Agent*—Marilyn Marlow, Curtis Brown Ltd., 10 Astor Place, New York, N.Y. 10003.

CAREER: Worked as a high school English teacher, radio announcer, and script writer. Member of board of directors, Concerned Berkeley Citizens.

MEMBER: League of American Penwomen, Authors Guild, Authors League of America, California Writer's Club (president, 1972-73), Berkeley City Club.

WRITINGS:

JUVENILE

Jambo, Sungura!: Tales from East Africa, illustrated by Robert Frankenberg, Norton, 1965.
When the Stones Were Soft: East African Fireside Tales, illustrated by Tom Feelings, Funk, 1968, reprinted, 1985.
Coat of the Earth: The Story of Grass, illustrated by husband, Harold F. Heady, Norton, 1968.
Brave Johnny O'Hare, illustrated by Steven Kellogg, Parents' Magazine Press, 1969.
Tales of the Nimipoo from the Land of the Nez Perce Indians, illustrated by Eric Carle, World Publishing, 1970.
(With H. F. Heady) *High Meadow: The Ecology of a Mountain Meadow,* illustrated by H. F. Heady, Grosset, 1970.
Safiri the Singer: East African Tales, illustrated by Harold James, Follett, 1972.

The Soil That Feeds Us, illustrated by Frankenberg, Parents' Magazine Press, 1972.

Sage Smoke: Tales of the Shoshoni-Bannock Indians, illustrated by Arvis Stewart, Follett, 1973.

Make Your Own Dolls, illustrated by H. F. Heady, Lothrop, 1974.

Plants on the Go: A Book about Seed Dispersal, illustrated by Susan Swan, Parents' Magazine Press, 1975.

Trees Are Forever: How They Grow from Seeds to Forests, illustrated by Gail Owens, Parents' Magazine Press, 1978.

(With H. F. Heady) *Range and Wildlife Management in the Tropics,* Longman, 1982.

Also contributor to *Cricket, Ranger Rick's Nature Magazine* and *Highlights for Children.*

BIOGRAPHICAL/CRITICAL SOURCES:

PERIODICALS

Christian Science Monitor, October 17, 1970.
New York Times Book Review, May 5, 1965.
Saturday Review, September 21, 1968, November 14, 1970.

[Sketch reviewed by husband, Harold F. Heady]

*   *   *

HEADY, Harold F(ranklin) 1916-

PERSONAL: Born March 29, 1916, in Buhl, Idaho; son of Orah Everett (a farmer) and Edith (Philbrick) Heady; married Eleanor Butler (a writer), June 12, 1940 (died, 1979); children: Carol Marie De Maria, Kent Arthur. *Education:* University of Idaho, B.S., 1938; New York State University College of Forestry, M.S., 1940; graduate study at University of Minnesota, 1940-41; University of Nebraska, Ph.D., 1947. *Politics:* Republican. *Religion:* Congregational.

ADDRESSES: Home—1864 Capistrano Ave., Berkeley, Calif. 94707. *Agent*—Marilyn Marlow, Curtis Brown Ltd., 10 Astor Place, New York, N.Y. 10003.

CAREER: U.S. Soil Conservation Service, White Salmon, Wash., range conservationist, 1941; New York State College of Forestry, Syracuse, assistant professor, 1942; Montana State University, Bozeman, assistant professor of range management and plant ecology, 1942-47; Texas A & M University, College Station, associate professor of range management, 1947-51; University of California, Berkeley, assistant professor and assistant plant ecologist at Experimental Station, 1951-56, associate professor and associate plant ecologist, 1956-62, professor of forestry and plant ecologist, 1962-77, associate dean of College of Natural Resources, 1974-77. Assistant vice president and associate director of agricultural experiment station, University of California, 1977-80; director of Wildland Resources Center, 1980-81. Fulbright professor at University of Queensland, 1966. Member of board of directors of Concerned Berkeley Citizens, 1971—; U.S. chairman of Australian American Rangeland Workshops, 1974-75.

MEMBER: Society for Range Management (founding member; first secretary-treasurer, 1947; president, 1980), Ecological Society of America, California Writers Club.

AWARDS, HONORS: Fulbright and Guggenheim scholar, East Africa, 1959-60; certificate of merit, 1969, and Renner Award, 1979, both from Society for Range Management; elected to University of Idaho Alumni Hall of Fame, 1988.

WRITINGS:

(With Robert P. Gibbens) *The Influence of Modern Man on the Vegetation of Yosemite Valley,* University of California Press, 1964.

Practices in Range Forage Production, University of Queensland Press, 1967.

Rangeland Management, McGraw, 1975.

JUVENILE

(Illustrator) Wife, Eleanor B. Heady, *Coat of the Earth: The Story of Grass,* Norton, 1968.

(With E. B. Heady, and illustrator) *High Meadow: The Ecology of a Mountain Meadow,* Grosset, 1970.

(Illustrator) E. B. Heady, *Make Your Own Dolls,* Lothrop, 1974.

(With E. B. Heady) *Range and Wildlife Management in the Tropics,* Longman, 1982.

OTHER

Also author of more than 160 scientific papers.

*   *   *

HEATH, William (Webster) 1929-

PERSONAL: Born July 1, 1929, in Buffalo, N.Y.; son of William and Elizabeth (Webster) Heath; married Mary Louise Townsend, June 21, 1952; children: Elizabeth Townsend, Emily Byron. *Education:* Amherst College, B.A., 1951; Columbia University, M.A., 1952; University of Wisconsin, Ph.D., 1956.

ADDRESSES: Home—36 Hunters Hill Circle, Amherst, Mass. 01002. *Office*—Department of English, Amherst College, Amherst, Mass. 01002.

CAREER: Amherst College, Amherst, Mass., instructor, 1956-59, assistant professor, 1959-64, associate professor, 1964-69, professor of English, 1969—, dean of freshmen, 1985-90. Visiting professor of English at University of Massachusetts, summers, 1962, 1964-68, and 1970.

AWARDS, HONORS: Grants from American Philosophical Society, 1967-68, 1972, and from American Council of Learned Societies, 1972.

WRITINGS:

Discussions of Jane Austen, Heath, 1961.

Elizabeth Bowen: An Introduction to Her Novels, University of Wisconsin Press, 1961.

Wordsworth and Coleridge: A Study of Their Literary Relations, 1801-1802, Clarendon Press, 1970.

(Editor) *Major British Poets of the Romantic Period,* Macmillan, 1972.

*   *   *

HEIDINGSFIELD, Myron S(amuel) 1914-1969

PERSONAL: Born February 3, 1914, in New York, N.Y.; died May 29, 1969, in Gainesville, Fla.; buried in West Hills Memorial Park, Gainesville, Fla.; son of Benjamin (a salesman) and Elsie (Byk) Heidingsfield; married Jane Cummins, February 17, 1946; children: Michael John. *Education:* College of the City of New York (now City College of the City University of New York), B.S., 1937; New York University, A.M., 1939, Ph.D., 1943. *Religion:* Episcopalian.

ADDRESSES: Home—415 Northwest 32nd St., Gainesville, Fla. 32601.

CAREER: College of William and Mary, Williamsburg, Va., assistant professor of economics, 1942-43; Temple University, Philadelphia, Pa., assistant professor, 1944-47, associate professor, 1947-49, professor and chairman of marketing department, 1949-58; manager of market research, Radio Corporation of America, Consumer Products Division, 1958-60; Villanova University, Villanova, Pa., associate dean and professor of marketing, 1960-63; University of Florida, College of Business Administration, Gainesville, Food Fair Foundation Professor of Marketing and director of International Marketing Resource Center, 1963-69. Marketing research consultant for variety of companies, 1945-58, for Radio Corporation of America, Rudd-Melikian, and others, 1960-69. A. B. Blankenship & Associates (market research), Philadelphia, Pa., associate director, 1949, executive vice president, 1950-51; education adviser, Charles Morris Price School of Advertising of Poor Richard Club, 1958-59; weekly business commentator, radio station WRUF, 1963-64. *Military service:* U.S. Army Service Forces, chief statistician, Management Control Division, Philadelphia Quartermaster Depot, 1943-44.

MEMBER: American Marketing Association, American Association for Advancement of Science (fellow), American Statistical Association, American Economic Association, American Association of University Professors, Beta Gamma Sigma, Phi Beta Kappa.

AWARDS, HONORS: Named national marketing educator of the year, Salesmen Marketing Executive International, 1966.

WRITINGS:

(With Albert B. Blankenship) *Market and Marketing Analysis,* Holt, 1947.
(With Blankenship) *Marketing, an Introduction,* Barnes & Noble, 1953, revised edition published as *Marketing,* 1959.
(With Frank H. Eby, Jr.) *Marketing and Business Research,* Holt, 1962, 3rd edition, 1974.
Changing Patterns in Marketing: A Study in Strategy, Allyn & Bacon, 1968.

Also author of *Social Engineering As Exemplified in Public-Health Achievement,* 1946. Contributor to professional journals.

AVOCATIONAL INTERESTS: Travel, French and Italian foods.

OBITUARIES:

PERIODICALS

New York Times, June 3, 1969.*

*   *   *

HEIMBERG, Marilyn Markham
See ROSS, Marilyn (Ann) Heimberg

*   *   *

HEINEMANN, Larry (Curtiss) 1944-

PERSONAL: Born January 18, 1944, in Chicago, Ill.; married Edie Smith (a mediator); children: Sarah, Preston. *Education:* Kendall College, Evanston, Ill., A.A., 1966; Columbia College, Chicago, Ill., B.A., 1971.

ADDRESSES: Home—1747 West Granville, Chicago, Ill. 60660.

CAREER: Columbia College, Chicago, Ill., instructor in writing, 1971-86; writer, 1971—. *Military service:* U.S. Army, Infantry,

1966-68, became sergeant; served in Vietnam; received Combat Infantryman's Badge.

AWARDS, HONORS: Best first novel citation from Society of Midland Authors, 1977, for *Close Quarters;* fellowships from National Endowment for the Arts, 1982 and 1987; National Book Award, Carl Sandburg Medal, and fiction prize from Society of Midland Authors, all 1987, all for *Paco's Story;* Guggenheim fellow, 1989.

WRITINGS:

Close Quarters (novel; portions appeared originally in *Penthouse* magazine), Farrar, Straus, 1977.
(Contributor) *Best American Stories in 1980,* Penguin, 1981.
(Contributor) *Best of TriQuarterly,* Washington Square Press, 1982.
Paco's Story (novel), Farrar, Straus, 1986.

Contributor of short stories to magazines, including *Harper's* and *Penthouse.*

WORK IN PROGRESS: A nonfiction book on post-traumatic stress disorder; a Chicago novel, *Cooler by the Lake.*

SIDELIGHTS: Larry Heinemann has said that he "came to writing with a story rather than the other way around." A Vietnam veteran whose tour of duty included more than a dozen deadly firefights, Heinemann has drawn from his experiences to produce two award-winning novels, *Close Quarters* and *Paco's Story.* The latter work, a tale of one wounded soldier's return to America, won the 1987 National Book Award as well as several prestigious regional prizes. *Washington Post Book World* reviewer Duncan Spencer calls Heinemann "the grunt's novelist of the Vietnam War," adding: "His is the storytelling of life and death between the laager and the tree line, a life of dirt, fear, dope, alcohol, brutality, curses and evil. He tells, from his own experience as a soldier, the results of fighting a war without will and without authority." In a Chicago *Tribune Books* piece, Gerald Nicosia notes that the author's novels expose "the primary fallacy of war, which comes from the notion that one can inflict pain without having pain inflicted upon one in return; and he shows this interconnectedness to be the primary truth of life itself."

The son of a Chicago bus driver, Heinemann grew up in an environment that did not include books. He earned average grades in high school and, after briefly aspiring to be an architect, seemed ready to follow in his father's blue-collar footsteps. In 1963 he enrolled in Kendall College, a two-year institution, principally to avoid the draft. After receiving his A.A. degree in 1966, however, he could not afford to continue his education; he was drafted and sent to Vietnam as an infantry soldier. In retrospect, he told the *Chicago Tribune Magazine,* he should have refused to cooperate, even if it meant being jailed. "There is no way I wanted to go [to war]," he said. "I saw it as a big waste of my time. . . . But in my family, there was no arguing. You just gritted your teeth and went."

Heinemann arrived in Vietnam March 17, 1967. *Chicago Tribune Magazine* contributor Jeff Lyon writes: "Stationed first at Cu Chi, then at Dau Tieng, almost always he was in the thick of the war. In the first nine months of his tour he was in 15 firefights. In the last three months he saw combat every day. Month by month he turned from a nice, unmotivated suburban kid into a self-preservation machine." Like many of the veterans of fighting in Southeast Asia, Heinemann returned to America to face a variety of stress-related emotional disorders. He differed from some of his comrades, though, because he found himself wanting to talk—and write—about what he had witnessed during his tour. Having gone back to school at Columbia College in Chicago, he enrolled in a writing workshop, and there he began to describe on paper the atrocities of the war. "I came to Columbia with a story already in mind," he told the *Chicago Tribune Magazine*. "But the workshop gave me the ability to train myself to see with a kind of vividness. It taught me how to organize my imagination. After a while I could recall everything that happened to me during the war, every shot fired, every breath."

Heinemann spent a number of years working on *Close Quarters,* his first novel. The work was published in 1977, and portions of it appeared as short stories in *Penthouse* magazine. *New York Times* correspondent Richard R. Lingeman calls the book "an unremittingly honest look into the black pit of war. . . . The descriptions are dead-on accurate, as is the language, a kind of obscene poetry of soldier talk." *Close Quarters* won the 1977 prize for best first novel from the Society of Midland Authors.

Paco's Story offers a different perspective on the war. The novel's hero, Paco Sullivan, returns to America wounded and disfigured, his company's only survivor. The ghosts of his fallen comrades narrate the story, in which Paco wanders into a small midwestern town where he finds work as a dish washer in a diner. Nicosia contends that while *Paco's Story* contains vivid descriptions of "some of the most brutal and gory incidents of the Vietnam war," it is also "the tale of one man's quest to be understood as a human being, and 'to discover a livable peace.' " Most critics have found the novel deeply affecting and have praised its imagery and unusual ghostly voice. Spencer calls *Paco's Story* "a nightmare in prose, perhaps the sliding kind, in which the sleeper finds himself slipping farther and farther into the pit in spite of every kind of struggle, a nightmare in which there is no rest, no safety, only the sure approach of an unknown doom."

The announcement that *Paco's Story* had won the 1987 National Book Award—the nation's most important citation for creative writing—took some members of the New York literary establishment by surprise. A few critics even suggested ungraciously that Heinemann did not deserve the award, and that his fellow nominees Toni Morrison and Philip Roth had both written better books. In the *Los Angeles Times Book Review,* editor Jack Miles defended Heinemann, noting: "The point is simply that Larry Heinemann richly deserved the prize that he won. . . . 'Paco's Story' was no fluke. It was, quite literally, a coast-to-coast success."

That "coast-to-coast success" for *Paco's Story* has allowed Heinemann to relinquish his duties as a college instructor in favor of full-time work as a writer. Heinemann told the *Chicago Tribune Magazine* that he is anxious to leave his Vietnam experiences behind now and that he is at work on other projects, including a novel about his hometown, Chicago. "For years I have been known as a Vietnam veteran who writes," he said. "Now all of a sudden I'm a writer who happens to be a Vietnam veteran."

CA INTERVIEW

CA interviewed Larry Heinemann by telephone on April 3, 1989, at his home in Chicago, Illinois.

CA: Before you won the 1987 National Book Award for Paco's Story, *there was the 1977 book* Close Quarters, *which you started not long after you came back from Vietnam. You'd had no previous writing experience and actually went to school to learn how to do it. How did you begin as a writer?*

HEINEMANN: First of all, I was never a very successful student, and I grew up in a house where there were no books. When I was overseas, I didn't keep a journal; the thought never occurred to me. The letters I wrote home were terrible. Before my wife and I were married, she was one of those people who wrote every day, amazingly enough, and her letters to me were much more interesting; they were real letters. My letters to her were junk. You would never think in a million years that the person who wrote those letters would be able to make his living writing.

I went back to school in '68 and had no ambition to be a writer whatever, but I took a writing course because I thought it was an easy A and wouldn't be any work. I got hooked. My teacher had been a medic in Korea during the Korean War. A lot of the kids I went to school with—this was in Chicago in 1968—had just been involved with the Democratic National Convention, at which there was a great deal of protest against the war in Vietnam—a riot of protest. To make a long story short, the man started putting books into my hand and telling me that I ought to write some of the things I knew, because I had started telling war stories right away. I worked on scenes—not really stories, but just scenes—for about three years when I was an undergraduate, and when I graduated he said, "You're really working on a novel. You ought to finish it."

In terms of a dramatic structure of a novel, the one-year combat tour is absolutely perfect because it begins with day one and it ends when Dosier goes home. There's a little spillover at the end. I always conceived of it as a novel, though two chapters were published as short stories in *Penthouse* in 1974 and 1975. Then in 1976 the novel was finished, and it was published in 1977.

CA: Did the Penthouse *acceptances provide some sort of encouragement you needed in order to keep working toward the novel?*

HEINEMANN: I knew I had a good story and a good chance for the novel to be published as a novel. I didn't "send out" the novel until 1975, and I published those chapters as short stories because that was the only way I knew to test-fly some of the material, just to see what it looked like in print. Before 1975, I have to say, it was clear to me and clear to other guys who were writing about the war that fiction or nonfiction written by the soldiers themselves was not very welcome. And I have had editors tell me that before 1975 that was true, although there was plenty of nonfiction by journalists, reporters, people like that, and books of history; Frances Fitzgerald's *Fire in the Lake* was published in 1972. But there was a tremendous resistance before 1975, before the war was over, to war novels. You can count on the fingers of one hand the number of good books written by soldiers. Since 1975 there have been well over three hundred novels about the war, and there are probably a like number of biographies and memoirs and extended essays. I never bothered sending *Close Quarters* out earlier than I did because it was clear to me that it would be rejected because of the material, not because of the quality of the writing.

CA: When you were finished with the book and had it safely placed with a publisher, did you have a feeling that your story wasn't told out?

HEINEMANN: I don't remember that. I remember being very tickled that all that work was actually going to amount to something; most first novels wind up in a drawer. It was after the book was out in 1977 and I sat down and read it that it occurred to me there was something more to the story. My wife encouraged me to write "something else," and a lot of people I hang out with said, "Well, now you've written your war novel and you can get on to something else." But that didn't happen, because I started *Paco's Story* in the summer of 1978, the next year. I didn't write anything for about six or eight months after *Close Quarters;* I decided to catch up on my family life and my reading. Then I started right in with *Paco's Story,* and it never occurred to me that it would take another eight years.

But I also knew that there was such a thing as what some people call the second-book let-down. It often occurs that a second novel will be somewhat diminished in quality from the first novel. So I felt I had nothing to lose by experimenting some with the sense of address and with the point of view and the language. I sat down and read some books that I had read before, but this time I really studied them: *Naked Lunch* by William S. Burroughs really impressed me, for example, and some of the work by Joseph Conrad, like *Lord Jim* and *The Nigger of the Narcissus. Michael Kohlhaas* by von Kleist. *Madame Bovary.* Kafka. Twain.

CA: You told Jeff Lyon for the Chicago Tribune Magazine *that* The Nigger of the Narcissus *gave you some of the inspiration for the unusual narrative device of* Paco's Story.

HEINEMANN: That's right. The reason I responded so strongly to Conrad is that here's a man writing in a second language, and his writing is very precise. He's an awful lot like Melville—he doesn't leave anything out. Here's a guy who thinks there's no such thing as a short story. I must have read those two Conrad books and *Naked Lunch* and *From Here to Eternity* and Christina Stead's *The Man Who Loved Children* a million times.

CA: Tell me more about how you arrived at the narrative voice of Paco's Story.

HEINEMANN: When I was teaching, we did an awful lot with the direct address of the letter form. When you sit down to write a letter, whether you know it consciously or not, you see in your mind the person you're addressing, or you bring to the writing some sort of attitude, or there's the history of the relationship, particularly if it's someone that you've known for a long time. And it can be a relationship that's good or bad—that doesn't matter. As you write a letter, you're telling a story to that person. What that does is set up a kind of immediacy with the reader. In a sort of odd way the reader is imaginatively involved in the story at basically the same emotional moment that you are telling the story to him or her. And this is where the James came from, to whom the narrative voice often says something directly. Jacob Bronowski said that writing is putting an image or an idea into the mind of an absent person. The matter of the James used throughout *Paco's Story* is just a way for me to keep establishing and re-establishing the relationship between myself, the story teller, and the reader. It happens the same way when I give readings too, that the James conveys a kind of attention-getting eye contact. *Paco's Story* is meant to be read out loud.

CA: It does have quite a cadence, I noticed reading it.

HEINEMANN: I worked very hard at that. I didn't make the discovery about the collective perception of the storyteller, which in the context of the novel is the guys who were killed in the company, until I had finished the first chapter. Then I realized that everybody in the company was dead except Paco, and here was this we telling what happened. It's intriguing, and it makes *Paco's Story* into a ghost story.

CA: A few reviewers commented that Paco wasn't well developed as a character. How would you respond to that criticism?

HEINEMANN: Commercial reviewers can be exasperating. I'm not sure what they mean by "well developed," but I think they're talking about the fact that he doesn't say very much, and that we don't know much about him or where he came from. First of all, I want to conceive any character as fully as possible so that it seems they have a life outside the story. They're less wooden and flat. On the other hand I always thought of *Paco's Story* in this way: Say you take a chair and set it some distance back from a doorway on a fairly busy street. When people pass in front of the door you see them head-to-toe for perhaps three or four paces. You see how they're dressed, what they're carrying; how they carry themselves, the look on their faces; you can size them up and make all kinds of surmises about them. What you don't know is where they came from or where they're going. In Paco's case I thought that who he was right then and there in the town of Boone was more important than any trivia about his childhood, etc. Paco comes into the town transformed anyway, as if he sprung up whole in the aftermath of the slaughter at Fire Base Harriette, so who or what he was before is virtually irrelevant. Ishmael, in *Moby Dick,* could be said to be not very "well developed" in that way. All we know about him is that as a child he was sent to his room without any supper on the longest day of the year. Paco doesn't talk much because he doesn't have much to say; he hasn't been able to discover the language he needs. And Paco recalls his father with great warmth, but in the context of receiving his medals. That's enough. I didn't see the point of slowing down the forward movement of the story by getting sidetracked with Paco's box scores.

CA: There's a third book on Vietnam in the works. Tell me something about that, and how the three books fit together from your perspective.

HEINEMANN: The one I'm working on is a book of nonfiction about post-traumatic stress disorder. In World War I they called it shell shock and neurasthenia. In World War II they called it combat fatigue. It's been in the last fifteen years that Robert Jay Lifton and Chaim Shatan and John Wilson and other people in the field of combat stress have developed this new thinking about it. Now it's a service-connected disability, just as if you were wounded. I've talked with some of the Vietnam veterans that I know of who live up on the Olympic Peninsula in Washington State, the peninsula west of Seattle, right across the Juan de Fuca Strait from Vancouver Island, about how they have struggled with settling the war for themselves, and what they did and what happened to them, coming to some sort of understanding about the good and the bad and the indifferent. It's called PTSD, or, more commonly, delayed stress. There are a lot of populations that suffer delayed stress: combat veterans, victims of rape, victims of incest or what's called family violence, survivors of the Nazi holocaust in World War II. I don't think you could call delayed stress an ailment; it's a set of psychological and emotional symptoms that are shared by a great many people. The kids out in Stockton, California, who survived the school yard massacre by that nut with the AK-47, for example—they're going to be suffering delayed stress.

Close Quarters and *Paco's Story* deal fictionally with delayed stress, and this third book (which will be done by the end of the year, and then I will finally have the war out of my house) is really an explanation of what delayed stress is. *Close Quarters* is a straight war story in almost a genre definition of a war story—what happened overseas. *Paco's Story* is somewhat more reflective; it has to do with the reverberations of the war and how being a soldier lingers in your life. The book on delayed stress is almost in a category by itself. It's much more explanatory. It's not scientific—I'm no scientist—more a straightforward, extended essay about the war.

CA: How much has writing the books helped you deal with your own experience in Vietnam?

HEINEMANN: When I first started writing, twenty years ago, it was very helpful. I think one of the things that Vietnam veterans did not have that guys from World War II, the men of my father's generation, had was a way to validate our experience. When I first started to write, it was cathartic. But after I'd been writing for three or four years it became a challenge to finish the novel and to see if I could sell it. It became less a matter of "healing" than simply a matter of learning a craft and seeing the challenge of writing a book all the way to the end—the last mile and then some. I can't tell you the number of times I abandoned the book, saying, I can't write this anymore; why keep mulling over it and beating myself to death? After a while it wasn't cathartic at all. It was actually something of an aggravation. *Paco's Story* was in no way cathartic. It was more a matter of craft and getting the story straight. The book on delayed stress I'm doing for the money. That's why it's going to be done by the end of the year!

CA: Though Close Quarters *had won a 1977 Society of Midland Authors award for best novel and a 1982 National Endowment for the Arts fellowship, the announcement that* Paco's Story *had won the National Book Award in 1987 surprised you and, judging from the furor, other people too. After things quieted down, how did the National Book Award victory affect you as a writer?*

HEINEMANN: I was tickled to death; I didn't know what to think of it. There was a great fuss made by the *New York Times* and by a lot of other people. I just read a snippet in *Spy* magazine, and they're still talking about it. Right away I understood the award as a great gift, because they don't have to give it to anybody. It also meant to me that all of a sudden I was regarded at the top of my profession, and it's the kind of recognition and approval that doesn't come to a person often in his life. I'm lucky to be working at a job where you can get those kinds of strokes. A lot of writers I know who work just as hard as I do and are just as talented don't get anything.

The difference that it's made is that people call me with work. It means that your reputation, deserved or not, precedes you into a room. For a while I was getting really carried away, smoking cigars in restaurants and being tongue-in-cheek obnoxious—much to the embarrassment of my wife, I must say. It's made my work easier in a way, and it's also made it harder in a way, because now everything I do is going to be compared to the award-winning work. But I'm also one of those people who thinks that when a good thing happens to you, you should just enjoy it, because something like the National Book Award is not going to happen again soon. So, one day at a time. Nobody is under any obligation to buy any book of mine.

CA: Have you had a large personal response to the two novels from readers who served in Vietnam or who are related to Vietnam veterans or fatalities?

HEINEMANN: Yes. More so when the books first appeared than two years later, but every once in a while I get a phone call or a letter, and that's very satisfying. I've never gotten a letter or a phone call about the books from somebody who wanted to bitch; the responses have always been very good. I think the people who don't agree with you or who have a negative response don't bother; they're really angry. But "Good Morning to You,

Lieutenant," the chapter from *Paco's Story* about a Vietcong girl who is captured by the Americans and raped by some of the guys in the company and then murdered, was originally published as a short story in *Harper's* in June, 1980, and I got a stack of letters from people who were positively irate. They wondered how I could write this. Half of the them were absolutely convinced that it was a real instance, which it was not, and half of them were outraged that *Harper's* would publish such "trash" and cancelled their subscriptions. When *Harper's* agreed to publish the story in the first place, I was flabbergasted. I didn't think they would consider it at all, because it is very strong. I will always speak well of Lewis Lapham, the editor of *Harper's,* because he was one of the people who supported my writing when I didn't think there was much support at all.

CA: You've taught creative writing along the way. Are you doing any teaching now?

HEINEMANN: No. I left teaching in January, 1986, and I was very surprised to find out I could make a living writing. Right then and there I got an Illinois Arts Council fellowship and then the next year I got a National Endowment for the Arts fellowship, which was very nice. I don't drive a cab, I don't wait tables, and I don't teach part-time. I just write. That's another reason why I regard myself as very lucky. I don't have to do those other things that take a lot of time and energy and effort from a person's writing.

CA: You mentioned your wife earlier. She seems to have been tremendously supportive of your writing, and I suspect from things I've read that you, in turn, are encouraging her in her work.

HEINEMANN: She's been great. We were married right after I got back from overseas, and except for when I was working during the summer while I was going to school, she supported us for about ten years. You don't often encounter that kind of loyalty and faith in a person. She typed all the manuscripts that left the house, and she has become a terrific editor. She worked a lot of dumb jobs: teaching physical education in a grammar school, being a clunky old secretary in an insurance office, working as the secretary in my English department for a year. The year my first book was published was really something. My wife quit work in December of 1976, got pregnant in January of 1977; the book was published in May, I got an offer to teach full-time, and then my daughter was born. Bingo! Also, the week *Close Quarters* was published, my father died. It was a big year; I'll never forget it.

Then I worked and my wife stayed home for ten years, more or less, raising kids. Now we have two, and they're old enough so when they come home from school, they don't have to be chased after. So my wife wants to go to graduate school and then become a mediator. She works for an outfit here in Chicago called Neighborhood Justice; she volunteers down at the courts to mediate neighborhood disputes—evictions and the like. She thought she might have to go to law school, but you don't need to go to law school to become a mediator. Basically you need law school so that when you talk to lawyers, they take you seriously. So she'll get a master's degree and continue working in the field.

CA: When you finish this third book and get Vietnam "out of the house," as you said, what direction will your work take?

HEINEMANN: Even as we speak, I'm working on a Chicago novel called *Cooler by the Lake.* I decided to write a purposely funny book, a Marx Brothers movie of a book. It will be, as the saying goes, a laugh riot; I need to lighten up. Also my wife has said (quite tongue-in-cheek, though) that she wouldn't believe I was a writer until I could write a book with a happy ending. I've put aside the book on delayed stress—it's very depressing—and started on the novel.

Last December I went with a group of Vietnam veterans to the U.S.S.R. to meet and talk with groups of Soviet veterans of the Afghan war, and I just got done writing an article about that for *Playboy* called "Brothers in Arms," coming out in July, 1989. That material is going into the delayed stress book. And apparently I've been invited to go to Hanoi in November with a delegation of Vietnam writers including Tim O'Brien and Bruce Weigl and Bob Mason and others. Mason and I, who happen to be really good friends, have decided that after the writers' conference in Hanoi, we want to travel south. He wants to go back to Pleiku and the A Shau Valley, where he was when he was there, and I want to go back to Tay Ninh and Cu Chi and that neck of the woods where I was. We'll probably stay a week or two. Whatever happens, that business will be the last chapter of the book on delayed stress. So I can spell myself a little here and have some fun.

BIOGRAPHICAL/CRITICAL SOURCES:

BOOKS

Contemporary Literary Criticism, Volume 50, Gale, 1988.

PERIODICALS

Booklist, November 15, 1986.
Chicago Tribune, November 11, 1987, December 2, 1987.
Chicago Tribune Magazine, February 7, 1988.
Kirkus Reviews, October 1, 1986.
Los Angeles Times, May 5, 1988.
Los Angeles Times Book Review, December 7, 1986, November 22, 1987.
Newsweek, June 6, 1977.
New York Review of Books, January 21, 1988.
New York Times, July 18, 1977, August 4, 1987, November 10, 1987, November 16, 1987.
New York Times Book Review, June 26, 1977, November 8, 1987.
Publishers Weekly, October 17, 1986, November 20, 1987.
Times Literary Supplement, February 26-March 3, 1988.
Tribune Books (Chicago), November 23, 1986.
Washington Post Book World, January 18, 1987.

—*Sketch by Anne Janette Johnson*

—*Interview by Jean W. Ross*

*　　*　　*

HELLER, Francis H(oward) 1917-

PERSONAL: Born August 24, 1917, in Vienna, Austria; came to the United States, 1938; naturalized U.S. citizen, 1943; son of Charles A. and Lily (Grunwald) Heller; married Donna De Munn, September 3, 1949; children: Denis Wayne. *Education:* Attended University of Vienna, 1935-37; University of Virginia, J.D., M.A., both 1941, Ph.D., 1948.

ADDRESSES: Home—3419 Seminole Dr., Lawrence, Kan. 66047. *Office*—School of Law, University of Kansas, Lawrence, Kan. 66045.

CAREER: College of William and Mary, Williamsburg, Va., assistant professor of government, 1947; University of Kansas, Lawrence, assistant professor, 1948-51, associate professor, 1951-56, professor of political science, 1956—, Roy A. Roberts Distinguished Professor of Law and Political Science, 1972—,

associate dean of faculties, 1966-67, dean of faculties, 1967-70, vice-chancellor for academic affairs, 1970-72. Visiting professor, Institute for Advanced Studies, Vienna, 1965, and University of Vienna Law School, 1985. Member, Kansas Governor's Commission on Constitutional Revision, 1957-61, and Lawrence City Planning Commission, 1957-63; Harry S Truman Library Institute, member of board of directors, 1958—, vice-president, 1962—; Benedictine College, member of board of directors, 1971-79, chairman, 1973-79. *Military service:* U.S. Army, 1942-47, 1951-52; became captain; awarded Silver Star and Bronze Star with oak leaf cluster. U.S. Army Reserve, 1956-65; retired as major.

MEMBER: American Political Science Association (executive council, 1958-60), American Association of University Professors, American Society for Legal History, Midwest Conference of Political Scientists, Phi Beta Kappa, Pi Sigma Alpha (executive council, 1958-60), Order of Coif.

AWARDS, HONORS: Higher Education Service Award, University of Kansas, 1973; Career Teaching award, University of Kansas Chancellor's Club, 1986; D.H.L., Benedictine College, 1988.

WRITINGS:

Virginia's State Government during the Second World War: Its Constitutional, Legislative, and Administrative Adaptations, Virginia State Library, 1949.
The Sixth Amendment to the Constitution of the United States: A Study in Constitutional Development, University of Kansas Press, 1951, reprinted, Greenwood Press, 1969.
Introduction to American Constitutional Law, Harper, 1952.
Our Stake in the Federal System, University of Kansas Governmental Research Center, 1954.
The Presidency, Random House, 1960.
Uniform State Laws in Kansas, University of Kansas Governmental Research Center, 1962.
(Editor) *The Korean War: A 25-Year Perspective,* Regents Press of Kansas, 1977.
(Compiler and editor) *Materials for the Study of the History, Method, and Process of the Law,* [Lawrence, Kan.], yearly editions, 1978-82.
(Editor) *The Truman White House: The Administration of the Presidency, 1945-1953,* Regents Press of Kansas, 1980.
(Editor) *Economics and the Truman Administration,* Regents Press of Kansas, 1981.
USA: Verfassung und Politik, Boehlau Verlag (Vienna), 1987.

Contributor to *Encyclopaedia Britannica,* political science reviews, and law journals.

*　　*　　*

HENNEMAN, John Bell, Jr. 1935-

PERSONAL: Born November 1, 1935, in New York, N.Y.; son of John Bell (a banker) and Esther Gracie (Ogden) Henneman; married Margery Meigs Clifford, September 17, 1960; children: John, Charles, Margery Lawrence. *Education:* Princeton University, A.B., 1957; Harvard University, A.M., 1961, Ph.D. (history), 1966; University of Iowa, M.A. (library science), 1982. *Politics:* Republican. *Religion:* Episcopalian.

ADDRESSES: Home—78 Shady Brook Lane, Princeton, N.J. 08540. *Office*—Princeton University Library, Princeton, N.J. 08544.

CAREER: McMaster University, Hamilton, Ontario, lecturer, 1965-66, assistant professor of history, 1966-69; University of

Iowa, Iowa City, associate professor, 1969-73, professor of history, 1973-83, chairman of department, 1980-83; Princeton University, Princeton, N.J., history bibliographer, 1983—. *Military service:* U.S. Navy, 1957-60; became lieutenant.

MEMBER: International Commission for the History of Representative and Parliamentary Institutions, American Historical Association, American Library Association, Mediaeval Academy of America, Society for French Historical Studies, Phi Beta Kappa.

AWARDS, HONORS: Woodrow Wilson fellowship, 1960-61; Guggenheim fellowship, 1976.

WRITINGS:

Royal Taxation in Fourteenth Century France: The Development of War Financing, 1322-1356, Princeton University Press, 1971.
(Editor) *The Medieval French Monarchy,* Dryden Press, 1973.
Royal Taxation in Fourteenth Century France: The Captivity and Ransom of John II, 1356-1370, American Philosophical Society, 1976.

Contributor to *Dictionary of the Middle Ages;* contributor and associate editor, *Medieval France: An Encyclopedia,* Garland Publishing. Contributor to *Speculum, Traditio, American Historical Review, Studia Gratiana,* and *Mediaeval Studies.*

WORK IN PROGRESS: Olivier de Clisson and Political Society in France under Charles V and Charles VI.

SIDELIGHTS: "Like many academics," John Bell Henneman, Jr., once told *CA,* "I was steered by my professor into my first project. I found that medieval taxation was not the dull, technical subject I had supposed it to be. As it does today, taxation aroused bitter passions, lengthy political debate, and dramatic litigation. The biggest cost was war, and the conduct of professional soldiers exerted a crucial influence on taxes. Many academic historians have turned their backs on event-oriented political history and have lost much of their reading public. At the risk of being old-fashioned, I still believe that the political behavior of the elite classes decisively affects human culture and remains the most fruitful subject for historical writing."

*   *   *

HENSLEY, Joe L. 1926-

PERSONAL: Born March 19, 1926, in Bloomington, Ind.; son of Ralph Ramon and Frances Mae (Wilson) Hensley; married Charlotte R. Bettinger, June 18, 1950; children: Michael Joseph. *Education:* Indiana University, A.B., 1950, LL.B., 1955. *Politics:* Democrat. *Religion:* Presbyterian.

ADDRESSES: Home—2315 Blackmore, Madison, Ind. 47250. *Office*—Fifth Judicial Circuit Courthouse, Madison, Ind. 47250.

CAREER: Admitted to State Bar of Indiana, 1955; Metford & Hensley, Attorneys at Law, Madison, Ind., associate, 1955-71; Ford, Hensley & Todd, Attorneys at Law, Madison, partner, 1971-73; Hensley, Todd & Castor, Madison, partner, 1973-75; Eightieth Judicial Circuit, Indiana, judge pro-tempore, 1975-76; Fifth Judicial Circuit, Indiana, judge, 1977-88; Hensley, Walro, Collins & Hensley, Madison, partner, 1988—. Member of Indiana General Assembly, 1961-62; prosecuting attorney of Fifth Judicial Indiana Circuit, 1963-66. *Military service:* U.S. Navy, hospital corpsman, 1944-46, journalist in Korea, 1951-52.

MEMBER: Mystery Writers of America, Science Fiction Writers of America, Indiana State Bar Association, Jefferson County Bar Association.

WRITINGS:

The Color of Hate, Ace, 1961.
Deliver Us to Evil, Doubleday, 1971.
Legislative Body, Doubleday, 1972.
The Poison Summer, Doubleday, 1974.
Song of Corpus Juris, Doubleday, 1974.
Rivertown Risk, Doubleday, 1977.
A Killing in Gold, Doubleday, 1978.
Minor Murders, Doubleday, 1980.
Outcasts, Doubleday, 1981.
Final Doors (short stories), 1981.
Robak's Cross, Doubleday, 1985.
Robak's Fire, Doubleday, 1986.
Color Him Guilty, Walker, 1987.
Robak's Firm (short stories), Doubleday, 1987.
Fort's Law, Doubleday, 1988.
Robak's Run, Doubleday, in press.

Contributor of more than fifty science fiction and suspense stories to magazines.

SIDELIGHTS: Joe L. Hensley, a judge and former attorney in Indiana, is creator of a series of whodunits featuring Don Robak. With a background similar to the author's, lawyer Robak defends the innocent and tries to identify the guilty in Indiana. Hensley "always uses his knowledge [of the state and its judicial system] . . . to enhance his well-woven novels of chicanery and murder," states Alice Cromie in the *Chicago Tribune Book World.*

Hensley told *CA:* "I'm a former judge who retired from the bench unbeaten and unbowed. Time is still difficult, but these days I try to find more of it for writing. My books and stories are part of my legal life. Although they usually take the suspense form, my books are about people who must live in this complicated and devious world all of us try our best to exist within. I find that I can't easily stop writing. So I get up earlier, work harder, and hope to get more done. It isn't fun anymore, but it's something I do. I'm glad I do it and I doubt that anything could make me stop."

BIOGRAPHICAL/CRITICAL SOURCES:

PERIODICALS

Chicago Tribune Book World, June 21, 1981.
New York Times Book Review, March 1, 1981, November 30, 1986.
Washington Post Book World, February 15, 1981, January 17, 1988.

*   *   *

HERGE
See REMI, Georges

*   *   *

HERMAND, Jost 1930-

PERSONAL: Born April 11, 1930, in Kassel, Germany (now West Germany); son of Heinz and Annelies (Hucke) Hermand; married Elisabeth Jagenburg, 1956. *Education:* University of Marburg, D.Phil., 1955.

ADDRESSES: Home—845 Terry Pl., Madison, Wis. 53711. *Office*—Department of German, University of Wisconsin, Madison, Wis. 53706.

CAREER: Free-lance writer, 1955-58; University of Wisconsin—Madison, assistant professor, 1958-61, associate professor,

1961-63, professor of German, 1963-67, Vilas Research Professor of German, 1967—. Visiting professor at U.S. and European universities, including Harvard University, Free University of Berlin, University of Freiburg, and University of Texas.

AWARDS, HONORS: American Council of Learned Societies fellowship, 1963.

WRITINGS:

(With Richard Hamann) *Deutsche Kunst und Kultur,* five volumes, Akademie, 1959-75.
Von Mainz nach Weimar, Metzler, 1969.
Pop International, Athenaeum (Frankfurt), 1971.
Unbequeme Literatur, Stiehm, 1971.
Der Schein des schoenen Lebens, Athenaeum, 1972.
Streitobjekt Heine, Fischer Athenaeum, 1975.
Der fruehe Heine, Winkler, 1976.
(With Evelyn T. Beck) *Interpretive Synthesis,* Ungar, 1976.
Stile, Ismen, Etiketten, Athenaeum, 1978.
(With Frank Trommler) *Die Kultur der Weimarer,* Nymphenburger, 1978.
Sieben Arten an Deutschland zu Leiden, Athenaeum, 1979.
Orte: Irgendwo, Athenaeum, 1981.
Konkretes Hoeren: Zum Inhalt der Instrumentalmusik, Argument, 1981.
Die Kultur der Bundesrepublik, Nymphenburger, Volume 1, 1985, Volume 2, 1988.
(With James Steakley) *Writings of German Composers,* Continuum, 1985.
Adolph Menzel, Rowohlt, 1986.
Der alte Traum vom neuen Reich, Athenaeum, 1988.
Arnold Zweig, Rowohlt, 1990.

*   *   *

HIGHAM, Robin (David Stewart) 1925-

PERSONAL: Born June 20, 1925, in London, England; United States citizen; son of Frank David (a literary agent and novelist) and Anne (Stewart) Higham; married Barbara Davies, 1950; children: Susan, Martha, Carol. *Education:* Attended University of New Hampshire, 1947-48; Harvard University, A.B. (cum laude), 1950, Ph.D., 1957; Claremont Graduate School, M.A., 1953. *Religion:* Presbyterian.

ADDRESSES: Home—2961 Nevada St., Manhattan, Kan. 66502. *Office*—History Department, Kansas State University, Manhattan, Kan. 66506-7186. *Agent*—Harold Ober Associates, 40 East 49th St., New York, N.Y. 10017.

CAREER: Instructor at Webb School of California, 1950-52, and University of Massachusetts, 1954-57; University of North Carolina at Chapel Hill, assistant professor, 1957-63; Kansas State University, Manhattan, associate professor, 1963-66, professor of history, 1966—, graduate faculty lecturer, 1971. Historian, British Overseas Airways Corp., 1960-66, 1976-78; archivist, American Committee on the History of the Second World War, 1977—. U.S. correspondent, *Histoire economie et societe,* 1984—. Vice chairman of editorial board, University Press of Kansas, 1967-71; military advisory editor, University Press of Kentucky, 1969-75, adviser to history committee, American Institute of Aeronautics and Astronautics, 1974—; founder, president, director, and publisher, Sunflower University Press, 1977—. *Military service:* Royal Air Force, 1943-47; became flight sergeant pilot; received Burma Star.

MEMBER: International Institute for Strategic Studies, American Aviation Historical Society, U.S. Naval Institute, American Military Institute, Air Force Historical Foundation, Organization of American Historians, Aviation/Space Writers Association, American Committee on the History of the Second World War (member of board of directors, 1980—), American Association for State and Local History, Society for History of Technology, Council of the Society for Army Historical Research (corresponding member), Conference on British Studies (member of publications committee, 1965—), Friends of the RAF Museum, Arnold Air Society (life member), Society for Scholarly Publishing, Conference of Historic Aviation Writers (organizer, 1982—), Riley County Historical Society (director, 1983-88).

AWARDS, HONORS: Social Science Research Council, National Security Policy Research fellowship, 1960-61; honorary colonel, Tar Heel Air Force, 1962; Samuel Eliot Morison Prize, American Military Institute, 1985; President's Award, Air Force Historical Foundation, 1988.

WRITINGS:

Britain's Imperial Air Routes, 1918-1939, G. T. Foulis, 1960, Archon Books, 1961.
The British Rigid Airship, 1908-1931: A Study in Weapons Policy, G. T. Foulis, 1961, Greenwood Press, 1976.
Armed Forces in Peacetime: Britain, 1918-1939, G. T. Foulis, 1963.
The Military Intellectuals in Britain: 1918-1939, Rutgers University Press, 1966, reprinted, Greenwood Press, 1981.
(With David H. Zook, Jr.) *A Short History of Warfare,* Twayne, 1966.
Air Power: A Concise History, St. Martin's, 1972, 3rd edition, Sunflower University Press, 1988.
The Complete Academic: Being an Informal Guide to the Ivory Tower, St. Martin's, 1975.
(Author of introduction with Donald J. Mrozek and Jeanne Louise Allen Newell) Franklin S. Allen *The Martin Marauder and the Franklin Allens: A Wartime Love Story,* Sunflower University Press, 1980.
(With Mary Crisper and Guy Dresser) *A Brief Guide to Scholarly Editing,* Sunflower University Press, 1982.
Diary of Disaster: British Aid to Greece, 1940-1941, University Press of Kentucky, 1986.

EDITOR

The Consolidated Author and Subject Index to the Journal of the Royal United Service Institution, 1857-1963, compiled by Karen Cox Wing, University Microfilms, 1964.
Bayonets in the Street, University Press of Kansas, 1969, enlarged edition, Sunflower University Press, 1989.
Official Histories: Essays in Historiography and Bibliographies of Official History and of Service Historical Sections around the World, Kansas State University Library, 1970.
Civil Wars in the Twentieth Century, University Press of Kentucky, 1972.
A Guide to the Sources of British Military History, University of California Press, 1972.
(Supervisory editor) John Greenwood, *American Defense Policy since 1945: A Preliminary Bibliography,* University Press of Kansas, 1973.
Intervention or Abstention: The Dilemma of U.S. Foreign Policy, University Press of Kentucky, 1975.
Flying Combat Aircraft of the USAAF-USAF, Iowa State University Press, Volume 1 (with Abigail T. Siddall), 1975, Volume 2 (with Carol Williams), 1978, Volume 3 (with Williams), Sunflower University Press, 1980.

Guide to the Sources of U.S. Military History, Archon Books, 1975, (with Mrozek), Supplement 1, 1981, Supplement 2, 1985, Supplement 3, 1990.

(With Carol Brandt) *The U.S. Army in Peacetime: Essays in Honor of the Bicentennial,* Freedom Park Press, 1975.

(With Jacob W. Kipp) *ACTA of the Washington ICMH Meeting: August, 1975,* Military Affairs/Aerospace Historian Publishing, 1976.

(With Kipp) *Soviet Aviation and Air Power,* Westview Press, 1978.

Keneth P. Werrell, *Eighth Air Force Bibliography: An Extended Essay and Listing of Published and Unpublished Materials,* Military Affairs/Aerospace Historian Publishing, 1981.

(With George Ham) *The Rise of the Wheat State: A History of Kansas Agriculture, 1861-1986,* Sunflower University Press, 1987.

(With daughter, Carol Lee Higham) George Stewart, *Morning in Kansas: A Near-Frontier Boyhood,* University Press of Kansas, c. 1988.

(With Williams and Tony Crawford) *Kansas State University—A Hundred and Twenty-fifth Anniversary Illustrated History,* Sunflower University Press, 1989.

Also editor of *ACTA of the Washington Meeting of the ICMH, 1985.*

CONTRIBUTOR

Joseph Dunner, editor, *Handbook of World History: Concepts and Issues,* Philosophical Library, 1967.

William Geffen, *Command and Commanders in Modern Warfare,* U.S.A.F. Academy, 1970.

The Normandy Invasion in Retrospect, University Press of Kansas, 1971.

Seemacht und Geschichte: Festschrift zum 80. Geburtstag von Friedrich Ruge, Deutsches Marine Institut, 1974.

ACTA of the ICMH at Athens, 1987, [Greece], 1988.

OTHER

Editor with Kipp, "International Military History" series, Garland, 1978—. Contributor, *Dictionary of Business Biography,* edited by David J. Jeremy, Butterworth & Co., 1982-84; contributor, *Encyclopedia Britannica, U.S. Naval Institute Proceedings,* and *Proceedings* of the American Society of Mechanical Engineers and New York Academy of Sciences. Contributor to *Christian Science Monitor, American Neptune,* and to other history, business, and military journals. Advisory editor, *Technology and Culture,* 1967-85; *Military Affairs,* editor, 1968-88, editor emeritus, 1989—; *Aerospace Historian,* editor, 1970-88, editor emeritus, 1988—; military advisory editor, University Press of Kentucky, 1970-75; editor, *Mandarin Memo,* 1974-80; *Revue international d'histoire militaire,* member of editorial board, 1976-85, president of consultative committee, 1981-85; editor, *Journal of the West,* 1977—; member of editorial advisory board, *Defense Analysis,* 1984—; member of advisory board, "Smithsonian History of Aviation" series, 1987—.

WORK IN PROGRESS: Peacekeeping; For Want of a Spanner; Essays on the RAF; The Aegean Basin: Its History, Battles, and Touchstones; BOAC; Nationalization in Policy and Practice; Production and Politics: The British Aircraft Industry; Military Frontiersmanship: World Wide Comparisons; a book on the history of the Royal Air Force.

SIDELIGHTS: Robin Higham once told *CA:* "Having grown up in Britain with a father who was an author's agent and a mother with an interest in history and an uncle who wrote, I always had as a goal publication. My first published work was my honor's thesis from Harvard. I wish to preserve and explain historical phenomenon and help people use history to solve present problems rather than to repeat past mistakes.

"I have to do my work when I can grab the time. I consequently normally now have to write whenever there is a break of even a few minutes, but I prefer to be able to have four hours at a time. As I am usually working on several books at once, including also other people's, the circumstances behind any book are hard to define, but usually it is because I see an opportunity to answer a question that has not yet been dealt with. A number of my books have been published on both sides of the Atlantic in Britain and America; one is used as a text at the Royal Swedish Staff College in Stockholm and [*A Short History of Warfare*] has been translated into Hebrew for the Israelis as their official text for the history of warfare, and into Chinese as a text there. *The British Rigid Airship* was the basis for an English Granada-TV presentation some years ago.

"Young writers should not be afraid to put pen to paper. I have followed Nevil Shute's advice, get a typewriter that works—and use it constantly. I write 70 to 80 letters a week and also try to make my classroom work a careful selection of words. I started out being a Samuel Eliot Morison student at Harvard and I have always admired his breadth and readability."

BIOGRAPHICAL/CRITICAL SOURCES:

PERIODICALS

Flying, February, 1976.
Times Literary Supplement, November 10, 1966, July 21, 1972, November 3, 1972, July 3, 1987.

*   *   *

HILL, Elizabeth Starr   1925-

PERSONAL: Born November 4, 1925, in Lynn Haven, Fla.; daughter of Raymond King (a science fiction novelist) and Gabrielle (Wilson) Cummings; married Russell Gibson Hill (a chemical engineer), May 28, 1949; children: Andrea van Waldron, Bradford Wray. *Education:* Attended Finch Junior College, New York, N.Y., and Columbia University. *Religion:* Episcopalian.

ADDRESSES: Home—Princeton, N.J.; and Winter Park, Fla. *Agent*—Harold Ober Associates, Inc., 40 East 49th St., New York, N.Y. 10017.

CAREER: Free-lance writer; actress in radio and summer stock productions.

AWARDS, HONORS: Evan's Corner was selected by the American Library Association as a Notable Book for Children.

WRITINGS:

JUVENILE

The Wonderful Visit to Miss Liberty, Holt, 1961.
The Window Tulip, Warne, 1964.
Evan's Corner, Holt, 1967, new edition, Penguin Books, 1990.
Master Mike and the Miracle Maid, Holt, 1967.
Pardon My Fangs, Holt, 1969.
Bells: A Book to Begin On, Holt, 1970.
Ever-After Island (Junior Literary Guild selection), Dutton, 1977.
Fangs Aren't Everything, Dutton, 1985.
When Christmas Comes (Junior Library Guild selection), Penguin Books, 1989.

Contributor to *Encyclopaedia Brittanica.* Contributor of stories and articles to *New Yorker, Reader's Digest, Harper's Bazaar, Seventeen, Woman's Day, Woman's Home Companion, Good Housekeeping, Collier's, Cricket, New World Writing, Faith Today,* and other magazines in the United States, Britain, and France.

MEDIA ADAPTATIONS: A movie version of *Evan's Corner* was produced by Stephen Bosustow Productions in 1969.

AVOCATIONAL INTERESTS: Music, theater, art, gardening.

*   *   *

HILL, Roger
  See PAINE, Lauran (Bosworth)

*   *   *

HILL, W. M.
  See DODD, Edward Howard, Jr.

*   *   *

HITE, Shere 1942-

PERSONAL: First name pronounced "share"; given name Shirley Diana; born November 2, 1942, in St. Joseph, Mo.; daughter of Paul Gregory (a flight controller); legally adopted by Raymond Hite (a truck driver); married Friedrich Hoericke (a concert pianist), 1985. *Education:* University of Florida, B.A. (cum laude), 1964, M.A., 1968; further graduate study at Columbia University, 1968-69.

ADDRESSES: Home—New York, N.Y.; and Laffont, 6 Place St., Sulpice, Paris 75006, France. *Office*—P.O. Box 5282, FDR Station, New York, N.Y. 10022.

CAREER: Model for Wilhelmina Agency, late 1960s; National Organization for Women (NOW), New York City, director of Feminist Sexuality Project, 1972-78; Hite Research International, New York City, director, 1978—. Instructor in female sexuality, New York University, 1977—; lecturer, Harvard University, McGill University, Columbia University, and women's groups, 1977-83. Member of advisory board, American Foundation of Gender and Genital Medicine, Johns Hopkins University.

MEMBER: National Organization for Women (NOW), American Historical Association, American Sociological Association, American Association for the Advancement of Science, Society for the Scientific Study of Sex, Women's Health Network, Academy of Political Science, Women's History Association.

WRITINGS:

(Compiler and editor) *Sexual Honesty: By Women for Women,* Warner Paperback Library, 1974.
The Hite Report: A Nationwide Study of Female Sexuality, Macmillan, 1976.
The Hite Report on Male Sexuality (Book-of-the-Month Club alternate selection), Knopf, 1981, published as *The Hite Report: A Study of Male Sexuality,* Ballantine, 1982.
Women and Love: A Cultural Revolution in Progress, Knopf, 1987.

Consulting editor, *Journal of Sex Education and Therapy* and *Journal of Sexuality and Disability.*

SIDELIGHTS: Shere Hite, who prefers to be called a cultural historian rather than a sex researcher or sexologist, has written three controversial, best-selling books on the topic of human sexuality—*The Hite Report: A Nationwide Study of Female Sexuality, The Hite Report on Male Sexuality,* and *Women and Love: A Cultural Revolution in Progress.* Each book was generated from lengthy questionnaires completed by either female or male respondents from across the nation, and each presents insightful, and even novel, information about this charged topic. With each of these publications, however, critics have called her research methods into question and some have criticized her for what they deem her strong feminist bias. Nevertheless, a thread of appreciation runs through the commentary, for many feel Hite has listened with compassion to the sexual frustrations of contemporary women and men. For instance, Arlie Russell Hochschild maintains in his *New York Times Book Review* assessment of *Women and Love* that "[Hite] sets us next to her in a kind of confessional booth to listen through the curtain. . . . She makes [the women] know they are not alone, she articulates their discontent."

Hite was born Shirley Diana Gregory in 1942 in St. Joseph, Missouri, but her mother and father divorced shortly after the end of World War II. When her mother remarried, Hite was legally adopted by Raymond Hite. This second marriage ended in divorce, as well, and for many years thereafter Hite lived on and off with her grandparents. Hite's earliest desire was to be a classical composer, "but how many women have you heard of becoming composers, right?," she asked *Chicago Tribune* interviewer Cheryl Lavin; accordingly, Hite says her second choice was "trying to figure out how society got where it is and why is it so irrational." Thus, after moving to Florida to stay with some relatives, Hite pursued her B.A. and M.A. degrees in history at the University of Florida. In 1968, she moved to New York City to further her study of history at Columbia University but withdrew early on and began modeling at the Wilhelmina Agency for the money. Her first link with the feminist movement developed shortly thereafter when she modeled as a secretary in a typewriter advertisement that proclaimed: "The typewriter is so smart she doesn't have to be," notes Martha Smilgis for *Time.* Because the ad incensed her, Hite joined the National Organization for Women (NOW) which was protesting the ad at the time. Then in 1971, according to Smilgis, "Hite read a pamphlet in the NOW office, *The Myth of Female Orgasm,* and decided to create a questionnaire on the issue for a NOW-sponsored 'speak up.' As she read the women's responses about their sexuality, 'a whole picture of the universe began to fall into place,' says Hite. 'Without feminism I don't know what I would be doing today. It gave me the belief in myself.' " It was this belief in herself and other women that motivated Hite to tap into the subject of contemporary sexual problems.

The first book in Hite's trilogy, *The Hite Report: A Nationwide Study of Female Sexuality,* was an immediate bestseller and was placed in the company of such classic works on sexuality as the Kinsey report and the Masters and Johnson reports. For a period of four years Hite distributed approximately 100,000 lengthy questionnaires to women through such sources as NOW, church newsletters, and *Mademoiselle, Oui,* and *Ms.* magazines. She based the resultant book on the responses of approximately 3,000 women ranging in age from fourteen to seventy-three, with representation from forty-nine states. According to Jean Seligmann for *Newsweek,* whereas the Kinsey and the Masters and Johnson reports were the product of interviews and laboratory research conducted by these authority figures, "the women themselves are presented as the authorities on their own sexuality" in *The Hite Report.* Thus, "reading *The Hite Report,*" notes Karen Durbin for *Mademoiselle,* "is rather like sitting in on a mass-consciousness raising session about female sexuality. Women talk in unusual detail about their sexual experiences and feelings—graphically, factually, rapturously, glumly, and sometimes brutally."

Hite's general conclusion in this first book is that current notions on sexuality must be revised if women are to achieve sexual fulfillment. Hite faults a male-oriented pattern of sexual expression for many of women's sexual difficulties: "There has rarely been any acknowledgement that female sexuality might have a complex nature of its own which would be more than just the logical counterpart of (what we think of as) male sexuality," she writes in the text. Hite also insists that the sexual revolution of the 1960s and 1970s created pressure for women to say "yes" to sex, but that it did not liberate women in any substantial way; that is, women did not find it any easier to say what they really wanted sexually from their partners.

Critical reaction to *The Hite Report,* as well as to the succeeding works in Hite's trilogy, is mixed. *Village Voice* contributor James Wolcott blasts the book, which he sees as a "feminist anthem. . . . *The Hite Report* is a bull session to which [the male writer] has not been invited. Nonetheless, I intend to intrude, for I think *The Hite Report* is a bum book, useful as a masturbation manual perhaps, but dubious as sociology, drear and dry as literature, and hopelessly muddled as polemic." Wolcott begins his criticism by questioning Hite's methodology. He feels the questionnaire Hite employed "bulges with questions so nebulous, so ludicrously open-ended, that it is a wonder the replies didn't run the riverrun length of *Finnegans Wake.*" He also questions the representativeness of Hite's sample after taking into consideration the organizations and magazines involved in distributing the questionnaire. He distrusts Hite's conclusions and proclaims that the "cant is never thicker than when Hite is chanting about the freedom to do your own you-know-what." Likewise, *Washington Post Book World* reviewer Barbara G. Harrison's analysis of the work is generally pessimistic. One of her chief complaints is Hite's overemphasis on the physiological: "I have no prudish objection to reading . . . about the sexual activities and preferences of the 3000 women Hite surveyed. I do, however, think it's daft to act, as Hite does, on the assumption that sex and love are unrelated phenomena. . . . With few exceptions, the questions call for bald physiological fact rather than for psychological nuance . . . which, as good sense ought to tell anybody, is boring." Harrison additionally feels that the many "fancy, flimsy, and unreadable statistical charts and appendices" included in the work as a means of assuring the book's scientific credibility instead "serve only to cast doubt on her methodology." However, Harrison goes on to maintain that doubtful methodology is not the book's main flaw: "What is more detrimental to the integrity of *The Hite Report* is the absence of any synthesizing, reflective intelligence to help us interpret the data . . . which is another way of saying that Hite did not know how to organize her material, or—which is worse—organized it according to her own transparent biases." In the end, though, Harrison recommends the book because she feels the authentic voices of the confused and pained women ought to be heard. "Read it," Harrison writes, "because the answers of many women transcend the limitations imposed on them by the nuts-and-bolts questions Hite asked. Read it because it is frequently provocative and affecting. . . . Read it because, while no one can swear to the honesty of all the answers, even the lies we tell one another are instructive."

Presenting the book from a more positive overall stance are Durbin for *Mademoiselle* and *New York Times Book Review* contributor Erica Jong. Durbin explains that "whatever the limitations of *The Hite Report,* its intentions are more than mechanistic he-

donism. If it lobbies for anything, it's for illumination and understanding of a dimension of women's experience that may always remain somewhat mysterious but has so far only been needlessly mystified." In turn, Jong optimistically comments that *The Hite Report* represents the culmination in terms of books that allow women to speak for themselves. According to Jong, women who read *The Hite Report* "will feel enormously reassured about their own sexuality and if enough young men read it, the quality of sex in America is bound to improve."

Hite followed her report on female sexuality with her equally controversial book *The Hite Report on Male Sexuality.* Like the previous work, this book chiefly presents verbatim questionnaire responses, but this time from men—more than 7,000 of them from ages thirteen to ninety-seven. Lynn Langway writes in her *Newsweek* commentary that this is a "larger [1,129 pages], more ambitious and provocative work than its predecessor" and she quotes Hite as saying: " 'I think it will definitely enrage and enlighten. The book was trying to ask how men feel about sexuality. The answer was they like it and they treasure it—but at the same time they dislike it and feel very put upon by it'. . . . Like the women depicted in her first book, many of the 7,239 men who participated in the second study said they felt trapped by sexual stereotypes, craved emotional intimacy—and found themselves unable to talk openly about their sexual angers, anxieties and desires."

Time reviewer John Leo thinks that Hite presents some bizarre theories on male sexuality in the book. For one, he says she "persistently applies a hard-line feminist interpretation. Most sexual problems and sexual differences, she argues, are the result of the 'patriarchal culture,' the age-old male suppression of women. Men like to have intercourse not because of biology, but because they are 'brought up to feel that [this is] a vital part of being a man.' " For another, according to Leo, Hite claims that many men have extramarital affairs because "they come to think of their wives as their mothers, and the incest taboo obviously inhibits sex with mothers." Leo concludes that occasionally "Hite descends from the soapbox long enough to notice what her men are saying. 'The basic feeling that comes through,' she writes, 'is that men feel they are not getting enough love, affection or appreciation.' "

Regarding critical reception to her second book, Hite commented in her interview with Lavin: "On my first book I had mostly women reviewers, and 95 percent of them liked it. On the second I had mostly men reviewers, and 95 percent of them didn't like it. I thought I was saying all these things about masculinity and the patterns of men's lives, and in the press all I'd see is, 'Is she scientific?' and 'Is she just trying to make money?' " According to Roger L. Gould in the *New York Times Book Review,* "For all her efforts, 'The Hite Report on Male Sexuality' is based on a nonrepresentative sample of the American male population. . . . Hite's book . . . informs us only about a specific fraction of our adult male population, and the professional therapist or counselor will find nothing new in it." Nevertheless, Gould goes on to say that "for the nonprofessional, [the book] may be an eye opener in the tradition of the original reports of Alfred Kinsey. . . . [It] pulverizes any remaining myths about 'normal' male sexuality that have not already been reduced to dust by earlier reports." And although Eliot Fremont-Smith claims in his *Village Voice* analysis that Hite overemphasizes what males dislike about sexual intercourse and downplays what they like, he does defend her feminist tone: "Hite's feminism . . . has to be accepted in the natural course of things—it's a contradiction of terms to think of her doing these books and *not* being feminist. It's dumb, too; I would say that a lot of critics of Hite are dumb, thinking she could be neuter or something." In turn, Langway concludes her review by quoting John Money, a Johns Hopkins University psychologist: "Hite has 'uncovered the extraordinary, romantic sentimentality of men who have been brainwashed to feel that they don't *have* these feelings.' " As Langway comments, "Such insights are profoundly important."

In her *Time* contribution, Claudia Wallis estimates that the first two books in Hite's trilogy garnered $2.5 million for the author and that the third, the 900-page "tome" *Women and Love,* is "characteristically grandiose in scope, murky in methodology—and right on target for commercial appeal." The book stirred up a controversy as surely as the previous two had, with some critics blasting Hite for being anti-male and others lauding her for relaying an important message about the disillusionment women experience in their relationships with men. Again, focus was on Hite's research methodology—with complaints centering on the small return rate of 4.5 percent, which many claim cannot provide a fair representation of the U.S. population as a whole, particularly when it is believed that only the most discontented would take the time to answer some 120 essay questions. In general, critics were split on this issue of methodology. For example, in the *Los Angeles Times,* Carol Tavris is especially judgmental of Hite's statistics: "The numbers are, to put it simply, a joke. . . . [Hite] devotes a chapter to defending subjective routes to truth, and then tries to convince the reader that her work is objective and scientifically accurate as well. . . . Well, what is wrong with subjective routes to truth? . . . The answer, I think, lies in the growing popularity of what Robert Asahina, a writer and editor, calls 'social-science fiction'—books that are not really social science but 'naive personal journalism'. . . . The impression that they are based on 'research' adds a veneer of respectability and seriousness, and supposedly elevates them above the authors' personal experiences." Also questioning Hite's statistical validity is *Los Angeles Times* staff writer Elizabeth Mehren who reports that the results of a Washington Post-ABC News public opinion survey are very much at odds with Hite's findings. Whereas Hite's statistics indicate that 98 percent of the women in her study are unhappy with some aspect of their relationship with men, this telephone survey of 1,505 men and women from across the nation found that 93 percent of the women called their relationships with men good or excellent.

Supportive viewpoints do abound, however, as evidenced by Mehren's commentary. She quotes University of Toronto psychiatrist Dr. Frank Sommers as saying that the debate surrounding Hite's book is "part of a defensive reaction where you shoot the messenger." Mehren further quotes Max Siegal, a former president of the American Psychiatric Association: "The big flaw I don't think is methodological. I think it's in society, in a society that is not willing to look at itself and the problems we have in relating to each other." Hite agrees, according to London *Times* reviewer Victoria McKee: "Hite believes that the attacks on her methods have been launched almost entirely by men in order to conjure up a smoke screen to obscure the 'real' issues raised by her book."

The "real" issues of *Women and Love* are summed up by *Ms.* contributor Lisa Duggan when she writes: "[Hite] argues that we are in a difficult phase of a cultural revolution, that women are extending the fight for meaningful equality into the innermost recesses of personal relationships, demanding that life be transformed to incorporate their deeply held values of equality, cooperation, communication, and caring." The chief complaint of the women in Hite's survey seems to be the failure of men to respond to their emotional needs. As Toronto *Globe and Mail* critic Michele Landsberg explains, "The voices of the women . . . are not

so much feminist or male-hating as puzzled, depressed, humorous, loving or rueful. But most of them agree: they're tired of doing all the emotional housework." Indeed, Hite reports that 87 percent of her respondents are emotionally closer to their women friends than to their husbands or lovers, and also that 70 percent of women married more than five years reported having extramarital affairs.

In the end, there are those who find Hite's work purposeful and compassionate, and there are those who challenge its very foundation. With respect to *Women and Love,* William Robertson for the *Chicago Tribune* calls it a "monument to dim-wittedness" and also a "bore. There's not an original thought anywhere in sight. . . . In the past, . . . the war between the sexes wasn't so carefully overburdened with mathematical evidence that attempts to convey the impression of truth. . . . She even ignores the evidence of her own research: The hopeless women in her survey don't seem to believe much is changing at all." The complaint that Mariana Valverde voices in her *Globe and Mail* analysis, which Robertson also shares, is that the book's structure obliterates the uniqueness of Hite's individual respondents: "The thousands of pages penned by women, often with great care, are simply put on the floor, cut into bits, and pasted into a mosaic without regard for the integrity of the person whose innermost feelings are . . . being utilized."

Those who are optimistic about *Women and Love* are generally so because Hite let the women themselves tell their stories of pain and disillusionment. "If 'Women and Love' isn't good social science," remarks Hochschild, "it is a valuable, provocative, loosely argued, searching meditation on how culture influences love, illustrated by many hypnotizing, sad, sweet, chilling and lurid stories." Although Hochschild believes that Hite is dealing with "fishy statistics," "what is wonderfully worthwhile about 'Women and Love' are the moving stories of women and the continuous stream of deep, probing questions Ms. Hite raises about them. . . . She also helps women make sense of their feelings. . . . She articulates their discontent." Landsberg also supports this work. She expresses her viewpoint that many critics "can't have read the book very seriously. Few researchers have ever listened so deeply to the innermost thoughts of their subjects. In fact, the . . . book . . . strikes me as a good deal more thorough and 'scientific' than the idiotic multiple-choice quizzes, the market surveys and opinion polls that reporters usually accept so reverentially. Scientific or not, the book is significant." Scientific or not, liked or not, Hite's trilogy on human sexuality has provided men and women the freedom to voice their opinions on this matter.

AVOCATIONAL INTERESTS: Playing and listening to music, old movies, reading Proust, interior decoration.

BIOGRAPHICAL/CRITICAL SOURCES:

BOOKS

Hite, Shere, *The Hite Report: A Nationwide Study of Female Sexuality,* Macmillan, 1976.
Hite, Shere, *The Hite Report on Male Sexuality,* Knopf, 1981, published as *The Hite Report: A Study of Male Sexuality,* Ballantine, 1982.
Hite, Shere, *Women and Love: A Cultural Revolution in Progress,* Knopf, 1987.

PERIODICALS

Chicago Tribune, November 28, 1982.
Globe and Mail (Toronto), January 2, 1988, January 9, 1988.

Los Angeles Times, October 29, 1987, November 1, 1987, November 16, 1987.
Maclean's, October 19, 1987.
Mademoiselle, January, 1977.
Ms., October, 1981, December, 1987.
Newsweek, October 18, 1976, June 15, 1981, October 19, 1987, November 23, 1987.
New York Times, November 13, 1987, November 15, 1987.
New York Times Book Review, October 3, 1976, July 21, 1981, November 15, 1987.
Psychology Today, December, 1976.
Spectator, March 12, 1988.
Time, October 25, 1976, June 15, 1981, October 12, 1987.
Times (London), November 16, 1987, February 19, 1988, February 25, 1988.
Tribune Books (Chicago), December 2, 1987.
Village Voice, November 1, 1976, June 24, 1981.
Washington Post, November 10, 1987, November 14, 1987.
Washington Post Book World, March 13, 1977, June 21, 1981.*

—*Sketch by Cheryl Gottler*

*   *   *

HOAGLAND, Edward   1932-

PERSONAL: Born December 21, 1932, in New York, N.Y.; son of Warren Eugene (an attorney) and Helen (Morley) Hoagland; married Amy J. Ferrara, 1960 (divorced); married Marion Magid, March 28, 1968; children: Molly. *Education:* Harvard University, A.B., 1954.

ADDRESSES: Home—P.O. Box 51, Barton, Vt. 05822. *Agent*—Robert Lescher, 155 East 71st St., New York, N.Y. 10021.

CAREER: Novelist and essayist, 1954—. Instructor at New School for Social Research, 1963-64, Rutgers University, 1966, City University of New York, 1967-68, University of Iowa, 1978 and 1982, Columbia University, 1980-81, Bennington College, 1987-89, and Brown University, 1988. *Military service:* U.S. Army, 1955-57.

MEMBER: American Academy and Institute of Arts and Letters.

AWARDS, HONORS: Houghton Mifflin literary fellowship, 1954, for *Cat Man;* Longview Foundation Award, 1961; American Academy of Arts and Letters travelling fellowship and Guggenheim fellowship, both 1964; O. Henry Award, 1971; New York State Council on the Arts award and Brandeis University Creative Arts Awards Commission citation in literature, both 1972; National Book Award nomination, 1974, for *Walking the Dead Diamond River;* Guggenheim fellowship, 1975; National Book Critics Circle Award nomination in nonfiction, 1979, for *African Calliope: A Journey to the Sudan;* Harold D. Vursell Award from American Academy and Institute of Arts and Letters, 1981; American Book Award nomination, 1982, for paperback edition of *African Calliope.*

WRITINGS:

NOVELS

Cat Man, Houghton, 1956.
The Circle Home, Crowell, 1960.
The Peacock's Tail, McGraw, 1965.
Seven Rivers West, Summit Books, 1986.

NONFICTION

Notes from the Century Before: A Journal from British Columbia, Random House, 1969, reprinted, North Point Press, 1982.

The Courage of Turtles: Fifteen Essays by Edward Hoagland, Random House, 1971, reprinted, North Point Press, 1985.
Walking the Dead Diamond River, Random House, 1973, reprinted, North Point Press, 1985.
The Moose on the Wall: Field Notes from the Vermont Wilderness, Barrie & Jenkins, 1974.
Red Wolves and Black Bears, Random House, 1976.
African Calliope: A Journey to the Sudan, Random House, 1979.
Geoffrey Wolff, editor, *The Edward Hoagland Reader,* Random House, 1979.
The Tugman's Passage, Random House, 1982.
City Tales, Capra, 1986.
(Editor) *The Penguin Nature Library,* 16 volumes, Penguin Books, 1985-90.
Heart's Desire: The Best of Edward Hoagland, Summit Books, 1988.

OTHER

Contributor to numerous periodicals, including *Esquire, New Yorker, New American Review, Transatlantic Review, Sports Illustrated,* and *New York Times.*

SIDELIGHTS: Edward Hoagland's award-winning essays explore the world of nature, the homely affairs of the human heart, and the dynamics of changing civilizations. Hoagland delights in presenting not only the sights of things but his insights into them as well, "trapping feeling and experience into an unexpected truth," to quote *New York Times Book Review* contributor Dan Wakefield. The author, a native of metropolitan New York, is best known for his closely-observed pieces on wild animals and natural phenomena; *Washington Post Book World* correspondent Edwin M. Yoder, Jr., notes that Hoagland "is one of New York City's important links with the wilderness." Yoder continues: "In the editorial columns of *The New York Times* the reader unnerved by nerve gas or frayed by the cost of living index may suddenly come upon [a Hoagland] editorial that begins, 'There's nothing like a canoe.'. . . And since the call of the wild is rarely heard in the 21 Club, or even on 43rd Street, Hoagland's nature prose is the next best thing. And it is a good thing indeed." In the *New York Review of Books,* R. W. Flint calls Hoagland's work "a gem of atmospheric figure painting and imaginative anthropology: thousands of anecdotes and small observations resolving themselves into a gallery of shaped figures."

The son of an oil corporation attorney, Hoagland grew up in Connecticut and Manhattan. A severe stammer restricted his social contacts, and he found himself most at home on long, solitary strolls or in the company of animals. Hoagland is quoted in the *Dictionary of Literary Biography* on the results of his affliction. "Words are spoken at considerable cost to me, so a great value is placed on each one," he declares. "That has had some effect on me as a writer. As a child, since I couldn't talk to people, I became close to animals. I became an observer, and in all my books, even the novels, witnessing things is what counts." In his youth Hoagland was able to enhance his conventional education by indulging in unconventional pursuits—he worked for a time as a Ringling Brothers and Barnum and Baily circus hand, tramped across the country hobo-style, and worked in an army morgue. His first novel, *Cat Man,* was accepted by Houghton Mifflin shortly before he graduated from Harvard University.

Hoagland published three novels between 1956 and 1965. In the *Village Voice,* Ross Wetzsteon characterizes these works as "marvelously rendered settings (the circus, a boxing gym, a welfare hotel) in futile search of narrative." The critic adds: "Even more problematic, all three novels dealt with confrontations between unequals in narrowly confined settings, and while this allowed the novels to explore the nature of power in human relationships, their inability to achieve any kind of narrative or emotional resolution meant that their attempts at compassion too often had overtones of something close to sadism." *Dictionary of Literary Biography* contributor James A. Hart finds much to admire in Hoagland's early fiction. "We appreciate the individuality of the chapters, the varied nature of the prose (Hoagland has a good ear for dialogue), and the sympathetic recreation of life among the misfits and the oddballs . . . ," writes Hart. "The primitivism of his fiction may exclude a Jamesian exploration of a character's psychology, but it leads nevertheless to deeply moving and disturbing scenes. . . . Throughout the fiction, . . . one senses in Hoagland an educated sensitivity, a sturdy intelligence, and a tenacious individualism."

A regular contributor to magazines, Hoagland began to concentrate almost exclusively on nonfiction in the late 1960s. Since then his interests have led him far and wide, from the waters surrounding Manhattan to the desert wastes of the Sudan. As James Kaufman notes in the *Los Angeles Times,* Hoagland has subsequently become "one of our best and most esteemed nature writers." A love of wild animals invests Hoagland's essays with both enthusiasm and elegy—he fears for the future of many species but avoids dogmatic assertions on the subject. "Hoagland is surely one of our most truthful writers about nature, one of the few who can be counted on to avoid the distracting theatricality of preaching or blaming or apocalypse-mongering," claims Thomas R. Edwards in the *New York Times Book Review*. "And his truthfulness doesn't rule out the pleasures of a brilliant image . . . or of passages of sustained inventive brio." *Newsweek* correspondent Peter S. Prescott writes: "Hoagland lives, diving from the city to Vermont to look for mountains, to Minnesota to stalk black bears, to Texas to see if the red wolf has a chance to survive. He seeks out the wildlife biologists and follows them through the woods. When he comes to write about what he has learned he writes complex essays in which a lot of good hard information is refracted through a distinctive, likable sensibility. . . . More than most writers, he seems to use everything that has ever happened to him, everything he has ever heard."

Subjects from nature often highlight Hoagland's essay collections, but a Hoagland book may also address an array of urban and personal topics. In the *New York Times Book Review,* Diane Johnson observes: "The best moments of [Hoagland's work] concern not actions or escapades but general matters of enduring interest—the death of a father, childbirth, the relation of man and animals, qualities of the human heart. These are subjects about which wisdom is of better use than wit, and rarer—wisdom and a lively sense of the role of the imagination in getting through life." Critic Alfred Kazin also contends in a *New York Times Book Review* piece that Hoagland is "one of the best 'personal essayists' in the business, a virtuoso of the reader-capsizing sentence, a splendid observer of city street, circus lot, go-go girls, freight trains, juries in the jury room plus, and especially, any and every surviving patch of North American wild he can get to moon around in."

Stylistically, writes Wetzsteon, Hoagland is "gifted at rescuing moribund adjectives and nursing them back to health, at combining the arcane with the colloquial, at guiding us through bewildering but suddenly gratifying digressions (like detours that turn out to save hours), and especially at jolting one's mind with abrupt, revelatory transitions. . . . He also rescues, combines, guides, and jolts, dealing with places and subjects we know little and care less about, . . . revealing that the universe can be glimpsed in a turtle or a tugboat as well as in a grain of sand." In the *National Review,* poet Donald Hall suggests that Hoag-

land's writing "combines world and self, or creates a self that we watch with delight as it observes and renders the world. He mostly describes or recounts matters external to himself—a tugboat, a lion tamer, a settlement on the Blue Nile—but which he observes very much in his own person. . . . Always Hoagland is *there;* we feel him, we listen to him examine himself, remember, and even think. One has the impression not of egotism but of restless self-examination—skeptical, alert, and intelligent."

Many critics have responded warmly to Hoagland's work. Edwards claims that the author's essays offer "the welcome companionship of an unusual personality, a man determined to know the worst of us so that he can find something helpful to say, a lover of animals who will not have them sentimentalized simply because they are endangered . . . an intelligence that's quiet, speculative, sensible." In the *Village Voice,* L. S. Klepp writes: "These essays, conveying an individuality both stubborn and serene, remind us that resolute curiosity is an offspring of vitality. What comes through above all is Hoagland's love of life and of beings, human and otherwise, intensely alive." Diane Johnson similarly states that throughout his essays, fiction, and travel books, "it is against the deadness of life that Edward Hoagland writes, or at least that is the effect of his writing. Beneath the wise and faintly elegiac tone of regret for this deadness there always lies a confidence about life that is reassuring." *Washington Post Book World* contributor L. J. Davis concludes that Hoagland's pieces "are richly particular and often luminously beautiful, conveying a love of vanishing things and doomed places that is poignant, intensely personal, and moodily level-headed. . . . One may quarrel with him, on occasion one may be embarrassed for him, but there is a quiet magnificence in the way he doggedly keeps plugging away despite the risks and the pain and the cost, persistently refusing to shun the unpleasantness of truth. In that task, he is among the best we have."

Hoagland told the *Washington Post Book World:* "I write to live. Alfred Kazin once wrote that he suspected I'd die if I didn't write. And he may have been correct. I might die from hurrying, worrying, and scurrying, if I didn't have something so worth hurrying about. I love life and believe in its goodness and rightness, but I seem not to be terribly well fitted for it—that is, not without writing. Writing is my rod and staff. It saves me, exults me."

BIOGRAPHICAL/CRITICAL SOURCES:

BOOKS

Contemporary Literary Criticism, Volume 28, Gale, 1984.
Dictionary of Literary Biography, Volume 6: *American Novelists since World War II, Second Series,* Gale, 1980.
Johnson, Diane, *Terrorists and Novelists,* Knopf, 1982.
Wolff, Geoffrey, editor, *The Edward Hoagland Reader,* Random House, 1979.

PERIODICALS

Book World, September 7, 1969, January 17, 1971.
Chicago Tribune, November 12, 1979, September 12, 1988.
Chicago Tribune Book World, September 23, 1979, April 4, 1982.
Commentary, September, 1969.
Detroit News, March 28, 1982, June 5, 1983.
Los Angeles Times, June 3, 1982.
Los Angeles Times Book Review, April 25, 1982.
National Review, May 30, 1980.
New Republic, December 29, 1979.
Newsweek, August 9, 1965, June 2, 1969, January 18, 1971, May 10, 1976, March 29, 1982.
New York Review of Books, September 11, 1969.

New York Times, January 15, 1971, September 11, 1979, March 17, 1982.
New York Times Book Review, January 15, 1956, June 8, 1969, February 7, 1971, March 25, 1973, June 13, 1976, September 16, 1979, March 21, 1982, September 21, 1986.
Saturday Review, May 29, 1976, September 15, 1979, March, 1982.
Sewanee Review, summer, 1980.
Time, May 3, 1976, September 10, 1979.
Village Voice, October 23, 1969, October 15, 1979.
Washington Post, January 14, 1971.
Washington Post Book World, May 16, 1976, September 23, 1979, February 28, 1982, October 12, 1986.

—*Sketch by Anne Janette Johnson*

* * *

HOLT, Helen
See PAINE, Lauran (Bosworth)

* * *

HONEY, Martha S(pencer) 1945-

PERSONAL: Born March 9, 1945, in Orange, N.J.; daughter of John C. (a professor) and Mary (a social worker; maiden name, Taber) Honey; married Peter Westover, January, 1967 (divorced, 1969); married Anthony Avirgan (a journalist), September 25, 1971; children: Shanti Hue, Jody Troi. *Education:* Oberlin College, B.A., 1967; Syracuse University, M.A., 1971; University of Dar es Salaam, Tanzania, Ph.D., 1983.

ADDRESSES: Home and office—Apartado 518, Centro Colon 1007, San Jose, Costa Rica.

CAREER: Friends Peace Committee, Philadelphia, Pa., youth director, 1967-68; National Action/Research on the Military-Industrial Complex (NARMIC), Philadelphia, researcher for American Friends Service Committee, 1968-70; Syracuse University, Syracuse, N.Y., research associate, 1970-73; University of Dar es Salaam, Dar es Salaam, Tanzania, research associate, 1973-75; free-lance journalist for the U.S., British, and Canadian press and broadcaster for radio and television, Dar es Salaam, 1975-82, and San Jose, Costa Rica, 1983—. Distinguished resident professor, California State University, Northridge, spring, 1989. Worked as antiwar organizer, 1968-70.

AWARDS, HONORS: Sell Foundation grant, 1973-75, for field research on a history of the Asian community in Tanzania and Zanzibar; Project Censored Award from Sonoma State University, 1987; Canadian Centre for Investigative Journalism Award, 1987; Elliott-Black Award from American Ethical Union, 1988.

WRITINGS:

(With husband, Tony Avirgan) *War in Uganda: The Legacy of Idi Amin,* Lawrence Hill, 1982.
(With Avirgan) *La Penca: Reporte de una investigacion,* Editorial Porvenir, 1985, translation published as *La Penca on Trial in Costa Rica,* 1987.
(With Avirgan) *John Hull: El Fingero de la CIA,* Varitec, 1989.
The Impact of U.S. Policies on Costa Rica: Undermining a Friend, University of Florida Presses, 1990.

Contributor of articles to newspapers, including *Times* (London), *Washington Post, New York Times,* and *London Guardian.*

SIDELIGHTS: Martha S. Honey told *CA:* "As a journalist, I have been writing mainly about politics, foreign affairs, and economic issues, first in East Africa and now in Central America. My husband and I wrote the book on Idi Amin after we were the only foreign journalists to accompany the Tanzanian troops into Uganda in the war that led to Amin's overthrow. My main attempt in my journalistic writings is to help explain Third World issues to American and British audiences."

* * *

HOPKINS, Jasper (Stephen, Jr.) 1936-

PERSONAL: Born November 8, 1936, in Atlanta, Ga.; son of Jasper Stephen, Sr. (a barber) and Willie Ruth (Sorrow) Hopkins; married Gabriele Voight, December 13, 1967. *Education:* Wheaton College, Wheaton, Ill., A.B., 1958; Harvard University, A.M., 1959, Ph.D., 1963.

ADDRESSES: Office—Department of Philosophy, University of Minnesota, 355 Ford Hall, 224 Church St. S.E., Minneapolis, Minn. 55455.

CAREER: Case Western Reserve University, Cleveland, Ohio, assistant professor, 1963-68; University of Massachusetts—Boston, associate professor, 1969-70; University of Minnesota, Minneapolis, associate professor, 1970-74, professor of philosophy, 1974—. Visiting associate professor, University of Arkansas, spring, 1969; visiting professor of philosophy, University of Graz, 1981-82, and University of Munich, winter, 1986-87. Visiting researcher, Instituto di Storia della Filosofia, University of Padua, spring, 1987.

AWARDS, HONORS: Fellowship for research in Munich, 1967-68, and translation fellowship, 1979, both from National Endowment for the Humanities; American Council of Learned Societies fellowship for research in Paris, 1973-74; Guggenheim fellowship for research in Paris, 1980-81; National Humanities Center fellowship, 1983-84.

WRITINGS:

(Editor, translator, and author of introduction with Herbert Richardson) St. Anselm of Canterbury, *Truth, Freedom, and Evil: Three Philosophical Dialogues,* Harper, 1967.
(Translator and author of introduction with Richardson) St. Anselm of Canterbury, *Trinity, Incarnation, and Redemption: Theological Treatises,* Harper, 1970.
A Companion to the Study of St. Anselm, University of Minnesota Press, 1972.
(Editor and translator with Richardson) *Anselm of Canterbury,* Edwin Mellin, Volume 1: *Monologion; Proslogion; Debate with Guanilo; A Meditation on Human Redemption,* 1974, Volume 2: *Philosophical Fragments; De Grammatico; On Truth; Freedom of Choice; The Fall of the Devil; The Harmony of the Foreknowledge, the Predestination, and the Grace of God with Free Choice,* 1976, Volume 3: *Two Letters Concerning Roscelin; The Incarnation of the Word; Why God Became a Man; The Virgin Conception and Original Sin; The Procession of the Holy Spirit; Three Letters on the Sacraments,* 1976, Volume 4 (sole author): *Hermeneutical and Textual Problems in the Complete Treatises of St. Anselm,* 1976.
A Concise Introduction to the Philosophy of Nicholas of Cusa, University of Minnesota Press, 1978, 3rd edition, Banning Press, 1986.
Nicholas of Cusa on God as Not-other: A Translation and an Appraisal of De Li Non Aliud, University of Minnesota Press, 1979, 3rd edition, Banning Press, 1987.

Nicholas of Cusa on Learned Ignorance: A Translation and an Appraisal of De Docta Ignorantia, Banning Press, 1981, 2nd edition, 1983.

Nicholas of Cusa's Debate with John Wenck: A Translation and an Appraisal of De Ignota Litteratura, and Apologia Doctae Ignorantiae, Banning Press, 1981, 3rd edition, 1988.

Nicholas of Cusa's Metaphysic of Contraction, Banning Press, 1983.

Nicolas of Cusa's Dialectical Mysticism: Text, Translation, and Interpretive Study of De Visione Dei, Banning Press, 1986.

Nicholas of Cusa's De Pace Fidei and Cribratio Alkorani: Translation and Analysis, Banning Press, in press.

*   *   *

HORNE, Howard
See PAYNE, (Pierre Stephen) Robert

*   *   *

HOUSTON, Will
See PAINE, Lauran (Bosworth)

*   *   *

HOWARD, C(hester) Jeriel 1939-

PERSONAL: Born March 14, 1939, in Wharton, Tex.; son of Chester (a service manager for B. F. Goodrich) and Alma Howard. *Education:* Union College, Lincoln, Neb., B.A., 1961; Texas Christian University, M.A., 1962; Ph.D., 1967.

ADDRESSES: Home—277 Biltmore Dr., North Barrington, Ill. 60010. *Office*—Department of English, Northeastern Illinois University, 5500 North St. Louis, Chicago, Ill., 60625.

CAREER: Southwestern Union College, Keene, Tex., instructor in English, 1962-64; Union College, Lincoln, Neb., assistant professor of English, 1964-66; Texas Christian University, Fort Worth, instructor in English, 1966-67; Tarrant County Junior College, Fort Worth, chairman of English department, 1967-69; Bishop College, Dallads, Tex., professor and chairman of English, 1970-79; Northeastern Illinois University, Chicago, Ill., professor of English, 1979—. Guest instructor, Texas Wesleyan College, 1967; guest professor, East Texas State University, summer, 1968.

MEMBER: National Council of Teachers of English, Conference on College Composition and Communication.

WRITINGS:

(With Coramea Thomas) *Contact: A Textbook in Applied Communications,* Prentice-Hall, 1970, 5th edition (with Richard F. Tracz), 1990.

(Compiler with Tracz) *The Responsible Man: Essays, Short Stories, Poems,* Canfield Press, 1970, 2nd edition published as *The Responsible Person,* 1975.

(With Tracz) *Tempo: A Thematic Approach to Sentence-Paragraph Writing,* Canfield Press, 1971.

(With Donald Gill) *Desk Copy: Modern Business Communications,* Canfield Press, 1971.

The Age of Anxiety, Allyn & Bacon, 1972.

Technique, Canfield Press, 1972, 2nd edition, 1977.

—30—A Journalistic Approach to Freshman Composition, Goodyear Publishing, 1973.

Reprise: A Review of the Basics in Grammar and Composition, Goodyear Publishing, 1975, 2nd edition, Scott, Foresman, 1980.

Writing Effective Paragraphs, Winthrop Publishers, 1976.

Writing for a Reason, Scott, Foresman, 1980.

(With Tracz) *The Paragraph Book,* Little, Brown, 1982.

(With Tracz) *The Essential English Handbook,* MacMillan, 1985.

(With Sheridan Baker) *The Practical Essayist,* Harper, 1985.

(With Tracz) *Paragraphs Plus: From Ideas to Paragraphs to Essays,* Scott, Foresman/Little, Brown, 1988.

*   *   *

HOWARD, Elizabeth
See PAINE, Lauran (Bosworth)

*   *   *

HOWARD, Maureen 1930-

PERSONAL: Born June 28, 1930, in Bridgeport, Conn.; daughter of William L. (a county detective) and Loretta (Burns) Kearns; married Daniel F. Howard (a professor of English), August 28, 1954 (divorced, 1967); married David J. Gordon (a professor), April 2, 1968 (divorced); married Mark Probst (a stockbroker and novelist), 1981; children: (first marriage) Loretta Howard. *Education:* Smith College, B.A., 1952.

ADDRESSES: Home—New York, N.Y. *Agent*—Gloria Loomis, Watkins, Loomis Agency, 150 East 35th St., Suite 530, New York, N.Y. 10016.

CAREER: Author of novels, literary criticism, and book reviews; editor. Worked in publishing and advertising, 1952-54; University of California, Santa Barbara, lecturer in English and drama, 1968-69; New School for Social Research, New York, N.Y., lecturer in English and creative writing, 1967-68, 1970-71, 1974—. Member of staff in English department, Columbia University. Visiting writer at Amherst College, Boston University, Brooklyn College, Princeton, and Yale.

AWARDS, HONORS: Guggenheim fellowship, 1967-68; fellow of Radcliffe Institute, 1967-68; National Book Critics Circle Award in general nonfiction, 1980, and American Book Award nomination in autobiography/biography, 1981, both for *Facts of Life;* PEN/Faulkner Award for Fiction nominations, 1983, for *Grace Abounding,* and 1987, for *Expensive Habits;* Ingram Merrill Fellowship, National Endowment of the Arts, 1988; D.Litt., Bridgeport University.

WRITINGS:

NOVELS

Not a Word about Nightingales, Atheneum, 1961, reprinted, Penguin, 1980.

Bridgeport Bus, Harcourt, 1966.

Before My Time, Little, Brown, 1975.

Grace Abounding, Little, Brown, 1982.

Expensive Habits, Summit Books, 1986.

OTHER

(Editor) *Seven American Women Writers of the Twentieth Century,* University of Minnesota Press, 1977.

Facts of Life (autobiography), Little, Brown, 1978.

(Author of introduction) Virginia Woolf, *Mrs. Dalloway,* centenial edition, Harcourt, 1981.

(Editor) *Contemporary American Essays,* Viking, 1984, published as *The Penguin Book of Contemporary American Essays,* Penguin, 1985.

Also author of a produced play and of screenplays. Represented in numerous anthologies, including *The Best American Short*

Stories, 1965, edited by Martha Foley and David Burnett, Houghton, 1965, and *Statements,* edited by Jonathan Baumbach, Braziller, 1975. Contributor to various periodicals, including *New York Times Book Review, New Republic, New Yorker, Hudson Review, Yale Review,* and *Vogue.*

WORK IN PROGRESS: Another novel.

AVOCATIONAL INTERESTS: Gardening, cooking.

SIDELIGHTS: Maureen Howard's literary talents are considered by many to be expansive. She is recognized as a thoroughly professional, perceptive, and sensitive literary critic and editor, and a much admired lecturer sharing her experience and thoughts on creative writing. Her novels are also praised for their clarity, linguistic precision, and character development. Peter S. Prescott declares in *Newsweek* that Howard is "a grand writer of English prose; she's witty and (a rarer quality in novelists) she's intelligent as well." Often compared to the writings of Henry James and Virginia Woolf, Howard's five novels, in addition to her autobiography, have been described as brilliantly sensitive commentaries on contemporary American society. Howard's books, according to Geoffrey Stokes in the *Voice Literary Supplement,* "are subtly scaffolded, intelligent, unsparing-shading-into-sneering chronicles of domestic and national madness."

Howard's first novel, *Not a Word about Nightingales,* portrays a family's unsuccessful attempt to achieve happiness and personal fulfillment. While on a research trip to Perguia, Italy, college professor Albert Sedgely discards his respected and secure middleclass life and family, and decides to remain in the small village. After completely changing his priorities and his lifestyle, Sedgely takes a mistress and strives to find inner peace and happiness. Meanwhile, his wife sends their eighteen-year-old daughter, Rosemary, to convince Sedgely to return home. While Rosemary quickly becomes enchanted with the colorful Italian life, Sedgely becomes increasing disenchanted. Back in the United States, Sedgely's wife is beginning to enjoy her new independence. However, Rosemary's attraction to her new lifestyle is short lived. Father and daughter return home and the three family members settle back into their safe and orderly life together. Doris Grumbach explains in the *New York Times Book Review* that Howard's intent in *Not a Word about Nightingales* is to write "about the deadly continuity of the marital condition," a condition from which "there is no permanent exit, only acceptance and repetition of marriage's inexorable routine."

Not a Word about Nightingales perfectly highlights a recurring theme found in most of Howard's works of fiction—that the individual must accept the fact that the events that make up and shape his or her life are predetermined. While no one can change their destiny, each one of us is free to grow, develop, and make choices within the limits our character allows. Remarks David M. Taylor in the *Directory of Literary Biography Yearbook: 1983,* "[Howard's] characters have limited control of their fates, but the exercise of will to effect change is championed rather than discouraged. It appears that the author believes that things will generally turn out badly, but the attempt at change is worthwhile." Howard explains her philosophy in a *Publishers Weekly* interview: "I want my characters to echo the excitement of real lives—lives that appear placid and ordinary on the surface but are really heroic efforts of will."

In *Bridgeport Bus,* Howard's second novel, a major life change comes for thirty-five-year-old, Mary Agnes Keely, an aspiring writer who after an argument with her stifling widowed mother, leaves the home they both share and moves to New York City.

Obtaining employment as a copywriter and showing real talent as a fledgling author, Mary Agnes takes in a troubled roommate, begins an affair with an advertising-agency artist, and keeps company with a group of bohemian artists. Towards the end of the book, she finds herself pregnant and totally alone. Mary Agnes accepts her situation, gives birth, and comes to the realization that being alone in this world is not as frightening or as tragic as she once thought.

While Elaine Ruben describes *Bridgeport Bus* in the *New Republic* as "a funny, sad work some readers were fortunate to discover and then eager to pass on to friends," Daniel Stern writes in the *Saturday Review,* "that such a diverse and sensitized imagination should exist in the captive body of an Irish Catholic spinster in fruitless rebellion against the paucity of experience to which she appears to be condemned is merely the cream of the irony." Stern continues: "In arriving at the concluding insight that 'it was no great sin to be, at last, alone,' the reader has been rewarded for his attention in a thousand subtle but tangible ways."

Writing novels populated with solid characters, such as Mary Agnes in *Bridgeport Bus,* and other strong-willed woman as Laura Quinn in *Before My Time,* Maud Dowd in *Grace Abounding,* and Margaret Flood in *Expensive Habits,* in addition to the powerful cast found in her autobiography, *Facts of Life,* Howard is referred to by some critics as a "woman's writer." These reviewers remark that her novels systematically revolve around women who are searching for their identity and their place within society's accepted boundaries. These female characters often work hard to grow and strive towards self-awareness even against seemingly very difficult odds. A reviewer for the *Washington Post Book World* describes Howard's novels as "meticulously observed and beautifully written short studies of women caught in the world of men, lost to themselves, and finding little meaning in what they do."

Other reviewers concede that while she does write about women trying to "find themselves," Howard should not be labeled solely a woman's writer since they feel her writings reflect all of contemporary society and not just women. "Howard is a writer in the feminist tradition only because the dominant sensibility is most often that of a woman," states Grumbach in the *Washington Post Book World.* "But she suffers no myopia when it comes to men: husbands, lover, priest-son are all very real and very central to the whole splendidly arranged and securely conceived structure. Women without men, to turn Hemingway's phrase about, is never her subject but rather women searching for their lost selves in a male world in which most of the men are also adrift." In seeming agreement with the premise that Howard's ability to mold and develop such full and deep personalitites is not limited only to her female characters, a reviewer writes in the *New Yorker,* "Maureen Howard has the knack of capturing the essence of people's lives in a shorter time than it takes most authors to usher their characters into a room."

Howard addresses the issue of being called a "woman's writer" in the *Voice Literary Supplement:* "You write a book at least partly because you feel these matters are so important that you want to bring them to life through your characters' stories, and then it's talked about as 'mothers and daughter' or 'a woman's book.' It's as though they decided they were not going to notice 'all that' because the lady writes pretty paragraphs."

Howard's third novel, *Before My Time,* tells the story of a woman forced to confront her past when her cousin's son stays with her family while awaiting arraignment on a drug charge. Laura Quinn attempts to frame a vision of the past for Jimmy Cogan in an effort to help him realize the error of his ways. As they trade stories of their pasts, each episode becomes a vignette of character development. A *New Yorker* critic observes that the book is "full of moral intelligence, wit, and fresh insights into the way people live," adding, "the sketches . . . are so rich that one can only wish they were twice as long." About the novel's content, Paul Gray writes in *Time,* "Without warning, what might have been just another serving of tea and sympathy has become a documentary on U.S. civilization and its discontents." Gray continues to note: "*Before My Time* conveys a range of details and events that would be impressive in a novel twice as long. Although the design appears casual, the book's power is in its language. Time and again, a part is successfully substituted for a whole."

Most critics seem to agree with Gray that one of Howard's most identifiable and admired talents lies in her ability to successfully shape and structure the language in each of her books. This task is accomplished without distracting attention away from her novel's other elements. "Certainly Miss Howard's stylistic virtuosity cannot be disputed," states Pearl K. Bell in the *New Leader,* "every inch of her prose . . . is trimmed and polished with meticulous skill." However, *Publishers Weekly*'s Sybil S. Steinberg observes "that critics have generally praised Howard's impeccable command of language, her exact and tartly humorous prose, somewhat surprises [Howard.]" As Howard explains to Steinberg: "Of course I am fascinated with language, but I don't think that is so unusual. I should think all writers who are serious about what they're doing *would* care a lot about language. I think it's very odd when I pick up a novel and see that language has not been honored or used well, or played with."

In her *New York Times Book Review* article on *Before My Time* Grumbach points to another element that seems constant in Howard's writings. Reviewers have longed praised her talent for delicately manipulating characters and plot, gently guiding the reader to the point where they will be required to interpret and draw their own conclusions concerning the characters and the story. As Grumbach writes of *Before My Time:* "Howard has the gift of being unobtrusively present in her fictions, like the good children who are neither seen nor heard. But her hand is felt, controlling events, keeping them in their assigned comic or poignant rings, preventing excess and promoting restrained yet agonized, circular movement. Reading her, one is made to return to the inevitable, to the conclusions that things do not end satisfactorily so much as they happen; they seem to mean something for the moment and then disappear into memory, which is what fiction is to this extraordinary talented writer." *Newsweek*'s Prescott also acknowledges Howard's talent: "Howard organizes each scene with artistry, expertly cutting in and out of her narrative and casting no words as she studs her prose with dour wit."

In her award-winning autobiography, *Facts of Life,* Howard recounts her life as daughter of Irish-Catholic parents, a college professor's wife, and tells of the experiences that have shaped her life. Karen Durbin writes in *Ms.:* "When I first read *Facts of Life,* I was immediately gripped by the sheer quality of the writing. Howard's memories of, among other things, her parents, her youth in Irish-Catholic Bridgeport, her experiences later as a faculty wife, are crouched in a vigorous, rushing prose. She uses words with the focused intensity and precision of a poet. . . . Her wit is everywhere. *Facts of Life* is at once painful and humorous." "Howard is a talented novelist who has never written anything so concentrated and properly disturbing as this memoir," states Alfred Kazin in the *New Republic.* "The style is very, very bright; the other characters are wonderfully alive; the suffering and resentment out of which the book was written stick to it like a burr. . . . A painfully strong, good book." And Walter Cle-

mons writes in *Newsweek* that *Facts of Life* "is brief, witty and utterly original. Its candor and conspicuous reticences are exciting and puzzling. . . . It exemplifies Howard's unsettling combination of elegance and earthiness."

In her fourth novel, *Grace Abounding,* Howard follows the path of Maud Dowd's life beginning with her very colorless and spiritless existence as a forty-three-year-old widow and mother of a teenage daughter, Elizabeth. Maud spends much of her time spying on her neighbors—a pair of spinster sisters—and visiting her dying mother. Maud's life dramatically changes after her mother dies and, after ending a brief and dreadful relationship with an unworthy man, she moves to New York City to pursue vocal training for the talented Elizabeth. Maud remarries a successful and loving man, earns a Ph.D. in psychology and becomes a children's therapist. Elizabeth, in turn, happily gives up her promising singing career to marry and have children. Life for Maud is not entirely golden however, as she copes with the death of a 3-year-old patient and wrestles with her own morality.

Robert Dawidoff writes in the *Los Angeles Times* that *Grace Abounding* "conveys a shrewd feeling for how life changes, how things affect and happen to people, how some stories have endings and meanings and some do not, staying, rather, unresolved in several memories—and how, where faith had best be, grace had better be." "It does give a sense of lives as they are really lived such as only a small minority of novelists in each generation can or even want to manage," remarks Noel Perrin in the *New York Times Book Review.* "Howard . . . is a writer to read. Here the sensibility. There the intelligence." Diane M. Ross comments in the *Chicago Tribune* that "meant to involve us in the irregular rhythms of particular lives, the structure of [*Grace Abounding*] allows for shifting points of view and for chronological gaps in the narrative," Ross continues: "[*Grace Abounding*] depends upon an accumulation of detail and a pattering of scenes rather than a straightforward plot. . . . Howard crosscuts between characters and locations, and blithely elides large chunks of time. . . . Her details are epiphanies, and they range from the ridiculous to the graceful."

At the beginning of Howard's most recent novel, *Expensive Habits,* seemingly successful and well-known writer, Margaret Flood, lays in a hospital room after learning she has a deteriorating heart disease. The forty-five-year-old returns to her Manhattan apartment and through a sequence of flashback scenes, the reader sees Margaret's life as a continual series of episodes—many involving loyalty and betrayal—that leave her searching for her true identity and self-worth. Margaret hopes this search will bring her the peace and contentment she so desperately desires.

Jonathan Yardley suggests in the *Washington Post Book World* that *Expensive Habits* "is a serious and accomplished piece of work. Here as in her other work Howard writes about the fads and fashions of the day, about a society eager to cash in on any passing joy or sorrow, but she is having none of that herself; she stands apart, observing 'the dumb glory of it all' with an eye that is sharp but kind. [*Expensive Habits*] is certainly a book rich in integrity and elegance, by a writer who matters." "Maureen Howard's fine fifth novel attempts more, and accomplishes more, than all the others, marking her steady progress toward the highest rank of American fiction writers," remarks Nora Johnson in the *Los Angeles Times Book Review.* "The prose in [*Expensive Habits*] is dense, complex, disturbing, authoritative. Its several voices suit her story and vividly demonstrate her literary intelligence. It's dazzling to see how deftly she wields her author's tools." And Gray writes in *Time:* "As she had done in her other novels and in the prizewinning autobiography *Facts of Life* . . . the author smuggles more subjects into a book than its length seems to allow. . . . [Howard] has skills that do not comfortably translate into screaming paperback covers and megabuck reprints. She is one of those rare contemporaries whose work demands, and deserves, rereadings."

Although her talent has long been acknowledged and applauded by reviewers and a loyal following, Howard has not yet achieved the measure of success many feel she deserves. "It is hard to understand how a writer of Maureen Howard's elegance, sharpness, sensibility and tenderness has escaped widespread public notice for so long," a critic states in the *Washington Post Book Review.* Durbin remarks in *Ms.:* "I can only hope that soon one of her books will achieve the kind of popular success that (via the publishing miracle of reissues) would rescue all of her work from the elite near-obscurity it now enjoys. Howard is too important a writer to miss. Talking about Willa Cather, Howard wrote: 'She had the nerve to confront big issues—the transience of youth and beauty, love relinquished for ambition, the bitter triumphs of success—what the past will yield if we are truthful.' She might have been describing herself."

CA INTERVIEW

CA interviewed Maureen Howard by telephone on March 7, 1989, at her home in New York, New York.

CA: In "The Making of a Writer" in the New York Times Book Review, *you talked about some of the things that made you a writer—a less important question, you said, than why you continue to write. Would you say something about when you actually started to write, and how?*

HOWARD: I think we all have experiences with writing when we're very young, the business of doing the essay that wins a little high school prize, that kind of thing. I suppose that puts ideas in one's head about a future. But I think in the long run that is fairly unimportant compared to what I think of as a second beginning, in which you realize that there is some real attachment to the process of telling stories and of dealing with words in a way that obviously is of enormous interest to you, and, you would hope, not just to you, but that the story can be given away, given out. I suppose that came to me when I was a young woman, out of college. One writes in college too, and these days, of course, there's much more teaching of writing in college. I have some problems with that: there is so much to learn, so much to read before we start to write. I teach with pleasure but I'm not sure that it isn't a strange, even dangerous way of encouraging the young to learn on the job. There were courses offered in writing when I went to Smith, but it certainly wasn't allowed as a major, absolutely not. But when I was a young faculty wife, it occurred to me that this was where my time, by which I guess I mean my life, should be going, though I had many other things to do: I did lots of research, I worked on a political campaign—I never lazed about the house. It just occurred to me naturally, as naturally as baking a cake. (I'm a very natural baker. I don't know why; I just am.) Writing seemed to me from the very beginning incredibly difficult and incredibly comfortable at once—an odd combination.

CA: Many women who came of age during the 1950s have had a hard time claiming a professional identity for themselves, though perhaps it isn't so true of writers. Was that a hurdle for you?

HOWARD: I don't think I ever had trouble with the idea that what I was doing was meant to be absolutely professional, not in any way dilettantish or amateurish. I wasn't in that way shy, though I think so many of us felt back then that we weren't quite entitled to a public personality. That's too bad, though I must say that seems a long time ago now and I don't have any chips on my shoulder about taking a back seat to my husband's academic career. No hard feelings about it. It's not only part of my personal history, but part of our social history.

CA: You've said that you sometimes begin a book and then go off to other things, and while you're doing those other things the book cooks in your mind so that you can finally come back to it and write it to the end. How much of the process takes place on a conscious level?

HOWARD: I suppose I have said that, but I probably should reinterpret it. I begin a book, but when I say "go to other things," I don't mean that I ever desert that book. I never go away from it completely; it's always in my head. I teach and I write articles and I go about my life, but the book is always there. I never have abandoned a work. Perhaps that's strange, not what I should have done. But I've never started something and thrown it aside. I know so many people who say that they started a book but it didn't work out. They have this legendary bottom drawer. Maybe my attitude comes from growing up in the Depression, when you had to use everything—I have no idea. Maybe it's left over from an era when you had to turn shirt collars, or goes back even further to a time I've only heard about, when a woman's dresses were inevitably ripped apart at the seams and resewn in the style of the current season.

CA: Was it your aim all along to be a novelist, rather than a poet or short story writer?

HOWARD: I've never written short stories; I think I've only published one in my life. Little pieces of novels have in the past been parceled out in short segments and published before the books, but it's not something I like to do. For some reason—maybe my Catholic background which accustomed me to large systems, inventive hierarchies—my head seems to work in terms of structure that goes on and becomes complicated and turns back on itself and unfolds as a longer piece of fiction. I love reading short stories; I love teaching short stories; I love reading the good short stories that my students sometimes write. But I don't do it.

CA: What you said about the story's turning back on itself is interesting. Especially in your later novels you've approached your story from several points of view and several time perspectives. Is that a method that has come more or less naturally to you?

HOWARD: It obviously does come naturally to me. One thing leads to another, and to another, and you revise the text. You revise various editions that have come earlier on within the story. It seems to me it's that process of discovery, of brushing away the dirt and the silt and all the encrustations to try and get at the center; as in an archaeological dig, to come up with the next shard that will fit the pattern.

CA: When Facts of Life *was published, in 1978, several critics commented on its likeness to fiction. And since its publication, there's been a strong tendency on the part of reviewers to examine your novels in the autobiography's light. Do you have any thoughts about the closeness of the two forms and the distance between them?*

HOWARD: Structurally there may be ways of saying there's a similarity between the autobiographical work and the novels, in the collage effect, in the working with pieces and building. But I see them as absolutely separate. To me, writing *Facts of Life* was a different process completely. I thought of that work as being only partially about me, as being about a whole world, about a time, very much about places, and a way of perceiving experience; the never ending process of putting it together, reconstructing the past. So I set up my sections in the book as an ironic tidying of life—culture, money, sex.

CA: I think Facts of Life *is so much about what parents give us and at the same time take away from us.*

HOWARD: Yes. And what we don't see, in our anger at them, at certain times in our lives is corrected by extraordinary revelations at other times about what they have given. I've always been bewildered by people who say, "Gosh, you hated your father." I say, "My God! No, no, no." The first take of that man would, I would hope, be balanced off by later takes. I remember way back, before I had finished writing that book, doing a reading from it at Massachusetts Institute of Technology. It was in one of the early waves of academic feminism, and there was a great feeling after I had done the reading that the opening of the book was an indictment of my mother; how precise I was, and how wonderfully cruel about my mother's loss of self. I suppose it's terribly sentimental of me, and foolish, but I still can't read that opening out loud without feeling that I've got to be a damned good actress not to start weeping at what happened to my mother, the way in which she spent all of her imagination on us, over-invested in her domestic life. To think that I had tramped over her by exposing her sad disappointments seems to me a terrible misreading.

CA: Facts of Life *has an unusual approach; it tells a great deal by telling so selectively. Were there things you set out not to do as an autobiographer?*

HOWARD: Yes. I think there's an awful lot of confessional stuff written which I find no artistic point in, no literary point to. Our lives are basically interesting to us, but why the hell should they be interesting to anybody else unless you shape your version and say, "This is my version now." I don't mean clean up the facts; I mean shape them, make them into something worth giving. As I'd shape fiction or cut you my prized delphiniums and lilies.

CA: Both Laura Quinn in Before My Time *and Margaret Flood in* Expensive Habits *are re-examining their lives, the latter by analyzing how she has dealt with her real experience in her fiction. Both those voices seem related to your own in* Facts of Life, *and very much a strong comment on the business of writing.*

HOWARD: I suppose I do have a voice going. I've been accused of it and I'm perfectly happy to stand by it; it doesn't bother me at all. I like strong voices in fiction, and I see that I often choose to begin at the crisis point, the moment at which Laura or Margaret feels she has lost herself, become something that seems all wrong, incorrect. We live now in such a world beholden to images that it is terrifying to think we can become some kind of mask or persona. I guess I can see that those two fictional creations do share my fear.

CA: There's something to be said for having the continuity of such a voice in a body of work.

HOWARD: A lot of writers I have admired have a discernable voice, certainly Virginia Woolf, Willa Cather, Eudora Welty, Flannery O'Connor, Joyce, Beckett, Milan Kundera. I don't see it as a limitation; I see it as liberating to find a voice. I'm perfectly happy to say, OK, that's my name on it. Anatole Broyard got on my case about that—he's always on my case—and that may have started the criticism on this point. But I don't really care. There was, and is, a whole lot of writing that started to come upon us in the seventies, in short stories particularly, in which there is a style of a certain kind, but there's no attitude, no mind discernable within the story. That doesn't interest me.

CA: I've missed some of your characters after I've finished the books—particularly those women I mentioned in the earlier question. You don't bring them back in later books, and one wonders what's happened to them.

HOWARD: Yes. Sometimes they're left at beginnings or at continuations. I don't tidy up at the end. I don't want to; I like the openness, the possibility. It's true that I never have brought a character back, and I can't imagine doing that, though I suppose one character will echo a character from an earlier novel.

CA: Two very interesting characters in your work are the little twins Siobhan and Cormac Cogan, from Before My Time. *Is there a story behind their evolution in your mind?*

HOWARD: Not really. I do have nieces who are twins, and it's fascinating to see how different twins will be. I think what I was playing with in that book was the sameness that was stamped upon those two, that extraordinary closeness that only twins can know, beyond even a sibling closeness. From the title on, that novel is concerned with the passing of time and our making our lonely contracts with that unalterable condition. But sexuality is what separates them, what breaks the coalition finally. That incredible united front is broken because they're aging, and that's the betrayal in a way. Girls almost always do begin to mature sexually earlier than boys, and once that lockstep is broken, the closeness is gone. It's a little bit like the loss in the Garden of Eden for those children.

CA: To that point they've closed the world out except as they see it jointly.

HOWARD: Yes, but the world has to begin to exist if Siobhan is going to exist sexually, which means separately.

CA: You told Sybil S. Steinberg in an interview for Publishers Weekly *that you recalled the days when it seemed you had leisure to read Charles Dickens and George Eliot. Are there particular kinds of books now that continue to fuel your creative imagination?*

HOWARD: Oh yes; I read constantly, and I can't understand how you can write without reading with enormous attention a great deal of the time. To see how it's done; to say there it is. I love finding writers new to me whom I enjoy greatly and learn from. It seems to me absolutely essential. Last spring I wrote a review of a book by Jay Cantor, *Krazy Kat;* and there's a young writer named Richard Powers, who wrote *Prisoner's Dilemma.* He's superb. I'm full of delight when I find books like that. I'm reading a book I've never read before by Steven Millhauser, *Portrait of an American Romantic.* He's terrific. I go back and re-read Dickens all the time, I re-read George Eliot. I worry when I have students who don't seem to be real readers; I wonder why they're in this trade. It's quite mystifying, and yet I believe that the primary impact on the young people I'm teaching now has been visual—it's been from the tube and the movies. They've been given at least equal time with the page. I'm not nay-saying and I don't want to turn back the clock, but this is what we have to work with. All reading, all viewing, of course, must be joined with our lives to live in the page.

CA: The influence of the visual certainly does seem to show up in a lot of fiction being written now.

HOWARD: Yes. There's a kind of passivity in much of both the writing and the reading now, a kind of acceptance of dullness, as though the story can just go on and on. Like sitcoms. I think it also shows up in a kind of writing that's done in segments. You can trace influences from the movies and television on fictional techniques from the early writings of this century, and unless they're brilliantly done, like Joyce who loved movies or the young writer Steve Erikson, or Pynchon, unless their transference into another medium is complete and fully realized, it can be very dull.

CA: A lot of readers seem not to have the attention span for the big novel, or so some critics feel.

HOWARD: Yes. I think the re-emergence of the short story is connected to that. But I find it something that we have to work with and deal with. I don't think we can throw up our hands and scold the audience: "Isn't that awful?" It isn't necessarily awful, not at all. Writers must both rise to the occasion and accept our limitations. There's a big world out there united by *signs* that are far more readable than pages of a demanding novel, united by "Dallas" or the camera's play over a street in Lebanon, the fragments of a plane scattered over Scotland.

CA: Your work as a reviewer and a critic must keep you closely in touch with new writing.

HOWARD: Yes, and for me it's healthy and good to write criticism at times, by which I mean more than just book reviews—to try and turn my attention away from myself and my work. After all, I don't want to become solipsistic; I don't want to get so enclosed that there isn't light and air. So it has always been profitable for me to try and understand what others are doing and to put it into print. It's incredibly important to keep the doors open. I worry terribly that American writers close themselves off into their own small stories too much. Maybe it's been very, very good for us to have to pay attention to European writers—not that they're necessarily better, but that their concerns are often broader because they have to be. I just read a wonderful book by Lars Gustafsson, *Bernard Foy's Third Castling.* It's a very fine book—playful, very bright, patterned after Hermann Brock's *The Sleepwalkers.* Gustafsson is funny about America. He teaches in Texas and I don't know very much more about him, but here's this extraordinary book that we won't pay much attention to. I think it's great to keep open and to have news coming in. I've done a lot of work with European writers, and with freedom-to-write issues. It's well worth doing.

CA: At some point you were working on a screenplay. Are you still doing that kind of writing?

HOWARD: No. I did write a play at one time that was produced. That was interesting to me, and I learned a lot. I've had two or three tiny flirtations with writing for the screen, but it's a totally different game. I've written part of a book that I call "Scenario," and I've written plays within novels. In the book I'm working

on now, I intend to have something very like a screenplay as the whole second section, but I don't mean it to be an honest-to-God producible screenplay; I mean it to be readable. That's another article completely.

CA: You also said in the Publishers Weekly *interview I quoted earlier that "the reader must fit the pieces [of the novels] together, with the author's discreet help. The most exciting thing in the world to me is the idea of audience." Do you hear much from good readers, members of your audience who approach your books with both an open mind and a personal sensibility?*

HOWARD: Yes, I do. People who bother to get in touch that way are always kind, and they seem to have been people who liked reading my fiction and putting it together as much as I enjoyed writing it and putting it together. I think that's terrific.

CA: Can you tell more about what you're working on?

HOWARD: I'm in the midst of a project that I thought was going to be fairly contained when it started out. Now it's turned large, encyclopedic, and I'm very caught up in history. It's not by any means an historical novel, but I'm concerned with P. T. Barnum and Tom Thumb and Mark Twain and the rise and fall of the city of Bridgeport, not the city of Mahagonny. And the showmanship of someone like Barnum, the great genius of the man. At this point I don't love him at all, but he was a genius. He gave us this century; he produced the show. He didn't live to see it, but he shaped a great deal of what America wants—entertainment, fun, amusement, distraction. He was an American genius with no dark side to him. Twain had the same instincts and was an equally fine showman, but he had that deep, terribly dark side. It's been a tremendously interesting book to work on. I went to look at Tom Thumb's little brown velvet suit that he wore when he went to visit Queen Victoria. It's in Bridgeport, about to be put on display again in a grand new museum they have up there. What are we preserving? What are we holding onto for dear life? It's very spooky stuff.

BIOGRAPHICAL/CRITICAL SOURCES:

BOOKS

Contemporary Literary Criticism, Gale, Volume 5, 1976, Volume 14, 1980, Volume 46, 1988.
Dictionary of Literary Biography Yearbook: 1983, Gale, 1984.
Howard, Maureen, *Facts of Life,* Little, Brown, 1978.

PERIODICALS

Chicago Tribune Book World, November 14, 1982.
Critics, February 1, 1979.
Harper's, November, 1978.
Los Angeles Times, December 7, 1982.
Los Angeles Times Book Review, May 18, 1986.
New Leader, January 20, 1975.
New Republic, February 8, 1975, September 9, 1978, October 4, 1982.
Newsweek, January 20, 1975, September 25, 1978, October 11, 1982.
New York Times Book Review, January 19, 1975, September 26, 1982, October 2, 1982, December 2, 1982, May 24, 1986, June 8, 1986.
Partisan Review, Volume 56, number 1, 1987.
Saturday Review, October 28, 1978.
Sewanee Review, winter, 1974-75.
Spectator, November 8, 1986.
Time, January 27, 1975.

Washington Post Book World, October 10, 1982, May 11, 1986.*

—*Sketch by Margaret Mazurkiewicz*

—*Interview by Jean W. Ross*

*   *   *

HOWARD, Troy
See PAINE, Lauran (Bosworth)

*   *   *

HUNT, James Gerald   1932-

PERSONAL: Born February 2, 1932, in Denver, Colo.; son of Newell M. and Rosalind G. Hunt; married, 1956; children: three. *Education:* Michigan Technological University, B.S., 1954; University of Illinois, M.A., 1957, Ph.D., 1966.

ADDRESSES: Office—College of Business Administration, Texas Tech University, Lubbock, Tex. 79409.

CAREER: General Motors Corp., Pontiac, Mich., project engineer in power development section of Pontiac Motor Division, 1954-56; U.S. Steel Corp., Detroit, Mich., personnel assistant at Michigan Limestone Division, 1957-58; West Virginia Institute of Technology, Montgomery, instructor in business administration, 1958-61; instructor, Millikan University, 1962-63; University of Illinois at Urbana-Champaign, Urbana, instructor in industrial administration, 1963-66, research associate, 1965-66; Southern Illinois University at Carbondale, assistant professor, 1966-69, associate professor, 1969-72, professor of administrative sciences, 1972-81; Texas Tech University, Lubbock, professor, 1981-84, Paul Whitfield Horn Professor of Management, 1984—, area coordinator of management, 1981-88. Visiting scholar, University of Aston, 1980. Management development consultant.

MEMBER: Academy of Management (vice-president of Midwest Division, 1974-75; president, 1976-77; president, Organizational Behavior Division, 1978-79; member of board of governors, 1978), Southern Management Association (president, 1988-89), Midwest Business Administration Association.

AWARDS, HONORS: Ford Foundation grant, summer, 1968; National Institute of Mental Health grant, 1970-73; grants from Office of Naval Research and Smithsonian Institution, 1973, 1975, 1977, 1979, and 1981, from Army Research Institute, 1973, 1975, 1977, 1980, 1983, and 1989, and from NATO, 1981.

WRITINGS:

(Editor with E. A. Fleishman, and contributor) *Current Developments in the Study of Leadership,* Southern Illinois University Press, 1973.
(Editor with Lars L. Larson) *Contingency Approaches to Leadership,* Southern Illinois University Press, 1974.

(Editor with Larson) *Leadership Frontiers,* Comparative Administration Research Institute, 1975.
(Editor with Larson) *Leadership: The Cutting Edge,* Southern Illinois University Press, 1977.
(Editor with Larson) *Crosscurrents in Leadership,* Southern Illinois University Press, 1979.
(With Richard N. Osborn and Lawrence R. Jauch) *Organization Theory: An Integrated Approach,* Wiley, 1980.
(Editor with others) *Leadership: Beyond Establishment Views,* Southern Illinois University Press, 1981.
(With Osborn and John R. Schermerhorn, Jr.) *Managing Organizational Behavior,* Wiley, 1982, 4th edition, 1991.
(Editor with others) *Leaders and Managers: International Perspectives on Managerial Behavior and Leadership Research,* Pergamon, 1984.
Managerial Behavior and Leadership, Science Research Associates, 1984.
(Editor with John D. Blair) *Leadership on the Future Battlefield,* Pergamon, 1985.
Emerging Leadership Vistas, Lexington, 1988.
Leadership: Top Down, Bottom Up, Inside Out, Sage Publications, 1990.

CONTRIBUTOR

M. S. Wortman and Fred Luthans, editors, *Emerging Concepts in Management,* Macmillan, 1969.
Gene Dalton, editor, *Motivation and Control in Organizations,* Irwin-Dorsey, 1970.
S. Chilton, editor, *Readings in Educational Administration,* MSS Educational Publishing, 1970.
W. K. Graham and Karlene Roberts, editors, *Comparative Studies in Organizational Behavior,* Holt, 1972.

OTHER

Also contributor to proceedings. Contributor to professional journals. Guest editor, *Organization and Administrative Sciences,* June, 1975; editor, *Journal of Management,* 1983-86; member of editorial board, *Journal of Business Research,* 1973—, and *Academy of Management Review,* 1975-80; manuscript reviewer, *Business Perspectives,* 1967-73, *Organization and Administrative Sciences, Journal of Applied Social Psychology,* and *Journal of Applied Psychology,* all 1973—, and for Dryden Press and Scott, Foresman, 1973—, and Richard D. Irwin, Inc., West Publishing, and Science Research Associates, all 1975—.

*   *   *

HUNT, John
See PAINE, Lauran (Bosworth)

I

IGNATOW, David 1914-

PERSONAL: Surname is accented on second syllable; born February 7, 1914, in Brooklyn, N.Y.; son of Max (a businessman) and Henrietta (Wilkenfeld) Ignatow; married Rose Graubert (an artist and writer), August 11, 1939; children: David, Jr., Yaedi (daughter). *Education:* High school graduate.

ADDRESSES: Home—P.O. Box 1458, East Hampton, N.Y. 11937.

CAREER: Free-lance writer and editor. Worked in family-owned butcher shop, and a bindery in Brooklyn, N.Y., which he later owned and managed; journalist, Writers Project of the Works Progress Administration, beginning 1932; New School for Social Research, New York City, instructor, 1962-64; University of Kentucky, Lexington, lecturer, 1964-65; University of Kansas, Lawrence, lecturer, 1966-67; Vassar College, Poughkeepsie, N.Y., instructor, 1967-68; Columbia University, New York City, adjunct professor, 1968-76, senior lecturer, 1977—; York College, City University of New York, New York City, poet in residence and associate professor, 1968-84, professor emeritus, 1984—.

MEMBER: PEN, Poetry Society of America (member of executive board, 1979; president, 1980-84; president emeritus, 1984—).

AWARDS, HONORS: National Institute and American Academy awards in literature, 1964, "for a lifetime of creative effort"; Guggenheim Memorial fellowships, 1965, 1973; Shelley Memorial Prize, Poetry Society of America, 1966; Rockefeller Foundation grant, 1968; National Endowment for the Arts grant, 1970, for "Against the Evidence"; Bollingen Prize, 1977; Wallace Stevens Fellowship, Yale University, 1977; D.Litt., Long Island University, 1987; poet in residence award, Walt Whitman Birthplace Association, 1986-87.

WRITINGS:

Poems, Decker Press, 1948.
The Gentle Weight Lifter, Morris Gallery, 1955.
(Editor) *Political Poetry,* Chelsea, 1960.
Say Pardon, Wesleyan University Press, 1961.
(Editor) *Walt Whitman: A Centennial Celebration,* Beloit College, 1963.
(Editor) *William Carlos Williams: A Memorial Chapbook,* Beloit College, 1963.

Figures of the Human, Wesleyan University Press, 1964.
Rescue the Dead, Wesleyan University Press, 1968.
Earth Hard: Selected Poems, Rapp & Whiting, 1968.
Poems, 1939-1969, Wesleyan University Press, 1970.
The Notebooks of David Ignatow, edited by Ralph Mills, Jr., Swallow Press, 1973, Sheep Meadow, 1981.
Facing the Tree: New Poems, Little, Brown, 1975.
Selected Poems, edited by Robert Bly, Wesleyan University Press, 1975.
The Animal in the Bush: Poems on Poetry, edited by Patrick Carey, Slow Loris Press, 1977.
Tread the Dark, Little, Brown, 1978.
Sunlight: A Sequence for My Daughter, BOA Editions, 1979.
Conversations, Survivors' Manual Books, 1980.
Open between Us, edited by Ralph J. Mills, Jr., University of Michigan Press, 1980.
Whisper to the Earth, Little, Brown, 1981.
Leaving the Door Open, Sheep Meadow, 1984.
New and Collected Poems, 1970-1985, Wesleyan University Press, 1987.
The One in the Many: A Poet's Memoirs, Wesleyan University Press, 1988.

Works represented in *Naked Poetry, A Big Jewish Book, News of the Universe,* and many other anthologies. Contributor of poems to *Quarterly Review of Literature, Sixties, Poetry, Kayak, Commentary, New Yorker, Saturday Review,* and other periodicals. Editor of *Beloit Poetry Journal,* 1949-59, guest editor, 1963; poetry editor, *Nation,* 1962-63; co-editor, *Chelsea,* 1967-76; associate editor, *American Poetry Review,* 1972-74.

WORK IN PROGRESS: Selected short stories; untitled new poetry collection.

SIDELIGHTS: David Ignatow once told *CA:* "My avocation is to stay alive; my vocation is to write about it; my motivation embraces both intentions and my viewpoint is gained from a study and activity in both ambitions. The book important to my career is the next one or two or three on the fire." Fidelity to the details and issues of daily life in Ignatow's poetry has won for him a widespread reputation for being "the most autobiographical of writers," suggests *Dictionary of Literary Biography* contributor Christopher Brown. Ignatow added, "The modern poet most influential in my work was William Carlos Williams. Earlier influences were the Bible, Walt Whitman, Baudelaire, Rimbaud, Hart Crane." In Williams, as in the works of Peruvian surrealist

Cesar Vallejo, Ignatow most appreciates "the language of hard living; the universal language," which is perceived "in the lines of the poets where you can feel the mind running like an electrical current through the muscles," he told *Paris Review* contributor Gerard Malanga. Ralph J. Mills observes in *Cry of the Human: Essays on Contemporary American Poetry* that Ignatow "has placed himself in the tradition of those genuine poets who have, in independent ways, struggled to create a living American poetry from the immediacies of existence in this country, from the tragedies and potentialities of its legacy, and from the abundant music and vitality of its language." The respected poet has edited several volumes of poetry and well-known poetry journals, including the *American Poetry Review.* He also addresses the topic of poetic theory in poems that discuss direct statement and clarity, the two objectives Ignatow keeps in mind when crafting a poem. Suggests Mills, "Authenticity speaks to us from every line of Ignatow's poetry, reaching into our lives with the force and deliberation of the seemingly unassuming art which he has subtly and skillfully shaped."

Critics trace several stages of development in the body of Ignatow's works. One line of development in the books is a gradual change in Ignatow's poetic technique. "His typical poem is a short lyric expressing what to all appearances are his genuine thoughts and feelings, yet he is expert at adopting personae, particularly those of insane businessmen and killers, to convey more effectively his vision of modern American life," notes Brown. As current events become increasingly macabre, Ignatow more frequently expresses his response to them in the form of the prose poem, which allows for the depiction of nightmarish sequences from a civilization reeling out of control. For example, in "A Political Cartoon," the President and cabinet members recklessly toss a gun around a conference room until two of them have been shot to death; backing a dump truck into the room, the poet arrives to bury them all under a load of grain.

Ignatow's poems—the lyrics and prose poems alike—are characterized by direct statement rendered with the minimum of poetic devices, achieving their effects through the poet's superb handling of the line, suggests Marvin Bell in the *American Poetry Review.* Coming from "a consciously skeletal aesthetic," says Bell, Ignatow's art is one "of apparent artlessness in the extreme." William Spanos, speaking to Ignatow in a *Boundary 2* interview, explains how the poet's spare, "flat" style of expression achieves maximum impact: unlike much modern poetry, which provides a release or escape from the tension or terror of life in the twentieth century, Ignatow's "poetry—and this is a stylistic as well as thematic matter—disintegrates the reader's expectation of release to demand a confrontation of the horror." The directness in the poems, Ignatow told Spanos, derives "from life itself and so they must always take into account the rawness with which life comes to me, its direct impact on my senses and the stance it alerts in me to keep myself from becoming overwhelmed by this direct impact." In the confessional volume *Leaving the Door Open,* a reflection on his performance as a husband and father, Ignatow is as relentless during self-evaluation as when diagnosing social ills. *Hudson Review* contributor James Finn Cotter admires both the "honesty . . . and the effort required to make such a confession."

Though events come to him without structure, in order to survive them, the poet "must try to structure [the poem] without losing the unstructured, random, elemental quality of things as they happen," Ignatow said in the *Boundary 2* interview. "I structure them through my person which is obliged to remain intact or consistent. . . . There is then a tension between myself and the world outside and it is on this tension that I build my

poems. . . . The world has an identity of its own with which I cannot associate myself altogether, especially at crucial points. . . . Clarity as I seek it in my poems is to distinguish my person from the rest of everything else. Clarity together with directness make my style."

Elaborating on his aesthetic, Ignatow told Spanos, "I use my materials without receiving from them any vote of confidence at all, nor do I have any confidence or trust in the materials, full of hidden and not so hidden traps. I may only trust myself and so I go carefully among my objects and events, picking and choosing from among them, letting myself be led only where I will go and so my line is spare, selective, concise, in search of form to hold all this disparate material together always about to fly apart." He compares his writing process to taking a walk through his native Brooklyn: "I have to watch my step around an open manhole, a drunk sprawled on the sidewalk, dog shit, a nodding drug addict. I have to glance behind me from time to time to be sure I'm not being followed. My poetry has this touch of paranoia, this tight alertness to dangers, this militant preparedness for the worst, and above all, the sense of absurdity that arises as we seek for a meaning in this kind of life." He does not provide a meaningful resolution in the poems, "nothing conclusive or definitive," however, because life itself provides no solutions, he said in the Spanos interview. As he explained to Malanga, the lyric form also seemed to require more closure than the prose poem; therefore, for Ignatow, breaking out of the strictures of composition by line was an important step toward fuller and more accurate expression.

In another line of development, Ignatow's themes follow a progression from reflections on individual causes of social ills to problems of wider scope, Brown observes. "Generally, the early work tends to concentrate upon the evils of business and money-grubbing, while the later presents a more surreal vision of social violence and insanity," summarizes Brown. Money, and how we acquire it, is the major topic of the early books and *The Notebooks of David Ignatow,* and, according to Ignatow, "is the central issue of our time."

Poems declaiming the evils of money stem from the poet's personal history. As Ignatow reveals in *Open between Us,* his early years were dominated by his parents' anxieties about the family business. At first fascinated by the intensity of their conversations, Ignatow began to recognize that he did not value material success as much as the kind of personal freedom exemplified by the poet Walt Whitman. Therefore, instead of joining the family business after graduating from high school, he left home to find employment that would allow him the peace and leisure to write poetry.

However, his idealism drew him repeatedly into conflict with his bosses. Moving from job to job, he found that the pressure to provide for himself displaced the time and energy he needed to continue writing. He entered the family business feeling resigned and guilty about imposing on the freedom of his workers in order to make a profit. They told him, however, that they voluntarily submitted to the unpleasant demands of industry in order to maintain a standard of living they equated with happiness. Seeing no alternative to making this kind of trade-off himself, Ignatow concluded, "And so there was poetry to be written, about this paradox of the perpetual search for personal happiness and freedom in things other than oneself." His struggles to earn a living without compromising his personal values is often expressed in the early volumes *Poems, The Gentle Weight Lifter,* and *Say Pardon.*

Other poems in the early volumes speak out against social problems such as urban crime, war, and economic collapse. "In the 1930s he wrote poems about the depression, in the 1940s about World War II, in the 1960s about Vietnam," notes Brown. In *Figures of the Human,* the poet "directs his creative rage toward the . . . subject of violence and social dissolution in the America of the Vietnam era," Brown relates. *Rescue the Dead* ironically holds out no hope of rescue for the poet who identifies himself in one poem as a man forced by a nation of killers to kill his neighbor. "We are more used to poets open to the personal unconscious," comments Robert Bly in the afterword to Ignatow's *Selected Poems.* "If the 'dark side' [of human energy] is thought of as part of the personal unconscious, we notice that David Ignatow sees his dark side clearly only after he has seen it reflected in the angers and frustrations of the collective, when he sees it embodied in a stabber moving through a subway car. He is a poet of the community, of people who work for a living, as Whitman was too, but he is also a great poet of the collective."

In subsequent books, Ignatow's focus on his social environment broadens to include his relationship with nature. More philosophical and imaginative than his other poetry, the poems in *Facing the Tree: New Poems* and *Whisper to the Earth* ask of nature the same questions Ignatow raises elsewhere, L. M. Rosenberg comments in Chicago's *Tribune Books.* In meditations on stones, plants, and weather, Ignatow asks how humans can live, and affirms consciousness of his membership in an ecology that unifies all forms of life, Rosenberg observes. Brown, like other critics, suggests that the poet thus reconciles himself to the inevitability of his death. Responding to these poems reprinted in *New and Collected Poems, 1970-1985,* *New York Times Book Review* contributor Peter Stitt remarks that they provide "a positive response to the threat of isolation, death, political cruelty, godlessness and meaninglessness. The answer is love. . . . Faced with the fact of a strictly physical universe, Mr. Ignatow chooses to love that universe for all he, and it, are worth."

Ignatow commented on another significant difference between his earlier and later work; regarding "my early concentration in my poetry on injustice and cruelty," he told *CA,* "these poems were written with the assumption that somewhere, somehow there was a social system, idealized in faith by me, that practised justice and decency consistently and with pleasure. I was wrong. At seventy-five years of age, I no longer have such hopes and expectations, though my heart still leaps at any and all pieces and fragments of good news. Nevertheless, I have fallen back upon my study of the individual, taking myself primarily as an example and revealing to myself my shortcomings, my failures. Like Whitman, I think of myself as representative, and so what I write about myself and quite often about others, is intended as, by extension, a comment on most of us. We live in one world."

"If I were to make of this litany a steady diet," he continued, "I don't think I could easily absorb it, and so you will find humor in the last four or five books, humor dealing with precisely those problems to which in my earlier books I gave my passionate concern. In other words, with humor I seem to be more at ease with the moral burdens I have taken on myself and I actually enjoy writing about them now with a sense of detachment, which humor affords." Ignatow elaborates on these changes in *The One in the Many: A Poet's Memoirs.*

Critical responses to Ignatow's work were more antagonistic than he expected, at first, but have gradually become more favorable. "After I had written the kind of poetry *I* thought deserved the respect and attention of people whose opinions *I* respected, I discovered to my dismay that I was writing a kind of poetry

which really did not relate to the taste or interests of my generation in any way," he told Malanga. Ignatow's poetic stance—one of direct confrontation with life—opposes the widespread attitude, coming down to us from romanticism, that in poetry, "language takes precedence over content," he explained. From Williams, Ignatow had learned to guard against "a romantic view of life. Against elevated language. Against trying to make a leap into something which didn't exist." In contrast, the prevailing trend fosters a "withdrawal from life" by concerning itself with imaginative poetic devices; a substantial number of influential poets and critics "think through language you learn of life. I say you learn of life through sensibility which then has to be translated into language," he continued. Being thus at odds with critical opinion, Ignatow has produced an important body of work largely without the support of his own generation of writers and without critical acclaim. Later generations have been more appreciative, honoring him with the Shelley Memorial Prize, the Wallace Stevens Fellowship at Yale University, and the Bollingen Prize.

Summing up Ignatow's lifetime accomplishment, which was recognized in 1964 by an award from the National Institute of Arts and Letters, Brown concludes, "Transmuting autobiography into art, he has examined the self's relationship with the environment over a long, productive career. He offers both the edifying spectacle of a man who has paid for his accommodation with life and a body of poetry combining deep-felt emotion, intellectual penetration, and a considerable technical facility."

BIOGRAPHICAL/CRITICAL SOURCES:

BOOKS

Contemporary Authors Autobiography Series, Volume 3, Gale, 1986.
Contemporary Literary Criticism, Gale, Volume 4, 1975, Volume 7, 1977, Volume 14, 1980, Volume 40, 1986.
Dickey, James, *From Babel to Byzantium,* Farrar, Straus, 1968.
Dickey, James, *The Suspect in Poetry,* Sixties Press, 1968.
Dictionary of Literary Biography, Volume 5: *American Poets since World War II,* Gale, 1980.
Ignatow, David, *The Notebooks of David Ignatow,* edited by Ralph J. Mills, Swallow Press, 1974.
Ignatow, David, *Selected Poems,* edited by Robert Bly, Wesleyan University Press, 1975.
Ignatow, David, *Open between Us,* edited by Ralph J. Mills, University of Michigan Press, 1980.
Ignatow, David, *The One in the Many: A Poet's Memoirs,* Wesleyan University Press, 1988.
Jackson, Richard, *Acts of Mind,* University of Alabama Press, 1983.
Mazzaro, J., *Postmodern American Poetry,* University of Illinois Press, 1980.
Mills, Ralph, J., Jr., *Cry of the Human: Essays on Contemporary American Poetry,* University of Illinois Press, 1975.
Smith, Robert A., *A Checklist of Writings,* University of Connecticut Library, 1966.

PERIODICALS

American Book Review, December/January, 1978-79, September/October, 1981.
American Poetry Review, March/April, 1974, January/February, 1976, March/April, 1976.
Boundary 2, spring, 1974 (interview), fall, 1975.
Contemporary Literature, summer, 1987 (interview).
Georgia Review, summer, 1979.
Hudson Review, autumn, 1984, autumn, 1985, spring, 1987.

Lamp in the Spine, spring, 1973.
New York Times Book Review, November 21, 1948, July 30, 1978, February 14, 1982, November 11, 1987.
Ontario Review, spring/summer, 1975.
Paris Review, fall, 1979 (interview).
Parnassus, fall/winter, 1975.
Poetry, April, 1976, June, 1980.
Salmagundi, spring/summer, 1973.
Sewanee Review, spring, 1976.
Some, winter, 1973 (interview).
Tennessee Poetry Journal, winter, 1970 (interview).

Times Literary Supplement, November 6, 1987.
Tribune Books (Chicago), April 12, 1987.
University Review, spring, 1968.
World Literature Today, summer, 1979.
Yale Review, autumn, 1955, summer, 1961.

—*Sketch by Marilyn K. Basel*

*   *   *

INGERSOL, Jared
  See PAINE, Lauran (Bosworth)

J

J. L.-M.
See LEES-MILNE, James

*   *   *

JACKSON, John N(icholas)   1925-

PERSONAL: Born December 15, 1925, in Nottingham, England; son of Alexander (a teacher and clergyman) and Phyllis E. (Oldfield) Jackson; married Kathleen M. Nussey, May, 1951; children: Andrew, Susan, Paul. *Education:* University of Birmingham, B.A., 1949; University of Manchester, Ph.D., 1960. *Religion:* Anglican.

ADDRESSES: Home—80 Marsdale Dr., St. Catharines, Ontario, Canada. *Office*—Department of Geography, Brock University, St. Catharines, Ontario, Canada.

CAREER: Herefordshire County Council, Herefordshire, England, research officer, 1950-53; Hull County Borough, Hull, England, senior planning assistant, 1954-56; University of Manchester, Manchester, England, lecturer in geography, 1956-65; Brock University, St. Catharines, Ontario, professor of applied geography, 1965—, head of department, 1965-70. *Military service:* Royal Navy.

MEMBER: Canadian Association of Geographers.

WRITINGS:

Surveys for Town and Country Planning, Hutchinson University Library, 1963.
Recreational Development and the Lake Erie Shore, Niagara Region Development Council, 1968.
The Industrial Structure of the Niagara Region, Brock University, 1971.
The Canadian City: Space, Form, Quality, McGraw-Ryerson, 1972.
(Editor with J. Forrester) *Practical Geography,* McGraw-Ryerson, 1972.
Welland and the Welland Canal, Mika, 1975.
St. Catharines, Ontario: Its Early Years, Mika, 1976.
A Planning Appraisal of the Welland Urban Community, Department of Public Works (Ottawa), 1976.
Land Use Planning in the Niagara Region, Niagara Region Study Review Commission, 1976.
(With John Burtniak) *Railways in the Niagara Peninsula,* Mika, 1976.

(Contributor) Lorne H. Russwurm and Ken B. Beesley, editors, *The Rural-Urban Fringe: Canadian Perspectives,* Department of Geography, Atkinson College, York University, 1981.
(With Fred A. Addis) *The Welland Canals: A Comprehensive Guide,* Welland Canals Foundation, 1982.
The Four Welland Canals: A Journey of Discovery in St. Catharines and Thorold, Vanwell Publishing, 1988.
Names across Niagara, Vanwell Publishing, 1989.
A River Divided: Landscape in Evolution at Niagara, Vanwell Publishing, 1990.

WORK IN PROGRESS: Urban Characteristics and the Changing Regional Format in the Niagara Peninsula, 1900 to Present; Urban Form, Regional Growth: Quality, Expectations and Reality in Western Europe and North America; St. Catharines, Our City: An Illustrated History.

*   *   *

JAKOBSON, Roman   1896-1982

PERSONAL: Surname is pronounce *Yaak*-aub-son; born October 11, 1896, in Moscow, Russia (now U.S.S.R.); died July 18, 1982, in Boston, Mass.; immigrated to Czechoslovakia, 1920; immigrated to United States, 1941, naturalized U.S. citizen, 1952; son of Osip J. (a chemist) and Anna (Volpert) Jakobson; married second wife, Svatana Pirkova; married third wife, Krystyna Pomorska (died December, 1986), September 28, 1962. *Education:* Lazarev Institute of Oriental Languages, B.A. (with silver medal), 1914; University of Moscow, M.A., 1918; University of Prague, Ph.D., 1930. *Religion:* Jewish.

ADDRESSES: Home—Cambridge, Mass. 02138. *Office*—301 Boylston Hall, Harvard University, Cambridge, Mass. 02138.

CAREER: University of Moscow, Moscow, Russia, research associate, 1918-20; Moscow Dramatic School, Moscow, Russia, professor of orthoepy, 1920; Masaryk University, Brno, Czechoslovakia, assistant professor, 1933-34, visiting professor, 1934-37, associate professor of Russian philosophy and old Czech literature, 1937-39; University of Copenhagen, Copenhagen, Denmark, visiting lecturer in phonology, 1939; University of Oslo, Oslo, Norway, visiting lecturer in linguistics, 1939-40; University of Uppsala, Uppsala, Sweden, visiting lecturer in Russian, 1940-41; Ecole Libre des Hautes Etudes, New York

City, professor of linguistics, 1942-46; Columbia University, New York City, visiting professor, 1943-46, T. G. Masaryk Professor of Czechoslovak Studies, 1946-49; Harvard University, Cambridge, Mass., Samuel Hazzard Cross Professor of Slavic Languages, Literatures, and General Linguistics, 1949-67, professor emeritus, 1967-82, fellow of Center for Cognitive Studies, 1967-69. T. G. Masaryk Professor at Institut de Philologie et d'Histoire Orientales et Slaves, 1943-46; professor at Massachusetts Institute of Technology, 1957-67, professor emeritus, 1967-82; visiting professor at Yale University, 1967, 1971, Princeton University, 1968, Brown University, 1969-70, Brandeis University, 1970, College de France, 1972, Catholic University of Louvain, 1972, New York University, 1973, and Bergen University, 1976. Fellow of Center for Advanced Study in the Behavioral Sciences, 1959, 1961; visiting fellow at Salk Institute for Biological Studies, 1966-69. President, International Council of Phonetic Sciences, 1948-61; vice president, International Committee of Slavists, 1958-76; honorary president, Tokyo Institute for the Advanced Study of Language, 1967-82. Consultant, Massachusetts Institute of Technology, 1967-82, and UNESCO. *Wartime service:* Served with the U.S.S.R. Red Cross mission to Czechoslovakia, 1920.

MEMBER: International Society of Phonetic Sciences (vice-president, 1970-82), Association Phonetique Internationale (honorary member), International Association for Semiotic Studies (vice president, 1969-82), Linguistic Society of America (president, 1956), American Anthropological Association, Acoustic Society of America, American Academy of Arts and Sciences (fellow), American Association for Armenian Studies and Research (honorary member), Academy of Aphasia (honorary member), Center for Byzantine Studies (honorary member), Norwegian Academy of Sciences (foreign member), Royal Danish Academy of Science and Letters (foreign member), Serbian Academy of Sciences (foreign member), Polish Academy of Science (foreign member), Royal Netherlands Academy of Sciences (foreign member), Irish Academy of Sciences (foreign member), Italian Academy of Sciences in Bologna (foreign member), British Academy (foreign member), Finnish Academy of Sciences (foreign member), Finno-Ugric Society (honorary member), Royal Society of Letters of Lund (honorary member), Associazione Italiana di Studi Semiotica (honorary member), Circolo Semiologico Siciliano (honorary member), Phonetic Society of Japan (honorary member), Philological Society (England; honorary member), Royal Anthropological Institute of Great Britain and Ireland (honorary member), Medieval Academy, Toronto Semeiotic Circle (honorary member).

AWARDS, HONORS: Chevalier de la Legion d'Honneur, 1947; honorary M.A., Harvard University, 1949; D.Litt. from Cambridge University, 1960, University of Chicago and University of Oslo, 1961, University of Uppsala and University of Michigan, 1963, University of Grenoble and University of Nice, 1966, University of Rome and Yale University, 1967, Charles University and Purkyne University, 1968, University of Zagreb, 1969, Ohio State University, 1970, University of Louvain, 1972, University of Tel Aviv and Harvard University, 1975, Columbia University, 1976, Oxford University, 1981, and Brandeis University, 1981; D.Sc., University of New Mexico, 1966, and Clark University, 1969; awards from American Council of Learned Societies, 1960, National Slavic Honor Society, 1967, and American Association for the Advancement of Slavic Studies, 1970; gold medal, Slovak Academy of Science, 1968; Johns Hopkins University centennial scholar, 1975; Boston College presidential bicentennial award, 1976; Antonio Feltrinelli Award for Philos-

ophy and Linguistics, 1980; Hegel Prize, International Hegel Society, 1982.

WRITINGS:

Remarques sur l'evolution phonologique du russe comparee a celle des autres langues slaves (title means "Remarks on the Phonological Evolution of Russian as Compared with That of Other Slavic Languages"), [Prague], 1929.

Kindersprache, Aphasie und allgemeine Lautgesetze, [Uppsala], 1941, 2nd edition, [Frankfurt], 1970, published as *Child Language, Aphasia and Phonological Universals,* Mouton, 1968.

(Editor with Ernest J. Simmons) *Russian Epic Studies,* American Folklore Society, 1949, reprinted, Kraus, 1976.

(With Gunnar M. Fant and Morris Halle) *Preliminaries to Speech Analysis: The Distinctive Features and Their Correlates,* MIT Press, 1952.

(With Halle) *Fundamentals of Language,* Mouton (Netherlands), 1956, revised edition, 1971.

(With Gerta Huettl-Worth and John Fred Beebe) *Paleosiberian Peoples and Languages: A Bibliographical Guide,* HRAF Press (New Haven), 1957, Greenwood Press, 1981.

(With Halle) *Grundlage der Sprache,* Akademie Verlag, 1960.

(With L. L. Hammerich) *Low German Manual of Spoken Russian, 1607,* Danish Academy of Sciences, Volume 1, 1961, Volume 2, 1970.

Selected Writings, Mouton, Volume 1: *Phonological Studies,* 1962, 2nd edition, 1971, Volume 2: *Word and Language,* 1971, Volume 3: *The Poetry of Grammar and the Grammar of Poetry,* 1981, Volume 4: *Slavic Epic Studies,* 1966, Volume 5: *On Verse, Its Masters and Explorers,* 1979, Volume 6: *Early Slavic Paths and Crossroads,* two parts, edited by Stephen Rudy, 1982, Volume 7: *Contributions to Comparative Mythology: Studies in Linguistics and Philology, 1972-1982,* edited by Rudy, preface by Linda R. Waugh, 1985.

Essais de linguistique generale (title means "Essays in General Linguistics"), Editions de Minuit (Paris), Volume 1, 1963, Volume 2, 1973.

(Editor with Dean S. Worth) *Sofonija's Tale of the Russian-Tatar Battle on the Kulikovo Field,* Mouton, 1963.

Principles of Phonology, translated by Christiane A. Baltaxe, University of California Press, 1969.

Language enfantin et aphasie (title means "Children's Language and Aphasia"), Editions de Minuit, 1969.

O cheshskom stikhe preimushchestvenno v sopostavlenii s russkin (title means "Czech Verse As Compared with Russian"), University Press of New England, 1969.

Linguistica, Poetica, Cinema (title means "Linguistics, Poetics, Cinema"), Editora Perspectiva, 1970.

(With L. G. Jones) *Shakespeare's Verbal Art in th'Experience of Spirit,* Mouton, 1970.

(Editor with Shigeo Kawamoto) *Studies in General and Oriental Linguistics, Presented to Shiro Hattori on the Occasion of His Sixtieth Birthday,* TEC (Tokyo), 1970.

Studies in Verbal Art: Texts in Czech and Slovak, Michigan Slavic Publications, 1971.

Studies on Child Language and Aphasia, Mouton, 1971.

Bibliography of Publications, Mouton, 1971.

Main Trends in the Science of Language, [New York], 1973.

Form und Sinn (title means "Form and Meaning"), W. Fink Verlag, 1973.

Questions de Poetique (title means "Questions of Poetics"), Editions de Seuil (Paris), 1973.

(Editor with C. H. van Schooneveld and Dean S. Worth) *Slavic Poetics: Essays in Honor of Kiril Taranovsky,* Mouton, 1973.

(With Claude Levi Strauss and others) *Results of the Conference of Anthropologists and Linguists* (originally published in *International Journal of American Linguistics,* April, 1953), University of Chicago Press, 1974.

(Editor, with others, and author of foreword) *N. S. Trubetzkoy's Letters and Notes,* Mouton, 1975.

Pushkin and His Sculptural Myth, edited by John Burbank, Mouton, 1975.

Coup d'oeil sur le developpement de la semiotique (title means "Glance on the Development of Semiotics"), Indiana University Press, 1975.

Premesse di storia letteraria Slava (title means "Foundations of Slavic Literary History"), Il Saggiatore (Milan), 1975.

Aufsaetze zur Linguistik und Poetik (title means "Contributions to Linguistics and Poetics"), Nymphenburger Verlag (Munich), 1976.

Six lecons sur le son et le sens, Editions de Minuit, 1976, translated by John Mepham as *Six Lectures on Sound and Meaning,* MIT Press, 1978.

Hoelderlin-Klee-Brecht: Zur Wortkunst dreier Gedichte (title means "Hoelderlin-Klee-Brecht: The Verbal Art of Three Poems"), Suhrkamp, 1976.

Der grammatische Aufbau der Kindersprache (title means "The Grammatical Structure of Children's Language"), Rheinisch-Westfaelische Akademie, 1977.

(With Stephen Rudy) *Yeats' "Sorrow of Love" through the Years,* Peter de Ridder Press, 1977.

(With Waugh) *The Sound Shape of Language,* Indiana University Press, 1978.

Lo sviluppo della semiotica (title means "Development of Semiotics"), Studi Bompiani (Milan), 1978.

Poetik: Ausgewaehlte Aufsaetze, 1921-1971, edited by Elmar Holenstein and Tarcisius Schelbert, Suhrkamp, 1979.

Brain and Language: Cerebral Hemispheres and Linguistic Structure in Mutual Light, Slavica, 1980.

(Contributor) Holenstein, *Von der Hintergehbarkeit der Sprache: Kognitive Unterlagen der Sprache,* Suhrkamp, 1980.

The Framework of Language, Michigan Slavic Publications, 1980.

(With wife, Krystyna Pomorska) *Dialogues,* Flammarion, 1980, translated from the French by Christian Hubert as *The Jakobson-Pomorska Dialogues,* MIT Press, 1983.

Russian and Slavic Grammar Studies, 1931-1981, edited by Waugh and Halle, Mouton, 1984.

(With Hans-Georg Gadamer and Holenstein) *Das Erbe Hegels II,* Suhrkamp, 1984.

Verbal Art, Verbal Sign, Verbal Time, edited by Pomorska and Stephen Rudy, University of Minnesota Press, 1985.

Language in Literature, edited Pomorska and Rudy, Harvard University Press, 1987.

Also author of *Noveyshaya russkaya poeziya* (title means "Contemporary Russian Poetry"), 1921, *Saggi di linguistica generale* (title means "Studies in General Linguistics"), 1966, and *Fonema e Fonologia* (title means "Phoneme and Phonology"), 1967. Co-author of *La geste du Prince Igor,* 1948. Co-editor, *Description and Analysis of Contemporary Standard Russian,* 1959, and *Poetics-Poetyka-Poetika, II: Problems of General Metrics and the Metrics of Slavonic Languages,* 1966. Contributor of poetry to *Zaumnaya Gniga.*

SIDELIGHTS: "Roman Jakobson, the father of modern structural linguistics, elaborated sophisticated theories of language and communication that had profound effects on such disciplines as anthropology, art criticism and brain research," according to a *New York Times* obituary. Strongly influenced by the structuralist theories of Ferdinand de Saussure, Jakobson passed along his theories on language to his disciple, Noam Chomsky, who is now well-known for his theories of generative grammar. Also a formalist critic of literature, Jakobson was more interested in the structure of literary works than he was in their meaning, favoring the analysis of technical form over the influence of historical and biographical considerations.

Jakobson's works have been translated into more than fifteen languages, including Portuguese, Swedish, Serbo-Croatian, Hungarian, Japanese, Korean, and Hebrew; he could read more than twenty-five languages and was fluent in Russian, French, Polish, German, Czech, and English.

BIOGRAPHICAL/CRITICAL SOURCES:

BOOKS

Armstrong, Daniel, and C. M. van Schooneveld, editors, *Roman Jakobson: Echoes of His Scholarship,* Lisse, 1977.
Halle, Morris, *Roman Jakobson: What He Taught Us,* Slavica, 1983.
Holenstein, Elmar, *Roman Jakobson's Approach to Language,* Indiana University Press, 1976.
Matejka, Ladislav, editor, *Sound, Sign, and Meaning,* University of Michigan, 1976.
Roman Jakobson: A Bibliography of His Writings, Mouton, 1971.
Waugh, Linda R., *Roman Jakobson's Science of Language,* Lisse, 1976.

PERIODICALS

Times Literary Supplement, April 17, 1987.

OBITUARIES:

PERIODICALS

Chicago Tribune, July 21, 1982.
Newsweek, August 2, 1982.
New York Times, July 20, 1982.
Washington Post, July 21, 1982.*

*   *   *

JAMES, Heather   1914-
(Heather Jenner)

PERSONAL: Born February 27, 1914, in London, England; daughter of Cyril Arthur (an army general) and Violet (Ellis) Lyon; married Michael George Cox, November 8, 1942; married Stephen Potter (a novelist and critic), May 20, 1955 (died, 1969); married Sir John Hastings James (deputy master and comptroller of the Royal Mint), June 30, 1971; children: (first marriage) Stella, James; (second marriage) Luke. *Education:* Educated in Bath, England.

ADDRESSES: *Home*—Flat 4, 86 Elm Park Gardens, London SW10 9PD, England. *Office*—Marriage Bureau, 124 New Bond St., London W.1, England.

CAREER: Marriage Bureau, London, England, owner and manager, 1939—.

MEMBER: Society of Authors.

WRITINGS:

UNDER PSEUDONYM HEATHER JENNER

(With Muriel Segal) *Marriage Is My Business,* Kimber & Co., 1953.
The Marriage Book, Duckworth, 1964.
Royal Wives, Duckworth, 1967, St. Martin's, 1971.

(With Segal) *Men and Marriage,* Putnam, 1970.
Marriages Are Made on Earth, David & Charles, 1979.

Author of column, "Heather Jenner Says," for *Evening News* (London), 1959-61; occasional contributor to other publications.

AVOCATIONAL INTERESTS: Music, reading, travel, the theater, bridge, picture galleries.

* * *

JENNER, Heather
See JAMES, Heather

* * *

JENTZ, Gaylord A. 1931-

PERSONAL: Born August 7, 1931, in Beloit, Wis.; son of Merlyn Adair and Delva (Mullen) Jentz; married JoAnn Mary Hornung, August 6, 1955; children: Katherine, Gary, Loretta and Rory (twins). *Education:* University of Wisconsin, B.A., 1953, J.D., 1957, M.B.A., 1958. *Religion:* Congregational.

ADDRESSES: Home—4106 North Hills Dr., Austin, Tex. 78731. *Office*—College of Business Administration 5.202, University of Texas, Austin, Tex. 78712.

CAREER: Admitted to Wisconsin Bar, 1957; University of Oklahoma, Norman, 1958-65, began as instructor, became associate professor of business law, 1968—, chairman of department of general business, 1968-74, 1980-86, Herbert D. Kelleher Professor of Business Law, 1982—. University of Wisconsin, 1957-65, began as visiting summer instructor, became visiting professor. *Military service:* U.S. Army, 1953-55.

AWARDS, HONORS: College of Business Administration Jack G. Taylor Teaching Excellence Award (undergraduate), 1971 and 1989; Joe D. Beasley Teaching Excellence Award (graduate), 1978; College of Business Administration Foundation Advisory Council Distinguished Contributions Award, 1979; American Business Law Faculty Award of Excellence, 1981; College of Business Administration and Student Council Service Award, 1983; James C. Scarboro Memorial Award from Colorado Graduate School of Banking, 1983.

WRITINGS:

Texas Uniform Commercial Code: Practical Aspects on Secured Transactions (monograph), Bureau of Business Research, University of Texas, 1966, revised edition, 1975.
(With others) *Business Law: Text and Cases,* 2nd edition, Allyn & Bacon, 1968.
(With others) *Business Law: Text and Cases,* Dryden, 1978.
(With others) *Business Law: Key Issues and Concepts,* Grid Publishing, 1978.
(With others) *West's Business Law: Text and Cases,* 2nd edition (Jentz was not associated with earlier edition), West, 1983, 4th edition, 1989.
(With others) *West's Business Law: Alternate UCC Comprehensive Edition,* 2nd edition (Jentz was not associated with earlier edition), West, 1983, 4th edition, 1990.
(With others) *Texas Family Law,* University of Texas Bureau of Business Research, 1987.
(Co-author) *Business Law Today,* West, 1988.
(With others) *Legal Environment of Business,* West, 1989.

Contributor to business and legal journals. *Social Science Quarterly,* deputy editor, 1966-82, member of editorial board, 1982—; *American Business Law Journal,* staff editor of case comments and digest section, 1967-69, editor in chief, 1969-74, advisory editor, 1974—.

* * *

JOHNSON, Harry Alleyn 1921-

PERSONAL: Born November 22, 1921, in Norfolk, Va.; son of O. L. (a businessman) and Blanche (Robinson) Johnson; married Mae Coleman (a college professor), August 15, 1953; children: Sharon Lynne, Jeffrey Alan. *Education:* Virginia State College for Negroes (now Virginia State College), B.S., 1942; Columbia University, M.A., 1948, Ed.D., 1952; post-doctoral study, Sorbonne, University of Paris, 1958. *Religion:* Protestant.

ADDRESSES: Home—4312 West River Rd., Ettrick, Va. 23803. *Office*—Department of Education, Virginia State College, Box 27, Petersburg, Va. 23803.

CAREER: Virginia State College, Petersburg, Va., instructor, 1949-50, assistant professor, 1950-52, associate professor, 1952-66, professor of education, 1966-85, professor emeritus, 1985—, associate dean, 1949-85, director of Learning Resources Center. Visiting professor at University of Maine, 1955, 1956, University of Oslo, 1959, 1962, 1965, 1967, University of California, Hayward, 1969, and Michigan State University, 1970; visiting lecturer at University of Puerto Rico, University of North Dakota, University of North Carolina, University of Nebraska, Howard University, Catholic University of America, and West Virginia State College. Member of board of directors, CINE International; member of advisory board, department of library and educational media, Stanford University; member, Commission Internationale pour le Developpement des Activites Educatives Culturelles en Afrique Italy. *Military service:* U.S. Army, 1942-45; became captain.

MEMBER: American Association of University Professors, Association for Supervision and Curriculum Development, National Education Association (member of board of directors and executive committee, 1966-69), Reserve Officers Association, Virginia Education Association, Kappa Delta Pi, Phi Delta Kappa, Kappa Alpha Psi.

AWARDS, HONORS: Fulbright fellowship to University of Paris, 1958-59; Outstanding Media Educator of the Year, 1975.

WRITINGS:

(Editor) *Multimedia Materials for Afro-American Studies: A Curriculum Orientation and Annotated Bibliography of Resources,* Bowker, 1971.
(Editor) *Ethnic American Minorities: A Guide to Media and Materials,* Bowker, 1976.
Selected Films and Filmstrips on Four Ethnic American Minorities: Afro, Indian, Oriental, and Spanish Speaking, School of Education, Stanford University, 1976.
(Editor) *Negotiating the Mainstream: A Survey of the Afro-American Experience,* American Library Association, 1978.

Member of editorial board of directors, *Journal of Instructional Media.*

* * *

JONES, J. Farragut
See LEVINSON, Leonard

JONES, Ken D(uane) 1930-

PERSONAL: Born July 10, 1930, in Hannibal, Mo.; son of Cliff G. (an accountant, musician, and grocer) and Clifton E. (Brown) Jones; married Nancy Johnston, December 21, 1952; children: Debra, Karen. *Education:* Hannibal LaGrange Junior College, A.A., 1950; attended Arizona State College, 1950-51; Culver-Stockton College, B.S., 1954. *Politics:* Democrat. *Religion:* Protestant.

ADDRESSES: Home—100 Manor Dr., Columbia, Mo. 65201. *Office*—State Farm Mutual Auto Insurance Co., Columbia, Mo. 65217.

CAREER: High school science teacher and basketball and baseball coach, Wright City, Mo., 1954-56; State Farm Mutual Auto Insurance Co., insurance agent, Warrenton, Mo., 1956-57, underwriting supervisor, Columbia, Mo., 1957—. *Military service:* U.S. Army, Intelligence, 1952-54.

MEMBER: International Brick Collector's Association (treasurer), Tin Container Collectors Association.

WRITINGS:

(With Alfred Twomey and Arthur McClure) *The Films of James Stewart,* A. S. Barnes, 1970.
(With McClure) *Western Films: Heroes, Heavies, and Sagebrush of the "B" Genre,* A. S. Barnes, 1972.
(With McClure) *Hollywood at War,* A. S. Barnes, 1973.
(With McClure) *Star Quality: Screen Actors from the Golden Age of Films,* A. S. Barnes, 1974.
(With McClure and Twomey) *Character People,* A. S. Barnes, 1976.
(With McClure and William T. Stewart) *International Film Necrology,* Garland Publishing, 1981.
(With McClure and Twomey) *More Character People,* Citadel, 1984.

Contributor of regular columns to *Film Collectors Registry* and *Western Film Collector.* Former co-editor, *Yesteryear,* beginning 1971.

AVOCATIONAL INTERESTS: Collecting movie memorabilia, tobacco tins, old name bricks, advertising items, and old toys; active in tennis, table tennis, and fishing.

*   *   *

JORDAN, Leonard
See LEVINSON, Leonard

*   *   *

JUERGENSMEYER, Jane Stuart
See STUART, (Jessica) Jane

K

KAISER, Robert G(reeley) 1943-

PERSONAL: Born April 7, 1943, in Washington, D.C.; son of Philip Mayer (a government official and diplomat) and Hannah (Greeley) Kaiser; married Hannah Jopling (a translator), April 14, 1965; children: Charlotte Jerome, Emily Eli. *Education:* Yale University, B.A., 1964; London School of Economics and Political Science, M.Sc., 1967; postgraduate study, Columbia University, 1970-71.

ADDRESSES: Office—Washington Post, 1150 15th St. N.W., Washington, D.C. 20071. *Agent*—John Hawkins, 71 West 23rd St., New York, N.Y. 10010.

CAREER: Washington Post, Washington, D.C., reporter, 1963—, correspondent in Saigon, 1969-70, bureau chief in Moscow, 1971-74, national correspondent, 1975-82, associate editor and columnist, 1982-85, assistant managing editor for national news, 1985—. Duke University, Durham, N.C., visiting professor, 1974-75, adjunct professor, 1980—.

MEMBER: Council on Foreign Relations, Elihu Club.

AWARDS, HONORS: Washington-Baltimore Newspaper Guild Front Page award, 1973; Overseas Press Club award for best foreign correspondence, 1974.

WRITINGS:

(With Dan Morgan) *The Soviet Union and Eastern Europe: New Paths, Old Ruts,* Foreign Policy Association, 1973.
Cold Winter, Cold War, Stein & Day, 1974.
Russia: The People and the Power, Antheneum, 1976, updated edition, Washington Square Press, 1984, abridged edition, Penguin, 1977.
(With Jon Lowell) *Great American Dreams: A Portrait of the Way We Are,* Harper, 1979.
(Author of text) *Russia from the Inside,* compiled and edited by wife, Hannah Jopling Kaiser, Dutton, 1980.

Contributor of articles to periodicals, including *Esquire, Foreign Affairs, New York,* and *Observer* (London).

SIDELIGHTS: A former Moscow bureau chief for the *Washington Post,* Robert G. Kaiser has parlayed his knowledge of the Soviet Union into several books on its people. *Russia: The People and the Power,* for example, "is a perfectly fascinating tour d'horizon of the Soviet Union," comments Erwin Canham in the *Christian Science Monitor.* "Not a page is dull. It is crammed

with first-hand precise reporting: episodes, anecdotes, events, observations. . . . Kaiser's account of the dead hand of bureaucratic mediocrity, bearing down on nearly everything, is persuasive." *New York Times Book Review* contributor Phillip Knightley similarly observes that Kaiser's book "tell[s] us how the Russians feel about [life]. . . . For the first time, I now know something about today's Russians as a people." *Russia,* which Lance Morrow of *Time* calls a "superb exercise . . . in political-travel journalism, give[s] Russia what it has always lacked for Americans: a complicated human reality."

Likewise, "Robert and Hannah Kaiser's *Russia from the Inside* is a real Russian book about the gritty Soviet reality that a casual tourist could never see," David Lapeza summarizes in the *Washington Post Book World.* A compilation of photographs, taken mostly by native Soviets, *Russia from the Inside* is "an exceptionally detailed and insightful look at modern Russian life," the critic continues. Kaiser's commentary, in particular, provides "a quick and deft course in the Soviet Union," writes *Christian Science Monitor* contributor Charlotte Saikowski, "touching on such aspects as schooling marriage, religion, village life, and the country's political system." "The text is not supplemental, as it often is with coffee table books" concludes Lapeza; "it is essential to an understanding of the photographs."

BIOGRAPHICAL/CRITICAL SOURCES:

PERIODICALS

Christian Science Monitor, February 10, 1976, September 8, 1980.
Newsweek, January 19, 1976.
New York Times, February 8, 1976, February 9, 1976.
New York Times Book Review, January 25, 1976.
Time, May 10, 1976.
Washington Post Book World, August 3, 1980.

*   *   *

KANE, Peter E(vans) 1932-

PERSONAL: Born February 27, 1932, in Beverly Hills, Calif.; son of Arthur G. and Eleanor I. (Evans) Kane; married Marguerite Coniff (a personal counselor); children: Emily Anne, Ellen Palmer, Amy Sara Forslind, Peter Jacob Barent. *Education:* Santa Barbara College (now University of California, Santa Barbara), B.A., 1954; University of California, Los Angeles, M.A., 1960; Purdue University, Ph.D., 1967.

ADDRESSES: Home—8 Chiswick Dr., Churchville, N.Y. 14428. *Office*—Department of Communication, State University of New York College at Brockport, Brockport, N.Y. 14420.

CAREER: Occidental College, Los Angeles, Calif., instructor in speech, 1957-60; Purdue University, West Lafayette, Ind., instructor in speech, 1960-61; St. Joseph's College, Rensselaer, Ind., assistant professor of speech, 1961-65; State University of New York at Binghamton, assistant professor of rhetoric, 1965-68; State University of New York College at Brockport, associate professor, 1968-74, professor of communication, 1974—.

MEMBER: Speech Communication Association, Rhetoric Society of America, Eastern Communication Association, New York State Speech Communication Association.

WRITINGS:

Speech Communication in a Democratic Society, Kendall/Hunt, 1975, 3rd edition, 1979.
(Contributor) Thomas Benson, editor, *Speech Communication in the Twentieth Century,* Southern Illinois University Press, 1985.
Murder, Courts, and the Press, Southern Illinois University Press, 1986.
(Contributor) Gerald Phillips and Julia Woods, editors, *Speech Communication: Essays to Commemorate the 75th Anniversary of the Speech Communication Association,* Southern Illinois University Press, 1989.

Editor of *Free Speech Yearbook,* 1979-81. Also contributor to periodicals, including *Choice* and *Philosophical Exchange.* Editor, *Communication Quarterly,* 1968-72, and *Free Speech,* 1973-76.

WORK IN PROGRESS: A book tentatively entitled *Errors, Lies, and Libels: Cases in Defamation.*

SIDELIGHTS: Peter E. Kane told *CA:* "All study of communication involves in one way or another analysis of constraints on communication. The very language of communication limits what can be said. Even the most intimate of interpersonal relationships involves rules that shape both form and content of communication.

"My research and writing involve the legal limitations on communication that are usually more easy to identify than the unwritten and other unacknowledged communication rules of interpersonal relationships. While the First Amendment to the United States Constitution seems to grant a totally unrestricted right to communicate, in reality that right is restricted by competing social claims.

"At present I am particularly interested in the conflict between freedom of communication and society's interest in protecting an individual's reputation. We attach great importance to maintaining our good name and naturally seek redress when false and injurious statements are made about us. I am working on a study of how our legal system attempts to protect freedom of expression while providing appropriate protection for reputation."

*   *   *

KARNOW, Stanley 1925-

PERSONAL: Born February 4, 1925, in New York, N.Y.; son of Harry (a businessman) and Henriette (Koeppel) Karnow; married Claude Sarraute, July 15, 1948 (divorced, 1955); married Annette Kline, April 12, 1959; children: Curtis Edward,

Catherine Anne, Michael Franklin. *Education:* Harvard University, A.B., 1947; additional study at the Sorbonne, University of Paris, 1947-48, and Ecole des Sciences Politiques, 1948-49.

ADDRESSES: Home—10850 Springknoll Dr., Potomac, Md. 20854. *Office*—1220 National Press Building, Washington, D.C. 20045. *Agent*—Ronald Goldfarb, 918 16th St. N.W., Washington, D.C. 20006; and Don Cutler, Sterling Lord Agency, 660 Madison Ave., New York, N.Y. 10021.

CAREER: Time, New York City, correspondent in Paris, France, 1950-57; Time-Life, New York City, bureau chief in North Africa, 1958-59, and Hong Kong, 1959-62; Time, Inc., New York City, special correspondent, 1962-63; *Saturday Evening Post,* Philadelphia, Pa., Far East correspondent, 1963-65; *Washington Post,* Washington, D.C., Far East correspondent, 1965-71, diplomatic correspondent, 1971-72; National Broadcasting Corp. (NBC) News, Washington, D.C., special correspondent, 1972-73; *New Republic,* Washington, D.C., associate editor, 1973-75; syndicated columnist, Register & Tribune Syndicate, 1974—, and King Features, 1975-87; correspondent for public television, 1975—; International Writers Service, Washington, D.C., editor in chief, 1975-86; writer. Chief correspondent for PBS-TV series "Vietnam: A Television History," 1983, and "The U.S. in the Philippines: In Our Image," 1989. Correspondent for *London Observer,* 1961-65; columnist for *Le Point,* Paris, 1976-83. Fellow, Institute of Politics, John F. Kennedy School of Government, and East Asian Research Center, Harvard University, both 1970-71. *Military service:* U.S. Army Air Forces, 1943-46.

MEMBER: Council on Foreign Relations, White House Correspondents Association, Authors Guild, Authors League of America, PEN American Center, Foreign Correspondents Club, Signet Society, Harvard Club, Century Association, Shek-O Club (Hong Kong).

AWARDS, HONORS: Citation from Overseas Press Club, 1966, and annual award for best newspaper interpretation of foreign affairs, 1968; Emmy Awards, Polk Award, and Dupont Award, all 1984, all for "Vietnam: A Television History"; Pulitzer Prize in history, 1990.

WRITINGS:

Southeast Asia, Time-Life Books, 1963.
Mao and China: From Revolution to Revolution, Viking, 1972, published as *Mao and China: Inside China's Cultural Revolution,* Penguin Books, 1984.
Vietnam: The War Nobody Won, Foreign Policy Association, 1983.
(With others) "Vietnam: A Television History" (multi-part documentary series; also see below), Public Broadcasting System (PBS-TV), 1983.
Vietnam: A History (companion volume to the television series), Viking, 1983.
(With others, and co-producer) "The U.S. in the Philippines: In Our Image" (multi-part documentary series; also see below), PBS-TV, 1989.
In Our Image: America's Empire in the Philippines (companion volume to the television series), Random House, 1989.

SIDELIGHTS: Stanley Karnow has a "well-earned reputation as one of the most diligent and disciplined reporters in Asian journalism," notes Allen S. Whiting in his *New Republic* review of *Mao and China: From Revolution to Revolution.* Karnow spent over twenty years in Asia as a reporter, "so it is hardly surprising that [he] has cut through the fog surrounding China with the skill of an acupuncturist and produced the finest, most objective, most comprehensive book on modern China yet to appear," states *Newsweek* contributor Arthur Cooper. *Mao and China* traces the development of China's Cultural Revolution of the mid-1960s, events which led to a major shift in the Communist party makeup and structure; the book focuses in particular on the actions of party leader Mao Tse-tung. Although China has been perceived in the West as a closed society, "amazingly, there was a continuous stream of information flowing out of China during those years of turmoil," including radio broadcasts, speeches, government documents, and eyewitness stories, as Charles Elliott observes in *Time.* "Karnow monitored enough of this material to be able to see it for what it really was—the first approximation of a free press ever in Communist China," Elliott explains. "His idea, brilliantly carried out, was to sort the mess into reliable narrative history."

Whiting concurs with this assessment, and relates that "Karnow mixes a lucid summary of the main events and contending factions with vivid first-hand accounts drawn from personal interviews with refugees and uniquely revealing Red Guard reports of mayhem." Although *Nation* contributor Bert Cochran faults the author for some of his historical interpretations and remarks that "Karnow does not go beyond the essential materials that have been gathered by American and British Sinologists," he admits that the author "has systematically organized these materials into a detailed brief, and has succeeded in fitting the events of 1966-69 into the story of the evolution of Chinese communism." As the critic summarizes, "Karnow's book is an important contribution to this history because it is the first comprehensive account of a unique and little understood insurrection." *Mao and China* is "a sobering reminder of how little the world knew about the clashes and crises which affected every province and most cities of China," concludes Whiting. The continuing mystery of Chinese society makes "especially valuable the sensitivity, patience and sheer effort by which Karnow [has] illuminated the central arena of politics at a critical juncture."

Karnow also uses his extensive Asian experiences as a background for *Vietnam: A History,* a book published in conjunction with the premiere of PBS-TV's documentary "Vietnam: A Television History." In profiling the background of this long-troubled country, Karnow examines its ancient conflicts with the Chinese as well as the era of French colonial rule before describing the clash Westerners term the "Vietnam War." "He supplements his rigorous research with interviewing of hundreds of participants in the war, including a number of present-day Communist leaders," Regina Millette Frawley describes in the *Christian Science Monitor.* "In so doing, Karnow corroborates many closely held perceptions but explodes others—to his credit, even his own." Karnow visited Vietnam in 1981 to interview the country's military leaders, and it is these "personal accounts, eyewitness reports, exclusive interviews—the nuances of history," comments *Detroit News* contributor Robert Pisor, "[which] give life to Karnow's book." In addition, as Bill Stout recounts in the *Los Angeles Times Book Review,* "Karnow goes back into the history of Vietnam—thousands of years, not mere decades as the U.S. and France had measured events there—and he reminds us again that we had virtually no understanding of the country and its people when our leaders decided to go in."

Indeed, many critics praise the large scope and comprehensiveness of *Vietnam: A History.* Even though "Karnow takes on the whole sweep of Vietnamese history," *Chicago Tribune Book World* writer Jack Fuller maintains that "the story does not overlook the personal, biographical forces that played into the tragedy [and] offers fascinating portraits of Vietnamese figures"

and "detailed narratives of controversial events and decisions" as well, including some accounts which are "riveting." Karnow's broad approach allows the reader to see that "America's war [was] merely an episode of the still continuing struggle," Richard West asserts in the *Spectator;* and not only are the Vietnamese and their history illuminated, "we feel, after reading Mr. Karnow, that we now know everything that is worth knowing on why decisions were taken about Vietnam by [the American government]."

These assessments notwithstanding, *New York Times Book Review* contributor Douglas Pike remarks that "despite a masterly effort to be comprehensive, Mr. Karnow's account comes out sketchy and abbreviated. Much important history is reduced to a sentence or two, and slightly less important history is ignored entirely." Harry G. Summers, however, believes that *Vietnam: A History* "is a landmark work. Exceptionally well researched and well written, it is the most complete account to date of the Vietnam tragedy." Stout also finds Karnow's work comprehensive, observing that "his is a rich and unusual mixture; he has the master reporter's eye for meaningful detail, an ear for the memorable quote, and he worked hard to give the Indochina epoch a historian's perspective." But what makes Karnow's work "so remarkable," Summers claims, "is its exceptional balance and objectivity."

Leslie H. Gelb concurs, writing in the *New Republic* that Karnow "draws the best [aspects from other histories], plus his own personal experience, and applies to it all a dispassionate and fair-minded attitude. Karnow himself was a critic of the war," the critic elaborates, "but he has the reportorial self-discipline to stand back now and tell the whole story in a manner that raises but does not answer the pivotal questions." Some reviewers are uncomfortable with Karnow's lack of political judgments—including *Nation* contributor Peter Biskind, who faults Karnow for "little analysis and much waffling"—but others feel this approach is effective. Frawley, for instance, explains that this ambiguity is intentional: "For the most part, [Karnow] is too much the scholar to violate his journalistic integrity. He presents an impressive array of facts and history, . . . but he deliberately stops short of conclusions." As Fuller reports, the author's opening with a description of Vietnam as it is today, impoverished and unable to deal with the legacy of war, "makes it impossible for the reader to choose sides with any conviction and creates a sense of sadness deeper than the mourning of the dead."

Arnold R. Isaacs comments in the *Washington Post Book World* that because of his impartiality, "Karnow makes clear that cruelty and callous strategies existed on all sides—as does the guilt." Gelb, a former supporter of the war, expresses a similar sentiment: "Karnow's book makes us stare these awful truths in the face once again. He does not judge those who gave us Vietnam, caught in a Greek tragedy as we were. He does not pronounce the war as right or wrong. Rather, he lets us see, as we must if we are to learn anything from that nightmare, that it was a tragic mistake." Commending in particular Karnow's "own skilled, personal observation," Frawley calls *Vietnam* "a major achievement, an important contribution, and a meaningful foundation for further research." As Isaacs concludes: "For a single, panoramic view of the [Vietnam] war and its setting, the best book is unquestionably Stanley Karnow's *Vietnam: A History.*"

The journalist has received similar acclaim for another study of an Asian country that has been closely linked to the United States; published in conjunction with a PBS-TV documentary special, *In Our Image: America's Empire in the Philippines* examines the complex history of the former U.S. colony. "While 'In

Our Image' covers recorded Philippine history from its discovery by Magellan in 1521 to America's annexation after the Spanish-American War," relates Garry Abrams of the *Los Angeles Times,* "the book is also a detailed account of recent events behind today's headlines," including the ouster of former president Ferdinand Marcos. Karnow uses the same approach as in *Vietnam,* and "in [his] sure hands, the formula is highly successful," Steve Lohr claims in the *New York Times.* "His implicit premise is that the present is ordained by the past. In the Philippines, as in Vietnam, American policy blunders were often explained by Washington's blinkered view or total ignorance of Philippine history and culture." The result of this, as *Time* contributor Howard G. Chua-Eoan observes, is an exploration of "two countries caught in an obsessive parent-child relationship." The critic explains: "It is a tale of how the U.S. tried to re-create itself in the malleable Philippines, . . . [and] also the story of how the U.S., though it succeeded in imbuing the archipelago with aspects of its likeness, failed at imparting its democratic spirit. In *In Our Image,* the sins of the creator are amply reflected in the faults of its creature."

In Our Image contains some of the same virtues as its predecessor, as Lohr recounts: "Karnow's achievement is in combining exhaustive research with the writing skill to fashion more than 450 years of the Philippine experience into a work that is both a page-turning story and authoritative history. It is hard to imagine anyone doing a better job." Although he thinks the author "is often over-detailed and occasionally irrelevant," *Washington Post Book World* contributor James Halsema similarly notes that Karnow "has written the best popular history of America's nine-decade relationship with the Philippines. It is a long book but never dull." "There is no other book even approaching Mr. Karnow's," concludes *New York Times Book Review* contributor Paul Kreisberg, "either in recounting with sensitivity and accuracy the long history of the Philippines or in leaving readers enormously satisfied with the tale. . . . 'In Our Image' is 22-karat gold, and worth the time of anyone interested not just in the Philippines or Asia or how Americans deal with their friends and their dependents, but simply in a terrific read."

BIOGRAPHICAL/CRITICAL SOURCES:

PERIODICALS

Chicago Tribune Book World, October 16, 1983.
Christian Century, November 16, 1983.
Christian Science Monitor, January 3, 1984.
Detroit News, November 13, 1983.
Los Angeles Times, April 24, 1989.
Los Angeles Times Book Review, November 6, 1983.
Nation, December 18, 1972, December 3, 1983.
New Republic, December 9, 1972, November 14, 1983.
Newsweek, November 6, 1972, October 3, 1983, April 10, 1989.
New York Times, March 29, 1989.
New York Times Book Review, October 29, 1972, October 16, 1983, April 2, 1989.
Spectator, April 27, 1985.
Time, November 6, 1972, April 17, 1989.
Tribune Books, April 30, 1989.
Washington Post Book World, October 2, 1983, April 21, 1985, April 2, 1989.

—*Sketch by Diane Telgen*

KEDOURIE, Elie 1926-

PERSONAL: Born January 25, 1926, in Baghdad, Iraq. *Education:* London School of Economics and Political Science, B.Sc., 1950; St. Antony's College, Oxford, graduate study, 1951-53.

ADDRESSES: Office—London School of Economics and Political Science, University of London, Houghton St., Aldwych, London W.C. 2, England.

CAREER: University of London, London School of Economics and Political Science, London, England, professor of politics, 1965—. Visiting professor, Princeton University, 1960-61, Monash University, Clayton, Victoria, Australia, 1967, 1989, Harvard University, 1968-69, Brandeis University, 1985-86. Visiting research fellow, All Souls College, Oxford, 1989-90.

MEMBER: British Academy (fellow).

WRITINGS:

England and the Middle East: The Destruction of the Ottoman Empire, 1914-1921, Bowes, 1956, revised edition, Mansell/Westview, 1987.
Nationalism, Praeger, 1960, new edition with afterword, Hutchinson, 1985.
Afghani and Abduh: An Essay on Religious Unbelief and Political Activism in Modern Islam, Cass & Co., 1966.
The Chatham House Version and Other Middle Eastern Studies, Weidenfeld & Nicolson, 1970, printed with new introduction, University Press of New England, 1984.
(Editor and author of introduction) *Nationalism in Asia and Africa,* New American Library, 1971.
Arabic Political Memoirs and Other Studies, Cass & Co., 1974.
In the Anglo-Arab Labyrinth: The McMahon-Husayn Correspondence and Its Interpretations, Cambridge University Press, 1976.
(Editor) *The Middle Eastern Economy: Studies in Economics and Economic History,* Cass & Co., 1976.
(Editor and contributor) *The Jewish World: History and Cultural Achievement,* Abrams, 1979.
(Editor with Sylvia G. Haim) *Modern Egypt: Studies in Politics and Society,* Cass & Co., 1980.
(Editor with Haim) *Towards a Modern Iran: Studies in Thought, Politics and Society,* Cass & Co., 1980.
Islam in the Modern World and Other Studies, Holt, 1980.
(Editor with Haim) *Zionism and Arabism in Palestine and Israel,* Cass & Co., 1982.
(Editor with Haim) *Palestine and Israel in the Nineteenth and Twentieth Centuries,* Cass & Co., 1982.
The Crossman Confessions and Other Essays in History, Religion and Politics, Mansell, 1984.
Diamonds into Glass: The Government and the Universities, Centre for Policy Studies, 1988.
(Editor with Haim) *Essays on the Economic History of the Middle East,* Cass & Co., 1988.
Perestroika in the Universities, Institute of Economic Affairs, 1989.

Founder and editor, *Middle Eastern Studies* (quarterly journal), 1964—.

WORK IN PROGRESS: Hegel.

SIDELIGHTS: In 1951, when Elie Kedourie first completed his doctoral thesis about the political relations between England and the Middle East, his examiner at Oxford University told him he must change his basic premise that the British Empire shirked its moral responsibilities toward the people once dominated by the Ottoman Empire. Kedourie, however, refused to comply, withdrew his paper, and never received his Ph.D. Since that time, the once optimistic view held by English historians toward that chapter of history has shifted toward Kedourie's perspective. "It is a striking tribute to [Kedourie]," declares one *Times Literary Supplement* critic, that his "version has advanced in thirty years from being regarded as a clever, but essentially perverse interpretation of Middle Eastern history to being accepted as the most authoritative account of the events it describes." Kedourie, now a respected professor of politics at the University of London, later published his thesis under the title *England and the Middle East: The Destruction of the Ottoman Empire, 1914-1921;* and the introduction of the 1987 edition of this book contains the author's arguments against his former examiner's opinions. Since *England and the Middle East* was first published, Kedourie has returned several times to the subject of Anglo-Arab relations in his books.

The political historian's view of the proper role of government, as he expresses it in *The Crossman Confessions and Other Essays in Politics, History and Religion,* is that its function should be restricted to the protection of its citizens and to mediation through laws. "Anything beyond this," asserts Kedourie, "the state cannot do well, or at all." It is just this premise that the British violated during their occupation of the Middle East, according to Kedourie. Thinking that they could improve upon the political practices of the Arabic people, British officials operated under the "assumption that the superficial adoption of such trappings of constitutionalism as written fundamental laws, political parties and nominally represented institutions meant that what were regarded as the bad old days of oriental despotism were gone forever," explains G. E. Wheeler in a *Times Literary Supplement* review of *Arabic Political Memoirs and Other Stories.* "Professor Kedourie," Wheeler continues, "is concerned to show the falsity of this assumption, which has resulted not only in a serious decline in East-West relations, but in ruin for most of the minorities in the Middle East, for whose security the West had explicitly accepted responsibility."

Kedourie's books have been praised by critics for their in-depth scholarly research. Wheeler observes that the academician makes use of "material virtually ignored by the great majority of historians and commentators on Middle East current affairs." And, in such works as *In the Anglo-Arab Labyrinth: The McMahon-Husayn Correspondence and Its Interpretations, Times Literary Supplement* contributor Douglas Dakin writes that "by clarity of style, by well-controlled repetition and recapitulation, [the author] helps the reader find his way through the documental labyrinth." Abbas Kelidar asserts in the *Times Literary Supplement* that "Kedourie's style is elegant, his interpretations are pungent, his conclusions are provocative. . . . He is now one of the world's most respected authorities on [Middle Eastern studies] and those concerned with it may either applaud or disapprove of his work, but they cannot ignore it."

BIOGRAPHICAL/CRITICAL SOURCES:

PERIODICALS

New York Review of Books, May 27, 1982.
Spectator, May 2, 1970.
Times Literary Supplement, September 8, 1966, May 14, 1970, January 10, 1975, April 30, 1976, January 30, 1981, May 1, 1981, February 22, 1985, September 27, 1985, April 22, 1988.
Washington Post Book World, May 31, 1981.

KELLEY, Ray
See PAINE, Lauran (Bosworth)

*   *   *

KELLY, Ray
See PAINE, Lauran (Bosworth)

*   *   *

KENNEDY, William 1928-

PERSONAL: Born January 16, 1928, in Albany, N.Y.; son of William J. (a deputy sheriff) and Mary (a secretary; maiden name, MacDonald) Kennedy; married Ana Daisy (Dana) Sosa (a former actress and dancer), January 31, 1957; children: Dana, Katherine, Brendan. *Education:* Siena College, B.A., 1949.

ADDRESSES: Office—New York State Writers Institute, Department of English, State University of New York at Albany, 1400 Washington Ave., Albany, N.Y. 12222. *Agent*—Liz Darhansoff, 1220 Park Ave., New York, N.Y. 10028.

CAREER: Post Star, Glen Falls, N.Y., assistant sports editor and columnist, 1949-50; *Times-Union,* Albany, N.Y., reporter, 1952-56; *Puerto Rico World Journal,* San Juan, assistant managing editor and columnist, 1956; Miami *Herald,* Miami, Fla., reporter, 1957; correspondent for Time-Life publications in Puerto Rico, and reporter for Dorvillier (business) newsletter and Knight Newspapers, 1957-59; San Juan *Star,* San Juan, Puerto Rico, founding managing editor, 1959-61; full-time fiction writer, 1961-63; *Times-Union,* Albany, special writer, 1963-70, and film critic, 1968-70; book editor of *Look* magazine, 1971; State University of New York at Albany, lecturer, 1974-82, professor of English, 1983—.

Writers Institute at Albany, founder, 1983, director, 1984—. Visiting professor of English, Cornell University, 1982-83. Cofounder, Cinema 750 film society, Rennselaer, N.Y., 1968-70; organizing moderator for series of forums on the humanities, sponsored by the National Endowment for the Humanities, New York State Library, and Albany Public Library. Panelist, New York State Council on the Arts, 1980-83. *Military service:* U.S. Army, 1950-52.

MEMBER: Writers' Guild of America, PEN.

AWARDS, HONORS: Award for reporting, Puerto Rican Civic Association (Miami, Fla.), 1957; Page One Award, Newspaper Guild, 1965, for reporting; the *Times-Union* won the New York State Publishers Award for Community Service, 1965, on the basis of several of Kennedy's articles on Albany's slums; NAACP award, 1965, for reporting; Writer of the Year Award, Friends of the Albany Public Library, 1975; D.H.L., Russell Sage College, 1980; National Endowment for the Arts fellowship, 1981; MacArthur Foundation fellowship, 1983; National Book Critics Circle Award, 1983, and Pulitzer Prize for fiction, 1984, both for *Ironweed;* New York State Governor's Arts Award; honored by the citizens of Albany and the State University of New York at Albany with a "William Kennedy's Albany" celebration, September 6-9, 1984; Before Columbus Foundation American Book Award, 1985, for *O Albany!;* Brandeis University Creative Arts Award, 1986.

WRITINGS:

The Ink Truck (novel), Dial Press, 1969, Viking, 1984.
Legs (novel), Coward, 1975.
(Contributor) *Gabriel Garcia Marquez* (criticism), Taurus Ediciones, 1982.

Billy Phelan's Greatest Game (novel), Viking, 1978.

Getting It All, Saving It All: Some Notes By an Extremist, New York State Governor's Conference on Libraries, 1978.

Ironweed (novel), Viking, 1983.

O Albany!: An Urban Tapestry (nonfiction), Viking, 1983, published as *O Albany! Improbable City of Political Wizards, Fearless Ethnics, Spectacular Aristocrats, Splendid Nobodies, and Underrated Scoundrels,* Penguin, 1985.

(Contributor of essay) *The Capitol in Albany* (photographs), Aperture, 1986.

(With son, Brendan Kennedy) *Charley Malarkey and the Belly Button Machine* (juvenile), Atlantic Monthly Press, 1986.

(With Francis Coppola and Mario Puzo) *The Cotton Club,* St. Martin's Press, 1986.

(Author of introduction) *The Making of Ironweed,* Penguin, 1988.

Quinn's Book, Viking, 1988.

SCREENPLAYS

(With Francis Ford Coppola) "The Cotton Club," Orion Pictures Corporation, 1984.

"Ironweed," Tri-Star Pictures, 1987.

Also author of screenplay "Legs" for Gene Kirkwood and "Billy Phelan's Greatest Game" for Pepper-Prince Company.

OTHER

Author of unpublished novel *The Angels and the Sparrows;* author of monographs and brochures for New York State Department of Education, New York State University System, New York Governor's Conference on Libraries, Empire State College, Schenectady Museum, and New York State Library. Contributor of short fiction to journals, including *Esquire, San Juan Review, Glen Falls Review, Epoch,* and *Harper's.* Contributor of articles, interviews, and reviews to periodicals, including *New York Times Magazine, New York Times Book Review, Washington Post Book World, New Republic,* and *Look.*

WORK IN PROGRESS: A novel about the Phelan family.

SIDELIGHTS: Novels by Irish-American writer William Kennedy did not receive much critical attention when they first appeared. He was known primarily as a respected and versatile journalist who had worked for Albany, New York's *Times-Union,* the Miami *Herald,* and Puerto Rico's San Juan *Star.* *Columbia Journalism Review* writer Michael Robertson cites former editor William J. Dorvillier's comment that Kennedy was "one of the best complete journalists—as reporter, editor, whatever—that I've known in sixty years in the business." But when Kennedy's 1983 novel *Ironweed* won the Pulitzer Prize, his fiction was given new life. Three early novels were reissued and became best sellers. Hollywood also took note. Francis Ford Coppola enlisted him to write the screenplay for *The Cotton Club,* and he wrote screen versions of his three other books.

Journalism plays an important role in most of Kennedy's books. Many of them present fictionalized newspapermen in narrating or supporting roles. The city of Albany, New York also figures prominently in the novels *Legs, Billy Phelan's Greatest Game, Ironweed,* and *Quinn's Book,* as well as his first novel, *The Ink Truck,* and his recent collection of essays, *O Albany!.* "Albany is to this gifted writer what the city of Paterson [, New Jersey] was to William Carlos Williams, and like our great laureate of urban plenitude, he wrests from an unlikely source a special kind of lyricism," Joel Conarroe states in *New York Times Book Review.*

O Albany! was written before *Ironweed*'s spectacular reception secured so much long-overdue literary recognition for Kennedy. *O Albany!* is based in part upon a series of articles Kennedy wrote about city neighborhoods for the *Times-Union* in the mid-1960s. *Publishers Weekly* reviewer Joseph Barbato maintains that the essays in *O Albany!* provide readers with a "nonfiction delineation of Kennedy's imaginative source—an upstate city of politicians and hoodlums, of gambling dens and ethnic neighborhoods, which for all its isolation remains, he insists 'as various as the American psyche' and rich in stories and characters." Christopher Lehmann-Haupt agrees in the *New York Times* that "even more absorbing than the detail and the enthusiasm is the raw material of Mr. Kennedy's fiction, present on every page [of the essays]. Even if one doesn't give a damn for Albany, it is always interesting to watch the author's imagination at play in the city and its history, for one is witnessing the first steps in a novelist's creative process." As Kennedy explains in his introduction to *O Albany!,* "I write this book not as a booster of Albany, which I am, nor as an apologist for the city, which I sometimes am, but rather as a person whose imagination has become fused with a single place, and in that place finds all the elements that a man ever needs for the life of the soul."

Kennedy didn't always think of Albany as a rich fictional source. He grew up in Albany, "the only child of a working-class couple from the Irish neighborhood of North Albany," according to a Toronto *Globe and Mail* article, and after graduation from college worked at a small daily before spending two years as a sports writer for an Army weekly. After leaving the Army, he worked for the Albany *Times-Union,* but grew restless with the job. One day, he told *Washington Post* reviewer Curt Suplee, "I got a great interview with Satchmo [Louis Armstrong]. And the editor threw it away. The guy said, 'What the hell, he's just another band leader.'. . . I knew I had to break out." Albany seemed too provincial, Kennedy told Suplee: "I really didn't like Albany—I felt it was an old man's town, moribund, no action."

After moving to Puerto Rico in search of more exotic material, Kennedy found his distance from Albany helped him to see its more interesting features. The author explained this process to Douglas Bauer of the *Washington Post Book World:* "[As a reporter in Albany] I wrote stories on my day off and they were set in Albany and they were lousy. Then I went away, and worked in Miami and Puerto Rico. In San Juan, I tried the same thing. I wrote stories about Puerto Rico, and I didn't like them, either. Finally, I said, the hell with it, I'm going to write about Albany and it was the first time a place truly engaged me. I think I needed to be in San Juan to sufficiently fictionalize Albany as a place. I started a novel, and every day I amazed myself at how much I knew about the people I was writing about. I had a concern for them. There was a substance to them that made some sense." As Kennedy told *New York Times* writer Susan Chira, "I felt I had probably outgrown Albany, the way you outgrow childhood. . . But I hadn't. When I was writing about Puerto Rico, it was o.k., but then I began to write about Albany, and it seemed to come far more easily, with a richness that was absent in the other work. It proved to me I really didn't need to go off to these exotic places. I felt like I didn't have to go anywhere else. It was really a young writer's education in discovering his own turf."

Legs, Billy Phelan's Greatest Game, and *Ironweed* are all set in the Albany of the 1930s. Margaret Croyden states in *New York Times Magazine* that the books "are inexorably linked to [Kennedy's] native city . . . during the Depression years, when Albany was a wide-open city, run by Irish bosses and their corrupt political machine. This sense of place gives Kennedy's work a rich texture, a deep sense of authenticity." Chira adds that Albany, "often dismissed by outsiders as provincial and drab, lives in Mr. Kennedy's acclaimed fiction as a raucous town that symbolizes all that was glorious and corrupt, generous and sordid in the America of the 20's and 30's."

The distinguishing mark of Kennedy as a writer, says *People* contributor Michael Ryan, is that he is "absolutely unsentimental and unsparing." Ryan explains, "In his fictional world, good deeds are not automatically rewarded, love is not eternal, and death is frequent, offhand and cruel. He demurs at the suggestion that he is preternaturally unkind to the gangsters, hoboes, has-beens and almost-were athletes and would-be entertainers who populate his fiction: 'I don't see how you can say that I'm more cruel than God. God is the cruelest cat in town.' " Though Kennedy, who won his success as a novelist despite numerous setbacks and disappointments, has had his share of troubled times, he told Ryan, "my observations and my characters are not equatable with my own life. People keep asking me now, 'Are you going to write books with happy endings?' My answer to that is no."

Kennedy's transition from reporter to novelist began in the 1960s. When master novelist Saul Bellow came to San Juan as writer-in-residence in 1963, Kennedy enrolled in the class. Bellow's encouragement prompted Kennedy to change his position from managing editor of the *Star* to part-time editor so that he could devote his time to writing novels. Publishers rejected the early novels, and when Kennedy returned to Albany to care for his ailing father, he wrote controversial articles for the *Times-Union.* His statements on the poverty and other social problems of the city were seen as criticisms of the local power structure and were branded "un-American." News writing occupied only half of his time; the rest was given to the novels, and finally in 1969, his first official novel *The Ink Truck* was published. He started his next novel, centered on gangster Jack "Legs" Diamond. When a publisher bought the book based on a few chapters, Kennedy immersed himself in exhaustive research for two years, seeking to authenticate the gangster world of the 1920s.

The Ink Truck is a novel about an Albany newspaper strike featuring a main character described by *Time* reviewer R. Z. Sheppard as "a columnist named Bailey, a highly sexed free spirit with a loud checkered sports jacket, a long green scarf and a chip on his shoulder as big as the state capitol." "It is my hope," Kennedy told *Library Journal* in 1969, that *The Ink Truck* "will stand as an analgesic inspiration to all weird men of good will and rotten luck everywhere." The novel, Sheppard relates, culminates in "a poignant conclusion, yet it does not show Kennedy at his full spellbinding power. Much of the book is inspired blarney, fun to read and probably fun to write."

When first published, *The Ink Truck* was generally ignored, but, as Kennedy indicates in *O Albany!,* he began to view his hometown as "an inexhaustible context for the stories I planned to write, as abundant in mythic qualities as it was in political ambition, remarkably consequential greed and genuine fear of the Lord. I saw it as being as various as the American psyche itself, of which it was truly a crucible: It was always a melting pot for immigrants as was New York or Boston, and it epitomizes today the transfer of power from the Dutch, to the English to the ethnic coalitions." Writing in *Village Voice Literary Supplement,* Mark Caldwell summarizes, Albany's "been run by the Dutch, the English, and the Irish, inhabited by trappers, Indians, soldiers, burghers, farmers, canal-workers, and bureaucrats. It's known every form of government from virtual fiefdom under the

Dutch patroons to an old-fashioned and still surviving ward-heeling Democratic machine."

This political landscape dominates Kennedy's novels. Kennedy wrote in *O Albany!* that "it was a common Albany syndrome for children to grow up obsessed with being a Democrat. Your identity was fixed by both religion and politics, but from the political hierarchy came the way of life: the job, the perpetuation of the job, the dole when there was no job, the loan when there was no dole, the security of the neighborhood, the new street-light, the new sidewalk, the right to run your bar after hours or to open a cardgame on the sneak. These things came to you not by right of citizenship. Republicans had no such rights. They came to you because you gave allegiance to Dan O'Connell and his party."

Kennedy's knowledge of Albany's political machinery is first-hand. A *Globe and Mail* reporter indicates that Kennedy's "father sold pies, cut hair, worked in a foundry, wrote illegal numbers, ran political errands for the Democratic ward heelers, and was rewarded by the Machine by being made a deputy sherriff." And, as Croyden explains, William Sr. "often took his son with him to political clubs and gambling joints where young Bill Kennedy, with his eye and ear for detail and for the tone and temper of Irish-Americans, listened and watched and remembered." Kennedy, writes Doris Grumbach in *Saturday Review,* "knows every bar, hotel, store, bowling alley, pool hall, and whorehouse that ever opened in North Albany. He knows where the Irish had their picnics and parties—and what went on at them; where their churches were; where they bet on horses, played the numbers, and bet on poker. He can re-create with absolute accuracy the city conversations."

One of the few Kennedy novels that does not rely heavily on firsthand experience is *Legs,* for which he did extensive research on the gangster era. *Legs,* according to Suplee, is a "fictional biography" of Jack 'Legs' Diamond, the "vicious" Irish-American ganster-bootlegger "who in 1931 was finally shot to death" at an Albany rooming house. Kennedy's novel chronicles "Legs' attempts to smuggle heroin, his buying of politicians, judges and cops," and his womanizing, relates W. T. Lhamon in *New Republic.* A bully and a torturer who frequently betrayed associates, Diamond made many enemies. Several attemps were made on his life, and to many people, he seemed unkillable. Legs Diamond, points out Suplee, "evolved into a national obsession, a godsend for copy-short newsmen, a mesmerizing topic in tavern or tearoom. Yet profoundly evil."

While writing the novel, Kennedy told Suplee, he tried to analyze Diamond's appeal: "So why do we like him? *That's* the thing." Kennedy said to Croyden, "Legs is another version of the American Dream—that you can grow up and shoot your way to fame and fortune. On the other hand, the people that live this kind of life are human beings like you or me. People did love Legs Diamond." Suplee notes that "among the book's many answers is Diamond's odd integrity: 'It is one thing to be corrupt. It is another to behave in a psychologically responsible way toward your own evil.' Legs becomes a litmus, huge and hugely awful, at whom folks could gape 'with curiosity, ambivalent benevolence, and a sense of mystery at the meaning of their own response.' "

Kennedy's second novel in the Albany cycle, *Billy Phelan's Greatest Game,* explores the same territory. *Newsweek* reviewer Peter S. Prescott relates, "the year is 1938, the time is almost always after dark, and the characters . . . are constantly reminded of times further past, of the floods and strikes, the scandals and murders of a quarter century before." The plot of the novel is related by reporter Martin Daugherty. Through his eyes, writes

Suplee, "we watch Billy—a pool shark, bowling ace and saloon-wise hustler with a pitilessly rigid code of ethics—prowl among Albany's night-town denizens. But when kidnappers abduct the sole child of an omnipotent clan (patterned on the family of the late Dan O'Connell, of Albany's Democratic machine), Billy is pushed to turn informer, and faces competing claims of conscience."

Billy Phelan's Greatest Game received a smattering of mildly favorable critical attention, as did *Legs,* but didn't sell particularly well; all three of the author's earlier novels sold only a few thousand copies. The first one hundred pages of *Ironweed,* the story of Billy's father who left the family when Billy was nine, were originally accepted by Viking, but the book later lost the marketing backing it needed. In 1979, Kennedy agreed it would be best to submit the novel elsewhere. It was rejected twelve more times, and the author was disillusioned—past fifty and in debt—when Saul Bellow wrote Viking, admonishing them for slighting Kennedy's talent and asking them to reconsider their decision not to publish *Ironweed.* Viking heeded Bellow's letter, in which the Nobel Prize-winner referred to Kennedy's "Albany novels," calling them "a distinguished group of books," Kennedy told *CA.* His editor at the house fell upon the idea of reissuing *Billy Phelan's Greatest Game* and *Legs,* then out of print, for simultaneous publication with *Ironweed,* and he made the occasion a publishing event, focusing on the author's long-standing plan to compose a "cycle" of novels.

By itself, *Ironweed* did not appear to be a good publishing risk. The subject matter is relentlessly downbeat. *Ironweed* portrays "the world of the down-and-outer, the man who drifts by the windows of boarding houses and diners with a slouch hat and a brain whose most vivid images are 20 years old," writes *Detroit News* critic James F. Veseley. Other editors had wanted Kennedy to rewrite *Ironweed* because of the book's unconventional use of language. *New York Review of Books* critic Robert Towers writes that, in *Ironweed,* Kennedy "largely abandons the rather breezy, quasi-journalistic narrative voice of his previous fiction and resorts to a more poetically charged, often surrealistic use of language as he re-creates the experiences and mental states of an alcoholic bum." As Kennedy told a Toronto *Globe and Mail* reporter, "They . . . objected that the book was overwritten, they didn't understand what I was doing in terms of language, they felt that no bum would ever talk like Francis does, or think like he does, that they thought of him only as a bum. They didn't understand that what I was striving for was to talk about the central eloquence of every human being. We all have this unutterable eloquence, and the closest you can get to it is to make it utterable at some point, in some way that separates it from the conscious level of life."

The figures in *Ironweed* are drawn from portraits Kennedy gathered for a nonfiction study of the street people of Albany, called *Lemon Weed.* Rejected by publishers, *Lemon Weed,* a collection of interviews with the winos, was set aside while Kennedy worked on *Billy Phelan's Greatest Game.* After concentrating on the character Francis Phelan, Billy Phelan's father, the author decided to reshape the *Lemon Weed* material using the fictional Francis's point of view. Thus, "the specifics in 'Ironweed'—the traction strike, professional baseball, Irish immigrant experiences, a vast Irish cemetery, an Irish neighborhood, the Erie Canal and so forth—are the elements of life in Albany," Kennedy told Croyden. "Some people say that 'Ironweed' might have had any setting, and perhaps this is true. But the values that

emerged are peculiar to my own town and to my own time and would not be the same in a smaller city, or a metropolis, or a city that was not Irish, or wasn't large enough to support a skid row." *Ironweed,* "which refers to a tough-stemmed member of the sunflower family," according to Lehmann-Haupt, "recounts a few days in the life of an Albany skid-row bum, a former major-league third-baseman with a talent for running, particularly running away, although his ambition now, at the height of the Depression, has been scaled down to the task of getting through the next 20 minutes or so." Once Phelan ran from Albany after he threw a rock at a scab and killed him during a trolley strike, setting off a riot, but he was later in the habit of leaving the town and his family to play in the leagues every baseball season. When he accidentally dropped his newborn son—breaking his neck and killing him—while attempting to change the child's diapers, Francis ran from town and abandoned his family for good.

Now Phelan is back in Albany after twenty-two years, reports Towers, "lurching around the missions and flophouses of the city's South End." On a cold Halloween night and the following All Saints' Day in 1938, the weekend of Orson Welles's "War of the Worlds" broadcast, Phelan "encounters the ghosts of his friends, relatives, and murder victims, who shout at him on buses, appear in saloons wearing [lapel flowers], talk with him from their graves in St. Agnes's cemetery," relates Caldwell. Kennedy tells two stories in *Ironweed,* Webster Schott observes in the *Washington Post Book World;* the first, he says, "is the gloriously checkered history of Francis Phelan as young lover of the neighbor lady in silk, star of baseball diamonds in Toronto and Dayton, wrathful killer of at least three men, and joyous victim of sin forever on the run. The other is of a newer Francis Phelan emerging during the crucial present of the novel—three days during which Francis moves from shoveling graves to picking rags, loses his Vassar-educated hobo girlfriend and a faithful drinking partner to the ravages of bumming, and finds himself face-to-face in his old house with the wife and children he left. The purpose of Kennedy's intertwining these narrative lines is to see whether he and we can locate a center around which order can be made of Francis' life. But none holds. What we see is the infinite complexity of personality, the effect of accident, and the awesome force of emotion on our lives."

Kennedy's next novel, *Quinn's Book,* set in pre-Civil War Albany, begins another cycle centered on residents of New York's capital city. In the beginning, pre-teen narrator Daniel Quinn witnesses a spectacular drowning accident on the banks of the Hudson River followed by a deviant sexual act in which a whore, presumed drowned, miraculously revives. It is also his first meeting with "Maud the wondrous," a girl he saves from drowning who becomes the love of his life. "The end is a whirl of events that include sketches of high life in Saratoga and accounts of horse races, boxing matches and a draft riot," Richard Eder relates in the *Los Angeles Times Book Review.* He continues, "Daniel shocks a fashionable audience with a bitterly realistic account of his Civil War experiences. Hillegond is savagely murdered; her murderer is killed by two owls jointly and mysteriously controlled by Maud and a magical platter owned by Daniel. The two lovers are lushly and definitively reunited." With these events, says Eder, *Quinn's Book* "elevates portions or approximations of New York history—Dutch, English, Irish—into legend."

Most reviews of *Quinn's Book* were favorable. Although George Garrett, writing in Chicago's *Tribune Books* calls *Quinn's Book* "one of the most bloody and violent novels" he has read, the gore is necessary to tell the whole truth about life in Albany, he adds. In this regard, Garrett elaborates, the author's "integrity is unflinching. Yet this is, too, a profoundly funny and joyous story, as abundant with living energy as any novel you are likely to read this year or for a long time to come." Some readers feel that the idiomatic language Kennedy uses to evoke a past era sometimes misses the mark; however, counters T. Coraghessan Boyle in the *New York Times Book Review*, "the language of 'Quinn's Book' rises above occasional lapses, and Quinn, as the book progresses, becomes increasingly eloquent, dropping the convoluted syntax in favor of a cleaner, more contemporary line. And if the history sometimes overwhelms the story, it is always fascinating. . . . Mr. Kennedy does indeed have the power to peer into the past, to breathe life into it and make it indispensible, and Quinn's battle to control his destiny and win Maud is by turns grim, amusing and deeply moving. In an era when so much of our fiction is content to accomplish so little, 'Quinn's Book' is a revelation. Largeminded, ardent, alive on every page with its author's passion for his place and the events that made it, it is a novel to savor." Concludes Toronto *Globe and Mail* reviewer H. J. Kirchhoff, "This is historical fiction suffused with mysticism and myth. . . . *Quinn's Book* is superlative fiction."

Kennedy's work in the movies has also succeeded, by charming audiences and attracting the industry's top performers. In *The Cotton Club*, co-authored with Francis Ford Coppola of "Godfather" fame, characters from gangster-wars of the 1930s cross paths with the stars of the Harlem night club scene. Its main characters are two sets of brothers. Richard Gere, who plays cornet at the club, falls in love with the mistress of mobster boss Dutch Schultz. Like Gere, tap dancer Gregory Hines has to leave his brother-partner behind and go solo to fulfill his ambitions. Both Gere and Hines try to avoid getting caught up in the mob on their way to stardom. The $50 million dollar film, says Sheila Benson in the *Los Angeles Times*, is carried less by the story line than by its "outrageous, joyous musical numbers by the singers, tap dancers, barbecue shouters and showgirls of the Cotton Club. . . . These numbers are integral to the action and each one of them may be show stoppers, but this show never stops." The film's remarkable scenes, of which there are many, include a state-of-the-art display of tap dancing performed by "a dozen emeritus tappers," love scenes that mix eroticism and the threat of violence, and a "dazzling" conclusion—"Hines' unaccompanied, bravura tap dance that becomes a montage of murder and farewell in which theatricality and reality are finally blurred," Benson notes. Toronto *Globe and Mail* contributor Jay Scott notes that this "mythic movie about movie myths" is as much about "the jazzy showmanship of movie-making" as it is about love and fame in the '30s. Scott explains that the film's effective use of cross-cutting, its "willingness to play with fantasy and reality, with movies and magic, results in one of the most technically exhilarating finales ever shot."

Since *The Cotton Club*'s success, Kennedy told *Esquire*, "I've been offered five or six other projects, but I'm not going to do them. I'd only go through all this for my own books." Argentinian film maker Hector Babenco took interest in Kennedy's Pulitzer winner and talked the author into making it his next feature film. Though generally opposed to foreign directors who try to make films having predominantly American themes, Kennedy was persuaded to work with Babenco because of the director's enthusiasm and complete understanding of the character Francis Phelan. Jack Nicholson plays Phelan opposite Meryl Streep in the film version of *Ironweed*. Haunted by the failures of his past into a life of dereliction, Phelan weaves in and out of the present, encountering ghosts from his past. Babenco excels at reproduc-

ing the "surreal dimension [that] is so important to the book and to the movie—the ghosts become materialized," Kennedy told Nina Darnton of the *New York Times*. Though not all reviewers agree with his assessment, the author is also pleased that the actors brought to the screen some of the "poetry" of the novel that was lost in the transition from print to film. He told Darnton, "Meryl and Jack had the ability to draw on elements of the book, to use throw-away lines from certain parts of the story, and with a look, a few words, a way of living in the past and present at the same time, which is what Helen does in the book, they were able to retain the interior life of the characters that might otherwise have been lost." The roles were challenging for the veteran stars, but "the risks paid off," Michael Ryan notes in a *People* article on the making of the film. Film critics in both New York and Los Angeles voted Nicholson Best Actor of 1988; Streep's performance was also highly acclaimed.

Explaining why characters like Francis Phelan interest him, Kennedy told Croyden, "When you take a character into his most extreme condition, you get extreme explanations, and you begin to discover what lurks in the far corners of the soul. I really do believe that that's the way a writer finds things out. I love the surrealistic, the mystical elements of life. There is so much mysteriousness going on in everybody's life." The author also admires the persistence that overcomes hopeless situations. In *Ironweed*, Phelan is the one derelict who is not overcome by the mean circumstances of street life. Kennedy told Suplee, "That's the kind of characters I've been writing about. The refusal to yield to what appears to be fate. If you don't die and you don't quit, then there's a chance."

MEDIA ADAPTATIONS: Ironweed became an Orion release in 1988.

CA INTERVIEW

CA interviewed William Kennedy by telephone on August 1, 1989, at his home in Averill Park, New York.

CA: In Quinn's Book *there's a point at which Daniel Quinn writes one sentence and "understands that he has just changed his life." Was there such a dramatic time for you, a specific moment when you discovered your own "control over the word" and felt Quinn's elation?*

KENNEDY: It kept happening to me all through my life as a journalist and as a writer of fiction. I remember the first time was when I was in the army. I had done a lot of interviews, news stories, sports columns, and I generally relied in subject matter on people of renown or well-known events. Then one day I went out and sat around with a club fighter who was coaching an army boxing team. I was writing for an army newspaper and I came back and wrote what I felt was a really good piece. It was a revelation that I could now write well about anything, or anybody. For a very young newsman, that was an interesting development.

Later, when I was a newspaperman in San Juan, I'd write fiction in the morning before going to work, and again in the evening after I came home. One morning I wrote something, and when I read it in the evening I was stunned that I had written it. It seemed to me quite unlike anything I had done up to that point. It had strength and an integrity that was not forced, not simple;

it had a complexity and a flow that proved to me I was getting better, and some day might even be good. Every once in a while in the writing of *Legs* and *Billy Phelan's Greatest Game* and *Ironweed,* the flood of language or ideas took me over and I felt a comparable strength, a leap forward into some new dimension. It happened also in *Quinn's Book.* I wonder if it will happen again.

CA: You told Larry McCaffery and Sinda Gregory for Alive and Writing *that much of the material for your subsequent books was present in an unpublished novel,* The Angel and the Sparrows. *Has that material easily suggested the shapes of the later novels that grew out of it?*

KENNEDY: In a broad sense, yes. Out of that book I extracted Francis when I began to write *Billy Phelan,* combined it with a character I had written about in journalism, and combined all that with the reinvention of the Phelan family—especially Francis's family; he wasn't even married in the book as I had written it in San Juan. Out of this new mix came the whole history of Billy and Peg and Annie and all the things that developed in the writing of *Billy Phelan.* And that in turn dictated the shape of *Ironweed.* I liked Francis so much I felt he had to have his own novel, and so I began to develop the family even further, in ways that had only been suggested in *Billy Phelan.* The book I'm writing now has some relevance to that first novel also. I suspect that I'll write a lot about the Phelans in the future, one way or another—I don't know whether they'll be minor characters or major characters—just as I suspect I'll write about the Quinns.

CA: Characters like Francis Phelan and his friend Helen in Ironweed *might seem unlikely subjects for fiction, and yet you make the reader care very much about them and about their world. What makes them heroic to you?*

KENNEDY: I never think of my characters as heroic in the conventional sense. I suppose Francis is a hero of survival and Legs is an antihero and Billy is a mythical hero in reverse and Bailey, in *The Ink Truck,* an unsung hero. These are characters who have behaved in ways that fascinated me as they developed in my imagination. They revealed something important about the extremes of human behavior that I felt was worth writing about: Francis going to the ends of the earth rather than face up to his shame; Billy ostracized for following his own peculiarly perverse code of ethics, yet helping to solve the kidnapping and maintaining his integrity by not being an informer. Legs Diamond was truly an extreme figure—a man living outside the law, at the edge of danger, and with such little regard for his own life and the lives of others. Yet he'd been liked by many people and loved by at least two women. Somehow he was able to maintain a public persona that was not entirely hateful. This anomaly is very appealing to me, and I write about it frequently.

CA: Reading your books, one is moved by the great exuberance of your language, your pleasure in words and sounds and rhythms. Does that poetry emerge so strongly in the first draft, or is it something you work at consciously in revisions and polishings?

KENNEDY: Sometimes it comes out in the first draft, but I don't think there's an untouched line in anything I've ever written; certainly not an untouched paragraph. I constantly polish and rewrite. I think of the Helen section, for instance, in *Ironweed,* and I remember back in the sixties, in an early version of that book, I sat down and it almost came out of my fingertips like automatic writing. I came back to it the next day and finished it—it was

done in two days. That is not what you now read in *Ironweed,* but it was the foundation for it; the style was there, the language and ideas all flowing easily, and setting the pattern for the internal dialogue Helen has with herself. I thought I understood the woman fairly well when I wrote that but when I wrote the novel as it now stands I revised it radically and expanded Helen considerably; she became far more complex than I originally created her.

That rush of language and ideas was a gift—from where I don't know, and I don't ask. Sometimes it happens and sometimes it doesn't. It's lovely when it does come along. Most of the time the prose is a product of spasmodic writing. A page in a day, two pages in a day is wonderful for me. I didn't write anything today; all I did was reread, and make notes and think about things. I revised two pages yesterday that I wrote one page of the day before. It's like that, constant polishing, expanding, contracting, revising, smoothing, intensifying—whatever is necessary, always with the sense that the language should be the best at my disposal.

CA: Might your obviously strong feelings about family have some bearing on your fascination with the Phelans and the related Quinns?

KENNEDY: Unlike a lot of people, I suppose, who are thrown out early and don't return home, I have been very close to all sides of my family for as long as they were alive. They're dead now; all my close antecedents are gone. I still have close friends who seem like family, and in-laws, and a few distant cousins— but very few. The monitoring of their behavior through the years has been a kind of fascination, and certainly it has fueled my imagination—there's no question about that. I feel that family is a way of grounding anything that I write about in Albany— people in a given place behaving in a given way—that helps me to shape the story, and to understand the matrix out of which these people have developed.

CA: Curt Suplee aptly described an important quality of your writing when he said in his Washington Post *article, "Each novel moves in liquid transit between reality and fantasy." Do the lines between those states sometimes seem indistinct to you?*

KENNEDY: I have had a few experiences when reality became confused with fantasy. Some people cite mystical occasions in their lives when something happens that they cannot understand; and they ascribe it to the supernatural. To me that's an extension of our dream life, and almost everybody lives in both of those worlds constantly. I move in and out of them regularly when I'm awake working, and when I'm asleep. Very often the dreams are powerful and compel me to record them. Then they find their way into these stories in which the dream life becomes important to the characters—or the daydreaming: the fantasizing that goes on in Francis's life, for instance, when he's remembering or reimagining history, imagining the ghosts of his past, creating a set of bleachers for them in the backyard from where they taunt him and prod him in ways that he doesn't understand. This is what we do to ourselves, what our minds do to us, and I believe a writer should reflect that complexity, and not settle for the mundane reality of waking consciousness only.

CA: Do you think the term "magical realism" adequately describes that quality not only in your writing but also in the work of such South American writers as Gabriel Garcia Marquez?

KENNEDY: "Magical realism" was coined by Alejo Carpentier, the Cuban novelist, but it's a very old genre; it's as old as Homer and the Greek playwrights and it's as new, in the nineteenth-century sense of newness, as Twain and Hawthorne and Dickens. In the modern world, Joyce and now any number of writers move in and out of the magical world at will. It's a convention now, hardly a radical departure. Kafka used it, which was very much an influence on me. Thornton Wilder used it in "Our Town." It's been used very successfully in movies by Fellini—"8 1/2," for instance—and Bergman used it in "The Seventh Seal" and "Wild Strawberries" and "Hour of the Wolf." So many filmmakers now have adopted this as a convention that I think it's a cliche to talk about it in terms of anybody's work anymore. It's like categorizing people as minimalists or black humorists; it doesn't serve much purpose. The distinction between the people who have moved in and out of those mystical realms is very great. Joyce is not at all like Dickens. Dickens is not at all like Fellini. Maybe they have some grounding in common, but the challenge is to discover the distinction and not the similarity.

*CA: You commented in the article "Be Reasonable—Unless You're a Writer" (*New York Times Book Review, *January 25, 1987) on the importance of "a serious reliance on intuition, and enduring reverence for the irrational."*

KENNEDY: Yes. Writers are writing something that they know is important, but they don't necessarily know what it is. You arrive at the importance only by writing. It takes its shape as you imagine it, as you intuit it, as you shape it from minute to minute to create something that is unlike anything you've ever known and therefore may be something new in the world and something that people might say is an original work. That is an important way to go, and the only way that any good work is ever done by me. If you willfully work out of tradition and genres, it's unlikely that there will be much originality in your work. It might be very entertaining and sell a lot of books because of its familiar form, but it will hardly be judged to be something original and worthy.

CA: Apart from giving you an understanding of the Catholicism inherent in the world you portray, what effect do you think your having grown up in the Catholic Church may have had on your fiction?

KENNEDY: The main effect is that I keep writing about Catholics. I've had, through the Church, an understanding of a mythical structure for my own life and other people's. I've understood the power of a social agency to change the world, change families, change the direction of societies. It's an extraordinarily powerful force; it was in the beginning, when it was merely an army of martyrs, and it's still very important. It's in constant transition, flux, waning power, crescendoing power, always changing its shape and its personalities but still capable of great influence on people's spirits. I'm not a champion entirely of the Church and its politics; sometimes it's very wrongheaded. Sometimes it hangs in with the dictators and ostracizes the wrong people. But sometimes it's a great leader of resistance and change for the better in the world. I'm constantly aware of its fascination as a force for social and spiritual change, in society and in the individual.

CA: After the exhaustive research you did for Legs, *you said you didn't want to do it again. Didn't you have to do it again for* Quinn's Book?

KENNEDY: I did indeed; I took years to do that book. I started to set it in both the nineteenth and twentieth centuries and do parallel Quinns, but that didn't work. The only thing I really liked about it was the nineteenth century, and once I had begun

it, I felt that I was onto something and I had to stay with it. So I broke my promise to myself and started to do some research. But it was not research in the conventional way, and certainly not in the way I did *Legs. Legs* dealt with a real, historical gangster, and there was the Jazz Age and prohibition and all that. I wanted to be accurate about it, so I had to understand it. I read a great deal about it in order to be specific, to reflect the real life of Legs Diamond. But I also invented freely. Not everything in that book is factual, obviously—it's a novel.

In *Quinn's Book* the story was vaguely moving from era to era, from the 1840s to the 1860s, from the Irish immigration and the Underground Railroad to the secret societies and bare-knuckle boxing and the draft riots in the Civil War. I did a certain amount of reading in and around these subjects, but I wasn't being specific about any particular character or any specific event in history, so I was able to be a lot more casual. But it was no less complicated. It took a great deal of time, because unless you know what you're talking about, it's very difficult to start inventing. One of my favorite lines is something Hemingway said, that you can't leave out what you don't know.

CA: You seem to have enjoyed tremendously collaborating with Francis Ford Coppola on "The Cotton Club" and turning Ironweed *into a movie. Are there movie projects in the works now that you can talk about?*

KENNEDY: I do have a project afoot, which is "Billy Phelan's Greatest Game." I've written a script for that and I'm hoping the film will be made one of these days. I'm going to be involved as a producer in order to maintain some semblance of control over it, but I have no real news to report—it's too premature. But the forward motion has begun. I've turned down any number of tempting invitations to write for some very good directors, but I don't want to do anything that's not my own work at this time. I'm very much involved in the new book, and the only thing I'll interrupt it for is to help develop the movie. But since I don't have a director's role, or anything like that, I'll continue to write the novel, no matter what happens.

CA: Do you feel director Hector Babenco brought something to the making of "Ironweed" that an American director couldn't have?

KENNEDY: Probably he did. He comes out of a European tradition. He knows a great deal about American films, but the feeling "Ironweed" creates is that of a European movie. What he brought to it was high seriousness, and a desire to make a movie on his terms and my terms. He wanted to be as faithful as he could to the book, which he loved very much and did his damndest to translate to the screen. What I think he brought was something that was not in the line of traditional commercial cinema, which we might have been forced into had we gone through a studio, or had some other director taken it on. You can't tell for sure; certainly there are first-rate American directors who might have done very well with it. But I think Babenco did a great job, and I'm very glad he wanted to do it.

CA: Some reviewers felt that the poetic quality of the novel Ironweed *didn't translate well to the screen. Did you consider that a particular concern in doing the movie?*

KENNEDY: I knew that the linguistics of the book, the poetic structures and fine tuning of the poetic insights of this brooding character, would never make it to the screen. That's the given. If you're going to translate a novel as abundant in language as *Ironweed* is, you know you're not ever going to get that on the screen. You could do it voice-over and hope for the best, but that's a very antique way of doing it. Also, it really is noncinematic—it's anticinematic—to think that you can just impose the language of the book on the screen. It's a liability. I've seen works where this has been done. You're hearing the voice-over while you're looking at these pictures, and the elements fight one another. You're trying to pay attention to the language that you're hearing, and the screen is giving you something else that doesn't conform to that—not unless it's coming out of the mouth of the person on screen. But then it's an exact rendering of what's on the page, and why not just film a reading? In making a film from a novel what you're doing is moving into another art form—creating a work of art in another medium. That's what Babenco and I tried very hard to do.

As for the critics who didn't like it, I think they're quite wrong-headed. Anybody who compares the book to the movie is being unjust and ultimately sappy. It's the oldest way in the world to put down a movie—or, if the movie is better than the book, to put down the book. But they don't compare. The story line is what may be followed and understood, and out of that story line comes the ensemble effect; and that's where the poetry of film lurks. I felt that Babenco did a wonderful job and that Nicholson and Streep were quite extraordinary, as was Tom Waits. Few writers come away from their movies with such a high degree of satisfaction. The negative criticism of the film seems to me quite mindless.

CA: Your books are all quite different from each other despite their links. Quinn's Book, *though, seems a remarkable leap from* Ironweed. *Did the writing of* Quinn's Book *feel somehow different to you?*

KENNEDY: It did. I had to go back and reimagine that century and invent a language that was compatible with it, yet wasn't an imitation of anybody in particular or even an evocation of anybody's style or syntax. That was difficult. Understanding the time period was also difficult. I remember Thornton Wilder saying that going into another country to write about it was child's play compared to going into another time era. That's the truth. Of course I chose a different style of writing—hyperbole—which went with the era of James, Melville, Hawthorne, Cooper. It was a revel, in a way, in newness—which was oldness, actually, but all new to me.

CA: What can you say about the book you're working on now?

KENNEDY: I'll only say that it is set in 1958 and is about the Phelan family. There are some familiar characters there, but there are new ones too.

CA: I wonder a great deal of the time now if Daniel Quinn's disk will reappear in the future. Can you say anything about that?

KENNEDY: I wouldn't give up on anything as complicated and magical as that disk. It could turn up anyplace.

BIOGRAPHICAL/CRITICAL SOURCES:

BOOKS

Contemporary Literary Criticism, Gale, Volume 6, 1976, Volume 28, 1984, Volume 34, 1985, Volume 53, 1989.
Dictionary of Literary Biography Yearbook 1985, Gale, 1986.
Kennedy, William, *Legs,* Coward, 1975.
Kennedy, William, *O Albany! An Urban Tapestry,* Viking, 1983.
McCaffery, Larry and Sinda Gregory, *Alive and Writing: Interviews with American Authors of the 1980s,* University of Illinois Press, 1987.

PERIODICALS

America, May 19, 1984.
Atlantic, June, 1978.
Best Sellers, October 15, 1969.
Book World, April 23, 1978.
Chicago Tribune, January 23, 1983.
Commonweal, October 13, 1978, September 9, 1983.
Detroit News, January 30, 1983, February 26, 1984.
Esquire, March, 1985.
Film Comment, April, 1985.
Globe and Mail (Toronto), September 1, 1984, December 15, 1984, May 21, 1988.
Hudson Review, summer, 1983.
Library Journal, October 1, 1969.
Listener, May 6, 1976.
Los Angeles Times, December 14, 1984.
Los Angeles Times Book Review, December 26, 1982, September 23, 1984, May 22, 1988.
New Republic, May 24, 1975, February 14, 1983.
Newsweek, June 23, 1975, May 8, 1978, January 31, 1983, February 6, 1984.
New Yorker, February 7, 1983.
New York Review of Books, March 31, 1983.
New York Times, January 10, 1983, September 17, 1983, December 23, 1983, September 22, 1984, March 12, 1987, July 19, 1987, September 18, 1987, December 13, 1987, May 16, 1988.
New York Times Book Review, January 23, 1983, November 13, 1983, January 1, 1984, September 30, 1984, October 2, 1986, May 22, 1988.
New York Times Magazine, August 26, 1984.
Observer, October 20, 1969.
People, December 24, 1984, January 18, 1988.
Publishers Weekly, December 9, 1983.
Saturday Review, April 29, 1978.
Time, January 24, 1983, October 1, 1984, December 17, 1984.
Times Literary Supplement, October 5, 1984.
Tribune Books (Chicago), May 8, 1988.
Village Voice Literary Supplement, February, 1983, October, 1984.
Washington Post, October 5, 1969, May 18, 1975, December 28, 1983.
Washington Post Book World, January 16, 1983, January 29, 1984, October 14, 1984, May 8, 1988.*

—Sketch by Marilyn K. Basel

—Interview by Jean W. Ross

*   *   *

KENNY, Shirley (Elise) Strum 1934-

PERSONAL: Born August 28, 1934, in Tyler, Tex.; daughter of Marcus Leon (a merchant) and Florence (Golenternek) Strum; married Robert Wayne Kenny (a professor), July 22, 1956; children: David Jack, Joel Strum, Daniel Clark, Jonathan Matthew, Sarah Elizabeth. *Education:* University of Texas, B.A. and B.J., 1955; University of Minnesota, M.A., 1957; University of Chicago, Ph.D., 1964.

ADDRESSES: Office—Queens College, Flushing, N.Y. 11367.

CAREER: University of Texas, Austin, instructor in English, 1955-56, 1958-59; Gallaudet College, Washington, D.C., assistant professor, 1962-64, associate professor of English, 1964-66; Catholic University of America, Washington, D.C., associate professor of English, 1966-71; University of Maryland, College Park, associate professor, 1971-73, professor of English, 1973, chairman of department, 1973-79, provost of arts and humanities department, 1979-85; Queens College, Flushing, N.Y., president, 1985—.

MEMBER: International Council of Fine Arts Deans, Modern Language Association of America, American Society for Eighteenth Century Studies (member of executive board, 1981-83), American Society for Theatre Research, American Handel Society (member of board), Academy of Literary Studies, South Atlantic Modern Language Association, Bibliographical Society of Virginia, Maryland Humanities Council, Maryland Handel Festival (member of executive board).

AWARDS, HONORS: Distinguished Alumnus Award, University of Chicago, 1980; named Outstanding Woman on Campus, University of Maryland, 1982; honorary doctorate, University of Rochester, 1988.

WRITINGS:

(Editor) *Richard Steele: The Conscious Lovers,* University of Nebraska Press, 1968, reprinted, 1983.
(Editor) *The Plays of Richard Steele,* Clarendon Press, 1971.
(Editor) *The Performers and Their Plays,* Garland Publishing, 1982.
British Theater and the Other Arts, 1660-1800, Folger Books, 1984.
(Editor) *The Works of George Farquhar,* Volumes 1-2, Oxford University Press, 1988.

Contributor to professional journals, including *Studies in Bibliography, Modern Philology, British Studies Monitor,* and *Theatre Notebook.* Book review editor, *South Atlantic Review,* 1981-83.

BIOGRAPHICAL/CRITICAL SOURCES:

PERIODICALS

Times Literary Supplement, October 1, 1971, January 3, 1986.*

* * *

KENYON, Kate
See ADORJAN, Carol (Madden)

* * *

KERMAN, Gertrude
See FURMAN, Gertrude Lerner Kerman

* * *

KETCHUM, Cliff
See PAINE, Lauran (Bosworth)

* * *

KETCHUM, Frank
See PAINE, Lauran (Bosworth)

* * *

KETCHUM, Jack
See PAINE, Lauran (Bosworth)

KEZYS, Algimantas 1928-

PERSONAL: Born October 28, 1928, in Vistytis, Lithuania; came to the United States in 1950, naturalized citizen, 1956; son of George (a government employee) and Eugenija (Kolytaite) Kezys. *Education:* Loyola University, Chicago, Ill., M.A., 1956.

ADDRESSES: Office—Galerija Art Gallery, 226 West Superior St., Chicago, Ill. 60610; (studio) 4317 South Wisconsin Ave., Stickney, Ill. 60402.

CAREER: Entered Society of Jesus (Jesuits), 1950, ordained Roman Catholic priest, 1961; editor in Chicago, Ill., 1964-67; founder of Lithuanian Photo Library in Chicago, 1966, president, 1966—; founder and director of Lithuanian Library Press, Chicago, 1976—. Director of Lithuanian Youth Center in Chicago, 1974-77. Photographer; first one-man show, 1963; exhibitions held at Art Institute of Chicago, 1965, and at other institutions in the United States and abroad.

WRITINGS:

(Editor and photographer) Francis Thompson, *I Fled Him, Down the Nights and Down the Days,* Loyola University Press, 1970.
Form and Content (photographs), M. Morkunas, 1972.
(Editor and photographer) *A Lithuanian Cemetery: St. Casimir Cemetery in Chicago, Ill.,* Lithuanian Photo Library, 1976.
(Photographer) Tom Collins, *The Search for Jimmy Carter,* Word Books, 1976.
Posters: Algimantas Kezys, Volume 1-4, Loyola University Press, 1978-79.
(Photographer) George Lane, *Chicago Churches and Synagogues,* Loyola University Press, 1981.
Chicago—Kezys: Sixty-four Photographs of Chicago, Loyola University Press, 1983.
Lithuania—Through the Wall, Loyola University Press, 1985.
Nature: Forms and Forces, Loyola University Press, 1986.
Variations on a Theme: World's Fairs of the Eighties, Loyola University Press, 1986.
Cityscapes, Loyola University Press, 1988.

Also author of *Portfolio '66,* 1966. Photos by Kezys appear in the monographs *Sventoji auka* (title means "The Holy Sacrifice"), Jesuit Fathers of Della Strada, 1965, and in *Photographs: Algimantas Kezys* by Bruno Markaitis, Loyola University Press, 1966. Contributor of photographs to *Famous Photographers Annual* and to various magazines, including *Camera.* Former editor, *Zvaigzde* (title means "The Star"), and *Sacred Heart Messenger.*

WORK IN PROGRESS: Double Prints and *Caged In.*

SIDELIGHTS: In the introduction to *Form and Content,* Algimantas Kezys writes: "I believe the camera is a mechanical tool for communication between individuals. The process of photographic communication begins with the photographer's inner self. It continues through the mechanics of photography, which act as transmitters of his thoughts, feelings, and vision to another individual. I have discovered that my pre-visualization powers are completely dormant and that my post-visualization dexterity is nonexistent. I can't be either an art director who tells photographers or himself what to shoot, nor a lab technician who produces marvels even from the most ordinary negative material. From my own observation of myself I know that my 'moment of glory' is the moment of seeing and discovering. For me this is the crucial point at which pictures are made or unmade."

BIOGRAPHICAL/CRITICAL SOURCES:

BOOKS

Kezys, Algimantas, *Form and Content,* M. Morkunas, 1972.

*   *   *

KIENZLE, William X(avier) 1928-
(Mark Boyle)

PERSONAL: Born September 11, 1928, in Detroit, Mich.; son of Alphonzo and Mary Louise (Boyle) Kienzle; married Javan Herman Andrews (an editor and researcher), 1974. *Education:* Sacred Heart Seminary College, B.A., 1950; also attended St. John's Seminary, 1950-54, and University of Detroit, 1968. *Politics:* Independent. *Religion:* Roman Catholic.

ADDRESSES: Home—2465 Middlebelt, West Bloomfield, Mich. 48033-1685.

CAREER: Ordained Roman Catholic priest, 1954; left priesthood, 1974; Roman Catholic Archdiocese of Detroit, Detroit, Mich., archdiocesan priest in five parishes, 1954-74, editor in chief of *Michigan Catholic,* 1962-74; *MPLS.* magazine, Minneapolis, Minn., editor in chief, 1974-77; Western Michigan University, Kalamazoo, associate director of Center for Contemplative Studies, 1977-78; University of Dallas, Irving, Tex., director of Center for Contemplative Studies, 1978-79; writer, 1979—.

MEMBER: Authors Guild, Authors League of America, Crime Writers Association, American Crime Writers League.

AWARDS, HONORS: Michigan Knights of Columbus journalism award, 1963, for general excellence; honorable mention from Catholic Press Association, 1974, for editorial writing.

WRITINGS:

MYSTERY NOVELS

The Rosary Murders, Andrews & McMeel, 1979.
Death Wears a Red Hat, Andrews & McMeel, 1980.
Mind over Murder, Andrews & McMeel, 1981.
Assault with Intent, Andrews & McMeel, 1982.
Shadow of Death, Andrews & McMeel, 1983.
Kill and Tell, Andrews & McMeel, 1984.
Sudden Death, Andrews, McMeel & Parker, 1985.
Deathbed, Andrews, McMeel & Parker, 1986.
Deadline for a Critic, Andrews, McMeel & Parker, 1987.
Marked for Murder, Andrews & McMeel, 1988.
Eminence, Andrews & McMeel, 1989.
Masquerade, Andrews & McMeel, 1990.

OTHER

Contributor under pseudonym Mark Boyle to *MPLS.* magazine.

WORK IN PROGRESS: A mystery novel for Andrews & McMeel.

SIDELIGHTS: Though he no longer delivers the sermons that captivated his parishioners, William X. Kienzle is still telling stories. After leaving the priesthood in 1974, he "exchanged his pulpit for a typewriter," as Bill Dunn describes in *Publishers Weekly,* and began writing the tales that have made him a bestselling mystery author. The twenty years he spent in the clergy now provide the raw material for his popular series involving Father Robert Koesler, an amateur sleuth and sharply defined priest who resembles Kienzle in several ways. "The fictitious Father Koesler divides his time between his pastoral duties within the Detroit archdiocese and his journalistic duties as an editor

of the area's Catholic newspaper, just as Kienzle spent his time during the 1960's," *Detroit News Magazine* writer Andrea Wojack observes.

Despite these similarities, Wojack does not envision Koesler as Kienzle in disguise. Rather, she sees him as a product of both Kienzle's background and "the tradition of clerical detectives in fiction, like Chesterton's Father Brown and Harry Kemelman's Rabbi Small." Andrew M. Greeley similarly observes in the *Los Angeles Times Book Review:* "William Kienzle is the Harry Kemelman of Catholicism, and his priest detective, Robert Koesler . . . is the Detroit response to Rabbi Small." The critic adds: "I am not suggesting that Kienzle is consciously imitating Kemelman—though there would be nothing wrong with such imitation. Rather I am arguing that religio-ethnic subcultures are fertile seedbeds for mystery stories. Kienzle's sensitivity to pathos and foolishness, shallow fads and rigid ideologies, mindless nonsense and deep faith of the contemporary Catholic scene compares favorably with Kemelman's vivid description of suburban Jewish life."

A native Detroiter, Kienzle also uses the city and its Catholic parishes as a backdrop for his fiction, reportedly drawing many of his characters from people he has known. "Kienzle's portrayals of various priests obviously [are] an insider's (or ex-insider's) work," a *Detroit News* contributor comments. "He seems accurate, yet relaxed, in his depictions of the clergy, and his genuine affection for many of them far outruns any tendency toward satiric thrust." In addition, Father Koesler's solutions rely on his knowledge of the Church and its workings; in the recent *Eminence,* for example, "Koesler's command of ecclesiastical detail is full and fascinating," *Los Angeles Times Book Review* critic Charles Champlin states, and "the uses of Latin and points of Canon law are significant clues."

Despite Kienzle's assertion that his novels are, as Dunn reports, "first of all thrillers," many critics find a deeper meaning in his work. In his review of *Mind over Murder,* for example, *Detroit Free Press* managing editor Neal Shine observes: "There has always been the sense that there's as much message as mystery in Kienzle's books. Kienzle is a former Detroit priest whose feelings about some of the ways in which the Catholic Church deports itself can hardly be called ambivalent. In *Mind over Murder* he goes to the heart of the matter for a lot of Catholics—marriage and the Church. The people with the clearest motives for rubbing out the monsignor are those who have run up against his incredibly inflexible rulings on marriage." *Chicago Tribune* writer Peter Gorner likewise remarks that in *Deadline for a Critic* "Kienzle addresses serious modern issues"; nevertheless, the author also "stops to digress and tell us his wonderful stories." The critic concludes that "Kienzle's books are more small morality plays than classic mysteries. He always is welcomed to my shelves."

Although Kienzle includes philosophical inquiries and religious asides in his books, his primary strength lies in the development of the mystery. In *Kill and Tell,* for example, "we're back to basics with a fascinating cast of three-dimensional characters who *act* like people caught up in a baffling case, a protagonist in Father Koesler who is both wry and intelligent, and an honest-to-badness murder at a tension-filled cocktail party that is truly puzzling," Don G. Campbell recounts in the *Los Angeles Times Book Review.* *Best Sellers* contributor Tony Bednarczyk likewise asserts that in *The Rosary Murders,* which he calls a "well paced, tightly written novel," the author, "more importantly, creates well defined characters that inhabit his story rather than decorate it." " 'The Rosary Murders' quickly established Father

Koesler as among the most likable and authentic of all recent sleuths and gave his wise and compassionate creator a midlife career and a new pulpit," Gorner concludes. "Since then, few mystery series have been more cozy and persuasive."

MEDIA ADAPTATIONS: The Rosary Murders was produced by Take One Productions in 1987.

CA INTERVIEW

CA interviewed William X. Kienzle by telephone on July 1, 1989, at his home in Southfield, Michigan.

CA: You became a mystery writer after twenty years in the priesthood. Besides the knack for storytelling that you've said you developed in the seminary, and the inspiration for some of your characters, how do you feel your work as a priest has enriched your writing?

KIENZLE: I don't think any experience in life, no matter what it is, is irrelevant to writing. Everything that you do has something to do with what you're writing, and certainly being a priest and caring for people in some of the most important times of their lives—birth, death, marriage and the failure of marriage—influences the way a person writes.

CA: You've said Father Bob Koesler, your detective, is you, a product of the old Church and now often at odds with its rigidity. Have you found some comfort in being able to express through his voice and his actions the dissatisfactions that led you to leave the priesthood?

KIENZLE: I think that was true early on, maybe in the first two, three, possibly four books. I was really never opposed to the Church as such. My only quarrel was with Church law, and I probably reflected that especially in the third book, *Mind over Murder.* Certainly after that it had very little to do with the writing.

CA: Did you ever have any reluctance to draw on your knowledge of the Catholic Church and your disagreements with Church law for material for your books?

KIENZLE: No. To forbid myself the use of that experience would be almost like telling a police officer that he couldn't use any of his experience as a police officer in writing a book. A police officer brings a very specialized technical knowledge to writing, an authenticity that would be almost impossible to capture if he hadn't lived that experience. You draw on your own life experience, and mine heavily has been well within the Catholic Church. I went to Catholic schools for the first eight grades, then a seminary for high school, college, and theology, and then spent twenty years as a priest. To take that whole package and throw it out the window would be to say that practically half of my life is irrelevant to what I'm doing now. I think somebody who has been a priest can bring a very special kind of authenticity and insight to writing—interest too, possibly, and humor.

CA: Detroit figures almost as a character in your books, it seems so integral to their plots. How do you manage to capture just the right physical details of the city to portray it as you do?

KIENZLE: I've spent fifty-five of my sixty years here, and that does give you a rather good idea of the town! That explains my familiarity with the topography, the different ethnic flavors of the neighborhoods and of suburbia, the sports arenas and theat-

rical facilities. I would like to make the point that, just as I'm writing stories that have to do with the Catholic Church but are not about the Catholic Church, so I am writing stories set in Detroit but not about Detroit. The neighborhood that I grew up in and some other places like it have almost disintegrated. If I wrote about the problems of Detroit, I'd be writing about Detroit. I'm setting the stories there, on the river front and the expressways, in the Renaissance Building, in the various sports facilities. But they don't really get into neighborhoods, at least not very frequently. *Marked for Murder* had quite a bit to do with the typical neighborhood in Detroit, but that's because it just fitted into the story.

CA: You must do some painful research for at least some of the books. To take an example from Eminence, *your latest as we speak, there's a lot of morgue detail at the beginning. Do you have friends in law enforcement to whom you can turn for help with such scenes or for access to places outsiders usually don't get into?*

KIENZLE: Yes, I do. I've often thought that if the reader were to take a look at the acknowledgments page, he would have a pretty good idea what the book's about. I need a lot of help with police procedural and, when it occurs, with morgue ritual; with the court system, when that figures in my stories, and with hospitals. Over the years I've built up friendships with a whole bunch of different people, and since I've been writing books, with a whole different cast of people that I can call on who are very generous in providing information.

CA: Other writers have commented on how helpful people can be in that way.

KIENZLE: Generally it's true. I'm afraid there are not an awful lot of people who read, so in the beginning, and even at the stage I'm at now, when you call and say that you're writing a book and need some resource material, a lot of people simply have no concept of what you're doing and who you are. I talked to Dick Francis once, and he attested to the fact that, when he was starting, he had a very difficult time getting people to understand what he was doing and to be willing to help. But now that he is DICK FRANCIS, people help him quite readily.

CA: The movie version of The Rosary Murders, *your first novel, was written by Elmore Leonard and starred Donald Sutherland as Father Bob Koesler. How did you feel about the story's adaptation for the screen?*

KIENZLE: I didn't see it. I don't want to see it. I think if you talk to authors who have been subjected to Hollywood, you'll find a pretty well unanimous body of people who've been disappointed. I don't think Elmore Leonard wrote the screenplay that was filmed. When the picture came out, he was credited with writing the screenplay along with the director of the film, Fred Walton, and I think it was the director's version that was used. I have heard about the movie almost frame by frame, so I know what's there. There are some parts of it people have told me about that I think were probably very effective, but other parts that were almost tragedies of poor research and amateurish work. For example, very shortly after the movie opens, the prime controversy in which they're trying to set up the characters is the baptism of an illegitimate baby. They have Father Koesler, who's going to be defined as a crashing liberal, who's ready to wave good-bye to the laws of the Church forbidding baptism of an illegitimate child. And there's Father Nabors, the pastor of the parish and the priest with whom Father Koesler lives in the rectory. He's going to be defined as a hard-line conservative priest, so he demands that the laws of the Church be enforced. Father Koesler proves that he is a liberal by baptizing the baby. Unfortunately, of the 1,752 laws in the Catholic Church, not one of them has to do with baptizing an illegitimate baby; there's no law against it. If the movie people didn't know that, all they had to do was call any rectory to find out. They not only changed the book, they changed it to an inauthentic kind of anecdote.

CA: Can I assume from your displeasure that there won't be any more movies based on the books?

KIENZLE: I don't know whether there will or won't; I have no way of telling. I had nothing to do with *The Rosary Murders* being turned into a movie anyway. The publisher, by contract—which I think is usually the case—had the right to negotiate ancillary rights like book clubs, softcover publications, foreign publications, movies, and television. So the publisher negotiated the movie—I didn't—and any future negotiations are in the hands of the publisher. I would like very much to be able to earn a sufficient living whereby I would be able to say that I don't want to have anything to do with Hollywood, but I don't think I'm ever going to get there.

CA: I would imagine that Father Koesler speaks for a great many Catholics, or certainly strikes a responsive chord in them. Do readers write to you to express their approval of your fictional character?

KIENZLE: Yes, sometimes they do write about him particularly. We're living in a Post-Vatican II Church. I remember one letter I got from a lady in New York who said that she was a lapsed Catholic and had no idea that there were so many interesting things going on in the Church; she was going to go back and find out about them. There have been people who have written to say they wish they had met a Father Koesler; they wish they could go to somebody like that who would be receptive and kind and forbearing.

CA: You told Roberta Schwartz for Michigan Magazine *just after the publication of* Deathbed, *your eighth novel, "I am really grateful that the readers are being so patient—because I am learning to write books." That seemed like a nice bit of modesty for someone whose books were already doing quite well. What do you feel the greatest hurdles have been for you as a writer?*

KIENZLE: I think a lot of writers have self-doubts about pacing. It's always difficult to know whether you've got enough action, enough dialogue, enough description, enough delineation. I think one of the great hurdles for me and everybody writing is that there is no feedback. If you're speaking—giving a sermon, for instance, or something like that—you know within a matter of seconds whether you've got the audience or not. But in a book you write for maybe five or six months and you don't have any feedback; you don't know how this thing is going over. The use of the device of pacing, I would imagine, might be one of the broader challenges to the writer, until you've perfected it.

CA: You've credited your wife, Javan, for extraordinary help in your work. Does she often disagree with you about points in the writing or provide you with insights that you might not otherwise have had?

KIENZLE: Definitely—not only in the writing, but in the re-writing. I write in longhand and she types the manuscript from

that, and finally types the entire manuscript three times. She was a copy editor in the *Detroit Free Press*'s features department, and each time through we talk about problems that might be occurring, loose ends that haven't been tied up, things like that. I spoke a little while ago about pacing. There isn't anything she can do about that, because that's an initiative that comes from me. But after that, the only feedback I get and the only feedback I really want is hers.

CA: Does each book usually grow out of the last, so that there's a fresh idea waiting by the time you've finished the book you're on?

KIENZLE: No, I don't think so. I'm in that spot as we speak now. Yesterday I finished the twelfth book, so I'm going to have to work over it with Javan and then with the publisher, but I'm really in the market for a new idea; I'm not exactly sure where I'm going to go. The process that seems to be pretty good for me is just opening the viaduct for ideas and letting them flood in and continuing to test them until I find one that is interesting to me and complex enough for a book. When I find one, I try and refine it to its first power, and then I tell the story to Javan. She will say, "I don't like that," or "I like that." If she says she doesn't like it, I'll go back and try for another one.

The books are sequels in that many of the same characters reappear and they're set in Detroit and they have a lot to do with the Catholic Church. The reason they do is because my clerical sleuth Father Koesler knows full well that he's not a policeman. He gets drawn into these cases because there's something Catholic happening, and it's his special expertise in Catholicism or in religion that usually spells his measure of aid to the investigating police. But that's about the extent of their similarity to each other. I might one time decide I'd like to investigate the fine arts scene in Detroit, and from that would come a book called *Deadline for a Critic*. Or I might like to think of professional sports in Detroit, and from that would come a book called *Sudden Death*. I might want to take a look at a hospital scene, and from that would come a book called *Deathbed*.

CA: So you're always learning something while you're writing, and, I assume, having a good time doing it.

KIENZLE: Yes. The learning part is very interesting for me, and I hope for the readers too. Generally they'll pick up some insights that maybe they didn't have before on various issues like theater or the symphony orchestra or a hospital or something like that.

CA: I think it's fair to say that, while your books are rousing mysteries first and foremost, they do deal with moral and social issues. When you're writing, do you ever find it difficult to keep your concern with issues in balance with the need to create good entertainment?

KIENZLE: I think there's an interesting and a dull way to treat anything. We've all had experiences of reading things that should have been very interesting but were very dull—and vice versa, things that we might suspect would be dull but were really quite interesting because of the way they were written. I don't think I have to fear about a subject being dull; I have to fear that I'm not telling an interesting story. To use the pulpit again as an example, how many times are we bored silly in church because somebody is talking about abstract ideas or telling us about the processions of the Trinity, or telling us about a very interesting thing but in a dull way? The thing I try to lean back on in any kind of presentation is stories. We start loving stories as children, and we never outgrow the feeling we get then when somebody says, "I'm going to tell you a story"—we sort of cuddle in and wait to hear it. If you get in the pulpit and say, "A funny thing happened to me on the way to church today . . ." people will be interested in what happened to you. Where the kind of book I write could get mired in a lot of mud is when I try to explain what this Catholic thing is that Father Koesler is an expert at. But if I can put it in the context of a story, something that happened to a priest or a nun, then it should be a fairly interesting treatment.

CA: There are obviously many Catholics who, like you, disagree with something in the Church and would like to see reforms, but can continue to be a part of the Church on their own terms. Does this involve a crisis of conscience, since the Catholic Church has traditionally demanded strict obedience from its members?

KIENZLE: It very seriously can. It depends on the attitude of the individual. There probably has never been, at least in recent history, such a division among Catholics as there has since the Second Vatican Council, and a lot of it has to do with what you mean by the Church. What a great number of people mean by the Church is the Pope. They still look at it as the triangle with the Pope on top, then bishops and priests, and then, on the bottom, the people. The way we grew up generally was believing that the Pope decides things and he tells the bishops, who tell the priests, who tell the people, who do it.

The Second Vatican Council came out with the definition of the Church as the people of God. While it is not, strictly speaking, a democracy, there can be a vast and vital difference in what people think of as the role of a person's conscience. The doctrine of the Church for as long as I can remember has been that an individual Catholic has an obligation to develop a true conscience and then follow it. But in practice, what's happened frequently is that the individual starts forming his or her conscience and the Pope and the bishops come in and say, "Wait a minute—we'll help you. This is the way your conscience ought to react." Then it becomes a kind of dictatorship. You can reply, "But my conscience doesn't react that way." They will then say, "Well, the Pope is pretty important." Then you can say, "Yes, to a Catholic, the Pope is extremely important and ought to be listened to, and his views and opinions should be very carefully considered. And if my conscience differs from the way the Pope's talking, I had better have awfully good reasons for disagreeing. But if in the final analysis I do have awfully good reasons, then I follow my conscience, not the Pope."

CA: What reforms do you think are likely to take place in the Church in the foreseeable future?

KIENZLE: I think we're headed back to the thirteenth century. My personal opinion is that the present Pope knows exactly what he's doing, and I think he sees the crisis in vocations and everything else to be a part of God's grand plan to remake the Church and back it up. I don't see any place on the horizon where the Church is advancing; we seem to be spending most of our time digging our heels in, retrenching. In Detroit, for example, at the moment the current crisis is closing churches in the core city. All of a sudden, instead of preaching the gospel or doing apostolic good things, everybody is just concerned about staying alive.

So it goes in theology. With the examples we have of Father Charlie Curran being dismissed from the faculty of Catholic University and his credentials as a theologian being withdrawn,

with Bishop Hunthausen out on the West Coast having four or five of his responsibilities as a bishop taken over by an auxiliary bishop—almost a contradiction in terms—we give the impression that what we're doing in the Catholic Church currently is trying to solidify positions instead of admitting that there are real problems in the world that we've got to face. We're just operating internally, not tackling the big tasks that need to be tackled.

Take a look at the Pope and the amount of influence he should have. The present Pope, John Paul II, is a charismatic figure with an absolutely astonishing knowledge of languages. He should be the headline maker, the directional father of everything. But where we look in the world for that role is not to the Pope but to Gorbachev. He is changing so much so vitally with the reduction of atomic weapons and things like that, he may make the greatest impression that's been made in the world in centuries. Catholics would like to see the Pope doing that.

CA: You got from your mother a talent for music that took the form of playing the piano and composing. Do you still enjoy those activities?

KIENZLE: I keep making good resolutions and keeping them for a short while, and then something always comes up. So I'm neglecting that. I should play the piano—even for my own amazement!—far more frequently than I do. As far as composing goes, that is kind of interesting: I can compose music, and it is very, very bad. When I was a reviewer of plays for a while for a couple of publications, I had an infallible way of dealing with the songs in a new musical. If in my wildest imagination I could imagine myself writing a song, I knew that it was bad. That always worked.

As a matter of fact, after the Second Vatican Council, when we went into vernacular languages in the liturgy, a whole bunch of new music was written, and most of it is extremely wretched. We'd had centuries of polyphony and Gregorian chant, some of the most beautiful music ever developed anywhere, but you can hardly even find that in the Church anymore. The only good music we've got now, we swiped from the Protestants. Who can do better now than "A Mighty Fortress Is Our God"? And that's Martin Luther.

CA: You've said you aren't sure about the next book. Is there anything you can say about the future for you and Father Bob Koesler?

KIENZLE: If history indicates anything, I will probably be writing another book every year for the rest of my life; it just depends on how long God gives me. I don't know if they're all going to be mystery stories. At the moment the publisher wants them, because they're working. And I'm not tired of them, or of Father Koesler. As a matter of fact, I have to try to make sure he doesn't dominate the scene. I try to concentrate on some figures who have cropped up more recently, like one I really enjoy, Alonzo Tully, whom everybody calls "Zoo." He's probably going to take a more and more dominant position in the future. But Koesler, of course, will always be there in the mysteries, because there will always be a Catholic element. Sometime in the future I'd like to get into some other kinds of novels; I have ideas for other kinds, and that may happen. But numerically, please God and as long as the reading public permits, I'll probably be writing a book a year.

BIOGRAPHICAL/CRITICAL SOURCES:

BOOKS

Contemporary Authors Autobiography Series, Volume 1, Gale, 1984.
Contemporary Literary Criticism, Volume 25, Gale, 1983.

PERIODICALS

Best Sellers, July, 1979.
Chicago Tribune, May 29, 1985, April 8, 1987, May 3, 1989.
Chicago Tribune Book World, July 11, 1982.
Detroit Free Press, February 22, 1980, April 26, 1981.
Detroit News, July 15, 1979, April 5, 1981.
Detroit News Magazine, March 16, 1980.
Los Angeles Times, April 24, 1981, May 7, 1987.
Los Angeles Times Book Review, June 22, 1980, May 23, 1982, August 5, 1984, May 7, 1987, April 9, 1989.
Michigan Magazine, August 11, 1985.
New York Times Book Review, June 15, 1980, June 21, 1981, May 23, 1982.
Publishers Weekly, April 18, 1980.

—*Interview by Jean W. Ross*

*   *   *

KILGORE, John
See PAINE, Lauran (Bosworth)

*   *   *

KIMBALL, Frank
See PAINE, Lauran (Bosworth)

*   *   *

KIMBALL, Ralph
See PAINE, Lauran (Bosworth)

*   *   *

KING, Deborah 1950-

PERSONAL: Born November 21, 1950, in Dorset, England; daughter of Alex (an inspector of shipping) and Joy King. *Education:* Hornsey School of Art Diploma in Art and Design (with honors), 1974.

ADDRESSES: Home—3 Harmony Ter., Studland, Dorset, England.

CAREER: Free-lance illustrator for publishers, periodicals, and newspapers, including Ladybird Books, Macdonald Educational, *Reader's Digest, Sunday Times* (London), and BBC Publications. Art work exhibited at Portal Gallery, London, England. Lecturer at Hornsey School of Art and Bournemouth College of Art.

WRITINGS:

(Illustrator) *The National History of Britain and Northern Europe,* Hodder & Stoughton, 1979.
(Co-illustrator) *The Herb and Spice Book,* Lincoln/Weidenfeld & Nicolson, 1979.
Rook (juvenile), Hamish Hamilton, 1980.
Sirius and Saba, Hamish Hamilton, 1981.
(With Naomi Lewis) *Puffin* (juvenile), Lothrop, 1984.
Swan (juvenile), Lothrop, 1985.
Jake (juvenile), Century/Hutchinson, 1988.

Cloudy (juvenile), Philomel/Putnam, 1989.
Custer (juvenile), Century/Hutchinson, 1990.

WORK IN PROGRESS: Water's Edge and *Passage of the Heron,* for adults; another children's book.

SIDELIGHTS: Deborah King told *CA:* "I always considered my books for all ages, but because they are first and foremost picture books they tend to be marketed as children's books. I have since been encouraged to work towards a younger age group, having been accused of writing rather 'too sophisticated' books for children. On my book *Puffin,* Naomi Lewis worked on my text and simplified my story for the benefit of younger readers. *Water's Edge* is a serious study of the coast where I live and will be for the adult market.

"It may be wise to point out that I am an artist first and a writer second, and my motivation is pure and simple: my fascination for the natural world. My paramount concern is conservation of the environment and wildlife. My aim is to educate the younger people about the wonders of the natural world in the hope that they will help preserve it for generations to come. One thing is for sure, I will *never* run out of inspiration and ideas." Many of King's books have appeared in Japanese, French, and Scandinavian editions.

BIOGRAPHICAL/CRITICAL SOURCES:

PERIODICALS

Observer, September 28, 1980.
Times Literary Supplement, November 21, 1980.

*   *   *

KING, Kimball 1934-

PERSONAL: Born February 5, 1934, in Trenton, N.J.; son of James and Virginia (Martin) King; married Harriet Richards Lowry, December 27, 1955; children: Scottow, Caleb, Virginia. *Education:* Johns Hopkins University, B.A., 1956; Wesleyan University, Middletown, Conn., M.A., 1960; University of Wisconsin—Madison, Ph.D., 1964.

ADDRESSES: Home—610 North St., Chapel Hill, N.C. 27514. *Office*—Department of English, University of North Carolina, Chapel Hill, N.C. 27514.

CAREER: University of North Carolina, Chapel Hill, assistant professor, 1964-68, associate professor, 1968-81, professor of English, 1981—.

MEMBER: Modern Language Association of America.

WRITINGS:

(Editor) Thomas Nelson Page, *In Old Virginia,* University of North Carolina Press, 1972.
Twenty Modern British Dramatists, Garland Publishing, 1977.
Ten Modern Irish Playwrights: A Comprehensive Annotated Bibliography, Garland Publishing, 1979.
Ten Modern American Playwrights: An Annotated Bibliography, Garland Publishing, 1982.
August Baldwin Longstreet, G. K. Hall, 1984.
Sam Shepard: A Casebook, Garland Publishing, 1989.

Contributor to literature journals. Managing editor, *Southern Literary Journal.*

KINGHORN, Kenneth Cain 1930-

PERSONAL: Born June 23, 1930, in Albany, Okla.; son of Kenneth (a businessman) and Eloise (Rye) Kinghorn; married Hilda Hartzler, June 4, 1955; children: Kathleen, Kenneth, Kevin, Kent. *Education:* Ball State University, B.S., 1952; Asbury Theological Seminary, B.D., 1962; Emory University, Ph.D., 1965.

ADDRESSES: Home—1083 The Lane, Lexington, Ky. 40504. *Office*—Office of the Dean, Asbury Theological Seminary, Wilmore, Ky. 40390.

CAREER: Ordained United Methodist minister, 1965; Asbury Theological Seminary, Wilmore, Ky., associate professor, 1965-70, professor of history of theology, 1970-82, dean, 1982—.

WRITINGS:

Contemporary Issues in Historical Perspective, Word Inc., 1970.
Dynamic Discipleship, Revell, 1973.
Fresh Wind of the Spirit, Abingdon, 1975.
Gifts of the Spirit, Abingdon, 1976.
Christ Can Make You Fully Human, Abingdon, 1979.
Celebration of Ministry, Francis Asbury, 1982.
Discovering Your Spiritual Gifts, Zondervan, 1984.
The Holy Spirit and You, University of the Air, 1987.
Secularism in America, Bristol Books, 1990.

Contributor of articles to periodicals.

*   *   *

KINKADE, Richard P(aisley) 1939-

PERSONAL: Born January 7, 1939, in Los Angeles, Calif.; son of Joseph Marion (a physician) and Elizabeth (Paisley) Kinkade; married Raquel Liebes, June 2, 1962 (divorced, 1977); married Kiki J. Gekas, August 27, 1986; children: (first marriage) Kathleen, Richard, Jr., Scott Philip; (second marriage) Mary Elizabeth. *Education:* Yale University, B.A., 1960, Ph.D., 1965.

ADDRESSES: Home—1200 Paseo Pavon, Tucson, Ariz. 85718. *Office*—Department of Spanish and Portuguese, University of Arizona, Tucson, Ariz. 85721.

CAREER: University of Arizona, Tucson, assistant professor, 1965-69, associate professor of Romance languages, 1969-71; Emory University, Atlanta, Ga., professor of Romance languages, 1971-77, chairperson of department, 1971-74, director of graduate studies in Spanish, 1971-75, chairperson of committee on foreign languages and classics, 1976-77; University of Connecticut, Storrs, professor of Romance languages and head of department of Romance and classical languages, 1977-82; University of Arizona, professor of Spanish and Portuguese, 1982—, dean of faculty of humanities, 1982-87. Member of international jury for Letras de Oro Prize, 1986—. Member of board of trustees, Greenfields Country Day School, 1983-89.

MEMBER: International Association of Hispanists, Modern Language Association of America (member of bibliography and research committee, 1972-75; chairperson of Spanish section, 1974, 1977; member of executive committee, 1974-78; divisional delegate to national delegate assembly, 1976-78), American Association of Teachers of Spanish and Portuguese, Medieval Academy of America, Academy of American Research Historians on Medieval Spain, South Atlantic Modern Language Association (chairperson of Medieval section, 1973; member of executive committee, 1973-76), Tucson Rotary Club (chairman of international student fellowships committee, 1987-88; member of board of directors, 1988-89).

AWARDS, HONORS: American Council of Learned Societies travel grant, 1974; National Endowment for the Humanities research grant, 1978-79.

WRITINGS:

Los "Lucidarios" espanoles (critical edition), Editorial Gredos (Madrid), 1968.
(Contributor) Staubach, Guerrero, and Bonilla, *Espanol,* Ginn, 1970.
(Contributor) *Estudios literarios de hispanistas norteamericanos dedicados a Helmut Hatzfeld,* HISPAM (Barcelona), 1974.
(Contributor with J. A. Zahner) *Homenaje a Agapito Rey,* Indiana University Press, 1980.
(Contributor) *Medieval, Renaissance and Folklore Studies in Honor of John Esten Keller,* Juan de la Cuesta Hispanic Monographs (Wilmington, Del.), 1980.
(With John E. Keller) *Iconography in Medieval Spanish Literature,* University Press of Kentucky, 1984.
(Contributor) *Selected Proceedings of the Sixth Louisiana Conference on Hispanic Languages and Literatures,* Tulane University Press, 1985.
(Editor with C. B. Faulhaber and T. A. Perry, and contributor) *Studies in Honor of Gustavo Correa,* Scripta Humanistica, 1986.
(Contributor) *Papers of the First International Symposium on the Cantigas de Santa Maria,* Hispanic Seminary of Medieval Studies (Madison, Wis.), 1987.

Also contributor to *Actas del primer congreso internacional sobre el arcipreste de Hita,* 1973, and *Actas del congreso internacional de hispanistas,* 1978. Contributor to professional journals, including *Speculum, Hispanic Review, Romance Philology, PMLA,* and *American Hispanist.* Member of editorial boards, *Scripta Humanistica,* 1975-82, *Revista de Estudios Hispanicos,* 1977-84, *Kentucky Romance Quarterly,* 1978-84, *Studia Humanitatis, Anuario Medieval,* and *Ideas '92.*

WORK IN PROGRESS: Dramatic Art Forms in Medieval Castile; Didactic Eroticism: Neoplatonic Patterns in Medieval Spanish Literature.

SIDELIGHTS: Richard P. Kinkade has travelled extensively in Mexico and Central America, and has lived in Spain.

*   *   *

KIRK, Philip
See LEVINSON, Leonard

*   *   *

KOBAYASHI, Masako Matsuno 1935-
(Masako Matsuno)

PERSONAL: Born July 12, 1935, in Niihama, Japan; daughter of Kiyokoto (a businessman) and Hideko (Nabeshima) Matsuno; married Toshiro Kobayashi (with Sanyo Electric Co. Ltd.), July 12, 1960; children: Ryosaku (son), Satoko (daughter), Kenjiro (son). *Education:* Waseda University, B.A., 1958; Columbia University, M.S., 1960.

ADDRESSES: Home—23-1, 1-chome, Furuedai, Suita-shi, Osaka, Japan.

CAREER: Writer for children, and translator. Lecturer on children's literature and library services for young people at Baika Women's College.

AWARDS, HONORS: Gozan Prize, 1984, for *Ohyakusho to meushi;* Robonoishi Bungaku Prize, 1987; Sankei Jido Shuppan Bunka Grand Prize for "Ryo chan to Satochan no Ohanashi" series.

WRITINGS:

JUVENILES; ALL UNDER NAME MASAKO MATSUNO

A Pair of Red Clogs, World Publishing, 1960.
Taro and the Tofu, World Publishing, 1962.
Fushigina Takenoko, Fukuinkan, 1963, translation published as *Taro and the Bamboo Shoot,* Pantheon, 1964.
Chie and the Sportsday, World Publishing, 1965.
Ryochan no Asa, Fukuinkan, 1968.
Okina Omiyage, Fukuinkan, 1970.
The Goldfish Vendor and the Two Boys, Doshinsha, 1972.
Nakitaro (picture book), Bunken Publishing, 1974.
Thunder-boy, Chibita, Rironsha Publishing, 1976.
Little Fox Kon and Little Badger Pon (picture book), Doshinsha Publishing, 1977.
The King Who Loved Keys, Doshinsha Publishing, 1979.
Momo to Kodanuki (title means "Momo and the Little Badger"), Dainihontosho Publishing, 1980.
Kousagi Kenta to Hottokeiki (title means "Stories about Little Rabbit Kenta"), Doshinsha Publishing, 1981.
Rabbit, Rabbit, What Are You Eating? (picture book), Fukuinkan, 1983.
Kowagari no Hashigosha (picture book), Fukuinkan, 1983.
Kuru-Kuru Guru-Guru (picture book), Doshinsha Publishing, 1984.
Cats (picture book), Doshinsha Publishing, 1984.
Apples (picture book), Doshinsha Publishing, 1984.
Kasa (title means "Umbrella"), Fukuinkan, 1985.
Kogitsune Kikko (title means "The Little Fox Kikko"), Doshinsha Publishing, 1985.
Chokomaka-Kumasan, Nossori-Kumasan, Hikarinokuni Publishing, 1985.
Tatsukun no Tanjobi (title means "Tatsukun's Birthday"), Fukuinkan, 1986.
Tatsukun no Omiseban (title means "Tatsukun Sells Balloons"), Fukuinkan, 1988.
Kogitsune Kikko, Ensoku no maki (title means "Kikko Goes Hiking"), Doshinsha Publishing, 1988.
Tatsukun to Kame (title means "Tatsukun and the Tortoise"), Fukuinkan, 1989.
Kogitsune Kikko, Sports Day, Doshinsha Publishing, 1989.

AUTHOR OF "RYO CHAN TO SATOCHAN NO OHANASHI" SERIES; PUBLISHED BY DAINIHONTOSHO PUBLISHING

Nendo no zo no Hanakurabe (title means "Which Clay Elephant Got the Longest Nose?"), 1985.
Mori no Usokuidori (title means "Strange Bird Who Eats Lies"), 1985.
Shabondama ni Notte (title means "Riding in Soap Bubbles"), 1985.
Tsumiki-no-Byoin (title means "What Happened in the Brick Hospital?"), 1986.
Dorotanuki Yukiusagi (title means "Mud Badger, Snow Rabbit"), 1986.

TRANSLATOR

Eriko Kishida, *Hippopotamus,* World Publishing, 1963.
A. H. White, *Junket,* Gakushu-Kenkyusha, 1969.
E. Johnson, *The Little Knight,* Gakushu-Kenkyusha, 1969.
M. Brown, *Cinderella,* Fukuinkan, 1970.

Ada and Frank Graham, *Jacob and Owl,* Dainihontosho Publishing, 1973.
Avery, *A Likely Lad,* Iwanami Publishing, 1977.
McNeill, *Umbrella Thursday,* Iwanami Publishing, 1979.
Robinson, *When Marnie Was There,* Iwanami Publishing, 1980.
Watts, *St. Francis and the Proud Crow,* Iwanami Publishing, 1988.

OTHER

Also author of *Rabbits in Flowers,* 1975, *Genta and the Mountain-Witch* (picture book), 1979, and *Ohyakusho to meushi;* also author or translator of other children's books.

WORK IN PROGRESS: Stories in English and Japanese.

SIDELIGHTS: Masako Matsuno Kobayashi told *CA* that she tries to write about the "real Japan and the real Japanese people. so that my country and people can be known and understood most truly by young foreign readers. . . . I am happy if even one boy or one girl would find anything warm, comforting, encouraging, or useful in my stories," adding, "I would like to write stories for children through my whole life."

AVOCATIONAL INTERESTS: Japanese Noh plays, Japanese tea ceremonies, gardening, reading, music, taking a walk.

BIOGRAPHICAL/CRITICAL SOURCES:

BOOKS

Jidobungku Annual, Kaiseisha, 1983, 1984.

PERIODICALS

Japan Times, September 1, 1963.
Student Times, June 30, 1961.

*   *   *

KOEHLER, Frank
   See PAINE, Lauran (Bosworth)

*   *   *

KOHAK, Erazim V.   1933-

PERSONAL: Born May 21, 1933, in Prague, Czechoslovakia; son of Miloslav (a journalist) and Zdislava (Prochazkova) Kohak; married Frances MacPherson, 1955 (divorced, 1976); married Sheree Dukes, 1981 (divorced, 1989); children: (first marriage) Mary Zdislava, Susan Bozena, Katherine MacPherson. *Education:* Colgate University, B.A., 1954; Yale University, M.A., 1957, Ph.D., 1958. *Religion:* Episcopalian.

ADDRESSES: Home—P.O. Box 355, Jaffrey, N.H. 03452. *Office*—Department of Philosophy, Boston University, 232 Bay State Rd., Boston, Mass. 02215.

CAREER: Gustavus Adolphus College, St. Peter, Minn., assistant professor of philosophy, 1958-60; Boston University, Boston, Mass., assistant professor, 1960-66, associate professor, 1966-71, professor of philosophy, 1971—, chairman of department, 1982-84. Visiting professor of philosophy, Bowling Green State University, 1971. Senior fellow, Institut fuer die Wissenschaften vom Menschen, Vienna, Austria.

MEMBER: American Philosophical Association, Society for Phenomenology and Existential Philosophy, Czechoslovak Society for Arts and Sciences, Husserl Circle, Personalistic Discussion Group (chairperson), Phi Beta Kappa.

WRITINGS:

(Translator and author of introduction) Paul Ricoeur, *Freedom and Nature,* Northwestern University Press, 1966.

(Editor and translator) Thomas G. Masaryk, *Masaryk on Marx,* Bucknell University Press, 1972.

(With Heda Kovaly) *The Victors and the Vanquished,* Horizon Press, 1972.

(With Kovaly) *Na vlastni kuzi,* Sixty-eight Publishers (Toronto), 1972.

Narod v nas, Sixty-eight Publishers, 1978.

Idea and Experience, University of Chicago Press, 1978.

The Embers and the Stars, University of Chicago Press, 1984.

Certorani s Misou, St. Michael Press, 1984.

Krize rozumu a prirozeny svet, Novecesty mysleni (Prague), 1987.

Jan Patocka, University of Chicago Press, 1989.

Contributor to *Commonweal* and *Harper's.* Member of editorial board, *Dissent* and *Philosophical Forum.*

WORK IN PROGRESS: Three Czech Thinkers: Masaryk, Radl, Patocka; a continuing series of philosophic/literary broadcasts for Radio Free Europe Czechoslovak Service.

SIDELIGHTS: Erazim V. Kohak told *CA:* "In a technological age, philosophy, too, tends to become a *techne,* the province of a technician. My aim as a writer is to return it to people. I write of the moral sense of nature to win a place for persons in an increasingly mechanized world, and of the world beyond the powerlines and paved roads, to rediscover nature as the dwelling place of moral subjects, not just a source of raw materials."

*   *   *

KRAMER, Rita 1929-

PERSONAL: Born April 30, 1929, in Detroit, Mich.; daughter of William R. and Sophie (Joffe) Blumenthal; married Yale Kramer (a physician), March 18, 1951; children: Deborah, Mimi. *Education:* University of Chicago, B.A., 1948. *Religion:* Jewish.

ADDRESSES: Agent—Michael Congdon, Don Congdon Associates Inc., 156 Fifth Ave., New York, N.Y. 10010.

CAREER: Free-lance writer, editor, and researcher, 1960—.

WRITINGS:

(With Lee Salk) *How to Raise a Human Being,* Random House, 1969.

Maria Montessori: A Biography, Putnam, 1976, published with a foreword by Anna Freud, Hamish Hamilton, 1989.

Giving Birth: Childbearing in America Today, Contemporary Books, 1978.

In Defense of the Family: Raising Children in America Today, Basic Books, 1983.

At a Tender Age: Violent Youth and Juvenile Justice, Holt, 1988.

Contributor to magazines, including *New York Times Magazine.*

WORK IN PROGRESS: A book on the education of teachers in America today, tentatively scheduled for publication in 1990.

SIDELIGHTS: In 1896, Maria Montessori became the first woman graduate of an Italian medical school; later she turned her talents to reforming the fields of early childhood and special education. "Thanks to Rita Kramer, Montessori's latest biographer," notes *Village Voice* contributor Donald M. Kaplan, "we now have a trustworthy and compelling account of the life and

career of this most brilliant educator, *Maria Montessori: A Biography.*" While Montessori's teaching methods have endured, many aspects of the professor's life have been overlooked; to rectify this, "Kramer has done some marvelous detective work in uncovering obscure facts about Montessori's life, and fitting them together to shed important light on her activities," remarks Barbara Castle in *Best Sellers.* Donald G. MacRae similarly observes in *New Statesman* that "Kramer has written a continually interesting book about Montessori and has not flagged in her researches into a life led in so many countries and an influence so widely exercised." The critic adds that *Maria Montessori* "is, as the author claims, something more than a life: it is also a contribution to intellectual and social history." "Kramer has captured precisely the circumstances of Montessori's achievement," maintains Kaplan. "For Kramer gives us not only a faithful portrait of a truly marvelous woman; Kramer's biography is also a travelogue, a chronicle of the first half of the century and, not least, a history of a social and intellectual struggle to liberate . . . the mind of the child."

Montessori was a natural subject for Kramer to investigate, for the author has been a long time child advocate. Her 1983 work *In Defense of the Family: Raising Children in America Today,* for example, proposes "that parents should and must reclaim for themselves the primary responsibility of nurturing, guiding and teaching their children," describes *Commonweal* contributor Janet Scott Barlow. The critic asserts that Kramer's book "does more than leave its mark; it scores a bullseye. . . . That this particular book will doubtless be viewed in some circles as either radical or reactionary says [something about our times]," adds Barlow. *In Defense of the Family's* suggestion that a parent (preferably the mother) remain at home with the child for at least its first three years has produced controversy among family advocates, researchers, and feminists. *New Republic* contributors Peter and Margaret O'Brien Steinfels, for example, believe that "it is no exaggeration to say that [Kramer's] book is a diatribe against feminism, which is never mentioned except disparagingly." The Steinfels elaborate, noting that "there is not the least acknowledgement that feminists have addressed any real problems"; Judith K. Davison similarly comments in the *New York Times Book Review* that "Kramer simply ignores many realities" about women's motives for remaining in the workplace after giving birth. Jane O'Reilly similarly criticizes Kramer for slighting issues such as the "feminization of poverty." Writing in the *Nation,* she asserts that it is "futile to suggest the solution [to family problems] lies is putting women back in the home—and, by unavoidable implication, keeping men out of it."

Kramer, however, responds in a *People* article that her book is directed toward a specific audience, not all parents. "I'm not prophesying doom for the offspring of every woman who doesn't have a man in the house and has to work to support her kids. . . . I'm addressing myself to the ambivalence of middle-class mothers who have options." *Commentary* contributor Chester E. Finn notes that while Kramer "harbors what many will deem old-fashioned views," *In Defense of the Family* "is not an exercise in finger-wagging or tradition mongering. Rather, Mrs. Kramer's image of the proper ordering of family and society is grounded in her understanding of child development, of human psychology, and of the requisites for the emergence of an autonomous young adult." Finn adds that the author does consider potential objections to her philosophy: "The objective reader will see that Mrs. Kramer has worked her way through these issues and is confident—I think justly so—of her conclusions." In addition, Kramer provides a theoretical basis for her assertions that a home environment with continuous parent involvement is crucial to a child's development; Elizabeth Cleland comments in the *Washington Post* that *In Defense of the Family* "offers 46 pages of detailed notes to reinforce her conclusions." "Rita Kramer suggests that parenthood is not only a noble, but an enobling task," contends Barlow. "She writes that one of the challenges of this task is to be 'tolerant while maintaining your standards.' True to her own advice, she has written a noble book which, like a good parent, provides the confidence of sure expectations and the safety of loving limits."

In another study involving children's issues, *At a Tender Age: Violent Youth and Juvenile Justice,* "Rita Kramer takes you to the edge of the abyss and lets you have a long, terrifying look," describes James Q. Wilson in *Commentary.* "The abyss is Family Court in New York City as it struggles to cope with violent, abused, and disorderly youth. The terror comes not only from seeing the violent ones," elaborates the critic, "but, worse, from seeing the inability of the court to do much except return them to the environment from which they came." Kramer's extensive research into the working of the juvenile justice system led her to encounter such subjects as a twelve-year-old who participated in the gang-rape and beating of an elderly woman and who had previously raped and murdered another; a year later he was released from rehabilitation and was soon spotted near the scene of a similar rape/beating. "Why was so obviously dangerous a boy left at large?," asks *Los Angeles Times Book Review* contributor George Cadwalader. "The answer, says longtime child advocate Rita Kramer in . . . her excellent and thought-provoking study . . ., lies in the 'obsolescent philosophy' behind a system that fails 'either to restrain or retrain the young.' "

This system, writes the author, has been undermined by conflicting court procedures. While the original concept of the juvenile justice system was to act in place of the parents when a child was "at risk," whether from abuse, criminal activity, or delinquency, later directives steered the court into an adversarial relationship where the focus is on the juvenile's "rights" and not his protection or rehabilitation. "[Kramer] has written an angry, unsettling book in which the impressive weight of her nuts-and-bolts reporting is to some extent undermined by an intemperate tone," remarks Susan Jacoby in the *New York Times Book Review.* The critic admits, however, that "anger is an understandable response to a system that fails to protect the community because it gives so much more weight to the age of the criminal than to the nature of the crime." Cadwalader concurs, noting that *At a Tender Age* "provides countless examples to prove that *parens patria,*" the concept of the court acting as parent, "doesn't work. . . . The sobering message implicit in this important book is that we must look instead at all the aspects of our society that contribute to producing [juvenile criminals]." "If a governor or mayor wants to make a lasting difference in New York City," concludes Wilson, "let him go with Mrs. Kramer and peek into the abyss of Family Court, and then set himself the task of reconstituting it along saner lines. If he is not willing to do this he should stop making speeches about crime."

BIOGRAPHICAL/CRITICAL SOURCES:

PERIODICALS

Best Sellers, July, 1976.
Commentary, May, 1983, July, 1988.
Commonweal, August 10, 1984.
Harper's, October, 1969.
Los Angeles Times, March 9, 1983.
Los Angeles Times Book Review, May 15, 1988.
Nation, July 9, 1983.
New Republic, May 16, 1983.

New Statesman, April 14, 1978.
New York Times Book Review, May 8, 1983, April 10, 1988.
People, March 14, 1983.
Times Literary Supplement, May 26, 1978.
Village Voice, August 16, 1976.
Washington Post, February 11, 1983.

—Sketch by Diane Telgen

*   *   *

KREEFT, Peter 1937-

PERSONAL: Surname is pronounced Krayft; born March 16, 1937, in Paterson, N.J.; son of John (an engineer) and Lucy (Comtobad) Kreeft; married Maria Massi, August 18, 1962; children: John, Jennifer, Katherine, Elizabeth. *Education:* Calvin College, A.B., 1959; graduate study at Yale University, 1959-60; Fordham University, M.A., 1961, Ph.D., 1965. *Religion:* Roman Catholic.

ADDRESSES: Home—44 Davis Ave., West Newton, Mass. 02165. *Office*—Department of Philosophy, Boston College, Chestnut Hill, Mass., 02167.

CAREER: Villanova University, Villanova, Pa., instructor in philosophy, 1961-65; Boston College, Chestnut Hill, Mass., assistant professor, 1965-69, associate professor of philosophy, 1969—.

AWARDS, HONORS: Woodrow Wilson fellowship, 1959-60; Danforth fellowship, 1966-67; *Love Is Stronger Than Death* was nominated for the American Book Award in the religion/inspirational category, 1980.

WRITINGS:

C.S. Lewis, Eerdmans, 1969, published as *C. S. Lewis: A Critical Essay,* Christendom College Press, 1988.
Love Is Stronger Than Death, Harper, 1979.
Heaven, the Heart's Deepest Longing, Harper, 1980.
Everything You Ever Wanted to Know about Heaven . . . but Never Dreamed of Asking, Harper, 1982.
Between Heaven and Hell, Inter-Varsity Press, 1982.
The Unaborted Socrates, Inter-Varsity Press, 1983.
The Best Things in Life, Inter-Varsity Press, 1984.
Yes or No?: Straight Answers to Tough Questions about Christianity, Servant Publications, 1984.
(With Richard Purtill and Michael MacDonald) *Philosophical Questions,* Prentice-Hall, 1984.
Prayer: The Great Conversation, Servant Publications, 1985.
The Source, Thomas Nelson, 1985.
For Heaven's Sake, Thomas Nelson, 1986.
Making Sense Out of Suffering, Servant Publications, 1986.
Socrates Meets Jesus, Inter-Varsity Press, 1987.
A Turn of the Clock, Ignatius Press, 1987.
Spiritual Journeys, Daughters of St. Paul, 1987.
The Reality of God's Love, Servant Publications, 1988.
Fundamentals of the Faith, Ignatius Press, 1988.
Letters to Jesus, Ignatius Press, 1989.
Three Philosophies of Life, Ignatius Press, 1989.

WORK IN PROGRESS: An introduction to St. Thomas Aquinas.

SIDELIGHTS: Peter Kreeft writes that his main interests are philosophy in literature, philosophy of religion, East-West dialogue, mysticism, and existentialism. His books sometimes dramatize both sides of a moral issue. For instance, *The Unaborted Socrates* is an imaginary dialogue between Socrates and a doctor, a lawyer, and a psychiatrist in an abortion clinic. Christian writer C. S. Lewis, statesman John F. Kennedy, and philosopher Aldous Huxley—who in real life all died on the same afternoon in 1963—meet in *Between Heaven and Hell* to discuss three world views (theism, humanism, and pantheism). And in *Socrates Meets Jesus,* Kreeft places the philosopher in Harvard Divinity School to dramatize a conversion through rational argument.

*   *   *

KREJCI, Jaroslav 1916-

PERSONAL: Surname rhymes with "Strachey"; born February 13, 1916, in Czechoslovakia; son of Jaroslav (a civil servant) and Zdenka (Dudova) Krejci; married Anna Cerna (a principal lecturer at Preston Polytechnic), May 11, 1940. *Education:* Charles University, Prague, D.Jur., 1945.

ADDRESSES: Office—Lonsdale College, University of Lancaster, Lancaster, England.

CAREER: State Planning Office, Prague, Czechoslovakia, secretary to chairman, 1945-48, head of department of national income, 1948-50; State Bank, Prague, research worker, 1950-53; Czechoslovak Academy of Sciences, Prague, research worker, 1968; University of Lancaster, Lancaster, England, lecturer in comparative social and cultural analysis, 1970-76, professor in School of European Studies, 1976-83, professor emeritus, 1983—. External associate professor, Graduate School of Political and Social Sciences, Prague, 1948-50, and Technological University, Prague, 1950-52; member of advisory body for economic analysis for Deputy Prime Minister, Prague, 1968.

MEMBER: International PEN, National Association of Soviet and East European Studies, University Association for Contemporary European Studies, Czechoslovak Society of Arts and Sciences.

AWARDS, HONORS: Received award for participation in Czech resistance movement during World War II.

WRITINGS:

Duchodove rozvrstveni (title means "Income Distribution"), [Prague], 1947.
Uvod do planovaneho hospodarstvi (title means "Introduction to the Planned Economy"), [Prague], 1949.
Volkseinkommensvergleich: Osterreich CSSR (title means "National Income Comparison: Austria-Czechoslovakia"),

Verlag des Osterreichischen Gewerkschaftsbundes (Vienna), 1969.
Social Change and Stratification in Postwar Czechoslovakia, Columbia University Press, 1972.
Social Structure in Divided Germany, St. Martin's, 1976.
(Editor) *Sozialdemokratie und Systemwandel,* Dietz, 1978.
(With V. Velimsky) *Ethnic and Political Nations in Europe,* St. Martin's, 1981.
National Income and Outlay in Czechoslovakia, Poland and Yugoslavia, St. Martin's, 1982.
Great Revolutions Compared, St. Martin's, 1983.
Before the European Challenge: The Great Civilizations of Asia and the Middle East, State University of New York Press, 1990.
Czechoslovakia at the Crossroads of European History, I. B. Tauris (London), 1990.

CONTRIBUTOR

M. S. Archer and L. S. Giner, editors, *Ethnic Problems in Contemporary Europe,* Routledge & Kegan Paul, 1978.
P. H. Merkl and Ninian Smart, editors, *Religion and Politics in the Modern World,* New York University Press, 1983.
L. Matejka and B. Stolz, editors, *Cross Currents,* Michigan Slavic Publications, 1983.
M. C. Kaser and E. A. Radice, editors, *The Economic History of Eastern Europe,* Clarendon Press, 1986.
A. Shtromas and M. A. Kaplan, editors, *The Soviet Union and the Challenge of the Future,* Paragon, 1989.
A. Graham and A. Sowden, editors, *Comparative Economic Performance,* Methuen, 1990.
L. Cheles, R. Ferguson, and M. Vaughan, editors, *Neo-Fascism in Europe,* Longman, 1990.

Contributor to *Review of Income and Wealth, Soviet Studies, Sociological Analysis, Journal of Religious History, Religion, History of European Ideas, Promeny, Journal of Communist Studies, Revue politique et parliamentaire,* and other periodicals.

WORK IN PROGRESS: Civilization and Social Structure.

SIDELIGHTS: Jaroslav Krejci spent the years from 1954-60 in a labor camp in Czechoslovakia.

*   *   *

KYLE, Duncan
See BROXHOLME, John Franklin

L

LaCOCQUE, Andre (Marie) 1927-

PERSONAL: Surname is pronounced La-*koke;* born October 26, 1927, in Liege, Belgium; came to the United States, 1966, naturalized citizen, 1983; son of Yehudah Arieh and Jeanne Henriette (Lurkin) LaCocque; married Claire Tournay (a professor of French), July 30, 1949; children: Michel, Pierre-Emmanuel, Elisabeth. *Education:* Protestant Theological Seminary, Montpellier, France, B.D., 1949; University of Strasbourg, D.Litt., 1957, D.Th., 1959.

ADDRESSES: Home—5555 South Everett, Chicago, Ill. 60637. *Office*—Department of Old Testament, Chicago Theological Seminary, 5757 University Ave., Chicago, Ill. 60637.

CAREER: Ordained minister of Reformed Church of Belgium, 1954; worked as pastor in France, 1955-57; Protestant Theological Seminary, Brussels, Belgium, professor of Old Testament, 1957-69; Chicago Theological Seminary, Chicago, Ill., professor of Old Testament and director of Jewish-Christian Studies Center, 1966—. Visiting professor at Spertus College of Judaica, 1969-73. *Military service:* Belgian Army, 1953-54; served as chaplain.

MEMBER: Society of Biblical Literature (president of Middle-West section, 1973-75), Council for Studies in Religion, American Academy of Religion.

AWARDS, HONORS: Award from American Jewish Committee, 1972, for service as co-director of the National Interreligious Task Force on Soviet Jewry; grant from the F.N.R.S., Belgium, 1976; grant from the F.N.S.R.S., Switzerland, 1979; grant from the American Theological Society, 1984.

WRITINGS:

Pentecost I: Proclamation, Fortress, 1975.
But as for Me: The Question of Election in the Life of God's People Today, John Knox, 1979.
THe Book of Daniel, John Knox, 1979.
(With son, Pierre-Emmanuel LaCocque) *The Jonah Complex,* John Knox, 1981.
(Contributor and editor with others) *Commentaire de l'Ancien Testament,* Labor et Fides (Geneva), 1981.
Daniel et son temps, Labor et Fides, 1983, translation by the author published as *Daniel in His Time,* University of South Carolina Press, 1988.

Jonah: The Prophet and the Complex, University of South Carolina Press, 1990.
The Feminine Unconventional in Israel's Tradition, Fortress, 1990.

SIDELIGHTS: Andre LaCocque told *CA:* "I became deeply concerned about the plight of the Jews during World War II, when my family sheltered Jews from the Nazis. Out of this experience I sought answers to the question 'Why should the Jews suffer?,' and I have researched Hebrew history emerging from the Old Testament from Rabbinic and pseudepigraphon literature.

"This first incentive has given an existential dimension to my scholarly quest. It is not foreign to my interest in the Jewish apocalyptic movement. Also, *The Jonah Complex* or *The Feminine Unconventional* are attempts at confronting again historic Israel's identity and destiny as they are mirrored in these ironic stories of the Bible."

*   *   *

LANDAU, Sol 1920-

PERSONAL: Born June 21, 1920, in Berlin, Germany; immigrated to the United States, 1940; naturalized U.S. citizen; son of Ezekiel (a rabbi) and Helene (Grynberg) Landau; married Gabriela Mayer, January 14, 1951; children: Ezra M., Tamara A. *Education:* Brooklyn College (now of the City University of New York), B.A., 1949; New York University, M.A., 1958; Jewish Theological Seminary, M.H.L. and Rabbi, 1951; Florida State University, Ph.D., 1977.

CAREER: Rabbi of Jewish congregations in Whitestone, N.Y., 1952-56, Cleveland, Ohio, 1956-60, 1963-65, and Wilmette, Ill., 1960-63; Beth David Congregation, Miami, Fla., rabbi, 1965-81, rabbi emeritus, 1981—; Midlife Service Foundation, Inc., Miami, Fla., president, 1981—. Adjutant professor of psychology, University of Miami, 1982-85. Chaplain, Homestead Air Force Base, 1974-77. President and founding member, Dade County Mental Health Association, 1973-81; president, Dade County Youth Advisory Board. Member of board of directors, Dropsie University. *Military service:* U.S. Army, 1942-45.

MEMBER: American Association of University Professors, National Academy of Adult Jewish Studies (member of board of directors), American Association of Counseling and Development,

Jewish Academy of Arts and Sciences (fellow), Orthopsychiatric Association, Adult Education Association, Jewish War Veterans of America (national deputy chairman), Rabbinical Assembly (president of Southeast Region), Rabbinical Association of Greater Miami (president, 1976-77, 1980-81).

AWARDS, HONORS: Liberation Award, Israel, 1967; Welfare Federation Council award, 1976; recipient of Jerusalem award, City of Miami citation, Dade County Mental Health Association award, and Rabbinic Community award.

WRITINGS:

Christian-Jewish Relations, Pageant, 1958.
Length of Our Days, Bloch Publishing, 1960.
Bridging Two Worlds (biography of Landau's father), J. David, 1969.
Turning Points, New Horizons Press, 1985.

Contributor to *Jewish Spectator, Adult Jewish Education, Torch, National Jewish Monthly,* and *United Synagogue Review.**

* * *

La PALOMBARA, Joseph 1925-

PERSONAL: Born May 18, 1925, in Chicago, Ill.; son of Louis (a tailor) and Helen (Teutonico) La Palombara; married Lyda Mae Ecke, June 22, 1947 (divorced); married Constance Ada Bezer, June, 1971; children: (first marriage) Richard Dean, David D., Susan Dee. *Education:* University of Illinois, A.B., 1947, M.A., 1950; Princeton University, M.A., 1952, Ph.D., 1954; University of Rome, graduate study, 1952-53. *Politics:* Democrat.

ADDRESSES: Home—8 Reservoir St., New Haven, Conn. 06511. *Office*—Department of Political Science, Yale University, New Haven, Conn. 06520.

CAREER: Oregon State College (now University), Corvallis, 1949-50, began as instructor, became assistant professor of political science; Princeton University, Princeton, N.J., instructor in politics, 1952; Michigan State University, East Lansing, assistant professor, 1953-56, associate professor, 1956-58, professor of political science and chairman of department, 1958-64; Yale University, New Haven, Conn., professor of political science, 1964-65, Arnold Wolfers Professor of Political Science, 1965—, chairman of department, 1974-78, 1982-84. Visiting professor of political science, University of Florence, Italy, 1957-58, University of California, Berkeley, 1962, and Columbia University, 1965-66.

Director of Michigan Citizenship Clearing House, 1955; member of staff, Social Science Research Council, 1966-73; senior research associate, Conference Board of New York, 1975-80; cultural attache and First Secretary, U.S. Embassy, Rome, Italy, 1980-81. Member of executive committee, Inter-University Consortium on Political Research, 1968-70; chairman of Western European foreign area fellowship program, Social Science Research Council/American Council of Learned Societies, 1972-76. Consultant to Federal Civil Defense Agency, 1956, Carnegie Corp., 1959, Brookings Institution, 1962, Ford Foundation, 1965-74, Twentieth-Century Fund, 1965-69, Agency for International Development, 1967-68, Foreign Service Institute, 1968-72, Educational Testing Service, 1970-76, and to several major U.S. corporations, 1975—.

MEMBER: International Political Science Association, American Political Science Association (vice-president, 1977-78), American Society for Public Administration, Society for Italian

Historical Studies, Italian Social Science Association, Societa Italiana di Studi Elettori, Phi Beta Kappa, Phi Kappa Phi, Phi Eta Sigma.

AWARDS, HONORS: Center for Advanced Study in the Behavioral Sciences fellow, 1961-62; Rockefeller fellow, 1963-64; Order of Merit, Republic of Italy, 1964; M.A., Yale University, 1964; Ford Foundation faculty fellow, 1969; Guggenheim fellow, 1971-72; named Knight Commander, Order of Merit, Republic of Italy, 1974; Guido Dorso Prize (Italy), 1985.

WRITINGS:

The Initiative and Referendum in Oregon, Oregon State College Press, 1950.
The Italian Labor Movement: Problems and Prospects, Cornell University Press, 1957.
Guide to Michigan Politics, Michigan State University, 1960.
(Co-editor) *Elezioni e comportamento politico in Italia,* Comunita, 1962.
Bureaucracy and Political Development, Princeton University Press, 1963.
Interest Groups in Italian Politics, Princeton University Press, 1964.
Italy: The Politics of Planning, Syracuse University Press, 1966.
(Editor with Myron Weiner) *Political Parties and Political Development,* Princeton University Press, 1966.
(With others) *Crises and Sequences in Political Development,* Princeton University Press, 1971.
Politics within Nations, Prentice-Hall, 1974.
(With Stephen Blank) *Multinational Corporations and National Elites,* Conference Board of New York, 1976.
(With Blank) *Multinational Corporations in Comparative Perspective,* Conference Board of New York, 1977.
(With Blank) *Multinational Corporations and Developing Countries,* Conference Board of New York, 1979.
(With others) *Assessing the Political Environment,* Conference Board of New York, 1980.
Democracy, Italian Style, Yale University Press, 1987.

CONTRIBUTOR

D.S. Piper and R.T. Cole, editors, *Post-Primary Education and Political and Economic Development,* Duke University Press, 1964.
L. Pyle and S. Verba, editors, *Political Culture and Political Development,* Princeton University Press, 1965.
H. Penniman, editor, *Italy at the Polls: 1976,* American Enterprise Institute for Public Policy Research, 1976.
A. Ranney and G. Sartori, editors, *Eurocommunism: The Italian Case,* American Enterprise Institute for Public Policy Research, 1978.
Pyle and Verba, editors, *The Citizen and Politics,* Greylock Press, 1978.
Penniman, editor, *Italy at the Polls: 1979,* American Enterprise Institute for Public Policy Research, 1981.
Penniman, editor, *Italy at the Polls: 1983,* American Enterprise Institute for Public Policy Research/Duke University Press, 1986.
Luigi Graziano, editor, *La scienza politica in Italia,* Franco Angeli (Milan), 1986.

OTHER

Contributor to numerous periodicals, including *Nation, Yale Review, Corriere della sera* (Milan), *La Repubblica* (Rome), *Times Literary Supplement, World Politics,* and *Pacific Spectator.*

WORK IN PROGRESS: Politics and the Multinational Corporation.

SIDELIGHTS: Joseph La Palombara has visited all of Europe, Japan, Vietnam, the Philippines, India, Pakistan, Israel, Mexico, and Brazil. *Avocational interests:* Book collecting, fishing.

* * *

LARSON, Calvin J(ames) 1933-

PERSONAL: Born September 25, 1933, in Oakland, Calif.; married wife, Edith S., February 6, 1959; children: Erik James, Adam Arthur. *Education:* University of California, Berkeley, B.A., 1956; San Jose State College (now California State University), M.S., 1960; University of Oregon, Ph.D., 1965.

ADDRESSES: Office—Department of Sociology, University of Massachusetts, Boston, Mass. 02125.

CAREER: Purdue University, Lafayette, Ind., assistant professor of sociology, 1965-70; University of Vermont, Burlington, associate professor, 1970-71; University of Massachusetts, Boston, associate professor of sociology, 1971—. *Military service:* U.S. Naval Reserve, 1956-58.

MEMBER: American Sociological Association.

WRITINGS:

(Editor with Philo Wasburn) *Power, Participation, and Ideology,* McKay, 1968.
(Editor with Jeffrey Hadden and Louis Massotti) *Metropolis in Crisis,* F. E. Peacock, 1971.
Major Themes in Sociological Theory, McKay, 1973.
(With Stan R. Nikkel) *Urban Problems: Perspectives on Corporations, Governments, and Cities,* Allyn & Bacon, 1979.
Crime, Justice, and Society, General Hall, 1984.
Sociological Theory: From the Enlightenment to the Present, General Hall, 1987.

Contributor to periodicals.

* * *

LAURENTI, Joseph L(ucian) 1931-

PERSONAL: Born December 10, 1931, in Hesperange, Luxembourg; naturalized U.S. citizen in 1953; son of Ernest (a lawyer) and Angelina (Dal Canton) Laurenti; married A(lice) Luellen Watson, June 10, 1967. *Education:* University of Illinois, B.A. (cum laude), 1958, M.A., 1959; University of Missouri, Ph.D., 1962. *Politics:* Democrat. *Religion:* Roman Catholic.

ADDRESSES: Office—Department of Spanish and Italian, Illinois State University, Normal, Ill. 61761.

CAREER: University of Illinois (now University of Illinois at Urbana-Champaign), Urbana, instructor in Spanish, 1958-59; University of Missouri—Columbia, instructor in Spanish, 1959-62; Illinois State University, Normal, assistant professor, 1962-63, associate professor, 1963-66, professor of Spanish and Italian, 1966—. *Military service:* U.S. Army, Intelligence, 1952-54.

MEMBER: International Association of Hispanists, International Association of Philologists, Modern Language Association of America, American Association of University Professors, American Association of Teachers of Spanish and Portuguese, Asociacion de Bibliografia Espanola (life member), Asosciacion de Cervantistas (life member), Midwest Modern Language Association, Illinois Association of Teachers of Modern Languages, Sigma Delta Pi (president of University of Illinois chapter, 1958-59).

WRITINGS:

Lazarillo de Tormes: Estudio critico de la segunda parte de Juan de Luna (title means "Lazarillo de Tormes: A Critical Study of the Second Part of Juan de Luna"), Studium, 1965.
Ensayo de una bibliografia de la novela picaresca espanola (title means "A Bibliographic Essay of the Spanish Picaresque Novel"), Consejo Superior de Investigaciones Cientificas, 1968.
Estudios sobre la novela picaresca espanola (title means "Studies in the Spanish Picaresque Novel"), Consejo Superior de Investigaciones Cientificas, 1970.
Los prologos en las novelas picarescas espanolas (title means "Critical Prefaces in the Spanish Picaresque Novel"), Castalia, 1971.
(With Alberto Porqueras Mayo) *Ensayo bibliografico del prologo en la literatura* (title means "A Bibliographic Essay of the Prologue in Literature"), Consejo Superior de Investigaciones Cientificas, 1971.
(With Joseph Siracusa) *Relaciones literarias entre Espana e Italia* (title means "Literary Relations between Spain and Italy"), G. K. Hall, 1972.
Bibliografia de la literature picaresca: Desde sus origenes hasta el presente, AMS Press, 1973, translation published as *A Critical Bibliography of Picaresque Literature,* G. K. Hall, 1973, revised edition published as *A Bibliography of Picaresque Literature from Its Origin to the Present,* AMS Press, 1981.
(With Siracusa) *The World of Federico Garcia Lorca,* Scarecrow, 1974.
(Editor with Mayo) *Antonio de Guevara en la biblioteca de la universidad de Illinois,* S.A. Impresores, 1974.
The Spanish Golden Age (1472-1700), G. K. Hall, 1979.
A Catalog of Rare Books in the Library of the University of Illinois and in Selected North American Libraries, G. K. Hall, 1979.
A Catalog of Spanish Rare Books (1701-1974) in the Library of the University of Illinois and in Selected North American Libraries, Peter Lang, 1984.
Hispanic Rare Books of the Golden Age (1470-1699) in the Newberry Library of Chicago and in Selected North American Libraries, Peter Lang, 1989.
(Editor with Vern Williamsen) *Varia hispanica estudios en los siglos de oro y literature moderna: Homenage a Alberto Porqueras Mayo,* Edition Reichenberger, 1989.

Contributor of articles and reviews to journals in France, Spain, Italy, Germany, Mexico, and United States. Editorial consultant to *Publications of Modern Language Association,* 1972—.

SIDELIGHTS: Joseph L. Laurenti told *CA:* "I believe that in this world there is something that is worth more than the joys derived from material possessions, better than fortunes, better than health itself, and that is the devotion to the arts and sciences. This has always been my motivation throughout life."

* * *

LEARY, William G(ordon) 1915-

PERSONAL: Born March 26, 1915, in Minneapolis, Minn.; son of Errol W. and Lillian (Giles) Leary; married Celia Graves (a reading specialist), June 10, 1940; children: Peter C., Jan E. (Mrs. Donald M. Burland). *Education:* University of California, Los Angeles, A.B., 1936, M.A., 1938; Stanford University, Ph.D., 1953. *Politics:* Democrat. *Religion:* None.

ADDRESSES: Home—55 Crest Dr., La Selva Beach, Calif. 95076. *Office*—Department of English, California State University, Los Angeles, Calif. 90032.

CAREER: Kern County Union High School, Bakersfield, Calif., teacher of English, 1938-41; University of Washington, Seattle, associate, 1941-42; California State Polytechnic University, San Luis Obispo, instructor, 1947-48, assistant professor, 1948-52; California State University, Los Angeles, associate professor, 1953-57, professor of English, 1957-78, emeritus professor, 1978—, associate dean of instruction, 1953-57. Visiting professor at Stanford University, summer, 1964; fellow in humanities at Educational Testing Service, summer, 1963. *Military service:* U.S. Navy, 1942-46; became lieutenant senior grade.

AWARDS, HONORS: James Nelson Raymond scholarship from Law School of University of Chicago, 1946, 1947; outstanding professor award from California State University, Los Angeles, 1965.

WRITINGS:

(With James Steel Smith) *Think Before You Write,* Harcourt, 1951.
(With Smith) *Thought and Statement,* Harcourt, 1955, 3rd edition (with Richard Blakeslee), 1969.
(With Lou LaBrant, Donald A. Bird, and Margaret Painter) *Your Language,* McGraw, Book Five, 1960, Book Six, 1962.
(Editor with Edgar H. Knapp) *Ideas and Patterns in Literature,* four volumes, Harcourt, 1970.
(With Wallace Graves) *From Word to Story,* Harcourt, 1971.
The World of Macbeth, Harper, 1975.
(Contributor) Edward Quinn, editor, *How to Read Shakespearean Tragedy,* Harper, 1978.
Shakespeare Plain: The Making and Performing of Shakespeare's Plays, McGraw, 1977.

Book reviewer and columnist for *Westwood Scene,* 1939, and *San Luis Obispo Telegram-Tribune,* 1948-50. Contributor to journals, including *Sewanee Review, Kenyan Review, Shenandoah, South Atlantic Quarterly, Southwest Review,* and *Western American Literature.*

WORK IN PROGRESS: A series of articles on Jean Stafford.

SIDELIGHTS: William G. Leary once told *CA:* "All of my books may be described as the direct result of the teacher's itch. I have spent nearly forty years attempting to devise strategies that will take the innocent, ignorant, unwary, and often recalcitrant student by surprise and teach him something about language and literature. When I succeed, it comes to him as both a surprise and a delight. My books are simply an effort to find a larger audience than the captive one I had in my own classrooms." Leary added that love of great paintings and architecture "has led to a helpless addiction—travel in Europe." He has managed to live nearly three full years in most of the countries of western Europe and said, "I stare, like Keats's explorer, with a wild surmise."

Leary recently told *CA:* "The first eighteen months following my retirement from the classroom were spent raising a grandson and a house—both 'firsts.' Discovering that I am much more at home with words than with woods, I'm starting on another book, but am leaving houses strictly alone."

Le DUC, Don R(aymond) 1933-

PERSONAL: Born April 7, 1933, in South Milwaukee, Wis.; son of Raymond Joseph (an engineer) and Roberta (Jones) Le Duc; married Alice Marie Pranica, October 24, 1959; children: Paul, Marie. *Education:* University of Wisconsin, B.A., 1959, Ph.D., 1970; Marquette University, J.D., 1962. *Politics:* Republican. *Religion:* Roman Catholic.

ADDRESSES: Home—1800 Fairhaven Dr., Cedarburg, Wis. 53012. *Office*— Department of Mass Communications, University of Wisconsin—Milwaukee, Milwaukee, Wis. 53201.

CAREER: Admitted to the Bar of Wisconsin, 1960, and the Bar of U.S. Supreme Court, 1969; Arnold, Murray & O'Neill (law firm), Milwaukee, Wis., 1962-63; private law practice in Green Bay, Wis., 1964-68; State of Wisconsin, Wisconsin Department of Insurance, Madison, chief counsel, 1967-69; University of Maryland, College Park, Md., assistant professor of communications law, 1970-71; Ohio State University, Athens, Ohio, associate professor, 1971-73; University of Wisconsin—Madison, Madison, associate professor, 1973-76, professor, 1976-84, chairman of West European studies program, 1979-84; University of Alabama, Tuscaloosa, Ala., Reagan professor of telecommunications and chairman of doctoral program, 1984-86; University of Wisconsin—Milwaukee, senior scholar, 1986—. Director of Comparative Telecommunications Research Center, Madison, 1974—. Ford Foundation fellow in comparative law, University of Wisconsin—Madison, 1963-64. Chief counsel, Wisconsin Governor's Task Force on Telecommunications, 1971-72; member of cable television advisory committee, Federal Communications Committee, 1972-76. *Military service:* U.S.Army, Counter Intelligence Corps, special agent, 1954-57.

MEMBER: International Institute of Communication, Federal Communications Bar Association, Broadcast Education Association, Wisconsin Bar Association.

AWARDS, HONORS: Research grant from Ohio State University, 1971; Wisconsin Alumni Research Foundation grants, 1974-75, 1977, 1979; American Philosophical Society grant, 1975, 1977; NATO fellowship, 1978; Council of European Studies research fellowship, 1979.

WRITINGS:

Cable Television and the FCC: A Crisis in Media Control, Temple University Press, 1973.
(Editor) *Issues in Broadcast Regulation,* Broadcast Education Association, 1974.
Beyond Broadcasting: Patterns in Policy and Law, Longman, 1987.
(With Dwight Teeter) *Law of Mass Communications,* Foundation Press, 1988.

Contributor to journals. Editor, *Client* (broadcast regulations newsletter), 1972-77; associate editor of *Journal of Broadcasting,* 1974—, and *Journal of Communication,* 1978—.

WORK IN PROGRESS: Comparative analysis of world broadcast systems; research on censorship in national and international communications; international and national direct broadcast satellite policies.

SIDELIGHTS: "I began writing plays in grade school, short stories in high school and novels in college," Don R. Le Duc told *CA.* "I still write fiction whenever I can and someday—. But for the present, my scholarly writing has to claim most of my attention and although I miss the flights of fancy that fiction allows, I can console myself with the knowledge that there is no more exciting area of scholarship today than that in which I am engaged, exploring the fascinating linkages between the processes of communication and law."

* * *

LEE, Dennis (Beynon) 1939-

PERSONAL: Born August 31, 1939, in Toronto, Ontario, Canada; son of Walter and Louise (Garbutt) Lee; married Donna Youngblut, June 24, 1962 (divorced); married Susan Perly, October 7, 1985; children: (first marriage) two daughters, one son. *Education:* University of Toronto, B.A., 1962, M.A., 1964.

ADDRESSES: Agent—MGA, 10 St. Mary's St., Suite 510, Toronto, Ontario, Canada M4Y 1P9.

CAREER: Writer. University of Toronto, Victoria College, Toronto, Ontario, lecturer in English, 1964-67; Rochdale College (experimental institution), Toronto, self-described "research person," 1967-69; House of Anansi Press, Toronto, co-founder and editor, 1967-72. Editorial consultant, Macmillan of Canada, 1973-78; poetry editor, McClelland & Stewart, 1981-84. Lyricist for television series, "Fraggle Rock," 1982-86.

AWARDS, HONORS: Governor-General's Award for Poetry, 1972, for *Civil Elegies;* Independent Order of Daughters of the Empire award, 1974; Canadian Association of Children's Librarians, Best Book Medals, 1974 and 1977, and English Medal, 1975, for *Alligator Pie;* named to Hans Christian Andersen Honour List and recipient of Canadian Library Association award, both 1976, both for *Alligator Pie;* Philips Information Systems Literary Award, 1984; Vicky Metcalf Award, Canadian Authors' Association, 1986, for body of work for children.

WRITINGS:

POETRY

Kingdom of Absence, House of Anansi, 1967.
Civil Elegies, House of Anansi, 1968, revised edition published as *Civil Elegies and Other Poems,* 1972.
Wiggle to the Laundromat (juvenile), New Press, 1970.
Alligator Pie (juvenile), Macmillan (Toronto), 1974, Houghton, 1975.
Nicholas Knock and Other People (juvenile; also see below), Macmillan, 1974, Houghton, 1975.
The Death of Harold Ladoo, Kanchenjunga Press, 1976.
Garbage Delight (juvenile), Macmillan, 1977, Houghton, 1978.
The Gods (also see below), McClelland & Stewart, 1979.
Jelly Belly (juvenile), Macmillan, 1983.
The Dennis Lee Big Book (anthology), Macmillan, 1985.
The Difficulty of Living on Other Planets (some poems already appeared in *Nicholas Knock and Other People* and *The Gods*), Macmillan, 1987.

OTHER

(Co-editor) *The University Game* (essays), House of Anansi, 1968.
(Editor) *T.O. Now: The Young Toronto Poets* (poetry anthology), House of Anansi, 1968.
Savage Fields: An Essay in Cosmology and Literature, House of Anansi, 1977.
The Ordinary Bath (juvenile), McClelland & Stewart, 1977.
Lizzy's Lion (juvenile), Stoddart, 1984.
(Editor and author of introduction) *New Canadian Poets, 1970-1985* (poetry anthology), McClelland & Stewart, 1985.

Also co-editor of two high school poetry anthologies.

WORK IN PROGRESS: Nightwatch, for McClelland & Stewart.

SIDELIGHTS: In a speech delivered at the 1975 Loughborough Conference in Toronto and reprinted in *Canadian Children's Literature,* Canadian author Dennis Lee examines the way his attitude toward children's verse evolved. As an adult and parent, he contemplates Mother Goose and discovers: "The nursery rhymes I love . . . are necessarily exotic. . . . But they were in no way exotic to the people who first devised them and chanted them. . . . The air of far-off charm and simpler pastoral life which now hangs over Mother Goose was in no way a part of those rhymes' initial existence. . . . The people who told nursery rhymes for centuries would be totally boggled if they could suddenly experience them the way children do here and now, as a collection of references to things they never see or do, to places they have never heard of and may never visit, told in words they will sometimes meet only in those verses."

Out of concern that his own children were learning that "the imagination leads always and only to the holy city of elsewhere," Lee decided to build his imaginary "city" from the language of familiar objects—elements of contemporary life made extraordinary by their unique use and sound in verse. Maintaining that "you are poorer if you never find your own time and place speaking words of their own," he believes the "fire hydrants and hockey sticks" of today can be the stuff of nursery rhymes, just as the curds and whey were for children of a previous time. Thus, he says, "to look for living nursery rhymes in the hockey-sticks and high-rises that [children know] first-hand [is not] to go on a chauvinistic trip, nor to wallow in a fad of trendy relevance. It [is] nothing but a rediscovery of what Mother Goose [has been] about for centuries."

Lee's poetic narratives, tongue-twisters, and riddles have been compared to the nonsense verse of Lewis Carroll and A. A. Milne. Lee, however, emphasizes the here-and-now objects of daily life in his work—things children may or may not recognize. Canadian places, history, politics, and colloquial diction, as well as purely invented words, all play a part in his pieces. Many critics feel the readability and repeatability of the poems—rather than references to far-away places—are what fascinates young children. As Betsy English writes in *In Review: Canadian Books for Children,* the strong rhythms, rhymes, and other sound devices in Lee's work produce "a sense of gaiety, an appeal that shouts for reading aloud."

MEDIA ADAPTATIONS: Co-author, with Jim Henson, of story adapted by Terry Jones for the screenplay of the Henson Associates Inc./Lucasfilm Ltd. production, "Labyrinth," 1985.

BIOGRAPHICAL/CRITICAL SOURCES:

PERIODICALS

Canadian Children's Literature, Number 4, 1976.
In Review: Canadian Books for Children, spring, 1971, winter, 1975.

* * *

LEE, Pali Jae 1929-
(Polly Jae Lee)

PERSONAL: Original name Polly Jae Lee; name legally changed in 1987; born November 26, 1929, in Toledo, Ohio; daughter of Jonathan Wheeler Stead (an electrical engineer) and Ona (a religious education director; maiden name, Grunder) Stead Gardiner; married Richard Lee (a clinical psychologist), April 7, 1945 (divorced, 1976); married John K. Willis, May 1, 1978; children: (first marriage) Lani Kay (original name Mary Kay; Mrs. Reginald Francis Lee); Karin Lin (Mrs. Benton Taylor Robinson), Ona Gwynne (Mrs. Sanford Yee), Laurie Brett (Mrs. Carlos Lam), Robin Lou (Mrs. Dennis Michael Halbert). *Education:* Attended University of Hawaii, 1944-46, and Michigan State University, 1971-72. *Religion:* "Unity."

ADDRESSES: Home—4462 Sierra Dr., Honolulu, Hawaii 96816. *Office*—Night Rainbow Publishing Co., P.O. Box 10706, Honolulu, Hawaii 96816.

CAREER: Ohio State University, Columbus, counselor, 1958-59; Annie Whittemyer Home (orphanage), Davenport, Iowa, writer of technical manuals, 1960; Grand Rapids Public Library, Grand Rapids, Mich., technical processor, 1960-61; Waterford Library, Waterford, Mich., director, 1962-65; Pontiac Public Library, Pontiac, Mich., acquisition librarian, 1965-68, reference librarian, 1968-70, director of East Side branch, 1970-71; free-lance writer, 1972-74; Bishop Museum, Honolulu, Hawaii, member of department of anthropology, 1975-77; free-lance writer, 1977-87; Night Rainbow Publishing Co., Honolulu, founder and president, 1987—. Member, Michigan Area Committee of American Friends Service Committee, 1965-68, Greater Detroit Area M.S. board, 1970-73, and Oakland County M.S. board, 1973. Vice-president, Friends of the Library, Pontiac, Mich., 1970-71.

MEMBER: Clergy and Laymen Concerned about Vietnam, Another Mother for Peace, Michigan Library Association, Fellowship of Reconciliation, American Folklore Society.

WRITINGS:

UNDER NAME POLLY JAE LEE

History of American Wine Making, Ohio Wholesale Wine Dealers, 1959.
House Parents' Manual, State of Iowa, 1960.
Giant: The Pictorial History of the Human Colossus, A. S. Barnes, 1970.
Twentieth-Century Saints, Exposition Press, 1971.
Mary Dyer: Child of Light, Friends General Conference, 1971.
Kane'ohe: History of Change, Bishop Museum Press, 1976, 2nd edition, 1980.
Tales from the Night Rainbow, Paia-Kapela-Willis 'Ohana, 1986, 4th edition, Night Rainbow Publishing, 1989.
Mo'olelo ona Pohukaina, Night Rainbow Publishing, 1986.

OTHER

Also author of plays and pageants for local schools and churches, and of short stories for children.

WORK IN PROGRESS: View from a Hawaiian Pathway; Tutu's Tales, a children's book of Hawaiian history.

SIDELIGHTS: Pali Jae Lee told *CA:* "Since I took the job of writing authentic Hawaiian history I have been riding a time elevator. More of my time has been spent in periods from 1200 A.D. to 1790 A.D. than in today's world; sometimes it's rapid trips back and forth. More and more I feel more at home in the early periods and less and less in what is termed 'the modern technological society.'"

AVOCATIONAL INTERESTS: Ecology, Hawaiian history, genealogy.

*   *   *

LEE, Polly Jae
    See LEE, Pali Jae

LEES-MILNE, James 1908-
  (J. L.-M.)

PERSONAL: Born August 6, 1908, in Worcestershire, England; son of George Crompton and Helen (Bailey) Lees-Milne; married Alvilde Bridges, 1951. *Education:* Attended Eton College, 1921-26, and Grenoble University, 1927-28; Magdalen College, Oxford, M.A., 1931. *Politics:* Conservative. *Religion:* Church of England.

ADDRESSES: Home—Essex House, Badminton, Gloucestershire, England.

CAREER: Private secretary to first Lord Lloyd of Dolobran, high commissioner to Egypt, 1931-34, and to Sir Roderick Jones, Chairman of Reuters, 1934-35; National Trust, London, England, secretary of Historic Buildings Committee, 1936-51, architectural advisor, 1951-66. *Military service:* British Army, Irish Guards, 1940-41; became second lieutenant; invalided.

MEMBER: Royal Society of Literature (fellow), Society of Antiquaries (fellow).

AWARDS, HONORS: Honorary fellowship, Trinity College of Music, 1948; Heinemann Award, 1956, for *Roman Mornings,* and 1982, for *Harold Nicolson: A Biography.*

WRITINGS:

(Editor and contributor) *The National Trust: A Record of Fifty Years' Achievement,* Batsford, 1945, 3rd edition, 1948.
The Age of Adam, Batsford, 1947, Scholarly Press, 1977.
National Trust Guide: Buildings, Batsford, 1948.
Tudor Renaissance, Batsford, 1951.
The Age of Inigo Jones, Batsford, 1953, Somerset, 1978.
Roman Mornings, Wingate, 1956.
Baroque in Italy, Batsford, 1959, Macmillan, 1960.
Baroque in Spain and Portugal, and Its Antecedents, Batsford, 1960.
Earls of Creation: Five Great Patrons of Eighteenth-Century Art, Hamish Hamilton, 1962, House & Maxwell, 1963, reprinted, Century, 1986.
(Author of introduction) Harold Busch and Bernhard Lohse, editors, *Baroque Europe,* translation by Peter George, Batsford, 1962.
Worcestershire: A Shell Guide, International Publications Service, 1964.
St. Peter's: The Story of St. Peter's Basilica in Rome, Little, Brown, 1967.
Another Self (autobiography), Coward, 1970, Faber, 1984.
English Country Houses: Baroque, 1685-1715, Country Life, 1970.
Heretics in Love (novel), Chatto & Windus, 1973.
Ancestral Voices (diaries, 1942-43), Scribner, 1975, Faber, 1984.
William Beckford, Compton Russell, 1976, Allanheld, Osmun, 1979.
Prophesying Peace (diaries, 1944-45), Scribner, 1977, Faber, 1984.
Round the Clock, Scribner, 1978.
Harold Nicolson, Chatto & Windus, Volume 1: *1886-1929,* 1980, Volume 2: *1930-1968,* 1981, Volume 1 published as *Harold Nicolson: A Biography,* Shoe String, 1982.
The Country House, Oxford University Press, 1982.
(With David Ford) *Images of Bath,* Saint Helena Press, 1982.
Caves of Ice (diaries, 1946-47), Chatto & Windus, 1983.
The Last Stuarts, Chatto & Windus, 1983.
Writers at Home, Trefoil, 1985.
Midway on the Waves (diaries, 1948-49), Faber, 1985.

The Enigmatic Edwardian, Sidgwick & Jackson, 1986.
Venetian Evenings, Collins, 1988.

Also author of *Some Cotswold Houses,* 1987.

BOOKLETS ON NATIONAL TRUST PROPERTIES

(With others) *Fenton House,* Hampstead, 1953.
(Under initials J. L.-M.) *Florence Court, Co. Fermanagh,* Country Life, 1954.
Melford Hall, Suffolk, 1961.

Also author, sometimes under initials J. L.-M., of more than a dozen shorter booklets on National Trust properties.

OTHER

Contributor of articles and reviews to periodicals, including *Times Literary Supplement, Connoisseur, Apollo, Country Life, Spectator,* and *Books and Bookmen.*

SIDELIGHTS: "In a modest way, almost in spite of himself," says Michael Holroyd in the *New York Times Book Review,* "James Lees-Milne could be counted a public figure. A distinguished historian of architecture, 'an aristocrat in mind and culture' as Harold Nicolson in his diary described him, [Lees-Milne] devoted all his energies and abilities, as adviser to the National Trust of Great Britain, to preserving the country houses of England." From 1941 on, reports Alastair Forbes in the *Times Literary Supplement,* Lees-Milne "was able, virtually single-handed, to run the Historic Buildings side of the National Trust and to lay the foundations for its rapid and revolutionary expansion at the end of the [Second World War]. Before it, the Trust had a membership of 6,000 and owned only six houses. Today the membership is not far off half a million and it owns almost as many acres, together with some 230 houses."

Pointing out that Lees-Milne "has become something of a Historic Monument himself," Forbes states that Lees-Milne "has led a very useful life. An architectural historian, . . . he has allowed houses rather the people who live in them to be his ruling passion. . . . He found his vocation before the Second World War in the National Trust which was then, as he writes, 'truly a vocation . . . not a profession.' " The critic concludes that "few men have striven so hard to save the architectural heritage and countryside of Britain from vandalism and destruction."

St. Peter's: The Story of St. Peter's Basilica in Rome has been translated into Italian, Spanish, and German.

MEDIA ADAPTATIONS: Another Self was serialized on the British Broadcasting Corp. radio program "Woman's Hour" with such success in 1970 that it was repeated in 1971.

BIOGRAPHICAL/CRITICAL SOURCES:

BOOKS

Lees-Milne, James, *Another Self,* Coward, 1970, Faber, 1984.
Lees-Milne, James, *Ancestral Voices,* Scribner, 1975, Faber, 1984.
Lees-Milne, James, *Prophesying Peace,* Scribner, 1977, Faber, 1984.
Lees-Milne, James, *Caves of Ice,* Chatto & Windus, 1983.
Lees-Milne, James, *Midway on the Waves,* Faber, 1985.

PERIODICALS

Modern Painters, Volume 2, number 1, 1989.
New York Times Book Review, January 10, 1971, September 16, 1984.

Times (London), November 13, 1980, March 3, 1983, December 1, 1983, September 8, 1984, November 21, 1985, February 4, 1988, May 20, 1988.
Times Literary Supplement, April 10, 1948, December 18, 1959, January 18, 1963, September 28, 1967, April 16, 1970, October 10, 1970, April 16, 1971, March 2, 1973, October 7, 1975, October 10, 1975, November 14, 1980, November 20, 1981, August 13, 1982, March 4, 1983, December 30, 1983, September 13, 1985, December 20, 1985, November 28, 1986.
Washington Post Book World, March 14, 1982, May 13, 1984, October 14, 1984, February 24, 1985.

*　　*　　*

le FORT, Gertrud (Petrea) von   1876-1971
(G. von Stark)

PERSONAL: Full name Gertrud Augusta Lina Elsbeth Mathilde Petrea von le Fort; born October 11, 1876, in Minden, Germany (now Federal Republic of Germany); died November 1, 1971, in Oberstdorf, Federal Republic of Germany; daughter of Lothar Friedrich (an army officer and baron) and Elsbeth Mathilde (von Wedel-Parlow) von le Fort. *Education:* Attended University of Heidelberg, 1908, 1910-14, and University of Berlin, 1916. *Religion:* Roman Catholic.

ADDRESSES: Home—Im Haslach 9, Oberstdorf im Allgaeu, Federal Republic of Germany.

CAREER: Writer. *Wartime service:* Served in the Red Cross.

MEMBER: Bayrische Akademie der Schoenen Kuenste, Akademie der Kuenste Berlin, Deutsche Akademie fuer Sprache und Dichtung.

AWARDS, HONORS: Munich Literature Prize, 1947; Annette von Droste-Huelshoff Prize, 1948; Gottfried Keller Prize (Switzerland), 1952; Great Service Cross (Federal Republic of Germany), 1953; Grosser Preis des Landes Nordrhein-Westfalen fuer Literatur, 1955; honorary doctorate in theology from University of Munich, 1956; Bayrischer Verdienstorden, 1959; Stern zum grossen Verdienstorden, 1959; Kultureller Ehrenpreis der Stadt Muenchen, 1969.

WRITINGS:

IN ENGLISH TRANSLATION

Hymnen an die Kirche (poetry), Theatiner (Munich), 1924, expanded edition, Koesel & Pustet (Munich), 1946, translation by Margaret Chanler published as *Hymns to the Church,* Sheed & Ward, 1938.
Das Schweisstuch der Veronika: Roman (novel; also see below), Koesel & Pustet, 1928, published as *Das Schweisstuch der Veronika,* Volume I: *Der Roemische Brunnen* (title means "The Roman Fountain"), Beckstein, 1946, translation by Conrad M. R. Bonacina of original German edition published as *The Veil of Veronica,* Sheed & Ward, 1932, reprinted, AMS Press, 1970.
Der Papst aus dem Ghetto: Die Legende des Geschlechtes Pier Leone—Roman (novel), Transmare (Berlin), 1930, reprinted, Ehrenwirth (Munich), 1959, translation by Bonacina published as *The Pope from the Ghetto: The Legend of the Family of Pier Leone,* Sheed & Ward, 1934.
Die Letzte am Schafott: Novelle, Koesel & Pustet, 1931, reprinted, Ehrenwirth, 1959, translation by Olga Marx published as *The Song at the Scaffold,* Holt, 1933, reprinted, Image Books, 1961, revised translation edited by Martin

McMurtrey and Robert Knopp and published under same title, Catholic Authors, 1954.

Die ewige Frau; Die Frau in der Zeit; [and] *Die zeitlose Frau* (essays), Koesel & Pustet, 1934, revised edition, 1960, translation by Marie Cecilia Buehrle published as *The Eternal Woman; Woman in Time;* [and] *Timeless Woman,* Bruce, 1954, translation of revised edition by Placid Jordan published under same title, 1962.

Madonnen: Eine Bilderfolge (in German, English, and French), Arche (Zurich), 1948, new edition, 1962.

Die Tochter Farinatas: Vier Erzaehlungen (four novellas; contains *Die Tochter Farinatas, Die Consolata, Das Gericht des Meeres,* and *Plus Ultra;* also see below), Insel (Weisbaden), 1950, translation by Isabel and Florence McHugh published as *The Judgement of the Sea: Four Novellas (The Gate of Heaven, The Tower of the Constant, The Judgement of the Sea,* and *Plus Ultra*), Regnery, 1962.

Die Frau des Pilatus: Novelle (also see below), Insel, 1955, translation by Buehrle published as *The Wife of Pilate,* Bruce, 1957.

(Author of introduction) Leonard von Matt, *Rom: Das Antlitz der ewigen Stadt,* Neptun (Kreuzlingen), 1955, translation by Wolf Friederich published as *Rome: The Eternal City,* Andermann (Munich), 1955.

IN GERMAN

(Under pseudonym G. von Stark) *Jacomino,* Weiman (Barmen), 1899.

(Under pseudonym G. von Stark) *Prinzessin Christelchen: Hofroman,* Vobach (Berlin), 1904.

(Editor) Ernst Troeltsch, *Glaubenslehre,* Duncker & Humblot, 1925.

Hymnen an Deutschland (title means "Hymns to Germany"; poetry), Koesel & Pustet, 1932.

Das Reich des Kindes: Legende der letzten Karolinger, Langen-Mueller (Munich), 1934.

Die Magdeburgische Hochzeit: Roman (title means "The Wedding in Magdeburg: Novel"), Insel (Leipzig), 1938, reprinted, 1973.

Die Opferflamme: Erzaehlung, Insel, 1938, new edition, Arche, 1962.

Die Abberufung der Jungfrau von Barby: Erzaehlung, Beckstein, 1940, reprinted, 1960.

Das Gericht des Meeres: Erzaehlung, Insel, 1943, reprinted, Insel (Frankfurt), 1975, new edition edited by Robert O. Roeseler and published under same title, Appleton, 1959.

Der Kranz der Engel (title means "The Wreath of Angels"; novel; sequel to *Das Schweisstuch der Veronika*) Beckstein, 1946, published as *Das Schweisstuch der Veronika,* Volume II: *Der Kranz der Engel,* 1962.

Die Consolata: Erzaehlung, Insel (Weisbaden), 1947.

Gedichte (poetry), Insel, 1949, expanded edition, 1953.

Unser Weg durch die Nacht: Eine Rede fuer meine Schweizer Freunde, Insel, 1949, published as *Unser Weg durch die Nacht: Worte an meine Schweizer Freunde,* Ehrenwirth, 1962.

Den Heimatlosen: Drei Gedichte, Ehrenwirth, 1950.

(Author of foreword) Graham Greene, *Vom Paradox des Christentums,* Arche, 1952.

(Author of preface) *Byzantinische Mosaiken: Torcello, Venedig, Monteale, Palermo, Cefalu,* Iris, 1952.

Am Tor des Himmels (title means "The Gate of Heaven"), Insel, 1954, new edition edited with introduction, notes and vocabulary by J. R. Foster and published under same title, Harrap, 1966.

Das kleine Weihnachtsbuch, Arche, 1954.

Die Brautgabe [Gedichte und Prosa], Arche, 1955.

Weihnachten: Das Fest der goettlichen Liebe, Evangelisches Verlagswerk (Stuttgart), 1956.

(Author of introduction) Leonard von Matt, *Rom: Das Antlitz der ewigen Stodt—Dreissig Farbaufnahmen,* Andermann, 1956.

Der Turm der Bestaendigkeit: Novelle, Insel, 1957.

Plus Ultra: Erzaehlung, Insel, 1957.

Die letzte Begegnung: Novelle, Insel, 1959.

Die Frau und die Technik, Arche, 1959.

Das fremde Kind: Erzaehlung (title means "The Foreign Child: Novella"), Insel (Frankfurt), 1961.

Aphorismen, Ehrenwirth, 1962.

Die Tochter Jephthas: Ein Legende (also see below), Insel, 1964.

Haelfte des Lebens: Erinnerungen, Ehrenwirth, 1965.

Das Schweigen: Ein Legende, Arche, 1967.

Die Verfemte: Mit einer autobiographischen Erinnerung "Heidelberg," Reclam (Stuttgart), 1967.

Der Dom: Erzaehlung, Ehrenwirth, 1968.

Unsere liebe Frau vom Carneval, Arche, 1975.

Der Kurier der Koenigen: Roman, Ehrenwirth, 1976.

COLLECTIONS IN GERMAN

Das Reich des Kindes [and] *Die Voeglein von Theres: Zwei Legenden,* Insel, 1950.

Aufzeichnungen und Erinnerungen (title means "Sketches and Memories"), Benziger (Einsiedeln), 1951.

Die Krone der Frau: Monographie in Selbstreugnissen (essays and occasional pieces), Arche, 1952.

Geloeschte Kerzen: Zwei Erzaehlungen (title means "Extinguished Candles: Two Novellas"; contains *Die Unschuldigen: Ein Erinnerungsblatt* and *Die Verfemte: Dem Andenken der toten Kinder des Weltkrieges*), Ehrenwirth, 1953.

Erzaehlende Schriften, three volumes, Ehrenwirth and Insel, 1966.

Die Erzaehlungen (fourteen novellas), Ehrenwirth and Insel, 1966.

Die Tochter Jephthas und andere Erzaehlungen (seven novellas: *Die Tochter Farinatas, Die Consolata, Plus Ultra, Am Tor des Himmels, Die Frau des Pilatus, Der Turm der Bestaendigkeit,* and *Die Tochter Jephthas*), Suhrkamp (Frankfurt), 1976.

Also author of *Mein Elternhaus* (title means "My Parents' House"; memoirs), 1941.

OTHER

Contributor to anthologies and to periodicals. Co-editor of "Das Literarische Deutschland," 1950-52.

SIDELIGHTS: Gertrud von le Fort, a prolific and popular German writer, was "a master of the historical novel as it develops out of her triad of themes—*die Kirche, die Frau,* [and] *das Reich,*" Frank Wood noted in *Studies in German Literature.* Her interest in the church appeared early in her writing and was already evident in her first volume of poetry, *Hymns to the Church.* A collection of psalm-like poems, the book was published when le Fort was nearly fifty and was her first work published under her real name. Her love for her homeland received equal attention in a similar cycle of poems entitled *Hymnen an Deutschland* (title means "Hymns to Germany") which proclaims the glories of her homeland. Women appear as the protagonists in most of le Fort's fictional works, usually in the form of young semi-autobiographical heroines who come to terms with their spiritual conflicts and go on to witness to their faith in the world. Commenting on le Fort's major themes in a *German Review* essay Eva C. Wunderlich asserted that "in none of her writings will the reader forget her Catholic-Christian attitude, nor her profound interest in women and in the past and present of her fatherland."

Le Fort's first important novel, *The Veil of Veronica,* and its sequel *Der Kranz der Engel* (title means "The Wreath of Angels"), are typical of her work. Both titles hint at the religious overtones found in the plot and character development in many of le Fort's novels: The first, set in pre-World War I Rome, deals with Veronika, a young girl whose conversion to Catholicism causes her aunt to attempt to kill her with a cross. The second follows Veronika's marriage to a writer who tries unsuccessfully to impose his anti-religious feelings on his young bride. Although the two volumes were widely read in their day, according to *Dictionary of Literary Biography* contributor Josef Schmidt, "neither the plots nor the styles of the novels are innovative, and long passages resound with an ecstatic expressionist pomposity that has a hollow ring for the modern reader." Schmidt observed that these novels, like most of le Fort's works, "appear dated" to the reader of today, because of their focus on themes and concerns more typical of nineteenth-century Germany than of contemporary society.

Le Fort's papers are held by the Deutsches Literatur archives at the Schiller-Nationalmuseum in Marbach am Neckar, Federal Republic of Germany.

MEDIA ADAPTATIONS: The Song at the Scaffold was adapted into a play, *Les Dialogues des Carmelites,* by Georges Bernanos, 1949, which was the basis for an opera, *Les Carmelites,* written by the French composer, Francis Poulenc, 1958, and made into a film, 1960; *The Song at the Scaffold* was adapted by Lavery Emmet into a two-act play of the same title which premiered in New York in 1949.

BIOGRAPHICAL/CRITICAL SOURCES:

BOOKS

Dictionary of Literary Biography, Volume 66: *German Fiction Writers, 1885-1913,* Gale, 1988.
Hammer, Carl, editor, *Studies in German Literature,* Louisiana State University, 1963.

PERIODICALS

German Review, 1952.

OBITUARIES:

PERIODICALS

New York Times, November 5, 1971.*

* * *

LEFTON, Robert Eugene 1931-

PERSONAL: Born September 4, 1931, in St. Louis, Mo.; son of Henry (a businessman) and Rose (Ivster) Lefton; married Marlene Shanfeld, June 6, 1954; children: Jeffrey, Cyntheia, Bradley. *Education:* Washington University, A.B., 1953, Ph.D., 1958.

ADDRESSES: Home—61 Ladue Estates Dr., St. Louis, Mo. 63141. *Office*—Psychological Associates, 8220 Delmer, St. Louis, Mo. 63124.

CAREER: Psychological Associates (industrial psychologists), St. Louis, Mo., director of management services, 1958—; Washington University Medical School, St. Louis, associate professor,

1958-70. Research consultant, Child Guidance Clinic, 1961-70; consulting medical psychiatrist, Department of Psychiatry and William Greenleaf Eliot Division of Child Psychiatry, 1970—. Member of board of directors, Direct Mail Corp. of America.

MEMBER: American Psychological Association, Missouri Psychological Association.

WRITINGS:

Dimensional Management Strategies, Behavioral Science Systems, 1968.
(With V. R. Buzzotta and Manuel Sherberg) *Effective Selling through Psychology: Dimensional Sales and Sales Management Strategies,* Wiley, 1972, new edition, Ballinger, 1982.
Dimensional Interviewing Strategies, Behavioral Science Systems, 1972.
(With others) *Effective Motivation through Performance Appraisal: Dimensional Appraisal Strategies,* Ballinger, 1977.
(With Buzzotta and Sherberg) *Improving Productivity through People Skills: Dimensional Management Studies,* Ballinger, 1980.

WORK IN PROGRESS: Conducting research projects on relating the concepts of the behavioral sciences to the development of mature organization and business enterprise.*

* * *

LEIGH, Mike 1943-

PERSONAL: Born February 20, 1943, in Salford, Lancashire, England; son of Alfred Abraham and Phyllis Pauline (Cousin) Leigh; married Alison Steadman (an actress), September 15, 1973; children: Toby, Leo. *Education:* Attended Royal Academy of Dramatic Art, 1960-62, Camberwell School of Arts and Crafts, 1963-64, Central School of Art and Design, 1964-68, and London Film School, 1965.

ADDRESSES: Agent—A. D. Peters & Co. Ltd., 10 Buckingham St., London WC2N 6BU, England.

CAREER: Dramagraph (a production company), London, England, co-founder, 1965; Midlands Art Centre for Young People, Birmingham, England, associate director, 1965-66; Victoria Theatre, Stoke-on-Trent, England, actor, 1966; assistant director of Royal Shakespeare Co., 1967-68; writer. Director of plays, including "Little Malcolm and His Struggle against the Eunuchs," 1965, and "The Knack," 1967. Lecturer, Sedgely Park College, 1968-69, De La Salle College, 1968-69, and London Film School, 1970-73.

AWARDS, HONORS: Golden Hugo Award, Chicago Film Festival, and Golden Leopard Award, Locarno Film Festival, both 1972, both for "Bleak Moments"; George Divine Award, 1973; Best Comedy Award, *Evening Standard,* and Best Comedy Award, *Drama,* both 1981, both for "Goose-Pimples"; *Evening Standard* award, 1982; People's Award, Berlin Film Festival, 1984, for "Meantime."

WRITINGS:

PLAYS

"The Box Play," first produced in Birmingham, England, at Midlands Art Centre Theatre, 1965.
"My Parents Have Gone to Carlisle," first produced in Birmingham, 1966.
"The Last Crusade of the Five Little Nuns," first produced at Midland Arts Centre Theatre, 1966.
"Waste Paper Guard," first produced in Birmingham, 1966.

"NENAA," first produced in Stratford-upon-Avon, England, 1967.

"Individual Fruit Pies," first produced in Loughton, England, at East-15 Acting School Theatre, 1968.

"Down Here and Up There," first produced in London at Theatre Upstairs, 1968.

"Big Basil," first produced in Manchester, England, at Manchester Youth Theatre, 1968.

"Epilogue," first produced in Manchester, 1969.

"Glum Victoria and the Lad with Specs," first produced at Manchester Youth Theatre, 1969.

"Bleak Moments" (also see below), first produced in London at Open Space Theatre, 1970.

"A Rancid Pong," first produced in London at Basement Theatre, 1971.

"Wholesome Glory," first produced at Theatre Upstairs, 1973.

"The Jaws of Death," first produced in Edinburgh, Scotland, at Traverse Theatre, 1973.

"Dick Whittington and His Cat," first produced in London, 1973.

"Babies Grow Old," first produced in Stratford-upon-Avon at the Other Place, 1974.

"The Silent Majority," first produced in London at Bush Theatre, 1974.

Abigail's Party (also see below; first produced in London at Hampstead Theatre, 1977), Samuel French, 1979.

"Ecstasy," first produced at Hampstead Theatre, 1979.

Goose-Pimples (also see below; first produced at Hampstead Theatre, 1981), Samuel French, 1982.

Abigail's Party and Goose-Pimples, Penguin, 1983.

TELEVISION SCREENPLAYS

"A Mug's Game," British Broadcasting Corp. (BBC-TV), 1973.

"Hard Labor," BBC-TV, 1973.

"The Permissive Society," BBC-TV, 1975.

"Knock for Knock," BBC-TV, 1976.

"Nuts in May," BBC-TV, 1976.

"The Kiss of Death," BBC-TV, 1977.

"Abigail's Party" (adapted from own play), BBC-TV, 1977.

"Who's Who," BBC-TV, 1978.

"Grown-Ups," BBC-TV, 1980.

"Home Sweet Home," BBC-TV, 1982.

"Meantime," BBC-TV, 1983.

"Four Days in July," BBC-TV, 1984.

OTHER

(And director) "High Hopes" (film screenplay), Skouras Pictures, 1989.

Also author of screenplays "Bleak Moments" (adapted from own play), 1971, and "The Short and Curlies," 1987. Author of "Five Minute Plays" for television, including "The Birth of the 2001 FA Cup Finale Goalie," "Old Chums," "Probation," "A Light Snack," and "Afternoon," all 1982.

SIDELIGHTS: Mike Leigh once told *CA:* "All my plays and films have evolved from scratch entirely by rehearsal through improvisation; thus it is inherent in my work that I always combine the jobs of author and director, and I never work with any other writers or directors. I have been pioneering this style of work in England, beginning with the 'Box Play' in 1965."

BIOGRAPHICAL/CRITICAL SOURCES:

BOOKS

Clements, Paul, *The Improvised Play: The Work of Mike Leigh*, Methuen, 1983.

PERIODICALS

Los Angeles Times, March 9, 1989.
New York Times, February 19, 1989.
Washington Post, April 7, 1989.*

*   *   *

LEITER, Samuel L(ouis) 1940-

PERSONAL: Surname is pronounced "lighter"; born July 20, 1940, in Brooklyn, N.Y.; son of Joseph and Frieda (Pekofsky) Leiter; married Marcia Frieda Lerner (a writer), February 3, 1963; children: Bambi Lani Leiter Falvo, Justin Leigh. *Education:* Brooklyn College of the City University of New York, B.A., 1962; University of Hawaii, M.F.A., 1964; New York University, Ph.D., 1968.

ADDRESSES: Home—137-29 79th St., Howard Beach, N.Y. 11414. *Office*—Department of Theatre, Brooklyn College of the City University of New York, Bedford Ave., Brooklyn, N.Y. 11210.

CAREER: Brooklyn College of the City University of New York, Brooklyn, N.Y., and Graduate Center of City University of New York, lecturer, 1965-68, assistant professor, 1968-73, associate professor, 1973-76, professor of theatre, 1977—.

MEMBER: American Society for Theatre Research, Association for Theatre in Higher Education.

AWARDS, HONORS: Grant from University of Hawaii's East-West Center, 1963, and Fulbright grant, 1974, both for study in Japan; PSC-CUNY grants, 1986-88, for study of New York theatre history.

WRITINGS:

(Translator and author of commentary) *The Art of Kabuki: Famous Plays in Performance*, University of California Press, 1979.

Kabuki Encyclopedia: An English Language Adaptation of "Kabuki Jiten," Greenwood Press, 1979.

(Editor) *The Encyclopedia of the New York Stage*, Greenwood Press, Volume 1: (with Holly Hill) *1920-1930*, 1985, Volume 2: (sole author) *1930-40*, 1989.

(Editor with Langdon Brown and others) *Shakespeare around the Globe: A Guide to Notable Postwar Revivals*, Greenwood Press, 1986.

Ten Seasons: New York Theatre in the Seventies, Greenwood Press, 1986.

Author of filmstrip series, "The Classical Theatre of Japan." Contributor to theatre journals. Editor, *Asian Theatre Bulletin*, 1970-78; book review editor, *Asian Theatre Journal* (Japan), 1983—.

WORK IN PROGRESS: From Belasco to Brook: Great Stage Directors of the Century, awaiting publication; *The Encyclopedia of the New York Stage, 1940-50.*

SIDELIGHTS: Samuel L. Leiter told *CA:* "Although my principal writing interest for many years was in the realm of Japanese theatre, especially *kabuki*, I was also seriously concerned with American theatre history, as noted in the various articles I wrote about the nineteenth-century theatre in Brooklyn. Subsequently, my American interests intensified and I began to work in the area of New York theatre history. This is most apparent in my *Encyclopedia of the New York Stage* series, which begins with the twenties, and plans to document and describe, decade by decade, for as long as my strength holds out, every professional theatre production in Manhattan. I would also like to do a series of books for a popular audience offering overviews of each of the decades more meticulously described in the show by show entries of the encyclopedia series. Meanwhile, my interests in *kabuki* and other forms of Japanese theatre continue, and I am still engaged in research and writing on the performance traditions of this wonderful old theatre style. "I continue to be actively engaged in theatre work and regularly direct plays at Brooklyn College. The forces, the people, the ideas that go into making theatre will continue to inspire me to write in this field."

* * *

LEONARD, Tom 1944-

PERSONAL: Born August 22, 1944, in Glasgow, Lanarkshire, Scotland; married, 1971; children: two. *Education:* University of Glasgow, B.A.

ADDRESSES: Home—56 Eldon St., Glasgow G3 6NJ, Scotland.

CAREER: Poet.

AWARDS, HONORS: Scottish Arts Council bursary, 1971, 1974; joint Scottish book of the year winner, Saltine Society, 1984, for *Intimate Voices.*

WRITINGS:

Six Glasgow Poems, Midnight Publications, 1969.
A Priest Came on at Merkland Street (poems), Midnight Publications, 1970.
Poems, E. & T. O'Brien, 1973.
Bunnit Husslin, [Glasgow], 1975.
(With Alex Hamilton and James Kelman) *Three Glasgow Writers: A Collection of Writings,* Molendinar Press, 1976.
If Only Bunty Was Here (radio playscript), Glasgow Print Studio Press, 1978.
My Name Is Tom (sound poem), Good Elf Publications, 1979.
Ghostie Men, Galloping Dog Press, 1980.
Intimate Voices: Selected Writings, 1965-1983, Galloping Dog Press, 1984.
Satires and Profanities, Scottish Trades Union, 1985.
Situations: Theoretical and Contemporary, Galloping Dog Press, 1986.
Two Members Monologues, Edward Polin Press, 1989.
(Editor) *Radical Renfrew: Renrewshire Poetry from the French Revolution to the First World War,* Polygon, 1989.

Contributor to *Edinburgh Review.*

SIDELIGHTS: Tom Leonard told *CA:* "My poetry is in English, and in a transcription of Glaswegian speech. The interest I have in the sound aspect of language led me to become involved in making sound-poems for tape recorder, sometimes accompanied by myself in performance as narrator/singer, and sometimes additionally using placards. In the past few years I've become interested in writing political satire for performance as well as poetry, and have written a series of articles for the *Edinburgh Review* mainly on language, accent, and power."

* * *

LEOPOLD, Luna B(ergere) 1915-

PERSONAL: Born October 8, 1915, in Albuquerque, N.M.; son of Aldo (a professor) and Estella (Bergere) Leopold; married Carolyn Clugston, September 6, 1940 (divorced, 1973); married Barbara Beck Nelson, 1973; children: (first marriage) Madelyn Dennette, Bruce Carl. *Education:* University of Wisconsin, B.S., 1936; University of California at Los Angeles, M.S., 1944; Harvard University, Ph.D., 1950.

ADDRESSES: Home—400 Vermont Ave., Berkeley, Calif. 94707. *Office*—Department of Geology, University of California, Berkeley, Calif. 94720.

CAREER: U.S. Soil Conservation Service, New Mexico, 1938-41, began as junior engineer, became associate engineer; U.S. Engineers Office, Los Angeles, Calif., associate engineer, 1941-42; U.S. Bureau of Reclamation, Washington, D.C., associate engineer, 1946; Pineapple Research Institute of Hawaii, Honolulu, head meteorologist, 1946-49; U.S. Geological Survey, hydraulic engineer, 1950-56, chief hydrologist, 1957-66, senior research hydrologist, 1966-73; University of California, Berkeley, professor of geology, 1973—. *Military service:* U.S. Army Air Forces, Air Weather Service, 1942-46; became captain.

MEMBER: American Meteorological Society, Geological Society of America (president, 1971), American Geophysical Union, American Society of Civil Engineers, American Academy of Arts and Sciences, American Philosophical Society, National Academy of Sciences, Sigma Xi, Tau Beta Pi, Phi Kappa Phi, Chi Epsilon, Cosmos Club (Washington, D.C.).

AWARDS, HONORS: Distinguished service award, U.S. Department of Interior, 1958; Kirk Bryan Award, Geological Society of America, 1958; Veth Medal, Royal Netherlands Geological Society, 1963; Liege University Medal, 1966; Cullum Geographical Medal, American Geographical Society, 1968; D.Geography, University of Ottawa, 1969; Rockefeller public service award, 1971; D.Sc., Iowa Wesleyan College, 1972, University of Wisconsin, 1980, St. Andrew's University, Scotland, 1981, and University of Murcia, Spain; Busk Medal, Royal Geographical Society, 1984; David Linton Award, British Geomorphological Research Group, 1986; Berkeley Citation, University of California.

WRITINGS:

(With Thomas Maddock, Jr.) *The Flood Control Controversy,* Ronald, 1954.
(With W. B. Langbein) *A Primer on Water,* U.S. Government Printing Office, 1960, enlarged edition by Leopold published as *Water: A Primer,* W. H. Freeman, 1974.
(With M. G. Wolman and J. P. Miller) *Fluvial Processes in Geomorphology,* W. H. Freeman, 1964.
(With Kenneth S. Davis and others) *Water,* Time-Life, 1965, revised edition, 1980.
(With William W. Emmett and Robert M. Myrick) *Channel and Hillslope Processes in a Semi-arid Area,* U.S. Government Printing Office, 1966.
(Editor) *Round River: From the Journals of Aldo Leopold,* Oxford University Press, 1972.
(With Thomas Dunne) *Water in Environmental Planning,* W. H. Freeman, 1978.
(With Dunne) *Flood and Sedimentation Hazards in the Toutle and Cowlitz River System as a Result of the Mt. St. Helens Eruption, 1980,* FEMA, Region X, 1981.
(Editor) *Field Trip Guidebook: 1982 Conference,* The Group, 1982.

Contributor of over one hundred papers to scientific journals.

LERNER, Alan Jay 1918-1986

PERSONAL: Born August 31, 1918, in New York, N.Y.; died June 14, 1986, in New York City; son of Joseph J. (founder of Lerner Stores, Inc.) and Edith Lerner; married Ruth O'Day Boyd, 1940 (divorced, 1947); married Marion Bell (a singer), 1947 (divorced, 1949); married Nancy Olson (an actress), 1950 (divorced, 1957); married Micheline Muselli (a lawyer), December, 1957 (divorced); also married Karen Gundersen (an editor), Sandra Paine (an actress), Nina Bushkin, and Liz Robertson (an actress, who survives him); children: Michael, Susan, Liza, Jennifer. *Education:* Attended Julliard School of Music, 1936-37; Harvard University, B.S., 1940.

CAREER: Lyricist, librettist, screenwriter, and producer of motion pictures and Broadway musicals. Worked as advertising copywriter for Lord & Thomas Agency, 1940-42. Member of President's Council for the Cultural Center in Washington, D.C., 1962.

MEMBER: Players, Lambs, Shaw Society.

AWARDS, HONORS: Received New York Drama Critics Circle Award, 1947, for "Brigadoon"; Academy Awards for best story and best screenplay, Academy of Motion Picture Arts and Sciences, 1951, for "An American in Paris"; Christopher Award, 1954; New York Drama Critics Circle Award, Donaldson award, and Antionette Perry ("Tony") Award, all 1956, all for "My Fair Lady"; Academy Awards for best screenplay and best song, 1958, for "Gigi"; Grammy Award, 1965, for "On a Clear Day You Can See Forever"; Choate Alumni Seal; elected to Songwriters Hall of Fame, 1971; co-winner, with Frederick Loewe, of Tony Award, 1974.

WRITINGS:

(Author of introduction) *Great Songs of Broadway*, Quadrangle, 1973.
(With George Bernard Shaw) *Pygmalion* (contains Shaw's "Pygmalion" and Lerner's "My Fair Lady"; also see below), New American Library, 1975.
On the Street Where I Live (autobiography), Norton, 1978.
The Musical Theatre: A Celebration, McGraw, 1986.

LYRICIST AND LIBRETTIST

"Life of the Party" (adapted from the play "The Patsy," by Barry Connor), first produced in Detroit, 1942.
"What's Up?," first produced on Broadway at National Theatre, November 11, 1943.
"The Day before Spring," first produced in 1945.
Brigadoon (musical play; first produced in 1947; also see below), music by Frederick Loewe, Coward, 1947.
"Love Life" (musical play), music by Kurt Weill, first produced in 1948.
Paint Your Wagon (musical play; first produced on Broadway, November, 1951; also see below), music by Loewe, Coward, 1952.
My Fair Lady (musical play; adapted from play "Pygmalion," by George Bernard Shaw; first produced on Broadway at Mark Hellinger Theatre, March 15, 1956; also see below), music by Loewe, Coward, 1956.
Camelot (musical play; adapted from the book *The Once and Future King* by T. H. White; first produced in 1960; also see below), music by Loewe, Random House, 1961.
Lerner & Loewe Song Book, music by Loewe, Simon & Schuster, 1962.
"On a Clear Day You Can See Forever" (also see below), music by Burton Lang, first produced in 1965.

"Coco," music by Andre Previn, produced at Mark Hellinger Theatre, December 18, 1969.
"Lolita, My Love" (adapted from the novel *Lolita*, by Vladimir Nabokov), music by John Barry, first produced in Philadelphia, 1971.
"Gigi" (also see below; adapted from own original screenplay), first produced in 1973.
"Music, Music," first produced in 1974.
"1600 Pennsylvania Avenue," first produced in 1975.
"Carmelina" (based on the movie "Buona Sera, Mrs. Campbell"), music by Barton Lane, produced on Broadway, April, 1978.
"Dance a Little Closer" (based on the play "Idiot's Delight," by Robert E. Sherwood), music by Charles Strouse, produced on Broadway at Minskoff Theatre, May, 1983.

SCREENWRITER AND LYRICIST

"Royal Wedding," Metro-Goldwyn-Mayer (MGM), 1951.
"An American in Paris," MGM, 1951.
"Brigadoon," MGM, 1954.
"Gigi" (adapted from the novel by Colette), MGM, 1958.
"My Fair Lady," Warner Brothers, 1967.
"Camelot," Warner Brothers, 1967.
"Paint Your Wagon," Paramount, 1969.
"On a Clear Day You Can See Forever," Paramount, 1970.

SIDELIGHTS: Through a career that spanned three decades, lyricist/librettist Alan Jay Lerner and his partner, composer Frederick Loewe, became virtually synonymous with the blockbuster Broadway musical. A list of their hits all but defines the genre: "Brigadoon," "Paint Your Wagon," "Camelot," the movie musical "Gigi," and their biggest triumph, "My Fair Lady."

The tuneful adaptation of George Bernard Shaw's "Pygmalion," "My Fair Lady" opened on Broadway in 1956 to rapturous notices and packed houses. Brooks Atkinson of the *New York Times*, for one, proclaimed "My Fair Lady" as "the most civilized play of its time and one of the finest of the century." On the occasion of Lerner's death, William A. Henry III of *Time* remembered how these classic lyrics "consistently matched ['Pygmalion's] wit, verve and acerbic class consciousness."

In the 1970s, after Loewe fell ill, Lerner continued writing with composers like Andre Previn and Charles Strouse, but such subsequent musicals as "Coco" and "Dance a Little Closer" never quite caught on with critics and playgoers. In 1978 Lerner produced his autobiography, *On the Street Where I Live*. By then he had quite a story to tell—the lyricist had been married a total of eight times—but as *New York Times* critic Mel Gussow noted, "The book is more professional than personal." He continued that the volume's delights include a look at Lerner and Loewe's labors with "My Fair Lady": "dashing off 'The Rain in Spain' in 10 minutes, agonizing over 'I Could Have Danced All Night' . . . and agreeing to eliminate 'With a Little Bit o' Luck' until it stopped the show at its first performance in New Haven."

BIOGRAPHICAL/CRITICAL SOURCES:

BOOKS

Engle, Lehmann, *Their Words Are Music*, Crown, 1975.
Ewen, David, *Great Men of Popular Song*, Prentice-Hall, 1970.
Lerner, Alan Jay, *The Street Where I Live*, Norton, 1978.
Lerner, Alan Jay, *The Musical Theatre: A Celebration*, Collins, 1987.

PERIODICALS

New York Times, March 16, 1956, March 9, 1958, November 25, 1978, April 10, 1979, November 8, 1987.
Time, July 14, 1986.

OBITUARIES:

PERIODICALS

Chicago Tribune, June 15, 1986.
Los Angeles Times, June 15, 1986.
New York Times, June 15, 1986.
Washington Post, June 15, 1986, June 16, 1986.*

*   *   *

LESTER, David 1942-

PERSONAL: Born June 1, 1942, in London, England; U.S. citizen; son of Harry (a bookie) and Kathleen (Moore) Lester; married Jean Mercer (a psychologist and author under names Gene Lester and Jean Mercer), April 15, 1967 (divorced, 1977); married Mary E. Murrell (a professor of criminal justice), July 20, 1979; married Bijou Yang (an economist), October 22, 1987; children: (first marriage) Simon. *Education:* Cambridge University, B.A., 1964, M.A., 1968; Brandeis University, M.A., 1966, Ph.D., 1968. *Politics:* None. *Religion:* None.

ADDRESSES: Home—RR 41, 5 Stonegate Ct., Blackwood, N.J. 08012. *Office*—Psychology Program, Richard Stockton State College, Pomona, N.J. 08240.

CAREER: Wellesley College, Wellesley, Mass., instructor, 1967-68, assistant professor of psychology, 1968-69; Suicide Prevention and Crisis Service, Buffalo, N.Y., research director, 1969-71; Richard Stockton State College, Pomona, N.J., associate professor, 1971-74, professor of psychology, 1975—, chairman of department, 1971-74. Instructor and clinical associate, State University of New York at Buffalo, 1969-71; research associate, Philadelphia General Hospital, 1971-75. Member of editorial advisory board, Institute for Scientific Information, 1969-70.

AWARDS, HONORS: Research grant, National Institute of Mental Health, 1967-68.

WRITINGS:

(Editor) *Explorations in Exploration,* Van Nostrand, 1969.
(With first wife, Gene Lester) *Suicide: The Gamble with Death,* Prentice-Hall, 1971.
Why Men Kill Themselves, C. C Thomas, 1972, 2nd edition published as *Why People Kill Themselves,* 1983.
(Editor with G. Brockopp) *Crisis Intervention and Counseling by Telephone,* C. C Thomas, 1973.
Comparative Psychology: Phyletic Differences in Behavior, Alfred Publishing, 1973.
A Physiological Basis for Personality Traits, C. C Thomas, 1974.
(With G. Lester) *Crime of Passion: Murder and the Murderer,* Nelson-Hall, 1975.
Unusual Sexual Behavior: The Standard Deviations, C. C Thomas, 1975.
The Use of Alternative Modes of Communication in Psychotherapy: The Computer, the Book, the Telephone, the Television, the Tape Recorder, C. C Thomas, 1977.
(Editor) *Gambling Today,* C. C Thomas, 1979.
(With B. H. Sell and K. D. Sell) *Suicide: A Guide to Information Sources,* Gale, 1980.
Psychotherapy for Offenders, Pilgrimage Press, 1981.
(Editor) *The Elderly Victim of Crime,* C. C Thomas, 1981.

(With second wife, Mary E. Murrell) *Introduction to Juvenile Delinquency,* Macmillan, 1981.
The Psychological Basis for Handwriting Analysis, Nelson-Hall, 1981.
THe Structure of the Mind, University Press of America, 1982.
Gun Control: Issues and Answers, C. C Thomas, 1984.
(With A. Levitt) *Insanity and Incompetence: Case Studies in Forensic Psychology,* Pilgrimage Press, 1984.
The Murderer and His Murder, AMS Press, 1986.
The Death Penalty, C. C Thomas, 1987.
Suicide as a Learned Behavior, C. C Thomas, 1987.
(With M. Braswell) *Correctional Treatment,* Anderson Publishing, 1987.
The Biochemical Basis of Suicide, C. C Thomas, 1988.
Suicide from a Psychological Perspective, C. C Thomas, 1988.
Why Women Kill Themselves, C. C Thomas, 1988.
Can We Prevent Suicide?, AMS Press, 1988.

Contributor of over five hundred articles to periodicals, including *Journal of Clinical Psychology, American Anthropologist, Journal of General Psychology, Nature,* and *Clinical Psychologist.* Founder and co-editor, *Crisis Intervention,* 1969-71; member of editorial advisory board, *Current Contents (Social and Behavioral Sciences);* member of editorial board, *Omega,* 1971—, and *Suicide and Life-Threatening Behavior,* 1981—.

SIDELIGHTS: David Lester told *CA:* "At this time in my life, I am growing tired of writing yet more books on psychological topics and social science issues. I am much more excited by my fledgling attempts to write [opinion-editorials] for newspapers, articles for magazines, and fiction. Even minor successes in these areas please me much more than my scholarly works. At present, I am in the midst of writing two detective stories, but I am still uncertain whether I will complete them and eventually see them in print."

*   *   *

Le TORD, Bijou 1945-

PERSONAL: Born January 15, 1945, in St. Raphael, France; immigrated to the United States, 1966; daughter of Jacques (an artist) and Paule (Pigoury) Le Tord. *Education:* Attended Ecole des Beaux Arts, Lyon, France. *Politics:* None. *Religion:* Protestant.

CAREER: Author and illustrator of children's books. Fashion Institute of Technology, New York, N.Y., instructor, 1978-1982.

ADDRESSES: Home—P.O. Box 2226, Sag Harbor, N.Y. 11963.

MEMBER: Society of Illustrators.

AWARDS, HONORS: American Institute of Graphic Arts Bookshow award, 1977, for *The Generous Cow; Joseph and Nellie* was named a "Notable Social Studies Trade Book of 1986"; *My Grandma Leonie* was chosen as one of *American Bookseller's* "Pick of the Lists" books, 1987.

WRITINGS:

SELF-ILLUSTRATED JUVENILES

A Perfect Place to Be, Parents Magazine Press, 1976.
The Generous Cow, Parents Magazine Press, 1977.
Rabbit Seeds, Four Winds, 1978.
Merry Christmas, Hooper Dooper, Random House, 1979.
Goodwood Bear, Bradbury, 1979.
Nice and Cozy, Four Winds, 1980.
Picking and Weaving, Four Winds, 1980.
Joseph and Nellie, Bradury, 1980.
Arf, Boo, Click: An Alphabet of Sounds, Four Winds, 1981.

My Grandma Leonie, Bradbury, 1981.
The Little Hills of Nazareth, Bradbury, 1988.
A Brown Cow, Little, Brown, 1989.
The Deep Blue Sea, Orchards Press, 1990.

AVOCATIONAL INTERESTS: Poetry, fine arts, music, people, travel in Europe.

* * *

LEVINE, Suzanne Jill   1946-

PERSONAL: Born October 21, 1946, in New York, N.Y.; daughter of Meyer and Elaine (Berger) Levine. *Education:* Vassar College, B.A., 1967; Columbia University, M.A., 1969; New York University, Ph.D., 1976.

ADDRESSES: Home—120 Hixon Rd., Santa Barbara, Calif. 93108. *Office*—Department of Spanish and Portuguese, University of California, Santa Barbara, Santa Barbara, Calif. 93106.

CAREER: Tufts University, Medford, Mass., assistant professor of Latin American literature and literary translation, 1977-84; University of Washington, Seattle, associate professor, 1984-88; University of California, Santa Barbara, Santa Barbara, 1988—. University of California Interdisciplinary Humanities Center fellow, spring, 1989; University of California Regents fellow, summer, 1989. Lecturer on literary translation, New York University, Hunter College and Graduate Center of the City University of New York, Yale University, and numerous other universities throughout the United States, Europe and Latin America. Freelance translator and writer. Judge, National Book Awards, 1978, and jurist, Letras de Oro Literary Translation Prize, University of Miami, 1987-89. Consultant to numerous publishers, including E.P. Dutton, Harper & Row, Brooklyn College Press, Wildman Press, and Adler & Adler.

MEMBER: American Literary Translators Association (member of executive council, 1981-84), PEN, International Board of Translators, Instituto Internacional de Literatura Iberoamericana.

AWARDS, HONORS: Mellon fellowship, Wellesley College, 1979; National Endowment for the Arts fellowship grant for literary translation, 1981, 1986; University of Washington Graduate School Research Fund summer grant, 1985.

WRITINGS:

TRANSLATOR

Manuel Puig, *Betrayed by Rita Hayworth,* Dutton, 1971.
Guillermo Cabrera Infante, *Three Trapped Tigers,* Harper, 1971.
Jose Donoso, Carlos Fuentes, and Severo Sarduy, *Triple Cross,* Dutton, 1972.
Julio Cortazar, *All the Fires, the Fire,* Pantheon, 1973.
Puig, *Heartbreak Tango,* Dutton, 1973.
Sarduy, *Cobra,* Dutton, 1975.
Adolfo Bioy Casares, *Plan for Escape,* Dutton, 1975.
Puig, *The Buenos Aires Affair,* Dutton, 1976.
Cabrera Infante, *View of Dawn in the Tropics,* Farrar, Straus, 1978.
Fuentes, *Holy Place,* Dutton, 1978.
Bioy Casares, *Asleep in the Sun,* Persea Books, 1978.
(With David Pritchard) Donoso, *A House in the Country,* Knopf, 1984.
(With the author) Cabrera Infante, *Infante's Inferno,* Harper, 1984.
Sarduy, *Maitreya,* Ediciones del Norte, 1987.
Bioy Casares, *Adventures of a Photographer,* Dutton, 1989.

Also translator of eight short plays for the Puerto Rican Traveling Theater, performed throughout New York City, summer, 1972. Contributor of translations of stories, poems, and essays by these and other authors, including Alejo Carpentier, Reinaldo Arenas, and Mario Benedetti, to numerous periodicals and anthologies, including *Other Fires: Short Fiction by Latin American Women,* edited by A. Manguel, C.N. Potter, 1986, and *The Renewal of the Vision: Voices of Latin American Women Poets, 1940-1980,* edited by M. Agosin, Spectacular Diseases, 1987.

OTHER

Latin America: Fiction and Poetry in Translation (bibliography), Center for Inter-American Relations, 1970.
El espejo hablado: A Study of Garcia Marquez's "One Hundred Years of Solitude," Monte Avila (Caracas), 1975.
Guia de Bioy Casares, Fundamentos (Madrid), 1982.
(Contributor) Agosin, editor, *Homage to Maria Luisa Bombal,* Bilingual Review/Press, 1987.
(Contributor) R. P. Warren, editor, *The Art of Translation: Voices from the Field,* Northwestern University Press, 1989.

Contributor to *Review, Revista de la Universidad de Mexico, World Literature Today* and numerous other periodicals. Guest editor of *Fiction, TriQuarterly,* and other journals. Consulting editor, *Handbook of Latin American Studies,* Library of Congress, 1985-86.

WORK IN PROGRESS: The Subversive Scribe: Translating Latin American Fiction; The Selected Stories of Adolfo Bioy Casares, an annotated translation; in collaboration with Julian Rios and Rick Francis, a translation of Rios's *Larva* for Dalkey Archive Press; essay on Adolfo Bioy Casares to be included in a forthcoming volume of *Dictionary of Literary Biography;* a translation of Manuel Puig's novel, *The Tropical Night Descends,* for Simon & Schuster.

SIDELIGHTS: Suzanne Jill Levine told *CA:* "Translation—an activity caught between the scholarly and the creative, between technique and intuition—is a route, a voyage if you like, through which a writer/translator may seek to reconcile fragments: fragments of texts, of language, of oneself. More than a moment of interpretation, translation is an act of passage."

* * *

LEVINSON, Leonard   1935-
(Nicholas Brady, Lee Chang, Glen Chase, Richard Hale Curtis, Gordon Davis, Clay Dawson, Nelson De Mille, Josh Edwards, Richard Gallagher, March Hastings, J. Farragut Jones, Leonard Jordan, Philip Kirk, John Mackie, Robert Novak, Philip Rawls, Bruno Rossi, Jonathan Scofield, Jonathan Trask, Cynthia Wilkerson)

PERSONAL: Born in 1935, in New Bedford, Mass.; married twice (first marriage ended by divorce, second by death); children: (first marriage) Deborah. *Education:* Michigan State University, B.A., 1961.

ADDRESSES: Agent—Barbara Lowenstein & Associates, Inc., Suite 601, 121 West 27th St., New York, N.Y. 10001.

CAREER: Writer, 1971—. Has also worked as a public relations representative, social worker, bartender, cab driver, and waiter. *Military service:* U.S. Army, 1954-57.

MEMBER: National Writers Union, Writers Guild of America (East).

WRITINGS:

UNDER PSEUDONYM NICHOLAS BRADY

Shark Fighter (adventure novel), Belmont-Tower, 1975.
Inside Job (crime novel), Belmont-Tower, 1978.

UNDER PSEUDONYM GORDON DAVIS

Death Train, Zebra Books, 1980.
Hell Harbor, Zebra Books, 1980.
Bloody Bush, Zebra Books, 1980.
The Goering Treasure, Zebra Books, 1980.
The Liberation of Paris, Bantam, 1981.
Doom River, Bantam, 1981.
Slaughter City, Bantam, 1981.
Bullet Bridge, Bantam, 1981.
Bloody Bastogne, Bantam, 1981.
The Battle of the Bulge, Bantam, 1981.

UNDER PSEUDONYM CLAY DAWSON

Gold Town, Charter, 1989.
Apache Dawn, Charter, 1989.

UNDER PSEUDONYM NELSON De MILLE

The Terrorists (crime novel), Leisure Books, 1974.
Word of Honor, Warner Books, 1985.

UNDER PSEUDONYM JOSH EDWARDS

Searcher, Charter/Diamond, 1990.
Hot Lead and Cold Blood, Charter/Diamond, 1990.
Tin Badge, Charter/Diamond, 1991.
Warpath, Charter/Diamond, 1991.
Last Stage to Santa Fe, Charter/Diamond, 1991.

UNDER PSEUDONYM J. FARRAGUT JONES

Forty Fathoms Down, Dell, 1981.
Tracking the Wolf Pack, Dell, 1981.

UNDER PSEUDONYM LEONARD JORDAN

Operation Perfidia (spy thriller), Warner Books, 1975.
The Bar Studs, Fawcett, 1976.
Hype!, Fawcett, 1977.
Cabby, Belmont-Tower, 1980.
The Last Buffoon, Belmont-Tower, 1980.
Without Mercy, Zebra Books, 1981.

UNDER PSEUDONYM PHILIP KIRK

The Hydra Conspiracy, Leisure Books, 1979.
Smart Bombs, Leisure Books, 1979.
The Slayboys, Leisure Books, 1979.
Chinese Roulette, Leisure Books, 1979.
Love Me to Death, Leisure Books, 1980.
Killer Satellites, Leisure Books, 1980.

UNDER PSEUDONYM JOHN MACKIE

Hit the Beach, Jove, 1983.
Death Squad, Jove, 1983.
River of Blood, Jove, 1983.
Meat Grinder Hill, Jove, 1984.
Down and Dirty, Jove, 1984.
Green Hell, Jove, 1984.
Too Mean to Die, Jove, 1984.
Hot Lead and Cold Steel, Jove, 1984.
Do or Die, Jove, 1984.
Kill Crazy, Jove, 1985.
Nightmare Alley, Jove, 1985.

Go for Broke, Jove, 1985.
Tough Guys Die Hard, Jove, 1985.
Suicide River, Jove, 1985.
Satan's Cage, Jove, 1985.
Go Down Fighting, Jove, 1986.

UNDER PSEUDONYM BRUNO ROSSI

The Worst Way to Die, Leisure Books, 1974.
Night of the Assassins, Leisure Books, 1974.
Headcrusher, Leisure Books, 1974.

UNDER PSEUDONYM CYNTHIA WILKERSON

Sweeter than Candy, Belmont-Tower, 1978.
The Fast Life, Belmont-Tower, 1979.

OTHER

(Under pseudonym March Hastings) *Private Sessions* (romantic comedy), Midwood Books, 1974.
(Under pseudonym Robert Novak) *The Thrill Killers* (crime novel), Belmont-Tower, 1974.
(Under pseudonym Lee Chang) *The Year of the Boar* (crime novel), Manor Publishing, 1975.
(Under pseudonym Philip Rawls) *Streets of Blood* (crime novel), Manor Publishing, 1975.
(Under pseudonym Glen Chase) *Where the Action Is* (crime novel), Leisure Books, 1977.
(Under pseudonym Jonathan Trask) *The Camp,* Belmont-Tower, 1977.
(Under pseudonym Richard Gallagher) *Doom Platoon* (war novel), Belmont-Tower, 1978.
(Under pseudonym Richard Hale Curtis) *Every Man on Eagle,* Dell, 1982.
(Under pseudonym Jonathan Scofield) *Bayonets in No-Man's Land,* Dell, 1982.

BIOGRAPHICAL/CRITICAL SOURCES:

PERIODICALS

Chicago Tribune Book World, February 2, 1986.
New York Times Book Review, December 1, 1985.
Time, December 9, 1985.

*   *   *

LEWIS, Michael
See UNTERMEYER, Louis

*   *   *

LEWIS, Thomas S(pottswood) W(ellford)   1942-

PERSONAL: Born May 29, 1942, in Philadelphia, Pa.; son of William Draper, Jr. (a field examiner for the National Labor Relations Board) and Belle (Wellford) Lewis; married Gillian Hollingworth (a librarian), August 29, 1964; children: Colin Geoffrey, Hilary Caroline. *Education:* University of New Brunswick, B.A., 1964; Columbia University, M.A., 1965, Ph.D., 1970.

ADDRESSES: Home—205 East Ave., Saratoga Springs, N.Y. 12866. *Office*—Department of English, Skidmore College, Saratoga Springs, N.Y. 12866.

CAREER: Iona College, New Rochelle, N.Y., instructor in English, summer, 1967; Skidmore College, Saratoga Springs, N.Y., instructor, 1968-70, assistant professor, 1970-75, associate professor of English, 1975—, director of summer school, 1978—.

MEMBER: Modern Language Association of America, American Association of University Professors.

AWARDS, HONORS: Woodrow Wilson fellow, 1968; American Philosophical Association grants, 1971, 1975; New York Council for the Humanities grant, 1977.

WRITINGS:

(Contributor) *Modern Irish Literature,* Twayne, 1972.
(Editor) *Letters of Hart Crane and His Family,* Columbia University Press, 1974.
(Editor) *Virginia Woolf,* McGraw, 1974.
(Contributor) *The Greek Vase,* Hudson-Mohawk Association of Colleges and Universities, 1981.
(Contributor) *Woolf Centennial Papers,* Whitson Press, 1982.

Also author of screenplay for film on the Brooklyn Bridge, 1979. Contributor to journals. Editor of special issue of *Salmagundi* highlighting the work of Lewis Mumford, 1980; member of editorial board of *Salmagundi* and *Hart Crane Newsletter.*

WORK IN PROGRESS: Books on the Bloomsbury Group and a biography of Lewis Mumford.

*   *   *

LIGGETT, Hunter
See PAINE, Lauran (Bosworth)

*   *   *

LINDQUIST, Emory Kempton   1908-

PERSONAL: Born February 29, 1908, in Lindsborg, Kan.; son of Harry Theodore and Augusta (Peterson) Lindquist; married Irma W. E. Lann, June 17, 1942; children: Beth, Kempton. *Education:* Bethany College, Lindsborg, Kan., A.B., 1930; Oxford University, B.A., 1930, M.A., 1933; University of Colorado, Ph.D., 1941. *Politics:* Democrat. *Religion:* Lutheran.

ADDRESSES: Home—3901 Pine Knot Ct., Wichita, Kan. 67208. *Office*—Clinton Hall, Wichita State University, Wichita, Kan. 67208.

CAREER: Bethany College, Lindsborg, Kan., assistant professor, 1933-38, professor of history, 1938-53, vice president, 1938-41, acting president, 1941-43, president, 1943-53; Wichita State University, Wichita, Kan., professor of history, 1953-55, 1961-63, 1968-78, president emeritus, 1978—, dean of faculty, 1955-61, president, 1963-68. Visiting professor, Wartburg College, 1968-69; visiting scholar, consortium for Iowa colleges, 1968-69.

MEMBER: National Education Association, American Historical Association, Kansas State Historical Society (member of board of directors, 1959—; president, 1963), Phi Beta Kappa, Pi Kappa Delta.

AWARDS, HONORS: Rhodes scholar at Oxford University, 1930-33; Royal Order of the North Star (Sweden), 1952, commander, 1978; LL.D., Augustana College, 1952; D.H.L., Bethany College, 1964, Wichita State University, 1983; D.Litt., Friends University, 1972; Carl Sandburg Medal, Swedish American Historical Society, 1986.

WRITINGS:

Smokey Valley People: A History of Lindsborg, Kansas, Augustana Historical Society, 1953.
Vision for a Valley: Olof Olsson and the Early History of Lindsborg, Augustana Historical Society, 1970.
Drommen om en Dal, Darlstad (Sweden), 1970.
An Immigrant's Two Worlds: A Biography of Hjalmar Edgren, Augustana Historical Society, 1972.

An Immigrant's American Odyssey: A Biography of Ernst Skarstedt, Augustana Historical Society, 1974.
Bethany in Kansas: The History of a College, Bethany College, 1975.
Shepherd of an Immigrant People: The Story of Erland Carlsson, Augustana Historical Society, 1978.
Hagbard Brasc: Beloved Music Master, edited by John A. Pearson, Bethany College, 1984.
G. N. Malm: A Swedish Immigrant's Varied Career, Smoky Valley Historical Association, 1989.

Contributor to *Kansas Historical Quarterly, Missouri Historical Review,* and *Swedish Pioneer Historical Review.*

*   *   *

LINEBACK, Richard H(arold)   1936-

PERSONAL: Born June 5, 1936, in Cincinnati, Ohio; son of Harold C. (a grocer) and Emma (Schoenberger) Lineback; married Carolyn M. Deckebach, August 24, 1957; children: Anna Marie, Lynn Renee. *Education:* University of Cincinnati, B.A., 1958; Indiana University, M.A., 1962, Ph.D., 1963.

ADDRESSES: Home—317 Knollwood Dr., Bowling Green, Ohio 43402. *Office*—Department of Philosophy, Bowling Green State University, Bowling Green, Ohio 43403.

CAREER: Wichita State University, Wichita, Kan., assistant professor of philosophy, 1963-65; Bowling Green State University, Bowling Green, Ohio, assistant professor, 1965-68, associate professor of philosophy and chairman of department, 1968—.

MEMBER: American Philosophical Association.

AWARDS, HONORS: National Endowments for the Humanities grant, 1976, 1977, 1978, 1979.

WRITINGS:

(Editor with Ramona Cormier and Ewing Chinn) *Encounter: An Introduction to Philosophy,* Scott, Foresman, 1970.
(Co-editor) *International Directory of Philosophy,* Philosophy Documentation Center, 1972, 4th edition, 1982.
(Editor) *The Philosopher's Index: A Retrospective to U.S. Publications from 1940,* Philosophy Documentation Center, three volumes, 1978, Volume XII: *Cumulative Edition, 1978,* 1979, Volume XIV: *Cumulative Edition, 1980,* 1981, Volume XV: *Cumulative Edition, 1981,* 1982, Volume XIX: *Cumulative Edition, 1985,* 1986, Volume XX: *Cumulative Edition, 1986,* 1987, Volume XXI: *Cumulative Edition, 1987,* 1988.
The Philosopher's Index: A Retrospective Index to Non-U.S. English Language Publications from 1940, three volumes, Philosophy Documentation Center, 1980.

Also editor of *The Philosopher's Index: Cumulative Edition, 1988.**

*   *   *

LIPTON, Dean   1919-

PERSONAL: Surname legally changed, 1943; born October 3, 1919, in Detroit, Mich.; son of Isadore and Dora Lipsitz; married Shirley Mills (a secretary), December 5, 1943 (divorced); children: Judy (Mrs. Bradley West), Linda (Mrs. Orville Perry). *Education:* Attended San Francisco City College, 1938-40;

Woodbury College, B.A., 1948. *Politics:* Democrat. *Religion:* Jewish.

ADDRESSES: Home—2348 Cabrillo, San Francisco, Calif. 94121.

CAREER: Los Angeles Daily News, Los Angeles, Calif., reporter, 1946-68; free-lance writer. Served as publicist for various political campaigns, 1948-68. Moderator, San Francisco Writer's Workshop, 1960-71. *Military service:* U.S. Army, historian, 1941-45.

MEMBER: San Francisco Press Club (1950-67, formerly historian and member of admissions committee).

WRITINGS:

Faces of Crime and Genius: The Historical Impact of the Genius-Criminal, A. S. Barnes, 1970.
Malpractice: Autobiography of a Victim, A. S. Barnes, 1978.
Blue Grass Frontier, Zebra Books, 1980.

Contributor to *National Review, General Politics, Editor & Publisher, Frontier, Industrial Marketing, Tomorrow, Science Digest, Freeman,* and other periodicals. Editor, *Truth* (newspaper), 1948-50, and *Engineer's Newsletter;* editor and publisher, *Jewish Record,* 1953-56; co-editor, *Machine Age.* Editorial writer and financial and economic correspondent for *Argonaut;* book reviewer for *San Francisco Chronicle* and *Berkeley Daily Gazette;* art critic for *Alameda Times-Star* and *San Francisco Progress.*

WORK IN PROGRESS: A novel titled *Land of the Canes;* revisions of three books, one about the Pueblo uprising in New Mexico, a satire on pacifism, and a publicist's guide.

SIDELIGHTS: Dean Lipton told *CA:* "It has been said that I am the only writer in the United States who has been both an art critic and a financial commentator. My published writings have ranged literally from A (art) to Z (zoology). This background made the writings of *Faces of Crime and Genius* possible. The book ranges from French poetic symbolism to Dampier's scientific discoveries. One of my main interests at the moment is an investigation into the possibility of silicon—instead of carbon—based life."

*   *   *

LOCRE, Peter E.
See COLE, E(ugene) R(oger)

*   *   *

LOTZ, James Robert   1929-
(Jim Lotz)

PERSONAL: Born January 12, 1929, in Liverpool, England; son of John Bowyer (a railway worker) and Mary (Hutcheon) Lotz; married Pat Wicks (a free-lance editor and librarian), December 12, 1959; children: Annette Mary, Fiona Suzanne. *Education:* University of Manchester, B.A. (with honors), 1952; McGill University, M.Sc., 1957; University of British Columbia, additional study, 1964-65 ("ejected from institution"). *Religion:* Christian.

ADDRESSES: Home—Box 3393, Halifax South P.O., Halifax, Nova Scotia, Canada B3J 3J1.

CAREER: Spent some time in Africa as trader after leaving England, and served with the special constabulary in the Kano riots in Nigeria, 1953; later wrote advertising copy in Ottawa, On-

tario; Canadian Government, Department of Indian Affairs and Northern Development, Ottawa, community planning officer, then research officer, 1960-66; Canadian Research Centre for Anthropology, Ottawa, associate director, 1966-71; St. Francis Xavier University, Coady International Institute, Antigonish, Nova Scotia, assistant professor of community development, 1971-73; freelance writer, teacher, research worker, and consultant, 1973—. *Military service:* Royal Air Force, radio technician, 1947-49.

MEMBER: Writer's Union of Canada.

AWARDS, HONORS: Queen's Commendation for Brave Conduct in Kano riots.

WRITINGS:

UNDER NAME JIM LOTZ

Northern Realities: Exploitation of the Canadian North, Follett, 1971.
(Editor with wife, Pat Lotz, and contributor) *Pilot, Not Commander: Essays in Memory of Diamond Jenness,* Canadian Research Centre for Anthropology, St. Paul University, 1971.
(Co-author) *Cape Breton Island,* David & Charles, 1974.
Understanding Canada: Regional and Community Development in a New Nation, NC Press, 1977.
Death in Dawson, PaperJacks, 1978.
Murder on the Mackenzie, PaperJacks, 1979.
Killing in Kluane, PaperJacks, 1980.
Sixth of December, PaperJacks, 1981.
History of Canada, Bison Books, 1984.
The Mounties, Bison Books, 1984.
Canadian Pacific, Bison Books, 1985.
Head, Heart and Hands, Braemar, 1986.
Prime Ministers of Canada, Bison Books, 1987.
Canadians at War, Brompton Books, 1990.

WORK IN PROGRESS: Caribou, Muskoxen, Lichen: Conflict, Confrontation, and Cooperation in Local Development; The First Disciple, a novel on the lost years of Jesus.

SIDELIGHTS: James Robert Lotz told *CA:* "I find that Canada resembles Shaw's description of marriage—'The maximum of temptation with the maximum of opportunity.' It's a country with large corporate concentrations in which individuals try to assert their individualism while striving for a sense of community. Under the prissy, moralistic, middle-class veneer of this country there are all kinds of interesting things bubbling up and creating a new society.

"Increasingly the centre cannot hold, and the country is polarizing between rich and poor, heartland and fringes, English and French. The media cover these divisions, and I'm more concerned with how healing is taking place between different groups in Canada and elsewhere in the world and how creativity and innovation are occurring as people come together and share their resources.

"Meanwhile, I'm retaining my sense of humor! Tragedy divides, comedy unites, and paradoxically, as W. B. Yeats put it, 'Until you realize that life is a tragedy, you can't start enjoying yourself.'"

BIOGRAPHICAL/CRITICAL SOURCES:

PERIODICALS

Windsor Star, February 21, 1981.

LOTZ, Jim
  See LOTZ, James Robert

                    *   *   *

LUCAS, J. K.
  See PAINE, Lauran (Bosworth)

                    *   *   *

LYON, Buck
  See PAINE, Lauran (Bosworth)

M

MA, John T(a-jen) 1920-

PERSONAL: Born February 22, 1920, in Wenchow, China; came to the United States in 1947, naturalized, 1962; son of Kung-yu (an artist) and Hsiang-chuan (Huang) Ma; married May Hoo, January 19, 1959; children: Averil, Carol, Debora. *Education:* National Central University, Chungking, China, Diploma, 1954; University of Wisconsin, M.A., 1948; Columbia University, M.S.L., 1958.

ADDRESSES: Home—138-10 Franklin Ave., Flushing, N.Y. 11355. *Office*—New York Public Library, Oriental Division, 5th Ave. and 42nd St., New York, N.Y. 10018.

CAREER: Yale University, New Haven, Conn., translator, Human Relations Area Files, 1955; University of Washington, Seattle, assistant editor of Chinese history project, 1955-56; Columbia University, New York, N.Y., associate librarian, Missionary Research Library, 1956-61; Cornell University Library, Ithaca, N.Y., Chinese cataloger-bibliographer, 1961-65; Hoover Institution on War, Revolution, and Peace, Stanford, Calif., curator-librarian, East Asian Collection, 1965-74; National Taiwan University, Taipei, visiting professor, 1975; Leiden University, Sinological Institute, Leiden, Netherlands, librarian, 1976-85. Peiping representative of Chinese Government Public Relations Office, 1945-46, and editor in International Department of Chinese Ministry of Information, 1945-47. *Military service:* Chinese First Army, volunteer, 1938-39. American Volunteers Group (Flying Tigers), interpreter-codeman, 1941-42; became first lieutenant.

MEMBER: Association for Asian Studies, American Association of Teachers of Chinese Language and Culture.

WRITINGS:

(With J. J. Dresher and Elaine L. Young) *A Test of Disputed Authorship: Ch'en Tzu-chia and Chu Tzu-chia,* Douglas Advanced Research Laboratories, 1968.
(With Dresher, Young, and R. E. Norton) *Power Spectral Densities of Literary Rhythms (Chinese),* Douglas Advanced Research Laboratories, 1968.
Elementary Chinese for American Librarians: A Simple Manual, Hanover (N.H.) Oriental Society, 1968.
(Contributor) Winston L. Y. Yang and T. S. Y. C. Yang, editors, *Asian Resources in American Libraries,* Foreign Area Mate-

rials Center, State University of New York, and National Council for Foreign Area Materials, 1968.
East Asia: A Survey of Holdings at the Hoover Institution on War, Revolution and Peace, Hoover Institution, 1971.
(Contributor) Yuan-li Wu, editor, *The Economic Condition of Chinese Americans,* Pacific/Asian American Mental Health Research Center, 1980.
Van Gulik Collection, Inter Documentation, 1982.
Chinese Collections in Western Europe, Inter Documentation, 1985.

Contributor to *Biographical Dictionary of Republican China* and to journals. Correspondent, *Chungking Reporter,* 1945-46.

* * *

MacDONNELL, Kevin 1919-

PERSONAL: Born November 25, 1919; son of Henry Lynch (a doctor) and Edith (Collin) MacDonnell; married Sheila Darragh (an aeronautical engineer). *Politics:* Irish Republican. *Religion:* Roman Catholic.

ADDRESSES: Home—Ten South Hill Park Gardens, Hampstead, London N.W.3, England.

CAREER: Worked as press photographer and journalist, 1936-39; conducted photographic research, 1939-45; ran film unit for aircraft company, 1945-48; researcher, lecturer, and television and publicity representative for photographic firm, 1948-69; photographer, publicity agent, and writer, 1969—.

MEMBER: Photographic Society of Ireland (honorary member), Institute of Incorporated Photographers.

WRITINGS:

Home Photography, Johnsons of Hendon, 1953, 10th edition, 1973.
35mm Cameraman, Johnsons of Hendon, 1963.
Better Photography, edited by Sheila Innes, British Broadcasting Corp., 1965.
Eadweard Muybridge: The Man Who Invented the Moving Picture, Little, Brown, 1972.
Looking Back at Transport, 1901-1939, EP Publishing, 1976.
(With Eric Hosking) *Eric Hosking's Birds: Fifty Years of Photographing Wildlife,* Pelham, 1979, published as *A Passion for*

Birds: Fifty Years of Photographing Wildlife, Coward, McCann, 1980.

Choosing and Using SLR Lenses, Euming, 1982.

An Amateur Photographer's Guide to Sussex, Wildwood House, 1984.

A Photographer's Guide to Kent, Gower, 1986.

A Photographer's Guide to London, Gower, 1986.

Freelance Photographer's Britain, BFP Books, 1988.

Also author of sixty television scripts. Author of monthly column in *Photography,* 1957—. Contributor of travel and photographic articles to journals.

WORK IN PROGRESS: Troubles in Ireland: 1916-1923; Taking Photographs; Victorian Photography.

AVOCATIONAL INTERESTS: Present-day life in Ireland, history of photography, air-to-air photography of antique aircraft, collecting old photographs, changes in the countryside of England, walking on footpaths, studying Victorian and Edwardian everyday life.

*   *   *

MacISAAC, David 1935-

PERSONAL: Born June 22, 1935, in Boston, Mass.; son of John L. (a marketing clerk) and Mary (a credit manager; maiden name, Mullen) MacIsaac; married Charlotte Wade, July 19, 1959; children: Donna Marie, Paul, Pamela, Patrick. *Education:* Trinity College, Hartford, Conn., A.B., 1957; Yale University, A.M., 1958; Duke University, Ph.D., 1970. *Politics:* "Eccentric."

ADDRESSES: Home and office—3411 Royal Carriage Dr., Montgomery, Ala. 36116.

CAREER: U.S. Air Force, career officer, 1958-81, retired as lieutenant colonel; freelance writer and consultant, 1981-82; Air University, Air Power Research Institute, Maxwell Air Force Base, Ala., senior research fellow and visiting professor, 1982-84; freelance writer and consultant, 1984-85; Air Power Research Institute, Maxwell Air Force Base, associate director, 1986—. Personnel officer with Strategic Air Command in Texas, 1959-61, and at Torrejon Air Base in Spain, 1961-64; Air Force Academy, instructor, 1964-66, assistant professor, 1968-70, associate professor, 1971-76, professor of history, 1976-78; member of Air Force advisory group in Vietnam, 1971; visiting professor at U.S. Naval War College, 1975-76; chief of history of warfare studies at Air War College, 1979-81. Adjunct teacher, University of Maryland, European Division (Madrid), 1962-63, and Far East Division (Saigon), 1971, Auburn University at Montgomery, 1981, University of Alabama, 1984-86. Fellow of Woodrow Wilson International Center for Scholars, Smithsonian Institution, 1978-79.

MEMBER: American Military Institute, Air Force Association, United States Naval Institute, American Committee on the History of the Second World War, Inter-University Seminar on the Armed Forces and Society, Phi Beta Kappa.

AWARDS, HONORS: Military—Air Force Commendation medals, 1961 and 1970; Bronze Star, 1971; Meritorious Service medals, 1976, 1978, and 1981. Civilian—Woodrow Wilson fellow, Yale University, 1958; best article awards, *Air University Review,* 1979, 1982, and 1984.

WRITINGS:

(Editor) *The Military and Society: Proceedings of the Fifth Military History Symposium,* U.S. Government Printing Office, 1975.

Strategic Bombing in World War II: The Story of the U.S. Strategic Bombing Survey, Garland Publishing, 1976.

(Editor and author of introductions) *The Defeat of the German Air Force: The U.S. Strategic Bombing Survey,* ten volumes, Garland Publishing, 1976.

(With Crayton E. Rowe) *Empathic Attunement: The "Technique" of Psychoanalytic Self Psychology,* Aronson, 1989.

CONTRIBUTOR

M. D. Wright and Lawrence Paszek, editors, *Soldiers and Statesmen: Proceedings of the Fourth Military History Symposium,* U.S. Government Printing Office, 1973.

David H. White, editor, *Proceedings of the Citadel Conference on War and Diplomacy,* Citadel, 1976.

A. F. Hurley and R. C. Erhart, editors, *Air Power and Warfare: Proceedings of the Eighth Military History Symposium,* U.S. Government Printing Office, 1979.

James Titus, editor, *Home Front and War in the Twentieth Century: Proceedings of the Tenth Military History Symposium,* U.S. Government Printing Office, 1984.

Peter Paret, editor, *Makers of Modern Strategy: New Edition,* Princeton University Press, 1986.

R. A. Mason, editor, *War in the Third Dimension,* Brassey's (London), 1986.

Paret, editor, *Makers of Modern Strategy from Machiavelli to the Nuclear Age,* Princeton University Press, 1986.

OTHER

Consultant, *Bombers over Japan,* by Kieth Wheeler, Time-Life, 1982. Contributor to *Dictionary of American History* and *Encyclopedia Britannica.* Contributor of more than fifty articles and reviews to history and military journals, including *Air University Review, Historian, Mid-America, Air Force Magazine, Naval War College Review, Military Review, Aerospace Historian, Wilson Quarterly, Washington Post Book World,* and *Journal of American History.*

SIDELIGHTS: "My writing has thus far been pretty straightforward stuff, history and all that, relating almost exclusively to military affairs," David MacIsaac told *CA.* "For the past several years it has centered increasingly on questions of nuclear weapons policy, indeed a dismal field of speculation. I'm about ready to start looking for a topic from the eighteenth century or so—before aircraft, before nukes, before security-classified documents, and before copying machines. Much of what I have written about of late so nearly fulfills the requirements for fiction that I might even give that a try."

*   *   *

MACKIE, John
See LEVINSON, Leonard

*   *   *

MACLEAN, Fitzroy (Hew) 1911-

PERSONAL: Born March 11, 1911, in Cairo, Egypt.; son of Charles Wilberforce (a British Army officer) and Gladys (Royle) Maclean; married Veronica Fraser (duaghter of 16th Baron of Lovat), January 12, 1946; children: Charles, James. *Education:* Cambridge University, M.A. (with first class honors), 1932. *Politics:* Conservative. *Religion:* Episcopal Church of Scotland.

ADDRESSES: Home—Strachur House, Strachur, Argyllshire, Scotland.

CAREER: Diplomatic Service, third secretary, 1933, transferred to Paris, 1934, transferred to Moscow, 1937, second secretary,

1938, transferred to Foreign Office, 1939; resigned from Diplomatic Service and enlisted ias private in Cameron Highlanders, 1941, became second lieutenant, joined First Special Air Service Regiment and became captain, 1942, lieutenant-colonel and brigadier, 1943, commander of British Military Mission to Yugoslav Partisans, 1943-45, head of Special Refugee Commission, Germany, Austria, and Italy, 1947; member of Parliament, Lancaster Division, 1941-59, Bute and North Ayrshire, 1959-74; War Office, parliamentary under-secretary of state and financial secretary, 1954-57. Lee Knowles Lecturer at Cambridge University, 1953. Member of United Kingdom delegation to North Atlantic Assembly, 1962-74; member, Council of Europe, 1972-74.

MEMBER: Cable Television Association (president), Great Britain—U.S.S.R. Association (past president), British Yugoslav Society (president).

AWARDS, HONORS: Military—Croix de Guerre (France), 1943; Commander, Order of the British Empire, 1944; Order of Kutusov (U.S.S.R.), 1944; Partisan Star 1st Class, 1945; Yugoslav Order of Merit, 1969; Yugoslav Order of the Flag, 1981. Civilian—Created Baronet of Dunconnel, 1957; LL.D., Glasgow University, 1969, and Dalhousie University; D. Litt., Acadia University, 1970.

WRITINGS:

Eastern Approaches (Book Society choice in England), J. Cape, 1949, published as *Escape to Adventure,* Little, Brown, 1950, special edition with new introduction by Charles W. Thayer, Time, 1964, reprinted, Atheneum, 1984.
The Heretic: The Life and Times of Josip Broz-Tito, Harper, 1957, published as *Tito, the Man Who Defied Hitler and Stalin,* Ballantine, 1957 (published in England as *Disputed Barricade: The Life and Times of Josip Broz-Tito, Marshal of Jugoslavia,* J. Cape, 1957).
A Person from England, and Other Travelers to Turkestan, Harper, 1958.
Back to Bokhara, Harper, 1959.
(Author of introduction) *Yugoslavia,* photographs by Toni Schneiders and others, Thames & Hudson, 1969.
A Concise History of Scotland, Viking, 1970.
The Battle of the Neretva, Panther Books, 1970.
To the Back of Beyond, Little, Brown, 1975.
To Caucasus: The End of All the Earth, Little, Brown, 1976.
Take Nine Spies, Atheneum, 1978.
Holy Russia, Atheneum, 1979.
Tito: A Pictorial Biography, McGraw, 1980.
The Isles of the Sea, Collins, 1985.
Bonnie Prince Charlie, Weidenfeld & Nicolson, 1988.
Portrait of the Soviet Union, Holt, 1988.

SIDELIGHTS: Fitzroy Maclean has traveled widely in the Balkans, the Caucasus, Near East, Middle East, Central Asia, Mongolia, and European Russia.

BIOGRAPHICAL/CRITICAL SOURCES:

PERIODICALS

New Yorker, May 30, 1970.
New York Times, October 21, 1980.
Times Literary Supplement, November 11, 1988.

*　　　*　　　*

MALKIEL, Burton Gordon　1932-

PERSONAL: Born August 28, 1932, in Boston, Mass.; son of Sol and Celia (Gordon) Malkiel; married former wife Judith Ather-

ton, July 16, 1954; married Nancy Weiss (dean of the College, Princeton University), July 31, 1988; children: (first marriage) Jonathan. *Education:* Harvard University, B.A., 1953, M.B.A., 1955; Princeton University, Ph.D., 1964.

ADDRESSES: Home—76 North Rd., Princeton, N.J. 08540. *Office*—Department of Economics, Princeton University, Princeton, N.J. 08544.

CAREER: Smith Barney & Co., New York, N.Y., associate, 1958-60; Princeton University, Princeton, N.J., assistant professor, 1964-66, associate professor, 1966-68, professor of economics, 1968-81, Gordon S. Rentschler Memorial Professor of Economics, 1969-81, chairman of department, 1974-75, 1977-81; Yale University School of Organization and Management, New Haven, Conn., dean, 1981-87; Princeton University, Chemical Bank Chairman's Professor of Economics, 1988—. Member of board of directors of several companies, including Prudential Insurance Company of America, 1973—, and Vanguard Group of Investment Companies, 1977—; member, President's Council of Economic Advisors, 1975-77; governor, American Stock Exchange, 1978—. *Military service:* U.S. Army, 1955-58; became first lieutenant.

MEMBER: American Economic Association, American Finance Association (president, 1979; member of board of directors, 1979-84).

AWARDS, HONORS: D.H.L., University of Hartford, 1971.

WRITINGS:

The Term Structure of Interest Rates: Expectations and Behavior Patterns, Princeton University Press, 1966.
(With Richard E. Quandt) *Strategies and Rational Decisions in the Securities Options Market,* MIT Press, 1969.
A Random Walk down Wall Street, Norton, 1973, 5th edition, 1990.
(With George M. von Furstenberg) *The Government and Capital Formation: A Survey of Recent Issues,* American Enterprise Institute, 1978.
The Inflation Beater's Investment Guide: Winning Strategies for the 1980s, Norton, 1980, new edition published as *Winning Investment Strategies: The Inflation-Beaters Guide,* 1982.
(With John G. Cragg) *Expectations and the Structure of Share Prices,* University of Chicago Press, 1982.

WORK IN PROGRESS: Research on securities markets.

*　　　*　　　*

MANCHESTER, William (Raymond)　1922-

PERSONAL: Born April 1, 1922, in Attleboro, Mass.; son of William Raymond and Sallie (Thompson) Manchester; married Julia Brown Marshall, March 27, 1948; children: John Kennerly, Julie Thompson, Laurie. *Education:* Massachusetts State College (now University of Massachusetts), A.B., 1946; University of Missouri, A.M., 1947.

ADDRESSES: Office—Wesleyan University, 329 Wesleyan Station, Middletown, Conn. 06457. *Agent*—Don Congdon Associates, Inc., 156 Fifth Ave., Suite 625, New York, N.Y. 10010.

CAREER: Daily Oklahoman, Oklahoma City, Okla., reporter, 1945-46; *Baltimore Sun,* Baltimore, Md., reporter, Washington correspondent, and foreign correspondent in the Middle East, India, and Southeast Asia, 1947-54; Wesleyan University, Middletown, Conn., managing editor of Wesleyan University Publications, 1955-64, member of university faculty, 1968-69, member of faculty of East College, 1968—, writer in residence, 1975—, adjunct professor of history, 1979—. Friends of the University of Massachusetts Library, president of board of trustees, 1970-72, trustee, 1970-74. *Military service:* U.S. Marine Corps, 1942-45; became sergeant; awarded Purple Heart.

MEMBER: American Historical Association, Society of American Historians, Authors Guild, Authors League of America, Williams Club, Century Club.

AWARDS, HONORS: Guggenheim fellow, 1959-60; Wesleyan Center for Advanced Studies fellow, 1959-60; L.H.D., University of Massachusetts, 1965; Prix Dag Hammarskjoeld au merite litteraire, 1967; Overseas Press Club citation for best book on foreign affairs, 1968; University of Missouri honor award for distinguished service in journalism, 1969; Connecticut Book Award, 1975; L.H.D., University of New Haven, 1979; National Book Award nomination, 1980, for *American Caesar: Douglas MacArthur, 1880-1964;* ALA Notable Book citation, 1980, for *Goodbye, Darkness: A Memoir of the Pacific War;* President's Cabinet Award, University of Detroit, 1981; Frederick S. Troy Award, University of Massachusetts, 1981; McConnaughty Award, Wesleyan University, 1981; *Los Angeles Times* Biography Prize nomination, 1983, and Union League/Abraham Lincoln Literary Award, 1984, both for *The Last Lion: Winston Spencer Churchill,* Volume 1: *Visions of Glory: 1874-1932;* Connecticut Bar Association Distinguished Public Service Award, 1985.

WRITINGS:

Disturber of the Peace: The Life of H. L. Mencken (originally serialized in *Harper's,* July-August, 1950), Harper, 1951, 2nd edition edited by Stephen B. Oates and Paul Mariani, University of Massachusetts Press, 1986.

The City of Anger (novel), Ballantine, 1953, reprinted, Little, Brown, 1987.

Shadow of the Monsoon (novel), Doubleday, 1956.

Beard the Lion (novel), Morrow, 1958.

A Rockefeller Family Portrait: From John D. to Nelson, Little, Brown, 1959.

(Contributor) Bredemier and Toby, editors, *Social Problems in America,* Wiley, 1960.

The Long Gainer: A Novel, Little, Brown, 1961.

Portrait of a President: John F. Kennedy in Profile, Little, Brown, 1962, 2nd edition, 1967.

(Contributor) Don Congdon, editor, *Combat World War I,* Dial, 1964.

(Contributor) Poyntz Tyler, *Securities Exchanges and the SEC,* Wilson, 1965.

The Death of a President: November 20-November 25, 1963 (originally serialized in *Look,* January 24-March 7, 1967; Book-of-the-Month Club selection), Harper, 1967, published with revised introduction, Arbor House, 1985, published with new addition by the author, Harper, 1988.

The Arms of Krupp, 1587-1968 (originally serialized in *Holiday,* November, 1964-February, 1965; Literary Guild selection), Little, Brown, 1968.

The Glory and the Dream: A Narrative History of America, 1932-1972 (Literary Guild selection), Little, Brown, 1974, reprinted, Bantam, 1989.

Controversy and Other Essays in Journalism, Little, Brown, 1976.

American Caesar: Douglas MacArthur, 1880-1964 (Book-of-the-Month Club selection), Little, Brown, 1978.

Goodbye, Darkness: A Memoir of the Pacific War (Book-of-the-Month Club selection), Little, Brown, 1980.

One Brief Shining Moment: Remembering Kennedy (Book-of-the-Month Club selection), Little, Brown, 1983.

The Last Lion: Winston Spencer Churchill, Volume 1: *Visions of Glory: 1874-1932* (Book-of-the-Month Club selection), Little, Brown, 1983, Volume 2: *Alone: 1932-1940* (Book-of-the-Month Club selection), Little, Brown, 1987.

(Contributor) *A Sense of History: The Best Writing from the Pages of American Heritage,* American Heritage/Houghton, 1985.

(Contributor) Annie Dillard and Robert Atwan, editors, *Best American Essays 1988,* Ticknor & Fields, 1988.

(Author of text) *In Our Time: The World as Seen by Magnum Photographers,* Norton, 1989.

Also author of introduction for *Thimblerigger: The Law v. Governor Marvin Mandel.* Contributor to *Encyclopaedia Britannica.* Contributor to *Atlantic, Harper's, Reporter, Saturday Review, Holiday, Nation, Esquire,* and *Saturday Evening Post.*

WORK IN PROGRESS: The Last Lion: Winston Spencer Churchill, Volume 3: *Defender of the Realm: 1940-1965.*

SIDELIGHTS: William Manchester's oeuvre ranges from structured novels to massive biographies. But his books, the author tells Stefan Kanfer of *People* magazine, all share one common theme—the study of power: "What exactly is power? Where are its roots? How do some people get it and others miss it entirely?" Using what Kanfer calls the "Manchester trademarks: unflagging energy, hundreds of interviews, monuments of detail and pounds of manuscript," Manchester, states Kenneth Atchity in the *Los Angeles Times,* has made himself "the [James] Michener of biographers."

Manchester's first book focused on the power of words. He was first attracted to the writings of H. L. Mencken, the famous critic and literary curmudgeon, while an undergraduate in college. After serving with the Marines in World War II, Manchester entered the graduate school of the University of Missouri and completed a thesis on Mencken. The critic read the thesis, authorized Manchester's proposed biography, and invited the young writer to join the staff of the Baltimore *Evening Sun,* Mencken's newspaper.

Disturber of the Peace: The Life of H. L. Mencken helped establish Manchester's reputation as a talented writer. Although some reviewers felt that Manchester's devotion to Mencken interfered with the story, many praised the young biographer's effort. *Saturday Review* critic Charles Angoff declared that *Disturber of the Peace* "is probably the most fully documented" of all Mencken studies and added that some of Manchester's remarks "display a refreshing critical independence." George Genzmer, writing in *Nation,* called the book "a generally well-proportioned narrative that . . . portrays [Mencken's] charm, vigor, and humor with notable effect." Manchester, Genzmer continued, "is slapdash in handling some details and in brushing in the background, but, such matters aside, the story is authentic."

Manchester then turned to fiction, and wrote four novels over the next few years. Many of these deal with the use and abuse of power and are based on Manchester's reporting experiences; for instance, *The City of Anger* traces corruption in an East Coast city very much like Baltimore, while *The Long Gainer* examines an academic and political scandal resembling one that "rocked the University of Maryland some years ago," reports Wirt Williams in the *New York Times Book Review. Beard the Lion* is a thriller involving politics in the Near East in the late 1950s, while *Shadow of the Monsoon* tells of post-Raj India, where Manchester served as a foreign correspondent.

Although they were generally favorably received, Manchester's novels are perhaps most significant because of the way they prefigure stylistic elements of his later nonfiction. The publisher's note that introduces the 1985 edition of *The City of Anger* explains, "The reviewers of each [of Manchester's four novels] commented on his skillful command of detail—accurate detail, for his eye has always been a lens, not a prism." "His use of detail is both Manchester's strength and his weakness," the publisher's note continues. "Those who dislike it, particularly in his nonfiction, criticize him as a collector of trivia. But to Manchester the skills of narration grow out of the mastery of detail. It is a matter of taste."

Manchester returned to biography in 1959 with *A Rockefeller Family Portrait: From John D. to Nelson,* and in 1962 with *Portrait of a President: John F. Kennedy in Profile.* Although different in many ways, the two books share several features: both were originally published as magazine articles, both reiterate Manchester's interest in power in their subjects (the family of then-governor Nelson Rockefeller of New York and then-President Kennedy), and critics gave both mixed reviews while recognizing that the two volumes were highly approving of their subjects. "Those who are looking for material to criticize the Rockefeller family or its individual members," writes Leo Egan in the *New York Times* about *A Rockefeller Family Portrait,* "would be well advised to look somewhere else." Tom Wicker remarks in the *New York Times Book Review,* that *Portrait of a President* "is what its title says it is—a portrait, not dishonest, but smitten, one in which the dazzled artist has gazed upon the subject with loving eyes and found redeeming beauty in his every flaw."

Yet several critics admit that Manchester's depictions of the Rockefellers and of Kennedy are appealing; in *Saturday Review,* Cleveland Amory calls *A Rockefeller Family Portrait* "skillfully and carefully" composed, and adds, "At least the first three-quarters of this book is as capably written as anything that has passed this writer's desk in some time." "In sum," declares G. W. Johnson in the *New Republic,* "what Manchester gives us [in *Portrait of a President*] is a picture of a brave, honorable and resolute man struggling with problems that may well be beyond his, or any human capacity to solve."

It was partly on the basis of *Portrait of a President* that, early in 1964, Jacqueline Kennedy asked Manchester to write an account of President Kennedy's assassination, offering him exclusive interviews with family members. Manchester had met Kennedy shortly after World War II when both of them were disabled veterans living in Boston, and he had since become a family friend. He agreed to write the book, and signed an agreement with Senator Robert Kennedy providing that most of the volume's royalties would go to the new Kennedy Memorial Library, and that Senator Kennedy and the President's widow would have the right to review the manuscript. When Manchester finished the book after two years of exhaustive research and writing, however, both Kennedys felt unable to read it. They sent representatives to review the manuscript instead, and, after some changes, the representatives unanimously approved publication of *The Death of a President: November 20-November 25, 1963.*

Controversy followed close behind the book's approval. After *Look* magazine made a record-setting bid of $665,000 for serialization rights, Jacqueline Kennedy, on the advice of several associates, withdrew her permission to publish the story. Her action was based on fears that Manchester's representation of Johnson's government would damage Senator Kennedy's presidential aspirations in 1968. However, both Manchester's publishers, *Look*

and Harper & Row, refused to stop publication and, in December of 1966, representatives of the Kennedy family filed suit. "We *couldn't* stop," Manchester told *CA.* "Contracts had been signed in 17 countries, [and] we (Bobby [Kennedy] and me) would have been sued into penury." The matter was settled out of court when the publishers' representatives persuaded Mrs. Kennedy to read the book for herself, and, after superficial changes, *The Death of a President* went to press early in 1967.

Although much of the media attention the book received centered on Mrs. Kennedy's suit rather than on its substance, reviewers noted several important characteristics of the work: Manchester's massive accumulation of facts, and his subjective treatment of the subject. "Had the Kennedy family merely wanted to set the record straight," states Margaret L. Coit in *Saturday Review,* "they should have approached some cut-and-dried academician who would have marshaled the facts with cold objectivity. Instead, their choice fell upon a highly emotional and subjective writer who identified himself with John F. Kennedy, his time, and his generation. They should have foreseen that the facts would not remain inert under his fingers, that the whole horror would blaze forth again with compounded intensity."

Manchester himself lends credibility to this interpretation of his work. In the introduction to the 1985 edition of *The Death of a President,* he writes: "Here . . . I have attempted to lead the reader back through historical events by recreating the sense of immediacy people felt at the time, so that he sees, feels, and hears what was seen, felt, and heard—mourns, rejoices, weeps, or loves with mourners, rejoicers, weepers, or lovers long since vanished: figures whose present has become our past." Finally, Manchester concludes, "*The Death of a President* was not written for Jackie or any of the others. I wrote it for the one Kennedy I had known well and deeply loved, the splendid man who had been cruelly slain at 12:30 p.m. Texas time on Friday, November 22, 1963."

After the furor surrounding *The Death of a President* died down, Manchester returned to the work he had abandoned for the Kennedy project: a history of the Krupp family, chief of the steel and munitions makers in Germany until 1967. Although Manchester's investigation begins in Renaissance Germany, the major portion of his study concentrates on the Krupps' role in Hitler's Third Reich. Alfried Krupp, who ran the business during the Second World War, was convicted at the Nuremburg trials of war crimes, including the exploitation of citizens of occupied countries and Jews as slave labor; he received a sentence of twelve years' imprisonment and the confiscation of all his property. However, Alfried served only three years of his term before the American High Commissioner in Germany released him and restored his property to him.

Many reviewers were impressed by the scope of *The Arms of Krupp.* "In this monumental study," declares *Saturday Review* commentator Henry C. Wolfe, "William Manchester has written a melodramatic, often macabre account of the Krupp empire that fascinates from beginning to ironical end." Christopher Lehmann-Haupt, writing in the *New York Times,* comments, "As research alone, the book is impressive. Manchester has unearthed material not known to the public before, and pieced it together in patterns that were not seen before." "The Krupps story, as Mr. Manchester tells it," states Geoffrey Barraclough in the *New York Review of Books,* "is a paradigm of German history."

Manchester chose an even broader range for his next book, *The Glory and the Dream: A Narrative History of America, 1932-*

1972. Manchester follows the generation that grew up during the Depression, chronicling its triumphs and tragedies, telling of its heroes and struggles: the Second World War, the loss of FDR, General MacArthur's resignation, Frank Sinatra and the Beatles, and the Bomb. Writing in the *New York Times Book Review,* Alfred Kazin calls *The Glory and the Dream* a "fluent, likeable, can't-put-it-down narrative history of America" that is "popular history in our special tradition of literary merchandising." "Reading Manchester," Kazin continues, "you run with the Bonus Army, lift up your chin like Roosevelt, put up the flag at Iwo Jima, and nervously dismiss MacArthur. You are against Communism and the Cold War. You participate!" "There is no fiction that can compare with good, gossipy, anecdotal history— the 'inside story' of who said or did what in moments of great tension or crisis," reports Anatole Broyard in the *New York Times.* "I think you ought to read this history and weep, read it and laugh, read it and make sure you don't repeat it."

The biography *American Caesar: Douglas MacArthur, 1880-1964,* Manchester's next book, brought wide acclaim from critics for its authoritative evocation of one of the most powerful and controversial figures in modern American history. Although MacArthur's military expertise defeated the Japanese in World War II's South Pacific theater with a minimum of casualties, his repeated disobedience of orders forced President Truman to remove him from command during the Korean War. "The personality and charisma of MacArthur are so successfully recreated in Manchester's biography that it is easy to forget that the book, unlike the man, had an author," remarks Orville Schell in *Saturday Review.* "This is to Manchester's credit. . . . [He] has written a thorough and spellbinding book. It is a dramatic chronicle of one of America's last epic heroes." Manchester's *American Caesar* "is exquisitely ambivalent," declares Broyard in the *New York Times,* "not so much torn as balanced between the two MacArthurs, whom he calls 'noble and ignoble, arrogant and shy, the best of men and the worst of men, the most protean, most ridiculous, and most sublime.'"

The author's own South Pacific experiences as a sergeant of Marines in World War II are the subject of *Goodbye, Darkness: A Memoir of the Pacific War.* Recalling his combat service, Manchester wonders what made his lightly-wounded younger self leave the hospital and return to his unit, only to receive an almost fatal injury. He believes that his gesture was partly an act of solidarity with his men, partly a desire to uphold family tradition, and partly a pride of country—feelings that, Manchester believes, have atrophied in post-war America. While not all critics agree with the author's analysis of the situation, many extol the power of his book. "Those sections of the book that are about the war itself are very well done," declares Broyard in the *New York Times.* "Manchester's combat writing is one of his book's strengths and stands comparison with the best" of the genre, adds *New York Times Book Review* contributor Ted Morgan. Clay Blair, writing in the *Chicago Tribune Book World,* states, "The reviewer is hard put to describe this intelligent, beautifully crafted but complicated work in a nutshell."

Most recently Manchester has examined the life of another important figure of the Second World War, Winston Churchill. The first two volumes of the biography *The Last Lion: Winston Spencer Churchill* trace Churchill's personal and political career from his early years to the time he became Prime Minister of Great Britain. Since Manchester's volumes have been preceded by many other studies, including Martin Gilbert's official Churchill biography, which runs eight and a half million words, some reviewers, in the words of *New York Review of Books* contributor Norman Stone, "simply do not see any need for Manchester's

book[s]." Others, however, recognize valuable elements in the author's work that sets his version of the Churchill epic apart from all others. Robert Conot writes in the *Chicago Tribune Book World* that "Churchill and Manchester were clearly made for each other." Manchester's "accumulated merits, of scrupulous research, sustained narrative lucidity, . . . [and] unabashed inquisitiveness, seem to me to outweigh most of the errors—of judgment, mainly—that [he] can be charged with," declares Alistair Cooke in the *New Yorker.* Finally, Cooke concludes, Manchester is able "to introduce us, by way of new and dramatic emphases, to many startling things we thought we knew."

MEDIA ADAPTATIONS: "The City of Anger," adapted from Manchester's novel of the same title, aired on NBC-TV in 1955. "American Caesar," a television miniseries based on Manchester's biography of Douglas MacArthur, was narrated by John Huston, produced by John McGreevey, aired on the Ted Turner cable network in 1985, and is presently available on videocassette.

BIOGRAPHICAL/CRITICAL SOURCES:

BOOKS

Authors in the News, Volume 1, Gale, 1976.
Corry, John, *The Manchester Affair,* Putnam, 1967.
Manchester, William, *The City of Anger* (novel), Ballantine, 1953, reprinted, Little, Brown, 1985.
Manchester, William, *The Death of a President: November 20-November 25, 1963,* revised edition, Arbor House, 1985.

PERIODICALS

Atlantic, May, 1967.
Boston Sunday Globe, October 23, 1988.
Chicago Tribune Book World, September 28, 1980, May 15, 1983, November 20, 1983.
Detroit Free Press, January 1, 1989.
Detroit News, June 26, 1983.
Los Angeles Times, November 6, 1983.
Los Angeles Times Book Review, May 8, 1983, November 27, 1983, December 11, 1988.
Nation, April 14, 1951, September 19, 1959, April 17, 1967.
National Review, May 30, 1967.
New Republic, October 8, 1962, April 22, 1967.
New Statesman, April 21, 1967.
Newsday, September 18, 1988, October 2, 1988.
Newsweek, November 25, 1974, September 11, 1978, December 12, 1988.
New Yorker, January 20, 1951, April 8, 1967, August 22, 1983.
New York Herald Tribune Book Review, January 7, 1951, July 19, 1953, August 2, 1959.
New York Review of Books, April 20, 1967, March 27, 1969, October 12, 1978, January 22, 1981, November 10, 1983.
New York Times, January 14, 1951, July 13, 1953, April 8, 1956, August 9, 1959, April 3, 1967, December 6, 1968, November 15, 1974, September 20, 1978, September 17, 1980, May 25, 1983.
New York Times Book Review, September 10, 1961, September 30, 1962, April 9, 1967, November 24, 1968, November 17, 1974, August 31, 1980, June 5, 1983, November 27, 1988.
People, November 27, 1978.
Saturday Review, July 11, 1959, January 21, 1967, April 15, 1967, December 21, 1968, January 11, 1975, October 14, 1978.
Saturday Review of Literature, January 6, 1951.
Time, January 8, 1951, December 20, 1968, November 18, 1974, September 11, 1978, October 31, 1988.

Times (London), November 24, 1988.
Times Literary Supplement, December 14, 1967, February 20, 1969, August 19, 1983.
Tribune Books (Chicago), September 18, 1988.
Washington Post Book World, October 30, 1983, November 10, 1985, October 16, 1988.

—Sketch by Kenneth R. Shepherd

* * *

MARCO

See CHARLIER, Roger H(enri)

* * *

MARKEN, Jack W(alter) 1922-

PERSONAL: Born February 11, 1922, in Akron, Ohio; son of James W. (a laborer) and Mary (Likens) Marken; married Martha Rose McVay, July 19, 1946; children: Janice (Mrs. John Hibbard), Roger, Harold. Education: University of Akron, B.A., 1947; Indiana University, M.A., 1950, Ph.D., 1953; also studied at Queen Mary College, London, 1951-52. Politics: Liberal Democrat.

ADDRESSES: Home—319 20th Ave., Brookings, S.D. 57006. Office—Department of English, South Dakota State University, Brookings, S.D. 57007.

CAREER: University of Kentucky, Lexington, instructor in English, 1952-54; Ohio Wesleyan University, Delaware, assistant professor of English and humanities, 1954-55; Central Michigan University, Mount Pleasant, assistant professor of English, 1955-60; Slippery Rock State College (now Pennsylvania State College), Slippery Rock, Pa., associate professor, 1960-63, professor of English, 1963-67; South Dakota State University, Brookings, professor of English, 1967—, chairman of department, 1967-76. Fulbright lecturer at University of Jordan, 1965-66; lecturer in Finland on the American Indian, under auspices of U.S. Information Service and Finnish-American Society, 1970. Military service: U.S. Army Air Forces, combat cameraman, 1943-45.

MEMBER: Modern Language Association of America, National Council of Teachers of English, American Association of University Professors (vice president of Pennsylvania Division, 1964-65), Keats-Shelley Society, Finnish-American Society, National Indian Education, Irish-American Institute, Midwest Modern Language Association, South Dakota Committee on the Humanities (chairman, 1971-74).

AWARDS, HONORS: Fulbright grant, 1951-52; American Philosophical Society grant, 1959, research grants, 1965, 1967; Distinguished Award in Humanities, South Dakota Committee on the Humanities, 1977.

WRITINGS:

(Editor and author of introduction) Imogen: A Pastoral Romance, New York Public Library, 1963.
(Editor with Burton R. Pollin) Uncollected Writings of William Godwin: 1785-1822, Scholars' Facsimiles & Reprints, 1968.
Bibliography of Books by and about the American Indian, Dakota Press, 1973.
The Indians and Eskimos of North America: A Bibliography of Books in Print through 1972, Dakota Press, 1973.
The American Indian: Language and Literature, AHM Publishing, 1978.
(With Herbert T. Hoover) Bibliography of the Sioux, Scarecrow, 1980.

(Editor with others) The Making of a Community: A History of Jerauld County to 1980, Wessington Springs Independent, 1982.

General editor, "Native American Bibliography Series," Scarecrow, 1980—. Contributor to professional journals, including Modern Language Notes, Yale University Library Gazette, Philological Quarterly, American Indian Quarterly, and Keats-Shelley Journal.*

* * *

MARKGRAF, Carl 1928-

PERSONAL: Born July 18, 1928, in Portland, Ore.; son of Carl Bertschi and Elizabeth (McNutt) Markgraf; married Mary Barbara Irene Fleming, November 13, 1952; children: Cecily B., Elinor M., Karl F., Lise M., Thomas B., Paul E., Anna D. Education: Attended University of California, Berkeley, 1946, and Multnomah College, 1947-48; University of Portland, A.B. (cum laude), 1951, M.A., 1954; University of California, Riverside, Ph.D., 1970. Politics: Democrat.

ADDRESSES: Home—2224 Northeast 26th Ave., Portland, Ore. 97212. Office—Department of English, Portland State University, Portland, Ore. 97207.

CAREER: High school teacher of English in Hood River, Ore., 1954-57; Marylhurst College, Marylhurst, Ore., instructor of English, 1957-60, director of drama, 1957-63, assistant professor of English, 1960-63; Portland State University, Portland, Ore., assistant professor, 1966-70, associate professor, 1970-75, professor of English, 1975—, assistant head of department, 1972—, acting head of department, 1973-74. New Theatre, Portland, member of board of directors, 1967-68, executive vice president, 1968-69, president, 1969-70. Military service: U.S. Navy, 1948-49. U.S. Army Reserve, 1956-64; became first lieutenant.

MEMBER: American Association of University Professors, Alpha Psi Omega, Delta Phi Alpha.

WRITINGS:

(Contributor) Herbert M. Schueller and Robert L. Peters, editors, The Letters of John Addington Symonds, Wayne State University Press, 1967.
(Editor)Problems in Usage, Teaching Research Commission, State of Oregon, 1969.
(Editor) Oscar Wilde's Anonymous Criticism, Xerox Corp., 1970.
(With Alex Scharbach) Making the Point: Challenge and Response, Crowell, 1975.
Punctuation, Wiley, 1979.

SCREENPLAYS FOR TELEVISION

"Marylhurst College" (documentary), broadcast on KGW-TV, November, 1957.
"A Woman Wrapped in Silence," broadcast on KGW-TV, December, 1957.
"The Play of Daniel," broadcast on KGW-TV, December, 1958.

OTHER

Adaptor of seven books into radio scripts, including Aeschylus' Agamemnon and William Shakespeare's Twelfth Night and Taming of the Shrew, all broadcast as part of the "Northwest Artists" series, 1951-52. Contributor of book reviews to South Atlantic Quarterly, Victorian Studies, and English Literature in Transition.

WORK IN PROGRESS: An annotated bibliography of writings about Jerome K. Jerome.

SIDELIGHTS: Carl Markgraf wrote *CA:* "From a childhood interest in writing plays and radio scripts came an interest in theatre that eventually led to an M.A. in theatre and ten years of theatre and radio production and direction. Pressure to acquire the Ph.D. led me back to graduate school in English, and there a specialization in Victorian literature focused on the later Victorians, especially Oscar Wilde and John Addington Symonds."

*   *   *

MARKS, Stan(ley)

PERSONAL: Born in London, England; taken to Australia at the age of two; son of Sidney and Sally Marks; married Eve Mass (a crafts lecturer and designer); children: Lee (daughter; deceased), Peter. *Education:* Attended University of Melbourne.

ADDRESSES: Home—348 Bambra Rd., Caulfield, Melbourne, Victoria, Australia 3162.

CAREER: Began working for an Australian country newspaper; later a reporter and theater critic for *Melbourne Herald,* Melbourne, Australia; reporter for newspapers in England, 1951, and in Montreal, Quebec, and Toronto, Ontario, 1952-53; correspondent for Australian newspapers in New York, N.Y., 1954-55; Australian Broadcasting Commission, Melbourne, public relations supervisor, 1958-64; public relations officer of Trans Australia Airlines, 1965-67; Australian Tourist Commission, Melbourne, public relations manager, 1968-86. Has given numerous radio talks in Australia, Canada, London, and the United States; has done a workshop with *Thunder on Anzac Grove.*

MEMBER: Australian Journalists Association, Australian Society of Authors, Society of Australian Travel Writers.

WRITINGS:

God Gave You One Face (novel), R. Hale, 1964.
(Contributor) *Walkabout's Book of Best Australian Stories,* Landsdowne Press, 1968.
Graham Is an Aboriginal Boy, photographs by Brian McArdle, Methuen, 1968, Hastings House, 1969.
Fifty Years of Achievement, Methuen, 1972.
Animal Olympics, Wren (Australia), 1972.
Rarua Lives in Papua New Guinea, Methuen, 1974.
Ketut Lives in Bali, Methuen, 1976.
Boy of Indonesia, Methuen, 1976.
(Author of text) William Andrew David Brodie, *St. Kilda Sketchbook,* Rigby, 1980.
Thunder on Anzac Grove (play), Methuen, 1980.
Malvern Sketchbook, Methuen, 1981.
Welcome to Australia, Methuen, 1981.
Out and About in Melbourne, Methuen, 1988.

Also author of plays, "Is She Fair Dinkum?," 1968, "When a Wife Strikes," 1970, and "Everybody Out"; also author of stories for two records for children, including *Montague the Mouse Who Sailed with Captain Cook.* Also contributor of short story to *Australia/New Zealand Yearbook,* 1985. Originator of a comic strip, "Ms.," for Australian newspapers, including *Melbourne Herald, Auckland Star,* and *Christchurch Star,* 1975-80. Contributor of feature stories and articles to Australian and overseas journals.

SIDELIGHTS: Stan Marks has a strong interest in the arts, youth, and in promoting better understanding between nations. As early as 1951 he suggested that an All-British Commonwealth Arts Festival should be held regularly; later he began urging that a Youth Council be established at the United Nations

to get the world's young closer to policy-making. A Commonwealth Arts Festival eventually did take place, and the Youth Council idea earned him an invitation to the 1960 White House Conference on Youth. Also in the 1960s, he advocated an "Ideas Bank" for international peace, where people might send suggestions to be sifted through for possible discussion ("just one good idea might save that button being pushed"). His books reflect these concerns as well as his interest in aborigines.

Marks told *CA* that his writings deal with topical themes. *God Gave You One Face* is about a woman in Australia who confronts the camp guard who killed her parents, in front of her, in a World War II camp, and *Thunder on Anzac Grove* explores what happens when an aboriginal family moves onto a diverse Melbourne street of ten homes, and what it means for the different groups with their different backgrounds, prejudices, and emotional reactions.

While researching *Graham Is an Aboriginal Boy,* Marks lived for ten days with the Arunta tribe near Alice Springs in Australia's Northern Territory, learning to hunt with a boomerang and to enjoy a diet of bush bananas and figs. He has also lived in other villages in New Guinea and Bali while researching his books. Marks told *CA* that these experiences have shown him that "all people really require [the] same things, especially [the] ability to survive with some dignity—a sense which over the centuries (I guess, since dawn of time) certain peoples, of all races, creeds, and self-righteousness, have felt they knew the answers and could dictate (or impose) their wills on others."

He adds: "I also worry about the international communications explosion. With all the power of good in our world-wide TV, radio, computer, satellite, and other links, we seem to be not using it effectively. Why this incredible leaning towards violence in our entertainments and leisure activities? Why? Is it really something inborn? Why are so many ready to die for something—is it easier than to TRY and live for it? Isn't it time we came together to give today's people a chance—not future generations? When do we start to think of all peoplekind? I hope, in some small way, my writings have sown some seeds of better understanding of each other, of the importance of each person, that no one has the only answer. With so much to live for, people seem bent on destruction."

Several of Marks's books have been published in Danish, Hebrew, and Braille.

MEDIA ADAPTATIONS: God Gave You One Face was optioned for a locally-made movie, 1988.

*   *   *

MARSHALL, J(ohn) D(uncan) 1919-

PERSONAL: Born April 2, 1919, in Ilkeston, Derbyshire, England; son of George (a civil servant) and Nellie (a nurse; maiden name, Osborn) Marshall; married Audrey F. Pullinger, 1948 (divorced, 1975); married Frances Sabina Harland, April 2, 1976; children: (first marriage) Celia Jane, Alison Rosalind, Edward. *Education:* University of Nottingham, B.Sc., 1950; University of London, Ph.D., 1956.

ADDRESSES: Home—Brynthwaite, Charney Rd., Grange-Over-Sands, Cumbria LA11 6BP, England. *Office*—University of Lancaster, Bailrigg, Lancaster, England.

CAREER: Teacher, Mansfield School of Art, 1950-54; assistant lecturer, Hucknall F. E. Centre, 1954-58; head of department of general subjects, Bolton College of Education, 1958-66; University of Lancaster, Bailrigg, Lancaster, England, senior lecturer, 1966-69, reader in regional history, 1969—, founder of Centre for North-West Regional Studies, 1971. Co-founder of Bolton's Community Relations Council, 1965. *Military service:* British Army, Royal Signals, 1942-46; served in European theater.

MEMBER: Royal Historical Society (fellow), Oral History Society (founding member; member of executive board, 1974; vice-chairman, 1977), Cumberland and Westmorland Antiquarian Society (vice-president and member of council), Conference of Regional and Local Historians (founding member; chairman, 1989—).

WRITINGS:

Furness and the Industrial Revolution, Barrow Corp., 1958, reprinted, 1981.
(Editor) *The Autobiography of William Stout,* Manchester University Press, 1966.
The Industrial Archaeology of the Lake Counties, David & Charles, 1969, revised edition, Michael Moon, 1977.
The Lake District at Work, David & Charles, 1972.
Old Lakeland, David & Charles, 1972.
Kendal, 1661-1801: The Growth of the Modern Town, Cumberland and Westmorland Antiquarian and Archaeological Society and the Curwen Trust, 1975.
(Editor) *The History of the Lancashire County Council, 1889-1974,* Martin Robertson, 1977.
The Lancashire Local Historian and His Theme, Federation of Local Historians in the County Palatine of Lancaster, 1977.
Portrait of Cumbria, Hale, 1981.
(With J. K. Walton) *The Lake Counties from 1830 to the Mid-Twentieth Century,* Longwood, 1982.
The Old Poor Law, 1795-1834, Macmillan, 1985.

Contributor to history journals.

WORK IN PROGRESS: A project on the development of regional and local history in England and Europe.

SIDELIGHTS: J. D. Marshall described himself to *CA* as being "among the pioneers in regional historical study." He was an "early worker in industrial archaeology (in the mid-1950's, before the term became accepted), and in regional population studies." He held the first readership in *regional* history to be conferred in British universities.*

* * *

MARSHALL, Percy
See YOUNG, Percy M(arshall)

* * *

MARTIN, Bruce
See PAINE, Lauran (Bosworth)

* * *

MARTIN, Tom
See PAINE, Lauran (Bosworth)

* * *

MASON, Bobbie Ann 1940-

PERSONAL: Born May 1, 1940, in Mayfield, Ky.; daughter of Wilburn A. (a dairy farmer) and Christianna (Lee) Mason; mar-

ried Roger B. Rawlings (a magazine editor and writer), April 12, 1969. *Education:* University of Kentucky, B.A., 1962; State University of New York at Binghamton, M.A., 1966; University of Connecticut, Ph.D., 1972.

ADDRESSES: Agent—Amanda Urban, International Creative Management, 40 West 57th St., New York, N.Y. 10019.

CAREER: Writer. *Mayfield Messenger,* Mayfield, Ky., writer, 1960; Ideal Publishing Co., New York, N.Y., writer for magazines, including *Movie Stars, Movie Life,* and *T.V. Star Parade,* 1962-63; Mansfield State College, Mansfield, Pa., assistant professor of English, 1972-79.

AWARDS, HONORS: National Book Critics Circle Award nomination and American Book Award nomination, both 1982, PEN-Faulkner Award for fiction nomination and Ernest Hemingway Foundation Award, both 1983, all for *Shiloh and Other Stories;* National Endowment for the Arts fellowship, 1983; Pennsylvania Arts Council grant, 1983; Guggenheim fellowship, 1984; American Academy and Institute for Arts and Letters award, 1984.

WRITINGS:

Nabokov's Garden: A Guide to Ada, Ardis, 1974.
The Girl Sleuth: A Feminist Guide to the Bobbsey Twins, Nancy Drew, and Their Sisters, Feminist Press, 1975.
Shiloh and Other Stories, Harper, 1982.
In Country (novel), Harper, 1985.
Spence + Lila (novel), Harper, 1988.
Love Life: Stories, Harper, 1989.

Also contributor of short stories to awards anthologies, including *Best American Short Stories,* 1981 and 1983, *The Pushcart Prize,* 1983, and *The O. Henry Awards,* 1986 and 1988. Contributor to numerous magazines, including *New Yorker, Atlantic,* and *Mother Jones;* frequent contributor to "The Talk of the Town" column, *New Yorker.*

WORK IN PROGRESS: Short stories and a novel; a television adaptation of *Spence + Lila.*

SIDELIGHTS: When Bobbie Ann Mason's first volume of fiction, *Shiloh and Other Stories,* was published in 1982, it established her reputation as a rising voice in Southern literature. "[But] to say that she is a 'new' writer is to give entirely the wrong impression, for there is nothing unformed or merely promising about her," emphasizes Anne Tyler in the *New Republic.* "She is a full-fledged master of the short story." Most of the sixteen works in *Shiloh* originally appeared in the *New Yorker, Atlantic,* or other national magazines, a fact surprising to several critics who, like Anatole Broyard in the *New York Times Book Review,* label Mason's work "a regional literature that describes people and places almost unimaginably different from ourselves and the big cities in which we live." Explains David Quammen in another *New York Times Book Review* piece: "Miss Mason writes almost exclusively about working-class and farm people coping with their muted frustrations in western Kentucky (south of Paducah, not far from Kentucky Lake, if that helps you), and the gap to be bridged empathically between her readership and her characters [is] therefore formidable. But formidable also is Miss Mason's talent, and her craftsmanship."

Most critics attribute Mason's success to her vivid evocation of a region's physical and social geography. "As often as not," Gene Lyons reports in *Newsweek,* the author describes "a matter of town—paved roads, indoor plumbing, and above all, TV—having come to the boondocks with the force of an unannounced social revolution." While the language of Mason's characters reflects their rural background, her people do not fit the Hollywood stereotype of backwoods hillbillies content to let the rest of the world pass by. Tyler notes that "they have an earnest faith in progress; they are as quick to absorb new brand names as foreigners trying to learn the language of a strange country they've found themselves in. It is especially poignant," she adds, "that the characters are trying to deal with changes most of us already take for granted." Mason's Kentucky is, reviewers note, a world in transition, with the old South fast becoming the new. As Suzanne Freeman comments in the *Washington Post Book World:* "Mason's characters are just trying not to get lost in the shuffle."

Mason often explores intensely personal events that lead to the acceptance of something new or the rejection—or loss—of something old. These adjustments in the characters' lives reflect a general uneasiness that pervades the cultural landscape; the forces of change and alienation are no less frightening because they are universal or unavoidable. "Loss and deprivation, the disappointment of pathetically modest hopes, are the themes Bobbie Ann Mason works and reworks," states Quammen. "She portrays the disquieted lives of men and women not blessed with much money or education or luck, but cursed with enough sensitivity and imagination to suffer regrets." The characters in Mason's fiction are caught between isolation and transience, and this struggle is reflected in their relationships, which are often emotionally and intellectually distant. "Some people will stay at home and be content there," the author noted in a *People* interview. "Others are born to run. It's that conflict that fascinates me." As a result, writes *Time* critic R. Z. Sheppard, "Mason has an unwavering bead on the relationship between instincts and individual longings. Her women have ambitions but never get too far from the nest; her men have domestic moments but spend a lot of time on wheels." Mason's characters "exist in a psychological rather than a physical environment," Broyard similarly contends, "one that has been gutted—like an abandoned building—by the movement of American life. They fall between categories, occupy a place between nostalgia and apprehension. They live, without history or politics, a life more like a linoleum than a tapestry."

Other critics, while noting Mason's ability to evoke psychological states, emphasize her skill at depicting the material details of her "linoleum" world. Tyler points out that readers know precisely what dishes constitute the characters' meals, what clothes hang in their closets, and what craft projects fill their spare time. Mason intones the brand names that are infiltrating her characters' vocabularies, and the exact titles of soap operas and popular songs provide an aural backdrop for Mason's own emotional dramas. Likewise, her characters' voices, according to Tyler, "ring through our living rooms." Freeman, however, cites Mason's use of colloquialisms as one of the book's few problems. "A couple of the stories have promising starts and clunky, disappointing endings," she writes. "And, here and there throughout the stories, Mason has overdone the country talk." Yet in the final analysis, the critic admits, "Mason has a vision and she makes us see it too—it is a glimpse straight into the heart of her characters' lives." "In true short-story tradition, [her] insights and epiphanies are spring-loaded," adds Sheppard. "Mason rarely says more than is necessary to convey what Hemingway called 'the real thing, the sequence of motion and fact which made the emotion.' "

In her first novel, *In Country,* "Mason returns to this same geographical and spiritual milieu" as her short fiction, notes *New York Times* critic Michiko Kakutani, "and she returns, too, to her earlier themes: the dislocations wrought on ordinary, blue-collar lives by recent history—in this case, recent history in the form of the Vietnam War." Seventeen-year-old Samantha

Hughes doesn't remember the war, but it has profoundly affected her life: her father died in Vietnam and her uncle Emmett, with whom she lives, still bears the emotional and physical scars of his service. In the summer after her high school graduation, Sam struggles to understand the war and learn about her father; "ten years after the end of the Vietnam War," summarizes Richard Eder of the *Los Angeles Times Book Review,* "in the most prosaic and magical way possible, she stubbornly undertakes the exorcism of a ghost that almost everything in our everyday life manages to bury." In addition, Mason shows the same concern for particulars that distinguishes her short fiction, as *Christian Science Monitor* contributor Marilyn Gardner observes: "She displays an ear perfectly tuned to dialogue, an eye that catches every telling detail and quirky mannerism. Tiny, seemingly insignificant observations and revelations accumulate almost unnoticed until something trips them, turning them into literary grenades explosive with meaning."

Detroit Free Press writer Suzanne Yeager similarly believes that the author's details contribute to the authenticity of the novel. "Mason's narrative is so extraordinarily rich with the sounds, smells and colors of daily life in the '80s that Sam and her family and friends take on an almost eerie reality." As a result, the critic adds, *In Country* "becomes less a novel and more a diary of the unspoken observations of ordinary America." Jonathan Yardley, however, faults the novel for the "dreary familiarity" of its Vietnam themes; writing in the *Washington Post Book World,* he asserts that Mason "has failed to transform these essentially political questions into the stuff of fiction; none of her characters come to life, the novel's structure is awkward and its narrative herky-jerky, her prose wavers uncertainly between adult and teenaged voices." But other critics find Mason's work successful; *Chicago Tribune Book World* contributor Bruce Allen, for instance, says that the novel's "real triumph . . . is Mason's deep and honest portrayal of her two protagonists," especially Sam. "More than any other character in our recent fiction," the critic continues, Sam "is a real person who grows more and more real the better we come to know her—and the novel that affords us the opportunity to is, clearly, the year's most gratifying reading experience." "[Mason's] first novel, although it lacks the page-by-page abundance of her best stories," concludes Joel Conarroe in the *New York Times Book Review,* "is an exceptional achievement, at once humane, comic and moving."

Spence + Lila, Mason's second novel, "is a love story that explores both human love and a love for life," writes Jill McCorkle in the *Washington Post.* "It is a short novel with a simple plot, the limited space enriched by characters whose voices and situations are realistic and memorable." Spence and Lila are a Kentucky farm couple who have been married for over forty years; Lila's upcoming surgery is forcing them to face the prospect of being separated for the first time since World War II. "The chapters alternate between Spence's and Lila's point of view, and such resonances [in their thoughts] range freely through the past and present," describes *Los Angeles Times Book Review* contributor Nancy Mairs. Despite the potential for sentimentality in the story, Mason "manages to avoid the gooey and patronizing muck that is usually described as heartwarming," remarks a *Time* reviewer. "Her account is funny and deft, with plenty of gristle."

Newsweek writer Peter S. Prescott, however, finds *Spence + Lila* a "gently tedious" book saved only by Mason's skillful writing. But Kakutani, although she acknowledges that the book "suffers from a melodramatic predictability absent from Ms. Mason's earlier works," thinks that the author treats her subject "without ever becoming sentimental or cliched." The critic goes on to praise Mason's "lean stripped-down language" and "nearly pitch-perfect ear for the way her characters speak," and adds that "mainly, however, it's her sure-handed ability to evoke Spence and Lila's life together that lends their story such poignance and authenticity." *New York Times Book Review* contributor Frank Conroy likewise commends Mason's dialogue, but admits that "one wishes she had risked a bit more in this book, taking us under the surface of things instead of lingering there so lovingly and relentlessly." "Awkward silence in the face of ideas and feelings is a common frailty," elaborates Mairs, "but it represents a limitation in 'Spence + Lila,' constraining Mason to rush her story and keep to its surface. . . . If I perceive any defect in 'Spence + Lila,' " the critic continues, "it's that this is a short novel which could well have been long." "As soon as [Mason's] characters open their mouths, they come to life and move to center stage," McCorkle similarly concludes. "If there is a weakness it would be the reader's desire to prolong their talk and actions before moving to an ending that is both touching and satisfying."

Despite the author's success with *In Country* and *Spence + Lila,* "Mason's strongest form may be neither the novel nor the story, but the story *collection,*" Lorrie Moore maintains in her *New York Times Book Review* assessment of *Love Life: Stories.* "It is there, picking up her pen every 20 pages to start anew, gathering layers through echo and overlap, that Ms. Mason depicts most richly a community of contemporary lives." Jack Fuller, however, believes that *Love Life* has a weakness: "Mason is a strong enough writer to make you believe her people, but she does not allow them any escape from the cliches that surround them," the Chicago *Tribune Books* writer notes, adding that her characters have "no exit" from their problems. While Kakutani likewise remarks that "few of Ms. Mason's characters ever resolve their dilemmas—or if they do, their decisions take place . . . beyond the knowledge of the reader," she asserts that the stories "are not simply minimalist 'slice-of-life' exercises, but finely crafted tales that manage to invest inarticulate, small-town lives with dignity and intimations of meaning." Mason's "stories work like parables, small in scale and very wise, tales wistfully told by a masterful stylist whose voice rises purely from the heart of the country," states Judith Freeman in the *Los Angeles Times Book Review.* As a *Chicago Tribune Book World* critic similarly concludes, "[Mason] is a writer of immense sensitivity, a true seer; technically, in terms of the making of sentences, she is a near virtuoso."

MEDIA ADAPTATIONS: In Country was made into a Warner Brothers film by director Norman Jewison in 1989.

CA INTERVIEW

CA interviewed Bobbie Ann Mason by telephone on March 9, 1989, at her home in Pennsylvania.

CA: You told Marianne Walker for the Louisville Courier-Journal Magazine *that you had to "leave a pretty sheltered life and find out about the outside world" before you could focus on writing. What did that learning process consist of, primarily, and what was the impediment to writing?*

MASON: I moved away from the South to the Northeast, first to work in New York right after college. Then I went to graduate school. The fact that I was in a strange culture was very stressful. I spent all of my energy for ten or fifteen years dealing with that. It was a tremendous culture shock.

CA: Was being a Southerner in a Northern environment the worst of it?

MASON: Yes. It's a familiar story, and I found it to be extremely difficult. In graduate school I felt intellectually unprepared, intimidated by the professors and the other graduate students. I was extremely shy and unsure of my own mind. So for years I was just having to fight that sense of inferiority. It was like it had dammed up my mind and I couldn't think creatively; I was much too concerned about writing my term papers and getting through classes. And not only going to classes, but teaching as a graduate assistant, which I found one of the most terrifying things I had ever done in my life, and I did it for years. It took me years to get through graduate school; I was going half-time because of being a graduate assistant. I was in shock that whole time.

CA: Was there a point at which it became clear to you that you could write, at which you had the confidence, or did it develop gradually?

MASON: It was pretty gradual. And too, as long as I was in graduate school, I didn't have time to write.

CA: How do you feel your concentrated study of literature shaped your own approach to writing?

MASON: I'm not sure there was any direct relationship. It was in graduate school that I really learned about reading, and that was valuable. But when it came to writing, I found it so completely different, it was as if none of my academic work had any bearing on it.

CA: It's refreshing that you not only feel you can *go home again, but you often do—both physically, to visit, and in all of your writing. Does living away from that setting somehow sharpen your creative perception of it?*

MASON: I think so. I think that distance is necessary, and it's made my fiction what it is, whatever it is. I'm sure it would have been completely different if I'd been totally inside it. It's the sharper awareness of everyday things, the small changes that people are going through and changes in the landscape that are so important.

CA: It must be a shock sometimes when you go back.

MASON: I don't think I've ever been away long enough for it to be shocking. The place where I come from has not changed as rapidly as some places, so in many ways things look just the same.

CA: The book you're soon off to be promoting, Love Life, *is dedicated to Roger Angell. Would you like to say something about the early encouragement he gave you and the part he has played in your work?*

MASON: It was very strong encouragement that was extremely important to me at just the right time. After I had been in graduate school and mostly avoiding writing but trying off and on, and then teaching and having difficulty with it, I gradually got back to writing stories and started sending them to the *New Yorker.* Roger Angell wrote me such wonderful encouraging letters that it gave me the right motivation and direction I needed at that point. He was virtually the first person who said to me, "You are a writer." That made a tremendous amount of difference.

CA: Somewhere you told a nice story about how the New Yorker *was still returning your manuscripts but said you didn't have to send return postage with them anymore.*

MASON: Yes. That happened after I had sent the *New Yorker* a dozen or so stories. For writers who mail off manuscripts time after time, it's such a nuisance to mail those return envelopes; it's really bothersome. To be freed from that was great.

CA: Comparing the stories that make up Love Life *to those in the 1982 collection,* Shiloh and Other Stories, *do you see any kind of difference in them, any progression, that might not be apparent to readers?*

MASON: It's hard for me to tell in terms of the writing itself. I hope the stories are more complex. On the surface I think, since my main theme probably is change, times have changed a bit since the first collection. In *Shiloh* the characters stayed home and watched network TV with the regular line-up. Now my characters are busting out of that because of the VCR and cable television and the satellite dish. So they have a lot of choices, and as a result—it's kind of interesting—TV has gotten boring to them. There are too many channels to choose from. But I think all those channels are also exposing the characters to a lot more possibilities, educating them more about the outside world. I think in a positive way it's throwing them back on themselves and their own resources, because TV isn't as satisfying as it once was when it was so regular and secure. Now the TV scene is as unstable and changing as anything else. I think also that, as they approach the mainstream, these characters are a little more prosperous as well as more mobile, partly because they have become more exposed to other places from television and the news. They're a little more restless and more willing to experiment and maybe a bit more unsettled.

CA: Did either your first novel, In Country, *or the second one,* Spence + Lila, *begin as a short story?*

MASON: I saw *Spence + Lila* pretty much from the beginning as a short novel. But *In Country* began as a short story and I couldn't figure it out. I tried to write it as a short novel and that didn't go anywhere either, so it just kept growing and changing.

CA: Have you had a response to In Country *from many people who were directly affected by Vietnam?*

MASON: Yes, I have—a fair number of people, including Vietnam vets and young girls whose fathers were in the war (some died in the war), and a number of wives of Vietnam vets. It's been personally very gratifying to hear from them, to know that they took the trouble to write me and tell me that the book meant something to them. Most of the Vietnam vets who wrote me didn't write at length; they just seemed to say thank you. It was very moving to hear from those people.

CA: Spence and Lila have, as a couple, a kind of stability that many of your younger characters lack. They're also closely tied to the land they've grown up on, with no regrets. It's a very affirmative novel. Were there inspirations for the book that you can talk about?

MASON: It is a very personal novel, and my family is in there in disguise. As in any fiction, some of it is stretched out of shape, but basically it's my parents' world, and I think my strong feelings about them helped me write about Spence and Lila in the way I did.

CA: Was it your sister who did the lovely illustrations for the book?

MASON: Yes, LaNelle Mason. I thought her work was perfect to illustrate it, because she understands the landscape and the people and knows what they look like. I like the wonderful faceless characters on the cover. It has been pointed out to me that they're perfect for a novel, because when you read a novel, you like for your own imagination to fill in what the characters look like.

CA: And the simplicity of the illustrations is perfectly suited to the story, too.

MASON: Yes. Also, her paintings are very colorful. You see that in the cover painting, but an earlier version she did was even more colorful. The color down there in the cornfields in western Kentucky in the summertime is so unbelievably green. And I like the way LaNelle does the tree lines. The landscape is fairly flat. There's cornfield after cornfield with tree lines in between. I like her perspective on those.

CA: One of the great strengths of your writing is the dialogue of your characters, which seems precise not only in its words and cadences, but also in what it tells about its speakers. Written dialogue, though, is rarely exactly the same as what's spoken in real life. How do you make the transformation?

MASON: It's a matter of trimming and shaping and zeroing in on just the right thing and trying not to make the dialogue go on for too long. I'm aware that with my characters, as with any people having conversation, if you wrote it down as it came out it would sound probably incoherent and certainly boring. In fiction people have to talk so that it sounds real and plausible, but it also has to carry the weight of the story. Real-life dialogue doesn't usually do that, so you have to be very careful with the shaping of it. But it's not something that has to be done so consciously.

The language—not only the dialogue, but the language itself—is one of the most important things to me in writing. You used the word *cadence*. The style of the narrative, the cadence of it, is very important to me. It imitates that country speech that I hear in my ear. It's not speech that's mellifluous or lilting or lovely; it's hard-edged, and I think that way of speaking comes out of hard times and lack of illusions. It's plain speech, matter-of-fact, not romantic language. I'm always aware of insisting on those stylistic characteristics because I think it creates the voice and the attitude that I have about the characters and the world. It's a way of cutting through things that are superfluous. Phrases catch my ear, and they're not pretty—like "a sack of doughnuts" or "a stack of videotapes on the sale table." It's all plain and flat, matter-of-fact. That's what my ear hears in the way people talk, and it also is an attitude.

Sometimes there are things that are funny about the language, like this drink that the characters have in the story "Memphis"—a fuzzy navel. I think words are funny. I had a family sitting on the living room floor on a quilt having a picnic and watching "Chitty-Chitty-Bang-Bang." I suppose they could have been watching "The Postman Rings Twice," but "Chitty-Chitty-Bang-Bang" seemed right.

CA: The subject of pop culture as it figures in your work comes into every review and every discussion of your writing. How would you explain its significance in your characters' lives?

MASON: It's very important to them what's on TV and what songs are on and what's on sale at the local store and what movies are playing. I think those kinds of things at one level or other are important to just about everybody. It's the news; it's what's going on in your life. Look at New York City: there are so many things to choose from there, and those cultural events are extremely important to many people living in New York. It's just the modern stuff that surrounds us, and we pay attention to it and care about it. My characters—although they're growing away from TV in a strange way, as I said—do care about TV. It brings them in touch with places outside their own small community. And they care about the products they buy because they like to go shopping and are concerned about getting something a little better at a bargain. That's natural. I try to use those references only when they're important to the characters, and not when they're important to me as some kind of judge. I'm not making a comment on their lives; I don't want to do that. I've started to realize that I have been talking a lot about pop culture in interviews because that's what readers and reviewers are seizing on in my work. So I've found myself explaining and defending it. But I don't think it's really the center of the work at all. It's not what I'm most concerned with.

CA: Your musical heroes include the Beatles, Bruce Springsteen, Elvis Presley—and, going way back, the Hilltoppers, a chapter in your life that you wrote about in "A World Unsuspected." What does music represent in your life, and what impact does it have on your work?

MASON: It was my earliest connection with the outside world, and the way I found of identifying with a strong feeling about life. The early music I listened to was rhythm and blues, and that grew into rock 'n' roll. I was also very fond of the big bands and the vocalists of the thirties and forties. Music speaks to people in a language there are no words for. I think rock 'n' roll in particular is a music of the people, and it speaks for people who don't have many choices. It's physical energy and it's sexual and it's rebellious, and I think for people who don't have much hope of gaining power over their lives economically or politically, rock 'n' roll is a very affirmative, expressive way of being alive and being joyous about it.

CA: You examine the lives and worries of older people in such stories as "The Ocean," collected in Shiloh and Other Stories, *and "Wish," from* Love Life; *and of course in the novel* Spence + Lila. *Will you be doing more of this in future work?*

MASON: I think I've tended to write about older people because I have more of an avenue into that culture I write about through older people than I do through younger people. Both the first story and the last story in *Love Life* are about older people, and I thought those framed the collection well. Both of those characters are looking back over lost loves, and they're both characters that had to live lives that were quite emotionally stressful and confining because of social conventions. My newer characters are not so constrained by those conventions, and I feel more obligated to write about younger characters right now. I think what's happening to them is both more exciting and more disturbing to write about. I kind of know the older people's scene now and it's distressing to me to see where old people are headed and the way they're treated in society. It's very poignant to me that all their values and conventions are up against enormous change. But they're sort of left there; I don't see much beyond that. With the younger characters it's not that their lives are more significant to me, but that it's more challenging to me to get into that area.

CA: How do you feel about writing short stories compared to writing novels?

MASON: Short stories are easier; they take less time. It's hard to get into a novel, hard to make that commitment. If short sto-

ries don't work I can literally toss them away. On the other hand, it turns out to be more rewarding to have written a novel than to have written a short story.

CA: There's a movie version of In Country *that will be out this fall, and you're writing a television adaptation of* Spence + Lila. *Do you have any great worries about these transformations of your books?*

MASON: I initially made a promise to myself that I wouldn't get emotionally tied up in whether or not they fit my vision of things, because I think it would be too easy to let oneself in for a great disappointment that way. As it turns out, however, I have great hopes that *In Country* will be pretty good because of the way it has been done. I'm impressed with the way the actors and director have gone about putting it together, and I'm looking forward to seeing it. I'm very excited to have a movie made of my work. I feel that the subject of the Vietnam War coming home to the American family is a significant one apart from my own work, so I'm very glad for that reason especially that it's being made into a movie.

CA: Do you find that very different types of people read and respond personally to your writing?

MASON: I think so. By and large, there's only a certain segment of the American public that reads literary fiction. Once in a while it falls into the hands of somebody who's not used to reading that sort of fiction. I've come across a few people like that, and they've been pleasantly surprised.

CA: Your husband, Roger Rawlings, is also a writer. Do you discuss your work in progress with each other, serve mutually as first readers or editors?

MASON: At some point we read each other's work, but not very early in the process. He's very helpful to me as an editor and gives me his responses. I'm not as good at that as he is.

CA: What do you consider your major concerns as a writer? What do you most want to do or to portray?

MASON: I guess what I think about what I'm trying to do at the time I'm trying to do it is very different from what I'd want the reader to get from it eventually. I'm not thinking about that, usually, when I'm writing. I'm always thinking about the challenge of coming up with something interesting and making it work out, so I don't go so far as to think in large terms what might emerge from the work by the time the reader gets to it. I'm often surprised by what comes out. The difficulty for me is the process— just getting the details, getting into the characters' world and shaping them, and coming up with something. After I do that, I would hope readers would feel that they know something about these characters and the world that they live in so that they're able to have some kind of insight into what makes them do what they do. I'd hope they would have some sympathetic understanding of them.

CA: Everybody who talks with you wonders if you'll move back to Kentucky. Can you say anything about that?

MASON: It's complicated, especially since I've been so busy— I've been doing a lot of traveling. My parents are there and I would like to, but it's easier said than done.

BIOGRAPHICAL/CRITICAL SOURCES:

BOOKS

Contemporary Literary Criticism, Gale, Volume 28, 1984, Volume 43, 1987.
Dictionary of Literary Biography Yearbook: 1987, Gale, 1988.
Prenshaw, Peggy Whitman, editor, *Women Writers of the South,* University Press of Mississippi, 1984.

PERIODICALS

Chicago Tribune Book World, January 23, 1983, September 1, 1985.
Christian Science Monitor, September 6, 1985.
Detroit Free Press, October 13, 1985.
Globe and Mail (Toronto), November 9, 1985, July 30, 1988.
Los Angeles Times Book Review, September 22, 1985, June 19, 1988, March 19, 1989.
Louisville Courier-Journal Magazine, January 29, 1989.
Nation, January 18, 1986.
New Republic, November 1, 1982.
Newsweek, November 15, 1982, September 30, 1985, August 1, 1988.
New York Review of Books, November 7, 1985.
New York Times, November 23, 1982, September 4, 1985, June 11, 1988, March 3, 1989.
New York Times Book Review, November 21, 1982, December 19, 1982, September 15, 1985, June 26, 1988, March 12, 1989.
New York Times Magazine, May 15, 1988.
People, October 28, 1985.
Publishers Weekly, August 30, 1985.
Time, January 3, 1983, September 16, 1985, July 4, 1988.
Times (London), August 11, 1983, March 6, 1986.
Times Literary Supplement, August 12, 1983, April 18, 1986.
Tribune Books (Chicago), June 26, 1988, February 19, 1989.
Voice Literary Supplement, November, 1982, February, 1986.
Washington Post, February 5, 1976, July 1, 1988.
Washington Post Book World, October 31, 1982, September 8, 1985, March 26, 1989.

—*Sketch by Diane Telgen*

—*Interview by Jean W. Ross*

*   *   *

MATES, Julian   1927-

PERSONAL: Born June 24, 1927, in New York, N.Y.; married Elaine Wollan, 1951 (divorced, 1973); married Barbara Richmond, 1975; children: (first marriage) Karen, Jessica; (second marriage) Ethan Saul. *Education:* Brooklyn College (now of the City University of New York), B.A., 1949; Columbia University, M.A., 1950, Ph.D., 1959.

ADDRESSES: Home—Two Poppy Lane, Glen Cove, N.Y. 11542. *Office*—Department of English, Long Island University, C. W. Post Campus, Brookville, Long Island, N.Y. 11548.

CAREER: City College (now of the City University of New York), New York, N.Y., lecturer in English, 1951-52; Hofstra College (now University), Hempstead, N.Y., lecturer, 1952-53, instructor, 1953-58; Long Island University, C. W. Post Campus, Brookville, N.Y., assistant professor, 1959-61, associate professor, 1961-67, professor of English, 1967—, dean of School of Arts and director of American Theatre Festival, 1968-87. *Military service:* U.S. Naval Reserve, 1945-47.

MEMBER: Theatre Library Association, American Society for Theatre Research, Sonneck Society.

AWARDS, HONORS: Hofstra College faculty fellowship; Oscar G. Sonneck Memorial Grant, Library of Congress; Long Island University Trustee Award for scholarly achievement.

WRITINGS:

The American Musical Stage before 1800, Rutgers University Press, 1962, reprinted, Greenwood Press, 1986.
(Editor with Eugene Cantelupe) *Renaissance Culture: A New Sense of Order,* Braziller, 1966.
(Contributor) *American Theatre: The Sum of Its Parts,* Samuel French, 1972.
(Contributor) *Europe Reborn: The Story of Renaissance Civilization,* New American Library, 1975.
(Contributor) *Discoveries and Considerations,* State University of New York, 1976.
(Editor) *William Dunlap: Four Plays,* Scholars' Facsimiles & Reprints, 1976.
(Editor) *Musical Works of William Dunlap,* Scholars' Facsimiles & Reprints, 1980.
America's Musical Stage: 200 Years of Musical Theatre, Greenwood Press, 1985.
(Editor and author of introduction) William Dunlap, *Adaptations of European Plays,* Scholars' Facsimiles & Reprints, 1988.

Contributor to professional journals.

*   *   *

MATHIS, (Gerald) Ray   1937-1981

PERSONAL: Born April 2, 1937, in Sanford, Miss.; died March 25, 1981; son of Paul M. (a machinist) and LaVerne (a teacher; maiden name, Morris) Mathis; married Mary Kathryn Pugh (a sociology instructor), December 28, 1958; children: John Paul, Charles Ray. *Education:* Snead Junior College, A.A., 1957; Birmingham-Southern College, B.A., 1958; Duke University, M.Div., 1962; University of Georgia, M.A., 1963, Ph.D., 1967.

ADDRESSES: Home—Route 1, Mathews, Ala. 36052. *Office*—Department of History, Troy State University, Troy, Ala. 36081.

CAREER: Snead Junior College, Boaz, Ala., instructor in history, 1964-65; Georgia Southern College, Statesboro, assistant professor, 1966-69; Troy State University, Troy, Ala., professor of history, 1969-80.

MEMBER: American Historical Association, Organization of American Historians, Southern Historical Association, Society for the Study of Southern Literature, Georgia Historical Society, Alabama Historical Society, Phi Beta Kappa, Phi Theta Kappa, Omicron Delta Kappa, Phi Kappa Phi, Phi Alpha Theta.

AWARDS, HONORS: American Philosophical Society grant, 1968; Certificate of Commendation, American Association for State and Local History, 1980, for *John Harry Dent: South Carolina Aristocrat on the Alabama Frontier;* James F. Salzby, Jr., Award, Alabama Historical Association, 1981.

WRITINGS:

John Harry Dent: South Carolina Aristocrat on the Alabama Frontier, University of Alabama, 1978.

EDITOR

Pilgrimage to Madison: Correspondence Concerning the Georgia Party's Inspection of the University of Wisconsin, November, 1904, University of Georgia, 1970.

T. W. Reed's History of the University of Georgia: 1885-89, University of Georgia Libraries, 1974.

College Life in the Reconstruction South, University of Georgia Libraries, 1974.

(With wife, Mary K. Mathis, and Douglas Clare Purcell) *John Harry Dent Farm Journals and Account Books, 1837-1892* (microfilm), University of Alabama, 1976, revised edition with an introduction and index my the author and M. K. Mathis entitled *John Harry Dent Farm Journals and Account Books, 1840-1892,* 1977.

(With Purcell) *In the Land of the Living: Wartime Letters by Confederates from the Chattahoochee Valley of Alabama and Georgia,* Troy State University Press, 1981.

Contributor to professional journals.

*WORK IN PROGRESS: Walter B. Hill and the Savage Ideal: Southern History and Myth as They Relate to the Search for National Character.**

*   *   *

MATSUNO, Masako
See KOBAYASHI, Masako Matsuno

*   *   *

MATTILL, A(ndrew) J(acob), Jr.   1924-

PERSONAL: Born August 2, 1924, in St. Joseph, Mo.; son of Andrew Jacob (an accountant) and Ruth Florence (Hanne) Mattill; married Mary Elizabeth Bedford, March 31, 1960. *Education:* University of Chicago, B.A. (with honors), 1949; Evangelical Theological Seminary, Naperville, Ill., B.D., 1952; Vanderbilt University, Ph.D., 1959.

ADDRESSES: Home—Route 2, Box 49, Gordo, Ala. 35466-9516.

CAREER: Armour & Co., South St. Joseph, Mo., assistant to paymaster, 1943-45; ordained to ministry of Evangelical United Brethren Church, 1952, transferred ordination and membership to Churches of God in North America, 1966, dropped ordination and membership, 1977, ordained to ministry of Unitarian Universalist Fellowship, Tuscaloosa, Ala., 1979; Evangelical United Brethren Church, Vassar, Kan., pastor, 1952-54; Berry College, Mount Berry, Ga., 1958-62, began as assistant professor, became associate professor of Bible; Livingstone College, Salisbury, N.C., professor of Bible, 1962-65; Winebrenner Theological Seminary, Findlay, Ohio, Bucher Professor of New Testament and registrar, 1965-75; private scholar, engaged in New Testament research on a farm near Gordo, Ala., 1975—. Part-time minister, Liberty Universalist Church, Louisville, Miss., 1977—, and Unitarian Universalist Fellowship, Tuscaloosa, 1979-84. Substitute letter carrier, U.S. Postal Service, Gordo, 1979—. *Military service:* U.S. Army, 1945-47; served in France; became sergeant.

MEMBER: Society of Biblical Literature.

AWARDS, HONORS: Scholarship through New York University for postdoctoral work in Israel, 1959; American Association of Theological Schools grant for sabbatical year in Germany, 1972-73.

WRITINGS:

The Wets Are All Wet (booklet), Christian Action League, 1965.
(With wife, Mary Elizabeth Mattill) *A Classified Bibliography of Literature on the Acts of the Apostles,* E. J. Brill, 1966.

(Translator) W. G. Kuemmel, *Introduction to the New Testament,* revised by Paul Feine and Johannes Behm, 14th revised edition, Abingdon, 1966.

The Church in a Revolutionary World (booklet), Central Publishing House of the Churches of God in North America, 1968.

(Contributor) W. W. Gasque and R. P. Martin, editors, *Apostolic History and the Gospel,* Paternoster, 1970.

A Religious Odyssey (booklet), Scott Recording Laboratory, 1977.

(Contributor) C. H. Talbert, editor, *Perspectives on Luke-Acts,* Association of Baptist Professors of Religion, 1978.

Luke and the Last Things: A Perspective for the Understanding of Lukan Thought, Western North Carolina Press, 1979.

A Christ for These Days, Church of the Larger Fellowship, 1979.

(Translator) Albert Schweitzer, *The Problem of the Lord's Last Supper,* Mercer University Press, 1982.

Jesus and the Last Things: The Story of Jesus the Suffering Servant, Flatwoods Free Press, 1983.

The Seven Mighty Blows to Traditional Beliefs, Flatwoods Free Press, 1986.

Ingersoll Attacks the Bible, Flatwoods Free Press, 1987.

The Art of Reading the Bible, Flatwoods Free Press, 1988.

A New Universalism for a New Century, Flatwoods Free Press, 1989.

Author of weekly column, "World of Religion," *Pickens County Advertiser,* 1982-83. Contributor of articles and reviews to religious journals.

SIDELIGHTS: A. J. Mattill, Jr., once told *CA* that his works are "free-thought studies [that] seek to show the inadequacy of traditional religions and set forth the basic elements of a rational religion." He more recently added: "I hope that my formulation of *A New Universalism for a New Century* will strike a responsive chord in the hearts and minds of at least a few of those persons who are searching for a satisfying rational religion without revelation to replace their former revealed religions which they now consider untenable."

*   *   *

McCARTHY, Martha M(ay)   1945-

PERSONAL: Born July 9, 1945, in Louisville, Ky.; daughter of James Warren (an engineer) and Martha (a teacher; maiden name, Adams) May; married George Dennis Kuh (a professor); children: Kari Ann, Kristian Randolph. *Education:* University of Kentucky, B.A. (with highest distinction), 1966, M.A., 1969; University of Florida, Specialist in Education, 1974, Ph.D., 1975.

ADDRESSES: Home—1903 East Winslow Rd., Bloomington, Ind. 47401. *Office*—241 School of Education, Indiana University, Bloomington, Ind. 47405.

CAREER: Teacher at public elementary schools in Lexington, Ky., 1966-69; Catherine Spalding College, Louisville, Ky., instructor in education, 1970; University of Kentucky, Lexington, instructor and coordinator of student teachers, 1970, instructor and field coordinator of Teacher Corps, 1970-71; Louisville Public Schools, Louisville, assistant director of "Project Focus," 1971-72, acting director, 1973, director of instructional planning and management, 1974-75; University of Florida, College of Education, Gainesville, fellow of Educational Resource Management Specialists program, 1973-74; Indiana University, Bloomington, assistant professor, 1975-78, associate professor, 1978-82, professor of education, 1982—, associate dean of faculties, 1982-84, director of Consortium on Educational Policy Studies, 1986—.

MEMBER: American Educational Research Association, National Organization on Legal Problems of Education (member of board of directors, 1979-82; vice-president, 1982-83; president elect, 1983-84; president, 1984-85), University Council for Education Administration (member of executive committee, 1984—; president, 1986), American Education Finance Association, Phi Delta Kappa, Kappa Delta Pi, Pi Lambda Theta.

AWARDS, HONORS: Wiles Memorial Award, University of Florida, 1975, for outstanding dissertation in education; grants from Bureau of Education for the Handicapped, 1975-76, 1976-78, Women's Educational Equity Act, 1976-79, Lilly Endowment and Phi Delta Kappa, 1978-79, Sex Desegregation Center, Indianapolis, Ind., 1979-81, and National Institute of Education, 1981; American Association of School Administrators Research Competition Award, 1980, for research presentation "Factors Related to Success in Urban Elementary Schools"; *Choice* "outstanding academic book" award, 1983, for *Public School Law: Teachers' and Students' Rights;* President's Award for service to the state, Indiana Association of Elementary and Middle School Principals, 1988.

WRITINGS:

(With William Patterson) *Law and the Indiana Educator,* Beanblossom, 1979.
How Can I Best Manage My Classroom? (monograph), Bet Yoats Library Services, 1980.
(With Nelda Cambron) *Public School Law: Teacher's and Student's Rights,* Allyn & Bacon, 1981, revised edition, 1987.
Judicial Interpretations of What Constitutes Appropriate Programs and Service for Handicapped Children (monograph), Council for Administrators of Special Education, 1981.
Federal Legislation on Behalf of Handicapped Children: Implications for Regular Educators, National In-Service Network, 1981.
(With Paul Deignan) *What Legally Constitutes an Adequate Public Education?,* Phi Delta Kappa, 1982.
Discrimination in Employment: The Evolving Law (monograph), National Organization on Legal Problems of Education, 1983.
A Delicate Balance: Church, State and the Schools, Phi Delta Kappa, 1983.
(Editor with Nelda Cambron-McCabe and Stephen Thomas) *Educators and the Law: Current Trends and Issues,* Institute for School Law and Finance, 1983.
(With D. Turner) *Competency Testing for Teachers: A Status Report* (monograph), Consortium on Educational Policy Studies, 1987.
(With L. D. Webb and Thomas) *Financing Elementary and Secondary Education,* Merrill, 1988.
(With husband, George Kuh, L. Jackson Newell, and Carla Iacona) *Under Scrutiny: The Educational Administration Professoriate,* University Council for Educational Administration, 1988.

CONTRIBUTOR

Thomas, K. Floyd, and M. Kivilighan, editors, *Critical Issues in Evaluation and Educational Adequacy,* Institute for Educational Finance, 1976.
Philip Piele, editor, *The Yearbook of School Law, 1978,* National Organization on Legal Problems of Education, 1978.
M. A. McGhehey, editor, *School Law Update, 1977,* National Organization on Legal Problems of Education, 1978.

Frank Aquila, editor, *School Desegregation: A Model at Work,* Training Institute, School of Education, Indiana University, 1978.
Piele, editor, *The Yearbook of School Law, 1979,* National Organization on Legal Problems of Education, 1979.
McGhehey, editor, *Contemporary Legal Issues in Education,* National Organization on Legal Problems of Education, 1979.
McGhehey, editor, *School Law in Contemporary Society,* National Organization on Legal Problems of Education, 1980.
Why Do Some Urban Schools Succeed?, Phi Delta Kappa, 1980.
K. F. Jordan and Cambron, editors, *Perspectives in State School Support Systems,* Ballinger, 1981.
McGhehey, editor, *School Law in Changing Times,* National Organization on Legal Problems of Education, 1982.
Joseph Beckham and Perry Zirkel, editors, *Legal Issues in Public School Employment,* Phi Delta Kappa, 1983.
Derek Burleson, editor, *Schools and the First Amendment,* Phi Delta Kappa, 1983.
David Alexander, editor, *The Principal and the Law,* National Organization on Legal Problems of Education, 1984.
L. Rudner and J. T. Sandefur, editors, *What's Happening in Teacher Testing?,* U.S. Department of Education, 1987.
G. Sorenson, editor, *Critical Issues in Education Law,* National Organization on Legal Problems of Education, 1988.

OTHER

Contributor of more than seventy articles and reviews to education and legal journals. Finance law co-editor, *Journal of Education Finance,* 1977—; law editor, *Journal of Educational Equity and Leadership,* 1981-88; member of editorial boards, *Education Law Reporter,* 1982—, *Issues in Education,* 1982—, *Educational Administration Quarterly,* 1985—, *Religion and Public Education,* and West's *Education Law Reporter;* legal columnist, *Educational Horizons,* 1984—.

WORK IN PROGRESS: Research on curriculum censorship, allegations that public schools are promoting "secular humanism," child abuse, and state education policymaking processes.

SIDELIGHTS: Martha M. McCarthy told *CA:* "A driving force behind my research and writing in educational law is my interest in equity issues and judicial interpretations of constitutional guarantees."

* * *

McCARTY, Doran Chester 1931-

PERSONAL: Born February 3, 1931, in Bolivar, Mo.; son of Bartie Lee (a tool and die setter) and Donta (an inventory controller; maiden name, Russell) McCarty; married Gloria Laffoon (a teacher), June 14, 1952; children: Gaye, Rise, Marletta, Beth. *Education:* Southwest Baptist College, A.A., 1950; William Jewell College, A.B., 1952; New Orleans Baptist Theological Seminary, graduate study, 1952-53; Southern Baptist Theological Seminary, B.D., 1956, Ph.D., 1963; also attended Indiana University.

CAREER: Pastor of Baptist churches in Springfield, Mo., 1949-50, Jameson, Mo., 1951-52, Elliston, Ky., 1953-56, Switz City, Ind., 1956-62, Pleasant Hill, Mo., 1962-65, and Independence, Mo., 1965-67; Midwestern Baptist Theological Semnary, Kansas City, Mo., associate professor, 1967-71, professor of theology and Christian philosophy and director of supervised ministry, 1971-81; Golden Gate Baptist Theological Seminary, Mill Valley, Calif., professor of ministry, 1981-87; Northeastern Baptist School of Ministry, New York, N.Y., coordinator, 1988—.

Instructor at William Jewell College, 1966-67, Metropolitan Junior College (Kansas City, Mo.), 1969, and Penn Valley Community College, 1969-74. Chairman, Missouri Baptist Historical Commission; member, executive committee of Indiana Baptist Convention. Consultant to Southern Baptist Board of Missions and Evangelism, 1981—.

MEMBER: Association for Theological Field Education (national chairman, 1979-81), Institute for Theological Reflection (executive director), Association for Clinical Pastoral Education.

WRITINGS:

(Co-author) *Invitation to Dialogue: The Professional World,* Broadman, 1970.
(Co-author) *These Missouri Baptists,* Missouri Baptist Press, 1970.
(Co-author) *Encyclopedia of Southern Baptists,* Volume III, Broadman, 1971.
Rightly Dividing the Word, Broadman, 1973.
The Marks of a Christian, Sunday School Board, 1974.
Social Implications for Churches with the Mobile American, Home Mission Board, 1975.
Sociological Aspects of Rural Urban Life in America Today, Home Mission Board, 1975.
(Co-author) *The Mobile American in Multi-Family Housing,* Home Mission Board, 1975.
Teilhard de Chardin, Word Publications, 1976.
A Collection of Key Resources, Association for Theological Field Education, Volume I: *Field Education,* 1977, Volume II: *Theological Reflection,* 1979, Volume III: *Religious Experience,* 1981, Volume IV: *Pastoral Hermeneutics,* 1983.
The Supervision of Ministry Students, Home Mission of the Southern Baptist Convention, 1978.
The Supervision of Mission Personnel, Home Mission, 1983.
The Inner Heart of Ministry, Broadman, 1986.
Working with People, Broadman, 1987.

Also author of *Supervising Ministry Students,* 1985; also co-author of *Adult Life and Work Annual Lessons,* Convention Press. Contributor to church periodicals. Co-editor of *Journal of Missouri Baptist History.*

WORK IN PROGRESS: Growing a Church in a Changing Community; Supervision in the Education of Ministers; co-editing "Leadership" series for Broadman.

*   *   *

McCLELLAND, Doug 1934-

PERSONAL: Born July 16, 1934, in Plainfield, N.J.; son of William Vincent and Elna (Whitlock) McClelland. *Education:* Attended Newark, N.J., public schools.

ADDRESSES: Home—704 Madison Ave., Bradley Beach, N.J. 07720.

CAREER: Office boy for *Newark Star-Ledger,* Newark, N.J., during late 1940s; *Newark Evening News,* Newark, arts editor, 1952-56; *Record World Magazine,* New York, N.Y., editor, 1961-72. Lecturer on motion pictures.

WRITINGS:

The Unkindest Cuts, A. S. Barnes, 1972.
(Contributor) *The Real Stars,* Curtis Publishing, 1973.
Susan Hayward: The Divine Bitch, Pinnacle, 1973.
Down the Yellow Brick Road, Pyramid Publications, 1976.
The Golden Age of "B" Movies, Charterhouse, 1978.

(Contributor) *Hollywood Kids,* Popular Library, 1978.
Hollywood on Ronald Reagan, Faber & Faber, 1985.
StarSpeak, Faber & Faber, 1987.
Blackface to Blacklist, Scarecrow Press, 1987.
Eleanor Parker: Woman of a Thousand Faces, Scarecrow Press, 1989.
Hollywood Talks Turkey, Faber & Faber, 1990.

Contributor of articles to *After Dark, Films and Filming, Films in Review, Filmograph, Screen Facts,* and *The Many Worlds of Music.* Author of jacket notes for record albums.

BIOGRAPHICAL/CRITICAL SOURCES:

PERIODICALS

Los Angeles Times Book Review, October 16, 1983.
People, June 8, 1987.

*   *   *

McCLOSKEY, Donald N(ansen) 1942-

PERSONAL: Born September 11, 1942, in Ann Arbor, Mich.; son of Robert Green (an academician) and Helen (a singer; maiden name, Stueland) McCloskey; married Joanne Comi (a nurse), June 19, 1965; children: Daniel, Margaret. *Education:* Harvard University, B.A. (magna cum laude), 1964, Ph.D., 1970. *Politics:* "Anarchist, registered Democrat." *Religion:* None.

ADDRESSES: Home—320 Melrose Ave., Iowa City, Iowa 52240. *Office*—Department of Economics, University of Iowa, Iowa City, Iowa 52242.

CAREER: University of Chicago, Chicago, Ill., assistant professor, 1968-73, associate professor of economics, 1973-80, associate professor of history, 1979-80; University of Iowa, Iowa City, professor of history and professor of economics, 1980—.

MEMBER: American Economic Association, American Economic History Association, Economic History Society (England).

AWARDS, HONORS: Guggenheim fellow, 1983; National Science Foundation grant; *The Rhetoric of Economics* was selected one of the Outstanding Academic Books of 1986 by *Choice.*

WRITINGS:

(Editor) *Essays on a Mature Economy: Britain after 1840,* Princeton University Press, 1972.
Economic Maturity and Entrepreneurial Decline: British Iron and Steel, 1870-1913, Harvard University Press, 1973.
Enterprise and Trade in Victorian Britain: Essays in Historical Economics, Allen & Unwin, 1981.
(Editor with Roderick Floud) *The Economic History of Britain since 1700,* Cambridge University Press, 1981, Volume I: *1700-1860,* Volume II: *1860 to the 1970s.*
The Applied Theory of Price, Macmillan, 1982, 2nd edition, 1985.
The Rhetoric of Economics, University of Wisconsin Press, 1985.
The Writing of Economics, Macmillan, 1987.
Econometric History, Macmillan, 1987.

Contributor to professional journals. Editor, *Journal of Economic History,* 1981-85.

WORK IN PROGRESS: How the Gold Standard Worked; Open Fields and Enclosures in England.

SIDELIGHTS: Donald N. McCloskey's books dealing with the economic history of Britain often challenge opinions held by many British historians. According to a *Times Literary Supplement* reviewer, in *Economic Maturity and Entrepreneurial Decline,* McCloskey "mounts a vigorous attack on the views of that historical school which has argued that a failure of entrepreneurship fostered the decline of the British iron and steel industries."

While McCloskey's writing as an economist often deals with statistical data, many critics comment on his prose style. In a discussion of McCloskey's work on Britain's iron industry, a *Choice* reviewer notes that the author writes in a way "that makes the book both good economics and good literature. . . . It illustrates an exercise in creative thinking, reasoning, and writing." Sidney Pollard of the *Times Literary Supplement* also remarks upon McCloskey's duplicate ease with economic information and readable prose, observing that he "is equally at home among the historical literature and the formulae of econometricians. He can . . . write elegantly and with wit."

McCloskey told *CA* that "he has recently scrutinized economics from a rhetorical perspective."

AVOCATIONAL INTERESTS: Latin, Greek, folk music.

BIOGRAPHICAL/CRITICAL SOURCES:

PERIODICALS

American Historical Review, June, 1973, June, 1975.
Business History Review, autumn, 1972, summer, 1974.
Choice, March, 1974.
Journal of Economic History, September, 1974.
Journal of Modern History, March, 1974.
Times Literary Supplement, March 24, 1972, August 16, 1974, August 7, 1981, August 1, 1986.
Washington Post Book World, May 17, 1987.

*   *   *

McCOMBS, Maxwell E(lbert)   1938-

PERSONAL: Born December 3, 1938, in Birmingham, Ala.; son of Max E. and Gertrude (Smith) McCombs; married Zoe Helen Collins (divorced March, 1988); children: Mary Elizabeth, Leslie Ann. *Education:* Tulane University, B.A., 1960; Stanford University, M.A., 1961, Ph.D., 1966.

ADDRESSES: Office—Department of Journalism, University of Texas at Austin, Austin, Tex. 78712.

CAREER: New Orleans Times-Picayune, New Orleans, La., general assignment reporter, 1961-62, state supreme court reporter, 1962-63; University of California, Los Angeles, lecturer, 1965-66, assistant professor of journalism, 1966-67; University of North Carolina, Chapel Hill, assistant professor, 1967-69, associate professor of journalism, 1969-73; Syracuse University, Syracuse, N.Y., John Ben Snow Professor of Newspaper Research, 1973-85, director of Communications Research Center, 1973-85; University of Texas at Austin, Jesse H. Jones Centennial Professor in Communication, 1985—, chairman of department of journalism, 1985—. Visiting lecturer at University of Wisconsin—Madison, summer, 1970, Northwestern University, summers, 1974-75, and University of Missouri, summer, 1980. *Military service:* U.S. Army Reserve, information officer, 1963-67.

MEMBER: World Association for Public Opinion Research (treasurer, 1985—), Association for Education in Journalism, American Newspaper Publishers Association (director of News Research Center, 1975—), A. G. Bell Association, American Association for Public Opinion Research.

WRITINGS:

Mass Communication on the Campus, Communication Board, University of California, Los Angeles, 1967.
Mass Media in the Marketplace, Journalism Monographs, 1972.
(Editor with Donald Shaw and David Gray, and contributor) *Handbook of Reporting Methods,* Houghton, 1976.
(Editor with Shaw, and contributor) *The Emergence of American Political Issues: The Agenda-Setting Function of the Press,* West, 1977.
(With George Comstock, Steven Chaffee, Natan Katzman, and Donald Roberts) *Television and Human Behavior,* Columbia University Press, 1978.
(With Lee Becker) *Using Mass Communication Theory,* Prentice-Hall, 1979.
(With David Weaver, Doris Graber, and Chaim Eyal) *Media Agenda-Setting in a Presidential Election: Issues, Images, Interests,* Praeger, 1981.
(With Garry Keir and Shaw) *Advanced Reporting: Beyond News Events,* Longman, 1986.
(Editor with Robert Picard, James Winter, and Stephen Lacy) *Press Concentration and Monopoly: New Perspectives on Newspaper Ownership and Operation,* Ablex Publishing, 1988.

CONTRIBUTOR

New Educational Media in Action: Case Studies for Planners, Volume III, UNESCO, 1967.
Phillip Tichenor and F. G. Kline, editors, *Current Perspectives in Mass Communication Research,* Volume I, Sage Publications, 1972.
D. M. Kovenock, J. W. Prothro, and others, editors, *Explaining the Vote: Presidential Choices in the Nation and the States, 1968,* Institute for Research in Social Science, University of North Carolina, Chapel Hill, 1973.
Roy Moore and others, editors, *Gathering and Writing News: Selected Readings,* College and University Press, 1975.
Steven Chaffee, editor, *Political Communication,* Sage Publications, 1975.
Ronald Ostman and Hamid Mowlana, editors, *International Yearbook of Drug Addiction and Society,* Volume III: *Communication Research and Drug Education,* Sage Publications, 1976.
James Grunig, editor, *Decline of the Global Village,* General Hall, 1976.
Jim Richstad, editor, *New Perspectives in International Communication,* East-West Center Communications Institute, 1977.
Laurily K. Epstein, editor, *Women and the News,* Hastings House, 1978.
Sidney Kraus, editor, *The Great Debates: Carter vs. Ford, 1976,* Indiana University Press, 1979.
Michael Emery and Ted Smythe, editors, *Readings in Mass Communication: Concepts and Issues in the Mass Media,* W. C. Brown, 1980.
Guido Stempel and Bruce Westley, editors, *Research Methods in Mass Communication,* Prentice-Hall, 1981, 2nd edition, in press.
Earl Newsom, editor, *The Newspaper,* Prentice-Hall, 1981.
G. C. Wilhoit, editor, *Mass Communication Review Yearbook,* Sage Publications, Volume II, 1981, Volume III (edited by Charles Whitney and Ellen Wartella), 1982.
Dan Nimmo and Keith Sanders, editors, *Handbook of Political Communication,* Sage Publications, 1981.

(Author of foreword) Shearon Lowery and Melvin DeFleur, *Milestones in Mass Communication Research,* Longman, 1983.

Karl Erik Rosengren, Lawrence Wenner, and Philip Palmgreen, editors, *Media Gratification Research: Current Perspectives,* Sage Publications, 1985.

Jennings Bryant and Dolf Zillman, editors, *Perspectives on Media Effects,* Lawrence Erlbaum, 1986.

Erik Barhouw, editor, *International Encyclopedia of Communications,* Oxford University Press, in press.

Pamela Shoemaker, editor, *Communication Campaigns about Drugs: Government, Media and the Public,* Lawrence Erlbaum, in press.

OTHER

Contributor of approximately fifty articles and reviews to periodicals.

WORK IN PROGRESS: The Art and Science of Advanced Reporting, with Donald Shaw and Garry Keir, for Longman.

* * *

McCREARY, Alf(red) 1940-

PERSONAL: Born September 26, 1940, in Bessbrook, Northern Ireland; married wife, Hilary-Anne (a physiotherapist), 1967; children: Emma Jane, Mark, Matthew. *Education:* Queens University of Belfast, B.A. (with honors), 1959, diploma in education, 1964. *Religion:* Christian.

ADDRESSES: Home—Belfast, Northern Ireland. *Office*—Queens University, University Rd., Belfast BT7 1NN, Northern Ireland.

CAREER: Journalist, beginning 1964, with positions as reporter, feature writer, critic, and columnist; formerly chief features writer, leader-writer, and columnist, *Belfast Telegraph,* Belfast, Northern Ireland; currently affiliated with Information Office, Queens University, Belfast. Fellow, Salzburg Seminar, 1981.

MEMBER: British National Union of Journalists.

AWARDS, HONORS: Named British Provincial Journalist, 1971, and British News Reporter of the Year, 1975; Rothmans Press award, 1979; certificate of merit, UNA Media Peace Prize, 1980; Rothmans Journalist of the Year, 1983.

WRITINGS:

Corrymeela: The Search for Peace, Christian Journal Ltd., 1975.
October 1976: Survivors (nonfiction), Century Books, 1976, published as *Survivors: A Documentary Account of the Victims of Northern Ireland,* Beekman Publications, 1977.
Corrymeela: Hill of Harmony in Northern Ireland, Hawthorn, 1976.
Up with People, Fount, 1979.
Profiles of Hope, Christian Journals, 1981, new edition published as *Tried by Fire: Finding Hope out of Suffering in Northern Ireland,* Marshall Pickering, 1986.
Spirit of the Age: Story of Old Bushmills, Blackstaff Press, 1983.
Ulster Journey, Greystone Books, 1986.

Also author of *Remember When,* 1987, *Princes, Presidents & Punters,* 1988, and *This Northern Land,* 1989. Contributor to magazines, including *Time, Worldview,* and *Good Housekeeping,* and to newspapers in Ireland, Scotland, England, and the United States; regular correspondent, *Christian Science Monitor.*

WORK IN PROGRESS: Traveling in Africa and Asia to conduct research for a book on the Third World.

SIDELIGHTS: Alf McCreary told *CA* that his work is "characterized by a human interest approach to complex subjects from peace to war and from problems of affluence to problems of starvation. I believe that people read books about people more readily than about abstract theories."

* * *

McCULLOUGH, David (Gaub) 1933-

PERSONAL: Born July 7, 1933, in Pittsburgh, Pa.; son of Christian Hax (a businessman) and Ruth (Rankin) McCullough; married Rosalee Ingram Barnes, December 18, 1954; children: Melissa (Mrs. John E. McDonald, Jr.), David, Jr., William Barnes, Geoffrey Barnes, Doreen Kane. *Education:* Yale University, B.A., 1955.

ADDRESSES: Home and office—4402 Westover Pl. N.W., Washington, D.C. 20016. *Agent*—Morton L. Janklow, 598 Madison Ave., New York, N.Y. 10022.

CAREER: Editor and writer for Time, Inc., New York City, 1956-61, U.S. Information Agency, Washington, D.C., 1961-64, and American Heritage Publishing Co., New York City, 1964-70; free-lance writer, 1970—. Host of television series "Smithsonian World," 1984—, and "The American Experience," 1988—, for Public Broadcasting Service Television (PBS-TV). Scholar in residence, University of New Mexico, 1979, Wesleyan University Writers Conference, 1982-83. Member, Bennington College Writers Workshop, 1978-79; member of advisory board, Center for the Book, Library of Congress; member, Harry S Truman Centennial Commission; trustee, Shady Side Academy, Pittsburgh, Pa.

MEMBER: Society of American Historians (fellow; vice-president), American Society of Civil Engineers (honorary).

AWARDS, HONORS: Special citation for excellence, Society of American Historians, 1973, Diamond Jubilee medal for excellence, City of New York, 1973, and certificate of merit, Municipal Art Society of New York, 1974, all for *The Great Bridge;* National Book Award for history, Francis Parkman Award from Society of American Historians, Samuel Eliot Morison Award, and Cornelius Ryan Award, all 1978, all for *The Path between the Seas;* Civil Engineering History and Heritage award, 1978; *Los Angeles Times* Award for biography, 1981, American Book Award for biography, 1982, and Pulitzer Prize nomination in biography, 1982, all for *Mornings on Horseback;* Emmy Award, for interview with Anne Morrow Lindbergh on "Smithsonian World"; honorary degrees include H.L.D., Rensselaer Polytechnic Institute, 1983, D.Eng., Villanova University, 1984, Litt.D., Allegheny College, 1984, and L.H.D, Wesleyan University, Middletown, Conn., 1984.

WRITINGS:

(Editor) C. L. Sulzberger, *The American Heritage Picture History of World War II,* American Heritage Press, 1967, revised edition published as *World War II,* McGraw, 1970, reprinted, Houghton, 1985.
(Editor) *Smithsonian Library,* six volumes, Smithsonian Institution Press/American Heritage Press, 1968-70.
The Johnstown Flood (*Reader's Digest* Condensed Book), Simon & Schuster, 1968.
The Great Bridge (*Reader's Digest* Condensed Book), Simon & Schuster, 1972.
The Path between the Seas: The Creation of the Panama Canal, 1870-1914 (Book-of-the-Month Club selection; *Reader's Digest* Condensed Book), Simon & Schuster, 1977.
Mornings on Horseback, Simon & Schuster, 1981.

(Contributor) *A Sense of History: The Best Writing from the Pages of American Heritage,* American Heritage Press/ Houghton, 1985.

(With others) William Zinsser, editor, *Extraordinary Lives: The Art and Craft of American Biography,* American Heritage Press, 1986.

(And host) "A Man, a Plan, a Canal—Panama" (episode of "Nova"), first broadcast on PBS-TV, November 3, 1987.

(Editor with others) Michael E. Shapiro and Peter H. Frederick, *Remington: The Masterworks,* Abrams, 1988.

Contributor to periodicals, including *Audubon, Architectural Forum, American Heritage, Geo, Smithsonian, New York Times, New Republic, Psychology Today,* and *Washington Post.* Senior contributing editor, *American Heritage;* contributing editor, *Parade.*

WORK IN PROGRESS: A biography of Harry S. Truman.

SIDELIGHTS: David McCullough is known to many Americans as an important disseminator of history not only through his award-winning books, but also through his appearances as host of the PBS television programs "Smithsonian World" and "The American Experience." Recognition for his abilities ranges from an Academy Award nomination for a film on the Brooklyn Bridge to a television Emmy Award for an interview he conducted on "Smithsonian World" to two National Book Awards for his narrative histories *The Path between the Seas* and *Mornings on Horseback.* Richard Robbins writes in the Pittsburgh *Tribune-Review* that in these histories, "David McCullough combines a powerful narrative style with an exhaustive concern for the details of a story."

McCullough began his first book, *The Johnstown Flood,* when he wanted to learn more about the 1889 bursting of a Pennsylvania dam that claimed the lives of more than two thousand people and was one of the most widely reported stories of the late nineteenth century. None of the volumes McCullough consulted proved satisfactory, however, and he finally decided he would have to write the book himself. Upon its publication, critics hailed *The Johnstown Flood* as an important addition to the field of social history. For example, Alden Whitman, writing in the *New York Times,* called it "a superb job, scholarly yet vivid, balanced yet incisive."

In 1972 McCullough published *The Great Bridge,* a history of the building of the Brooklyn Bridge. Considered by contemporaries and historians to be the greatest engineering feat of America's "Gilded Age," the Brooklyn Bridge was the dream of one man—John Roebling, a wealthy steel cable manufacturer. When he died in 1869, before construction of the bridge actually began, his son Washington A. Roebling became chief engineer, and, over the next thirteen years, saw the bridge completed. McCullough traces the dangers that the younger Roebling faced and the problems he overcame, ranging from corrupt politicians in Boss Tweed's Tammany Hall to cases of the "bends" that afflicted workers and left Roebling himself a semi-invalid for the rest of his life.

The Great Bridge covers both the engineering and social aspects of the bridge's construction. "The whole story is told in David McCullough's admirably written, definitive and highly entertaining book," remarks L. J. Davis in the *Washington Post Book World.* "He is especially adept at weaving in those disparate but relevant details that bring an age to life, from the Cardiff giant to the scandal of Henry Ward Beecher's infidelity. It is hard to see how the story could be better or more thoroughly told." "McCullough does justice to this gamy background," declares

Justin Kaplan in *Saturday Review,* "but never allows it to get the better of his subject or his narrative or to turn into that familiar historical stereotype that obscures the fact that the Gilded Age was a period of enormous achievement in virtually every area of activity."

McCullough shifted settings from Brooklyn to Panama for *The Path between the Seas: The Creation of the Panama Canal, 1870-1914.* Once again the author mixes engineering with social, political, and economic history, this time to create a panorama of the canal project from its origins to the day it finally opened. Beginning with the dream of Suez Canal entrepreneur Ferdinand de Lesseps, McCullough describes how political corruption, disease, anti-Semitism, and bankruptcy put an end to French efforts to dig a sea-level canal across the isthmus of Panama. Later, McCullough continues, the Americans under the leadership of Theodore Roosevelt connived to "liberate" Panama from an uncooperative Colombia, conquered the yellow fever and malaria that had plagued the French, and over a ten-year period created the largest and costliest engineering project the world had ever seen—and, as R. Z. Sheppard reminds us in *Time,* completed it "six months ahead of schedule and below the estimated cost."

The Path between the Seas won the National Book Award as well as several important awards from historical associations. Critics hailed the book for its vivid portrayal of the many issues that surrounded the canal's construction. "There are scores of previous volumes on the subject," reports *New York Times Book Review* contributor Gaddis Smith, "but none is so thorough, readable, fair or graceful in the handling of myriad intricately connected elements: French national pride and humiliation, personal courage and corruption, disease and death, medical and engineering genius, political and financial chicanery, and the unsung contribution of tens of thousands of black laborers recruited from the West Indies to do the heavy work." McCullough, declares Walter Clemons in *Newsweek,* "is a storyteller with the capacity to steer readers through political, financial and engineering intricacies without fatigue or muddle. This is grand-scale, expert work."

In his next book, *Mornings on Horseback,* McCullough examines the early years of the Panama Canal's greatest supporter—Theodore Roosevelt. Unlike many biographies of the Republican Roosevelt, however, McCullough's work encompasses the entire family: Theodore, Sr., philanthropic scion of an old New York Dutch clan, his wife Martha ("Mittie") Bulloch, a Georgia belle whose family mansion may have been the inspiration for Tara in Margaret Mitchell's *Gone with the Wind,* their daughters Anna ("Bamie") and Corinne ("Conie"), and sons Theodore, Jr. and Elliott. Moreover, in its depiction of the Roosevelts, *Mornings on Horseback* affords a glimpse of American society in the years following the Civil War, "a period that has always seemed remote and cartoonlike," explains James Lardner in the *New Republic.* "It introduces us to a collection of fascinating people and makes their society vivid, plausible, and even a tempting destination for anyone planning a trip back in time."

McCullough also breaks new ground by exploring neglected aspects of Theodore Jr.'s youth, including his bouts of psychosomatic illness and his fascination with killing and mounting animals. As a child "Teedie" suffered from violent attacks of asthma, probably brought on by feelings of inadequacy, that occurred "almost invariably on a Saturday night [in order] to secure a Sunday with his father," reports John Leonard in the *New York Times Book Review.* McCullough notes that the boy's asthma disappeared as soon as he left home to begin studying at Harvard. Roosevelt's enchantment with shooting and the Wild

West, the author suggests, in part stemmed from his mother's stories about the Old South and his relatives' exploits in the Confederate Army. McCullough combines these images to create a portrait of a man who, as *Saturday Review* contributor Gary Wills puts it, "never felt more alive than when killing something."

In all his work McCullough emphasizes the value history has for modern Americans. "We're not being quite selfish enough if we don't know history, not that history is likely to repeat itself," McCullough tells Robbins. "Besides, there is the matter of commiserating in the agonies and basking in the glories of our fellow human beings from long ago, of not being provincial, of opening our minds and hearts to generations once alive. . . . Why should we deny ourselves the chance to experience life in another time if it's available to us? There is a wonderful world called the past, and for heaven's sake don't miss it, because if you do you'll be denying yourself a big part of being alive."

BIOGRAPHICAL/CRITICAL SOURCES:

PERIODICALS

Atlantic, July, 1977.
New Republic, July 4, 1981.
Newsweek, June 13, 1977, June 22, 1981.
New Yorker, June 20, 1977.
New York Times, April 24, 1968, May 24, 1977, June 18, 1981.
New York Times Book Review, October 15, 1972, June 19, 1977, July 26, 1981.
Saturday Review, September 30, 1972, June 11, 1977, June, 1981.
Time, June 6, 1977, July 20, 1981.
Tribune-Review (Pittsburgh), November 11, 1984.
Washington Post Book World, October 1, 1972, June 12, 1977, June 14, 1981, July 15, 1986.

—*Sketch by Kenneth R. Shepherd*

*   *   *

McDONALD, Jerry N(ealon) 1944-

PERSONAL: Born August 15, 1944, in Newark, Ohio; son of Oscar Matthew (an electrician) and Elma Grayce (Powell) McDonald; married Beverly Childers Kerger, June 7, 1965 (marriage ended, January 30, 1978); children: Christian Herendon, Jay Ian. *Education:* Muskingum College, B.A., 1970; University of Texas, M.A., 1972; University of California, Los Angeles, Ph.D., 1978.

ADDRESSES: Office—McDonald & Woodward Publishing Co., P.O. Box 10308, Blacksburg, Va. 24062-0308.

CAREER: University of Texas, El Paso, visiting assistant professor of geography, 1978-79; Radford University, Radford, Va., assistant professor, 1979-84, associate professor of geography, 1984-86. Managing partner, McDonald & Woodward Publishing Co., beginning 1986. Smithsonian Institution, post-doctoral fellow, 1982-83, research associate, 1989—. *Military service:* U.S. Marine Corps, 1965-67.

MEMBER: Association of American Geographers, American Society of Mammalogists, American Quaternary Association, American Minor Breeds Conservancy, Society of Vertebrate Paleontology.

WRITINGS:

North American Bison: Their Classification and Evolution, University of California Press, 1981.
(Contributor) P. S. Martin and R. G. Klein, editors, *Quaternary Extinctions,* University of Arizona Press, 1984.

(With Susan L. Woodward) *Indian Mounds of the Middle Ohio Valley: A Guide to Adena and Ohio Hopewell Sites,* McDonald & Woodward, 1986.
(Co-editor and contributor) *The Quaternary of Virginia,* Virginia Department of Mineral Resources, 1986.
(With Woodward) *Indian Mounds of the Atlantic Coast: A Guide to Sites from Maine to Florida,* McDonald & Woodward, 1987.

Contributor to scientific journals.

WORK IN PROGRESS: Scientific research focusing on the biological systematics of North American ovibovines (musk and shrub oxen), and on the paleoecology of large mammals of the last Ice Age; writing a book on the Blue Ridge Parkway and publicly accesible, interpreted fossil localities for McDonald & Woodward.

SIDELIGHTS: Jerry N. McDonald told *CA:* "I resigned my faculty position at Radford University effective September 1, 1986, in order to manage a new publishing company formed by myself and Susan L. Woodward. We searched in vain for an appropriate fictitious name for our company, but concluded that all of the good names had been taken already and those that were left really didn't lend themselves to our intended purpose. So we settled upon the unimaginative name 'McDonald and Woodward Publishing Company.' We plan to publish high quality guide books to selected themes in the natural and cultural history of Anglo-America, as well as general trade books for adults and children. Our first book, *Indian Mounds of the Middle Ohio Valley: A Guide to Adena and Ohio Hopewell Sites,* was issued on December 18, 1986. Presently six writers are working on additional volumes that will be published in a series we call 'Guides to the American Landscape.' Publishing (and writing) guides of this type has been an idea I've nurtured for a long time; now it's happening and it's *fun!*

"I expect to continue with my paleoecological research also, particularly my study of late Quaternary large-mammal ecology, evolution, and taxonomy. Excavation activity at the Saltville, Virginia, paleoecological site will also be continued, since this very productive site still has many secrets to divulge."

BIOGRAPHICAL/CRITICAL SOURCES:

PERIODICALS

Redford University Magazine, winter, 1981, December, 1984.

*   *   *

McDONALD, Walter (Robert) 1934-

PERSONAL: Born July 18, 1934, in Lubbock, Tex.; son of Charles Arthur (a house painter) and Vera Belle (Graves) McDonald; married Carol Ham, August 28, 1959; children: Cynthia, David, Charles. *Education:* Texas Technological College (now Texas Tech University), B.A., 1956, M.A., 1957; University of Iowa, Ph.D., 1965. *Religion:* Christian.

ADDRESSES: Office—Department of English, Texas Tech University, Lubbock, Tex. 79409.

CAREER: U.S. Air Force, career officer, 1957-71, instructor at U.S. Air Force Academy, 1960-62, 1965-66, assistant professor, 1966, associate professor of English, 1967-71, retired as major; Texas Tech University, Lubbock, associate professor, 1971-75, professor of English, 1975-87, Paul Whitfield Horn Professor of English, 1987—, director of creative writing, 1972—. Member of literature advisory panel, Texas Commission on the Arts, 1986-88. Poetry consultant, Texas Tech Press, 1977—.

MEMBER: P.E.N., Modern Language Association of America, Conference of College Teachers of English (member of council, 1977-80; president, 1985-86), South Central Modern Language Association, Texas Institute of Letters, Texas Association of Creative Writing Teachers (president, 1974-76).

AWARDS, HONORS: Voertman's Poetry Award, Texas Institute of Letters, 1976, for *Caliban in Blue and Other Poems;* best story award, Texas Institute of Letters, 1976, for "The Track"; Amoco Outstanding Teaching Award, Texas Tech University, 1983-84; creative writing fellowship, National Education Association, 1984; poetry award co-winner, Texas Institute of Letters, for *Witching on Hardscrabble,* and 1987, for *The Flying Dutchman;* PEN Syndicated Fiction Award, February, 1985, for "The Track," and August, 1985, for "Memorial Day"; George Elliston Poetry Prize, 1986, for *The Flying Dutchman;* Juniper Prize for Poetry, University of Massachusetts Press, 1987, for *After the Noise of Saigon;* Distinguished Alumnus Award, Texas Tech University Ex-Students Association, 1988.

WRITINGS:

(Editor with Frederick Kiley) *A "Catch-22" Casebook,* Crowell, 1973.
Caliban in Blue and Other Poems, Texas Tech Press, 1976.
(Editor with James White) *Texas Prize Stories and Poems,* Texas Center for Writers Press, 1978.
One Third Leads to Another, Cedar Rock Press, 1978.
Anything, Anything, L'Epervier, 1980.
Burning the Fence, Texas Tech Press, 1981.
Working against Time, Calliope Press, 1981.
Witching on Hardscrabble, Spoon River Poetry Press, 1985.
The Flying Dutchman, Ohio State University Press, 1987.
Splitting Wood for Winter (trilobite poetry chapbook), University of North Texas Press, 1988.
After the Noise of Saigon, University of Massachusetts Press, 1988.
Night Landings, Harper, 1989.

Contributor of stories, poems, and articles to literature journals, including *TriQuarterly, Poetry, American Poetry Review, Antioch Review, Kenyon Review, Atlantic,* and *North American Review.*

WORK IN PROGRESS: Poetry; fiction.

*   *   *

McKINLEY, (Jennifer Carolyn) Robin 1952-

PERSONAL: Born November 16, 1952, in Warren, Ohio; daughter of William (in U.S. Navy and Merchant Marine) and Jeanne Carolyn (a teacher; maiden name, Turrell) McKinley. *Education:* Attended Dickinson College, 1970-72; Bowdoin College, B.A. (summa cum laude), 1975. *Politics:* "Few affiliations, although I belong to MADD and NOW, and have strong feelings pro-ERA and pro-freedom—and anti-big-business and anti-big-government." *Religion:* "You could call me a lapsed Protestant."

ADDRESSES: Home—Maine and New York, N.Y. *Agent*—Merrilee Heifetz, Writers House, Inc., 21 West 26th St., New York, N.Y. 10010.

CAREER: Writer. Ward & Paul (stenographic reporting firm), Washington, D.C., editor and transcriber, 1972-73; Research Associates, Brunswick, Me., research assistant, 1976-77; worked as a clerk in a Maine bookstore, 1978; teacher and counselor at

private secondary school, Natick, Mass., 1978-79; Little, Brown, & Co., Boston, Mass., editorial assistant, 1979-81; barn manager on horse farm, Holliston, Mass., 1981-82; Books of Wonder, New York, N.Y., clerk, 1983; free-lance reader, copy- and line-editor, and "general all-purpose publishing dogsbody," 1983—.

AWARDS, HONORS: Horn Book honor list citation, 1978, for *Beauty: A Retelling of the Story of Beauty and the Beast,* and 1985, for *The Hero and the Crown;* Best Books for the Teen Age citation, New York Public Library, 1980, 1981, and 1982, all for *Beauty;* Best Young Adult Books citation, American Library Association, 1982, and Newbery Honor citation, 1983, both for *The Blue Sword;* Newbery Medal, 1985, for *The Hero and the Crown;* honorary Ph.D., Bowdoin College, 1986; World Fantasy Award for best anthology, 1986, for *Imaginary Lands.*

WRITINGS:

Beauty: A Retelling of the Story of Beauty and the Beast (novel), Harper, 1978.
The Door in the Hedge (short stories), Greenwillow, 1981.
The Blue Sword (novel), Greenwillow, 1982.
(Contributor) Terri Windling and Mark Alan Arnold, editors, *Elsewhere Volume II,* Ace Books, 1982.
The Hero and the Crown (novel), Greenwillow, 1984.
(Contributor) Windling and Arnold, editors, *Elsewhere Volume III,* Ace Books, 1984.
(Editor and contributor) *Imaginary Lands,* Greenwillow, 1985.
(Adapter) Rudyard Kipling, *Jungle Book Tales,* Random House, 1985.
(Contributor) Windling, editor, *Faery,* Ace Books, 1985.
(Adapter) Anna Sewell, *Black Beauty,* Random House, 1986.
(Adapter) George MacDonald, *The Light Princess,* Harcourt, 1988.
(Contributor) Jane M. Bingham, editor, *Writers for Children,* Scribner, 1988.
The Outlaws of Sherwood (novel), Greenwillow, 1988.

Contributor of book reviews to numerous periodicals. Also author of column, "In the Country," for *New England Monthly,* 1987—.

WORK IN PROGRESS: A book laid in a different part of *Sword* and *Hero*'s world; an adult fantasy; "other miscellaneous bits and pieces that may or may not come to something."

SIDELIGHTS: Robin McKinley "populates her novels and stories with some of the most civilized, decent, honorable, and well-rounded heroes and villains in modern fiction," write Terri Windling and Mark Alan Arnold in *Horn Book.* "She eschews not only helpless heroines and hapless swains but also the one-dimensional, rotten-to-the-core villains of other fantasies." "More than adventure, more than romance, more even than her determination to write stories about 'girls who do things,'" Windling and Arnold conclude, "her tales are about honor—which is perhaps the key to the 'real' Robin McKinley, just as the complexity and vividness of her created worlds resonate from the strength and vibrancy of her own life."

Many of McKinley's stories and two of her novels—*The Blue Sword* and *The Hero and the Crown*—are set in the land of Damar, a land based in part on the Rudyard Kipling story "The Man Who Would Be King"—and on John Huston's movie of that story. *The Blue Sword,* the first book that explores Damar, has "its roots in Rudyard Kipling and Rider Haggard and P. C. Wren—and, for that matter, in E. M. Hull's *The Sheik,* though I suppose I should blush to admit it," McKinley states in *Horn Book.* Marilyn H. Karrenbrock declares in the *Dictionary of Literary Biography* that *The Blue Sword* "is definitely reminiscent of Kipling's India. . . . It is a fresh and interesting setting for a novel of high fantasy." The Newbery Award-winning *The Hero and the Crown* takes place in an earlier Damar, and is less Kiplingesque than *The Blue Sword.* Karrenbrock concludes, "*The Hero and the Crown* is a rousing story which convincingly makes McKinley's point: girls can be heroes, too."

Robin McKinley told *CA:* "Storytelling has always been the other side of reading for me; it's the way my mind works. I can't remember a time when I wasn't telling myself stories. When I learned to write I started trying to write them down, but for many years they were only fragments; the first thing I finished that I was halfway content with was *Beauty,* which became my first published novel.

"I read a lot of fairy tales when I was a child, and a lot of horse stories, both of which show in my work now—and I have never grown out of being horse-mad, as girls are expected to. I still want to grow up to be a sort of combination of the best bits of Rudyard Kipling, Joseph Conrad, Raymond Chandler, and J. R. R. Tolkien, though I haven't figured out quite how yet. Meanwhile I write what and as I can. I am very preoccupied with female heroes, however; the heroes of all the books I loved best seemed to be men; and the imbalance is changing far more slowly that I would like. I don't object to male heroes, I just want female heroes too.

"I was an only child and a Navy brat, so I grew up travelling, and I still do a lot of travelling and still enjoy it. I am invited to speak at schools and libraries all over this country, and whenever possible use such gigs as an excuse to do some sightseeing afterwards; occasionally I can find a legitimate business excuse to go farther. I visit England as often as I can, where I feel my most important literary roots are. But even when I am 'home' I divide my time between a little house in a village on the coast of Maine and a co-op in New York City."

BIOGRAPHICAL/CRITICAL SOURCES:

BOOKS

Children's Literature Review, Volume 10, Gale, 1986.
Dictionary of Literary Biography, Volume 52: *American Writers for Children since 1960: Fiction,* Gale, 1986.
Kingman, Lee, editor, *Newbery and Caldecott Medal Books, 1976-1985,* Horn Book, 1986.
Moorcock, Michael, *Wizardry and Wild Romance: A Study of Epic Fantasy,* Gollancz, 1987.
Spivack, Charlotte, *Merlin's Daughters: Contemporary Women Writers of Fantasy,* Greenwood Press, 1987.

PERIODICALS

Fantasy Review, March, 1985, February, 1986.
New York Times Book Review, January 27, 1985, November 13, 1988.
Science Fiction Review, spring, 1982.
Times Literary Supplement, November 25, 1983, August 30, 1985, August 7, 1987.
Washington Post Book World, November 6, 1988.
Wilson Library Bulletin, January, 1987.
Writing, December, 1989.

*   *   *

McLEOD, Wallace (Edmond)   1931-

PERSONAL: Born May 30, 1931, in Toronto, Ontario, Canada; son of Angus Edmond (a printing pressman) and Mary A. E. (Shier) McLeod; married Elizabeth M. Staples (a teacher), July 24, 1957; children: Betsy, John, James, Angus. *Education:* University of Toronto, B.A., 1953; Harvard University, A.M., 1954, Ph.D., 1966; American School of Classical Studies, Athens, additional study, 1957-59. *Politics:* Conservative. *Religion:* Presbyterian.

ADDRESSES: Home—399 St. Clements Ave., Toronto, Ontario, Canada M5N 1M2. *Office*—Victoria College, University of Toronto, Toronto, Ontario, Canada M5S 1K7.

CAREER: Trinity College, Hartford, Conn., instructor in classical languages, 1955-56; University of British Columbia, Vancouver, instructor in classics, 1959-61; University of Western Ontario, London, lecturer in classics, 1961-62; University of Toronto, Victoria College, Toronto, Ontario, assistant professor, 1962-66, associate professor, 1966-74, professor of classics, 1974—, associate chairman, 1975-78, acting chairman of classics department, 1978-79. Prestonian lecturer, 1986. Member of Society of Blue Friars, 1984; fellow of Philalethes Society, 1986.

MEMBER: Classical Association of Canada, American Philological Association, Archaeological Institute of America, Society of Archer-Antiquaries, Ancient Free and Accepted Masons.

AWARDS, HONORS: Canada Council fellowship, 1970-71.

WRITINGS:

Composite Bows from the Tomb of Tut'ankhamun, Oxford University Press, 1970.
(Editor and contributor) *Beyond the Pillars: More Light on Freemasonry,* Grand Lodge of Canada, 1973.
(Editor and contributor) *Meeting the Challenge: The Lodge Officer at Work,* Grand Lodge of Canada, 1976.
(Editor and author of introduction) *The Sufferings of John Coustos: A Facsimile Reprint of the First English Edition, Published at London in 1746,* Masonic Book Club, 1979.
(Editor and contributor) *Whence Came We?: Freemasonry in Ontario, 1764-1980,* Grand Lodge of Canada, 1980.
Self Bows and Other Archery Tackle from the Tomb of Tut'ankhamun, Griffith Institute, 1982.
(Editor and author of introduction) *The Old Gothic Constitutions: Facsimile Reprints of Four Early Printed Texts of the Masonic Old Charges,* Masonic Book Club, 1985.
The Old Charges: The Prestonian Lecture for 1986, privately printed, 1986.
(Editor and author of introduction) *Wellins Calcott, a Candid Disquisition: A Facsimile Reprint of the First English Edition, Published at London in 1769,* Masonic Book Club, 1989.

Contributor of articles and reviews to professional journals. *Phoenix,* associate editor, 1965-70, acting editor, 1973, acting review editor, 1976-77, 1989-90, acting associate editor, 1985-86.

WORK IN PROGRESS: Inscribed Pottery from the Middle Bronze Age at Lerna; Crusaders' Castles of the Argolid.

SIDELIGHTS: Wallace McLeod participated in archaeological excavations at Lerna, Greece, and Gordion, Turkey, in 1958.

*   *   *

McPHERSON, James M(unro)   1936-

PERSONAL: Born October 11, 1936, in Valley City, N.D.; son of James Munro (a high school teacher) and Miriam (a teacher; maiden name, Osborn) McPherson; married Patricia A. Rasche, December 28, 1957; children: Joanna Erika. *Education:* Gustavus Adolphus College, B.A., 1958; Johns Hopkins University, Ph.D., 1963. *Politics:* Democratic. *Religion:* Presbyterian.

ADDRESSES: Home—15 Randall Rd., Princeton, N.J. 08540. *Office*—Department of History, Princeton University, Princeton, N.J. 08544.

CAREER: Princeton University, Princeton, N.J., instructor, 1962-65, assistant professor, 1965-66, associate professor, 1966-72, professor of history, 1972—, Edwards Professor of American History, 1982. Fellow, Behavioral Sciences Center, Stanford University, 1982-83. Consultant, Social Science program, Educational Research Council, Cleveland, Ohio; elder, Nassau Presbyterian Church, 1976-79.

MEMBER: American Historical Association, Association for the Study of Negro Life and History, Organization of American Historians, Southern Historical Association, Phi Beta Kappa.

AWARDS, HONORS: Danforth fellow, 1958-62; Proctor & Gamble faculty fellowship; Anisfield Wolff Award in Race Relations, 1965, for *The Struggle for Equality: Abolitionists and the Negro in the Civil War and Reconstruction;* Guggenheim fellow, 1967-68; National Endowment for the Humanities-Huntington fellowship, 1977-78; Huntington-Seaver Institute fellow, 1987-88; National Book Award nomination, 1988, National Book Critics Circle nomination, 1988, and Pulitzer Prize in history, 1989, all for *Battle Cry of Freedom: The Civil War Era.*

WRITINGS:

The Struggle for Equality: Abolitionists and the Negro in the Civil War and Reconstruction, Princeton University Press, 1964.

(Editor) *The Negro's Civil War: How American Negroes Felt and Acted in the War for the Union,* Pantheon, 1965, reprinted, University of Illinois Press, 1982.

(Contributor) Martin B. Duberman, editor, *The Anti-Slavery Vanguard: New Essays on Abolitionism,* Princeton University Press, 1965.

(Editor) *Marching Toward Freedom: The Negro in the Civil War, 1861-1865,* Knopf, 1968.

(Contributor) Barton J. Bernstein, editor, *Towards a New Past: Dissenting Essays in American History,* Pantheon, 1968.

(With others) *Blacks in America: Bibliographical Essays,* Doubleday, 1971.

The Abolitionist Legacy: From Reconstruction to the NAACP, Princeton University Press, 1976.

Ordeal by Fire: The Civil War and Reconstruction, Knopf, 1981.

(Editor with J. Morgan Kousser) *Region, Race, and Reconstruction: Essays in Honor of C. Vann Woodward,* Oxford University Press, 1982.

Battle Cry of Freedom: The Civil War Era (volume 6 of "The Oxford History of the United States"), Oxford University Press, 1988.

Contributor of articles to *American Historical Review, Journal of American History, Journal of Negro History, Caribbean Studies, Phylon, Mid America,* and other publications. Member of editorial board, *Civil War History.*

WORK IN PROGRESS: Abraham Lincoln and the Second American Revolution, a collection of essays.

SIDELIGHTS: When James M. McPherson's *Battle Cry of Freedom: The Civil War Era,* the sixth volume of the "Oxford History of the United States," appeared in 1988 it caused a sensation among reviewers and readers alike—Ballantine Books made a record-setting bid of $504,000 for the paperback rights, and the book appeared on the *New York Times* bestseller chart from March to July of 1988. Critics noted that the volume made few

new revelations about the war: "The Civil War," declared Hugh Brogan in the *New York Times Book Review,* "is the most worked-over topic in United States history, one of the most written about in the history of the world"; and Peter S. Prescott, writing in *Newsweek,* stated that "the more than 50,000 books already written about the Civil War have left the field as thoroughly turned over as the ground was at Antietam." What they admired about the book was its expert synthesis of the period's history, incorporating political, social, economic, and military factors to present a portrait of this most central event in U.S. history.

Civil War historiography has a long and distinguished history of its own. Although critics have acclaimed other single-volume histories of the Civil War—among them Bruce Catton's *This Hallowed Ground* and McPherson's own *Ordeal by Fire: The Civil War and Reconstruction*—generally the most prominent works have been multi-volume efforts. One of the earliest interpretations of the war appeared in George Bancroft's *History of the United States from the Discovery of the American Continent to the Present Time.* Bancroft, considered by many contemporaries to be the preeminent nineteenth-century American historian, lived through the events leading up to the War, through the war itself, and through most of the period of Reconstruction that followed it. His ten-volume work presented one of the first attempts to understand the war as the triumph of Unionism (right) over Secessionism (wrong). James Ford Rhodes, writing his seven-volume *History of the United States from the Compromise of 1850* around the turn of the century, was among the first historians to emphasize the importance of race as an issue in nineteenth-century politics. Allan Nevins, writing after World War II, completed eight volumes on *The Ordeal of the Union,* in which he challenged the then-held view that the Civil War had been unnecessary, forced on the South by fanatical Northern abolitionists. More recently, Bruce Catton and Shelby Foote have published narrative histories describing the military conflict from Northern and Southern perspectives—Catton's "Army of the Potomac" and "Centennial History of the Civil War" trilogies, and Foote's *The Civil War: A Narrative.*

Critical opinion gives *Battle Cry of Freedom* a distinguished place among its precursors. Historian Thomas L. Connelly, writing in the *Washington Post Book World,* calls *Battle Cry* the "finest single volume on the [Civil] war and its background." *New York Review of Books* contributor Richard E. Beringer declares, "It is the only recent book I know of that effectively integrates in one volume social, political, and military events from the immediate aftermath of the Mexican War through the sectional strife of the 1850s, the secession movement, and the Civil War." In the *Los Angeles Times Book Review,* Huston Horn calls *Battle Cry* "the finest compression of that national paroxysm ever fitted between two covers." Brogan states that the book "is the best one-volume treatment of its subject that I have ever come across. It may actually be the best ever published. It is comprehensive yet succinct, scholarly without being pedantic, eloquent but unrhetorical. It is compellingly readable. I was swept away, feeling as if I had never heard the saga before."

McPherson also offers a reassessment of the outcome of the war, believing that the Union victory was by no means as preordained as some historians would have it. He examines three reasons often cited for the South's defeat: 1. the South was overwhelmed by superior numbers; 2. Southern soldiers lost the will to fight; and 3. Union leadership proved better able to manage the new industrial warfare. While acknowledging that each interpretation has its strengths, McPherson notes in his epilogue to *Battle Cry of Freedom* that "most attempts to explain southern defeat or northern victory lack the dimension of *contingency*—the recognition that at numerous critical points during the war things might have gone altogether differently." "Northern victory and southern defeat in the war," he concludes, "cannot be understood apart from the contingency that hung over every campaign, every battle, every election, every decision during the war." "This is historical writing of the highest order," Brogan states, "conveying perhaps the most important lesson of all: that we are not always masters of our fate, even when we most need to be."

Another of McPherson's major themes concerns the war's revolutionary nature. He sees the Civil War as a turning point in American history, as do many other historians: a point in which American society turned away from Southern agrarianism to Northern capitalism and industrialization. However, he writes, "until 1861, it was the North that was out of the mainstream, not the South. . . . The South more closely resembled a majority of the societies in the world than did the rapidly changing North during the antebellum generation." Many southerners, McPherson explains, viewed the new "competitive, egalitarian, free-labor capitalism" in the North with alarm, seeing in its power a threat to their traditional liberties and property rights. When the Republican party won the election of 1860, the South figured "that the northern majority had turned irrevocably toward this frightening, revolutionary future," and accordingly began what McPherson calls "a pre-emptive counterrevolution"—a term Beringer defines as "a revolution launched to prevent the real revolution from occurring."

The war wrought as well a profound change in the way Americans perceived themselves and their government. "Before 1861," McPherson explains, "the two words 'United States' were generally rendered as a plural noun: 'the United States *are* a republic.' The war marked a transition of the United States to a singular noun. The 'Union' also became the nation, and Americans now rarely speak of their Union except in an historical sense." McPherson points out that before the war, most citizens were unaffected by the federal government in their daily lives, except through the postal service. By the war's end, however, a U.S. citizen had to deal with a federal income tax, the Internal Revenue Service, the draft, a national paper currency, and the first national welfare system. "At the end" of the book, declares Prescott, McPherson ". . . demonstrates a point he made firmly at the start: this country went into the war a union and came out a nation. What that difference is, is what this book is about."

CA INTERVIEW

CA interviewed James M. McPherson by telephone on May 23, 1989, in Princeton, New Jersey.

CA: According to Something about the Author, *both of your parents were teachers. Did they encourage you to follow in their footsteps?*

McPHERSON: Their example probably did have some influence on me. My father was a high school teacher and administrator for many years. My mother went back to finish her education after her children grew up and then became an elementary school teacher. I know that when I first went to college, I had only dim and vague ideas of career possibilities, but the one model I had before me was their role as teachers. Later on in college I was encouraged by the influence of two or three of my professors to think in terms of becoming a college teacher.

CA: You lived your first six years in Valley City, North Dakota, and from then through college in Minnesota. Those areas don't

have large concentrations of blacks. How did you come by your interest in black history?

McPHERSON: That happened in graduate school. I went to Baltimore to do my graduate work at Johns Hopkins, and I was there from 1958 to 1962, which were the early years of the civil rights movement. The combination of studying Southern history and Civil War history in Baltimore and being surrounded by the activities of the early years of the civil rights movement turned my interest to the role of earlier civil rights activists and black leaders in the Civil War period. That's what launched my interest in the subject.

CA: While you were at Johns Hopkins, did you ever go down into the Deep South to work with the civil rights activists?

McPHERSON: I did go to the Deep South for research trips and to visit a friend. I wasn't involved in civil rights demonstrations in the Deep South, but I was involved in activities in the Baltimore area. Baltimore was then half or more than half a Southern city, or a border city. My civil rights participation was concentrated in the Baltimore area.

CA: Are you satisfied by the progress made by blacks in the last thirty years?

McPHERSON: Satisfied would not be the correct verb in this case, though I think enormous strides have been made. The difference between what I saw and knew about in the South, and even in a border area like Maryland, thirty years ago and today is enormous. But there are still a lot of problems, and a lot of improvements that need to be made.

CA: You have been teaching and writing at Princeton for almost thirty years now. Have you noticed much of a change in the quality of students over that period?

McPHERSON: I think overall there hasn't been any dramatic change in the academic and intellectual quality of students, but during my time at Princeton there have been dramatic changes in the social makeup of the students. For one thing, we went coeducational in 1969. When I first came here it was entirely a men's school. Now nearly forty percent of our undergraduate students are women. The same kind of dramatic changes have taken place in the graduate student constituency. Also there were very few black students, or indeed students from any minority group, when I first came here. Now blacks make up about seven percent of the undergraduate student body, and there's a wider representation from the whole social spectrum.

I think in the sixties and early seventies the graduate students were very good. When the bottom dropped out of the job market for college teachers, there was an overnight shrinkage in the number of people coming to graduate school here, and I think also some decline in the quality. But that has turned around in the past few years as the job market has improved, and there's been an upsurge in both quality and quantity.

CA: In The Closing of the American Mind, *University of Chicago professor Allan Bloom described what he feels is a serious lack of interest among college students in such areas as literature and music, and his belief that students today are driven mainly by the hope of material gain. How do you feel about his points?*

McPHERSON: I think what he said was exaggerated, at least according to my experience. For a while there was some decline in the preparation of students in their ability to write and in their knowledge of the fundamentals. In that respect I suppose there was some accuracy to what Professor Bloom had to say. But I didn't think the decline was dramatic. I've noticed relatively little change among undergraduates over the years. I think more of the change, as I suggested, occurred among graduate students, and that was for different reasons than Allan Bloom mentioned. I think it was just because the perceived career opportunities for professional historians and college teachers declined for a decade or so, and the better students were going elsewhere: they were going to law school or somewhere else. Now we're seeing them return.

CA: In the last twenty-five years, have there been any new findings in Civil War studies that have supplanted our accepted understanding of the Civil War?

McPHERSON: There's been a great deal of activity in several areas of scholarship in nineteenth-century history that impinge on our understanding of the Civil War. There have been radical changes in our perception of slavery, for example, and the experience of both blacks and whites in slavery. That has meant a difference in the way we look at the experience of emancipation and the transition from a slave society to a free society in the South during and after the Civil War. That's one area, and an area that I've been involved in to some extent. There's been a greater emphasis on the initiative that slaves themselves took in winning their own freedom, both by escaping from the plantations to Union lines during the Civil War and thereby forcing the question of slavery and emancipation on the Union government and for that matter on the South as well; and in the role that blacks played in the war effort for both the North and the South, but especially, as time went on, as soldiers for the Union in the Civil War. That's been an area of considerable research and some new findings and many new interpretations.

Another area of research that has focused a lot of new viewpoints on the Civil War is the study of the non-slaveholding whites in the South, the so-called yeoman farmers, their attitude toward the plantation and toward slavery, what stake they had in the Civil War, their roles in the post-war period. Some of them became supporters of the Republican Party, but the tension between this white yeoman constituency in the Republican Party in the South and the black constituency in the Republican Party in the South, both of them allied with a different group of Northerners who were Republicans, has formed an area of interesting research and some new findings in the Reconstruction period. One of the things I've been interested in in the Civil War is the prisoner-of-war exchange program and the reasons it broke down and the responsibility for the suffering and deaths in prison camps, especially in the last year of the war. These are some of the areas in which there have been, if not major new findings, at least some new perspectives.

CA: I read with interest the Civil War article in U.S. News & World Report *in which you figured prominently. It was stated in the opening paragraph that there's more interest in the Civil War today than there has been since* Gone with the Wind *was so popular in the 1930s. What explains the resurgence of interest now?*

McPHERSON: That question has very much occupied my mind in the last year and a half since I wrote *Battle Cry of Freedom* because I think I've been one beneficiary of this interest in the Civil War. There are various explanations for it, and I'm not sure that any single one is adequate to understand the phenomenon. One thing is that right now we're in the midst of the 125th anni-

versary of the war. That does not seem like a good reason for interest to be sparked, but in fact there have been conferences, reenactments of Civil War battles, and all that sort of publicity that's associated with anniversary commemorations, and I think that has aroused some interest.

There have also been cycles of interest in the Civil War over the past hundred and twenty-five years. For a generation or so after the war, as happens after most wars, the participants wanted to put it behind them and get on with their lives. It wasn't until the 1880s, when the memories of the hardships and suffering and chaos and trauma of the war began to fade and be overlain by a kind of romantic haze, that veterans of the Civil War began to write their memoirs and write articles about it and form veterans' associations. There was a very high rate of interest in the Civil War in the late nineteenth and early twentieth centuries. Then there was a decline in the teens and twenties, partly because another major war came along, World War I, and reminded everyone again of the horrors of war and brought about a preoccupation with a different war.

But then with the Depression and *Gone with the Wind* and the kind of romanticization of the past that was done in that book, there was another revival of interest in the Civil War. In the forties and fifties there was a decline again, partly associated with World War II. There was a sharp rise of interest in the 1960s with the centennial observation of the Civil War, but then with Vietnam and with the turning against any kind of interest in the military and military history, there was a sharp decline in the late sixties and seventies. We're on the upswing from that again right now.

So it is partly a cyclical phenomenon, but I wouldn't want to attribute it entirely to that. I think that with the civil rights movement of the 1960s and the continuing concern about the question of race relations in this country there's an ongoing interest in the history of race relations. The most vivid and dramatic moment in that history in the United States was the Civil War and Emancipation. That clearly means that there's going to be a great deal of research and writing and interest focused on that aspect of American history. And because the Civil War was such a traumatic, virtually revolutionary experience in American history, destroying a whole society and trying to create a new one out of the ashes of the old and transforming the constitutional and political and economic structure of the United States, there's going to be an ongoing fascination with the process and the problems associated with this revolutionary transformation.

CA: In your preface to Battle Cry of Freedom *you say that you adopted a narrative form instead of a topical approach; you found that the best way to do justice to the Civil War in recounting it. As a historian, do you feel the narrative approach is generally the most desirable one if you're taking a period in history like World War I or the American Revolution?*

McPHERSON: I think that depends on what the historian hopes to accomplish. In my case, I was going to try to tell the story of the causes of the Civil War and of the war itself, and try to explain the reasons why these things happened. I think a narrative form was best both to convey the complexity and the passion of that period, and to explain the cause-effect relationships between the events that were crucial to determining what happened during the period. That would probably be true for an historian who had the same goals in mind with the Revolution or with other important events in American history if the main focus were on a series of events, and that's especially true with a war and the political events that surround a war. But if an historian starts out to try to explain different kinds of problems or phenomena in history, it may be that a different kind of format would best fit that purpose. I think the narrative format best fits my purpose.

CA: Considering that new scholarship is incorporated into the texts of such recent books as Battle Cry of Freedom, *do you feel students can profit from reading the older books by such historians as James Ford Rhodes, George Bancroft, and Allan Nevins?*

McPHERSON: Yes, I think so. Sometimes I'm a little reluctant to send students to some of them because they're multi-volume histories. You mentioned Rhodes: he has seven volumes on the whole period of the war, the causes of the war, Reconstruction. Allan Nevins has eight large volumes on the same period that I cover in one volume, which is the period from the Mexican War to the Civil War. Those volumes are eminently readable, very detailed, and I profited from them a great deal in my research. There is some value in sending students to them if they're going to do the same kind of thoroughgoing research, but if I'm just recommending to a student a book on some aspect of the Civil War, I'm not sure I would send him to the multi-volume studies. I would try to pick out what I consider to be the most challenging and important study, which might be a single volume or might be more, on the particular aspect the student was interested in. But if a student had a lot of time—the whole summer—I could provide a reading list that would include several multi-volume studies that would be of considerable value, going all the way back to Rhodes or up to books as recent as Shelby Foote's on the military history of the Civil War, which is three very large but extremely readable volumes.

CA: Do you think that, at the beginning of the Civil War, there was a chance that either side could have won, or was it pretty much a foregone conclusion that the North was destined to win?

McPHERSON: I think either side could have won the war, not only at the beginning but at almost any time up until the fall of 1864. It was by no means a foregone conclusion that the North would win, any more than it was a foregone conclusion that Britain would suppress the insurrection in the colonies in 1776 or that the mighty United States would put down the Vietnamese in 1965. Certainly Britain thought that it would have no trouble in '76, and the United States thought that it would have no trouble in 1965 and 1966, and many people in the North thought they would have no trouble in putting down this insurrection in 1861. But in fact, of course, that was not true in any of the three cases.

There were many times during the Civil War when the South came quite close to victory, partly because what victory meant for the South was much different from what it was for the North. The South merely had to compel the North to give up its attempt to put down the insurrection, give up its attempt to invade, conquer, occupy, and suppress the war of independence by the Southerners, in the same way that the United States in 1776 had to persuade Britain merely to give up. But the North in 1861 did have to invade, conquer, occupy, and basically destroy the infrastructure that supported the Confederate war effort. That's a much larger undertaking, and that was why the South, even with a smaller population and far inferior industrial resources, had a good chance to win its independence a number of times between the beginning of the war and the fall of 1864.

The fall of 1864 was the crucial, final turning point because of the capture of Atlanta and several Union victories in Virginia which ensured the re-election of Abraham Lincoln in that year, which was very much in jeopardy earlier in the summer. If Lin-

coln had not been re-elected, I think that would have been taken as a sign that the North was not willing to continue this war on to victory. Lincoln's re-election was an endorsement by the Northern electorate of his policy of unconditional victory, his demand for unconditional surrender of the Confederacy. And that's what eventually happened in 1865.

CA: You hear so often that if only one factor had been different, the South might have won. In fact, you said in your 1985 lecture "How Lincoln Won the War with Metaphors" that if Lincoln had been president of the South and Jefferson Davis had been president of the North, the South would have won the war.

McPHERSON: That was a quotation I took from the late David Potter, who was an eminent historian. I went on in the lecture to analyze different contingencies in the Civil War and to argue that if one factor or a combination of factors had been different, it's quite possible that the outcome would have been different. My major theme in that lecture, and I think in *Battle Cry of Freedom* too, was that Northern victory in the Civil War was not inevitable, and indeed, by implication, that nothing in history is inevitable. That's another reason I think the narrative format is the best way to tell this story, because the narrative format does not assume any inevitability. It tries to tell the story of how and why things happened the way they did without starting out with the assumption that they had to happen that way.

CA: In your research and writing on the Civil War, have you discovered any new heroes, individuals who in your opinion have not received due recognition?

McPHERSON: I would not say that I have discovered any new heroes, but my own appreciation and admiration for certain individuals has deepened as a result of my research. One, and a fairly obvious one, I suppose, is Abraham Lincoln himself, an extraordinarily complex man and one who cannot be understood at a superficial level. The more I've come to know about him, the more I've come to appreciate the complexity of the problems he faced and the pressures he was under and how he dealt with them, the deeper my admiration has become. The same is true of Ulysses S. Grant, who is often underrated both as an individual and as a general. I've come to appreciate him in both respects more as a result of my study and writing.

But neither Lincoln nor Grant is an undiscovered hero by any means. One person less well known that I've come to admire a great deal is a man named Joshua Lawrence Chamberlain, who was made famous in our own time by Michael Shaara's novel *The Killer Angels,* about the Battle of Gettysburg. Chamberlain was a colonel who commanded the 20th Maine Regiment, which defended Little Round Top on the second day. He was a college professor from Bowdoin College in Maine who joined the army in the summer of 1862 and rose eventually to become a major general and one of the heroes of Northern victory. He's a name that I think is unknown to all but the more dedicated Civil War buffs. I came to understand and appreciate him too.

CA: You look upon Shaara's The Killer Angels *as one of the better novels on the Civil War, I believe.*

McPHERSON: I do. I assign it in my undergraduate course because I think it is not only an accurate account of the Battle of Gettysburg, but a wonderful novel to get at what the men who fought at Gettysburg thought they were fighting for. That in turn is a way of presenting a variety of perspectives on what the Civil War was all about and what it meant to America.

CA: You adapted one of your books, The Negro's Civil War, *for high school students. Are you thinking of adapting some of your other work for younger students?*

McPHERSON: I don't have any present plans to do that, but I have heard from a number of high school students and teachers that *Battle Cry of Freedom* is being used in advanced elective high school history courses on the Civil War. I've been quite gratified by that, because the book is aimed at an adult audience and I know it is being used quite widely also in colleges. I'm happy for it to be used in high schools, and I'm glad that some high school students find it interesting and readable.

CA: The wide response to your book must be very exciting. I don't think I've ever before read such an enthusiastic review on the front page of the New York Times Book Review *as Hugh Brogan gave* Battle Cry of Freedom *on February 14, 1988.*

McPHERSON: Yes, that launched the book, without question. I have been astonished by the response to it and by the letters I get from people all over the country, from all walks of life, who have read it and have found something worthwhile in it.

CA: I would imagine that one of the most difficult things about writing about the Civil War is that so much has already been written about it.

McPHERSON: Yes. A lot of times I'm asked, Why one more book, when we already have so many? What I tried to do was package between one pair of covers the whole story of how and why the war happened. I start with 1848 and the end of the Mexican War and go to the 1850s, and then try to tell the story of the war itself. As I mentioned a few minutes ago, most of the really fine accounts of either this whole period or parts of it are multi-volume accounts. The great complexity and great intensity of the issues in this period seem to force people to write multi-volume accounts. I tried to put it all in one volume, and I think that's been one reason for the popularity of the book.

CA: What are your writing plans for the immediate future?

McPHERSON: Over the past several years, in addition to finishing this book, I have on one occasion or another given public lectures or written essays on a couple of themes revolving around Abraham Lincoln and his leadership during the war, and on the question of the Civil War as a kind of second American revolution. So I'm putting those essays together in a book which I will call *Abraham Lincoln and the Second American Revolution.* It will be a much shorter book than *Battle Cry of Freedom,* probably no more than two hundred pages, and a much different kind of book. It won't be a narrative history, but a series of separate but related brief interpretive essays.

BIOGRAPHICAL/CRITICAL SOURCES:

BOOKS

Dictionary of Literary Biography, Gale, Volume 17: *Twentieth-Century American Historians,* 1983, Volume 30: *American Historians, 1607-1865,* 1984, Volume 47: *American Historians, 1866-1912,* 1986.
McPherson, James M., *Battle Cry of Freedom: The Civil War Era,* Oxford University Press, 1988.
Shaara, Michael, *The Killer Angels,* McKay, 1974.
Something about the Author, Volume 16, Gale, 1979.

PERIODICALS

Book World, May 5, 1968.

Chicago Tribune, March 20, 1988.
Chicago Tribune Book World, October 17, 1982.
Commonweal, May 24, 1968.
Los Angeles Times Book Review, March 20, 1988.
National Observer, November 4, 1968.
Newsweek, April 11, 1988.
New York Review of Books, June 2, 1988.
New York Times Book Review, February 14, 1988.
U.S. News & World Report, August 15, 1988.
Washington Post Book World, March 13, 1988.

—Sketch by Kenneth R. Shepherd

—Interview by Walter W. Ross

*   *   *

MELDRUM, James
See BROXHOLME, John Franklin

*   *   *

MENKUS, Belden   1931-

PERSONAL: Born May 6, 1931, in Sacramento, Calif.; son of Julian (a sales manager) and Ida (Dunnevitz) Menkus; married JoAnn Bozarth (a researcher), December 14, 1952; children: Neal, Belden, Jr., Donald, Juli Ann. *Education:* Attended Bob Jones University, 1949-1951, and Tennessee Temple College, 1952. *Politics:* Independent Democrat. *Religion:* Southern Baptist.

ADDRESSES: Home—Route 3, Box 3493, Harpole Rd., Manchester, Tenn. 37355.

CAREER: U.S. Air Force, records management technician at various locations, 1953-57; Southern Baptist Sunday School Board, Nashville, Tenn., records manager, 1957-1962; Prentice-Hall, Inc., Englewood Cliffs, N.J., senior editor, 1962-64; Kennecott Copper Corp., New York City, senior management analyst, 1965-66; REA Express, New York City, director of administrative services, 1967-68; independent management consultant, 1968—. Certified as Records Manager, 1973, Information Systems Auditor, 1976, Systems Professional, 1983, and Office Automation Professional, 1986. Member of faculty, New York University Management Institute, 1965-67, and U.S. Civil Defense Staff College, 1970-76. Judge of graphic arts competition, Printing Industries of America, 1974; member of Emmett Leahy Memorial Award Selection Committee, 1974.

MEMBER: Society of Professional Management Consultants (vice president, 1975-76), Society of Magazine Writers, Association for Systems Management, Society of American Archivists, National Microfilm Association, Association for State and Local History, EDP Auditors Association, American Records Management Association (regional vice president, 1962-63), Near East Archaeological Society, National Conference of Christians and Jews, Interfaith Affairs Advisory Council, Conference on Faith and History, Association for the Development of Religious Information Systems, Business Forms Management Association, Conference on Jewish Social Studies, British Administrative Management Institute, British Institute of Reprographic Technology, Evangelical Theological Society.

AWARDS, HONORS: Silver Medallion, American Management Association, 1968, 1972; distinguished service citations, Association of Records Executives and Administrators, 1968, National Microfilm Association, 1974, New York Chamber of Commerce and Industry, 1978, Association for Systems Management, 1980, and Institute of Internal Auditors, 1982; Life Honorary Faculty Member, U.S. Civil Defense Staff College, 1973.

WRITINGS:

Meet the American Jew, Broadman, 1963.
Study Guide to Meet the American Jew, Convention Press, 1966.
(Contributor) John Macquarrie, editor, *Dictionary of Christian Ethics,* Westminster, 1967, new edition published as *The Westminster Dictionary of Christian Ethics,* 1986.
(Contributor) Carl Heyel, editor, *Handbook of Modern Office Management and Administrative Services,* McGraw, 1972.
(Contributor) Heyel, editor, *Encyclopedia of Management,* 2nd edition, Van Nostrand, 1973.
(Contributor) Douglas Hoyt, editor, *Computer Security Handbook,* Macmillan, 1974.
(Editor) *Handbook of Management for the Growing Business,* Van Nostrand, 1986.

Contributor to professional and religious journals in the United States and Canada. Editor, *Management Letter,* 1962-64, *Records Management Journal,* 1963-67, *Computer Security Letter,* 1974-77, *Data Processing Auditing Report,* 1983-86, and *EDPACS: EDP Audit, Control and Security,* 1988; contributing editor, *Baptist Watchman-Examiner,* 1966-69, *Business Forms Reporter,* 1968, *Canadian Office Administrator,* 1968-70, *Business Graphics,* 1969-75, *Administrative Management,* 1973-85, *Modern Office Technology,* 1986—, and *Computers and Security,* 1986—.

* * *

MENTON, Seymour 1927-

PERSONAL: Born March 6, 1927, in New York, N.Y.; son of Alexander (a windowtrimmer) and Mildred (Sahr) Menton; married Catherine Conrad, June 7, 1958; children: Tim Rudolph, Allen Walter. *Education:* City College (now City College of the City University of New York), B.A., 1948; Universidad Nacional Autonoma de Mexico, M.A., 1949; New York University, Ph.D., 1952.

ADDRESSES: Home—2461 Basswood St., Newport Beach, Calif. 92660. *Office*—Department of Spanish and Portuguese, University of California, Irvine, Calif. 92717.

CAREER: Public school teacher in New York, N.Y., 1949-52; Dartmouth College, Hanover, N.H., instructor in Spanish, 1952-54; Dartmouth College, Hanover, N.H., instructor in Spanish, 1952-54; University of Kansas, Lawrence, assistant professor, 1954-58, associate professor, 1958-62, professor of Spanish and Portuguese, 1962-65; University of California, Irvine, professor of Spanish and Portuguese, 1965—, chairman of department of foreign languages, 1965-68, chairman of department of Spanish and Portuguese, 1968-70 and 1979—. *Military service:* U.S. Navy, 1945-46.

MEMBER: International Institute of Iberoamerican Literature, American Association of Teachers of Spanish and Portuguese (president, 1971), Modern Language Association of America, Phi Beta Kappa.

AWARDS, HONORS: Smith-Mundt grant to Brazil, 1960-61.

WRITINGS:

Saga de Mexico (title means "Saga of Mexico"), Appleton, 1955, reprinted, Irvington, 1979.
Historia critica de la novela guatemalteca (title means "Critical History of the Guatemalan Novel"), University of San Carlos, 1960.
El cuento hispanoamericano (title means "The Spanish American Short Story"), Fondo de Cultura Economica, 1964, 4th edition, 1972.

El cuento costarricense (title means "The Costa Rican Short Story"), Studium (Mexico), 1964.
(Editor with Wilson Martins) *Teatro Brasileiro contemporaneo* (title means "Contemporary Brazilian Theatre"), Appleton, 1966, 2nd edition, revised, Irvington, 1978.
(Editor) *Frutos de mi tierra,* Instituto Cara y Cuervo (Bogota), 1972.
Prose Fiction of the Cuban Revolution, University of Texas Press, 1975.
La novela colombiana: planetas y satelites, Plaza y Janes (Bogota), 1978.
(Compiler) *The Spanish American Short Story: A Critical Anthology,* University of California Press, 1980.
Magic Realism Rediscovered, 1918-1981, Art Alliance, 1983.

Contributing editor, *Handbook of Latin American Studies,* 1960-72, and *Books Abroad;* editor, *Hispania,* 1963-65; advisory editor, *Revista Iberoamericana,* 1969-73.

SIDELIGHTS: Seymour Menton has traveled extensively throughout Latin America.

BIOGRAPHICAL/CRITICAL SOURCES:

PERIODICALS

Los Angeles Times Book Review, August 24, 1980.*

* * *

MERTON, Robert K(ing) 1910-

PERSONAL: Born July 5, 1910, in Philadelphia, Pa.; son of Jewish, working-class, immigrant parents from eastern Europe; married Suzanne M. Carhart (a social worker), September 8, 1934 (separated, 1968); children: Stephanie (Mrs. Thomas A. Tombrello, Jr.), Robert C., Vanessa H. *Education:* Temple University, A.B., 1931; Harvard University, M.A., 1932, Ph.D., 1936.

ADDRESSES: Office—Fayerweather Hall 415, Columbia University, New York, N.Y. 10027.

CAREER: Harvard University, Cambridge, Mass., tutor and instructor in sociology, 1936-39; Tulane University, New Orleans, La., associate professor, 1939-40, professor of sociology and chairman of department, 1940-41; Columbia University, New York, N.Y., assistant professor, 1941-44, associate professor, 1944-47, professor, 1947-63, Giddings Professor of Sociology, 1963-74, University Professor, 1974-79, University Professor Emeritus, 1979—, Special Service Professor, 1979-84, associate director, Bureau of Applied Social Research, 1942-71. Adjunct professor, Rockefeller University, 1979—; resident scholar, Russell Sage Foundation, 1979—; George Sarton Professor of the History of Science, University of Ghent, 1986-88. Distinguished or special lecturer to numerous universities, institutes, and organizations in the United States and overseas.

Member of first official delegation of behavioral scientists to U.S.S.R. Academy of Sciences, 1961; vice-president, National Commission for the Study of Nursing and Nursing Education, 1967-69; chairman, Committee on the Social Organization of Science, Social Science Research Council, 1968-70. Trustee, Center for Advanced Study in the Behavioral Sciences, 1953-75, Institute for Scientific Information, 1968—, and American Nurses Foundation, 1969-71; Guggenheim Foundation Educational Advisory Board, member, 1963-79, chairman, 1971-79. Member, Committee on Human Rights, National Academy of Sciences, 1977—, advisory committee, program of science books, Alfred P. Sloan Foundation, 1978—, and commission on monographs of the 1980 U.S. Census, Social Science Research Council, 1980-89.

MEMBER: International Sociological Society (council, 1971-73), American Sociological Association (president, 1957), Sociological Research Association (president, 1968), Society for Social Studies of Science (president, 1975-76), Authors Guild (council member, 1974-78), Authors League of America, History of Science Society, Tocqueville Society.

AWARDS, HONORS: Prize for distinguished scholarship in the humanities, American Council of Learned Societies, 1962; Guggenheim fellow, 1962; distinguished alumni award, Temple University, 1964; fellow, Center for Advanced Study in the Behavioral Sciences, 1973; fellow, Institute of Medicine, National Academy of Sciences, 1973; merit award, Eastern Sociological Society, 1978; Talcott Parsons Prize for Social Science, American Academy of Arts and Sciences, 1979; Common Wealth Award for distinguished service, 1979, and Career of Distinguished Scholarship Award, 1980, both from American Sociological Association; Memorial Sloan-Kettering Cancer Center Award, 1981; J. D. Bernal Award for outstanding scholarly contributions, Society for Social Studies of Science, 1982; MacArthur Prize Fellow, 1983-88; first recipient of Who's Who in America Achievement Award in Social Science, 1984. Numerous honorary degrees from universities in the United States and overseas. Member of honorary societies, including National Academy of Sciences, American Philosophical Society, American Academy of Arts and Sciences, Royal Swedish Academy of Sciences, National Academy of Education, and World Academy of Art and Science.

WRITINGS:

(Contributor) *Osiris: Studies on the History and Philosophy of Science, and on the History of Learning and Culture* (contains monograph "Science, Technology and Society in Seventeenth-Century England"), Bruges (Belgium), 1938, monograph published with new introduction as *Science, Technology and Society in Seventeenth-Century England,* Harper, 1970, reprinted, Howard Fertig, 1988.

(With Marjorie Fiske and Alberta Curtis) *Mass Persuasion: The Social Psychology of a War Bond Drive,* Harper, 1946, reprinted, Greenwood Press, 1971.

Social Theory and Social Structure: Toward the Codification of Theory and Research, Free Press, 1949, 3rd edition, 1968.

(With Patricia S. West and Marie Jahoda) *Patterns of Social Life: Explorations in the Sociology of Housing,* Columbia University Bureau of Applied Social Research, 1951.

(With Fiske and Patricia M. Kendall) *The Focused Interview: A Manual of Problems and Procedures,* Free Press, 1956, new edition, 1990.

(With R. P. McKeon and Walter Gellhorn) *The Freedom to Read: Perspective and Program,* Bowker, 1957.

On the Shoulders of Giants: A Shandean Postscript, Free Press, 1965, vicennial edition, Harcourt, 1985.

On Theoretical Sociology: Five Essays, Old and New, Free Press, 1967.

Social Theory and Functional Analysis, translation by Togo Mori, Yoshio Mori, and Minoru Kanazawa, Aoki Shoten (Tokyo), 1969.

The Sociology of Science: Theoretical and Empirical Investigations, University of Chicago Press, 1973.

Sociological Ambivalence and Other Essays, Free Press, 1976.

The Sociology of Science: An Episodic Memoir, University of Southern Illinois Press, 1979.

Social Research and the Practicing Professions, edited by Aaron Rosenblatt and Thomas F. Gieryn, Abt Books, 1982.

EDITOR

(With Paul F. Lazarsfeld) *Continuities in Social Research: Studies in the Scope and Methods of "The American Soldier,"* Free Press, 1950, reprinted, Arno, 1974.

(With A. P. Gray, Barbara Hockey, and Hanan Selvin) *Reader in Bureaucracy,* Free Press, 1952.

(With George G. Reader and Kendall) *The Student-Physician: Introductory Studies in the Sociology of Medical Education,* Harvard University Press, 1957.

(With Leonard Broom and L. S. Cottrell, Jr.) *Sociology Today: Problems and Prospects,* Basic Books, 1959.

(With Robert A. Nisbet) *Contemporary Social Problems: An Introduction to the Sociology of Deviant Behavior and Social Disorganization,* Harcourt, 1961, 4th edition, 1976.

(With Jerry Gaston) *The Sociology of Science in Europe,* University of Southern Illinois Press, 1977.

(With Yehuda Elkana, Joshua Lederberg, Arnold Thackray, and Harriet Zuckerman) *Toward a Metric of Science: The Advent of Science Indicators,* Wiley, 1978.

(With James S. Coleman and Peter H. Rossi) *Qualitative and Quantitative Social Research: Papers in Honor of Paul F. Lazarsfeld,* Free Press, 1979.

(With Thaddeus J. Trenn) Ludwik Fleck, *Genesis and Development of a Scientific Fact* (translated from the German), University of Chicago Press, 1979.

(With Matilda W. Riley) *Sociological Traditions from Generation to Generation: Glimpses of the American Experience,* Ablex, 1980.

(With Peter M. Blau) *Continuities in Structural Inquiry,* Sage Publications, 1981.

OTHER

(Compiler with Aron Halberstam) *Perspectives in Social Inquiry: Classics, Staples, and Precursors in Sociology,* 40 volumes, Arno, 1974.

(Compiler with Elkana, Thackray, and Zuckerman) *History, Philosophy, and Sociology of Science,* 60 volumes, Arno, 1975.

(Compiler with Zuckerman) *Dissertations on Sociology,* 61 volumes, Arno, 1980.

Contributor of many articles in journals and symposia. Member of editorial advisory boards to *International Encyclopedia of the Social Sciences, Webster's International Unabridged Dictionary, International Encyclopedia Britannica, World Book Encyclopedia,* and *Dictionary of Scientific Biography.* Consulting editor to Harcourt, Brace & Jovanovich.

Merton's work has been translated into many foreign languages, including French, Italian, Japanese, Spanish, Hebrew, German, Russian, Portuguese, Czechoslovakian, Hungarian, Polish, Rumanian, and Chinese.

SIDELIGHTS: A preeminent American sociologist, Robert K. Merton is an articulate and well-known defender of sociology as a genuine science. In *The Sociology of Science: Theoretical and Empirical Investigations,* Merton "shows that sociology can only do what science can do, namely reduce a subject to its logical components, where emotions disappear, and the problem becomes amenable to analysis in the light of empirical evidence," observes Joseph Ben-David for the *New York Times Book Review.* "This requires the renouncement of immediate practical solutions and the willingness to follow unexpected leads. But it is the only way in which social science can ever become really useful. There are very few other books in sociology that teach this lesson as well as the present one. And none that teaches it with such meticulous scholarship, or in so elegant a style." Alden Whitman, in a *New York Times* review of *Sociological Ambivalence and Other Essays,* finds Merton "has a knack for straightforward English and a fondness for the witty, illuminating phrase, as this collection of his occasional essays over almost 40 years attests. He has a tart mind, too. . . . Dr. Merton's book will profit almost anyone who troubles to peruse it with a modicum of interest and intelligence." An earlier essay collection by Merton, *Social Theory and Social Structure: Toward a Codification of Theory and Research,* is considered by many to be a classic text. In a review of its second edition published in 1958, K. D. Naegele in *American Sociological Review* deemed it a "magnificent and demanding book, written and rewritten by a man who was and is among the very best of teachers."

Merton is also noted for his intellectual versatility. His 1965 book, *On the Shoulders of Giants: A Shandean Postscript* was praised by Sean French in the *Times Literary Supplement* as "the delightful apotheosis of donmanship: Merton parodies scholarliness while being faultlessly scholarly; he scourges pedantry while brandishing his own abstruse learning on every page." Described by John Gross in the *New York Times* as "a masterpiece of wit and erudition," the book began in response to a colleague's inquiry into the origins and usages of the phrase "on the shoulders of giants." French comments: "In his other work, Merton has been much concerned with the sociology of science, dealing with such topics as plagiarism, priority of scientific discovery, collaboration and rivalry between contemporaries, the relation of scientists to their past. The aphorism stands at the heart of these concerns, a multi-edged weapon that can be used for a variety of purposes, and under Merton's learned gaze it becomes a rich and revealing tool for uncovering a whole range of attitudes."

BIOGRAPHICAL/CRITICAL SOURCES:

BOOKS

Clark, Jon, editor, *Robert K. Merton: Consensus and Controversy,* Falmer Press, 1990.
Cohen, I. Bernard, editor, *Puritanism and the Rise of Modern Science: The Merton Thesis,* Rutgers University Press, 1990.
Coser, Lewis A., editor, *The Ideas of Social Structure: Papers in Honor of Robert K. Merton,* Harcourt, 1975.
Crothers, Charles, *Robert K. Merton: A Key Sociologist,* Tavistock Publications, 1987.
Garcia, Jesus L., *Merton: La estructura precaria,* Editorial Edicol (Mexico City), 1979.
Gieryn, Thomas F., editor, *Science and Social Structure: A Festschrift for Robert K. Merton,* New York Academy of Sciences, 1980.
Mongardini, Carlo and Simonetta Tabboni, editors, *L'Opera di Robert K. Merton e la sociologia contemporanea,* Acig (Genoa, Italy), 1989.
Patel, Pravin, *Sociology of Robert K. Merton,* Gujarat University Press (Ahmedabad, India), 1976.
Sztompka, Piotr, *Robert K. Merton: An Intellectual Profile,* St. Martin's, 1986.

PERIODICALS

American Sociology Review, December, 1957.
Contemporary Sociology, Volume 6, 1977.
Current Contents, July 11, 1977.
New Yorker, January 28, 1961.
New York Review of Books, May 6, 1971.
New York Times, March 4, 1977, April 25, 1985.

New York Times Book Review, November 11, 1973.
Science in Context, 1989.
Teaching Sociology, July, 1984.
Times Literary Supplement, April 16, 1971, April 26, 1974, July 25, 1986.

*   *   *

MESSENGER, Charles (Rynd Milles) 1942-

PERSONAL: Born May 11, 1942, in Fulmer, England; married Anne Falconer; children: Emma, Rawdon, Harriet. *Education:* Oxford University, B.A. (with honors), 1965, M.A., 1973.

ADDRESSES: Office—c/o Williams & Glyns Bank Ltd., Holts Farnborough Branch, 31-37 Victoria Rd., Farnborough, Hampshire, England.

CAREER: British Army, Royal Tank Regiment, career officer, 1959-80, retired as major; military historian and defence analyst, 1980—. Served as lecturer in the Near East, Germany, and the United States, and held technical and non-technical positions with Ministry of Defence. Historical and defence lecturer and editorial consultant.

MEMBER: Royal United Service Institute (research fellow, 1982-83), Army and Navy Club.

WRITINGS:

Trench Fighting, 1914-1918, Ballantine, 1972.
The Art of Blitzkrieg, Ian Allan, 1976.
THe Blitzkrieg Story, Scribner, 1976.
Blitzkrieg, Gustav Lubbe, 1978.
The Observer's Book of Tanks, Warne, 1981.
Terriers in the Trenches: The Post Office Rifles at War, 1914-1918, Picton Publishing, 1982.
The First One Thousand Raid, Ian Allan, 1982.
The Unknown Alamein, Ian Allan, 1982.
The Tunisian Campaign, 1942-1943, Hippocrene, 1982.
The New Observer's Book of Tanks, Warne, 1984.
"Bomber": Sir Arthur Harris and the Strategic Bombing Offensive, 1939-1945, Arms & Armour, 1984.
Combat Aircraft (juvenile), F. Watts, 1984.
Helicopters (juvenile), F. Watts, 1985.
Anti-Armour Warfare, Ian Allan, 1986.
The History of the British Army, Presidio Press, 1986.
The Second World War (juvenile), F. Watts, 1987.
Pictorial History of World War II, Smith Publications, 1987.
(Editor) *The Middle East* (juvenile), F. Watts, 1988.
The Chronological Atlas of World War II, Macmillan, 1989.

Also author of *Armies of World War III,* Bison/Hamlyn, *Twentieth-Century Weapons: Combat Aircraft,* Aladdin Books, and *The Steadfast Gurkha: A History of the Sixth Queen Elizabeth's Own Gurkha Rifles, 1948-1982,* Leo Cooper/Secker & Warburg. Also contributor to *Purnell's History of the First World War.* United Kingdom/North Atlantic Treaty Organization correspondent for *Defence Update International.* Contributor of articles and book reviews to various historical and military journals. Co-editor, *Current Military List.*

WORK IN PROGRESS: The Anti-Armour Battle, for Ian Allan; *A Commando Anthology,* for Kimber; *The Military Campaign in North Ireland,* for Ian Allan; *The British Army in the Future,* for Ian Allan; *The Dark Tunnel: British High Technology Military Aircraft Procurement from 1957,* for Royal United Services Institute/Buchan & Enright.

SIDELIGHTS: Charles Messenger told *CA:* "Since my last appearance in *Contemporary Authors,* my life has undergone a dramatic change, having decided to forsake the sword for the pen. My original ambition to combine fact with fiction writing has not as yet been realised and is unlikely to be for some time, as I find that fact and the analysis of it takes up all my waking hours. I still remain a twentieth-century military historian, but, as you can see from my titles, I have diversified. Indeed, I enjoy tackling unfamiliar subjects and find the research into these exhilarating. Key to this is extensive reading of primary sources and avoiding hindsight, which has made me realise the extent to which myths are regurgitated time and again.

"I am very conscious of the increasing interest in defence matters in the past few years, but believe that ignorance born of understandable emotion can only too easily distort the real issues. I believe that my knowledge of history and my own military service make me well-equipped to tackle the defence issues of today. Regrettably, aggression is part of the human being's make-up. Only by understanding this and using the lessons of the past can we make the world of tomorrow a safer place in which to live."

BIOGRAPHICAL/CRITICAL SOURCES:

PERIODICALS

Times Literary Supplement, October 12, 1984.

*   *   *

MICHAELS, Molly
   See UNTERMEYER, Louis

*   *   *

MICHEL, Georges 1926-

PERSONAL: Born March 4, 1926, in Paris, France; married March 5, 1951.

CAREER: Watch-repairer; writer.

MEMBER: Society of Authors.

AWARDS, HONORS: Ibsen Prize, 1967.

WRITINGS:

Les Jouets (play; first produced in Paris at Theatre Gramont, March, 1964), Gallimard, 1963.
Les Timides aventures d'un laveur de carreaux (novel), Grasset, 1966, translation by Helen Weaver published as *The Timid Adventures of a Window Washer,* Doubleday, 1969.
La Promenade du dimanche (play; first produced in Paris at Studio des Champs-Elysees, February, 1966), preface by Jean-Paul Sartre, Gallimard, 1967, translation by Jean Benedetti published as *The Sunday Walk,* Methuen Playscripts, 1968.
L'Agression (play; first produced in Paris at Theatre National Populaire, March, 1967), Gallimard, 1968.
Les Bravos (novel), Gallimard, 1968.
Arbaletes et vieilles rapieres (play), Gallimard, 1969.
Un petit nid d'amour (play; first produced on radio by France-Culture, April, 1969), Gallimard, 1970.
Les Bancs (novel), Grasset, 1970.
"La Ruee vers l'ordre" (play), first produced in Geneva, 1971.
"J'ai vingt ans et je veux mourir" (play), first produced on radio, 1971.
"Mange pour faire plaisir a ta mere" (play), first produced on radio, 1971.
Le Lit-cage (play; first produced in Paris at Theatre de la Cour des Miracles, April 10, 1975), Galilee, 1975.
"Tiens le coup jusqu'a la retraite" (play), first produced in Paris, 1976.

Mes annees Sartre: Histoire d'une amitie, Hachette, 1981.

Also author of television play "Le Bar," play "L'Escalier C," and novel *Le Grouillement.*

SIDELIGHTS: "I try in my novels, as well as in my plays, to write about the obscure, the classless, and to bring to light the inconsistencies and alienation of our time, through comedy and provocation," Georges Michel told *CA.* The author's books and plays have been widely reviewed.

BIOGRAPHICAL/CRITICAL SOURCES:

PERIODICALS

Books Abroad, spring, 1968, winter, 1970, spring, 1971.
London Review of Books, May 20, 1982.
Nation, July 28, 1969.
New York Times Book Review, August 3, 1969.
Prompt, Number 12, 1968.
Saturday Review, July 5, 1969.
Times Literary Supplement, September 19, 1968.
Washington Post, July 18, 1969.*

*   *   *

MIDDLEBROOK, (Norman) Martin 1932-

PERSONAL: Born January 24, 1932, in Boston, England; married Mary Sylvester, September 7, 1954; children: Jane, Anne, Catherine. *Education:* Attended schools in England "and the University of Life." *Politics:* Independent. *Religion:* Agnostic.

ADDRESSES: Home and office—48 Linden Way, Boston, Lincolnshire, England. *Agent*—A. P. Watt & Son, 20 John St., London, England.

CAREER: Poultry farmer in Boston, England, 1956-81. *Military service:* British Army, 1950-52.

WRITINGS:

The First Day on the Somme, Allen Lane, 1971, Norton, 1972.
The Nuremberg Raid, Allen Lane, 1973, Morrow, 1974.
Convoy, Allen Lane, 1976, Morrow, 1977.
(Contributor) Edward Marshal and Michael Carver, editors, *The War Lords,* Weidenfeld & Nicolson, 1976.
(With Patrick Mahoney) *Battleship,* Allen Lane, 1977, Scribner, 1979.
The Kaiser's Battle, Allen Lane, 1978.
(Editor) *Private Bruckshaw's Diaries,* Scolar Press, 1979.
The Battle of Hamburg, Allen Lane, 1980.
The Peenemunde Raid, Bobbs-Merrill, 1982.
The Schweinfurt-Regensburg Mission, Scribner, 1983.
Operation Corporate, Viking, 1984.
De Bamber Command War Diaries, Viking, 1985.
The Berlin Raids, Viking, 1985.
The Fight for the "Malvinas," Viking, 1989.

WORK IN PROGRESS: The Somme Battlefields.

SIDELIGHTS: Martin Middlebrook told *CA,* "In my opinion there is no such thing as a 'last word' in history, and anyone who thinks he/she has written a 'definitive' book is a fool."

AVOCATIONAL INTERESTS: Golf, bowls ("a la Francis Drake"), travel, giving guided tours of the Western Front battlefields.

BIOGRAPHICAL/CRITICAL SOURCES:

PERIODICALS

Times Literary Supplement, December 26, 1980.

Washington Post Book World, May 18, 1986.

* * *

MIKHAIL, E(dward) H(alim) 1926-

PERSONAL: Born June 29, 1926, in Cairo, Egypt; emigrated to Canada in 1966; son of Halim and Mathilda (Phares) Mikhail; married Isabelle Bichai, July 22, 1954; children: May, Carmen. *Education:* Cairo University, B.A. (with honors), 1947, B.Ed., 1949; Trinity College, Dublin, D.E.S., 1959; University of Sheffield, Ph.D., 1966. *Politics:* Conservative. *Religion:* Christian.

ADDRESSES: Home—6 Coachwood Pt. W., Lethbridge, Alberta, Canada. *Office*—Department of English, University of Lethbridge, Lethbridge, Alberta, Canada.

CAREER: Cairo University, Cairo, Egypt, 1949-66, began as lecturer, became assistant professor; University of Lethbridge, Lethbridge, Alberta, associate professor, 1966-72, professor of English, 1972—.

MEMBER: International Association for the Study of Anglo-Irish Literature, Canadian Association for Irish Studies, Modern Language Association of America, Association of Canadian University Teachers of English, British Drama League, American Committee for Irish Studies.

AWARDS, HONORS: Nine Canada Council and SSHRCC research grants, 1967-85.

WRITINGS:

Social and Cultural Setting of the 1890s, Garnstone Press (London), 1969.
John Galsworthy the Dramatist: A Bibliography of Criticism, Whitston Publishing, 1971.
Sean O'Casey: A Bibliography of Criticism, University of Washington Press, 1972.
Comedy and Tragedy: A Bibliography of Critical Studies, Whitston Publishing, 1972.
A Bibliography of Modern Irish Drama, 1899-1970, University of Washington Press, 1972.
Dissertations on Anglo-Irish Drama, Rowman & Littlefield, 1973.
(Editor with John O'Riordan) *The Sting and the Twinkle: Conversations with Sean O'Casey,* Barnes & Noble, 1974.
J. M. Synge: A Bibliography of Criticism, Rowman & Littlefield, 1975.
Contemporary British Drama, 1950-1976: An Annotated Critical Bibliography, Rowman & Littlefield, 1976.
J. M. Synge: Interviews and Recollections, two volumes, Barnes & Noble, 1977.
English Drama, 1900-1950: A Guide to Information Services, Gale, 1977.
Lady Gregory: Interviews and Recollections, Rowman & Littlefield, 1977.
Oscar Wilde: An Annotated Bibliography of Criticism, Rowman & Littlefield, 1978.
A Research Guide to Modern Irish Dramatists, Whitston Publishing, 1979.
Oscar Wilde: Interviews and Recollections, two volumes, Barnes & Noble, 1979.
The Art of Brendan Behan, Barnes & Noble, 1979.
Brendan Behan: An Annotated Bibliography of Criticism, Barnes & Noble, 1979.
An Annotated Bibliography of Modern Anglo-Irish Drama, Whitston Publishing, 1981.
Lady Gregory: An Annotated Bibliography of Criticism, Whitston Publishing, 1982.

Brendan Behan: Interviews and Recollections, two volumes, Barnes & Noble, 1982.
Sean O'Casey and His Critics, Scarecrow, 1985.
The Abbey Theatre: Interviews and Recollections, Barnes & Noble, 1988.
Sheridan: Interviews and Recollections, St. Martin's, 1989.

Also author of *James Joyce: Interviews and Recollections* and *The Letters of Brendan Behan.*

WORK IN PROGRESS: Goldsmith: Interviews and Recollections; A Dictionary of English Adjectives.

BIOGRAPHICAL/CRITICAL SOURCES:

PERIODICALS

Times Literary Supplement, April 18, 1980, April 22, 1983.

* * *

MILLER, Marc S(cott) 1947-

PERSONAL: Born December 27, 1947, in Mount Vernon, N.Y.; son of Ben and Ruth (Ash) Miller. *Education:* Attended Lehigh University, 1965-66; Massachusetts Institute of Technology, B.S., 1969; Boston University, M.A., 1973, Ph.D., 1978. *Politics:* Anarchist.

ADDRESSES: Home—15 Bishop St., Jamaica Plain, Mass. 02130. *Office*—*Technology Review,* Massachusetts Institute of Technology, Cambridge, Mass. 02139.

CAREER: Citywide Coordinating Committee, Boston, Mass., desegregation monitor, 1975-76; Institute for Southern Studies, Durham, N.C., research director, 1977-85; *Technology Review,* Cambridge, Mass., senior editor, 1986—. Assistant director of oral history program, Massachusetts Institute of Technology, 1975-77, and Boston University and Boston Center for Adult Education, both 1977. Member of Massachusetts Committee on Occupational Safety and Health.

MEMBER: Organization of American Historians, American Civil Liberties Union.

WRITINGS:

(Editor and contributor) *Working Lives: The "Southern Exposure" History of Labor in the South,* Pantheon, 1981.
(Editor with Pat Bryant) *Militarism and Human Needs,* Institute for Southern Studies, 1982.
(Editor) *Elections: A User's Manual,* Institute for Southern Studies, 1984.
(Editor with Peter Wood and Bob Hall) *Liberating Our Past: Four Hundred Years of Southern History,* Institute for Southern Studies, 1984.
The Irony of Victory: World War II and Lowell, Massachusetts, University of Illinois Press, 1988.

Contributor of articles and reviews to magazines and newspapers, including *Radical Teacher, Boston after Dark,* and *New England Quarterly.* Editor, *Southern Exposure,* 1977-85, and *Dollars and Sense,* 1986—.

SIDELIGHTS: Marc S. Miller once told *CA:* "Writing is no excuse for doing; thinking is no excuse for acting; sidelights do not make a life."*

* * *

MITCHELL, Don(ald Earl) 1947-

PERSONAL: Born October 15, 1947, in Chicago, Ill.; son of Wayne Treleven (an electrical engineer) and Elizabeth (Bowker)

Mitchell; married Cheryl Warfield, November 29, 1969; children: Ethan, Anais. *Education:* Swarthmore College, A.B., 1969. *Politics:* Democrat. *Religion:* Protestant.

ADDRESSES: Home—R.D. 2, Vergennes, Vt. 05491. *Agent*—Blanche C. Gregory, Inc., 2 Tudor City Pl., New York, N.Y. 10017.

CAREER: American Baptist Board of Education and Publication, Valley Forge, Pa., staff member, 1971; The New School, Wayne, Pa., high school teacher, 1972; writer, and sheep breeder at Treleven Farm in Vermont, 1973—; Middlebury College, Middlebury, Vt., lecturer in creative writing, 1986—.

WRITINGS:

Thumb Tripping (also see below), Little, Brown, 1970.
Four-Stroke, Little, Brown, 1973.
The Souls of Lambs, Houghton, 1979.
Moving UpCountry, Yankee, Inc., 1984.
Living UpCountry, Yankee, Inc., 1986.
(Contributor) *The Bread Loaf Anthology of Contemporary American Essays,* University Press of New England, 1989.

Also author of "Thumb Tripping," Avco Embassy Pictures, 1969-70. Columnist, *Boston Magazine,* 1979—. Contributor to *Harper's, Atlantic, Esquire, Shenandoah, Viva, Country Journal,* and *Yankee.*

WORK IN PROGRESS: Second Nature, a novel; *Growing Up-Country,* essays.

SIDELIGHTS: Don Mitchell told *CA:* "For many years I used to say: 'Well, I've had my ups and downs as a writer, and at times I've supported my writing by unlikely occupations—sheep farming, carpentry—but at least I've never had to teach creative writing for a living.' As though that were the lowest one could go, a retreat from serious engagement with the 'real' world. My time came around, though, and once I got into the classroom, it was love at first sight. Writing *can* be taught in the college writing-workshop situation; it just takes one heck of a lot of time and dedication on everybody's part.

"I continue trying to live a life that tests the proposition that modern artists need a strong measure of bohemianism, ruthlessness, self-possession and mania—not to say schizophrenia—in order to succeed at their creative labors. I wouldn't *mind* a bit more success, I suppose, but not at the cost of these essentially boring, old-fashioned pleasures: one wife of twenty years, two growing kids, a house I built myself on a farm where I perform certain menial chores day in, day out, and follow such seasonal routines as birthing spring lambs, summer hay-making, and autumn wood-cutting. As writers go, I think I'm far more rooted than most.

"I think I'm entering a more productive phase of my career as a writer, too. I'm finding I can do 15-20 magazine pieces per year—essays, mostly, often having to do with the sociology of rural life—as well as keep a major project, e.g. a novel, cooking away on the back burner and periodically getting hot. I feel past the age of false-starts on novels, too; I've learned how to bring to fruition the projects I undertake. My hunch is that some long apprenticeship is over. It would be especially nice now, therefore, to get some of my more recent fiction published. But that, as they say, is a whole 'nother story."

BIOGRAPHICAL/CRITICAL SOURCES:

PERIODICALS

Best Sellers, August 15, 1970.

New York Times Book Review, August 2, 1970, October 26, 1986.
Wall Street Journal, April 23, 1979.

*   *   *

MNACKO, Ladislav   1919-

PERSONAL: Surname is pronounced M-natch-ko; born January 29, 1919, in Val Klobouky, Czechoslovakia; married. *Politics:* Former member of Communist Party in Czechoslovakia (expelled in 1967).

ADDRESSES: Home—c/o Molden Verlag, A-1190, Vienna, Soudgasse 33, Austria.

CAREER: Czech journalist and author, now living in exile; former editor-in-chief of *Kwlturny Zivot* at different times; was stripped of his Czech citizenship when he denounced anti-Semitism in his country and made an unauthorized trip to Israel in 1967; returned to Czechoslovakia in 1968 but left again after the invasion by Russian military forces later that same year.

AWARDS, HONORS: Klement Gottwald Prize (highest state award for literature in Czechoslovakia); named the outstanding writer in Czechoslovakia.

WRITINGS:

IN SLOVAK, WITH SOME BOOKS TRANSLATED FOR PUBLICATION IN CZECH THE SAME YEAR

Albanska reportaz, [Bratislava], 1950.
Vpad Rok na stavbe HUKO, [Bratislava], 1952.
Co nebolo v novinach (on the Communist coup d'etat), Slovenske Vydavatel'stvo Politickej Literatury, 1958.
Daleko je do Whampoa (on China travels), Slovenske Vydavatel'stvo Politickej Literatury, 1958.
U 2 (on the U-2 incident), Statni Nakladatelstvi Politickej Literatury, 1960.
Smrt' sa vola Engelchen (published in Czech as *Smrt si rika Engelchen),* Slovenske Vydavatel'stvo Politickej Literatury, c. 1960, translation by George Theiner published as *Death Is Called Engelchen,* Artia (Prague), 1961.
Vystavba Slovenska, 1945-1960, edited by Kamil Gross, Vydavatel'stvo ROH, 1960.
Ja, Adolf Eichmann, Slovenske Vydavatel'stvo Politickej Literatury, 1961.
Marxova ulica (short stories; title means "Marx's Street"), Mlade Leta, 1962.
Oneskorene reportaze (published in Czech as *Opozdene reportare),* Vydavatel'stvo Politickej Literatury, 1963.
Kde koncia prasne cesty (published in Czech as *Kde donci prasne cesty),* Osveta, 1963.
Rozpraval ten kapitan (on Danube travels; published in Czech as *Kapitan mi vypravel),* Vydavatel'stvo Politickej Literatury, 1965.
Dlha, biela prerusovana ciara (on German travels; published in Czech as *Dlouha bila prerusovana cara),* Slovensky Spisovatel, 1965.
Nocny rozhovor (published in Czech as *Nocni rozhovor),* Vydavatel'stvo Politickej Literatury, 1966.
Jizvy, zustaly, Nase Vojsko, 1966.

IN GERMAN

Wie die Macht schmeckt (novel; written in Slovak as "Jak chutna moc" but only excerpts were published in Czechoslovakia in two issues of the monthly *Plamen,* 1966, prior to an expurgated edition, 1968; translated into German for first complete edition), Molden (Vienna), 1967, English translation from the original Slovak by Paul Stevenson published as *A Taste of Power,* Praeger, 1967.

Die siebente Nacht (autobiographical; written in Slovak and translated into German for initial publication), Molden, 1968, English translation from the original Slovak manuscript published as *The Seventh Night,* Dutton, 1969.

Die Aggressoren (on Israel; written in Slovak and translated into German for initial publication), Molden, 1968.

Der Vorgang (novel), Kindler Verlag, 1970.

Genosse Muenchhausen (satirical novel), Kindler Verlag, 1973.

Hanoi, Holsten Verlag, 1973.

Einer wird ueberleben, List Verlag, 1974.

Die Festrede, List Verlag, 1976.

Jenseits von Intourist: satir. Reportagen, Lange-Mueller, 1979.

OTHER

Also author of *Partyzani,* 1945, *Piesne ingotov,* 1950, *Mosty na vychod,* 1952, *Bubny a cinely,* 1954, *Ziva voda,* 1954, *Vody Orava,* 1955, *Aj taky clovek,* 1960, and *Sudruh Muenchhausen,* 1972; also author of filmscript of *Smrt' sa vola Engelchen (Death Is Called Engelchen).*

SIDELIGHTS: Some of Ladislav Mnacko's books have been translated into as many as twenty-two languages.

MEDIA ADAPTATIONS: Smrt' sa vola Engelchen was made into a successful film; *Der Vorgang* was filmed for German television in 1971; an adaptation of *Einer wird ueberleben* was also filmed for German television.

BIOGRAPHICAL/CRITICAL SOURCES:

PERIODICALS

Books and Bookmen, July, 1967.

L'Express (Paris), September 8-14, 1969.

National Review, October 17, 1967.

Newsweek, August 28, 1967.

New York Review of Books, October 12, 1967, June 19, 1969.

New York Times, August 12, 1967, August 17, 1967, April 7, 1968.

New York Times Book Review, May 28, 1967, September 10, 1967, October 13, 1968.

Time, March 17, 1967.

Times Literary Supplement, June 29, 1967, June 5, 1969.*

*　　*　　*

MOORE, James T. III　1939-
(Jimmy Moore)

PERSONAL: Born October 1, 1939; son of James T., Jr., and Olean Moore; married Ava Jean Nelson; children: Pamela, Steve, Kimberly Lynn.

ADDRESSES: Home—P.O. Box 974, Lawrenceburg, Tenn. 38464.

CAREER: Photographer, writer, and actor. Director of photography, Union Carbide Corp., 1960-67; official American Broadcasting Co. photographer, *ABC/TV GUIDE,* 1968-70; vice president, New World Photography, 1969-72; Aesthetics, Inc., Nashville, Tenn., co-owner and vice president, 1972-75; director, Lawrenceburg-Lawrence County Emergency Management Agency, 1975-78; Atlantic-Creek Organization, Spring Hill, Tenn., president, 1978-80; director of photography, Tennessee Emergency Management Agency, 1984-87. Photography displayed at numerous exhibitions. Photographer of LP album covers for major recording companies, including RCA, Capitol, Electra-Asylum, and Columbia. Photographer of character portraits, including Everett Dirkson, Thomas De La Cruz, Winfield Dunn, Chet Atkins, Louis Armstrong, and Dame Vera Lynn. Writer and producer of and actor in television series, "Hee Haw." Writer and producer of and actor in television commercials. Writer, director, and cameraman of videos. Producer of music video "I Like Bread and Butter," performed by The Newbeats, and "Luckenback, Texas," performed by Waylon Jennings. Civil Defense Rescue, Lawrenceburg, Tenn., captain, 1954, deputy director, 1957.

MEMBER: National Academy of Recording Arts and Sciences, American Federation of Television and Radio Artists, Gospel Music Association.

AWARDS, HONORS: Dove Award for best album cover, Gospel Music Association, 1969, for "What's Happening"; award for best album cover, *Billboard,* 1970, for "Back Where It's At"; awards for best book cover and best book design, Nashville Art Directors, 1970, for *A Value of Time.*

WRITINGS:

A Value of Time (poetry), Impact Books, 1971.

(Photographer) Jesse Burt and Robert Ferguson, *Indians of the Southeast: Then and Now,* Abingdon Press, 1973.

(Photographer) Jake Butcher and Mil Leonard, *A Man from Butcher Holler,* Goodrum, 1978.

"Lawrenceburg: A Nice Place to Be" (screenplay), broadcast on Public Broadcasting Systems (PBS-TV), 1981.

Also author of screenplays, "Knoxville Police" (documentary), produced in 1973, "Daybreaker," 1975, option held by Twentieth-Century Fox, and "You Are My Sunshine." Author of album liner notes for Willie Nelson's "The Willie Way," RCA, 1972, and Chet Atkins's "Alone," RCA, 1973.

*　　*　　*

MOORE, Jimmy
See MOORE, James T. III

*　　*　　*

MOREY, Walt(er Nelson)　1907-

PERSONAL: Born February 3, 1907, in Hoquiam, Wash.; son of Arthur Nelson (a carpenter) and Gertrude (Stover) Morey; married Rosalind Ogden (a teacher and secretary), July 8, 1934 (died February, 1977); married Peggy Kilburn, June 26, 1978. *Education:* Attended schools in Oregon, Washington, Montana, and Canada; attended Benkhe Walker Business College.

ADDRESSES: Home—10830 Southwest Morey Lane, Wilsonville, Ore. 97070. *Agent*—Lenniger Literary Agency, 437 Fifth Ave., New York, N.Y. 10016.

CAREER: Writer, 1928—. Millworker, construction worker, professional boxer, and theatre manager in Oregon and Washington during the 1930s and 1940s; filbert farmer, 1938—; Kaiser Shipyards, Vancouver, Wash., shipbuilder and supervisor of burners, 1940-45; deep sea diver and fish trap inspector in Alaska, 1951. Director of Oregon Nut Growers Cooperative, 1960-61.

MEMBER: Oregon Freelance Club.

AWARDS, HONORS: Dutton Junior Animal Book Award, 1965, Sequoyah Children's Book Award, 1967, Yippee Award,

1970, and American Library Association (ALA) Notable Book selection, all for *Gentle Ben;* Dutton Junior Animal Book Award, 1968, Northwest Bookseller's Award, 1968, Tonawanda (N.Y.) School Children's Award, 1968, Dorothy Canfield Fisher Memorial Children's Book Award, 1970, and William Allen White Children's Book Award, 1971, all for *Kavik, the Wolf Dog;* Children's Books of the Year citations, Children's Book Committee for the Child Study Association, 1968, for *Kavik, the Wolf Dog,* 1973, for *Canyon Winter* and *Runaway Stallion,* 1974, for *Run Far, Run Fast,* and 1976, for *Year of the Black Pony;* Evelyn Sibley Lampman Award, Oregon Library Association, 1982, for significant contribution to children's literature.

WRITINGS:

JUVENILES

Gentle Ben, Dutton, 1965.
Home Is the North, Dutton, 1967.
Kavik, the Wolf Dog, Dutton, 1968.
Angry Waters, Dutton, 1969.
Gloomy Gus, Dutton, 1970, reprinted, Blue Heron Publishing, 1989.
Deep Trouble, Dutton, 1971.
Scrub Dog of Alaska, Dutton, 1971, reprinted, Blue Heron Publishing, 1989.
Canyon Winter, Dutton, 1972.
Runaway Stallion, Dutton, 1973, reprinted, Blue Heron Publishing, 1989.
Run Far, Run Fast, Dutton, 1974.
Year of the Black Pony, Dutton, 1976.
Sandy and the Rock Star, Dutton, 1979.
The Lemon Meringue Dog, Dutton, 1980.

OTHER

(With Virgil Burford) *North to Danger* (adult), John Day, 1954, revised and enlarged edition, Caxton, 1969.
Operation Blue Bear: A True Story (adult nonfiction), Dutton, 1975.

Also author of novel, *No Cheers, No Glory, 1945,* published in *Blue Book* magazine. Contributor to men's magazines, 1930-1950, including *Saga, True, Argosy,* and others.

WORK IN PROGRESS: Death Wall, a novel about three men who flee to Alaska to avoid criminal prosecution; *The Further Adventures of Gentle Ben;* books on pre-statehood Alaska, the fishing industry, and associated activities; a juvenile book on the Snake River area of Oregon and Utah.

SIDELIGHTS: For over twenty years, Walt Morey had been writing solely for an adult audience; he was a regular contributor of stories to pulp magazines and had published *North to Danger,* a chronicle of the adventures of his longtime friend and companion Virgil Burford, a deep-sea diver, bear hunter, prospector, and cohort of fish pirates in Alaska. After the market for pulp fiction fell in the 1950s, however, Morey stopped writing entirely to concentrate on his filbert nut farm—until his wife, who had read some of his stories to her middle school students, suggested he try his hand at young adult novels. "She hectored me for the better part of ten years," the author told Marguerite Feitlowitz in a *Something about the Author* interview, "and to get her off my back—to prove that I couldn't do it—I began the story that became *Gentle Ben.*" The tale of an Alaskan bear and the young boy who gains his trust, *Gentle Ben* was an instant hit, selling millions of copies and spawning a movie and television series.

Morey's subsequent novels have also been successful; *Books and Bookmen* contributor Jessica Jenkins, for example, calls *Home*

Is the North "a story in which the fascination of the wild is inseparably bound up with the realities of living. It makes compelling reading, not only on account of its irresistible setting (a remote homestead on the Alaskan shore) but because the variety of events and the characters make it an absorbing story." "Animal stories are best when they avoid attributing human qualities to the animal world," a reviewer for the *Times Literary Supplement* remarks about *Kavik, the Wolf Dog.* "Although it is scarcely possible to make an animal the main figure in a story without using a good deal of imagination on its behalf, it can be done objectively and in a credible way. *Kavik, the Wolf Dog* by Walt Morey is a sound example of this." *Book World* contributor Helen Renthal likewise concludes that "once again the author of *Gentle Ben* has worked a kind of verbal thaumaturgy, mixing some familiar ingredients with a few fresh ones and a knowledge of the Alaskan wilderness to produce an animal story that is something more than the sum of its parts."

MEDIA ADAPTATIONS: Gentle Ben was the inspiration for both the motion picture, "Gentle Giant," Paramount, 1967, and the CBS television series, "Gentle Ben," 1967-69; "Sultan and the Rock Star," based on *Sandy and the Rock Star,* and "The Courage of Kavik, the Wolf Dog," based on *Kavik, the Wolf Dog,* were both broadcast on NBC in 1980; *Year of the Black Pony* was made into a film titled "The Wild Pony"; Disney Studios owns the rights to *Run Far, Run Fast.*

BIOGRAPHICAL/CRITICAL SOURCES:

BOOKS

Something about the Author, Volume 51, Gale, 1988.
Something about the Author Autobiography Series, Volume 9, Gale, 1989.

PERIODICALS

Books and Bookmen, November, 1968.
Book World, November 3, 1968.
Times Literary Supplement, June 26, 1969.*

*   *   *

MORGAN, Angela
    See PAINE, Lauran (Bosworth)

*   *   *

MORGAN, Arlene
    See PAINE, Lauran (Bosworth)

*   *   *

MORGAN, Frank
    See PAINE, Lauran (Bosworth)

*   *   *

MORGAN, John
    See PAINE, Lauran (Bosworth)

*   *   *

MORGAN, Valerie
    See PAINE, Lauran (Bosworth)

MORRIS, (Murrell) Edward 1935-

PERSONAL: Born September 21, 1935, in Elkview, W.Va.; son of Charles Sennet (a laborer) and Mary Elizabeth (a laborer; maiden name, Pauley) Morris; married Norma Chapman (a textbook author), February 6, 1960; children: Erin, Christopher (deceased), Jason, Rachel. *Education:* Morris Harvey College, B.A., 1958; Ohio University, M.S., 1959. *Politics:* Socialist. *Religion:* None.

ADDRESSES: Home—1710 Clough St., Bowling Green, Ohio 43402. *Office—Billboard,* 49 Music Sq. W., Nashville, Tenn. 37203.

CAREER: Findlay College, Findlay, Ohio, instructor in English, 1960-63; Alice Lloyd College, Pippa Passes, Ky., assistant professor of English, 1965-66; Edinboro State College, Edinboro, Pa., assistant professor of English, 1967-70; Brookside Children's Home, Charleston, W.Va., childcare worker, 1971-72; Appalachia Educational Laboratory, Charleston, W.Va., staff writer and editor, 1972-74; free-lance writer, 1974-76; *Writer's Digest,* Cincinnati, Ohio, assistant editor, 1976-78; free-lance writer, 1978-81; *Billboard,* Nashville, Tenn., writer and editor, 1981—.

WRITINGS:

(Contributor of poetry) Frederick Eckman, editor, *Poems from Bowling Green* (anthology), Winesburg Editions, 1967.
(Contributor of poetry) William Plumley, editor, *Poems from the Hills, 1970* (anthology), Morris Harvey College Press, 1970.
(With Freida Gregory) *TV: The Family School,* Avatar Press, 1976.
(With wife, Norma Morris) *Free and Low-Cost Publicity for Your Musical Act,* Media Modes, 1978.
Alabama, Contemporary Books, 1985.
In Charge: Music Row's Decision Makers, Music Row Publications, 1987.
(Contributor) *Country: The Music and the Musicians,* Abbeville Press, 1988.

Also author of publicity releases for CBS/Epic Records, RCA Records, and Warner Brothers Records. Contributor to numerous periodicals, including *International Musician, Journal of Country Music, Writer's Digest, Mechanix Illustrated, Amusement Business, Mother Earth News,* and *Advertising Age.*

SIDELIGHTS: Edward Morris told *CA:* "Writing is appealing to me because it allows me to earn a living without going out-of-doors. As much as I enjoy good writing (doing it or reading it) I have almost no faith in its ability to change people's lives. And I have identical qualms about teaching. Had I been a religious man, I would have tried to sell my soul to write like Peter DeVries or S. J. Perelman."

*   *   *

MOYERS, Bill 1934-

PERSONAL: Given name legally changed from Billy Don; born June 5, 1934, in Hugo, Okla.; son of John Henry (a laborer) and Ruby (Johnson) Moyers; married Judith Suzanne Davidson, December 18, 1954; children: William Cope, Alice Suzanne, John Davidson. *Education:* Attended North Texas State University, 1952-54; University of Texas, Austin, B.J. (with honors), 1956; attended University of Edinburgh, 1956-57; Southwestern Baptist Theological Seminary, B.D., 1959.

ADDRESSES: Office—Public Affairs TV, Inc., 524 West 57th St., New York, N.Y. 10019.

CAREER: News Messenger, Marshall, Tex., reporter and sports editor, 1949-54; KTBC Radio and Television, Austin, Tex., assistant news editor, 1954-56; assistant pastor of churches in Texas and Oklahoma, 1956-59; special assistant to Senator Lyndon B. Johnson, 1959-60; executive assistant for vice-presidential campaign, 1960-61; Peace Corps, Washington, D.C., director of public affairs, 1961, deputy director, 1962-63; special assistant to President Lyndon B. Johnson, 1963-65, White House press secretary, 1965-67; *Newsday,* Garden City, N.Y., publisher, 1967-70; television executive and series host, 1970—; host of "This Week," National Educational Television, 1970, and of "Bill Moyers' Journal," Educational Broadcasting Corp., 1971-76, 1978-81; editor and chief correspondent, "CBS Reports," Columbia Broadcasting System, 1976-80, senior news analyst and commentator, "CBS News," 1981-86; executive editor, Public Affairs TV, Inc., 1987—. President, Florence and John Schumann Foundation and Schumann Fund of New Jersey.

AWARDS, HONORS: Emmy Awards from National Academy of Television Arts and Sciences for outstanding broadcaster, 1974, 1978, 1980, 1982, 1983, 1984, 1985, 1986, and 1987; George Peabody Awards, 1976, 1980, 1985, and 1986; DuPont Columbia awards, 1979 and 1986; George Polk awards, 1981, 1986, and 1987; Medal of Excellence from University of the State of New York, 1984; Ralph Lowell medal for contributions to public television; Silver Gavel Award from American Bar Association.

WRITINGS:

Listening to America: A Traveler Rediscovers His Country, Harper Magazine Press, 1971.
A World of Ideas: Conversations with Thoughtful Men and Women about American Life Today and the Ideas Shaping Our Future, Doubleday, 1989.

TELEVISION SERIES

"Creativity," first broadcast by the Public Broadcasting System (PBS), January, 1982.
"A Walk through the Twentieth Century," first broadcast by PBS, January, 1984.
"In Search of the Constitution," first broadcast by PBS, April, 1987.
"Joseph Campbell and the Power of Myth," first broadcast by PBS, 1987.
"Facing Evil," first broadcast by PBS, March, 1988.
"Moyers: The Power of the Word," first broadcast by PBS, September, 1989.

SIDELIGHTS: Broadcast journalist Bill Moyers is well known for providing American television audiences with "news of the mind." His political commentaries, historical essays, and series on such erudite subjects as myth and evil challenge the limits of television programming and offer educational alternatives to standard prime-time fare. "The conventional wisdom is that ideas and intelligent conversation make bad TV," writes Geoffrey C. Ward in *American Heritage* magazine. "Within the industry, human beings with something to say are dismissed as 'talking heads.' Moyers knows better and has proved it time and again. His is an earnest presence . . . but it is also intelligent, humane, and intensely curious. He seems genuinely affected by what he sees and hears, and more important, he possesses the mysterious power to pass along his amusement or astonishment or horror intact to the viewer." Most of Moyers's work, including his series "Creativity," "A Walk through the Twentieth Century," and "Facing Evil," have appeared on public television, a forum well suited to his intellectual style and scope. He has also served as a commentator and investigative reporter for CBS Television, both on the nightly news and in special shows. According to a *Saturday Review* correspondent, Moyers "asks the questions we ourselves would like to [ask] and, unlike most of us, never interrupts the answer. His passing comment seems designed not to draw attention to himself, . . . but to bring out something in the interviewee that a direct question might not evoke. . . . He's an intellectual. . . . He's a man of political acuity. . . . He's moral but not a preacher, political but not a politician."

Moyers was born in 1934 and christened Billy Don. The younger of two sons, he grew up in Marshall, Texas, where his father held a variety of blue collar jobs. In *People* magazine, Moyers reminisced about his youth. Marshall, he said, "was a wonderful place to be poor if you had to be poor. It was a genteel poverty in which people knew who you were and kind of looked after you. Status was important in Marshall, but more important was being part of the community." As a child during the Second World War, Moyers was particularly drawn to the overseas broadcasts of journalist Edward R. Murrow. "This stout voice coming across the ocean night after night, describing the horrors of war," he told *People.* "He brought history alive for me." A good student who also found time to work and engage in extracurricular activities, Moyers began his own journalism career at the Marshall *News Messenger* in 1949. He changed his name to Bill because he thought the name more appropriate for a budding sports writer. After graduating from high school he enrolled at North Texas State College, where he met his future wife, Judith Suzanne Davidson.

In the spring of his sophomore year of college, Moyers wrote to Senator Lyndon B. Johnson, offering to help with Johnson's reelection campaign. Johnson hired Moyers for a summer internship, then, impressed with the young man's work habits, persuaded Moyers to transfer to the University of Texas at Austin. There Moyers studied journalism and theology, worked as assistant news director at KTBC-TV, and preached at two small Baptist churches two Sundays per month. He received his Bachelor's degree in journalism in 1956 and spent the following year at the University of Edinburgh in Scotland as a Rotary International fellow. In 1957 he entered the Southwestern Baptist Theological Seminary to train for the ministry, and he earned another Bachelor's degree with honors in 1959. Moyers never served as a full-time minister, however. He told *People:* "I knew I couldn't be a preacher. I thought that my talents lay elsewhere." Apparently Lyndon Johnson agreed with that assessment, offering Moyers a position as special assistant in Washington, D.C. Soon after Johnson was elected vice-president, Moyers was appointed associate director of public affairs of the newly-created Peace Corps. He was made deputy director in 1962—one of the youngest presidential appointees ever approved by Congress.

Moyers returned to the White House in 1963, when John F. Kennedy's assassination elevated Johnson to the presidency. First Moyers served as one of Johnson's advisors on domestic affairs, overseeing the far-reaching Great Society legislation. Then, in 1964, he became White House chief of staff, and in 1965 he assumed the position of press secretary. As the *Saturday Review* reporter notes, the Washington press corps "was fascinated by the young man who seemed to have Lyndon Johnson's full confidence. Part of the appeal was his background—son of an East Texas dirt farmer, former divinity student, and ordained Baptist teacher. Part was his age—30. Part was his already impressive political credentials. . . . And part was his character—he was bright, and he was calm and efficient. This inner fortitude took its toll. Moyers suffered from a chronic ulcer when he worked

for Johnson, and the strain is obvious even in photographs, which show a tense, skinny young man with heavy, black-rimmed glasses." Indeed, Moyers became increasingly disillusioned as Johnson intensified America's military involvement in Southeast Asia while placing less stress on domestic improvements. In 1967 he left public service, over Johnson's strenuous objections, to become publisher of *Newsday,* one of the nation's largest suburban daily newspapers.

Under Moyers's tenure at *Newsday,* the paper garnered thirty-three major journalism awards, including two Pulitzer Prizes. Still Moyers quit *Newsday* in the summer of 1970 for a more leisurely adventure. He boarded a bus with a notebook and tape recorder and embarked on a 13,000-mile trip across the United States. Claiming that he had been out of touch with Americans for too long, he interviewed numerous ordinary folk from all walks of life and described his subjects in *Listening to America: A Traveler Rediscovers His Country,* published in 1971. The book was a best-seller as well as a critical success.

Moyers also began his long association with public television in 1970. He recognized the then-fledgling medium as the perfect forum for a free and unhurried discussion of important issues. "You know that your [public television] viewer has a tolerance for ideas, a willingness to be patient, a mind that wants to be stretched," Moyers commented in *Saturday Review.* "Commercial television paces itself so rapidly that it's hard to absorb. It's racing—it wants to keep the action flowing like the Indianapolis speedway. . . . My work on public broadcasting wants to almost infiltrate—to insinuate itself into the consciousness of the viewer." In 1971 Moyers became host of "Bill Moyers' Journal," a weekly show that addressed the political and social issues of the time. To quote the *Saturday Review* reporter, the program "epitomized public-affairs broadcasting at its best"; it won its host a total of five Emmy Awards. "Bill Moyers' Journal" ran from 1971 until 1976 and again from 1978 to 1981. His appreciation of public television notwithstanding, Moyers has also worked with CBS on a regular basis. From 1976 until 1980 he was chief correspondent of "CBS Reports," and for five years between 1981 and 1986 he was a senior analyst and commentator for "CBS News." He has since returned to public television because, as he put it in the *Chicago Tribune,* "I've always thought there's no limit to what you can do in this world if you don't want to get rich or gain credit. . . . I've done 500 hours of television or more by staying loose, by going to where I could create the opportunity."

Critical acclaim and viewer support from a surprising cross-section of the population has assured Moyers a lasting berth on public television. As Jane Hall notes in *People,* Moyers "has been honored as perhaps the most insightful broadcast journalist of our day, an astute interviewer to whom philosophers, novelists and inarticulate workers have revealed their deepest dreams." *Newsweek* contributor Harry F. Waters writes that Bill Moyers "looks at America and sees freeways of the mind connecting great and complex issues, a landscape of ethical cloverleafs that affords a natural habitat for the journalist as moralist. . . . Along with his gifts of insight and eloquence, this Texas populist and former Baptist preacher possesses a special knack for bringing big issues down to human dimension." Waters concludes: "Besides choosing fertile thematic terrain, Moyers always brings a point of view to his craft that . . . at least dares to challenge and provoke. Agree with him or not, he never leaves your mind in neutral."

BIOGRAPHICAL/CRITICAL SOURCES:

BOOKS

Authors in the News, Volume 1, Gale, 1976.

PERIODICALS

American Heritage, December, 1983.
Chicago Tribune, March 28, 1988.
Harper's, October, 1965.
Los Angeles Times, April 20, 1987.
Newsday, June 4, 1974.
Newsweek, March 1, 1965, April 15, 1974, October 21, 1974,
   July 4, 1983.
New York Times Magazine, April 3, 1966.
People, February 22, 1982, August 1, 1983.
Saturday Review, February, 1982.
Time, July 15, 1974, June 13, 1977.
Washington Magazine, July/August, 1974.

—*Sketch by Anne Janette Johnson*

*   *   *

MUELLER, Claus 1941-

PERSONAL: Born July 23, 1941, in Berlin, Germany; came to the United States in 1964; son of Wilhelm (a secret service agent) and Dorothea Elisabeth (Milsch) Mueller; married second wife, Martha A. Link (a flight attendant), June 5, 1976 (divorced). *Education:* University of Cologne, B.A., 1964; New School for Social Research, M.A., 1966, Ph.D., 1970; Institut Etudes Politiques, C.E.P., 1967; attended Ecole Pratique des Hautes-Etudes, 1968-69.

ADDRESSES: Home—420 East 64th St., W2H, New York, N.Y. 10021. *Office*—Department of Sociology, Hunter College of the City University of New York, 695 Park Ave., New York, N.Y. 10021.

CAREER: City College of the City University of New York, New York City, adjunct lecturer in sociology, summer, 1968; Hunter College of the City University of New York, New York City, adjunct assistant professor, 1970-71, assistant professor, 1971-74, associate professor of sociology, 1974—, director of masters' program in social research, 1976—. Reviewer for Random House, 1974-75. Photographic editor for West German television, Cologne, 1963-64; executive producer of "VideoSociology" for Manhattan Cable Television, New York City, 1974-76; partner, Media Resource Associates, New York City, 1978—; has exhibited videotapes at Artists' Space. Consultant.

MEMBER: Institut International de Sociologie, International Beaux Arts Society (honorary member), National Academy of Television Arts and Sciences, American Sociological Association, Association of Independent Video and Filmmakers, Center for Inter-American Relations, Experimental Television Cooperative, Special Citizens Futures Unlimited (honorary board member), University Film and Video Association.

WRITINGS:

(Contributor) Peter Dreitzel, editor, *Recent Sociology II,* Macmillan, 1970.
(Contributor) Dorothy Flapan, editor, *American Social Institutions,* Behavioral Publications, 1972.
(Contributor) C. Conway and Nelson Foote, editors, *Social Institutions,* Kendal/Hunt, 1973.
The Politics of Communication: A Study in the Political Sociology of Language, Socialization, and Legitimation, Oxford University Press, 1973.

American Media and Mass Culture, California University Press, 1987.
Access of Third World Television to U.S. Media, Friedrich Naumann Foundation, 1989.
(Contributor) *The European Film in the World,* Organisation Catholique Internationale du Cinema (Brussels), 1989.

WORK IN PROGRESS: Temporary Man, on identity problems in contemporary society, for Oxford University Press; *Crosscurrent,* a historical novel about Berlin and Paris in the late 1930s and early 1940s; research on the psychopathology of the family and the impact of children's television.

SIDELIGHTS: Claus Mueller once wrote *CA:* "Underlying my academic and fictional writing is a strong biographical concern. I hope to explore and clarify the world in and around me."

*   *   *

MURPHY, Warren B. 1933-

PERSONAL: Born September 13, 1933, in Jersey City, N.J.; married Dawn Walters, June 25, 1955 (divorced, 1973); married Mariko Cochran, February 14, 1984; children: (first marriage) Deirdre, Megan, Brian, Ardath, (second marriage) Devin. *Education:* Attended St. Peter's College, 1968-69. *Religion:* Methodist.

ADDRESSES: Agent—Margaret McBride Literary Agency, P.O. Box 8730, La Jolla, Calif. 92038.

CAREER: Reporter and editor. Acting director of community affairs, Jersey City, N.J., 1971; member of Hackensack Meadowlands Development Commission. *Military service:* U.S. Air Force, Alaskan Air Command, 1952-56; became sergeant.

MEMBER: American Newspaper Guild.

AWARDS, HONORS: Freedoms Foundation award, 1955; public relations award, National League of Cities, 1963; scroll award, Mystery Writers of America, 1984, for *Trace;* Shamus Award, Private Eye Writers of America, 1985, for *The Ceiling of Hell;* Edgar award, Mystery Writers of America, 1985, for *Grandmaster,* and 1986, for *Pigs Get Fat;* five Private Eye Writers of America special awards.

WRITINGS:

(Editor) *The Road to Anarchy,* New Jersey Patrolmen's Benevolent Association, 1968.
Dead End Street, Pinnacle Books, 1973.
Subways Are for Killing, Pinnacle Books, 1973.
One Night Stand, Pinnacle Books, 1973.
City in Heat, Pinnacle Books, 1973.
Down and Dirty, Pinnacle Books, 1974.
Lynch Town, Pinnacle Books, 1974.
On the Dead Run, Pinnacle, 1975.
Leonardo's Law, Carlyle, 1978.
(With Frank Stevens) *Atlantic City* (novelization of a screenplay), Pinnacle Books, 1979.
(With Robert J. Randisi) *Midnight Man,* Pinnacle Books, 1981.
(With Richard Sapir) *The Assassin's Handbook,* Pinnacle Books, 1982.
The Red Moon, Fawcett, 1983.
The Ceiling of Hell, Ballantine, 1984.
Remo Williams and the Secret of the Sinanju, New American Library, 1985.
(With others) *Murder in Manhattan,* Morrow, 1986.
Old Fashioned War, New American Library, 1987.
The Sure Thing, [Windsor, N.Y.], 1988.

"THE DESTROYER" SERIES; WITH RICHARD SAPIR

The Destroyer, No. 1: Created the Destroyer, Pinnacle Books, 1971.

. . . *No. 2: Death Check,* Pinnacle Books, 1972.
. . . *No. 3: The Chinese Puzzle,* Pinnacle Books, 1972.
. . . *No. 4: Mafia Fix,* Pinnacle Books, 1972.
. . . *No. 5: Dr. Quake,* Pinnacle Books, 1972.
. . . *No. 6: Death Therapy,* Pinnacle Books, 1972.
. . . *No. 7: Union Bust,* Pinnacle Books, 1973.
. . . *No. 8: Summit Chase,* Pinnacle Books, 1973.
. . . *No. 9: Murder's Shield,* Pinnacle Books, 1973.
. . . *No. 10: Terror Squad,* Pinnacle Books, 1973.
. . . *No. 11: Kill or Cure,* Pinnacle Books, 1973.
. . . *No. 12: Slave Safari,* Pinnacle Books, 1973.
. . . *No. 13: Acid Rock,* Pinnacle Books, 1973.
. . . *No. 14: Judgment Day,* Pinnacle Books, 1974.
. . . *No. 15: Murder Ward,* Pinnacle Books, 1974.
. . . *No. 16: Oil Slick,* Pinnacle Books, 1974.
. . . *No. 17: Last War Dance,* Pinnacle Books, 1974.
. . . *No. 18: Funny Money,* Pinnacle Books, 1975.
. . . *No. 19: Holy Terror,* Pinnacle Books, 1975.
. . . *No. 20: Assassin's Play-Off,* Pinnacle Books, 1975.
. . . *No. 21: Deadly Seeds,* Pinnacle Books, 1975.
. . . *No. 22: Brain Drain,* Pinnacle Books, 1976.
. . . *No. 23: Child's Play,* Pinnacle Books, 1976.
. . . *No. 24: King's Curse,* Pinnacle Books, 1976.
. . . *No. 25: Sweet Dreams,* Pinnacle Books, 1976.
. . . *No. 26: In Enemy Hands,* Pinnacle Books, 1977.
. . . *No. 27: The Last Temple,* Pinnacle Books, 1977.
. . . *No. 28: Ship of Death,* Pinnacle Books, 1977.
. . . *No. 29: The Final Death,* Pinnacle Books, 1977.
. . . *No. 30: Mugger Blood,* Pinnacle Books, 1977.
. . . *No. 31: The Head Men,* Pinnacle Books, 1977.
. . . *No. 32: Killer Chromosomes,* Pinnacle Books, 1978.
. . . *No. 33: Voodoo Die,* Pinnacle Books, 1978.
. . . *No. 34: Chained Reaction,* Pinnacle Books, 1978.
. . . *No. 35: Last Call,* Pinnacle Books, 1978.
. . . *No. 36: Power Play,* Pinnacle Books, 1979.
. . . *No. 37: Bottom Line,* Pinnacle Books, 1979.

"THE DESTROYER" SERIES; SOLE AUTHOR

. . . *No. 38: Bay City Blast,* Pinnacle Books, 1979.
. . . *No. 39: The Missing Link,* Pinnacle Books, 1980.
. . . *No. 40: Dangerous Game,* Pinnacle Books, 1980.
. . . *No. 41: Firing Line,* Pinnacle Books, 1980.
. . . *No. 42: Timber Line,* Pinnacle Books, 1980.
. . . *No. 43: Midnight Man,* Pinnacle Books, 1981.
. . . *No. 44: Balance of Power,* Pinnacle Books, 1981.
. . . *No. 45: Spoils of War,* Pinnacle Books, 1981.
. . . *No. 46: Next of Kin,* Pinnacle Books, 1981.
. . . *No. 47: Dying Space,* Pinnacle Books, 1982.
. . . *No. 48: Profit Motive,* Pinnacle Books, 1982.
. . . *No. 49: Skin Deep,* Pinnacle Books, 1982.
. . . *No. 50: Killing Time,* Pinnacle Books, 1982.
. . . *No. 51: Shock Value,* Pinnacle Books, 1983.
. . . *No. 52: Fool's Gold,* Pinnacle Books, 1983.
. . . *No. 53: Time Trial,* Pinnacle Books, 1983.
. . . *No. 54: Last Drop,* Pinnacle Books, 1983.
. . . *No. 55: Master's Challenge,* Pinnacle Books, 1984.
. . . *No. 56: Encounter Group,* Pinnacle Books, 1984.
. . . *No. 57: Date with Death,* Pinnacle Books, 1984.
. . . *No. 58: Total Recall,* Pinnacle Books, 1984.
. . . *No. 59: The Arms of Kali,* New American Library, 1984.
. . . *No. 60: The End of the Game,* New American Library, 1985.

. . . *No. 61: Lords of the Earth,* New American Library, 1985.
. . . *No. 62: The Seventh Stone,* New American Library, 1985.
. . . *No. 63: The Sky Is Falling,* New American Library, 1986.
. . . *No. 64: The Last Alchemist,* New American Library, 1986.
. . . *No. 65: Lost Yesterday,* New American Library, 1986.
. . . *No. 66: Sue Me,* New American Library, 1986.
. . . *No. 67: Look into My Eyes,* New American Library, 1987.
. . . *No. 69: Blood Ties,* New American Library, 1987.
. . . *No. 70: Eleventh Hour,* New American Library, 1987.
. . . *No. 71: Return Engagement,* New American Library, 1988.
. . . *No. 72: Sole Survivor,* New American Library, 1988.
. . . *No. 73: Line of Succession,* New American Library, 1988.

"DIGGER" SERIES

Smoked Out, Pocket Books, 1982.
Fool's Flight, Pocket Books, 1982.
Dead Letter, Pocket Books, 1982.
Lucifer's Weekend, Pocket Books, 1982.

"TRACE" SERIES

Trace, No. 1, New American Library, 1983.
. . . *No. 2: Trace and Forty-Seven Miles of Rope,* New American Library, 1984.
. . . *No. 3: When Elephants Forget,* New American Library, 1984.
. . . *No. 4: Once A Mutt,* New American Library, 1984.
. . . *No. 5: Pigs Get Fat,* New American Library, 1985.
. . . *No. 6: Too Old A Cat,* New American Library, 1986.
. . . *No. 7: Getting Up with Fleas,* New American Library, 1987.

WITH MOLLY COCHRAN

Grandmaster, New American Library, 1985.
The High Priest, New American Library, 1987.
The Hand of Lazarus, New American Library, 1988.
The Temple Dogs, New American Library, 1988
Sons of the Wave, New American Library, 1988.

SCREENPLAYS

(With Hal Dresner and Rod Whitaker) "The Eiger Sanction," Universal Pictures, 1975.

Also creator of "Murphy's Law" television series, 1989.

SIDELIGHTS: "The Destroyer" series, written by Warren B. Murphy and Richard Sapir, began when the two men were both working in New Jersey, Murphy in politics and Sapir as a newspaper reporter. Sapir, who cared more about expressing particular concerns than action, wrote the first half of each book; Murphy finished up with the action writing. Their first "Destroyer" book was finished in 1963, but they were unable to find a publisher for it until 1971. Once the series caught on, however, the new "Destroyer" books were published at a steady rate. In 1978, Sapir dropped out of the series to write suspense novels and while Murphy has started two new series with new partners, he has continued the "Destroyer" series alone. There are now seventy-five books in the series and over thirty million copies have been sold.

The series concerns the adventures of Remo Williams, an assassin for the U.S. National Security Agency who has been listed as "officially dead," and Chiun, an aged Korean martial arts expert who serves as Remo's teacher. According to Dick Lochte in the *Los Angeles Times Book Review,* those who have not read one of the series' books are "unaware of the oddball, satiric nature of the exploits." "There's a wry, deadpan humor to the writing," a *Publishers Weekly* reviewer states, "and asides are made on everything from American soap operas to global politics."

Writing in *Crime and Mystery Writers,* Will Murray notes that "individual novels satirize such topics as black supremacists (*Mugger Blood*), white supremacists (*Chained Reaction*), hippies (*Acid Rock*), gurus (*Holy Terror*), liberal politicians (*In Enemy Hands*), and even other action heroes (*Bay City Blast*)."

Speaking to Lochte for *Armchair Detective,* Murphy cites Doc Savage, a pulp magazine hero of the 1930s, as one inspiration for the "Destroyer" books, but "we didn't set out to rip off Doc Savage," Murphy states. "The homage we owe him is that we were going to do a book about a superhero who was bigger than life and who fights the world on those terms." But Murphy points out that unlike other series heroes, Remo and Chiung are not restricted by a rigid plot formula or inflexible personalities. "We allowed ourselves the freedom to write anything we want to," he says, "to let our characters roam anywhere." In *The Assassin's Handbook,* Murphy and Sapir provide a realistic-sounding guide to the "Destroyer" series, including such items as Chiun's "obscure Ung poetry" and "The Assassin's Quick Weight-Loss Diet," Lochte relates. Lochte describes the tongue-in-cheek guide as "unbridled nonsense."

Murphy's other books, mostly thrillers and mystery novels, have been well-received by the critics. *Smoked Out,* the first in his "Digger" series about Julian Burroughs, a claims investigator for an insurance company, is described by a *Publishers Weekly* critic as "snappily written, witty, sometimes laughing-out-loud funny." *The Red Moon,* a thriller about a former CIA agent investigating his father-in-law's murder, is called by Henry Zorich of the *West Coast Review of Books* a "blockbuster suspense thriller. . . . Few books are as powerful and as exciting."

A number of Murphy's books have been translated into Spanish, including *Dead End Street, City in Heat,* and *One Night Stand.*

MEDIA ADAPTATIONS: Remo Williams: The Adventure Begins, a 1985 film produced by Orion Pictures, was based on the characters in "The Destroyer" series.

BIOGRAPHICAL/CRITICAL SOURCES:

BOOKS

Crime and Mystery Writers, St. James, 1984.

PERIODICALS

Armchair Detective, July, 1978.
Los Angeles Times Book Review, November 14, 1982.
New Republic, November 4, 1978.
Publishers Weekly, July 14, 1975, January 22, 1982.
West Coast Review of Books, November, 1982.

*   *   *

MURRAY, John E(dward), Jr. 1932-

PERSONAL: Born December 20, 1932, in Philadelphia, Pa.; son of John E. and Mary Catherine (Small) Murray; married Isabelle A. Bogusevich, April 11, 1955; children: Bruce, Suzanne, Timothy, Jacqueline. *Education:* La Salle College, B.S., 1955; Catholic University of America, J.D., 1958; University of Wisconsin, S.J.D., 1959. *Politics:* Democrat. *Religion:* Roman Catholic.

ADDRESSES: Home—6009 Parkvue Dr., Pittsburgh, Pa. 15236. *Office*—Duquesne University, Administration Building, Pittsburgh, Pa. 15282.

CAREER: Admitted to Wisconsin Bar, 1959, and Pennsylvania Bar, 1986. Duquesne University, Pittsburgh, Pa., assistant professor, 1959-62, associate professor, 1962-63, professor of law, 1965-67, acting dean of School of Law, 1967; Villanova University, Villanova, Pa., professor of law, 1964-65; University of Pittsburgh, Pittsburgh, professor of law, 1967-84, acting dean, 1976-77, dean, 1977-84; Villanova University, professor of law and dean, 1984-86; University of Pittsburgh, professor of law, 1986-88; Duquesne University, president, 1988—. Lecturer, Pennsylvania Bar Institute, 1970; mayor of Pleasant Hills, Pa., 1970-74. Chairman, Pennsylvania Chief Justice's committee on comprehensive judicial and lawyer education; consultant to law firms.

MEMBER: American Law Institute, Pennsylvania State Mayors Association (member of executive committee), Allegheny County Bar Association.

WRITINGS:

(Editor) *Grismore on Contracts,* Bobbs-Merrill, revised edition, 1965, 2nd revised edition published as *Murray on Contracts,* 1974, 3rd edition, Michie Co., 1990.
Cases and Materials on Contracts, Bobbs-Merrill, 1969, 3rd edition, Michie Co., 1983.
Purchasing and the Law, Purchasing Management Association of Pittsburgh, 1973, 2nd edition, 1980.
Problems and Materials on Commercial Law, West Publishing, 1975.
(With Robert J. Nordstrom and Albert L. Clovis) *Problems and Materials on Sales,* West Publishing, 1982.
(With Nordstrom and Clovis) *Problems and Materials on Secured Transactions,* West Publishing, 1987.

Contributor of articles to law journals. Editor, *Catholic University Law Review,* 1958, and *Journal of Legal Education,* 1971-83.

SIDELIGHTS: John E. Murray, Jr. told *CA* that throughout deanships and now a presidency, he continues to pursue his scholarship in books and articles because he is convinced that "writing is a dimension that has a pervasive influence in every aspect of one's work including administration. It is the most difficult and most rewarding of all my activities."

N

NARANG, Gopi Chand 1931-

PERSONAL: Born January 1, 1931, in Dukki, Baluchistan, India; son of Dharam Chand (a civil servant) and Tekan (Bai) Narang; married Tara Rani (a teacher; divorced, 1972); married second wife, Manorma (a teacher); children: Arun, Tarun. *Education:* Punjab University, B.A. (with honors in Persian), 1950; University of Delhi, M.A. (with honors in Urdu), 1954, Ph.D., 1958, Diploma in Linguistics, 1961.

ADDRESSES: *Home*—D 252 Sarvodaya Enclave, New Delhi-17, India. *Office*—Department of Urdu, Delhi University, New Delhi, 110017 India.

CAREER: University of Delhi, Delhi, India, 1957-74, began as lecturer, associate professor of Urdu language and literature, 1961-74; Jamia Millia University, New Delhi, India, professor of Urdu and chairman of department, 1974—. Visiting professor in department of Indian studies, University of Wisconsin, 1963-65, 1968-70. Regular broadcaster on All India Radio and Delhi Television; member of baord of directors, Jamia Publishing House; member of executive board and convener of Urdu advisory board, Sahitya Academi; chairman of Urdu committee, National Council of Educational Research and Training (India); convener, Bharatiya Jnanpith Literary Award committee. Member of Indian Government delegation to 27th Orientalist International Congress, University of Michigan, 1967.

MEMBER: Urdu Association of India (member of executive committee), American Oriental Society, Linguistic Society of America, Modern Language Association of America, Association for Asian Studies, Linguistic Society of India, Royal Asiatic Society of London (fellow), All India PEN.

AWARDS, HONORS: Ghalib Prize of Indian Government for best scholarly work of 1962, for *Urdu Masnawiyan;* Commonwealth fellowship, 1963; U.P. Urdu Academy Prize, 1972, for *Karbal Katha ka Lisaniyati Mutaliya;* Mir Award for total literary services, 1976; President of Pakistan's Gold Medal, 1978, for distinguished scholarly work on the poet Iqbal; national award from National Council of Educational Research and Training, 1980; Association for Asian Studies award, 1982, for services to Urdu language and literature; award from Aligarh Alumni Association, Washington, D.C., 1982, for Urdu scholarship; Ghalib Memorial Award, 1983; special award from Bihar Urdu Academy, 1983; Sahitya Kala Parishad Award, 1984; Khusrau Award, AKSA Chicago, 1987.

WRITINGS:

(Editor) *Miraj ul-Ashiqeen,* Azad Kitab Ghar, 1957.

Teaching Urdu as a Foreign Language, Azad Kitab Ghar, 1960, 2nd edition, 1963.

Urdu Masnawiyan, Maktaba Jamia, 1962.

Karkhandari Dialect of Delhi Urdu, Munshi Ram Manohar Lal, 1963.

(Editor) *Adabi Tahreerin,* Sab Ras Kitab Ghar, 1964.

Readings in Literary Urdu Prose, University of Wisconsin Press, 1968.

(Editor) *Manshurat,* Anjuman taraqqi-e-Urdu, 1968.

(Co-author) *Karbal Katha ka Lisaniyati Mutaliya,* Maktaba Shahrah, 1970.

(Editor) *Aemughan-e-Malik,* Maktaba Jamia, 1973.

(Editor) *Imla Namah,* Urdu Development Board, 1974.

Puranon ki Kahaniyan, National Book Trust (India), 1976.

(Editor) *Iqbal Jamia ke Musannifin ki Nazar men,* Maktaba Jamia, 1978.

(Co-author) *Wazahati Kitabiyat,* Urdu Promotion Bureau, 1979.

(Editor and translator) *Indian Poetry Today,* Volume 4: *Modern Urdu Poetry,* Indian Council for Cultural Relations, 1980.

(Editor) *Urdu Afsanah: Riwayat aur Masail,* Educational Publishers, 1981.

Anis Shanasi, Educational Publishers, 1981.

Safar Ashna, Educational Publishers, 1982.

Iqbal Ka Fann, Educational Publishers, 1983.

Usloobiyat-e-Mir, Educational Publishers, 1984.

Saniha-e-Karbala bataur Sheri Istiara, Educational Publishers, 1986.

Amir Khusrau ka Hindavi Kalaam, Amir Khusrau Society of America (Chicago), 1987.

Adabi Tanqeed aur Usloobiyat, Educational Publishers, 1989.

(Editor) *Selected Short Stories of Rajinder Singh Bedi,* Sahitya Akademi, 1989.

Urdu ki Nai Kitab, National Council of Educational Research and Training, 1989.

WORK IN PROGRESS: An anthology of Urdu short stories in English translation; *Urdu Zaban aur Lisaniyat; Ababi Tanqeed aur Sakhtiyat; Studies in Urdu Literature and Linguistics.*

NASKE, Claus-M(ichael) 1935-

PERSONAL: Born December 18, 1935, in Stettin, Germany; son of Alfred (an army officer) and Kaethe (Salomon) Naske; married Dinah Ariss (a teacher), May 20, 1960; children: Natalia-Michelle Nau-geak, Nathaniel-Michael Noah. *Education:* University of Alaska, B.A., 1961; University of Michigan, M.A., 1964; Washington State University, Ph.D., 1970. *Politics:* Independent.

ADDRESSES: Office—Department of History, University of Alaska Fairbanks, Fairbanks, Alaska 99775.

CAREER: Farm laborer in Palmer, Alaska, 1954-56; surveyor in Palmer and Fairbanks, Alaska, 1957-61, and Monterey, Calif., 1962; Bureau of Indian Affairs, Barrow, Alaska, teacher, 1964-65; Juneau-Douglas Community College, Juneau, Alaska, instructor in history and political science, 1965-67; University of Alaska Fairbanks, 1969—, began as assistant professor, professor of history, 1981—, head of department of history, 1986—, executive director of University of Alaska Press. Member of board of directors of Pacific Northwest History Conference, 1970—. Consultant to Bureau of Land Management, Alaska Department of Transportation and Public Facilities. *Military service:* U.S. Army Reserve.

MEMBER: Association for Canadian Studies in the United States, Canadian Historical Association, Alaska Historical Society, Tanana-Yukon Historical Society (past president).

WRITINGS:

An Interpretive History of Alaskan Statehood, Alaska Northwest Publishing, 1973, 2nd revised edition published as *A History of Alaskan Statehood,* University Press of America, 1985.
(With Herman Slotnick) *Alaska: A History of the Forty-Ninth State,* Eerdmans, 1979, 2nd edition, Oklahoma State University Press, 1987.
(With William R. Hunt and Lael Morgan) *Alaska,* Abrams, 1979.
Edward Lewis "Bob" Bartlett of Alaska: A Life in Politics, University of Alaska Press, 1980.
(With Ludwig J. Rowinski) *Anchorage: A Pictorial History,* Donning, 1981.
(With Rowinski) *Fairbanks: A Pictorial History,* Donning, 1981.
(With Rowinski) *Alaska: A Pictorial History,* Donning, 1983.
(With Hans Blohm) *Alaska,* Oxford University Press, 1984.
Paving Alaska's Trails: The Work of the Alaskan Road Commission, University Press of America, 1986.

Also contributor to *Proceedings* of the 27th and 29th Alaska Science Conference, 1976 and 1978. Contributor to numerous periodicals, including *American Historical Review, Pacific Northwest Quarterly, Alaska Journal, Choice, Journal of the West, Military Affairs,* and *Pacific Historian.*

WORK IN PROGRESS: Ernest Gruening: Alaska's Territorial Governor, 1939-1953.

SIDELIGHTS: Claus-M. Naske told *CA:* "I am damn glad I made it to America and was able to leave Europe behind. American society is fascinating—I wake up each morning, realizing with great joy that I am doing what I want to do, and getting paid for it on top of it all. What a life!"

*   *   *

NEE, Kay Bonner

PERSONAL: Born in Plummer, Minn.; daughter of David Thomas (a teacher) and Helena (Franken) Bonner; married William J. Nee (engaged in public relations), April 19, 1947; children: Christopher, Nicole, Lisa, Rachel. *Education:* College of St. Catherine, B.A.; University of Minnesota, graduate study, 1947. *Politics:* Democrat. *Religion:* Roman Catholic.

ADDRESSES: Home—219 Logan Park Way, Fridley, Minn. 55432. *Office*—Pederson-Herzog & Nee, Advertising and Public Relations, P.O. Box 32007, Northeast Minneapolis, Minn. 55432.

CAREER: Dayton Co., Minneapolis, Minn., emcee of radio show, 1945-50; Manson-Gold-Miller, Inc., Minneapolis, radio-television director, 1951-53; WCCO-TV, Minneapolis, writer, director, and producer, 1954-56; White-Herzog-Nee, Inc., Minneapolis, radio and television writer and producer, 1956-65; North State Advertising Agency, Minneapolis, president, 1966-70; Minnesota Association of Voluntary Social Service Agencies, St. Paul, executive director, 1972-81; Pederson-Herzog & Nee, Minneapolis, vice president, 1981—. Television director of McCarthy for President campaign, 1968, and director of television and radio for other political campaigns. Member, Minnesota Governor's Committee on Status of Women, 1966.

MEMBER: American Federation of Television and Radio Artists (AFTRA), Northwest Advertising Council, Minnesota Press Club, North Suburban Center for the Arts (president), The Loft, Delta Phi Lambda.

AWARDS, HONORS: Citation, United States Holocaust Memorial Council, 1981; North Metro "Business Woman of the Year" award, Business and Professional Woman's Club, 1983.

WRITINGS:

(With husband, William Nee) *Eugene McCarthy: United States Senator,* Gilbert Press, 1964.
Powhatan: The Story of an American Indian, Dillon, 1971, revised edition, 1978.
"Old Man Jar" (one-act play), first produced in Minneapolis, Minn., at Hansberry Theatre, 1983.
"Une Affaire Pour Deux" (play), first produced in St. Paul, Minn., at King Theater, 1984, produced for television by Nortel Cable TV (Minn.), 1985.

JUVENILE ONE-ACT PLAYS

"Rhymes Ago-go," first produced in Anoka, Minn., at Logan Theatre, 1967.
"Land of the Moogazoos," first produced in Fridley, Minn., at Riverwood Theatre, 1969.
"The Winner," first produced in Fridley at District 14 Theater, 1971.
"Hey Joe!," first porduced in Blaine, Minn., at The Playhouse, 1972.
"The Time Machine," first produced for the Minnesota State Fair, 1976.
"My Friend the Box," first produced in Coon Rapids, Minn., at Community Playhouse, 1978.
"How to Hold Up a Lamp Post," first produced in Fridley at Hayes Theatre, 1982.

OTHER

Writer of weekly radio show "Soda Set," 1945-50, and for television series "Your Child's World," 1967-68, "Preparing Children for the 21st Century," 1973, "Living Married," 1974-75, and "People Who Care," 1979. Former columnist for *Catholic Miss.*

WORK IN PROGRESS: Fifth Row Center, a children's book that is being considered for a television series; "How Can You

Do It without Me?," a two-act play; *Stelle,* a novel; *Please Believe Me,* a romance novel.

SIDELIGHTS: Kay Bonner Nee told *CA:* "Living is, I think, a form of writing waiting to be recorded. Many times the person bursting with ideas gets so busy living their story, novel, play, that they never take that disciplined time needed to put it all down on paper. Then there is the grey door of self doubt. Writing is, for most of us, a statement of self confidence—a belief that what we have to say is important or at least interesting. Without this belief the writer never really gets started. Perhaps this is just as well."

*   *   *

NELKIN, Dorothy 1933-

PERSONAL: Born July 30, 1933, in Boston, Mass.; daughter of Henry and Helen (Fine) Wolfers; married Mark Nelkin (a physicist and professor at Cornell University), August 31, 1952; children: Lisa, Laurie. *Education:* Cornell University, B.A., 1954.

ADDRESSES: Office—Department of Sociology, New York University, New York, N.Y. 10003.

CAREER: Cornell University, Ithaca, N.Y., senior research associate in science, technology, and society program, 1969-72, professor of sociology, 1972-89; New York University, New York, N.Y., professor of sociology and affiliated professor of law, 1989—. Clare Booth Luce visiting chair, 1988-90.

AWARDS, HONORS: Guggenheim fellowship, 1983; Russell Sage Fellow, 1984.

WRITINGS:

On the Season: Aspects of the Migrant Labor System, New York State School of Industrial and Labor Relations Press, 1970.
(With William H. Friedland) *Migrant: Farm Workers in America's Northwest,* Holt, 1971.
Nuclear Power and Its Critics: The Cayuga Lake Controversy, Cornell University Press, 1971.
The Politics of Housing Innovation: The Fate of the Civilian Industrial Technology Program, Cornell University Press, 1971.
The University and Military Research: Moral Politics at M.I.T., Cornell University Press, 1972.
Methadone Maintenance: A Technological Fix, Braziller, 1973.
Science Textbook Controversies, MIT Press, 1977.
Technological Decisions and Democracy, Sage Publications, 1977.
The Atom Besieged, MIT Press, 1982.
The Creation Controversy: Science or Scripture in the Schools, Norton, 1982.
Workers at Risk, University of Chicago Press, 1984.
Selling Science: How the Press Covers Science and Technology, W. H. Freeman, 1987.
(With Laurence Tancredi) *Dangerous Diagnostics: The Social Power of Biological Information,* Basic Books, 1989.

AVOCATIONAL INTERESTS: Playing cello, tennis.

BIOGRAPHICAL/CRITICAL SOURCES:

PERIODICALS

Chicago Tribune, September 20, 1989.
Los Angeles Times, May 5, 1987.

NELSON, Ruben F(rederick) W(erthenbach) 1939-

PERSONAL: Born May 15, 1939, in Calgary, Alberta, Canada; son of Charles Gordon and Dorothy Ester (Werthenbach) Nelson; married Heather Mae Ross (a registered nurse), May 22, 1961; children: Michael Christopher Werthenbach, Miriam Alexandra Jean. *Education:* Queen's University, Kingston, Ontario, B.A. (with honors), 1961; Queen's Theological College, Kingston, Testamur, 1964; attended United Theological College, Bangalore, India, and University of Calgary.

ADDRESSES: Home and office—P.O. Box 2699, Canmore, Alberta, Canada T0L 0M0.

CAREER: Queen's University, Kingston, Ontario, senior instructor in philosophy, 1966-68; University of Calgary, Calgary, Alberta, director of MacEwan Hall, 1968-70; Canadian Government, Ottawa, Ontario, consultant to privy council office, 1970-71, consultant to citizenship branch, secretary of state, 1971-72, special assistant to assistant deputy minister, developmental programs, health, and welfare, 1972-74; Square One Management Ltd., Ottawa, president, 1974—. President of Transformation Research Network, 1983—; futurist, strategist, and facilitator; conducts management development seminars; public speaker; consultant on change and its implications to all types of organizations. Ottawa chairperson of Les Petits Ballets, 1977-83; member of Public Social Responsibility Unit of Anglican Church of Canada, 1977-83.

MEMBER: Canadian Association for Futures Studies (president, 1978-79), Association for Humanistic Psychology (member of board of directors, 1983—; president, 1989-90).

WRITINGS:

(Contributor) Harold Bailey, editor, *You Have a Right to Be Here,* United Church of Canada (Toronto), 1973.
The Illusions of Urban Man, Macmillan, 1976, 2nd edition, Square One Management (Ottawa), 1981.
Preparing for a Changing Future: A Networkers Catalogue of Futures-Oriented Work in Canada, Square One Management, Volume 1, 1984, volume 2, 1986.
The Future of Work, Transformation Research Network (Ottawa), 1984.
Canadian Directory of Futures Services and Resources, Square One Management, 1986.
The Post-Industrial Future Papers, Square One Management, 1989.

Contributor to magazines, including *Futures Conditional, Earthrise Newsletter, Social Sciences in Canada, Recreation Canada, Report,* and *Futures Canada.*

WORK IN PROGRESS: How to Think about the Future.

SIDELIGHTS: Ruben F. W. Nelson has described himself as a futures-oriented adviser to cabinet ministers, a public and corporate affairs consultant, social researcher, conference designer, philosopher, and theologian. He informed *CA* that his goal is "to assist those with whom I work to face, explore, and understand the nature and implications of the profound social, economic, and technological changes which are now taking place in Canada and around the world. I seek to shape rather than be shaped by the future. The essential focus is the importance of recognizing and grasping the fact that ours is a time of personal and cultural change. The future will not and cannot be a mere extension of the past. Our future hangs on our ability to become and act as responsible persons and organizations who live in, with, and for (and not merely on) the earth and for one another."

NEWMAN, Barbara
  See NEWMAN, Mona Alice Jean

*   *   *

NEWMAN, Mona Alice Jean
  (Barbara FitzGerald, Barbara Newman, Jean
  Stewart)

PERSONAL: Born in Sydney, Australia; daughter of William (a financier) and Mary Elizabeth (Maunsell) Stewart; married John FitzGerald Newman (a military colonel), August 19, 1944; children: Patrick FitzGerald. *Education:* Prince Henry's Hospital, S.R.N., 1932. *Religion:* Church of England.

ADDRESSES: Home—St. Fillans, 88 Shipton Rd., York YO3 6RJ, England. *Agent*—Rosemary Gould, Laurence Pollinger Ltd., 18 Maddox St., London W1R 0EU, England.

CAREER: Cedars Private Nursing Home, Sydney, Australia, theatre sister, 1931-34; D. M. Bembaron Ltd., London, England, industrial nurse, 1934-39; King James School, Knaresborough, England, tutor, 1974-79; writer, 1979—. Past nursing officer with St. John Ambulance Brigade; member and past county borough organizer for Women's Royal Volunteer Service; member of executive committee of Soldiers, Sailors, Air Force Association; past member of Yorkshire Area Mental Health Executive Committee. *Military service:* Queen Alexandra's Imperial Military Nursing Service, nurse, 1940-45; served in Africa, the Pacific, and Burma.

MEMBER: Romantic Novelists Association, Authors' North, York Writers' Circle (past chairman), York Ladies Luncheon Club (past president).

WRITINGS:

History of Clifton and Clifton Parish Church (nonfiction), Vicar & Parochial Church Council, 1967.
Centenary Souvenir, [England], 1967.
Tenderly Touch My Cheek (novel), [England], 1967.
Night of a Thousand Stars (novel), [England], 1968, Aston Hall Publications, 1979.
The Faithful Heart (novel), [England], 1969, reprinted as *Two Faces of a Spy,* Fratelli Fabbri Editora, 1970.
Softly Shines the Moon (novel), R. Hale, 1970.
Harbour of Dreams (novel), R. Hale, 1970.
Stranger in the Wolds (novel), R. Hale, 1971.
Hills of the Purple Mist (novel), R. Hale, 1973.
Love Be Not Proud (novel), R. Hale, 1974.
Dr. Cherrill's Dilemma (novel), R. Hale, 1976.
The Surgeon's Choice (novel), R. Hale, 1976.
The Substance Not the Dream (novel), Woman's Weekly, 1976.
Conflict in Berlin (novel), R. Hale, 1979.
To Vienna with Love (novel), R. Hale, 1980.
Hong Kong Triangle (novel), R. Hale, 1981.

UNDER PSEUDONYM BARBARA NEWMAN

Military Hospital Nurse, Mills & Boon, 1978.
Striking a Balance: Dancers Talk about Dancing, Houghton, 1982.
(With Barbara Rogan) *The Covenant: Love and Death in Beirut* (novel), Crown, 1989.

UNDER NAME JEAN STEWART

Where Love Could Not Follow (novel), Woman's Weekly, 1977.
Nurse in Istanbul (novel), R. Hale, 1979.
Escape to Hong Kong (novel), R. Hale, Hamlyn, 1981.

(Translator) Georges Simenon, *The Man with the Little Dog,* Harcourt, 1989.

OTHER

(Under pseudonym Barbara FitzGerald) *We Are Besieged,* Putnam, 1946.

Contributor of articles and stories to magazines and newspapers, including *Lady* and *Women's Story.*

WORK IN PROGRESS: In the Steps of the Emperor, under name Jean Stewart; a historical novel set in early nineteenth-century Australia.

SIDELIGHTS: Mona Newman wrote: "I have been extremely lucky to be able to do so much traveling and to actually live in so many foreign countries. This has helped my writing tremendously, not only with experiences, but in providing exotic backgrounds for my books. I lived in India three years, Nigeria three and a half years, Ghana three and a half years, and Egypt eighteen months. I have visited most western European countries, and the Far East, including Turkey, Ceylon, and Iraq.

"*Night of a Thousand Stars* was born years ago when I came down from a holiday in Darjeeling, having seen range upon range of the mighty Himalayas. That in itself was an experience, but the night I came down by the small mountain train along torturous winding tracks from nine thousand feet to the plains at Siliguri was my night of nights. Above us the sky was peppered with large, shining stars, larger than ever seen in nontropical areas; below us on the ground were scattered thousands of glow worms and all around us fireflies, their lights flashing on and off in a constant rhythm. It was impossible to see where the sky finished and the earth began. I always remember that as my 'Night of a Thousand Stars' so, when I started writing several years later, a novel was born.

"Incidents in other countries have also inspired my novels. In the early fifties I had a weekly radio program in Nigeria. I wrote, produced, and presented it. It was great fun and brought me into contact with many Nigerians I would not otherwise have met. Some of these inspired my first novel, *Tenderly Touch My Cheek.*

"I enjoy my writing, but I will not write any form of pornography. I feel very strongly on this subject, as I think it does far more harm than good. Everyone has imagination, but not one is being asked to exercise it these days."

AVOCATIONAL INTERESTS: Travel, painting (oils), reading, photography, natural history, collecting stamps, public speaking.

BIOGRAPHICAL/CRITICAL SOURCES:

PERIODICALS

Los Angeles Times Book Review, April 23, 1989.
Washington Post Book World, May 30, 1982.

*   *   *

NICHOLS, Stephen G(eorge, Jr.) 1936-

PERSONAL: Born October 24, 1936, in Cambridge, Mass.; son of Stephen George (a manufacturer) and Marjorie (Whitney) Nichols; married Mary Winn Jordan, June 22, 1957 (divorced, 1972); married Edith Karetzky (a public relations specialist), March 23, 1972; children: (first marriage) Stephen Frost, Sarah Winn; (stepchildren) Laura Natalie Karetzky, Sarah Alexandra Karetzky. *Education:* Dartmouth College, A.B. (cum laude),

1958; Universite d'Aix-Marseille, graduate study, 1958-59; Yale University, Ph.D., 1963.

ADDRESSES: Home—200 St. Mark's Sq., Philadelphia, Pa. 19104. *Office*— Department of Romance Languages, University of Pennsylvania, Philadelphia, Pa. 19104.

CAREER: University of California, Los Angeles, assistant professor of French and member of faculty at Center for Medieval and Renaissance Studies, 1963-65; University of Wisconsin—Madison, associate professor, 1965-68, professor of comparative literature, 1968, chairman of department, 1967-68, fellow at Institute for Research in the Humanities, 1966-67; Dartmouth College, Hanover, N.H., professor of Romance languages and comparative literature, 1968-84, Edward Tuck professor of French, 1984-85, chairman of department of comparative literature program, 1969-71, 1974, 1979-82, chairman of Romance languages department, 1974-77, chairman of French and Italian department, 1982-85, associate director of foreign study program, 1969-71, director of French foreign study program, 1970-78, faculty member, 1980-85, and faculty director, 1984-85, of Dartmouth Institute, liaison officer, School of Criticism and Theory, 1983-85; University of Pennsylvania, Philadelphia, professor of Romance languages, 1985—. Visiting professor at universities in Europe, Israel, and the United States; Phi Beta Kappa visiting scholar, 1983-84. Member of advisory boards, Institute d'Etudes Francaises d'Avignon, Bryn Mawr, 1965—, and Princeton University comparative literature department, 1982—. National Endowment for the Humanities Summer Seminar, director, 1975, 1979, review panelist, 1979-81. Danforth associate, 1969—.

MEMBER: International Comparative Literature Association, Association International des Etudes Francaises, Modern Language Association, American Association of Teachers of French (vice-president, Southern California branch, 1964-65), Academy of Literary Studies (secretary-treasurer, 1978—), Medieval Academy of America, Dante Society, Societe Rencesvals (secretary-treasurer, American section, 1964-69), Eastern Comparative Literature Conference (executive committee), New England Medieval Association (advisory committee, 1981—).

AWARDS, HONORS: American Council of Learned Societies grant, 1968-69; National Endowment for the Humanities fellow, 1978-79, summer grant, 1986-87; James Russell Lowell Prize, Modern Language Association of America, 1984, for *Romanesque Signs: Early Medieval Narrative and Iconography.*

WRITINGS:

Formulaic Diction and Thematic Composition in the Chanson de Roland, University of North Carolina Press, 1961.
(Editor with Galm Giamatti and others, and author of introduction and notes) *The Songs of Bernart de Ventadorn,* University of North Carolina Press, 1962.
(Editor) Rene Wellek, *Concepts of Criticism,* Yale University Press, 1963.
(Contributor of translation) Angel Flores, editor, *The Medieval Age,* Dell, 1963.
(Contributor) Will Matthews, editor, *Medieval Secular Literature,* University of California Press, 1965.
(Editor) Guillame de Lorris, *Le roman de la rose,* Appleton, 1967.
(Editor with R. B. Vowles) *Comparatists at Work,* Ginn-Blaisdell, 1968.
(Contributor) L. S. Dembo, editor, *Criticism: Speculative and Analytical Essays,* University of Wisconsin Press, 1968.

(Contributor) Peter Demetz, Thomas Greene, and Lowry Nelson, editors, *The Disciplines of Criticism,* Yale University Press, 1968.
(Contributor) John Graham, editor, *Studies in Second Skin,* C. E. Merrill, 1971.
(Editor with Frank Robinson) *The Meaning of Mannerism,* University Press of New England, 1972.
(Editor and author of introduction with John D. Lyons) *Mimesis: From Mirror to Method, Augustine to Descartes,* University Press of New England, 1982.
Romanesque Signs: Early Medieval Narrative and Iconography, Yale University Press, 1983.
(Editor with Kevin Brownlee) *Images of Power: Medieval History-Discourse-Literature,* Yale University Press, 1986.

Contributor to honorary volumes and to *Encyclopedia of World Literature* and *Reader's Dictionary.* Contributor of articles, poetry essays, and reviews to *Nation, Los Angeles Times,* and to literature journals, including *Quixote, Romance Notes, Contemporary Literature,* and *New Literary History.* Advisory editor, "Old French Text Series," Appleton. Assistant literature editor, *French Review,* 1968—; member of editorial committee, *PMLA,* 1969-74, 1980-85; member of editorial boards, *Olifant,* 1974—, *Medievalia et Humanistica,* 1974—, and *Medievalia,* 1974—.*

*　　*　　*

NIVEN, (James) David (Graham)   1910-1983

PERSONAL: Born March 1, 1910, in Kirriemuir, Scotland; died July 29, 1983, in Chateau-d'Oex, Vaud, Switzerland, of Lou Gehrig's disease; son of William Edward Graham Niven (a military officer) and Henriette Etta (Degacher) Niven; married Primula Rollo (an officer in the Women's Auxiliary Air Force), 1940 (died May 21, 1946); married Hjoerdis Tersmeden (a model), January 4, 1948; children: (first marriage) David, James Graham; (stepchildren) Kristina, Fiona. *Education:* Royal Military College, Sandhurst, graduate, 1929.

CAREER: Actor, 1935-83. Worked in Canada at a lumber camp, as a member of a road-building crew, and as a journalist, 1932-33; worked as a representative for a London wine merchant, New York, N. Y., as an agent for the Indoor American Pony Express Association, Atlantic City, N. J., and as a laundryman, 1933-35. Co-founder with Charles Boyer and Dick Powell of Four Star Television (a television production company), 1952. Appeared in over 100 films, including: "The Charge of the Light Brigade," 1936, "The Dawn Patrol," 1938, "Wuthering Heights," 1939, "Bachelor Mother," 1939, "Raffles," 1939, "Stairway to Heaven," 1945, "The Bishop's Wife," 1947, "Enchantment," 1948, "The Moon Is Blue," 1953, "Court Martial," 1954, "Around the World in Eighty Days," 1956, "Separate Tables," 1958, "Ask Any Girl," 1959, "Please Don't Eat the Daisies," 1960, "The Guns of Navarone," 1961, "55 Days at Peking," 1963, "The Pink Panther," 1964, "Where the Spies Are," 1965, "Casino Royale," 1967, "Murder by Death," 1976, "Death on the Nile," 1978, "The Trail of the Pink Panther," 1982. Television appearances included: "Four Star Playhouse," 1952-56, "Alcoa Theatre," 1957-58, "The David Niven Show," 1959-64, "The Rogues," 1964-65, and the mini-series "A Man Called Intrepid," 1979. *Military service:* Highland Light Infantry, 1929-32, served in Malta; became lieutenant. British Army, 1939-45, served with the Rifle Brigade, Phantom Reconnaissance Regiment, and British Liberation Army, in Belgium, Holland, Germany, and Normandy; became lieutenant colonel; received Legion of Merit from the United States, 1945.

AWARDS, HONORS: Golden Globe Award for best comedy performance, 1953, for "The Moon Is Blue"; Academy Award for best performance by an actor, 1958, and New York Film Critics' Circle Award, 1958, both for "Separate Tables."

WRITINGS:

Once Over Lightly (novel), Prentice-Hall, 1951 (published in England as *Round the Rugged Rocks,* Cresset Press, 1951).
The Moon's a Balloon (memoir), Putnam, 1971.
Bring on the Empty Horses (memoir), Putnam, 1975.
Go Slowly, Come Back Quickly (novel), Doubleday, 1981.

WORK IN PROGRESS: At the time of his death in 1983, Niven was reportedly working on a romantic-adventure novel entitled *From Dawn Until Dusk.*

SIDELIGHTS: During a film and television career lasting over forty years, actor David Niven epitomized for many people the suave, sophisticated English gentleman, a character a London *Times* writer described as "witty, debonair, immaculate in dress and behaviour but with mischief lurking not far from the surface." Usually cast as a soldier, aristocrat, or thief, Niven appeared in over 100 films, including such hits as "Around the World in 80 Days," "Separate Tables," "The Guns of Navarone," and "The Pink Panther." Niven's unfailing charm, wit, and gentlemanly good manners won him popular and critical acclaim. For his portrayal of a retired officer in "Separate Tables" he received an Academy Award in 1958, an award he attributed not to his own talents but to the efforts of his two female co-stars. The modesty was typical of Niven, who always claimed to have limited acting talent. He once said: "I always expect a little man to tap me on the shoulder and say: 'Sorry chum, you've been found out.'" Niven proved to be a successful businessman as well as actor. He was a co-owner with Charles Boyer and Dick Powell of Four Star Television, a production company which at one time had seventeen series airing on network television. As a writer, too, Niven enjoyed great success; his books *The Moon's a Balloon* and *Bring on the Empty Horses,* amusing accounts of his personal life and Hollywood career, sold over eleven million copies. His novel *Go Slowly, Come Back Quickly,* based in part on his own life, was also a bestseller.

Niven came from a long line of Scottish military officers. His father, an officer in the British army, was killed in action during the Gallipoli campaign of the First World War. Following his death, Niven's mother moved the family to London, where she eventually married a member of parliament and became Lady Comyn-Platt. Niven's stepfather sent the boy to a series of military schools, from which he frequently ran away or was expelled. In *The Moon's a Balloon* he wrote about Elstree, the first of several schools he was to attend: "Sadistic masters and the school bullies tying small boys to hot radiators . . . mad matrons . . . ex-naval cooks with fingernails like toenails doling out their nauseous confections. . . . Thus began a long and multi-phased career of occasional study and frequent expulsions." Niven's mischievous behavior in school helped cause many of these expulsions. While in charge of the bellows for one school's church organ, for example, he devised a way to sneak in a "rude noise" during Sunday service. At another school Niven aided his schoolmates' shoplifting sprees by noisily dropping a bag of marbles at the crucial moment, spilling them on the floor and distracting store clerks from the thievery. Niven later claimed that he was lonely as a child; one of his few friends was a teenaged prostitute whom he befriended at the age of 14.

Despite his unruly behavior and personal loneliness, Niven's academic record sufficed to qualify him for the Royal Military College at Sandhurst, England's equivalent of West Point. He graduated from the school in 1929 and took a commission in the Highland Light Infantry, serving three years in Malta before deciding that military life was not for him. Along with a friend, Niven left for North America in 1933 to make his fortune. In Canada, he worked odd jobs as a lumberjack and road crew member before selling a couple of articles to a Toronto newspaper. The money for the articles paid his way to New York, where Niven became a representative for a London wine merchant. (Some sources say he worked as a bootlegger at this time.) A stint with a New Jersey pony racing firm followed, as well as a brief trip to Cuba, where he allegedly gave military training to a band of rebels before being expelled from the country.

By 1935, Niven was in California to try his hand at acting. There was a great interest in British actors at the time, so he wryly registered himself with Central Casting as "Anglo-Saxon type #2008," but his first job was playing a Mexican extra in a Hopalong Cassidy film. He appeared as an extra in some twenty-seven other Westerns before graduating to talking parts. His British accent and impeccable manners soon became his trademarks. By the late 1930s he was starring in light comedies and war adventures and sharing a beach house with close friend Errol Flynn. The two actors nicknamed the house "Cirrhosis by the Sea." Early Niven hits included the military adventure films "The Charge of the Light Brigade" and "The Dawn Patrol," the film adaptation of the classic "Wuthering Heights," and "Raffles," in which he played a suave thief.

With the outbreak of the Second World War in 1939, Niven was "the first star to return from Hollywood to join the British forces," according to a writer for the *Chicago Tribune.* Because of his earlier military experience Niven was called upon to serve for a time as a major in the Phantom Reconnaissance Regiment, a secret British commando unit. He saw action in Normandy, Belgium, Holland, and Germany and suffered several war injuries. On two occasions he was given leave to make British war propaganda films. At war's end, Niven was a lieutenant colonel and one of only twenty-five Britons to receive the Legion of Merit from the United States government.

With the end of the war, Niven returned to Hollywood to pick up the pieces of his film career. But he suffered both personal and business setbacks. In 1946, while playing hide-and-seek during a party at Tyrone Powers' house, Niven's wife entered what she thought was a closet. The door led to the basement steps instead; she fell in the dark and later died from her injuries, leaving Niven to raise two small sons on his own. His film career was also in a shambles. Michael Seiler of the *Los Angeles Times* reported that when Niven came back to Hollywood he mistakenly confronted his studio boss in a bid for more money. "I went to Sam Goldwyn," Niven explained, "said I was being underpaid, and asked how soon I could get out of my contract. 'The minute you reach the street,' he told me." For several years Niven was without a studio and took whatever work he could find. Roles in such films as "Stairway to Heaven" and "The Bishop's Wife" brought little critical attention, although his work in "The Moon Is Blue" won a Golden Globe Award. He made his Broadway debut with Gloria Swanson in "Nina" in 1951, but the play failed.

While Niven's acting career was floundering, his business ventures prospered. In 1952 he co-founded Four Star Television, a production company Seiler described as "hugely successful" despite its competition with the major studios. Such television programs as "The Rifleman" and "Zane Grey Theater" were among the company's biggest hits. By the early 1960s Niven was "one of the richest men in Hollywood," according to Seiler. He moved his family to Europe (he had married the Swedish model Hjoerdis Tersmeden in 1948), buying a house on the French Riviera and another one in the Swiss Alps.

Only in the late 1950s did Niven's film career pick up again. His role in 1956's "Around the World in Eighty Days" was his biggest success in many years. Based on the Jules Verne adventure story about a record-breaking journey done on a bet, "Around the World in Eighty Days" won the Academy Award for best picture of the year. The film was shot in the Todd-AO process, similar to Cinerama and other enlarged-screen techniques, and was projected onto a 26 foot by 60 foot curved screen. The process greatly enhanced the film, a nearly three hour-long extravaganza featuring a jungle safari, a hot-air balloon voyage, a bullfight, an Indian attack, and much more. Niven played the lead role of adventurer Phileas Fogg, while some 40 stars, including Peter Lorre, Frank Sinatra, Marlene Deitrich, and Buster Keaton, made cameo appearances. "It is, undeniably, quite a show," Bosley Crowther admitted in the *New York Times.* Crowther found Niven to be "excellent as the punctual Phileas Fogg." Henry Hart wrote in *Films in Review* that "Around the World in Eighty Days" was a "landmark of motion picture history. . . . There is not anywhere on this earth *any* entertainment in *any* medium that approaches the range and variety of pleasurable experiences afforded [by the film.] The human race has never before seen entertainment such as this." Hart claimed that "David Niven as Phileas Fogg suits *anyone's* conception of Fogg."

Niven followed up this success with his Academy Award-winning performance in "Separate Tables" in 1958. Set at an English seaside boarding house, the film explores the lives of several lonely and isolated people who have come to the resort to hide away. Niven played a charming retired major who, it is revealed, accosts young women in public moviehouses. After his arrest in a nearby town is reported in the local paper, the major is also revealed to be a liar; he is not a war hero or a major at all. A *Chicago Tribune* writer claimed that Niven gave a "moving portrayal of a pathetic loser." In his review of the film, Crowther wrote: "As the breezy British major who turns out to be a fraud and a particularly sad sort of person, David Niven starts weakly and gains strength, so that his final scene of gathering valor is one of the best in the film."

During the late 1950s and early 1960s Niven appeared in a string of successful films, enjoying the greatest popularity of his career. He played opposite Shirley MacLaine in the comedy "Ask Any Girl" and with Doris Day in "Please Don't Eat the Daisies." He played Corporal Miller in the World War II adventure "The Guns of Navarone," Sir Arthur Robertson in "55 Days at Peking," and the sophisticated jewel thief Sir Charles Lytton in "The Pink Panther." Several commentators have noted, however, that Niven also took roles in many films of a lesser quality, something the actor freely admitted as being necessary to pay the bills. In the eyes of some critics, this practice lowered Niven's professional status. But most observers ranked his work highly, praising his ability to bring a touch of sophisticated charm and self-deprecating humor to any part he played. As J. Y. Smith noted in the *Washington Post,* Niven "played officers, gentlemen, lovers and thieves with a charm and lightheartedness that are sure to be remembered when many of his films are not." "An enjoyable and polished film star of the second magnitude," as Gary Arnold described him in the *Washington Post,* "Niven was highly valued as a refining, finishing class attraction." A London *Times* writer called Niven "a popular star of the traditional type, establishing a screen persona that became instantly recognizable and was repeated, more or less, through film after film."

In *The Moon's a Balloon* and *Bring on the Empty Horses,* Niven recounted the story of his life and career, focusing especially on amusing anecdotes about his many friends and associates in entertainment, politics, and the arts. "I apologize for the name-dropping . . . ," he explained in *The Moon's a Balloon.* "People in my profession, who, like myself, have the good fortune to parlay a minimal talent into a long career, find all sorts of doors opened that would otherwise have remained closed. Once behind those doors, it makes little sense to write about the butler if Chairman Mao is sitting down to dinner."

Niven's storytelling skills were widely praised by the critics. John F. Baker in *Publishers Weekly* called Niven "a magnificent raconteur" in person, explaining that he "tells stories effortlessly, with superb timing, and with irresistible sound effects and mime thrown in, and it is not hard to believe, as he claims, that the writing comes easily to him, though he polishes away at it all the same." Seiler noted that the books "confirmed Niven's reputation as a raconteur. More than that, the books attested to the fact that Niven—a man of considerable charm, wit and sophistication—had an extraordinary life." Writing in the *New York Times Book Review,* William F. Buckley, Jr., described *Bring on the Empty Horses* as "what might easily be the best book ever written about Hollywood." Although pleased with the success of his books—they were both enormous bestsellers—Niven told Janet Graham of *Holiday:* "Writing scares the pants off me—it's so difficult." He explained his writing technique to Graham: "I used to wake and remember things in the middle of the night and jot them on a pad by my bed. I found it fascinating to lift up a stone in my memory and find that all sorts of little things would wriggle out that I had entirely forgotten about." When turning his hand to fiction, Niven found equal success; his novel *Go Slowly, Come Back Quickly,* the story of a married couple in the television industry and largely based on Niven's own life, was acclaimed by critics and became a bestseller.

The debonair style that endeared Niven to millions of his fans around the world was still evident at the end of his life. His nephew, Michael Wrangdah, was with Niven at the time of his death in 1983. According to the *Chicago Tribune,* Wrangdah reported that Niven's "last gesture a few minutes before he died had been to give the thumbs up sign." The gesture was typically Niven. As actress Mae West once remarked, according to Seiler, "Niven has charm where other men only have cologne."

BIOGRAPHICAL/CRITICAL SOURCES:

BOOKS

Morley, Sheridan, *The Other Side of the Moon: The Life of David Niven,* Harper, 1985.
Niven, David, *The Moon's a Balloon,* Putnam, 1971.
Niven, David, *Bring on the Empty Horses,* Putnam, 1975.

PERIODICALS

Biography News, March, 1975.
Chicago Tribune Book World, November 8, 1981.
Films and Filming, November, 1978.
Films in Review, November, 1956.
Holiday, January, 1973.
National Review, January 23, 1976.
New Yorker, October 27, 1956.
New York Times, October 18, 1956, December 19, 1958.
New York Times Book Review, September 21, 1975, December 27, 1981.
Publishers Weekly, August 25, 1975.
Times Literary Supplement, December 18, 1981.
Washington Post Book World, November 22, 1981.

OBITUARIES:

PERIODICALS

Chicago Tribune, July 30, 1983.
Detroit News, July 31, 1983.
Films and Filming, September, 1983.
Los Angeles Times, July 30, 1983.
Maclean's, August 8, 1983.
National Review, August 19, 1983.
Newsweek, August 8, 1983.
New York Times, July 30, 1983.
Time, August 8, 1983.
Times (London), July 30, 1983.
Washington Post, July 30, 1983.*

—*Sketch by Thomas Wiloch*

*   *   *

NORTON, Andrew
   See NORTON, Andre

*   *   *

NORTON, Andre 1912-
   (Andrew North; Allen Weston, a joint pseudonym)

PERSONAL: Given name Alice Mary Norton; name legally changed, 1934; born February 17, 1912, in Cleveland, Ohio; daughter of Adalbert Freely and Bertha (Stemm) Norton. *Education:* Attended Western Reserve University (now Case Western Reserve University), 1930-32. *Politics:* Republican. *Religion:* Presbyterian.

ADDRESSES: Home and office—1600 Spruce Ave., Winter Park, Fla. 32789. *Agent*—Russell Galen, Scott Meredith Literary Agency, 845 Third Ave., New York, N.Y. 10022.

CAREER: Cleveland Public Library, Cleveland, Ohio, children's librarian, 1930-41, 1942-51; Mystery House (book store and lending library), Mount Ranier, Md., owner and manager, 1941; free-lance writer, 1950—. Worked as a special librarian for a citizenship project in Washington, D.C., and at the Library of Congress, 1941. Editor, Gnome Press, 1950-58.

MEMBER: American Penwomen, Science Fiction Writers of America, American League of Writers, Swordsmen and Sorcerers Association.

AWARDS, HONORS: Award from Dutch government, 1946, for *The Sword Is Drawn;* Ohioana Juvenile Award honor book, 1950, for *Sword in Sheath;* Boys' Clubs of America Medal, 1951, for *Bullard of the Space Patrol;* Hugo Award nominations, World Science Fiction Convention, 1962, for *Star Hunter,* 1964, for *Witch World,* and 1968, for "Wizard's World"; Headliner Award, Theta Sigma Phi, 1963; Invisible Little Man Award, Westercon XVI, 1963, for sustained excellence in science fiction; Boys' Clubs of America Certificate of Merit, 1965, for *Night of Masks;* Phoenix Award, 1976, for overall achievement in science fiction; Gandalf Master of Fantasy Award, World Science Fiction Convention, 1977, for lifetime achievement; Andre Norton Award, Women Writers of Science Fiction, 1978; Balrog Fantasy Award, 1979; Ohioana Award, 1980, for body of work; named to Ohio Women's Hall of Fame, 1981; Fritz Leiber Award, 1983, for work in the field of fantasy; E. E. Smith Award, 1983; Nebula Grand Master Award, Science Fiction Writers of America, 1984, for lifetime achievement; Jules Verne Award, 1984, for work in the field of science fiction; Second Stage Lensman Award, 1987, for lifetime achievement.

WRITINGS:

SCIENCE FICTION

(Editor) Malcolm Jameson, *Bullard of the Space Patrol,* World Publishing, 1951.
Star Man's Son, 2250 A.D., Harcourt, 1952, reprinted, Del Rey, 1985, published as *Daybreak, 2250 A.D.* (bound with *Beyond Earth's Gates,* by C. M. Kuttner), Ace Books, 1954.
Star Rangers ("Central Control" series), Harcourt, 1953, reprinted, Del Rey, 1985, published as *The Last Planet,* Ace Books, 1955.
(Editor) *Space Service,* World Publishing, 1953.
(Editor) *Space Pioneers,* World Publishing, 1954.
The Stars Are Ours! ("Astra" series), World Publishing, 1954, reprinted, Ace Books, 1983.
(Under pseudonym Andrew North) *Sargasso of Space* ("Solar Queen" series), Gnome Press, 1955, published under name Andre Norton, Gollancz, 1970.
Star Guard ("Central Control" series), Harcourt, 1955, reprinted, 1984.
(Under pseudonym Andrew North) *Plague Ship* ("Solar Queen" series), Gnome Press, 1956, published under name Andre Norton, Gollancz, 1971.
The Crossroads of Time ("Time Travel" series), Ace Books, 1956, reprint edited by Jim Baen, 1985.
(Editor) *Space Police,* World Publishing, 1956.
Sea Siege, Harcourt, 1957, reprinted, Del Rey, 1987.
Star Born ("Astra" series), World Publishing, 1957.
Star Gate, Harcourt, 1958.
The Time Traders ("Time War" series), World Publishing, 1958, reprinted, Ace Books, 1987.
Galactic Derelict ("Time War" series), World Publishing, 1959, reprinted, Ace Books, 1987.
(Under pseudonym Andrew North) *Voodoo Planet* ("Solar Queen" series; also see below), Ace Books, 1959.
Secret of the Lost Race, Ace Books, 1959, (published in England as *Wolfshead,* Hale, 1977).
The Beast Master ("Beast Master" series), Harcourt, 1959.
Storm over Warlock ("Planet Warlock" series), World Publishing, 1960, reprinted, Gregg Press, 1980.
The Sioux Spaceman, Ace Books, 1960, reprinted, 1987.
Star Hunter (also see below), Ace Books, 1961.
Catseye, Harcourt, 1961, reprinted, Del Rey, 1984.
Eye of the Monster, Ace Books, 1962, reprinted, 1987.
Lord of Thunder ("Beast Master" series), Harcourt, 1962.
The Defiant Agents ("Time War" series), World Publishing, 1962, reprinted, Ace Books, 1987.
Key out of Time ("Time War" series), World Publishing, 1963, reprinted, Ace Books, 1987.
Judgment on Janus, ("Janus" series), Harcourt, 1963, reprinted, Del Rey, 1987.
Ordeal in Otherwhere ("Planet Warlock" series), Harcourt, 1964, reprinted, Gregg Press, 1980.
Night of Masks, Harcourt, 1964, reprinted, Del Rey, 1985.
The X Factor, Harcourt, 1965, reprinted, Del Rey, 1984.
Quest Crosstime ("Time Travel" series), Viking, 1965, reprinted, Ace Books, 1981 (published in England as *Crosstime Agent,* Gollancz, 1975).
Moon of Three Rings ("Moon Magic" series; Junior Literary Guild selection), Viking, 1966, reprinted, Ace Books, 1987.
Victory on Janus ("Janus" series), Harcourt, 1966, reprinted, Del Rey, 1984.
Operation Time Search, Harcourt, 1967, reprinted, Del Rey, 1985.
Dark Piper, Harcourt, 1968.

The Zero Stone ("Zero Stone" series), Viking, 1968, reprinted, Ace Books, 1985.

Uncharted Stars ("Zero Stone" series), Viking, 1969.

Postmarked the Stars ("Solar Queen" series), Harcourt, 1969, reprinted, Fawcett, 1985.

Ice Crown, Viking, 1970.

Android at Arms, Harcourt, 1971, reprinted, Del Rey, 1987.

Exiles of the Stars ("Moon Magic" series), Viking, 1971.

Breed to Come, Viking, 1972.

Here Abide Monsters, Atheneum, 1973.

Forerunner Foray (Science Fiction Book Club selection), Viking, 1973.

(Editor with Ernestine Donaldy) *Gates to Tomorrow: An Introduction to Science Fiction,* Atheneum, 1973.

Iron Cage, Viking, 1974.

The Many Worlds of Andre Norton (short stories), edited by Roger Elwood, Chilton, 1974, published as *The Book of Andre Norton,* DAW Books, 1975.

Outside, Walker & Co., 1975.

(With Michael Gilbert) *The Day of the Ness,* Walker & Co., 1975.

Knave of Dreams, Viking, 1975.

No Night without Stars, Atheneum, 1975.

Perilous Dreams (short stories), DAW Books, 1976.

Voor Loper, Ace Books, 1980.

Forerunner ("Forerunner" series), Tor Books, 1981.

Voodoo Planet [and] *Star Hunter,* Ace Books, 1983.

Forerunner: The Second Venture ("Forerunner" series), Tor Books, 1985.

Flight in Yiktor ("Moon Magic" series), Tor Books, 1986.

"STAR KA'AT" SCIENCE FICTION SERIES; WITH DOROTHY MADLEE

Star Ka'at, Walker & Co., 1976.

Star Ka'at World, Walker & Co., 1978.

Star Ka'ats and the Plant People, Walker & Co., 1979.

Star Ka'ats and the Winged Warriors, Walker & Co., 1981.

FANTASY

Rogue Reynard (juvenile), Houghton, 1947.

Huon of the Horn (juvenile), Harcourt, 1951, reprinted, Del Rey, 1987.

Steel Magic, World Publishing, 1965, published as *Gray Magic,* Scholastic Book Service, 1967.

Octagon Magic, World Publishing, 1967.

Fur Magic, World Publishing, 1968.

Dread Companion, Harcourt, 1970.

High Sorcery (short stories), Ace Books, 1970.

Dragon Magic, Crowell, 1972.

Garan the Eternal (short stories), Fantasy Publishing, 1973.

Lavender-Green Magic, Crowell, 1974.

Merlin's Mirror, DAW Books, 1975.

Wraiths of Time, Atheneum, 1976.

Red Hart Magic, Crowell, 1976.

Yurth Burden, DAW Books, 1978.

Quag Keep, Atheneum, 1978.

Zarthor's Bane, Ace Books, 1978.

(With Phyllis Miller) *Seven Spells to Sunday,* McElderry, 1979.

Iron Butterflies, Fawcett, 1980.

Moon Called, Simon & Schuster, 1982.

Wheel of Stars, Simon & Schuster, 1983.

Were-Wrath, Cheap Street, 1984.

(Editor with Robert Adams) *Magic in Ithkar,* Tor Books, 1985.

(Editor with Adams) *Magic in Ithkar, Number 2,* Tor Books, 1985.

(Editor with Adams) *Magic in Ithkar, Number 3,* Tor Books, 1986.

(Editor with Adams) *Magic in Ithkar, Number 4,* Tor Books, 1987.

The Magic Books, Signet, 1988.

Moon Mirror, Tor Books, 1989.

(Editor with Martin H. Greenberg) *Catfantastic,* DAW Books, 1989.

"WITCH WORLD" FANTASY SERIES

Witch World, Ace Books, 1963, reprinted, 1978.

Web of the Witch World, Ace Books, 1964, reprinted, 1983.

Three against the Witch World, Ace Books, 1965.

Year of the Unicorn, Ace Books, 1965, reprinted, 1989.

Warlock of the Witch World, Ace Books, 1967.

Sorceress of the Witch World, Ace Books, 1968, reprinted, 1986.

Spell of the Witch World (short stories), DAW Books, 1972, reprinted, 1987.

The Crystal Gryphon (first volume in "Gryphon" trilogy), Atheneum, 1972.

The Jargoon Pard, Atheneum, 1974.

Trey of Swords (short stories), Ace Books, 1977.

Lore of the Witch World (short stories), DAW Books, 1980.

Gryphon in Glory (second volume in "Gryphon" trilogy), Atheneum, 1981.

Horn Crown, DAW Books, 1981.

'Ware Hawk, Atheneum, 1983.

(With A. C. Crispin) *Gryphon's Eyrie* (third volume in "Gryphon" trilogy), Tor Books, 1984.

The Gate of the Cat, Ace Books, 1987.

(Editor) *Tales of the Witch World,* Tor Books, 1987.

Four from the Witch World, Tor Books, 1989.

HISTORICAL NOVELS

The Prince Commands, Appleton, 1934.

Ralestone Luck, Appleton, 1938, reprinted, Tor Books, 1988.

Follow the Drum, Penn, 1942, reprinted, Fawcett, 1981.

The Sword Is Drawn (first volume of "Swords" trilogy; Junior Literary Guild selection), Houghton, 1944, reprinted, Unicorn-Star Press, 1985.

Scarface, Harcourt, 1948.

Sword in Sheath (second volume of "Swords" trilogy), Harcourt, 1949, reprinted, Unicorn-Star Press, 1985 (published in England as *Island of the Lost,* Staples Press, 1954).

At Sword's Points (third volume of "Swords" trilogy), Harcourt, 1954, reprinted, Unicorn-Star Press, 1985.

Yankee Privateer, World Publishing, 1955.

Stand to Horse, Harcourt, 1956.

Shadow Hawk, Harcourt, 1960, reprinted, Del Rey, 1987.

Ride Proud, Rebel!, World Publishing, 1961, reprinted, Juniper, 1981.

Rebel Spurs, World Publishing, 1962.

OTHER

(With Grace Hogarth, under joint pseudonym Allen Weston) *Murder for Sale* (mystery), Hammond, 1954.

(With mother, Bertha Stemm Norton) *Bertie and May* (biography), World Publishing, 1969.

(Editor) *Small Shadows Creep: Ghost Children,* Dutton, 1974.

The White Jade Fox (gothic), Dutton, 1975.

(Editor) *Baleful Beasts and Eerie Creatures,* Rand McNally, 1976.

Velvet Shadows (gothic), Fawcett, 1977.

The Opal-Eyed Fan (gothic), Dutton, 1977.

Snow Shadow (mystery), Fawcett, 1979.

Ten Mile Treasure (juvenile mystery), Pocket Books, 1981.

(With Enid Cushing) *Caroline,* Pinnacle, 1982.

(With Miller) *House of Shadows* (mystery), Atheneum, 1984.

Stand and Deliver, Tor Books, 1984.

(With Miller) *Ride the Green Dragon* (mystery), Atheneum, 1985.

Contributor to numerous periodicals and anthologies.

WORK IN PROGRESS: The Black Trillium, a novel, with fellow fantasists Marion Zimmer Bradley and Julian May.

SIDELIGHTS: Although she has penned numerous books of historical fiction and mystery, among other kinds, Andre Norton is best known and admired for her science fiction and fantasy. Although women writers were rare in the genre when she published *Star Man's Son, 2250 A.D.* in 1952, Norton quickly became a popular favorite, with some of her books selling over a million copies each. Despite frequent critical dismissal of her work as lacking complexity, both Norton's fans and peers have recognized her contributions to science fiction: she is one of the few writers to be awarded both the Science Fiction Writers of America's Grand Master Award and science fiction fandom's equivalent, the Gandalf Award.

"Those who know Miss Norton's work well appreciate her highly," notes a *Times Literary Supplement* writer. "She belongs to the group of writers whose books appear on the list for the young as a result of shrinkage in the adult novel, although her readers might be of any age over twelve." The critic adds that "the background of her stories is a literary one and includes myth and legend and the high tone and seriousness of epic, the dark and brooding matters of tragedy." Indeed, many critics have observed that solid research is the foundation of a Norton novel, a product of her early career as a librarian. As Francis J. Molson remarks in a *Dictionary of Literary Biography* essay: "The excitement and zest of great deeds or intrepid voyaging across galactic distances readers sense in Norton's science fiction and fantasy originate within her creative and prolific imagination, especially as it draws inspiration from and refashions material she has discovered in her extensive reading and research in history and related fields."

While critics may debate Norton's literary significance, many agree that her work has been overlooked for a variety of reasons. For instance, her first books were marketed toward juvenile readers, much as the early work of Robert Heinlein had been; thus, although they were read by all ages, Norton's novels were dismissed as relatively unimportant. Charlotte Spivack, however, proposes another explanation for Norton's lack of critical attention: "Her wide reading public has simply taken Andre Norton for granted, not as the author of a single masterpiece but rather as a steadily dependent writer who is always there with a couple of entertaining new paperbacks every year," as she writes in *Merlin's Daughters: Contemporary Women Writers of Fantasy.* "The would-be critic, on the other hand, is likely to be intimidated by the vast output and remarkable variety of this prolific writer."

Donald Wollheim similarly remarks in his introduction to *The Many Worlds of Andre Norton* that while science fiction and fantasy readers "may spend a lot of time discussing the sociology and speculations of the other writers, Andre Norton they read for pleasure. This is not to say that her works lack the depth of the others, because they do not," explains the critic. "But it is that these depths form part of the natural unobtrusive background of her novels." "It is possible that the pace and suspense of Norton's storytelling may so ensnare readers that they may overlook the themes or concerns her narratives embody," states Molson. But, the critic claims, "Norton's science fiction is actually serious on the whole—sometimes even explicitly earnest and didactic—as it dramatizes several themes and concerns. In fact, one theme, above all others, is pervasive in Norton's [work]: the centrality of passage or initiation in the lives of many of her protagonists."

Elisa Kay Sparks believes this theme figures prominently in Norton's work; in a *Dictionary of Literary Biography* essay, Sparks characterizes Norton's writings as "almost always . . . center[ing] on the process by which a somehow displaced, exiled, or alienated hero or heroine finds a new home or sense of community. From the first to the last her books insist on the necessity of cooperation between equals." "Frequently," relates Roger Schlobin in the introduction to his *Andre Norton: A Primary and Secondary Bibliography,* "the protagonists must undergo a rite of passage to find self-realization." The story of *Star Man's Son, 2250 A.D.* exemplifies this theme: a young mutant, scorned by a post-war society because of his differences, quests on his own to fulfill his father's legacy; in doing so, he discovers his own self-worth. As Molson describes it, the book "speaks directly and forcefully . . . through its convincing story of a boy's passage from a questioning, unsure adolescence to confident, assured young manhood."

It is this focus on the internal struggles of her characters that makes Norton's work interesting, suggests Schlobin in *The Feminine Eye: Science Fiction and the Women Who Write It.* "Norton's reverence for the self, especially as it seeks to realize its potentials . . . is one of the major reasons why her plots are always so exciting. Her protagonists have to deal not only with dangerous external forces but also with their own maturation and personal challenges," states the critic. One such protagonist appears in *Forerunner: The Second Venture,* a 1985 work. While *Fantasy Review* contributor Carl B. Yoke finds other aspects of the story disappointing, the main character Simsa "is one of those stubbornly-independent, highly resourceful, intuitive, and intelligent characters that many of us fans have come to expect and admire in Norton's work."

In resolving this theme of self-fulfillment, Norton's work frequently expresses another idea of importance to her work: that to understand oneself, a person must come to understand and accept others. "In Norton's novels the heroic quest for self-realization ends typically in union with another," maintains Spivack. "The resolution of inner conflict is androgynous. For Norton the integration of Self and Other is of supreme importance, whether the Other is gender or species." The critic elaborates, observing that in the "Magic" series of books for younger readers, "in each case the self-knowledge of the protagonist results not only from the admission of one's own weaknesses but also from the discovery of the Other as worthy of respect." Schlobin similarly comments in his bibliography that Norton's "resolutions are androgynous: within themselves or in union with another, [Norton's characters] find the ideal combination of male and female characteristics. Most of all," continues the critic, "they discover a sanctity of ideas and ethics, and they recognize their own places within the patterns and rhythms of elemental law and carry that recognition forward into a hopeful future."

For instance, in what is her most popular series, the novels of the "Witch World," the resolution of many of the books lies in the cooperation of male and female aspects. The Witch World includes a society of female witches who remain virginal as a means of sustaining their power; this dictate is later shown to be unnecessary and even detrimental to the witches. As Spivack interprets this, "in Norton's view neither sex is complete without the other; self-fulfillment involves union with the opposite sex. Furthermore," she adds, "the relationship between the sexes should be based on equality, not domination. . . . Wholeness through balanced union of male and female, especially on the plane of values, tends to eliminate the need for aggression. Norton is thus the first of the women fantasists to combine the themes of the renunciation of power, the depolarization of values, and the vindication of mortality." Characters who reject such compromises make up a great number of Norton's antagonists, states Sparks: "Norton consistently associates evil with the denial of such bonds, or with a lack of appreciation for individuality and liberty; opportunism, willful destructiveness, and the urge to dominate through the imposition of mechanized forms of control are characteristic attributes of her villains."

Indeed, it is the mechanical, non-individualistic aspects of science that frequently provide the conflict in Norton's work; "though many of her novels are set in the future," remarks Schlobin, "she has no special affection for the technological and, in fact, science is most often the antagonist in her fiction." Rick Brooks similarly notes in *The Many Worlds of Andre Norton* that "in the battle between technology and nature, Miss Norton took a stand long before the great majority of us had any doubts. . . . Technology is a necessary evil [in her work] to get there for the adventure and to get some of the story to work. And the adventure is as much to mold her universe to her views as to entertain," adds the critic. Norton revealed the reasons behind her distrust of technology to Charles Platt in *Dream Makers Volume II: The Uncommon Men and Women Who Write Science Fiction:* "I think the human race made a bad mistake at the beginning of the Industrial Revolution. We leaped for the mechanics, and threw aside things that were just as important. We made the transition too fast. I do not like mechanical things very much," the author explained. "And I don't like a lot of the modern ways of living. I prefer to do things with my hands; and I think everybody misses that. People need the use of their hands to feel creative." Brooks further notes: "Norton consistently views the future as one where the complexity of science and technology have reduced the value of the individual. . . . So Miss Norton is actually wrestling with the prime problem, that of human worth and purpose."

While some critics, such as Brooks, observe a higher purpose in Norton's writing, they consistently remark upon the author's ability to craft an entertaining tale. "Norton is above all committed to telling a story, and she tells it in clear, effective prose," asserts Spivack. "Not given to metaphors or lyricism, her style is focused on narrative movement, dialogue, and descriptive foreground. . . . Her scenes are moving and vivid, and both the outward action and inward growth are drawn convincingly and absorbingly." Molson concurs, calling Norton "a skilled teller of stories. . . . Characteristically, her stories, either science fiction or fantasy, are replete with incident; take place in the near or far future; feature alien or bizarre life forms, futuristic technology or exotic settings." In addition, the author not only provides her readers with new and exciting concepts but also with an opportunity to visualize these notions for themselves. As *Riverside Quarterly* contributor Barry McGhan summarizes, "[one critic] claims that a prime attraction of this author's writing is that she introduces many intriguing ideas that are never completely wrapped up at the end of the book, thus leaving something to be filled in by the reader's own imagination."

Yet for all Norton's skill in creating and presenting universes to her readers, she always includes ideas of substance in her fiction.

"The sheer size of [Norton's] world, which is infinitely extended in time and space, and in which nothing is outside the bounds of possibility, is matched by the size of the themes she tackles," claims John Rowe Townsend in *A Sense of Story: Essays on Contemporary Writers for Children*. In a Norton novel, he adds, "there is always something beyond the immediate action to be reached for and thought about." Because of the breadth and scope of her work, maintains Brooks, "the chief value of Andre Norton's writing may not lie in entertainment or social commentary, but in her 're-enchanting' us with her creations that renew our linkages to all life." "Not only does she succeed in holding her reader," observes Spivack, "but her cosmos lingers in the mind, with its unforgettable images of alien species, jewels and talismans resonant with psychic powers, and magical transcendence of time and space. At the center of this original universe, with its startling variety of life forms, is the individual, alone, heroic, supremely important."

Another quality that makes Norton's science fiction memorable, as Wollheim states, is her ability to evoke the "sense of wonder" that characterizes much of the genre. "Andre Norton is at home telling us wonder stories. She is telling us that people are marvelously complex and marvelously fascinating. She is telling us that all life is good and that the universe is vast and meant to enhance our life to infinity. She is weaving an endless tapestry of a cosmos no man will ever fully understand, but among whose threads we are meant to wander forever to our personal fulfillment." The critic continues: "Basically this is what science fiction has always been about. And because she has always understood this, her audience will continue to be as ever-renewing and as nearly infinite as her subjects." Schlobin similarly concludes in *The Feminine Eye:* "Andre Norton, then, like all special writers, is more than just an author. She is a guide who leads us, the real human beings, to worlds and situations that we might very well expect to live in were we given extraordinary longevity. . . . The Norton future is an exciting realm alive with personal quests to be fulfilled and vital challenges to be overcome," Schlobin continues. "Is it any wonder that millions upon millions of readers, spanning three generations, have chosen to go with her in her travels?"

AVOCATIONAL INTERESTS: Collecting fantasy and cat figurines and paper dolls, needlework.

BIOGRAPHICAL/CRITICAL SOURCES:

BOOKS

Contemporary Literary Criticism, Volume 12, Gale, 1980.
Crouch, Marcus, *The Nesbit Tradition: The Children's Novel in England, 1945-70,* Benn, 1972.
Dictionary of Literary Biography, Gale, Volume 8: *Twentieth-Century American Science Fiction Writers,* 1981, Volume 52: *American Writers for Children since 1960: Fiction,* 1986.
Elwood, Roger, editor, *The Many Worlds of Andre Norton,* introduction by Donald Wollheim, Chilton, 1974, published as *The Book of Andre Norton,* DAW Books, 1975.
Magill, Frank N., editor, *Survey of Science Fiction Literature,* Volumes 1-5, Salem Press, 1979.
Platt, Charles, *Dream Makers Volume II: The Uncommon Men and Women Who Write Science Fiction,* Berkley Publishing, 1983.
Schlobin, Roger C., *Andre Norton,* Gregg, 1979.
Schlobin, Roger C., *Andre Norton: A Primary and Secondary Bibliography,* G. K. Hall, 1980.
Shwartz, Susan, editor, *Moonsinger's Friends: An Anthology in Honor of Andre Norton,* Bluejay Books, 1985.

Spivack, Charlotte, *Merlin's Daughters: Contemporary Women Writers of Fantasy,* Greenwood Press, 1987.
Staicar, Tom, editor, *The Feminine Eye: Science Fiction and the Women Who Write It,* Ungar, 1982.
Townsend, John Rowe, *A Sense of Story: Essays on Contemporary Writers for Children,* Lippincott, 1971.

PERIODICALS

Extrapolation, fall, 1985.
Fantasy Review, September, 1985.
Los Angeles Times, December 27, 1984.
New York Times Book Review, September 20, 1970, February 24, 1974, January 25, 1976.
Riverside Quarterly, January, 1970.
School Librarian, July, 1967.
Times Literary Supplement, June 6, 1968, June 26, 1969, October 16, 1969, July 2, 1971, April 18, 1972, April 6, 1973, September 28, 1973, July 16, 1976.

—*Sketch by Diane Telgen*

* * *

NOVAK, Robert
   See LEVINSON, Leonard

* * *

NUESSEL, Frank H(enry)   1943-

PERSONAL: Born January 22, 1943, in Evergreen Park, Ill.; son of Frank Henry and Rita Elizabeth (Aspel) Nuessel. *Education:* Thornton Junior College, A.A., 1963; Indiana University, A.B., 1965; Michigan State University, M.A., 1967; University of Illinois, Ph.D., 1973.

ADDRESSES: Home—New Albany, Ind. *Office*—Department of Classical and Modern Languages, University of Louisville, Louisville, Ky. 40292.

CAREER: Northern Illinois University, DeKalb, instructor in Spanish, 1967-70; Indiana State University, Terre Haute, assistant professor of Spanish and director of language laboratory, 1973-75; University of Louisville, Louisville, Ky., assistant professor, 1975-78, associate professor, 1978-82, professor of modern languages and linguistics, 1982—, Oppenheimer Fellow, 1985—, associate dean, College of Arts and Sciences, 1986-88.

MEMBER: Linguistic Society of America, American Association of Teachers of Spanish and Portuguese, Modern Language Association of America, Understanding Aging, Inc.

WRITINGS:

(Editor) *Linguistic Approaches to the Romance Lexicon,* Georgetown University Press, 1978.
(Editor) *Contemporary Studies in Romance Languages,* Linguistics Club, Indiana University, 1980.
(Contributor) *MLA International Bibliography,* Volume 3, Italic Linguistics, 1980-88.
(Editor) *Current Issues in Hispanic Phonology and Morphology,* Linguistics Club, Indiana University, 1985.
Theoretical Studies in Hispanic Linguistics, Linguistics Club, Indiana University, 1988.
Onomastics: An Introduction to the Study of Names, University of Toronto Press, 1989.

Contributor of about 100 articles to language, linguistic, and gerontology journals.

SIDELIGHTS: Frank H. Nuessel once told *CA:* "Many of my writings deal directly or indirectly with the topics of discrimination and censorship. In order to live in a free society, it is necessary to be vigilant against such encroachments upon personal liberty."

BIOGRAPHICAL/CRITICAL SOURCES:

PERIODICALS

Canadian Journal of Italian Studies, Volume 5, number 3, 1982.
Canadian Modern Language Journal, Volume 38, number 2, 1982.
Canadian Modern Language Review, Volume 40, number 5, 1986.
Estudios filologicos, Volume 21, 1986, Volume 23, 1988.
Hispanic Linguistics, Volume 2, number 1, 1984.
Language, Volume 56, number 1, 1980, Volume 60, number 2, 1984.
Romance Philology, Volume 35, number 2, 1981.
Year's Work in Modern Language Studies, Volume 42, 1981.

O

O'CONNER, Bert
See PAINE, Lauran (Bosworth)

*   *   *

O'CONNER, Clint
See PAINE, Lauran (Bosworth)

*   *   *

O'CONNOR, Mark 1945-

PERSONAL: Born March 19, 1945, in Melbourne, Australia; son of Kevin J. (a magistrate) and Elaine (a journalist; maiden name, Riordan) O'Connor; married Janet Eagleton (a university administrator), September 28, 1988. *Education:* University of Melbourne, B.A. (with first class honors), 1965. *Politics:* "Humanist." *Religion:* "Biologist."

ADDRESSES: Home—8 Banjine St., O'Connor, 2601, Canberra, Australia. *Agent*—Curtis Brown Ltd., P.O. Box 19, Paddington, Sydney NSW 2021, Australia.

CAREER: University of Western Australia, Perth, lecturer in English, 1966; Australian National University, Canberra, lecturer in English, 1967-68; writer, 1968—. Writer in residence, James Cook University, 1983. Has appeared or been featured on numerous Australian radio and television programs; lecturer at international conferences and festivals.

MEMBER: Australian Society of Authors (regional vice-president, 1976), Poets' Union, Australian Capital Territory Fellowship of Australian Authors (vice-president, 1974-75), Wildlife Preservation Society of Queensland.

AWARDS, HONORS: Farmers International Poetry Prize, *Poetry Australia,* 1973, for "Flight Poem," and 1975, for "Turtle Hatching"; Marten Bequest travelling scholarship for poetry, 1977; Shell-Artlook Prize for poetry, 1979; British Commonwealth Short Story Prize, 1979, for "The Black Cabaret"; Kenneth Allsop Memorial Prize for prose, London *Times,* 1980; John Shaw Nielson Poetry Prize, 1981; Canning Literary Award, 1982; Tom Collins Poetry Prize, 1983; SPACLALS Short Story Prize, 1983, for "Hunting and Living"; Charles Thatcher Prize, 1985; Sir Thomas Ramsay fellowship, 1987.

WRITINGS:

(Contributor) Harold Love, editor, *Essays in Restoration Literature,* Methuen, 1972.
"Cure of the Ring" (one-act play), first produced in Canberra, Australia, at Street Theatre Locations, March, 1973.
"Reft" (one-act play), first produced in Canberra at Act IV Festival, August, 1974.
"Dillion" (four-act play), first produced in Melbourne, Australia, at Melbourne Theatre, August, 1974.
"Scenes" (four-act play), first produced in Canberra at Australian National University, September, 1976.
Reef Poems, University of Queensland Press, 1976.
The Eating Tree (poetry), Angus & Robertson, 1980.
The Fiesta of Men (poetry), Hale & Iremonger, 1983.
Modern Australian Styles (criticism), James Cook University (Queensland, Australia), 1983.
Words on Paper (theory), James Cook University, 1983.
(Contributor) Paul Cavanagh, editor, *A Bundle of Yarns: Australian Short Stories,* Oxford University Press, 1986.
Selected Poems, Dent, 1986.
Poetry of the Mountains, Megalong, 1988.
(Editor) *Two Centuries of Australian Poetry,* Oxford University Press, 1988.

Also author of *Poetry in Pictures: The Great Barrier Reef.* Contributor of poems to numerous anthologies, including *The New Oxford Book of Australian Verse,* 1986, and *The Penguin Book of Modern Australian Verse;* contributor of articles and stories to periodicals, including the London *Times* and *Canberra Times.* Associate editor, *Canberra Poetry,* 1973-75.

WORK IN PROGRESS: A book on Europe, entitled *Journey to the Northern Antipodes;* a revision of *Words on Paper,* for Oxford University Press; poetry.

SIDELIGHTS: Australian Mark O'Connor told *CA* that in writing, "the only absolute rule, whether in prose or verse, is to say something interesting, something new, something important, and to say it memorably and well." He added that he has "a particular interest in biology, ecology, conservation, and islands," and has "spent much time on the Great Barrier Reef." This interest is reflected in such works as *Reef Poems* and *Poetry of the Mountains,* which combines photographs and verse.

AVOCATIONAL INTERESTS: Diving, gardening.

OETTINGER, Anthony Gervin 1929-

PERSONAL: Born March 29, 1929, in Nuremberg, Germany (now West Germany); immigrated to the United States, 1941; naturalized citizen, 1947; son of Albert and Marguerite (Bing) Oettinger; married Marilyn Tanner, June 20, 1954; children: Douglas, Marjorie. *Education:* Harvard University, A.B. (summa cum laude), 1951, Ph.D., 1954.

ADDRESSES: Home—65 Elizabeth Rd., Belmont, Mass. 02178. *Office*—33 Oxford St., Cambridge, Mass. 02138.

CAREER: Harvard University, Cambridge, Mass., instructor, 1955-56, assistant professor, 1957-60, associate professor, 1960-63, Gordon McKay Professor of Applied Mathematics, 1963—, professor of linguistics, 1963-75, member of government faculty, 1973—, professor of information resources policy program, 1975—, chairman of program, 1972—. Chairman, Computer Science and Engineering Board, National Academy of Sciences, 1968-73; Massachusetts Community Antenna Television Commission, commissioner, 1972-79, chairman, 1975-79; member of research advisory board, Committee for Economic Development, 1975-79; member of command control communications and intelligence board, U.S. Navy, 1978-83; member of science advisory group, Defense Communications Agency, 1979—. Consultant, Executive Office of the President of the United States, Office of Science and Technology, 1960-73, and National Security Council, 1975-81, President's Foreign Intelligence Advisory Board, 1981—; consultant to business organizations. Member of board of visitors, Defense Intelligence College, 1986—.

MEMBER: American Academy of Arts and Sciences (fellow), American Association for the Advancement of Science (fellow), Institute of Electrical and Electronics Engineers (fellow), Association for Computing Machinery (member of council, 1961-68, president, 1966-68), Society of Industrial and Applied Mathematics (member of council, 1963-67), Council on Foreign Relations, Cosmos Club (Washington), Harvard Club (New York, N.Y.), Phi Beta Kappa, Sigma Xi.

AWARDS, HONORS: Henry fellowship, Cambridge University, 1951-52; Litt.D., University of Pittsburgh, 1984.

WRITINGS:

(Contributor) W. N. Locke and A. D. Booth, editors, *Machine Translation of Language,* Wiley, 1955.
(Contributor) Reuben A. Brower, editor, *On Translation,* Harvard University Press, 1959.
Automatic Language Translation: Lexical and Technical Aspects, Harvard University Press, 1960.
(Editor) *Proceedings of a Harvard Symposium on Digital Computers,* Harvard University Press, 1962.
(With Sema Marks) *Run, Computer, Run: The Mythology of Educational Innovation,* Harvard University Press, 1969.
High and Low Politics: Information Resources for the 80's, Ballinger, 1977.
Stakes in Telecommunications Cost and Prices, Center for Information Policy Research, Harvard University, 1980.
(With Carol Weinhaus) *Players, Stakes and Politics of Regulated Competition in the Communications Infrastructure of the Information Industry,* Program on Information Resources Policy, Harvard University, 1981.
(With Weinhaus) *Behind the Telephone Debates,* Ablex Publishing, 1988.

Contributor of articles and reviews to journals in fields of machine translation, data processing, mathematics, and linguistics.

Editor, *Communications,* Association for Computing Machinery, 1964-66.

BIOGRAPHICAL/CRITICAL SOURCES:

PERIODICALS

Nation, September 1, 1969.
New York Times Book Review, September 14, 1969.

* * *

O'HARA, John (Henry) 1905-1970
(Franey Delaney)

PERSONAL: Born January 31, 1905, in Pottsville, Pa.; died of a heart attack April 11, 1970, in Princeton, N.J.; son of Patrick Henry (a physician) and Katherine Elizabeth (Delaney) O'Hara; married Helen Pettit, 1931 (divorced, 1933); married Belle Mulford Wylie, December 3, 1937 (died January, 1954); married Katherine Barnes Bryan, January 31, 1955; children: (second marriage) Wylie Delaney (Mrs. Dennis J. D. Holahan). *Education:* Attended Niagara Preparatory School, Niagara Falls, N.Y. *Religion:* None; raised as a Roman Catholic.

ADDRESSES: Home—Linebrook, R.D. 2, Princeton, N.J.

CAREER: Novelist and short story writer. *Pottsville Journal,* Pottsville, Pa., reporter, 1924-26; worked in Chicago, Ill., as an evaluating engineer, a boat steward, a steel mill worker, a soda jerk, an amusement park guard, a call boy and freight clerk for the Pennsylvania Railroad, and as a gas meter reader; worked in New York, N.Y., for various periodicals, including jobs as a rewrite man for the *Daily Mirror,* radio columnist (under pseudonym Franey Delaney) and movie critic for *Morning Telegraph,* staff member of *Time* magazine, reporter for *Herald Tribune,* and secretary to Heywood Broun; managing editor of *Pittsburgh Bulletin-Index;* became a press agent for Warner Bros., Hollywood, Calif.; film-writer, 1934 until mid-1940s. Appeared briefly as a reporter in the film "The General Died at Dawn," Paramount, 1936.

MEMBER: National Institute of Arts and Letters, Authors Guild, Dramatists Guild, Authors League of America, Screen Writers Guild, National Press Club, Silurians, Nassau Club (Princeton, N.J.), Field Club (Quogue, Long Island), Century Association, The Leash (New York), Raquet Club (Philadelphia), Beach Club (Santa Barbara), Loyal Legion (Pennsylvania commandery), National Golf Links of America (Southhampton, N.Y.), Kew-Teddington Observatory Society (Princeton), Hessian Relief Society (Princeton), Sigma Delta Chi.

AWARDS, HONORS: New York Critics Circle and Donaldson awards, 1952, both for musical "Pal Joey"; National Book Award, 1956, for *Ten North Frederick;* named honorary citizen of City of Philadelphia, 1961; Gold Medal Award of Merit for the Novel, 1964, American Academy of Arts and Letters.

WRITINGS:

NOVELS

Appointment in Samarra (also see below), Harcourt, 1934, reprinted with a new foreword by the author, Modern Library, 1953, Random House, 1982.
Butterfield 8 (also see below), Harcourt, 1935, Random House, 1982.
Hope of Heaven (also see below), Harcourt, 1938, Popular Library, 1973.
Pal Joey (also see below), Duell, 1940, Popular Library, 1976.
A Rage to Live, Random House, 1949, Popular Library, 1974.

The Farmers Hotel (novella; also see below), Random House, 1951, Popular Library, 1973.

Ten North Frederick, Random House, 1955, Popular Library, 1975.

A Family Party (novella), Random House, 1956.

From the Terrace, Random House, 1958, Popular Library, 1974.

Ourselves to Know, Random House, 1960.

The Big Laugh, Random House, 1962, Popular Library, 1977.

Elizabeth Appleton, Random House, 1963.

The Lockwood Concern, Random House, 1966.

The Instrument, Random House, 1967.

Lovey Childs: A Philadelphian's Story, Random House, 1969.

The Ewings, Random House, 1972.

The Second Ewings (fragment), Bruccoli Clark, 1977.

SHORT STORY COLLECTIONS

The Doctor's Son, and Other Stories (also see below), Harcourt, 1935, Hearst Books, c. 1962.

Files on Parade (also see below), Harcourt, 1939.

Pipe Night (also see below), preface by Wolcott Gibbs, Duell, 1945, Popular Library, 1974.

Hellbox, Random House, 1947, Popular Library, 1975.

Stories of Venial Sin, from Pipe Night, Avon, 1947.

The Great Short Stories of John O'Hara: Stories from The Doctor's Son, and Other Stories and Files on Parade, Bantam, 1956, Popular Library, 1973.

Selected Short Stories, Modern Library, 1956.

Assembly, Random House, 1961.

The Cape Cod Lighter: 23 New Short Stories, Random House, 1962.

49 Stories, Modern Library, 1962.

The Hat on the Bed, Random House, 1963.

The Horse Knows the Way, Random House, 1964.

Waiting for Winter, Random House, 1967.

And Other Stories, Random House, 1968.

The O'Hara Generation, Random House, 1969.

The Time Element, and Other Stories, Random House, 1972.

The Good Samaritan, and Other Stories, Random House, 1974.

OTHER

(Author of libretto) "Pal Joey" (two-act musical; based on O'Hara's novel of the same title; also see below), lyrics by Lorenz Hart, music by Richard Rogers, first produced on Broadway at Ethel Barrymore Theatre, December 25, 1940.

"Moontide" (screenplay), Twentieth Century-Fox, 1942.

Here's O'Hara (contains novels *Butterfield 8, Hope of Heaven,* and *Pal Joey;* and twenty short stories), Duell, 1946.

"On Our Merry Way" (screenplay; based on a story by Arch Oboler), Miracle Productions, 1948.

(With Hart) *Pal Joey: The Libretto and Lyrics,* Random House, 1952.

Sweet and Sour (essays), Random House, 1954, Popular Library, 1974.

Three Views of the Novel (lectures), [Washington], 1957.

Sermons and Soda-Water (three novellas), Volume 1: *The Girl on the Baggage Truck,* Volume 2: *Imagine Kissing Pete,* Volume 3: *We're Friends Again,* Random House, 1960.

Five Plays (also see below; contains "The Farmers Hotel," based on O'Hara's novel of the same title, "The Searching Sun," "The Champagne Pool," "Veronique," and "The Way It Was"), Random House, 1961.

Appointment in Samarra, Butterfield 8, [and] *Hope of Heaven,* Random House, 1963 (published in England as *Hope of Heaven, and Other Stories,* Hamish Hamilton, 1963).

My Turn (newspaper columns), Random House, 1967.

A Cub Tells His Story, Windhover/Bruccoli Clark, 1974.

"An Artist Is His Own Fault": John O'Hara on Writers and Writing, edited and with an introduction by Matthew J. Bruccoli, Southern Illinois University Press, 1977.

Remarks on the Novel (cassette recording), Bruccoli Clark, 1977.

The Selected Letters of John O'Hara, edited by Bruccoli, Random House, 1978.

Two by O'Hara (contains the unproduced play "Far from Heaven," and the unproduced screenplay "The Man Who Could Not Lose"), edited by Bruccoli and Carol Meyer, Harcourt/Bruccoli Clark, 1979.

Also author of play, "The Searching Sun," first produced in 1952. Author of columns "Entertainment Week," for *Newsweek,* 1940-42, "Appointment with O'Hara," for *Collier's,* 1954-56, and a column for *Holiday,* 1966. Contributor of over three hundred short stories to *New Yorker;* contributor to other periodicals.

SIDELIGHTS: The name of novelist and short story writer John O'Hara is not widely recognized today, but in the 1950s and 1960s he was one of the most popular, prolific, and financially successful authors in the United States. In the opinion of the majority of his critics, however, O'Hara's stories about upper-middle-class American social life in the first half of the twentieth century lacked the thematic depth and characterization of other authors whom he emulated: Ernest Hemingway, Sinclair Lewis, John Steinbeck, and F. Scott Fitzgerald. "Despite the great merit of his first novel [*Appointment in Samarra*] and his admirable accomplishments in the short-story form, including the *Pal Joey* sequence, O'Hara's reputation has been firmly nailed in place among the lower rungs on the ladder of literary prestige," remarked *Profiles of Modern American Authors* writer Bernard Dekle. A realist-naturalist writer, O'Hara emphasized complete objectivity in his books, writing frankly about the materialistic aspirations and sexual exploits of his characters. In order to simulate reality as much as possible, he also filled his novels with superfluous details, action, and characters. Critics often complemented the novelist on his "remarkable ear for language," as *John O'Hara* author Charles Child Walcutt called it, but felt his attention to details unimportant to plotting caused his books to lose focus. O'Hara biographer, Matthew J. Bruccoli, criticized this viewpoint of the author in his *The O'Hara Concern: A Biography of John O'Hara:* "The more-or-less grudging acknowledgement of O'Hara's 'surface reality,' " Bruccoli stated, "is intended to signal the absence of more profound qualities in his work. Fashionable critics look in vain for evidence of his commitment to relevant issues. O'Hara knew that such things have nothing to do with literature. His concern was to write truthfully and exactly about life and people." But "if it is impossible to say he was profound," as critics like *New York Times* contributor Robert F. Moss maintained, "[O'Hara] was something that, for a writer, is almost as important: irresistibly readable."

O'Hara was born to Irish Catholic parents in Pottsville, Pennsylvania, "a town dominated by a Protestant elite," according to *Dictionary of Literary Biography* contributor Charles W. Bassett. Patrick Henry O'Hara was a successful surgeon and prominent citizen in his community; his son John soon noticed, however, that there existed in Pottsville certain places where Irishmen, no matter how successful, were unwelcome. "O'Hara's Catholic faith declined in the face of Pottsville's elaborate demarcation according to wealth, class, and religion," Bassett related. Envious of the wealthy Protestants who were educated at Ivy League schools, O'Hara wanted to attend Yale himself, but was denied the opportunity when his father died unexpectedly and left the family with no money for such expenses. Instead, the future author spent a number of years working odd jobs, drinking heavily, and suffering through a brief, turbulent marriage with Helen R. Petit. His first break came when the *New Yorker* accepted some of his story submissions, which eventually encouraged O'Hara to begin his first novel. Although *Appointment in Samarra* was a great success and led to a lucrative career as a writer, O'Hara would never forget the social prejudices of Pottsville, and so this theme became dominant in his novels and short stories. "In one sense," commented James W. Tuttleton in his *The Novel of Manners in America,* "O'Hara's novels may thus be seen as the means by which he worked out his own ethnic resentment against the high and mighty in southeastern Pennsylvania."

Appointment in Samarra illustrates the tensions between the Irish Catholics and elite Protestants of the fictional town of Gibbsville, Pennsylvania, a city modeled after the author's own hometown, and in which many of his later stories would come to be set. The novel, which takes place in the 1920s, is about a Protestant Cadillac dealer, Julian English, who breaks the established social code of manners by throwing a drink in the face of an Irish bartender. This key turning point in the story marks the beginning of the end for English. He loses his other Irish customers, who regard English's behavior as an insult to their people, as well as his status as a true gentleman. The resulting loss of financial and social prestige eventually lead English to commit suicide. *Appointment in Samarra* was an instant popular success for the author, and went into five printings in its first year.

Reviewers in the 1930s, however, were shocked by the author's frank treatment of sex and social snobbery. In a 1934 *Saturday Review of Literature* article by Henry Seidel Canby, for example, the reviewer complained of a "thoroughgoing vulgarity in this book." Even one of O'Hara's literary idols, Sinclair Lewis, wrote in a following *Saturday Review of Literature* issue that "this book, for all the cleverness of is observation, the deftness of its tempo, the courage of its vocabulary, was inherently nothing but infantilism." Today, however, critics consider *Appointment in Samarra* one of O'Hara's best works, often praising the concise plotting that the author would later sacrifice in his longer, more ambitious books. As a character study, *Appointment in Samarra* is also a stronger work than later O'Hara efforts. As Edmund Wilson, author of *Classics and Commercials: A Literary Chronicle of the Forties,* remarked: "*Appointment in Samarra* is a memorable picture both of a provincial snob, a disorganized drinking-man of the twenties, and of the complexities of the social organism in which he flourished and perished."

O'Hara's success with *Appointment in Samarra* opened a door for him as a writer for Paramount Studios in Hollywood, where his ability to write smooth dialogue was put to good use. Reviewers often praised O'Hara's talent in writing dialogue. Dekle, for instance, once noted that O'Hara "hears American speech with such unparalled accuracy and authenticity that his dialogue seems to have been recorded from life rather than written." According to Bassett, however, when it came to applying this skill to the screen "O'Hara was never . . . outstanding." Nevertheless, the experiences he had while in Hollywood proved to provide valuable material for his best-selling novels *Butterfield 8* and *Hope of Heaven.* Again, these works were unfavorably reviewed by critics. *Butterfield 8,* a book about a promiscuous woman whose desire to become respectable is thwarted by her bad reputation, was called "either pointless or puerile" by *Nation* reviewer Lionel Trilling. Interestingly, Trilling later changed his mind in a *New York Times Book Review* article. As other critics had noted, he complimented O'Hara this time on his understanding of "the complex, contradictory, asymmetrical society in which we live."

O'Hara's first attempt to write for the Broadway stage received more attention than his work for the film studios. "Pal Joey," an adaptation of the author's book of the same title, featured music by Richard Rodgers and Lorenz Hart, and was an immediate hit. Its 1952 revival, which won the New York Critics Circle and Donaldson awards, was an even bigger smash and has had more performances than any other Broadway revival. "Pal Joey"'s popularity was shared among critics and audiences alike this time, and O'Hara began to believe that he had "the right stuff for the stage, particularly the musical drama," related Bassett. "Potential directors and collaborators disagreed. . . . [His following plays] turn out to be alternately talky and dull, or melodramatic and incredible."

Between the publication of *Hope of Heaven* and *A Rage to Live,* O'Hara concentrated on his short story writing for the *New Yorker,* where his abilities were more appreciated. But the author, whose life had stabilized somewhat with his marriage to Belle Mulford Wylie and the birth of his daughter, became "restive under the widely held critical estimate that he was the master only of the stereotypically oblique *New Yorker* short story," reported Bassett. Therefore, he composed what became one of his most ambitious books, *A Rage to Live.* A lengthy novel about a marriage that is destroyed after the wife commits adultery, this novel addresses almost all of the author's concerns about social stratification, materialism, and the dangers of sexual passion. In a *New York Times Book Review* interview with Harvey Breit, the novelist asserted that *A Rage to Live* was a departure from all his previous work in that the "earlier books were special books about specialized people; but this is the big one, the overall one."

But many critics felt that the novel was poorly plotted and contained too many unnecessary details. One reviewer, Brendan Gill, called the book "discursive and prolix" and that it resembled "one of those 'panoramic,' three-or-four generation novels that writers of the third and fourth magnitude turn out in such disheartening abundance." The article, which appeared in the *New Yorker,* enraged O'Hara and caused him to break relations with the magazine for eleven years. *A Rage to Live* marked the beginning of a new phase in O'Hara's career in which his novels grew increasingly in length in his effort to, as he put it in his introduction to *Imagine Kissing Pete* in *Sermons and Soda-Water,* "devote my energy and time to the last, simple, but big task of putting it [the early twentieth-century American experience] all down as well as I knew how." Many reviewers, such as *Contemporaries* author Alfred Kazin, felt that the result of this objective was a book filled with irrelevant details and characters and demonstrated that O'Hara could no longer "keep a book under control." O'Hara considered himself a realist and repeatedly defended his approach by arguing that "actuality itself, the object of his mimetic art, lacked symmetry and 'discipline,' " reported Bassett. "Because O'Hara correlated his characters so closely with their milieu and its values," Bassett later added, "he expected his readers to *want* to understand that milieu as thoroughly as possible—hence, the 'irrelevancies.' "

Of the many lengthy novels that O'Hara wrote in the 1950s and 1960s, Bassett and other critics believed *Ten North Frederick* to be his "most successful 'big' novel"; and *New York Herald Tribune Book Review* contributor Milton Rugoff was impressed by "the evident maturity of the artist who composed it." The novel "is in a way a summation of O'Hara's concern with social status," related Rugoff. *Ten North Frederick,* concerns the life of Joseph Chapin, a successful lawyer whose career, marriage, and political aspirations to become Governor of Pennsylvania have all been predetermined by his family's prominent social status. When Chapin overreaches the status that has been determined for him by aspiring to the presidency and having an affair with a woman half his age, he is destroyed. By the end of the novel, social pressures have forced him to break off his extramarital relationship, he has been cheated out of a one hundred thousand dollar campaign contribution, and he spends the rest of his life drinking himself to death. As Deborah A. Forczek observed in the *John O'Hara Journal, Ten North Frederick* clearly illustrates the novelist's belief that "social class distinctions were critical in determining an individual's fate."

Despite the fact that *Ten North Frederick* won a National Book Award, the sexual content of the novel caused it to be banned as obscene in Detroit and Albany. Sexuality had always been an important thematic part of O'Hara's works. Norman Podhoretz pointed out in his *Doings and Undoings* that the author believed "that a man is exhaustively defined by his observable behavior—by what is usually called his manner—and beyond that, by his sexual habits." But according to Bassett, the author's "vision of the mantislike female, ever ready to pounce on her sex-bewitched mate, waxes in the later fiction," as does "the sterile exploitiveness of lesbianism." The main female characters in such books as *From the Terrace, Ourselves to Know, Elizabeth Appleton,* and *Lovey Childs: A Philadelphian's Story* are drawn as conniving, snobbish, lubricious, and deadly in their ability to lure men toward self-destruction. In a 1975 *New Yorker* issue, however, a much more sympathetic Brendan Gill attributed O'Hara's treatment of his female characters to the novelist's Catholic upbringing. "Few of O'Hara's female characters are able to remain chaste for long," Gill observed; "he wrote about women and their sexual failings so often and with such relish that many reviewers accused him of seeing all women as nymphomaniacs. The truth is that his gloomy view of their weakness was but a manifestation of a profound and typically Irish Catholic disappointment" that women were not all virgins.

As O'Hara's emphasis on the sexual relationships of his characters increased, so did his concern for providing all the details he could about life in the first half of the twentieth century. This is especially evident in such works as *The Lockwood Concern* and *The Ewings,* both of which were critical failures. In a *Life* review of *The Lockwood Concern,* a book about the vision of a family's patriarchs to establish an enduring family dynasty, Conrad Knickerbocker averred that O'Hara's attention to "detail has become merely catalogue, and when the ephemera are stripped away his tales are lifeless." Characterization also became flatter in these books, according to a number of critics like Granville Hicks. "Except possibly in their sex lives," declared Hicks in a *Saturday Review* article, O'Hara's later characters "are dull people."

In his effort to write down everything he knew about twentieth century America, O'Hara's "output of words outran his considerable powers of invention," remarked *New York Times Book Review* critic Malcolm Cowley. A number of O'Hara's evaluators believed, therefore, that his shorter fiction was superior to his later novels. Short story collections like the author's *The Doctor's Son, and Other Stories* were highly acclaimed over the years. John Chamberlain, for example, glowingly reviewed *The Doctor's Son* in the *New York Times,* where he stated that in "any number of these stories, the transition from mimetic reporting to a turn of events that sharply illuminates basic character is very unobtrusively and skillfully made." Most of the stories in O'Hara's collections had been previously published in the *New Yorker,* and so when he broke relations with the magazine his short story output also diminished considerably. It was not until the publication of the three novellas comprising *Sermons and Soda-Water, The Girl on the Baggage Truck, Imagine Kissing*

Pete, and *We're Friends Again,* that the writer returned to the *New Yorker* and the short story form.

Reviewers viewed these novellas to be some of the author's finest efforts. In the *Village Voice,* for instance, Sally O'Driscoll remarked that *Imagine Kissing Pete* "is probably his best work. . . . [It] has all O'Hara's important themes, distilled and condensed, without a wrong note anywhere." Douglas Robillard similarly asserted in an *Essays in Arts and Sciences* article that the last two novellas "should stand with the best fiction that O'Hara has written." *Sermons and Soda-Water* marked a new and superior phase in O'Hara's short story writing, according to critics like Robillard, who noted that the "stories he now wrote were exciting, moving, full of a great storyteller's most polished artistry." Books like *The Cape Cod Lighter, The Hat on the Bed,* and *The Horse Knows the Way* show the author's "practiced ease with the [short story] form," said Bassett, "and . . . the quality of all three of these collections is high, higher indeed than the achievement of his novels of the same era."

Many O'Hara critics now believe that it will be for his shorter works of fiction that the author will be remembered. Robert F. Moss, for one, concluded in the *New York Times Book Review* that the author's "lean, compact short stories have generally been more admired than his poorly focused novels"; and Robillard wrote that O'Hara's short fiction "will establish O'Hara in that great storytelling tradition that is very nearly the best thing in American literature." But in the opinion of other critics, one aspect of the writer's work that exists in both his short stories and his novels makes him a significant American author: his documentation of American social history. "Even those who disliked O'Hara's work," noted *New Republic* contributor Stanley Kauffman, "conceded that he was a sharp social historian, a ruthless investigator of sexual mores and a connoisseur of cultural data." "No one," declared George Steiner in the *Yale Review,* "has captured the relevant tones and shapes of American life with greater fidelity." O'Hara, however, disliked the label of social historian, and once said in a speech he gave in London in 1967, quoted in the *Dictionary of Literary Biography Documentary Series,* that being called a social historian was dangerous "because an author so described may begin to think of himself as a social historian and fall into the habit of writing like one."

O'Hara never got over the fact that he won few awards for his work, but he was proud that his books were frequently on the best seller lists. He told his audience in 1967 that "you must not expect modesty from me. I am just as aware as anyone else that my books have sold something like 15 million copies, and I could not have attained that circulation if I had not been readable." "O'Hara was given to immodest appraisals of his talent," reported *New York Times Book Review* critic James Atlas, "but his convictions about the scope and value of his work were by no means unjustified." John O'Hara, summed up a *Time* obituary, "was indisputably one of the major figures of 20th century American literature, but as indisputably, he was an author who never quite fulfilled the promise of his talent." But even though O'Hara was not a revolutionary writer, Christopher Lehmann-Haupt argued that it is not necessarily the "path-finders" and "experimenters" who will be remembered as it is "those who stake out their own territories and draw them so accurately as to give them lives of their own. If [this] is so, then John O'Hara's huge body of work may be around much longer than we had predicted."

The largest collection of John O'Hara's manuscripts and letters is kept at the John O'Hara study of Pattee Library at Pennsylvania State University.

MEDIA ADAPTATIONS: Three of O'Hara's novels have been adapted as films: "Ten North Frederick," starring Gary Cooper, 20th Century-Fox, 1958, "Butterfield 8," starring Elizabeth Taylor, Metro-Goldwyn-Mayer, 1960, and "From the Terrace," starring Paul Newman, 20th Century-Fox, 1960.

AVOCATIONAL INTERESTS: Golf, music.

BIOGRAPHICAL/CRITICAL SOURCES:

BOOKS

Aldridge, John W., *Time to Murder and Create: The Contemporary Novel in Crisis,* McKay, 1966.
Allen, Walter, *The Modern Novel,* Dutton, 1964.
Auchincloss, Louis, *Reflections of a Jacobite,* Houghton, 1961.
Breit, Harvey, *The Writer Observed,* World Publishing, 1956.
Bruccoli, Matthew J., *The O'Hara Concern: A Biography of John O'Hara,* Random House, 1975.
Carson, E. Russell, *The Fiction of John O'Hara,* University of Pittsburgh Press, 1961.
Concise Dictionary of American Literary Biography: The Age of Maturity, 1929-1941, Gale, 1989.
Contemporary Literary Criticism, Gale, Volume 1, 1973, Volume 2, 1974, Volume 3, 1975, Volume 6, 1976, Volume 11, 1979, Volume 42, 1987.
Dekle, Bernard, *Profiles of Modern American Authors,* Tuttle, 1969.
Dictionary of Literary Biography, Volume 9: *American Novelists, 1910-1945,* Gale, 1982.
Dictionary of Literary Biography Documentary Series, Volume 2, Gale, 1982.
Grebstein, Sheldon Norman, *John O'Hara,* Twayne, 1966.
Kazin, Alfred, *Contemporaries,* Atlantic/Little, Brown, 1962.
Kazin, Alfred, *Bright Book of Life: American Novelists and Storytellers from Hemingway to Mailer,* Atlantic/Little, Brown, 1973.
Long, Robert Emmet, *John O'Hara,* Ungar, 1983.
Madden, David, editor, *Tough Guy Writers of the Thirties,* Southern Illinois University Press, 1968.
O'Hara, John, *Sermons and Soda-Water,* Random House, 1960.
O'Hara, John, *Collected Stories of John O'Hara,* Random House, 1984.
Podhoretz, Norman, *Doings and Undoings,* Farrar, Strauss, 1964.
Tuttleton, James, *The Novel of Manners in America,* Norton, 1972.
Vidal, Gore, *Reflections Upon a Sinking Ship,* Little, Brown, 1969.
Voss, Arthur, *The American Short Story: A Critical Survey,* University of Oklahoma Press, 1973.
Walcutt, Charles Child, *John O'Hara,* University of Minnesota Press, 1969.
Wilson, Edmund, *Classics and Commercials: A Literary Chronicle of the Forties,* Farrar, Strauss, 1950.

PERIODICALS

America, October 12, 1985.
Books and Bookmen, April, 1968, August, 1970, May, 1974.
Chicago Tribune Book World, February 3, 1985.
Christian Science Monitor, November 30, 1967, December 19, 1968.
Detroit News, January 5, 1972.
Esquire, August, 1969, May, 1972.
Essays in Arts and Sciences, May, 1979.
John O'Hara Journal, winter, 1979-80.
Life, November 26, 1965.

Los Angeles Times, September 10, 1985.
Los Angeles Times Book Review, February 3, 1985.
Nation, November 6, 1935, January 20, 1969, October 6, 1969.
National Observer, January 1, 1967, December 23, 1968.
New Republic, April 13, 1938, November 11, 1940, February 26, 1972, October 5, 1974.
Newsweek, April 20, 1970.
New Yorker, August 20, 1949, September 15, 1975.
New Yorker Magazine, November 6, 1978.
New York Herald Tribune, November 25, 1958, November 24, 1961.
New York Herald Tribune Book Review, November 27, 1955, April 8, 1962.
New York Times, February 21, 1935, January 4, 1952, February 27, 1960, November 13, 1967, November 27, 1968, July 8, 1970, February 29, 1972, August 9, 1978, May 14, 1984, February 18, 1985.
New York Times Book Review, March 18, 1945, September 4, 1949 (interview), November 27, 1966, November 13, 1967 (interview), November 26, 1967, November 24, 1968, November 30, 1969, February 27, 1972, March 18, 1973, August 18, 1974, October 26, 1975.
Partisan Review, March, 1950.
Publishers Weekly, November 3, 1958 (interview).
Saturday Review, November 27, 1965, November 25, 1967, November 30, 1968, August 9, 1969, March 4, 1972.
Saturday Review of Literature, August 18, 1934, October 6, 1934.
Sewanee Review, summer, 1975.
Spectator, April 27, 1974.
Times Literary Supplement, August 24, 1967, May 28, 1976.
Village Voice, December 16, 1981, February 19, 1985.
Washington Post, July 16, 1969, February 25, 1972.
Washington Post Book World, November 19, 1967, November 24, 1968, February 20, 1972, February 10, 1985.
Yale Review, spring, 1961.

OBITUARIES:

PERIODICALS

Christian Science Monitor, April 23, 1970.
New York Times, April 12, 1970, April 13, 1970.
Publishers Weekly, April 20, 1970.
San Francisco Examiner, May 25, 1970.
Time, April 20, 1970.
Variety, April 15, 1970.
Washington Post, April 12, 1970, April 29, 1970.*

—*Sketch by Kevin S. Hile*

* * *

O'KEEFE, Patrick E.
See GRACE, John Patrick

* * *

OLSON, Elder (James) 1909-

PERSONAL: Born March 9, 1909, in Chicago, Ill.; son of Elder James and Hilda (Schroeder) Olson; married Ann Elisabeth Jones, 1937 (divorced, 1948); married Geraldine Louise Hays, 1948; children: (first marriage) Ann, Elder; (second marriage) Olivia, Shelley. *Education:* University of Chicago, B.A., 1934, M.A., 1935, Ph.D., 1938.

ADDRESSES: Home—1501 Los Alamos Ave., Albequerque, N.M. 87104.

CAREER: Armour Institute of Technology, Chicago, Ill., 1935-42, instructor, 1935-39, assistant professor, 1939-42; University of Chicago, Chicago, assistant professor, 1942-48, associate professor, 1948-53, professor of English, 1954-71, distinguished service professor, 1971-77, professor emeritus, 1977—; Mahlon Powell Professor of Philosophy, University of Indiana, 1955; Patten Lecturer, Indiana University, 1965; M. D. Anderson Distinguished Professor, University of Houston, 1978-79. Rockefeller visiting professor and lecturer at other universities and colleges in the United States and abroad.

MEMBER: Societe Europeenne de Culture, International PEN.

AWARDS, HONORS: Witter Bynner Award, 1927; Guarantor's Award, *Poetry,* 1931; Friends of Literature Award, 1935, for *Thing of Sorrow;* Eunice Tietjens Memorial Award for poetry, 1953; Poetry Society of America Chap-book Award for a notable work dealing with poetry, 1955, for *The Poetry of Dylan Thomas;* joint award, Academy of American Poets and the Columbia Broadcasting System, 1986, for verse radio play "The Carnival of Animals"; Longview Foundation Award for poetry, 1958; Emily Clark Balch Award, *Virginia Quarterly Review,* 1965; Quantrell Award, University of Chicago, 1966; Academy of American Poets award, 1966; University of the Philippines distinguished service award, 1967; Society of Midland Authors award, 1976; Mary Elinore Smith Prize, *The American Scholar,* 1986; John Billings Fiske award.

WRITINGS:

General Prosody: Rhythmic, Metric, Harmonics, University of Chicago Press, 1938.
(Author of introduction) *Longinus on the Sublime, an English Translation by Benedict Einarson, and Sir Joshua Reynolds Discourses on Art,* Packard, 1945.
(Contributor) *English Institute Essays,* Columbia University Press, 1951.
(Contributor) R. S. Crane, editor, *Critics and Criticism, Ancient and Modern,* University of Chicago Press, 1952.
The Poetry of Dylan Thomas, University of Chicago Press, 1954, 2nd edition, 1961.
Tragedy and the Theory of Drama, Wayne State University Press, 1961.
The Theory of Comedy, Indiana University Press, 1968.
On Value Judgments in the Arts, and Other Essays, University of Chicago Press, 1976.

POETRY

Thing of Sorrow, Macmillan, 1934.
The Cock of Heaven, Macmillan, 1940.
The Scarecrow Christ and Other Poems, Noonday Press, 1954.
Plays and Poems: 1948-1958, University of Chicago Press, 1958, reprinted, 1975.
Collected Poems, University of Chicago Press, 1963.
Olson's Penny Arcade, University of Chicago Press, 1975.
Last Poems, University of Chicago Press, 1984.

EDITOR

American Lyric Poems: From Colonial Times to the Present, Appleton, 1964.
Aristotle's Poetics and English Literature: A Collection of Critical Essays, University of Chicago Press, 1965.
Major Voices: Twenty British and American Poets, McGraw, 1973.

OTHER

Also author of plays, "Faust: A Masque," published in *Measure: A Critical Journal,* summer, 1951, "The Sorcerer's Apprentices," published in *Western Review,* autumn, 1956, "A Crack in the Universe," published in *First Stage,* spring, 1962, and "The Abstract Tragedy: A Comedy of Masks," published in *First Stage,* summer, 1963. Author of radio verse play, "Carnival of Animals," 1958. Contributor to *Encyclopedia Britannica.* Contributor of articles and poems to *New Yorker, Poetry, Pedagogia, Modern Philology,* and other publications.

WORK IN PROGRESS: Poems; a mini-autobiography for Gale's *Contemporary Authors Autobiography Series.*

SIDELIGHTS: As a prominent member of what has been called the neo-Aristotelian school which emerged at the University of Chicago in the 1940s, the poet Elder Olson has expressed in his criticism the group's belief that the principles set down by Aristotle in the *Poetics* could be applied to contemporary literature. The group was "not exclusively Aristotelian," Olson states in *American Scholar;* to suggest otherwise, he told *CA,* "is absurd." His colleagues held a variety of critical opinions while holding in common "a concern with certain problems and a general agreement about methods we might use to solve them." He adds, "We were unanimous only in our view that Aristotle—in our interpretations of him—had certainly offered one of the many possible methods of criticism."

Olson's *Poetry of Dylan Thomas,* "the first considerable attempt to evaluate the whole body of [Thomas's] verse" as Dudley Fitts of *Saturday Review* describes it, is widely praised for its critical insights. Paul Engle of the *Chicago Tribune* finds the book "always helpful and often brilliant, making discoveries in the poetry of Thomas which not only illuminate the poems under discussion, but throw a revealing light on poetry in general." Nicholas Joost of *Commonweal* considers the study a "just and intelligent and dignified appraisal." "Olson," Jacob Korg of *Nation* writes, "leaves little doubt that he has discovered the key to an understanding of these poems."

In *The Theory of Comedy,* Olson applies Aristotelian theory to a study of comedy in literature and drama. A reviewer for *Yale Review* finds the study "Aristotelian in rigor and intended exclusiveness . . . yet freely expansive and liberally applied over a wide panorama of comic examples." He concludes that the result, unfortunately, is often "one obvious statement after another [and] a repeated pedagogic buttonholing and patronage of the reader." In contrast to this view, Kenneth Burke of the *New Republic* calls *The Theory of Comedy* "an unusually able and superior work." In the *Dictionary of Literary Biography: Modern American Critics,* James L. Battersby observes that the critic Longinus and the philosopher David Hume lend as much to the groundwork of his theories as Aristotle does. "With his pluralist convictions about the powers and limitations of all methods, Olson knows that an Aristotelian poetics *can* explain how a composite system of differentiable artistic parts—plot, character, thought, diction—achieves a particular effect, but *cannot* deal directly with, say, the faculties of artists, the nature of audiences, or the political and social functions of art." Battersby sums up Olson's accomplishment as a critic by saying Olson did more than most of his peers "to make the study of criticism and critical theory a rigorous, intellectual enterprise."

Olson's poetry, written in "strict and formal lyric forms" as Louise Bogan of the *New Yorker* states, is particularly noted for its superb craftsmanship and intelligence. Olson has avoided many of the current literary trends in favor of his own poetic concerns.

M. E. Rosenthal of the *New York Times Book Review,* in an evaluation of *Collected Poems,* writes that Olson "gives us some exquisitely sculptured, intense poems, and some others that are . . . robust. . . . Taken all together, Mr. Olson's poems are not quite a continuum, not quite in concentrated focus. Taken one at a time, they yield not only hard gems but plain human revelations." Speaking of the same collection, George Garrett of *Virginia Quarterly Review* believes that Olson's work is a "considerable achievement over a sustained period of time, and this is the sign of the true poet." Although Gilbert Sorrentino of *Book Week* finds some of the poems in the collection "hopelessly marred by archaic syntax and verbiage," he thinks that Olson's "moods and interests are varied and rich, and his intelligence is remarkable."

Critics find *Olson's Penny Arcade,* containing a verse play and poems, impressive, as well. A reviewer for *Choice* describes the play as "strong, sententious, and filled with vigor, intensity, and keen insight, characteristics usually present in all of Olson's work." The critic for *Hudson Review,* after calling the book "a rather oddly assorted volume ([but] some very good books of verse are oddly assorted)," writes that "many of the poems are excellent." He judges Olson's comic verse "Four Immensely Moral Tales" as "delightfully told." "Olson's *Penny Arcade,*" Paul Ramsey states in the *Sewanee Review,* "is a fine book, not with the fineness of gossamer, or sighs, but of ivory, of steel, of the true scholar's eyes focusing on the page. It is a privilege to be in the presence of so much intelligence, integrity, and fully controlled poetic skill."

Olson told *CA* that although some critics have identified the influence of Aristotle's *Poetics* in his poetry, he defines himself as not "exclusively 'Aristotelian.' It is equally absurd to suppose that I must have an 'innocent eye' or a 'personal voice,' or any of the other shibboleths that reviewers blindly cling to. As a poet, I am a narrative and dramatic lyricist, and I try to do whatever the poem commands me to do, whether it be in archaic or illiterate language or whatever." He composes poems according to the terms that his statements require, not according to an outside standard. He explains, "If the poem demanded that I write it in Chinese, I should have to learn Chinese. I will also compose in the strictest and most elaborate forms or the most irregular, exactly as the poem requires." Other suppositions about his writing process, he says, are "nonsense."

Speaking of Olson's stature as a poet, Joost writes in the *Chicago Tribune:* "Olson is one of those American poets who never receives publicity and the adulation awarded to flashier talents among us. But his kind of poet keeps doggedly on, developing what he has to say until we recognize it immediately as the expression of a real person and not a literary fashion."

BIOGRAPHICAL/CRITICAL SOURCES:

BOOKS

Battersby, James L., *Elder Olson: An Annotated Bibliography,* Garland, 1983.
Burke, Kenneth, *A Grammar of Motives,* Prentice-Hall, 1945.
Contemporary Poets, St. James Press, 1985.
Dictionary of Literary Biography, Gale, Volume 48: *American Poets, 1880-1945,* 1986, Volume 63: *Modern American Critics,* 1988.
Holloway, John, *The Charted Mirror: Literary and Critical Essays,* Routledge & Kegan Paul, 1960.
Lucas, Thomas E., *Elder Olson,* Twayne, 1972.
Ransom, John Crowe, *Poems and Essays,* Knopf, 1955.

PERIODICALS

American Scholar, spring, 1984.
Book Week, March 1, 1964.
Canadian Forum, September, 1954.
Catholic World, November, 1954.
Chicago Tribune, May 2, 1954, May 27, 1955, January 4, 1959.
Choice, March, 1976.
Christian Science Monitor, May 6, 1954.
Commonweal, May 14, 1954, May 21, 1976.
Comparative Literature, spring, 1963, summer, 1970.
Hudson Review, spring, 1976.
Journal of Aesthetics and Art Criticism, December, 1953.
Kenyon Review, spring, 1953.
Nation, April 24, 1954.
New Republic, March 15, 1969.
New Yorker, April 30, 1955.
New York Herald Tribune Book Review, May 23, 1954.
New York Times, May 22, 1955.
New York Times Book Review, March 8, 1964.
Poetry, June, 1955, August, 1959, June, 1964.
Quarterly Journal of Speech, October, 1969.
San Francisco Chronicle, June 13, 1954.
Saturday Review, May 1, 1954, June 18, 1955.
Spectator, August 20, 1954.
Times Literary Supplement, May 7, 1964.
Virginia Quarterly Review, spring, 1964, summer, 1976.
Yale Review, summer, 1955, summer, 1969.

—*Sketch by Marilyn K. Basel*

*　　*　　*

OLSON, Toby 1937-

PERSONAL: Name at birth, Merle Theodore Olson; born August 17, 1937, in Berwyn, Ill.; son of Merle T. Olson and Elizabeth (Skowbo) Olson Potokar (a telephone company supervisor); married Ann Yeomans, September 10, 1963 (divorced, 1965); married Miriam Meltzer (a social worker), November 27, 1966. *Education:* Occidental College, B.A., 1965; Long Island University, M.A., 1967.

ADDRESSES: Home—329 South Juniper St., Philadelphia, Pa. 19107. *Office*—Department of English, Temple University, Philadelphia, Pa. 19122.

CAREER: Long Island University, Brooklyn, N.Y., assistant professor of English, 1966-74; Friends Seminary, New York, N.Y., writer in residence, 1974-75; Temple University, Philadelphia, Pa., 1975—, began as associate professor, currently professor of English. Associate director and instructor, Aspen Writers' Workshop, 1964-67; member of faculty, New School for Social Research, 1967-75; poet in residence, State University of New York College at Cortland, 1972. Has given poetry readings all over the United States. *Military service:* U.S. Navy, surgical technician, 1957-61.

MEMBER: Coordinating Council of Literary Magazines, Poets and Writers, PEN.

AWARDS, HONORS: Creative Artists Public Service Program award, New York State Council on the Arts, 1975; Pennsylvania Governor's Award nomination, 1980; PEN/Faulkner Award, 1983, for *Seaview;* fellowships from Pennsylvania Council on the Arts, 1983, Yaddo Corporation, 1985, National Endowment for the Arts, 1985, Guggenheim Foundation, 1985, and Rockefeller Foundation, 1987.

WRITINGS:

POETRY

The Hawk-Foot Poems, Abraxas Press, 1968.
Maps, Perishable Press, 1969.
Worms into Nails, Perishable Press, 1969.
The Brand, Perishable Press, 1969.
Pig's Book, Dr. Generosity Press, 1969.
(Contributor) Robert Vas Dias, editor, *Inside Outer Space,* Doubleday, 1970.
Vectors, Membrane Press, 1972.
(Contributor) Marguerite Harris, editor, *Loves, Etc.,* Doubleday, 1973.
Fishing, Perishable Press, 1974.
The Wrestlers and Other Poems, Barlenmir House, 1974.
City, Membrane Press, 1974.
(Contributor) George Quasha, *Active Anthology,* Sumac Press, 1974.
Changing Appearance: Poems 1965-1970, Membrane Press, 1975.
Home, Membrane Press, 1976.
Three and One, Perishable Press, 1976.
Doctor Miriam, Perishable Press, 1977.
The Florence Poems, Permanent Press, 1978.
Aesthetics, Membrane Press, 1978.
Birdsongs, Perishable Press, 1980.
Two Standards, Salient Seedling Press, 1982.
Still/Quiet, Landlocked Press, 1982.
We Are the Fire: A Selection of Poems, New Directions, 1984.

OTHER

(Author of introduction) Carl Thayler, *Goodrich,* Capricorn Books, 1972.
(Author of introduction) Helen Saslow, *Arctic Summer,* Barlenmir House, 1974.
(Author of introduction) Annette Hayn, *One Armed Flyer,* Poets Press, 1976.
The Life of Jesus: An Apocryphal Novel, New Directions, 1976.
Seaview (novel), New Directions, 1982.
(Editor with Muffy E. Siegel) *Writing Talks: Views on Teaching Writing from Across the Professions,* Boynton Cook, 1983.
The Woman Who Escaped from Shame (novel), Random House, 1986.
Utah (novel), Simon & Schuster, 1987.
Dorit in Lesbos (novel), Simon & Schuster, 1990.

Also author of numerous poetry broadsides; editor of *Margins 1976* (anthology); contributor to *New Directions 25, 29, 35, 40,* and *50.* Also contributor of articles, stories, poems, and reviews to more than one hundred journals, including *Nation, Washington Post, New York Quarterly, Choice, Confrontation, Ohio Review, American Poetry Review, Caterpillar, Temblor,* and *Ninth Decade.*

SIDELIGHTS: "Toby Olson writes talk poems," asserts *Voice Literary Supplement* critic Geoffrey O'Brien, poems which are "lightly swinging conversational riffs . . . [that] move with deceptive casualness from dreams to sex to cancer to fishing." While Olson's work often uses a formal, stylized approach, his poetry deals in everyday experience, as Robert Vas Dias observes in *Poetry Information:* "Though the occasion [of Olson's verse] may at first glance seem literary, the poetry is the poetry of experience and conveys always a strong sense of place and circumstance. In fact, this is the source of the poetry's power." The critic elaborates: "The language of the poems is . . . 'natural'—not casual or sloppy, but the language of a man

talking to you or thinking aloud, having paced himself and concentrating on particulars." Thomas Meyer similarly praises the speech of Olson's poems, writing in the *American Book Review* that "I admire their language, its cadence and self-assured grammatical vigor, its bid for permanence. . . . I mean that I admire the meaningfulness of the language," the critic continues, explaining that "[*when*] these things are said in [Olson's work] is equal in worth to the act of saying them." "Olson's voice has developed into an instrument," concludes Vas Dias, "capable of giving shape in an extended form to the range of the experience of living with others (and himself)."

Olson's unique voice also distinguishes his fiction; the author's PEN/Faulkner Award-winning *Seaview,* for example, "is a very inventive work, unlike any other recent American novel in the freshness of its approach and vision," Ronald De Feo comments in the *New York Times Book Review.* Seaview is a golf course and the focus of a cross-country journey by Allen, a professional golf hustler, and his wife Melinda, who is dying of cancer and wishes to return to her birthplace in Cape Cod. The couple is being pursued by Richard, a drug dealer who supplies Melinda with her cancer medication and who wants to kill Allen for bungling a cocaine drop; the confrontation between the two men occurs at Seaview in the midst of demonstrators, protestors, nude sunbathers, and a golf tournament. In relating the progress of the journey and of Melinda's disease, Olson uses passages that "are notable for their restraint, the way they subtly suggest the cancer's steady wasting effects rather than blatantly emphasize it," states De Feo. "They are, in fact, representative of the method Mr. Olson employs throughout much of the book: a kind of intense indirectness, a concentration not so much on inner life as on externals—gestures, movements, landscapes, interiors—that reveal that life. Some of the loveliest, most affecting moments in the book simply take the form of descriptions of Allen's careful and tender handling of his wife."

Tova Reich concurs with this assessment, noting in the *New Republic* that *Seaview* "is very much a poet's novel. The images that are captured, the patterns they form, and the ideas they yield are the basic materials, and the final structure stands or falls by them." The critic remarks, however, that this poetic abundance of detail and description in Olson's novel occasionally overcomes the story: "While this technique of piling details on top of each other often produces a rich impact, the effect can also be congested and tedious, shallow and forced." This criticism notwithstanding, Reich admits that sometimes "Olson's packing of visual details builds to an effect that is just right." As De Feo relates, Olson "creates dreamlike scenes by magnifying the smallest details and actions until they appear unreal and nightmarish." Despite the power of the author's descriptions, Jamie James claims in the *American Book Review* that "it is Olson's sensitive portrayal of Allen and Melinda's relationship that makes the novel work as well as it does. He goes beyond the conventional assertion of contemporary fiction that there are unbridgeable spaces between lovers, and defines those spaces, giving them [sharp and clear] contours." James continues: "The uncommunicable is expressed as surely as the blatant," and Olson "creates scenes of powerful beauty." In their awarding statement, the PEN/Faulkner Award judges similarly applauded the author's work, as Edwin McDowell reports in the *New York Times:* "In 'Seaview,' Toby Olson has sustained with a loving attention to detail one long ending of such beauty, courage and tenderness that it is more than a match for the concluding apocalyptic assault."

In *The Woman Who Escaped from Shame,* Olson likewise "takes his start right in the middle of the ordinary, as a good writer always will, and worries his material and struggles with it to make it reveal the splendors and austerities our fantasies try to persuade us do proliferate from every common act," states *New York Times Book Review* contributor Robert Kelly. Consisting of various linked episodes, the novel traces the exploits of Paul, a surgical instrument salesman who goes to Mexico to rescue a pair of miniature horses from a pornographer. The result "is an action-adventure story, complete with cliffhangers and chases," Holly Prado describes in the *Los Angeles Times Book Review,* "but that's only the beginning. The novel weaves its way through complexities of mythology . . . [and] philosophical excursions into storytelling itself." Kelly also finds the novel's "nest of stories" revealing, for while it seems loosely linked, "the nest turns out instead to be a network, meaningfully interconnected, fascinating. We are reading a well-constructed plot where we had imagined only fable." Richard Peabody, however, believes that in its confrontational climax "the novel falters . . . [for] the final scenes are—perhaps inevitably—unconvincing." Nevertheless, the critic admits in the *Washington Post Book World* that *The Woman Who Escaped from Shame* is "nine-tenths" of a great novel, for "Olson [is] getting better and better." As Clarence Petersen notes in the *Chicago Tribune Book World,* this "invigorating combination of pursuit thriller and metaphysical novel . . . [is] the only American novel I can think of that genuinely resembles D. H. Lawrence's fiction."

Like its predecessors, Olson's novel *Utah* "starts off so unassumingly—it seems for a while that the reader is in for a string of anecdotes—that few who pick it up will be prepared for the virtuoso performance that follows," Bob Halliday maintains in the *Washington Post Book World.* The author "loves to develop ideas by playing them off against subtle variants of themselves," the critic recounts; in this novel, "Olson uses this method to weave familiar ideas and seemingly familiar plot-strands into an original and bizarrely contemporary parable." *Utah* is another story of a journey, this time of David, a masseur in search of his ex-wife and the grave of his dead roommate. Along the way David encounters several old friends, each seeking something lost of their own; the resolutions to all their searches somehow end in Utah. "But the Utah Olson describes is not the one on the map," Halliday observes. "It is a magical territory where all the novel's characters can realize gifts and possibilities that have eluded them in the past." But *New York Times Book Review* contributor Charles Johnson feels that "overexplanation" and the coincidences bringing all the characters together "strain credibility" and weaken the ending of the novel. Nevertheless, the critic acknowledges that "nothing can detract from Mr. Olson's ability to conjure gorgeous prose passages that celebrate the healing powers of friendship, the pleasures of love and lovemaking, and the inborn mystery and beauty of things in this world." "Nature is seldom more simply or convincingly evoked," comments Judith Freeman in the *Los Angeles Time Book Review,* adding that *Utah* "is, above all, a novel of immense beauty." Paul Stuewe likewise concludes in his *Quill & Quire* review that "this subtly nuanced story is almost excruciatingly sensitive and digs far deeper than [most fiction]. . . . It is highly recommended to anyone prepared to listen to a distinctive and different literary voice."

BIOGRAPHICAL/CRITICAL SOURCES:

BOOKS

Contemporary Literary Criticism, Volume 28, Gale, 1984.
Polak, Maralyn Lois, *The Writer as Celebrity: Intimate Interviews,* M. Evans, 1986.

PERIODICALS

American Book Review, February, 1980, November-December, 1982.
Chicago Tribune Book World, June 1, 1986.
Los Angeles Times Book Review, May 18, 1986, June 14, 1987.
New Republic, July 4, 1983.
New York Times, May 22, 1983.
New York Times Book Review, June 19, 1983, June 1, 1986, August 9, 1987.
Poetry Information, winter, 1976-77.
Quill & Quire, August, 1987.
Voice Literary Supplement, November, 1983, December, 1984.
Washington Post, May 22, 1983, May 23, 1983.
Washington Post Book World, June 29, 1986, August 2, 1987.

—*Sketch by Diane Telgen*

*   *   *

O'MALLEY, William J(ohn) 1931-

PERSONAL: Born August 18, 1931, in Buffalo, N.Y.; son of William John (a food distributor) and Beatrice (an office manager; maiden name, Foley) O'Malley. *Education:* Attended College of the Holy Cross, 1949-51; attended seminaries in New York, 1951-55; Fordham University, B.A., 1956, M.A., 1957; Woodstock College, B.Th., 1963, M.Div., 1964; graduate study at St. Bueno's College, 1964-65, Royal Academy of Dramatic Art, 1967, Northwestern University, 1969, and Jesuit School of Theology (Berkeley), 1974.

ADDRESSES: Home—Faber Hall, Fordham University, Bronx, N.Y. 10458.

CAREER: Entered Society of Jesus (Jesuits), 1951, ordained Roman Catholic priest, 1963; high school teacher in New York, N.Y., 1957-60; McQuaid Jesuit High School, Rochester, N.Y., English and theology teacher, 1965-86; Georgetown University, Washington, D.C., lecturer, 1986-87; Boston College, Boston, Mass., lecturer, 1986-87; Fordham Preparatory, Bronx, N.Y., English and theology teacher, 1987—. Played the role of Father Joe Dyer in film "The Exorcist," released by Warner Brothers, 1973; has acted in and directed numerous plays. Consultant to American Education Publications, 1964-68, Education Testing Service, and National Assessment of Writing, 1971-72.

AWARDS, HONORS: Best article of 1981-82, Catholic Press Association, 1982, for "Carl Sagan's Gospel of Scientism" in *America.*

WRITINGS:

An Approach to English (syllabus and teaching manuals), Buffalo Province Educational Association, 1965.
(Contributor) Robert Beauchamp, editor, *The Structure of Literature,* American Education Publications, 1969.
Meeting the Living God, Paulist/Newman, 1973, revised edition, Paulist Press, 1983.
The Fifth Week, Loyola University Press, 1976.
The Roots of Unbelief, Paulist Press, 1976.
A Book about Praying, Paulist Press, 1976.
The Living Word, Paulist Press, Volume I: *Scripture and Myth,* 1980, Volume II: *How the Gospels Work,* 1980.
The Voice of Blood, Orbis, 1980.
Phoenix: Twenty-Five Years of McQuaid Jesuit High School, Northeastern Publications, 1980.
Love and Justice, Loyola University Press, 1985.
Why Not?: Daring to Live the Challenge of Christ, Alba House, 1986.

Recruiting Christian Subversives, Communication Works, 1988.

Also author of nine unpublished books; also author of several musical adaptations of plays. Contributor to *English Journal, America, Media and Methods, National Catholic Reporter, Catholic Digest, Columbia,* and *Notre Dame Magazine.*

WORK IN PROGRESS: "I've completed: three novels about the 2,700 priests who were interned by the Nazis in Dachau from 1938 to 1945; two books on meditation; a book on ethics for public school students (which never mentions God or religion), and a book trying to explain to students that being an active Catholic does not automatically make you a slave, an idiot, or a dweeb; two novels, one about escalating pranks in a suburban school, the other about a group of monks who aren't what they seem and a band of Heavy Metal rockers into satanism."

SIDELIGHTS: William J. O'Malley told *CA:* "After 22 years, I was uprooted from a place I'd taught [in] and loved, and I thought it was the biggest tragedy of my life. Dumb. Quite the contrary, it was a most liberating gift in disguise, like getting booted out of Eden—which I would have found a deadly dull amusement park." He says he is expending every effort to "come out of my shell."

O'Malley has acted in twelve plays, directed sixty, and appeared on several national television shows in connection with his role in "The Exorcist." About his completed, but as yet unpublished, books, he adds: "All nine manuscripts make periodic stops back in my room—after spending six months each on someone's slush pile. If somebody doesn't pick one up soon, it's going to look as if the Collier brothers just moved out."

The Fifth Week has been translated into Thai, while *The Voice of Blood* has been translated into Spanish and Portuguese.

* * *

ORBEN, Robert 1927-

PERSONAL: Born March 4, 1927, in New York, N.Y.; son of Walter August and Marie (Neweceral) Orben; married Jean Louise Connelly, July 25, 1945. *Religion:* Unitarian.

ADDRESSES: Home—1200 North Nash St. #1122, Arlington, Va. 22209. *Office*—The Comedy Center, 700 Orange St., Wilmington, Del. 19801.

CAREER: Writer and consultant, 1946—; lecturer on humor in communications, 1977—. Comedy writer for Jack Paar, 1962-63, Red Skelton, 1964-70, and Dick Gregory; speechwriter for President Gerald Ford, 1974-76, director of White House speechwriting department, 1976-77. President of Comedy Center, Inc., 1971-73.

MEMBER: Writers Guild, National Press Club (Washington, D.C.).

WRITINGS:

(Editor) Dick Gregory, *From the Back of the Bus,* Dutton, 1962.
The Joke-Teller's Handbook, or 1,999 Belly Laughs, Doubleday, 1966.
The Ad-Libber's Handbook: 2000 New Laughs for Speakers, Doubleday, 1969, published as *2000 New Laughs for Speakers: The Ad-Libber's Handbook,* Gramercy, 1978.
The Encyclopedia of One-Liner Comedy, Doubleday, 1971.
2500 Jokes to Start 'Em Laughing, Doubleday, 1979.
2100 Laughs for All Occasions, Doubleday, 1983.
2400 Jokes to Brighten Your Speeches, Doubleday, 1984.
2000 Sure-Fire Jokes for Speakers and Writers, Doubleday, 1986.

Also author of more than forty humor books in the "Orben Comedy Series," including *The Encyclopedia of Patter, Patter Parade, The Emcee's Handbook, The Working Comedian's Gag-File, The Best of Current Comedy, If You Have to Be a Comic, Belly Laughs, Big Big Laughs, Calendar Comedy, Classified Comedy, Comedian's Gag File, Comedian's Professional Source-Book, Ad Libs, Bits, Boffs and Banter, Blue Ribbon, Caravan, Emcee Blockbusters, Fillers, Flip Lines, Jackpot, Laugh Package, M.C. Bits, Magic Dotes, Quickies, Showstoppers, Sight Bits, Comedy Technique, Gag Bonanza, Gag Showcase, Screamline Comedy, Spotlight on Comedy,* and *Rapid Fire Comedy.*

Contributor to magazines. Editor of *Orben's Current Comedy,* 1958-79.

WORK IN PROGRESS: A book of speech humor.

SIDELIGHTS: For over forty years, Robert Orben has provided comedy material for public speakers, entertainers, and leaders in business, politics, and community affairs through his books and his magazine, *Orben's Current Comedy.* The author began his career at the age of eighteen, when he saw a need for material for professional comedians and published *The Encyclopedia of Patter;* he progressed to writing for such show business luminaries as Red Skelton and Dick Gregory, and eventually branched out into advising political and business leaders, becoming a writer for President Gerald Ford. As Orben told Janine Ragan in *USA Today,* humor is useful to people in business and other traditionally "serious" occupations: "Laughter is an ideal tension breaker. An apt joke gives everybody involved enough time to draw back, rethink a position or reconsider an action." Orben also recognizes the importance of laughter to political candidates, commenting in *Time* that a sense of humor "is one of the attributes a good candidate must have. The good will engendered by humor goes a long way in covering his gaffes." "Humor is one of the best forms of communication known to man," the author revealed to Marjorie Hunter in the *New York Times.* "It can sooth, heal and build. If you can put someone at ease," he concluded, "you have a friend."

AVOCATIONAL INTERESTS: Travel, theater.

BIOGRAPHICAL/CRITICAL SOURCES:

PERIODICALS

Los Angeles Times, January 19, 1983.
New York Times, June 5, 1977, June 1, 1982.
Time, August 15, 1983.
USA Today, August 6, 1984.
U.S. News and World Report, December 17, 1979.

* * *

O'REILLY, Jane 1936-

PERSONAL: Born April 5, 1936, in St. Louis, Mo.; daughter of Archer (an insurance executive) and Mary Margaret (Conway) O'Reilly; children: Jan Fischer. *Education:* Radcliffe College, B.A., 1958.

ADDRESSES: Agent—Lois Wallace, Wallace & Sheil Agency, Inc., 177 East 70th St., New York, N.Y. 10021.

CAREER: New York, New York City, contributing editor, 1968-76; *Time,* New York City, contributing editor, beginning 1979. Free-lance writer, 1959—.

MEMBER: Society of American Travel Writers, National Book Critics Circle, Workers Guild of America.

AWARDS, HONORS: Missouri School of Journalism/J. C. Penney Award, 1970.

WRITINGS:

The Girl I Left Behind: The Housewife's Moment of Truth, and Other Feminist Ravings, Macmillan, 1980.

Author of weekly newspaper column, "Jane O'Reilly," for Enterprise Features, 1976-79. Contributor to periodicals, including *Atlantic, House and Garden, Ms., New Republic, Oui,* and *New York Times Book Review.*

SIDELIGHTS: A close friend to Gloria Steinem and one of the women at the center of the feminist movement, Jane O'Reilly has actively supported women's rights since the early 1970s. She has contributed articles concerning this subject to many magazines over the years, including the premier issue of *Ms.* magazine; and her book, *The Girl I Left Behind: The Housewife's Moment of Truth, and Other Feminist Ravings,* is a collection of these writings from the 1970s. But according to John Leonard of the *New York Times,* this work "is much more than a collection of her articles and columns; it is a superbly edited anthology of connections between self and society."

"The strength of the collection," comments *New York Times Book World* contributor Abigail McCarthy, "lies in Miss O'Reilly's frank introspection and her clear insights into the ambivalence, longings, discoveries, joys and fears of the woman who has chosen to live alone. Many of her personal revelations are funny and will evoke a shock of recognition in her readers." In a *Publishers Weekly* interview with Stella Dong, O'Reilly advises that "men should read *The Girl I Left Behind* from back to front because it ends with essays on political issues but starts on a personal level. And that's how men move, from being distant, objective and intellectual to the world of their emotions. Women, on the other hand, should read it from front to back because we are moving from our emotions and inner experience to try to grasp the general experience and apply it to our lives. That's what politics and public policy is all about. We can't let others take care of it for us anymore. We have to take care of that too."

BIOGRAPHICAL/CRITICAL SOURCES:

PERIODICALS

Los Angeles Times, October 8, 1980.
New York Times, September 29, 1980.
New York Times Book Review, October 12, 1980.
Publishers Weekly, October 31, 1980.
Washington Post, September 22, 1980.*

P

PAGE, Malcolm 1935-

PERSONAL: Born June 4, 1935, in York, England; son of Arthur Stanley (a bank officer) and Hilda (Jennings) Page; married Angela Maclennan, December 21, 1961; children: Christopher, Jonathan, Antony, Amanda. *Education:* Christ's College, Cambridge, B.A., 1958, M.A., 1962; Barnett House, Oxford, Dip.P. and S.A., 1959; McMaster University, M.A., 1964; University of California, Riverside, Ph.D., 1966. *Politics:* New Democratic Party.

ADDRESSES: Office—Department of English, Simon Fraser University, Burnaby, British Columbia, Canada V5A 1S6.

CAREER: Adult Education Centre, Letchworth, Hertfordshire, England, warden, 1959-63; Simon Fraser University, Burnaby, British Columbia, assistant professor, 1966-70, associate professor, 1970-86, professor of English, 1986—. *Wartime service:* National Service as conscientious objector in Friends Ambulance Unit International Service, 1953-55.

MEMBER: Association of Canadian University Teachers of English, Association for Canadian Theatre History, Canadian Association for Commonwealth Literature and Language Studies.

WRITINGS:

John Arden, Twayne, 1984.
(Compiler) *Arden on File,* Methuen, 1985.
(Compiler) *File on Stoppard,* Methuen, 1986.
Richard II, Macmillan, 1987.
(Co-compiler) *File on Sheffer,* Methuen, 1987.
(Compiler) *File on Osborne,* Methuen, 1988.
(Compiler) *File on Ayckbourn,* Methuen, 1989.

Contributor to *Contemporary Novelists* and *Contemporary Dramatists,* St. Martin's. Contributor to journals, including *Modern Drama, Theatre Quarterly, Quarterly Journal of Speech, Journal of Popular Culture, Twentieth Century Literature, Literature/Film Quarterly,* and *Novel.* Associate editor, "Writers on File"; member of editorial board, *Canadian Drama* and *Theatre History in Canada.*

WORK IN PROGRESS: A book on E. M. Forster.

PAGE, Norman 1930-

PERSONAL: Born May 8, 1930, in Kettering, England; son of Frederick Arthur and Theresa Ann (Price) Page; married Jean Hampton, March 29, 1958; children: Camilla, Benjamin, Barnaby, Matthew. *Education:* Emmanuel College, Cambridge, B.A., 1951, M.A., 1955; University of Leeds, Ph.D., 1968.

ADDRESSES: Office—Department of English Studies, University of Nottingham, Nottingham NG7 2RD, England.

CAREER: High school teacher of English in England, 1951-60; Ripon College of Education, Yorkshire, England, principal lecturer in English and head of department, 1960-69; University of Alberta, Edmonton, assistant professor, 1969-70, associate professor, 1970-75, professor of English, 1975-85; University of Nottingham, professor of modern English literature, 1985—, head of department, 1987—.

AWARDS, HONORS: Canada Council research grants, 1971, 1973, and 1975; Guggenheim fellowship, 1979-80; University of Leicester honorary visiting research fellow, 1979-80, 1982; Royal Society of Canada fellow, 1982.

WRITINGS:

(Editor) Charles Dickens, *Bleak House,* Penguin Books, 1971.
The Language of Jane Austen, Blackwell, 1972.
Speech in the English Novel, Longman, 1973, 2nd revised edition, Humanties, 1988.
(Editor) *Wilkie Collins: The Critical Heritage,* Routledge & Kegan Paul, 1974.
Thomas Hardy, Routledge & Kegan Paul, 1977.
E. M. Forster's Posthumous Fiction, University of Victoria, 1977.
(Editor) Thomas Hardy, *Jude the Obscure,* Norton, 1978.
(Editor) *Thomas Hardy: The Writer and His Background,* St. Martin's, 1980.
(Editor) *D. H. Lawrence: Interviews and Recollections,* Macmillan, 1981.
(Editor) *Nabokov: The Critical Heritage,* Routledge & Kegan Paul, 1982.
(Editor) *A Thomas Hardy Annual,* five volumes, Humanities, 1982-87.
A. E. Housman: A Critical Biography, Schocken, 1983.
(Editor) *Tennyson: Interviews and Recollections,* Barnes & Noble, 1983.

(Editor) *Henry James: Interviews and Recollections,* St. Martin's, 1984.
(Editor) *The Language of Literature,* Macmillan, 1984.
A Dickens Companion, Schocken, 1984.
A Kipling Companion, Macmillan, 1984.
(Editor) *William Golding: Novels, 1954-67,* Macmillan, 1985.
(Editor) *Byron: Interviews and Recollections,* Humanities, 1985.
A Conrad Companion, St. Martin's, 1986.
(Editor) *Dr. Johnson: Interviews and Recollections,* Barnes & Noble, 1987.
E. M. Forster, St. Martin's, 1988.
A Dickens Chronology, Macmillan, 1989.
The Thirties in Britain, Humanities, 1990.

General editor, Macmillan "Modern Novelists" and "Author Chronologies" series. Contributor of chapters to scholarly books. Contributor of articles and book reviews to professional and scholarly journals.

BIOGRAPHICAL/CRITICAL SOURCES:

PERIODICALS

Los Angeles Times Book Review, February 19, 1984.
New York Review of Books, March 15, 1984.
Times Literary Supplement, September 6, 1974, September 9, 1977, March 18, 1983, February 10, 1984, April 6, 1984, October 17, 1986, December 18, 1987, February 17, 1989.
Washington Post Book World, February 5, 1984, February 7, 1988.

*   *   *

PAINE, Lauran (Bosworth)   1916-
  (Ray Ainsbury, Roy Ainsbury, Ray Ainsworth, Roy Ainsworth, Roy Ainsworthy, Clay Allen, Rosa Almonte, A. A. Andrews, Dennis Archer, John Armour, Carter Ashby, Kathleen Bartlett, Reg Batchelor, Harry Beck, Kenneth Bedford, Will Benton, Martin Bishop, Lewis H. Bond, Jack Bonner, Frank Bosworth, Ruth Bovee, Will Bradford, Concho Bradley, Buck Bradshaw, Will Brennan, Charles Burnham, Mark Carrel, Nevada Carter, Claude Cassady, Badger Clark, Richard Clarke, Robert Clarke, Clint Custer, Amber Dana, Richard Dana, Audrey Davis, J. F. Drexler, Antoinette Duchesne, John Durham, Margot Fisher, Betty Fleck, George Flynn, Harry Foster, Joni Frost, Donn Glendenning, James Glenn, Angela Gordon, Beth Gorman, Fred Harrison, Francis Hart, Travis Hartley, Jay Hayden, Roger Hill, Helen Holt, Will Houston, Elizabeth Howard, Troy Howard, John Hunt, Jared Ingersol, Ray Kelley, Ray Kelly, Cliff Ketchum, Frank Ketchum, Jack Ketchum, John Kilgore, Frank Kimball, Ralph Kimball, Frank Koehler, Hunter Liggett, J. K. Lucas, Buck Lyon, Bruce Martin, Tom Martin, Angela Morgan, Arlene Morgan, Frank Morgan,

John Morgan, Valerie Morgan, Bert O'Conner, Clint O'Conner, Leland Rhodes, Arthur St. George, Helen Sharp, Jim Slaughter, Buck Standish, Margaret Stuart, Bruce Thomas, Buck Thompson, Russ Thompson, Barbara Thorn, P. F. Undine)

PERSONAL: Born February 25, 1916, in Duluth, Minn.; married Mona Lewellyn; children: Lauran, Jr., Robert T. (deceased). *Education:* Attended private schools in California and Illinois.

ADDRESSES: Home—P. O. Box 130, Greenview, Calif. 96037.

CAREER: Writer, 1950—. Rancher.

WRITINGS:

Adobe Empire, Hamilton & Co. (London), 1950.
The Apache Kid, Hamilton & Co., 1950.
Geronimo!, Hamilton & Co., 1950.
The Modoc War, Hamilton & Co., 1950.
Timberline, Hamilton & Co., 1950.
The Bounty Hunter, Hamilton & Co., 1955.
Californios, Hamilton & Co., 1955.
Decade of Deceit, Hamilton & Co., 1955, published as *Dakota Deathtrap,* Belmont, 1979.
Greed at Gold River, Hamilton & Co., 1955.
Kiowa-Apache, Hamilton & Co., 1955.
Lawman, Hamilton & Co., 1955.
Lord of the South Plains, Hamilton & Co., 1955.
Six-Gun Atonement, Hamilton & Co., 1955.
The Story of Buckhorn, Hamilton & Co., 1955.
Valour in the Land, Hamilton & Co., 1955.
Wake of the Moon, Hamilton & Co., 1955.
Arrowhead Rider, Arcadia House, 1956.
The Hangrope, Hamilton & Co., 1956.
Land beyond the Law, Hamilton & Co., 1956.
The Long Years, Transworld Publishers, 1956.
Rogue River Cowboy, Arcadia House, 1956.
Trail of the Freighters, Arcadia House, 1956.
Trail of the Sioux, Arcadia House, 1956.
Trail of the Hunter, Hamilton & Co., 1956.
Apache Trail, Arcadia House, 1957.
The Farthest Frontier, Transworld Publishers, 1957.
The Forbidding Land, Hamilton & Co., 1957.
Man from Butte City, Arcadia House, 1957.
The Manhunter, Hamilton & Co., 1957.
The Past Won't End, Hamilton & Co., 1957.
The Rawhiders, Hamilton & Co., 1957.
Texas Revenge, Foulsham, 1957.
Wilderness Road, Ward, Lock, 1957.
The Long War Trail, Transworld Publishers, 1957.
Man behind the Gun, Arcadia House, 1958.
Return of the Hunted, Hamilton & Co., 1958.
The San Luis Range, Ward, Lock, 1958.
The Texan Rides Alone, Foulsham, 1958.
Vengeance Trail, Foulsham, 1958.
Western Vengeance, Foulsham, 1958.
The Massacre at Mountain Meadows, Transworld Publishers, 1958.
The Fifth Horseman, Foulsham, 1959.
Range War, Foulsham, 1959.
Conquest of the Great Northwest, Robert M. McBride, 1959, (published in England as *Northwest Conquest,* Foulsham, 1959).
The Long Law Trail, Arcadia House, 1960.
Wyoming Trail, Foulsham, 1960.
The General Custer Story: The True Story of the Little Big Horn, Foulsham, 1960.

Tom Horn: Man of the West, John Long (London), 1962, Barre Publishing, 1963.

This Time Tomorrow, World Distributors, 1963.

Outpost, Ward, Lock, 1963.

The Sheepmen, Ward, Lock, 1963.

Benedict Arnold: Hero and Traitor, R. Hale, 1965.

Viet-Nam, Roy Publishers, 1965.

Texas Ben Thompson, Westernlore Press, 1966.

Warm Beer and Cold Comfort: A Yank's Eye View of Britain, R. Hale, 1968.

Bolivar, the Liberator, Roy Publishers, 1970.

A Gaggle of Ghosts, R. Hale, 1971.

The Hierarchy of Hell, Hippocrene Books, 1972.

Sex in Witchcraft, Taplinger, 1972.

Witches in Fact and Fantasy, Taplinger, 1972.

Captain John Smith and the Jamestown Story, R. Hale, 1973.

Gentleman Johnny: The Life of General John Burgoyne, R. Hale, 1973.

Saladin: A Man for All Ages, R. Hale, 1974.

The Assassin's World, Taplinger, 1975, (published in England as *The Assassins,* R. Hale, 1975).

The Terrorists, R. Hale, 1975.

Witchcraft and the Mysteries: A Grimoire, Taplinger, 1975.

The Invisible World of Espionage, R. Hale, 1976.

Mathilde Carre: Double Agent, R. Hale, 1976.

The C.I.A. at Work, R. Hale, 1977.

Double Jeopardy, R. Hale, 1978.

The Technology of Espionage, R. Hale, 1978.

Frontier Doctor, R. Hale, 1979.

Britain's Intelligence Service, R. Hale, 1979.

The Hammerhead, R. Hale, 1981.

Punchbowl Range, R. Hale, 1981.

D-Day, R. Hale, 1981.

Adobe Wells, R. Hale, 1982.

The Lord of Lost Valley, R. Hale, 1982.

Scarface, R. Hale, 1982.

Thunder Valley, R. Hale, 1982.

High Ridge Range, R. Hale, 1983.

The South Desert Trail, R. Hale, 1983.

The Trail Drive, R. Hale, 1983.

The Bordermen, R. Hale, 1984.

Skye, Walker & Co., 1984.

Tanner, Walker & Co., 1984.

The War-Wagon, R. Hale, 1984.

Zuni Country, R. Hale, 1984.

German Military Intelligence in World War II: The Abwehr, Stein & Day, 1984, (published in England as *The Abwehr,* R. Hale, 1984).

America and the Americans, R. Hale, 1984.

The Horseman, Walker & Co., 1986.

The Marshall, Walker & Co., 1986.

Silicon Spies, St. Martin's, 1986.

The Blue Basin Country, Walker & Co., 1987.

The Medicine Bow, R. Hale, 1987.

The New Mexico Heritage, Walker & Co., 1987.

Spirit Meadow, Walker & Co., 1987.

The Trail of the Hawks, R. Hale, 1987.

Nightrider's Moon, Walker & Co., 1988.

Custer Meadow, Walker & Co., 1988.

The Guns of Summer, Fawcett, 1988.

The Sheridan Stage, Fawcett, 1989.

The Taurus Gun, Walker & Co., 1989.

The Catch Colt, Fawcett, 1989.

Also author of *All Men Are Strangers, Buckskin Buccaneer, Moon Prairie, The Outcast,* and *The Renegade,* all published by Hamilton & Co.

UNDER PSEUDONYM RAY AINSBURY

When the Moon Ran Wild, World Distributors, 1962.

UNDER PSEUDONYM ROY AINSWORTHY

Focolor, R. Hale, 1973.

UNDER PSEUDONYM CLAY ALLEN

Apacheria, World Distributors, 1962.

The Tombstone Range, R. Hale, 1965.

The Guns of Bitter Creek, R. Hale, 1966.

The Iron Stirrup, R. Hale, 1966.

The Steeldust Hills, R. Hale, 1966.

Cheyenne Range, R. Hale, 1972.

Sixguns and Saddleguns, R. Hale, 1978.

Range Trouble, R. Hale, 1979.

Cougar Canyon, R. Hale, 1980.

Piute Range, R. Hale, 1981.

Oxyoke, R. Hale, 1981.

The Wagon Road, R. Hale, 1982.

UNDER PSEUDONYM ROSA ALMONTE

Love in the Clouds, R. Hale, 1967.

UNDER PSEUDONYM A. A. ANDREWS

Thunderbird Range, Gresham Books, 1963.

Under the Gun, Gresham Books, 1963.

The Six-Gun Brand, Gresham Books, 1965.

Gun Country, Gresham Books, 1965.

The Short Guns of Texas, R. Hale, 1965.

Skull Valley, Gresham Books, 1968.

The Bald Hills, Gresham Books, 1969.

The Guns of Lincoln, R. Hale, 1973.

The Cannonball Cattle Company, R. Hale, 1973.

Connall's Valley, R. Hale, 1975.

Land of Barbed Boundaries, R. Hale, 1975.

April's Guns, R. Hale, 1976.

Buffalo Township, R. Hale, 1977.

Four Aces, R. Hale, 1977.

Devil's Meadow, R. Hale, 1980.

Sixkiller, R. Hale, 1983.

Marshal Redleaf, R. Hale, 1988.

UNDER PSEUDONYM DENNIS ARCHER

Cannon's Law, R. Hale, 1978.

The Vermilion Hills, R. Hale, 1978.

Juniper Range, R. Hale, 1979.

Cloud Prairie, R. Hale, 1987.

UNDER PSEUDONYM JOHN ARMOUR

The Love of a Banker, R. Hale, 1969.

Run with the Killer, R. Hale, 1969.

A Killer's Category, R. Hale, 1973.

Murder in Hawthorn, R. Hale, 1975.

The Saturday Night Massacre, R. Hale, 1976.

The Longlance Plain, R. Hale, 1981.

Carter Valley, R. Hale, 1982.

Paloverde, R. Hale, 1983.

The Witness Tree, R. Hale, 1983.

UNDER PSEUDONYM CARTER ASHBY

Pine Ridge, R. Hale, 1980.

The Timber Trail, R. Hale, 1982.
Tenino, R. Hale, 1983.

UNDER PSEUDONYM KATHLEEN BARTLETT

Love and a Rusty Moon, R. Hale, 1968.
The Love Match, R. Hale, 1971.
Love of an Heiress, R. Hale, 1971.
Love Takes Its Choice, R. Hale, 1971.
Lovers in Autumn, R. Hale, 1972.
Love Has a Hard Heart, R. Hale, 1972.
Love in a Glass Suit, R. Hale, 1973.
The Hemstead Women, R. Hale, 1978.

UNDER PSEUDONYM REG BATCHELOR

Blue Sea and Yellow Sun, R. Hale, 1967.
The Time of Assassins, R. Hale, 1969.
Murderer's Row, R. Hale, 1970.
The Murder Game, R. Hale, 1970.
Inspector Cole, R. Hale, 1970.
The Twilight People, R. Hale, 1970.
A Legacy of Shadows, R. Hale, 1972.
The Triangle Murder, R. Hale, 1973.
Achilles' Isle, R. Hale, 1974.
Cody Jones, R. Hale, 1979.
Stolen Gold, R. Hale, 1981.
The Nighthawks, R. Hale, 1982.
Crow Range, R. Hale, 1983.
Guns of the Hunters, R. Hale, 1983.

UNDER PSEUDONYM HARRY BECK

Centre-Fire Country, R. Hale, 1965.
Desert Guns, Gresham Books, 1965.
The Blazed Trail, Gresham Books, 1966.
The Scarlet Hills, Gresham Books, 1967.
Colorado Guns, R. Hale, 1975.
Cain's Trail, R. Hale, 1976.
The Long-Rope Riders, R. Hale, 1976.
Sawgrass Range, R. Hale, 1976.
Utah Summer, R. Hale, 1977.
The Lawbreaker, R. Hale, 1977.
Casadora, R. Hale, 1977.
West of Tucumcari, R. Hale, 1978.
The Longhorns, R. Hale, 1978.
Colt's Law, R. Hale, 1978.
Baylor's Bounty, R. Hale, 1979.

UNDER PSEUDONYM KENNETH BEDFORD

The Merchant of Menace, R. Hale, 1968.
The Mathematics of Murder, Roy, 1969.
Solitaire, R. Hale, 1978.
Saddle Mountain, R. Hale, 1979.
The Hideout, R. Hale, 1980.
The Mexican Treasure, R. Hale, 1981.
The Piegan Range, R. Hale, 1982.
Eagle Valley, R. Hale, 1983.

UNDER PSEUDONYM WILL BENTON

The Man without a Gun, Gresham Books, 1961.
Rainy Valley, Gresham Books, 1962.
The Brush Country, Gresham Books, 1962.
Bushwhacker Vengeance, Gresham Books, 1964.
The Drifter, Gresham Books, 1964.
Bushwhacker's Moon, Gresham Books, 1965.
Cheyenne Pass, R. Hale, 1965.
The Buckskin Hills, Gresham Books, 1966.

Wild Horse Mesa, Gresham Books, 1967.
The Last Ride, R. Hale, 1972.
Wild Horse Pass, R. Hale, 1973.
Trouble at Lansing Ferry, R. Hale, 1973.
The Outlaw, R. Hale, 1974.
Buffalo Butte, R. Hale, 1975.
Horsethief!, R. Hale, 1975.
The Long Sleep, R. Hale, 1975.
The Horsetrader, R. Hale, 1976.
Big Mesa, R. Hale, 1976.
Cayuse Country, R. Hale, 1977.
Indian Summer, R. Hale, 1977.
Logan's Guns, St. Martin's, 1978.
The Lodgepole Trail, R. Hale, 1979.
Vaso Valley, R. Hale, 1980.
Secret Valley, R. Hale, 1982.
Rye Meadow Range, R. Hale, 1983.

UNDER PSEUDONYM MARTIN BISHOP

Evergreen, R. Hale, 1980.
Knight's Meadow, R. Hale, 1982.
Hardin's Valley, R. Hale, 1983.
The Fourth Horseman, R. Hale, 1989.

UNDER PSEUDONYM LEWIS H. BOND

Ohlund's Raiders, R. Hale, 1979.
Black Rock, R. Hale, 1982.

UNDER PSEUDONYM JACK BONNER

Red Autumn, R. Hale, 1979.
The Lalo Trail, R. Hale, 1980.
Surprise Attack, R. Hale, 1981.
The Trail Rider, R. Hale, 1982.
The Fenwick Stage, R. Hale, 1983.
The Cache Hunter, R. Hale, 1984.
Buffalo Grass, R. Hale, 1986.
The Evening Gun, R. Hale, 1987.
The Trail to Nowhere, R. Hale, 1987.
The Shadow Horseman, R. Hale, 1988.

UNDER PSEUDONYM FRANK BOSWORTH

Hangtown, R. Hale, 1964.
Trail to Deming, R. Hale, 1965.
The Purple Plain, R. Hale, 1966.
The Loser, R. Hale, 1967.
Bags and Saddles, R. Hale, 1967.
The Guns of Big Valley, R. Hale, 1967.
Murder Now, Pay Later, R. Hale, 1969.
The Long-Riders, R. Hale, 1971.
Mustang Mesa, R. Hale, 1971.
The Singing Wind Trail, R. Hale, 1971.
Rainey Valley, R. Hale, 1971.
The South Slope, R. Hale, 1972.
Sunday's Guns, R. Hale, 1972.
Bear-Claw Range, R. Hale, 1973.
Riders in the Dusk, R. Hale, 1974.
The Rogue Hills, R. Hale, 1976.
Stranger's Trail, R. Hale, 1978.
Barling's Guns, R. Hale, 1980.
The Bountymen, R. Hale, 1981.
Rawhide, R. Hale, 1982.
The Brand Tree, R. Hale, 1986.
The Oxyoke, R. Hale, 1987.

UNDER PSEUDONYM RUTH BOVEE

Angelina, R. Hale, 1967.
Antoinette, R. Hale, 1968.
The Lady and the Moon, R. Hale, 1968.
Love and a Dark Night, R. Hale, 1971.
A Heart of Shadows, R. Hale, 1974.

UNDER PSEUDONYM WILL BRADFORD

The Time of the Texan, Gresham Books, 1962.
Range of the Winter Moon, Gresham Books, 1964.
Rustler's Moon, R. Hale, 1964.
The Last Gun, Gresham Books, 1965.
Ambush Canyon, Gresham Books, 1965.
The Fast-Draw Men, Gresham Books, 1966.
Avenger's Trail, Gresham Books, 1967.
The Left-Hand Gun, R. Hale, 1972.
Land of Low Hills, R. Hale, 1973.
Cache Valley Guns, R. Hale, 1973.
Squatter's Rights, R. Hale, 1973.
The Dawnrider, R. Hale, 1974.
Gunhill, R. Hale, 1975.
The Butte Country, R. Hale, 1975.
The Legend of Lost Valley, R. Hale, 1975.
Lodgepole Range, R. Hale, 1976.
The Sundowners, R. Hale, 1976.
Lightning Strike, R. Hale, 1977.
Outlaw Town, R. Hale, 1977.
Buffalo Gun, R. Hale, 1980.
The Hangrope Posse, R. Hale, 1982.
The Prisoner of Lonesome Valley, R. Hale, 1984.
The Squaw Blanket, R. Hale, 1987.
The Sand Painting, R. Hale, 1987.
High Lift Trail, R. Hale, 1987.

UNDER PSEUDONYM CONCHO BRADLEY

Lynch Law, R. Hale, 1964.
Guns of Arizona, R. Hale, 1965.
Johnny Colt, R. Hale, 1966.
Land of Long Rifles, R. Hale, 1966.
The Scattergun Men, R. Hale, 1967.
Winchester Hills, R. Hale, 1967.
The Cactus Country, R. Hale, 1972.
A Gunman's Code, R. Hale, 1974.
The Guns of San Angelo, R. Hale, 1975.
The Killer's Legacy, R. Hale, 1975.
Culpepper County, R. Hale, 1975.
Carleton's Meadow, R. Hale, 1976.
The Blue Hills, R. Hale, 1976.
Raider's Moon, R. Hale, 1976.
The Juniper Shadow, R. Hale, 1977.
Return to the South Desert, R. Hale, 1980.
Wyoming Springtime, R. Hale, 1980.
Copperdust Valley, R. Hale, 1982.
Moon Meadow, R. Hale, 1986.

UNDER PSEUDONYM BUCK BRADSHAW

Forbes Prairie, R. Hale, 1984.
Sweetwater, R. Hale, 1984.
Graveyard Meadow, R. Hale, 1985.
Pine Mountain, R. Hale, 1986.
The Tomahawk, R. Hale, 1986.
Trouble at Valverde, R. Hale, 1987.

UNDER PSEUDONYM WILL BRENNAN

The Flint Hills, Gresham Books, 1963.

Jubelo Junction, Gresham Books, 1964.
The Savage Land, Gresham Books, 1964.
Way of the Outlaw, Gresham Books, 1965.
The Guns of Nevada, Gresham Books, 1966.
Gunman's Moon, Gresham Books, 1967.
Muleshoe Range, R. Hale, 1972.
Black Rock Range, R. Hale, 1973.
Rustler's Law, R. Hale, 1973.
The Gunsight Incident, R. Hale, 1974.
Scarface, R. Hale, 1975.
The Ghost Rider, R. Hale, 1977.
The Border Pawn, R. Hale, 1977.
Quade, R. Hale, 1980.
Cowman's Vengeance, R. Hale, 1982.
Round Rock Range, R. Hale, 1986.
The Hourglass, R. Hale, 1987.
Cheyenne Dawn, R. Hale, 1987.
Wolf Country, R. Hale, 1987.

UNDER PSEUDONYM CHARLES BURNHAM

Montana Moon, R. Hale, 1980.
Blackfeet Country, R. Hale, 1982.
The Mustang, R. Hale, 1987.
Sage City, R. Hale, 1987.

UNDER PSEUDONYM MARK CARREL

Comancheria, Hamilton & Co., 1950.
El Vengador!, Hamilton & Co., 1950.
Land of the Harmattan, Hamilton & Co., 1955.
Last of the Balfreys, Hamilton & Co., 1955.
The Oldest Treachery, Hamilton & Co., 1955.
The Sinister Horde, Hamilton & Co., 1955.
Case of the Hollow Man, Foulsham, 1958.
The Hangrope's Shadow, Ward, Lock, 1959.
Case of the Innocent Witness, Foulsham, 1959.
The Case of the Perfect Alibi, Foulsham, 1960.
Carry a Gun, Foulsham, 1961.
The Blood-Pit, R. Hale, 1967.
The Dark Edge of Violence, R. Hale, 1967.
Shadow of a Hawk, R. Hale, 1967.
A Sword of Silk, R. Hale, 1967.
Tears of Blood, R. Hale, 1967.
The Steel Mask, R. Hale, 1968.
Kill and Be Damned, R. Hale, 1970.
The Emerald Heart, R. Hale, 1971.
A Crack in Time, R. Hale, 1971.
Another View, R. Hale, 1972.
The Undine, R. Hale, 1972.
Counsel for the Killer, R. Hale, 1972.
Bannister's Z-Matter, R. Hale, 1973.
One Last Time, R. Hale, 1973.
Murder without Motive, R. Hale, 1974.
The Octopus' Shadow, R. Hale, 1974.
Assignment for Trouble, R. Hale, 1974.
The Underground Men, R. Hale, 1975.

Also author, under pseudonym Mark Carrel, of *Comanche Trail,* *The Hate Trail,* and *Wagon Train,* all published by Hamilton & Co.

UNDER PSEUDONYM NEVADA CARTER

Texan Fast Gun, Gresham Books, 1963.
Perdition Wells, Gresham Books, 1964.
Perdition Range, Gresham Books, 1964.
Frontier Steel, Gresham Books, 1965.
Hangtown Sheriff, Gresham Books, 1966.

The Chaparral Trail, Gresham Books, 1967.
The Outsiders, Gresham Books, 1968.
The Gunsight Range, R. Hale, 1972.
The Green Hills, R. Hale, 1973.
A Man Called Faro, R. Hale, 1974.
The Badlands Trail, R. Hale, 1975.
Fugitive Trail, R. Hale, 1975.
The Lost Trail, R. Hale, 1977.
Buffalo Range, R. Hale, 1980.
The Horse Camp, R. Hale, 1986.

UNDER PSEUDONYM CLAUDE CASSADY

The Prairie Fighter, R. Hale, 1963.
The Law of Langley Valley, R. Hale, 1964.
The Outriders, R. Hale, 1965.
The Man from Cody County, R. Hale, 1966.
Sunset Guns, R. Hale, 1966.
Sunset Marshal, R. Hale, 1966.
Monday's Guns, R. Hale, 1967.
Bounty Hunters' Range, R. Hale, 1967.
The Hideout, R. Hale, 1977.
The Man from Tucson, R. Hale, 1978.

UNDER PSEUDONYM BADGER CLARK

Cow-Country Killer, R. Hale, 1976.
Round Mountain Range, R. Hale, 1976.
Trouble at Fenmore, R. Hale, 1976.
Pawnee Dawn, R. Hale, 1977.
Phantom Canyon, R. Hale, 1977.
Secret Mesa, R. Hale, 1977.
Singleton, R. Hale, 1978.

UNDER PSEUDONYM RICHARD CLARKE

Identity of a Lover, R. Hale, 1969.
The Shoshone Trail, R. Hale, 1980.
The Copperdust Hills, Walker & Co., 1983.
Pinon Country, R. Hale, 1983.
The Homesteaders, Walker & Co., 1986, published under name
    Lauran Paine, Thorndike Press, 1986.
The Peralta Country, Walker & Co., 1987.
The Arrowhead Cattle Company, Walker & Co., 1988.
The Arizona Panhandle, Walker & Co., 1989.

UNDER PSEUDONYM ROBERT CLARKE

The Case of the Gambler's Corpse, R. Hale, 1969.
Murderers Are Silent, R. Hale, 1969.
Love in New England, R. Hale, 1970.
Death of a Flower Child, R. Hale, 1970.
The 13th Lover, R. Hale, 1970.
A Synonym for Murder, R. Hale, 1972.

UNDER PSEUDONYM CLINT CUSTER

Apache Wells, Gresham Books, 1964.
Ute Peak Country, Gresham Books, 1964.
Webb County Sheriff, Gresham Books, 1965.
Night of the Gunman, Gresham Books, 1966.
Sixguns and Sam Logan, Gresham Books, 1966.
The Wells of San Saba, R. Hale, 1967.
Gila Bend, R. Hale, 1976.
Matanzas, R. Hale, 1986.

UNDER PSEUDONYM AMBER DANA

Love and Company, R. Hale, 1969.
Love Is a Red Rose, R. Hale, 1969.
Love Is Forever, R. Hale, 1969.

One Love for Summer, R. Hale, 1969.
The Widow Is a Temptress, R. Hale, 1969.
Helen of Troydon, R. Hale, 1970.
Love Is Triumph, R. Hale, 1970.
A Rich Girl's Love, R. Hale, 1970.
The Queen of Hearts, R. Hale, 1971.
A Rose without Love, R. Hale, 1973.
A Scarlet Dawn, R. Hale, 1978.
The Kiss of Life, R. Hale, 1980.
The Jade Moon, R. Hale, 1981.

UNDER PSEUDONYM RICHARD DANA

Death of a Millionaire, R. Hale, 1969.
Murder in Paradise, R. Hale, 1969.
Murderer's Moon, R. Hale, 1969.
Death Was the Echo, R. Hale, 1975.
The Long Ride, R. Hale, 1980.
Mandan Valley, R. Hale, 1981.
Shadow Valley, R. Hale, 1982.

UNDER PSEUDONYM AUDREY DAVIS

Love by Starlight, R. Hale, 1968.
Love In Eden, R. Hale, 1973.
A Favoured Dawn, R. Hale, 1974.
An Autumn to Remember, R. Hale, 1976.

UNDER PSEUDONYM J. F. DREXLER

The Anonymous Assassin, R. Hale, 1968.
The Fire Ant, R. Hale, 1975.
The Unsuspecting Victim, R. Hale, 1976.

UNDER PSEUDONYM ANTOINETTE DUCHESNE

Love Is a Triangle, R. Hale, 1967.
Decision to Love, R. Hale, 1968.
Love Is the Enemy, R. Hale, 1968.

UNDER PSEUDONYM JOHN DURHAM

Hate Trail to Idaho, Gresham Books, 1963.
Shoot-Out, Gresham Books, 1963.
Caprock Vengeance, Gresham Books, 1964.
The Border Guns, Gresham Books, 1965, published as *Arizona
    Drifter,* Arcadia House, 1966.
Catch and Kill!, Gresham Books, 1966.
Guns Along the Border, Gresham Books, 1966.
The Killer-Gun, Gresham Books, 1967.
Apache Moon, R. Hale, 1972.
Sundown, R. Hale, 1973.
The Buckaroo, R. Hale, 1974.
The Cowtown Debt, R. Hale, 1974.
The Purple Mesa, R. Hale, 1975.
Caine's Range, R. Hale, 1975.
The Arapahoe Trail, R. Hale, 1976.
Circle H Range, R. Hale, 1976.
Signal Rock Range, R. Hale, 1977.
Tomahawk Meadow, R. Hale, 1977.
Nightrider's Moon, R. Hale, 1977.
The Reluctant Partner, St. Martin's, 1978.
Bound Out, R. Hale, 1979.
Cottonwood, R. Hale, 1980.
The Horsebreaker, R. Hale, 1981.
The Tennyson Rifle, R. Hale, 1982.

UNDER PSEUDONYM MARGOT FISHER

The Maltese Moon, R. Hale, 1968.

UNDER PSEUDONYM BETTY FLECK

Under a Dark Moon, R. Hale, 1967.
Love and a Winter Moon, R. Hale, 1968.
The Love Thief, R. Hale, 1968.
A Rose for Love, R. Hale, 1968.
The Love That Never Was, R. Hale, 1969.
A Different Kind of Marriage, R. Hale, 1970.

UNDER PSEUDONYM GEORGE FLYNN

Rancheria, St. Martin's, 1979.
Colorado Stage, R. Hale, 1982.
The Titusville Country, R. Hale, 1989.

UNDER PSEUDONYM HARRY FOSTER

The Gunbearers, R. Hale, 1979.
Canbyville, R. Hale, 1980.
The Mud Wagon, R. Hale, 1981.
The Mexican Gun, R. Hale, 1989.

UNDER PSEUDONYM JONI FROST

A Girl in Blue, R. Hale, 1968.
To Face the Sun, R. Hale, 1968.

UNDER PSEUDONYM DONN GLENDENNING

The Border Country, R. Hale, 1963.
The Hashknife, R. Hale, 1964.
Thunder Pass, R. Hale, 1966.
Salt-Lick Range, R. Hale, 1967.
Shadow Valley, R. Hale, 1976.
High Ridge Country, R. Hale, 1977.
The Hunter of Faro Canyon, R. Hale, 1977.

UNDER PSEUDONYM JAMES GLENN

The Law Behind the Gun, Gresham Books, 1962.
Last of the Gunmen, Gresham Books, 1963.
Gun Town, Gresham Books, 1964.
Guns of the Hunter, Gresham Books, 1965.
Longhorn Trail, Gresham Books, 1966.
Oregon Guns, Gresham Books, 1966.
The Border Men, Gresham Books, 1967.
The Guns of Autumn, Gresham Books, 1967.
Broken Wheel Range, Gresham Books, 1968.
The Big Sky Trail, R. Hale, 1976.
Stedman's Law, R. Hale, 1977.
The Tumbleweed Stage, R. Hale, 1977.
The Law Trail, R. Hale, 1978.

UNDER PSEUDONYM ANGELA GORDON

Fate of the Lovers, R. Hale, 1968.
Heart of a Widow, R. Hale, 1968.
The Little Goddess, R. Hale, 1968.
Love Has Many Faces, R. Hale, 1969.
Love Is a Tempest, R. Hale, 1969.
Not without Love, R. Hale, 1969.
A Game Called Love, R. Hale, 1970.
Jacqueline, R. Hale, 1970.
Love in Her Life, R. Hale, 1970.
The Love of Damocles, R. Hale, 1971.
Love on the Moors, R. Hale, 1973.
The Love Harvest, R. Hale, 1974.
Stranger in the Shadows, R. Hale, 1974.
Carlotta, R. Hale, 1976.
Autumn Gold, R. Hale, 1978.
The House on Sorrel Lane, R. Hale, 1978.
Forbidden Autumn, R. Hale, 1979.

A Gentle Spring, R. Hale, 1980.
Misty's Mother, R. Hale, 1980.

UNDER PSEUDONYM BETH GORMAN

Lanterns in the Night, R. Hale, 1967.
Gentle Lover, R. Hale, 1968.
Love Is a Stranger, R. Hale, 1968.
Love Has a Golden Touch, R. Hale, 1969.
Love Has a Double, R. Hale, 1973.
Lover's Valley, R. Hale, 1974.

UNDER PSEUDONYM FRED HARRISON

Horse Mesa, R. Hale, 1980.
Horsethief's Moon, R. Hale, 1980.
The Long Rope, R. Hale, 1982.

UNDER PSEUDONYM FRANCIS HART

Red Autumn, R. Hale, 1967.
Doctor Blaydon's Dilemma, R. Hale, 1968.
Love Is a Secret, R. Hale, 1968.
Once There Was a Golden Moon, R. Hale, 1968.
The Gulls of Autumn, R. Hale, 1974.
Lover's Dilemma, R. Hale, 1974.
Topaz, R. Hale, 1974.

Also author, under pseudonym Francis Hart, of *Moment of Truth,* R. Hale.

UNDER PSEUDONYM TRAVIS HARTLEY

Longlance Range, R. Hale, 1980.
Shawnee County, R. Hale, 1980.
The Bronc Buster, R. Hale, 1982.

UNDER PSEUDONYM JAY HAYDEN

The Canada Kid, Gresham Books, 1964.
The Ridge Runners, Gresham Books, 1965.
Cimarron Guns, Gresham Books, 1966.
The Long Trail Back, Gresham Books, 1966.
Sonora Pass, Gresham Books, 1967, Lenox Hill Press, 1970.
Pinon Range, R. Hale, 1976.
Wanderer of the Open Range, R. Hale, 1977.

UNDER PSEUDONYM ROGER HILL

Red Rock, R. Hale, 1979.
Navajo Country, R. Hale, 1980.
Redstone, R. Hale, 1981.
Round-Up, R. Hale, 1981.
The Trinity Brand, R. Hale, 1986.

UNDER PSEUDONYM HELEN HOLT

Dilemma for the Doctor, R. Hale, 1968.
Only with Love, R. Hale, 1971.
June Love, R. Hale, 1973.
One Love Lost, R. Hale, 1973.
A Troubled Heart, R. Hale, 1973.

UNDER PSEUDONYM WILL HOUSTON

Iron Marshal, Gresham Books, 1964.
Outlaw Range, R. Hale, 1965.
Sixshooter Trail, Gresham Books, 1965.
Stranger in Canebrake, Gresham Books, 1965.
Night of the Outlaws, Gresham Books, 1966.
The Sixgun Judge, R. Hale, 1972.
Ride to Battle Mountain, R. Hale, 1974.
The Professionals, R. Hale, 1975.
The Gunman's Grave, R. Hale, 1975.

The Shotgun Sheriff, R. Hale, 1976.
Colorado Trail, R. Hale, 1977.
Gila Pass, R. Hale, 1977.
Howe, R. Hale, 1977.
The Loner, R. Hale, 1978.
Death of a Gambler, R. Hale, 1982.
The Springfield Stage, R. Hale, 1984.
Sam's Valley, R. Hale, 1986.

UNDER PSEUDONYM ELIZABETH HOWARD

Love Has Two Faces, R. Hale, 1968.

UNDER PSEUDONYM TROY HOWARD

The Black Light, R. Hale, 1968.
The Harbinger, R. Hale, 1972.
The Kernel of Death, R. Hale, 1973.
The Misplaced Psyche, R. Hale, 1973.
Longbow Range, R. Hale, 1978.
Iron Mountain range, R. Hale, 1980.
Carrigan's Law, R. Hale, 1984.
The Black Colt, R. Hale, 1985.
Buffalo Run, R. Hale, 1986.
Eagle Trail, R. Hale, 1986.
Big Blue Canyon, R. Hale, 1987.
The Big High Desert, R. Hale, 1987.

UNDER PSEUDONYM JOHN HUNT

Guns of Revenge, Gresham Books, 1963.
The Sagebrush Sea, Gresham Books, 1963.
The Kansas Kid, R. Hale, 1964.
Larkspur Range, Gresham Books, 1964.
Fast Guns of Deadwood, Gresham Books, 1965.
Thunder Guns, Gresham Books, 1966.
Rebel Guns, Gresham Books, 1967.
The Bushwhackers, Gresham Books, 1968.
A Town Called Centrefire, R. Hale, 1972.
Bitterbrush Range, R. Hale, 1975.
Colt Country, R. Hale, 1975.
Oxbow, R. Hale, 1975.
Outlaw's Moon, R. Hale, 1976.
Roundup, R. Hale, 1976.
Seven Bullets, R. Hale, 1976.
Law Along the Border, R. Hale, 1977.
The Skyline Trail, R. Hale, 1977.
Cannonball Canyon, St. Martin's, 1978.
Cantrell, R. Hale, 1978.
The Long Autumn, R. Hale, 1978.
Shawnee Valley, R. Hale, 1979.
Shepler's Spring, R. Hale, 1981.
The Pine Cone Ranch, R. Hale, 1985.
Lee's Meadow Country, R. Hale, 1986.
The Guns of Summer, R. Hale, 1987.
A Town Named Meridian, R. Hale, 1987.
The Expedition, R. Hale, 1988.
Charley Choctaw, R. Hale, 1989.

UNDER PSEUDONYM JARED INGERSOL

The Night of the Crisis, R. Hale, 1968.
A Game Called Murder, R. Hale, 1969.
A Rose Can Kill, R. Hale, 1969.
The Beautiful Murder, R. Hale, 1970.
Diamond Fingers, R. Hale, 1970.
The Jade Eye, R. Hale, 1970.
The Steel Garrotte, R. Hale, 1970.
The Killer's Conscience, R. Hale, 1971.

The Man Who Stole Heaven, R. Hale, 1971.
The Money Murder, R. Hale, 1971.
The Man Who Made Roubles, R. Hale, 1972.
The Non-Murder, R. Hale, 1972.
The Golden Gloves, R. Hale, 1973.
A Fine Day for Murder, R. Hale, 1974.
The Witchcraft Murder, R. Hale, 1975.

UNDER PSEUDONYM RAY KELLEY

The Long-Riders, R. Hale, 1964.
The Guns of El Paso, R. Hale, 1965.
High Desert Guns, R. Hale, 1966.
The High Plains, R. Hale, 1966.
The Mankiller, R. Hale, 1967.
Shotgun Rider, R. Hale, 1967.
The Gunsight Affair, R. Hale, 1975.
Cane's Mesa, R. Hale, 1976.
A Gunman's Shadow, R. Hale, 1976.
Justice in New Mexico, R. Hale, 1976.
Blue Grass Range, R. Hale, 1977.
Johnny Centavo, R. Hale, 1977.
Sixgun Assassin, R. Hale, 1977.
Blue Rock Range, St. Martin's, 1978.

UNDER PSEUDONYM CLIFF KETCHUM

The Border Men, R. Hale, 1977.
Rustler's Raid, R. Hale, 1978.
Gunnison Valley, R. Hale, 1980.

UNDER PSEUDONYM FRANK KETCHUM

Idaho Trail, R. Hale, 1978.
The Kiowa Plains, R. Hale, 1978.
The Guns of Parral, R. Hale, 1984.
Ghost Meadow, R. Hale, 1986.
The Last Ride, R. Hale, 1987.
The Renegade's Moon, R. Hale, 1988.

UNDER PSEUDONYM JACK KETCHUM

The Laramie Plains, R. Hale, 1964.
Winchester Pass, R. Hale, 1965, Arcadia House, 1966.
Dead or Alive, R. Hale, 1966.
The Guns of Amarillo, R. Hale, 1966.
The Guns of Buck Elder, R. Hale, 1967.
The Trail without End, R. Hale, 1973.
Cactus Country, R. Hale, 1975.
Border Dawn, R. Hale, 1976.
Guns of the South Desert, R. Hale, 1976.
Open Range, R. Hale, 1981.
Off Season, Ballantine, 1981.

UNDER PSEUDONYM JOHN KILGORE

Return of the Fast Gun, R. Hale, 1961.
Sheriff of Cow County, R. Hale, 1962.
The Short-Gun Man, R. Hale, 1962.
The Gunfighter, R. Hale, 1963.
The Man from Secret Valley, R. Hale, 1964.
The Hidden Hills, R. Hale, 1965.
Man from the Cherokee Strip, R. Hale, 1966.
Nightrider's Moon, R. Hale, 1966.
Oklahoma Fiddlefoot, Arcadia House, 1966.
Lynch Town, R. Hale, 1967.
Some Die Young, R. Hale, 1970.
Murder to Music, R. Hale, 1972.
Pawnee Butte, R. Hale, 1975.
The Painted Pony, R. Hale, 1976.

The Partnership, R. Hale, 1976.
Southwest Law, R. Hale, 1976.
Topar Rim, R. Hale, 1979.
The Shadow Gunman, R. Hale, 1986.
The Sun Devils, R. Hale, 1987.
Three Silver Bullets, R. Hale, 1987.
The Deadwood Stage, R. Hale, 1987.

UNDER PSEUDONYM FRANK KIMBALL

Saginaw Hills, R. Hale, 1981.

UNDER PSEUDONYM RALPH KIMBALL

Buckeye, R. Hale, 1980.
Manning, R. Hale, 1981.
The Bushwhacker, R. Hale, 1989.

UNDER PSEUDONYM FRANK KOEHLER

Trouble Valley, R. Hale, 1982.
Buffalo Range, R. Hale, 1985.

UNDER PSEUDONYM HUNTER LIGGETT

Murder for Money, R. Hale, 1969.
The Murder Maze, R. Hale, 1969.
The Victim Died Twice, R. Hale, 1969.
The Unknown Murderer, R. Hale, 1975.
The Ragheads, R. Hale, 1980.

UNDER PSEUDONYM J. K. LUCAS

Haight Is the Killer, R. Hale, 1969.
The Born Survivor, R. Hale, 1975.

UNDER PSEUDONYM BUCK LYON

Trail of the Hunted, Gresham Books, 1967.
Sundown, R. Hale, 1978.
Sandrock, R. Hale, 1979.
Cow Camp, R. Hale, 1979.
Bear Valley, R. Hale, 1980.
Carver Valley, R. Hale, 1981.
The Rain-Maker, R. Hale, 1983.

UNDER PSEUDONYM BRUCE MARTIN

Fighting Marshall, Gresham Books, 1963.
Guns of the Law, Mills & Boon, 1963.
The Top Lash, Gresham Books, 1963.
Badland Guns, Gresham Books, 1964.
The Men from Tombstone, Mills & Boon, 1964.
The Texas Twister, Gresham Books, 1965, Arcadia House, 1966.
The Raw Country, Gresham Books, 1966, Arcadia House, 1967.
Arizona Ambush, Gresham Books, 1967, Lenox Hill Press, 1971.
The Pinon Hills, R. Hale, 1978.

UNDER PSEUDONYM TOM MARTIN

Land of Long Shadows, Gresham Books, 1963.
Lone Trail to Puma, Gresham Books, 1964.
The Oxbow Range, Gresham Books, 1964.
The Texas Trail, R. Hale, 1964.
Deadwood, Gresham Books, 1965.
Vengeance in Hangtown, Gresham Books, 1966.
The Lone Pine Trail, Gresham Books, 1966.
Dead Man Canyon, Gresham Books, 1967.
Gunsight Pass, R. Hale, 1967, Arcadia House, 1969.
Guntown Justice, R. Hale, 1976.
Long Lance, R. Hale, 1977.
The Men from El Paso, R. Hale, 1977.

UNDER PSEUDONYM ANGELA MORGAN

Two Loves for Sue, R. Hale, 1974.

UNDER PSEUDONYM ARLENE MORGAN

Ten Days to Remember, R. Hale, 1967.
Starfire, R. Hale, 1974.
A Time for Lovers, R. Hale, 1974.

UNDER PSEUDONYM FRANK MORGAN

A Fortune for Love, R. Hale, 1971.
The Desert Riders, R. Hale, 1978.
Trail Guns, R. Hale, 1980.
Tomahawk Range, R. Hale, 1981.
San Saba Trail, R. Hale, 1982.
Farnham's War, R. Hale, 1987.

UNDER PSEUDONYM JOHN MORGAN

Death to Comrade X, R. Hale, 1969.
Murderers Don't Smile, R. Hale, 1969.
Spy in the Tunnel, R. Hale, 1969.
To Kill a Hero, R. Hale, 1969.
The Nicest Corpse, R. Hale, 1970.
The Perfect Frame, R. Hale, 1970.
The Midnight Murder, R. Hale, 1971.
The Killer's Manual, R. Hale, 1972.
The Ivory Penguin, R. Hale, 1974.
Windriver Hills, R. Hale, 1980.
Harper's Trail, R. Hale, 1981.
Bluegrass Range, R. Hale, 1982.

UNDER PSEUDONYM VALERIE MORGAN

The Ides of Love, R. Hale, 1968.
The Lovers, R. Hale, 1981.

UNDER PSEUDONYM BERT O'CONNER

Morgan Valley, R. Hale, 1980.

UNDER PSEUDONYM CLINT O'CONNER

The Tall Texans, R. Hale, 1964.
Dead Man's Range, R. Hale, 1965.
Thieves' Trail, R. Hale, 1966.
Cooper's Moon, R. Hale, 1973.
Guns of Black Rock, R. Hale, 1975.
Mule-Train, R. Hale, 1978.
Broken Bow Range, R. Hale, 1982.
The Paloverde Tree, R. Hale, 1984.
White Stone, R. Hale, 1984.

UNDER PSEUDONYM LELAND RHODES

The Danger Trail, R. Hale, 1981.
Eagle Mountain Range, R. Hale, 1981.
Morning Gun, R. Hale, 1982.

UNDER PSEUDONYM ARTHUR ST. GEORGE

A Race with Love, R. Hale, 1969.

UNDER PSEUDONYM HELEN SHARP

Ward Nurse, R. Hale, 1968.
Love and Heather, R. Hale, 1969.
The Image of Love, R. Hale, 1970.
Love Came Slowly, R. Hale, 1970.
A Girl Named Gardenia, R. Hale, 1971.
Love and a Half Moon, R. Hale, 1971.
The Love Token, R. Hale, 1971.
Love the Second Time, R. Hale, 1972.

The Huntress, R. Hale, 1973.
Love Is a New World, R. Hale, 1973.
Lover from Another Time, R. Hale, 1973.
The Sunday Lover, R. Hale, 1973.

UNDER PSEUDONYM JIM SLAUGHTER

The Free-Graze War, R. Hale, 1964.
Rustler's Trail, R. Hale, 1965.
The Sonora Plains, R. Hale, 1965.
The Guns of Johnny Dalton, R. Hale, 1966.
The Guns of Fortune, R. Hale, 1967, Arcadia House, 1969.
The Stage to Amarillo, R. Hale, 1967.
Lariat Law, R. Hale, 1974.
The Mustangers, R. Hale, 1974.
Gun Country, R. Hale, 1975.
Gunnison Butte, R. Hale, 1975.
Shadow Range, R. Hale, 1975.
Boone's Law, R. Hale, 1976.
The Gunman's Choice, R. Hale, 1976.
Rendezvous on the South Desert, R. Hale, 1976.
Blue Star Range, R. Hale, 1977.
The Guns of Summer, R. Hale, 1977.
The Hangtree, R. Hale, 1977.
The Legend of Chilili, R. Hale, 1978.
Montana Trail, R. Hale, 1978.
Deuce, St. Martin's, 1979.
Mandan Meadow, R. Hale, 1983.
The Bordermen, R. Hale, 1987.
Horse Canyon, R. Hale, 1989.

UNDER PSEUDONYM BUCK STANDISH

The Durango Kid, Gresham Books, 1963.
Gunsight, Gresham Books, 1963.
Incident at Alturas, R. Hale, 1964.
Prairie Town, R. Hale, 1965.
Montana Trail, Gresham Books, 1966.
Brothers of Vengeance, Gresham Books, 1966.
Eagle Pass, Arcadia House, 1967.
Gundown, R. Hale, 1973.
The Guns of High Meadow, R. Hale, 1973.
Custer County, R. Hale, 1974.
The Guns of Dawn, R. Hale, 1974.
Custer Meadow, R. Hale, 1975.
The Jayhawker, R. Hale, 1975.
Squatter's Guns, R. Hale, 1976.
White Mountain Range, R. Hale, 1976.
Shipman's Meadow, R. Hale, 1976.
Riders of the Law, R. Hale, 1977.
The Land of Buffalo Grass, R. Hale, 1977.
The Gunman's Legacy, R. Hale, 1978.
Phantom Trail, R. Hale, 1979.
The Line Riders, R. Hale, 1982.
The Lodgepole Trail, R. Hale, 1983.
Hardin County, R. Hale, 1985.
The Rim Rock Country, R. Hale, 1986.

UNDER PSEUDONYM MARGARET STUART

April Is Our Time, R. Hale, 1968.
A Doctor in Exile, R. Hale, 1968.

UNDER PSEUDONYM BRUCE THOMAS

Sioux Autumn, St. Martin's, 1979.
Blue Sage Country, R. Hale, 1982.
Mormon Meadow, R. Hale, 1985.
Men for Boot Hill, R. Hale, 1986.

The Horse Trap, R. Hale, 1987.
Arrowhead Range, R. Hale, 1987.
The Moccasin Trail, R. Hale, 1987.

UNDER PSEUDONYM BUCK THOMPSON

Starfire Range, R. Hale, 1975.
The Juniper Hills, R. Hale, 1976.
Shiloh, R. Hale, 1978.
Harmon Valley, R. Hale, 1979.
Bull Mountain Range, R. Hale, 1981.
The Warbonnet, R. Hale, 1982.
The Yucca Cattle Company, R. Hale, 1984.
The Camp Robbers, R. Hale, 1985.
The Bob-Tailed Horse, R. Hale, 1986.
Stranger to Dogwood, R. Hale, 1986.

UNDER PSEUDONYM RUSS THOMPSON

Trail Town, R. Hale, 1963, published as *West of Sioux Pass,* Arcadia House, 1965.
The Night-Riders, R. Hale, 1964.
Riders in the Night, R. Hale, 1964.
Tumbleweed Trail, R. Hale, 1965.
Winchester Plains, R. Hale, 1966.
Bitterbrush Basin, Arcadia House, 1966.
Green River Marshal, R. Hale, 1966, Arcadia House, 1968.
A Pair of Aces, R. Hale, 1967.
Carson City, R. Hale, 1968, Lenox Hill Press, 1970.
The Copperhead, R. Hale, 1973.
Laramie Stage, R. Hale, 1974.
The Man Called Corbett, R. Hale, 1974.
The Top Whip, R. Hale, 1975.
A Lawman's Choice, R. Hale, 1975.
The Gun Brand, R. Hale, 1976.
Range Law, R. Hale, 1976.
The Iron Mountains, R. Hale, 1977.
Desert Journey, R. Hale, 1978.
The Patterson Stage, R. Hale, 1978.
Gundown, R. Hale, 1979.
Solablo, R. Hale, 1983.
The Last Fugitive, R. Hale, 1987.

UNDER PSEUDONYM BARBARA THORN

Beyond This Valley, Bouregy, 1964.
From Karen with Love, R. Hale, 1967.
Love Is a Crescent Moon, R. Hale, 1967.
Nurse for a Night, R. Hale, 1968.
To Sandy with Love, R. Hale, 1968.
Love Once, Love Twice, R. Hale, 1970.
Midsummer Love, R. Hale, 1970.
One Woman's Heart, R. Hale, 1971.
The Doctors Nelson, R. Hale, 1973.
Love and the Blue Moon, R. Hale, 1973.

WORK IN PROGRESS: Alamo Jefferson, The Mars Gun, The Sun Devils, Six Silver Bullets, Sam Coyote, The Outlaw's Trap, Beyond the Law, The Autumn Hunter, and *April D'auriac,* all for R. Hale; *The Bandoleros* and *The Young Maurauders,* both for Fawcett; *Open Range Men, Riders of the Trojan Horse,* and *The Squaw Men,* all for Walker & Co.; books of fiction: *The Sundown Murders, An Un-Simple Murder, A Butterfly Moon, The Undertaker,* and *The Floor of Heaven;* books of nonfiction: *The Mexican-American War, Mexico and Santa Anna,* and *God's Gunman.*

SIDELIGHTS: As the author of some 900 books, Lauran Paine is arguably the most prolific writer of our time. "In terms of book-length works published," Allen J. Hubin notes in *Armchair Detective,* "he may well be the most prolific author in history." Paine concentrates on three popular genres; he has written over 600 Westerns, 125 romance novels, and 75 mysteries, in addition to numerous nonfiction works of history and biography, and on modern espionage and the occult.

Speaking to Jack Friedman of *People,* Paine recalls that he first began writing fiction back in the late 1940s after reading a number of popular Western novels. "They had a vocabulary of roughly 300 words, the longest maybe eight letters," Paine tells Friedman. "I thought, 'My God, people make money writing this baloney.' " He soon tried his own hand at it. Because of the low pay rates for Western fiction, he had to write "one a week just to make a living," he tells Friedman. Paine's background as a cowboy in Wyoming and a rancher in northern California gave him an excellent firsthand knowledge of the West and its tradition that has served him well in his Westerns.

Ironically, most of Paine's Westerns have been published in England, primarily by the firm of Robert Hale in London. "I started writing for that market because that's where I encountered first and total acceptance of my book-lengthers," Paine tells Hubin. He now has an agreement with the firm's owner, John Hale, who, Paine tells Hubin, "takes everything I send him."

The key to Paine's phenomenal production lies in his ability to write entire novels in one draft. "You lose something" when you rewrite, he tells Friedman. "I write," he explains to Hubin, "the way some people 'do' sums in their heads: from ideas interwoven or inter-related, or inter-actioned. . . . I suppose most of my books have started out created around a character and have gone on from there to specific situations which I have had in mind at the first sitting."

Paine's books have been translated into German, French, Spanish, Italian, Swedish, Swahili, Danish, Norwegian, and Portuguese. Several of his Westerns have been bought for television. *The Hierarchy of Hell,* a nonfiction study, has been a bestseller in France and Belgium.

BIOGRAPHICAL/CRITICAL SOURCES:

PERIODICALS

Armchair Detective, Volume 15, number 1, 1982.
Globe, July 16, 1985.
People, May 13, 1985.
Roundup, April, 1982.

*   *   *

PALMER, (Nathaniel) Humphrey 1930-

PERSONAL: Born November 6, 1930, in Keighley, England; son of William Nathaniel (a teacher) and Dorothy (Procter) Palmer; married Elizabeth Packiam Theophilus (a lecturer), December 20, 1956; children: Jeremy Mohan. *Education:* Christ Church, Oxford, B.A. (in classics and philosophy; with first class honors), 1953, M.A., 1956, B.A. (in theology), 1958; University of Wales, Ph.D., 1966.

ADDRESSES: Office—School of English Journalism and Philosophy, University College, University of Wales, P.O. Box 94, Cardiff CF1 3XE, Wales.

CAREER: Christ Church College, Kanpur, India, lecturer in philosophy and English, 1956-58; University of Wales, University College, Cardiff, assistant lecturer, 1958-60, lecturer,

1960-68, senior lecturer, 1968-74, reader, 1974-86, professor of philosophy, 1986—, assistant dean of Faculty of Theology, 1968-70, head of religious studies department, 1984—. Visiting professor and Miller Memorial Lecturer, University of Madras, 1977. Lecturer, Madras Christian College, 1962-64; lecture tour, western India, 1972, northern and eastern India, 1977, and Sri Lanka, 1980. External examiner in theology, University of Bristol. *Military service:* National service as conscientious objector, 1953-55.

WRITINGS:

(With wife, Elizabeth Palmer) *Common Tamil Words,* Christian Literature Society, 1964.
The Logic of Gospel Criticism: An Account of the Methods and Arguments Used by Textual, Documentary, Source and Form Critics of the New Testament, St. Martin's, 1968.
(Translator from the German) L. Nelson, *Progress and Regress in Philosophy,* Basil Blackwell, Volume I, 1970, Volume II, 1971.
Analogy: A Study of Qualification and Argument in Theology, St. Martin's, 1973.
(Editor with A. F. Thyagaraju) J. R. Macphail, *The Parables of Jesus King and Teacher,* Christian Literature Society, 1976.
Religion, Language and Philosophy, Dr. S. Radhakrishnan Institute for Advanced Study in Philosophy, University of Madras, 1977.
(Editor) Macphail, *The Sermons of Jesus King and Teacher,* Christian Literature Society, 1977.
(Editor) Macphail, *The Kingdom and the King,* Christian Literature Society, 1977.
Arguing, for Beginners (also see below), University College Cardiff Press, 1979.
(Translator from the German) Immanuel Kant, *Kant's Critique of Pure Reason: An Introductory Text,* University College Cardiff Press, 1983.
(Contributor) C. Wickramasinghe, editor, *Fundamental Studies and the Future of Science,* University College Cardiff Press, 1984.
(With D. M. Evans) *Understanding Arguments* (includes *Arguing, for Beginners*), Department of Extra-Mural Studies, University College Cardiff, 1983, new edition, University of Wales Press, 1986.
Presupposition and Transcendental Inference, Croom Helm, 1985.
At Home with Greek: A Short Home-Study Course, Church in Wales Publications, 1985.

Also author of numerous tapes and computer utility programs. Also contributor to *Proceedings of the C. S. Peirce Bicentennial International Congress,* 1981. Contributor to many periodicals, including *Reason Papers, Listener, New Testament Studies, Theology, Mind, Philosophy,* and *Journal of the Madras University.*

WORK IN PROGRESS: Deeming Everybody Selfish; a book on work-sharing, with rostering to increase employment without reducing utilization of capital (plant and machinery).

SIDELIGHTS: Humphrey Palmer told *CA:* "My teaching and research have been mainly in the field of applied logic. In teaching, I try to equip people to tackle difficult books on their own, to seek consistency in their ideas and beliefs, and to attempt rational evaluation of these and other sets of ideas. In my writing I have ventured such assessments of some schemes for literary and historical re-creation (*Logic of Gospel Criticism*), of qualification in metaphysical reasoning (*Analogy*), and of Kant's program for justifying science (*Presupposition and Transcendental Inference*); [I have] offered comments on some debated points in logical theory and produced with a colleague a text on elementary logic, for use in schools."

He adds, "I have also been keen that the study of religions—and not just Christianity—should continue to form part of a humane education."

AVOCATIONAL INTERESTS: Simple gadgetry.

* * *

PARKER, Barry (Richard) 1935-

PERSONAL: Born April 13, 1935, in Penticton, British Columbia, Canada; immigrated to the United States, 1961; naturalized citizen, 1980; son of Gladstone (a garage owner) and Olive (Young) Parker; married Gloria Haberstock, 1962; children: David. *Education:* University of British Columbia, B.A. (with honors), 1959, M.Sc., 1961; Utah State University, Ph.D., 1967.

ADDRESSES: Home—750 Fairway Dr., Pocatello, Idaho 83201. *Office*—Department of Physics, Idaho State University, Pocatello, Idaho 83209.

CAREER: Weber State College, Ogden, Utah, lecturer, 1963-65, assistant professor of physics, 1965-66; Idaho State University, Pocatello, associate professor, 1967-75, professor of physics, 1975—.

MEMBER: American Physical Society, Sigma Xi (president, 1974-75), Sigma Pi Sigma.

AWARDS, HONORS: Science writing prize, McDonald Observatory, 1980, for article "The Gravitational Lens."

WRITINGS:

(Contributor) Michael Seeds, editor, *Astronomy: Selected Readings,* Benjamin-Cummings, 1980.
Concepts of the Cosmos: An Introduction to Astronomy, Harcourt, 1983.
Einstein's Dream: The Search for a Unified Theory of the Universe, Plenum, 1986.
Search for a Supertheory: From Atoms to Superstrings, Plenum, 1987.
Creation: The Story of the Origin and Evolution of the Universe, Plenum, 1988.
Invisible Matter and the Fate of the Universe, Plenum, 1989.
Colliding Galaxies, Plenum, 1990.

Contributor to *Encyclopedia Britannica.* Contributor to scientific journals and popular magazines, including *Astronomy, Star and Sky, Fly Fisherman, Fishing World, High Country,* and *Angler.*

WORK IN PROGRESS: Writing with a Flair, a guide to dramatic nonfiction.

SIDELIGHTS: Barry Parker once told *CA:* "It's difficult to say why one writes, but in my case I suppose it's because I thoroughly enjoy the challenge of taking a scientific subject—or any difficult subject, for that matter—and making it understandable and enjoyable for a popular audience. The emphasis here should, I firmly believe, be placed on the word 'enjoyable'; it's not enough just to make the material understandable.

"My first book, *Concepts of the Cosmos,* resulted from many years of teaching astronomy and writing popular articles on the subject. I felt that the majority of astronomy books on the market were not enjoyed by most students, and I hoped I could produce a book that would at least partially overcome this. Once I had completed it I found I was hooked—well hooked—and I im-

mediately started a second book. It is also oriented, to some degree, towards astronomy, but it is much narrower in scope than the previous book. Titled *Einstein's Dream,* it is the story of man's search for a unified theory of the universe.

"Although much of my writing has been in the area of popular science, I am also an enthusiastic outdoorsman and have published many articles on fishing, backpacking, and so on. 'Write about the things that you enjoy most,' someone once said to me. And I guess I've taken that advice."

BIOGRAPHICAL/CRITICAL SOURCES:

PERIODICALS

Los Angeles Times, November 20, 1987, October 11, 1988.
New York Times Book Review, January 10, 1988.

* * *

PAYACK, Paul J. J. 1950-

PERSONAL: Born January 3, 1950, in Morristown, N.J.; son of Peter Paul (a trucking company owner) and Florence (a teacher; maiden name, Marcello) Payack; married Millie Lorenzo, April 19, 1974; children: Rebecca Ashley, Elisabeth Lauren. *Politics:* Democrat. *Religion:* Unitarian-Universalist. *Education:* Attended Bucknell University, 1968-71; Harvard University, A.B., 1974, C.A.G.S., 1984.

ADDRESSES: Home—448 Beaumont Circle, West Chester, Penn. 19380. *Office*—Unisys Corporation, P.O. Box 500, Blue Bell, Penn. 19424.

CAREER: Newbury College, Boston, Mass., admissions counselor, 1975, senior admissions counselor, 1976, assistant director of admissions, 1977, assistant to the president, 1978; Digital Equipment Corporation, Maynard, Mass., software writer, 1978-79; Wang Laboratories, Lowell, Mass., senior software writer, 1980-82; Apollo Computer, Chelmsford, Mass., software engineer, 1981-84, senior promotional specialist, 1984, manager of promotional writing group, 1985, marketing manager, sales promotion, 1986; Unisys Corporation, Blue Bell, Penn., corporate director, marketing communications, 1987—. Editor, Chthon Press, 1973-82. Lecturer at University of Lowell, Babson College, Massachusetts State College system, University of Texas at Arlington, Harvard University, and other schools.

WRITINGS:

A Ripple in Entropy, Chthon Press, 1973.
Legend of the Shaman, Free Books, 1974.
Solstice; or, Star-Tales, Samisdat Press, 1975.
The Unexpected Twist Series, Chthon Press, 1976.
Solstice II, Samisdat Press, 1976.
Mythomania, New York Culture Review Press, 1977.
Solstice III, Samisdat Press, 1977.
The Black List, Chthon Press, 1977.
Microtales, Quark Press, 1977.
Land of Orth, Chthon Press, 1978.

Also author of *A Short History of Chess, Mortality Tales, Shortest Tomes, Upon the Birth of a First Child, Worlds to Shatter, Shattered Worlds, Upon the Birth of a Second Child, Children of the Mind, The Book of Hours,* and *The Divine Comedy: A Post-Modern Commentary.* Contributor of metafictions, prose poems, and collages to over one hundred publications, including *Paris Review, Wisconsin Review, New York Culture Review, Omni, New Letters, Isaac Asimov's Science Fiction Magazine, Kansas City Star,* and *Creative Computing.*

SIDELIGHTS: Paul J. J. Payack told CA: "I consider all my work metafiction." In her introduction to Mythomania, Sylvia Berkman calls Payack "a writer of great originality, seriousness, and imaginative zest, to the highest degree intellectually curious." She finds that "what continues to distinguish even more forcibly Paul Payack's later work, is the nature of the creative intelligence from which it stems. This is an intelligence cool yet engaged, composed, witty, immensely concerned with the broad pivotal elements of human experience . . . as well as the minute arcane details of human behavior through uncounted centuries."

* * *

PAYNE, (Pierre Stephen) Robert 1911-1983
(Richard Cargoe, John Anthony Devon, Howard Horne, Valentin Tikhonov, Robert Young)

PERSONAL: Born December 4, 1911, in Saltash, Cornwall, England; came to the United States, 1946; naturalized in the 1950s; died February 18, 1983, while on vacation in Bermuda, of complications from a stroke and heart attack; son of Stephen (a naval architect) and Mireille Antoinette (Dorey) Payne; married Rose Hsiung (daughter of Hsiung Hseling, former prime minister of China), 1942, divorced, 1951; married Sheila Lawani, 1981. Education: Attended Diocesan College, Rondebosch, South Africa, 1929-30, University of Capetown, 1931-32, University of Liverpool, 1933-36, University of Munich, 1937, and Sorbonne, University of Paris, 1938.

ADDRESSES: Home—New York, N.Y. Agent—Bertha Klausner International Literary Agency, Inc., 71 Park Ave., New York, N.Y. 10016.

CAREER: Author, 1936-83. Shipwright's apprentice, Liverpool, England, 1932-33; Singapore Naval Base, Singapore, China, shipwright, 1939-41, armament officer, 1941; British Ministry of Information in Chungking, China, translator, 1941-42; Lienta University, China, professor of English poetry and lecturer in naval architecture, 1943-46; Alabama College, Montevallo, head of English department, 1949-54. War correspondent in Spain, 1938, and correspondent for London Times in Changsha, China, 1942. Founding director of Columbia University Translation Center.

MEMBER: PEN (chairman of translation committee).

AWARDS, HONORS: M.A., Asia Institute (New York), 1951; Gold Medal, Columbia University Translation Center, 1986, for excellence in translation.

WRITINGS:

FICTION

(Under pseudonym Valentin Tikhonov) The Mountains and the Stars, Little, Brown, 1938.
(Under pseudonym Robert Young) The War in the Marshes, Faber, 1938.
(Under pseudonym Robert Young) The Song of the Peasant, Heinemann, 1939.
Singapore River, Heinemann, 1942.
David and Anna, Heinemann, 1943, Dodd, 1947.
The Chinese Soldier, and Other Stories, Heinemann, 1945.
Love and Peace, Heinemann, 1945, published as Torrents of Spring, Dodd, 1946, reprinted, Queens House, 1976.
A Bear Coughs at the North Pole, Dodd, 1947.
The Blue Nigger, and Other Stories, Grey Walls Press, 1947.
The Lion Roars, Heinemann, 1949.

(Under pseudonym Richard Cargoe) The Tormentors, Gollancz, 1949, Sloane, 1950, published under own name, Hillman Books, 1959, reprinted, 1980.
The Young Emperor, Macmillan, 1950 (published in England as The Great Mogul, Heinemann, 1950).
The Lovers, Heinemann, 1951.
Red Lion Inn, Prentice-Hall, 1951.
(Under pseudonym Richard Cargoe) Maharajah, World Publishing, 1951.
Blood Royal, Prentice-Hall, 1952.
(Under pseudonym Howard Horne) Concord Bridge, Bobbs-Merrill, 1952.
The Emperor, Heinemann, 1953.
The Chieftain: A Story of the Nez Perce People, Prentice-Hall, 1953.
Alexander, the God, A. A. Wyn, 1954, abridged edition published as Alexander and the Camp Follower, Paul Elek, 1961.
(Editor) The Deluge: A Novel by Leonardo da Vinci (based on da Vinci's notes), Twayne, 1954.
(Under pseudonym Richard Cargoe) Brave Harvest, Ballantine, 1954 (published in England as Harvest, Heinemann, 1955).
The Roaring Boys, Doubleday, 1955 (published in England as The Royal Players, R. Hale, 1956).
A House in Peking: A Novel of 18th-Century China, Doubleday, 1956 (published in England as Red Jade, Heinemann, 1957).
The Shepherd, Heinemann, 1957, Horizon, 1959.
(Under pseudonym John Anthony Devon) O Western Wind, Putnam, 1957.
The Barbarian and the Geisha (novelization of screenplay by Ellis St. Joseph), Pan Books, 1958, New American Library, 1977.
Trumpet in the Night, Hale, 1961.
(Under pseudonym Richard Cargoe) The Back of the Tiger, Belmont Books, 1961.
The Lord Jesus (novel), Abelard, 1964.
Caravaggio, Little, Brown, 1968.
The Tortured and the Damned, Vigward Limited, 1979.

Also author of novel The Palace in Peking.

POETRY

The Granite Island, and Other Poems, J. Cape, 1945.
The Rose Tree, Dodd, 1947.
Songs, Heinemann, 1948.
Peking Elegies, Blue Dolphin Press, 1978.

NONFICTION

(Under pseudonym Robert Young) A Young Man Looks at Europe, Heinemann, 1938.
Forever China (diary; also see below), Dodd, 1945 (published in England as Chungking Diary, December 1941-April 1944, Heinemann, 1945).
Journey to Red China, Heinemann, 1947, reprinted, Hyperion Press (Westport, Conn.), 1977.
The Revolt of Asia, Day, 1947.
China Awake (diary, 1944-46; also see below), Dodd, 1947.
The Changing Face of China (booklet), Bureau of Current Affairs (London), 1949.
Report on America, Day, 1949 (published in England as Fabulous America, Gollancz, 1949).
Zero: The Story of Terrorism, introduction by Pearl S. Buck, Day, 1950.
The Fathers of the Western Church, Viking, 1951.
Journey to Persia, Heinemann, 1951, Dutton, 1952.

The Wanton Nymph: A Study in Pride, Heinemann, 1951, revised edition published as *Hubris: A Study in Pride,* Harper, 1960.

Red Storm over Asia, Macmillan, 1951.

The Splendor of Persia, illustrations by Leonard Everett Fisher, Knopf, 1957.

The Terrorists: The Story of the Forerunners of Stalin, Funk, 1957.

The Island: Being the Story of the Fortunes and Vicissitudes and Triumphs of the Island, Once Known as Monchonaka . . . Now Known as Gardiner's Island . . . Now Faithfully Related from Original Documents and Presented to the Public, Harcourt, 1958.

The Holy Sword: The Story of Islam from Muhammad to the Present, Harper, 1959.

The Canal Builders: The Story of Canal Engineers through the Ages, Macmillan, 1959.

The Splendor of Greece, Harper, 1960, unabridged edition, Pan Books, 1964.

The White Rajahs of Sarawak, Funk, 1960, reprinted, Oxford University Press, 1987.

(Compiler and annotator) *The Civil War in Spain, 1936-1939* (personal narratives), Putnam, 1962.

Lost Treasures of the Mediterranean World, Thomas Nelson (New York), 1962.

The Roman Triumph, Hale, 1962, Abelard-Schuman, 1963.

(Author of text) *Sun, Stones and Silence,* photographs by Dorothy Hales Gary, Simon & Schuster, 1963.

The Splendor of Israel, Harper, 1963.

The Splendor of France, Harper, 1963.

Ancient Greece: The Triumph of a Culture, Norton, 1964 (published in England as *The Triumph of the Greeks,* Hamish Hamilton, 1964).

(Author of text) *The Isles of Greece,* photographs by Alexander Artemakis, Simon & Schuster, 1965, reprinted, 1983.

(Author of text) *The Splendors of Asia: India, Thailand, Japan,* photographs by Gary, Viking, 1965.

The Christian Centuries from Christ to Dante, Norton, 1966.

(Author of text) William Harlan Hale, editor, *The Horizon Book of Ancient Rome,* American Heritage Press, 1966, reprinted, Doubleday, 1987, revised edition published as *Ancient Rome,* 1970.

(Author of text) *The Splendors of Byzantium,* photographs by Gary, Viking Press, 1967.

(Author of text) *Mexico City,* photographs by Dick Davis, Harcourt, 1968.

Chinese Diaries, 1941-1946 (condensed versions of *Forever China* and *China Awake*), Weybright & Talley, 1969, abridged one-volume edition, 1969.

Eyewitness: A Personal Account of a Tumultuous Decade, 1937-1946, Doubleday, 1972.

The World of Art, Doubleday, 1972.

Massacre, Macmillan, 1973.

The Corrupt Society: From Ancient Greece to Present-Day America, Praeger, 1975.

The Splendor of the Holy Land: Egypt, Jordan, Israel, Lebanon, Harper, 1976.

A Rage for China, Holt, 1977.

The Dream and the Tomb: A History of the Crusades, Stein and Day, 1984.

BIOGRAPHIES

(With Stephen Chen) *Sun Yat-sen: A Portrait,* Day, 1946.

The Yellow Robe (novel on the life of Buddha), Dodd, 1948 (published in England as *The Lord Comes,* Heinemann, 1948).

Mao Tse-tung: Ruler of Red China, Schuman, 1950, revised edition published as *Portrait of a Revolutionary: Mao Tse-tung,* Abelard, 1961, 3rd edition published as *Mao Tse-tung,* Weybright & Talley, 1969.

The Marshall Story: A Biography of General George C. Marshall, Prentice-Hall, 1951 (published in England as *General Marshall: A Study in Loyalties,* Heinemann, 1952).

The Great God Pan: A Biography of the Tramp Played by Charles Chaplin, Hermitage House, 1952 (published in England as *The Great Charlie,* Deutsch, 1952, revised edition with foreword by G. W. Stonier, Pan Books, 1957, reprinted, 1988).

The Holy Fire: The Story of the Fathers of the Eastern Church, Harper, 1957, reprinted, 1980.

The Three Worlds of Albert Schweitzer, Thomas Nelson (New York), 1957 (published in England as *Schweitzer: Hero of Africa,* R. Hale, 1958).

The Gold of Troy: The Story of Heinrich Schliemann and the Buried Cities of Ancient Greece, Scientific Book Club (London), 1958, Funk, 1959, published as *The Gold of Troy: The True Story of the Greatest Treasure Hunt in History,* Paperback Library, 1961.

Gershwin, Pyramid Books, 1960.

Dostoyevsky: A Human Portrait, Knopf, 1961.

The Three Worlds of Boris Pasternak, Coward, 1961.

Lawrence of Arabia: A Triumph, Pyramid Books, 1962, revised edition, Hale, 1966.

The Life and Death of Lenin, Simon & Schuster, 1964, reprinted, Grafton, 1987.

The Rise and Fall of Stalin, Simon & Schuster, 1965.

The Fortress, Simon & Schuster, 1967, reprinted, 1986.

Marx (biography of Karl Marx), Simon & Schuster, 1968.

Chiang Kai-shek, Weybright & Talley, 1969.

The Life and Death of Mahatma Gandhi, Dutton, 1969.

Portrait of Andre Malraux, Prentice-Hall, 1970.

(Editor) *The Unknown World of Karl Marx,* New York University Press, 1971.

The Life and Death of Adolph Hitler, Praeger, 1973.

The Great Man: A Portrait of Winston Churchill, Coward and Geoghegan, 1974.

(With Nikita Romanoff) *Ivan the Terrible,* Crowell, 1975.

The Great Garbo, Praeger, 1976.

The Life and Death of Trotsky, McGraw, 1977.

Leonardo, Doubleday, 1978.

By Me, William Shakespeare, Everest House, 1980.

TRANSLATOR

Yuri Olyesha, *Envy,* Hogarth Press (London), 1936.

Soren Kierkegaard, *Fear and Trembling* (original title, *Frygt og Baeven*), Oxford University Press, 1939.

Boris Pasternak, *Childhood,* [Singapore], 1941.

Boris Pasternak: The Collected Prose Works, Drummond, 1945.

(And editor with Chia-hua Yuan), *Contemporary Chinese Short Stories,* N. Carrington, 1946.

(And editor) *Contemporary Chinese Poetry,* Routledge & Kegan Paul, 1947.

(And editor) *The White Pony: An Anthology of Chinese Poetry from the Earliest Times to the Present Day,* Day, 1947, reprinted, New American Library, 1960.

(With Ching Ti, and editor) Shen Tsung-wen, *The Chinese Earth,* Allen & Unwin, 1948, reprinted, Columbia University Press, 1982.

(And editor) *The Image of Chekhov: 40 Stories in the Order in Which They Were Written,* Knopf, 1963.

Yuri Olyesha, *Love and Other Stories,* Washington Square Press, 1967.

OTHER

(Author of libretto) "Open the Gates" (opera), produced in New York at Blackfriars Theatre, 1951.

Also author of several documentary films during the 1950s. Contributor to *New York Times* and *Saturday Review*. Editor, *Montevallo Review,* 1950-52. General editor, "Russian Library," Washington Square Press, 1963-83.

SIDELIGHTS: Referring to Robert Payne as "more than anything a phenomenon of prolificity," a London *Times* contributor added that "probably no author of this century has produced so many books at such a relatively high level of scholarship." A novelist and poet, a professor of literature and lecturer in naval architecture, a playwright and journalist, Payne authored more than one hundred books on a diversity of subjects during a career that spanned forty years. Payne is well-known for his myriad biographies of such literary figures as Fyodor Dostoyevsky, Andre Malraux, and William Shakespeare, political figures such as Mahatma Gandhi, Winston Churchill, Chiang Kai-shek, Mao Tse-tung, Karl Marx, and Adolf Hitler, or film stars such as Charlie Chaplin and Greta Garbo. However, Payne was also a linguist fluent in Latin, Greek, French, Italian, German, Russian, Polish, Danish, and Chinese, among other languages. The founding director of the Columbia University Translation Center, Payne was posthumously awarded its Gold Medal for excellence in translation.

Well-travelled, Payne had much to say about other countries, including India, Greece, Israel, France, Italy, as well as the United States, his adopted country. In his 1949 *Report on America,* a study of American politics, housing, and education, he praised the country's machinery and production but condemned its treatment of minority groups, and even suggested a forerunner of the Peace Corps—a 'peace army.' The book was greeted by mixed critical reaction, however. While a *San Francisco Chronicle* reviewer found that "Payne writes with great passion, with firm conviction, and with beautiful simplicity," a *Nation* critic, for example, called the report "confused and opinionated." And according to Oscar Handlin in the *Saturday Review of Literature:* "His argument is wrapped up in an involved, cushiony prose that only the most persistent reader will penetrate. . . . These stylistic difficulties are directly related to a fundamental gap in Mr. Payne's thinking. In this book, he deals entirely with the realm of what should be done, as if that were altogether independent of considerations of feasibility and probability." But according to Henry Sowerby in the *Christian Science Monitor,* "Payne reports on America in much the same way that Herman Melville reports on whaling. His subject broadens out to embrace the universe. His picture of the fabulous, machine-driven American giant—groping uncertainly around to find his destiny in a distraught world that looks to him for salvation—is reporting with true poetic insight."

While Payne's global travels provided subjects for many books, he possessed an abiding interest in China, especially the relationship between East and West. And throughout his life, he attempted to convey a sense of that country and its people in a variety of genres. *Forever China* and *China Awake* recount in diary form his early years in that country. Consistently praised for the eloquence and grace of his prose, Payne was also lauded for the understanding he brought to his subject. For instance, in *Weekly Book Review,* Thomas Sugrue mentioned the "lovely, sensitive prose" in *Forever China,* calling Payne "a writer to remember." And of *China Awake,* D. G. Bennett remarked in *Catholic World:* "Payne writes of China with a superlative skill and a sound knowledge of the country he greatly loves. He has the

heightened perception of a poet, a warm human understanding." Or as Eleanor Breed observed in the *San Francisco Chronicle:* "Payne's writing has a special charm. It is leisurely, philosophical, reflective, like the country he describes. It is in part sensitivity of eye to color and to the mists and mystery of China, and in part a sheer love of words."

Payne will also be remembered for editing in 1947 what Jeremy Ingalls called in the *Saturday Review of Literature,* "the most comprehensive selection of Chinese poetry in English so far available"—*The White Pony: An Anthology of Chinese Poetry from the Earliest Times to the Present Day.* In the *New York Times,* Marguerite Young praised Payne's introduction, in particular, as "a learned study of Chinese poetry in its relation to Chinese culture." But Payne also depicted China in poetry and novels of his own. His "remarkable fecundity of prose in praise of China is equally remarkable for its fecund beauty of language," noted Starr Nelson in the *Saturday Review of Literature* about *The Rose Tree,* a collection of Payne's own poetry published that same year. Nelson suggested that, although the author's best writing may perhaps be found in "the distinguished prose" of his diary, *Forever China,* to read Payne's book of poems "straight through is an exciting experience. Here, at last, as a poet with a tongue of gold!" His 1945 novel, *Love and Peace,* published in the United States as *Torrents of Spring* and reviewed in the *New Yorker* as "a restrained, beautifully written, unromantic novel about China," relates the story of three upper-class Chinese children who mature into political awareness around the turn of the twentieth century. His 1956 novel *A House in Peking* portrays life in eighteenth-century China and presents "an engrossing picture of one of China's great courts—its magnificence, its ceremonies, its officials, its eunuchs, its pleasures and its intrigues," wrote Peggy Durdin in the *New York Times.* And at the time of his death, Payne had just completed work on another novel, *The Palace in Peking,* about an imperial Chinese family.

Payne chronicled the history of China biographically through the lives of its political leaders as well. Writing about *Sun Yat-sen: A Portrait,* Payne's 1946 biography of the father of the Chinese republic, Guenther Stein stated in the *Christian Science Monitor:* "There is somewhat more in this book about the man himself than in former books on Sun Yat-sen; and what little fresh information the authors are able to give is so well presented in Robert Payne's eloquent English prose that there are at least some glimpses of the living human being behind the legendary figure." About the 1950 biography, *Mao Tse-tung: Ruler of Red China,* Conrad Brandt commented in *New Republic:* "Payne is a gifted author-poet with extensive experience in China; he is a non-Communist who understands the appeal of Communism to Asiatics. His book has the great merit of being neither a diatribe nor a hagiography. It is also highly readable, fluent and assertive." A *San Francisco Chronicle* contributor called the biography "superb" and "a major contribution to our understanding of the Chinese revolution." Although in a *Library Journal* review, W. S. Wong considered the revised 1969 edition still "a literary description rather than a documentary interpretation," Marvin Kalb described it in the *Saturday Review* as "well written, broadly stroked, highly professional," adding that the adjective "professional" also described Payne himself.

"A prolific writer with pronounced opinions on the controversial Chinese problem," noted E. O. Reischauer in the *New York Times,* Payne also wrote of China's political climate. For example, suggesting that *Red Storm over Asia,* an examination of the spread of communism throughout that continent, had been written in 1951 "at white hot speed with white hot passions," Reischauer found the book "repetitious and at times contradictory." And while he estimated that "much of what [Payne] has to say is half smothered by rhetorical bombast and irritating overstatement," Reischauer added, "And yet, perhaps because of these very imperfections, the book carries a strong emotional impact." In the estimation of Hallett Abend, writing in the *Saturday Review of Literature,* "Payne's brief but vivid summary of how the Communist triumph in China came about is an excellent piece of clear and informative writing." In 1977, Payne continued his examination of that country in *A Rage for China.* "A graceful, sensitive prose modulates his rage at the overbearing bureaucracy and the dogmatic emptiness of recent literature," remarked E. A. Teo in *Library Journal.* "The result is a perceptive report which unlocks part of the puzzle of contemporary China." And according to F. B. Randall in *National Review:* "He writes beautifully about Hangchow's Western Lake and mountains, and movingly about ancient heroes such as Yo Fei, who is buried there." Finding "vivid accounts of [Payne's] extraordinary past," which included living in a Peking palace, Randall deemed it "a fine book!"

According to Ursula Schoenhelm in the *Library Journal,* Payne wrote books "faster than most people read them." Edwin McDowell noted in the *New York Times* that Payne produced approximately two books annually, "many of them massive studies," using a portable typewriter and working between the very early morning hours of two and eight. "He almost always demanded total solitude," wrote McDowell, "but in the last two years he allowed his cat, Ashley Aurangzeb, to curl up on his lap as he worked in his living room. Bertha Klausner, his literary agent for more than 35 years, said: 'He was a workaholic who just lived to write. That was his whole life.' "

BIOGRAPHICAL/CRITICAL SOURCES:

PERIODICALS

Catholic World, December, 1947.
Christian Science Monitor, July 11, 1946, March 10, 1949.
Library Journal, April 1, 1964, April 15, 1969, September 15, 1977.
Nation, March 26, 1949.
National Review, December 23, 1977.
New Republic, December 25, 1950.
New Yorker, May 11, 1946.
New York Times, October 19, 1947, December 21, 1947, April 1, 1951, May 20, 1956, February 22, 1983.
San Francisco Chronicle, October 26, 1947, July 17, 1949, November 26, 1950.
Saturday Review, August 2, 1969.
Saturday Review of Literature, October 4, 1947, December 27, 1947, March 5, 1949, April 14, 1951.
Times (London), February 22, 1983.
Weekly Book Review, October 7, 1945.

OBITUARIES:

PERIODICALS

AB Bookman's Weekly, March 7, 1983.
Los Angeles Times, February 24, 1983.
Maclean's, March 7, 1983.
Newsweek, March 7, 1983.
New York Times, February 22, 1983.
Publishers Weekly, March 11, 1983.
Time, March 7, 1983.
Times (London), February 22, 1983.

Washington Post, February 26, 1983.*

—*Sketch by Sharon Malinowski*

* * *

PEARCE, Mary E(mily) 1932-

PERSONAL: Born December 7, 1932, in London, England; daughter of Francis James (a works manager) and Catherine (Lewis) Pearce. *Education:* Attended elementary schools in London, England. *Politics:* "Uncertain." *Religion:* Agnostic.

ADDRESSES: Home—Owls End, Shuthonger, Tewkesbury, Gloucestershire, England.

CAREER: Writer, 1960—.

MEMBER: Society of Authors, National Book League.

WRITINGS:

Apple Tree Lean Down (also see below), Macdonald & Co., 1973.
Jack Mercybright (also see below), Macdonald & Jane's, 1974.
The Sorrowing Wind (also see below), Macdonald & Jane's, 1975.
Apple Tree Lean Down (trilogy; includes *Apple Tree Lean Down, Jack Mercybright,* and *The Sorrowing Wind*), St. Martin's, 1976 (published in England as *Apple Tree Saga,* Macdonald & Jane's, 1977).
Cast a Long Shadow, St. Martin's, 1977.
The Land Endures, Macdonald & Jane's, 1978.
Seedtime and Harvest, Macdonald Futura, 1980.
Polsinney Harbour, St. Martin's, 1983.
The Two Farms, St. Martin's, 1985.

Contributor of stories to publications in England, the Netherlands, Sweden, and Denmark.

WORK IN PROGRESS: A novel.

SIDELIGHTS: "A quiet, unsentimental but not uneventful slice of [country] life has been preserved for us who know it and revealed for those who do not" in Mary E. Pearce's series *Apple Tree Lean Down,* notes *Washington Post Book World* writer Brigitte Weeks. Consisting of *Apple Tree Lean Down, Jack Mercybright,* and *The Sorrowing Wind,* the trilogy follows three rural families in England from the 1880s through World War I. Katha Pollitt states in the *New York Times Book Review* that "Pearce writes fluently and draws her characters broadly but well. The many details she provides of English folkways ring absolutely true." Although the critic comments that at its best, the trilogy "even has a touch of the poetic and inevitable quality of Thomas Hardy," she faults *Apple Tree Lean Down* for a "patent wholesomeness" which lacks introspection. Weeks, however, believes that the work "escapes being an extravaganza of nostalgia by its firm realism and clear assessment of both the strengths and the weaknesses of . . . rural society."

Pearce's other novels also make the most of her provincial subjects; in *The Land Endures,* for example, "Pearce brings to eloquent life the English countryside of 20th century and the people who farm it," Jack Sullivan remarks in the *Washington Post Book World.* The critic adds that "whether describing landscapes or the feelings of struggling farmers, . . . [Pearce] writes with unfailing musicality." "In a time when most writers have finessed the problem of making the ordinary interesting by choosing to write instead about the extraordinary, author Mary Pearce succeeds by a quiet layering of a familiar plot and characters with the detail of humaneness," Maude McDaniel observes in her *Washington Post* review of *The Two Farms.* With her unsentimental style and "no pretensions to profundity," the critic concludes, "Pearce evokes a way of life that really was less complicated, if not always more innocent. It is a good story."

Pearce told *CA:* "I am fascinated by the past; by the working and domestic lives of country people in particular. I live in a rural area rich in old house cottages, barns. I like to find out as much as I can about the people who lived in such places in the past, and who worked the land round about; I like to imagine their lives and loves, etc.; I like to weave stories around them."

BIOGRAPHICAL/CRITICAL SOURCES:

PERIODICALS

Christian Science Monitor, September 22, 1976.
Los Angeles Times, June 12, 1981.
New York Times Book Review, October 3, 1976, March 16, 1986.
Washington Post, January 28, 1986.
Washington Post Book World, September 12, 1976, May 3, 1981.

*   *   *

PEARSALL, Ronald   1927-

PERSONAL: Surname is pronounced *Peer*-sall; born October 20, 1927, in Birmingham, England; son of Joseph (an engineer) and Elsie Caroline (Rawlins) Pearsall. *Education:* Studied art, 1950-52, and attended Birmingham College of Art, 1952-54. *Religion:* Church of England.

ADDRESSES: Home—Sherwell, St. Teath, Cornwall PL30 3JB, England.

CAREER: Writer. Traveled about England, 1954-61, working variously as bank clerk, cinema manager, wine waiter, dance hall musician, private detective, composer, and at other short-term jobs in twenty cities; dealer in art and antiques. Exhibited abstract paintings, New Vision Gallery, London, 1956, and surrealist paintings, Lambray's, Cornwall, 1989. Lecturer in Sweden for British Council, 1964. *Military service:* British Army, Royal Corps of Signals, 1945-48.

WRITINGS:

Scarlet Mask (spy thriller), Lloyd Cole, 1941.
Is That My Hook in Your Ear?, Stanley Paul, 1966.
Worm in the Bud, Macmillan, 1969, published as *The Worm in the Bud: The World of Victorian Sexuality,* Penguin, 1983.
The Table-Rappers, St. Martin's, 1972.
The Possessed, Sphere Books, 1972.
The Exorcism, Sphere Books, 1972.
Diary of Vicar Veitch, Bruce & Watson, 1972.
Victorian Sheet Music Covers, Gale, 1973.
Victorian Popular Music, Gale, 1973.
The Wizard and Elidog, Pitman, 1973.
A Day at the Big Top, Pitman, 1973.
Collecting Mechanical Antiques, Gale, 1973.
Edwardian Life and Leisure, St. Martin's, 1973.
Collecting Scientific Instruments, Gale, 1974.
(With Graham Webb) *Inside the Antique Trade,* Reid & Son, 1974.
Edwardian Popular Music, Fairleigh Dickinson University Press, 1975.
Night's Black Angels: The Forms and Faces of Victorian Cruelty, McKay, 1975.
Collapse of Stout Party, Weidenfeld & Nicolson, 1975.
Popular Music of the Twenties, Gale, 1976.
Public Purity, Private Shame: Victorian Sexual Hypocrisy Exposed, Weidenfeld & Nicolson, 1976.
The Alchemists, Weidenfeld & Nicolson, 1976.

The Belvedere, Dial, 1976.
Conan Doyle: A Biographical Solution, St. Martin's, 1977.
Antique Hunter's Handbook, David & Charles, 1978.
Tides of War, M. Joseph, 1978.
The Iron Sleep, M. Joseph, 1979.
Making and Managing an Antique Shop, David & Charles, 1979, revised edition, 1986.
Tell Me, Pretty Maiden: The Victorian and Edwardian Nude, Webb & Bower, 1981.
Practical Painting, W. H. Smith, 1984, published in four volumes, Trodd, 1989.
Joy of Antiques, David & Charles, 1988.
The Murder in Euston Square, David & Charles, 1989.
Antique Furniture for Pleasure and Profit, David & Charles, 1990.
Being a Special Constable, David & Charles, 1990.
Painting Abstract Pictures, David & Charles, 1990.

Contributor to *Punch, Quarterly Review, Motoring, Homes and Gardens, Field History Today, Books & Bookmen, Ideal Home, Music Review,* and other periodicals in Britain, United States, Canada, and Australia.

SIDELIGHTS: Scarlet Mask, a spy thriller, was published in paperback when Ronald Pearsall was just fourteen and, as Pearsall told *CA,* "the firm decamped without paying me any royalties." The author added that he is "looking for an adventurous publisher (is there such an animal?) to commission an encyclopedia of spiritualism of 250,000 words."

*   *   *

PEAVY, Linda   1943-

PERSONAL: Born November 5, 1943, in Hattiesburg, Miss.; daughter of Wyatt Gaines (a forest products dealer) and Claribel (a teacher; maiden name, Hickman) Sellers; married Howard Sidney Peavy (a professor of environmental engineering), December 21, 1962; children: Erica, Don. *Education:* Mississippi College, B.A., 1964; University of North Carolina, M.A., 1970.

ADDRESSES: Home—521 South Sixth, Bozeman, Mont. 59715. *Office*—P.S., A Partnership, 1104 South Fifth, Bozeman, Mont. 59715.

CAREER: High school teacher of English and journalism in Jackson, Miss., 1964-66, and Baton Rouge, La., 1966-69; Oklahoma Baptist University, Shawnee, instructor in English, 1970-74; P.S., A Partnership, Bozeman, Mont., partner and writer, 1974—. Poet/writer with Montana Arts Council, 1982—. Gives readings and workshops on poetry, fiction, and nonfiction.

MEMBER: Authors Guild, Authors League of America, National Women's Studies Association, American Association of University Women, Society of Children's Book Writers, Western History Association, Women's History Network, Montana Institute of the Arts.

WRITINGS:

(With Jere Day) *The Complete Book of Rockcrafting,* Drake, 1976.
Have a Healthy Baby: A Guide to Prenatal Nutrition and Nutrition for Nursing Mothers, Drake, 1977.
Canyon Cookery: A Gathering of Recipes and Recollections from Montana's Scenic Bridger Canyon, Artcraft, 1978.
(With Andrea Pagenkopf) *Grow Healthy Kids!: A Parents' Guide to Sound Nutrition,* Grosset, 1980.

Allison's Grandfather (picture storybook), illustrations by Ron Himler, Scribner, 1981.

(With Ursula Smith) *Food, Nutrition, and You* (young adult), Scribner/Macmillan, 1982.

(With Smith) *Women Who Changed Things* (young adult), Scribner/Macmillan, 1983.

(WIth Smith) *Dreams into Deeds: Nine Women Who Dared* (young adult), Scribner/Macmillan, 1985.

(Author of libretto with Smith) "Pamelia" (opera), first performed in Billings, Mont., August 25, 1989; choral suite from opera performed at Carnegie Hall, May 29, 1989.

(With Smith) *The Widows of Little Falls,* Minnesota Historical Society Press, 1990.

Also author of *Women in Waiting: The Home Frontier in the Westward Movement.* Work represented in anthologies, including *With Joy: Poems for Children,* edited by T. E. Wade, Jr., *The Poetry of Horses,* edited by William Cole, *Rapunzel, Rapunzel,* edited by Katharyn Machan Aal, *Word of Mouth,* edited by Irene Zahaua, and *Cracks in the Ark,* edited by Richard Morgan and Phyllis Fischer. Contributor of poems and stories to magazines, inducing *Texas Review, Cottonwood Review, South Dakota Review,* and *Antigonish Review.*

WORK IN PROGRESS: A Tangle of Kudzu and *Something Worth Saying,* stories for adults; *More than Muse,* a book on friendships between women writers.

SIDELIGHTS: Linda Peavy once wrote *CA:* "Poetry and fiction allow me to express the feelings that are mine during one small moment in time. The poem or story that results from this expression of feeling about a single event, person, or place represents my own personal perspective on this one aspect of life. It is simply that—a single person's view on a single aspect of life. Only when it is shared with others does the intensely personal expression take on another dimension.

"Different kinds of sharing bring different rewards. Since readers seldom correspond with authors, I have only the reactions of editors, critics, and friends by which to judge whether my published work has spoken to others. Conversely, readings, workshops, and work in schools and communities all allow for a more direct sharing. It is in that sharing that I realize my poems have value for those fellow travelers who seem to need to have their private perceptions expressed by a writer. It is as if such an expression somehow validates the worth of the inward journey for us all.

"For two of my nonfiction books, I was the writer and another woman was the expert, and I thoroughly enjoyed both projects. But I've found my greatest satisfaction in working with another writer whose love of research, writing, and editing are equal to my own. Though my writing partner and I have worked together (as well as separately) on many nonfiction projects, working on women's biographies has become our obsession. We're fierce admirers of those women whose accomplishments show that they never regarded overwhelming odds against success as insurmountable obstacles. In our most recent work, we've become fascinated with the extraordinariness of ordinary lives and have turned our attention to researching and writing the stories of women whose everyday accomplishments formed the backdrop against which the more spectacular events of history were played out.

"Though many beginning writers seem to see writing for children as an 'easy' way to break into print, I consider writing for children and young adults as one of the greatest challenges a serious writer can accept."

AVOCATIONAL INTERESTS: Hiking, birdwatching, backpacking, cross-country skiing.

*   *   *

PECK, Richard E(arl)   1936-

PERSONAL: Born August 3, 1936, in Milwaukee, Wis.; son of Earl Mason (a machinist) and Mary (Fry) Peck; married Donna Krippner, August 13, 1970; children: Mason, Laura. *Education:* Carroll College, B.A., 1961; University of Wisconsin—Madison, M.S., 1962, Ph.D., 1964.

ADDRESSES: Home—1938 East Hackamore St., Mesa, Ariz. 85203. *Office*—Administration, Arizona State University, Tempe, Ariz. 85287.

CAREER: University of Virginia, Charlottesville, assistant professor of English, 1964-67; Temple University, Philadelphia, Pa., assistant professor, 1967-68, associate professor, 1968-77, professor of English, 1977-84; dean of arts and sciences at University of Alabama, 1984-88; Arizona State University, Tempe, provost and vice-president for academic affairs, 1988-89, interim president, 1989-90. *Military service:* U.S. Marine Corps, helicopter pilot, 1954-59; became captain.

MEMBER: Screen Writers Guild of America (West), Dramatists Guild.

AWARDS, HONORS: Ruth Wallerstein Award, Carroll College, 1961, for poetry; *Final Solution* nominated by Science Fiction Research Association for John Campbell Award as best American science fiction novel, 1973.

WRITINGS:

(Editor) *Nathaniel Hawthorne, Poems,* University Press of Virginia, 1967.
(Editor) *Floyd Stovall, Poems,* privately printed, 1967.
Final Solution (novel), Doubleday, 1973.
Something for Joey (novel; based on teleplay by Jerry McNeely), Bantam, 1978.

PLAYS

"Sarah Bernhardt and the Bank," first produced in September, 1972.
Don't Trip over the Money Pail (three-act; first produced in Ridley Park, Pa., at The Barnstormers, April 1, 1976), privately printed, 1977.
"The Cubs Are in Fourth Place and Fading" (three-act), first produced in Swarthmore, Pa., at The Players Club of Swarthmore, December 1, 1977.
"Bathnight," first produced in October, 1978.
"Prodigal Father" (three-act), first produced in Swarthmore at The Players Club of Swarthmore, December, 1978.
"Lovers, Wives and Tennis Players," first produced in December, 1979.
"Curtains," first produced in November, 1980.
"A Party for Wally Pruett," first produced in February, 1982.
"Allergy Tests," first produced in March, 1982.
"Your Place or Mine," first produced in February, 1987.

OTHER

Also author of scripts, for "Owen Marshall," 1972, and "Tutte le Strade Portano a Roma" (title means "All Roads Lead to Rome"), 1975, and of story for "Indict and Convict," 1973. Also contributor of short stories to anthologies, including *Best SF: 1971,* edited by Harrison and Aldiss, Putnam, 1972.

WORK IN PROGRESS: A play, "Heartland"; a novel; a play (comedy); a nonfiction book on university administration.

SIDELIGHTS: Richard E. Peck told *CA:* "I spent two years in Rome as director of Temple University's center there, picked up basic Italian, and visited about eighteen countries. My recent writing has focused on plays (comedies, principally), with several successful productions and others pending. Drama interests me most because of its immediacy and constant freshness (each single performance is 'new'), and comedy because it earns an unfeigned emotional response. It can be more serious than portentous 'serious drama'—an opinion obviously valid to some but one that cannot be made persuasive to others. I intend to continue with plays as time allows, short stories as they occur . . . no more poetry."

*   *   *

PECK, Robert Newton   1928-

PERSONAL: Born February 17, 1928, in Vermont; son of Haven (a farmer) and Lucile (Dornburgh) Peck; married Dorothy Anne Houston, 1958; children: Christopher Haven, Anne Houston. *Education:* Rollins College, A.B., 1953; Cornell University, law student.

ADDRESSES: Home—500 Sweetwater Club Circle, Longwood, Fla. 32779.

CAREER: Writer. Director of Rollins College Writers Conference, 1978—. *Military service:* U.S. Army, Infantry, 1945-47; served with 88th Division in Italy, Germany, and France; received commendation.

AWARDS, HONORS: Mark Twain Award, 1982, for *Soup for President.*

WRITINGS:

FICTION

A Day No Pigs Would Die, Knopf, 1972, reprinted, ABC-Clio, 1987.
Millie's Boy, Knopf, 1973.
Soup, Knopf, 1974.
Fawn, Little, Brown, 1975.
Wild Cat, Holiday House, 1975.
Soup and Me, Knopf, 1975.
Hamilton, Little, Brown, 1976.
Hang for Treason, Doubleday, 1976.
Rabbits and Redcoats, Walker & Co., 1976.
Trig, Little, Brown, 1977.
Last Sunday, Doubleday, 1977.
The King's Iron, Little, Brown, 1977.
Patooie, Knopf, 1977.
Soup for President, Knopf, 1978.
Mr. Little, illustrations by Ben Stahl, Doubleday, 1978.
Eagle Fur, Knopf, 1978.
Trig Sees Red, Little, Brown, 1978.
Basket Case, Doubleday, 1979.
Hub, illustrations by Ted Lewin, Knopf/Random House, 1979.
Clunie, Knopf/Random House, 1979.
Soup's Drum, illustrations by Charles Robinson, Knopf/Random House, 1980.
Trig Goes Ape, illustrations by Pamela Johnson, Little, Brown, 1980.
Soup on Wheels, illustrations by Robinson, Knopf/Random House, 1981.
Justice Lion, Little, Brown, 1981.
Kirk's Law, Doubleday, 1981.

Trig or Treat, illustrations by Johnson, Little, Brown, 1982.
Banjo, illustrations by Andrew Glass, Knopf/Random House, 1982.
Soup in the Saddle, Knopf/Random House, 1983.
The Seminole Seed, Pineapple Press, 1983.
Soup's Goat, Knopf, 1984.
Dukes, Pineapple Press, 1984.
Soup on Ice, Knopf, 1985.
Jo Silver, Pineapple Press, 1985.
Spanish Hoof, Knopf, 1985.
Soup on Fire, Delacorte, 1987.
Soup's Uncle, Delacorte, 1988.
The Horse Hunters, Random House, 1988.
Hallapoosa, Walker & Co., 1988.
Arly, Walker & Co., 1989.
Soup's Hoop, Delacorte, 1989.
Higbee's Halloween, Walker & Co., 1990.

OTHER

Path of Hunters: Animal Struggle in a Meadow (nonfiction), Knopf, 1973.
Bee Tree and Other Stuff (poems), Walker & Co., 1975.
King of Kazoo (musical), Knopf, 1976.
Secrets of Successful Fiction (nonfiction), Writer's Digest Books, 1980.
Fiction Is Folks (nonfiction), Writer's Digest Books, 1983.
My Vermont (nonfiction), two volumes, Peck Press, 1985.

Also adapter of novels *Soup and Me, Soup for President,* and *Mr. Little* for television's "Afterschool Specials," American Broadcasting Companies, Inc. (ABC-TV).

SIDELIGHTS: Many of Robert Newton Peck's well-known novels are set in his own boyhood era of the 1930s, evoking a rural America that few of his readers know today. Among his most notable works are his first novel, *A Day No Pigs Would Die,* the story of how family hardship forces a young boy to give up his pet pig for slaughter, and the comical series of "Soup" tales focusing on a mischievous boy and his pals.

Of *A Day No Pigs Would Die* Jonathan Yardley says in a *New York Times Book Review* article: "[It] will appeal to readers who are hooked on easy nostalgia. But there is more to it than that. It is sentiment without sentimentality—no easy feat—and it is an honest, unpretentious book." In his *New York Times* column, Christopher Lehmann-Haupt takes a similar view, calling the novel "a stunning little dramatization of the brutality of life on a Vermont farm. . . . [And while in the book] there is no rhetoric about love . . . love nevertheless suffuses every page."

Peck told *CA:* "I didn't start out to write for any particular age group. I only write about what I know, and if my books turn out to be right for teenagers and/or younger kids as well as for adults, it just happens that way. My first book, *A Day No Pigs Would Die,* was influenced by my father, an illiterate farmer and pig-slaughterer whose earthy wisdom continues to contribute to my understanding of the natural order and the old Shaker beliefs deeply rooted in the land and its harvest." Peck added that his *Soup* books reflect his boyhood on a farm in Vermont: "I believe that educators are akin to farmers—both are custodians of the green and growing. My first schoolteacher, Miss Kelly, used to say that her garden came to her each morning. In the *Soup* books, Rob and Soup, though abrim with rascality, respect their beloved Miss Kelly, her Vermont virtue—and her ruler."

BIOGRAPHICAL/CRITICAL SOURCES:

BOOKS

Contemporary Literary Criticism, Volume 17, Gale, 1981.
Something About the Author Autobiography Series, Volume 1, Gale, 1986.

PERIODICALS

New York Times, January 4, 1973.
New York Times Book Review, May 13, 1973.

* * *

PENN, John
See HARCOURT, Palma

* * *

PENNINGTON, Lee 1939-

PERSONAL: Born May 1, 1939, in White Oak, Ky.; son of Andrew Virgil (a farmer) and Mary Ellen (Lawson) Pennington; married Joy Stout (a teacher), January 28, 1962. *Education:* Attended Baldwin Wallace College, 1958, and San Diego State University, 1961; Berea College, B.A., 1962; University of Iowa, M.A., 1965; University of Kentucky, graduate study, 1966.

ADDRESSES: Home—11905 Lilac Way, Middletown, Ky. 40243. *Office*—Jefferson Community College, First & Broadway, Louisville, Ky. 40202.

CAREER: Writer and storyteller. Newburgh Free Academy, Newburgh, N.Y., instructor in English, 1962-64; Southeast Community College, Cumberland, Ky., chairperson of English department, 1965-67; Jefferson Community College, Louisville, Ky., professor of English, 1967—. Manager of Bingham Trio (musical group), 1963; instructor in Upward Bound program, 1966; poetry instructor, Murray State University, summers, 1969-72 and 1975-77. Presenter at writers' workshops.

MEMBER: World Poetry Society Intercontinental, International Order of E.A.R.S. (chairman of board), National Association for the Preservation and Perpetuation of Storytelling (member of executive board, 1975-77), Appalachian Consortium (member of advisory board), Kentucky State Poetry Society, Kentucky Council of Teachers of English.

AWARDS, HONORS: Has received many awards for poetry, including four awards from Kentucky State Poetry Society; Pulitzer Prize nomination in poetry, 1977, for *I Knew a Woman;* D.Litt., World University, 1979; Mildred A. Dougherty Award for Literature, 1982; poet laureate of Kentucky, 1984.

WRITINGS:

The Dark Hills of Jesse Stuart (criticism), Harvest Press, 1967.
Scenes from a Southern Road (poetry), Judson R. Dicks Publishing, 1969.
Wildflower . . . Poems for Joy, Poetry Prevue, 1970.
April Poems, Poetry Prevue, 1971.
Songs of Bloody Harlan (poetry), Westburg Associates, 1975.
Spring of Violets (poetry), Love Street Books, 1976.
Creative Composition (textbook), Jefferson Community College, 1976.
I Knew a Woman (poetry), Love Street Books, 1977.
Janus Collection (poetry/photography book), Louisville Graphique, 1982.
Appalachian Newground (poetry, prose and drama), Kentucky Imprints, 1983.

Also author of unpublished books of poetry, including *Hornet Wings, Segovia's Fingernail, Song for a Huckster, Thigmotropism, Moon Breath,* and *Does Anybody Live Here with the Crushed Down Mailbox Anymore.*

PLAYS

Appalachia, My Sorrow (for voices; first produced in New York City at Riverside Theatre, October, 1969), Love Street Books, 1971.
The Porch (one-act; first produced in Berea, Ky., at Berea College, March, 1962), Love Street Books, 1976.
The Spirit of Poor Folk (one-act; first produced at Cumberland, Ky., at Southeast Community College, October, 1966), Love Street Books, 1976.
Coalmine (for voices; first produced in Louisville, Ky., at Jefferson Community College, April, 1976), Love Street Books, 1976.
The Scotian Women (first produced in Kentucky at Guignol Theatre, University of Kentucky, February, 1981), Aran Press (Louisville), 1984.
Appalachian Quartet, Aran Press, 1984.

Also author of "Ragweed," 1980, "Foxwind," 1984.

OTHER

"The Moonshine War" (screenplay), Metro-Goldwyn-Mayer, 1970.

Also author of unpublished books, including *Bloody Bones and Bloody Harlan* (folktales), *Wind and Foxes* (short stories), *To Wake the Water* (novel), and *Letters to April* (essays). Contributor of over 1,000 poems, stories, and articles to more than 300 magazines, including *Southern Poetry Review, North American Mentor, Appalachian Review, American Bard,* and *Poet.* Author of column, "Have Yarn, Will Ravel," for *Greenup News,* 1970-72.

SIDELIGHTS: One of the first, and most active, proponents of art and culture in his native Appalachia, Lee Pennington has become known as a poet, playwright, and college instructor who "refused to accept the stereotype of Appalachian students as helpless, backward products of a depressed region, unworthy of serious teaching," as Jean W. Ross notes in a *Dictionary of Literary Biography* article on the writer. Pennington once told *CA:* "Students everywhere, young and old, need to be given the freedom to write, to create—the same right we afford our great writers. Every person is a unique entity in the universe and thus capable of creating something no one else can. I sincerely believe if we permit students to dream, if we encourage their dreaming and if we give them total freedom to create, they will loose on the world a love and lasting art never witnessed before by any age."

As a result of his efforts, Pennington has helped carve a niche for Appalachian letters, culminating in a Pulitzer Prize nomination for his 1977 poetry collection *I Knew a Woman.* Among the writer's inspirations is Jesse Stuart, an early mentor of Pennington's who himself was a voice of the South for many years. The author also cites the Spanish poet Frederico Garcia Lorca—"he may be the largest influence on me," Pennington tells Ross. "I'm fascinated with Lorca because the common people in Spain can relate to him as well as people in the highest academic circles."

Undoubtedly, though, Pennington's most personal inspiration comes from his wife, Joy Stout, for whom he has written several poetry collections. Among them is the lauded *I Knew a Woman,* a work in which Pennington, according to Ross (who quotes the author), "successfully writes about [women] on both a personal level and a timeless and universal level—so that on the one hand, 'an ordinary woman could pick up the book and glean some pleasure of it,' and on the other, 'Women in the book represented not just women but the concept of woman, the creative concept.' "

In 1981 Pennington wrote *The Scotian Women,* a play that, though based on a real-life coal mine disaster, takes its dramatic format from the ancient Greeks. As the author explains to Ross, "I feel very close to the classical Greek dramatists—Sophocles, Aristophanes, and others—but I also feel very close to Greek culture as a whole. When [my wife and I] were in Athens and traveling over other parts of Greece, I felt that if I weren't in heaven I certainly must be in the front yard."

BIOGRAPHICAL/CRITICAL SOURCES:

BOOKS

Dictionary of Literary Biography Yearbook, 1982, Gale, 1983.

PERIODICALS

Kentucky Living, May, 1989.
Small Press Review, March, 1976.
Southern Quarterly, fall, 1981.
Writer's Digest, August, 1981, May, 1983.

*   *   *

PERRIN, Noel 1927-

PERSONAL: Born September 18, 1927, in New York, N.Y.; son of Edwin Oscar (an advertising executive) and Blanche Browning (Chenery) Perrin; married Nancy Hunnicutt, November 26, 1960 (divorced, 1971); married Annemarie Price, June 20, 1975 (divorced, 1980); married Anne Spencer Lindbergh, December 26, 1988; children: (first marriage) Elisabeth, Amy. *Education:* Williams College, B.A., 1949; Duke University, M.A., 1950; Trinity Hall, Cambridge, M.Litt., 1958. *Religion:* Episcopalian.

ADDRESSES: Home—R.R. Box 8, Thetford Center, Vt. 05075. *Office*—Department of English, Dartmouth College, Hanover, N.H. 03755.

CAREER: Daily News, New York, N.Y., copy boy, 1950-51; *Medical Economics,* Oradell, N.J., associate editor, 1953-56; University of North Carolina, Woman's College, Chapel Hill, instructor, 1956-59; Dartmouth College, Hanover, N.H., assistant professor, 1959-64, professor of English, 1964—, chairman of department, 1972-75. *Military service:* U.S. Army, Artillery, 1945-46, 1950-51; became first lieutenant; served in Korea; received Bronze Star.

MEMBER: Phi Beta Kappa.

AWARDS, HONORS: Guggenheim fellowships, 1970, 1985.

WRITINGS:

A Passport Secretly Green (essays), St. Martin's, 1961.
Dr. Bowdler's Legacy: A History of Expurgated Books in England and America, Atheneum, 1969, Macmillan, 1970.
Amateur Sugar Maker, University Press of New England, 1972.
Vermont: In All Weathers, Viking, 1973.
(Editor) *The Adventures of Jonathan Corncob, Legal American Refugee,* David Godine, 1976.
First Person Rural: Essays of a Sometime Farmer, illustrated by Stephen Harvard, David Godine, 1978.
Giving up the Gun: Japan's Reversion to the Sword, 1543-1879, David Godine, 1979.
Second Person Rural: More Essays of a Sometime Farmer, illustrated by F. Allyn Massey, David Godine, 1980.

Third Person Rural: Further Essays of a Sometime Farmer, woodcuts by Robin Brickman, David Godine, 1983.
A Reader's Delight, University Press of New England, 1988.
(With Kenneth Breisch) *Mills and Factories of New England: Essays,* photographs by Serge Hambourg, Abrams, 1988.

Columnist for *Vermont Life,* 1976-81, *Boston Magazine,* 1978-79, and *Washington Post Book World,* 1981—. Contributor to periodicals, including *New Yorker, Country Journal, Vermont Life,* and *Horticulture.*

SIDELIGHTS: Noel Perrin is an English professor at Dartmouth College and author of such scholarly works as *Dr. Bowdler's Legacy: A History of Expurgated Books in England and America* and *Giving Up the Gun: Japan's Reversion to the Sword, 1543-1879.* Since his move to the Vermont countryside at the age of thirty, however, Perrin has written several books about his experiences as a part-time farmer there. Three of these books, *First Person Rural: Essays of a Sometime Farmer, Second Person Rural: More Essays of a Sometime Farmer,* and *Third Person Rural: Further Essays of a Sometime Farmer,* contain essays previously published in magazines like *Country Journal* and *Vermont Life* and have been highly praised for their unaffected style, wit, and abstention from the pitfalls of idealizing life in a bucolic setting.

In *First Person Rural,* Perrin fills most of the book's pages with practical advice for the novice or part-time farmer on how to tend grounds, buy supplies, and keep pipes from bursting during the bitter-cold Vermont winters. The essays in *Second Person Rural,* notes *Washington Post Book World* contributor Stephen Goodwin, "are more reflective, less concerned with *How-to* than with the meatier question, *Why?*" The answer to this question, at least for Perrin, "is that he likes what he's doing." Extolling the joys of raising animals and crops, making one's own butter, and tapping trees for real maple syrup, the author is nevertheless "no rustic romantic," according to Doris Grumbach's *Saturday Review* article. "When he writes about rural existence he sees all the flies in the idyllic ointment . . . [and the] interesting thing is, Noel Perrin has never become indifferent to the pleasures of the city."

The author does insist, however, on the importance of keeping the rural separate from the urban so that the countryside might be spared the fate of becoming a mere tract of city suburbs; and in *Second Person Rural* he proposes an immigration test in which new-comers to the countryside would be issued one-year visas that would be revoked by a board of native farmers should candidates prove incapable of raising their own livestock. In this way, a large outflow of urbanites might be prevented from settling the farmlands. As for Perrin himself, by the time he wrote *Third Person Rural* he felt confident enough in his assimilation into country life to declare: "I am so deeply into rurality that my own [suburban] childhood conditioning has almost been overcome."

As an expounder of the delights of rural living, Perrin has been favorably compared to another well-known writer on the subject. "No writer since E. B. White," avers Goodwin, "can make puttering around a small farm sound so satisfying. Perrin's prose style is as unaffected as White's, and he is always deft, droll, and thoroughly civilized." Another *Washington Post Book World* critic, Peter Davison, similarly remarks that "like E. B. White, [Perrin] can make amusing what we wood-splitters, hay-makers, pig-sloppers encounter as dreary labor." "He is to farming," Davison also asserts, "what that eloquent physician, Lewis Thomas, is to medicine." After the positive reception of all three of these books, Robert W. Glasgow laments in the *Los Angeles Times Book Review* that "Perrin says that [*Third Person Rural*] is the last volume in his trilogy of published essays. I am among the readers who implore him not to stop."

BIOGRAPHICAL/CRITICAL SOURCES:

BOOKS

Perrin, Noel, *Third Person Rural: Further Essays of a Sometime Farmer,* David Godine, 1983.

PERIODICALS

Los Angeles Times Book Review, December 18, 1983.
New York Review of Books, October 11, 1979.
New York Times Book Review, November 9, 1969, July 23, 1978, July 15, 1979, October 26, 1980, January 8, 1984, April 17, 1988.
Saturday Review, October 14, 1978.
Time, October 3, 1969, July 24, 1978.
Times Literary Supplement, May 7, 1970, December 4, 1981.
Washington Post Book World, August 12, 1979, November 2, 1980, November 27, 1983.

* * *

PFEFFER, Susan Beth 1948-

PERSONAL: Born February 17, 1948, in New York, N.Y.; daughter of Leo (a lawyer and professor) and Freda (a secretary; maiden name, Plotkin) Pfeffer. *Education:* New York University, B.A., 1969.

ADDRESSES: Home—14 South Railroad Ave., Middletown, N.Y. 10940. *Agent*—Curtis Brown, 575 Madison Ave., New York, N.Y. 10022.

CAREER: Writer.

AWARDS, HONORS: Dorothy Canfield Fisher Award, and Sequoya Book Award, both for *Kid Power;* South Carolina Young Adult Book Award, for *About David.*

WRITINGS:

NOVELS FOR YOUNG PEOPLE

Just Morgan, Walck, 1970.
Better Than All Right, Doubleday, 1972, reprinted, 1987.
Rainbows and Fireworks, Walck, 1973.
The Beauty Queen, Doubleday, 1974.
Whatever Words You Want to Hear, Walck, 1974.
Marly the Kid, Doubleday, 1975.
Kid Power, illustrations by Leigh Grant, F. Watts, 1977.
Starring Peter and Leigh, Delacorte, 1978.
Awful Evelina, illustrations by Diane Dawson, A. Whitman, 1979.
Just Between Us, illustrations by Lorna Tomei, Delacorte, 1980.
What Do You Do When Your Mouth Won't Open?, illustrations by Tomei, Delacorte, 1981.
A Matter of Principle, Delacorte, 1982.
Starting with Melodie, Four Winds, 1982.
About David, Dell, 1982.
Courage, Dana, illustrations by Jenny Rutherford, Delacorte, 1983.
Truth or Dare, Macmillan, 1983.
Fantasy Summer, Putnam, 1984.
Kid Power Strikes Back, F. Watts, 1984.
Paperdolls, Dell, 1984.
On the Move, Berkley Publishing, 1985.
Take Two and Rolling, Putnam, 1985.
The Friendship Pact, Scholastic, 1986.
Hard Times High, Berkley Publishing, 1986.

Love Scenes, Berkley Publishing, 1986.
Getting Even, Berkley Publishing, 1987.
Prime Time, Berkley Publishing, 1987.
Wanting It All, Berkley Publishing, 1987.
The Year without Michael, Bantam, 1987.
Rewind to Yesterday, Delacorte, 1988.
Turning Thirteen, Scholastic, 1988.
Future Forward, Delacorte, 1989.
Dear Dad, Love Laurie, Scholastic, 1989.

"SEBASTIAN SISTERS" SERIES

Evvie at Sixteen, Bantam, 1988.
Thea at Sixteen, Bantam, 1988.
Claire at Sixteen, Bantam, 1989.
Sybil at Sixteen, Bantam, 1989.

SIDELIGHTS: A prolific author of young-adult novels, Susan Beth Pfeffer has garnered praise for her handling of controversial subjects within the dramatic form. A *Publishers Weekly* critic, for instance, calls the author "a natural storyteller with an acute ear" in a review of *Whatever Words You Want to Hear,* a realistic tale of teenage romance. Other novels take a lighter view of life. In *Children's Book Review Service* critic Glenda Broughton's opinion, Pfeffer's *What Do You Do When Your Mouth Won't Open?* is "another delightful story," this one about a 12-year-old who, though terrified of public speaking, finds her courage when she has to present an essay at a school contest. "Probably lots of kids will identify with [the protagonist's] problems and cheer her strength and perseverance," Broughton concludes.

AVOCATIONAL INTERESTS: U.S. movie history.

BIOGRAPHICAL/CRITICAL SOURCES:

BOOKS

Children's Literature Review, Volume 11, Gale, 1986.

PERIODICALS

Children's Book Review Service, March, 1981.
Publishers Weekly, September 23, 1974.

* * *

PHILLIPS, Irv(ing W.) 1905-

PERSONAL: Born November 29, 1905, in Wilton, Wis.; son of Mary Ellen (Willis) Phillips; married Lucille D. Defnet; children: Arden. *Education:* Attended Chicago Academy of Fine Arts and Columbia Music College.

ADDRESSES: Home—2807 East Sylvia St., Phoenix, Ariz. 85032.

CAREER: Cartoonist, illustrator, and writer. *Esquire Magazine,* New York, N.Y., cartoon humor editor, 1937-39; Chicago *Sun-Times* Syndicate, Chicago, Ill., cartoon staff member, 1940-52; Phoenix College, Phoenix, Ariz., instructor in cartooning and humor writing, 1976-81. Former playwright in residence, University of California, Los Angeles. Has had motion picture assignments with Warner Brothers, RKO, Charles Rodgers Productions, and United Artists. Work has been shown across the United States at fairs and exhibits, including National Cartoonist Society exhibits; Arizona State University, "Comedy in Art" (one-man show); New York Worlds Fair exhibits; Cartoon Council traveling exhibits; Smithsonian Institute (permanent collection); El Prado Gallery, Sedona, Ariz.; and Phoenix College Gallery, Phoenix. Once painted under the name of Sabuso.

MEMBER: Writers Guild, Dramatists Guild, Authors League of America, National Cartoonists Society, Magazine Cartoonists

Guild, Newspaper Cartoon Council, American Society of Composers, Authors, and Publishers.

AWARDS, HONORS: Certificate of Appreciation from President of the United States, 1944, 1971; Honorary Bartender, Dodge City Chamber of Commerce, 1966; International first prize and cup, Salone dell'Umorismo of Bordighera, Italy, 1969; Television Ruggles Family Awards from Parent-Teachers Association, National Kids Day Foundation, Kiwanis International, Sister Elizabeth Kenny Foundation, *Time,* and *American.*

WRITINGS:

"Caricature" (play), first produced in Los Angeles, Calif., at the Ebony Showcase, 1948.
(With Charles Previn) "La Belle Lulu" (operetta), first produced in Dallas, Tex., at Margo Jones Theatre, 1950.
"Rumple" (play), first produced in New York, N.Y., at Alvin Theatre, 1956.
(Self-illustrated) *The Strange World of Mr. Mum* (juvenile), Putnam, 1965.
The Twin Witches of Fingle Fu (juvenile), Random House, 1969.
No Comment by Mr. Mum (juvenile), Popular Library, 1971.

Also author of plays "Mother Was a Bachelor," 1954, *One Foot in Heaven,* Dramatic Publishing, "Gown of Glory," "Two Adams for Eve," "Hurlyburly," first produced at the University of California, Los Angeles, "The Wayward Kiss," first produced at Bucks County Playhouse, "Rehearsal for Spring," first produced in Pasadena, Calif., at Pasadena Playhouse, and "The Lady Forgot," first produced at Pasadena Playhouse; author or co-author of over two hundred sixty television scripts, including one hundred four episodes of "The Ruggles Family," scripts for "Hollywood Opening Night," "Hollywood Theater Time," "Four Star Playhouse," "The Ray Milland Show," and "Pride of the Family"; contributor of scripts and animation to American Broadcasting Corp. (ABC-TV) children's program, "Curiosity Shop"; author-illustrator of syndicated cartoon strip "The Strange World of Mr. Mum," appearing in one hundred eighty newspapers in twenty-two countries. Contributor to periodicals, including *Saturday Evening Post, Changing Times, Colliers, Gourmet, Wall Street Journal, New Yorker,* and *National Enquirer.* Former humor editor, *Esquire* and *Coronet.*

WORK IN PROGRESS: A musical fantasy for children; an autobiography; two plays.

*　　*　　*

PIAGET, Jean 1896-1980

PERSONAL: Surname is pronounced pee-ah-jhay; born August 9, 1896, in Neuchatel, Switzerland; died September 16, 1980, in Geneva, Switzerland; son of Arthur (a professor) Piaget; married Valentine Chatenay (a psychologist), 1923; children: Jacqueline, Lucienne, Laurent. *Education:* Universite de Neuchatel, B.A., 1915, Ph.D., 1918; postgraduate study at Universitaet Zurich, Universite de Paris, and the Sorbonne.

ADDRESSES: Office—Faculty of Psychology and Educational Sciences, University of Geneva, 3 Place de l'Universite, 1211 Geneva 4, Switzerland.

CAREER: Institut Jean Jacques Rousseau, Geneva, Switzerland (now Institut des Sciences de l'Education, University of Geneva), research psychologist, 1921-33, co-director, 1933-71; Universite de Neuchatel, Neuchatel, Switzerland, professor of philosophy, 1925-29; Universite de Geneve, Geneva, associate professor of the history of scientific thought, 1929-39, professor of sociology, 1939-52, professor of experimental psychology, 1940-71, professor emeritus, 1971-80; International Center of Genetic Epistemology, Geneva, founder and director, 1955-80. Director of International Bureau of Education, Geneva, 1929-67; professor of psychology at Universite de Lausanne, Lausanne, Switzerland, 1937-51; professor of psychology at the Sorbonne, 1952-63. Visiting lecturer at numerous universities in Europe and the United States.

MEMBER: Academie Internationale de Philosophie des Sciences, Institut Internationale de Philosophie, Union Internationale de Psychologie Scientifique, New York Academy of Science, Boston Academy of Arts and Sciences, Academie dei Lincei, Academie des Sciences de Bucarest, Academie des Sciences et Lettres de Montpellier, Academie Royale de Belgique, Association de Psychologie Scientifique de Langue Francaise, Societe Suisse de Logique et de Philosophie des Sciences, Societe de Psychologie de Espagne, Societe Suisse de Psychologie, Societe Neuchateloise des Sciences Naturelles, Federacion Columbiana de Psicologia.

AWARDS, HONORS: Prix de la Ville de Geneve, 1963; American Research Association award, 1967; American Psychological Association award, 1969; Prix Foneme, 1970; Erasmus Prize, 1972; Prix de l'Institut de la Vie, 1973. Honorary degrees from numerous universities, including Harvard University, 1936, the Sorbonne, 1946, University of Brussels, 1949, University of Oslo, 1960, Cambridge University, 1960, University of Moscow, 1966, Yale University, 1970, Temple University, 1971, and Yeshiva University, 1973.

WRITINGS:

IN ENGLISH TRANSLATION

Le Langue et la pensee chez l'enfant, Delachaux & Niestle, 1923, 7th edition, 1968, translation by Marjorie Worden published as *The Language and Thought of the Child,* Harcourt, 1926, 3rd revised edition, Humanities, 1959, reprinted, 1971.
(With others) *Le Jugement et le raisonnement chez l'enfant,* Delachaux & Niestle, 1924, 5th edition, 1963, translation by Worden published as *The Judgment and Reasoning in the Child,* Harcourt, 1928, published as *The Judgment and Reason in the Child,* 1929, reprinted, Littlefield, 1976.
Le Representation du monde chez l'enfant, Delachaux & Niestle, 1926, translation by Jean Tomlinson and Andrew Tomlinson published as *The Child's Conception of the World,* Harcourt, 1929, reprinted, Littlefield, 1975.
La Causalite physique chez l'enfant, Delachaux & Niestle, 1927, translation by Marjorie Worden Gabain published as *The Child's Conception of Physical Causality,* Harcourt, 1930.
Le Jugement moral chez l'enfant, Presses universitaires de France, 1932, 4th edition, 1973, translation by Gabain published as *The Moral Judgment of the Child,* Harcourt, 1932, reprinted, Free Press of Glencoe, 1966.
La Naissance de l'intelligence chez l'enfant, Delachaux & Niestle, 1936, 5th edition, 1966, translation by Margaret Cook published as *The Origins of Intelligence in Children,* International Universities Press, 1952, published as *The Origin of Intelligence in the Child,* Routledge & Kegan Paul, 1953, Norton, 1963.
La Construction du reel chez l'enfant, Delachaux & Niestle, 1937, 3rd edition, 1963, translation by Cook published as *Child's Construction of Reality,* Routledge & Kegan Paul, 1953, published as *The Construction of Reality in the Child,* Basic Books, 1954, reprinted, Ballantine, 1986.

(With Barbel Inhelder) *Le Developpement des quantites chez l'enfant: Conservation et atomisme,* Delachaux & Niestle, 1940, 2nd augumented edition, 1962, translation by Arnold J. Pomerans published as *The Child's Construction of Quantities: Conservation and Atomism,* Routledge & Kegan Paul, 1974.

(With Alina Szeminska) *La Genese du nombre chez l'enfant,* Delachaux & Niestle, 1941, 3rd edition, 1964, translation by C. Gattegno and F. M. Hodgson published as *The Child's Conception of Number,* Routledge & Kegan Paul, 1952, Norton, 1965.

La Formation du symbole chez l'enfant: Imitation jeu et reve, image et representation, Delachaux & Niestle, 1945, 2nd edition, 1959, translation by Gattegno and Hodgson published as *Play, Dreams, and Imitation in Childhood,* Norton, 1951, reprinted, Peter Smith, 1988.

(With others) *Les Notions de mouvement et de vitesse chez l'enfant,* Presses universitaires de France, 1946, translation by G. E. T. Holloway and M. J. Mackenzie published as *The Child's Conception of Movement and Speed,* Basic Books, 1970, reprinted, Ballantine, 1986.

(With Esther Bussmann, Edith Meyer, Vroni Richi, and Myriam van Remoortel) *Le Developpement de la notion de temps chez l'enfant,* Presses universitaires de France, 1946, 2nd edition, 1973, translation by Pomerans published as *The Child's Conception of Time,* Routledge & Kegan Paul, 1969, Ballantine, 1985.

La Psychologie de l'intelligence, Colin, 1947, translation by M. Piercy and D. E. Berlyne published as *The Psychology of Intelligence,* Routledge & Kegan Paul, 1950, Littlefield, 1976.

(With Inhelder) *La Representation de l'espace chez l'enfant,* Presses universitaires de France, 1948, translation by F. J. Langdon and J. L. Lunzer published as *The Child's Conception of Space,* Humanities, 1956.

(With Inhelder and Szeminska) *La Geometrie spontanee de l'enfant,* Presses universitaires de France, 1948, 2nd edition, 1973, translation by E. A. Lunzer published as *The Child's Conception of Geometry,* Basic Books, 1960.

(With Inhelder) *La Genese de l'idee de hasard chez l'enfant,* Presses universitaires de France, 1951, translation by Lowell Leake, Paul Burrell, and Harold Fishbein published as *The Origin of the Idea of Chance in Children,* Norton, 1975.

Logic and Psychology, translation by Wolfe Mays and F. Whitehead, Manchester University Press, 1953, Basic Books, 1957.

(With Inhelder) *De la logique de l'enfant a logique de l'adolescent,* Presses universitaires de France, 1955, translation by Anne Parson and Stanley Milgrom published as *The Growth of Logical Thinking from Childhood to Adolescence: An Essay on the Construction of Formal Operational Structures,* Basic Books, 1958.

Le Genese des structures logique elementaire: Classifications et seriations, Delachaux & Niestle, 1959, translation by Lunzer and D. Papert published as *The Early Growth of Logic in the Child: Classification and Seriation,* Harper, 1964.

Les Mecanismes perceptifs, Presses universitaires de France, 1961, translation by G. N. Seagrim published as *The Mechanisms of Perception,* Basic Books, 1969.

Comments on Vygotsky's Critical Remarks Concerning "The Language and Thought of the Child," and "Judgment and Reasoning in the Child," translated by Parson, M.I.T. Press, 1961.

(With Evert W. Beth) *Epistemologie mathematique et psychologie: Essai sur les relations entre la logique formelle et la pensee reele,* Presses universitaires de France, 1961, translation published as *Mathematical Epistemology and Psychology,* Gordon & Beech, 1966.

(With Paul Fraisse and Maurice Reuchlin) *Histoire et methode,* Presses universitaires de France, 1963, 3rd edition, 1970, translation by Judith Chambers published as *History and Method,* Basic Books, 1968.

(Editor with Fraisse) *Traite de psychologie experimentale,* Presses universitaires de France, 1963, 3rd edition, 1970, translation published as *Experimental Psychology: Its Scope and Method,* Basic Books, 1968.

Six etudes de psychologie, Gonthier, 1964, translation by Anita Tenzer and David Elkind published as *Six Psychological Studies,* Random House, 1967.

Sagesse et illusions de la philosophie, Presses universitaires de France, 1965, 3rd edition, 1972, translation by Wolfe Mays published as *Insights and Illusions of Philosophy,* World Publishing, 1971.

(With Inhelder) *L'Image mentale chez l'enfant,* Presses universitaires de France, 1966, translation by P. A. Chilton published as *Mental Imagery in the Child: A Study of the Development of Imaginal Representation,* Basic Books, 1971.

(With Inhelder) *La Psychologie de l'enfant,* Presses universitaires de France, 1966, 6th edition, 1975, translation by Helen Weaver published as *The Psychology of the Child,* Basic Books, 1969.

Biologie et connaissance: Essai sur les relations entre les regulations organiques et les processes cognitifs, Gallimard, 1966, reprinted, 1973, translation by Beatrix Walsh published as *Biology and Knowledge: An Essay on the Relations between Organic Regulations and Cognitive Processes,* University of Chicago Press, 1971.

On the Development of Memory and Identity, translation by Eleanor Duckworth, Barre, 1968.

John Amos Comenius on Education, Teachers College, 1968.

Le Structuralisme, Presses universitaires de France, 1968, 6th edition, 1974, translation by Chaninah Maschler published as *Structuralism,* Basic Books, 1970.

(With Inhelder) *Memoire et intelligence,* Presses universitaires de France, 1968, translation by Arnold J. Pomerans published as *Memory and Intelligence,* Basic Books, 1973.

L'Epistemologie genetique, Presses universitaires de France, 1970, translation by Duckworth published as *Genetic Epistemology,* Basic Books, 1972.

(With R. Garcie) *Les Explications causales,* Presses universitaires de France, 1971, translation by Donald Miles and Marguerite Miles published as *Understanding Causality,* Norton, 1974.

Science of Education and the Psychology of the Child, translation by Derek Coltman, Viking, 1971, reprinted, Penguin, 1977.

Psychology and Epistemology: Towards a Theory of Knowledge, translation by P. A. Wells, Viking, 1972.

The Principles of Genetic Epistemology, translation by Mays, Basic Books, 1972.

Ou va education, Denoel/Gonthier, 1973, translation by George-Anne Roberts published as *To Understand Is To Invest: The Future of Education,* Grossman, 1973.

The Child and Reality: Problems of Genetic Psychology, translation by Arnold Rosin, Grossman, 1973.

Main Trends in Interdisciplinary Research, Harper, 1973.

Main Trends in Psychology, Harper, 1973.

The Place of the Sciences of Man in the System of Sciences, Harper, 1974.

(With others) *Recherches sur la contradiction,* two volumes, Presses universitaires de France, 1974, translation by Derek

Coltman published as *Experiments in Contradiction,* University of Chicago Press, 1981.

Adaptation vitale et psychologie de l'intelligence: Selection organique et phenocopie, Hermann, 1974, translation by Stewart Eames published as *Adaptation and Intelligence: Organic Selection and Phenocopy,* University of Chicago Press, 1980.

L'Equilibration des structures cognitives: Probleme central du developpement, Presses universitaires de France, 1975, translation by Arnold Rosin published as *The Development of Thought: Equilibration of Cognitive Structures,* Viking, 1977.

(With M. Amann) *Reussir et comprendre,* Presses universitaires de France, 1978, translation by Pomerans published as *Success and Understanding,* Harvard University Press, 1978.

The Grasp of Consciousness: Action and Concept in the Young Child, translation by Susan Wedgwood, Harvard University Press, 1976.

Sarah F. Campbell, editor, *Piaget Sampler: An Introduction to Jean Piaget through His Own Words,* Wiley, 1976, J. Atonson, 1977.

Howard E. Gruber and J. Jacques Voneche, editors, *The Essential Piaget,* Basic Books, 1977.

Behavior and Evolution, translation by Donald Nicholson-Smith, Pantheon, 1978.

Howard E. Gruber and J. Jacques Voneche, editors, *The Essential Piaget: An Interpretive Reference and Guide,* Basic Books, 1978.

Jeanette McCarthy Gallagher and J. A. Easley, Jr., editors, *Piaget and Education,* Plenum, 1978.

Jean-Claude Bringuier, *Conversations with Jean Piaget,* University of Chicago Press, 1980.

Massimo Piattelli-Palmarini, editor, *Language and Learning: The Debate between Jean Piaget and Noam Chomsky,* Harvard University Press, 1980.

Intelligence and Affectivity: Their Relationship during Child Development, translation by T. A. Brown and C. E. Kaegi, Annual Reviews, 1981.

Possibility & Necessity, two volumes, translation by Helga Feider, University of Minnesota Press, 1987.

(With Rolando Garcia) *Psychogenesis & the History of Science,* translation by Feider, Columbia University Press, 1988.

IN FRENCH

Recherche (novel), Edition la Concorde, 1918.

Classes, relations et nombres: Essai sur les groupements de la logistique et sur la reversibilite de la pensee, Vrin, 1942.

(With Marc Lambercier, Ernest Boesch and Barbara von Albertini) *Introduction a l'etude des perceptions chez l'enfant et analyse d'une illusion relative a la perception visuelle de cercles concentriques,* Delachaux & Niestle, 1942.

(With Lambercier) *La Comparaison visuelle des hauteurs a distances variables dans la plan fronto-parallele,* Delachaux & Niestle, 1943.

(With others) *Essai d'interpretation probabliste de la loi de Weber et de celles des concentrations relatives,* Delachaux & Niestle, 1945.

(With Inhelder) *Experiences sur la construction projective de la ligne droite chez les enfants de 2 a 8 ans,* Delachaux & Niestle, 1946.

Etude sur la psychologie d'Edouard Claparede, Delachaux & Niestle, 1946.

Le Droit a l'education dans le monde actuel, UNESCO, 1949.

(With M. Boscher) *L'Initiation au calcul: Enfants de 4 a 7 ans,* Bourrelier, 1949.

Traite de logique: Essai de logistique operatoire, Colin, 1949, 2nd edition published as *Essai de logique operatoire,* Dunod, 1972.

Introduction a l'epistemologie genetique, three volumes, Presses universitaires de France, 1950, 2nd edition, 1973.

Essai sur les transformations des operations logiques: Les 256 operations ternaires de la logique bivalente des propositions, Presses universitaires de France, 1952.

Les Relations entre l'affectivite et l'intelligence dans le developpement mental de l'enfant, Centre de Documentation Universitaire, 1954.

(With others) *L'Enseignement des mathematiques,* Delachaux & Niestle, 1955.

(Editor) *Etudes d'epistemologie genetique,* Presses universitaires de France, 1957.

(With Inhelder) *Le Developpement des quantites physiques chez l'enfant,* Delachaux & Niestle, 1962.

(With Fraisse, Elaine Vurpillot, and Robert Frances) *La Perception,* Presses universitaires de France, 1963.

(Editor with Maurice Patronnier de Gandillac) *Entretiens sur les notions de genese et de structure,* Mouton, 1965.

Etudes sociologiques, Librarie Droz, 1965.

Logique et connaissance scientifique, Gallimard, 1967.

La Psychologie de l'intelligence, A. Colin, 1967, 2nd edition, 1973.

Epistemologie et psychologie de l'identite, Presses universitaires de France, 1968.

(With others) *Epistemologie et psychologie de la fonction,* Presses universitaires de France, 1968.

Epistemologie des sciences de l'homme, Gallimard, 1970.

(With others) *Les Theories de la causalite,* Presses universitaires de France, 1971.

(With J. Bliss) *Les Directions des mobiles lors de chocs et de poussees,* Presses universitaires de France, 1972.

(With Bliss) *La Transmission des mouvements,* Presses universitaires de France, 1972.

La Formation de la notion de force, Presses universitaires de France, 1973.

(With Bliss) *La composition des forces et le probleme des vecteurs,* Presses universitaires de France, 1973.

(With A. Blanchet) *La Prise de conscience,* Presses universitaires de France, 1974.

Les Mecanismes perceptifs: Modeles probabilistes, analyse genetique, relations avec l'intelligence, 2nd edition, Presses universitaires de France, 1975.

Le Comportement, moteur de l'evolution, Gallimard, 1976.

(With Gil Henriques and I. Berthoud-Papandropoulou) *Recherches sur la generalisation,* Presses universitaires de France, 1978.

Recherches sur les correspondances, Presses universitaires de France, 1980.

CONTRIBUTOR

Troisieme cours pour le personnel enseignant, Bureau International d'Education, 1930.

Quatrieme cours pour le personnel enseignant, Bureau International d'Education, 1931.

C. Murchison, editor, *Handbook of Child Psychology,* Clark University Press, 1931.

Le Self-Government a l'ecole, Bureau International d'Education, 1934.

Le Travail par equipes a l'ecole, Bureau International d'Education, 1935.

UNESCO, Freedom and Culture, Columbia University Press, 1951.

(And author of introduction) *Conference internationale de l'instruction publique,* [Geneva], 1951.

E. G. Boring and others, *History of Psychology in Autobiography,* Volume 4, Clark University Press, 1952.

Swanson, Newcomb, and Hartley, editors, *Readings in Social Psychology,* Holt, 1952.

(And author of introduction) R. Girod, *Attitudes collectives et relations humaines,* Presses universitaires de France, 1952.

H. E. Abramson, *Conference on Problems of Consciousness,* Josiah Macy Foundation, 1954.

P. Osterrieth and others, *Le Probleme des stades en psychologie de l'enfant,* Presses universitaires de France, 1955.

P. H. Hock and J. Zubin, editors, *Psychopathology of Childhood,* Grune & Stratton, 1955.

J. de Ajuriaguerra and others, *Aktuelle Problem der Gestalttheorie,* Hans Huber, 1955.

J. Tanner and Inhelder, editors, *Discussions on Child Development,* Volumes 1-4, Tavistock, 1956, International Universities Press, 1958.

(And author of introduction) Jan Comenius, *Pages Choisies,* UNESCO, 1957, also published as *Selections,* UNESCO [Paris], 1957.

D. Katz, *Handbuch der Psychologie,* 2nd edition, Benno Schwabe, 1959.

(Author of introduction) M. Margot, *L'Ecole operante,* Delachaux & Niestle, 1960.

(And author of introduction) M. Nassefat, *Etude quantitative sur l'evolution des operations intellectuals,* Delachaux & Niestle, 1963.

(And author of introduction) Elaine Vurpillot, *L'Organisation perceptive,* Vrin, 1963.

(And author of introduction) Inhelder, *Le Diagnostic du raisonnement chez les debiles mentaux,* 2nd edition, Delachaux & Niestle, 1963.

(And author of introduction) John H. Flavell, *The Developmental Psychology of Jean Piaget,* Van Nostrand, 1963.

Richard E. Ripple and Verne N. Rockcastle, editors, *Piaget Rediscovered,* Cornell University School of Education, 1964.

(And author of introduction) T. Gouin Decarie, *Intelligence and Affectivity in Early Childhood,* translation by Elisabeth Brandt and Lewis Brandt, International Universities Press, 1965.

(And author of introduction) Millie Almy and others, *Young Children's Thinking: Studies of Some Aspects of Piaget's Theory,* Teacher's College Press, 1966.

(And author of introduction) *Dictionnaire d'epistemologie genetique,* Presses universitaires de France, 1966.

Marcia W. Piers, editor, *Play and Development: A Symposium,* Norton, 1972.

Richard I. Evans, *Jean Piaget: The Man and His Ideas,* Dutton, 1973.

OTHER

Contributor to *Proceedings of the International Congresses of Psychology,* Harvard Tercentenary Conference. Co-editor of *Revue Suisse de Psychologie* and *Archives de Psychologie.* Contributor to numerous periodicals, including *Mind, British Journal of Psychology, Initiation au Calcul, Scientific American, Enfance, British Journal of Educational Psychology, Revue Suisse Psychologie, Synthese, Methados, Diogene Traite de Psychologie Experimentale, Etudes d'Epistemologie Genetique, Journal de Psychologie Normale et Pathologique, Archives de Psychologie* (Geneva), *American Journal of Mental Deficiency, Acta Psychologica,* and *Annee Psychologique.*

SIDELIGHTS: Psychologist Jean Piaget spent most of his long and productive career studying the development of intelligent thinking in children. *Times Literary Supplement* contributor Keith Lovell called Piaget "one of the giants in the history of psychology," a tireless worker who gave the world "a wealth of brilliant and penetrating insights into the intellectual growth of children." In an era when much attention focused on abnormal or pathological behavior, Piaget became known for his descriptions of the normal processes that transform infants into rational, creative adults. His work took into account biological functions, environmental stimuli, and even philosophical theory to create a detailed picture of the stage development of human intellectual life. According to Howard Gardner in the *New York Times Book Review,* Piaget "realized a scientific career of unsurpassed fecundity" that is still gaining approval among modern educators and social scientists. Margaret A. Boden expressed a similar opinion in her work *Jean Piaget.* The psychologist's influence, noted Boden, "has been enormous, especially in his later years, by which time American experimental psychology had moved toward a philosophical base more congruent with his approach." Jerome S. Bruner put it more simply in a *New York Times Book Review* essay. To quote Bruner, Piaget remains "one of the two towering figures of 20th-century psychology."

Ironically, Piaget did not consider himself a child psychologist. He preferred the title "genetic epistemologist"—one who studies the mechanisms by which an organism learns. Richard Evans explained the term in *Jean Piaget: The Man and His Ideas.* "Genetic epistemology deals with the formation and meaning of knowledge and with the means by which the human mind goes from a lower level of knowledge to one that is judged to be higher," Evans wrote. "It is not for psychologists to decide what knowledge is lower or higher but rather to explain how the transition is made from one to the other. The nature of these transitions is a factual matter. They are historical, or psychological, or sometimes even biological." *New York Review of Books* essayist Rosemary Dinnage claimed that Piaget's "mighty project," the one that consumed him for sixty years, was "to trace, right into adulthood, the growth of all the major concepts that structure our world: time, space, causality, substance, number." By this means Piaget discovered that learning is not something poured into a child, but rather something a child helps to create through his or her own activities. In the *New Republic,* Robert Coles concluded: "His studies are meant to give us clues about how we get to be the somewhat knowing, thoughtful people we are. . . . [Piaget was] ever anxious to learn how it is we obtain our knowledge of the world—an acquisition that begins during the first days of life."

Piaget was born and raised in Neuchatel, Switzerland, the son of a college professor who specialized in the history of the Middle Ages. In *Jean Piaget: The Man and His Ideas,* Piaget described his childhood as not particularly happy; his mother suffered from mental illness, and partly out of fear of her condition he threw himself into rigorous scientific study at an early age. He was only eleven when he published his first paper—a short account of a rare part-albino sparrow he observed in his garden. From there he undertook the biological study of mollusks, a genera of great variety in Switzerland. While still in his early teens he was invited to assist the curator of Neuchatel's museum, and he began writing a series of papers on the mollusks in the museum's collection. His reputation became such that at the tender age of sixteen he was offered the directorship of another of Switzerland's mollusk collections—the board of trustees were not aware that he had yet to finish high school. In *Jean Piaget: The Man and His Ideas,* Piaget reminisced about the lasting importance of his work on mollusks, which he continued in college: "These studies, premature as they were, were nevertheless of great value for my scientific development; moreover, they functioned, if I may say so, as instruments of protection against the demon of philosophy. Thanks to them, I had the rare privilege of getting a glimpse of science and what it stands for, before undergoing the philosophical crises of adolescence. To have had early experience with these two kinds of problematic approaches constituted, I am certain, the hidden strength of my later psychological activity."

Eventually Piaget became less interested in pure biology and more consumed by the philosophical/psychological dilemma of "how we know." He turned to psychological study as a means to the end of developing a biologically-oriented theory on the nature and origins of knowledge. As Howard E. Gruber noted in the *New York Times Book Review,* Piaget "took up the study of the child as an approach to fundamental epistemological questions. To his surprise, this became a never-ending enterprise." In the 1920s, many people held the view that children were merely "little adults," who reasoned like grownups. While administering intelligence tests on his young subjects, Piaget came to realize that the "wrong" answers children gave to some questions were quite revealing. Boden explained: "These errors were not merely insignificant mistakes due to childish ignorance and uninformed guessing; rather, they suggested to Piaget's amazement that the logical structures of the child's mind are importantly different from those of adult knowledge. . . . Piaget decided to explore children's thinking further for the light it might throw on the nature and development of human knowledge in general: psychology, he thought, was 'the embryology of intelligence.' " Evans described the aim of Piaget's early experiments: "By testing the child's understanding of the physical, biological, and social worlds at successive age levels, Piaget hoped to find an answer to the question of how we acquire knowledge. In effect Piaget had created an experimental philosophy that sought to answer philosophical questions by putting them to empirical test."

Piaget summarized his findings on juvenile cognition in a series of books, beginning in 1923 with *Le langue et la pensee chez l'enfant* (translated into English as *The Language and Thought of the Child*). Although he later wrote that his early publications were premature—merely the groundwork for future theories—they "made Piaget's name and have probably been more widely read than anything he subsequently wrote," to quote Dinnage. In 1925 Piaget and his wife began their own family, and with the birth of their daughter Jacqueline, they embarked on a program of detailed observation of infant behavior. Boden declared that the result of this observation "was the theory of sensorimotor intelligence, published through the 1930s, which described the spontaneous development (well before the appearance of language) of a practical intelligence based in action, an intelligence that forms and is formed by the infant's nascent concepts of permanent objects, space, time, number, and cause." Put more simply, Piaget suggested that such humble infant acts as sucking and looking constitute the earliest manifestations of intellect, and that babies are born possessing structures with which to organize experience. Dinnage concluded that the birth of his own children made Piaget aware "of how much happened in children's lives before they even started to talk, and one of the main themes in all his work since then has been that intelligence can only grow through actual physical as well as mental engagement with the environment." The critic added that Piaget's books on his children's growth "make up the only coherent account we have of the human being's experience in the first year of life."

"Piaget set himself the task of explaining how the mental structures of the newborn baby become the structures of the adolescent intellect," wrote P. G. Richmond in *An Introduction to Piaget.* "He knew these extreme conditions were not the same and that there must be changes in between which would explain how the first condition became the last." Taking issue with conceptions of heredity and passive accumulation of knowledge as the formative processes in children's cognition, Piaget contended that youngsters of all ages were active agents in their personal intellectual development. According to Evans, Piaget "spoke of learning as, in part, 'the modification of experience as the result of behavior.' He argued that the child's actions upon the world changed the nature of his experience. This is another way of stating the relativity of nature and nurture. If experience is always a product (to some extent) of the child's behavior, any modification of behavior as a result of experience must be relative to the child's actions. Human experience, then, must be relative to human action. . . . Piaget [argued] that the mind never copies reality but instead organizes it and transforms it, reality, in and of itself being . . . unknowable." Bruner felt that Piaget "made a profound mark on modern psychology by refocusing attention on man's sources of rationality, on the processes by which he achieves that rationality, and by showing how human intelligence at all levels of development can be described precisely and rigorously in terms of the underlying logic of the action through which intelligence expresses itself."

As his experience with children of all ages accumulated, Piaget was able to formulate a series of four major stages of mental growth. In the first, the "sensory-motor period," the infant is chiefly concerned with the mastery of objects—toys, blocks, and household items. This phase lasts roughly from birth to two years. The second stage, the "preoperational period," concerns the mastery of symbols, including those occurring in language, fantasy, play, and dreams. This period generally lasts until age six. From six to twelve, the child undergoes the "concrete operational period," during which he or she learns to master the concepts of numbers, classes, and relations, and how to reason about them. Finally, the adolescent enters the "formal operational period," a stage dominated by logical thought and the understanding of others' thinking. "One of Dr. Piaget's major contributions was his development of a theory that children pass through distinct stages of mental and emotional development," wrote J. Y. Smith in the *Washington Post.* "This home truth has been observed by other psychologists—and by numerous parents—but Dr. Piaget gave it a coherence that has had enormous implications not only for the development of clinical child psychology, but also for education." Piaget was criticized for the formality of his stage development plan, but he himself was careful not to tie the stages too closely to chronological ages, recognizing that individual children develop at different rates. Coles summarized Piaget's formulation: "If Freud has taught us how hard and even fierce a struggle each child must wage for sanity, emotional stability, self-respect, Piaget has given us a glimpse of the work that goes into the gradually obtained victory we all too readily tend to think of as a flat given: intelligence—meaning competence, judgment and perceptiveness with respect to the things of this world."

Because he was trained first as a biologist, Piaget sought to explain the development of intelligence as a biological adaptation to the environment—the human organism's way of maximizing its genetic potential. Boden contended that the scholar's "genetic structuralism in biology attempted a synthesis of the Darwinian stress on the organism's autonomy and the Lamarckian emphasis on the organism's adaptive response to the environment."

Piaget's guiding principle was the movement toward "equilibrium," achieved through the two components of adaptation he called "assimilation" and "accommodation." Henry W. Maier explained the concepts in *Thinkers of the Twentieth Century.* "In Piagetian formulation," Maier stated, "equilibration involves the adaptive processes of assimilation and accommodation. A process of feedback and forecasting leads to an advancement in thinking. To put it in another way, events are understood or adjusted at first within the context of ongoing comprehension in order to make sense out of one's experience. Assimilation occurs at the expense of the input. Accommodation, in contrast, changes a person's understanding (and eventually the structure of comprehending) in order to adapt more fully and potentially reorganize one's conception of the world." Evans put it thus: "Piaget's answer . . . was that the child's ideas about the world were 'constructions' that involved both mental structures and experience. . . . While the changes with age imply the role of experience, their orderliness reflects an interaction between nature and nurture." Dinnage, too, concluded that "the crown of the theory . . . is that precisely as the individual's thinking evolves from infancy, so do species themselves evolve—both are concerned in a process of constant re-equilibration, of balancing accommodation to the environment with assimilation of it."

To quote Whitman, "the unfolding of Dr. Piaget's explanations occurred over a lifetime, so there were refinements as new evidence was sifted; but these did not alter his basic theories." Piaget was a prolific writer who spent at least four hours every day composing new text; his lifetime output has been estimated at more than one hundred books, chapters of books, published papers, and edited volumes. As Piaget's explorations of juvenile cognition became more complicated over the years, however, so did his writings. In the *New York Times Book Review,* David Elkind declared that as he did less of the interviewing of children himself, and as his theory became more systematic, Piaget's style "became more abstract and difficult to read. Moreover, he [made] no concessions to readers and [assumed] that they [would] understand his integration of biological, logical, philosophical and psychological concepts." Gardner similarly observed that Piaget's publications "are workaday at best, and often pose difficulties for colleagues and translators." Elkind added, though, that despite their difficulty, "the books are rewarding because on almost every page there are fresh insights into the ways children think about and see the world. For those who have the time and are willing to put in the effort, reading Piaget himself more than repays the investment."

Piaget's work has had broad implications for the fields of psychology, education, and philosophy. "Many experienced or gifted teachers have long applied Piaget's concepts in the classroom without giving conscious consideration to the matter," wrote Richmond. "In such cases Piaget's work lends systematic support to what is intuitively understood. In another sense, however, Piaget's work has greater value. The generality of his concepts, and the panoramic view of intellectual development he offers, can comment upon a diversity of educational matters." Boden addressed a different dimension of Piaget's study. "Psychologists," she claimed, "have given much attention to his theory of intelligence as interiorized action, to his vision of the mind as a continuously developing system of self-regulating structures that actively mediate and are transformed by the subject's interaction with the environment." Dinnage looked at Piaget's work from its philosophical perspective in her essay. The critic observed that from Piaget's perspective, "childhood is a long process of 'decentering,' abandoning the egocentric position until gradually 'the self is freed from itself and assigns itself a place

as a thing among things, an event among events.' For Piaget this is noble: the great act of intellect, as central for the individual as when 'Copernicus ceased to believe in geocentrism and Einstein in Newtonian absolutes.' " Here, concluded Dinnage, "we find the unacknowledged moral mainspring of all [Piaget's] work."

If the intellectual establishment was slow to accept Piaget's theories, subsequent decades have enhanced the scholar's reputation. According to Evans, Piaget retained "the ambiguous position of the intellectual innovator" throughout his life, and therefore "it will probably be decades before his ideas become firmly rooted within the canons of psychology." Evans explained, however, that Piaget will be remembered just as Sigmund Freud has been, and for many of the same reasons. "The findings he . . . gleaned, and the theory he . . . constructed after more than forty years of studying the development of intelligence, are effecting a veritable Copernican revolution in our understanding of the growth and functioning of the human mind," Evans wrote. Boden likewise stated that modern developmental psychology "would be very different without him and, surely, considerably poorer." She added: "For all the criticisms that can justly be made of him, there is no question that Piaget is a modern master. At both observational and theoretical levels, his work has provided a stimulus to (or more appropriately perhaps, a seed of) our understanding of the development of intelligence that is without equal." *New York Times* correspondent John Leonard concluded that Piaget "asked the right questions and . . . what he observed of children getting to know space, time, cause and objectivity is an indispensable starting point for thinking about how the mind constructs the world." To quote Leonard further, Piaget's "is at least a humane psychology, stressing curiosity and competence."

BIOGRAPHICAL/CRITICAL SOURCES:

BOOKS

Atkinson, Christine, *Making Sense of Piaget: The Philosophical Roots,* Routledge & Kegan Paul, 1983.

Boden, Margaret, *Jean Piaget,* Viking, 1979.

Brainerd, J., *Piaget's Theory of Intelligence,* Prentice-Hall, 1978.

Brearly, Molly and Elizabeth Hitchfield, *A Teacher's Guide to Reading Piaget,* Routledge & Kegan Paul, 1966.

Bruner, Jerome S., *The Process of Education,* Harvard University Press, 1960.

Bruner, Jerome S., *Towards a Theory of Instruction,* Harvard University Press, 1966.

Butterworth, George, editor, *Infancy and Epistemology: An Evaluation of Piaget's Theory,* St. Martin's, 1982.

Cohen, David, *Piaget: Critique and Reassessment,* Croom Helm, 1983.

Dasen, Pierre R., editor, *Piagetian Psychology: Cross Cultural Contributions,* Gardner Press, 1976.

Egan, Kieran, *Education and Psychology: Plato, Piaget, and Scientific Psychology,* Columbia Teachers College Press, 1983.

Elkind, David and John Flavell, editors, *Studies in Cognitive Development: Essays in Honor of Jean Piaget,* Oxford University Press, 1969.

Evans, Richard I., *Jean Piaget: The Man and His Ideas,* Dutton, 1973.

Evans, Richard I., *Dialogue with Jean Piaget,* Praeger, 1981.

Flavell, John H., *The Developmental Psychology of Jean Piaget,* Van Nostrand, 1963.

Furth, Han, *Piaget and Knowledge: Theoretical Foundations,* Prentice Hall, 1969.

Gallagher, J. M. and Reid, D. K., *The Learning Theory of Piaget and Inhelder,* Brooks/Cole, 1981.

Geber, Beryl A., *Piaget and Knowing: Studies in Genetic Epistemology*, Routledge & Kegan Paul, 1977.

Gruber, Howard E. and J. Jacques Voneche, *The Essential Piaget: An Interpretive Reference and Guide*, Basic Books, 1978.

Holloway, G. E. T., *An Introduction to "The Child's Conception of Geometry,"* Routledge & Kegan Paul, 1967.

Hunt, J. McVicker, *Intelligence and Experience*, Ronald, 1961.

Inhelder, Barbel and Harold H. Chipman, editors, *Piaget and His School: A Reader in Developmental Psychology*, Springer-Verlag, 1976.

Kessen, William and Clementina Kuhlman, *Thought in the Young Child: Report with Particular Attention to the Work of Piaget*, Child Development Publications, 1960.

Kitchener, Richard F., *Piaget's Theory of Knowledge: Genetic Epistemology and Scientific Reason*, Yale University Press, 1986.

Labinowicz, E., *The Piaget Primer*, Addison-Wesley, 1980.

Liben, Lynn S., editor, *Piaget and the Foundations of Knowledge*, Erlbaum, 1983.

Maier, Henry, *Three Theories of Child Development*, Harper, 1965.

Malerstein, A. J., *A Piagetian Model of Character Structure*, Human Sciences Press, 1982.

Modgil, Sohan and Celia Modgil, *Jean Piaget: Consensus and Controversy*, Praeger, 1982.

Modgil, Sohan, and others, editors, *Jean Piaget: An Interdisciplinary Critique*, Routledge & Kegan Paul, 1983.

New Directions in Piagetian Theory and Practice, Erlbaum, 1981.

Phillips, J. L., *Piaget's Theory: A Primer*, W. H. Freeman, 1980.

Piattelli-Palmarini, Massimo, *Language and Learning: The Debate between Jean Piaget and Noam Chomsky*, Harvard University Press, 1980.

Pulaski, M. A. S., *Understanding Piaget*, revised edition, Harper, 1980.

Richmond, P. G., *An Introduction to Piaget*, Basic Books, 1971.

Ripple, Richard E. and Verne N. Rockcastle, editors, *Piaget Rediscovered*, Cornell University School of Education, 1964.

Seltman, Muriel and Peter Seltman, *Piaget's Logic: A Critique of Genetic Epistemology*, Allen and Unwin, 1985.

Shulman, Valerie L., and others, editors, *The Future of Piagetian Theory: The Neo-Piagetians*, Plenum, 1985.

Silverman, Hugh J., editor, *Piaget, Philosophy, and the Human Sciences*, Humanities Press, 1980.

Thinkers of the Twentieth Century, Gale, 1983.

Varma, Ved P. and Phillip Williams, editors, *Piaget, Psychology and Education: Papers in Honor of Jean Piaget*, Hodder & Stoughton, 1976.

Wadsworth, B. J., *Piaget's Theory of Cognitive Development*, Longman, 1979.

Wolff, Peter H., *The Developmental Psychologies of Jean Piaget and Psychoanalysis*, International Universities Press, 1960.

PERIODICALS

American Sociological Review, February, 1966.
Commonweal, April 5, 1968.
Education Digest, March, 1968.
New Republic, March 18, 1978.
New York Review of Books, December 21, 1978, October 23, 1980.
New York Times, January 25, 1980.
New York Times Book Review, February 11, 1968, August 1, 1976, May 14, 1978, October 19, 1980.
New York Times Magazine, May 26, 1968.
Saturday Review, May 20, 1967, April 20, 1968.

Times Educational Supplement, December 6, 1957.
Times Literary Supplement, August 22, 1968, September 4, 1969, June 25, 1970, March 17, 1972, June 2, 1972, August 11, 1972, June 29, 1973, August 19, 1977.
Yale Review, winter, 1987.

OBITUARIES:

PERIODICALS

Newsweek, September 29, 1980.
New York Times, September 17, 1980.
Time, September 29, 1980.
Times (London), September 18, 1980.*

—*Sketch by Anne Janette Johnson*

*   *   *

PIERCE, Glenn
  See DUMKE, Glenn S.

*   *   *

PINSKER, Sanford   1941-

PERSONAL: Born September 28, 1941, in Washington, Pa.; son of Morris David (a salesman) and Sonia (Molliver) Pinsker; married Ann Getson (a teacher), January 28, 1968; children: Matthew, Beth. *Education:* Washington and Jefferson College, B.A., 1963; University of Washington, Seattle, M.A., 1965, Ph.D., 1967. *Religion:* Jewish.

ADDRESSES: Home—700 North Pine St., Lancaster, Pa. 17603. *Office*—Department of English, Franklin and Marshall College, Lancaster, Pa. 17604.

CAREER: Franklin and Marshall College, Lancaster, Pa., assistant professor, 1967-73, associate professor, 1974-84, professor of English, 1984-88, Shadek Humanities Professor, 1988—. Visiting professor, University of California, Riverside, 1973, 1975.

MEMBER: Modern Language Association of America, Multi-Ethnic Literature of the United States, James Joyce Society, Northeast Modern Language Association.

AWARDS, HONORS: Graduate Institute of Modern Letters fellowship, 1968; National Endowment for the Humanities Younger Humanist Award, 1970-71, Seminar in American Humor, 1978-79; Fulbright senior lecturer, Belgium, 1984-85; Pennsylvania Humanist Award, 1985-87.

WRITINGS:

The Schlemiel as Metaphor: Studies in the Yiddish and American-Jewish Novel, Southern Illinois University Press, 1971.
Still Life and Other Poems (chapbook), Greenfield Review Press, 1975.
The Comedy That "Hoits": An Essay on the Fiction of Philip Roth, University of Missouri Press, 1975.
Between Two Worlds: The American Novel in the 1960s, Whitston Publishing, 1978.
The Languages of Joseph Conrad, Rodopi (Amsterdam), 1978.
Philip Roth: Critical Essays, G. K. Hall, 1982.
Memory Breaks Off and Other Poems, Northwoods Press, 1984.
(Co-author) *America and the Holocaust*, Penkevill Publishing, 1985.
Conversations with Contemporary American Writers, Rodopi, 1985.
Whales at Play and Other Poems of Travel, Northwoods Press, 1986.

Three Pacific Northwest Poets: Stafford, Hugo, and Wagoner, G. K. Hall, 1987.

The Uncompromising Fictions of Cynthia Ozick, University of Missouri Press, 1987.

Also contributor to numerous books and anthologies. Co-editor, *Holocaust Studies Annual* and *Encyclopedia of Jewish-American History and Culture.* Contributor of numerous articles, reviews, and poems to periodicals, including *Virginia Quarterly Review, Commonweal, Saturday Review, Poetry Now, Ball State University Forum, Christian Science Monitor,* and *New York Times.* Member of editorial board, *Studies in American Jewish Literature, Critique,* and *Journal of Modern Literature.*

WORK IN PROGRESS: The Achievement of the Jewish-American Novel, 1917-1987, for G. K. Hall; *Understanding Joseph Heller,* for University of South Carolina Press; other books on Irving Hawe and American humor.

SIDELIGHTS: Sanford Pinsker told *CA:* "Auden once said that the important things to learn were how to laugh and how to pray. For me, poetry seems an ideal place to do both. Criticism, on the other hand, happens when ideas are clear enough to fit into prose."

*   *   *

POMORSKA, Krystyna 1928-1986

PERSONAL: Born April 5, 1928, in Lwow, Poland; died December, 1986; daughter of Juliusz (a lawyer) and Maria (Ziemba) Pomorski; married Roman Jakobson (died July 18, 1982), September 28, 1962. *Education:* Slowacki College, Warsaw, Poland, B.A., 1951; Warsaw University, M.A., 1955; University of Chicago, Ph.D., 1962.

ADDRESSES: Home—Cambridge, Mass. 02138. *Office*—Department of Humanities, Massachusetts Institute of Technology, Cambridge, Mass. 02139.

CAREER: State Publishing House, Warsaw, Poland, editor, translator, and consultant, 1952-59; Warsaw University, Warsaw, assistant to the chair of literary theory, 1956-59; Massachusetts Institute of Technology, Center for Communication Sciences, Cambridge, visiting scholar, 1960-61; University of Chicago, Chicago, Ill., assistant professor in Slavic department, 1961-62; Massachusetts Institute of Technology, assistant professor of modern languages, 1963-64, associate professor, 1964-70, professor of foreign literatures and linguistics, 1970—.

MEMBER: American Association for the Advancement of Slavic Studies.

WRITINGS:

Russian Formalist Theory and Its Poetic Ambience, Mouton, 1968.

(Editor) *Fifty Years of Russian Prose: From Pasternak to Solzhenitsyn,* MIT Press, 1971.

(Editor with Ladislav Matejka) *Readings in Russian Poetics: Formalist and Structuralist Views,* MIT Press, 1971.

Themes and Variations in Pasternak's Poetics, Peter De Ridder Press (Lisse), 1975.

Pasternak and Futurism, Peter De Ridder Press, c. 1975.

(Editor with Andrei Kodjak and Kiril Taranovsky) *Alexander Puskin Symposium II,* Slavica, 1980.

(Editor with Kodjak and Michael J. Connolly) *The Structural Analysis of Narrative Texts: Conference Papers,* Slavica, 1980.

(With husband, Roman Jakobson) *Dialogues,* Flammarion, 1980, translated from the French by Christian Hubert as *The Jakobson-Pomorska Dialogues,* MIT Press, 1983.

(Editor with Kodjak and Stephen Rudy) *Myth in Literature,* Slavica, 1984.

(Editor with Rudy) Jakobson, *Verbal Art, Verbal Sign, Verbal Time,* University of Minnesota Press, 1985.

(With Rudy) Jakobson, *Language in Literature,* Harvard University Press, 1987.

(With others) *Language, Poetry, and Poetics: The Generation of the 1890s: Jakobson, Trubetzkoy, Majakovski—Proceedings of the First Roman Jakobson Colloquim,* Mouton, 1987.

BIOGRAPHICAL/CRITICAL SOURCES:

PERIODICALS

Times Literary Supplement, August 28, 1969.*

*   *   *

PRESLEY, Delma E(ugene) 1939-

PERSONAL: Born May 16, 1939, in Tallulah Lodge, Ga.; son of W. F. (a barber) and Addie (a textile worker; maiden name, Franklin) Presley; married Beverly Bloodworth, June 17, 1961; children: Jonathan Worth, Susan Franklin, Edwin Brockman. *Education:* Mercer University, A.B., 1961; Southern Baptist Theological Seminary, B.D., 1964; Emory University, Ph.D., 1969. *Religion:* Presbyterian.

ADDRESSES: Home—106 South Edgewood Dr., Statesboro, Ga. 30458. *Office*—Georgia Southern Museum, Georgia Southern College, Statesboro, Ga. 30460.

CAREER: Columbia College, Columbia, S.C., instructor in English and religion, 1967-69; Georgia Southern College, Statesboro, assistant professor, 1969-73, associate professor, 1973-79, professor of English, 1979—, director of Georgia Southern Museum, 1982—. Exchange program executive with Piggly Wiggly Southern, Inc., 1974. Director, Project RAFT: Restoring Altamaha Folklife Traditions, 1981-82.

MEMBER: American Association of Museums, Association of Science-Technology Centers, Southeastern Museums Conference, Coastal Museums Association (vice-president, 1987-88), Georgia Historical Society, Georgia Association of Museums and Galleries (president, 1988-89), Bulloch County Historical Society (president, 1982), Phi Delta Kappa.

AWARDS, HONORS: National Endowment for the Humanities fellow, 1974-75; Professor of the Year award, Georgia Southern University, 1981; Georgia Governor's Award for the Humanities, 1986.

WRITINGS:

(Editor and author of introduction) James Holmes, *Dr. Bullies' Notes: Reminiscences of Early Georgia and of Philadelphia and New Haven in the 1800s,* Cherokee, 1976.

(With Francis Harper) *Okefinokee Album,* University of Georgia Press, 1981.

(Author of introduction) Brainard Cheney, *Lightwood,* Burr Oak Press, 1983.

Piggly Wiggly Southern Style, PWS Publishers, 1986.

The Glass Menagerie: An American Memory, Twayne, 1990.

Contributor to literature and history journals and literary magazines, including *American Literature, Mississippi Quarterly, Journal of Popular Culture, Georgia Review,* and *South Atlantic Review.*

WORK IN PROGRESS: Exhibit and exhibit catalog of photographs and artifacts from the Okefenokee Swamp and the Altamaha River Valley.

SIDELIGHTS: Delma E. Presley told *CA:* "Becoming a museum director in 1982 was the pivotal moment in my career as a teacher and writer. For the previous fifteen years I had taught literature, published articles, essays and two books, and had made those predictable transitions through the ranks to full professor. However, I also had spent a great deal of time doing what I also enjoy: interpreting and communicating ideas to the public in an informal setting. My interest in folklore and regional history led me toward the museum field. Here I have renewed a commitment to interdisciplinary scholarship that I found inspiring as a student in Emory University's Graduate Institute of the Liberal Arts in the mid-1960s. The museum directorship has also enabled me to reconcile, at least for my satisfaction, the intellectual debate concerning idea vs. reality. I have learned to appreciate the importance of focusing attention on the artifact, the work of art, the real thing. I had been involved in museum work for six years when I wrote *The Glass Menagerie: An American Memory.* I discovered myself much more at home in the literary world of Tennessee Williams than I had been earlier. I saw more 'things' in this great play, and I realized the thematic significance of objects, facts, and dialogue I previously overlooked when I had approached the work along the lines of conventional literary criticism. The basic task of a museum professional is not unlike that of a teacher, my original calling. Like a good book, a museum can provide the means for people to fulfill the universal desire both for adventure and for understanding. Helping people become explorers is no little task, and good museums encourage exploration and help explorers along their way."

* * *

PRITCHETT, V(ictor) S(awdon) 1900-

PERSONAL: Born December 16, 1900, in Ipswich, England; son of Sawdon (a businessman) and Beatrice (Martin) Pritchett; married second wife, Dorothy Roberts, October 2, 1936; children: (second marriage) Josephine (Mrs. Brian Murphy), Oliver. *Education:* Attended secondary school in Dulwich, England.

ADDRESSES: Home—12 Regents Park Terr., London N.W. 1, England. *Agent*—A. Peters, 10 Buckingham St., London WC2N 6BU, England.

CAREER: Writer, 1921—. Bookkeeper in the leather trade, London, England, 1916-20; freelance journalist for the *Christian Science Monitor* in France, Ireland, Spain, Morocco, and the United States, 1923-26; *New Statesman,* London, and *Nation,* New York, N.Y., literary critic, 1926-65, director, 1951-75. Christian Gauss Lecturer, Princeton University, 1953; Beckman Professor, University of California, Berkeley, 1960; writer in residence, Smith College, 1966; Zisskind Professor, Brandeis University, 1968; Clark Lecturer, Cambridge University, 1969; visiting professor, Columbia University, 1970.

MEMBER: PEN International (president, 1974-75), English PEN Club (president, 1970), Society of Authors (president), American Academy of Arts and Sciences (honorary foreign member), American Academy and Institute of Arts and Letters (honorary foreign member), Royal Society of Literature (fellow), Savile Club, Beefsteak Club.

AWARDS, HONORS: Royal Society of Literature Award, 1967, and Heinemann Award, 1969, both for *A Cab at the Door: A Memoir;* Commander of the British Empire, 1968, knighted,

1975; PEN Award for biography, 1974, for *Balzac;* "notable book of 1979" citation from *Library Journal,* 1980, for *The Myth Makers: Literary Essays.* Honorary degrees from Leeds University, 1971, Columbia University, Harvard University, and University of Sussex.

WRITINGS:

NONFICTION

Marching Spain, Benn, 1928.
In My Good Books, Chatto & Windus, 1942, reprinted, Kennikat, 1970.
The Living Novel, Chatto & Windus, 1946, Reynal, 1947, revised and expanded edition published as *The Living Novel, And Later Appreciations,* Random House, 1964.
(With Elizabeth Bowen and Graham Greene) *Why Do I Write?,* Percival Marshall, 1948.
Books in General, Harcourt, 1953, reprinted, Greenwood Press, 1981.
The Spanish Temper, Knopf, 1954, reprinted, Hogarth, 1984.
London Perceived, Harcourt, 1962, 2nd edition, 1963.
The Offensive Traveller, Knopf, 1964 (published in England as *Foreign Faces,* Chatto & Windus, 1964).
New York Proclaimed, Harcourt, 1965.
The Working Novelist, Chatto & Windus, 1965.
Shakespeare: The Comprehensive Soul, British Broadcasting Corporation (BBC), 1965.
Dublin: A Portrait, Harper, 1967.
A Cab at the Door: A Memoir (autobiography), Random House, 1968 (published in England as *A Cab at the Door: An Autobiography, Early Years,* Chatto & Windus, 1968).
George Meredith and English Comedy, Random House, 1970.
Midnight Oil (autobiography), Chatto & Windus, 1971, Random House, 1972.
Balzac (biography), Random House, 1974.
The Gentle Barbarian: The Life and Work of Turgenev (biography), Random House, 1977.
The Myth Makers: Literary Essays, Random House, 1979 (published in England as *The Myth Makers: Essays on European, Russian, and South American Novelists,* Chatto & Windus, 1979).
The Tale Bearers: Literary Essays, Random House, 1980 (published in England as *The Tale Bearers: Essays on English, American, and Other Writers,* Chatto & Windus, 1980).
(With Reynolds Stone) *The Turn of the Years,* Random House, 1982.
The Other Side of the Frontier: A V. S. Pritchett Reader, Robin Clark, 1984.
Man of Letters: Selected Essays, Chatto & Windus, 1985, Random House, 1986.
Chekhov: A Spirit Set Free (biography), Random House, 1988.
At Home and Abroad, North Point Press, 1989.

NOVELS

Clare Drummer, Benn, 1929.
Elopement into Exile, Little, Brown, 1932 (published in England as *Shirley Sanz,* Gollancz, 1932).
Nothing Like Leather, Macmillan, 1935.
Dead Man Leading, Macmillan, 1937, reprinted, Oxford University Press, 1985.
Mr. Beluncle, Harcourt, 1951, reprinted, Postway Press, 1972.

SHORT STORIES

The Spanish Virgin and Other Stories, Benn, 1930.
You Make Your Own Life, Chatto & Windus, 1938.

It May Never Happen and Other Stories, Chatto & Windus, 1945, Reynal, 1947.

The Sailor, Sense of Humor, and Other Stories, Knopf, 1956 (published in England as *Collected Stories,* Chatto & Windus, 1956), also published as *The Saint and Other Stories,* Penguin, 1966.

When My Girl Comes Home, Knopf, 1961.

The Key to My Heart: A Comedy in Three Parts (contains "The Key to My Heart," "Noisy Flushes the Birds," and "Noisy in the Doghouse"), Chatto & Windus, 1963, Random House, 1964.

Blind Love and Other Stories, Chatto & Windus, 1969, Random House, 1970.

(Contributor) *Penguin Modern Stories 9,* Penguin, 1971.

The Camberwell Beauty, Random House, 1975.

Selected Stories, Random House, 1978.

The Fly in the Ointment, Cambridge University Press, 1978.

On the Edge of the Cliff, Random House, 1979.

Collected Stories, Random House, 1982.

More Collected Stories, Random House, 1983.

A Careless Widow and Other Stories, Random House, 1989.

EDITOR

Robert Louis Stevenson, *Novels and Stories: Selected,* Duell, Sloan & Pearce, 1946.

Turnstile One: A Literary Miscellany from the New Statesman and Nation, Turnstile, 1951.

Robert Southey, *The Chronicle of the Cid,* J. Enschede en Zonen for Limited Editions Club, 1958.

The Oxford Book of Short Stories, Oxford University Press, 1981.

Also editor of periodicals *This England, New Statesman,* and *Nation,* 1937.

OTHER

"Essential Jobs" (screenplay), 1942.

Author of weekly column, "Books in General," in the *New Statesman.* Contributor of essays to numerous periodicals, including *Nation, New York Times, New York Times Book Review, New York Review of Books, Holiday, English Review, New Yorker, Playboy,* and *Atlantic Monthly.*

SIDELIGHTS: Many observers consider V. S. Pritchett England's premier living man of letters. Pritchett's phenomenal career spans six decades and includes numerous volumes of literary criticism, fiction, biography, and nonfiction—all crafted for the discerning general reader. *New York Times Book Review* contributor Penelope Mortimer calls Pritchett "a veteran of the international literary establishment: a humanitarian and one of the greatest stylists in the English language." Mortimer adds that the author's "position in the world of letters is unassailable. . . . [His] reputation for excellence is unquestionable and secure." Knighted in 1975 for his service to British literature, Pritchett has spent a lifetime studying—and adding to—the Continental literary canon. According to Helen Muchnic in the *Saturday Review,* he is "the most cosmopolitan of literary critics. His range is broad, and he is always at home in the work he is writing about, whatever its place of origin, language, or century. . . . He likes to detect a writer's individuality in his work and to examine the special quality of his skill. His approach is essentially humanistic, and he writes with unassuming wisdom, perceptiveness, and charm." *Los Angeles Times Book Review* essayist Charles Champlin expresses a similar opinion: "V. S. Pritchett," writes Champlin, "Sir Victor since 1975, is the wise, foxy and kindly grandfather of present English letters: critic, biographer, essayist, novelist and, above all, one of the masters of the short

story. . . . Pritchett is a matchless observer, but more: an appreciator of what he observes and, accordingly, a writer to be appreciated, profoundly."

Washington Post Book World correspondent Michael Dirda calls Pritchett's achievement "a triumph of the work ethic." Indeed, Pritchett has managed to write full-length books while maintaining a substantial schedule of monthly reviewing for a number of British and American periodicals. Such industry, writes Richard Locke in the *New York Times Book Review,* "suggests the preternatural energy of genius, and almost all this . . . work exhibits a fresh, compulsive curiosity and a vigorous prose style." Pritchett's career is characterized by its unusual length and also by the author's unconventional background. Largely self-educated, the son of working-class parents, Pritchett "rose by talent and force of will to gentility, a high personal civilization, and a distinguished literary career," to quote *Sewanee Review* contributor B. L. Reid. Walter Sullivan praises Pritchett in the *Sewanee Review* for his ability "to create a variety of backgrounds: he is not tied, as so many writers are, to a single and usually restricted world." Locke likewise contends that Pritchett "has the lower-middle-class Londoner's quick eye and sharp tongue and appetite for comedy. He's quick to spot pride, the cover-up, flummery, snobbery, cant. From his work he appears to be an emotional, intensely curious man—plucky, blunt, generous." Pritchett "seems to have been a virtuoso all his working life," writes Lynne Sharon Schwartz in the *Washington Post Book World.* "[He is] a luminous example of what it means to be timeless."

Pritchett himself has documented his unorthodox childhood in an award-winning narrative entitled *A Cab at the Door: A Memoir.* By his own account, his youth was not the sort which portended a career in letters. He was born in 1900 into genteel London poverty; his father, a constantly failing businessman, moved the family often in order to outrun debt collectors. Pritchett's schooling was consequently haphazard, although he did manage to learn French and German and cultivate a taste for literature. While still a young teen he came under the influence of a school teacher who encouraged him to write, and the youngster determined that he wanted to be a professional author. This career choice was unacceptable to his family—*New York Review of Books* essayist John Gross comments that Pritchett's father "jeered at his ambitions and grumbled about his ingratitude." At the age of fifteen Pritchett was forced to leave school for a position with a London leather wholesaler. The tedious office work was made bearable by the opportunity to observe the various colorful characters in the leather trade, and Pritchett spent most of his off-hours reading classical English and European literature. Finally, when he was twenty, Pritchett was granted a trip to Paris after a long illness that forced him out of work. He left for France secretly vowing never to return.

Reid writes: "All lives are hard but Pritchett's was harder than most. His family created him and by their lights nurtured him, but they very nearly killed him. . . . Writing . . . is something one must do for oneself, but few writers can have been so utterly self-made. Pritchett learned to write by reading and writing. No master, no old boys, pulled him along." Once out of sight of his family, Pritchett found life on his own in Paris an exhilarating experience. While working a number of odd jobs, he absorbed the culture and ambience of the city and continued his solitary regimen of reading. In 1921 his first three submitted pieces of writing were accepted by the *Christian Science Monitor.* Pritchett chose that particular periodical because his father was a Christian Scientist and because he himself had followed the faith—without much enthusiasm—for some years. With the promise of further work from the *Monitor,* he quit his regular jobs; however, assignments came slowly and paid low wages, so he eventually had to return to London, nearly penniless. *Dictionary of Literary Biography* contributor Harry S. Marks notes that Pritchett "left Paris after a two-year stay, having gained a large degree of freedom, self-confidence, and an expanded awareness of different cultures and national characteristics." He was to put this awareness to good use in the ensuing years, as the *Monitor* sent him to Ireland, Spain, and the Appalachian Mountain region of America as an investigative reporter.

Still in his mid-twenties, Pritchett began writing regular articles from the various countries to which he was assigned by the *Monitor.* He then began to use his impressions in books such as the nonfiction *Marching Spain* and the collection *The Spanish Virgin and Other Stories.* Meanwhile, he began to sell his travel essays and book reviews to the *Manchester Guardian* and the *New Statesman,* both prestigious forums for such a young writer. According to Champlin, Pritchett's "range of information and his perfect command of style stay constant, which is to say they were achieved early." Modest success also came early to Pritchett; both *Marching Spain* and *The Spanish Virgin* sold in excess of three thousand hardback copies, a much better showing than the publishers had anticipated. Marks observes, however, that the critics "were less than kind to Pritchett's early efforts at writing fiction." For several years Pritchett concentrated on writing novels rather than stories, and it is these works that received such cool reviews. Between 1929 and 1937 he published four novels, after which he opted almost exclusively for the short story format. As Valentine Cunningham notes in the *Times Literary Supplement,* by his own and his century's thirties, "Pritchett was well into his stride: a pace that, astonishingly, he's been able to maintain ever since. . . . From the start his trademark has been making human moments into epiphanies through memorable phrases, vivid tags and scraps of ideolect captured by roaming and plundering the language registers of an extraordinary breadth of classes and sects, odd social crannies, dark and curious corners of behavior."

Pritchett's youth may not have prepared him for a conventional career in literary criticism, but it certainly gave him ample material from which to draw for fiction. To quote *Time* magazine correspondent Timothy Foote, the author's short stories "regularly throb with the same grotesque scenes and sensuous memories as his life, recollected with a comic clarity and shrewd indulgence." Many of Pritchett's stories chronicle the mundane lives of England's lower middle class, especially its older, more eccentric members. In *Books and Bookmen,* Jean Stubbs maintains that the writer "has a lively affection for the oddballs: seldom successful, physically and mentally scarred, stupid and shrewd, mean and kind and predatory, unconsciously ridiculous, tripped up by their virtues and hounded by their vices. But never once does he allow his compassion to slither into sentimentality, nor his listening eyes and seeing ears to persuade him into mere cleverness." Cunningham notes that what Pritchett celebrates "is the heroicism of banal life [as well as] ordinary people, made marginal and socially insignificant by provinciality or lack of intelligence, or by the chosen exiles of enthusiastic religiosity." Eudora Welty elaborates in the *New York Times Book Review:* "These are *social* stories," Welty writes. "Life goes on in them without flagging. The characters that fill them—erratic, unsure, unsafe, devious, stubborn, restless and desirous, absurd and passionate, all peculiar unto themselves—hold a claim on us that is not to be denied. They demand and get our rapt attention, for in their revelation of their lives, the secrets of our own lives come into view. How much the eccentric has to tell us of what is central!" Robert Kiely also observes in the *New York Times Book Review*

that Pritchett's characters "are often middle-aged or old and living in moderate-to-desperate circumstances." The critic adds, however, that Pritchett "resists the temptation (possibly is not even tempted) to blast them off the face of the earth or transform them into heroes. But he shows us, and, furthermore, delights us, by making us believe in the human capacity to change and, particularly, to love." *New Republic* essayist William Trevor concludes that a foreign reader wishing to understand the English people "might profitably turn first to the stories of V. S. Pritchett. . . . He would meet the prejudices and pettinesses of that extraordinary island, the subtleties of its class system, the trailing mists of an empire that will not quite go away."

Some reviewers feel that Pritchett's stories offer scathing criticism of British middle-class mores. Others find the author preoccupied with individual lives, with the fantasies, illusions, and longings that transcend class or education. "Typically," declares Benjamin DeMott in the *New York Times Book Review,* "a Pritchett tale offers a minimum of two vividly defined, sprightly-tongued characters, much observable incident, and authoritative views of contemporary manners. . . . But Pritchett's creative energy usually spends itself not upon narrative ingenuities but upon climaxes in which surprising configurations of feelings stand revealed, born naturally from the movement of events, and unobtrusively correcting simplistic versions of our emotional insides. The effect is often that of ironic comedy, never harsh but never gullible." In the *New York Review of Books,* Denis Donoghue writes: "Mr. Pritchett's stories are invariably written in search of a character. They end when the character has been disclosed. Usually the story presents the character at one revealing moment, and it rarely concerns itself with other possibilities, later chapters, for instance, in a character's life. The short story is a happy form for Mr. Pritchett because he identifies character and nature; a man's character is his nature and it may be disclosed in a flash, the significant circumstances of a moment." *New York Times Book Review* correspondent Guy Davenport likewise observes that Pritchett's characters "are human wills desperately on their own; their dogged independence being the source of the comedy they generate. And it is the comedy of tolerant understanding, for Mr. Pritchett is a sane and immensely civilized writer. He is also a wonderfully invisible writer. Accomplished as he is with books and ideas . . . nothing resembling a thesis or political stance or philosophical notion appears in these stories. Mr. Pritchett is all eye, all ear. That an author so congenial and wise can tell such tales of human folly with never a blush nor a grumble is a triumph of good nature."

Stylistically, Pritchett's stories combine economical language and descriptive passages with a strong sense of the comic in human language and gesture. Pritchett "can peek and tell with the best of them," according to Carole Cook in the *Saturday Review.* "His hallmark is the airy gentleness of his touch as he lifts the veils." *New York Review of Books* essayist Jonathan Raban offers a more detailed appraisal. "The moral philosophy and the literary artifice by which [Pritchett's] characters are brought into being are cunningly hidden from the reader," Raban writes. "The seemingly inconsequential talkiness of tone, together with Pritchett's habitual air of just being a plain man with an anecdote to tell, are devices that conceal an art as rigorous and deeply thought out as that of Henry James. Beware of Pritchett's homespun manner: it is an elaborate camouflage." Similarly, *New Republic* contributor Edith Milton observes that underlying Pritchett's simple narratives and familiar settings "is the suggestion of wildly tangled contradiction. Pritchett's stories are full of mysteries and the unexplained fragments of relationships, which we are asked to intuit rather than understand. . . . These are stories which so delicately suggest the unseen, inner core by its shadow cast against the visible outside surface, that they succeed not only as works of fiction but as achievements of a profoundly poetic imagination." In the *New York Review of Books,* Frank Kermode calls Pritchett "in the best sense, very knowing. . . . He always knows how people speak, with their bodies as well as their tongues. Yet it seems wrong to say, as people do, that his primary concern is with the progressive unveiling of character. . . . [A] literal transfiguration of the commonplace seems to be Pritchett's central theme."

Recent compilations of Pritchett's fiction, including *Collected Stories, More Collected Stories,* and *On the Edge of the Cliff,* have introduced the author to a new generation of readers and have enhanced his reputation amongst his peers. "Pritchett's literary achievement is enormous, but his short stories are his greatest triumph," claims Paul Theroux in the *Saturday Review.* "And one can say with perfect confidence that there is nothing like them in the language, because every short story writer of brilliance makes the form his own." Welty writes: "Any Pritchett story is all of it alight and busy at once, like a well-going fire. Wasteless and at the same time well fed, it shoots up in flame from its own spark like a poem or a magic trick, self-consuming, with nothing left over. He is one of the great pleasure-givers in our language." In the *Washington Post Book World,* Robertson Davies concludes that Pritchett's fictions "are all illuminated by understanding, and have the ring of truth. Every word and situation, every queer turn of events, carries conviction. This is literary achievement on a very high level, and what a relief it is from the tedious stream of stories about privileged people who have time and inclination for foolish mischief, usually of a sexual kind, and who are so frequently authors, or artists, or simply rich idlers, but who are invariably self-indulgent dullards." *New Republic* contributor William Trevor suggests that Pritchett "has probably done more for the English short story than anyone has ever done."

As a literary journalist, Pritchett strives to keep his essays free of academic cant and pedantic assertions—these, he feels, obscure literature and quell curiosity. His criticism, most of which has appeared initially in periodicals, has been collected in *The Myth Makers: Literary Essays, The Tale Bearers: Literary Essays,* and *Man of Letters: Selected Essays,* among others. Locke calls Pritchett the critic "a surviving link with the great tradition of English and European literature. Neither a scholar nor an intellectual in the New York or Continental sense, Pritchett is the supreme contemporary virtuoso of the short literary essay. . . . Pritchett is informal but never clubby, witty but never snide or snobbish, precise and always full of gusto—a true descendant of William Hazlitt." Reid likewise notes that no writer in years "has talked so clearly and wisely about the craft of writing and what might be called the moral psychology of the writer." *Times Literary Supplement* reviewer D. J. Enright sees Pritchett as the consummate teacher, offering his audience fresh insights. "In truth he does teach," Enright declares, "and by the direct method: journeying through literature, exploring, recording and sharing his findings in their immediate (though never naive) freshness and concreteness. He doesn't write down to the common reader; he writes at his own level, which *seems* to be that of the common reader, a figure whose actual existence in flesh and blood we may doubt but of whose nature and capacities we somehow have a pretty good idea." *Chicago Tribune* correspondent Stevenson Swanson concludes that Pritchett's "resourcefulness never flags in finding ways to communicate what it feels like to read a particular author, one of the most difficult tasks of a critic."

Pritchett enjoys probing the unity of a writer's life and art in his critical essays. He has also explored this theme in full-length biographies such as *Balzac, The Gentle Barbarian: The Life and Work of Turgenev,* and *Chekhov: A Spirit Set Free.* According to George Core in the *Sewanee Review,* to read Pritchett's criticism "is to understand the relation of the author's world to the life of his writing—or the writer's life to the world of his characters. Pritchett enters so thoroughly into the mind and work of the writer he criticizes that he all but vanishes." In Bayley's view, such perceptions "are fresh and invariably good-natured for it is by his kindliness and fellow-feeling that [Pritchett] goes on to reveal the real qualities of the writers under discussion. Of course he favors writers who take a real interest in human beings and the performances they create around themselves, because that is what, as a novelist and short-story writer, he does so well himself." *New Statesman* contributor A. S. Byatt states that the critic "likes to take the great, the outstanding, the enduring book and isolate the qualities that make it so. If biography helps, he tells us what we need to know; if political or cultural history is more useful, we have that; if perfectly chosen examples of style and pace are required, he provides them. He is supremely tactful, and never superfluous." A *Times Literary Supplement* reviewer similarly concludes that Pritchett's essay subjects "exist in their environments, writer and circumstance explaining each other, and these cross-explanations are surely what any reader wants to know about a writer. But there is also another and most compelling question that one practitioner inevitably puts to another: How did you do it? Mr. Pritchett has a keen professional eye for the technical tricks of his craft, the management and mismanagement of effects."

Pritchett's essays show the same straightforward prose and clarity of style that can be found in his fiction. To quote Core, the life of art "is conveyed by the vitality of V. S. Pritchett's prose and by his unflagging curiosity. The critical prose is less metaphorical, less involved with the idiom of the times and its walks. . . . In the criticism Pritchett speaks directly to the reader in a unique voice—quiet, measured, compelling." Dirda praises Pritchett for his qualities of "modesty, judiciousness, and good sense," adding: "The essays are clearly written and jargon-free; they emphasize the biographical and are sprinkled with apt quotations. . . . Throughout, one senses that Pritchett has done enormous homework, that he has read an author entire, and that he brings to bear, appropriately and illuminatingly, a lifetime of reading." John Gross in the *New York Times* notes a "prose at once ruminative and succinct, close-packed and compressed without being congested," and suggests that half of Pritchett's secret "lies in a style which does not only illumine or take on the color of its surroundings, but which provides its own satisfactions as well. It is as satisfying to come across the right words in the right order in a critical essay as it would be anywhere else." *London Magazine* correspondent John Mellors also cites Pritchett's essays for their careful use of the *mot juste.* "The best of Pritchett's reviews and criticisms are as enthralling as his short stories," Mellors writes. "Nothing is either a priori or ex cathedra. . . . He observes and describes, simplifies and sympathizes, and finally illuminates by a combination of common sense and brilliant insight. . . . Above all, he has the knack of helping the common reader . . . to clarify apparent obscurities and discrepancies in an author's work."

It can be argued that Pritchett is best known as a critic and that his essays are widely read and respected by others in his field. *Chicago Tribune Book World* contributor Robert W. Smith contends that Pritchett's criticism "still stands unsurpassed. It has sweep and cogency and charm. And always surprise." Davies feels that Pritchett's nonfiction work "is a fine balance in the hurly-burly of weekly publishing. Critics like Pritchett belong to the small body of serious lovers of literature who will not compromise with standards that reach beyond the enthusiasms of the immediate present." Cunningham writes: "Matured long ago past the stage of having to strain for a young reviewer's smartness, V. S. Pritchett's criticism practices wisdom. Wisdom comes so naturally to his reviewing pen, in fact, that we end up taking his crisply sage reflections, his most assentable asides, the continual evidencing of hard-schooled and well-tried gumption, almost for granted. Well-put insights pile up." R. W. B. Lewis offers perhaps the most cogent appreciation of Pritchett in a *New Republic* review. "Pritchett's well-modulated prose is a constant pleasure," Lewis declares; "it is never self-admiring and never out of keeping with its subject. . . . He occupies today a nearly solitary position as a literary critic in the great tradition—standing between literature and human society to greet the books as they come, passing the word back and forth."

Few workers in any line of business sustain careers into their seventies. Pritchett has labored well into his late eighties, publishing a biography of Chekhov and continuing his reviewing almost on a full-time basis. Theroux observes that the affable Pritchett "has a hiker's obvious health, a downright manner, an exuberant curiosity and the sort of twinkle that puts one in mind of a country doctor—that spirit-boosting responsiveness that works cures on malingerers." In the *Detroit News,* Sheldon Frank also notes that Pritchett is "a man invigorated by growing old, alive and open to the world in a way a child should envy." Pritchett lives in the Camden Town district of London, and although he sometimes complains about his work load, he is still able to communicate enthusiasm for his surroundings, his essay subjects, and the world of letters in general. According to William Abrahams in the *New Republic,* the pleasure Pritchett takes in writing "translates itself into the pleasure one takes in reading him—the opportunity to acquaint oneself with a temperament that is humane, an intelligence that is acute and a technique that is masterly." Locke calls Pritchett "incontestably one of the happy few, a man seemingly blessed in life and work. He still regards literature as a personal communication, a social act, a performance and a mark of character. This is certainly not the only way to read and write, but it carries the cultural momentum and authority of a great tradition with it; and Pritchett deserves our warmest homage and thanks, particularly in an age of rising literary technocrats and declining literary culture and continuity."

BIOGRAPHICAL/CRITICAL SOURCES:

BOOKS

Contemporary Fiction in America and England, 1950-70, Gale, 1976.
Contemporary Literary Criticism, Gale, Volume 5, 1976, Volume 13, 1980, Volume 15, 1980, Volume 41, 1987.
Dictionary of Literary Biography, Volume 15: *British Novelists, 1930-1959,* Gale, 1983.
Pritchett, V. S., *A Cab at the Door: A Memoir,* Random House, 1968 (published in England as *A Cab at the Door: An Autobiography, Early Years,* Chatto & Windus, 1968).
Pritchett, V. S., *Midnight Oil,* Chatto & Windus, 1971, Random House, 1972.
Solotaroff, Theodore, *The Red Hot Vacuum and Other Pieces on Writing in the Sixties,* Atheneum, 1970.

PERIODICALS

Atlantic, August, 1971.
Books and Bookmen, December, 1969, November, 1985.

Chicago Tribune, July 9, 1986.
Chicago Tribune Book World, May 27, 1979, May 23, 1982.
Detroit News, May 30, 1982, October 30, 1983.
Listener, July 19, 1979, August 5, 1982.
London Magazine, April/May, 1975, July, 1980.
Los Angeles Times, March 16, 1983.
Los Angeles Times Book Review, May 23, 1982, September 11, 1983, June 29, 1986.
Modern Fiction Studies, summer, 1978.
Nation, October 2, 1967, May 8, 1972, December 31, 1973, May 10, 1975, August 16-23, 1986.
New Leader, December 31, 1979.
New Republic, May 11, 1968, May 6, 1972, October 19, 1974, April 23, 1977, July 8, 1978, July 19, 1980, August 2, 1982.
New Statesman, May 18, 1979.
Newsweek, April 22, 1968, May 16, 1977, May 29, 1978, May 10, 1982.
New Yorker, May 1, 1965, October 29, 1973, May 30, 1977, June 11, 1979, June 9, 1980, June 28, 1982, April 8, 1985, June 9, 1986.
New York Herald Tribune Book Review, April 25, 1954.
New York Review of Books, July 1, 1965, September 14, 1967, February 13, 1969, March 12, 1970, July 20, 1972, October 4, 1973, March 20, 1975, September 15, 1977, August 17, 1978, February 7, 1980, June 12, 1980, June 24, 1982, June 26, 1986.
New York Times, May 5, 1977, May 28, 1979, June 28, 1979, October 31, 1979, April 24, 1982, August 31, 1983, December 16, 1985.
New York Times Book Review, April 25, 1954, April 18, 1965, August 13, 1967, April 28, 1968, December 1, 1968, January 25, 1970, April 30, 1972, October 14, 1973, September 15, 1974, May 22, 1977, June 25, 1978, June 3, 1979, November 18, 1979, June 29, 1980, May 30, 1982, September 18, 1983, May 4, 1986.
New York Times Magazine, December 14, 1980, March 13, 1983.
Observer, June 21, 1970, December 15, 1985.
Publishers Weekly, April 10, 1972.
Saturday Review, June 26, 1965, April 6, 1968, May 4, 1968, March 14, 1970, May 6, 1972, October 19, 1974, May 14, 1977, July 8, 1978, December, 1979, May, 1982.
Sewanee Review, summer, 1975, spring, 1977, spring, 1981.
Spectator, October 12, 1974, June 25, 1977, January 7, 1984.
Time, May 17, 1968, August 3, 1970, September 16, 1974, May 23, 1977, November 12, 1979, May 5, 1980.
Times (London), June 25, 1981, February 11, 1984, June 4, 1988.
Times Literary Supplement, February 4, 1965, April 1, 1965, August 17, 1967, February 22, 1968, November 6, 1969, December 18, 1970, October 22, 1971, September 14, 1973, October 25, 1974, June 24, 1977, May 12, 1978, January 18, 1980, February 29, 1980, September 26, 1980, June 25, 1982, November 4, 1983, August 17, 1984, November 22, 1985.
Tribune Books (Chicago), October 16, 1988.
Washington Post Book World, April 30, 1972, June 12, 1977, May 27, 1979, November 18, 1979, December 9, 1979, May 25, 1980, April 25, 1982, October 9, 1983, June 22, 1986, October 23, 1988.

—Sketch by Anne Janette Johnson

*   *   *

PROXMIRE, William 1915-

PERSONAL: Born November 11, 1915, in Lake Forest, Ill.; son of Theodore Stanley (a doctor) and Adele (Flanigan) Proxmire;

married Ellen Hodges (an author), December 1, 1956; children: Theodore Stanley, Elsie Stillman, Douglas Clark. *Education:* Yale University, B.A., 1938; Harvard University, M.B.A., 1948. *Politics:* Democrat. *Religion:* Episcopalian.

ADDRESSES: Home—4613 East Buckeye Rd., Madison, Wis. 53704. *Agent*—Donald MacCampbell, Inc., 12 East 41st St., New York, N.Y. 10017.

CAREER: Reporter for *Capital Times,* 1949, and *Madison Union Labor News,* 1950, both Madison, Wis.; assemblyman, Wisconsin State Legislature, 1951-52; Artcraft Press, Waterloo, Wis., president, 1953-57; U.S. Senate, Washington, D.C., senator from Wisconsin, 1957-88, served on Appropriations Committee, Banking and Currency Committee, and numerous other committees and subcommittees, chairman of Senate Banking Committee, Joint Economic Committee, Consumer Credit Subcommittee, and others. Unsuccessful Democratic candidate for governor of Wisconsin, 1952, 1954, 1956. Commentator, CNBC (cable television network), 1989—. *Military service:* U.S. Army, served in Counterintelligence Corps, 1941-46; became first lieutenant.

MEMBER: American Legion, Madison Press Club.

WRITINGS:

Can Small Business Survive?, Regnery, 1964.
Report from Wasteland: America's Military-Industrial Complex, foreword by Paul H. Douglas, Praeger, 1970.
Uncle Sam—The Last of the Bigtime Spenders, Simon & Schuster, 1972.
You Can Do It!, Simon & Schuster, 1973.
The Fleecing of America, Houghton, 1980.

SIDELIGHTS: In his three decades as a member of the U.S. Senate, William Proxmire made a name for himself as an active voice in such organizations as the Appropriations Committee, the Defense Production Committee, and the Banking Committee. His record on fiscal matters is well documented: Proxmire "wrote laws that require lenders to tell actual costs of loans," notes Rogers Worthington in a *Chicago Tribune* article, "that give consumers access and correction power to their credit reports; that prohibit discrimination based on sex, race or religion; that make real estate red-lining [a form of discrimination] more difficult by requiring lenders to disclose the geographic patterns of their loans," and many more.

But the Wisconsin Democrat is perhaps best known to his countrymen as the originator of the monthly "Golden Fleece Awards"—a wry look at apparent excess in government spending, usually in the form of grants. These dubious honors have in the past been granted "to such notorious big spenders as the military and public works agencies," explains *Nation* critic James R. McDonald. "From time to time, however, the Senator has selected scientific research projects funded by such Federal agencies as the National Science Foundation or the National Institutes of Health, and the 'Golden Fleeces' bestowed on these occasions have led him into deeper waters."

Indeed, the studies targeted by Golden Fleece honors have often appeared bizarre: a Law Enforcement Assistance Administration grant to study why inmates wish to escape from jail, or a study on the physiques of flight attendants for the Federal Aviation Administration. But at the same time, Proxmire's decrying of certain science-based grants has led to charges that the senator doesn't realize the long-range importance behind such studies. Reviewing Proxmire's book *The Fleecing of America,* a collection of Golden Fleece honorees over the years, Norman J. Orn-

stein claims that the author never "discusses the grant-review process, or offers serious suggestions for reform. Instead, [he] simply ridicule[s] study after study with funny titles (those with any kind of sexual connotation are especially vulnerable), which of course are quite common in biological and psychological research," as Ornstein writes in *Washington Post Book World.* "On the other hand, the child who observed that the king had no clothes was doubtless written off as a philistine by the king's courtiers," counters *New York Times Book Review* critic Walter Goodman, adding that in *The Fleecing of America,* Proxmire "does not argue that such endeavors are altogether without merit, only that the taxpayer ought not to be subsidizing them. He calls for 'proportion, moderation, common sense' in Federal spending."

On the occasion of Proxmire's announcement that he would not seek another term in the Senate following the 1988 season, Worthington recalled the politician as a "steel-disciplined workaholic and loner who would rather read a book than gab with colleagues unless one could teach him something. He is also remembered by some as a senator who would not play team politics with his party or the state's congressional delegation, and who did little, say his political enemies, to bring public works projects and federal dollars to the state." But Worthington adds that "the polls rated [Proxmire] high in name recognition and job approval. On a more personal level, he says he feels fine. . . . He runs 5 miles and does 100 pushups each day."

BIOGRAPHICAL/CRITICAL SOURCES:

BOOKS

Proxmire, William, *The Fleecing of America,* Houghton, 1980.

PERIODICALS

Atlantic, December, 1970.
Chicago Tribune, August 30, 1987.
Los Angeles Times, August 29, 1987.
Nation, June 28, 1980.
National Review, November 3, 1970, October 13, 1972.
New Republic, April 25, 1970.
New York Times Book Review, May 24, 1970, June 15, 1980.
Saturday Review, April 25, 1970.
Washington Post Book World, June 1, 1980.*

*   *   *

PUHVEL, Jaan 1932-

PERSONAL: Surname is pronounced *Puh*-vel; born January 24, 1932, in Tallinn, Estonia; naturalized U.S. citizen; son of Karl (a civil engineer) and Meta Elisabeth (Paern) Puhvel; married Sirje Madli Hansen (a research immunologist), June 4, 1960; children: Peter Jaan, Andres Jaak, Markus Juri. *Education:* Received secondary education in Sweden; McGill University, B.A., 1951, M.A., 1952; Harvard University, Ph.D., 1959. *Politics:* Democrat.

ADDRESSES: Home—15739 High Knoll Rd., Encino, Calif. 91316. *Office*—Department of Classics, University of California, Los Angeles, Calif. 90024.

CAREER: McGill University, Montreal, Quebec, lecturer in classics, 1955-56; University of Texas at Austin, instructor in classical languages, 1957-58; University of California, Los Angeles, assistant professor, 1958-61, associate professor of classics and Indo-European linguistics, 1961-64, professor of Indo-European studies, 1964—, director of Center for Research in Languages and Linguistics, 1962-67, vice-chairman of Indo-

European studies, 1964-68, chairman of department of classics, 1968-75. Collitz Professor of Indo-European Comparative Philology, State University of New York at Buffalo, 1971.

MEMBER: Linguistic Society of America, American Oriental Society, American Philological Association, Association for the Advancement of Baltic Studies (president, 1971-72).

AWARDS, HONORS: Governor General's gold medal, Canada, 1951; Moyse travelling fellow, 1952; American Council of Learned Societies fellow, 1961-62; Officer First Class, Order of the White Rose (Finland), 1967; Guggenheim fellow, 1968-69.

WRITINGS:

(Reviser with others, under direction of Joshua Whatmough) *Pierre Guiraud: Bibliographie critique de la statistique linguistique,* Editions Spectrum (Utrecht), 1954.

Laryngeals and the Indo-European Verb, University of California Press, 1960.

(Editor with Henrik Birnbaun, and contributor) *Ancient Indo-European Dialects,* University of California Press, 1966.

(Editor) *Substance and Structure of Language,* University of California Press, 1969.

(Editor and contributor) *Myth and Law among the Indo-Europeans: Studies in Indo-European Comparative Mythology,* University of California Press, 1970.

(Editor and contributor) *Baltic Literature and Linguistics,* Association for the Advancement of Baltic Studies, 1973.

Myth in Indo-European Antiquity, University of California Press, 1974.

(Editor with Ronald Stroud) *California Studies in Classical Antiquity,* eight volumes, University of California Press, 1976.

(Editor) Georges Dumezil, *The Stakes of the Warrior,* University of California Press, 1983.

Hittite Etymological Dictionary, two volumes, Mouton, 1984.

(Editor with David Weeks) Dumezil and others, *The Plight of a Sorcerer,* University of California Press, 1986.

Comparative Mythology, Johns Hopkins University Press, 1987.

CONTRIBUTOR

Ernst Pulgram, editor, *Studies Presented to Joshua Whatmough,* Mouton, 1957.

E. L. Bennett, editor, *Mycenaean Studies,* University of Wisconsin Press, 1964.

Werner Winter, editor, *Evidence for Laryngeals,* Mouton, 1965.

George Cardona and others, editors, *Indo-European and Indo-Europeans,* University of Pennsylvania Press, 1970.

OTHER

Contributor to festschrifts and symposia. Contributor to *Encyclopaedia Britannica, Encyclopedia Americana, Books Abroad, Western Folklore,* and to philological, linguistic, and literary journals in the United States and other countries.

BIOGRAPHICAL/CRITICAL SOURCES:

PERIODICALS

American Journal of Philology, summer, 1973.
American Journal of Sociology, January, 1972.
Choice, November, 1987.
Classical World, October, 1974.
Journal of American Folklore, July, 1988.
Library Journal, July, 1987.
Times Literary Supplement, May 31, 1985, April 15, 1988.

R

RAMKE, Bin 1947-

PERSONAL: Born February 19, 1947, in Port Neches, Tex.; son of Lloyd Binford (an engineer) and Melba (Guidry) Ramke; married Linda Keating (a teacher), May 31, 1967. *Education:* Louisiana State University, B.A., 1970; University of New Orleans, M.A., 1971; Ohio University, Ph.D., 1975.

ADDRESSES: Home—2042 South High St., Denver, Colo. 80210. *Office*—Department of English, University of Denver, Denver, Colo. 80208.

CAREER: Columbus College, Columbus, Ga., assistant professor of English, beginning 1975; University of Denver, Denver, Colo., currently professor of English.

MEMBER: Modern Language Association of America, P.E.N., Associated Writing Programs.

AWARDS, HONORS: Yale Younger Poets Award, Yale University Press, 1977, for *The Difference between Night and Day.*

WRITINGS:

Any Brass Ring (poetry chapbook), Ohio Review, 1977.
The Difference between Night and Day (poems), Yale University Press, 1978.
The Language Student, Louisiana State University Press, 1981.
White Monkeys (poems), University of Georgia Press, 1984.
The Erotic Light of Gardens, Wesleyan University Press, 1989.

Associate editor, *Denver Quarterly;* assistant editor, *Ohio Review,* 1973-75.

WORK IN PROGRESS: The Man Whose Mother Was Beautiful.

SIDELIGHTS: "In *The Difference between Night and Day,* Bin Ramke shows an unusual maturity in both vision and technique," asserts Peter Stitt in the *Georgia Review.* A critic for the *New York Times Book Review,* however, feels that "Ramke's poems embody many of the strengths and failings brought to mind by the phrase 'younger poet': he has a rich imagination, and he often overspends it wastefully." Stitt perceives Ramke's creativity differently, commenting that "his manipulation of images and figures of speech gives his poems a striking density of texture and complexity of theme." In addition, Stitt believes Ramke's "command of the formal elements of verse is truly impressive—his strong supple rhythms reflect the movement our poets have recently made away from, up from, the plain style," concluding, "Bin Ramke is a poet of very large talent."

About his own writing, Ramke told *CA:* "My early interest and training was in mathematics and physics. Curiously, my movement away from those disciplines paralleled the major movements *within* them during the same time—toward cosmology, toward the large unanswerable, the first and last questions: toward a concern for a *logos.* I still admire accuracy, discipline, precision, and seek those qualities in my own work. And yet *The Difference between Night and Day* is a book about where to stand, not in order to move the world, but to be moved by it. I still stand, if not by, at least in the vicinity of [this] book, but have moved more, in my third book, into *personae,* more interesting, more outrageous, versions of myself. And since the death of my father, my work has become a quarrel with him, an *apologia.*"

BIOGRAPHICAL/CRITICAL SOURCES:

PERIODICALS

Georgia Review, fall, 1978.
New York Times Book Review, November 12, 1978.
Times Literary Supplement, October 20, 1978.

*　　*　　*

RASKY, Harry 1928-

PERSONAL: Born May 9, 1928, in Toronto, Ontario, Canada; son of Louis (a teacher) and Perl (Krazner) Rasky; married Ruth Arlene Werkhoven (a researcher), March 20, 1965; children: Holly Laura, Adam Louis. *Education:* University of Toronto, B.A., 1949.

ADDRESSES: Home—Toronto, Ontario, Canada. *Office*—Canadian Broadcasting Corp., Box 500, Terminal A, Toronto, Ontario, Canada. *Agent*—Lucinda Vardey, 97 Maitland, Toronto, Ontario, Canada M4Y 1E3.

CAREER: Canadian Broadcasting Corp., Toronto, Ontario, producer, director, and writer, 1952-55; Columbia Broadcasting System, New York City, producer, director, and writer, 1955-60; National Broadcasting Co., New York City, producer, director, and writer, 1961; American Broadcasting Companies, Inc., New York City, producer, director, and writer, 1961-71; Canadian Broadcasting Corp., producer, director, and writer, 1971—. President, Harry Rasky Productions, Inc. Lecturer at universities, including Columbia University, Ohio State University, and New School for Social Research.

MEMBER: Directors Guild of America (member of board of directors), Writers Guild of America (East), National Academy of Television Arts and Sciences, Association of Canadian Television and Radio Artists.

AWARDS, HONORS: Emmy Award, Academy of Television Arts and Sciences, 1966, for "Hall of Kings"; Venice Film Festival award, 1970, for "Upon This Rock"; Association of Canadian Television and Radio Artists awards, 1973, for "Tennessee Williams' South," 1974, for "Next Year in Jerusalem," and 1981, for "Africa Week"; International Emmy Award, Academy of Television Arts and Sciences, 1975, for "Travels through Life with Leacock," and 1978, for "Homage to Chagall: The Colours of Love"; Oscar nomination, Motion Picture Academy of Arts and Sciences, 1978, for "Homage to Chagall: The Colours of Love"; Minneapolis Film Festival Award, 1980; LL.D., University of Toronto, 1982; best non-fiction director award, Directors Guild of America, 1986; Emmy Award for best documentary director, 1986; Silver Award, New York International Film and Television Festival, 1986, for "Karsh—The Searching Eye"; grand prize, New York International Film and Television Festival; silver prize, Festival of Americas; New York Mayor's Citation; special jury prize, San Francisco International Film Festival; awards from American Council for Better Broadcasters, Writers Guild of America, Freedom Foundation, Montreal World Film Festival, Toronto Festival of Festivals, Ohio State University, Overseas Press Club, and Australian National Advisory Board; other awards include Peabody Award, Sylvania Award, Jerusalem Medal, Hollywood International Television Award, Canadian Wilderness Award, and International Golden Eagle Award.

WRITINGS:

Nobody Swings on Sunday: The Many Lives and Films of Harry Rasky, (autobiography), P. Collier, 1980.
Tennessee Williams: A Portrait in Laughter and Lamentation, Dodd, 1986.
Stratas, Oxford University Press, 1988.

Also author of unpublished works *Lower Than the Angels, Tales of Aculpulco Ladies,* and *TV Bitch.*

TELEVISION SCRIPTS

"Hall of Kings," American Broadcasting Co. (ABC-TV), 1966.
"The Legend of Silent Night," ABC-TV, 1968-69.
"Upon This Rock," National Broadcasting Co. (NBC-TV), 1971.
"The Wit and World of George Bernard Shaw," Canadian Broadcasting Corp. (CBC-TV), 1971.
"Tennessee Williams' South," CBC-TV, 1972.
"Homage to Chagall: The Colours of Love," CBC-TV, 1977.
"Arthur Miller on Home Ground," CBC-TV, 1979.
"The Song of Leonard Cohen," CBC-TV, 1980.
"The Man Who Hid Anne Frank," CBC-TV, 1980.
"The Spies Who Never Were," CBC-TV, 1981.
"Karsh—The Searching Eye," CBC-TV, 1986.
"To Mend the World," CBC-TV, 1987.
"The Secret of Degas," CBC-TV, 1988.
"The Great Teacher: Northrop Frye," CBC-TV, 1989.

Also author of "An Invitation to the Wedding," 1972; "Next Year in Jerusalem," 1974; "Baryshnikov," 1974; "The Peking Man Mystery," 1977; "The Lessons of History," 1978; "Being Different," 1981; "Thorn of Plenty," ABC-TV; "This Proud Land," ABC-TV; "The Lion and the Cross," Columbia Broadcasting System (CBS-TV); "The African Revolution" series, CBS-TV; "Panama: Danger Zone," NBC-TV; "Cuba and Castro Today," ABC-TV; "The Forty-ninth State," CBS-TV; "A Child Is to Love"; "Travels through Life with Leacock"; and "The Twentieth Century." Contributor to "CBC Newsmagazine" series, CBC-TV.

OTHER

Author of scripts for Canadian radio, including "George the Good." Contributor to United Features and to magazines and newspapers, including *Nation, Saturday Night,* and *Toronto Telegram.*

SIDELIGHTS: Harry Rasky once told *CA:* "I make literary films of compassion, a mixture of drama and documentary that the *Los Angeles Times* called 'Raskymentary.' I also broadcast and write works of love."

Rasky received international recognition in 1978 as author of "Homage to Chagall: The Colours of Love," a documentary on the ninety-year-old creator of numerous works celebrating Jewish traditions. For more than two years, Rasky conducted interviews with Chagall and studied the artist's writings as well as his work in painting, stained glass, tapestries, and other media. A *Saturday Review* critic calls the film "a paean to life and the glories of living" and praises its "spiritual refreshment."

BIOGRAPHICAL/CRITICAL SOURCES:

PERIODICALS

Globe and Mail (Toronto), December 20, 1986.
Saturday Review, June 25, 1977.

*   *   *

RAVITCH, Diane 1938-

PERSONAL: Born July 1, 1938, in Houston, Tex.; daughter of Walter Cracker (a businessman) and Ann Celia (Katz) Silvers; married Richard Ravitch (a lawyer and businessman), June 26, 1960 (divorced December, 1986); children: Joseph, Steven (deceased), Michael. *Education:* Wellesley College, B.A., 1960; Columbia University, Ph.D., 1975.

ADDRESSES: Office—Teachers College, Columbia University, Box 177, New York, N.Y. 10027.

CAREER: Columbia University, Teachers College, New York, N.Y., assistant professor, 1975-78, adjunct associate professor, 1978-84, adjunct professor of history and education, 1984—. Director, Educational Excellence Network, 1982—, and Encyclopaedia Britannica Corporation, 1985—. Chairman, Secretary of Education's Research Priorities Panel, 1985. Member, Second Circuit Judicial Nominating Commission, as appointed by President Carter, 1978-79, 1980; member, Secretary of Education's Study Group on the Elementary School, 1985-86. Delegate, International Seminar on Educational Reform, Tokyo and Kyoto, Japan, 1985. Lifetime trustee of New York Public Library. Consultant to several university presses, including Princeton University Press, Harvard University Press, and Johns Hopkins University Press.

MEMBER: PEN International, National Academy of Education, American Educational Research Association, American Academy of Arts and Sciences, American Historical Association, Society of American Historians, Organization of American Historians, Woodrow Wilson National Fellowship Foundation (trustee, 1988—), Council for Basic Education (director, 1989—).

AWARDS, HONORS: Delta Kappa Gamma Educators' Award, 1975, for *The Great School Wars, New York City, 1805-1973,* and 1984, for *The Troubled Crusade: American Education, 1945-1980;* Doctor of Humane Letters, Williams College, 1984, Reed College, 1985, Amherst College, 1986, and State University of New York, 1988; Phi Beta Kappa visiting scholar, 1984-85; Ambassador of Honor Award from English-Speaking Union, 1984, for *The Troubled Crusade,* and 1985, for *The Schools We Deserve: Reflections on the Educational Crises of Our Times;* Phi Beta Kappa visiting scholar, 1984-85; Henry Allen Moe Prize from American Philosophical Society, 1986; designated honorary citizen by State of California Senate Rules Committee, 1988, for work on state curriculum; Alumnae Achievement Award from Wellesley College, 1989.

WRITINGS:

The Great School Wars, New York City, 1805-1973, Basic Books, 1974.

The Revisionists Revised: A Critique of the Radical Attack on the Schools, Basic Books, 1978.

(Editor with Ronald Goodenow) *Educating an Urban People: The New York City Experience,* Holmes & Meier, 1981.

The Troubled Crusade: American Education, 1945-1980, Basic Books, 1983.

(Editor with Goodenow) *The School and the City: Community Studies in the History of American Education,* Holmes & Meier, 1983.

(Editor with Chester E. Finn, Jr., and Robert Fancher) *Against Mediocrity: The Humanities in America's High Schools,* Holmes & Meier, 1984.

The Schools We Deserve: Reflections on the Educational Crises of Our Times (essays), Basic Books, 1985.

(Editor with Finn and Holley Roberts) *Challenges to the Humanities,* Holmes & Meier, 1985.

(With Finn) *What Do Our Seventeen-Year-Olds Know?: A Report on the First National Assessment of History and Literature,* foreword by Lynne V. Cheney, Harper, 1987.

Also author, with Charlotte Crabtree, of *California K-12 History: A Social Science Framework.*

CONTRIBUTOR

Jane Newitt, editor, *Future Trends in Education,* D. C. Heath, 1979.

Derrick A. Bell, Jr., editor, *Shades of Brown: New Perspectives on School Desegregation,* Teachers College Press, Columbia University, 1980.

Adam Yarmolinsky and Lance Leibman, editors, *Race and Schooling in the City,* Harvard University Press, 1981.

John H. Bunzel, editor, *Challenge to American Schools: The Case for Standards and Values,* Oxford University Press, 1985.

Winthrop Knowlton and Richard Zeckhauser, editors, *American Society: Public and Private Responsibility,* Harvard University Press, 1986.

OTHER

Contributor of more than a hundred articles and reviews to such periodicals as *New York Times Magazine, American Scholar,* and *Harvard Educational Review.* Editor, *Notes on Education,* 1974-75.

SIDELIGHTS: As an historian of American education, Diane Ravitch has authored a number of reputable historiographies that explore the successes and failures played out in the Ameri-can school system through the years. The widely reviewed *The Troubled Crusade: American Education, 1945-1980,* for instance, is considered by *Los Angeles Times Book Review* critic David Savage to be "a fascinating history of 35 years of conflict and turmoil in the nation's schools and universities. Whether the issue was the McCarthy crusades (Joe's or Gene's), racial desegregation, rights for women and the handicapped, bilingual education or affirmative action, each has been fought out, to a greater or lesser degree, on school and college campuses."

According to Savage, the underlying theme of *The Troubled Crusade* is that "social scientists, political activists and compliant educators have often combined to lead the schools astray. If educational history does resemble a pendulum swinging, it has swung further right or left . . . because educators have been too willing to follow any fad, Ravitch says." In support of this theme, Ravitch addresses the issue of education for all. Immediately after World War II, teachers and administrators were adamant about providing equal opportunity education for all students and they hoped to do this through federal financial aid. According to reviewer Stanley Aronowitz for the *Village Voice Literary Supplement,* this effort was, "as Ravitch sees it, derailed by reformers' meddling in the educational process. . . . Things went wrong, according to Ravitch, when the simple claim that local taxes were not sufficient to deliver first-class education to millions of blacks and rural whites got tangled up with the idea that the federal government should use its financial clout to regulate curriculum, college entrance requirements, and other matters of policy. Rank amateurs—civil rights groups, radical students, militant feminists—began to demand a say in decisions best left to professionals; the inevitable result was mediocrity." *New York Times* critic Christopher Lehmann-Haupt believes that, on the whole, "what is recounted in 'The Troubled Crusade' is every conservative's fear of what befalls a freely functioning community system when Big Government gets its hands on it. For in the 35-year history that Mrs. Ravitch covers, the long-deferred dream of Federal aid to education could be said to have been corrupted into a nightmare of bureaucratic meddling and muddling." Apart from her critique of the federal government's expanding influence on school policy matters, Ravitch analyzes the damaging effects other faddish ideas, from both the political left and right, have had on students. Because she has viewed such issues from both political perspectives, Ravitch objects to the neo-conservative label some critics have given her. She told *CA,* "I find that I am conservative in some matters, liberal in some others, and radical in a few more. Therefore it is obnoxious to me to have one or several people hang a political label on me which does not reflect my own thinking about my views and life."

With regard to critical acceptance, Hechinger claims *The Troubled Crusade* "does what American historiography usually does not: it places education near the center of national affairs instead of near the periphery. It is thus indispensable for a full understanding of the critical postwar period. . . . One may argue with Mrs. Ravitch's less than enthusiastic view of the federal and judicial role in education; but she is surely justified, in the light of past history, in her suspicion of panaceas and her ardent and intelligent defense of 'piecemeal change'. . . . This . . . holds a lesson for today. The air is crowded with calls for school reform, and generally such a mood is cause for celebration. But once again, there is a temptation for politicians to demand miracles." Aronowitz, in contrast, faults what he sees as Ravitch's limited view of the role of the American education system: "She really wants to persuade us that there's only one royal road to success—acquiring the skills and values of the dominant culture while learning the three Rs. Within those bounds, Ravitch supports piecemeal reform, but her perspective is profoundly antiutopian. . . . *The Troubled Crusade* could serve as the autobiography of a generation of former social critics and disillusioned radicals convinced by the turbulent struggle of the postwar era that profound social change inevitably leads to totalitarianism." In his *Newsweek* assessment, Gene Lyons is similarly harsh, for he feels *The Troubled Crusade* "is less a history of American schools than of intellectual fashion, government studies, federal court decisions and the sorts of books and periodicals mentioned regularly in The New York Times. If Ravitch has so much as entered an elementary classroom, a junior-high teachers' lounge or attended a high-school football game in the course of her studies, there's no sign of it here." As for Lehmann-Haupt, his is a mixed analysis. Accordingly, he writes that "at times her narrative assumes the aspect of a very dark comedy, and one fully expects her to pronounce some dire moral at the end. But she never does. . . . She discovered that there really are no villains. Everyone behaved with the best of motives, she seems to be saying. . . . It was just that the winds of history kept shifting and changing the landscape." In his conclusion, Lehmann-Haupt notes that *The Troubled Crusade* "leaves the reader with a refreshingly clear and objective review that lends valuable perspective to a confusing period in the very recent past."

Two additional works by Ravitch that address the troubles of American education are *The Schools We Deserve: Reflections on the Educational Crises of Our Time* and, with Chester E. Finn, Jr., *What Do Our Seventeen-Year-Olds Know?: A Report on the First National Assessment of History and Literature.* Regarding the former, *New York Times Book Review* critic Philip W. Jackson explains that whereas *The Troubled Crusade* "offered a panoramic view of education in the United States[,] . . . in 'The Schools We Deserve,' [Ravitch] concentrates with equal skill on more sharply defined issues, ranging from the . . . debate over tuition tax credits to the place of history in today's elementary schools, from aspects of school desegregation to the uses and misuses of tests. No matter what the focus of her concern, Mrs. Ravitch brings to bear a keen intelligence working in the service of a neoconservative educational outlook." Jackson continues that "even though its central message has been sounded many times before . . . , 'The Schools We Deserve' demands to be read all the same by every citizen who cares about our schools and would like to see them better than they are."

In the *Washington Post,* Paul Piazza calls *What Do Our Seventeen-Year-Olds Know?* "a statistical description of a generation, a 'snapshot in time.' " The book, more specifically, is an analysis of how nearly eight thousand high school juniors fared on a multiple choice examination on American history and English literature that the National Assessment of Educational Progress, a major testing organization, devised and distributed in 1986. Cleverly put by Piazza, "the results are, as one might expect, abysmal. Mediocrity has been quantified. We have met ignorance, Ravitch and Finn might declare, and it is ourselves." Although both Piazza and the authors admit that multiple-choice examinations have shortcomings, overall Piazza is encouraged by the undertaking: "Recognizing one's ignorance is the beginning of wisdom. To Ravitch and Finn we owe a great deal for starting us down the road, if not to wisdom, at least to a knowledge of our failure." Alternately, Deborah Meier and Florence Miller for *Nation* sense that Ravitch and Finn's "view of ignorance is familiar and fruitless. They miss the vital connection between knowing and not knowing, and because they do so, not knowing is failure, or bad schooling. . . . Given the influence of Ravitch and Finn, new curriculums are probably already in

the making. If so, we will have foreclosed on the real debate and be witness to one more cycle of alarm and reform, swinging from fad to fad and never digging deep." Even though *New York Times* critic John Gross detects that "none of their conclusions are particularly earthshaking . . . they do make a lengthy series of recommendations on how to improve things. . . . A few are fairly vague, but others could in principle be acted on quite quickly. . . . The chief value," continues Gross, "of 'What Do Our 17-Year-Olds Know?' lies in its documentation of existing conditions," and he concludes that the same type of study should be conducted in Western Europe for the sake of comparison.

BIOGRAPHICAL/CRITICAL SOURCES:

BOOKS

Finn, Chester E., Jr., and Diane Ravitch, *What Do Our Seventeen-Year-Olds Know?: A Report on the First National Assessment of History and Literature,* Harper, 1987.
Ravitch, Diane, *The Troubled Crusade: American Education, 1945-1980,* Basic Books, 1983.

PERIODICALS

Chicago Tribune, October 13, 1983.
Harper's, June, 1985.
Los Angeles Times Book Review, September 11, 1983, November 29, 1987.
Nation, September 2, 1978, January 9, 1988.
New Republic, June 1, 1974, October 17, 1983.
Newsweek, November 28, 1983.
New York Times, July 6, 1978, September 7, 1983, October 2, 1987.
New York Times Book Review, May 12, 1974, June 18, 1978, September 18, 1983.
Times Literary Supplement, July 6, 1984.
Village Voice Literary Supplement, May, 1985.

—*Sketch by Cheryl Gottler*

* * *

RAWLS, Philip
See LEVINSON, Leonard

* * *

REID, Sue Titus 1939-

PERSONAL: Born November 13, 1939, in Bryan, Tex.; daughter of Andrew Jackson, Jr., and Lorraine (Wylie) Titus. *Education:* Texas Woman's University, B.S. (with honors), 1960; University of Missouri, M.A., 1962; University of Iowa, J.D., 1972.

ADDRESSES: Office—Dean's Office, School of Criminology, Florida State University, Tallahassee, Fla. 32306.

CAREER: Cornell College, Mount Vernon, Iowa, instructor, 1963-65, assistant professor, 1965-69, associate professor of sociology, 1969-72, acting chairman of department, 1969-72; admitted to Iowa State Bar, 1972; Coe College, Cedar Rapids, Iowa, associate professor of sociology and chairman of department, 1972-74; University of Washington, School of Law, Seattle, associate professor, 1974-78; University of Tulsa, College of Law, Tulsa, Okla., professor of law, beginning 1978; Florida State University, School of Criminology, Tallahassee, currently dean. Visiting summer professor, University of Nebraska, 1970; visiting distinguished professor of law and sociology, University of Tulsa, 1977-78; visiting professor, University of San Diego

School of Law, 1981-82; George Beto Professor of Criminal Justice, Sam Houston State University, 1984-85.

MEMBER: American Sociological Association (executive associate, 1976-77), American Society of Criminology, American Bar Association, Midwest Sociological Society (member of board of directors, 1970-72), Iowa Bar Association.

WRITINGS:

Crime and Criminology, Holt, 1976, 5th edition, 1988.
(Editor with David L. Lyon) *Population Crisis: An Interdisciplinary Perspective,* Scott, Foresman, 1976.
The Correctional System: An Introduction, Holt, 1981.
(Contributor with Lorna Keltner) *Encyclopedia of Crime and Justice,* Macmillan, 1984.
Criminal Justice, West Publishing, 1987, 2nd edition, Macmillan, 1990.
Criminal Law, Macmillan, 1989.

* * *

REIMAN, Donald H(enry) 1934-

PERSONAL: Born May 17, 1934, in Erie, Pa.; son of Henry Ward (a teacher) and Mildred A. (a teacher; maiden name, Pearce) Reiman; married Mary Warner (a rare book restorer and conservator), September 21, 1958 (divorced); married Helene Dworzan (a writer and teacher), October 3, 1975; children: (first marriage) Laurel Elizabeth. *Education:* College of Wooster, B.A., 1956; University of Illinois, M.A., 1957, Ph.D., 1960. *Politics:* Democrat. *Religion:* Presbyterian.

ADDRESSES: Home—6495 Broadway, Bronx, N.Y. 10471. *Office*—Room 226, New York Public Library, Fifth Ave. and 42nd St., New York, N.Y. 10018.

CAREER: Duke University, Durham, N.C., instructor, 1960-62, assistant professor of English, 1962-64; University of Wisconsin—Milwaukee, associate professor of English, 1964-65; Carl H. Pforzheimer Library, New York, N.Y., editor of *Shelley and His Circle,* 1965—. Adjunct professor of English, City University of New York, 1967-68; adjunct professor of English and senior research associate, Columbia University, 1969-74; visiting professor of English, St. Johns University, 1974-75, and University of Washington, 1981; James P. R. Lyell Reader in Bibliography, Oxford University, 1988-89.

MEMBER: Modern Humanities Research Association, Modern Language Association of America, Keats-Shelley Association of America (treasurer, 1973—), Charles Lamb Society, Byron Society, Wordsworth-Coleridge Association, Society for Textual Scholarship, Association for Documentary Evidence, Bibliographical Society of America, Better World Society, American Association of University Professors, Common Cause, Phi Beta Kappa, Phi Kappa Phi.

AWARDS, HONORS: American Council of Learned Societies grant, 1961-62, study fellow, 1963-64; associate fellow, Center for Advanced Study, Wesleyan University, 1963-64; National Endowment for the Humanities summer stipend, 1978; Litt.D., College of Wooster, 1981; National Endowment for the Humanities editing grants, 1983-86, 1986-88, 1988-90.

WRITINGS:

Shelley's "Triumph of Life": A Critical Study, University of Illinois Press, 1965.
Percy Bysshe Shelley, Twayne, 1968.
(Editor) *Shelley and His Circle, 1773-1822,* Harvard University Press, Volumes 5-6, 1973, Volumes 7-8, 1986.

(Editor) *The Romantics Reviewed,* nine volumes, Garland Publishing, 1972.
(With Doucet Devin Fischer) *Byron on the Continent,* New York Public Library, 1974.
(Editor) *The Romantic Context: Poetry,* 128 volumes, Garland Publishing, 1976-79.
(With Sharon B. Powers) *Shelley's Poetry and Prose,* Norton, 1977.
English Romantic Poetry, 1800-1835, Gale, 1979.
(Editor) *The Bodleian Shelley Manuscripts: A Facsimile Edition, with Full Transcriptions and Scholarly Apparatus,* Garland Publishing, Volume 1: *Peter Bell the Third, the Press-Copy Transcript . . . and "The Triumph of Life",* 1984, Volume 7: *Shelley's Last Notebook and Other MSS: Bodleian MS Shelley add. e. 15 and adds. e. 20, together with Additional Portions of the Holograph MSS. of "A Defence of Poetry" from Shelley adds. c. 4.,* 1989.
(Editor) *The Manuscripts of the Younger Romantics: A Facsimile Edition, with Scholarly Introductions, Bibliographical Descriptions, and Annotations,* Garland Publishing, 1985.
(Editor) *The Esdaile Notebook: A Facsimile of the Holograph Copybook in the Carl H. Pforzheimer Library,* Garland Publishing, 1985.
(Editor) *The Mask of Anarchy: Facsimiles of the Intermediate Fair-Copy Holograph in the . . . British Library: The Press-Copy Transcription by Mary W. Shelley in the Library of Congress; Proofs of the First Edition, 1832 (Corrected by Leigh Hunt) in the . . . University of Iowa; and a Holograph Addition to Leigh Hunt's Preface in . . . the British Library,* Garland Publishing, 1985.
(Editor) *Hellas: A Lyrical Drama: A Facsimile of the Press-Copy Transcript,* Garland Publishing, 1985.
Romantic Texts and Contexts, University of Missouri Free Press, 1987.
Intervals of Inspiration: The Skeptical Tradition and the Psychology of Romanticism, Penkevill Publishing, 1988.
(Editor) *The Harvard Shelley Manuscripts: Facsimiles of Two Fair-Copy Notebooks of Shelley's Poetry and the Houghton Library, Harvard University, with Other Related Manuscripts at Harvard in the Pierpont Morgan Library and the Bodleian Library, Oxford,* Garland Publishing, 1990.

CONTRIBUTOR

Frank Jordan, editor, *The English Romantic Poets: A Review of Research and Criticism,* 3rd revised edition (Reiman was not associated with earlier editions), Modern Language Association of America, 1972.
John D. Baird, editor, *Editing Texts of the Romantic Period,* Hakkert (Toronto), 1972.
M. H. Abrams, editor, *Norton Anthology of English Literature,* Norton, 1974.
(And editor with others) *The Evidence of the Imagination,* New York University Press, 1978.
Robert A. McCown, editor, *The Life and Times of Leigh Hunt,* Friends of the University of Iowa Libraries, 1985.
Richard Landon, editor, *Editing and Editors, A Retrospect: Papers Given at the Twenty-First Annual Conference on Editorial Problems, University of Toronto, 1-2 November 1985,* AMS Press, 1988.

Also contributor to several other books on literary criticism and teaching the Romantic poets.

OTHER

Also contributor to *The Reader's Encyclopedia of English Literature, New Catholic Encyclopedia,* and *Encyclopedia Americana.*

Contributor of more than one hundred articles and reviews on English and American literature to scholarly journals. Member of editorial board, *Keats-Shelley Journal*, 1968-73, *PMLA*, 1969-70; member of advisory board, *Milton and the Romantics*, 1975-80, *Studies in Romanticism*, 1977—, *Romanticism Past and Present*, 1980-86, *Nineteenth-Century Contexts*, 1987—, *Nineteenth-Century Literature*, 1986—.

WORK IN PROGRESS: Volumes 9-10 and 11-12 of *Shelley and His Circle;* further volumes in both *The Manuscripts of the Younger Romantics* and *The Bodleian Shelley Manuscripts: Public, Confidential, and Private;* essays on sociological and contextual issues associated with the Romantic tradition from the early nineteenth century to the present, to be collected in a volume with the working title, *Romantic Society;* essays on major English and American writers from Chaucer to the Postmodernists, to be collected in a volume with the working title, *Ethical Continuity and the Literary Canon;* and a critical edition of Shelley's poetry.

SIDELIGHTS: Donald H. Reiman told *CA:* "My basic belief is that scholars and critics are servants of the creative writers they study, though no reader of *Romantic Texts and Contexts* will doubt that I also see a place for the humanistic expression of the scholar-critic's personal values and aspirations. No critic can totally escape the subjectivity of the human condition, or evade errors and unintentional distortions in descriptions of the works of others, but we needn't wallow in those limitations. If critics would study and struggle to represent the great writers and their works as fully and forthrightly as those writers have depicted nature and society, our inevitably partial perspectives would blend to provide our contemporaries with portraits of the artists that are *true*—at least for our time."

* * *

REINHARDT, Richard W. 1927-

PERSONAL: Born March 25, 1927, in Oakland, Calif.; son of Emil C. and Eloise (Rathbone) Reinhardt; married Joan Maxwell, December 15, 1951; children: Kurt, Paul, Andrew. *Education:* Stanford University, B.A., 1949; Columbia University, M.S., 1950; Princeton University, graduate study, 1957-58.

ADDRESSES: Home—712 Lake St., San Francisco, Calif. 94118.

CAREER: San Francisco Chronicle, San Francisco, Calif., reporter, 1951-57; employed in public relations and campaign management in San Francisco, 1960-66; free-lance writer, 1966—. Lecturer in Graduate School of Journalism, University of California, Berkeley, 1961—; staff member, Squaw Valley (Calif.) Community of Writers, 1976—. President of Foundation for San Francisco's Architectural Heritage; director of California Tomorrow. Member of several San Francisco organizations. *Military service:* U.S. Naval Reserve, active duty, 1945-46.

MEMBER: Authors Guild, California Historical Society (trustee).

AWARDS, HONORS: Pulitzer traveling scholarship, Columbia University, 1950; award for outstanding news story of the year, San Francisco Press Club, 1954; fellowship in Near East area studies, Ford Foundation, 1957-60; first prize, Fabilli-Hoffer Essay, 1982-83.

WRITINGS:

Out West on the Overland Train, American West, 1967.
(Editor and author of commentary) *Workin' on the Railroad*, American West, 1970.

The Ashes of Smyrna: A Novel of the Near East, Harper, 1971 (published in England as *The Ashes of Smyrna: A Novel of the Greco-Turkish War*, Macmillan, 1972).
(Contributor) *The Ultimate Highrise*, San Francisco Bay Guardian, 1971.
Treasure Island, 1939-40: San Francisco's Exposition Years, Scrimshaw Press (San Francisco, Calif.), 1973.
(With William Bronson) *The Last Grand Adventure*, McGraw, 1977.
(With Paul C. Johnson) *San Francisco as It Is, as It Was*, Doubleday, 1979.
(Contributor) *Three Centuries of Notable American Architects*, American Heritage Publishing, 1981.
(Contributor) *California from the Air: The Golden Coast*, Squarebooks, 1981.
(Principal author) *California 2000: The Next Frontier*, California Tomorrow, 1982.
(With Peter Perkins) *Chinatown San Francisco*, Lancaster-Miller, 1982.
(Contributor) *The New Book of California Tomorrow*, William Kaufmann, 1984.
(Contributor) *A Sense of History*, American Heritage Publishing, 1985.

Contributor to periodicals, including *Look, Venture, Columbia Journalism Review, Westways, American Heritage*, and *New York Times*. Associate editor, *San Francisco Magazine*, 1963-67; contributing editor, *American West*, 1965-75, and *World's Fair*, 1981—.

WORK IN PROGRESS: A novel set in California; a book about American entertainments.

* * *

REMI, Georges 1907-1983
(Herge)

PERSONAL: Surname listed in some sources as Remy; born May 5, 1907, in Brussels, Belgium; died March 3, 1983, in Brussels, Belgium, of leukemia; son of Alexis Remy; married.

ADDRESSES: Office—Studios Herge, Avenue Louise 162/Bte. 7, 1050 Brussels, Belgium.

CAREER: Le Boy-Scout Belge, Brussels, Belgium, cartoonist, 1923-26, author of the periodical's comic strip, "The Adventures of Totor, Troop Leader," 1926; *Le Vingtieme Siecle* (newspaper), Brussels, creator of comic strip "Tintin" for weekly supplement *Le Petit Vingtieme*, 1929-83, which was syndicated in newspapers throughout the world. Also creator of comic strips "Jo, Zette et Jocko" and "Quick et Flupke."

WRITINGS:

ALL UNDER PSEUDONYM HERGE; CARTOON BOOKS

Tintin au pays des Soviets, Casterman, 1930.
Tintin au Congo, Casterman, 1931, published as *Les aventures de Tintin, reporter du petit 'Vingtieme,' au Congo*, 1982.
Tintin en Amerique, Casterman, 1932, translation by Leslie Lonsdale-Cooper and Michael Turner published as *Tintin in America*, Little, Brown, 1979.
Les Cigares du pharaon, Casterman, 1934, translation by Lonsdale-Cooper and Turner published as *The Cigars of the Pharaoh*, Little, Brown, 1975.
Le Lotus bleu, Casterman, 1936, translation by Lonsdale-Cooper and Turner published as *The Blue Lotus*, Little, Brown, 1984.

L'Oreille cassee, Casterman, 1937, translation by Lonsdale-Cooper and Turner published as *Tintin and the Broken Ear,* Methuen, 1975, published in America as *The Broken Ear,* Little, Brown, 1978.

L'Ile noire, Casterman, 1938, translation by Lonsdale-Cooper and Turner published as *The Black Island,* Methuen, 1966, Little, Brown, 1975.

Le Sceptre d'Ottokar, Casterman, 1939, translation by Lonsdale-Cooper and Turner published as *King Ottokar's Sceptre,* Methuen, 1958.

Le Crabe aux pinces d'or, Casterman, 1941, translation by Lonsdale-Cooper and Turner published as *The Crab with the Golden Claws,* Methuen, 1958, Little, Brown, 1974.

L'Etoile mysterieuse, Casterman, 1942, translation by Lonsdale-Cooper and Turner published as *The Shooting Star,* Methuen, 1961, Little, Brown, 1978.

Le Secret de la licorne, Casterman, 1943, translation by Lonsdale-Cooper and Turner published as *The Secret of the Unicorn,* Methuen, 1959, Little, Brown, 1974.

Le Tresor de Rackham le Rouge, Casterman, 1945, translation by Lonsdale-Cooper and Turner published as *Red Rackham's Treasure,* Methuen, 1959.

Les Sept Boules de Cristal, Casterman, 1948, translation by Lonsdale-Cooper and Turner published as *The Seven Crystal Balls,* Methuen, 1963, Little, Brown, 1975.

Le Temple du soleil, two volumes, Casterman, 1949, translation by Lonsdale-Cooper and Turner published as *Prisoners of the Sun,* Methuen, 1962, Little, Brown, 1975.

Tintin au pays de l'Or Noir, Casterman, 1951, translation by Lonsdale-Cooper and Turner published as *The Land of Black Gold,* Methuen, 1972, Little, Brown, 1975.

Objectif Lune, Casterman, 1953, translation by Lonsdale-Cooper and Turner published as *Destination Moon,* Methuen, 1959, Little, Brown, 1976.

On a marche sur la Lune, two volumes, Casterman, 1954, translation by Lonsdale-Cooper and Turner published as *Explorers on the Moon,* Methuen, 1959, Little, Brown, 1976.

L'Affaire Tournesol, Casterman, 1956, translation by Lonsdale-Cooper and Turner published as *The Calculus Affair,* Methuen, 1960, Little, Brown, 1976.

Les Exploits de Quick et Flupke, Casterman, 1956, reprinted, 1982.

Coke en Stock, Casterman, 1958, translation by Lonsdale-Cooper and Turner published as *The Red Sea Sharks,* Methuen, 1960.

Tintin au Tibet, Casterman, 1960, translation by Lonsdale-Cooper and Turner published as *Tintin in Tibet,* Methuen, 1962, Little, Brown, 1975.

Les Bijoux de la Castafiore, Casterman, 1963, translation by Lonsdale-Cooper and Turner published as *The Castafiore Emerald,* Methuen, 1963, Little, Brown, 1975.

Tintin and the Golden Fleece, Methuen, 1965.

Vol 714 pour Sydney, Casterman, 1968, translation by Lonsdale-Cooper and Turner published as *Flight 714,* Methuen, 1968, Little, Brown, 1975.

Popol Out West, Methuen, 1969.

Destination New York, Casterman, 1971.

Tintin et le Lac aux Requins (also see below; based on Herge's screenplay of the same title), Casterman, 1973, translation by Lonsdale-Cooper and Turner published as *Tintin and the Lake of Sharks,* Methuen, 1973.

Tintin et moi: Entretiens avec Herge, Casterman, 1975.

Tintin et les Picaros, Casterman, 1976, translation by Lonsdale-Cooper and Turner published as *Tintin and the Picaros,* Methuen, 1976, Little, Brown, 1978.

Archives Herge (contains *Totor, C.P. des Hannetons, Tintin au pays des Soviets, Tintin au Congo, Tintin en Amerique, L'Ile noire, Le sceptre d'Ottokar,* and *Le crabe aux pinces d'or*), Casterman, 1980.

The Making of Tintin (contains *The Secret of the Unicorn, Red Rackham's Treasure,* and an art section by Benoit Peeters explaining how the two books were created), Methuen Children's Books, 1983.

Special Herge: Vive Tintin!, Casterman, 1983.

L'Oeuvre integrale de Herge, Rombaldi, 1984—.

Le Musee imaginaire de Tintin, Le Chateau (Angillon, France), 1984.

The Making of Tintin in the World of the Incas (contains *Prisoners of the Sun* and *The Seven Crystal Balls*), Methuen Children's Books, 1984.

(Illustrator) *Ils ont marche sur la Lune, de la fiction a la realite: Exposition au Centre Wallonie Bruxelles a Paris,* Casterman, 1985.

Tintin et l'Alph-Art, Casterman, 1986.

The Valley of the Cobras, Methuen, 1986.

The Tintin Games Book, translated from the French by Lonsdale-Cooper and Turner, Methuen, 1986.

OTHER

Also author of screenplay "Tintin et le Lac aux Requins," produced in 1972, and of book *Popol et Virginie au pays des Lapinos.*

SIDELIGHTS: For over fifty years cartoonist Georges Remi, better known under his pseudonym of Herge, chronicled the far-flung adventures of boy reporter Tintin, his trusty dog Snowy, and their companions Captain Haddock, Professor Calculus, and the twin detectives Thomson and Thompson. The never-aging Tintin made Herge "the most influential cartoonist of our century," Martin Spence reported in the London *Times.* Tintin's many adventures were translated into 33 languages, including Chinese, Welsh, Icelandic, Indonesian, Basque, Hebrew, Esperanto, and five Indian dialects. Some 300 million people are said to have followed the saga worldwide.

Tintin began in 1929 as a comic strip in the weekly children's supplement of the Brussels newspaper *Le Vingtieme Siecle.* Herge had previously been a cartoonist for a Belgian boy scout periodical, a position he had held from the age of sixteen, and many of the boy scouts' values were reflected in his character Tintin, a young boy reporter who battled gun runners, smugglers, corrupt politicians, and pirates in the course of covering a story. Tintin has a tuft of yellow hair sticking from the top of his head, a round, naive face, perpetually raised eyebrows, and is dressed in slightly ridiculous-looking baggy pants. His white fox terrier Snowy accompanies him on all of his adventures, providing companionship and comic relief. Snowy is able to speak, although only the reader can understand him, and he enjoys making snide comments on the story's development. Tintin's friend Captain Haddock is a gruff, tough, and salty fellow who swears colorful oaths in original and yet ultimately acceptable language, while the brilliant Professor Calculus is absent-minded, gentle, and a bit deaf. The bumbling twin detectives Thomson and Thompson, indistinguishable save for a slight difference in the twirl of their moustaches, rounded out the team. Together, the group solved mysteries and pursued adventure in such exotic locales as Tibet, Arabia, India, and even on the moon. Most of the plots revolved around such staples as hidden treasure, stolen jewels, and nefarious criminal plots.

The first book-length Tintin adventure, entitled *Tintin au pays des Soviets,* appeared in 1930 and took the intrepid boy reporter to the Soviet Union. A sixty-four-page, over-sized volume, this first adventure reprinted a year's worth of the comic strip. Later Tintin books followed the same format and approach. Some critics lambasted *Tintin au pays des Soviets* as bitterly anticommunist, perhaps because Tintin believed the Soviet Union to be a "stinking cesspool" and claimed that Lenin, Trotsky, and Stalin were "amassing the treasures stolen from the people." Controversy greeted Tintin's second adventure, *Tintin au Congo,* as well, this time for alleged racism and colonialism; Herge portrayed the story's African natives as dull-witted, comic figures. And the third book in the series, *Tintin en Amerique* (translated as *Tintin in America*), was called anti-American because of its portrayal of violent Chicago gangsters during Prohibition. But such criticism did not hurt sales. And Herge brushed aside the objections: "The Left has said I'm Right, and the Right has said I'm Left. I don't like to contradict either." Michael Dobbs of the *Washington Post* noted that "Tintin was accused at various times of being racist, fascist and even homosexual. . . . His true ethos was that of the boy scout who never grew up." "Tintin," Aidan Chambers explained in *Children's Book News,* "is an upholder of all things traditional, established, and legal."

As the Tintin saga unfolded in following years, the strip became noted for its keen mysteries, gentle humor, and outstanding graphic achievement. Adults as well as children were fans. Brigitte Bardot, Charles de Gaulle, and Madame Chiang Kaishek counted themselves among Tintin's admirers. "The world of Tintin offers satisfactions to the most sophisticated adult," as John Rodenbeck remarked in *Children's Literature.* A reviewer for *Junior Bookshelf* claimed that "there are no other strip-cartoons in this class. Tintin enjoys the benefit of meticulous drawing, excellent colour-printing, tireless invention, enormous humour, a gallery of memorable characters. . . . the catalogue might be extended indefinitely." Nicholas Pease commented in *Lion and the Unicorn* that "while no claims can (or should) be made for the series as serious literature, [the Tintin saga] uniquely demonstrates that comic book comedy need not be incompatible with the tastes of those who take literature seriously."

As graphic art, Herge's drawings are among the finest examples to be found in the comic strip genre. Although finding the early strips less competent, Peter Mikelbank of the *Washington Post* described Herge's later work as "vibrant imagery" comparable to that of "pioneer American cartoon artist Windsor McCay. Like a cross between the work of Walt Disney and Roy Lichtenstein, Herge's later strips, rich in texture, pop color definition and mythology, weave detailed tapestries around their familiar, clean-lined characters." To Sherwin D. Smith of the *New York Times Book Review,* "the most striking thing about the Tintin books is their art work. . . . People and animals are drawn very simply, flatly, little more than a firm outline. . . . Machines—especially airplanes and ships—are done with . . . precise detail and loving care. . . . Suddenly, there will be a set piece—a full-page pastiche of a Persian miniature, a 17th-century sea battle, a parrot-filled jungle, a Transylvanian town, an aerial panorama, an under-seascape. The shifts are dramatically and esthetically effective, and, I think, unique." After recounting the many virtues of the Tintin strip, a *Times Literary Supplement* reviewer remarked that "even considered just as illustration this is among the most interesting work being done to-day. . . . Herge has justified an interesting and immensely popular medium, made it vastly more entertaining and turned it into an art."

Herge's artwork borrowed much from the cinema, incorporating close-ups, sight gags, and the same narrative pace and sequences found in films. "One does not drop a Tintin any more than one walks out in the middle of a good film," Olivier Todd explained

in the *Listener.* Herge's work had a tremendous influence on other cartoonists, creating what was called a "Brussels school" of comic strip artists, named after Herge's hometown in Belgium. The art of this school stresses an attention to realistic detail, a meticulous rendering of color tones, and a controlled, sustained, narrative pace.

Several critics pointed out that the strip's enduring appeal, especially for children, was its ever-present humor. Herge often said that he tried to fit as many "gags" into his stories as possible, and the number of comic scenes, and their variety, was undeniable. "On any given page," Pease recounted, "[Herge] may give us sparkling wit, low farce, ingenious situation comedy, or whatever other curiosities he wishes to pull from his ragbag of humor." Much of the humor came from the interplay of the strip's characters. Crusty Captain Haddock was known for exclaiming complex, alliterative, but pure oaths when roused to anger, such as "Billions of blistering blue barnacles!" Haddock also had a sailor's weakness for the liquor bottle, and periodic scenes exploited the comic potentials of his tipsiness. Thomson and Thompson "symbolize bureaucratic inefficiency and stupidity," according to Todd, and their futile attempts to solve the mystery at hand provided many comic opportunities.

Tintin's popularity was always phenomenal, particularly in the French-speaking countries. In France and Belgium alone, the Tintin books sold some 70 million copies. Tintin also appeared in several films over the years, in two series of cartoons, and even in a London stageplay. A measure of the character's enormous appeal can be seen from the reaction at the time of Herge's death in 1983. Dobbs reported that in Paris, the event was treated "with the solemnity normally reserved for the passing of a great national hero or statesman. Newspapers have come out with black borders, cabinet ministers have been asked to make statements, and philosophers have been pondering the question of how Tintin changed their lives." The Belgian minister of finance, when questioned about Herge's death and the importance of Tintin, claimed that he had always identified more with Snowy, Tintin's terrier, because "I, too, lead the life of a dog." In the years since Herge's death a statue of Tintin has been erected in Belgium, and the Centre du Bande Dessine, a comic strip museum housed in a former luxury hotel and featuring Herge's original artwork, has been opened in Brussels. In addition, as Mikelbank noted, more than two dozen books have been published "discussing Tintin in terms of cartoon psychoanalysis, literary criticism, astrological and numerological appreciation. There are Tintin dictionaries, Tintin quizzes, and a coffee-table-sized treatment documenting the strip's influence on contemporary filmmakers and graphic artists." Le kiki, a Tintin-style haircut popular among young Europeans, was also inspired by the comic strip.

Since Herge's death the Tintin oeuvre has been managed by the Foundation Herge in Belgium, a nonprofit foundation devoted to the saga. The foundation handles the reprinting of Herge's many books, and it oversees the marketing and merchandising of the strip's characters. The various Tintin products still enjoy millions of dollars in sales annually. Despite the continuing popularity of Herge's character, no new artist has been allowed to continue the Tintin comic strip. Herge insisted that Tintin should die with him, and the Foundation Herge has respected his wish. As Dobbs reported, Herge explained his reason for ending the strip in these words: "Tintin, c'est moi."

MEDIA ADAPTATIONS: The Crab with the Golden Claws was made into an animated puppet feature in 1948; an animated cartoon series was produced in England by the publisher of *Tintin Weekly* in 1957; another animated cartoon series appeared in

1960; *Prisoners of the Sun* was made into an animated cartoon feature in 1969; the film "Moi, Tintin," was released by Elan Films of Brussels in 1976; and "Tintin's Great American Adventure," a play based on Herge's character, was produced at the Arts Theater in London in 1977.

BIOGRAPHICAL/CRITICAL SOURCES:

BOOKS

Butler, Francelia, editor, *Children's Literature,* Volume 1, Temple University Press, 1972.
Children's Literature Review, Volume 6, Gale, 1984.
Couperie, Pierre, Maurice C. Horn, and others, *A History of the Comic Strip,* Crown, 1967.
Hurlimann, Bettina, *Three Centuries of Children's Books in Europe,* Oxford University Press, 1967.

PERIODICALS

Children's Book News, January-February, 1969.
Choice, October, 1974.
Guardian, October 29, 1976.
Junior Bookshelf, October, 1958, July, 1959.
Lion and the Unicorn, Volume 1, number 1, 1977.
Listener, October 3, 1957.
New York Times Book Review, August 11, 1974.
Studio International, October, 1974.
Time, December 23, 1974.
Times (London), December 4, 1986.
Times Literary Supplement, December 5, 1958, May 19, 1966, October 3, 1968, December 4, 1969, October 22, 1971, December 8, 1972.
Washington Post, March 7, 1983, December 28, 1987.
Washington Post Book World, May 19, 1974.

OBITUARIES:

PERIODICALS

AB Bookman's Weekly, February 6, 1984.
Chicago Tribune, March 6, 1983.
Maclean's, March 14, 1983.
New York Times, March 5, 1983.
Time, March 14, 1983.
Times (London), March 5, 1983.
Washington Post, March 5, 1983.*

—*Sketch by Thomas Wiloch*

*   *   *

RESTON, James (Barrett) 1909-

PERSONAL: Born November 3, 1909, in Clydebank, Scotland; naturalized U.S. citizen, 1927; son of James (a machinist) and Johanna (Irving) Reston; married Sarah Jane Fulton, December 24, 1935; children: Richard Fulton, James Barrett, Jr., Thomas Busey. *Education:* University of Illinois, B.A., 1932.

ADDRESSES: Home—Washington, D.C. *Office*—*New York Times,* 1627 I St. N.W., Washington, D.C. 20006.

CAREER: Springfield Daily News, Springfield, Ohio, sports editor, 1932-33; Ohio State University, Columbus, head of publicity for athletic department, 1933-34; Associated Press (AP), sports writer in New York City, 1934-37, and London, England, 1937-39; *New York Times,* New York City, reporter in London, 1939-45, diplomatic correspondent in Washington, D.C., 1945-53, columnist, 1945-87, author of "Washington" column, 1953-87, chief of Washington, D.C., bureau, 1953-64, associate

editor in Washington, D.C., 1964-68, executive editor in New York City, 1968-69, vice-president in Washington, D.C., 1969-73, director of company and consultant, 1973—. Cochairman of board, *Vineyard Gazette,* 1968—.

MEMBER: National Press Club (Washington), Century Club (New York), Chevy Chase (Md.) Club.

AWARDS, HONORS: Pulitzer Prize, 1945, 1957, both for national reporting; Overseas Press Club awards, 1949, 1951, 1955; George Polk Memorial Award, Long Island University, 1953, for reporting, and 1987, for career achievement; University of Missouri medal, 1961; John Peter Zenger Award, University of Arizona, 1964; Elijah Parish Lovejoy fellowship, Colby College, 1974; Regents Medal, University of the State of New York, 1984; Presidential Medal of Liberty, 1986; Helen B. Bernstein Award for Excellence in Journalism, 1988; Order of the British Empire (commander); chevalier of the Legion d'Honneur (France); Order of St. Olav (Norway); Order of Merit (Chile); Order of Leopold (Belgium); honorary degrees from over twenty universities and colleges in the United States and Scotland, including Harvard University, Yale University, University of Illinois, and University of Glasgow.

WRITINGS:

Prelude to Victory, Knopf, 1942.
(Editor with Marquis William Childs) *Walter Lippmann and His Times,* Harcourt, 1959.
Sketches in the Sand, Knopf, 1967.
Artillery of the Press, Council on Foreign Relations, 1967.
(With Tillman Durdin and Seymour Topping) *The New York Times Report from Red China,* edited by Frank Ching, Quadrangle, 1971.
Washington, Macmillan, 1986.

SIDELIGHTS: During his heyday as a reporter for the *New York Times* in the forties and fifties, James "Scotty" Reston was considered, as *New Yorker* contributor Alistair Cooke describes him, "the most agile filcher of confidential agreements, the most alert, the most probing, the most knowledgeable—the best—of all Washington correspondents." Reston won his first Pulitzer Prize in 1945 for his exclusive series of articles on the plans for creating the United Nations, and as Washington, D.C., bureau chief was the first to interview President Kennedy after his historic meeting with Soviet leader Nikita Khrushchev. As he became more involved in the running of the *Times,* Reston contributed to and supported the controversial decision to publish the "Pentagon Papers," an incriminating government study of U.S. involvement in Vietnam—a decision which led to a Supreme Court case reaffirming the rights of the press.

Despite the long-time reporter's participation in some of the biggest news stories of his time, "Reston knew that the story was more important than the storyteller, and that the sensation of the scoop was trivial by comparison with the dogged pursuit of the truth," notes the *Washington Post*'s Jonathan Yardley in a farewell tribute to Reston. His "Washington" column, which ran in the *Times* for thirty-five years, has also added to his professional stature, as David K. Willis attests in the *Christian Science Monitor:* "I regard James Reston as one of the most thoughtful, most sensible, drollest columnists this country has produced. To read [*Sketches in the Sand*]—a collection of his writings between 1941 and 1967—is to be impressed anew with the elements of his appeal, to recognize the roots of his enduring popularity and stature." The critic adds that while Reston has been successful as a columnist, he has never forgotten his roots as a reporter: "This is not a man writing conscious 'columns' filled with literary flourishes and a pretense to omniscience but an informed reporter, . . . looking beyond the words of the speeches and the surface brilliance of large events to underlying common-sensical matters." Reston, he concludes, "writes primarily as a concerned and thinking newsman, with an ear for the actual sounds, feel, and impact of events."

Richard D. Heffner likewise states in the *Saturday Review* that Reston's columns "are so free from pretension as to be pure delight, not only in the vigor and distinction of his style, but in the sheer relevance and import of his observations on the pressing questions that were with us yesterday and will be with us tomorrow." Commenting on Reston's individual approach, *New York Times Book Review* contributor Penn Kimball explains that the columnist's "virtue in a capital where all eyes are usually fastened on the scramble to grab hold of the levers of power is his insistence on trying to clarify the purposes for which this exhausting effort is expended." "It is in this process of cool analysis in the midst of the event that Reston is at his best," remarks Richard C. Wald in *Book World.* "He is capable of stepping aside from the fashionable to see the thing differently—maybe not as it really is, but certainly in a light that is persuasive and conducive to thought."

Sketches in the Sand, while it takes its title from famed journalist Walter Lippmann's description of a commentator as "a puzzled man . . . drawing sketches in the sand, which the sea will wash away," is proof to the contrary, Gene Graham asserts: "Mr. Reston is an analyst," the critic observes in *Commonweal.* "With clean reason and reasonably simple prose, he has spent a distinguished career picking his way between the messy affairs of the world and mankind's hope to clean it up. Almost invariably, Mr. Reston sees a light at the end of the tunnel. His optimism has cheered millions." Graham concludes that while Reston's hopeful brand of journalism might be on the wane, "those of us who still cling to logic and naively await its salvation will cherish Mr. Reston, confident that what he has sketched—and built—is not upon sand."

Washington, a second collection of Reston columns published shortly before his retirement in 1987, also demonstrates the newsman's skill in combining observation with opinion, as Cooke maintains: "It is [Reston's] continuing strength, in his rude old age, that on both big and little issues of the day he does his own digging: he gets to the characters in the play, and finds out at first hand what they think and what they did. Only then does he sit back and, like a veteran drama critic, compare the plot and its treatment with a clutch of plays remembered from the past. This is Mr. Reston's notable distinction," Cooke explains. "He has been there before, and has pretty much total recall of the way the protagonists handled similar problems of government in the past forty or fifty years; he rarely fails to see today in the light of yesterday and the day before that." "[Reston has] had neither the training nor the true inclination for philosophical reflection," concludes Yardley in his article on the columnist's retirement. "He was, instead, a reporter and an analyst, and no one in his time was better than he at either. Which is to say that he was the first and only Reston, and that is quite enough distinction for anyone to claim."

BIOGRAPHICAL/CRITICAL SOURCES:

BOOKS

Authors in the News, Volumes 1-2, Gale, 1976.

PERIODICALS

Akron Beacon Journal (Ohio), November 4, 1973, February 8, 1976.
Book Week, April 16, 1967.
Book World, September 24, 1967.
Christian Science Monitor, September 23, 1967.
Commonweal, March 15, 1968.
National Review, May 16, 1967.
New Republic, April 29, 1967.
New Yorker, February 9, 1987.
New York Review of Books, May 4, 1967.
New York Times Book Review, April 2, 1967, October 8, 1967.
Saturday Review, April 8, 1967, November 11, 1967.
Time, August 31, 1987.
Washington Post, August 17, 1987.
Washington Post Book World, November 30, 1986.

—*Sketch by Diane Telgen*

* * *

RESTON, James B(arrett), Jr. 1941-

PERSONAL: Born March 8, 1941, in New York, N.Y.; son of James Barrett (a journalist) and Sarah Jane (a journalist; maiden name, Fulton) Reston; married Denise Brender Leary, June 12, 1971. *Education:* Attended Oxford University, 1961-62; University of North Carolina at Chapel Hill, B.A., 1963.

ADDRESSES: Home—4714 Hunt Ave., Chevy Chase, Md. 20815. *Agent*—Timothy Seldes, Russell & Volkening, 50 West 29th St., New York, N.Y. 10001.

CAREER: U.S. Department of the Interior, Washington, D.C., speech writer for Secretary of the Interior Udall, 1964-65; *Chicago Daily News,* Chicago, Ill., reporter, 1964-65; University of North Carolina at Chapel Hill, lecturer in creative writing, 1971-1981; writer. *Military service:* U.S. Army, Military Intelligence, 1965-68; became sergeant.

MEMBER: Authors Guild, PEN, Dramatists Guild.

AWARDS, HONORS: Dupont-Columbia Award, and Prix Italia (Venice), both 1982, both for "Father Cares: The Last of Jonestown"; National Endowment for the Arts grant, 1982.

WRITINGS:

To Defend, to Destroy (novel), Norton, 1971.
The Amnesty of John David Herndon, McGraw, 1973.
(With Frank Mankiewicz) *Perfectly Clear: Nixon from Whittier to Watergate,* Quadrangle, 1973.
The Knock at Midnight (novel), Norton, 1975.
The Innocence of Joan Little: A Southern Mystery (nonfiction), Quadrangle, 1977.
"Sherman, the Peacemaker" (play), first produced in Chapel Hill, N.C., by the Playmakers Repertory, 1979.
Our Father Who Art in Hell: The Life and Death of Jim Jones, Quadrangle, 1981.
"Father Cares: The Last of Jonestown" (radio documentary), first aired on National Public Radio, May, 1981.
88 Seconds in Greensboro (documentary; first aired on PBS-TV's "Frontline" series, 1983), WGBH Transcripts, 1983.
"Jonestown Express" (play), first produced in Providence, R.I., by Trinity Square Repertory Company, May 22, 1984.
Sherman's March and Vietnam, Macmillan, 1985.
"The Real Stuff" (documentary), first aired on PBS-TV's "Frontline," 1987.
"The Mission of Discovery" (documentary), first aired on PBS-TV, 1988.

The Lone Star: The Life of John Connally, Harper, 1989.

Scriptwriter for David Frost, "The Nixon Interviews," 1976-77. Contributor of articles to *New Yorker, Saturday Review, New York Times Magazine, Washington Post Magazine, Omni, Esquire, New York Times Book Review,* and other periodicals. Regular fiction reviewer, *Chronicle of Higher Education,* 1976-77.

SIDELIGHTS: James B. Reston, Jr., has explored the Jonestown mass suicide-murder of 1978 in three different forms: as a documentary on public radio; in a book-length study of Jim Jones's commune; and in a semi-fictionalized play. Winning access to a series of recordings of the Jonestown colony's proceedings, Reston "has succeeded in extracting startling connections and meanings from the transcripts of these tapes," observes Malcolm Boyd in the *Los Angeles Times Book Review.* In addition, remarks Robert Coles in his *Washington Post Book World* review, Reston "tries hard in *Our Father Who Art in Hell* to give us some philosophical distance on this recent horror." The critic elaborates: "Reston's eye is novelistic; he has followed the tracks of a movement's downward slide, and is in a position to give us careful details. . . . He strains to explain. And he does so, at times, with the good judgment of a writer willing to avoid certain faddish modes of analysis." While Peter Schrag faults the book as "flawed both by uncertain purpose and by an excessive tendency to . . . speculations of various obvious sorts," he admits in the *Nation* that the tape transcriptions are invaluable and the "book makes clear how much of a tall tale Jonestown really was." Reston's play "Jonestown Express" conveys this same idea, as Richard Zoglin suggests in *Newsweek:* "At a time when dramatists are shying away from 'big' social issues . . ., [in 'Jonestown Express'] the message comes through with clarity and power: it could happen again; it could happen here."

In *Sherman's March and Vietnam,* Reston "unearths unusual and thoughtful metaphorical parallels between William Tecumseh Sherman's way of war [during the Civil War] and the conduct of the war in Vietnam," writes Brian Burns in the *Los Angeles Times Book Review. Washington Post Book World* contributor Russell F. Weigley relates: "By breaking down one of the major limits restraining the violence of war, Reston contends, Sherman accustomed American soldiers to regarding such limits lightly. [Sherman's march] pointed the way to subsequent, larger violations, destroying lives as well as property." In pursuing this theory, the author "traces Sherman's march, seeking to find out what the man was like and to measure his impact on the ethics of modern war," summarizes Stephen W. Sears in the *New York Times Book Review.*

In addition, Reston contrasts the resolutions of the two wars, pointing out that while dissenters in the Civil War were given amnesty, neither side involved in the Vietnam debate was given a substantial resolution. Sears finds this portion of Reston's account, which "examines why a dozen years after the Paris peace accords . . . the wounds of the Vietnam era are still unhealed," more convincing. Weigley likewise notes that "some of the most eloquent passages of Reston's book return to searching the Civil War for possible guidance toward escaping the divisive emotional legacy of Vietnam." While the critic faults the author for "indulg[ing] in ambivalence and complexity," he concludes that *Sherman's March and Vietnam* is "stimulating," for "the lasting damage that Sherman perpetrated against restraint in war is a theme worth emphasizing."

AVOCATIONAL INTERESTS: Woodcrafting on a lathe.

BIOGRAPHICAL/CRITICAL SOURCES:

PERIODICALS

Boston Globe, February 10, 1985.
Los Angeles Times Book Review, April 26, 1981, March 17, 1985.
Nation, May 2, 1981.
National Review, April 16, 1982.
Newsweek, June 1, 1981, June 4, 1984.
New York Times, May 25, 1984.
New York Times Book Review, February 17, 1985.
Washington Post Book World, April 5, 1981, February 10, 1985.

*   *   *

REUTHER, David L(ouis) 1946-

PERSONAL: Born November 2, 1946, in Detroit, Mich.; son of Roy L. (a labor leader) and Fania (Sonkin) Reuther; married Margaret Miller (a photographer), July 21, 1973; children: Katherine Anna, Jacob Alexander Louis. *Education:* University of Michigan, B.A. (with honors), 1968.

ADDRESSES: Home—271 Central Park W., New York, N.Y. 10024. *Office*—William Morrow & Co., Inc., 105 Madison Ave., New York, N.Y. 10016.

CAREER: Lewis-Wadhams School, Westport, N.Y., teacher of humanities, 1968-70; Children's Book Council, Inc., New York City, editor, 1972-75; Scholastic Book Services, New York City, senior editor of Four Winds Press, 1975-82; William Morrow & Co., Inc., New York City, vice-president and editor in chief of Morrow Junior Books, 1982—.

MEMBER: Authors Guild, Authors League of America, American Library Association.

WRITINGS:

(With Roy Doty) *Fun to Go: A Take-Along Activity Book* (juvenile), Macmillan, 1982.
Save-the-Animals Activity Book (juvenile), Random House, 1982.
(Editor with John Thorn) *The Armchair Quarterback,* Scribner, 1982.
(Editor with Thorn) *The Armchair Aviator,* Scribner, 1983.
(Editor with Thorn) *The Armchair Mountaineer,* Scribner, 1984.
(With Thorn) *The Hidden Game of Baseball: A Revolutionary Approach to Baseball and Its Statistics,* Doubleday, 1984.
(Editor with Terry Brykczynski) *The Armchair Angler,* Scribners, 1985.
(With Thorn) *The Complete Book of the Pitcher,* Prentice-Hall, 1988.
(Editor with Thorn) *The Armchair Traveler,* Prentice-Hall, 1988.
(With Thorn) *Total Baseball,* Warner, 1989.

WORK IN PROGRESS: With John Thorn, several books sponsored by the National Baseball Hall of Fame and Major League baseball, publication by Simon & Schuster expected in April 1990 and 1991.

*   *   *

RHODES, Leland
See PAINE, Lauran (Bosworth)

*   *   *

RICHARDS, Norman 1932-

PERSONAL: Born March 14, 1932, in Winchendon, Mass.; son of Burton W. (in business) and Berthalene (a nurse; maiden name, Webster) Richards; married wife, Robin (a writer, editor, and photographer); children: Gary, Gayle, Gregory. *Education:* Boston University, B.S., 1958; Harvard University, graduate study, 1959.

ADDRESSES: Home—93 Stonehenge Dr., Washington, Pa. 15301. *Office*—Public Affairs, USX Corp., 600 Grant St., Pittsburgh, Pa. 15219.

CAREER: United Airlines, Chicago, Ill., managing editor of monthly travel magazine *Mainliner*, 1962-68; *Chicago* (magazine), Chicago, editor, 1968-69; *Patient Care* (medical magazine), Greenwich, Conn., member of editorial staff, 1969-71; Exxon Corp., New York, N.Y., managing editor of magazine *The Lamp*, 1971-79; Marathon Oil Co., Findlay, Ohio, manager of publications, 1979-88; USX Corp., Pittsburgh, Pa., publications manager, 1988—. *Military service:* U.S. Navy, served as aircraft crew member and control tower operator during Korean War.

WRITINGS:

JUVENILES

Douglas MacArthur, Childrens Press, 1967.
Giants in the Sky (a Junior Literary Guild selection; illustrated by Robert Borja and Corinne Borja), Childrens Press, 1967.
(With John P. Reidy) *John F. Kennedy*, Childrens Press, 1967.
The Story of Old Ironsides (a Junior Literary Guild selection; illustrated by Tom Dunnington), Childrens Press, 1967.
The Story of the Mayflower Compact (illustrated by Darrell Wiskur), Childrens Press, 1967.
Ernest Hemingway, Childrens Press, 1968.
Helen Keller, Childrens Press, 1968.
Robert Frost, Childrens Press, 1968.
The Story of the Declaration of Independence (illustrated by Dunnington), Childrens Press, 1968.
Dag Hammerskjoeld, Childrens Press, 1969.
Pope John XXIII, Childrens Press, 1969.
The Story of the Bonhomme Richard (illustrated by Dunnington), Childrens Press, 1969.
The Story of Monticello (illustrated by Chuck Mitchell), Childrens Press, 1970.
The Story of the Alamo (illustrated by Dunnington), Childrens Press, 1970.
Jetport, Doubleday, 1973.
The Complete Beginner's Guide to Soaring and Hang Gliding, Doubleday, 1976.
Tractors, Plows, and Harvesters: A Book about Farm Machines, Doubleday, 1978.
(With Pat Richards) *Trucks and Supertrucks*, Doubleday, 1980.
Dreamers and Doers: Inventors Who Changed the World, Atheneum, 1984.

ADULT BOOKS

Cowboy Movies, Bison Books, 1984.
Heart to Heart: A Guide to Understanding Heart Disease and Open-Heart Surgery, Atheneum, 1987.

OTHER

Contributor of articles to periodicals, including *Gentleman's Quarterly, Reader's Digest,* and *Family Circle.*

*   *   *

RICHLER, Mordecai 1931-

PERSONAL: Born January 27, 1931, in Montreal, Quebec, Canada; son of Moses Isaac and Lily (Rosenberg) Richler; married

Florence Wood, July 27, 1960; children: Daniel, Noah, Emma, Martha, Jacob. *Education:* Attended Sir George Williams University, 1949-51. *Religion:* Jewish.

ADDRESSES: Home and office—1321 Sherbroake St. W., Apt. 80C, Montreal, Quebec, Canada H3G 1J4. *Agent*—Lynn Nesbit, International Creative Management, 40 West 57th St., New York, N.Y. 10019; (for films) William Morris Agency, 1350 Avenue of the Americas, New York, N.Y. 10019.

CAREER: Author and screenwriter. Left Canada in 1951 to become free-lance writer in Paris, France, 1952-53, and London, England, 1954-72; returned to Canada, 1972. Writer in residence, Sir George Williams University, 1968-69; visiting professor, Carleton University, 1972-74. Member of editorial board, Book-of-the-Month Club, 1972—.

AWARDS, HONORS: President's medal for nonfiction, University of Western Ontario, 1959; Canadian Council junior art fellowships, 1959 and 1960, senior arts fellowship, 1967; Guggenheim Foundation creative writing fellowship, 1961; *Paris Review* humor prize, 1967, for section from *Cocksure;* Canadian Governor-General's award for literature and London Jewish Chronicle literature award, both 1972, both for *St. Urbain's Horseman;* Berlin Film Festival Golden Bear, Academy Award nomination, and Screenwriters Guild of America award, all 1974, all for the screenplay, "The Apprenticeship of Duddy Kravitz"; Canadian Bookseller's award for best children's book and Canadian Librarian's medal, both 1976, both for *Jacob Two-Two Meets the Hooded Fang;* London *Jewish Chronicle*/H. H. Wingate award for fiction, 1981, for *Joshua Then and Now.*

WRITINGS:

The Acrobats (novel; also see below), Putnam, 1954, published as *Wicked We Love,* Popular Library, 1955.
Son of a Smaller Hero (novel), Collins (Toronto), 1955, Paperback Library, 1965.
A Choice of Enemies (novel), Collins, 1957.
The Apprenticeship of Duddy Kravitz (novel; also see below), Little, Brown, 1959.
The Incomparable Atuk (novel), McClelland & Stewart, 1963, published as *Stick Your Neck Out,* Simon & Schuster, 1963.
Cocksure (novel), Simon & Schuster, 1968.
Hunting Tigers under Glass: Essays and Reports, McClelland & Stewart, 1969.
The Street: Stories, McClelland & Stewart, 1969, New Republic, 1975.
(Editor) *Canadian Writing Today* (anthology), Peter Smith, 1970.
St. Urbain's Horseman (novel; Literary Guild featured alternate), Knopf, 1971.
Shoveling Trouble (essays), McClelland & Stewart, 1973.
Notes on an Endangered Species and Others (essays), Knopf, 1974.
Jacob Two-Two Meets the Hooded Fang (juvenile), Knopf, 1975.
Images of Spain, photographs by Peter Christopher, Norton, 1977.
The Great Comic Book Heroes and Other Essays, McClelland & Steward, 1978.
Joshua Then and Now (novel; also see below), Knopf, 1980.
(Editor) *The Best of Modern Humor,* Knopf, 1984.
Home Sweet Home: My Canadian Album (nonfiction), Knopf, 1984, published in paperback as *Home Sweet Home,* Penguin, 1985.
Jacob Two-Two and the Dinosaur (juvenile), Knopf, 1987.
Solomon Gursky Was Here, (novel), Viking, 1989.

SCREENPLAYS

(With Nicholas Phipps) "No Love for Johnnie," Embassy, 1962.

(With Geoffrey Cotterell and Ivan Foxwell) "Tiara Tahiti," Rank, 1962.

(With Phipps) "The Wild and the Willing," Rank, 1962, released in United States as "Young and Willing," Universal, 1965.

"Life at the Top," Royal International, 1965.

"The Apprenticeship of Duddy Kravitz" (adapted from his novel), Paramount, 1974.

(With David Giler and Jerry Belson) "Fun with Dick and Jane," Bart/Palevsky, 1977.

"Joshua Then and Now" (adapted from his novel), Twentieth Century-Fox, 1985.

TELEVISION AND RADIO SCRIPTS

"The Acrobats" (based on his novel), Canadian Broadcasting Corp. (CBC), 1956 (radio), 1957 (television).

"Friend of the People," CBC-TV, 1957.

"Paid in Full," ATV (England), 1958.

"Benny, the War in Europe, and Myerson's Daughter Bella," CBC-Radio, 1958. "The Trouble with Benny" (based on his short story), ABC (England), 1959.

"The Apprenticeship of Duddy Kravitz" (based on his novel), CBC-TV, 1960.

"The Spare Room," CBC-Radio, 1961.

"Q for Quest" (excerpts from his fiction), CBC-Radio, 1963.

"The Fall of Mendel Krick," British Broadcasting Corp. (BBC-TV), 1963.

"It's Harder to Be Anybody," CBC-Radio, 1965.

"Such Was St. Urbain Street," CBC-Radio, 1966.

"The Wordsmith" (based on his short story), CBC-Radio, 1979.

OTHER

"The Suit" (animated filmstrip), National Film Board of Canada, 1976.

(Author of Book) "Duddy" (play; based on his novel *The Apprenticeship of Duddy Kravitz*), first produced in Edmonton, Alberta, at the Citadel Theatre, April, 1984.

Contributor to Canadian, U.S., and British periodicals. Richler's papers are collected at the University of Calgary Library in Alberta.

SIDELIGHTS: "To be a Canadian and a Jew," as Mordecai Richler wrote in his book *Hunting Tigers under Glass: Essays and Reports,* "is to emerge from the ghetto twice." He refers to the double pressures of being in both a religious minority and the cultural enigma that is Canada. Yet in his decades as a novelist, screenwriter, and essayist, Richler has established himself as one of the few representatives of Canadian Jewry known outside his native country.

That many of his fictional works feature Jewish-Canadian protagonists in general (most notably in his best-known book *The Apprenticeship of Duddy Kravitz*), and natives of Montreal in particular, denotes the author's strong attachment to his early years. Richler was born in the Jewish ghetto of Montreal to a religious family of Russian emigres. "In his teens, however, he abandoned Orthodox customs, gradually becoming more interested both in a wider world and in writing," relates R. H. Ramsey in a *Dictionary of Literary Biography* article on Richler. After a stint at a university, Richler cashed in an insurance policy and used the money to sail to Liverpool, England. Eventually he found his way to Paris, where he spent some years emulating such expatriate authors as Ernest Hemingway and Henry Miller,

then moved on to London, where he worked as a news correspondent.

During those early years, Richler produced his first novel, *The Acrobats,* a book he now characterizes as "more political than anything I've done since, and humorless," as he tells Walter Goodman in a *New York Times* interview, adding that the volume, published when he was twenty-three, "was just a very young man's novel. Hopelessly derivative. Like some unfortunate collision of [Jean-Paul] Sartre and Hemingway and [Louis-Ferdinand] Celine, all unabsorbed and undigested. I wasn't writing in my own voice at all. I was imitating people." But Richler found his voice soon after, with novels like *Son of a Smaller Hero, A Choice of Enemies,* and *The Incomparable Atuk.* Ramsey finds that from these efforts on, "two tendencies dominate Richler's fiction: realism and satire. [Much of the early work is] realistic, their plots basically traditional in form, their settings accurately detailed, their characters motivated in psychologically familiar ways." At the other extreme, Ramsey continues, there is "pure satiric fantasy, [with] concessions to realism slight. In [such works] Richler indulges the strong comic vein in his writing as he attacks Canadian provincialism and the spurious gratifications of the entertainment medium."

Richler gained further notice with three of his best-known titles, *The Apprenticeship of Duddy Kravitz, St. Urbain's Horseman,* and *Joshua Then and Now.* These books share a common theme—that of a Jewish-Canadian protagonist at odds with society—and all three novels revolve around the idea of the way greed can taint success. *The Apprenticeship of Duddy Kravitz* presents its eponymous hero as a ghetto-reared youth on a never-ending quest to make a name for himself in business. It is also "the first of Richler's novels to exhibit fully his considerable comic talents, a strain that includes much black humor and a racy, colloquial, ironic idiom that becomes a characteristic feature of Richler's subsequent style," according to Ramsey.

Comparing *The Apprenticeship of Duddy Kravitz* to other such coming-of-age stories as James Joyce's *Portrait of the Artist as a Young Man* and D. H. Lawrence's *Sons and Lovers,* A. R. Bevan, in a new introduction to Richler's novel, finds that the book, "in spite of its superficial affinity with the two novels mentioned above, ends with [none of their] affirmation." The character of Duddy, "who has never weighted the consequences of his actions in any but material terms, is less alone in the physical sense than the earlier young men, but he is also much less of a man. . . . He is a modern 'anti-hero' (something like the protagonist in Anthony Burgess's *A Clockwork Orange*) who lives in a largely deterministic world, a world where decisions are not decisions and where choice is not really choice." In *Modern Fiction Studies,* John Ower sees *The Apprenticeship of Duddy Kravitz* as "a 'Jewish' novel [with] both a pungent ethnic flavor and the convincingness that arises when a writer deals with a milieu with which he is completely familiar." For the author, Ower continues, "the destructive psychological effects of the ghetto mentality are equalled and to some extent paralleled by those of the Jewish family. Like the society from which it springs, this tends to be close and exclusive, clinging together in spite of its intense quarrels. The best aspect of such clannishness, the feeling of kinship which transcends all personal differences, is exemplified by Duddy. Although he is in varying degrees put down and rejected by all of his relatives except his grandfather, Duddy sticks up for them and protects them."

For all its success, *The Apprenticeship of Duddy Kravitz* was still categorized by most scholars as among Richler's early works. By the time *St. Urbain's Horseman* was published in 1971, the author had all but sealed his reputation as a sharp cultural critic. In this work, a character named Jacob Hersh, a Canadian writer living in London, questions "not only how he rose to prominence but also the very nature and quality of success and why, having made it, [he] is dissatisfied," as Ramsey puts it. Hersh's success as a writer "brings with it a guilt, a sense of responsibility, and an overwhelming paranoia, a belief that his good fortune is largely undeserved and that sooner or later he will be called to account," Ramsey adds. In his guilt-based fantasies, Hersh dreams that he is a figure of vengeance protecting the downtrodden, a character based on the Horseman, a shadowy figure from Hersh's past. "Richler prefaces *St. Urbain's Horseman* with a quotation from [British poet W. H.] Auden which suggests that he does not wish to be read as a mere entertainer, a fanciful farceur," notes David Myers in *Ariel.* "What is there in the *Horseman* that would justify us as regarding it as such a[n affirming] flame? Certainly the despair that we find there is serious enough; the world around Jake Hersh is sordid and vile." The author accords sympathy "to only two characters in his novel, Jake and his wife Nancy," Myers says. "They are shown to feel a very deep love for one another and the loyalty of this love under duress provides the ethical counterbalance to the sordidness, instability, lack of integrity, injustice, and grasping materialism that Richler is satirizing in this book."

In the opinion of Kerry McSweeney, writing in *Studies in Canadian Literature,* the novel "gives evidence everywhere of technical maturity and full stylistic control, and combines the subjects, themes and modes of Richler's earlier novels in ways that suggest—as does the high seriousness of its epigraph—that Richler was attempting a cumulative fictional statement of his view on the mores and values of contemporary man. But while *St. Urbain's Horseman* is a solid success on the level of superior fictional entertainment, on the level of serious fiction it must be reckoned a considerable disappointment. It doesn't deliver the goods and simply does not merit the kind of detailed exegesis it has been given by some Canadian critics." Elaborating on this thesis, McSweeney adds that everything in the novel "depends on the presentation of Jake, especially of his mental life and the deeper reaches of his character, and on the intensity of the reader's sympathetic involvement with him. Unfortunately, Jake is characterized rather too superficially. One is told, for example, but never shown, that he is charged with contradictions concerning his professional life; and for all the time devoted to what is going on in his head he doesn't really seem to have much of a mental life. Despite the big issues he is said to be struggling with, *St. Urbain's Horseman* can hardly claim serious attention as a novel of ideas."

Robert Fulford offers a different view. In his *Saturday Night* article, Fulford lauds *St. Urbain's Horseman* as "the triumphant and miraculous bringing-together of all those varied Mordecai Richlers who have so densely populated our literary landscape for so many years. From this perspective it becomes clear that all those Richlers have a clear purpose in mind—they've all been waiting out there, working separately, honing their talents, waiting for the moment when they could arrive at the same place and join up in the creation of a magnificent *tour de force,* the best Canadian book in a long time."

The third of Richler's later novels, *Joshua Then and Now,* again explores a Jewish-Canadian's moral crises. Joshua Shapiro, a prominent author married to a gentile daughter of a senator, veers between religious and social classes, and withstands family conflicts, especially as they concern his father Reuben. It is also a novel full of mysteries. Why, asks *Village Voice* critic Barry Yourgrau, "does the book open in the present with this 47-year-

old Joshua a rumple of fractures in a hospital bed, his name unfairly linked to a scandalous faggotry, his wife doped groggy in a nuthouse and he himself being watched over by his two elderly fathers?" The reason, Yourgrau continues, "is Time. The cruelest of fathers is committing physical violence on Joshua's dearest friends (and crucial enemies)."

Joshua, sometimes shown in flashback as the son of the ever-on-the-make Reuben and his somewhat exhibitionist mother (she performed a striptease at Joshua's bar mitzvah), "is another one of Richler's Jewish *arrivistes,* like Duddy Kravitz [and] Jacob Hersh," says *New Republic* critic Mark Shechner. After noting Joshua's unrepentant bragging, Shechner finds the character "a fairly unpleasant fellow, and indeed, though his exploits are unfailingly vivid and engaging—even fun—they rarely elicit from us much enthusiasm for Joshua himself. He is as callow as he is clever, and, one suspects, Richler means him to be an anti-type, to stand against the more common brands of self-congratulation that are endemic to Jewish fiction. From Sholom Aleichem and his Tevye to [Saul] Bellow and [Bernard] Malamud, . . . Jewish fiction has repeatedly thrown up figures of wisdom and endurance, observance and rectitude. . . . Richler, by contrast, adheres to a tradition of dissent that runs from Isaac Babel's Odessa stories through Daniel Fuchs's *Williamsburg Trilogy* and Budd Schulberg's *What Makes Sammy Run?,* which finds more color, more life, and more fidelity to the facts of Jewish existence in the demimonde of hustlers, heavies, strong-arm types and men on the make than in the heroes of *menschlichkeit* [Yiddish slang for the quality of goodness]."

But whatever message *Joshua Then and Now* might deliver, the lasting appeal of the novel, to John Lahr, is that "Richler writes funny. Laughter, not chicken soup, is the real Jewish penicillin. . . . Richler's characters enter as philosophers and exit as stand-up comics, firing zingers as they go," as Lahr explains in a *New York* article. On the other hand, *New York Times Book Review* writer Thomas R. Edwards, while acknowledging the novel's humor, finds it "dangerously similar in theme, situation and personnel to a number of Mordecai Richler's other novels—'Son of a Smaller Hero,' 'The Apprenticeship of Duddy Kravitz,' 'Cocksure' and 'St. Urbain's Horseman.' It's as if a rich and unusual body of fictional material had become a kind of prison for a writer who is condemned to repeat himself ever more vehemently and inflexibly." *Joshua Then and Now* brought much more critical debate. Mark Harris, on one hand, faults the novel for its style, "resplendent with every imaginable failure of characterization, relevance, style or grammar," in his *Washington Post Book World* review. An *Atlantic* critic, on the other hand, saw the book as "good enough to last, perhaps Richler's best novel to date."

Among his nonfiction works, Richler's *Home Sweet Home: My Canadian Album* drew some attention. It's "a different sort of book, but no less direct and pungent in its observations about what makes a society tick," according to a Toronto *Globe and Mail* writer. In this volume the author uses essays to examine Canadian culture, addressing subjects from nationalism to hockey. In another *Globe and Mail* article, Joy Fielding sees the book as "a cross-country tour like no other, penetrating the Eastern soul, the Western angst, and the French-Canadian spirit." *Home Sweet Home* drew admiring glances from American as well as Canadian critics. Peter Ross, of the *Detroit News,* writes, "Wit and warmth are constants and though Richler can temper his fondness with bursts of uncompromising acerbity, no reader can fail to perceive the depth of his feelings as well as the complexities of Canada." And *Time*'s Stefan Kanfer observes that "even as he celebrates [Canada's] beauties, the author never loses sight of his country's insularity: when Playboy Films wanted to produce adult erotica in Toronto, he reports, officials wanted to know how much Canadian content there would be in the features. But Richler also knows that the very tugs and pulls of opposing cultures give the country its alternately appealing and discordant character."

"Throughout his career Richler has spanned an intriguing gulf," concludes Ramsey in his *Dictionary of Literary Biography* piece. "While ridiculing popular tastes and never catering to popular appeal, he has nevertheless maintained a wide general audience. Though drawing constantly on his own experience, he rejects the writer as personality, wishing instead to find acceptance not because of some personal characteristic or because of the familiarity of his subject matter to a Canadian reading public but because he has something fresh to say about humanity and says it in a well-crafted form, which even with its comic exuberance, stands firmly in the tradition of moral and intellectual fiction."

MEDIA ADAPTATIONS: Richler's children's book *Jacob Two-Two Meets the Hooded Fang* was filmed in 1977 by Cinema Shares International. Film rights have been sold for both *Stick Your Neck Out* and *Cocksure.* A reading by Christopher Plummer of *Jacob Two-Two Meets the Hooded Fang* was recorded by Caedmon Records in 1977.

BIOGRAPHICAL/CRITICAL SOURCES:

BOOKS

Authors in the News, Volume 1, Gale, 1976.
Contemporary Literary Criticism, Gale, Volume 3, 1975, Volume 5, 1976, Volume 9, 1978, Volume 13, 1980, Volume 18, 1981, Volume 46, 1987.
Dictionary of Literary Biography, Volume 53: *Canadian Writers since 1960, First Series,* Gale, 1986.
Klinck, Carl F., and others, editors, *Literary History of Canada: Canadian Literature in English,* University of Toronto Press, 1965.
New, W. H., *Articulating West,* New Press, 1972.
Northey, Margot, *The Haunted Wilderness: The Gothic and Grotesque in Canadian Fiction,* University of Toronto Press, 1976.
Ramraj, Victor J., *Mordecai Richler,* Twayne, 1983.
Richler, Mordecai, *The Apprenticeship of Duddy Kravitz,* introduction by A. R. Bevan, McClelland & Stewart, 1969.
Richler, Mordecai, *Hunting Tigers under Glass: Essays and Reports,* McClelland & Stewart, 1969.
Sheps, G. David, editor, *Mordecai Richler,* McGraw-Hill/Ryerson, 1971.
Woodcock, George, *Mordecai Richler,* McClelland & Stewart, 1970.

PERIODICALS

Ariel, January, 1973.
Atlantic, July, 1980.
Books in Canada, August-September, 1984.
Canadian Literature, spring, 1973, summer, 1973.
Commentary, October, 1980.
Detroit News, July 29, 1984.
Esquire, August, 1982.
Globe and Mail (Toronto), May 5, 1984, June 24, 1985, June 13, 1987.
Los Angeles Times Book Review, August 19, 1984.
Maclean's, May 7, 1984.
Modern Fiction Studies, autumn, 1976.
Nation, July 5, 1980.
New Republic, May 18, 1974, June 14, 1980, December 5, 1983.

Newsweek, June 16, 1980, February 3, 1986.
New York, June 16, 1980.
New York Review of Books, July 17, 1980.
New York Times, June 22, 1980.
New York Times Book Review, May 4, 1975, October 5, 1975, June 22, 1980, September 11, 1983, February 5, 1984, June 3, 1984, October 18, 1987.
Saturday Night, June, 1971, March, 1974.
Spectator, August 25, 1981.
Studies in Canadian Literature, summer, 1979.
Time, June 16, 1980, November 7, 1983, April 30, 1984.
Times Literary Supplement, April 2, 1976, September 26, 1980, August 3, 1984, December 21, 1984.
Village Voice, June 2, 1980, May 1, 1984.
Washington Post, November 9, 1983.
Washington Post Book World, June 29, 1980.*

　　　　　　　　　　　　　　　　—*Sketch by Susan Salter*

*　　　*　　　*

RIVERS, Elfrida
　See BRADLEY, Marion Zimmer

*　　　*　　　*

ROBERTS, Myron　1923-

PERSONAL: Born September 6, 1923, in Los Angeles, Calif.; son of Harry and Rose (Kessler) Roberts; married Estelle Caloia, 1944; children: Cathy, Victoria. *Education:* Los Angeles State College (now California State University, Los Angeles), B.A., 1949, M.A., 1967.

CAREER: Former reporter for *Honolulu Star Bulletin,* Honolulu, Hawaii, *Los Angeles Examiner,* Los Angeles, Calif., and *Savannah Morning News,* Savannah, Ga.; teacher of history and English in California junior and senior high schools, 1949-55; Chaffey College, Alta Loma, Calif., associate professor of English, 1956—. Executive secretary to Lieutenant Governor of California, 1962-64. Has worked as general manager and columnist, Advertiser-Press Newspapers, Hawthorne, Calif. Frequently appears on radio and television public affairs shows. *Military service:* U.S. Army Air Forces, 1942-45.

WRITINGS:

A Nation of Strangers and Other Essays, W. C. Brown, 1967.
(With Lincoln Haynes and Sasha Gilien) *The Begatting of a President,* Ballantine, 1969.
The Roots of Rebellion, W. C. Brown, 1970.
(With Michael Malone) *Pop to Culture* (English literature text), Holt, 1971.
Writing under Thirty (English literature text), Scott, Foresman, 1971.
(With John Moore) *American Politics,* Macmillan, 1976.
(With Moore) *The Pursuit of Happiness: Government and Politics in America,* Macmillan, 1978, 3rd edition, 1985.
(With Haynes and Malone) *The Begatting of Ronald Reagan,* Palos Verdes/Triad Associates, 1982.
(With Moore) *Essays in American History and Culture,* American Studies Press, 1983.

Columnist, *Theater Arts,* 1969—. Contributor to *Saturday Review, West Magazine,* and to U.S. Information Service publications abroad. Associate editor, *Los Angeles Magazine,* 1960-71; former editor and publisher, *West Covina News* and *Manhattan Beach Tide;* former editor, *Pomona Today.*

SIDELIGHTS: Myron Roberts, Lincoln Haynes, and Sasha Gilien printed and marketed *The Begatting of a President* themselves when their "ugly child," as one local distributor called the book, failed to find a market. Ultimately, California reviewers began to notice the book, but the trio claims that forty-four New York publishers turned them down before Ballantine offered a contract. Since then, *The Begatting,* a biblical parody of the Johnson and Nixon administrations, has been produced as a comedy record with Orson Welles as narrator and condensed for United Features syndication to newspapers.*

*   *   *

ROBERTS, Robert C(ampell) 1942-

PERSONAL: Born January 28, 1942, in Wichita, Kan.; son of Arthur Verne (a lawyer) and Elisabeth (Euwer) Roberts; married Elizabeth Vanderkooy (a teacher), December 18, 1976; children: Nathan, Maria. *Education:* Wichita State University, B.A., 1965, M.A., 1970; Yale University, B.D., 1970, Ph.D., 1973; attended University of Paris, 1962-63, Princeton Theological Seminary, 1965-66, and Oxford University, 1970-71. *Religion:* Christian.

ADDRESSES: Office—J. Omar Good Office, Juniata College, Huntingdon, Penn. 16652.

CAREER: Western Kentucky University, Bowling Green, instructor of philosophy, 1973-74, assistant professor, 1974-79, associate professor, 1979-83, professor, 1983-84; Wheaton College, Wheaton, Ill., professor of philosophy and psychological studies, 1984-89; Juniata College, Huntingdon, Penn., J. Omar Visiting Professor, 1989-90.

MEMBER: American Philosophical Association, Society of Christian Philosophers (member of executive committee).

AWARDS, HONORS: Grants from Institute for Advanced Christian Studies, 1980-81, 1987-88; fellow, Institute for Ecumenical and Cultural Research, 1980-81.

WRITINGS:

Rudolf Bultmann's Theology: A Critical Interpretation, Eerdmans, 1976.
Spirituality and Human Emotion, Eerdmans, 1983.
The Strengths of a Christian, Westminster, 1984.
(Contributor) *Psychology and the Christian Faith,* edited by Stanton L. Jones, Baker Book House, 1986.
(Editor with Robert B. Kruschwitz) *The Virtues: Contemporary Essays on Moral Character,* Wadsworth, 1986.
Faith, Reason, and History: Rethinking Kierkegaard's "Philosophical Fragments," Mercer University Press, 1986.
(Contributor) *The Grammar of the Heart: New Essays in Moral Philosophy and Theology,* edited by Richard H. Bell, Harper, 1988.

Contributor to *International Kierkegaard Commentary,* Mercer University Press, 1984, 1985, and 1988. Contributor to popular and scholarly journals, including *Christian Century, Christianity Today, American Philosophical Quarterly,* and *Journal of Religion;* contributor of book reviews for journals, including *International Journal for Philosophy of Religion* and *Christian Scholar's Review.*

WORK IN PROGRESS: Taking the Word to Heart: Relationships in an Age of Therapies; Passions and Virtues: An Essay in Moral Psychology "a discussion of the nature of the virtues insofar as it can be characterized independently of an particular tradition"; *Therapy and Virtue,* "a comparative study of virtues with respect to features peculiar to one or another moral tradition."

ROCHARD, Henri
See CHARLIER, Roger H(enri)

*   *   *

ROMERO, Patricia W. 1935-
(Patricia Romero Curtin)

PERSONAL: Born July 28, 1935, in Columbus, Ohio; daughter of Warren Arthur Watkins (a farmer); children: Stephen, Arthur, Jeffrey. *Education:* Central State College (now University), B.A., 1964; Miami University, Oxford, Ohio, M.A., 1965; Ohio State University, Ph.D., 1971. *Politics:* Democrat. *Religion:* Episcopalian.

ADDRESSES: Home—3831 Fenchurch Rd., Baltimore, Md. 21218.

CAREER: Central State University, Wilberforce, Ohio, instructor in history, 1964-65; Association for the Study of Negro Life and History, Washington, D.C., research associate, 1965-68, 1970-72; United Publishing Corp., Washington, D.C., editor in chief, 1968-70; Outdoor Books, Nature Series, Inc., Baltimore, Md., president, 1982—; Towson State University, Baltimore, assistant professor, 1989—. Visiting lecturer, Findlay College, 1969, and University of South Florida, Tampa, 1972-74; visiting fellow, Johns Hopkins University, 1976-89.

MEMBER: American Historical Association, Organization of American Historians, African Studies Association, Southern Historical Association, Phi Alpha Theta.

AWARDS, HONORS: Negro history research grant, Southern Historical Association, 1965-66; Ford Foundation grant, 1969.

WRITINGS:

(With Charles H. Wesley) *Negro Americans in the Civil War,* Publishers, 1967.
(Editor) *I, Too, Am America,* Publishers, 1968, revised edition, 1970.
(Editor) *In Black America,* United Publishing, 1969.
In Pursuit of African Culture, United Publishing, 1972.
(Under name Patricia Romero Curtin) *Michael Shows off Baltimore* (for children), Outdoor Books, 1982.
(Under name Patricia Romero Curtin) *Tippet Shows off Washington* (for children), Outdoor Books, 1983.
E. Sylvia Pankhurst: Portrait of a Radical, Yale University Press, 1987.
(Editor) *Life Histories of African Women,* Ashfield Press, 1988.

Research editor, *Negro Life and History,* ten volumes, International Library; associate editor, *Negro History Bulletin,* 1966-68.

WORK IN PROGRESS: Cultural History of Lamu from 1873-1960.

SIDELIGHTS: Patricia W. Romero's *E. Sylvia Pankhurst: Portrait of a Radical* is the first biography about the radical British suffragette who moved from cause to cause with enthusiasm and flair. "Filled with fascinating material from many sources," as *Christian Science Monitor* contributor Merle Rubin writes, Romero's book presents "an objective, balanced view of a woman who could be erratic, inspiring, foolish, one-sided, altruistic, infuriatingly stubborn, and incredibly courageous." Pankhurst's complex and mercurial personality could also be exasperating, however, which *Times Literary Supplement* reviewer Jose Harris sees as a problem in the biography: "Romero confesses to a mounting irritation with Sylvia, and this feeling lends a certain air of disenchantment to her whole book." In contrast,

Fiona MacCarthy believes that "this book is very good on analysing [Pankhurst's] extremism, her insistence on the most dramatic and exaggerated version of whatever current ideology she was espousing," as the critic states in the London *Times.* Including research done "with immense thoroughness and energy," MacCarthy concludes, *E. Sylvia Pankhurst* "is a rivetingly interesting study of female immaturity."

BIOGRAPHICAL/CRITICAL SOURCES:

PERIODICALS

Christian Science Monitor, June 4, 1987.
Spectator, March 21, 1987.
Times (London), March 5, 1987.
Times Literary Supplement, April 10, 1987.

*   *   *

ROOS, Stephen (Kelley) 1945-

PERSONAL: Born February 9, 1945, in New York, N.Y.; son of William Ernest (a writer) and Audrey (a writer; maiden name, Kelley) Roos. *Education:* Yale University, A.B., 1967.

ADDRESSES: Home—Canal Rd., High Falls, N.Y. 12440.

CAREER: Harper & Row Publishers, Inc., New York, N.Y., in promotion department, 1968-76, assistant editor, 1976-80; writer, 1980—.

AWARDS, HONORS: Charlie May Simon Award, 1986, for *My Horrible Secret.*

WRITINGS:

My Horrible Secret, Delacorte, 1983.
The Terrible Truth, Delacorte, 1983.
My Secret Admirer, Delacorte, 1984.
(With Kelley Roos) *The Incredible Cat Caper,* Delacorte, 1985.
Confessions of a Wayward Preppie, Delacorte, 1986.
The Fair-Weather Friends, Atheneum, 1987.
Thirteenth Summer, Atheneum, 1987.
My Favorite Ghost, Atheneum, 1988.
You'll Miss Me When I'm Gone, Delacorte, 1988.
And the Winner Is . . ., Atheneum, 1989.
Twelve-Year-Old Vows Revenge after Being Dumped by Extraterrestrial on First Date, Delacorte, in press.

WORK IN PROGRESS: "Gone fishin'!"

SIDELIGHTS: Stephen Roos told *CA:* "In March I finished the revisions on my eleventh novel for kids and it seemed like the time to take several deep breaths and find out where I am now with my writing. It's July now and I still haven't come up with anything definitive, but I'm working in collaboration on a play this summer and enjoy it a lot. I know I'm becoming more enthusiastic about the writer's ability to entertain—and considerably less enthusiastic about the ability to influence. I plan to start a new story for kids in September."

*   *   *

ROSEN, George 1910-1977

PERSONAL: Born June 23, 1910, in New York, N.Y.; died July 28, 1977, in Oxford, England; son of Morris and Rose (Hendleman) Rosen; married Beate Caspari (an ophthalmologist), July 6, 1933; children: Paul Peter, Susan Joan Rosen Kosglow. *Education:* City College (now of the City University of New York),

B.S., 1930; University of Berlin, M.D., 1935; Columbia University, Ph.D., 1944, M.P.H., 1947.

ADDRESSES: Home—1480 Ridge Rd., New Haven, Conn. 06510.

CAREER: Beth-El Hospital, Brooklyn, N.Y., intern, 1935-36; practicing physician, New York City, 1937-42; New York City Health Department, health officer, 1947-49, director, bureau of public health education, 1949-50; Health Insurance Plan of Greater New York, New York City, associate medical director, 1950-57. Columbia University, New York City, lecturer, 1949-50, professor of health education, 1951-69; Yale University, New Haven, Conn., professor of history of medicine, epidemiology, and public health, 1969-77. Visiting lecturer at Harvard University, 1956-60; Victor Robinson Memorial lecturer at Temple University, 1958; Fielding H. Garrison lecturer at American Association for the History of Medicine, 1961; Beaumont Lecturer at Yale University, 1962 and 1964; Benjamin Rush Lecturer at American Psychiatric Association, 1967; Hideyo Noguchi Lecturer at Johns Hopkins University, 1968. Consultant to National Institutes of Health, 1959-64. *Military service:* U.S. Medical Corps, 1943-46; became medical intelligence officer.

MEMBER: International Academy of the History of Medicine (president), American Association for the History of Medicine (vice-president, 1962-64; president, 1964-66), American Public Health Association, American Sociological Association (fellow), Society for Social History of Medicine (past president), Association of Teachers of Preventive Medicine, New York Academy of Medicine (fellow).

AWARDS, HONORS: Grant Squires Award, Columbia University, 1945; William H. Welch Medal, American Association for the History of Medicine, 1961; Elizabeth Severance Prentiss Award, Cleveland Health Museum, 1964; Edgar C. Hayhow Award, American College of Hospital Administrators, 1964; Hafner Award, American Association for the History of Medicine and Medical Library Association, 1966.

WRITINGS:

The Reception of William Beaumont's Discovery in Europe, foreword by John F. Fulton, Schuman's, 1942, reprinted, 1983.
The History of Miners' Diseases: A Medical and Social Interpretation, introduction by Henry E. Sigerist, Schuman's, 1943.
The Specialization of Medicine with Particular Reference to Ophthalmology, Froben Press, 1944, reprinted, Arno Press, 1972.
Fees and Fee Bills: Some Economic Aspects of Medical Practice in Nineteenth Century America, Johns Hopkins Press, 1946.
(Editor with wife, Beate Caspari-Rosen) *400 Years of a Doctor's Life,* Schuman, 1947, reprinted, 1983.
(Translator and editor) *Einstein: His Life and Times,* Knopf, 1947.
A History of Public Health, MD Publications, 1958.
The Hospital: Historical Sociology of a Community Institution, privately printed, c. 1962.
Madness in Society: Chapters in the Historical Sociology of Mental Illness, University of Chicago Press, 1968.
(Compiler) *From Medical Police to Social Medicine: Essays on the History of Health Care,* Science History Publications, 1974.
Preventive Medicine in the United States, 1900-1975: Trends and Interpretations, Watson Publishers International, 1976.
The Structure of American Medical Practice, 1875-1941, University of Pennsylvania Press, 1983.

Also author of *Democracy and Socialism,* 1939. Contributor of articles to medical and historical journals, including *Journal of the History of Medicine and Allied Sciences.* Editor, *Ciba* symposia, 1938-44, and *Journal History of Medicine,* 1946-52; *American Journal of Public Health,* member of editorial board, 1948-57, board chairman, 1957, editor, 1957-73.

BIOGRAPHICAL/CRITICAL SOURCES:

PERIODICALS

American Historical Review, February, 1969.
American Journal of Sociology, Volume 74, 1969.
New York Times Book Review, July 21, 1968.
Observer, February 4, 1968.
Times Literary Supplement, January 9, 1969.

OBITUARIES:

PERIODICALS

AB Bookman's Weekly, October 17, 1977.
New York Times, August 6, 1977.*

*   *   *

ROSS, Marilyn (Ann) Heimberg 1939-
(Marilyn Markham Heimberg)

PERSONAL: Born November 3, 1939, in San Diego, Calif.; daughter of Glenn J. (a businessman) and Dorothy (a real estate broker; maiden name, Scudder) Markham; married T. M. Ross (an advertising executive), May 25, 1977; children: Scott, Steve, Kevin, Laurie. *Education:* Attended San Diego State University. *Religion:* Church of Religious Science.

ADDRESSES: Home—P.O. Box 909, Buena Vista, Colo. 81211.

CAREER: Manager of a women's ready-to-wear business, 1959-69; San Diego-South Bay Trade Schools, San Diego, Calif., director of marketing, 1969-74; marketing consultant, advertising copywriter, and writer, 1974-80; co-founder of About Books, Inc. (nationwide writing and publishing consulting service), 1980—. President, Communication Creativity, Buena Vista, Colo., beginning 1978; co-founder and director, Copy Concepts, beginning 1978. Instructor, San Diego Community College District, 1975-77. Member of board of directors of Research Electronics Co.

MEMBER: Authors League of America, Authors Guild, San Diego Women in Business (founding member of board of directors).

AWARDS, HONORS: First place in nonfiction from Southern Division of California Press Women, 1977, for "Business Bites Back at Internal Crime," 1978, for *Creative Loafing: Shoestring Guide to New Leisure Fun,* and 1979, for *Encyclopedia of Self-Publishing: How to Successfully Write, Publish, Promote and Sell Your Own Work.*

WRITINGS:

(Under name Marilyn Markham Heimberg) *Discover Your Roots: A New, Easy Guide for Tracing Your Family Tree,* Communication Creativity, 1977.
(Under name Marilyn Markham Heimberg) *Finding Your Roots: How to Trace Your Ancestors and Record Your Family Tree,* Dell, 1978.
Creative Loafing: A Shoestring Guide to New Leisure Fun, Communication Creativity, 1978.
(With husband, T. M. Ross) *The Encyclopedia of Self-Publishing: How to Successfully Write, Publish, Promote and*

Sell Your Own Work, Communication Creativity, 1979, 2nd edition, 1980.
Be Tough or Be Gone, Northern Trails Press, 1984.
The Complete Guide to Self-Publishing, Writer's Digest Press, 1985, 2nd edition, 1989.
How to Make Big Profits Publishing City and Regional Books, Communication Creativity, 1987.
Big Marketing Ideas for Small Service Businesses, Dow Jones/ Irwin, 1990.

Ghost writer and editor. Contributor to over fifteen magazines, including *Essence, Modern Maturity, Coronet, Catholic Digest,* and *Westways.* Editor of *People in Motion* (company newsletter), 1971-74.

WORK IN PROGRESS: Business in the Boonies.

SIDELIGHTS: Marilyn Heimberg Ross writes: "To me, communication is a vital facet of life. It is the catalyst that helps us understand ourselves and others better. I hope to use the written and spoken word to enlighten and empower people on a broad scope. It is important to me that others be encouraged to enjoy the abundance in life that I have discovered. Towards this goal, I lecture and consult on various aspects of marketing writing and publishing, and find great personal satisfaction in assisting promising writers."

AVOCATIONAL INTERESTS: Dancing, horses, reading.

*   *   *

ROSSI, Bruno
See LEVINSON, Leonard

*   *   *

ROTHCHILD, Donald (Sylvester) 1928-

PERSONAL: Born August 11, 1928, in New York, N.Y.; son of Sylvester E. (a businessman) and Alice (Levy) Rothchild; married Edith Lee White (a psychiatric social worker), 1953; children: Derek, Maynard. *Education:* Kenyon College, B.A. (with high honors), 1949; University of California, Berkeley, M.A., 1954; Johns Hopkins University, Ph.D., 1958. *Politics:* Democrat.

ADDRESSES: Office—Department of Political Science, University of California, Davis, Calif. 95616.

CAREER: Colby College, Waterville, Me., instructor, 1957-59, assistant professor, 1959-62, associate professor of political science, 1962-65; University of California, Davis, associate professor, 1965-69, professor of political science, 1969—. Fulbright lecturer, Makerere University, 1962-64; senior lecturer, University of Nairobi, 1966-67; Ford Foundation visiting professor, University of Zambia, 1970-71; director, Ghana Study Center, University of Ghana, 1975-77; visiting scholar, Institute of U.S.A. and Canada, Moscow, 1984; USIS visiting professor, University of Ghana, winter, 1985; USIA visiting scholar, University of the West Indies, 1989. *Military service:* U.S. Army, 1960-62.

MEMBER: African Studies Association, American Political Science Association, International Studies Association, International Political Science Association, Western Political Science Association, Phi Beta Kappa.

AWARDS, HONORS: Fellow, Hebrew University of Jerusalem, 1980.

WRITINGS:

Toward Unity in Africa, Public Affairs Press, 1960.

(Contributor) Gwendolen M. Carter, editor, *Politics in Africa: Seven Cases,* Harcourt, 1966.

(Contributor) Carter, editor, *National Unity and Regionalism in Eight African States,* Cornell University Press, 1966.

(Editor) *Politics of Integration: An East African Documentary,* East African Publishing House, 1968.

(Editor with C. J. Gertzel and Maure Goldschmidt) *Government and Politics in Kenya,* East African Publishing House, 1969, International Publications Service, 1972.

Racial Bargaining in Independent Kenya: A Study of Minorities and Decolonization, Oxford University Press, for Institute of Race Relations, 1973.

(Co-author) *Scarcity, Choice, and Public Policy in Middle Africa,* University of California Press, 1978.

(Co-editor) *Eagle Entangled,* Longman, 1979.

(Co-editor) *State Versus Ethnic Claims,* Westview, 1983.

(Co-editor) *Eagle Defiant,* Little, Brown, 1983.

(Co-editor) *Eagle Resurgent?,* Little, Brown, 1987.

(Co-editor) *Afro-Marxist Regimes,* Lynne Rienner, 1987.

(Co-author) *The Precarious Balance,* Westview, 1988.

(Co-author) *Politics and Society in Contemporary Africa,* Lynne Rienner, 1988.

Contributor to *Harper's* and to political science and African studies journals.

WORK IN PROGRESS: Ethnicity and Public Policy.

*   *   *

ROYLE, Trevor 1945-

PERSONAL: Born January 26, 1945, in Mysore, India; son of Kenneth Brooke (an army officer) and Kathleen Beatrice (Page) Royle; married Jane Bonnie Sibbald, August 26, 1967 (divorced, 1973); married Hannah Mary Rathbone (a doctor), April 23, 1973; children: Sebastian, George, Patrick. *Education:* Attended Madras College, 1957-63; University of Aberdeen, M.A. (honors), 1967.

ADDRESSES: Home—6 James St., Edinburgh, EH15 2DS, Scotland. *Agent*—Scott Ferris, 15 Gledhow Gardens, London SW5 0AY, England.

CAREER: William Blackwood (publishers), Edinburgh, Scotland, editor, 1968-70; Scottish Arts Council, Edinburgh, literature director, 1971-79; writer, 1979—. Editorial consultant to Paul Harris Publishing, 1980-85.

MEMBER: International PEN (member of Scottish committee, 1983-84), Society of Authors (member of Scottish committee, 1981-83, 1985-88), National Union of Journalists.

AWARDS, HONORS: Award from Scottish Arts Council, 1982, for *Death before Dishonour.*

WRITINGS:

(With Ian Archer) *We'll Support You Ever More: The Impertinent Saga of Scottish Fitba',* Souvenir Press, 1976.

Jock Tamson's Bairns (essays), Hamish Hamilton, 1977.

Precipitous City: The Story of Literary Edinburgh, Mainstream, 1980.

A Diary of Edinburgh, Polygon Books, 1981.

Edinburgh, Spurbooks, 1982.

Death before Dishonour: The True Story of the Fighting Mac, Mainstream, 1982, St. Martin's, 1983.

The Macmillan Companion to Scottish Literature, Gale, 1983.

James and Jim: A Biography of James Kennaway, Mainstream, 1983.

The Kitchener Enigma: A Biographical Study of Field Marshall Lord Kitchener of Khartoum, M. Joseph, 1985.

The Best Years of Their Lives: The National Service Experience, 1945-1963, M. Joseph, 1986.

War Report: The War Correspondent's View of Battle from the Crimea to the Falklands, Mainstream, 1987.

The Last Days of the Raj, M. Joseph, 1989.

A Dictionary of Military Quotations, Routledge, 1989.

The Welsh Guards: Anatomy of a Regiment, M. Joseph, 1990.

RADIO SCRIPTS; ALL BROADCAST BY BBC-RADIO

"The Mostest of the Bestest," 1979.

"A Portrait of David Daiches," 1979.

"Ring Out Ye Crystal Spheres: A Celebration of Christmas in Poetry and Music," 1979.

"Glasgow's Whistlers: A Portrait of the Hunterian Gallery in Glasgow," 1980.

"Summer's Seamless Haze: A Celebration of Summer in Poetry and Music," 1980.

"Ode to the North Wind: A Portrait of the Artist William Johnstone," 1980.

"The Art of Patronage," 1981.

"Magnificat: A Play," 1984.

"Old Alliances: A Play," 1984.

"Paying the Piper: The Subsidized Arts in Scotland," 1985.

"In Flanders Fields: Scottish Literature of the Great War," 1985.

"Awa for a Sojer: The History of the Scottish Soldier," 1986.

"Going Home: The Last Days of the Raj," 1987.

"Foreigners: A Play," 1987.

"On the Border: A View of the Scottish-English Border," 1988.

"Huntingtower: An Adaptation of John Buchan's Novel," 1988.

"The Spirit of Angus: The Fifth Black Watch during the Second World War," 1988.

"General Sikorski's Tourists: The Polish Forces during the Second World War," 1988.

"A Man Flourishing: A Play Based on Sam Hanna Bell's Novel," 1988.

OTHER

Editor, *Lines Review,* 1982-88; literary editor, *Scotland on Sunday,* 1988—.

WORK IN PROGRESS: The Last Pasha, a biography of Sir John Bagot Glubb, the last British commander of the Arab Legion ("far more interesting than the more famous soldier-scholar with whom he is often compared—T. E. Lawrence, 'Lawrence of Arabia' "), for Macdonald/Futura.

SIDELIGHTS: Trevor Royle's nonfiction on contemporary issues and historical figures is frequently heard on British radio. The author of more than a dozen scripts and plays for radio and television, Royle is also the author of fifteen books that apply a journalistic approach to topics from British and Scottish history. *Precipitous City* chronicles literary activity in Edinburgh, Scotland, from the Middle Ages to the present time. His subjects include Robert Fergusson, a writer whose calamitous end hastened his obscurity, the popular poet Robert Burns, novelists Walter Scott and Robert Louis Stevenson, and the contemporary writer Hugh MacDiarmid. James Campbell, reviewing this early Royle book in the *Times Literary Supplement,* deems it "amiable" and describes the author as an "Englishman propelled by a genuine love for Scottish literature." The more recent work *The Last Days of the Raj,* which looks back at the end of British rule in

India, elicits higher praise from a London *Times* reviewer: "Trevor Royle writes in a most attractive style, showing himself to be an unusual and successful blend of journalist and historian—a journalist, because he is continually quoting real people, with varying points of view and at different levels, witnessing and taking part in significant happenings." As a historian, Royle provides "a comprehensive picture . . . together with a discussion now and again of the social science side of things," the reviewer adds. Hilary Mantel, writing in the *Weekend Telegraph,* comments, "The observations of his missionaries, industrialists and soldiers are strikingly perceptive and interesting. The general reader would probably like more of them to break up the solidity of the exposition, but Royle's calm and even-handed treatment sees us safely through the complex excitements of the era."

Death before Dishonour: The True Story of Fighting Mac is the story of Major-General Sir Hector Macdonald, a British hero of the Boer War who killed himself after being implicated in a scandal involving homosexuality. The winner of a Scottish Arts Council award in 1982, the book aroused debate concerning Macdonald's demise. Denis Judd, in a *Times Literary Supplement* review, expresses impatience with Royle's speculation that Macdonald did not actually die in 1903—Royle considered and finally disproved the rumors that Macdonald cheated death to become Field-Marshal von Mackensen of the Imperial German Army. However, Judd also writes that Royle "has done his best with this rather pathetic and cautionary tale." He calls *Death before Dishonour* "a trim, very readable book."

Royle told *CA* that he took courage to become a full-time writer at the age of thirty-four. The author of two books by then, he was commissioned to write a companion to Scottish literature. More recently he said, "Ten years on, I can find no reason for regretting the choice. If anything, though, the writing process has become much more difficult and infinitely more complex. Whereas in the beginning the need to write was a powerful and all-absorbing impetus I no longer feel so satisfied with the early drafts. More careful and more cautious revision has replaced the earlier frenetic attempts and as a result I think that I have attained a more ordered and more calm literary style. Radio remains a major influence on my work and I still enjoy the precision and the need for inventiveness of language that radio writing requires.

"My books now deal more or less exclusively with military history. The warm critical reception accorded to my biography of Kitchener [*The Kitchener Enigma*] was the first encouragement but it was the success of *The Best Years of Their Lives,* an oral history of post-war conscription in Britain, that finally decided me. It was a nonfiction bestseller and became a film under the title 'Kilroy Was There.' It also formed the basis for a successful exhibition at the Imperial War Museum in London. Since then I have written a study of the war correspondent's view of battle and a book which took me back to my roots, *The Last Days of the Raj,* a study of the end of empire in India as witnessed by the people who lived through the experience. As my parents left India at that time their story gave me the first encouragement to write the book.

"My next book is an anatomy, or social history, of the Welsh Regiment of Foot Guards, one of the exclusive regiments of the Household Division. I lived with the regiment for extended periods, including their posting to Belize in Central America, and was given a unique introduction to its officers and men—the first time that an outsider has been accorded the privilege."

MEDIA ADAPTATIONS: "Kilroy Was There," a film based on *The Best Years of Their Lives,* was broadcast on Channel 4.

BIOGRAPHICAL/CRITICAL SOURCES:

PERIODICALS

Daily Mail, October 2, 1986.
Listener, October 30, 1986.
New Statesman, February 25, 1983.
Observer, September 22, 1985.
Scotsman, October 5, 1985.
Spectator, September 28, 1985.
Times (London), June 17, 1989.
Times Literary Supplement, July 25, 1980, December 3, 1982, August 26, 1983, December 13, 1985, January 23, 1987.
Weekend Telegraph, July 8, 1989.

*   *   *

RUARK, Gibbons 1941-

PERSONAL: Born December 10, 1941, in Raleigh, N.C.; son of Henry Gibbons (a minister) and Sarah (Jenkins) Ruark; married Kay Stinson, October 5, 1963; children: Jennifer Kay, Emily Westbrook. *Education:* University of North Carolina at Chapel Hill, A.B., 1963; University of Massachusetts, M.A., 1965.

ADDRESSES: Office—Department of English, University of Delaware, Newark, Del. 19711.

CAREER: University of North Carolina at Greensboro, instructor in English, 1965-68; University of Delaware, Newark, assistant professor, 1968-73, associate professor, 1973-83, professor of English, 1983—.

AWARDS, HONORS: National Arts Council awards for poetry, 1968, and 1971, for *A Program for Survival;* National Endowment for the Arts fellowships, 1979 and 1986.

WRITINGS:

(Editor with Robert Watson) *The Greensboro Reader,* University of North Carolina Press, 1968.
A Program for Survival (poems), University of Virginia, 1971.
Reeds (poems), Texas Tech Press, 1978.
Keeping Company (poems), Johns Hopkins University Press, 1983.
Small Rain (poems), The Center for Edition Works, 1984.

CONTRIBUTOR

American Literary Anthology #1, Farrar, Strauss, 1968.
Lionel Steveson and others, editors, *Best Poems of 1968,* Pacific Books, 1969.
X. J. Kennedy, editor, *Messages,* Little, Brown, 1973.
Stevenson and others, editors, *Best Poems of 1974,* Pacific Books, 1975.
Kennedy, editor, *Introduction to Poetry,* Little, Brown, 1982.
Kennedy, editor, *Introduction to Literature,* Little, Brown, 1983.
1984 Anthology of Modern Poetry, Monitor Book, 1984.
Dave Smith and David Bottoms, editors, *The Morrow Anthology of Younger American Poets,* Morrow, 1984.
Leon Stokesbury, *The Made Thing,* Arkansas, 1987.
Robert Richman, editor, *The Direction of Poetry,* Houghton, 1988.
Robert Wallace, *Vital Signs,* Wisconsin, 1989.

WORK IN PROGRESS: Poems.

SIDELIGHTS: Gibbons Ruark is described by James Whitehead in *Saturday Review* as "quiet, reflective; in fact nostalgia is his vision, particularly in memories of his dead father. . . . Ruark accepts and loves the family that raised him, and he accepts and loves the family he is raising in turn. Affirming family and friends, he makes marvelous poetry in the process."

The poems in *A Program for Survival* are, according to Michael Hefferan's review in *Midwest Quarterly,* "of a high and difficult sort, not easily achieved and less easily contrived. These poems took a long time: nothing here was slapped down unrevised, nothing here depends for its effects on cryptic, half-digested talk to obfuscate same basic vacancy. . . . There is an emotional authenticity about all these poems that makes them almost overpowering with a kind of uncanny, unrelenting force. They stay in the mind because they have been, many of them, driven there so deeply they will not pry loose."

A tape recording of Ruark's poems has been placed in the archives of the Library of Congress.

BIOGRAPHICAL/CRITICAL SOURCES:

BOOKS

Contemporary Literary Criticism, Volume 3, Gale, 1975.

PERIODICALS

Midwest Quarterly, Volume 12, 1971.
Saturday Review, December 18, 1971.
Virginia Quarterly Review, autumn, 1971.

*   *   *

RUSHING, Francis W(illard) 1939-

PERSONAL: Born July 30, 1939, in Savannah, Ga.; married; children: four. *Education:* University of Georgia, A.B. (magna cum laude), 1961; University of North Carolina, Ph.D., 1967.

ADDRESSES: Home—26 Walker Terrace, N.E., Atlanta, Ga. 30309. *Office*—Department of Economics, College of Business Administration, Georgia State University, Atlanta, Ga. 30303.

CAREER: University of Georgia, Athens, assistant professor of economics, 1968-72; College of William and Mary, Williamsburg, Va., associate professor of economics, 1972-74; Georgia State University, Atlanta, associate professor, 1974-80, professor of economics, 1980—, chairman of department, 1980-86, director of Center for Business and Economic Education, 1974-81, associate dean for research and director of International Center for Entrepreneurship, 1986—. Visiting assistant professor, University of North Carolina, summers, 1969-71; public speaker in the United States and the Soviet Union. SRI International, consultant, 1972-75, senior economics consultant, Science Policy Program, International Policy Center, 1976—, program manager in economics, 1976-77; economist, Consumer Economics Institute for College and University Professors, 1979. Economist, National Science Foundation team advising Saudi Arabian National Center on Science and Technology, 1981; member, National Committee on U.S.-China Relations Technology Transfer, 1987. Executive director of Georgia Council on Economic Education, 1974-81. *Military service:* U.S. Air Force, economic analyst for U.S. Department of Defense, 1965-68.

MEMBER: Society of Economics Educators (president, 1987-89), Association of Private Enterprise Education (vice-president, 1989-90).

AWARDS, HONORS: Grants from National Science Foundation, 1975, 1979-80, 1989, U.S. Office of Education, 1976-77, and Brazil-U.S. Business Council of the U.S. Chamber of Commerce, 1989.

WRITINGS:

(Contributor) S. Stowell Symmes, editor, *Economic Education: Links to the Social Studies,* National Council of the Social Sciences and Joint Council on Economic Education, 1981.
(With Catherine P. Ailes) *The Science Race: Education and Employment of Scientists and Engineers, U.S. and U.S.S.R.,* Crane, Russak, 1982.
(With Arnold Heertje and Felicity Skidmore) *Economics,* Dryden, 1983.
(Editor) *National Policies for Developing High Technology Industries: International Comparisons,* Westview Press, 1986.
(Editor with Hu Gentles) *The Role of the Market in Economic Development: The Case of Jamaica,* Georgia State University, College of Business Administration, 1989.
(Contributor) Calvin Kent, editor, *Entrepreneurship Education,* Quorum Press, 1989.
(Editor with Carol Ganz Brown) *Intellectual Property Protection in Science and Technology and Economic Performance: International Comparisons,* Westview Press, 1990.
(With Ailes) *Soviet Mathematics and Science Education,* Westview Press, 1990.

Contributor to proceedings; contributor of articles and reviews to social studies and economic journals, and to *Atlanta.* Guest editor, *Georgia Social Studies Journal,* November, 1976; member of editorial board, *Journal of Comparative Strategy.*

WORK IN PROGRESS: Research on Soviet science and math education for precollege and university levels, on economic policy developments in the Soviet Union and the People's Republic of China, and on teaching entrepreneurship in elementary and secondary schools.

*   *   *

RUSS, Joanna 1937-

PERSONAL: Born February 22, 1937, in New York, N.Y.; daughter of Evarett I. (a teacher) and Bertha (a teacher; maiden name, Zinner) Russ. *Education:* Cornell University, B.A., 1957; Yale University, M.F.A., 1960. *Politics:* Feminist. *Religion:* None.

CAREER: Queensborough Community College, Bayside, N.Y., lecturer in speech, 1966-67; Cornell University, Ithaca, N.Y., instructor, 1967-70, assistant professor of English, 1970-72; State University of New York at Binghamton, assistant professor of English, 1972-75; University of Colorado, Boulder, assistant professor of English, 1975-77; University of Washington, Seattle, associate professor, 1977-84, professor of English, 1984—. Member of New York University Hall of Fame Players, 1964-66.

MEMBER: Modern Language Association of America, Science Fiction Writers of America.

AWARDS, HONORS: Nebula Award, Science Fiction Writers of America, 1972, for short story "When It Changed"; National Endowment for the Humanities fellow, 1974-75; Hugo Award, World Science Fiction Convention, 1983, and Nebula Award, 1983, both for novella "Souls."

WRITINGS:

Picnic on Paradise (also see below), Ace Books, 1968.
And Chaos Died, Ace Books, 1970.
The Female Man, Bantam, 1975.
(Author of introduction) Mary Shelley, *Tales and Stories,* G. K. Hall, 1975.
Alyx (includes *Picnic on Paradise*), G. K. Hall, 1976.
We Who Are about To . . ., Dell, 1977.

The Two of Them, Berkeley, 1978.
Kittatinny: A Tale of Magic, Daughters Publishing, 1978.
On Strike against God: A Lesbian Love Story, Out & Out, 1979.
How to Suppress Women's Writing, University of Texas, 1983.
The Zanzibar Cat, Arkham, 1983.
Extra (Ordinary) People, (short story collection; includes "Souls"), St. Martin's, 1984.
(Contributor) Sandra Gilbert and Susan Gubar, editors, *The Norton Anthology of Literature by Women: The Tradition in English,* W. W. Norton, 1985.
Magic Mommas, Trembling Sisters, Puritans and Perverts: Feminist Essays, Crossing Press, 1985.
The Hidden Side of the Moon, St. Martin's, 1988.
Houston, Houston, Do You Read? [and] *Souls,* Tor Books, 1989.

Contributor of short stories, articles, and poetry to *Sinister Wisdom, Thirteenth Moon, Sojourner, Journal of Homosexuality, Ms.,* and other periodicals.

SIDELIGHTS: Joanna Russ combines a feminist perspective with a sophisticated style to write science fiction novels which, Marge Piercy states in the *American Poetry Review,* "are interesting beyond the ordinary. They ask nasty and necessary questions [and] offer a gallery of some of the most interesting female protagonists in current fiction." Gerald Jonas of the *New York Times Book Review* notes that in her early work, "Russ used science fiction as a vehicle for the most intelligent, hard-minded commentary on feminism that you are likely to find anywhere."

The Female Man is perhaps the novel in which Russ's feminist ideas are most completely expressed. The book's four heroines—each from a different time and place—represent different possibilities for women in society. "Each of these fictional realities," writes Barbara Garland in the *Dictionary of Literary Biography,* "makes a statement about the self versus society and about male versus female: and each has a distinctive style." In their book *Science Fiction: History, Science, Vision,* Robert Scholes and Eric S. Rabkin find that in *The Female Man,* Russ "has used the visionary potential of science fiction to convey the contrast between life as it is presently lived by many women and life as it might be. Among other things, Russ has demonstrated the unique potential of science fiction for embodying radically different life styles, which can hardly be conveyed in fiction bound by the customs of present literature."

Not all critics judge *The Female Man* to have successfully presented its feminist ideas. Jonas, for example, thinks that Russ, "with her obvious grasp of the biological givens and her command of so many science-fictional weapons, . . . might have produced a truly provocative study of 'woman's fate.' Unfortunately, she keeps slipping into the easy rhetoric of mainstream feminist tracts." Michael Goodwin of *Mother Jones* claims that *The Female Man* "is not a novel—it's a scream of anger. . . . It's unfair, it's maddening, it's depressing. I hated it. . . . And yet, a year after reading it, *The Female Man* remains perfectly clear in my mind—seductive, disturbing and hateful. I'm not sure whether that makes it a good book or not, but I think it makes it an important one."

In an article for *Extrapolation,* Natalie M. Rosinsky analyzes *The Female Man* as "a model of the ways in which feminist humor can operate within a literary text" and sees Russ concerned primarily with "the ways in which humor has been used as a weapon against women." Although each female character in the novel comes from a different time and place, Rosinsky states, "all live in worlds in which humor is used as a weapon against women. Only Janet, the visitor from the all-female universe of Whileaway, has freely experienced and created a differ-

ent kind of humor, one that does not wound or function to maintain a hierarchical status quo."

Rosinsky sees this difference in humor as pivotal to an understanding of the novel. "We can transcend and transform our lives," she states, "take what has been male-identified and make it female-identified or gender-free. Redefining what is or is not truly funny is one way to begin. And thus, humor in *The Female Man* is not peripheral to either its themes or structure, but is instead an integral, though often undervalued, component of its composition." Rosinsky calls the book "a classic of feminist polemical literature," while Ellen Morgan of *Radical Teacher* judges it "the truest, most complete account available of what it feels like to be alienated as a woman and a feminist."

The collection *The Hidden Side of the Moon* represents nearly thirty years of Russ's work in short fiction. Fred Pfeil, writing in the *Washington Post Book World,* says that in some of the stories, her "writing is incandescent, bordering on the visionary." The other pieces show the author reworking similar images and themes to heightened effect. *New York Times Book Review* contributor John Clute relates that all of the stories seem to directly address the reader with challenges about women's roles in contemporary society. "And because she is a writer of such energetic clarity," adds Clute, "Ms. Russ is very easy to read, which is to say very hard not to read, even though it may hurt. She lets no one off the hook. However hilarious, the pointed urgency of her anger can scathe." Russ excels when describing the complex relations between parents and children, he says of this "major writer within the science fiction genre, and beyond it."

Validating her status is her role as a pathfinder for women writers of science fiction, Pfeil observes. Her novel *The Female Man,* he explains, with its "dazzling play of points of view and narrative forms (from drama to fable and essay to epic) on the one hand, and its unapologetically explicit feminist politics and visions on the other, have helped to inspire a new generation of women writers within science fiction."

BIOGRAPHICAL/CRITICAL SOURCES:

BOOKS

Contemporary Literary Criticism, Volume 15, Gale, 1980.
Dictionary of Literary Biography, Volume 8: *Twentieth Century American Science Fiction Writers,* Gale, 1980.
Scholes, Robert and Eric S. Rabkin, *Science Fiction: History, Science, Vision,* Oxford University Press, 1977.
Walker, Paul, *Speaking of Science Fiction: The Paul Walker Interviews,* Luna Press, 1978.

PERIODICALS

Algol, summer, 1975.
American Poetry Review, May-June, 1977.
Booklist, November 1, 1977.
Extrapolation, spring, 1982.
Fantasy Newsletter, April, 1983.
Frontiers, spring, 1979.
Magazine of Fantasy and Science Fiction, August, 1975, February, 1978, April, 1979.
Mother Jones, August, 1976.
New York Times Book Review, May 4, 1975, September 25, 1977, June 25, 1978, January 31, 1988.
Radical Teacher, Number 10, 1978.
Science Fiction Review, May, 1975, May, 1978.
Washington Post Book World, February 28, 1988.

S

SAFILIOS-ROTHSCHILD, Constantina 1936-

PERSONAL: Born November 25, 1936, in Jannina, Greece; daughter of Constantine (a judge) and Anne (Fondaras) Safilios; married Walter G. Rothschild (a research chemist), September 15, 1960. *Education:* Agricultural College, Athens, Greece, diploma, 1957; Ohio State University, M.S., 1959, Ph.D., 1963.

ADDRESSES: Office—Population Council, One Dag Hammarskjold Plaza, New York, N.Y. 10017.

CAREER: Lafayette Clinic, Detroit, Mich., research associate in social psychiatry, 1961-62; Merrill-Palmer Institute, Detroit, senior research associate in family sociology, 1963-70; Wayne State University, Detroit, adjunct professor, 1968-72, professor of sociology, beginning 1972, director of Family Research Center, beginning 1970; currently affiliated with Population Council, New York, N.Y. Visiting professor at various international universities, including Case Western Reserve University, 1967, and University of Zurich, 1973. Research associate, Center for Population Studies, Harvard University, 1966-68, and National Center for Social Research, Athens, 1969—. Consultant to UNICEF, Ford Foundation, and Center for Mental Health and Research, Athens.

MEMBER: International Family Research Committee, International Scientific Commission on the Family, International Union for the Scientific Study of Population, International Federation for Parent Education, Social Commission of Rehabilitation International, American Sociological Association (fellow; member of executive council), National Council on Family Relations, Alpha Kappa Delta, Gamma Epsilon Delta.

AWARDS, HONORS: Fulbright exchange student, 1957; Foundations' Fund for Research in Psychiatry grant, 1964; National Institute for Mental Health grant, 1965-66; National Science Foundation fellowship, 1967; Greek National Center for Social Research grant, 1967-73; Lee Franklin Memorial Lecturer Award, 1976.

WRITINGS:

(Contributor) E. M. Rogers, editor, *Social Change in Rural Sociology,* Appleton, 1960.
(Contributor) *Promena structure savremenog Jugoslovenskog drustrva* (title means "Changes in Class Structure of the Present Day Jugoslav Society"), Yugoslavian Sociological Association, 1967.

(Contributor) Marvin Sussman, editor, *Sourcebook in Marriage and the Family,* 3rd edition, Houghton, 1968.
(Contributor) Ivar Berg, editor, *The Business of America,* Harcourt, 1968.
(Contributor) Gerhard Neubeck, editor, *The Dynamics of Extra-Marital Relations,* Prentice-Hall, 1969.
(Contributor) Reuben Hill and Rene Konig, editors, *Families East and West,* Mouton & Co., 1970.
The Sociology and Social Psychology of Disability and Rehabilitation, Random House, 1970.
Children and Adolescents in Slums and Shanty-Towns in Developing Countries, UNICEF Executive Board, 1971.
(Contributor) Pamela Roby, editor, *Child Care: An International Perspective,* Basic Books, 1972.
(Contributor) Paul Roman and Harry Trice, editors, *Current Perspectives in Psychiatric Sociology,* Science House, 1972.
(Editor) *Toward a Sociology of Women,* Ginn, 1972.
(Contributor) Jacob Christ and Henry Grunebaum, editors, *Marriage Problems and Their Treatment,* Little, Brown, 1973.
Women and Social Policy, Prentice-Hall, 1973.
The Modern Greek Family, Volume I: *The Dynamics of the Husband-Wife Interaction,* Volume II: *Parent-Child Interaction: Dimensions of Family Modernity-Cross-Cultural Comparisons,* National Center for Social Research (Athens), 1973.
Love, Sex, and Sex Roles, Prentice-Hall, 1977.
Sex Role Socialization and Sex Discrimination: A Synthesis and Critique of the Literature, U.S. Department of Health, Education, and Welfare, 1979.
Sex Role Socialization/Sex Discrimination: A Bibliography, U.S. Department of Health, Education, and Welfare, 1979.
Relationships: Special Issue Psychology of Women Quarterly, Human Sciences, 1981.
Socioeconomic Indicators of Women's Status in Developing Countries, 1970-1980, Population Council, 1986.

OTHER

Also author of *Slums and Social Policy,* Quadrangle, and *Myths and Realities about the Family: A Cross-Cultural Perspective,* Dorsey. Contributor to conferences and proceedings; contributor to professional journals, including *Human Relations, International Journal of the Sociology of the Family, New Horizons, International Journal of Social Psychiatry,* and *American Sociolo-*

gist. Associate editor, *Journal of Marriage and the Family, Journal of Comparative Family Studies, International Journal of Family Sociology,* and *Journal of Health and Human Behavior.**

*   *   *

SAFIRE, William 1929-

PERSONAL: Born William Safir, December 17, 1929; name legally changed to Safire; son of Oliver C. and Ida (Panish) Safir; married Helene Belmar Julius (a jewelry-maker), December 16, 1962; children: Mark Lindsey, Annabel Victoria. *Education:* Attended Syracuse University, 1947-49. *Politics:* Libertarian conservative.

ADDRESSES: Office—*New York Times,* 1627 Eye St. N.W., Washington, D.C. 20006. *Agent*—Morton Janklow, 598 Madison Ave., New York, N.Y. 10036.

CAREER: New York Herald-Tribune Syndicate, reporter, 1949-51; WNBC-WNBT, correspondent in Europe and Middle East, 1951; WNBC, New York City, radio-TV producer, 1954-55; Tex McCrary, Inc., vice-president, 1955-60; Safire Public Relations, Inc., New York City, president, 1961-68; The White House, Washington, D.C., special assistant to the President and speechwriter, 1968-73; *New York Times,* Washington, D.C., columnist, 1973—. *Military service:* U.S. Army, 1952-54.

AWARDS, HONORS: Pulitzer Prize for distinguished commentary, 1978, for articles on Bert Lance.

WRITINGS:

The Relations Explosion, Macmillan, 1963.
(With M. Loeb) *Plunging into Politics,* McKay, 1964.
The New Language of Politics, Random House, 1968, 3rd edition published as *Safire's Political Dictionary: The New Language of Politics,* Random House, 1978.
Before the Fall, Doubleday, 1975, published as *Before the Fall: An Inside View of the Pre-Watergate White House,* Da Capo, 1988.
Full Disclosure (novel; Literary Guild selection), Doubleday, 1977, limited edition with illustrations by George Jones, Franklin Library, 1977.
On Language, Times Books, 1980.
Safire's Washington, Times Books, 1980.
What's the Good Word?, Times Books, 1982.
(With brother, Leonard Safir) *Good Advice,* Times Books, 1982.
I Stand Corrected: More on Language, Times Books, 1984.
Take My Word for It: More on Language, Times Books, 1986.
Freedom (Book-of-the-Month Club main selection), Doubleday, 1987.
You Could Look It Up: More on Language, Times Books, 1988.
Words of Wisdom, Fireside Books, 1990.

Author of political column "Essay," in *New York Times,* and "On Language" column in *New York Times Magazine.* Contributor to *Harvard Business Review, Cosmopolitan, Playboy, Esquire, Reader's Digest, Redbook,* and *Collier's.*

SIDELIGHTS: William Safire has worn several hats in his varied career: speechwriter for President Nixon, language commentator for the Sunday *New York Times Magazine,* political commentator for the *New York Times,* novelist, and historian. Safire does not pull his punches, and has made both friends and enemies on all sides of political and linguistic issues. According to J. A. Barnes in the *National Review,* "whether you love [Safire] or you hate him, you cannot afford to skip over him." *Time* contributor Paul Gray appreciates Safire's lack of rigidity: "William

Safire has largely made his reputation through epigrammatic feistiness and hit-and-run repartee. . . . His twice-a-week columns continue to display reportorial zeal and refreshing unpredictability." Safire is also quick to alert his readers to governmental figures who run amuck. *Washington Post* contributor Eleanor Randolph notes: "The years in public relations and the White House seem to have given [Safire] an ear for sour notes on both sides—among those in power in the government and those in power in the press." And when speaking of his commentaries on English-language usage, some critics view Safire as an institution. David Thomas in the *Christian Science Monitor* observes that "in the absence of a thoughtful but unthinkable French Academy to tell Americans how they must express themselves, Safire may be the closest we have to a clearinghouse for hearing, seeing, and testing how we're doing with the language."

Safire began his career as a public relations writer, took a job as speechwriter for Spiro Agnew in the 1968 presidential campaign, and eventually became a senior speechwriter for President Nixon. He left his position, however, before the bugging of Watergate and was finishing his memoir of the Nixon White House when the president resigned. Because of the timing of its completion, *Before the Fall* almost missed publication entirely. The book painted a fairly positive view of the administration and was rejected by William Morrow, who also demanded back their advance. But eventually the book was published by Doubleday.

Newsweek's Walter Clemons calls *Before the Fall* "a puffy, lightweight concoction, served up for the faithful." Clemons complains that "Safire is protective of Nixon, reserving his harshest judgment for the deviousness and drive for power he attributes to Henry Kissinger." But *Atlantic* contributor Richard Todd gives the book credit for being "full of interesting data on the theme that Safire identifies as crucial to the Nixon Administration: its sense of the world as 'us' against 'them.' " And Daniel Schorr, in the *New York Times Book Review,* recounts Safire's description of Nixon's desire for "understanding and perspective," and notes: "If Nixon gets the kind of understanding he wants, this book will surely have helped a lot. In any event [*Before the Fall*] . . . will still be an enormous contribution to understanding the phenomenon called Nixon. This is, after all . . . the first real post-Watergate view of Nixon by someone who was both there and innocent."

Safire's first novel, *Full Disclosure,* also deals with a president in danger of losing his office. His fictional leader, Sven Ericson, has been blinded from a bump on the head received while closeted in a Pullman berth with a female member of the White House press corps. The plot's concerns whether the Twenty-fifth Amendment, concerning disabled presidents, will be used to oust Ericson. *New Republic* contributor Stephen Hess says *Full Disclosure's* strength comes from the fact that it "is about presidential politics by a man who intimately knows presidential politics." But a *Saturday Review* contributor questions the work's literary value, claiming that the story's political puzzle is "the book's one redeeming feature." The critic adds, however, that by exploring Ericson's uncertain position, "Safire not only cooks up a fiery stewpot of political ambitions, but produces a dramatic warning of the [Twenty-fifth Amendment's] possible abuse."

Safire's columns on language are widely read and enjoyed. In several books, he has reprinted column selections and his readers' replies. *On Language* gives examples of correct and incorrect usage, and explores word origins as well. In the *Saturday Review,* John Ciardi explains Safire's position toward communication in "On Language" as "neither an [etymologist] nor an expert on usage. He is a keen reporter at his splendid best in such reports as the one here labeled 'Kissingerese,' a star coverage of the idiom of Henry the Pompous." Ciardi continues: "I am engaged and rewarded by this maculate Safire, and even more so when he is attended by his letterwriters." Other reviewers also enjoy Safire's interaction with his readers. "Although what Safire has discovered about word origins and their current usage made good reading, the inclusion of what his readers have to add makes them even more so," states *Christian Science Monitor* contributor Maria Lenhart. And, according to D. J. Enright in the *Encounter*, "Safire's relations with his 'Irregulars' are highly interesting, and help to generate much of the comedy in this almost continuously entertaining book."

Freedom, a heavily-detailed historical novel, is the author's largest work. When Safire submitted the manuscript to his publisher after working on it for seven years, the triple-spaced copy ran 3300 pages. As Doubleday found the book too large to bind, Safire had to cut at least one section; still, the final product was 1152 pages. In *Freedom,* Safire again uses his Washington experience to describe the city between June, 1861, and January 1, 1863. The story opens with Lincoln's issue of the Emancipation Proclamation, and focuses on the president's role during the early Civil War years. *New York Review of Books* contributor C. Vann Woodward describes Safire's Lincoln as "a Lincoln racked by debilitating depression (which he called melancholia), agonizing over the daily choice of evils, and seeking relief in one of his that-reminds-me stories. He is by turns Saint Sebastian, Machiavelli, Pericles, and an oversize, countrified Puck."

Safire explains his attitude toward Lincoln to Alvin P. Sanoff for *U.S. News & World Report:* "It's impossible to approach Lincoln honestly with a spirit of reverence and awe. He is a secular and not a religious figure. He wasn't martyred; he was assassinated. Approaching Lincoln as a political figure, which is what he was, you can appreciate him." Still, Safire concludes that "searching through [Lincoln's] life, putting myself in the shoes of a cabinet member or a reporter covering him, I've come to the conclusion that he was, indeed, the greatest President, with the possible exception of Washington, because he was so complex and so purposeful. When you see him with all the warts, when you see his drawbacks and his failures and his shortcomings, then you see his greatness." The author explains to *Publishers Weekly* contributor Trish Todd that one of the greatest issues facing the U.S. government at that time is the contemporary problem of "how much freedom must be taken away from individuals in order to protect the freedom of the nation." And while Safire feels that Lincoln occasionally went too far in suspending individual liberties, he told Eleanor Randolph for the *Washington Post:* "If [Lincoln] were running today, I'd vote for him. I think he had his priorities straight." Randolph continues, "straight priorities mean having a core of beliefs that are worth all the harassment and trouble that come with leadership."

While *Freedom* has received much popular and critical acclaim, some reviewers dislike the book's focus. Woodward feels Safire has almost neglected the presence of blacks in the Civil War: "One book of the nine into which the novel is divided is indeed entitled 'The Negro,' but it is largely concerned with other matters, with only four or five pages on blacks, and most of that is what whites said or did about them, not what they said and did themselves." Woodward adds, "as a whole [blacks] are granted fewer than twenty-five lines of their own to speak. None of their prominent leaders are introduced, and Frederick Douglass is not mentioned. . . . Nowhere does this huge book face up squarely to the impact of slavery and the complexities of race." Other critics have found the book too lengthy and detailed. But while *Los Angeles Times Book Review* contributor Winston Groom finds

the book "often ponderous, tedious and maddening to plow through," he feels that reading *Freedom* is worth the effort: "It's a story that ought to be read by every American, and for that matter everyone else in the world, because it so graphically presents how our grand experiment in democracy has actually worked in a time of extreme stress. . . . [*Freedom*] enlivens and elucidates a period of American history that remains crucial for anyone with the faintest interest in what we, the American people, are all about." And Chicago *Tribune Books* contributor John Calvin Batchelor calls *Freedom* "a mountain to dazzle and assault," states that it is "loving, cogent, bottomlessly researched, [and] passionately argued," and claims the book "is guaranteed to exhaust the reader like no other intellectual endeavor, yet in the end it delivers a miracle."

BIOGRAPHICAL/CRITICAL SOURCES:

BOOKS

Contemporary Literary Criticism, Volume 10, Gale, 1979.

PERIODICALS

Atlantic, July, 1975, March, 1979.
Chicago Tribune, August 4, 1988.
Christian Science Monitor, January 12, 1981, December 31, 1984.
Encounter, April, 1981.
Los Angeles Times Book Review, August 30, 1987.
National Review, November 28, 1980.
New Republic, July 9-16, 1977, February 16, 1987.
New York Review of Books, September 24, 1987.
New York Times Book Review, February 23, 1975.
Newsweek, March 3, 1975, August 31, 1987.
Publishers Weekly, April 30, 1982, March 29, 1987.
Saturday Review, July 9, 1977, November, 1980.
Time, August 31, 1987.
Tribune Books (Chicago), August 9, 1987.
U.S. News & World Report, August 24, 1987.
Washington Post, August 24, 1987.

—*Sketch by Jani Prescott*

*   *   *

St. GEORGE, Arthur
   See PAINE, Lauran (Bosworth)

*   *   *

SALISBURY, Ray(mond Eric) 1942-

PERSONAL: Born May 27, 1942, in Hindhead, Surrey, England; son of Eric (in government) and Ida (Patterson) Salisbury; married Elizabeth Rampton (a secretary), October 3, 1964 (divorced March, 1970); married Sally Haigh (a secretary), April, 1971 (divorced May, 1983); children: (first marriage) Mark, Timothy; (second marriage) Benjamin, Daniel. *Education:* Attended Worthing Technical College.

ADDRESSES: Home—11 Delves Close, Ringmer, Lewes, Sussex, England. *Office*—London Borough of Greenwich, Nelson House, 50 Wellington St., Woolwich, London S.E.18, England.

CAREER: West Sussex County Council, Chichester, administrator, 1958-68; Wigan Borough Council, Lancashire, England, administrator, 1967-68; East Sussex County Council, East Sussex, England, administrator, 1968-81; London Borough of Bromley, Bromley, Kent, England, assistant director of social services, 1981-85; London Borough of Greenwich, London, England, member of administrative staff, 1985—.

MEMBER: Institute of Chartered Secretaries and Administrators.

WRITINGS:

NOVELS

Close the Door behind You, Deutsch, 1982.
When the Boys Came out to Play, Deutsch, 1984.
Birds of the Air, Deutsch, 1988.
Sweet Thursday, Deutsch, 1990.

WORK IN PROGRESS: A novel.

SIDELIGHTS: Ray Salisbury's *Close the Door behind You* is a novel of rural childhood set in a Sussex village at the end of World War II. A four-year-old boy, Simon, who is living happily with his grandparents when the story begins, provides the book's point-of-view. When Simon's father, a former prisoner of war whom the boy has never seen, returns to Sussex, however, Simon must go and live with his parents. The drama of the tale lies in Simon's struggle to adjust to a new life with his mother and father in a house he dislikes. "Ray Salisbury manages to catch both the limpid perception of childhood and its awful bewilderment," observes critic Lewis Jones in the *New Statesman,* adding that the book is "in a class . . . with Laurie Lee." In a *Spectator* review, Miranda Seymour describes the work as "leisurely, evocative and curiously moving . . . one of the most engaging first novels I have read this year."

When the Boys Came out to Play and *Birds of the Air* continue Simon's story through primary school, recounting his developing experience as life unfolds around him. *Sweet Thursday* sees Simon plucked from his village school and set down into a large comprehensive school in the local town where he has to meet the requirements of a more demanding and threatening sub-culture.

About his writing background, Ray Salisbury told *CA:* "As a child I enjoyed reading Dickens and most of the British children's classics. I read Steinbeck and Hemingway compulsively in my later teens and still relate to them. I wanted to write from the age of fifteen, but I was pretentious and tended to overwrite. When I was in my mid-thirties and getting too old for playing soccer and cricket and spending daylight time with my children, I felt the need for a substitute hobby. One day I was doing some woodwork at home and not making a very good job of it. My family suggested that I take lessons, but when I went up to the Evening Institute, woodwork was fully subscribed and so was woodcarving. I noticed Creative Writing in the prospectus and decided to try that.

"My course tutor, author Carol Filby, welcomed me to the class, but I fully expected her to let me go when I handed in my first short story. By the time she gave it back I had a firm ambition to write, but I was so apprehensive I couldn't look at her comments. Carol pressed me to read her criticism, and I was surprised at how encouraging it was.

"*Close the Door behind You* followed a selection of short stories about children which I had sent to Andre Deutsch to see if he'd like a novel of the same type. He encouraged me, and the book was published two years later. *When the Boys Came out to Play,* published by Deutsch in May, 1984, was followed by *Birds of the Air* four years later. *Sweet Thursday* takes Simon mid-way through secondary education, and further novels in the series are planned.

"I like to write about relationships and the impact of individuals and groups on each other. Children, particularly, often feel and think differently from the image they portray. Feelings and emotions are better watched than judged.

"I would like to write full-time and branch out into short stories and television, but my work in social welfare provides a stable income and a wealth of life experiences from which I am not yet ready to withdraw."

AVOCATIONAL INTERESTS: "I spend my time looking after my boys and their innumerable friends and our home and garden. We like walking on the Downs, swimming, tennis, and badminton, and I play soccer and cricket when I get the opportunity. I like the countryside and take an interest in political activities and their impact on some of our more pressing social problems."

BIOGRAPHICAL/CRITICAL SOURCES:

PERIODICALS

New Statesman, August 20, 1982.
Spectator, August 21, 1982.
Times Literary Supplement, September 10, 1982, June 29, 1984.

*   *   *

SALKELD, Robert J(ohn)   1932-

PERSONAL: Born July 26, 1932, in Glen Rock, N.J.; son of Charles Feagles and Doris (Cheney) Salkeld. *Education:* Attended California Institute of Technology, 1950-52; Princeton University, A.B., 1954; Harvard University, M.B.A., 1956. *Politics:* Republican.

CAREER: Ramo-Wooldridge Corp., Los Angeles, Calif., administrative assistant, 1956-58; Space Technology Labs, Inc., Los Angeles, assistant project engineer, 1958-60; Aerospace Corp., Los Angeles, project engineer, 1960-62, manager of Advanced Manned Systems, 1962-64; United Aircraft Corp., Los Angeles, technical director of Military and Space Systems Planning, 1964-67; president, R. J. Salkeld and Associates, 1967—; Systems Development Corp., Santa Monica, Calif., planning director, 1971-75, consultant, 1975—. Consultant to United Aircraft, Aerospace Corp., Aerojet-General, and National Aeronautics and Space Administration (NASA), 1967-71. Member of space panel, Project Forecast, U.S. Air Force, 1963-64. Patentee in the field of strategic missiles and space vehicles.

MEMBER: American Association for the Advancement of Science (fellow), American Institute of Aeronautics and Astronautics (associate fellow), American Astronautical Society (senior member), American Physics Society, British Interplanetary Society (fellow).

WRITINGS:

War and Space, foreword by B. A. Schriever, Prentice-Hall, 1970.
(Editor with Donald W. Patterson and Jerry Grey) Christopher J. Cohan and others, *Space Transportation,* American Institute of Aeronautics and Astronautics, 1978.
(Editor with Frank P. Davidson and L. J. Giacoletto) *Macro-Engineering and the Infrastructure of Tomorrow,* Westview, 1978.
(Editor with Davidson and C. Lawrence Meador) *How Big and Still Beautiful?: Macro-Engineering Revisited,* Westview, 1980.
(Editor with Davidson and Meador) *Macroengineering: The Rich Potential,* American Institute of Aeronautics and Astronautics, 1981.

WORK IN PROGRESS: A second edition of *War and Space.* *

* * *

SAMPSON, R(obert) Neil 1938-

PERSONAL: Born November 29, 1938, in Spokane, Wash.; son of Robert Jay (an electrician) and Juanita Cleone (an artist; maiden name, Hickman) Sampson; married Jeanne L. Stokes (a teacher), June 7, 1960; children: Robert W., Eric S., Christopher B., Heidi L. *Education:* University of Idaho, B.S., 1960; Harvard University, M.P.A., 1974. *Religion:* Presbyterian.

ADDRESSES: Home—5209 York Rd., Alexandria, Va. 22310. *Office*—American Forestry Association, 1516 P St. N.W., Washington, D.C. 20005.

CAREER: U.S. Soil Conservation Service, Boise, Idaho, soil conservationist in Burley, Idaho, 1960-61, work unit conservationist in Orofino, Idaho, 1962-65, agronomist in Idaho Falls, Idaho, 1967-68, information specialist, 1968-70, area conservationist, 1970-72; State of Idaho, Boise, director of land use program, 1971-73; U.S. Soil Conservation Service, Washington, D.C., land use specialist, 1974-78, director of environmental services, 1977; National Association of Conservation Districts, Washington, D.C., executive vice-president, 1978-84; American Forestry Association, Washington, D.C., executive vice-president, 1984—. Director, American Land Forum, Washington, D.C., 1978-88.

MEMBER: Soil Conservation Society of America (fellow, 1979), Society of American Foresters, American Society of Association Executives, Outdoor Writers Association of America, Society for the Preservation of Barbershop Quartet Singing in America (chapter president, 1970-72), Clearwater [Idaho] Sheriffs Posse (president, 1964-65), Orofino [Idaho] Golf Association (president, 1966).

AWARDS, HONORS: Boise Federal Civil Servant of the Year, 1972; president's citation, Soil Conservation Society of America, 1978.

WRITINGS:

"Look to the Land" (documentary film), Idaho Department of Planning and Community Affairs, 1973.
(Contributor) *The American Land,* Smithsonian Institution Press, 1979.
(Contributor) Max Schnepf, editor, *Farmland, Food and the Future,* Soil Conservation Society of America, 1979.
Farmland or Wasteland: A Time to Choose, Rodale Press, 1981.
(Contributor) Frederick R. Steiner and John E. Theilacker, editors, *Protecting Farmlands,* AVI, 1984.
For Love of the Land: A History of the National Association of Conservation Districts, National Association of Conservation Districts, 1985.
(Contributor) John Cairns, Jr. and Ruth Patrick, editors, *Managing Water Resources,* Praeger, 1986.
(Contributor) Carla Carlson, editor, *Soil Conservation: Assessing the National Resources Inventory,* Volume 2, National Academy Press, 1986.
(Contributor) Gary Moll and Sara Ebenreck, editors, *Shading Our Cities: A Resource Guide for Urban and Community Forests,* Island Press (Covelo, Calif.), 1989.
(Editor with Dwight Hair) *Natural Resources for the 21st Century,* Island Press (Covelo, Calif.), 1989.

Also contributor of short stories and articles to periodicals, including *Soil Conservation, Scouting, All Outdoors, Environmental Comment, Snowmobiling, Audubon, American Forests,* and *Journal of Soil and Water Conservation.*

SIDELIGHTS: R. Neil Sampson's book *Farmland or Wasteland: A Time to Choose* deals with soil erosion and the possible threat it poses to farming. Noting that the U.S. grain export market has grown into a $40 billion per year industry, Sampson writes that farmers are tending to grow cash crops, such as soybeans, which leave the land depleted of material to hold the soil after a harvest, hence causing erosion. Sampson also examines land damage due to surface mining and irrigating, predicting that ruined farmland will lead to resource scarcity and exorbitant food prices. According to Ken Cook of the *Washington Post,* Sampson "provides an especially lucid discussion of the powerful economic forces working against soil and water conservation down on the farm."

Sampson told *CA:* "My writings have attempted to illuminate the relationships between people and the environment. Whether short stories on outdoor subjects, how-to pieces on conservation, or essays on ethics, I have tried to convey a feeling for the bond between modern humans and the natural world around them. In addition to writing, I give between ten and twenty paid lectures per year, along with dozens of speeches on soil and water conservation, land use, and other environmental issues. My main goal is to help people see that stewardship of the natural environment is, at its roots, the most humanitarian and civilized manner in which any society can behave."

BIOGRAPHICAL/CRITICAL SOURCES:

PERIODICALS

Christian Science Monitor, January 15, 1982.
New York Tribune, February 2, 1982.
Washington Post, February 2, 1982.

* * *

SANDLER, Irving (Harry) 1925-

PERSONAL: Born July 22, 1925, in New York, N.Y.; son of Harry (a teacher) and Diana (Drori) Sandler; married Lucy Freeman (a professor of art history), September 4, 1958; children: Catherine Harriet. *Education:* Attended Franklin and Marshall College, 1943-44; Temple University, B.A., 1948; University of Pennsylvania, M.A., 1950; New York University, Ph.D., 1976.

ADDRESSES: Home—100 Bleecker St., New York, N.Y. 10012. *Office*—Division of Visual Arts, State University of New York College at Purchase, Purchase, N.Y. 10577.

CAREER: Tanager Gallery, New York City, director, 1956-59; *Art News,* New York City, senior critic, 1956-62; *New York Post,* New York City, art critic, 1961-64; New York University, New York City, instructor in art history, 1963-72; State University of New York College at Purchase, Purchase, N.Y., professor of art history, 1972—. President of board of directors, Committee for the Visual Arts, New York City. Consultant, National Endowment for the Arts. *Military service:* U.S. Marine Corps, 1943-46; became second lieutenant.

MEMBER: International Association of Art Critics (president of American section, 1959—), College Art Association (member of the board, 1985-89), Institute for the Study of Art in Education.

AWARDS, HONORS: Tona Shepard grant to travel in Germany and Austria, 1960; Guggenheim fellow, 1965-66; National Endowment for the Arts fellowship, 1977.

WRITINGS:

(With E. C. Goossen and Robert Goldwater) *Three American Sculptors,* Grove, 1959.

(Contributor) B. H. Friedman, editor, *School of New York: Some Younger Artists,* limited edition, Grove, 1960.

Paul Burlin (exhibit catalogue), American Federation of Arts, 1962.

(Contributor) Maurice Tuchman, *American Sculpture of the Sixties,* New York Graphics Society, 1967.

The Triumph of American Painting: A History of Abstract Expressionism, Praeger, 1970.

(Contributor) *Contemporary Art, 1942-1972: Collection of the Albright-Knox Art Gallery,* Praeger, 1973.

(Contributor) Gregory Battcock, editor, *New Ideas in Art Education,* Dutton, 1973.

(Contributor) Dore Ashton and others, editors, *The Hirshhorn Museum and Sculpture Garden,* Abrams, 1974.

The New York School: Painters and Sculptors of the Fifties, Harper, 1978.

Alex Katz, Abrams, 1979.

(Contributor) Holliday T. Day, *Shape of Space: The Sculpture of George Sugarman,* The Arts Publisher (New York, N.Y.), 1981.

Twenty Artists: Yale School of Art, 1950-1970, Yale Art Gallery, 1981.

Concepts in Construction: 1910-1980, Indiana Curators, 1982.

Al Held, Hudson Hills, 1984.

(Editor with Amy Newman) *Defining Modern Art: Selected Writings of Alfred H. Barr,* Abrams, 1986.

American Art in the 1960s, Harper, 1988.

Contributor to *Saturday Review* and art journals. Art critic and contributing editor, *Art in America,* 1971—; member of editorial board, *Art Journal.*

WORK IN PROGRESS:

Further writing on contemporary art.

BIOGRAPHICAL/CRITICAL SOURCES:

PERIODICALS

Nation, December 23, 1978, December 29, 1979.
New York Times Book Review, December 6, 1970, November 25, 1979.
Saturday Review, November 28, 1970, November 24, 1979.
Times Literary Supplement, August 6, 1971.
Washington Post Book World, November 29, 1970, December 3, 1978.

*   *   *

SANDLER, Lucy Freeman   1930-

PERSONAL: Born June 7, 1930, in New York, N.Y.; daughter of Otto and Frances (Glass) Freeman; married Irving Harry Sandler (an art historian), September 4, 1958; children: Catherine Harriet. *Education:* Queens College, B.A., 1951; Columbia University, M.A., 1957; New York University, Ph.D., 1964.

ADDRESSES: Home—100 Bleecker St., New York, N.Y. 10012. *Office*—Department of Fine Arts, New York University, Washington Square, New York, N.Y. 10003.

CAREER: New York University, New York City, assistant professor, 1964-70, associate professor, 1970-75, professor, 1975-85, Helen Gould Sheppard Professor of Art History, 1985—, chairman of department, 1975-89.

MEMBER: American Association of University Professors, College Art Association (president, 1981-84).

AWARDS, HONORS: National Endowment for the Humanities fellowship, 1967-68, 1977; Guggenheim fellowship, 1988-89.

WRITINGS:

(Editor) *Essays in Memory of Karl Lehmann,* Institute of Fine Arts, New York University, 1964.

The Peterborough Psalter in Brussels and Other Fenland Manuscripts, New York Graphic Society, 1974.

(Editor) *Art, the Ape of Nature: Studies in Honor of H. W. Janson,* Abrams, 1981.

The Psalter of Robert de Lisle in the British Library, Oxford University Press, 1982.

Gothic Manuscripts, 1285-1385, Oxford University Press, 1986.

Assistant editor, *Art Bulletin,* 1964-67; editor, *Monograph Series,* 1970-75, 1986-89; member of editorial board, *Journal of Jewish Art,* 1978; editorial consultant, *Viator,* 1983—.

BIOGRAPHICAL/CRITICAL SOURCES:

PERIODICALS

Los Angeles Times, June 7, 1981.
Times Literary Supplement, July 3, 1987.

*   *   *

SARAH, Robyn   1949-

PERSONAL: Born October 6, 1949, in New York, N.Y.; daughter of Leon Lipson and Toby (Palker) Belkin; married Fred Louder (a graphic designer and printer), 1970; children: two. *Education:* McGill University, B.A., 1970, M.A., 1974; Conservatoire de Musique du Quebec, Concours Diploma in Clarinet, 1972.

ADDRESSES: Home—Montreal, Quebec, Canada.

CAREER: Editions Villeneuve, Montreal, Quebec, co-founder, 1976, publisher, 1976-87. Member of English faculty at Champlain Regional College, 1975—.

AWARDS, HONORS: Canada Council arts grant, 1984, 1985, 1988.

WRITINGS:

POETRY

Shadowplay, Fiddlehead Poetry Books, 1978.
The Space Between Sleep and Waking, Editions Villeneuve, 1981.
Three Sestinas, Editions Villeneuve, 1984.
Anyone Skating on That Middle Ground, Vehicule Press, 1984.
Becoming Light, Cormorant Books, 1987.

CONTRIBUTOR TO ANTHOLOGIES

Dennis Lee, editor, *The New Canadian Poets, 1970-1985,* McClelland & Stewart, 1985.

Helwig and Martin, editors, *Best Canadian Stories 86,* Oberon, 1986.

Sullivan, editor, *More Stories by Canadian Women,* Oxford University Press, 1987.

Geddes, editor, *Fifteen Canadian Poets X 2,* Oxford University Press, 1988.

Sullivan, editor, *Poetry by Canadian Women,* Oxford University Press, 1989.

SIDELIGHTS: Robyn Sarah told *CA:* "I think the music of words, the sound and rhythm of them, is above all what informs my writing, whether it is poetry or fiction. My poems most often germinate from a combination of words—a phrase, maybe a line or two—with a sound that pleases me. I call these 'tinder words.' The rest of the poem evolves from them, sometimes at once, sometimes months or years later."

BIOGRAPHICAL/CRITICAL SOURCES:

PERIODICALS

Globe & Mail (Toronto), March 30, 1985, June 18, 1988.

* * *

SATTLER, Helen Roney 1921-

PERSONAL: Born March 2, 1921, in Newton, Iowa; daughter of Louie Earl (a farmer) and Hazel (Cure) Roney; married Robert E. Sattler (a chemical engineer), September 30, 1950; children: Richard, Kathryn. *Education:* Southwest Missouri State College (now University), B.S., 1946; Famous Artist's School, Certificate in Commercial Art, 1960. *Politics:* Democrat. *Religion:* Christian.

ADDRESSES: Home—Bartlesville, Okla.

CAREER: Elementary teacher in Aldrich, Mo., 1941-42, Norwood, Mo., 1942-45, and Marshfield, Mo., 1945-48; Kansas City Public Library, Kansas City, Mo., children's librarian, 1948-49; Standard Oil of New Jersey, elementary teacher at company school on Aruba (Dutch island off Venezuelan coast), 1949-50.

MEMBER: Authors League of America, Authors Guild, Society of Children's Book Writers, Oklahoma Writers Federation, Bartlesville Writer's Association (chairman, 1967-68 and 1981-82).

AWARDS, HONORS: American Library Association Book of Interest, 1973, for *Recipes for Art and Craft Materials;* Oklahoma Cherubim Award, 1978, for *Nature's Weather Forecasters;* Golden Kite Award honor book, 1981, for *Dinosaurs of North America;* Children's Choice Award, 1982, for *No Place for a Goat;* Golden Kite Award, 1983, for *The Illustrated Dinosaur Dictionary;* Oklahoma Book Award, 1989, for *Tyrannosaurus Rex and Its Kin: The Mesozoic Monsters;* numerous outstanding children's book citations from many organizations.

WRITINGS:

Kitchen Carton Crafts, Lothrop, 1970.
A Beginning to Read Book of Puzzles, Denison, 1971.
Holiday Gifts, Favors and Decorations, Lothrop, 1971.
The Eggless Cookbook, A. S. Barnes, 1972.
Sockcraft, Lothrop, 1972.
Jewelry from Junk, Lothrop, 1973.
Recipes for Art and Craft Materials, Lothrop, 1973, revised edition, 1987.
Jar and Bottle Craft, Lothrop, 1974.
Train Whistles, Lothrop, 1977, revised edition, 1985.
Bible Puzzle Collection, Baker Book, 1977.
Bible Puzzle Pack, Baker Book, 1977.
Nature's Weather Forecasters, Dutton, 1978.
Dollars from Dandelions, Lothrop, 1979.
Bible Puzzles for Teens, Concordia 1979.
Brain Busters, Scholastic Book Services, 1980.
Dinosaurs of North America, Lothrop, 1981.
No Place for a Goat, Dutton, 1981.
The Smallest Witch, Dutton, 1981.
Charley le mulet, Harlequin, 1981, translation published as *Morgan the Mule,* Ideals Publishing, 1982.
Noses Are Special, Abingdon, 1982.
The Illustrated Dinosaur Dictionary, Lothrop, 1983.
Fish Facts and Bird Brains, Dutton, 1984.

Baby Dinosaurs, Lothrop, 1984.
Sharks: The Superfish, Lothrop, 1985.
Pterosaurs: The Flying Reptiles, Lothrop, 1985.
Whales: The Nomads of the Sea, Lothrop, 1987.
Hominids: A Look Back at Our Ancestors, Lothrop, 1988.
Tyrannosaurus Rex and Its Kin: The Mesozoic Monsters, Lothrop, 1989.
The Book of Eagles, Lothrop, 1989.
Giraffes: Sentinels of the Savannas, Lothrop, 1990.

Contributor of puzzles, how-to articles, stories, and verse to more than forty magazines, including *Child Life, Junior Discoveries, Jack and Jill, Boys' Life, Cricket,* and *Highlights for Children.*

WORK IN PROGRESS: Our Patchwork Planet: The Story of Plate Tectonics and *The Earliest Americans.*

SIDELIGHTS: Helen Roney Sattler told *CA:* "I love books and I love children, a perfect combination for either writing or teaching. When I retired from teaching to raise my family, I turned to writing as a natural second career. Many years of experience working with children as a teacher, mother, and Scout leader led to my creating crafts and puzzles, first for magazine publication, then in books. I believe that puzzles stimulate their minds and that most children can be taught to work with their hands and be creative if shown a few basic designs to get them started. A toy or gift made by themselves is more valuable than an expensive one bought in a store. Creative work need not be expensive. This is what I try to show in my craft books. As my own children matured and left home, it became the role of my grandchildren to inspire my books. I wrote *Train Whistles* for my grandson who could never find enough train books in the library. Then when he was four, he asked me to write him a book about dinosaurs that 'didn't have any mistakes in it.' This resulted in *Dinosaurs of North America.*

"When I began research for this book, I knew very little about dinosaurs. I soon realized the need for a book like *The Illustrated Dinosaur Dictionary.* A book that would define all of those words that I could not find in a regular dictionary. A book that would give the pronunciation of each dinosaur and one that would distinguish between dinosaurs and non-dinosaurian Mesozoic animals. So I wrote one.

"I know that all children, like my grandson, want the facts in their books to be accurate, so I take great pains to research my books carefully. The research for *The Illustrated Dinosaur Dictionary* spanned five years. I read more than one hundred fifty references and visited excavations. I also talked to and corresponded with paleontologists all over North America. My fascination with these creatures has never waned and I never tire of reading about them. I am delighted when I learn something new.

"While researching the book on sharks, I interviewed shark experts and visited a dozen aquariums both in the United States and in Canada. My research on whales [involved] a whale watch trip to Baja California where I played with the grey whales [and] I had to go to Kenya to get first hand experience with wild giraffes while writing *Giraffes: The Sentinels of the Savannas.* It was a totally different experience than seeing these magnificent animals in a zoo.

"Writing nonfiction for children is almost as much fun as reading [it]. I strive to write books that will capture the interest of all children, especially the reluctant readers." Sattler has visited most of the fifty states, in addition to Canada, Mexico, Haiti, Cuba, and Aruba.

AVOCATIONAL INTERESTS: Painting, drawing, cooking, crafts, puzzle solving, and travel.

BIOGRAPHICAL/CRITICAL SOURCES:

PERIODICALS

New York Times Book Review, November 15, 1981, November 13, 1983.
Tribune Books (Chicago), May 14, 1989.

* * *

SAVORY, Teo 1907-1989

PERSONAL: Given name is pronounced Tay-o; born December 27, 1907, in Hong Kong; died November 14, 1989, in Greensboro, N.C.; daughter of Lambert and Elizabeth (Lyons) Dunbar; married Alan Brilliant (director and co-owner of the Unicorn Press), February 20, 1958. *Education:* Studied with private tutors in Hong Kong; Royal Academy of Music, London, graduate, 1929; attended Paris Conservatoire and University of London.

ADDRESSES: Office—Unicorn Press, P.O. Box 3307, Greensboro, N.C. 27402.

CAREER: Novelist, poet, and translator. Unicorn Press, Greensboro, N.C., general editor, 1968-72, editor-in-chief, 1972-89. Former producer and script reader, American National Theatre and Academy, New York, N.Y.

AWARDS, HONORS: National Endowment for the Arts grant, 1969, 1979.

WRITINGS:

NOVELS

The Landscape of Dreams, Braziller, 1960, reprinted, Unicorn Press, 1987.
The Single Secret, Braziller, 1961, reprinted, Unicorn Press, 1988.
A Penny for the Guy, Gollancz, 1963, published as *A Penny for His Pocket,* Lippincott, 1964.
To a High Place, Unicorn Press, 1971.
Stonecrop: The Country I Remember, Unicorn Press, 1977.
A Childhood, Unicorn Press, 1978.
To Raise a Rainbow, Unicorn Press, 1980.

POETRY

Seed Under Mulch, [New York], 1963.
The House Wrecker, Unicorn Press, 1967.
Traveler's Palm: A Poetry Sequence, Unicorn Press, 1967.
A Christmas Message Received During a Car Ride, Grace Hoper Press, 1967.
Snow Vole: A Poetry Sequence, Unicorn Press, 1968.
Transitions, Unicorn Press, 1971.
Dragons of Mist and Torrent, Unicorn Press, 1974.

SHORT FICTION

A Clutch of Fables, Unicorn Press, 1976.
West to East: Collected Short Fiction, 1948-1988, with introduction by Robert Peters, Unicorn Press, 1988.

TRANSLATOR

Corbiere, Unicorn Press, 1967.
Prevert I, Unicorn Press, 1967.
Prevert II, Unicorn Press, 1967.
Supervielle, Unicorn Press, 1967.
Michaux, Unicorn Press, 1967.

Jammes, Unicorn Press, 1967.
Guillevic, Unicorn Press, 1968.
Queneau, Unicorn Press, 1971.
Guenter Eich, Unicorn Press, 1971.
Katrina von Hutten, *eleven visitations,* [Munich], 1971.
(With Ursula Mahlendorf) Horst Bienek, *The Cell,* Unicorn Press, 1972.
Guillevic, *Selected Poems,* Penguin, 1974.
Guillevic, *Euclidians,* Unicorn Press, 1975.
(With Vo-Dinh) Nhat Hanh, *Zen Poems,* Unicorn Press, 1976.
Paul Eluard, *Liberte,* Unicorn Press, 1977.
Words for All Seasons: Selected Poems of Jacques Prevert, Unicorn Press, 1979.
Raymond Queneau, *Pataphysical Poems,* Unicorn Press, 1984.

OTHER

Editor, *Unicorn Journal,* beginning 1968.

SIDELIGHTS: Teo Savory's novels concerning the small Massachusetts town of Stonecrop have been praised for their authenticity and graceful style. The first of these novels, *Stonecrop: The Country I Remember,* is structured around a writer's talks with the residents of a small town in the Berkshires, an area of western Massachusetts where Savory herself spent much of her time from 1956 to 1986. Each resident of Stonecrop tells his story in his own words. These stories are then interwoven to create a literary tapestry of the town, its people, and their lives together. Fae K. Hamilton, in her review for *Library Journal,* refered to *Stonecrop* as "a fascinating portrait of an American town—its history, its present, and how it has been affected by events in the larger American society." "Stonecrop and its quixotic inhabitants," wrote the reviewer for *Booklist,* "possess an authenticity only a master storyteller could evoke." Doris Grumbach, writing in *Saturday Review,* called the book a "series of affectionate vignettes about eccentric and likable New England citizens."

In addition to her books set in Stonecrop, Savory wrote several novels drawing on her own experiences. *Landscape of Dreams* traced the early life of a girl who has lived in both China and the Western United States and who feels at home in neither location. Her struggle to break free of her family and its constraints results in a confrontation with her mother. The *Booklist* reviewer described the novel as "a delicate evocation of an unusual childhood," while Caroline Tunstall of the *New York Herald Tribune Book Review* called it "a convincing and smoothly written story." In *The Single Secret,* Savory wrote of a young woman who battles schizophrenia. Frank G. Slaughter in the *New York Times Book Review* found *The Single Secret* to be "a remarkable novel, both in concept and discipline." He concluded that it is the work of "an exceptionally skilled and perceptive novelist." *A Penny for His Pocket* told of a young man whose love for a ballet dancer leads him to a brief and unrewarding film career in Hollywood. R. D. Spector in *Book Week* believed that the novel displays a "rich prose, evocative landscapes . . ., and tragicomic portraits." He concluded that *A Penny for His Pocket* is "an altogether original literary experience."

Savory also wrote poetry and worked as a translator. Many of her works were published by the Unicorn Press, which she owned and operated with her husband, Alan Brilliant. Writing in *Library Journal,* Bill Katz claimed that "few small presses combine excellent printing and book production with equally fine translations. The outstanding one in this twin field is Teo Savory's and Alan Brilliant's Unicorn Press. The infinitely painstaking work which goes into each book should be evident even to the uninitiated."

BIOGRAPHICAL/CRITICAL SOURCES:

PERIODICALS

America, March 28, 1964.
Booklist, March 1, 1960, December 15, 1977.
Book Week, March 15, 1964.
Library Journal, December 15, 1975, November 15, 1977.
New York Herald Tribune Book Review, February 14, 1960.
New York Times Book Review, March 19, 1961.
Saturday Review, February 4, 1978.

[Sketch verified by husband, Alan Brilliant]

* * *

SCARLETT, Susan
See STREATFEILD, (Mary) Noel

* * *

SCHAAR, John H(omer) 1928-

PERSONAL: Born July 7, 1928, in Lock Haven, Pa.; son of John Homer and Pearl (Benson) Schaar; married Karin Hustvedt, 1954. *Education:* University of California, Los Angeles, B.A., 1950, M.A., 1952, Ph.D., 1954.

ADDRESSES: Office—Department of Political Science, University of California, Santa Cruz, Calif. 95064.

CAREER: University of California, Los Angeles, instructor of political science, 1953-54; Mount Holyoke College, South Hadley, Mass., assistant professor, 1954-55; Human Relations Area Files, Washington, D.C., research associate, 1955-56; University of California, Berkeley, 1957-70, began as assistant professor, became professor; University of California, Santa Cruz, professor of political science, 1970—. *Military service:* Psychological Warfare, nearly two years.

MEMBER: American Political Science Association.

AWARDS, HONORS: Rockefeller grant, University of California, Berkeley, 1961-62; Guggenheim fellow, 1964-65.

WRITINGS:

Loyalty in America, University of California Press, 1957, reprinted, Greenwood Press, 1982.
Escape from Authority: The Perspectives of Erich Fromm, Basic Books, 1961.
Legitimacy in the Modern State, Transaction Books, 1979.

Contributor of articles to professional journals.

WORK IN PROGRESS: Studies in American Political Thought.

* * *

SCHACHT, Richard (Lawrence) 1941-

PERSONAL: Surname is pronounced "shocked"; born December 19, 1941, in Racine, Wis.; son of Robert Hugo and Alice (Munger) Schacht; married Marsha Ruth Clinard, 1963 (divorced, 1989); children: Eric Lawrence, Marshall Robert. *Education:* Harvard University, B.A., 1963; Princeton University, M.A., 1965, Ph.D., 1967; University of Tuebingen, graduate study, 1966-67.

ADDRESSES: Office—Department of Philosophy, 105 Gregory Hall, University of Illinois, 810 S. Wright St., Urbana, Ill. 61801.

CAREER: University of Illinois at Urbana-Champaign, Urbana, assistant professor, 1967-71, associate professor, 1971-80, professor of philosophy, 1980—, chair of department, 1979—. Visiting professor, University of Oregon, 1969, University of Pittsburgh, 1973, University of Michigan, 1979; visiting scholar, University of Tuebingen, 1975.

MEMBER: International Sociological Association (vice president), American Association of University Professors, American Philosophical Association (chairman of committee on the status and future of the profession, 1990-93), North American Nietzsche Society (executive director).

WRITINGS:

Alienation, Doubleday, 1970, reprinted, University Press of America, 1985.
Hegel and After: Studies in Continental Philosophy between Kant and Sartre, University of Pittsburgh Press, 1975.
Nietzsche, Routledge & Kegan Paul, 1983.
Classical Modern Philosophers: Descartes to Kant, Routledge & Kegan Paul, 1984.

WORK IN PROGRESS: Human Nature, a book to appear in Routledge & Kegan Paul's series "The Problems of Philosophy."

SIDELIGHTS: Contemporary analyzers of Friedrich Nietzsche's writings have contended that the nineteenth-century philosopher's reasoning was unsound, and "have gone on to argue that soundness is not all that it has been cracked up to be," according to *Times Literary Supplement* contributor Richard Rorty. "They claim that the traditions which embody philosophical soundness need to be overthrown, and that Nietzsche helps us see how to get out from under those traditions." But Richard Schacht's *Nietzsche,* "is untypical. He urges that we judge Nietzsche's views on the basis of 'soundness and adequacy.' " In doing so, notes Rorty, the author interprets Nietzsche in a way that appears to vary from Nietzsche's own notion that there are no absolute truths. Despite this difficulty, "Schacht does an honest and thorough job of sorting out Nietzsche's thought and offering it for our inspection."

BIOGRAPHICAL/CRITICAL SOURCES:

PERIODICALS

Times Literary Supplement, October 1, 1971, June 17, 1983.

* * *

SCHAFFER, Ulrich 1942-

PERSONAL: Born December 17, 1942, in Germany; son of Otto and Agathe (Beyer) Schaffer; married Waltraud Gursche, September 6, 1965; children: Kira, Silya. *Education:* University of British Columbia, B.A., 1965, M.A., 1970; additional study at University of Hamburg, 1965-66.

ADDRESSES: Home—7320 Ridge Dr., Burnaby, British Columbia, Canada V5A 1B5. *Office*—Douglas College, New Westminster, British Columbia, Canada.

CAREER: Douglas College, New Westminster, British Columbia, instructor in European literature, 1970—.

WRITINGS:

IN ENGLISH

A Growing Love (meditations; self-illustrated with photographs and calligraphy by author), Harper, 1977.
Searching for You (self-illustrated with photographs by author), Harper, 1978.
Surprise by Light, Harper, 1980.
Into Your Light, Inter-Varsity, 1980.

For the Love of Children, Lion Publishing, 1981.
Greater Than Our Hearts: Prayers and Reflections, Harper, 1981.
With Open Eyes, Harper, 1982.
Growing into the Blue, Harper, 1984.

IN GERMAN

Trotz meiner Schuld (title means "In Spite of My Guilt"), Oncken/Brockhaus, 1971.
Kreise Schlagen (title means "Making Rings"), Oncken/Brockhaus, 1974.
Ich will dich Lieben, Oncken/Brockhaus, 1974, translation published as *Love Reaches Out: Meditations for People in Love,* Harper, 1976.
Umkehrungen (title means "Reversals"), Oncken/Brockhaus, 1975.
Gott, was willst du?, Oncken/Brockhaus, 1976.
Wurzeln schlagen, Oncken, 1981.
Das Schweigen dieser unendlichen Raeume, Brockhaus, 1982.
Wachsende Liebe, Oncken, 1984.
Das Zarte Lieben, Oncken, 1984.
Uberrascht vom Licht, Oncken, 1984.
Der Turm, Oncken, 1983.
Ein Lied von Licht und Leben, Oncken, 1983.
Im Aufwind: Meditations-Fotoband, Onken, 1984.
Jesus, Ich bin traurig froh (title means "Jesus, I Am Happy, Sad"), Brockhaus, 1984.
Neues Umarmen, Kreuz Stgt, 1984.
Umkehrunger, Oncken, 1985.
Mit Kindern wachsen, Oncken, 1985.
Ich ahne den wechselnden Weg: Im Tagebuch sich selbst begegnen, Kreuz Stgt, 1985.
Sammle mir Kiesel am Fluss, Quell-Verlag, 1986.
Sehnsuct nach Naehe, Kreuz Stgt, 1986.
Winter de Gefuehle, Kreuz Stgt, 1986.

WORK IN PROGRESS: Another book of meditations.

SIDELIGHTS: Ulrich Schaffer once told *CA:* "Most of my writing is concerned with relating the life of faith as a Christian to the everyday questions of living. I am trying to express the relevancy of faith." A number of reviewers have praised Schaffer's books for their inspirational quality. A critic for *Booklist* writes that Schaffer "articulates the questionings and longings of every thoughtful Christian in his relevant and skillfully written prayers and reflections." And Malcolm Boyd remarks in *Christian Century* that Schaffer "is at his best as he writes a prayer that is so specific it becomes universal. . . . His unfettered awareness of human weakness coupled with stabbing honesty of expression give the best of Schaffer's work a uniqueness."

BIOGRAPHICAL/CRITICAL SOURCES:

PERIODICALS

Booklist, November 15, 1981.
Christian Century, May 26, 1982.*

*   *   *

SCHLACHTER, Gail Ann 1943-

PERSONAL: Born April 7, 1943, in Detroit, Mich.; daughter of Lewis E. (an attorney) and Helen (Blitz) Goldstein; married Alfred S. Schlachter, June 18, 1964 (divorced, 1973); married Stuart Hauser, 1986; children: (first marriage) Sandra Elyse, Eric Brian. *Education:* Attended Santa Monica City College, 1960-62; University of California, Berkeley, B.A., 1964; University of Wisconsin—Madison, M.A. (history and education),

1966, M.A. (library science), 1967; University of Minnesota, Ph.D., 1971; University of Southern California, M.P.A., 1979.

ADDRESSES: Home—1 Tulip Lane East, San Carlos, Calif. 74070. *Office*—Reference Service Press, 1100 Industrial Rd., Suite 9, San Carlos, Calif. 94070.

CAREER: University of Wisconsin—Madison, director of Industrial Relations Reference Center and Social Science Graduate Reference Center, 1967-68; University of Minnesota, Minneapolis, lecturer in library science, 1969-70; University of Southern California, Los Angeles, assistant professor of library science, 1971-74; California State University Library, Long Beach, head of department of social sciences, 1974-76; University of California, Davis, assistant university librarian, 1976-81; American Bibliographical Center, ABC-Clio Information Services, Santa Barbara, Calif., director, 1981-82, vice-president for publications, 1982-83, vice-president and general manager, 1983-85; Reference Service Press, San Carlos, Calif., president, 1985—.

MEMBER: American Library Association (president, reference and adult services division, 1988-89), Publishers Marketing Association, Committee of Small Magazine Editors and Publishers, California Library Association (chapter president, 1977-78), Beta Phi Mu, Alpha Gamma Sigma, Alpha Mu Gamma.

AWARDS, HONORS: Ford Foundation Area fellowship, 1965; Higher Education Act fellowship, 1968-70.

WRITINGS:

Library Science Dissertations, 1925-1972: An Annotated Bibliography, Libraries Unlimited, 1974.
Directory of Internships, Work Experience Programs, and On-the-Job Training Opportunities, Ready Reference Press, 1976.
Minorities and Women: A Guide to Reference Literature in the Social Sciences, Reference Service Press, 1977.
Directory of Financial Aids for Women (with biennial revisions), Reference Service Press, 1978.
The Service Imperative for Libraries: Essays in Honor of Margaret E. Monroe, Libraries Unlimited, 1982.
Library Science Dissertations, 1973-1981, Libraries Unlimited, 1983.
Directory of Financial Aids for Minorities, 1984/85 (with biennial revisions), Reference Service Press, 1984.
Directory of Financial Aids for the Disabled (with biennial revisions), Reference Service Press, 1988.
Financial Aid for Veterans, Military Personnel, and Their Dependents (with biennial revisions) Reference Service Press, 1988.
Financial Aid for Research, Study, and Travel Abroad (with biennial revisions), Reference Service Press, 1990.

Editor of "Facsimile Reprint Series," California State University. Editor of *Critique: Journal of Southern California Public Policy,* 1976, and of *CARL Newsletter;* book review editor of *Reference Quarterly,* 1978-88.

*   *   *

SCHWED, Peter 1911-

PERSONAL: Surname is pronounced Schwade; born January 18, 1911, in New York, N.Y.; son of Frederick (a stockbroker) and Bertie (Stiefel) Schwed; married Antonia Holding (an enamelist), March 6, 1947; children: Katharine (Mrs. Eric F. Wood), Peter Gregory, Laura, Roger. *Education:* Attended Princeton University, 1929-31. *Politics:* Democrat. *Religion:* Jewish.

ADDRESSES: Home—151 West 86th St., New York, N.Y. 10024. *Agent*—Scott Meredith Literary Agency, Inc., 845 Third Ave., New York, N.Y. 10022.

CAREER: Provident Loan Society of New York, New York City, assistant vice president, 1932-41; Simon & Schuster, Inc., New York City, editor, 1945-65, vice president and executive editor, 1957-62, publisher of trade books, 1966-71, chairman of editorial board, 1972-82, chairman emeritus, 1982—. Trustee of Lawrenceville School. *Military service:* U.S. Army, Field Artillery, 1942-45; became captain; received Bronze Star and Purple Heart.

MEMBER: Century Association.

WRITINGS:

(Compiler) *The Cook Charts,* Simon & Schuster, 1949.
(Editor with Herbert Warren Wind) *Great Stories from the World of Sport,* Simon & Schuster, 1958.
(Editor with Allison Danzig) *The Fireside Book of Tennis,* Simon & Schuster, 1972.
Sinister Tennis: How to Play against and with Left-Handers, Doubleday, 1975.
God Bless Pawnbrokers, Dodd, 1975.
Hanging in There!, Houghton, 1977.
(With Nancy Lopez) *The Education of a Woman Golfer,* Simon & Schuster, 1979.
Test Your Tennis I.Q., Simon & Schuster, 1981.
Turning the Pages: An Insider's Story of Simon & Schuster, 1924-1984, Macmillan, 1984.
Overtime!: A Twentieth Century Sports Odyssey, Beaufort Books, 1987.
How to Talk Tennis, Dembner, 1988.
Enjoy Playing Quality Tennis after Fifty, St. Martin's, 1990.

Contributor to periodicals, including *Esquire, New York Times, Runner, Saturday Review, Sports Illustrated,* and *Tennis.*

SIDELIGHTS: Peter Sched's *God Bless Pawnbrokers* is an account of the years he worked for the Provident Loan Society of New York, prior to entering the publishing business. A prosperous company, the Provident Loan Society was established in 1894 by wealthy New Yorkers primarily to help victims of the panic of 1892 and the following depression. Later the company's employees became expert gemstone appraisers. *New York Times* reviewer Christopher Lehman-Haupt comments that "everyone who reads [*God Bless Pawnbrokers*] will come away with a favorite anecdote or two. Perhaps it will be the one about the musician who played the William Tell Overture over the telephone to the expert at Schirmer's to prove that the piccolo he was trying to pledge actually worked." Readers will "find Mr. Schwed's book a little mine of entertainment," indicates Lehman-Haupt, "with a vein of gentle nostalgia for the days when a dollar was a dollar, a working week was five-and-a-half days, and Hubert's Flea Circus, at Times Square, housed Jack Johnson, Grover Cleveland Alexander, and real-live fleas that performed tricks."

Schwed takes a similar anecdotal approach to his book about the publishing company Simon & Schuster, for which he worked over thirty years and edited over five hundred books. *Turning the Pages: An Insider's Story of Simon & Schuster, 1924-1984* discusses the important people who helped to chart the course of one of the largest publishing firms in the United States, as well as revealing what Elaine Kendall calls in the *Los Angeles Times* "the often turbulent relationships with the continuously growing list of writers" with whom Simon & Schuster dealt. "Ostensibly the literary and corporate account of a publishing empire, *Turning the Pages* expands into a social history of American phenom-

ena, fads and trends during the last half-century, told by a man in a superb position to observe, record and sometimes influence change."

BIOGRAPHICAL/CRITICAL SOURCES:

PERIODICALS

Commonweal, March 24, 1967.
Los Angeles Times, November 13, 1984.
New Yorker, January 12, 1976.
New York Times, November 17, 1975, December 22, 1977.

*   *   *

SCHWEIK, Robert C(harles)   1927-

PERSONAL: Born August 5, 1927, in Chicago, Ill.; son of Charles Anthony (a candy broker) and Eleanor (Waters) Schweik; married Joanne Lovell (a free-lance writer), December 27, 1954; children: Susan, Charles. *Education:* Loyola University, Chicago, Ill., A.B., 1951; University of Notre Dame, Ph.D., 1957.

ADDRESSES: Home—27 Newton St., Fredonia, N.Y. 14063. *Office*—Department of English, State University of New York, Fredonia, N.Y. 14063.

CAREER: Marquette University, Milwaukee, Wis., instructor, 1953-58, assistant professor, 1958-65, associate professor of English, 1965-69; State University of New York at Fredonia, professor of English literature, 1969-78, Distinguished Teaching Professor, 1978—. Visiting professor, Wisconsin State University—Superior, 1969, Universitaet Trier-Kaiserslautern, 1972-73, and University of Stockholm, 1979. Faculty exchange scholar, State University of New York, 1982. *Military service:* U.S. Navy, 1944-45; became seaman first class.

MEMBER: International Association of University Professors of English, Modern Language Association of America, Victorian Studies Association, Thomas Hardy Society (vice president, 1988—).

AWARDS, HONORS: American Philosophical Society grant, 1966; SUNY Research Foundation grant, 1970; Deutsche Forschungsgemeinschaft grant, 1972; National Endowment for the Humanities fellowship, 1981; Fulbright-Hays Program senior fellowship, 1982;

WRITINGS:

(Editor and author of introduction) Emily Bronte, *Wuthering Heights,* Cambridge Book Co., 1968.
(With Joseph Schwartz) *Hart Crane: A Descriptive Bibliography,* University of Pittsburgh Press, 1972.
(Contributor) Ronald P. Draper, editor, *Hardy: The Tragic Novels,* Macmillan (London), 1975.
(Contributor) F. B. Pinion, editor, *Budmouth Essays on Thomas Hardy,* Thomas Hardy Society, 1976.
(With Dieter Riesner) *English and American Literature: A Guide to Reference Materials,* Adler's Foreign Books, 1976.
(With Riesner) *Reference Sources in English and American Literature: An Annotated Bibliography,* Norton, 1977.
(Contributor) Lance St. J. Butler, editor, *Thomas Hardy: After Fifty Years,* Rowman & Littlefield, 1977.
(Editor) Thomas Hardy, *Far from the Madding Crowd,* Norton, 1986.
(Contributor) Om Brack, editor, *Twilight of Dawn: Studies in English Literature in Transition,* Arizona University Press, 1987.

(Contributor) Paula Kepos and Dennis Poupard, editors, *Twentieth Century Literary Criticism,* Volume 32, Gale, 1989.

Contributor to professional journals, including *Browning Institute Studies, Nineteenth Century Fiction, Victorian Newsletter, Philological Quarterly, Cithara, College English, English Studies, Quarterly Journal of Speech, Modern Language Notes, Notes and Queries, Papers of the Bibliographical Society of America,* and *Texas Studies in Literature and Language;* also contributor to *Ellery Queen's Mystery Magazine.* Member of editorial board, *English Literature in Transition,* 1972—, *Literary Research Newsletter,* 1978—, and *Cithara,* 1979—.

AVOCATIONAL INTERESTS: Writing detective stories, chess.

* * *

SCOFIELD, Jonathan
    See LEVINSON, Leonard

* * *

SCOTT
    See CHARLIER, Roger H(enri)

* * *

SEIDE, Diane   1930-
    (Diane Seidner)

PERSONAL: Born June 15, 1930, in New York, N.Y.; daughter of Alvin (a salesman) and Sylvia (an artist; maiden name, Kessler) Seide; married Joseph Seidner, May 28, 1960 (divorced January, 1971); children: Michael David, Sabrina Jennifer. *Education:* Attended Ithaca College, 1948-50; Adelphi University, B.S., 1953; also attended New School for Social Research.

CAREER: Registered nurse; St. Vincent's Hospital, New York City, head nurse of psychiatry, 1957-58; Mount Sinai Hospital, New York City, instructor in nursing and delivery room head nurse, 1958-59; free-lance writer and editor, 1959-71; St. Luke's Hospital, New York City, head nurse, 1971-72; *Parents' Magazine,* New York City, associate editor, 1973; writer, 1973—; currently field nurse supervisor, United Jewish Council Home Attendant Program, New York City.

WRITINGS:

(Under name Diane Seidner) *Young Nurse in New York* (young adult), Dial, 1967.
Careers in Medical Science, Thomas Nelson, 1972, revised edition published as *Careers in Health Services,* Lodestar Books, 1982.
Looking Good: Your Everything Guide to Beauty, Health, and Modeling (young adult), Thomas Nelson, 1977.
(With Mark Traynor) *Mark Traynor's Beauty Book,* Doubleday, 1980.
Nurse Power, Lodestar Books, 1986.
Physician Power, Lodestar Books, 1989.

Also author of novels under pseudonyms. Contributor of articles to *Parents' Magazine* and other periodicals. Associate editor, *R.N.,* 1960.

WORK IN PROGRESS: The Lamp in front of the Picture, fiction; studying with Chandler Brossard.

SIDELIGHTS: Diane Seide told *CA:* "Now that I am freed from financial constraints I have returned to writing fiction. It is liberating to be able to linger with my characters in the world of the Lower East Side. My novel is concerned with the Jewish past, the Jewish present, identity, values, growing old, illness, death, and affirmation. My literary guides are Isaac Babel, Bruno Schultz, Tadeusz Bornuski, Natalia Ginzburg, [and] Primo Levi."

* * *

SEIDNER, Diane
    See SEIDE, Diane

* * *

SHARP, Helen
    See PAINE, Lauran (Bosworth)

* * *

SHELBOURNE, Cecily
    See GOODWIN, Suzanne

* * *

SHIMBERG, Elaine Fantle   1937-

PERSONAL: Born February 26, 1937, in Yankton, S.D.; daughter of Karl S. (in real estate) and Alfreda (Edelson) Fantle; married Mandell Shimberg, Jr. (a developer), October 1, 1961; children: Karen, Scott, Betsy, Andrew, Michael. *Education:* Northwestern University, B.S., 1958.

ADDRESSES: Office—1013 South Skokie, Tampa, Fla. 33629.

CAREER: WFLA-Radio, Tampa, Fla., director of continuity, 1959-61; free-lance writer, 1961—. Former co-hostess of "Women's Point of View," a talk show on WXFL-TV. Teacher of writing courses and seminars at Hillsborough Community College and University of South Florida. Member of board of directors, St. Joseph's Hospital Development Council; member of public information committee for Florida Division of American Cancer Society.

MEMBER: American Society of Journalists and Authors, American Medical Writers Association, Tampa Athena Society (vice-president, 1980).

AWARDS, HONORS: National Honor citation from American Cancer Society, 1982, for booklet "Living in a Strange World."

WRITINGS:

How to Be a Successful Housewife/Writer, Writer's Digest, 1979.
(With Dore Beach) *Two for the Money: A Woman's Guide to Double-Career Marriage,* Prentice-Hall, 1981.
(Contributor) Glen Evans, editor, *The Complete Guide to Writing Nonfiction,* Writer's Digest, 1983.
(With Linda Albert) *Coping with Kids and Vacation,* Ballantine Books, 1986.
Relief from Irritable Bowel Syndrome, M. Evans Publishers, 1989.
What Families Should Know about Stroke, Ballantine Books, 1990.

Contributor to magazines, including *Highlights for Children, Screen Star, Lady's Circle, Seventeen, Glamour,* and *Essence.*

SIDELIGHTS: "I've always felt more comfortable 'speaking' by typewriter," Elaine Shimberg told *CA,* "rather than in person.

My first book was born out of the frustration of trying to do what was important to me—writing. It was good therapy. It incorporated and clarified my feelings on the subjects that are important to me: family, finding and expressing myself, humor, and organizing one's life so it could be enjoyed to the fullest. I find these topics permeating my other writings. For instance, I have used humor in most of my articles and books.

"I also believe that life is filled with excitement and challenge. I enjoy writing about those people (in fiction and nonfiction) who have taken whatever gifts they had and pushed themselves to the fullest. I find humor in daily living, even when others cannot, and hope to have written on my tombstone: 'She wasn't ready.' "

*   *   *

SHLEMON, Barbara Leahy 1936-

PERSONAL: Born March 6, 1936, in Canton, Ohio; daughter of Thomas E. (an engineeer) and Margaret J. (Christy) Leahy; married Ben Shlemon (a recreation therapist), September 7, 1957 (divorced, 1988); children: Christopher, Steven, Beth, Amy, David. *Education:* St. Francis School of Nursing, Diploma in Nursing, 1957. *Religion:* Roman Catholic.

ADDRESSES: Home—22307 Kent Ave., Torrance, Calif. 90505. *Office*—P.O. Box 1587, Torrance, Calif. 90505.

CAREER: Victory Memorial Hospital, Waukegan, Ill., staff nurse, 1957-61; Condell Memorial Hospital, Libertyville, Ill., staff nurse, 1961-64; Downey Veterans Administration Hospital, North Chicago, Ill., psychiatric nurse, 1965-68; free-lance writer and public speaker, 1969—; Our Lady of Divine Providence House of Prayer, Clearwater, Fla., co-founder and member of staff, 1980-88; Be-Loved Ministry, Torrance, Calif., founder and president, 1988—. Member of advisory committee for national service committee of Catholic Charismatic Renewal.

MEMBER: Association of Christian Therapists (chairman of board of directors).

WRITINGS:

Healing Prayer, Ave Maria Press, 1975.
(With Matthew Linn and Dennis Linn) *To Heal as Jesus Healed,* Ave Maria Press, 1977.
Healing the Hidden Self, Ave Maria Press, 1983.
Living Each Day by the Power of Faith, Servant Publications, 1986.

Contributor to *New Covenant* and *Linacre Quarterly.* Editor of *Association of Christian Therapists Journal,* 1977-80.

SIDELIGHTS: Barbara Leahy Shlemon told *CA:* "Writing spiritual literature in the form of books and magazine articles has been a very rewarding experience. It has put me in touch with the great need for meaning and hope in today's society. I encourage those who want to write on this topic to share much from their own experiences with sincerity and simplicity. The ordinary people who buy our books are not looking for theological rhetoric. They want practical advice that will give them the courage to explore their own inner beings. Knowledge of the Scriptures is certainly helpful, too."

Healing Prayer has been translated into sixteen languages.

*   *   *

SIEGMAN, Gita 1939-

PERSONAL: Born March 20, 1939, in Montreal, Quebec, Canada; daughter of Abraham and Sarah (Friedman) Perel; married Charles J. Siegman (a senior associate director in international finance with the Federal Reserve Board), September 3, 1962; children: Atara, Naomi, Dafna, Dov Aaron. *Education:* Sir George Williams University, B.A., 1961; University of Maryland, M.L.S., 1971.

ADDRESSES: Home—Silver Spring, Md. *Office*—GS Associates, P.O. Box 1456, Wheaton, Md. 20902.

CAREER: Institute for Jewish Policy Planning and Research, Washington, D.C., librarian, 1972-78; Gale Research Co. (now Gale Research, Inc.), Detroit, Mich., member of editorial staff, 1978-82, managing editor, 1982—; Reference Services, Inc., Wheaton, Md., president, 1983-86; GS Associates, Wheaton, sole proprietor, 1987—.

WRITINGS:

(Associate editor) *Consumer Sourcebook,* Gale, 3rd edition, 1980, 4th edition, 1983.
(Associate editor) *Awards, Honors, and Prizes,* Volume I, 5th edition, Gale, 1982.
(Managing editor) *Awards, Honors, and Prizes,* Gale, Volume I, 6th edition, 1985, Volume II, 8th edition, 1989.

WORK IN PROGRESS: Editor of *Awards, Honors, and Prizes,* 9th edition, for Gale; editor of *World of Winners,* 2nd edition, for Gale.

*   *   *

SILITCH, Clarissa MacVeagh 1930-

PERSONAL: Surname is pronounced *Sill*-itch; born December 18, 1930, in New York, N.Y.; daughter of Charlton and Adele Katte (Merrill) MacVeagh; married; children: Ian M., Nicholas C. *Education:* Bryn Mawr College, B.A., 1952.

ADDRESSES: Office—Yankee Books, Yankee Publishing, Inc., Dublin, N.H. 03444.

CAREER: Free-lance artist and translator, and teacher, 1952-70; Yankee, Inc., Dublin, N.H., assistant editor of *Yankee,* 1970-73, associate editor, 1973-75, editor of book department, 1975-83, senior editor, 1983-84, acquisitions editor, 1984-88; free-lance artist (portraits in oil) and writer, 1988—.

WRITINGS:

EDITOR

Mad and Magnificent Yankees: A New England Portrait Gallery, Yankee Books, 1973.
Danger, Disaster, and Horrid Deeds, Yankee Books, 1974.
(With Laurie Armstrong) *A Treasury of New England Short Stories,* Yankee Books, 1974.
Yankee's Book of Whatsits, Yankee Books, 1975.
The Old Farmer's Almanac Book of Old Fashioned Puzzles, Yankee Books, 1976.
The Old Farmer's Almanac Colonial Cookbook, Yankee Books, 1976, 2nd edition, 1982.
Yankees Remember, Yankee Books, 1976.
A Little Book of Yankee Humor, Yankee Books, 1977.
The Forgotten Arts: Making Old-Fashioned Jellies, Jams, Preserves, Conserves, Marmalades, Butters, Honeys and Leathers, Yankee Books, 1977.
(With Cherry Pyron) *Making Old-Fashioned Pickles, Relishes, Chutneys,* Yankee Books, 1978.
Yankee Church Supper Cookbook, Yankee Books, 1980.
The Yankee Magazine Cookbook, Harper, 1981.
The Old Farmer's Almanac Heritage Cookbook, Yankee Books, 1982.

The Forgotten Arts: Yesterday's Techniques Adapted to Today's Materials, Book 5, Yankee Books, 1982.

Yankee Magazine's Good Neighbors U.S.A. Cookbook, Yankee Books, 1985.

The Perilous Sea, Yankee Books, 1985.

WORK IN PROGRESS: Downstairs to Death; Ring around a Horse Show; A Victorian Fairy Tale.

SIDELIGHTS: Clarissa MacVeagh Silitch told *CA* that since she retired from editing in 1988, she has "more time for horses, independent writing projects, and painting commissions." She also said, "The word processor and printer (*when* they're working) are the greatest mechanical inventions since the sewing machine—the only other machine of our technological revolution I can make work."

*   *   *

SILVER, Ruth
   See CHEW, Ruth

*   *   *

SILVERSTEIN, Josef   1922-

PERSONAL: Born May 15, 1922, in Los Angeles, Calif.; son of Frank and Betty (Heymanson) Silverstein; married Marilyn Cooper, June 20, 1954; children: Frank Stephen, Gordon Alan. *Education:* University of California, Los Angeles, B.A. (with honors), 1952; Cornell University, Ph.D., 1960. *Politics:* Democrat. *Religion:* Jewish.

ADDRESSES: Home—93 Overbrook Dr., Princeton, N.J. 08540. *Office*—Department of Political Science, Rutgers University, New Brunswick, N.J. 08903.

CAREER: U.S. Merchant Marine, 1942-53; became licensed second officer; Wesleyan University, Middletown, Conn., instructor and assistant professor of political science, 1958-64; Rutgers University, New Brunswick, N.J., professor of political science, 1967—, chairman of department, 1977-80. Fulbright lecturer, Burma, 1961-62, and Malaysia, 1967-68. Director of Institute of Southeast Asian Studies, Singapore, 1970-72; member of board of trustees, Princeton in Asia.

MEMBER: Association for Asian Studies, American Political Science Association, American Association of University Professors, Burma Studies Foundation.

WRITINGS:

(Contributor) G. M. Kahin, editor, *Government and Politics of Southeast Asia,* Cornell University Press, 1959, revised edition, 1964.

(Editor and contributor) *Southeast Asia in World War II: Four Essays,* Yale University Southeast Asian Studies, 1966.

(Contributor) S. Lipset and P. Altbach, editors, *Students in Revolt,* Houghton, 1969.

(Editor and author of introduction) *The Political Legacy of Aung San,* Southeast Asia Program, Cornell University, 1972.

(Editor and author of introduction) *The Future of Burma in Perspective: A Symposium,* Center for International Studies, Ohio University, 1974.

(Contributor) R. M. Smith, editor, *Southeast Asia: Documents of Political Development and Change,* Cornell University Press, 1974.

Burma: Military Rule and the Politics of Stagnation, Cornell University Press, 1977.

Burmese Politics: The Dilemma of National Unity, Rutgers University Press, 1980.

(Contributor) *Southeast Asian Affairs 1986,* Institute of Southeast Asian Studies (Singapore), 1986.

(Contributor) Snitwongse and Sukhumbhand Paribatra, editors, *Durable Stability in Southeast Asia,* Institute of Southeast Asian Studies, 1987.

(Contributor) R. Ghose, editor, *Protest Movements in South and Southeast Asia,* Centre of Asia Studies, University of Hong Kong, 1987.

(Editor and contributor) *Independent Burma at Forty Years: Six Assessments,* Southeast Asia Program, Cornell University, 1989.

Also author of "Asia, the One and the Many," 20 programs produced on National Broadcasting Co. (NBC) television, 1967.

WORK IN PROGRESS: Civil War and Revolution in Burma; The Burma Communist Party Speaks Out.

SIDELIGHTS: Josef Silverstein told *CA:* "My writings center around the common theme of national unity and the development of a national mentality in an area where people too often think of themselves first as members of a religious group, second a linguistic group and lastly as members of a nation state. While most of my writings have centered on Burma, I have sought to broaden my scope by examining common questions in neighboring states. Lately, I have been studying the impact of international law and new legal concepts on the region of Southeast Asia.

"It pleases me that some of my writings have been translated into Burmese and Indonesian so that scholars and laymen alike in the region can read what I have written and thereby broaden the dialogue I have enjoyed with Asians who know me both personally and through my writings."

*   *   *

SIMMEL, Edward C(lemens)   1932-

PERSONAL: Born January 30, 1932, in Berlin, Germany; naturalized U.S. citizen; son of Ernst (a psychoanalyst) and Herta (Bruggeman) Simmel; married Marilyn J. Reed, December 26, 1950 (divorced, 1980); married Wendy Taylor, January 4, 1983; children: (first marriage) Gregg Chace, Cassandra Anne, Kristina. *Education:* University of California, Berkeley, A.B., 1955; Washington State University, Ph.D. (experimental psychology), 1960.

ADDRESSES: Home—P.O. Box 759, Borrego Springs, Calif. 92004.

CAREER: Western Washington State College, Bellingham, assistant professor of psychology, 1960-62; California State College (now University), Los Angeles, assistant professor of psychology, 1962-65; Miami University, Oxford, Ohio, assistant professor, 1965-67, associate professor, 1967-71, professor of psychology, 1971-90, professor emeritus, 1990—, director of behavior genetics laboratory, 1977-84. Visiting investigator, Jackson Laboratory, Bar Harbor, Me., summers, 1970, 1973, 1975, 1982; visiting professor, University of Victoria, summer, 1971. *Military service:* U.S. Air Force, 1951-52.

MEMBER: American Psychological Society, Association of Aviation Psychologists, Behavior Genetics Association, Aerospace Medical Association, Western Psychology Association, Sigma Xi.

AWARDS, HONORS: Outstanding Research Contribution Award, Sigma Xi (Miami University chapter), 1976; National Science Foundation research grant.

WRITINGS:

(Editor with R. A. Hoppe and G. A. Milton) *Social Facilitation and Imitative Behavior,* Allyn & Bacon, 1968.

(Editor with Hoppe and Milton) *Early Experiences and the Processes of Socialization,* Academic Press, 1970.

(Editor with Martin E. Hahn) *Communicative Behavior and Evolution,* Academic Press, 1976.

(Editor) *Early Experiences and Early Behavior: Implications for Social Development,* Academic Press, 1980.

Aggressive Behavior: Genetic and Neural Approaches, Lawrence Erlbaum, 1983.

(Editor with John L. Fuller) *Behavior Genetics: Principles and Applications,* Lawrence Erlbaum, 1983.

(With Fuller) *Perspectives in Behavior Genetics,* Lawrence Erlbaum, 1986.

Contributor to *Aviation, Space, and Environmental Medicine, Developmental Psychobiology, Experimental Aging Research, Behavior Genetics,* and other journals.

WORK IN PROGRESS: Research on behavior genetics, aviation psychology, and human stress.

*　　*　　*

SIMMONS, Paul D(ewayne) 1936-

PERSONAL: Born July 18, 1936, in Troy, Tenn.; son of Dewey Benjamin (a salesman) and LaVerne (Brown) Simmons; married Betty Kinlaw, December 15, 1963; children: Brent, Brian, Catherine Anne. *Education:* Southwest Baptist College, A.A., 1956; Union University, B.A., 1958; Southeastern Baptist Seminary, B.D., 1962, Th.M., 1967; Southern Baptist Theological Seminary, Ph.D. (Christian ethics), 1970; graduate study at Princeton University and Cambridge. *Politics:* Democrat.

ADDRESSES: Home—2006 Bainbridge Row Dr., Louisville, Ky. 40207. *Office*—Department of Christian Ethics, Southern Baptist Theological Seminary, P.O. Box 1906, 2825 Lexington Rd., Louisville, Ky. 40280.

CAREER: First Baptist Church, Liberty, N.C., minister, 1961-66; Edmonton Baptist Church, Edmonton, Ky., minister, 1968-69; Southern Baptist Theological Seminary, Louisville, Ky., assistant professor, 1970-76, associate professor, 1976-80, professor of Christian ethics, 1980—, acting dean, 1983, director of Clarence Jordan Center for Ethics, 1985—.

MEMBER: American Academy of Religion, American Association of University Professors (AAUP), Society of Christian Ethics, Association of Baptist Professors of Religion.

WRITINGS:

(With Kenneth Crawford) *Growing Up with Sex,* Broadman, 1973.

(Contributor) *A Matter of Life and Death,* Broadman, 1977.

(Contributor) *Struggle for Meaning,* Judson Press, 1977.

(Editor and contributor) *Issues in Christian Ethics,* Broadman, 1980.

(Contributor) Edward Batchelor, Jr., editor, *Abortion: The Moral Issues, Pilgrim, 1982.*

Birth and Death, Westminster, 1983.

A Theological Response to Fundamentalism on Abortion, Religious Coalition of Abortion Rights, 1985.

(Contributor) Earl E. Shelp, editor, *Sexuality and Moral Medicine,* Volume 2, Kluwer Academic, 1985.

Personhood, the Bible and the Abortion Debate, Religious Coalition of Abortion Rights, 1987.

(Contributor) Stephen E. Lammers and Allen Verhey, editors, *On Moral Medicine: Theological Perspectives in Medical Ethics,* Fortress, 1987.

(Contributor) E. Doerr and J. Prescott, editors, *Abortion Rights and Fetal "Personhood,"* Centerline, 1989.

(Contributor) James W. Cox, editor, *Best Sermons,* Number 2, Harper, 1989.

Contributor to *Baker's Dictionary of Christian Ethics* and *Mercer Dictionary of the Bible.* Contributor to periodicals, including *Review and Expositor, Perspectives in Religious Studies, Church and State, Report from the Capital,* and *Annals of Clinical and Laboratory Science.*

WORK IN PROGRESS: The Minister and the Abortion Debate; Dimensions of Violence: Christian Perspective.

*　　*　　*

SKEI, Allen B(ennet) 1935-1985

PERSONAL: Surname is pronounced "Sky"; born November 5, 1935, in Fargo, N.D.; died of cancer July 23, 1985, in Fresno, Calif.; son of Andrew (a druggist) and Helen (a druggist; maiden name, Swensen) Skei; married Carolyn Iverson, July 5, 1957 (divorced, 1974); married Nancy Cousins (a cellist), July 20, 1974; children: Rachel Iverson, Philip Andrew. *Education:* Attended Concordia College, 1956 and 1957; St. Olaf College, B.A., 1957; University of Michigan, M.Mus., 1959, Ph.D., 1965.

ADDRESSES: Office—Department of Music, California State University, 6241 North Maple Ave., Fresno, Calif. 93740-0077.

CAREER: Gustavus Adolphus College, St. Peter, Minn., instructor in music, 1961-62; Lewis and Clark College, Portland, Ore., instructor in music, 1962-65; Georgia College, Milledgeville, assistant professor, 1965-66, associate professor of music, 1966-70; California State University, Fresno, associate professor, 1970-77, professor of music, 1977-85.

MEMBER: American Musicological Society, Music Library Association, Music Critics Association, United Professors of California, Fresno Free College Foundation.

WRITINGS:

(Editor) Jacob Handl, *The Moralia of 1596,* A-R Editions, 1970.

(Editor) Stefano Rossetti, *Sacrae cantiones* (title means "Sacred Songs"), A-R Editions, 1973.

(Editor) Rossetti, *Il primo libro de madregali a quatto voci* (title means "First Book of Madrigals for Four Voices"), A-R Editions, 1978.

Musicology and Other Delights, Lingua, 1978.

Heinrich Schuetz: A Guide to Research, Garland Publishing, 1981.

Woodwind, Brass and Percussion Instruments of the Orchestra: A Bibliographic Guide, Garland Publishing, 1984.

Also author of Volumes 66 and 67 of *Recent Researches in the Music of the Renaissance,* madrigal collections by Rossetti. Contributor to *Grove's Dictionary of Music and Musicians;* contributor to music, education, and library journals, including *Music Quarterly, Music Review, Music Educators Journal, Journal of the American Musicological Society, Journal of Research in Music Education,* and *Notes.* Music critic, *Fresno Bee* (Calif.), 1971-85.

WORK IN PROGRESS: Editing three- to eight-voice madrigals by Stefano Rossetti, for A-R Editions.

SIDELIGHTS: Allen B. Skei once told *CA:* "The thing that distinguishes my work from that of most academics is its apparent schizophrenia. On the one hand there are discussions and editions of music from sixteenth-century Italy and Bohemia, and on the other hand there are reviews of concerts in present-day California. I've compiled an annotated bibliography of books and articles about the seventeenth-century composer Heinrich Schuetz; I've contributed to a series given over mostly to publications of new music; I've written about musical settings of Virgil; I've reported on the recent activities of Little Richard.

"It's almost as if I've not been able to decide who my audience is or what my metier should be. That's always been my problem. In college I was first a chemistry major, next an English major, then a prospective high school music teacher, and finally a hopeful music historian. I've been a clarinet player (in one competition taking second place to a baton twirler), a band director, and a teacher of all kinds of music courses.

"In a way, I suppose, my work—past and present—defines me, and words aren't necessary. What matters is that the work has never become boring. What matters even more is that it always carries some satisfaction and, often enough, a bit of fun as well."*

*   *   *

SLAATTE, Howard A(lexander) 1919-

PERSONAL: Surname is pronounced *Slah*-te; born October 18, 1919, in Evanston, Ill.; son of Iver T. (a clergyman) and Esther Elina (Larsen) Slaatte; married Mildred Gegenheimer, June 20, 1952; children: Elaine (Mrs. Tu Van Tran), Mark Edwin, Paul Andrew. *Education:* Kendall College, A.A., 1940; University of North Dakota, B.A. (cum laude), 1942, graduate study, 1941-42; Drew University, B.D. (cum laude), 1945, Ph.D., 1956; Oxford University, graduate study, 1949-50.

ADDRESSES: Home—407 Grand Blvd., Huntington, W. Va. 25705. *Office*—Department of Philosophy, Marshall University, Huntington, W.Va. 25701.

CAREER: Bethelship Methodist Church, Brooklyn, N.Y., co-pastor, 1942-45; minister of education at Methodist churches in New Jersey and Long Island, N.Y., 1945-49; Detroit Conference, Detroit, Mich., pastor of Methodist churches, 1950-56; Temple University, Philadelphia, Pa., associate professor of systematic theology, 1956-60; McMurry College, Abilene, Tex., visiting professor, 1960-63, professor of philosophy, 1963-65; Marshall University, Huntington, W.Va., professor of philosophy, 1965—, chairman of department, 1966-84. Member of West Virginia Conference of United Methodist Church, 1966—. Member of board, Institute for Advanced Philosophical Research, Boulder, Colo.

MEMBER: American Philosophical Society, American Academy of Religion, American Ontoanalytical Society, West Virginia Philosophical Society (president, 1966-67, 1983-84).

AWARDS, HONORS: Pilling traveling fellow from Drew University to Oxford University, 1949-50; alumni award, Kendall College, 1964; grant, National Science Foundation, 1965, 1971; grant, Marshall University, 1977, 1978.

WRITINGS:

Time and Its End, Vantage, 1962.
Fire in the Brand, Exposition, 1963.
The Pertinence of the Paradox, Humanities, 1968.
The Paradox of Existentialist Theology, Humanities, 1971.
Modern Science and the Human Condition, Intelman, 1974.
The Arminian Arm of Theology, University Press of America, 1977.

The Dogma of Immaculate Perception: A Critique of Positivism, University Press of America, 1979.
Discovering Your Real Self, University Press of America, 1980.
The Seven Ecumenical Councils, University Press of America, 1980.
The Creativity of Consciousness, University Press of America, 1983.
Martin Heidegger's Philosophy, University Press of America, 1984.
Modern Philosophies of Religion, University Press of America, 1986.
A Critical Survey of Ethics, University Press of America, 1988.
Religious Issues in Contemporary Philosophy, University Press of America, 1988.
Time, Existence, and Destiny, Peter Call, 1989.

Also general editor, *Existentialism,* Peter Call. Contributor to philosophy and theology journals.

WORK IN PROGRESS: "A Critical Re-appraisal of Kierkegaard."

SIDELIGHTS: Howard A. Slaatte told *CA:* "Basic to my professional work has been a pro-religious concern for the meaning of life. I have found Christian existential thought to be the most relevant and provocative in this respect. Yet I am respectful of all the major Western and some of the Eastern philosophies from 600 B.C. to today. Writing is to me a means of clarifying and dialectically expressing my views both objectively and subjectively, largely as supplemental to my lectures as a professor of philosophy. Each book is a *specialized* study, some in areas much too neglected.

"My first books called for eighteen hours per day at my desk, three to four days per week, when at Temple University. Reading many works by philosophers and theologians has been stimulating. *Time and Its End* on the meaning and fulfilled end of time has close to five hundred sources. Currently Western civilization is on a decline because of much moral debauchery. Writers must turn to themes that are more than realistic, to use [those] which bespeak constructive possibilities and destiny-making commitments."

AVOCATIONAL INTERESTS: Singing (as baritone soloist and in operettas), collecting limestone fossils, drama, sports.

*   *   *

SLAUGHTER, Jim
See PAINE, Lauran (Bosworth)

*   *   *

SMITH, Adam
See GOODMAN, George J(erome) W(aldo)

*   *   *

SNYDER, John P(arr) 1926-

PERSONAL: Born April 12, 1926, in Indianapolis, Ind.; son of Ralph W. (an accountant) and Freda (Parr) Snyder; married Jeanne Kallmeyer (a social worker), May 3, 1952; children: Barbara, Carolyn. *Education:* Purdue University, B.S.Ch.E., 1948; Massachusetts Institute of Technology, S.M.Ch.E.P., 1949.

ADDRESSES: Home—2370 Trail Dr., Reston, Va. 22091. *Office*—U.S. Geological Survey, National Center, MS 521, Reston, Va. 22092.

CAREER: CIBA-GEIGY Corp., Summit, N.J., chemical project engineer, 1956-78, part-time chemical project engineer, 1978-80; research physical scientist specializing in map projections and related cartography, U.S. Geological Survey, 1978—.

MEMBER: American Society of Photogrammetry, American Congress on Surveying and Mapping.

AWARDS, HONORS: Award of merit from American Association for State and Local History, 1970, for *The Story of New Jersey's Civil Boundaries, 1606-1968;* John Wesley Powell Award for U.S. Geological Survey, 1978.

WRITINGS:

The Story of New Jersey's Civil Boundaries, 1606-1968, New Jersey Bureau of Geology and Topography, 1969.
The Mapping of New Jersey: The Men and the Art, Rutgers University Press, 1973.
The Mapping of New Jersey in the American Revolution, New Jersey Historical Commission, 1975.
Space Oblique Mercator Projection—Mathematical Development, U.S. Geological Survey, 1981.
Map Projections Used by the U.S. Geological Survey, U.S. Geological Survey, 1982.
Computer-Assisted Map Projection Research, U.S. Geological Survey, 1985.

Contributor of articles on map projections to various journals.

SIDELIGHTS: John P. Snyder wrote *CA:* "Most of my writing relates to an interest in maps which dates to childhood. In high school I began a hobby of map projections (mapping the round earth on a flat surface mathematically). My first pocket calculator, obtained over thirty years later, reawakened the interest in projections and led to a full time profession, replacing my work as a chemical engineer. Since I never took a course which involved map projections, I am fortunate that the number of such specialists is quite small, even worldwide. This enhances the acceptability of what I write."

*   *   *

SOBEL, Robert 1931-

PERSONAL: Born February 19, 1931, in New York, N.Y.; son of Philip (an artist) and Blanche (Levinson) Sobel; married Carole Ritter (a teacher), July 31, 1958; children: David, Barbara. *Education:* City College (now of the City University of New York), B.S.S., 1951; New York University, M.A., 1952, Ph.D., 1957. *Politics:* Independent. *Religion:* Jewish.

ADDRESSES: Home—21 Division Ave., Massapequa, N.Y. 11758. *Office*—Department of Economics, New College, Hofstra University, Hempstead, N.Y. 11550.

CAREER: New York University, New York, N.Y., instructor, 1956-57; Hofstra University, Hempstead, N.Y., 1957-76, began as assistant professor, became associate professor, professor of history, 1976—. Business history editor, Greenwood Press, 1966—; principal, Winthrop Group, 1987—. *Military service:* U.S. Army, 1953-55.

MEMBER: American Historical Association, American Economic Association, Business History Association, Phi Alpha Theta.

AWARDS, HONORS: Cordell Hull fellow, 1961-63; Economics-in-Action fellow, 1962; New York State fellow in African history, 1966-67.

WRITINGS:

The Origins of Interventionism: The United States and the Russo-Finnish War, Bookman Associates, 1961.
The Collier Quick and Easy Guide to American History, Collier, 1962.
Basic Facts of U.S. History, Collier, 1963.
Review Notes and Study Guide to "The Peleponnesian War" by Thucydides, Monarch, 1964.
The Big Board: A History of the New York Stock Market, Free Press, 1965.
The Putnam Collegiate Guide to American History, two volumes, Putnam, 1965, published as *American History: College Level,* American R.D.M. Corp., 1968.
Niccolo Machiavelli's "The Prince"; also "The Discourses," and Other Works, Monarch, 1965.
Voltaire, including "Candide" and "The Philosophes," Monarch, 1965.
The Federalist Papers, Monarch, 1965.
The Putnam Collegiate Guide to Western Civilization, Volume 2, Putnam, 1966, published as *World History,* Volume 2, American R.D.M. Corp., 1968.
(Editor) D. N. Alloway, *Economic History of the United States,* Monarch, 1966.
The American Revolution: A Concise History and Interpretation, Ardmore, 1967.
The French Revolution: A Concise History and Interpretation, Ardmore, 1967.
The Great Bull Market: Wall Street in the 1920s, Norton, 1968.
Panic on Wall Street: A History of America's Financial Disasters, Macmillan, 1968, new edition published as *Panic on Wall Street: A Classic History of America's Financial Disasters—With a Timely Exploration of the Crash of 1987,* Dutton, 1988.
Study Master Notes in American History, American R.D.M. Corp., 1968.
Study Master Notes in the History of Western Civilization, American R.D.M. Corp., 1968.
(With Paul Sarnoff) *The Automobile Makers,* Putnam, 1969.
The Curbstone Brokers: The Origins of the American Stock Exchange, Macmillan, 1970.
Conquest and Conscience: The 1840s, Crowell, 1971.
(Editor in chief) *Biographical Directory of the United States Executive Branch, 1774-1971,* Greenwood Press, 1971, 2nd edition published as *Biographical Directory of the United States Executive Branch, 1774-1977,* 1977.
The Age of Giant Corporations: A Microeconomic History of American Business, 1914-1970, Greenwood Press, 1972, 2nd edition published as *The Age of Giant Corporations: A Microeconomic History of American Business, 1914-1984,* 1984.
Amex: A History of the American Stock Exchange, 1921-1971, Weybright & Talley, 1972.
For Want of a Nail . . . : If Burgoyne Had Won at Saratoga, Macmillan, 1973.
Machines and Morality: The 1850s, Crowell, 1974.
The Money Manias: The Eras of Great Speculation in America, 1770-1970, Weybright & Talley, 1974.
The Entrepreneurs: Explorations within the American Business Tradition, Weybright & Talley, 1974.
Herbert Hoover at the Onset of the Great Depression, 1929-1930, Lippincott, 1975.
N.Y.S.E.: A History of the New York Stock Exchange, 1935-1975, Weybright & Talley, 1975.
The Manipulators: America in the Media Age, Doubleday, 1976.
The Fallen Colossus, Weybright & Talley, 1977.

Inside Wall Street: Continuity and Change in the Financial District, Norton, 1977.
(Editor with John Raimo) *Biographical Directory of the Governors of the United States, 1789-1978,* Meckler, 1978.
They Satisfy: The Cigarette in American Life, Doubleday, 1978.
The Last Bull Market: Wall Street in the 1960s, Norton, 1980.
The Worldly Economists, Macmillan, 1980.
IBM: Colossus in Transition, Times Books, 1981.
ITT: The Management of Opportunity, Times Books, 1982.
The Rise and Fall of the Conglomerate Kings, Stein & Day, 1984.
Car Wars: The Battle for Global Supremacy, Dutton, 1984.
IBM vs. Japan: The Struggle for the Future, Stein & Day, 1986.
Salomon Brothers 1910-1985: Advancing to Leadership, Salomon Brothers, 1986.
RCA, Stein & Day, 1986.
(With David B. Sicilia) *The Entrepreneurs: An American Adventure,* Houghton, 1986.
The New Game on Wall Street, Wiley, 1987.
(Editor with Bernard S. Katz) *Biographical Directory of the Council of Economic Advisers,* Greenwood Press, 1988.
Trammell Crow, Master Builder: The Story of America's Largest Real Estate Empire, Wiley, 1989.

WORK IN PROGRESS: Dillon Read: A History; Anheuser Busch: King of Beers.

SIDELIGHTS: Though Robert Sobel's academic specialty is American business history, his books on the subject are written with a popular (rather than scholarly) audience in mind. Downplaying the role of complex analysis and detailed statistical evidence, Sobel instead relies on biographical vignettes, anecdotes, and reminiscences to produce studies many critics find unusually brisk and entertaining. Commenting in the *New York Times Book Review* on *Panic on Wall Street: A History of America's Financial Disasters,* for example, Gerald Carson notes that "the author's eye for the revealing anecdote and his evident gift for projecting social history" are talents that "enliven matters that might otherwise remain somewhat abstract." Another *New York Times Book Review* contributor, Andrew Tobias, has similar words of praise for *The Last Bull Market: Wall Street in the 1960s:* "You might not think that a history of the United States whose principal figure is the Dow Jones Industrial Average would hold a reader's interest," he begins. "But [*The Last Bull Market*] does this and more. . . . Mr. Sobel has managed to weave a fine narrative. It is as though you are walking through a historical theme park, with this engaging man at your side pointing out the sights." Similarly, the author's *RCA,* the story of David Sarnoff and the development of his communications company, "is a fascinating study of an innovative thinker who foresaw the impact of radio in 1916 and of television in 1924," observes Jim Quinlan in the *New York Times Book Review.* The book "has the stuff of a smash television mini-series," the critic concludes; *RCA* "is a catalogue of amazing stories."

BIOGRAPHICAL/CRITICAL SOURCES:

PERIODICALS

Chicago Tribune, December 6, 1978.
Christian Science Monitor, November 5, 1976, October 15, 1984.
New Yorker, February 20, 1978.
New York Times Book Review, February 9, 1969, October 27, 1974, September 7, 1975, November 6, 1977, February 19, 1978, June 15, 1980, July 8, 1984, March 1, 1987.
Washington Post, November 24, 1978, January 8, 1985.

SOLTIS, Jonas F(rancis) 1931-

PERSONAL: Born June 11, 1931, in Norwalk, Conn.; son of Jonas J., Jr. (a realtor) and Margaret (Soltes) Soltis; married Nancy Schaal (a teacher), September 10, 1955; children: Susan Soltis Shaw, Robin Lee Davis. *Education:* University of Connecticut, B.A. (with honors), 1956; Wesleyan University, M.A.T., 1958; Harvard University, Ed.D., 1964.

ADDRESSES: Home—15 Bank St., Mystic, Conn. 06355. *Office*—Division of Philosophy and Social Sciences, Teachers College, Columbia University, New York, N.Y. 10027.

CAREER: University of Connecticut, Waterbury, instructor in history and philosophy, 1958-60; Wesleyan University, Middletown, Conn., instructor in education, 1962-64; Columbia University, Teachers College, New York, N.Y., professor of philosophy and education, 1964-79, William Heard Kilpatrick Professor of Philosophy and Education, 1979—, director of Division of Instruction, 1971-75, director of Division of Philosophy and the Social Sciences, 1977-79. Consultant to the Addison-Wesley Publishing Company, Reading, Mass., 1965-68. *Military service:* U.S. Air Force, 1950-54.

MEMBER: Philosophy of Education Society (president, 1975), American Philosophical Association, National Society for the Study of Education, American Educational Research Association, John Dewey Society (president, 1990-91), Phi Beta Kappa, Phi Delta Kappa.

AWARDS, HONORS: U.S. Office of Education post-doctoral fellowship in education research, 1968-69.

WRITINGS:

Seeing, Knowing, and Believing, Allen & Unwin, 1966.
Introduction to the Analysis of Educational Concepts, Addison-Wesley, 1968, 2nd edition, 1978.
(Editor with B. Chazan) *Moral Education,* Teachers College Press, 1974.
(Editor) *Philosophy of Education since Mid-Century,* Teachers College Press, 1980.
(Editor) *Philosophy of Education,* National Society for the Study of Education/University of Chicago Press, 1981.
(With Kenneth A. Strike) *The Ethics of Teaching,* Teachers College Press, 1984.
(With D. C. Phillips) *Learning Theories,* Teachers College Press, 1985.
(With Walter Feinberg) *School and Society,* Teachers College Press, 1985.
(With Decker Walker) *Curriculum and Aims,* Teachers College Press, 1986.
(With Gary Fenstermacher) *Approaches to Teaching,* Teachers College Press, 1986.
(With Strike and E. Haller) *The Ethics of School Administration,* Teachers College Press, 1988.

Editor, "Problems in Education" series, 1970, and "Thinking about Education" series, 1984, both published by Teachers College Press. Editor, *Teachers College Record,* 1984-90; member of editorial board, *Educational Theory,* 1969-74, and *Studies in Philosophy and Education,* 1971-75.

*   *   *

SOLWOSKA, Mara
See FRENCH, Marilyn

SORESTAD, Glen (Allan) 1937-

PERSONAL: Surname is pronounced *Sor*-stad; born May 21, 1937, in Vancouver, British Columbia, Canada; son of John (a salesman) and Myrtle (Dalshaug) Sorestad; married Sonia Diane Talpash (in business), September 17, 1960; children: Evan, Mark, Donna, Myron. *Education:* University of Saskatchewan, B.Ed. (with distinction), 1963, M.Ed., 1976.

ADDRESSES: Home—668 East Place, Saskatoon, Saskatchewan, Canada S7J 2Z5.

CAREER: Yorkton Public Schools, Yorkton, Saskatchewan, elementary school teacher, 1957-60, vice-principal, 1963-67; Saskatoon Board of Education, Saskatoon, Saskatchewan, elementary school teacher, 1967-69, high school teacher of English, 1969-81; writer, 1981—. Instructor in creative writing at Saskatoon Community College, 1976-81, and University of Saskatchewan—Extension, 1984. Co-founder, publisher, and director of Thistledown Press, 1975—. Executive member of Literary Press Group, 1983-84; president of Prairie Publishers Group, 1984-85. Writer-in-residence at numerous schools, libraries, and writing programs.

MEMBER: League of Canadian Poets (executive member), Saskatchewan Writers Guild, University of Saskatchewan Alumni Association (vice-president, 1966), Saskatchewan Teachers Federation (member of council, 1957, 1963, 1965, 1966).

AWARDS, HONORS: Hilroy fellowship from Canadian Teachers Federation, 1976, for innovative teaching project, "Prairie Writers Workshop"; Canada Council grant, 1976, for completion of *Prairie Pub Poems.*

WRITINGS:

POETRY

Wind Songs, Thistledown Press, 1975.
Prairie Pub Poems, Thistledown Press, 1976.
Pear Seeds in My Mouth, Sesame Press, 1977.
Ancestral Dances, Thistledown Press, 1979.
Jan Lake Poems, Harbour Publishing, 1984.
Hold the Rain in Your Hands, Coteau Books, 1985.
(With Jim Harris and Peter Christensen) *Stalking Place: Poems Across Borders,* Hawk Press, 1988.
Air Canada Owls, Harbour Publishing, 1989.
West Into Night, Thistledown Press, 1990.

EDITOR

(With James A. MacNeill) *Strawberries and Other Secrets,* Nelson Canada, 1970.
(With MacNeill) *Tigers of the Snow,* Nelson Canada, 1973.
(With MacNeill) *Sunlight and Shadows,* Nelson Canada, 1974.
(With Christine McClymont and Clayton Graves) *Contexts: Anthology Three,* Nelson Canada, 1984.
(With Allan Forrie and Paddy O'Rourke) *The Last Map Is the Heart,* Thistledown Press, 1989.

OTHER

Work is included in numerous anthologies, including *Number One Northern,* Coteau Books, 1978, *The Maple Laugh Forever,* Hurtig, 1981, and *Fishing North America,* Hawk Press, 1989. Contributor of poetry and short stories to many periodicals.

WORK IN PROGRESS: The Windsor Hotel; The Chalkboard Poems, a book of poems about teaching high school; a collection of longer narrative poems; a growing manuscript of short prose pieces which may be both prose-poems and mini-fictions.

SIDELIGHTS: Glen Sorestad wrote *CA:* "I continue to write because I can't imagine what else I would rather do and because if I didn't write I would be a miserable creature, intolerable to live with. As Alden Nowlan once said when asked why he wrote: 'What else would I do?'

"I am more and more fascinated by the phenomenon of human memory, what we remember and why, and by the discoveries memory holds for the writer in that amazing creative act by which memory is unlocked and manifests itself into poems or stories. So often, it seems, the poem or story is for me a voyage of discovery; this is both the challenge and the reward, the pain and the pleasure."

AVOCATIONAL INTERESTS: "I am a constantly amazed traveller who loves to see new places, to meet new people and find new friends in the unlikeliest places. I always want to know what lies over the next mountain."

BIOGRAPHICAL/CRITICAL SOURCES:

BOOKS

Hillis, Doris, editor, *Voices and Visions,* Coteau Books, 1985.

*   *   *

SORIN, Gerald 1940-

PERSONAL: Born October 23, 1940, in Brooklyn, N.Y.; son of John (a foreman) and Ruth (a secretary; maiden name, Gass) Sorin; married Myra Cohen (a language teacher), June 9, 1962; children: Anna Bess. *Education:* Columbia University, A.B., 1962, Ph.D., 1969; Wayne State University, M.A., 1964. *Politics:* Democratic Socialist. *Religion:* Jewish.

ADDRESSES: Home—28 Woodland Dr., New Paltz, N.Y. 12561. *Office*—Department of History, State University of New York College at New Paltz, New Paltz, N.Y. 12561.

CAREER: State University of New York College at New Paltz, assistant professor, 1965-70, associate professor, 1970-77, professor of history, 1977—, director of Jewish studies, 1983—.

MEMBER: Association for Jewish Studies, American Jewish Historical Society, Organization of American Historians, American Studies Association, Social Science History Association, Group for the Use of Psychology in History, Southern Historical Association.

AWARDS, HONORS: Danforth associate, 1970; State University of New York Foundation fellowships, 1970, 1971, and 1979.

WRITINGS:

New York Abolitionists: A Case Study of Political Radicalism, Greenwood Press, 1971.
Abolitionism: A New Perspective, Praeger, 1972.
The Prophetic Minority: American Jewish Immigrant Radicals, 1880-1920, Indiana University Press, 1984.

SIDELIGHTS: In an article *Abolitionism: A New Perspective,* a reviewer for *Choice* states that Sorin's study "is a fair and useful summary of very recent scholarship." The reviewer goes on to write that "Sorin traces the colonial roots of the 19th-century movement and clearly discusses means and ends of moral suasionists and political abolitionists (who, he points out, shared motivations and commitments)." And David Brion Davis remarks in *Reviews in American History* that Sorin "gives us a clear and admirable account of the 'rise of immediatism.' He correctly points to the evangelical background of the majority of abolitionists, and arrays a good bit of evidence to oppose the well known theses of David Donald and Stanley Elkins. He gives detailed attention to the black abolitionists, who have so often been ignored by white historians. If Sorin's *Abolitionism* is something less than an imaginative synthesis, it is probably the most readable and informative survey now available."

Gerald Sorin once remarked to *CA:* "History gives me a weapon with which to negotiate a tentative peace with a chaotic universe."

BIOGRAPHICAL/CRITICAL SOURCES:

PERIODICALS

Choice, November, 1972.
Reviews in American History, March, 1973.

*   *   *

SORKIN, Alan Lowell 1941-

PERSONAL: Born November 2, 1941, in Baltimore, Md.; son of Martin and Sally (Steinberg) Sorkin; married Sylvia Jean Smardo, September 9, 1967; children: David Lowell, Suzanne Elizabeth. *Education:* Johns Hopkins University, B.A. (with honors), 1963, M.A., 1964, Ph.D., 1966. *Politics:* Republican. *Religion:* Lutheran.

ADDRESSES: Home—1694 Campbell Rd., Forest Hill, Md. 21050. *Office*—Department of Economics, University of Maryland, Baltimore County, 5401 Wilkens Ave., Baltimore, Md. 21228.

CAREER: Bureau of Labor Statistics, Washington, D.C., economist, summers, 1963-64; Research Analysis Corp., McLean, Va., economic analyist, 1966-67; Brookings Institution, Washington, D.C., research associate in economics, 1967-69; Johns Hopkins University, Baltimore, Md., assistant professor, 1969-72, associate professor of international health and economics, 1972-74; University of Maryland, Baltimore County, Baltimore, professor of economics and chairman of department, 1974—. Lecturer at Goucher College and George Washington University, 1966-67; part-time professor of health economics, University of Maryland Medical School, 1974—.

MEMBER: American Economic Association, Phi Beta Kappa.

WRITINGS:

American Indians and Federal Aid, Brookings Institution, 1971.
(With others) *Health and Economic Development: An Annotated, Indexed Bibliography,* Department of International Health, Johns Hopkins University, 1972.
Education, Unemployment, and Economic Growth, Heath Lexington, 1974.
Health Economics: An Introduction, Heath Lexington, 1975, 2nd revised edition, 1984.
Health Economics for Developing Nations, Heath Lexington, 1976.
Health Manpower: An Economic Perspective, Heath Lexington, 1977.
The Urban American Indian, Heath Lexington, 1978.
The Economics of the Postal Service, Heath Lexington, 1980.
Economic Aspects of Natural Hazards, Heath Lexington, 1982.
(Editor with David Salkever and Ismail Sirageldin) *Health and Economic Development,* Volume 3: *Research in Human Capital and Development,* JAI Press, 1983.
Health Economics: An Introduction, 2nd edition (Sorkin not associated with first edition), Heath Lexington, 1984.
Health Care and the Changing Economic Environment, Heath Lexington, 1986.

Monetary and Fiscal Policy and the Postwar Business Cycles, Heath Lexington, 1988.
(With Sirageldin) *Public Health and Development,* JAI Press, 1988.

Contributor of more than thirty articles and reviews to education and social science journals, including *Journal of Negro Education, Growth and Change: A Journal of Regional Development, Social Forces, College and University, Monthly Labor Review, American Journal of Economics and Sociology, Journal of Economic Studies, Journal of Economic Literature,* and *Journal of Health Administration Education.*

WORK IN PROGRESS: Research on correlates of declining birth rates in Punjab; a monograph on the economic aspects of health manpower; a study of the economic and social position of American Indians living in cities.

*   *   *

SOUTHERN, Eileen 1920-

PERSONAL: Born February 19, 1920, in Minneapolis, Minn.; daughter of Walter Wade (a teacher) and Lilla (Gibson) Jackson; married Joseph Southern (a college professor), August 22, 1942; children: April, Edward. *Education:* University of Chicago, B.A., 1940, M.A., 1941; New York University, Ph.D., 1961; studied piano at Chicago Musical College, Boston University, and Juilliard School.

ADDRESSES: Home—115-05 179th St., St. Albans, N.Y. 11434. *Office*—Department of Music, Harvard University, Cambridge, Mass. 02138.

CAREER: Concert pianist, 1940—; Prairie View State Normal and Industrial College (now Prairie View A&M University), Prairie View, Tex., instructor in music, 1941-42; Southern University, Baton Rouge, La., assistant professor of music, 1943-45; Claflin College, Orangeburg, S.C., instructor in music, 1947-49; Southern University, assistant professor of music, 1949-51; secondary school music teacher in public schools of New York, N.Y., 1954-60; Brooklyn College of the City University of New York, Brooklyn, N.Y., instructor, 1960-64, assistant professor of music, 1964-68; York College of the City University of New York, Jamaica, N.Y., associate professor, 1968-71, professor of music, 1972-75; Harvard University, Cambridge, Mass., professor of music and Afro-American studies, 1976-87, professor emerita, 1987—. Active in Girl Scouts of America, 1954-63.

MEMBER: International Musicological Society, American Musicological Society (member of board of directors, 1973-75), Association for the Study of Negro Life and History, Music Library Association, Sonneck Society for American Music (member of board of directors, 1985-87), Renaissance Society, Authors Guild, National Association for the Advancement of Colored People, National Association of Negro Business and Professional Women's Clubs, Phi Beta Kappa, Alpha Kappa Alpha, Mu Sigma, Young Women's Christian Association (chairperson of management committee for Queens chapter, 1970-73).

AWARDS, HONORS: Citation from Voice of America for activities in promoting black music and culture; achievement award from National Association of Negro Musicians, 1971; award from American Society of Composers, Authors, and Publishers, 1973, for *The Music of Black Americans: A History;* honorary D. Arts from Columbia College (Chicago), 1985.

WRITINGS:

The Buxheim Organ Book, Institute of Medieval Music, 1963.

(Contributor) Jan LaRue, editor, *Aspects of Medieval and Renaissance Music,* Norton, 1966.
(Contributor) Dominique-Rene de Lerma, editor, *Black Music in Our Culture,* Kent State University Press, 1970.
The Music of Black Americans: A History, Norton, 1971, revised edition, 1983.
(Editor) *Readings in Black American Music,* Norton, 1971, revised edition, 1983.
(Contributor) *The New Grove Dictionary of Music,* Grove, 1980.
Anonymous Pieces in the Ms. El Escorial IV. a.24, American Institute of Musicology, 1981.
Biographical Dictionary of Afro-American and African Musicians, Greenwood Press, 1982.
(Contributor) *The New Grove Dictionary of American Music,* Grove, 1986.
(Contributor) *A Celebration of American Music,* University of Michigan Press, 1989.
(With Josephine Wright) *Afro-American Traditions in Song, Sermon, Tale and Dance, 1630-1920: An Annotated Bibliography,* Greenwood Press, 1990.

Also contributor to *Baker's Biographical Dictionary of Musicians,* 1976; also contributor to encyclopedias. Contributor to scholarly journals. Founder and editor, *Black Perspective in Music,* 1973—.

WORK IN PROGRESS: Computer-Assisted Index of Anonymous Chansons of the Mid-Fifteenth Century.

BIOGRAPHICAL/CRITICAL SOURCES:

PERIODICALS

New York Post, July 22, 1971.

* * *

SPENDER, Stephen (Harold) 1909-

PERSONAL: Born February 28, 1909, in London, England; son of Edward Harold (a journalist and lecturer) and Violet Hilda (Schuster) Spender; married Agnes Marie Pearn, 1936 (divorced); married Natasha Litvin (a pianist), 1941; children: (second marriage) Matthew Francis, Elizabeth. *Education:* Attended University College, Oxford, 1928-30.

ADDRESSES: Home—15 Loudoun Rd., London NW8, England (winters); Maussane-Les-Alpieles, Provence, France (summers).

CAREER: Writer. University of London, University College, London, England, professor of English, 1970-77, professor emeritus, 1977—. Counselor in Section of Letters, UNESCO, 1947. Holder of Elliston Chair of Poetry, University of Cincinnati, 1953; Beckman Professor, University of California, 1959; visiting lecturer, Northwestern University, 1963; Clark lecturer, Cambridge University, 1966; Northcliffe lecturer, University of London, 1969; visiting professor at University of Connecticut, 1969, Vanderbilt University, 1979, and University of South Carolina, 1981. Fellow of Institute of Advanced Studies, Wesleyan University, 1967. Consultant in poetry in English, Library of Congress, Washington, D.C., 1965. *Wartime service:* National Fire Service, fireman, 1941-44.

MEMBER: PEN International (president, English Centre, 1975—); American Academy of Arts and Letters and National Institute for Arts and Letters (honorary), Phi Beta Kappa (Harvard University; honorary member), Beefsteak Club.

AWARDS, HONORS: Commander of the British Empire, 1962; Queen's Gold Medal for Poetry, 1971; named Companion of Lit-

erature, 1977; knighted by Queen Elizabeth II, 1983; nominated for 1986 *Los Angeles Times* Book Award in poetry for *Collected Poems, 1928-1985;* honorary fellow, University College, Oxford; D.Litt. from University of Montpelier, Cornell University, and Loyola University.

WRITINGS:

POETRY

Nine Experiments: Being Poems Written at the Age of Eighteen, privately printed, 1928.
Twenty Poems, Basil Blackwell, 1930.
Poems, Faber, 1933, Random House, 1934, revised edition, Faber, 1934.
Perhaps (limited edition), privately printed, 1933.
Poem (limited edition), privately printed, 1934.
Vienna, Faber, 1934, Random House, 1935.
At Night, privately printed, 1935.
The Still Centre, Faber, 1939.
Selected Poems, Random House, 1940.
I Sit by the Window, Linden Press, c. 1940.
Ruins and Visions: Poems, 1934-1942, Random House, 1942.
Poems of Dedication, Random House, 1947.
Returning to Vienna, 1947: Nine Sketches, Banyan Press, 1947.
The Edge of Being, Random House, 1949.
Sirmione Peninsula, Faber, 1954.
Collected Poems, 1928-1953, Random House, 1955, reprinted, 1975, revised edition published as *Collected Poems, 1928-1985,* Faber, 1985.
Inscriptions, Poetry Book Society (London), 1958.
Selected Poems, Random House, 1964.
The Generous Days: Ten Poems, David Godine, 1969, enlarged edition published as *The Generous Days,* Faber, 1971.
Descartes, Steam Press (London), 1970.
Art Student, Poem-of-the-Month Club (London), 1970.
Recent Poems, Anvil Press Poetry (London), 1978.

PLAYS

Trial of a Judge: A Tragedy in Five Acts (first produced in London at Rupert Doone's Group Theatre on March 18, 1938), Random House, 1938.
(Translator and adapter with Goronwy Rees) *Danton's Death* (first produced in London, 1939; adaptation of a play by Georg Buechner), Faber, 1939.
"To the Island," first produced at Oxford University, 1951.
(Adapter) "Lulu" (adaptation from plays by Frank Wedekind; also see below), produced in New York, 1958.
(Translator and adapter) *Mary Stuart* (adaptation of a play by Johann Christoph Friedrich von Schiller; produced on the West End at Old Vic, 1961; produced on Broadway at Vivian Beaumont Theatre, November 11, 1971), Faber, 1959, reprinted, Ticknor & Fields, 1980.
(Translator and adapter) *The Oedipus Trilogy—King Oedipus, Oedipus at Colonos, Antigone: A Version by Stephen Spender* (three-act play; revision of play produced at Oxford Playhouse, 1983), Faber, 1985.

ESSAYS

The Destructive Element: A Study of Modern Writers and Beliefs, J. Cape, 1935, Houghton, 1936, reprinted, Folcroft, 1970.
Forward from Liberalism, Random House, 1937.
The New Realism: A Discussion, Hogarth, 1939, Folcroft, 1977.
Life and the Poet, Secker & Warburg, 1942, Folcroft, 1974.
European Witness, Reynal, 1946.
(Contributor) Richard H. Crossman, editor, *The God that Failed: Six Studies in Communism,* Harper, 1950.

Learning Laughter, Weidenfeld & Nicolson, 1952, Harcourt, 1953.

The Creative Element: A Study of Vision, Despair, and Orthodoxy among Some Modern Writers, Hamish Hamilton, 1953, Folcroft, 1973.

The Making of a Poem, Hamish Hamilton, 1955, Norton, 1962.

The Imagination in the Modern World: Three Lectures, Library of Congress, 1962.

The Struggle of the Modern, University of California Press, 1963.

Chaos and Control in Poetry, Library of Congress, 1966.

The Year of the Young Rebels, Random House, 1969.

Love-Hate Relations: A Study of Anglo-American Sensibilities, Random House, 1974.

Eliot, Fontana, 1975, published as *T. S. Eliot,* Viking, 1976.

Henry Moore: Sculptures in Landscape, Studio Vista (London), 1978, C. N. Potter, 1979.

The Thirties and After: Poetry, Politics, People, 1933-1970, Random House, 1978.

(Contributor) *America Observed,* C. N. Potter, 1979.

(With David Hockney) *China Diary,* with illustrations by Hockney, Thames & Hudson, 1982.

In Irina's Garden with Henry Moore's Sculpture, Thames and Hudson, 1986.

EDITOR

W. H. Auden, *Poems,* privately printed, 1928.

(With Louis MacNeice) *Oxford Poetry 1929,* Basil Blackwell, 1929.

(With Bernard Spencer) *Oxford Poetry 1930,* Basil Blackwell, 1930.

(With John Lehmann and Christopher Isherwood) *New Writing, New Series I,* Hogarth, 1938.

(With Lehmann and Isherwood) *New Writing, New Series II,* Hogarth, 1939.

(With Lehmann and author of introduction) *Poems for Spain,* Hogarth, 1939.

Spiritual Exercises: To Cecil Day Lewis (poems), privately printed, 1943.

(And author of introduction) *A Choice of English Romantic Poetry,* Dial, 1947, reprinted, Books for Libraries Press, 1969.

(And author of introduction) Walt Whitman, *Selected Poems,* Grey Walls Press (London), 1950.

Martin Huerlimann, *Europe in Photographs,* Thames & Hudson, 1951.

(With Elizabeth Jennings and Dannie Abbse) *New Poems 1956: An Anthology,* M. Joseph, 1956.

(And author of introduction) *Great Writings of Goethe,* New American Library, 1958.

(And author of introduction) *Great German Short Stories,* Dell, 1960.

(And author of introduction) *The Writer's Dilemma,* Oxford University Press, 1961.

(With Irving Kristol and Melvin J. Lasky) *Encounters: An Anthology from the First Ten Years of "Encounter" Magazine,* Basic Books, 1963.

(With Donald Hall) *The Concise Encyclopedia of English and American Poets and Poetry,* Hawthorn, 1963, revised edition, Hutchinson, 1970.

(And author of introduction) *A Choice of Shelley's Verse,* Faber, 1971.

(And author of introduction) *Selected Poems of Abba Kovne* [and] *Selected Poems of Nelly Sachs,* Penguin, 1971.

The Poems of Percy Bysshe Shelley, Limited Editions Club (Cambridge), 1971.

D. H. Lawrence: Novelist, Poet, Prophet, Harper, 1973.

W. H. Auden: A Tribute, Macmillan (New York), 1975.

TRANSLATOR

(And author of introduction and, with J. B. Leishman, commentary) Rainer Maria Rilke, *Duino Elegies* (bilingual edition), Norton, 1939, 4th edition, revised, Hogarth, 1963.

(With Hugh Hunt) Ernst Toller, *Pastor Hall* (three-act play; also see below), John Lane, 1939.

(With Hunt) Toller, *Pastor Hall* (bound with *Blind Man's Buff* by Toller and Denis Johnson), Random House, 1939.

(With J. L. Gili) Federico Garcia Lorca, *Poems,* Oxford University Press (New York), 1939.

(With Gili) *Selected Poems of Federico Garcia Lorca,* Hogarth, 1943.

(With Frances Cornford) Paul Eluard, *Le Dur desir de Durer,* Grey Falcon Press, 1950.

(And author of introduction) Rilke, *The Life of the Virgin Mary (Das Marien-Leben)* (bilingual edition), Philosophical Library, 1951.

(With Frances Fawcett) Wedekind, *Five Tragedies of Sex,* Theatre Arts, 1952.

(With Nikos Stangos) C. P. Cavafy, *Fourteen Poems,* Editions Electo, 1977.

Wedekind, *Lulu Plays and Other Sex Tragedies,* Riverrun, 1979.

OTHER

The Burning Cactus (short stories), Random House, 1936, reprinted, Books for Libraries Press, 1971.

The Backward Son (novel), Hogarth, 1940.

(With William Sansom and James Gordon) *Jim Braidy: The Story of Britain's Firemen,* Lindsay Drummond, 1943.

(Author of introduction and notes) *Botticelli,* Faber, 1945, Pitman, 1948.

(Author of introduction) Patrice de la Tour du Pin, *The Dedicated Life in Poetry* [and] *The Correspondence of Laurent de Cayeux,* Harvill Press, 1948.

World Within World: The Autobiography of Stephen Spender, Harcourt, 1951.

Engaged in Writing, and The Fool and the Princess (short stories), Farrar, Straus, 1958.

(With Nicholas Nabokov) *Rasputin's End* (opera), Ricordi (Milan), 1963.

(Contributor with Patrick Leigh Fermor) *Ghika: Paintings, Drawings, Sculpture,* Lund, Humphries, 1964, Boston Book and Art Shop, 1965.

(Reteller) *The Magic Flute: Retold* (juvenile; based on the opera by Mozart), Putnam, 1966.

(Author of introduction) *Venice,* Vendome, 1979.

Letters to Christopher: Stephen Spender's Letters to Christopher Isherwood, 1929-1939, with "The Line of the Branch"—Two Thirties Journals, Black Sparrow, 1980.

(Author of introduction) *Herbert List: Photographs, 1930-1970,* Thames & Hudson, 1981.

(Contributor) Martin Friedman, *Hockney Paints the Stage,* Abbeville Press, 1983.

The Journals of Stephen Spender, 1939-1983, Random House, 1986.

The Temple (novel), Grove, 1988.

Contributor to numerous anthologies. Editor, with Cyril Connolly, of *Horizon,* 1939-41; co-editor, with Melvin J. Lasky, 1953-66, and corresponding editor, 1966-67, *Encounter;* co-founder of *Index on Censorship* (bimonthly magazine).

SIDELIGHTS: Stephen Spender is the last surviving member of the generation of British poets who came to prominence in the

1930s, a group that included W. H. Auden, Christopher Isherwood, D. Day Lewis, and Louis MacNeice. In *World within World: The Autobiography of Stephen Spender* the author speculates that the names of the members of the group became irreversibly linked in the minds of critics for no other reason other than having their poems included in the same important poetic anthologies of the early thirties. However, in *The Angry Young Men of the Thirties* Elton Edward Smith finds that the poets had much more in common and states that they shared a "similarity of theme, image, and diction." According to Smith, the poets also all rejected the writing of the immediately preceding generation. Gerald Nicosia reaches the same conclusion in his *Chicago Tribune Book World* essay on Spender's work. "While preserving a reverence for traditional values and a high standard of craftsmanship," Nicosia writes, "they turned away from the esotericism of T. S. Eliot, insisting that the writer stay in touch with the urgent political issues of the day and that he speak in a voice whose clarity can be understood by all." Comparing the older and younger generations of writers, Smith notes that while the poets of the 1920s focused on themes removed from reality, "the poets of the 1930s represented a return to the objective world outside and the recognition of the importance of the things men do together in groups: political action, social structure, cultural development."

Spender's name is most frequently associated with that of W. H. Auden, perhaps the most famous poet of the thirties; yet some critics, including Alfred Kazin and Helen Vendler, find the two poets dissimilar in many areas. In the *New Yorker,* for example, Vendler observes that "at first [Spender] imitated Auden's self-possessed ironies, his determined use of technological objects. . . . But no two poets can have been more different. Auden's rigid, brilliant, peremptory, categorizing, allegorical mind demanded forms altogether different from Spender's dreamy, liquid, guilty, hovering sensibility. Auden is a poet of firmly historical time, Spender of timeless nostalgic space." In the *New York Times Book Review* Kazin similarly concludes that Spender "was mistakenly identified with Auden. Although they were virtual opposites in personality and in the direction of their talents, they became famous at the same time as 'pylon poets'—among the first to put England's gritty industrial landscape of the 1930's into poetry."

The term "pylon poets" refers to "The Pylons," a poem by Spender which many critics describe as typical of the Auden generation. The much-anthologized work, included in one of Spender's earliest collections, *Poems,* as well as in his compilation of a lifetime's accomplishments, *Collected Poems, 1928-1985,* is characteristic of the group's imagery and also reflects the political and social concerns of its members. Smith recognizes that in such a poem "the poet, instead of closing his eyes to the hideous steel towers of a rural electrification system and concentrating on the soft green fields, glorifies the pylons and grants to them the future. And the nonhuman structure proves to be of the very highest social value, for rural electrification programs help create a new world of human equality."

The decade of the thirties was marked by turbulent events that would shape the course of history: the world-wide economic depression, the Spanish Civil War, and the beginnings of the Second World War. Seeing the established world crumbling around them, the writers of the period sought to create a new reality to replace the old which in their minds had become obsolete. According to D. E. S. Maxwell, commenting in his *Poets of the Thirties,* "the imaginative writing of the thirties created an unusual *milieu* of urban squalor and political intrigue. This kind of statement—a suggestion of decay producing violence and leading to

change—as much as any absolute and unanimous political partisanship gave this poetry its marxist reputation. Communism and 'the communist' (a poster-type stock figure) were frequently invoked." For a time Spender, like many young intellectuals of the era, was a member of the Communist party. "Spender believed," Smith notes, "that communism offered the only workable analysis and solution of complex world problems, that it was sure eventually to win, and that for significance and relevance the artist must somehow link his art to the Communist diagnosis." Smith describes Spender's poem, "The Funeral" (included in *Collected Poems: 1928-1953* but omitted from the 1985 revision of the same work), as "a Communist elegy" and observes that much of Spender's other works from the same early period as "The Funeral," including his play, "Trial of a Judge," his poems from *Vienna,* and his essays in *The Destructive Element: A Study of Modern Writers and Beliefs* and *Forward from Liberalism* deal with the Communist question.

Washington Post Book World contributor Monroe K. Spears finds "The Funeral," one of Spender's least successful poems, but, nevertheless acknowledges that it reveals some of the same characteristics of the poet as his better work: "an ardent idealism, an earnest dedication that leaves him vulnerable in his sympathy for the deprived and exploited, his hopes for a better world, [and] his reverence for greatness and heroism, especially in art." Critics note that Spender's attitudes, developed in the thirties, have continued to influence the poet throughout his life. As Peter Stansky points out in the *New Republic:* "The 1930s were a shaping time for Spender, casting a long shadow over all that came after. . . . It would seem that the rest of his life, even more than he may realize, has been a matter of coming to terms with the 1930s, and the conflicting claims of literature and politics as he knew them in that decade of achievement, fame, and disillusion." Stansky also observes, as do other reviewers, that Spender is at his best when he is writing autobiography. The poet himself seems to point out the truth in this statement when he writes in the postscript to *Thirties and After: Poetry, Politics, People, 1933-1970:* "I myself am, it is only too clear, an autobiographer. Autobiography provides the line of continuity in my work. I am not someone who can shed or disclaim his past."

The past has often become the subject of Spender's recent writing. His books of the eighties—particularly *The Journals of Stephen Spender, 1939-1983, Collected Poems, 1928-1985,* and *Letters to Christopher: Stephen Spender's Letters to Christopher Isherwood, 1929-1939, with "The Line of the Branch"—Two Thirties Journals*—place a special emphasis on autobiographical material that reviewers find reveal Spender as both an admirable personality and a notable writer. In a *New York Times Book Review* commentary by Samuel Hynes on the collection of Spender's letters, for instance, the critic expresses his belief that "the person who emerges from these letters is neither a madman nor a fool, but an honest, intelligent, troubled young man, groping toward maturity in a troubled time. And the author of the journals is something more; he is a writer of sensitivity and power." Discussing the same volume in the *Times Literary Supplement* Philip Gardener notes, "If, since the war, Spender's creative engine has run at less than full power, one remains grateful for his best work, the context of which is fascinatingly provided by these letters and journals." "Some of Spender's poems, criticism, memoirs, translations have contributed to the formation of a period, which to some extent, they now represent . . . ," Robert Craft observes in his *New York Review of Books* critique of *The Journals of Stephen Spender, 1939-1983.* "Yet Spender himself stands taller than his work. The least insular writer of his generation and the most generous, he is a kinder man—*hypocrite lecteur!*—than most of us deserve."

Collections of Spender's papers can be found at Northwestern University in Evanston, Illinois, and in the Bancroft Library at the University of California at Berkeley.

BIOGRAPHICAL/CRITICAL SOURCES:

BOOKS

Contemporary Literary Criticism, Gale, Volume 1, 1973, Volume 2, 1974, Volume 5, 1976, Volume 10, 1979, Volume 41, 1987.
Dictionary of Literary Biography, Volume 20: *British Poets, 1914-1945,* Gale, 1983.
Maxwell, D. E. S., *Poets of the Thirties,* Barnes & Noble, 1969.
Smith, Elton Edmund, *The Angry Young Men of the Thirties,* Southern Illinois University Press, 1975.
Spender, Stephen, *World Within World: The Autobiography of Stephen Spender,* Harcourt, 1951.
Spender, Stephen, *The Thirties and After: Poetry, Politics, People, 1933-1970,* Random House, 1978.

PERIODICALS

Chicago Tribune Book World, January 12, 1986.
New Republic, September 23, 1978.
New Yorker, November 10, 1986.
New York Review of Books, January 25, 1979, April 24, 1986.
New York Times Book Review, February 1, 1981, January 26, 1986.
Times Literary Supplement, April 17, 1981.
Washington Post Book World, January 12, 1986.*

—*Sidelights by Marian Gonsior*

*   *   *

SPILHAUS, Athelstan (Frederick) 1911-

PERSONAL: Born November 25, 1911, in Rondeborsch, near Cape Town, South Africa; came to United States, 1931, naturalized, 1946; son of Karl Antonio (a merchant) and Nellie (Muir) Spilhaus; married Mary Atkins, 1935; married Gail T. Griffin, 1964; married Kathleen FitzGerald, 1978; children: (first marriage) Athelstan F., Jr., Mary Muir, Eleanor, Margaret Ann, Karl Henry. *Education:* University of Cape Town, B.Sc., 1931, D.Sc., 1948; Massachusetts Institute of Technology, S.M., 1933.

ADDRESSES: Home—P.O. Box 1063, Middleburg, Va. 22117.

CAREER: Massachusetts Institute of Technology, Cambridge, research assistant, 1933-35; Woods Hole Oceanographic Institution, Woods Hole, Mass., research assistant, 1936-37, investigator in physical oceanography, 1938-60, associate, 1960, honorary staff member, 1960—; New York University, New York, N.Y., assistant professor, 1937-38, associate professor, 1939-42, professor of meteorology, 1942-48, organizer, and chairman of department of meteorology, 1938-47, director of research, 1946-48; University of Minnesota, Institute of Technology, Minneapolis, dean, 1949-66, professor of physics, 1966-67; Franklin Institute, Philadelphia, Pa., president, 1967-69; president of Aqua International, Inc., 1969-70; Smithsonian Institution, International Center for Scholars, Washington, D.C., fellow, 1971-74; National Oceanic and Atmospheric Administration of U.S. Department of Commerce, Washington, D.C., special assistant to the administrator, 1974-80. University visiting professor, Texas A & M University, 1974, 1975; distinguished visiting professor of marine sciences, University of Texas at Austin, 1977, 1978; distin-

guished scholar, Annenberg Center, University of Southern California, 1981; visiting fellow, Institute for Marine and Coastal Studies, University of Southern California, 1981—. Meteorological adviser, government of South Africa, 1947; member of various advisory committees to several government agencies, including U.S. Department of Interior, Department of Commerce, Army, and Air Force. Scientific director of weapons effects on two Nevada atomic tests, 1951; U.S. representative on executive board of UNESCO, 1954-58; member of U.S. National Committee for the International Geophysical Year, 1955-58; U.S. commissioner in charge of science exhibit, Seattle World's Fair, 1961-63; member of National Space Board, 1966-72.

Inventor of bathythermograph, Spilhaus space clock, and other oceanographic, aircraft, and meteorological instruments. Director of Pergamon Press and of several business firms. Scientific posts include committee on extent of air space, International Astronautical Federation, chairman of National Academy of Sciences-National Research Council Committee on pollution, and former chairman of committee on oceanography. Trustee of Science Service, Inc., International Oceanographic Foundation, Woods Hole Oceanographic Institution, Pacific Science Center Foundation; director of American Museum of Archaeology and North Star Research and Development Institute. *Military service:* Union of South Africa Defense Forces, assistant director of Technical Services, 1933-35, became lieutenant. U.S. Army Air Forces, 1943-46; became lieutenant colonel; received Legion of Merit.

MEMBER: Royal Meterological Society (fellow), American Meteorological Society, American Society of Limnology and Oceanography, American Society for Engineering Education, American Philosophical Society, American Geophysical Union, American Institute of Aeronautics and Astronautics (fellow), American Association for the Advancement of Science (fellow; president, 1970; chairman of board of directors, 1971), American Newspaper Publishers Association, Marine Technology Society (member of board of directors), Royal Society of South Africa, Sigma Xi, Tau Beta Pi, Iota Alpha, Cosmos Club (Washington, D.C.), Explorers Club, Bohemian Club.

AWARDS, HONORS: Exceptional Civilian Service Medal from U.S. Air Force, 1952; Patriotic Civilian Service Award from U.S. Army, 1959; Berzelius Medal, 1962; Proctor Prize from Scientific Research Society of America, 1968; Marine Technology Society, 1977, Fifteenth Anniversary Award, 1981, Compass Distinguished Achievement Award; D.Sc. from Coe College, 1961, Rhode Island University, 1968, Hahnemann Medical College, 1968, Philadelphia College of Science, 1968, Hamilton College, 1970, Southeastern Massachusetts University, 1970, Durham University, 1970, University of South Carolina, 1971, Southwestern University at Memphis, 1972, and University of Maryland, 2; L.L.D. from Nova University, 1970.

WRITINGS:

(With James E. Miller) *Workbook in Meteorology,* McGraw, 1942.
Report on the Meteorological Services for the Union of South Africa, Union of South Africa Government Printer, 1948.
Weathercraft (juvenile), Viking, 1951.
(With W. E. K. Middleton) *Meteorological Instruments,* 3rd edition, University of Toronto Press, 1953.
(With Joseph J. George and others) *Weather Is the Nation's Business,* U.S. Government Printing Office, 1953.
Satellite of the Sun (juvenile), Viking, 1958.
Turn to the Sea, National Academy of Sciences, 1959, revised children's edition, Whitman Publishing Co., 1962.

Waste Management and Control, National Academy of Sciences, 1966.
The Ocean Laboratory (juvenile), Creative Educational Society, Inc., 1967.
The Experimental City: Utopia, Charlatan Publishers, 1967.
Daring Experiments for Living, Science Service, 1968.
Up Your Alley: Selections from Spilhaus, St. Martin's, 1974.
Stories from a Snowy Meadow, Seabury, 1976.

CONTRIBUTOR

The Nation Looks at Its Resources, Resources for the Future, Inc., 1954.
Morton Alperin and H. F. Gregory, editors, *Vistas in Aeronautics,* Volume 2, Pergamon, 1959.
M. Bailey and U. Leavell, editors, *A World to Discover,* American Book Co., 1963.
Francois Leydet, editor, *Tomorrow's Wilderness,* Sierra Club, 1963.
E. John Long, editor, *Ocean Sciences,* U.S. Naval Institute, 1964.
Our World in Peril: An Environment Review, Fawcett, 1971.
The Restless Americans, Xerox College Publishing, 1971.

OTHER

Creator of illustrated strip on science, "Our New Age," published as a Sunday feature in U.S. and several foreign newspapers, 1958-62, as daily feature in U.S. newspapers, 1962-73. Contributor of more than two hundred articles to periodicals, mainly in engineering, geographic, and meteorological fields. Member of honorary editorial board of *Underwater Yearbook;* member of advisory board of *Industrial Research, Oceanology, Planetary and Space Physics,* World Book Encyclopedia Science Service, and Industrial Research.

SIDELIGHTS: As a young scientist Athelstan Spilhaus became internationally known for inventing the bathythermograph, a device for measuring depth and temperature of ocean waters from a moving craft. This instrument revolutionized oceanography and was extremely valuable for submarine detection during World War II. Spilhaus also play an important part in developing several other oceanographic, aircraft, and meteorological instruments or tools.

*   *   *

SPILKA, Mark   1925-

PERSONAL: Born August 6, 1925, in East Cleveland, Ohio; son of Harvey Joseph (a lawyer) and Zella (a poet; maiden name, Fenberg) Spilka; married Ellen Potter, May 6, 1950 (divorced December 14, 1965); married Ruth Dane Farnum (a weaver), January 18, 1975; children: Jane, Rachel, Aaron; (stepchildren) Betsey, Polly. *Education:* Brown University, B.A., 1949; Indiana University, M.A., 1953, Ph.D., 1956.

ADDRESSES: Home—294 Doyle Ave., Providence, R.I. 02906. *Office*—Department of English, Brown University, Providence, R.I. 02912.

CAREER: American Mercury, New York, N.Y., editorial assistant, 1949-51; University of Michigan, Ann Arbor, instructor, 1954-58, assistant professor of English, 1958-63; Brown University, Providence, R.I., associate professor, 1963-67, professor of English, 1967—, head of department, 1968-73. Visiting professor at Indiana University, autumn, 1961, summer, 1976, Hebrew University of Jerusalem, spring, 1972, and University of Tulsa, summer, 1975. Director of National Endowment for the Hu-

manities Summer Seminar, 1974. *Military service:* U.S. Army Air Forces, 1944-46; became sergeant.

MEMBER: Modern Language Association of America (president of Conference of Editors of Learned Journals, 1974-75), American Association of University Professors, Dickens Society (vice-president, 1984; president, 1985).

AWARDS, HONORS: Fellow of Indiana School of Letters, 1963; Guggenheim fellow, 1967-68; director of National Endowment for the Humanities fellow, 1978-79.

WRITINGS:

The Love Ethic of D. H. Lawrence, Indiana University Press, 1955.
Dickens and Kafka: A Mutual Interpretation, Indiana University Press, 1963.
(Editor) *D. H. Lawrence: A Collection of Critical Essays,* Prentice-Hall, 1963.
(Editor) *Toward a Poetics of Fiction,* Indiana University Press, 1977.
Virginia Woolf's Quarrel with Grieving, University of Nebraska Press, 1980.
(Editor) *Pagliacci's Piano: Selected Late Poems by Grandma Goda,* Providence, 1983.

Editor of *Novel: A Forum on Fiction,* 1967—.

WORK IN PROGRESS: Hemingway's Quarrel with Androgyny, which will be published as part of an ongoing study on the taboo on tenderness in modern fiction, to be called *New Literary Quarrels with Tenderness.*

SIDELIGHTS: Of Mark Spilka's collection of essays inquiring into the nature of fiction, Philip Stevick remarks in the *Journal of Aesthetics:* "In our culture, a collection like Spilka's is all the poetics we will ever have, a group of 'approaches,' assessments, and analyses, none of them exclusive of the others, all of them done with wit, grace, and a profound respect for the art of the novel. It is a brilliant collection and anyone who cares about the novel and the forms with which one may discourse about it will find it consistently impressive." And a reviewer for *Choice* writes: "This impressive collection . . . constitutes a debate on the possibilities of a 'poetics' of fiction. . . . Anyone interested in recent critical methods, and their application to classic fiction, will find herein competent—and even a few brilliant—essays."

Mark Spilka told *CA:* "I hold the dubious distinction of receiving in 1953 the world's first master's degree in literary criticism from the School of Letters (now defunct) at Indiana University. My mentors there were Leslie Fiedler, Francis Fergusson, and the philosophical anthropologist David Bidney. From Fiedler I leaned to combine my penchant for new critical exegesis with psychological speculations and a certain measure of artistry. From Fergusson I learned how to diagnose dramatic actions in fiction. From Bidney I learned to look for definitions of human nature by which writers' works and worlds were governed. Most of my published criticism reflects these lessons."

BIOGRAPHICAL/CRITICAL SOURCES:

PERIODICALS

Choice, March, 1978.
Journal of Aesthetics, fall, 1978.

SPINOSSIMUS
See WHITE, William, Jr.

*   *   *

STAFFORD, Gilbert Wayne   1938-

PERSONAL: Born December 30, 1938, in Portageville, Mo.; son of Dawsey Calvin (a minister) and Orell Elvesta (Smith) Stafford; married Darlene Dawn Covert, December 30, 1962; children: Matthew Wayne, Heather Noelle, Anne Elizabeth, Joshua Wayne Covert. *Education:* Anderson College and Theological Seminary (now Anderson University), B.A. (with honors), 1961; Andover Newton Theological School, M.Div., 1964; Boston University, Th.D., 1973; attended Institute of Holy Land Studies, Jerusalem, Israel, 1975-76.

ADDRESSES: Home—2424 Albert St., Anderson, Ind. 46012. *Office*—Department of Christian Theology, Anderson University, School of Theology, Anderson, Ind. 46012-3462.

CAREER: Ordained minister of Church of God, 1965; pastor of Church of God in Malden, Mass., 1962-66; Boston University, School of Theology, Boston, Mass., teaching fellow, 1966-68; Hyde Park Congregational Church, Boston, Mass., director of Christian education, 1968-69; East Ashman Church of God, Midland, Mich., pastor, 1969-76; Anderson University, School of Theology, Anderson, Ind., assistant professor, 1976-79, professor of Christian theology and associate dean, 1980—, dean of the chapel, 1984—, convener of the International Dialogue on Doctrinal Issues, 1980—. Feature writer for *Vital Christianity,* 1986—. Chair of Commission on Christian Unity of the Church of God, 1985—; member of Mass Communications Board of the Church of God and speaker for the Christian Brotherhood Hour—English, 1986—. Visiting scholar, Cambridge University, 1985; senior associate, Westminster Theological College, Cambridge, 1985. Protestant chaplain of Malden Fire Department, 1964-65; leader of pastors' conferences in Kenya, 1983.

MEMBER: American Academy of Religion, Wesleyan Theological Society.

AWARDS, HONORS: Bethany Heritage Award, 1982.

WRITINGS:

Living as Redeemed People: Studies in James and Jude, Warner Press, 1976.
Beliefs That Guide Us, Center for Pastoral Studies (Anderson, Ind.), 1977.
The People of God, Center for Pastoral Studies, 1977.
The Person and Work of the Holy Spirit, Center for Pastoral Studies, 1977.
The Seven Doctrinal Leaders of the Church of God Movement, Center for Pastoral Studies, 1977.
The Life of Salvation, Warner Press, 1979.
(Contributor) John E. Hartley and R. Larry Shelton, editors, *An Inquiry into Soteriology from a Biblical Theological Perspective,* Warner Press, 1981.
(Contributor) Charles W. Carter, R. Duane Thompson, and Charles R. Wilson, editors, *A Contemporary Wesleyan Theology,* Volume I, Zondervan, 1983.
(Contributor) James Earl Massey, editor, *Educating for Service: Essays Presented to Robert H. Reardon,* Warner Press, 1984.

Also author of study guide "James: A Practical Handbook for Believers," Women of the Church of God (Anderson, Ind.), 1981; also contributor to reports. Contributor of articles to periodicals, including *Centering on Ministry, Christian Leadership, Colloquium,* and *Seminary Today.*

WORK IN PROGRESS: Orderly Thinking about the Church's Faith.

SIDELIGHTS: Gilbert Wayne Stafford told *CA:* "Several years ago I dealt with personal goals by asking myself, 'When I die, what do I hope to leave as a contribution?' My answer fell into four categories: 1) a family, each member of which would realize his or her fullest potential under the lordship of Jesus Christ; 2) a congregation to which I had given my best pastoral leadership; 3) theological students with whom I had a relationship of both mutual respect and common commitment to Christ's mission; and 4) published works of scholarly and spiritual integrity.

"Writing, therefore, is one of my four major goals in life. *Living as Redeemed People,* a study of James and Jude, represents the excitement of a first published work. *The Life of Salvation,* which considers all major doctrines of the Christian faith from the perspective of salvation, represents a community effort in that it was written in connection with a seminary class that critiqued every paragraph.

"I have contributed to three other works: 'Salvation in the General Epistles' is in Volume I of the four-volume *Wesleyan Theological Perspectives,* the first being on the biblical doctrine(s) of salvation. This contribution represents some theological reflections that continue to be of great interest to me: the nature of Christian perfection, the universal work of the Holy Spirit, and entire sanctification in the sense of having passed the point of no return in our commitment to Christ.

"In *A Contemporary Wesleyan Theology,* the first chapter is entitled 'Frontiers in Contemporary Theology' and represents my most extensive research for any writing outside of my doctoral dissertation.

" 'What the Church Does with Its Eyes,' an essay in *Educating for Service,* represents my attempt to address the church in such a way that I encourage depth of thinking and warmth of feeling. I develop six modes of operation found among modern Christian churches, under the rubrics of the backward, the forward, the upward, the downward, the inward, and the outward foci. My thesis is that the church of Pentecost had a multidirectional focus. I see this essay as a discussion piece for church renewal."

AVOCATIONAL INTERESTS: Travel (has traveled widely throughout Europe, Japan, China, the Far East, Canada, Jamaica, the Cayman Islands, Kenya, Greece, and Israel).

*   *   *

STAINBACK, Susan Bray   1947-

PERSONAL: Born May 22, 1947, in Baltimore, Md.; daughter of William DeVaughn (an optician) and Cleo (Selig) Bray; married William Clarence Stainback (a university professor), December 16, 1967. *Education:* Radford College, B.S., 1968; University of Virginia, M.Ed., 1971, Ed.D., 1973. *Religion:* Catholic.

ADDRESSES: Home—2922 Minnetonka Dr., Cedar Falls, Iowa 50613. *Office*—College of Education, University of Northern Iowa, Cedar Falls, Iowa 50613.

CAREER: Albemarle County (Va.) public schools, teacher of intermediate age educable mentally retarded students, 1968-70; held part-time positions as consultative specialist, behavior modification consultant, research assistant, and research associate at various school systems in Virginia, 1971-73; Hope Haven Children's Hospital, Jacksonville, Fla., educational and behavioral specialist, 1973-74; University of Northern Iowa, Cedar Falls, assistant professor, 1974-78, associate professor of special education, 1978-79; Florida Atlantic University, Center of Excellence, Boca Raton, associate professor, 1979-80; University of Northern Iowa, associate professor, 1980-83, professor of special education, 1983—. Visiting lecturer in special education, University of Virginia, summer, 1973; visiting professor, Syracuse University, 1988; endowed chair professor, California State University at Los Angeles, 1988-89. Lecturer throughout the United States and Canada; consultant to numerous national, state, and local organizations.

MEMBER: American Association for the Severely and Profoundly Handicapped, Council for Exceptional Children, Council for Children with Behavioral Disorders, Teacher Educators in Severe Behavior Disorders, Canadian Association for Community Living, Phi Delta Kappa.

WRITINGS:

WITH HUSBAND, WILLIAM STAINBACK

(And with J. S. Payne and R. A. Payne) *Establishing a Token Economy in the Classroom,* C. E. Merrill, 1973.
Classroom Discipline: A Positive Approach, C. C Thomas, 1974.
Educating Children with Severe Maladaptive Behavior, Grune, 1980.
Integrating Students with Severe Handicaps into Regular Schools, Council for Exceptional Children, 1985.
Understanding and Conducting Qualitative Research, Council for Exceptional Children, 1988.
How to Help Your Child Succeed in School, Meadowbrook, 1988.
(And with M. Kidd) *Making the Grade,* McPhee Gribble, 1989.
(Editor, and with Marsha Forrest) *Educating All Students in the Mainstream of Regular Education,* Paul Brookes, 1989.
Support Systems for Inclusive Schooling, Paul Brookes, 1990.

OTHER

(With Harriet Healy) *The Severely Motorically Impaired Child,* C. C Thomas, 1980.
(With Healy) *Teaching Eating Skills,* C. C Thomas, 1983.

Also author, with W. Stainback, of numerous monographs and textbook chapters; contributor, with W. Stainback, to professional publications, including *Education and Training of the Mentally Retarded, Journal of Abnormal Child Psychology, Teacher Educator,* and *Behavioral Disorders.* Consulting editor for numerous journals, including *Journal for the Association of the Severely Handicapped, Education and Training of the Mentally Retarded, Education Review, Exceptional Children, Teacher Education and Special Education, Journal of Education and Treatment of Children, Behavioral Disorders,* and *Teaching Exceptional Children.*

WORK IN PROGRESS: Research and advocacy activities with William Stainback regarding inclusive schools and communities and including all children into the mainstream of the educational system.

SIDELIGHTS: Susan Bray Stainback told *CA:* "In education, writing activities provide a great deal of personal satisfaction. They provide an opportunity to contribute ideas and varying perspectives as well as keep in touch with the work of other professionals in a critical, ever-changing field. They also provide for me personally an opportunity to work closely with my husband in attempting to produce a product we can both be proud of, though never allowing either of us to become stagnant in our profession or our friendship."

AVOCATIONAL INTERESTS: Family, friends, animals, animal advocacy, vegetarianism.

* * *

STAINBACK, William (Clarence) 1943-

PERSONAL: Born April 13, 1943, in Emporia, Va.; son of Willard T. and Maybelle (Moore) Stainback; married Susan Bray (a professor of education), December 16, 1967. *Education:* Atlantic Christian College, B.S., 1966; Radford College, M.S., 1967; University of Virginia, Ed.D., 1971. *Politics:* Democrat.

ADDRESSES: Home—2922 Minnetonka Dr., Cedar Falls, Iowa 50613. *Office*—College of Education, University of Northern Iowa, Cedar Falls, Iowa 50613.

CAREER: Virginia State College (now University), Petersburg, assistant professor of special education, 1971-73; University of Florida, Gainesville, assistant professor of special education, 1973-74; University of Northern Iowa, Cedar Falls, professor of special education, 1974—.

MEMBER: Association for Persons with Severe Handicaps, Council for Exceptional Children.

WRITINGS:

WITH WIFE, SUSAN BRAY STAINBACK

(And with J. S. Payne and R. A. Payne) *Establishing a Token Economy in the Classroom,* C. E. Merrill, 1973.
Classroom Discipline: A Positive Approach, C. C Thomas, 1974.
Educating Children with Severe Maladaptive Behavior, Grune, 1980.
Integrating Students with Severe Handicaps into Regular Schools, Council for Exceptional Children, 1985.
Understanding and Conducting Qualitative Research, Council for Exceptional Children, 1988.
How to Help Your Child Succeed in School, Meadowbrook, 1988.
(And with M. Kidd) *Making the Grade,* McPhee Gribble, 1989.
(Editor, and with Marsha Forrest) *Educating All Students in the Mainstream of Regular Education,* Paul Brookes, 1989.
Support Systems for Inclusive Schooling, Paul Brookes, 1990.

Also co-author of monographs and textbook chapters; contributor, with S. B. Stainback, to professional publications, including *Exceptional Children* and *Journal of the Association for the Severely Handicapped.*

* * *

STANDISH, Buck
See PAINE, Lauran (Bosworth)

* * *

STARRETT, (Charles) Vincent (Emerson) 1886-1974

PERSONAL: Born October 26, 1886, in Toronto, Ontario, Canada; died January 5, 1974; son of Robert Polk and Margaret Deniston (Young) Starrett. *Education:* Attended public schools in Toronto and Chicago, Ill.

ADDRESSES: Home—Chicago, Ill.

CAREER: Newspaperman, *Chicago Inter-Ocean,* 1905-06; *Chicago Daily News,* Chicago, Ill., newspaperman, 1906-16, war correspondent in Mexico, 1914-15; *Chicago Wave,* Chicago, editor, 1921-22; *Chicago Tribune,* Chicago, author of column "Books

Alive" in Sunday edition, beginning 1942. Instructor, Medill School of Journalism, 1922-23.

MEMBER: Society of Midland Authors (president, 1933-34), Mystery Writers of America (president, 1961), Arthur Machen Society, Sherlock Holmes Society of England, Baker Street Irregulars (founding member).

AWARDS, HONORS: Award for nonfiction, Friends of Literature, 1966, for *Born in a Bookshop;* received first Edgar Award presented by Mystery Writers of America.

WRITINGS:

Arthur Machen: A Novelist of Ecstasy and Sin, W. M. Hill, 1918.
The Escape of Alice: A Christmas Fantasy, privately printed, 1919.
Ambrose Bierce, W. M. Hill, 1920, reprinted, Kennikat, 1969.
The Unique Hamlet: A Hitherto Unchronicled Adventure of Mr. Sherlock Holmes, privately printed, 1920.
Ebony Flame (poems), Covici-McGee, 1922.
Banners in the Dawn: Sixty-Four Sonnets, W. M. Hill, 1923.
Stephen Crane: A Bibliography, Centaur, 1923.
Buried Caesars: Essays in Literary Appreciation, Covici-McGee, 1923, reprinted, AMS Press, 1970.
Coffins for Two, Covici-McGee, 1924.
Flame and Dust, Covici, 1924.
Seaports in the Moon: A Fantasia on Romantic Themes, Doubleday, Doran, 1928.
Penny Wise and Book Foolish, Covici Friede, 1929.
Murder on "B" Deck, Doubleday, Doran, 1929.
The Blue Door: Murder, Mystery, Detection in Ten Thrill-Packed Novelettes, Doubleday, Doran, 1930.
All about Mother Goose, Apellicon Press, 1930.
Dead Man Inside, Doubleday, Doran, 1931.
The End of Mr. Garment, Doubleday, Doran, 1932.
The Private Life of Sherlock Holmes, Macmillan, 1933, reprinted, Pinnacle Books, 1975, revised and enlarged edition, Macmillan, 1960.
The Great Hotel Murder (originally appeared in *Redbook* magazine under the title *Recipe for Murder),* Doubleday, Doran, 1935.
Snow for Christmas, [Glencoe, Ill.], 1935.
Midnight and Percy Jones, Covici Friede, 1936.
Persons from Porlock, and Other Interruptions (essays), Normandie House, 1938.
Oriental Encounters: Two Essays in Bad Taste, Normandie House, 1938.
Books Alive, Random House, 1940, reprinted, Books for Libraries, 1969.
Bookman's Holiday: The Private Satisfactions of an Incurable Collector, Random House, 1942, reprinted, 1971.
Autolycus in Limbo (poems), Dutton, 1943.
The Case Book of Jimmie Lavender, Gold Label Books, 1944, reprinted, Bookfinger, 1973.
Murder in Peking, Lantern Press, 1946.
(With Ames W. Williams) *Stephen Crane: A Bibliography,* J. Valentine, 1948.
Sonnets, and Other Verse, Dierkes Press, 1949.
Best-Loved Books of the Twentieth Century, Bantam, 1955.
The Great All-Star Animal League Ball Game (juvenile), illustrated by Kurt Wiese, Dodd, 1957.
Book Column, Caxton Club, 1958.
The Quick and the Dead, Arkham House, 1965.
Born in a Bookshop: Chapters from the Chicago Renascence (autobiographical), University of Oklahoma Press, 1965.
Late, Later and Possibly Last: Essays, Autolycus Press, 1973.

An Essay on Limited Editions, Black Cat Press, 1982.

EDITOR

In Praise of Stevenson, Bookfellows, 1919, reprinted, R. West.
(And author of introduction) Stephen Crane, *Men, Women, and Boats,* Boni & Liveright, 1921, reprinted, Books for Libraries, 1970.
Et Cetera: A Collector's Scrap-Book, Covici, 1924.
Fourteen Great Detective Stories, Modern Library, 1928.
A Modern Book of Wonders: Amazing Facts in a Remarkable World, University of Knowledge, 1938.
(With Christopher Morley, Elmer Davis, and others) *221B: Studies in Sherlock Holmes,* Macmillan, 1940, reprinted, Biblo & Tannen, 1969.
World's Great Spy Stories, World Publishing, 1944.

OTHER

Also author of *Brillig,* 1949, *Poems,* 1951, *The Old Dog and Other Essays,* reissued, 1971, and *Books and Bipeds.*

SIDELIGHTS: Born in Toronto of Scottish-Irish parentage, Vincent Starrett was the grandson of famous Canadian publisher and bookseller John Young. Starrett wanted to be an illustrator, but began writing stories instead. A $75 check from *Collier's Weekly* for the publication of a mystery story decided his literary future. An authority on Sherlock Holmes, he wrote prolifically, including poetry, short stories, detective novels, humorous sketches, biographies, and novels.

Commenting on Starrett's *Books Alive,* a *Commonweal* critic noted: "Mr. Starrett has, apparently, written without any serious intent: he succeeds admirably in giving us an entertaining book. It is a volume of literary gossip, a book not for students or bibliographers, but for those literary ladies—and gentlemen—who appreciate a fund of anecdote and chatty comment. The anecdotes are not, by any means, new; in fact, their familiarity is the chief charm of some: known trivia have a power of solacing by again distracting, which, especially today, many a reader will find welcome."

About *221B: Studies in Sherlock Holmes,* a *Books* reviewer observed: "In this branch of biography nobody ever uses the word definitive. It is an appetite that grows as it eats, and Holmesians will not only feed upon but fall upon this feast, opening the book with a gesture like tucking a napkin under the chin." A *Books* writer also commented upon Starrett's *The Private Life of Sherlock Holmes,* describing the original edition as "a book for pleasure, for such peaceful slippered contentment as the two friends found together in Baker Street." A *Chicago Tribune* review of the 1960 revised edition of *The Private Life of Sherlock Holmes* noted, "The volume is rich with enlightenment on every aspect of the lore of Holmes and the period in which he flourished as the world's only consulting detective. The author's scholarship in Holmesiana is supreme, and he writes as if communicating a happy sense of enchantment. The format is a masterpiece of decorative design."

A leading member of the Chicago Literary Renaissance, Starrett lived all over the world, including such cities as St. Louis, Reno, New York, London, Paris, Rome, and Peking. When he died at age 87, he was interred in Chicago's well-known Victorian resting place Graceland Cemetery, which holds the remains of numerous Chicago luminaries. The *AB Bookman's Weekly* remarks in a retrospective on the centennial anniversary of his birth that he was "one of the most dedicated bookmen of this century—in the finest sense of Eugene Field's acronym, a DOFAB—a 'damned old fool about books.' " The critic concludes by commending Starrett's "bookworld dedication and achievements, his personal generosity, gentle nature and his consuming lifelong focus on literature and scholarship."

MEDIA ADAPTATIONS: The Great Hotel Murder was produced as a film of the same title by the Fox Film Corp., 1935.

BIOGRAPHICAL/CRITICAL SOURCES:

BOOKS

Rubber, Peter A., *Last Bookman: A Journey into the Life and Times of Vincent Starrett, Author, Journalist, Bibliophile,* Candlelight Press, 1968.

Starrett, Vincent, *Born in a Bookshop: Chapters from the Chicago Renascence* (autobiographical), University of Oklahoma Press, 1965.

PERIODICALS

AB Bookman's Weekly, January 28, 1974, October 20, 1986.
Books, October 22, 1933, March 31, 1940.
Chicago Sunday Tribune, May 1, 1960.
Commonweal, December 6, 1940.
New York Times, January 6, 1974.
Publishers Weekly, February 4, 1974.
Washington Post, January 13, 1974.*

* * *

STEDMAN JONES, Gareth 1942-

PERSONAL: Born December 17, 1942, in London, England; son of Lewis (a teacher) and J. O. (Legros) Stedman Jones. *Education:* Lincoln College, Oxford, B.A. (with first class honors), 1964; Nuffield College, Oxford, D. Phil., 1970. *Politics:* Socialist. *Religion:* None.

ADDRESSES: Home—91 Alderney St., London S.W.1, England. *Agent*—John Wolfers, 3 Regent Sq., London W.C.2, England.

CAREER: Oxford University, Nuffield College, Oxford, England, research fellow, 1967-70; Cambridge University, Cambridge, England, university lecturer in history, 1979—. Fellow, King's College, Cambridge, 1976—.

AWARDS, HONORS: Humboldt Award, West Germany, 1973-74.

WRITINGS:

Outcast London, Oxford University Press, 1971.
(Editor with Raphael Samuel) *Culture, Ideology, and Politics: Essays for Eric Hobabawn,* Methuen, 1983.
Languages of Class: Studies in English Working Class History, Cambridge University Press, 1984.

Contributor of articles to periodicals, including *New Left Review, Modern Occasions, Times Literary Supplement, New Statesman,* and *History Workshop Journal.*

WORK IN PROGRESS: A biography of Fredrich Engels.*

* * *

STEIN, Joseph 1912-

PERSONAL: Born May 30, 1912, in New York, N.Y.; son of Charles and Emma (Rosenblum) Stein; married Sadie Singer (died, 1974); married Elisa Loti (an actress), 1976; children: Daniel, Harry, Joshua. *Education:* City College (now City Col-

lege of the City University of New York), B.S.S., 1935; Columbia University, M.S.W., 1937.

ADDRESSES: Office—250 West 57th St., New York, N.Y. 10019. *Agent*—Paramuse Artists, 1414 Avenue of the Americas, New York, N.Y. 10019.

CAREER: Playwright. Consultation Center of Jewish Family Service, New York, N.Y., psychiatric social worker, 1939-44; Jewish Board of Guardians, New York City, public relations director, 1945-47; writer for radio, television, and stage, beginning 1947, including work for radio's "Henry Morgan Show" and "Kraft Music Hall," and television's "Your Show of Shows," "Sid Caesar Show," and others.

MEMBER: Dramatists Guild of the Authors League of America.

AWARDS, HONORS: Antoinette Perry (Tony) Award of American Theatre Wing for best musical, New York Drama Critics Award, and Newspaper Guild Award, all 1965, all for "Fiddler on the Roof"; Tony Award nomination for best musical, 1969, for "Zorba," and 1987, for "Rags."

WRITINGS:

PLAYS

(With Will Glickman) "Lend an Ear," produced in New York City at National Theatre, 1948.
(With Glickman) *Mrs. Gibbons' Boys* (produced on Broadway at Music Box Theatre, 1949), Samuel French, 1958.
(With Glickman) "Alive and Kicking," produced on Broadway at Winter Garden Theatre, 1950.
(With Glickman) "Inside U.S.A.," produced in New York City at Century Theatre, 1951.
(With Glickman) *Plain and Fancy* (produced on Broadway at Mark Hellinger Theatre, 1955), Random House, 1955.
(With Glickman) *Mr. Wonderful* (produced on Broadway at Broadway Theatre, 1956), Hart Stenographic Bureau, 1956.
(With Glickman) *The Body Beautiful* (produced on Broadway at Broadway Theatre, 1958), Samuel French, 1958.
Juno (based on Sean O'Casey's play "Juno and the Paycock"; produced on Broadway at Winter Garden Theatre, 1959), Hart Stenographic Bureau, 1959.
(With Robert Russell) "Take Me Along," produced on Broadway at Shubert Theatre, 1959.
Enter Laughing (based on the autobiography by Carl Reiner; produced on Broadway at Henry Miller's Theatre, 1963), Samuel French, 1963, reprinted, 1984; film version produced by Columbia, 1967.
Fiddler on the Roof (based on short stories by Sholom Aleichem; produced on Broadway at Imperial Theatre, 1964; film version produced by United Artists, 1971), Crown, 1965.
Zorba (based on Nikos Kazantzakis' book *Zorba the Greek;* produced on Broadway at Imperial Theatre, 1968), Random House, 1969.
(With Hugh Wheeler and others) "Irene," produced on Broadway at Minskoff Theatre, 1973.
"King of Hearts" (based on the film of the same name), produced on Broadway at Minskoff Theatre, 1978.
(With Alan Jay Lerner) "Carmelina" (based on the film "Buona Sera, Mrs. Campbell"), produced on Broadway at St. James Theatre, April, 1979.
"The Baker's Wife" (based on a 1937 French film), produced in New York at York Theatre Company, 1985.
"Before the Dawn" (adaptation of the play "A Ladies' Tailor" by Aleksandr Borshchagovsky), produced in New York at American Place Theatre, 1985.

"Rags," produced on Broadway at Mark Hellinger Theatre, 1986.

SIDELIGHTS: Playwright Joseph Stein, in a career that spans four decades, has been connected with some of Broadway's biggest hits (like "Fiddler on the Roof," "Zorba," and "Irene") as well as some of its major disappointments (most notably in his most recent projects, the musicals "Carmelina" and "Rags"). Much of his work focuses on Jewish themes and the immigrant experience in America. In one of his few nonmusical productions, the play "Before the Dawn," Stein looks at the same sort of Soviet anti-Semitism that propelled his musical comedy "Fiddler on the Roof."

Another musical, 1986's "Rags," was notable both for the presence of an opera star, Teresa Stratas, in the lead role as a turn-of-the-century Jewish immigrant to New York, and for the production's last-minute rally to gain financial support after critics lambasted the musical during previews. As Stephen Holden relates in a *New York Times* article, the production had been cursed from the beginning with few backers and "no central characters or stars." Even in its early stages, according to lyricist Stephen Schwartz in the same article, "there was always the question of whether to tell more of a story or less of one." The show toured the country on tryouts to mixed reviews. Then, on its Broadway debut, "Rags" had "already used up its initial $4.5 million capitalizations," according to Holden. "Prior to opening night . . ., the box-office for 'Rags' had been a meager $25,000 a day. The day after, on Friday, only $11,000 worth of tickets were sold."

But the "Rags" company was determined not to see a closing notice posted in the Mark Hellinger Theatre. Producer Lee Guber, who had already realized that, barring a miracle, the show would close within a week, "decided to face the cast and tell them in person," as he tells Holden. Guber first approached star Stratas. "She said she would do anything for the show and offered to defer her salary. When I told the cast of her offer, they agreed to do the same." After the closing curtain that night, Stratas and other cast members held a curtain speech for the audience, exhorting them to promote the financially struggling "Rags." The audience responded in kind, as Holden notes. "Chanting, 'Keep Rags open, keep Rags open!' several hundred people paraded down Broadway and circled the ticket booth."

But it was all to no avail. By early the next week, the producers were able to raise only another $450,000, less than half of what was needed to keep the production running for another month, and ticket sales remained sluggish. The show closed Tuesday, August 26, just five days after opening. "Crucial to the failure of 'Rags' was a deep philosophical conflict between 'art' and entertainment," Holden concludes. "The show's semi-operatic score, and its formidable star, . . . suggested a high-minded conceptual show—a musicalized 'Mother Courage.' Mr. Stein and [director Gene] Saks, on the other hand, have had their biggest Broadway successes in works that told warmhearted stories in a more traditional, populist style."

BIOGRAPHICAL/CRITICAL SOURCES:

BOOKS

Otis L. Guernsey, Jr., editor, *Broadway Song and Story: Playwrights/Lyricists/Composers Discuss Their Hits,* Dodd, Mead, 1986.

PERIODICALS

New York Times, April 10, 1979, April 22, 1979, March 25, 1985, August 17, 1986, August 22, 1986, September 21, 1986.

Washington Post, March 4, 1979, April 22, 1979.*

*   *   *

STEINER, George 1929-

PERSONAL: Born April 23, 1929, in Paris, France; came to the United States in 1940, naturalized citizen, 1944; son of Frederick George (a banker) and Elsie (Franzos) Steiner; married Zara Alice Shakow (a university professor), July 7, 1955; children: David Milton, Deborah Tarn. *Education:* University of Chicago, B.A., 1948; Harvard University, M.A., 1950; Oxford University, Ph.D., 1955.

ADDRESSES: Home—32 Barrow Rd., Cambridge, England.

CAREER: Economist, London, England, member of editorial staff, 1952-56; Princeton University, Princeton, N.J., fellow of Institute for Advanced Study, 1956-58, Gauss Lecturer, 1959-60; Cambridge University, Cambridge, England, fellow of Churchill College, 1961-69, Extraordinary Fellow, 1969—; University of Geneva, Geneva, Switzerland, professor of English and comparative literature, 1974—. Visiting professor at New York University, 1966-67, University of California, 1973-74, and at Harvard University, Yale University, Princeton University, and Stanford University.

MEMBER: English Association (president, 1975), Royal Society of Literature (fellow), German Academy of Literature (corresponding member), Athenaeum Club (London), Savile Club (London), Harvard Club (New York).

AWARDS, HONORS: Bell Prize, 1950; Rhodes scholar, 1955; Fullbright professorship, 1958-59; O. Henry Short Story Prize, 1959; Morton Dauwen Zabel Award from National Institute of Arts and Letters, 1970; Guggenheim fellowship, 1971-72; Cortina Ulisse Prize, 1972; Remembrance Award, 1974, for *The Language of Silence;* PEN-Faulkner Award nomination, 1983, for *The Portage to San Cristobal of A. H.;* named Chevalier de la Legion d'Honneur, 1984. Numerous honorary degrees, including University of East Anglia and Mount Holyoke College.

WRITINGS:

Tolstoy or Dostoevsky: An Essay in the Old Criticism, Knopf, 1959, reprinted, University of Chicago Press, 1985.
The Death of Tragedy, Knopf, 1961, reprinted, Oxford University Press, 1980.
(Editor with Robert Fagles) *Homer: A Collection of Critical Essays,* Prentice-Hall, 1962.
Anno Domini: Three Stories, Atheneum, 1964.
(Editor and author of introduction) *The Penguin Book of Modern Verse Translation,* Penguin Books, 1966, reprinted as *Poem into Poem: World Poetry in Modern Verse Translation,* 1970.
Language and Silence: Essays on Language, Literature, and the Inhuman, Atheneum, 1967.
Extraterritorial: Papers on Literature and the Language Revolution, Atheneum, 1971.
In Bluebeard's Castle: Some Notes towards the Redefinition of Culture, Yale University Press, 1971.
Fields of Force: Fischer and Spassky in Reykjavik, Viking, 1973 (published in England as *The Sporting Scene: White Knights in Reykjavik,* Faber, 1973).
After Babel: Aspects of Language and Translation, Oxford University Press, 1975.
On Difficulty and Other Essays, Oxford University Press, 1978.
Martin Heidegger, Viking, 1978 (published in England as *Heidegger,* Fontana, 1978).

The Portage to San Cristobal of A. H. (novel), Simon & Schuster, 1981.

George Steiner: A Reader, Oxford University Press, 1984.

Antigones: How the Antigone Legend Has Endured in Western Literature, Art, and Thought, Oxford University Press, 1984.

Real Presences, University of Chicago Press, 1989.

Columnist and book reviewer for the *New Yorker;* contributor of essays, reviews, and articles to numerous periodicals, including *Commentary, Harper's,* and *Nation.*

SIDELIGHTS: "George Steiner is the most brilliant cultural journalist at present writing in English, or perhaps in any language," a *Times Literary Supplement* reviewer writes. Steiner, who teaches at Cambridge University and the University of Geneva, is known on two continents for his literary criticism and far-ranging essays on linguistics, ethics, translation, the fine arts, and science. According to Pearl K. Bell in the *New Leader,* few present-day literary critics "can match George Steiner in erudition and sweep. Actually, he resists confinement within the fields of literature, preferring more venturesome forays into the history of ideas. . . . Steiner has proceeded on the confident assumption that no activity of the human mind is in any way alien or inaccessible to his own." Steiner writes for the educated general reader rather than for the academic specialist; London *Times* contributor Philip Howard calls the author "an intellectual who bestrides the boundaries of cultures and disciplines." In addition to his numerous books, including *Language and Silence: Essays on Language, Literature, and the Inhuman* and *After Babel: Aspects of Language and Translation,* Steiner produces regular columns for the *New Yorker* magazine, where he serves primarily as a book reviewer. Almost always controversial for his bold assertions and assessments of highly specialized theories, Steiner "has been called both a mellifluous genius and an oversimplifying intellectual exhibitionist," to quote Curt Suplee in the *Washington Post.* *National Review* correspondent Scott Lahti claims, however, that most readers find Steiner's "provocative manner of expression . . . by turns richly allusive, metaphoric, intensely concerned, prophetic, apocalyptic—and almost always captivating."

Much of Steiner's criticism reflects his own sensitivity to the shaping events of modern history. "One way or another," writes a *Times Literary Supplement* reviewer, "in his view, the word has been pushed into a corner; non-verbal forms of discourse have taken over so many fields where writing once reigned supreme. . . . There is also the terrible cloud that has been cast over language and literature by the actions of a thoroughly literate and cultured people between 1933 and 1945. This bears doubly on the critic: first there is the need to expose all such dehumanization of the word . . . and secondly the changed sense of proportion and perspective that it must give to any concern with literature, however ancient or academic." In the *New Republic,* Theodore Solotaroff proposes that Steiner, himself a Jew who escaped France just before the Nazi atrocities descended, regards himself as heir to a European intellectual community that was annihilated by the Holocaust. Solotaroff suggests that Steiner stands "in a deep sense for the whole generation of his peers— these children who did not survive, who left this great tradition bereft of its natural proteges, who make such a haunting absence today in the life of the European mind. . . . There is a driving, obsessive quality to Steiner's acquisitiveness, a fever in his point of view which goes beyond curiosity and self-assertion." Indeed, one of Steiner's central preoccupations, discussed in both his fiction and his nonfiction, is the relation between high culture and barbarism—how, for instance, a concentration camp guard could enjoy a novel or a symphony after sending people to the gas chambers. *Punch* contributor Melvyn Bragg writes: "The drive, the necessity, the fate which kept Sisyphus going has been, with Steiner, the Holocaust. In that blaze, he has written, not only did a people burn, but words turned to ashes, meaning and value were powdered to be ground into dirt by the heels of vacant inheritors." Steiner himself told the *New York Times Book Review* that central to everything he is and believes and has written "is my astonishment, naive as it seems to people, that you can use human speech both to bless, to love, to build, to forgive and also to torture, to hate, to destroy and to annihilate."

Rootlessness—or, as he puts it, extraterritoriality, also serves as a foundation for Steiner's essays on language and literature. *Dictionary of Literary Biography* contributor Bruce Robbins sees in Steiner "the willed trace of a radical homelessness that he has made a personal motif for almost thirty years." Steiner was born in Paris to Viennese parents; he was only eleven when his family fled to the United States in 1940. Thus he grew up with a full command of three languages—English, French, and German— and his adult life has included extensive work on the nature and limitations of human communication. "The recent preoccupation of all thoughtful practitioners of the humanities with language is [Steiner's] preoccupation," writes David H. Stewart in the *Western Humanities Review.* "Semantics, semiotics, psycholinguistics, structuralist literary criticism: these are his concerns. These he orchestrates into his continuing effort to explain how human beings communicate and what their *manner* of communication does to the content and style of their minds." In *Book World,* Richard Freedman contends that Steiner's interests have led him to investigate "the very roots of communication: . . . how the special patterns of the some 4,000 languages now spoken in the world determine not only the course of the literature, but of the psychology, philosophy, and even the physiology of the people who speak and write them." As Malcolm Bradbury puts it in the London *Times,* part of Steiner's appeal is that he "celebrates, and *is,* the great scholar-reader for whom endless reinterpretation of major ideas and myths is fundamental to existence. He becomes himself the case in point: native in three languages, read in many more, learned over a massive range, requiring of those who study or debate with him an unremitting dedication. All this is expressed with a charismatic power which makes even difficulty seem easy, and invites rebellion against low educational standards, intellectual simplifications, and false prophesy."

Steiner was educated on two continents, having studied at the University of Chicago, Harvard, and Oxford University on a Rhodes scholarship. His first book, published the year he turned thirty, concerns not English literature but the works of two great Russian writers, Tolstoy and Dostoevsky. Entitled *Tolstoy or Dostoevsky: An Essay in the Old Criticism,* the book "announces the particular place Steiner has assigned himself," writes Robbins. "Neither Europe nor America, his Russia is a no-man's-land that permits him to remain, to use his term, unhoused." In addition to offering an analysis of the two writers' lives, thoughts, and historical milieux, the work challenges the *au courant* "New Criticism" by assigning moral, philosophical, and historical worth to the texts. A *Times Literary Supplement* correspondent observes that Steiner "is concerned not with a catalogue of casual, incidental parallels between life and fiction but with the overmastering ideas which so preoccupied the two men that they could not help finding parallel expression in their lives and their works." Another *Times Literary Supplement* reviewer likewise declares that Steiner "feels he is addressing not professional scholars merely, safely shut in the confines of one particular discipline, but all thinking men who are aware of the larger world of social and political realities about them. Dr. Steiner's style derives part of its force from his seeing intellectual questions against the background of historical crises and catastrophes."

In 1967 Steiner published *Language and Silence,* a collection of essays that establish the author's "philosophy of language." The book explores in depth the vision of the humanely educated Nazi and the diminution of the word's vitality in an audio-visual era. Solotaroff maintains that *Language and Silence* "casts a bright and searching light into the murky disarray of current letters and literacy: it looks back to a darkness and disruption of Western culture that continues to plague and challenge the moral purpose of literature, among other fields, and it looks forward to possibilities of art and thought that may carry us beyond our broken heritage. It provides an articulate and comprehensive discussion of the impact of science and mass communications on the ability of language to describe the realities of the earth and the world." Steiner's conclusion—that silence and the refusal to write is the last-resort moral act in the face of bestiality—has aroused conflicting opinions among his reviewers. In the *New York Times Book Review,* Robert Gorham Davis suggests that the author "displaces onto language many of his feelings about history and religion. He makes it an independent living organism which can be poisoned or killed." The critic adds, however, that throughout the volume, "thoughts are expressed with such a fine and knowledgeable specificity that when we are forced to disagree with Steiner, we always know exactly upon what grounds. He teaches and enlightens even where he does not convince." *New York Times* contributor Eliot Fremont-Smith concludes that *Language and Silence* "will confirm, if confirmation is necessary, [Steiner's] reputation as one of the most erudite, resourceful and unrelentingly serious critics working today."

Most observers agree that *After Babel* is Steiner's monumental work, a "deeply ambivalent hymn to language," as Geoffrey H. Hartman puts it in the *New York Times Book Review.* The book offers a wide-ranging inquiry into the fields of linguistics and translation, with commentary on the vagaries of communication both inside and between languages. *Washington Post Book World* reviewer Peter Brunette explains that in *After Babel* Steiner proposes "the radical notion that the world's many diverse languages (4000 plus, at last count) were created to disguise and hide things from outsiders, rather than to assist communication, as we often assume. A corollary is that the vast majority of our day-to-day language production is internal, and is not meant to communicate at all." In *Listener,* Hyam Maccoby contends that Steiner's predilection is for a view "that a language is the soul of a particular culture, and affects by its very syntax what can be said or thought in that culture; and that the differences between languages are more important than their similarities (which he calls 'deep but trivial')." The book has brought Steiner into a debate with linguists such as Noam Chomsky who are searching for the key to a "universal grammar" that all human beings share. Many critics feel that in *After Babel* Steiner presents a forceful challenge to the notion of innate, universal grammar. According to Raymond Oliver in the *Southern Review,* the book "is dense but lucid and often graceful; its erudition is balanced by sharpness of insights, its theoretical intelligence by critical finesse; and it pleads the cause of poetry, language, and translation with impassioned eloquence. . . . We are ready to be sustained and delighted by the sumptuous literary feast [Steiner] has prepared us." *New Yorker* columnist Naomi Bliven likewise points out that Steiner's subject "is extravagantly rich, and he ponders it on the most generous scale, discussing how we use and misuse, understand and misunderstand words, and so,

without always being aware of what we are doing, create art, history, nationality, and our sense of belonging to a civilization. . . . He is frequently ironic and witty, but for the most part his language and his ideas display even-handedness, seriousness without heaviness, learning without pedantry, and sober charm."

"Steiner's performance is mindful of a larger public," writes Robbins. Not surprisingly, therefore, the author does not shy from forceful communication or controversial conclusions. For instance, in his novel *The Portage to San Cristobal of A. H.,* Steiner gives readers an opportunity to ponder world history from Adolf Hitler's eloquent point of view. Some critics have found the novel morally outrageous, while others cite it for its stimulating—if not necessarily laudable—ideas. Steiner's essays also have their detractors. Bradbury suggests that his nonfiction has "a quality of onward-driving personal history, and it is not surprising that they have left many arguments in their wake." Bradbury adds that Steiner's impact "in provoking British scholars to a much more internationalist and comparative viewpoint has been great, but not always gratefully received." Lahti, for one, finds Steiner's conclusions "often fragmentary, and his frequent resort to extravagant assertions and perverse generalizations lessens the force of his arguments." Similarly, *New York Review of Books* essayist D. J. Enright faults Steiner for "a histrionic habit, an overheated tone, a melodramatization of what (God knows) is often dramatic enough, a proclivity to fly to extreme positions. The effect is to antagonize the reader on the brink of assent."

Other reviewers suggest that Steiner intends to challenge his audience, deliberately provoking strong opinions. In the *New Republic,* Robert Boyers writes: "Readers will sense, on every page, an invitation to respond, to argue, to resist. But so nimble and alert to possibility is the critic's articulating voice that one will rather pay careful attention than resist. Ultimately, no doubt, 'collaborative disagreement' may seem possible, but few will feel dismissive or ungrateful. . . . No reader will fail to feel Steiner's encouragement as he moves out on his own." According to Edward W. Said in *Nation,* Steiner "is that rare thing, a critic propelled by diverse enthusiasms, a man able to understand the implications of trends in different fields, an autodidact for whom no subject is too arcane. Yet Steiner is to be read for his quirks, rather than in spite of them. He does not peddle a system nor a set of norms by which all things can be managed, every text decoded. He writes to be understood by nonspecialists, and his terms of reference come from his experience—which is trilingual, eccentric and highly urbane—not from something as stable as doctrine or authority. This is the other side of his egotism: that he, George Steiner, conscientiously tries to register every response accurately, work through every difficulty, test every feeling, authenticate each experience of the best that is known and thought. As such, then, the critic functions as a real if very unusual person, not an academic abstraction." Bradbury states that what can always be said of Steiner "is that what he questions and quarrels with, he reads and knows. And, whatever the quarrels, Steiner is a major figure, who has sustained a profoundly enquiring philosophy of literature." Fremont-Smith expresses a similar opinion. "Whether or not one agrees with Mr. Steiner's analyses," the reviewer concludes, "he does set one thinking, and thinking, moreover, about issues that are paramount."

MEDIA ADAPTATIONS: The Portage to San Cristobal of A. H. was adapted for the stage under the same title by Christopher Hampton, first produced in America at Hartford Stage, Hartford, Connecticut, January 7, 1983.

AVOCATIONAL INTERESTS: Music, chess, hiking.

BIOGRAPHICAL/CRITICAL SOURCES:

BOOKS

Contemporary Literary Criticism, Volume 24, Gale, 1983.
Dictionary of Literary Biography, Volume 67: *American Critics since 1955,* Gale, 1988.

PERIODICALS

Book World, January 2, 1972.
Christian Science Monitor, May 25, 1975.
Commentary, October, 1968, November, 1975.
Commonweal, May 12, 1961, October 27, 1967.
Detroit News, April 25, 1982.
Listener, April 27, 1972, January 30, 1975, March 22, 1979, July 3, 1980.
London Magazine, December, 1967.
Los Angeles Times, October 23, 1980.
Los Angeles Times Book Review, April 11, 1982, November 18, 1984.
Nation, March 2, 1985.
National Review, December 31, 1971, August 31, 1979, June 11, 1982, July 26, 1985.
New Leader, June 23, 1975.
New Republic, May 13, 1967, January 27, 1979, May 12, 1979, April 21, 1982, November 19, 1984.
New Statesman, November 17, 1961, October 20, 1967, October 22, 1971, January 31, 1975, December 1, 1978, June 27, 1980.
Newsweek, April 26, 1982.
New Yorker, January 30, 1965, May 5, 1975.
New York Review of Books, October 12, 1967, November 18, 1971, October 30, 1975, April 19, 1979, August 12, 1982, December 6, 1984.
New York Times, March 20, 1967, June 22, 1971, July 1, 1974, May 7, 1975, April 16, 1982, January 7, 1983.
New York Times Book Review, May 28, 1967, August 1, 1971, October 13, 1974, June 8, 1975, January 21, 1979, May 2, 1982, December 16, 1984.
Observer, December 17, 1978.
Punch, June 17, 1981.
Southern Review, winter, 1978.
Spectator, April, 1960, December 2, 1978, July 19, 1980.
Time, July 26, 1971, March 29, 1982.
Times (London), March 20, 1982, June 23, 1984, June 28, 1984.
Times Literary Supplement, March 11, 1960, September 28, 1967, December 17, 1971, May 19, 1972, May 18, 1973, January 31, 1975, November 17, 1978, June 12, 1981.
Voice Literary Supplement, April, 1982, December, 1984.
Washington Post, May 13, 1982.
Washington Post Book World, January 14, 1979, May 2, 1982, December 30, 1984, January 19, 1986.
Western Humanities Review, autumn, 1979.
Yale Review, autumn, 1967.*

—*Sketch by Anne Janette Johnson*

*   *   *

STEWART, Jean
See NEWMAN, Mona Alice Jean

*   *   *

STONE, Robert B.   1916-

PERSONAL: Born February 26, 1916, in New York, N.Y.; son of David and Freida (Corenthal) Blustein; married Athalie Tit-

man, 1950; married second wife, Lola Solomon, March 13, 1953; children: (second marriage) Dennis. *Education:* Massachusetts Institute of Technology, S.B., 1937.

ADDRESSES: Agent—Curtis Brown Ltd., Ten Astor Place, New York, N.Y. 10003.

CAREER: Writer. Publisher of house plans magazines, Huntington, N.Y., 1950-59; worked in public relations, specializing in school and community relations, Huntington, 1960-69. Conductor of awareness and sensitivity workshops sponsored by Huntington Public Library and other Huntington groups. Founder, past president, and director, 1957-59, Huntington Township Mental Health Clinic; past president, Huntington Town Forum. *Military service:* U.S. Army, Signal Corps, 1943-45; became master sergeant.

MEMBER: National School Public Relations Association, Authors Guild, Authors League of America.

WRITINGS:

(With Samuel Paul) *Complete Book of Home Modernizing,* Stuttman, for Literary Guild, 1953.
(With Paul) *Homes for Living,* Simmons-Boardman, 1953.
(With Sidney Petrie) *How to Reduce and Control Your Weight with Self-Hypnotism,* Prentice-Hall, 1964.
(With Petrie) *Martinis and Whipped Cream,* Parker Publishing, 1965.
(With Petrie) *How to Strengthen Your Life with Mental Isometrics,* Parker Publishing, 1966.
(With Petrie) *What Modern Hypnotism Can Do for You,* Hawthorn, 1968.
(With Christopher R. Vagts) *Anatomy of a Teacher Strike,* Parker Publishing, 1969.
(With Petrie) *The Lazy Lady's Easy Diet,* Parker Publishing, 1969.
(With Petrie) *The Truth about Hypnotism,* Frewin, 1969.
(With Petrie) *The Miracle Diet for Fast Weight Loss,* Parker Publishing, 1970.
(With Christopher Hills) *Conduct Your Own Awareness Sessions,* New American Library, 1971.
Jesus Has a Man in Waikiki: The Story of Bob Turnbull, Revell, 1973.
(With Giraud Campbell) *A Doctor's Proven New Home Cure for Arthritis,* Prentice-Hall, 1973.
(With Petrie) *Hypno-Cybernetics: Helping Yourself to a Rich New Life,* Prentice-Hall, 1973.
(With Petrie) *Hypno-Dietetics,* Peter H. Wyden, 1975.
(With Connie Haines) *For Once in My Life,* Warner Paperback, 1976.
The Power of Miracle Metaphysics, Parker Publishing, 1976.
(With L. L. Schneider) *Old Fashioned Health Remedies that Work Best,* Prentice-Hall, 1977.
The Magic of Psychotronic Power, Parker Publishing, 1978.
(With Norman Goldstein) *The Skin You Live In: How to Recognize and Prevent Skin Problems and Keep Your Skin Youthful and Attractive,* Hart Publishing, 1978.
(With Petrie) *The Wonder Protein Diet: Miracle Way to Better Health and Longer Life,* Parker Publishing, 1979.
(With Constance Reed) *How to Be Beautiful after the Baby Comes,* F. Watts, 1979.
(With wife, Lola Stone) *Hawaiian and Polynesian Miracle Health Secrets,* Parker Publishing, 1980.
(With Judith Stransky) *The Alexander Technique: Joy in the Life of Your Body,* Beaufort Books, 1981.
(With Petrie) *Helping Yourself with Autogenics,* Parker Publishing, 1983.

(With Jose Silva) *The Silva Mind Control Method for Business Managers,* Prentice-Hall, 1983.

Also author, with Silva, of forthcoming *Man the Healer,* for Institute of Psychorientology. Architectural editor, *Popular Science Do-It-Yourself Encyclopedia,* 1954.

SIDELIGHTS: Robert B. Stone once commented that he "evolved from home improvement, to body improvement, to mind improvement" and is "getting close to the human spirit."*

*   *   *

STOVER, Marjorie Filley 1914-

PERSONAL: Born June 23, 1914, in Lincoln, Neb.; daughter of H. Clyde (a college professor) and Creta (Warner) Filley; married John F. Stover, August 21, 1937; children: John C., Robert V., Charry E. *Education:* University of Nebraska, A.B., 1935. *Religion:* Methodist.

ADDRESSES: Home—615 Carrolton Blvd., West Lafayette, Ind. 47906.

CAREER: Nebraska School of Agriculture, Curtis, instructor in English and speech, 1935-37; Bergen Junior College, Teaneck, N.J., instructor in speech and drama, 1937-41.

MEMBER: Chicago Round Table, Creative Writers, Society of Children's Book Writers.

AWARDS, HONORS: Dorothy Canfield Fisher master award list, 1973-74.

WRITINGS:

JUVENILE

Trail Boss in Pigtails, Atheneun, 1972.
Chad and the Elephant Engine, Atheneum, 1975.
Patrick and the Great Molasses Explosion, Dillon, 1985.
When the Dolls Woke, edited by Abby Levine, Albert Whitman, 1985.
Midnight in the Doll House, Albert Whitman, 1990.

SIDELIGHTS: Marjorie Filley Stover told *CA:* "I have a basically optimistic viewpoint of life, and I regret the dark and pessimistic trend that has crept into children's books in recent years. Life is never perfect, but surely love and kindness are just as real as violence and despair. It is important that children have an upbeat swing to life. They need heroes and heroines whom they can admire. They need the challenge of working toward a better life."

Stover also added that "excerpts from *Trail Boss in Pigtails* have also appeared in five elementary readers published by Laidlaw, Ginn, Macmillan, Scribner, and Harcout Brace Jovanovich."

BIOGRAPHICAL/CRITICAL SOURCES:

PERIODICALS

Washington Post Book World, November 5, 1972.

*   *   *

STOWERS, Carlton 1942-

PERSONAL: Born April 14, 1942, in Brownwood, Tex.; son of Ira (in sales) and Fay (a secretary; maiden name, Stephenson) Stowers; married Betty Darby, October 7, 1962; married Lynne Livingston, November 30, 1975; married Pat Cruce, March 2, 1981; children: Anson, Ashley. *Education:* Attended University of Texas, 1961-63. *Religion:* Episcopalian.

ADDRESSES: Home—1015 Randy Rd., Cedar Hill, Tex. 75104.

CAREER: Associated with *Amarillo Daily News,* Amarillo, Tex., 1966-69, and *Lubbock Avalanche Journal,* Lubbock, Tex., 1970-73; free-lance writer, 1974-76; *Dallas Morning News,* Dallas, Tex., sportswriter and columnist, 1976-81; affiliated with *Dallas Cowboys Weekly,* 1981-89. Writer for and associate producer of weekly television series "Countdown to '84," USA Cable network, 1984.

MEMBER: International Association of Crime Writers, Authors Guild, Mystery Writers of America, Professional Football Writers Association, Texas Sportswriters Association.

AWARDS, HONORS: Edgar Allan Poe Award for Best Fact Crime Book, Mystery Writers of America, and Oppie Award for Reporting, Southwestern Booksellers, both 1986, both for *Careless Whispers;* recipient of other national and state awards for magazine and newspaper journalism.

WRITINGS:

The Randy Matson Story, Tafnews, 1971.
Spirit, Berkley, 1973.
(With Wilbur Evans) *Champions,* Strode, 1978.
The Overcomers, Word Books, 1978.
(With Trent Jones) *Where the Rainbows Wait,* Playboy Press, 1978.
(Editor) *Happy Trails to You* (autobiography of Roy Rogers and Dale Evans), Word Books, 1979.
Journey to Triumph, Taylor Publishing, 1982.
The Unsinkable Titanic Thompson, Eakin Press, 1982.
Dallas Cowboys Bluebook III, Taylor Publishing, 1982.
Friday Night Heroes, Eakin Press, 1983.
Partners in Blue, Taylor Publishing, 1983.
Dallas Cowboys Bluebook IV, Taylor Publishing, 1983.
(With Billy Olson) *Reaching Higher,* Word Books, 1984.
The Dallas Cowboys: The First 25 Years, with foreword by James Michener, Taylor Publishing, 1984.
The Cowboys Chronicles, Eakin Press, 1984.
Careless Whispers: The True Story of a Triple Murder and the Determined Lawman Who Wouldn't Give Up, Taylor Publishing, 1984.
The Cotton Bowl: The First 50 Years, Host Communications, 1986.
(With William C. Dear) *Please . . . Don't Kill Me* (nonfiction), Houghton, 1989.
(With Larry Wansley) *The FBI Undercover,* Pocket Books, 1989.
Innocence Lost, Pocket Books, 1990.

Contributor to periodicals, including *Good Housekeeping, Sports Illustrated, TV Guide, Inside Sports,* and *People.*

SIDELIGHTS: Carlton Stowers told *CA:* "The greatest enjoyment I receive from my work is the variety of projects I'm involved in. A newspaper background has provided me with the kind of work habits necessary to work swiftly and on more than one project at a time. In recent years I've dealt more attention to nonfiction books and have also found that television writing provides me a welcome respite from the long narrative of print journalism on occasion. I'm fortunate that a variety of subjects interests me; therefore I don't devote my efforts to a particular field even though I continue to do a considerable amount of sportswriting."

BIOGRAPHICAL/CRITICAL SOURCES:

PERIODICALS

New York Times Book Review, October 15, 1989.

* * *

STREATFEILD, (Mary) Noel 1895(?)-1986
(Susan Scarlett)

PERSONAL: Born December 24, 1895 (some sources say 1897), in Amberley, near Arundel, Sussex, England; died September 11, 1986, in London, England; daughter of William Champion (the Bishop of Lewes) and Janet Mary (Venn) Streatfeild. *Education:* Attended Laleham in Eastbourne, Hastings College, St. Leonards College, and Royal Academy of Dramatic Art, London.

ADDRESSES: Home—Vicarage Gate, London W8, England. *Agent*—A. M. Heath, 40-42 William IV St., London WC2N 4DD, England.

CAREER: Began as an actress with a Shakespearean repertory company in England; later appeared in a variety of theatrical productions in South Africa and Australia; writer and editor, beginning 1930; became a book critic for *Elizabethan* magazine; presented book talks for BBC radio.

AWARDS, HONORS: Carnegie Medal, 1938, for *The Circus Is Coming; A Young Person's Guide to the Ballet* was chosen as a Children's Book of the Year, 1975, by the Child Study Association, and as a 1976 Children's Book Showcase Title by the Children's Book Council; Officer, Order of the British Empire, 1983.

WRITINGS:

FICTION

The Whicharts, Heinemann, 1931, Brentano's, 1932.
Parson's Nine, Heinemann, 1932, Doubleday, Doran, 1933.
Tops and Bottoms, Doubleday, Doran, 1933.
Shepherdess of Sheep, Heinemann, 1934, Reynal & Hitchcock, 1935.
Creeping Jenny, Heinemann, 1936.
It Pays to Be Good, Heinemann, 1936.
Caroline England, Heinemann, 1937, Reynal & Hitchcock, 1938.
Dennis the Dragon, Dent, 1939.
Luke, Heinemann, 1939.
The House in Cornwall, illustrated by D. L. Mays, Dent, 1940, published as *The Secret of the Lodge,* illustrated by Richard Floethe, Random House, 1940.
The Winter Is Past, Collins, 1940.
The Stranger in Primrose Lane, illustrated by Floethe, Random House, 1941 (published in England as *The Children of Primrose Lane,* illustrated by Marcia Lane Foster, Dent, 1941).
I Ordered a Table for Six, Collins, 1942.
Harlequinade, illustrated by Clarke Hutton, Chatto & Windus, 1943.
Myra Carrel, Collins, 1944.
Saplings, Collins, 1945.
Grass in Piccadilly, Collins, 1947.
Mothering Sunday, Coward, 1950.
Osbert, illustrated by Susanne Suba, Rand McNally, 1950.
The Theatre Cat, illustrated by Suba, Rand McNally, 1951.
Aunt Clara, Collins, 1952.
The Fearless Treasure: A Story of England from Then to Now, illustrated by Dorothea Braby, M. Joseph, 1953.
Judith, Collins, 1956.

The Grey Family, illustrated by Pat Marriott, Hamish Hamilton, 1957.
Bertram, illustrated by Margery Gill, Hamish Hamilton, 1959.
Christmas with the Chrystals, Basil Blackwell, 1959.
The Silent Speaker, Collins, 1961.
Lisa Goes to Russia, illustrated by Geraldine Spence, Collins, 1963.
The Children on the Top Floor, illustrated by Jillian Willett, Collins, 1964, Random House, 1965.
Let's Go Coaching, illustrated by Peter Warner, Hamish Hamilton, 1965.
The Growing Summer (Junior Literary Guild selection), illustrated by Edward Ardizzone, Collins, 1966, published as *The Magic Summer,* Random House, 1967.
Old Chairs to Mend, illustrated by Barry Wilkinson, Hamish Hamilton, 1966.
Caldicott Place (Junior Literary Guild selection), illustrated by Betty Maxey, Collins, 1967, published as *The Family at Caldicott Place,* Random House, 1968.
Gemma, illustrated by Maxey, May Fair Books, 1968.
Gemma and Sisters, illustrated by Maxey, May Fair Books, 1968.
The Barrow Lane Gang, BBC Publications, 1968.
Gemma Alone, Armada, 1969.
Goodbye Gemma, Armada, 1969.
Red Riding Hood, illustrated by Svend Otto S., Benn, 1970.
Thursday's Child, illustrated by Peggy Fortnum, Random House, 1970.
When the Siren Wailed, illustrated by Gill, Collins, 1974, American edition illustrated by Judith Gwyn, Random House, 1976.
Gran-Nannie, illustrated by Charles Mozley, M. Joseph, 1976.
Far to Go, illustrated by Mozley, Collins, 1977.
Meet the Maitlands, illustrated by Anthony Maitland, W. H. Allen, 1978.
The Maitlands: All Change at Cuckly Place, illustrated by Maitland, W. H. Allen, 1979.

"SHOES" SERIES

Ballet Shoes: A Story of Three Children on the Stage, illustrated by Ruth Gervis, Dent, 1936, published as *Ballet Shoes,* illustrated by Floethe, Random House, 1937, reprinted, Dell, 1979.
Tennis Shoes, illustrated by Mays, Dent, 1937, reprinted, 1965, American edition illustrated by Floethe, Random House, 1938.
The Circus Is Coming, illustrated by Steven Spurrier, Dent, 1938, revised edition, illustrated by Clarke Hutton, 1960, published as *Circus Shoes,* illustrated by Floethe, Random House, 1939.
Curtain Up, Dent, 1944, published as *Theatre Shoes: or, Other People's Shoes,* illustrated by Floethe, Random House, 1945.
Party Frock, illustrated by Anna Zinkeisen, Collins, 1946, published as *Party Shoes,* illustrated by Zinkeisen, Random House, 1947.
Movie Shoes, illustrated by Suba, Random House, 1949 (published in England as *Painted Garden,* Collins, 1949), new edition illustrated by Shirley Hughes, Penguin, 1961.
Skating Shoes, illustrated by Floethe, Random House, 1951 (published in England as *White Boots,* Collins, 1951), new edition illustrated by Milein Cosman, Penguin, 1976.
Family Shoes, illustrated by Floethe, Random House, 1954 (published in England as *The Bell Family,* illustrated by Hughes, Collins, 1954).

Wintle's Wonders, illustrated by Richard Kennedy, Collins, 1957, published as *Dancing Shoes,* illustrated by Floethe, Random House, 1958.

New Shoes, illustrated by Hughes, Random House, 1960 (published in England as *New Town: A Story about the Bell Family,* illustrated by Hughes, Collins, 1960).

Traveling Shoes, illustrated by Reisie Lonette, Random House, 1962 (published in England as *Apple Bough,* illustrated by Gill, Collins, 1962).

Ballet Shoes for Anna, illustrated by Mary Dinsdale, Collins, 1976.

NOVELS; UNDER PSEUDONYM SUSAN SCARLETT

Clothes-Pegs, Hodder & Stoughton, 1939.
Sally-Ann, Hodder & Stoughton, 1939.
Peter and Paul, Hodder & Stoughton, 1940.
Ten Way Street, Hodder & Stoughton, 1940.
The Man in the Dark, Hodder & Stoughton, 1941.
Baddacombe's, Hodder & Stoughton, 1941.
Under the Rainbow, Hodder & Stoughton, 1942.
Summer Pudding, Hodder & Stoughton, 1943.
Murder While You Work, Hodder & Stoughton, 1944.
Poppies for England, Hodder & Stoughton, 1948.
Pirouette, Hodder & Stoughton, 1948.
Love in a Mist, Hodder & Stoughton, 1951.

NONFICTION

The Picture Show of Britain, illustrated by Ursula Koering, edited by Helen Hoke, Bell Publishing, 1951.

The First Book of Ballet, illustrated by Moses Soyer, F. Watts, 1953, revised edition, illustrated by Stanley Houghton and Soyer, Edmund Ward, 1963.

The First Book of England, illustrated by Gioia Fiammenghi, F. Watts, 1958, revised edition, Edmund Ward, 1963.

Magic and the Magician: E. Nesbit and Her Children's Books, Abelard, 1958.

Queen Victoria, illustrated by Robert Frakenberg, Random House, 1958.

The Royal Ballet School, Collins, 1959.

Look at the Circus, illustrated by Constance Marshall, Hamish Hamilton, 1960.

A Vicarage Family: An Autobiographical Story (first book of a trilogy), illustrated by Mozley, F. Watts, 1963.

The Thames: London's River, illustrated by Kurt Wiese, Garrard, 1964.

Away from the Vicarage (second book of an autobiographical trilogy), Collins, 1965.

On Tour: An Autobiographical Novel of the 20's, F. Watts, 1965.

The First Book of the Opera, illustrated by Hilary Abrahams, F. Watts, 1966 (published in England as *Enjoying Opera,* Dobson, 1966).

Before Confirmation, Heinemann, 1967.

The First Book of Shoes, illustrated by Jacqueline Tomes, F. Watts, 1967.

Beyond the Vicarage (third book of an autobiographical trilogy), Collins, 1971, F. Watts, 1972.

The Boy Pharaoh: Tutankhamen, M. Joseph, 1972.

A Young Person's Guide to the Ballet, illustrated by Georgette Bordier, Warne, 1975.

EDITOR

The Years of Grace, Evens Brothers, 1950, revised edition, 1956.

By Special Request: New Stories for Girls, Collins, 1953.

Growing up Gracefully, illustrated by John Dugan, A. Barker, 1955.

The Day before Yesterday: Firsthand Stories of Fifty Years Ago, illustrated by Dick Hart, Collins, 1956.

Confirmation and After, Heinemann, 1963.

Merja Otava, *Priska,* translated by Elizabeth Portch, Benn, 1964.

Marlie Brande, *Nicholas,* translated by Elisabeth Boas, Follett, 1968.

M. Brande, *Sleepy Nicholas,* Follett, 1970.

Also editor of "Noel Streatfeild Holiday" books, illustrated by Sara Silcock, five volumes, Dent, 1973-77.

OTHER

"Them Wings" (play), produced in London, 1933.

Children's Matinees (plays), illustrated by Gervis, Heinemann, 1934.

Wisdom Teeth (three-act play), Samuel French, 1936.

(With Roland Pertwee) *Many Happy Returns,* (two-act play; first produced in Windsor, 1950), English Theatre Guild, 1953.

Also author of the "Baby Books" series, published by A. Barker, beginning 1959; also author, with Jack Whittingham, of "Welcome Mr. Washington" (screenplay), 1944; author of radio plays based on her "Bell Family" books, 1949-51, on her "New Town" books, of "Kick Off," 1973, and others. Editor of *Noel Streatfeild's Ballet Annual,* beginning 1959.

SIDELIGHTS: Noel Streatfeild, the daughter of a bishop, lived a full and varied life, much of which she shared in her scores of children's books. A former dancer and actress, Streatfeild was best known for her tales of the Fossil girls in *Ballet Shoes.* This story was an instant sensation on its publication in 1936. "The author had no idea of the excitement her book was causing until she saw Bumpus's bookshop in London with one window full of pairs of ballet shoes," noted a London *Times* obituary. "[Another store] in Piccadilly rationed the queue of customers to one copy each."

Streatfeild, the *Times* article continued, "had a sense of humour and the ability to laugh at herself. Her greatest delight was to escape into the country and look for wild flowers, a passion she inherited from her mother. Whatever she did was done with complete thoroughness and professionalism. Children on both sides of the Atlantic will recall with pleasure hearing her speak to them on one of the many occasions when she visited a school or library or an exhibition of children's books."

MEDIA ADAPTATIONS: Ballet Shoes was adapted into a television series in 1976; *New Town: A Story about the Bell Family* was adapted as the television series "The Bell Family." In addition, many of the author's books have been read for BBC radio.

BIOGRAPHICAL/CRITICAL SOURCES:

BOOKS

Contemporary Literary Criticism, Volume 21, Gale, 1982.

Streatfeild, Noel, *Vicarage Family: An Autobiographical Story,* F. Watts, 1963.

Streatfeild, Noel, *Away from the Vicarage,* Collins, 1965.

Streatfeild, Noel, *On Tour: An Autobiographical Novel of the 20's,* F. Watts, 1965.

Streatfeild, Noel, *Beyond the Vicarage,* Collins, 1971, F. Watts, 1972.

Wilson, Barbara Ker, *Noel Streatfeild,* Bodley Head, 1961, Walck, 1964.

PERIODICALS

Saturday Review, November 9, 1968.
Washington Post Book World, September 8, 1985, April 13, 1986.

OBITUARIES:

PERIODICALS

Times (London), September 12, 1986.*

* * *

STUART, (Jessica) Jane 1942-
(Jane Stuart Juergensmeyer)

PERSONAL: Born August 20, 1942, in Ashland, Ky.; daughter of Jesse Hilton (a writer) and Naomi Deane (Norris) Stuart; married Julian Conrad Juergensmeyer (a professor of law), August 20, 1963; children: Conrad Stuart, Erik Markstrom. *Education:* Attended American University at Cairo, 1961-62, and University of Kentucky, 1962; Western Reserve University (now Case Western Reserve University), A.B. (magna cum laude), 1964; Indiana University, M.A. (classics), 1967, M.A. (Italian), 1969, Ph.D., 1971; also attended Anglo-American Cultural Institute for Modern Greek (Athens), summer, 1966, and Universite d'Aix-Marseilles, spring, 1968; studied independently in Italy, Kenya, and Uganda.

CAREER: Everglades School for Girls, Miami, Fla., Latin teacher, 1962; Haile Selassie I University, Addis Ababa, Ethiopia, lecturer in Italian, 1968-69; writer, lecturer, and translator, 1969—. Has also taught in the elementary schools of Greysbranch and Wurtland, Ky., the British School in Addis Ababa, and the University of Florida.

MEMBER: Phi Beta Kappa, Eta Sigma Phi.

WRITINGS:

A Year's Harvest (poems), Landmark House, 1957.
Eyes of the Mole (poems), Staunton & Lee, 1967.
White Barn (poems), Whippoorwill, 1973.
Yellowhawk (novel), McGraw-Hill, 1973.
Passerman's Hollow (novel), McGraw-Hill, 1974.
Land of the Fox (novel), McGraw-Hill, 1975.
Gideon's Children (stories), McGraw-Hill, 1976.
Transparencies: Remembrances of My Father, Jesse Stuart, Archer Editions, 1985.

CONTRIBUTOR TO ANTHOLOGIES

Kentucky Contemporary Poetry: I & II, Bean Publishing, 1965-66.
Fire, Sleet and Candlelight, Staunton & Lee, 1963.
Short Stories for Discussion, Scribner, 1965.
Poems from the Hills: 1971, M. H. C. Publications, 1971.
Voices from the Hills: Selected Readings from Southern Appalachia, Ungar, 1976.

OTHER

Book reviewer, *Louisville Courier Journal,* 1967. Contributor of stories, poems, translations, and reviews to magazines and newspapers, including *Lyric, Educational Forum, Progressive Farmer, Activist, Ladies' Home Journal, Pegasus, National Wildlife, Literature East and West,* and *Discourse.* Contributing editor, *Playgirl,* 1973.

WORK IN PROGRESS: Translating *Poems of Alcaeus* and the poetry of Eugenio Montale.

AVOCATIONAL INTERESTS: Travel (Eastern and Western Europe, Africa, and Central America.

STUART, Jesse (Hilton) 1906-1984

PERSONAL: Born August 8, 1906, in W-Hollow, near Riverton, Ky.; died of complications following a series of strokes, February 17, 1984, in Ironton, Ohio; son of Mitchell (a tenant farmer) and Martha (Hilton) Stuart; married Naomi Dean Norris (a teacher), October, 1939; children: Jessica Jane. *Education:* Lincoln Memorial University, A.B. 1929; attended Vanderbilt University, 1931-32, and Peabody College. *Politics:* Republican. *Religion:* Methodist.

ADDRESSES: Home and office—W-Hollow, Greenup, Ky. 41144. *Agent*—Annie Laurie Williams, 18 East 41st St., New York, N.Y. 10017.

CAREER: Writer, 1929—. Teacher in Greenup County, Ky., 1929-30, superintendent of schools, 1932-34; principal of McKell High School, 1933-37 and 1956-57. Visiting professor at University of Nevada, Reno, 1958, The American University, Cairo, Egypt, 1960-61, and Eastern Kentucky University, 1965-66. U.S. Information Service lecturer for Bureau of Educational and Cultural Affairs, 1962-63, serving Egypt, Iran, Greece, Lebanon, Pakistan, the Philippines, Formosa, and Korea. *Military service:* U.S. Naval Reserve, 1943-46; became lieutenant (junior grade).

AWARDS, HONORS: Jeannette Sewal Davis prize from *Poetry* magazine, 1934, for *Man with a Bull-Tongue Plow;* Guggenheim fellowship, 1937; Academy of Arts and Sciences award, 1941, for *Men of the Mountains;* Thomas Jefferson Memorial Award, 1943, for *Taps for Private Tussie;* "best book" citation from National Education Association, 1949, for *The Thread That Runs So True;* named poet laureate of Kentucky, 1954; Berea College Centennial Award for literature, 1955, for body of work; Academy of American Poets award, 1955, for "distinguished service to American poetry"; Academy of American Poets fellowship, 1960; a high school in Louisville, Ky. was named after Stuart, 1966; Pulitzer Prize nomination, 1975, for *The World of Jesse Stuart.* Recipient of numerous honorary degrees, including D.Litt., University of Kentucky, 1944, D.H.L., Lincoln Memorial University, 1950, LL.D., Baylor University, 1954, and LL.D., Ball State University, 1975.

WRITINGS:

FICTION

Head o' W-Hollow, Dutton, 1936, reprinted, University Press of Kentucky, 1979.
Trees of Heaven, Dutton, 1940, reprinted, University Press of Kentucky, 1980.
Men of the Mountains, Dutton, 1941, reprinted, University Press of Kentucky, 1979.
Taps for Private Tussie, Dutton, 1943 (published in England as *He'll Be Coming Down the Mountain,* Dobson, 1947).
Foretaste of Glory, Dutton, 1946, reprinted, University Press of Kentucky, 1986.
Tales from the Plum Grove Hills, Dutton, 1946.
Hie to the Hunters, McGraw-Hill, 1950.
Clearing in the Sky and Other Stories, McGraw-Hill, 1950, reprinted, University Press of Kentucky, 1984.
The Good Spirit of Laurel Ridge, McGraw-Hill, 1953.
Plowshare in Heaven, McGraw-Hill, 1958.
Save Every Lamb, McGraw-Hill, 1964.
Daughter of the Legend, McGraw-Hill, 1965.
My Land Has a Voice, McGraw-Hill, 1966.
Mr. Gallion's School, McGraw-Hill, 1967.
Stories by Jesse Stuart, McGraw-Hill, 1968.
Tim, Kentucky Writers Guild, 1968.
Come Gentle Spring, McGraw-Hill, 1969.

Come Back to the Farm, McGraw-Hill, 1971.
Come to My Tomorrow Land, Aurora, 1971.
Dawn of Remembered Spring, McGraw-Hill, 1972.
The Land beyond the River, McGraw-Hill, 1973.
32 Votes before Breakfast, McGraw-Hill, 1974.
The Kingdom Within, McGraw-Hill, 1979.
The Best-Loved Short Stories of Jesse Stuart, McGraw-Hill, 1982.
Cradle of the Copperheads, McGraw-Hill, 1988.

POETRY

Harvest of Youth, Scroll Press, 1930.
Man with a Bull-Tongue Plow, Dutton, 1934, reprinted, AMS Press, 1988.
Album of Destiny, Dutton, 1944.
Kentucky Is My Land, Dutton, 1952.
Hold April, McGraw-Hill, 1962.
The World of Jesse Stuart: Selected Poems, McGraw-Hill, 1975.
The Seasons of Jesse Stuart: An Autobiography in Poetry 1907-1976, Archer Editions, 1976.

JUVENILES

Mongrel Mettle: The Autobiography of a Dog, Dutton, 1944.
The Beatinest Boy, McGraw-Hill, 1953.
A Penny's Worth of Character, McGraw-Hill, 1954.
Red Mule, McGraw-Hill, 1955.
The Rightful Owner, McGraw-Hill, 1960.
Andy Finds a Way, McGraw-Hill, 1961.
A Ride with Huey the Engineer, McGraw-Hill, 1966.
Old Ben, McGraw-Hill, 1970.

NONFICTION

Beyond Dark Hills (autobiography), Dutton, 1938.
The Thread That Runs So True (autobiography), Scribner, 1949.
The Year of My Rebirth (autobiography), McGraw-Hill, 1956.
God's Oddling, McGraw-Hill, 1960.
To Teach, To Love, World, 1970.
My World: Jesse Stuart's Kentucky, University Press of Kentucky, 1975.
Up the Hollow from Lynchburg, photographs by Joe Clark, McGraw-Hill, 1975.
Dandelion on the Acropolis: A Journal of Greece, Archer Editions, 1978.
Lost Sandstones and Lonely Skies and Other Essays, Archer Editions, 1979.
If I Were Seventeen Again and Other Essays, Archer Editions, 1980.

OTHER

A Jesse Stuart Reader (omnibus volume), McGraw-Hill, 1963.
(Editor, with others, and contributor) *Outlooks through Literature,* Scott, Foresman, 1964.
(Editor with A. K. Ridout) *Short Stories for Discussion,* Scribner, 1965.
(Author of foreword) *Tomorrow's People,* Harvest Press, 1968.

Contributor of numerous stories, poems, and articles to periodicals, including *Commonweal, Christian Science Monitor, Progressive Farmer, American Mercury, Yale Review, Saturday Review, Today's Health, Audubon Magazine, New Republic, Women's Day, Harper's,* and *Esquire.*

SIDELIGHTS: The late Jesse Stuart was an Appalachian regional writer whose publications included poetry, fiction, essays, and children's stories. Once named poet laureate of Kentucky, Stuart compiled a staggering list of works over his lifetime, most of them exploring life in his native Greenup County. As Frank

Levering observed in the *Los Angeles Times Book Review,* Stuart "stands as the lone giant in the literary forest of rural Appalachia. . . . He has long been an inspiration to generations of younger Appalachian writers who, as with Stuart, have struggled against poverty, provincialism and the colonization of Appalachia by corporate America." In the *Dictionary of Literary Biography Yearbook,* H. Edward Richardson declared that Stuart "was the bardic chronicler of Appalachia—its poet and storyteller. . . . Commencing as a regional writer, Stuart brought to his sources an original, evocative language, at once authentic and stylistically apt and broadly assimilative, because he knew his people from the inside out and was so close to the soil. In time, he successfully transmuted the shadowy figures of local legends into the consciously communicated personae of literary art."

Jesse Hilton Stuart was born in a one-room log cabin in Greenup County, Kentucky. His father worked a number of jobs, including tenant farming, coal mining, and railroad construction. Neither of Stuart's parents had completed even an elementary school education, and Stuart himself was often pulled from classes to help with the chores. When he was twelve his family finally settled down on a fifty acre farm, and several years thereafter he entered Greenup High School. Stuart's early education was so piecemeal that he found high school a great struggle. He persisted because he discovered a love for literature, especially the poetry of Robert Burns, Carl Sandburg, and Walt Whitman. After graduating in 1926, he worked briefly in a Kentucky steel mill before deciding to attend college.

Stuart knew his chances for acceptance were slim, so he was delighted when he was admitted to Lincoln Memorial University in Harrogate, Tennessee. He worked his way through and earned a bachelor's degree in 1929. That same year he began teaching and serving as principal at high schools in his home region. "Though he made his living teaching," claimed Richardson in *Arizona Quarterly,* "he was writing whenever he could, not so much because he wanted to, but because he was compelled to; and he was living on the [family] farm in W-Hollow with a hoe in his hands, in more ways than in lyrical themes getting back close to the soil again." After a brief sojourn at Vanderbilt University—where he penned a 310-page autobiography for a term paper assignment—Stuart returned to Greenup County. His first major publication, a volume of more than 700 sonnets entitled *Man with a Bull-Tongue Plow,* was published in 1934.

Dictionary of Literary Biography contributor J. R. LeMaster has noted that Stuart "first established his literary reputation as a poet." Although *Man with a Bull-Tongue Plow* was by no means an unqualified success, it did receive favorable reviews from such notable critics as Mark Van Doren, Malcolm Cowley, and Horace Gregory. In that work and subsequent poetry volumes, according to LeMaster, Stuart "began creating a mythical Appalachia which he would continue to shape throughout his career as a writer. . . . The style he achieved was peculiarly his own. The sonnet proved to be a convenient form—a canvas on which he could paint his scenes of life in W-Hollow . . . and its surroundings. He used a large number of voices, and . . . he succeeded in lifting his part of Appalachia to a literary level." Stuart's best-known volume of poetry, *Album of Destiny,* addresses two of his central concerns: his pioneer ancestors and the contrast between the rural life of the golden past and the debilitating urban existence of the twentieth century. "Viewing himself in a modern wasteland," wrote LeMaster, "the poet [celebrated] his ancestry and [admonished] others to sing because art is the only surviving means of creating values worth bothering about."

Stuart was one author who heeded the axiom "write what you know." Almost all of his fiction, nonfiction, and poetry is set in or near W-Hollow, the tiny Kentucky community where he lived most of his life. Stuart observed his neighbors and turned to fiction their foibles and strengths, their families' tribulations and joys. He wrote of moonshiners, horse traders, and proud tenant farmers, creating "a living world in which the connection between people and the land is close and organic, in which people are aware of their dependence on the land," to quote Jim Wayne Miller in *Jesse Stuart: Essays on His Work.* The author's themes were as diverse as his prolific output might suggest—everything from bigotry and drunken violence to faithfulness, love and marriage—but his most enduring motif was the relationship between man and nature. Frank H. Leavell offered an explanation in *Jesse Stuart:* "A man draws his strength from the land. Its produce feeds his body as its poetry feeds his soul. He thrives when he is close to the soil; he withers when he forsakes it and sojourns in the city. . . . Through his communion with the land he finds a mystic communion with God. Yet this view of the land stops short of pantheism. Nature remains inanimate; God remains transcendent."

Although bound to his region, Stuart still managed to craft works with universal significance. "To an outlander the people of Eastern Kentucky must have appeared culturally retarded, primitive, and definitely odd," wrote Wade Hall in *Jesse Stuart.* "However, Stuart has never written with the intention of ridiculing them because of their way of life. When he sketches a man drunk in a cow stall, he is holding up a mirror in which his readers may see their own absurd excesses. It is the way of serious humor that first one laughs at someone else, then gradually realizes that he is laughing at an aspect of himself. The accidents of language, looks, and dress—as all humorists know—derive from a common human nature." Hall added that from regional raw materials Stuart shaped "fiction and nonfiction that transcend locale and speak to man's comic (and tragic) condition everywhere." Also in *Jesse Stuart,* J. R. LeMaster contended that, having arrested the frontier in his consciousness, Stuart "held Appalachia before the remainder of America as a model for national existence."

Critics of Stuart's work have faced a daunting task. During a half-century of continuous publishing, the author penned more than fifty-five book-length works, some 2,000 poems, nearly 500 short stories, and 260 essays. At one point Stuart estimated that he wrote an astonishing 30,000 words per day. Even a series of heart attacks failed to diminish his output, and his occasional teaching duties and lecture tours only provided him with more experiences about which to write. In the *Arizona Quarterly,* Richardson observed that Stuart "required no induced mood, incentive, or inspiration; something as natural as breathing took hold of him and he wrote, as he had from the time he was eight." *Dictionary of Literary Biography Yearbook* contributor Ruel E. Foster concluded that the author "was a maker, a poet who said 'yes' to life as he matured. He knew sickness, injustice, and death, but he still said 'yes' to the bone-deep sweetness and diversity of life."

Addressing himself to Stuart's literary legacy, LeMaster wrote that Stuart's works "remain to remind us that the world has not changed for the better. . . . In his fifty or more volumes Jesse Stuart gave us a vision of a world he perceived as a viable alternative to the one in which we live, and that vision remains. Using his beloved W-Hollow as a microcosm he spoke to the common lot of humanity all over the world; he never had time for pretense or sham." In a book-length critique entitled *Jesse Stuart,* Foster concluded that the author, "in the timeless vignettes of his . . .

stories, has done what every great writer longs to do. He has created a *place* and wedged it everlastingly in the imagination of America. His stories have given a voice to the far and lost land of the Appalachians, a voice which calls us ever and delightedly into the outdoor world. The reader of any volume of Stuart . . . opens the book and feels immediately the fine mist of nature blowing into his face. This is the world that Stuart has made, . . . and it can no longer be ignored by serious critics."

Jesse Stuart died after a long illness early in 1984. He once told *CA:* "I live on a farm, I have lived here all my life. I am interested in farming and, up until the year I had a heart attack (1954), I did considerable farm work. I am interested in conservation of land and people too; my land is covered in grass or trees and without any erosion. I am interested in teaching. . . . I am also interested in travel and have traveled quite extensively in all states in the Union but Alaska; have traveled in 94 countries. About my writing, I do the writing and let others make the comments."

Stuart has had more stories published in *Esquire* magazine than any other writer—"fifty-nine, I believe," he estimated for *CA,* "(or sixty-nine)." His works have been translated into numerous languages, including Arabic, Danish, German, French, Spanish, Japanese, Czechoslovakian, Chinese, Polish, Russian, Bengali, Dutch, Italian, Norwegian, Swedish, West Pakistani, and Telegu. Stuart's papers are housed at Murray State University, Murray, Kentucky.

BIOGRAPHICAL/CRITICAL SOURCES:

BOOKS

Blair, Everetta Love, *Jesse Stuart: His Life and Works,* University of South Carolina Press, 1967.

Clarke, Mary Washington, *Jesse Stuart's Kentucky,* McGraw-Hill, 1967.

Contemporary Literary Criticism, Gale, Volume 1, 1973, Volume 8, 1978, Volume 11, 1979, Volume 14, 1980, Volume 34, 1985.

Dictionary of Literary Biography, Gale, Volume 9: *American Novelists, 1910-1945,* 1981, Volume 48: *American Poets, 1880-1945, Second Series,* 1986.

Dictionary of Literary Biography Yearbook 1984, Gale, 1985.

Foster, Ruel E., *Jesse Stuart,* Twayne, 1968.

LeMaster, J. R., and Mary Washington Clarke, *Jesse Stuart: Essays on His Work,* University Press of Kentucky, 1977.

LeMaster, J. R., *Jesse Stuart: Selected Criticism,* Valkyrie Press, 1978.

LeMaster, J. R., *Jesse Stuart: A Reference Guide,* G. K. Hall, 1979.

LeMaster, J. R., *Jesse Stuart: Kentucky's Chronicler-Poet,* Memphis State University Press, 1980.

Peden, William, *The American Short Story: Continuity and Change, 1940-1975,* Houghton, 1975.

Pennington, Lee, *The Dark Hills of Jesse Stuart,* Harvest Press, 1967.

Perry, Dick, *Reflections of Jesse Stuart,* McGraw-Hill, 1971.

Reality and Myth: Essays in American Literature, Vanderbilt University Press, 1964.

Spurlock, John Howard, *He Sings for Us: A Socio-linguistic Analysis of the Appalachian Subculture and of Jesse Stuart as a Major American Author,* University Press of America, 1980.

Woodbridge, Hensely C. *Jesse and Jane Stuart: A Bibliography,* Murray State University, 1979.

PERIODICALS

American Book Collector, September, 1958, February, 1963.

Arizona Quarterly, summer, 1984.
Chicago Tribune, December 22, 1985.
College English, March, 1942.
Detroit News, April 9, 1972.
Los Angeles Times Book Review, June 12, 1988.
Newsweek, November 26, 1956.
New York Times Book Review, July 16, 1950, September 22, 1963, October 20, 1963, November 6, 1966, October 27, 1968, August 17, 1969, August 8, 1971, March 26, 1972, April 15, 1973.
Saturday Evening Post, March 28, 1959, July 25, 1959.
Southwest Review, summer, 1971.
University of Kansas City Quarterly, June, 1958.
Virginia Quarterly Review, spring, 1976.
Washington Post Book World, October 24, 1982.
Writers Digest, July, 1957, June, 1984.

OBITUARIES:

PERIODICALS

Chicago Tribune, February 20, 1984.
New York Times, February 20, 1984.
Publishers Weekly, March 9, 1984.
Washington Post, February 19, 1984.*

—Sketch by Anne Janette Johnson

* * *

STUART, Margaret
  See PAINE, Lauran (Bosworth)

* * *

SUBAK-SHARPE, Genell J(ackson) 1936-

PERSONAL: Born May 9, 1936, in Great Falls, Mont.; daughter of Martin (a farmer) and Agnes (Hagadon) Jackson; married Gerald Subak-Sharpe (a professor of electrical engineering), November 23, 1963; children: David, Sarah and Hope (twins). Education: Attended University of Montana, 1954-57; Butler University, B.S., 1959; Columbia University, B.M.S., 1961.

ADDRESSES: Office—G. S. Sharpe Communications, 606 West 116th St., New York, N.Y. 10027. Agent—Barbara Lowenstein Associates, Inc., 121 West 27th St., New York, N.Y. 10003.

CAREER: New York Times, New York City, copy editor, 1962-72; Family Health (now Health), New York City, managing editor, 1973-75; Medical Opinion, New York City, editor in chief, 1975-77; Biomedical Information Corp., New York City, vice-president and editor, 1977-83; president, G. S. Sharpe Communications, New York City.

MEMBER: National Association of Science Writers, New York Newswomen's Club.

AWARDS, HONORS: Magazine writing awards from Arthritis Foundation, 1974, for article "New Victories against Arthritis," and American Dental Society, 1977, for article "Fighting Periodontal Disease"; Blakeslee Award, American Heart Association, 1985, for *Surviving Your Heart Attack.*

WRITINGS:

(With Kathryn Schrotenboer) *Freedom from Menstrual Cramps,* Pocket Books, 1982.
(Editor with Morton D. Bogdonoff and Rubin Bressler) *Physicians' Drug Manual: Prescription and Nonprescription Drugs,* Doubleday, 1982.
(Editor) *The Physicians' Manual for Patients,* Times Books, 1984.

Surviving Your Heart Attack, Doubleday, 1984.
Living with Diabetes, Doubleday, 1984.
The Cancer Book of the American Cancer Society, Doubleday, 1984.
The Columbia University College of Physicians and Surgeons Complete Home Health Guide, Crown, 1985, 2nd edition, 1989.
(With Elizabeth Randolph) *The Complete Book of Dog Health,* Macmillan, 1986.
(With Randolph) *The Complete Book of Cat Health,* Macmillan, 1986.
Managing Hypertension, Doubleday, 1986.
(With Robert Weiss) *The Columbia University School of Public Health Complete Guide to Health and Well-Being after 50,* Times Books, 1987.
Surviving Breast Cancer, Doubleday, 1987.
(With Lois Jovanovic) *Hormones, the Woman's Answer Book,* Atheneum, 1987.
Breathing Easy, Doubleday, 1988.
(Editorial director) *The Columbia University College of Physicians and Surgeons Complete Guide to Pregnancy,* Crown, 1988.
(Editor with Victor Herbert) *The Mount Sinai Nutrition Book,* St. Martin's, 1990.
(Editorial director) *The Columbia University College of Physicians and Surgeons Complete Guide to Early Childcare,* Crown, 1990.
(With Edward Frohlich) *Overcoming Your Odds of a Heart Attack,* Crown, in press.

Former editor, *Drug Therapy;* founding editor, *Rx Being Well, Off Hours,* and *Physicians Lifestyle Magazine.*

SIDELIGHTS: Genell J. Subak-Sharpe wrote CA: "My specialty is working with leading health professionals and institutions to produce books for both the lay public and medical professionals. My purpose is to give people reliable and authoritative information to make their own health care decisions. Since my books are prepared in collaboration with leading academic physicians, they have the support of the medical community. I think most doctors recognize the advantages of treating well-informed, cooperative patients, but many have lacked the time and/or communicative skills for effective patient education. *The Physicians' Manual for Patients* is a collection of two hundred illustrated and highly informative patient guides, many of which are now being used by more than 150 thousand physicians nationwide."

* * *

SUDA, Zdenek (Ludvik) 1920-

PERSONAL: Born October 7, 1920, in Pelhrimov, Czechoslovakia; naturalized U.S. citizen; son of Ludvik (director of an agricultural cooperative) and Marie (Chudoba) Suda; married Maria Kerstens, August 23, 1952; children: Maria Svatava, Sybilla Adriana, Petra Mojmira, Ludvik Zdenek. Education: Charles University, Ph.D., 1948; University of Geneva, License es Sciences Economiques, 1950; College of Europe, Certificat d'Etudes Europeenes, 1951.

ADDRESSES: Home—15 Highmeadow Rd., Pittsburgh, Pa. 15215. Office—Department of Sociology, University of Pittsburgh, Pittsburgh, Pa. 15260.

CAREER: International Secretariate of the European Movement, Paris, France, assistant head of department, 1951-54, supervisor of education program, Free Europe Committee, Inc., 1954-68; University of Pittsburgh, Pittsburgh, Pa., associate professor of sociology, beginning 1968.

WRITINGS:

La division internationale socialiste du travail, Sijthoff, 1967.

The Czechoslovak Socialist Republic, edited by Jan F. Triska, Johns Hopkins Press, 1969.

(Editor with Jiri Nehnevajsa) *Czechoslovakia 1968: The Spring That Turned to Autumn,* XYZYX Publication, 1971.

Zealots and Rebels: A History of the Communist Party in Czechoslovakia, Hoover Institution Press, 1980.

(Editor with Mustafa O. Attir and Burkart Holzner) *Directions of Change: Modernization Theory, Research, and Realities* (essays), Westview Press, 1981.

Also author of *Occupational Satisfaction of Graduates under Conditions of Overqualification,* published by European Centre for Work and Society. Contributor to periodicals, including *Est & Ouest, Neue Zuercher Zeitung,* and *American Sociological Review.*

WORK IN PROGRESS: Research on the disintegrative processes within totalitarian control structures; comparative research on social changes occasioned by modernization.

SIDELIGHTS: Zdenek Suda speaks, reads, and writes French and German, in addition to Czech and English; he also reads Italian, Dutch, Russian, and Spanish.*

* * *

SWANN, Brian (Stanley Frank) 1940-

PERSONAL: Born August 13, 1940, in Wallsend, Northumberland, England; son of Stanley and Lilyan (Booth) Swann; married; wife's name, Roberta. *Education:* Queens' College, Cambridge, B.A., 1963, M.A., 1965; Princeton University, Ph.D., 1970.

ADDRESSES: Office—Faculty of Humanities and Social Sciences, Cooper Union, Cooper St., New York, N.Y. 10003.

CAREER: Manchester Grammar School, Manchester, England, assistant English master, 1963-64; Princeton University, Princeton, N.J., instructor in English, 1965-66; University of Arizona, Tucson, instructor, 1966; Rutgers University, New Brunswick, N.J., instructor in English, 1966-67; lecturer at the British Council, 1966; teacher at the London School, Rome, Italy, at Magistero, Cassino, Italy, and at the University of Rome, 1967; special language advisor, Esso Standard Italiano, 1967; Princeton University, assistant in instruction, 1968-69, assistant professor of English, 1970-72; Cooper Union, New York, N.Y., assistant professor, 1972-76, associate professor, 1976-81, professor of English, 1981—. Director, Bennington Writing Workshops, 1987—. Has also taught at Touro College, the New School for Social Research, the Poetry Center (YM/YWHA), and Columbia University.

MEMBER: Rights for American Indians Now, Indian Rights Association, Association for the Study of American Indian Literatures, Sierra Club, Friends of the Earth, National Wildlife Federation, Natural Resources Defense Council, Audubon Society, American Museum of Natural History, American Literary Translators Association, Associated Writing Programs, PEN (member of translation committee, 1983—).

AWARDS, HONORS: Foundation fellow, Queens' College; Proctor fellow, Princeton University, 1964-65; John Florio Prize, 1977, for *Shema: Collected Poems of Primo Levi;* National Endowment for the Arts fellowship in fiction, 1979; Creative Artists in Public Service grant, 1981.

WRITINGS:

POEMS

The Whale's Scars, New Rivers Press, 1975.
Roots, New Rivers Press, 1976.
Living Time, Quarterly Review of Literature, 1978.
Paradigms of Fire, Corycian Press, 1981.
The Middle of the Journey, University of Alabama Press, 1982.

FICTION

The Runner, Carpenter Press, 1979.
Unreal Estate, Toothpaste Press, 1981.
Elizabeth, Penmaen Press, 1981.
Another Story, Adler Publishing, 1984.
The Plot of the Mice, Capra, 1986.

JUVENILE

The Tongue Dancing, Rowan Tree, 1984.
The Fox and the Buffalo, Green Tiger Press, 1985.
A Basket Full of White Eggs: Riddle-Poems, Orchard Books, 1988.
Der Rote Schwan, translation by Kaethe Recheis, Herder Verlag (Vienna), 1989.

EDITOR

Smoothing the Ground: Essays on Native American Oral Literature, University of California Press, 1982.

(With Arnold Krupat) *Recovering the Word: Essays on Native American Literature,* University of California Press, 1987.

(With Krupat) *I Tell You Now: Autobiographical Essays by Native American Writers,* University of Nebraska Press, 1987.

TRANSLATOR

(And editor, with Ruth Feldman) *The Collected Poems of Lucio Piccolo,* Princeton University Press, 1972.

(With Feldman) *Shema: Collected Poems of Primo Levi,* Menard (London), 1975.

(With Michael Impey) *Primele Poeme/First Poems of Tristan Tzara,* New Rivers Press, 1975.

(And editor, with Feldman) *Selected Poetry of Andrea Zanzotto,* Princeton University Press, 1976.

(With Impey) *Selected Poems of Tudor Arghezi,* Princeton University Press, 1976.

(With Feldman) *The Dawn Is Always New: Selected Poems of Rocco Scotellaro,* Princeton University Press, 1979.

(And editor, with Feldman) *Currents and Trends: Italian Poetry Today,* New Rivers Press, 1979.

(With Feldman) *The Dry Air of the Fire: Selected Poems of Bartolo Cattafi,* Ardis/Translation Press, 1981.

(With Peter Burian) *Euripedes' Phoenissae,* Oxford University Press, 1981.

(With Feldman) *The Hands of the South: Selected Poems of Vittorio Bodini,* Charioteer Press, 1981.

(With Talat Halman) *Rain One Step Away: Selected Poems of Milih Cevdat Anday,* Charioteer Press, 1981.

Rafael Alberti, *Rome: Danger to Pedestrians,* Quarterly Review of Literature, 1984.

Song of the Sky: Versions of Native American Poetry, Four Zoas Press, 1985.

(With Feldman) *Collected Poems of Primo Levi,* Faber, 1988.

OTHER

Contributor of translations to anthologies, including *The Prose Poem,* Dell, 1976, *The Penguin Anthology of Women Poets,* Weaver, 1979, *Contemporary Eastern European Poetry,* Ardis, 1982, and *Women on War,* Simon & Schuster, 1988. Contributor of poems, stories, essays, translations, and drawings to over 400 magazines, including *New Yorker, Poetry, Paris Review, Virginia Quarterly Review, Partisan Review, Harper's, Triquarterly,* and *Kenyon Review.* Contributor to *Columbia Dictionary of Modern European Literature* and to *Dictionary of Literary Biography Yearbook, 1982.* Former poetry editor, *La Fusta;* poetry editor, *Amicus;* associate editor, *Chelsea.*

MEDIA ADAPTATIONS: Some of Swann's poems were set to music by Doris Hays and performed by the Thompson Trio at the Symphony Space, New York City, March 22, 1982.

T

TALBERT, Charles H(arold) 1934-

PERSONAL: Born March 19, 1934, in Jackson, Miss.; son of Carl E. (a minister) and Audrey (Hale) Talbert; married Betty Weaver, June 30, 1961; children: Caroline O'Neil, Charles Richard. *Education:* Howard College (now Samford University), B.A., 1956; Southern Baptist Theological Seminary, B.D., 1959; Vanderbilt University, Ph.D., 1963. *Politics:* Democrat. *Religion:* Baptist.

ADDRESSES: Home—3091 Prytania Rd., Winston-Salem, N.C. 27106. *Office*—Box 7212, Wake Forest University, Winston-Salem, N.C. 27109.

CAREER: Wake Forest University, Winston-Salem, N.C., assistant professor, 1963-68, associate professor, 1969-74, professor of religion, 1974-89, Wake Forest Professor of Religion, 1989—.

MEMBER: Society of Biblical Literature, Society for New Testament Studies, Catholic Bible Association, Society for Values in Higher Education, National Association of Baptist Professors of Religion.

AWARDS, HONORS: Cooperative Program in Humanities fellowship, 1968-69; Society for Religion in Higher Education fellowship, 1971-72; Reynolds Research leaves, 1979 and 1986.

WRITINGS:

Luke and the Gnostics, Abingdon, 1966.
Reimarus: Fragments, Fortress, 1970, Scholars Press, 1985.
Literary Patterns, Theological Themes, and the Genre of Luke-Acts, Scholars Press, 1974.
What Is A Gospel?, Fortress, 1977.
(Editor) *Perspectives on Luke-Acts,* Association of Baptist Professors of Religion, 1978.
Reading Luke, Crossroad Publishing, 1982.
Luke-Acts: New Perspectives from the Society of Biblical Literature Seminar, Crossroad Publishing, 1983.
Acts: Knox Preaching Guides, John Knox, 1984.
(Editor) *Perspectives on the New Testament,* Mercer, 1985.
(Editor) *Perspectives on I Peter,* Mercer, 1986.
Reading Corinthians, Crossroad Publishing, 1987.
Learning through Suffering, Michael Glazier, 1990.

Member of editorial board, *Journal of Biblical Literature,* 1981-83. Editor of dissertation series, National Association of Baptist Professors of Religion, 1981-83, and Society of Biblical Literature, 1984-89.

WORK IN PROGRESS: Commentary on the gospel of John, for Crossroad Publishing.

SIDELIGHTS: Charles Talbert's book *Literary Patterns, Theological Themes, and the Genre of Luke-Acts* has been translated into Japanese. Talbert is competent in Hebrew, Greek, Latin, French, German, and Italian.

*   *   *

TARSKY, Sue 1946-

PERSONAL: Born July 26, 1946, in New York, N.Y.; daughter of George and Virginia Krawchick. *Education:* Cedar Crest College, B.A., 1968.

ADDRESSES: Home—London, England. *Office*—Aurum Books for Children, 33 Museum St., London WC1A 1LO, England.

CAREER: Simon & Schuster, Inc., New York City, editorial assistant of adult books, 1968-71; Random House, Inc., New York City, editorial assistant of adult books, 1971-73, assistant editor of children's books, 1973-75; Usborne Publishing Ltd., London, England, editor of children's books, 1976-77; Marshall Cavendish Books Ltd., London, editor, 1977-78; Walker Books Ltd., London, editor of children's books, 1978-84; Creative Books Ltd., London, co-founder and director, 1984-86; Aurum Books for Children, London, publishing director, 1986—.

AWARDS, HONORS: The Prickly Plant Book was selected as one of the outstanding science books for children, 1981, by the National Teachers Association/Children's Book Council Joint Committee.

WRITINGS:

JUVENILE

The Nature Trail Book of Wild Flowers, edited by Sue Jaquemier and others, illustrated by David Ashby and others, Usborne, 1977.
(With Malcolm Hart and Ingrid Selberg) *The Children's Book of the Countryside,* illustrated by Ashby and others, Usborne, 1978.
(With Michael Raine) *The Spectrum Book of Subroutines,* Grisewood & Dempsey, 1985.

"LOOK AND SAY" SERIES

Apple and Pear, illustrated by Clive Scruton, Simon & Schuster, 1983.
Cup and Bowl, illustrated by Scruton, Simon & Schuster, 1983.
Doll and Drum, illustrated by Scruton, Simon & Schuster, 1983.
Table and Chair, illustrated by Scruton, Simon & Schuster, 1983.

"TIME TO TALK" SERIES

Playtime, illustrated by David Bennett, Simon & Schuster, 1983.
Shopping, illustrated by Bennett, Simon & Schuster, 1983.

"CHATTERBOX" SERIES

Who Goes Moo?, illustrated by Deborah Ward, Walker Books, 1984.
Open the Door, illustrated by Ward, Walker Books, 1984.
I Can, illustrated by Katy Sleight, Walker Books, 1984.
What Goes Beep?, illustrated by Sleight, Walker Books, 1984.
Who Goes Splash?, illustrated by Sleight, Walker Books, 1985.

"TAKING A WALK" SERIES

Taking a Walk in the Town, illustrated by Grahame Corbett, Marshall Cavendish, 1979.
. . . in the Park, illustrated by Corbett, Marshall Cavendish, 1979.
. . . on the Seashore, illustrated by Jane Walton, Marshall Cavendish, 1979.
. . . in the Countryside, illustrated by Walton, Marshall Cavendish, 1979.

"HOW DOES YOUR GARDEN GROW?" SERIES

The Prickly Plant Book, illustrated by Corbett and Will Giles, Little, Brown, 1980.
The Window Box Book, illustrated by Corbett and Amanda Severne, Walker Books, 1980.
The Potted Plant Book, illustrated by Barbara Firth and Jane Wolsak, Walker Books, 1980, Little, Brown, 1981.

"MY STICKER BOOKS" SERIES

My Farm, illustrated by Leon Baxter, Methuen, 1986.
My House, illustrated by Baxter, Methuen, 1986.
My Playground, illustrated by Baxter, Methuen, 1986.
My Holiday, illustrated by Baxter, Methuen, 1986.

EDITOR

(With Eleanor Ehrhardt) *Love Themes: Selected Writings on the Many Meanings of Love* (for adults), Random House, 1974.
(With Jaquemier) Peter Hoden, *Spotter's Guide to Birds* (juvenile), illustrated by Trevor Boyer, Usborne, 1978.
Alfred Leutscher, *A Walk through the Seasons* (juvenile), illustrated by Graham Allen and others, Walker Books, 1981.
Never a Dull Moment (juvenile), illustrated by Scruton and others, Schocken, 1983.*

* * *

TAYLOR, Henry (Splawn) 1942-

PERSONAL: Born June 21, 1942, in Loudoun County, Va.; son of Thomas Edward (a farmer and teacher) and Mary (an economist and teacher; maiden name, Splawn) Taylor; married second wife, Frances Ferguson Carney (an accountant), June 29, 1968; children: (second marriage) Thomas Edward, Richard Carney. *Education:* University of Virginia, B.A., 1965; Hollins College, M.A., 1966. *Religion:* Society of Friends.

ADDRESSES: Home—Box 85, Lincoln, Va. 22078-0085. *Office*—Literature Department, American University, 4400 Massachusetts Ave. N.W., Washington, D.C. 20016.

CAREER: Roanoke College, Salem, Va., instructor in English, 1966-68; University of Utah, Salt Lake City, assistant professor of English, 1968-71; American University, Washington, D.C., associate professor of literature, 1971-76; professor of literature, 1976—; co-director of creative writing program, 1982—, director of American studies program, 1983-85. Director, University of Utah Writers' Conference, 1969-72. Writer in residence, Hollins College, 1978.

MEMBER: Agricultural History Society.

AWARDS, HONORS: Academy of American Poets prize, University of Virginia, 1962, 1964; Utah State Institute of Fine Arts poetry prize, 1969, 1971; creative writing fellowships, National Endowment of the Arts, 1978-87; research grant, National Endowment for the Humanities, 1980-81; Witter Bynner Prize for poetry, American Academy and Institute of Arts and Letters, 1984; Pulitzer Prize in poetry, 1986, for *The Flying Change: Poems.*

WRITINGS:

The Horse Show at Midnight (poems), Louisiana State University Press, 1966.
Breakings (poems), Solo Press, 1971.
(And editor) *Poetry: Points of Departure* (textbook), Winthrop Publishing, 1974.
An Afternoon of Pocket Billiards (poems), University of Utah Press, 1975.
(Editor) *The Water of Light: A Miscellany in Honor of Brewster Ghiselin,* University of Utah Press, 1976.
Desperado (poems), Unicorn, 1979.
(Translator with Robert A. Brooks) Euripides, *The Children of Herakles,* edited by William Arrowsmith, Oxford University Press, 1981.
The Flying Change: Poems, Louisiana State University Press, 1985.
Landscape with Tractor (cassette recording), Watershed Foundation, 1985.

Also author of *Writing for Computers: A Real Book for Real Writers.* Contributor to anthologies, including *The Girl in the Black Raincoat,* edited by George Garrett, Duell, Sloan & Pearce, 1966; *Introduction to Poetry,* edited by X. J. Kennedy, Little, Brown, 1971; *Contemporary Southern Poetry: An Anthology,* edited by Guy Owen and Mary C. Williams, Louisiana State University Press, 1979; *The Pure Clear Word: Essays on the Poetry of James Wright,* edited by Dave Smith, Illinois University Press, 1982; *The Morrow Anthology of Younger American Poets,* edited by Smith and David Bottoms, Morrow, 1985; *The Norton Book of Light Verse,* edited by Russell Baker, Norton, 1986; and other anthologies. Contributor to periodicals, including *Plume and Sword, Shenandoah, Encounter, Ploughshares and Poetry, Nation, Georgia Review, Southern Review, Virginia Quarterly Review, Hollins Critic,* and others. *Magill's (Masterplots) Literary Annual,* Salem Press, contributor, 1967—, editorial consultant, 1971—. Contributing editor, *Hollins Critic,* 1970-77; poetry editor, *New Virginia Review,* 1989.

WORK IN PROGRESS: Research on the history of rural Loudoun County, Virginia; a collection of essays on recent American poets; new poems.

SIDELIGHTS: After winning the Pulitzer Prize in 1986 for his book, *The Flying Change: Poems,* poet Henry Taylor remarked to Joseph McLellan of the *Washington Post:* "The Pulitzer has a funny way of changing people's opinions about it. If you haven't won one, you go around saying things like 'Well, it's all political' or 'It's a lottery' and stuff like that. I would like to go on record as saying that although I'm deeply grateful and feel very honored, I still believe that it's a lottery and that nobody deserves it." Despite his disbelief that he could earn such a prestigious award, the Pulitzer is not the first major prize Taylor has won. He was also given the Witter Bynner Prize for poetry in 1984. Critics, too, have recognized Taylor's technical skill, which is traditional in its form, and his aptitude for poetic insight. "Taylor," declares George Garrett in the *Dictionary of Literary Biography,* "was from the first a skilled and demanding craftsman"; and his poems have "all the ring and authority of an American Hardy, intensely aware of the darkness that moves around us and in us," writes Richard Dillard in the *Hollins Critic.*

In addition to this awareness, however, Taylor also has a sense for the comic. Indeed, the poet has remarked that he was first recognized as the author of several verse parodies which he submitted to the magazine *Sixties.* "I was mildly nettled to find that they were better known, at least among poets, than anything else I had done," Taylor reflects in the *Contemporary Authors Autobiography Series.* These parodies, along with other poems, appear in the author's first poetry collection, *The Horse Show at Midnight.* This book also contains poems concerned with the unavoidable changes people must go through in life, a theme which dominates many of Taylor's verses. Dillard explains: "Henry Taylor has for all his poetic career been drawn inexorably to questions of time and mutability, of inevitable and painful change in even the most fixed and stable of circumstances." The conflict between a desire for life to remain constant and predictable and the realization of the necessity for change in the form of ageing, personal growth, and death creates a tension in Taylor's poems that is also present in his other collections, including *An Afternoon of Pocket Billiards.* Dillard calls this third collection, which contains all the poems previously published in *Breakings,* Taylor's "best work" up to that time, "clearly marking growth and progress to match his own changes in the years since *The Horse Show at Midnight.*"

A lover of horses since his childhood in rural Virginia, Taylor uses an equestrian term for the title of his fifth book of poems, *The Flying Change.* The name refers to the mid-air change of leg, or lead, a horse may sometimes make while cantering. Several of the poems contained in the collection describe similarly unexpected changes that occur in the course of otherwise predictable lives spent in relaxed, countryside settings. "Thus in the best poems here," comments *New York Times Book Review* contributor Peter Stitt, "we find something altogether different from the joys of preppy picnicking. Mr. Taylor seeks for his poetry [a] kind of unsettling change, [a] sort of rent in the veil of ordinary life." Some examples of this in *The Flying Change* are the poems "Landscape with Tractor," in which the narrator discovers a corpse in a field, and "At the Swings," in which the poet reflects on his cancer-stricken mother-in-law, while pushing his sons on a swing set. Other poems in the book explore the effects of such incidents as a small herd of deer suddenly interrupting the peace of a lazy day in which the narrator has been reflecting on his old age, or the surprise of seeing a horse rip its neck on a barbed wire fence.

A number of critics, like *Washington Times* reviewer Reed Whittemore, laud Taylor's calm thoughtfulness in these and other poems, comparing it to the tone of other current poets. "Much contemporary verse is now so flighty," says Whittemore, "so persistently thoughtless, that in contrast the steadiness of [*The Flying Change*], its persistence in exploring the mental dimensions of a worthwhile moment, is particularly striking, a calmness in the unsettled poetic weather." Other critics, like *Poetry* contributor David Shapiro, also compliment the writer on his sensitivity to the atmosphere of the countryside. "Taylor is a poet of white clapboard houses that have existed 'longer / than anyone now alive,'" observes Shapiro, who quotes the poet. "That is why Taylor can be such a satisfactory poet," the reviewer concludes.

But even though he has written award-winning verses, Taylor remains relatively unnoticed among his peers. According to Garrett and others, this lack of popularity is due to Taylor's nonconformist approach. The critic continues: "In forms and content, style and substance, he is not so much out of fashion as deliberately, determinedly unfashionable. His love of form is (for the present) unfashionable. His sense of humor, which does not spare himself, is unfashionable. His preference for country life, in the face of the fact that the best known of his contemporaries are bunched up in several urban areas, cannot have made them, the others, feel easy about him, or themselves for that matter. They have every good reason to try to ignore him." Whittemore compares Taylor's technically well-ordered style and leisurely reflections of life to the poetry of Robert Frost and Howard Nemerov. "Among 20th-century poets," Whittemore concludes, "Mr. Taylor is . . . trying to carry on with this old and honorable, but now unfavored, mission of the art. He enjoys such reflections, reaching (but modestly) for what, remember, we even used to call wisdom."

BIOGRAPHICAL/CRITICAL SOURCES:

BOOKS

Contemporary Authors Autobiography Series, Volume 7, Gale, 1988.
Contemporary Literary Criticism, Volume 44, Gale, 1987.
Dictionary of Literary Biography, Volume 5: *American Poets since World War II,* Gale, 1980.

PERIODICALS

Hollins Critic, April, 1986.
Hudson Review, fall, 1986.
New York Times Book Review, May 4, 1986.
Poetry, March, 1987.
Times Literary Supplement, August 18, 1966, April 30, 1982.
Virginia Quarterly Review, summer, 1966.
Washington Post, April 19, 1986.
Washington Times, March 24, 1986.

—*Sketch by Kevin S. Hile*

*   *   *

TERRY, Margaret
See DUNNAHOO, Terry

*   *   *

TEZLA, Albert 1915-

PERSONAL: Born December 13, 1915, in South Bend, Ind.; son of Michael and Lucia (Szenasi) Tezla; married Olive Anna Fox (a psychiatric nurse), July 26, 1941; children: Michael William, Kathy Elaine. *Education:* University of Chicago, B.A., 1941, M.A., 1947, Ph.D., 1952.

ADDRESSES: Home—5412 London Rd., Duluth, Minn. 55804.

CAREER: Employed during his early career as shipping clerk, lathe operator, and secondary teacher; Indiana University, South Bend, instructor in English literature in Extension Division, 1946-48; University of Minnesota, Duluth, instructor, 1949-53, assistant professor, 1953-56, associate professor, 1956-61, professor of English, 1961-83, professor emeritus, 1983—. Columbia University, visiting professor of Hungarian literature, 1966, visiting scholar, 1975. *Military service:* U.S. Navy, 1942-46; became lieutenant; received Purple Heart and Commendation medal.

MEMBER: International Association of Hungarian Studies (member of executive committee).

AWARDS, HONORS: Faculty-staff award from University of Minnesota Student Association, 1958, for contributions to student life outside the classroom; Fulbright research fellow in Vienna, 1959-60; American Council of Learned Societies grants, 1961, 1968; Inter-University Committee research fellow in Budapest, 1963-64; Outstanding Teacher Award, University of Minnesota Student Association, Duluth, 1965; commemorative medal from Institute of Cultural Relations (Budapest), 1970, for contributions to the knowledge of Hungarian culture in the United States; International Research and Exchanges Board research fellowship, 1978; National Endowment for the Humanities research grant, 1978-81; award from ARTISJUS, Agence Litteraire, Theatrale et de Musique (Budapest), 1982, for translations of Hungarian literature; Hungarian Publisher's annual award, 1985, for *Ferenc Santa: The Fifth Seal, A Novel,* and *Ferenc Santa: God in the Wagon (Ten Short Stories);* award from Presidium of the Hungarian PEN Center, 1986, for his lifework and contributions to Hungarian studies; John Lotz memorial award, International Association of Hungarian Studies, 1986, for contributions to Hungarian literary scholarship; Hungarian Publishers annual award, 1988, for *Ivan Mandy: On the Balcony, Selected Short Stories;* honorary membership in Hungarian PEN Centre, Budapest, for work in Hungarology and Hungarian literature, 1989.

WRITINGS:

An Introductory Bibliography to the Study of Hungarian Literature, Harvard University Press, 1964.
(Contributor) *East Central Europe: A Guide to Basic Publications,* University of Chicago Press, 1969.
Hungarian Authors: A Bibliographical Handbook, Belknap Press, 1970.
(Editor and contributor) *Ocean at the Window: Hungarian Prose and Poetry since 1945,* University of Minnesota Press, 1981.
(Contributor) Paul Varnai, editor, *Hungarian Short Stories,* Exile Editions (Toronto), 1983.
(Contributor) *William Rose Benet: The Reader's Encyclopedia,* Crowell, 1984, 3rd edition, Harper, 1987.
Ferenc Santa: God in the Wagon (Ten Short Stories), Corvina Publishing House, 1985.
Ferenc Santa: The Fifth Seal, A Novel, Corvina Publishing House, 1986.
(With daughter, Kathy Elaine Tezla) *Valahol tul, meseorszagban; Az amerikas magyarok, 1895-1920: Somewhere in a Distant Fabled Land,* two volumes, Europa (Budapest), 1987.
(Translator) *Ivan Mandy: On the Balcony, Selected Short Stories,* Corvina Publishing House, 1988.
(Translator) *Istvan Lazar, Hungary: A Brief History,* Corvina Publishing House, 1990.
Three Recent Hungarian Plays, Corvina Publishing House, 1991.

The Hazardous Quest: Hungarian Immigrants in the United States, 1895-1920, Corvina Publishing House, 1991.

Also contributor to *Academic American Encyclopedia,* Arete Publications, 1980, *World Authors, 1975-1980,* H. W. Wilson, 1985 and 1991, and *Austrian History Yearbook.* Contributor to *New Hungarian Quarterly, Valosag, Hungarian PEN,* and other periodicals.

WORK IN PROGRESS: Translating *Miklos Meszoely: Once Upon a Time There Was a Central Europe,* Corvina Publishing House, expected 1994.

SIDELIGHTS: The University of Minnesota, Duluth, has established the Albert Tezla Scholar/Teacher Award in honor of the author. The award recognizes "faculty members who excel in bringing to the classroom a teaching style that emphasizes the worth of research," Tezla told *CA.*

*   *   *

THIHER, Allen 1941-

PERSONAL: Surname rhymes with "fire"; born April 4, 1941, in Fort Worth, Tex.; son of Ottah A. (a salesman) and Helen (Massy) Thiher. *Education:* University of Texas, B.A., 1963; University of Wisconsin, M.A., 1964, Ph.D., 1968.

ADDRESSES: Home—105 Meadow Ln., Columbia, Mo. 65203. *Office*—Department of Romance Languages, 143 Arts and Science Building, University of Missouri, Columbia, Mo. 65211.

CAREER: Duke University, Durham, N.C., assistant professor of French, 1967-69; Middlebury College, Middlebury, Vt., assistant professor of French, 1969-76; University of Missouri—Columbia, associate professor, 1976-81, professor of French, 1982—. Middlebush Chair for Romance Languages, 1985-89.

MEMBER: Modern Language Association of America, American Association of Teachers of French, American Association of University Professors, Phi Beta Kappa.

AWARDS, HONORS: University of Wisconsin fellowships, 1963-66; Fulbright scholarship, 1966-67; Middlebury College faculty research grant, 1971; Shell Foundation grant, 1973; Guggenheim fellowship, 1976-77; University of Missouri summer research fellowship, 1978, travel grants, 1979 and 1981, and Chancellor's Award for outstanding research in the humanities and the arts, 1981.

WRITINGS:

Celine: The Novel as Delirium, Rutgers University Press, 1972.
The Cinematic Muse: Critical Studies in the History of French Cinema, University of Missouri Press, 1979.
(Contributor) *Actes du Colloque international d'Oxford,* Societe des etudes celiniennes, 1981.
(Contributor) Morris Beja, S. E. Gontarski, and Pierre Astier, editors, *Samuel Beckett: Humanistic Perspectives,* Ohio State University Press, 1983.
Words in Reflection: Modern Language Theory and Postmodern Fiction, University of Chicago Press, 1984, 2nd edition, 1987.
Raymond Queneau, Twayne, 1985.
Franz Kafka: A Study of the Short Fiction, Twayne, 1989.

Also contributor to a volume on Franz Kafka, published by Indiana University Press. Contributor of book reviews and essays to journals, including *Modern Fiction, Modern Drama, PMLA, Philological Quarterly, Literature/Film Quarterly, Romance Notes,* and *Kentucky Quarterly of Romance Studies.*

SIDELIGHTS: Allen Thiher told *CA,* "Like one of Beckett's heroes, I keep trying to make sense of the senseless, which is, I suppose, the central task of literary studies today."

*   *   *

THOMAS, Bruce
See PAINE, Lauran (Bosworth)

*   *   *

THOMAS, J(ames) D(avid) 1910-

PERSONAL: Born July 20, 1910, in Holliday, Tex.; son of William Albert (a clerical worker) and Angie Belle (Wisdom) Thomas; married Mary Katherine Payne, February 22, 1931; children: Deborah Gayle, Thomas Fish (deceased), Hannah Belle (Mrs. Dwayne Kissick), John Paul. *Education:* Attended University of Texas, 1926-28; Abilene Christian College (now University), A.B., 1943; Southern Methodist University, M.A., 1944; University of Chicago, Ph.D., 1957.

ADDRESSES: Home—1334 Ruswood, Abilene, Tex. 79601.

CAREER: Clergyman of Church of Christ, 1937—; City of Lubbock, Tex., assistant city manager, 1939-42; Northwest Church of Christ, Chicago, Ill., minister, 1945-49; Abilene Christian University, Abilene, Tex., associate professor, 1949-57, professor of the Bible, 1957-82, professor emeritus, 1982—, head of department, 1970-79, lectureship director, 1952-70. Elder, University Church of Christ, Abilene, 1955-86. Publisher, owner, manager, and editor, Biblical Research Press (now Abilene Christian University Press), Abilene, Tex., 1958-84. Lecturer in Japan, Korea, Taiwan, Hong Kong, and the Philippines, 1958, and in thirty countries during world tour in 1969. President of corporation board, *Restoration Quarterly,* 1974-79.

MEMBER: Society of Biblical Literature (former president of Southwestern section), American Bible Society (member of advisory board), American Academy of Religion, American Scientific Affiliation, Evangelical Theological Society, Southwestern Philosophical Society.

AWARDS, HONORS: Century Book Award, Family Book Club, 1966, for *Facts and Faith,* Volume 1; Christian journalism award, *Twentieth Century Christian,* 1966; named outstanding educator by *Twentieth Century Christian,* 1981.

WRITINGS:

We Be Brethren, Biblical Research Press, 1958.
Evolution and Antiquity, Biblical Research Press, 1961.
Facts and Faith, Biblical Research Press, Volume 1, 1966, Volume 2: *The Bible and Faith,* 1980.
The Spirit and Spirituality, Biblical Research Press, 1967, 2nd edition, 1982.
(Editor) Frank Pack and Prentice A. Meador, Jr., *Preaching to Modern Man,* Biblical Research Press, 1969.
Self-Study Guide to Galatians and Romans, Biblical Research Press, 1971.
Self-Study Guide to the Corinthian Letters, Biblical Research Press, 1972.
(Editor) *Spiritual Power: Great Single Sermons,* Biblical Research Press, 1972.
Heaven's Window, Biblical Research Press, 1975.
(Editor) *What Lack We Yet?,* Biblical Research Press, 1977.
The Biblical Doctrine of Grace, Biblical Research Press, 1977.
Divorce and Remarriage, Biblical Research Press, 1977.
The Message of the New Testament: Romans, Biblical Research Press, 1982.

The Message of the New Testament: First Corinthians, Abilene Christian University Press, 1984.
Second Corinthians: The Message of the New Testament, Abilene Christian University Press, 1986.
The Well-Spring of Morality, Abilene Christian University Press, 1987.
Hebrews-James: The Message of the New Testament, Abilene Christian University Press, 1988.
(Editor) *Evolution and Faith,* Abilene Christian University Press, 1988.

EDITOR; "GREAT PREACHERS OF TODAY" SERIES

Sermons of Batsell Barrett Baxter, Biblical Research Press, 1960.
Sermons of George W. Bailey, Biblical Research Press, 1961.
Sermons of Frank Pack, Biblical Research Press, 1963.
Sermons of John H. Banister, Biblical Research Press, 1965.
Sermons of Gus Nichols, Biblical Research Press, 1966.
Sermons of William S. Banowsky, Biblical Research Press, 1967.

Also editor of six other volumes in the series.

EDITOR; "TWENTIETH-CENTURY SERMONS" SERIES

Reuel Lemmons, *The King and His Kingdom,* Biblical Research Press, 1968.
John A. Chalk, *Jesus' Church,* Biblical Research Press, 1969.
Robert C. Douglas, *Freedom in Christ,* Biblical Research Press, 1970.
C. E. McGaughey, *The Hope of the World,* Biblical Research Press, 1971.
Akio Limb, *Because of Jesus,* Biblical Research Press, 1972.
Anthony L. Ash, *The Word of Faith,* Biblical Research Press, 1973.
Joe R. Barnett, *Live, with Peace, Power and Purpose,* Biblical Research Press, 1978.

Also editor of six other volumes in the series.

OTHER

Editor, "Sermons for Today" series, three volumes, 1981—. Contributor to *Journal of Biblical Literature.* Member of board, *Restoration Quarterly,* 1957-89; former staff writer, *Gospel Advocate* and *Twentieth Century Christian.*

SIDELIGHTS: J. D. Thomas told *CA* that his motivation "is to teach Christians, primarily, so that they in turn may teach others. The time is short and the need is great. The masses do not have the intellectual grasp they should have on the basic issues and the meanings in life. Writing should be done as a contribution to the education of humanity in matters spiritual, for these are the important matters."

His first book, *We Be Brethren,* was written to help solve a problem of interpretation that had developed among his colleagues, and since he had business experience, Thomas decided to publish it himself. This launched his publishing career, which now includes over eighty titles. Several of his books have been translated into other languages.

*   *   *

THOMPSON, Buck
See PAINE, Lauran (Bosworth)

*   *   *

THOMPSON, Russ
See PAINE, Lauran (Bosworth)

THORN, Barbara
See PAINE, Lauran (Bosworth)

*   *   *

THORNBROOK, Bill
See TURNBAUGH, William A(rthur)

*   *   *

TIKHONOV, Valentin
See PAYNE, (Pierre Stephen) Robert

*   *   *

TODD, Ian A(lexander) 1941-

PERSONAL: Born September 24, 1941, in West Kirby, Cheshire, England; came to the United States in 1969, naturalized citizen, 1979; son of Alexander Henry Turnbull (a bank officer) and Jessie Margaret (Lloyd) Todd; married Alison Katharine South, June 12, 1981. *Education:* University of Birmingham, B.A. (with honors), 1963, Ph.D., 1967.

ADDRESSES: Home—Waltham, Mass. *Office*—Department of Classical and Oriental Studies, Brandeis University, P.O. Box 9110, Waltham, Mass. 02254-9110.

CAREER: Brandeis University, Waltham, Mass., assistant professor, 1969-77, associate professor, 1977-86, professor of classical and Oriental studies, 1986—, chairman of department, 1981-84. Director of Vasilikos Valley Project in Larnaca District, Cyprus, 1976—; director of Cyprus American Archaeological Research Institute, Nicosia, 1979-80; member of executive committee of American Schools of Oriental Research, 1980-82. Has conducted archaeological field work in England, Turkey, Greece, Cyprus, Western Europe, and the Middle and Near East.

MEMBER: International Institute for the Conservation of Historic and Artistic Works, Archaeological Institute of America (first vice-president of Boston Society, 1979), Association Paleorient, American Friends of Cyprus (founding member), British Institute of Archaeology at Ankara (fellow, 1964-69), British Institute of Persian Studies, British School at Athens, British School of Archaeology in Iraq, British School of Archaeology in Jerusalem, Israel Exploration Society, Palestine Exploration Society, Prehistoric Society.

AWARDS, HONORS: Tweedie Fellowship from University of Edinburgh, 1968; grant for excavation in Cyprus from National Science Foundation, 1976, 1977, 1978, and 1979, from National Endowment for the Humanities, 1982, 1983, and 1984, and from the Mazer Fund, 1982, 1984, and 1985; senior Fulbright grant for excavation in Cyprus, 1979-80 and 1986-87.

WRITINGS:

Catal Huyuk in Perspective, Cummings, 1976.
The Prehistory of Central Anatolia I: The Neolithic Period, Paul Aastroems Foerlag, 1980.
(Editor) *Vasilikos Valley Project I: The Middle Bronze Age Cemetery in Kalavasos Village,* Paul Aastroems Foerlag, 1985.
Vasilikos Valley Project 6: Excavations at Kalavasos-Tenta, Volume I, Paul Aastroems Foerlag, 1987.
Vasilikos Valley Project 8: Excavations at Kalavasos-Ayious, Paul Aastroems Foerlag, 1989.
Vasilikos Valley Project 7: Excavations at Kalavasos-Tenta, Volume II, Paul Aastroems Foerlag, 1990.

Vasilikos Valley Project 9: The Field Survey of the Vasilikos Valley, Volume I, Paul Aastroems Foerlag, 1990.

Contributor of about fifty articles and reviews to archaeology and classical studies journals.

SIDELIGHTS: Ian A. Todd told *CA* that a trip he made to Turkey following his first year at the University of Birmingham sparked his interest in Near Eastern archaeology and prompted him to apply to attend an excavation in that country. He recalls: "I was lucky—the first excavation I ever attended in the Near East was the site of Catal Huyuk, one of the most important earlier prehistoric sites to be excavated in many years. I first went to Cyprus in 1969 and immediately loved it. Conditions for excavation there are so much better than elsewhere in the Near East that I decided I would like to run an excavation there. After the necessary period of working in Cyprus with other projects, I was granted my excavation license for the summer of 1976.

"Previous projects in Cyprus and elsewhere have frequently concentrated on a single archaeological site. I wanted to take a small area, rather than one specific site, and cover it in detail to understand the changes in the way of life through various periods. This approach requires excavations at a number of sites of different periods, as well as various studies of the modern environment.

"Our major discoveries to date are a Neolithic village (c. 6000 B.C.) consisting of circular mud brick and stone buildings, and a very impressive Late Bronze Age town (thirteenth century B.C.) strategically located astride a major route of communication and close to important copper mines. Our overall aim is to recover, as completely as possible, a picture of all aspects of life in the Vasilikos Valley from the earliest occupation (c. 7000 B.C.) to c. 1000 B.C. We are especially interested in any evidence for gaps in the archaeological sequence. If such exist, what happened to cause the abandonment of the valley? In the case of one apparent gap (from c. 5000 B.C. until c. 3500 B.C.) environmental deterioration may be the cause, but this remains to be confirmed."

Todd adds: "After thirteen seasons of fieldwork our efforts are now being concentrated on the completion of the field survey (looking for archaeological sites of all periods) and the publication of all excavations carried out to date. We expect to be back in the field excavating our Late Bronze Age town in 1990 and hope to undertake the excavation of a site of another period thereafter. Although the Vasilikos Valley covers quite a small area, it seems that its archaeological resources are sufficient to last us a lifetime!!"

*   *   *

TODSICHER, J(ohn) Edgar 1926-

PERSONAL: Born December 26, 1926, in Yahoo, Kan.; son of Andrew Jackson (an intinerant preacher) and Thelma (Thanatogenes) Todsicher; married Inocencia B. Engkopf, June 26, 1944 (divorced, 1972); married Amelia Whitbread, July 4, 1973 (divorced, 1975); married Nancy Snake Bear (a souvenir retailer), June 25, 1976 (divorced, 1980); children: (first marriage) John (deceased), Carrie Nation (Mrs. Gerry C. Mander), Bob Jones, Aimee Semple, Mercury and Apollo (twin sons; deceased), Richard Spiro; (second marriage) Cosmo Milhous; (third marriage) Joyce Loud Snake. *Education:* Attended God's Peace and Power Baptist Seminary, 1944; Gopher Junction Community College, A.A., 1947; also studied Kranshaw Correspondence Course in salesmanship, 1949, and attended Betsy Barnes Business College, Gopher Junction, 1951. *Politics:* "Liberty." *Religion:* "Native Pantheism."

ADDRESSES: Home—9568 Columbia, Redford, Mich. 48239.

CAREER: Employed as door-to-door vacuum cleaner salesman in Haggard County, Kan., 1950-51; Heep Collection Agency, St. Louis, Mo., collector, 1952-56; Eddie Scheister's Used Parts and Service (used car dealer), St. Louis, Mo., salesman, 1956-59, sales trainer, 1959-62; Sado & Miasma Life Insurance, Inc., Grand Rapids, Mich., broker, 1963-69; Caveat Emptor Life Insurance, Detroit, Mich., founder and president, 1969-76; Todsicher-Bear Wild West Novelty Products, Grosse Shores, Ohio, vice-president, 1976-80; free-lance writer, 1980—. Organizer of evangelical meetings for Amazing Grace Baptist Union throughout southern United States, 1952-62; founder and treasurer of Metropolitan Brothers of the New Kingdom, Detroit, Mich.; founder of Great Native Future Church of the Everlasting Love, Detroit, Mich., 1976. *Military service:* U.S. Army, chaplain's assistant, 1947-49.

MEMBER: Sons of Business Association (founder and president, 1968), National Association of Itinerant Preachers.

AWARDS, HONORS: Sons of Business Award, 1968, for outstanding service to the life insurance community; George Lincoln Rockwell Memorial Award, Sweet Jesus Press, 1970, for "New Kingdom" series; Pearly Bridle Award, 1978, for *Plains Tuxedos: A History of Fringed Leather Attire;* award of merit, Western Merchants and Clothiers Association, 1978.

WRITINGS:

The Christian Car Salesman: Moral Merchandising (booklet), Betsy Barnes Business Press, 1958.
(With father, Andrew Jackson Todsicher) *Armageddon Trilogy,* Schweinkopf Publishers, Book 1: *Armageddon and You,* 1959, Book 2: *Armageddon Revisted,* 1961, Book 3: *Son of Armageddon,* 1961.
Redemption in Our Time: How Life Insurance Can Save America, Palm Tree Press, 1975.
Life Insurance and the Hereafter: How You Can Collect on Your Own Policy, Palm Tree Press, 1975.
From Right to Left: One Man's Personal and Political Odyssey through the American Socio-Political Landscape, New Morality Publications, 1976.
Buying Back Manhattan: American Souvenirs as a Force to Be Reckoned With in the National Marketplace, Todsicher-Bear Books, 1977.
Plains Tuxedos: A History of Fringed Leather Attire, Todsicher-Bear Books, 1978.
Marketing Western Products: A Guide to Manufacturing and Distribution, Western Merchants and Clothiers Association, 1979.
Buying Junk, Selling Antiques, Todsicher-Bear Books, 1979.
Recovering from Divorce, or, Re-Entering the Singles Market during Retirement, Todsicher Books, 1981.

Also author of "New Kingdom" series of pamphlets, 1964-74.

WORK IN PROGRESS: Creatively Coping with Child Support Claims, expected 1991.

SIDELIGHTS: J. Edgar Todsicher told *CA:* "The turns in my career reflect the turns in my life, from a long personal obsession with right-wing extremist politics and religious fundamentalism to cultural activism and then on to a period of reorientation which I can only say I hope will result in a few good short stories, or maybe a best selling novel. It will probably be about the power of women. Women have been the catalysts at every turn in my

life; women have razed my consciousness. Though I was once committed to the enterprise of selling back to the Americans artifacts from their past, I am now venturing to reacquaint women with the sense of their true power, which is mostly in their relationships with men and children. Deep down inside, I suspect that the driving motivation behind the writing is money.

"I would also like to leave something for my children, maybe a few picture books about a character I've had in mind for some time now—an angel on furlough who tries to learn what it means to be human from watching people. He thinks he has to hide his origins to make friends. It doesn't work, of course, and that provides the humor. But the field of spy thrillers interests me, too. Plus, the supernatural. I have notes for a novel about an agent for a secret organization who decides he likes it better among the people he's spying on. I'm currently looking for a partner to share my motor home while I'm traveling for research."

AVOCATIONAL INTERESTS: The stock market, outdoor cooking.

BIOGRAPHICAL/CRITICAL SOURCES:

BOOKS

Slarom, Seymour, *A Christian Interpretation of "The Armageddon Trilogy,"* Sweet Jesus Press, 1963.

PERIODICALS

Garment Marketing Newsletter, December, 1980.
Supremacist Quarterly, spring, 1968.
Yahoo Daily Record (Kan.), November 17, 1970.

*   *   *

TOLEDANO, Ralph de 1916-

PERSONAL: Surname is pronounced Toe-leh-*dah*-no; born August 17, 1916, in International Zone, Tangier, Morocco; son of Haim (a foreign correspondent and businessman) and Suzanne (Nahon) de Toledano; married Nora Romaine, July 6, 1938 (divorced, 1968); married Eunice Marshall, April 19, 1979; children: (first marriage) James, Paul Christopher. *Education:* Columbia University, B.A., 1938; language studies at Cornell University, 1943-44.

ADDRESSES: Home and office—825 New Hampshire Ave. N.W., Washington, D.C. 20037.

CAREER: Lex Publications, New York City, editor, 1938-39; *New Leader,* New York City, associate editor, 1940-43; *Plain Talk,* New York City, managing editor, 1946-47; International Ladies Garment Workers Union, New York City, publicity director of Dress Joint Board, 1947-48; *Newsweek,* New York City, assistant editor, 1948, associate editor, 1949, national reports editor, 1950-60, Washington bureau, 1956-60; Taft Broadcasting Co., Washington, D.C., Washington bureau chief, 1960; syndicated columnist with King Features Syndicate, 1960-71, National News-Research Syndicate, 1971-74, Copley News Service, 1974-89, and Heritage Features Syndicate, 1989—. Former radio and television commentator; lecturer; photographer. Publisher, Anthem Books. *Military service:* U.S. Army, 1943-46; served as artillery gunner and with Office of Strategic Services; became staff sergeant.

MEMBER: American Conservative Union (vice-chairman, 1965-66), Sigma Delta Chi, National Press Club, Dutch Treat Club.

AWARDS, HONORS: Philolexian Prizes for Poetry, Columbia University (two); Freedoms Foundation Awards, 1950, 1961,

1974, for books and columns; Americanism award, Veterans of Foreign Wars, 1953; distinguished journalism fellow, Heritage Foundation.

WRITINGS:

(Editor) *Frontiers of Jazz,* Oliver Durrell, 1947, 2nd edition, Ungar, 1962.
Seeds of Treason: The True Story of the Hiss-Chambers Tragedy, Funk, 1950, revised and updated edition, Regnery, 1962.
Spies, Dupes and Diplomats, Duell, Sloan & Pearce, 1952, new edition, Arlington House, 1967.
Day of Reckoning (novel), Holt, 1955.
Nixon, Holt, 1956, revised and expanded edition, Duell, Sloan & Pearce, 1960.
Lament for a Generation, foreword by Richard Nixon, Farrar, Straus, 1960.
The Greatest Plot in History, Duell, Sloan & Pearce, 1963, new edition, Arlington House, 1977.
The Winning Side: The Case for Goldwater Republicanism, Putnam, 1963, revised and updated edition, Macfadden, 1964.
(Editor with Karl Hess) *The Conservative Papers,* Anchor, 1964.
R.F.K., the Man Who Would Be President, Putnam, 1967.
America, I Love You, National Press, 1968.
One Man Alone: Richard Nixon, Funk, 1969.
(With Philip V. Brennan, Jr.) *Claude Kirk—Man and Myth,* Pyramid Publications, 1970.
(Author of introduction) William F. Buckley, Jr., editor, *Odyssey of a Friend,* Putnam, 1970.
Little Cesar, Anthem Books, 1971.
J. Edgar Hoover: The Man in His Time, Arlington House, 1973.
Hit and Run: The Ralph Nader Story, Arlington House, 1974.
Let Our Cities Burn, Arlington House, 1975, reprinted as *The Municipal Doomsday Machine,* Green Hill, 1976.
Poems: You and I, Pelican, 1979.
Devil Take Him (novel), Putnam, 1980.

Also author of *The Goldwater Story,* 1964. Contributor to *Commentary, American Scholar, American Mercury, Commonweal, Collier's, Saturday Review, Chicago Tribune,* and other periodicals and newspapers. Contributing editor, *National Review,* 1960—; editor in chief, *Washington World,* 1961-62.

WORK IN PROGRESS: No Road to Damascus, an autobiography; a novel; two collections of poems.

SIDELIGHTS: Ralph de Toledano, a music critic and political writer who has been writing professionally since the age of 16 and who turns out about three hundred thousand words a year, told *CA:* "Writing is hard work. . . . My advice to my own children has always been 'stay out of this profession; there are better ways to make a living.' But this kind of advice won't keep out those who really want to write. And they don't ask for advice."

BIOGRAPHICAL/CRITICAL SOURCES:

BOOKS

Authors in the News, Volume 1, Gale, 1976.

PERIODICALS

National Review, May 2, 1967, October 22, 1968, January 13, 1970, June 29, 1971, May 30, 1980.
New York Review of Books, June 1, 1967.
New York Times, December 12, 1969.
New York Times Book Review, November 23, 1969, June 17, 1973, August 10, 1975.
Time, May 19, 1967.

TRASK, Jonathan
See LEVINSON, Leonard

*   *   *

TREBING, Harry M(artin)   1926-

PERSONAL: Born September 14, 1926, in Baltimore, Md.; son of Harry A. (a chemist) and Bess (Shore) Trebing; married Joyce Christie, 1958; children: Evan, David. *Education:* University of Maryland, B.A., 1950, M.A., 1952; University of Wisconsin, Ph.D., 1958. *Religion:* Protestant.

ADDRESSES: Home—4568 Manitou Dr., Okemos, Mich. 48864. *Office*—101 Marshall Hall-Economics, Michigan State University, East Lansing, Mich. 48824.

CAREER: University of Maryland, College Park, instructor in economics, 1951-52; University of Nebraska, Lincoln, assistant professor of economics, 1957-62; Indiana University, Bloomington, associate professor of public utilities and transportation, 1962-66; Michigan State University, East Lansing, professor of economics and director of Institute of Public Utilities, 1966—. Federal Communications Commission, supervisory industry economist in Common Carrier Bureau, 1963-65, chief of Economic Studies Division, 1965-66. Consultant to government commissions, including President's Task Force on Communications Policy, 1968. Chief economist, U.S. Postal Rate Commission, 1971-72; conference administrator for Annual Regulatory Studies Program, National Association of Regulatory Utility Commissioners, 1973—. *Military service:* U.S. Naval Reserve, 1945-46.

MEMBER: American Economic Association (past president of Transportation and Public Utilities Group), Association for Evolutionary Economics (vice-president, 1972; president, 1973), National Academy of Engineering, National Research Council, Midwest Economics Association, Midwest Business Administration Association, Economics Society of Michigan, Beta Gamma Sigma.

AWARDS, HONORS: University of Nebraska summer research fellow, 1958; National Science Foundation grant, 1976-78.

WRITINGS:

EDITOR

Performance under Regulation, Institute of Public Utilities, Michigan State University, 1968.
(With R. H. Howard) *Rate of Return under Regulation: New Directions and Perspectives,* Institute of Public Utilities, Michigan State University, 1969.
The Corporation in the American Economy, Quadrangle, 1970.
Essays on Public Utility Pricing and Regulation, Institute of Public Utilities, Michigan State University, 1971.
(And author of introduction) *New Dimensions in Public Utility Pricing,* Michigan State University, Bureau of Business and Economic Research, 1976.
Issues in Public Utility Regulation, Division of Research, Graduate School of Business Administration, Michigan State University, 1979.
Challenges for Public Utility Regulation in the 1980s, Division of Research, Graduate School of Business Administration, Michigan State University, 1981.
(With Patrick C. Mann) *Changing Patterns in Regulation, Markets, and Technology: The Effect on Public Utility Pricing,* Division of Research, Graduate School of Business Administration, Michigan State University, 1984.

(With Mann) *The Impact of Deregulation and Market Forces on Public Utilities: The Future Role of Regulation,* Division of Research, Graduate School of Business Administration, Michigan State University, 1985.

CONTRIBUTOR

(With Manley R. Irwin) H. Edward English, editor, *Telecommunications for Canada,* Methuen (Canada), 1973.

William G. Shepherd and Thomas G. Gies, editors, *Regulation in Further Perspective,* Ballinger, 1974.

(With W. H. Melody) Michael W. Klass and Shepherd, editors, *Regulation and Entry,* Michigan State University, Bureau of Business and Economic Research, 1976.

W. J. Samuels, editor, *The Chicago School of Political Economy,* Association for Evolutionary Economics and Michigan State University, Bureau of Business and Economic Research, 1976.

Werner Sichel, editor, *Salvaging Public Utility Regulation,* Lexington Books, 1976.

OTHER

Also author of government reports on communications and regulated industries. Contributor to professional journals. Member of editorial board, *Nebraska Journal of Economics and Business,* 1961-62, and *Land Economics,* 1969—.

WORK IN PROGRESS: Competition and Regulatory Reform in the Energy Utilities, a project funded by the National Science Foundation.*

*   *   *

TROJANOWICZ, John M.
See TROYANOVICH, John M(ichael)

*   *   *

TROJANOWICZ, Robert C(hester) 1941-

PERSONAL: Born May 25, 1941, in Bay City, Mich.; son of Chester R. (a detective) and Loretta (Duffy) Trojanowicz; married Susan E. Schell, December 30, 1961; children: Eric, Elise. *Education:* Michigan State University, B.S., 1963, M.S.W., 1965, Ph.D., 1969. *Politics:* Independent. *Religion:* Roman Catholic.

ADDRESSES: Office—School of Criminal Justice, Michigan State University, East Lansing, Mich. 48824.

CAREER: Michigan State University, East Lansing, assistant professor, 1969-71, associate professor of juvenile delinquency, deviant behavior, and the community, 1971—, dean of the College of Social Science, 1973—. *Military service:* U.S. Army Reserve, 1961-62.

MEMBER: International Criminal Justice Association (member of board of trustees, 1971—).

WRITINGS:

Juvenile Delinquency: Concepts and Control, Prentice-Hall, 1973, 4th edition, with Merry Morash, 1987.
(With Samuel L. Dixon) *Criminal Justice and the Community,* Prentice-Hall, 1974.
(With brother, John M. Trojanowicz, and Forrest M. Moss) *Community Based Crime Prevention,* Goodyear Publishing, 1975.
(With J. M. Trojanowicz) *Police Supervision,* Prentice-Hall, 1980.
The Environment of the First-Line Supervisors, Prentice-Hall, 1980.

(With others) *An Evaluation of the Neighborhood Foot Patrol in Flint, Michigan,* Michigan State University, c. 1982.

Contributor to professional journals.

WORK IN PROGRESS: Research in comparing college-educated policemen with non-college policemen, and on diversionary programs for youngsters in lieu of court commitment.*

*   *   *

TROYANOVICH, John M(ichael) 1936-
(John M. Trojanowicz)

PERSONAL: Surname is pronounced Troy-a-*no*-vich; original surname, Trojanowicz, legally changed, 1966; born August 22, 1936, in Bay City, Mich.; son of Chester R. (a detective) and Loretta (Duffy) Trojanowicz; married Kathleen Gallagher (a bookkeeper), September 1, 1956; children: John L., Stephan J., Mark M., Rita M., Josef G. *Education:* University of Michigan, B.A., 1960; University of Illinois, M.A., 1961; Michigan State University, Ph.D., 1964.

ADDRESSES: Home—7383 Deerhill Dr., Clarkston, Mich. 48016. *Office*—Chrysler Corp., 11631 Mack Ave., Detroit, Mich. 48214.

CAREER: Michigan State University, East Lansing, instructor, 1962-64, assistant professor of German, 1964-68; University of Kansas, Lawrence, associate professor of German and education, 1968-71; Illinois Wesleyan University, Bloomington, professor of modern languages and education, 1971-77, chairman of department of foreign languages, 1971-74; Volkswagen of America, New Stanton, Pa., training and communications administrator, 1977-79, Troy, Mich., coordinator of engineering liaison, 1979-81, purchasing agent, 1981-84; Chrysler Corp., Detroit, Mich., quality specialist and manufacturing liaison in Mexico, 1984-86, training manager, 1986—. Professor of business, Oakland Community College, 1983—. President of board of directors, McLean County Mental Health Center, Center for Human Resources. *Military service:* U.S. Army, Security Agency, interpreter and translator in German and Rumanian, 1955-58.

MEMBER: American Management Association.

AWARDS, HONORS: Woodrow Wilson fellow, 1960; study grant at University of Tuebingen, Germanistic Society of America, 1964; travel grant from Republics of West Germany and Austria.

WRITINGS:

(With Kurt W. Schild) *German Conversational Reader,* American Book Co., 1969.
German: From Language to Literature, Van Nostrand, 1972.
(Author of instructor's manual for brother's book) Robert C. Trojanowicz, *Juvenile Delinquency: Concepts and Control,* Prentice-Hall, 1973, 4th edition, with Merry Morash, 1987.
(Author of instructor's manual) R. C. Trojanowicz and Samuel L. Dixon, *Criminal Justice and the Community,* Prentice-Hall, 1974.
(Under name John M. Trojanowicz; R. C. Trojanowicz, and Forrest M. Moss) *Community Based Crime Prevention,* Goodyear Publishing, 1975.
(With R. C. Trojanowicz) *Police Supervision,* Prentice-Hall, 1980.

Contributor to periodicals, including *American Foreign Language Teacher, Foreign Language Annals, Die Unterrichtspraxis,*

Public Personnel Review, Classical Outlook, Bereavement, and *Texas Foreign Language Bulletin.*

WORK IN PROGRESS: Research in German-American cross-cultural contrasts, especially in the area of business practices and automobile manufacturing.

*　　*　　*

TRUDEAU, G(arretson) B(eekman) 1948-
(Garry B. Trudeau)

PERSONAL: Born in 1948, in New York, N.Y.; married Jane Pauley (a television journalist), June 14, 1980; children: Rachel and Ross (twins), Jack. *Education:* Yale University, received degree, 1970, received M.F.A.

ADDRESSES: Office—c/o Universal Press Syndicate, 4400 Johnson Dr., Fairway, Kan. 66205.

CAREER: Cartoonist and writer, primarily of comic strip "Doonesbury," currently syndicated to almost 850 newspapers. Formerly operated a graphics studio in New Haven, Conn.

AWARDS, HONORS: Pulitzer Prize for editorial cartooning, 1975; D.H.L. from Yale University, 1976; Academy Award nomination and Cannes Film Festival special jury prize, both 1977, both for the animated film "A Doonesbury Special"; Drama Desk nominations for book and lyrics, 1983, for musical "Doonesbury"; various honorary degrees from colleges and universities.

WRITINGS:

Doonesbury, foreword by Erich Segal, American Heritage Press, 1971.

Still a Few Bugs in the System, Holt, 1972, selections published as *Even Revolutionaries Like Chocolate Chip Cookies* and as *Just a French Major from the Bronx,* Popular Library, 1974.

The President Is a Lot Smarter Than You Think, Holt, 1973.

But This War Had Such Promise, Holt, 1973, selections published as *Bravo for Life's Little Ironies,* Popular Library, 1975.

(Under name Garry Trudeau) *Doonesbury: The Original Yale Cartoons,* Sheed, 1973.

Call Me When You Find America, Holt, 1973.

(With Nicholas von Hoffman) *The Fireside Watergate,* Sheed, 1973.

Guilty, Guilty, Guilty!, Holt, 1974.

(Under name Garry Trudeau) *Joanie,* afterword by Nora Ephron, Sheed, 1974.

(Under name Garry Trudeau) *Don't Ever Change, Boopsie,* Popular Library, 1974.

Dare to Be Great, Ms. Caucus, Holt, 1975.

"What Do We Have for the Witness, Johnnie?," Holt, 1975.

The Doonesbury Chronicles, introduction by Garry Wills, Holt, 1975.

(Under name Garry Trudeau) *We'll Take It from Here, Sarge,* afterword by Chuck Stone, Sheed, 1975.

(Under name Garry Trudeau) *I Have No Son,* Popular Library, 1975.

Wouldn't a Gremlin Have Been More Sensible?, Holt, 1975.

(With von Hoffman) *Tales from the Margaret Mead Taproom: The Compleat Gonzo Governorship of Doonesbury's Uncle Duke,* Sheed, 1976.

"Speaking of Inalienable Rights, Amy . . . ," Holt, 1976.

You're Never Too Old for Nuts and Berries, Holt, 1976.

An Especially Tricky People, Holt, 1977.

(With David Levinthal) *Hitler Moves East: A Graphic Chronicle, 1941-43,* Sheed, 1977.

(Under name Garry Trudeau) *As the Kid Goes for Broke,* Holt, 1977.

Stalking the Perfect Tan, Holt, 1978.

(Under name Garry Trudeau) *Any Grooming Hints for Your Fans, Rollie?,* Holt, 1978.

Doonesbury's Greatest Hits, introduction by William F. Buckley, Holt, 1978.

We're Not out of the Woods Yet, Holt, 1980.

"But the Pension Fund Was Just Sitting There," Holt, 1980.

A Tad Overweight, but Violet Eyes to Die For, Holt, 1980.

And That's My Final Offer!, Holt, 1980.

Guess Who, Fish-Face!, Fawcett Crest, 1981.

Do All Birders Have Bedroom Eyes, Dear?, Fawcett Crest, 1981.

He's Never Heard of You, Either, Holt, 1981.

Ask for May, Settle for June (also see below), Holt, 1982.

In Search of Reagan's Brain (also see below), Holt, 1982.

Gotta Run, My Government Is Collapsing, Fawcett, 1982.

Unfortunately, She Was Also Wired for Sound, Holt, 1982.

We Who Are About to Fry, Salute You: Selected Cartoons from In Search of Reagan's Brain, Volume 1, Fawcett, 1982.

Is This Your First Purge, Miss? Selected Cartoons from In Search of Reagan's Brain, Volume 2, Fawcett, 1982.

The People's Doonesbury: Notes from Underfoot, Holt, 1982.

You Give Great Meeting, Sid, Holt, 1983.

The Wreck of the Rusty Nail, Holt, 1983.

It's Supposed to Be Yellow, Pinhead: Selected Cartoons from Ask for May, Settle for June, Volume 1, Fawcett, 1983.

The Thrill Is Gone, Bernie, Fawcett, 1983.

Doonesbury Dossier, Holt, 1984.

Confirmed Bachelors Are Just So Fascinating, Fawcett, 1984.

Doonesbury: A Musical Comedy (also see below), Holt, 1984.

Dressed for Failure, I See, Fawcett, 1984.

Sir, I'm So Worried about Your Mood Swings, Fawcett, 1984.

Check Your Egos at the Door, Holt, 1985.

(Contributor) *Comic Relief: Drawings from the Cartoonists' Thanksgiving Day Hunger Project,* Holt, 1986.

Death of a Party Animal, Holt, 1986.

Rap Master Ronnie (also see below), deluxe edition, Lord John, 1986.

That's Doctor Sinatra, You Little Bimbo!, Holt, 1986.

Doonesbury Deluxe: Selected Glances Askance, Holt, 1987.

Downtown Doonesbury, Holt, 1987.

Calling Dr. Whoopee!, Holt, 1987.

Talkin' about My G-G-Generation, Holt, 1988.

We're Eating More Beets!, Holt, 1988.

PLAYS AND TELEVISION SCRIPTS

"A Doonesbury Special" (animated film), produced for television, 1977.

(Author of book and lyrics) "Doonesbury" (stage musical), produced on Broadway at Biltmore Theatre, November 21, 1983.

(Author of lyrics) "Rap Master Ronnie" (stage musical), produced in New York at Top of the Gate, October 3, 1984.

"Tanner '88" (television series), produced for Home Box Office, 1988.

OTHER

Editor of "Cartoons for New Children" series for Sheed. Contributor of articles to *Rolling Stone, New York, Harper's,* and *New Republic.*

SIDELIGHTS: When G. B. (Garry) Trudeau's comic strip "Doonesbury" debuted in syndication, Richard Nixon was president, U.S. troops were fighting in Viet Nam, and campus unrest made headlines across America. The popularity of the seven-days-a-week strip earned Trudeau a Pulitzer Prize in 1975, a *Time* cover story in 1976, and almost three dozen book compilations. But at the same time, "Doonesbury" has come to represent the controversial nature of editorial cartooning; throughout its history, the comic has been argued over and even pulled from the comics section of some papers and put into the opinion pages. At times, the strip was pulled out altogether by disapproving editors.

"Doonesbury" was born as "Bull Tales," a strip Trudeau produced while still a student at Yale University. Even then, the subject matter drew attention: the strip poked "sophomoric fun at mixers, campus revolutionaries, Yale President Kingman Brewster—but mostly at the football huddles of 'B.D.' Yalies recognized the jock as Brian Dowling, standout Yale quarterback," according to the *Time* cover story. Other recognizable figures from the early days include Yale's Reverend William Sloane Coffin, Jr., now known as the Reverend W. S. Sloan, Jr., the spiritual center of "Doonesbury's" Walden Puddle, and campus activist Mark Zanger, a.k.a. the opinionated "Megaphone" Mark Slackmeyer. But perhaps the most well-known early figure parodied by Trudeau is the "gonzo" journalist Hunter S. Thompson, author of *Fear and Loathing in Las Vegas.* His pen-and-ink incarnation is the mysterious Uncle Duke.

And then there is the low-keyed optimist Michael J. Doonesbury, a character not unlike Trudeau himself, *Time* suggests. Certainly the cartoonist's early years gave little indication of his famous future. As the article notes, Trudeau was born in New York City of Canadian background (a distant relative is former Canadian Prime Minister Pierre Trudeau), and the family moved to upstate New York when Garry was five. "It was a real Christopher Robin existence," recalls Trudeau, referring to the best friend of Winnie-the-Pooh. "I was well schooled in fantasy and Beatrix Potter." But as a budding artist in a school full of football players, young Trudeau "took a lot of grief," as a former classmate tells *Time.* "Adolescence is, I think, an unpleasant time of life no matter where you spend it and with whom you spend it. I didn't like being a teenager," says Trudeau to *Washington Post* writer Lloyd Grove. "I didn't like teenagers when I was one. And I still don't like them. It's a very selfish time of life."

So when the acerbic "Bull Tales" caught on in the Yale community, Trudeau, not a natural celebrity, kept a safe distance from reporters (one legend has him hiding in his bathroom for three hours to avoid a persistent newsman) and still grants only a rare interview today. Universal Press Syndicate took an interest in "Bull Tales" in 1970 and, after Trudeau "erased the Y on B.D.'s helmet, clothed all the naked girls, deleted expletives, and completely redrew nearly an entire year's worth of strips to lend them a universal appeal," as *Time* puts it, "Doonesbury" first appeared in 28 newspapers. The rise of "Doonesbury" in popularity and controversy reflects its readers' growing sophistication about politics and society. Thus has the strip explored America's involvement in Viet Nam, Watergate, women's rights, several presidential elections, and other hot topics. For many years, the action centered on the Walden Puddle Commune, a haven for characters like Michael, Mark, B. D., the 1960s throwback Zonker Harris, and their friends. In the early years, Trudeau introduced a fortyish wife and mother, Joanie Caucus, who soon became one of Walden's most popular residents. Joanie left her husband and enrolled in law school when one night Mr. Caucus put his arm around her and declared, "My wife. I think I'll keep her." "I broke his nose," says Joanie. "Trudeau's dislikes are am-

bidextrous," as *Time* has noted. "Neither radicals nor reactionaries are safe from his artillery. Stuffed shirts of Oxford broadcloth or frayed denim receive the same impudent deflation. Yet Trudeau attacks with such gentle humor that even hard-nosed presidential aides can occasionally be heard chuckling over the daily White House news summary—when it includes a *Doonesbury.*"

Trudeau dealt his fans a severe blow in 1983, when he abruptly announced a sabbatical from "Doonesbury" in order to give the characters a chance to grow up and out of Walden Puddle. "Editors across the nation were outraged that I could be so presumptuous as to take control of my own career," the artist recalls to Rick Kogan of *Chicago Tribune Book World.* "People regard their comics pages as sacrosanct. Stopping them is like an interruption of a public utility. I knew editors would think I was frivolous, that I was being a dilettante [in trying] my hand at other endeavors." He used the interim to pursue another of his great loves. "Theatre was my earliest life's passion," Trudeau tells Kogan. "I formed a theatre group at the ripe old age of seven. At first, I wrote the shows. Then at 10 I decided it was time to stop doing amateurish pieces and get on with the real business of theatre. I sent away for the catalog of Samuel French plays, and I'll never forget the rush when my first package of plays arrived. I devoured them."

And so Trudeau ventured onto Broadway with a musical version of "Doonesbury," for which he wrote the book and lyrics. The story draws several of Walden's denizens in a plot that finds perennial student Zonker finally graduating, Uncle Duke attempting to bulldoze Walden Puddle into condominiums, and Mike wooing Joanie Caucus's daughter J. J., a new-wave artist. Overall, the musical garnered lukewarm reviews, with Benedict Nightingale of the *New York Times* representing several critics' opinions: "True, there are some ruefully amusing encounters, . . . [but] even the most astringent passages don't seem ideally suited to that extrovert medium, the musical theatre. Often you can see the drawings in your mind's eye, each framed, each part of a deftly composed series of four or six, each reaching its tiny climax, each ready for the press."

The musical of "Doonesbury" had a short run. But Trudeau fared better a few years later with "Rap Master Ronnie," a self-proclaimed "partisan revue" of President Reagan's career. As Frank Rich sees it in a *New York Times* article, " 'Rap Master Ronnie' doesn't merely mock the President's style, 'evil empire' rhetoric and factual misstatements. . . . [Trudeau and composer Elizabeth Swados] also wish to make a concerted ideological statement of how, in their view, the Administration's policies have corroded the nation in the last four years. This is an ambitious task—roughly akin to adapting the Democratic Party platform into a musical—and the writing is not always up to it." Still, Rich lauds Trudeau's "ingenious lyrics [and] bristling polemical wisecracks."

At about the same time "Rap Master Ronnie" was premiering, the "Doonesbury" strip resumed original publication. Following its 19-month hiatus, the comic's return focused new attention on its contents, with some critics wondering how such archetypically 1970s characters would survive in the age of Yuppies and leveraged buyouts. David Ignatius, for one, worried about a slacking of "Doonesbury's" bite. In a 1986 *Washington Post* piece, Ignatius complained that the strip now "involves something different: the gradual disappearance of ordinary people and experience . . . since its characters moved from Walden Commune into the real world two years ago." Trudeau, Ignatius continues, "seems at time to have lost touch with the simple pleasures and absurdities of ordinary life. As a result, his once-delicate satirical touch has become, too often, leaden and heavy-handed."

Certainly the biggest controversies of the era came to the fore. When, for instance, Trudeau lampooned anti-abortion advocates with his own version of their film "The Silent Scream," which purports to show a fetus reacting to an abortion, the syndicate handling "Doonesbury" convinced the artist to cancel that series of strips. (In Trudeau's version, "Silent Scream II: The Prequel," his correspondent shows not a fetus, but a dividing cell whom he dubs Timmy.) In another series, Trudeau got personal with Frank Sinatra when the singer was cited by President Reagan with a Medal of Freedom. A set of "Doonesbury" strips showed actual photographs of Sinatra in the company of organized-crime figures, and featured sardonic comments on the singer's plaudits. As had happened several times before, a number of papers pulled the Sinatra series, fearing libel suits. "Sinatra is fair game," argues *Newsweek*'s Jonathan Alter. "His association with mob bosses is beyond dispute, and Trudeau had every right to question the propriety of his being honored at the White House and elsewhere."

As the decade neared an end, Trudeau embarked on yet another satirical project, this time focusing on the 1988 Presidential campaign. In association with film director Robert Altman, Trudeau wrote a cable-television series called "Tanner '88," a show unique in that it featured up-to-the-minute coverage of the real campaign as seen through the eyes of a fictional contender, Senator Jack Tanner, democrat from Michigan. Tanner and his staff covered the same ground as the real candidates, going on location around the country and even filming scenes with Gary Hart, Robert Dole, and Pat Robertson. The series, which ends with Tanner's defeat at the Democratic National Convention, "has become a cult favorite among those who have watched it being filmed," according to *New Republic* writer Maureen Dowd. "Ironically, the small cadre of political junkies who can best appreciate the program live in the nation's capital, where cable television isn't available. It is hard to imagine what a traveling salesman from Akron, flipping on HBO in his hotel room hoping for a mildly erotic movie, could make of this fantastic voyage into the inner arteries of politics."

Reacting to his reputation as a recluse (notwithstanding his well-publicized marriage to television reporter Jane Pauley), Trudeau notes to *Washington Post*'s Grove that he could "quite happily have continued on with my preference not to do interviews for the rest of my life. I'd rather have people come to the strip and read it in the clear, without any preconceived notions of the personality behind it." In the same article, the artist amusedly reacted to one charge that has dogged his entire career—that he can't draw. "I'm still working on it," Trudeau says. "I have always felt that I'm not much of a writer and I'm not much of an artist but I reside at the intersection of those two disciplines and that's where I make my contribution, such as it is . . . I think [Doonesbury] has a unique look, for lack of a better word." Going on, Trudeau states that his comic strip "has always been a kind of Rorschach test for its readers. To the extent to which it is a diary for a certain generation, it becomes a way of mirroring both change in the culture and change in the individual who is reading the strip."

BIOGRAPHICAL/CRITICAL SOURCES:

BOOKS

Authors in the News, Volume 2, Gale, 1976.
Contemporary Literary Criticism, Volume 12, Gale, 1980.

PERIODICALS

Chicago Tribune, September 16, 1981, September 14, 1985.
Chicago Tribune Book World, November 24, 1985.
Christian Science Monitor, January 27, 1982.
Esquire, December, 1985.
Los Angeles Times, October 29, 1984, February 20, 1985, November 26, 1987.
New Republic, August 1, 1988.
Newsweek, June 24, 1985.
New York Times, February 28, 1980, November 22, 1983, November 27, 1983, September 30, 1984, October 4, 1984.
New York Times Book Review, December 7, 1975.
Time, February 9, 1976, June 24, 1985, December 8, 1986.
Washington Post, January 1, 1983, August 24, 1986, November 12, 1986, May 9, 1987, July 21, 1988.*

—Sketch by Susan Salter

* * *

TRUDEAU, Garry B.
See TRUDEAU, G(arretson) B(eekman)

* * *

TURNBAUGH, William A(rthur) 1948-
(Bill Thornbrook)

PERSONAL: Born June 1, 1948, in Williamsport, Pa.; son of William Hugh and Louise Elizabeth (Muller) Turnbaugh; married Sarah Ropes Peabody, October 12, 1974. *Education:* Lycoming College, A.B. (history; summa cum laude), 1970, A.B. (Spanish; summa cum laude), 1970; Harvard University, Ph.D., 1973.

ADDRESSES: Office—Department of Sociology/Anthropology, University of Rhode Island, Kingston, R.I. 02881.

CAREER: Harvard University, Cambridge, Mass., research assistant at Peabody Museum of Archaeology and Ethnology, 1973-74; University of Rhode Island, Kingston, assistant professor, 1974-78, associate professor, 1978-83, professor of anthropology, 1983—, archaeologist, 1974—. Has done fieldwork in the U.S., Canada, and the Near East, 1968-74. Has given over 35 presentations at professional meetings and colloquia. Designer of official flag of Lycoming County, Pa., 1970. Consultant to National Science Foundation, National Endowment for the Humanities, National Geographic Society, Commonwealth of Massachusetts, Museum of American Life, Institute for Conservation Archaeology (Harvard University), Public Archaeology Laboratory (Brown University), Rhode Island Historical Preservation Commission, Rhode Island State Education Department, and to numerous publishers and journals.

MEMBER: Society of Professional Archaeologists, Society for American Archaeology, Society for Historical Archaeology, American Association of University Professors, Society for Pennsylvania Archaeology, Lycoming County Historical Society (member of board of directors; acting president, 1966-70), Explorers Club, Sigma Xi, Phi Alpha Theta, Phi Kappa Phi.

AWARDS, HONORS: Woodrow Wilson fellowship, 1970-71; National Science Foundation fellowship, 1970-73; National Endowment for the Arts travel grant, 1985; distinguished alumnus award, Lycoming College, 1987.

WRITINGS:

Man, Land, and Time: Cultural Prehistory and Demographic Patterns of North-Central Pennsylvania, Unigraphic, 1975, 2nd edition, 1977.

(With Robert Jurmain and Harry Nelson) *Understanding Physical Anthropology and Archaeology,* West Publishing, 1981, 4th edition, revised, 1990.

The Material Culture of RI-1000, a Mid-17th-Century Narragansett Indian Burial Site in North Kingstown, Rhode Island, University of Rhode Island, 1984.

(With wife, Sarah Peabody Turnbaugh) *Indian Baskets,* Schiffer, 1986.

(With S.P. Turnbaugh) *Indian Jewelry of the American Southwest,* Schiffer, 1988.

(With S.P. Turnbaugh; under pseudonyms Bill and Sarah Thornbrook) *R.F.D. Country! Mailboxes and Post Offices of Rural America,* Schiffer, 1988.

CONTRIBUTOR

J.E. Ericson and B.A. Purdy, editors, *Prehistoric Quarries and Lithic Production,* Cambridge University Press, 1984.

G. Horse Capture and G. Ball, editors, *Plains Indian Seminar,* Buffalo Bill Historical Center, 1984.

J. Rogers and S. Wilson, editors, *Perspectives on Change: Ethnohistorical and Archaeological Approaches to Culture Contact,* Cambridge University Press, in press.

OTHER

Also author of technical and completion reports. Also contributor to A. McMullen and R. Handsmen, editors, *A Key into the Language of Woodsplint Baskets,* 1987. Contributor to anthropology and archaeology journals, including *American Anthropologist, Journal of Anthropological Research, Numismatist, Journal of American Indian Culture and Research, Explorers Journal, Journal of Political and Military Sociology,* and *Choice.* Editor, Society for Pennsylvania Archaeology *Newsletter,* 1963-68; associate editor, *Anthropological Journal of Canada,* 1966-74, and *Historical Archaeology,* 1986—; review editor, *Pennsylvania Archaeologist,* 1981—; special publications editor, Society for Historical Archaeology, 1987-88.

WORK IN PROGRESS: Research on contact between American Indian and European cultures, especially intercultural trade and its effects on native arts; compiling a volume on the early colonial period in southern New England.

SIDELIGHTS: William A. Turnbaugh told *CA:* "Some early encouragement from Pulitzer Prize-winning novelist Conrad Richter, a fellow Pennsylvanian and a patient correspondent, helped focus my scholarly interests. His sensitivity to the people and events of the frontier infused his carefully researched literary works. His personal letters further inspired me to explore those dramatic episodes of human contact fueled by the conflict of cultures in the American wilderness. Much of my fieldwork and publication activity continues to examine the many facets of this confrontation, which, as Conrad Richter recognized, is one of the universal themes of humanity."

*   *   *

TURNER, Ann W(arren) 1945-

PERSONAL: Born December 10, 1945, in Northampton, Mass.; daughter of Richard Bigelow (a printer) and Marian (an artist; maiden name, Gray) Warren; married Richard E. Turner (a teacher), June 3, 1967. *Education:* Attended University of Manchester, 1965-66; Bates College, B.A., 1967; University of Massachusetts, M.A.T., 1968. *Politics:* Liberal Democrat. *Religion:* Protestant.

ADDRESSES: Home and office—Briar Hill Rd., Williamsburg, Mass. 01036. *Agent*—Marilyn Marlow, Curtis Brown Ltd., 575 Madison Ave., New York, N.Y. 10022.

CAREER: High school English teacher in Great Barrington, Mass., 1968-69; writer, 1969—.

AWARDS, HONORS: First prize, *Atlantic Monthly* college creative writing contest, 1967, for "Athinai"; American Library Association notable book citations, 1980, for *A Hunter Comes Home,* and 1985, for *Dakota Dugout.*

WRITINGS:

Vultures (nonfiction for children), McKay, 1973.
Houses for the Dead (nonfiction), McKay, 1976.
A Hunter Comes Home (novel for children), Crown, 1980.
The Way Home (novel for children), Crown, 1982.
Dakota Dugout (poem for children), Macmillan, 1985.
Tickle a Pickle (poems for children), Macmillan, 1986.
Street Talk (poems), Houghton, 1986.
Third Girl from the Left (novel), Macmillan, 1986.
Nettie's Trip South (historical poem), Macmillan, 1987.
Time of the Bison (fiction), Macmillan, 1988.
Heron Street (picture book), Harper, 1989.
Grasshopper Summer (novel), Macmillan, 1989.
Hedgehog for Breakfast (picture book), Macmillan, 1989.
Through Moon and Stars and Night Skies (picture book), Harper, 1990.
Mathilda's Revenge (novel), Harper, 1991.
Stars for Sarah (picture book), Harper, 1991.

Also author of *Rituals of Birth* (nonfiction).

WORK IN PROGRESS: No Maybes, a novel for Harper; two picture books for Macmillan, due 1993 or 1994; illustrations for *Apple Valley Year,* for Macmillan.

SIDELIGHTS: Ann W. Turner told *CA:* "My upbringing influenced my writing. Possibly because my liberal family was somewhat 'different' from the New Englanders of our town, I grew up being interested in different peoples and cultures. Living in the country and having an artist for a mother gave me a certain way of seeing, an eye for beauty and interest in what others might think ugly or dull; dead weeds, old men and women, fat ladies at the beach, ancient and venerable crows, and vultures. I still live in the country, draw nourishment from it, and write about the seasons in my journal.

"I am concerned with the things that make each culture individual, and the traits that hold us together. To understand ourselves now, I feel we must know the Eskimos, the Aborigines, the ancient Chinese, and Paleolithic man. We are that strange tribe in the jungle; we are the people so old that only their bones and amulets are left. In strange and beautiful ways we are the same, yet different. That is what I write of, and will probably continue writing of for a long, long time."

The author later added: "Writers write for the same reasons that readers read—to find out the end of the story. I never know how my stories will end. Will it be a happy ending? Will there be disaster along the way? I must just push along, writing as often as I can and as well as I can, to get the same answers that you look for.

"Most of the time, writing is fun—although there are times when I want to burn my manuscript in the driveway. But I always come back to it for that delicious sense of surprise: What will come out today? There is the same satisfaction in writing a book as there is in doing other things well."

U

UNDINE, P. F.
   See PAINE, Lauran (Bosworth)

* * *

UNTERMEYER, Bryna Ivens   1909-

PERSONAL: Born April 27, 1909, in New York, N.Y.; daughter of Benjamin F. (a lawyer) and Millie (Drescher) Isaacs; married Louis Untermeyer (author and editor), July 23, 1948 (died December 19, 1977); married Emanuel E. Raices, June 9, 1979. *Education:* Hunter College (now Hunter College of the City University of New York), B.A., 1930.

ADDRESSES: Home and office—Great Hill Rd., Newtown, Conn. 06470. *Agent*—McIntosh & Otis, Inc., 475 Fifth Ave., New York, N.Y. 10017.

WRITINGS:

(Editor) *The Seventeen Reader,* Lippincott, 1951.
(Editor) *Nineteen from Seventeen,* Lippincott, 1952.
(Editor) *Stories from Seventeen,* Lippincott, 1955.
(Editor with husband Louis Untermeyer) Jakob Ludwig Karl Grimm and Wilhelm Karl Grimm, *Fairy Tales: The Complete Household Tales of Jakob and Wilhelm Grimm,* Limited Editions Club, 1962.
Memoir for Mrs. Sullavan, Simon & Schuster, 1966.
(Editor) *Sorry, Dear,* Golden Press, 1968.
(Editor with L. Untermeyer) *Animal Stories,* Golden Press, 1968.
(Editor with L. Untermeyer) *Words of Wisdom* (quotations), Golden Press, 1968.
(Editor with L. Untermeyer) *Favorite Classics,* Golden Press, 1968.
(Editor with L. Untermeyer) *Tales and Legends,* Golden Press, 1968.
(Editor with L. Untermeyer) *Stories and Poems for the Very Young,* Golden Press, 1973.
(Editor with L. Untermeyer) *A Galaxy of Verse,* M. Evans, 1978.

"GOLDEN TREASURY OF CHILDREN'S LITERATURE" SERIES; EDITOR WITH L. UNTERMEYER

Big and Little Creatures, Golden Press, 1961.
Beloved Tales, Golden Press, 1962.
Fun and Fancy, Golden Press, 1962.
Old Friends and Lasting Favorites, Golden Press, 1962.
Wonderlands, Golden Press, 1962.
Unfamiliar Marvels, Golden Press, 1963.
Creatures Wild and Tame, Golden Press, 1963.
Adventures All, Golden Press, 1963.
Legendary Animals, Golden Press, 1963.
Tall Tales, Golden Press, 1963.
The Golden Treasury of Children's Literature, Golden Press, 1966 (published in England as *The Children's Treasury of Literature in Colour,* Hamlyn, 1966).

WORK IN PROGRESS: Cats as Cats Can; Comedy of Eros, a novel.

SIDELIGHTS: Bryna Ivens Untermeyer told *CA:* "Although my ambition to work in some editorial or writing capacity goes as far back as grammar school days, the break into publishing was the result of the Second World War. Women finally were getting a chance at men's jobs: I became editor of a large liquor company's external house organ. From there, it was an easy transition to *She* and then *Seventeen.* When I left *Seventeen,* I began the exciting, active editorial collaboration with my late husband, Louis Untermeyer [see sketch elsewhere in this volume]."

AVOCATIONAL INTERESTS: Raising orchids, cats, and dogs, travel.

* * *

UNTERMEYER, Louis   1885-1977
(Michael Lewis, Molly Michaels)

PERSONAL: Born October 1, 1885, in New York, N.Y.; died December 18, 1977, and cremated in Newtown, Conn.; son of Emanuel (a manufacturing jeweler) and Julia (Michael) Untermeyer; married Jean Starr (a poet), 1907 (divorced, 1926, remarried, 1927, divorced, 1933); married Virginia Moore (a poet), 1926 (divorced, 1927); married Esther Antin (a lawyer), 1933 (divorced, 1948); married Bryna Ivens (an editor of children's books), 1948; children: (first marriage) Richard Starr (deceased), Laurence Starr (adopted), Joseph Louis (adopted); (second marriage) John Moore. *Education:* Left high school before graduating; awarded high school diploma, 1965.

ADDRESSES: Office—Bryna Ivens Untermeyer (literary executor), Great Hill Road, Newton, Conn. 06470.

CAREER: Untermeyer-Robbins Co. and Charles Keller & Co. (a jewelry manufacturing enterprise), began in sales in 1902, became vice-president and manager of factory at Newark, N.J., resigned, 1923; writer, editor, and lecturer, 1923-77. Cultural editor, Decca Records, 1943-56. Poet in residence, University of Michigan, 1939-40, University of Kansas City, Mo., 1939, and Iowa State College, 1940. U.S. representative at conferences in India, 1961. Conducted seminars in American poetry in Japan, 1962. Consultant in English poetry, Library of Congress, 1961-63, and honorary consultant in American Humanities. *Wartime service:* U.S. Office of War Information, publications editor, 1942; Armed Services Editions, editor, 1944.

MEMBER: PEN, National Institute of Arts and Letters, Phi Beta Kappa.

AWARDS, HONORS: Henry Ward Beecher Lecturer, Amherst College, 1937; Hannold Lecturer, Knox College, 1937; Gold Medal, Poetry Society of America, for services to poetry, 1956; Sarah Josepha Hale Award, 1965; Golden Rose Trophy, New England Poetry Club, 1966; D.H.L., Union College, 1967.

WRITINGS:

The New Era in American Poetry (essays), Holt, 1919, reprinted, Scholarly Press, 1970.

Heavens (parodies), Harcourt, 1922.

American Poetry since 1900 (essays), Holt, 1923, reprinted, Folcroft, 1977.

The Forms of Poetry: A Pocket Dictionary of Verse, Harcourt, 1926, reprinted, Darby Books, 1982, latest revised edition, Harcourt, 1967.

Collected Parodies, Harcourt, 1926.

Moses (novel), Harcourt, 1928.

Blue Rhine, Black Forest, a Hand- and Day-Book (travel journal), Harcourt, 1930.

The Donkey of God (short stories), Harcourt, 1932.

Chip: My Life and Times, as Overheard by Louis Untermeyer (fiction; self-illustrated with Vera Neville), Harcourt, 1933.

(With Carter Davidson) *Poetry: Its Appreciation and Enjoyment,* Harcourt, 1934.

The Last Pirate: Tales from the Gilbert and Sullivan Operas, Harcourt, 1934.

(With Clara Mannes) *Songs to Sing to Children,* Harcourt, 1935.

Heinrich Heine: Paradox and Poet, Volume 1: *The Poems,* Volume 2: *The Life,* Harcourt, 1937, reprinted, R. West, 1980.

(With others) *Doorways to Poetry* (textbook), Harcourt, 1938.

Play in Poetry (Henry Ward Beecher Lectures), Harcourt, 1938, Arden Library, 1980.

From Another World: The Autobiography of Louis Untermeyer, Harcourt, 1939.

(Reteller) *The Wonderful Adventures of Paul Bunyan,* Heritage, 1945.

(Reteller) Charles Perrault, *French Fairy Tales Retold,* illustrated by Gustave Dore, Didier, 1945.

(Reteller) Perrault, *All the French Fairy Tales,* illustrated by Dore, Didier, 1945.

(Reteller) Perrault, *More French Fairy Tales Retold,* illustrated by Dore, Didier, 1946.

A Century of Candymaking, 1847-1947, privately printed, 1947.

Makers of the Modern World (biography), Simon & Schuster, 1955.

Lives of the Poets: The Story of 1000 Years of English and American Poetry, Simon & Schuster, 1959.

The Kitten Who Barked (fiction), Golden Press, 1962.

Edwin Arlington Robinson: A Reappraisal, Library of Congress, 1963.

The Letters of Robert Frost to Louis Untermeyer, Holt, 1963.

Lives of the Poets 1963, Simon & Schuster, 1963.

The Second Christmas, Hallmark Cards, 1964.

The World's Greatest Stories: Fifty-Five Legends that Live Forever, Evans, 1964, published as *The Firebringer, and Other Great Stories: Fifty-Five Legends that Live Forever,* Evans, 1968.

Robert Frost: A Backward Look, Library of Congress, 1964.

Bygones: The Recollections of Louis Untermeyer (autobiography), Harcourt, 1965.

The Paths of Poetry: Twenty-Five Poets and Their Poems, Delacorte, 1966.

Merry Christmas, Golden Press, 1967.

Lift up Your Heart (consolation), Golden Press, 1968.

Your Lucky Stars (juvenile), Golden Press, 1968.

The Pursuit of Poetry: A Guide to Its Understanding and Appreciation with an Explanation of Its Forms and a Dictionary of Poetic Terms, Simon & Schuster, 1969.

Plants of the Bible (juvenile), paintings by Anne O. Dowden, Golden Press, 1970.

Cat o' Nine Tales (fiction), Heritage, 1971.

Said I to Myself, Said I: Reflections and Reappraisals, Digressions and Diversions, privately printed, 1978.

POETRY

The Younger Quire (parodies), Mood Publishing, 1911.

First Love, French, 1911.

Challenge, Century, 1914.

—and Other Poets (parodies), Holt, 1916.

These Times, Holt, 1917.

Including Horace, Harcourt, 1919.

The New Adam, Harcourt, 1920.

Roast Leviathan, Harcourt, 1923, reprinted, Arno, 1975.

(With son, Richard Untermeyer) *Poems,* privately printed, 1927.

Burning Bush, Harcourt, 1928.

Adirondack Cycle, Random House, 1929.

Food and Drink, Harcourt, 1932.

First Words before Spring, Knopf, 1933.

Selected Poems and Parodies, Harcourt, 1935.

For You with Love (juvenile), Golden Press, 1961.

Long Feud: Selected Poems, Harcourt, 1962.

One and One and One (juvenile), Crowell-Collier, 1962.

This Is Your Day (juvenile), Golden Press, 1964.

Labyrinth of Love, Simon & Schuster, 1965.

Thanks: A Poem (juvenile), Odyssey, 1965.

Thinking of You (juvenile), Golden Press, 1968.

A Friend Indeed, Golden Press, 1968.

You: A Poem, (juvenile), illustrations by Martha Alexander, Golden Press, 1969.

EDITOR OR COMPILER

Modern American Verse, Harcourt, 1919, published as *Modern American Poetry* (also see below), 1921, revised edition, 1969.

A Miscellany of American Poetry, Granger, 1920, reprinted, 1978.

Modern British Poetry (also see below), Harcourt, 1920, revised edition, 1969.

Modern American and British Poetry, Harcourt, 1922, 9th revised edition, 1962.

American Poetry, 1922: A Miscellany, Granger, 1922, reprinted, 1976.

This Singing World, Harcourt, Volume 1: *An Anthology of Modern Poetry for Young People,* 1923, Volume 2: *Junior Edition,* 1926, Volume 3: *For Younger Children,* 1926.

American Poetry 1925: A Miscellany, Granger, 1925, reprinted, 1977.

Walt Whitman, Simon & Schuster, 1926.

Yesterday and Today: A Comparative Anthology of Poetry, Harcourt, 1926, revised edition published as *Yesterday and Today: A Collection of Verse (Mostly Modern) Designed for the Average Person of Nine to Nineteen and Possibly Older,* 1927.

American Poetry, 1927: A Miscellany, Granger, 1927, reprinted, 1978.

Emily Dickinson, Simon & Schuster, 1927.

Conrad Aiken, Simon & Schuster, 1927.

(With Clara and David Mannes) *New Songs for New Voices* (poems; juvenile), Harcourt, 1928.

A Critical Anthology: Modern American Poetry, Modern British Poetry (contains revised editions of *Modern American Poetry* and *Modern British Poetry*), Harcourt, 1930.

American Poetry from the Beginning to Whitman, Harcourt, 1931.

The Book of Living Verse: English and American Poetry from the Thirteenth Century to the Present Day, Harcourt, 1932, 2nd revised edition published as *The Book of Living Verse: Limited to the Chief Poets,* 1939, text edition, 1949.

The New Treasury of Verse, Odhams Press, 1934.

Rainbow in the Sky (poems; juvenile), Harcourt, 1935, reprinted, 1980.

Stars to Steer By (poems; juvenile), Harcourt, 1941.

A Treasury of Great Poems: English and American, Simon & Schuster, 1942, revised edition published as *A Concise Treasury of Great Poems, English and American, from the Foundations of the English Spirit to the Outstanding Poetry of Our Own Time,* 1955, revised and enlarged edition published as *A Treasury of Great Poems, English and American, with Lives of the Poets and Historical Settings Selected and Integrated by Louis Untermeyer,* two volumes, 1964.

Edgar Allen Poe, *Complete Poems,* Heritage, 1943.

Henry W. Longfellow, *Poems,* Heritage, 1943.

Robert Frost, *Come In, and Other Poems,* Holt, 1943, revised and enlarged edition published as *The Road Not Taken: An Introduction to Robert Frost,* 1951.

Great Poems from Chaucer to Whitman, Editions for the Armed Services, 1944.

Ralph Waldo Emerson, *Poems,* Heritage, 1945.

(And author of introduction) *The Pocket Book of Story Poems,* Pocket Books, 1945, revised and enlarged edition published as *Story Poems: An Anthology of Narrative Verse,* Washington Square Press, 1957.

John Greenleaf Whittier, *Poems,* Heritage, 1945.

(And author of foreword) *Love Poems of Elizabeth Barrett Browning and Robert Browning,* Rutgers University Press, 1946.

A Treasury of Laughter, Simon & Schuster, 1946.

The Book of Noble Thoughts, American Artists Group, 1946.

William Cullen Bryant, *Poems,* Heritage, 1947.

(With others) *The Pocket Treasury* (prose selections), Pocket Books, 1947.

Omar Khayyam, *Rubaiyat,* Random, 1947.

Anthology of the New England Poets from Colonial Times to the Present Day, Random, 1948.

The Love Poems of Robert Herrick and John Donne, Rutgers University Press, 1948.

The Pocket Book of American Poems from the Colonial Period to the Present Day, Pocket Books, 1948.

The Inner Sanctum Walt Whitman, Simon & Schuster, 1949.

(With R. E. Shikes) *The Best Humor of 1949-50,* Holt, 1951.

(With Shikes) *The Best Humor of 1951-52,* Holt, 1952.

Emily Dickinson, *Poems,* Heritage, 1952.

The Magic Circle: Stories and People in Poetry, Harcourt, 1952.

Early American Poets, Literary Publishers, 1952, reprinted, Books for Libraries, 1970.

The Book of Wit and Humor (prose selections), Mercury Books, 1953.

(And author of commentary) *A Treasury of Ribaldry,* Hanover House, 1956.

The Golden Treasury of Poetry (juvenile), Golden Press, 1959.

The Britannica Library of Great American Writing (prose selections), two volumes, Britannica Press, 1960.

Albatross Book of Verse: English and American Poetry from the 13th Century to the Present Day, Collins, 1960, revised and enlarged edition, 1978.

(And author of commentary) *Lots of Limericks, Light, Lusty and Lasting,* Doubleday, 1961.

(With wife, Bryna Untermeyer) Jakob Ludwig Karl Grimm and Wilhelm Karl Grimm, *Fairy Tales; the Complete Household Tales of Jakob and Wilhelm Grimm,* Limited Editions Club, 1962.

(With B. Untermeyer) *Legendary Animals* (juvenile), Western, 1963.

An Uninhibited Treasury of Erotic Poetry, Dial, 1963.

The Pan Book of Lymericks, Pan Books, 1963.

Love Sonnets, Odyssey, 1964.

(And adapter) *Aesop's Fables,* Golden Press, 1965.

Love Lyrics, Odyssey, 1965.

(With B. Untermeyer) *The Golden Treasury of Children's Literature,* Western, 1966 (published in England as *The Children's Treasury of Literature in Colour,* Hamlyn, 1966).

Songs of Joy: Selections from the Book of Psalms (juvenile), World Publishing, 1967.

(With B. Untermeyer) *Words of Wisdom* (quotations), Golden Press, 1968.

(With B. Untermeyer) *Tales and Legends,* Golden Press, 1968.

(With B. Untermeyer) *Adventure Stories,* Golden Press, 1968.

(With B. Untermeyer) *Animal Stories,* Golden Press, 1968.

(With B. Untermeyer) *Favorite Classics,* Golden Press, 1968.

(And adaptor) *Tales from the Ballet,* Golden Press, 1968.

A Time for Peace: Verses from the Bible, World Publishing, 1969.

The Golden Book of Fun and Nonsense, Golden Press, 1970.

Roses: Selections, paintings by Dowden, Golden Press, 1970.

Men and Women: The Poetry of Love, American Heritage Press, 1970.

The Golden Book of Poems for the Very Young, Golden Press, 1971.

The Golden Treasury of Animal Stories and Poems, Golden Press, 1971.

Treasury of Great Humor: Including Wit, Whimsy and Satire from the Remote Past to the Present, McGraw, 1972.

Fifty Modern American and British Poets, 1920-1970, McKay, 1973.

(With B. Untermeyer) *Stories and Poems for the Very Young,* Golden Press, 1973.

(With B. Untermeyer) *A Galaxy of Verse,* Evans, 1978.

New Enlarged Anthology of Robert Frost's Poems, Washington Square Press, 1982.

Also editor of *The Poems of Anna Wickham,* 1921.

TRANSLATOR

Heinrich Heine, *Poems,* Harcourt, 1923.

(And adapter) Gottfried Keller, *Fat of the Cat, and Other Stories,* Harcourt, 1925.

Heine, *Poetry and Prose,* Citadel, 1948.

Edmond Rostand, *Cyrano de Bergerac,* Limited Editions Club, 1954.

(And editor) Heine, *The Poems of Heinrich Heine,* Limited Editions Club, 1957.

OTHER

Editorial consultant, "Prose and Poetry" series of recordings, L. W. Singer Co., 1963. Contributor to periodicals, including *New Republic, Yale Review, Saturday Review,* and others. Contributing editor, *The Liberator,* 1918-24; poetry editor, *American Mercury,* 1934-37; co-founder and contributing editor, *Seven Arts.*

SIDELIGHTS: Louis Untermeyer was the author, editor or compiler, and translator of more than one hundred books for readers of all ages. He will be best remembered as the prolific anthologist whose collections have introduced students to contemporary American poetry since 1919. The son of an established New York jeweler, Untermeyer's interest in poetry led to friendships with poets from three generations, including many of the century's major writers. His tastes were eclectic. Martin Weil related in the *Washington Post* that Untermeyer once "described himself as 'a bone collector' with 'the mind of a magpie.' " He was a liberal who did much to allay the Victorian myth that poetry is a high-brow art. "What most of us don't realize is that everyone loves poetry," he was quoted by Weil as saying, pointing out the rhymes on the once-ubiquitous Burma Shave road signs as an example.

Untermeyer developed his taste for literature while still a child. His mother had read aloud to him from a variety of sources, including the epic poems "Paul Revere's Ride" and "Hiawatha." Bedtime stories he told to his brother Martin combined elements from every story he could remember, he revealed in *Bygones: The Recollections of Louis Untermeyer.* When he learned to read for himself, he was particularly impressed by books such as Alfred Lord Tennyson's *Idylls of the King* and Dante's *Inferno.* Gustave Dore's illustrations in these books captivated him and encouraged his imagination toward fantasy. Almost fifty years later, Untermeyer published several volumes of retold French fairy tales, all illustrated by the famous French artist.

In addition to children's books and anthologies, Untermeyer published collections of his own poetry. He began to compose light verse and parodies during his teen years after dropping out of school to join his father's business. With financial help from his father, he published *First Love* in 1911. Sentiments of social protest expressed in the 1914 volume *Challenge* received disapproval from anti-communist groups forty years later; as a result of suspicion, Untermeyer lost his seat on the "What's My Line" game show panel to publisher Bennett Cerf. During the 1970s, he found himself "instinctively, if incongruously, allied with the protesting young," he wrote in the *New York Times.* In the same article he encouraged the spirit of experiment that characterized the decade, saying, "it is the non-conformers, the innovators in art, science, technology, and human relations who, misunderstood and ridiculed in their own times, have shaped our world." Untermeyer, who did not promote any particular ideology, remained a popular speaker and lecturer, sharing criticism of poetry and anecdotes about famous poets with audiences in the United States and as far away as India and Japan.

Untermeyer resigned from the jewelry business in 1923 in order to give all his attention to literary pursuits. Friendships with Robert Frost, Ezra Pound, Arthur Miller, and other literary figures provided him with material for books. For example, *The Letters of Robert Frost to Louis Untermeyer* contains letters selected from almost fifty years of correspondence with the New England poet. The anthologist's autobiographies *From Another World* and *Bygones* relate as much about other writers as they

do about his personal life. *Bygones* provides his reflections on the four women who were his wives. Jean Starr moved to Vienna with Untermeyer after he became a full-time writer; Virginia Moore was his wife for about a year; Esther Antin, a lawyer he met in Toledo, Ohio, married him in 1933; fifteen years later, he married Bryna Ivens, with whom he edited a dozen books for children.

In his later years, Untermeyer, like Frost, had a deep appreciation for country life. He once told *CA:* "I live on an abandoned farm in Connecticut . . . ever since I found my native New York unlivable as well as unlovable. . . . On these green and sometimes arctic acres I cultivate whatever flowers insist on growing in spite of my neglect; delight in the accumulation of chickadees, juncos, cardinals, and the widest possible variety of songless sparrows; grow old along with three pampered cats and one spoiled cairn terrier; season my love of home with the spice of annual travel, chiefly to such musical centers as Vienna, Salzburg, Milan, and London; and am always happy to be home again."

BIOGRAPHICAL/CRITICAL SOURCES:

BOOKS

Untermeyer, Louis, *From Another World: The Autobiography of Louis Untermeyer,* Harcourt, 1939.
Untermeyer, Louis, *Bygones: The Recollections of Louis Untermeyer,* Harcourt, 1965.

PERIODICALS

Best Sellers, November 15, 1969.
New York Times, October 1, 1970.

OBITUARIES:

PERIODICALS

Detroit Free Press, December 20, 1977.
Newsweek, January 2, 1978.
New York Times, December 20, 1977.
Publishers Weekly, December 26, 1977.
Time, January 2, 1978.
Washington Post, December 20, 1977.*

*   *   *

UROFSKY, Melvin I. 1939-

PERSONAL: Born February 7, 1939, in New York, N.Y.; son of Philip and Sylvia (Passow) Urofsky; married Susan Linda Miller (the Commissioner of Rehabilitative Services for Commonwealth of Virginia), August 27, 1961; children: Philip Eric, Robert Ian. *Education:* Columbia University, A.B., 1961, M.A., 1962, Ph.D., 1968; University of Virginia, J.D., 1984. *Politics:* "Democratic-Independent." *Religion:* Jewish.

ADDRESSES: Home—14301 Spring Gate Ct., Midlothian, Va. 23112. *Office*—Department of History, Virginia Commonwealth University, Richmond, Va. 23284.

CAREER: New York State Employment Service, New York City, interviewer, 1962; Robert Saudek Associates, New York City, researcher, 1963; Ohio State University, Columbus, instructor in history, 1964-67; State University of New York at Albany, assistant professor of history and education, 1967-70, assistant dean for innovative education, 1970-72, lecturer in history in Allen Center, 1972-74; Virginia Commonwealth University, Richmond, beginning 1974, currently professor of history. Chairman, Zionist Academic Council, 1976-79. Consultant to Institute for the Advancement of Urban Education.

MEMBER: Organization of American Historians, American Jewish Historical Society (chairman, academic council, 1980-83), American Historical Association, American Legal History Society.

AWARDS, HONORS: National Endowment for the Humanities, grants for editing Louis D. Brandeis letters, 1967-74 and 1984-86, senior fellowship, 1976-77; American Council of Learned Societies grants-in-aid, 1972, 1978; Jewish Book Council Kaplun Award, 1976.

WRITINGS:

Big Steel and the Wilson Administration: A Study in Business-Government Relations, Ohio State University Press, 1969.
(Editor) *Why Teachers Strike: Teachers' Rights and Community Control,* Doubleday-Anchor, 1970.
(Editor with David W. Levy) *Letters of Louis D. Brandeis,* State University of New York Press, Volume 1: *Urban Reformer, 1870-1907,* 1971, Volume 2: *People's Attorney, 1907-1912,* 1972, Volume 3: *Progressive and Zionist, 1913-1915,* 1973, Volume 4: *Elder Statesman, 1922-1941,* 1978.
A Mind of One Piece: Brandeis and American Reform, Scribner, 1971.
(Editor) *Perspectives on Urban America,* Doubleday, 1973.
American Zionism from Herzl to the Holocaust, Doubleday, 1975.
We Are One! American Jewry and Israel, Doubleday, 1978.
Essays on American Zionism, Herzl Press, 1978.
Louis D. Brandeis and the Progressive Tradition, Little, Brown, 1980.
A Voice that Spoke for Justice: The Life and Times of Stephen S. Wise, State University of New York Press, 1981.
A March of Liberty, Knopf, 1987.
Documents of American Constitutional and Legal History, two volumes, Knopf, 1988.

(Editor with son, Philip E. Urofsky) *The Douglas Letters: Selections from the Private Papers of Justice William O. Douglas,* Adler & Adler, 1988.
The Continuity of Change, Wordsworth, 1990.

Contributor of numerous articles to scholarly journals and popular periodicals. Member of editorial board, *Midstream,* 1978-86.

WORK IN PROGRESS: A study of the courts and the right to die.

SIDELIGHTS: Melvin I. Urofsky's *Louis D. Brandeis and the Progressive Tradition* "is not a full-blown biography moving into the inner person of a truly great man," states Philip Allan Friedman in the *Los Angeles Times.* "Rather, it is a fine study . . . of Brandeis' crusading public career—as the people's defender against the 'curse of bigness' in business, as the great dissenter along with Justice Holmes on the highest court of the land, and as the leader of the American Zionist Organization." Opposing monopolies and working for wage-earners' rights, Brandeis became a top adviser to President Woodrow Wison, a Supreme Court justice, and a renowned professor of law. Credited with upgrading the teaching of law "by popularizing the case-study method," according to Friedman, Brandeis often researched cases independently while serving on the bench. In addition to writing the biography of Brandeis, Urofsky, with David W. Levy, has edited and published Brandeis letters spanning more than seventy years.

BIOGRAPHICAL/CRITICAL SOURCES:

PERIODICALS

Chicago Tribune, December 9, 1987.
Los Angeles Times, February 12, 1981.
New York Times, November 29, 1987.
New York Times Book Review, February 21, 1988.
Washington Post Book World, October 4, 1987.

V

VANGELISTI, Paul 1945-

PERSONAL: Born September 17, 1945, in San Francisco, Calif.; son of Nicholas Thomas (an accountant) and Josephine (a saleswoman; maiden name, Zangani) Vangelisti; married Margaret Dryden, December 31, 1966 (divorced, 1980); children: Tristan, Simone. *Education:* University of San Francisco B.A., 1967; graduate study at Trinity College, Dublin, 1967-68; University of Southern California, M.A., 1971, doctoral study, 1972.

ADDRESSES: Home—3132 Berkely Circle, Los Angeles, Calif. 90026. *Office*—Otis Art Institute of Parsons School of Design, 2401 Wilshire Blvd., Los Angeles, Calif. 90057.

CAREER: San Francisco Department of Recreation and Parks, San Francisco, Calif., recreation director, 1967-68; University of Southern California, Los Angeles, assistant instructor in English, 1968-72; *Hollywood Reporter,* Hollywood, Calif., assignment editor, 1972-73; KPFK-Radio, North Hollywood, Calif., cultural affairs director, 1974-82; part-time instructor at colleges in Los Angeles, 1980—; Otis Art Institute of Parsons School of Design, Los Angeles, instructor, 1984—.

AWARDS, HONORS: Coordinating Council of Little Magazines' Editors fellowship, 1981, for magazine *Invisible City;* National Endowment for the Arts translators fellowship, 1981, and poetry fellowship, 1988.

WRITINGS:

POETRY

Communion, Red Hill, 1970.
Tender Continent, Chatterton's Bookstore, 1974.
Air, Red Hill, 1973.
Pearl Harbor, Isthmus, 1975.
Il tenero continente (bilingual; title means "The Tender Continent"), Edizione Geiger, 1975.
The Extravagant Room, Red Hill, 1976.
Two by Two, Red Hill, 1977.
Remembering the Movies, Red Hill, 1977.
Another You, Red Hill, 1980.
Un grammo d'oro, Cervo Volante (Rome), 1981.
Ora blu, Telai del Bernini (Modena), 1981.
Abandoned Latitudes, Red Hill, 1983.
Rime, Red Hill, 1983.
Domain, Red Hill, 1986.
Portfolio, Edizioni TamTam (Parma), 1989.

EDITOR

(With Charles Bukowski) *Anthology of Los Angeles Poets,* Red Hill, 1973.
Specimen 73 (catalogue and anthology), Pasadena Museum, 1973.
(And translator with Milne Holton) *New Polish Poetry,* University of Pittsburgh Press, 1978.
BreathingSpace 79 (international anthology of sound poetry), Black Box, 1979.
(With Adriano Spatola and translator) *Italian Poetry, 1960-1980: From Neo to Post Avant-Garde,* Red Hill, 1982.

Co-editor, *Invisible City* (literary magazine).

TRANSLATOR

Sixteen Poems of Vittorio Sereni, Red Hill, 1971.
Spatola, *Mayakovskiiiiiiiij,* Red Hill, 1975.
Guilia Niccolai, *Substitutions,* Red Hill, 1975.
Corrado Costa, *Our Positions,* Red Hill, 1975.
Rocco Scotellaro, *The Sky with Its Mouth Wide-Open,* Red Hill, 1976.
Franco Beltrametti, *Another Earthquake,* Red Hill, 1977.
Antonio Porta, *As If It Were a Rhythm,* Red Hill, 1978.
(With Carol Lettieri) Mohammed Dib, *Omneros,* Red Hill, 1978.
Spatola, *Various Devices,* Red Hill, 1978.
Costa, *The Complete Films,* Red Hill, 1983.
Sereni, *Algerian Diary,* Red Hill, 1986.
Porta, *Invasions,* Red Hill, 1986.
Foresta ultra naturam, Red Hill, 1989.
Spatola, *Material, Materials, Recovery of,* Sun & Moon Press, 1990.

*   *   *

van OORT, Jan 1921-
(Jean Dulieu)

PERSONAL: Born April 13, 1921, in Amsterdam, Netherlands; married M. M. Sijmons (died April 12, 1986), July 8, 1943; children: Dorinde, Annelies, Francesco. *Education:* Studied at Conservatorium for Music, Amsterdam, 1935-40.

CAREER: Violinist in Amsterdam, Netherlands, playing for opera orchestra, 1941-44, and with Concertgebouw Orkest,

1944-46; free-lance writer, radio actor, and puppeteer, 1946-86; free-lance illustrator, 1946—.

MEMBER: PEN, Vereniging van Letterkundigen (writer's organization; member of board, 1960-65), Maatschappy van Letterkunde.

AWARDS, HONORS: Prize from Youth Friends Association (New York), 1956, and Diploma of Merit in International Hans Christian Andersen Awards, 1958, both for *Francesco; Paulus de hulpsinterklaas* was named best children's book of the year in the Netherlands, 1962; Edison award for best recording for children, 1962.

WRITINGS:

UNDER PSEUDONYM JEAN DULIEU; JUVENILE; SELF-ILLUSTRATED

Het winterboek van Paulus, Arbeiderspers, 1948.
Francesco (biography of Saint Francis of Assisi), van der Peet, 1956.
Paulus en Kenarrepoere, van der Peet, 1957.
Paulus en Priegeltje, van der Peet, 1957.
De verrassing, van der Peet, 1959.
Het ei, van der Peet, 1959.
Het klaaghemd, van der Peet, 1959.
Puntnik en andere verhalen, van der Peet, 1960.
Paulus de hulpsinterklaas, Ploegsma, 1962.
Paulus en Eucalypta, Ploegsma, 1962.
Paulus en het levenswater, Ploegsma, 1962.
Paulus en Joris het vispaard, Ploegsma, 1962.
Paulus en Mol, Ploegsma, 1962, translation by Marian Powell published as *Paulus and Mole,* World's Work (England), 1965.
Paulus en Wawwa, Ploegsma, 1962, reprinted, Leopold, 1982.
Paulus en de 3 rovers, Ploegsma, 1963, tranlsation by Powell published as *Paulus and the Three Robbers,* World's Work, 1965.
Paulus en Pieter, Ploegsma, 1963.
Paulus en Salomon, Ploegsma, 1963, translation by Powell published as *Paulus and Solomon,* World's Work, 1965.
Paulus en het draakje, [Netherlands], 1964, translation by Vivien Visser published as *Paulus and the Dragon,* Crossing Press, 1978.
Paulus en schipper Makreel, Ploegsma, 1964.
Paulus en de eikelmannetjes, Ploegsma, 1965, translation by the author, assisted by T. D. R. Thomason and Patricia Tracy Lowe, published as *Paulus and the Acornmen,* World Publishing, 1966.
Poetepoet, Ploegsma, 1965.
De zeven wonderdaden van Kevertje Plop, van Goor Zoznen, 1966, translation by the author, assisted by Thomason and Lowe, published as *The Adventures of Beetlekin the Brave,* World Publishing, 1966.
Het eukelknijn, Van Holkema en Warendorf, 1970.
Japie de eenhoorn, Van Holkema en Warendorf, 1970.
Het oliebollenfeest, Van Holkema en Warendorf, 1970.
De rokomobiel, Van Holkema en Warendorf, 1970.
Heksenvakantie, Van Holkema en Warendorf, 1970.
De reus worrelsik, Van Holkema en Warendorf, 1970.
De beren, Van Holkema en Warendorf, 1971.
Het boomspook, Van Holkema en Warendorf, 1971.
De bruiloft, Van Holkema en Warendorf, 1971.
De bergbouters, Van Holkema en Warendorf, 1971.
De zeurboom en andere verhalen van Paulus de Boskabouter, Van Holkema en Warendorf, 1978.
Paulus en de insekten, Leopold, 1981.

Paulus en het beest van Ploemariac, Leopold, 1982.
Paulus en de toverhoed, Leopold, 1983.

Also author of scripts, including 750 short radio plays for children, and forty puppet films for television. Creator and illustrator of a daily comic strip appearing in *Vrije Volk* (Amsterdam) for more than twelve years; writer of weekly illustrated stories for *Eva* (Leiden) for six years, and for *Margriet* (Amsterdam) for two years; currently author and illustrator of a daily comic strip appearing in twenty journals; also author and illustrator of stories for *Bobo* (weekly publication); contributor of more than 150 illustrated short stories for *Kris Kras* (children's journal published in Amsterdam).

SIDELIGHTS: Jan van Oort once produced puppet films, writing the scripts, making puppets, and creating the animation with the assistance of his wife, M. M. van Oort; he was also a prolific writer of children's books. But, since his wife's death in 1986, the author told *CA:* "I no longer write children's stories, but I make drawings every day."

Jan van Oort's books have been translated for publications in Indonesia, Sweden, South Africa, Japan, and Germany.

*   *   *

Van RIPER, Paul P(ritchard) 1916-

PERSONAL: Born July 29, 1916, in LaPorte, Ind.; son of Paul and Margaret (Pritchard) Van Riper; married Dorothy Ann Dodd Samuelson (a lecturer), May 11, 1964; children: Michael Scott Samuelson (stepson). *Education:* DePauw University, A.B. (highest distinction and honors), 1938; University of Chicago, Ph.D., 1947; graduated from U.S. Army Command and General Staff College, Ft. Leavenworth, Kan., 1960. *Politics:* Republican. *Religion:* Baptist.

ADDRESSES: Home—713 East 30th St., Bryan, Tex. 77803. *Office*—Department of Political Science, Texas A & M University, College Station, Tex. 77843.

CAREER: International Personnel Management Association, Chicago, Ill., research assistant, 1939-40; Northwestern University, Evanston, Ill., instructor, 1947-49, assistant professor of political science, 1949-52; Civil Administration Division, Office of Military Government, Germany, consultant, 1949; U.S. Army, Office of Comptroller, Washington, D.C., management analyst and military services section chief, 1951-52; George Washington University, Washington, D.C., lecturer in public administration, 1951-52; Cornell University, Graduate School of Public and Business Administration, Ithaca, N.Y., associate professor, 1952-57, professor of public administration, 1957-70, secretary to university faculty, 1960-65, acting dean, 1961; Texas A & M University, College Station, Tex., professor of political science, 1970-81, professor emeritus, 1981—, head of department, 1970-77, coordinator of M.P.A. program, 1979-81. Visiting professor at universities in the United States and the United Kingdom, including University of Oklahoma, 1968—. Member of historical advisory committee to National Aeronautics and Space Administration (NASA), 1964-66; member of Brazos County Historical Commission, 1975—. Member of board of directors, Brazos Valley Community Action Agency, 1975-78; elected Republican precinct chairman, Brazos County, 1976-80. *Military service:* U.S. Army, Quartermaster Corps, 1942-46; became major; received Croix de Guerre. U.S. Army Reserve; became lieutenant colonel in 1958.

MEMBER: International Personnel Management Association, Institute of Management Sciences, American Association of

University Professors, American Society for Public Administration (advisory committee, 1957-60), American Political Science Association, American Association for the Advancement of Science, Reserve Officers Association, Southern Political Science Association, Southwestern Political Science Association (executive committee, 1975-77), Phi Beta Kappa, Phi Kappa Phi, Sigma Delta Chi, Pi Sigma Alpha, Beta Theta Pi (vice president and trustee, 1962-63; general secretary, 1963-65).

AWARDS, HONORS: Alumni citation, DePauw University, 1966; Dimock Prize, 1983, for best commissioned essay in *Public Administration Review.*

WRITINGS:

(With Irving Sheffel) *Civil Service Agencies: A 1940 Census,* Civil Service Assembly, 1940.

Handbook of Practical Politics, Holt, 1952, 3rd edition, Harper, 1967.

History of the United States Civil Service, Row, Peterson, 1958, reprinted, Greenwood Press, 1976.

Some Educational and Social Aspects of Fraternity Life at Cornell University, Cornell Association of Resident Fraternity Advisers, 1961.

(With W. Lloyd Warner, Norman H. Martin, and Orvis F. Collins) *The American Federal Executive,* Yale University Press, 1963.

(Editor and co-author) *The Wilson Influence on Public Administration: From Theory to Practice,* American Society for Public Administration, in press.

Author of pamphlets and special studies reports. Contributor to professional journals. Member of editorial board, *Federal Accountant,* 1958-60; editorial consultant, *Public Personnel Review,* 1959-74.

WORK IN PROGRESS: A monograph on the administrative and political writings of Dr. Luther P. Gulick.

AVOCATIONAL INTERESTS: Bridge, antiques, golf, tennis, swimming, squash.

*   *   *

von le FORT, Gertrud (Petrea)
  See le FORT, Gertrud (Petrea) von

*   *   *

von STARK, G.
  See le FORT, Gertrud (Petrea) von

W

WALLACE, David Rains 1945-

PERSONAL: Born August 10, 1945, in Charlottesville, Va.; son of Sebon Rains (a psychologist) and Sarah (Hahn) Wallace; married Elizabeth Ann Kendall (an artist), July 3, 1975. *Education:* Wesleyan University, Middletown, Conn., B.A. (cum laude), 1967; graduate study at Columbia University, 1967-68; Mills College, M.A., 1974. *Politics:* Democrat.

ADDRESSES: Home—1568 San Lorenzo, Berkeley, Calif. 94707.

CAREER: Metropolitan Park District of Columbus and Franklin County, Columbus, Ohio, public information specialist, 1974-78; free-lance writer, 1978—. Creative writing teacher at extension centers, University of California, Berkeley, 1988, 1989; Ohio University summer seminars, 1988-89. Writing consultant, Oakland Museum Human Ecology exhibit, 1987—.

MEMBER: Wilderness Society, Sierra Club, National Audubon Society, Nature Conservancy, California Native Plant Society.

AWARDS, HONORS: National Endowment for the Arts fellowship, 1979-80; Silver Medal, Californiana category, Commonwealth Club of California, 1979, for *The Dark Range: A Naturalist's Night Notebook* and 1984, for *The Klamath Knot: Explorations of Myth and Evolution;* Ohioana Award, science category, 1981, for *Idle Weeds: The Life of a Sandstone Ridge;* John Burroughs Medal for Nature Writing, 1984, for *The Klamath Knot.*

WRITINGS:

The Dark Range: A Naturalist's Night Notebook, illustrations by Roger Bayless, Sierra Books, 1978.
Idle Weeds: The Life of a Sandstone Ridge, Sierra Books, 1980.
The Klamath Knot: Explorations of Myth and Evolution, Sierra Books, 1983.
The Wilder Shore, Sierra Books, 1984.
The Turquoise Dragon (a novel), Sierra Books, 1985.
The Untamed Garden and Other Personal Essays, Ohio State University Press, 1986.
Life in the Balance (companion volume to "Audubon Specials" television series), Harcourt, 1987.
Dryland, Harcourt, 1987.
Bulow Hammock: Mind in a Forest, Sierra Books, 1989.
The Vermillion Parrot: A Novel, Sierra Books, 1990.
The Curious Naturalists, National Geographic Books, in press.

Contributor to conservation journals and newspapers, including *New York Times Book Review, Sierra, Wilderness, Country Journal, Ohio Sierran, Mother Jones, Pacific Discovery,* and *Image.*

SIDELIGHTS: David Rains Wallace "is a mature, professional nature writer at the height of his analytical and interpretive powers, an author who has crafted a prose style that enables him to write with ease and facility on subjects as diverse as the Okefenokee Swamp, the wilds of Alaska, nature in Japan, the hills of Ohio, and the forests of northern California," John Murray relates in the *Bloomsbury Review.* A number of Wallace's books have won literary prizes—including two silver medals in the Californiana category from the Commonwealth Club of California—and critical acclaim.

The Klamath Knot: Explorations of Myth and Evolution, Wallace's second Silver medal winner, explores a unique tract of wilderness along the California-Oregon border. Commenting on Wallace's work, Clifford D. May writes in the *New York Times Book Review,* "He spins intriguing scientific tales and tosses out some delightful tidbits of arcana." A *Publishers Weekly* reviewer adds, "This is a rare and imaginative introduction to a wilderness that links past and present; Wallace belongs to the first rank of science writers."

Of Wallace's chosen genre, Murray comments, "At its best, nature writing is capable of achieving the qualities of all good literature: universality, depth of feeling, and personal revelation. Nature writers like Wallace are more than interpreters and field guides, they are highly skilled artists creating with a deceptive simplicity in a form that has not even come close to being exhausted. . . . Gifted writers like Wallace . . . are trying to transcend our cultural alienation from nature, and often they succeed brilliantly."

Life in the Balance, a collection of essays about nature under seige, also succeeds, David M. Graber notes in the *Los Angeles Times Book Review.* "Although Wallace makes every effort to be upbeat, to teach the lesson that nature can be saved and is worth saving, the sickening destruction that our species has wrought and continues to wreak on this planet is hard to present cheerfully," Graber writes. Despite their often depressing subject matter, Graber feels these essays constitute "an excellent argument for conservation."

In *Bulow Hammock: Mind in a Forest* Wallace looks at an unpopular Florida swamp with an eye to what it can reveal about the human brain. *Washington Post Book World* reviewer Dennis Drabelle relates that in this "challenging book," Wallace suggests that "the human mind has an innate receptivity to shadowy, fecund places like hammocks." *New York Times Book Review* contributor Jack Rudloe appreciates other aspects of the book more than the analogy. Rudloe particularly recommends the author's vivid descriptions of local wildlife, and his extended comparison of John Audubon's and John Muir's perceptions of the Florida ecosystem.

Wallace told *CA:* "My writing arises from a fascination with this planet—its climate, waters, rocks, soils, plants, and animals. I want to awaken readers to the fact that we remain a part of the biosphere, that we cannot destroy it without destroying ourselves." More recently, he commented, "In the five or so years since I wrote the above, the fact of human-natural interdependence has become increasingly, frighteningly obvious. But I want to show that this fact is not only cause for fear, but also for joy that we can't *save* the planet without saving ourselves."

BIOGRAPHICAL/CRITICAL SOURCES:

PERIODICALS

Bloomsbury Review, July, 1988.
Cleveland Plain Dealer, November 17, 1980.
Columbus Dispatch, August 14, 1988.
Los Angeles Times Book Review, September 6, 1987,
Los Angeles Times View (Sunday magazine), January 3, 1988.
New York Times Book Review, April 7, 1985, April 16, 1989.
Philadelphia Enquirer, July 17, 1983.
Publishers Weekly, December 3, 1982.
San Francisco Chronicle Review (Sunday magazine), April 16, 1989.
San Francisco Guardian, November 9, 1978.
Wall Street Journal, February 14, 1983.
Washington Post Book World, March 13, 1983, April 9, 1989.

*   *   *

WALLACE, Roger
    See CHARLIER, Roger H(enri)

*   *   *

WALLER, G(ary) F(redric)   1944-
    (Gary Waller)

PERSONAL: Born January 3, 1944, in Auckland, New Zealand; came to the United States in 1983; son of Fred and Joan Elsie (Smythe) Waller; married Jennifer Robyn Denham, 1966 (marriage ended); married Linda Levine, 1982 (marriage ended); married Kathleen McCormick, 1988; children: Michael, Andrew, Philip. *Education:* University of Auckland, B.A., 1965, M.A., 1966; Cambridge University, Ph.D., 1969.

ADDRESSES: Office—Department of English, Carnegie-Mellon University, 5000 Forbes Ave., Pittsburgh, Pa. 15213.

CAREER: Cambridge University, Cambridge, England, fellow of Magdalene College, 1968-70; University of Auckland, Auckland, New Zealand, 1970-72, began as lecturer, became senior lecturer in English; Dalhousie University, Halifax, Nova Scotia, 1972-78, began as assistant professor, became associate professor of English; Wilfred Laurier University, Waterloo, Ontario, professor of English and chairman of department, 1978-83; Carnegie-Mellon University, Pittsburgh, Pa., professor of English and chairman of department, 1983—.

MEMBER: Modern Language Association of America, Renaissance Society of America, Modern Humanities Research Association.

WRITINGS:

The Strong Necessity of Time: Time in Shakespeare and the Elizabethans, Mouton, 1976.
(Editor) Mary Wroth, *Pamphilia to Amphilanthus,* University of Salzburg, 1977.
(Editor) Mary Sidney, *The Triumph of Death and Other Poems,* University of Salzburg, 1977.
Dreaming America: Obsession and Transcendence in the Fiction of Joyce Carol Oates, Louisiana State University Press, 1979.
Mary Sidney, Countess of Pembroke, University of Salzburg, 1979.
(Under name Gary Waller) *Impossible Futures, Indelible Pasts* (poems), Kellner/McCaffery, 1983.
Sir Philip Sidney in His Time and Ours, Croom Helm, 1984.
Sixteenth-Century Poetry, Longman, 1986.
Reading Texts, Heath, 1986.
Lexington Introduction to Literature, Heath, 1987.
Shakespeare's Comedies: A Critical Reader, Longman, in press.
Edmund Spenser: A Literary Life, Macmillan, in press.

Contributor to literature journals.

WORK IN PROGRESS: The Sidney Family Romance; writing a second volume of poems.

SIDELIGHTS: "Poetry is a very intense sideline to the rest of my life," Gary Waller commented to Linda Fording in *Focus.* A critic, scholar, and teacher, Waller considers poetry "a rigorous form of relaxation." He recalled a ten-to-twelve-year period of his career when he had devoted all of his time to writing literary criticism and teaching and "did no serious creative writing at all." In retrospect, he feels the experiences of those years have shaped his poetry. "Working with language in other written forms made me more aware of language's poetic possibilities and gave me more ability to control and manipulate words," he explained to Fording. He also reflected that is it more important for a writer or poet to have "intense involvement with and command of language" than to have "intense experiences," adding that "if you can write authentically, you need not be authentic: poetry is drama, not autobiography." Some of the authenticity of Waller's works comes from overheard bits of conversation. A self-admitted eavesdropper in restaurants, Waller takes detailed notes and incorporates interesting idioms into his poems.

BIOGRAPHICAL/CRITICAL SOURCES:

PERIODICALS

Focus, May, 1984.
Times Literary Supplement, December 21, 1979.

*   *   *

WALLER, Gary
    See WALLER, G(ary) F(redric)

*   *   *

WARDE, Alan   1949-

PERSONAL: Born August 18, 1949, in Newcastle upon Tyne, Northumberland, England; son of Ernest (a railway clerk) and Nancy (a music teacher; maiden name, Smurthwaite) Warde.

Education: Downing College, Cambridge, B.A., 1971; University of Durham, M.A., 1972; University of Leeds, Ph.D., 1976.

ADDRESSES: Home—28, Lunesdale Court, Derwent Rd., Lancaster LA1 3ET, England.

CAREER: University of Leeds, Leeds, Yorkshire, England, temporary lecturer in sociology, 1975-78; Lancaster University, Lancashire, England, lecturer in sociology, 1978—.

MEMBER: British Sociological Association.

WRITINGS:

Consensus and Beyond: The Development of Labour Party Strategy Since the Second World War, Manchester University Press, 1982.
(With Linda Murgatroyd and others) *Localities, Class, and Gender,* Pion, 1985.
(With Nicholas Abercrombie) *Contemporary British Society,* Polity, 1988.
(With Paul Bagguley and others) *Restructuring: Place, Class, and Gender,* Sage, in press.

CONTRIBUTOR

D. Gregory and J. Urry, editors, *Social Relations and Spatial Structures,* Macmillan, 1985.
H. Newby, J. Bujra, P. Littlewood, G. Rees, and T. Rees, editors, *Restructuring Capital: Recession and Reorganisation in Industrial Society,* Macmillan, 1986.
K. Hoggart and E. Kofman, editors, *Politics, Geography, and Social Stratification,* Croom Helm, 1986.
P. Cooke, editor, *Localities: The Changing Face of Urban Britain,* Unwin Hyman, 1989.
J. Anderson and A. Cochrane, editors, *A State of Crisis: The Changing Face of British Politics,* Hodder & Stoughton, 1989.

OTHER

Contributor of articles in scholarly journals, including *Political Geography Quarterly, International Journal of Urban and Regional Research,* and *Work Employment and Society.*

SIDELIGHTS: In *Consensus and Beyond: The Development of Labour Party Strategy Since the Second World War,* Alan Warde argues that throughout post-World War II history Britain's unions have had the determining power over the directions the Labour party should take. Warde chronicles the party's history from the years of the "social reformists" who supported a mixed economy, through the rise of the "technocratic-collectivists" who wanted a more efficient mixed economy, to the early 1980's when the unions abandoned the traditional party leadership in favor of an alliance with leftist Labour.

In his *Times Literary Supplement* review of *Consensus and Beyond,* Ben Pimlott noted that "Alan Warde rightly stresses that the crucial factor in Labour's internal history has not been the bogus dilemma of Left-versus-Right, but the shifting attitudes and alliances of the trade unions." Pimlott found the book to be "interesting though infuriatingly jargon-ridden" and concluded by observing that "wisely . . . Warde makes no predictions, and instead provides a thoughtful examination of trends in post-war Labour thinking and policy, delving beneath ideologies and traditions and looking at the social forces which lie beyond them."

BIOGRAPHICAL/CRITICAL SOURCES:

PERIODICALS

Times Literary Supplement, October 15, 1982.

WARWICK, Jarvis
See GARNER, Hugh

*   *   *

WATERMAN, Andrew (John)   1940-

PERSONAL: Born May 28, 1940, in London, England; son of Leonard and Olive (Smith) Waterman; married Angela Marilyn Hannah Eagle, May 21, 1982 (divorced, 1985); children: Rory John Nolan. *Education:* Leicester University, B.A. (first class honors), 1966; graduate study at Oxford University, 1966-68.

ADDRESSES: Home—15 Hazelbank Rd., Coleraine, Londonderry, Northern Ireland, U.K. *Office*—University of Ulster, Coleraine, Londonderry, Northern Ireland, U.K.

CAREER: University of Ulster (formerly New University of Ulster), Coleraine, Norther Ireland, lecturer, 1968-78; senior lecturer in English literature, 1978—.

MEMBER: Poetry Society, Association of University Teachers.

AWARDS, HONORS: Cholmondeley Award for Poets, 1977; second prize in Arvon Foundation Poetry Competition, 1981, for *Out for the Elements.*

WRITINGS:

POETRY

Living Room: Poems, (Poetry Book Society choice in England), Marvell Press, 1974.
Last Fruit, Mandeville Press, 1974.
From the Other Country, Carcanet Press, 1977.
Over the Wall, Carcanet Press, 1980.
Out for the Elements (Poetry Book Society recommendation in England), Carcanet Press, 1981.
(Editor) *The Poetry of Chess,* Anvil Press Poetry, 1981.
Selected Poems, Carcanet Press, 1986.

OTHER

(Contributor) Michael Schmidt and Peter Jones, editors, *British Poetry since 1970,* Carcanet Press, 1980.

Contributor of articles and reviews to journals and newspapers, including *London Magazine, Poetry Wales, P.N. Review,* and *Times Literary Supplement.*

WORK IN PROGRESS: Further poems; a critical book on British poetry since 1910; a novel.

SIDELIGHTS: In a *Times Literary Supplement* article, Grevel Lindop characterized Waterman's *Out for the Elements* as "an autobiography framed in a diary: the past recaptured through the preoccupations of the present." The book begins with an introductory set of twenty lyrics titled "Given Worlds," which are memories and insights into Waterman's personal experience; the book continues with another group of "Shorter Poems," and closes with the major works. These include "Anglo-Irish," a discussion of the situation in Northern Ireland from the author's perspective, and "Out for the Elements," a wide-ranging account of the author's travels in England and Ireland during 1979 and 1980.

Reflecting on the poetic achievement in *Out for the Elements* and some of Waterman's earlier efforts, Lindop declared, "One has the impression of a poet who has found his proper direction, and has begun to produce important work." He continued, " 'Out for the Elements' is a rare thing: a long poem which is highly readable, as well as thoroughly contemporary in its techniques and its mode of intelligence. It also goes with sensitivity to the heart of several problems that beset modern Britain."

Waterman told *CA,* "Life provides sufficient motivation for writing poetry; that is, one is nagged to articulate response, to use language to explore and try to clarify various areas of experience. Obviously one could enlarge enormously on this."

AVOCATIONAL INTERESTS: Hill-walking, chess, good conversation.

BIOGRAPHICAL/CRITICAL SOURCES:

BOOKS

Dictionary of Literary Biography, Volume 40: *Poets of Great Britain and Ireland since 1960,* Gale, 1985.
Michael Schmidt and Peter Jones, editors, *British Poetry since 1970,* Carcanet Press, 1980.

PERIODICALS

Encounter, January, 1982.
Listener, April 15, 1976.
London Review of Books, February 18, 1982.
Times Literary Supplement, April 16, 1982.

*   *   *

WATKINS, T(homas) H(enry) 1936-

PERSONAL: Born March 29, 1936, in Loma Linda, Calif.; son of Thomas F. (a newspaper worker) and Orel (Roller) Watkins; married Elaine Otakie, January 26, 1957 (divorced); married Ellen J. Parker, June 12, 1976; children: (first marriage) Lisa Lynn, Kevin Blair. *Education:* Attended San Bernardino Valley College, 1954-56; University of Redlands, B.A., 1958; San Francisco State College (now University), graduate study, 1963-64. *Politics:* Democrat. *Religion:* "Former Catholic, now militantly ecumenical Christian."

ADDRESSES: Home—2226 Decatur Pl. N.W., Washington, D.C. 20008. *Office*—The Wilderness Society, 1400 Eye St. N.W., Washington, D.C. 20005.

CAREER: American West Publishing Co., Palo Alto, Calif., *American West* (magazine), managing editor, 1966-69, editor, 1969-70, associate editor, 1970-76; *American Heritage* (magazine), New York, N.Y., member of board of editors, 1976-79, senior editor, 1979-82; *Wilderness* (magazine), Washington, D.C., editor, 1982—.

WRITINGS:

San Francisco in Color, Hastings House, 1968.
(With Roger R. Olmsted) *Here Today: San Francisco's Architectural Heritage,* San Francisco Chronicle, 1968.
(With others) *The Grand Colorado: The Story of a River and Its Canyons,* American West, 1969.
California in Color: An Essay on the Paradox of Plenty, Hastings House, 1970.
(With others) *The Water Hustlers,* Sierra Club, 1971.
Gold and Silver in the West: The Illustrated History of an American Dream, American West, 1971.
California: An Illustrated History, American West, 1973.
On the Shore of the Sundown Sea, Sierra Club, 1973.
Mark Twain's Mississippi: The Pictorial History of America's Greatest River, American West, 1974.
(With Charles S. Watson, Jr.) *The Lands No One Knows: America and the Public Domain,* Sierra Club, 1975.
John Muir's America, illustrated with photographs by DeWitt Jones, American West, 1976.

(With Olmsted) *Mirror of the Dream: An Illustrated History of San Francisco,* Scrimshaw Press, 1976.
Taken by the Wind: Vanishing Architecture of the West, illustrated with photographs by Ronald Woodall, New York Graphic Society, 1977.
Gold Country, illustrated with photographs by Stanly Truman, California Historical Society, 1982.
(Author of introduction) John Wesley Powell, *Lands of the Arid Region of the United States,* new edition, Harvard Common Press, 1983.
American Landscape, illustrated with photographs by David Muench, Graphic Arts Center, 1987.
Vanishing Arctic: Alaska's National Wildlife Refuge, Aperture and Wilderness Society, 1988.
Time's Island: The California Desert, Peregrine Smith and Wilderness Society, 1989.
Righteous Pilgrim: The Life and Times of Harold L. Ickes, 1874-1952, Henry Holt, 1990.

Contributor of more than 250 articles to numerous periodicals.

SIDELIGHTS: T. H. Watkins told *CA:* "Some people call me an historian, some a journalist, some an environmentalist—they're all wrong. I'd prefer to think of myself *first* as a writer—a writer who happens to work in all these areas, as well as anything else which presents itself. I'm in love with words, with the sound and muscularity of phrases. . . . At the same time, I cannot deny a profound dependence upon the historical view, for it seems to me that it provides the essential key to understanding—and understanding is the only shield we have against fate and all its consequences. I learned this essential fact, among other things, from the one writer who has influenced my work, such as it is, more than any other: Wallace Stegner, the novelist and historian who needs no encomiums from me to place him at or very near the head of the small list of this century's major American writers."

BIOGRAPHICAL/CRITICAL SOURCES:

PERIODICALS

Los Angeles Times Book Review, October 15, 1989.
New York Times Book Review, December 14, 1969, December 18, 1977.

*   *   *

WATTS, (Anna) Bernadette 1942-
(Bernadette)

PERSONAL: Born May 13, 1942, in Northampton, England; daughter of Bert (a surveyor) and Josephine (Roberts) Watts; children: Nywell. *Education:* Maidstone College of Art, National Diploma in Design. *Politics:* Socialist. *Religion:* None.

ADDRESSES: Home—11/12 Stockwell St., Colchester CO1 18N, England.

CAREER: Free-lance illustrator and author.

AWARDS, HONORS: Premio Graphico (Bologna, Italy), 1969, for illustrations in James Reeves' *One's None: Old Rhymes for New Tongues;* Best New Children's Book award, 1975, for *Little Red Riding Hood.*

WRITINGS:

JUVENILE; ILLUSTRATOR

Ruth Ainsworth, *Look, Do and Listen,* F. Watts, 1969.
James Reeves, editor, *One's None: Old Rhymes for New Tongues,* F. Watts, 1969.

Alfred Tennyson, *Lady of Shallott,* F. Watts, 1969.

Reinhold Ehrhardt, *Kikeri; or, The Proud Red Rooster,* World Publishing, 1969.

Kathleen Arnott, *Animal Folk Tales around the World,* Blackie & Son, 1970, Walck, 1971.

Rhoda D. Power, *The Big Book of Stories from Many Lands,* F. Watts, 1970.

Ehrhardt, *Die Turmuhr* (title means "The Clock Tower"), Nord-Sued Verlag, 1971.

George Mendoza, *The Christmas Tree Alphabet Book,* World Publishing, 1971.

Arthur Scholey, *Sallinka and the Golden Bird,* Evans (London), 1978.

Margaret Rogers, *Green Is Beautiful,* R. Rourke, 1982.

Brigitte Hanhart, adapter, *Shoemaker Martin: Based on a Story by Leo Tolstoy,* translated by Michael Hale, North-South Books, 1986.

Gerda Marie Scheidl, *George's Garden,* translated by Rosemary Lanning, North-South Books, 1986.

ADAPTER AND ILLUSTRATOR OF BROTHERS GRIMM FAIRY TALES

Little Red Riding Hood, Oxford University Press, 1968, World Publishing, 1969.

Jorinda and Joringel, World Publishing, 1970.

Mother Holle (retelling of *Frau Holle*), Crowell, 1972.

Haensel und Gretel, Nord-Sued Verlag, 1973.

Rapunzel, Crowell, 1975.

Three Tales, Little, Brown, 1980.

Snow White, Faber, 1983.

Goldilocks and the Three Bears, Abelard-Schuman, 1984, North-South Books, 1985.

The Elves and the Shoemaker, North-South Books, 1986.

The Magic Ring, Knopf, 1987.

JUVENILE; AUTHOR AND ILLUSTRATOR UNDER NAME BERNADETTE

Hans the Miller Man, McGraw, 1969 (published in England as *Hans Millerman,* Oxford University Press, 1969).

Varenka, Oxford University Press, 1970.

The Proud Crow, edited by Caroline Rubin, Albert Whitman, 1975.

The Little Flute Player, Abelard-Schuman, 1975, published as *Brigette and Ferdinand: A Love Story,* Prentice-Hall, 1976.

Christmas Story, Abelard-Schuman, 1982.

OTHER

David's Waiting Day (juvenile), Prentice-Hall, 1975.

(Illustrator under name Bernadette) Arthur Scholey, *Der Wunschvogel: eine Geschichte,* Nord-Sued Verlag, 1978.

Also illustrator of *Cinderella,* C. A. Watts, and *The Lord's Prayer,* Parents Magazine Press. Also illustrated little "zig-zag" books for Kauffmann Verlag, posters, book jackets, and educational materials.

WORK IN PROGRESS: Writing more children's short stories; *Ashputtel,* and two other full color books.

SIDELIGHTS: Bernadette Watts has a great interest in the people of Africa, their culture, music, and stories, and spent four months in South Africa in 1969. She attends the Bologna and Frankfurt book fairs annually, and also visits other European countries regularly. Watts told *CA:* "[I'm] interested, more and more, in producing books toward the universal understanding of all peoples in the world." She is also currently interested in illustrating small books for schools in the Welsh language.

BIOGRAPHICAL/CRITICAL SOURCES:

PERIODICALS

Young Readers Review, October, 1969.

* * *

WEINSTEIN, Norman Charles 1948-

PERSONAL: Born January 26, 1948, in Philadelphia, Pa.; son of Emanuel (a florist supplier) and Gertrude (Zamarin) Weinstein; married to Julie Hall. *Education:* Bard College, B.A., 1969; State University of New York at New Paltz, M.A.T., 1975.

MEMBER: Modern Language Association, Association for Third World Studies, National Academy of Recording Arts and Sciences.

AWARDS, HONORS: Deems Taylor Award, American Society of Composers, Authors, and Publishers (ASCAP), 1989, for excellence in music writing.

WRITINGS:

Gertrude Stein and the Literature of the Modern Consciousness, Ungar, 1970.

Nigredo: Selected Poems 1970-1980, Station Hill, 1982.

Albedo, North Atlantic Books, 1984.

WORK IN PROGRESS: Rubedo, a poem.

SIDELIGHTS: A music critic, poet, and literary critic, Norman Charles Weinstein told *CA* that his "current writing focuses upon the impact of African ritual rhythms and tones upon American poetries and music."

* * *

WEIR, Joan 1928-

PERSONAL: Born April 21, 1928, in Calgary, Alberta, Canada; daughter of L. Ralph (an archbishop) and Carolyn (a musician; maiden name, Gillmor) Sherman; married Ormond Weir (a surgeon), May 14, 1955; children: Ian, Paul, Michael, Richard. *Education:* University of Manitoba, B.A., 1948. *Religion:* Anglican.

ADDRESSES: Home—463 Greenstone Dr., Kamloops, British Columbia, Canada V2C 1N8. *Agent*—J. Kellock & Associates, 11019 80th Ave., Edmonton, Alberta, Canada T6G 0R2.

CAREER: T. Eaton Co. (retail chain), Winnipeg, Manitoba, director of radio programming for children, author and producer of weekly fantasy programs, 1948-55, assistant fashion coordinator, 1955-56; free-lance writer, 1956-73; CFJC-TV, Kamloops, British Columbia, author, host, and producer of "Story Corner," a weekly half-hour series for children, 1973-77; Cariboo College, Kamloops, lecturer in English and creative writing, 1978—. Conducts weekend workshops in creative writing throughout British Columbia, Alberta, and Manitoba; gives readings to schools and adult groups in Canadian cities, including Surrey, Vancouver, Winnipeg, and Kamloops. President of Kamloops Music Festival, 1968-70; member of Western Canada Theatre Co. board of directors, 1975-80.

MEMBER: Writers' Union of Canada, Canadian Authors Association, Canadian Society of Children's Authors, Illustrators, and Performers, British Columbia Federation of Writers.

WRITINGS:

Three Day Challenge (juvenile novel), Scholastic/TAB, 1976.

Sherman (biography), Anglican Book Centre, 1976.

Exile of the Rocking Seven (teenage novel), Macmillan, 1977.

The Caledonians (history), Peerless Press, 1977.
Career Girl (juvenile novel), Tree Frog Press, 1979.
The Secret at Westwind (juvenile mystery), Scholastic/TAB, 1981.
So, I'm Different (juvenile novel), Douglas & McIntyre, 1981.
Walhachin: Catastrophe or Camelot (adult history), Hancock House, 1984.
Canada's Gold Rush Church (adult history), Anglican Church, 1986.
Storm Rider (young adult novel), Scholastic/TAB, 1987.
Ski Lodge Mystery (juvenile novel), Overlea House, 1988.
Balloon Race Mystery (juvenile novel), Overlea House, 1988.
Sixteen Is Spelled O-U-C-H (young adult novel), Stoddart, 1988.
Mystery at Lighthouse Rock (juvenile novel), Overlea House, 1989.

JUVENILE STAGE PLAYS

"The Ladder of Golden Arrows" (one-act), first produced in British Columbia, 1976.
"Guardian Spirits" (one-act), first produced in British Columbia, 1977.
"Winnie the Pooh Stories" (one-act; adapted from Alan Alexander Milne's book *Winnie the Pooh*), first produced in Kamloops, British Columbia, at Sagebrush Theatre, 1977.

OTHER

Also author of "Christmas Fantasies" (five short plays), first broadcast by Canadian Broadcasting Corp. (CBC), 1948. Also contributor to *Canadian Children's Annual 1988* (anthology). Contributor to periodicals, including *Discovery, Friend, Trials,* and *Kamloops Sentinel.*

WORK IN PROGRESS: Men of God, an historical study "of the spread of the Church in British Columbia and its effect on the social and political development of the province."

SIDELIGHTS: Joan Weir told *CA:* "Talent, of course, is absolutely essential, but the successful writer needs other things too—one of them is a driving sense of self-motivation. Another is the ability to step over disappointment and start again.

"Aspiring writers seem to ask the same standard questions. The first is, 'What is it like to be a writer?' To this my answer is simple: 'It is exciting; it is demanding; it is often lonely; it is even more often frustrating; but it is the greatest craft in the world.' The second question, which invariably follows, is 'Where do you get your ideas?' I am often tempted to reply, 'At dollar-forty-nine-day,' but I curb the urge and answer instead that having more ideas than time to write about them is one sure proof that a person is indeed a 'writer.' And that leads to the third question, namely, 'How can I tell if my work is any good?' To this query I can reply with conviction and assurance. If your characters come to life as the story is unfolding and start to take the plot twists into their own hands, arguing back at you when you try to force them into a set mold or pattern, then you can be pretty sure that your story is going to be 'good.' It may still require seventeen rewrites, but there is life in it, and that is the vital ingredient."

AVOCATIONAL INTERESTS: Dogs, jogging, "keeping up with my four grown sons."

*   *   *

WERTSMAN, Vladimir (F.) 1929-

PERSONAL: Born April 6, 1929, in Secureni, Romania; immigrated to the United States, 1967; naturalized U.S. citizen, 1972;

son of Filip and Anna Wertsman. *Education:* University of A. I. Cuza, LL.M. (legal sciences; summa cum laude), 1953; Columbia University, M.S.L.S., 1969.

ADDRESSES: Home—330 West 55th St., Apt. 3G, New York, N.Y. 10019. *Office*—Learner's Advisory Service and Job Information Center, Mid-Manhattan Library, 455 Fifth Ave., New York, N.Y. 10016.

CAREER: Lawyer with practice in criminal and civil law in Romania, 1953-67; First National City Bank, New York City, stock certificates examiner, 1967-68; Brooklyn Public Library, Brooklyn, N.Y., reference librarian in Science and Industry Division, 1969-74, assistant branch librarian at Canarsie Branch, 1974-77, and at Greenpoint Branch, 1977-80, branch librarian at Leonard Branch, 1980-82; New York Public Library, New York City, senior librarian and Slavic and Romanian languages specialist at Foreign Language Library, Donnell Library Center, 1982-86, senior librarian at Learner's Advisory Service and Job Information Center, Mid-Manhattan Library, 1987—.

MEMBER: American Library Association, Public Library Association (chair of multilingual materials and library service committee, 1985-87, and Leonard Wertheimer multilingual award committee, 1988—), American Association for the Advancement of Slavic Studies, American Romanian Academy of Arts and Sciences, American Society of Writers, Independent Press Association, Ethnic Materials Information Exchange, Round Table (chair of publications committee), Slavic American Cultural Association (member of board of directors), Delta Tau Kappa.

AWARDS, HONORS: Distinguished Literary Achievement Award, American Society of Writers, 1977, for article "Dracula's Revenge: 500 Years of Facts, Fiction, and Mystery"; Special Merit Award, Public Library Association, 1988, for "services contributing to the continuing success of America's public libraries in serving their communities."

WRITINGS:

The Romanians in America, 1748-1974, Oceana, 1975.
The Ukrainians in America, 1608-1975, Oceana, 1976.
The Russians in America, 1727-1970, Oceana, 1977.
The Armenians in America, 1618-1976, Oceana, 1978.
(Editor) *The Romanians in America and Canada: A Guide to Information Sources,* Gale, 1980.
(Co-author) *The Ukrainians in Canada and the United States,* Gale, 1981.
(With Bosiljka Stevanovic) *Free Voices in Russian Literature, 1950s-1980s,* Russica, 1986.
(Contributor) *Proceedings of the Second International Conference of Slavic Librarians,* Russica, 1986.
(Contributor) *The Immigrant Labor Press in North America, 1840s-1970s,* Greenwood, 1987.
Librarian's Companion: A Handbook of Facts and Figures on Books, Libraries, and Librarians, Greenwood Press, 1987.
Multilingual America: Directory of Education and Employment Resources for Job Hunters with Language Skills, Scarecrow, 1990.

Editorial consultant for *Harvard Encyclopedia of American Ethnic Groups,* Harvard University Press, 1980. Contributor of over forty articles and book reviews to periodicals, including *Booklist, Ethnic Forum, Law Books in Review, Topical Time,* and *What's New in Scholarly Books.* Editor, *EMIE Bulletin,* 1982-86.

WORK IN PROGRESS: "A comprehensive reference book—with over 3,500 annotated items—helping researchers to locate educational resources for learning foreign languages, and also to identify American and foreign employers interested in hiring American professionals and para-professionals with language skills."

SIDELIGHTS: Vladimir Wertsman once told *CA:* "As a book lover since early school days, I view my present professions—librarian and author—as twin brothers, two happy companions who inspire and supplement each other. Being an ethnic American and multilingual, I have devoted my writings to various ethnic American groups and languages. Multi-ethnicity (multiculture) is the spice of America, and American history is, in essence, multi-ethnic."

Wertsman is fluent in Russian, Romanian, and Ukrainian, and has a working knowledge of all the Slavic and Romance languages.

AVOCATIONAL INTERESTS: Chess, stamp-collecting, music, travel (including Europe, Asia, South America, Africa, and Central America).

BIOGRAPHICAL/CRITICAL SOURCES:

PERIODICALS

American Romanian Review, May, 1980.
Choice, January, 1988.
Ethnic American News, October, 1975.
Ethnic Forum, spring, 1982.
National Genealogical Inquirer, summer, 1980.
National Genealogical Society Quarterly, June, 1981.
RQ, spring, 1988.
Solia, May, 1980.
Unirea, May, 1980.

*   *   *

WEST, Anthony C(athcart Muir) 1910-

PERSONAL: Born July 1, 1910, in County Down, Ulster (now Northern Ireland); married Olive Mary Burr, 1940; children: seven daughters, four sons. *Education:* "The 4 R's." *Religion:* Christian.

ADDRESSES: Home—London, England. *Office*—c/o Midland Bank Ltd., Castle St., Beaumaris, Anglesey, Gwynedd LL58 8AR, North Wales.

CAREER: Novelist; worked as a jack-of-all-trades in the United States and Canada. *Military service:* Royal Air Force, 1939-45; served as a meteorological air observer and navigator-bomber in the Pathfinder Force.

MEMBER: Aosdana, Society for Irish Artists.

AWARDS, HONORS: Rockefeller Atlantic Award, 1946.

WRITINGS:

River's End and Other Stories, McDowell & Obolensky, 1957.
The Native Moment (novel), McDowell & Obolensky, 1959.
Rebel to Judgement (novel), McDowell & Obolensky, 1962.
The Ferret Fancier (novel), MacGibbon & Kee, 1962, Simon & Schuster, 1963, reprinted, Devin-Adair, 1983.
As Towns with Fire (novel), MacGibbon & Kee, 1968, Knopf, 1970, reprinted, Blackstaff (Belfast), 1985.
All the King's Horses and Other Stories, Poolbeg Press (Dublin), 1981.

Contributor of numerous short stories and articles to magazines in the United States, Great Britain, and East and West Germany.

WORK IN PROGRESS: The Casual Comedy, a novel; a rewrite of a novel about the Irish immigrant in the depression-era United States.

SIDELIGHTS: "The fiction of Anthony C. West is filled with poignant and great tenderness, yet it is not just lyric," asserts William Bittner in *Contemporary Novelists.* "The main characters of his [fiction] are all very much attuned to nature, yet *in* the world if not entirely *of* it." In the collection *River's End and Other Stories,* for example, the author uses a prose which is "not merely rich and precise," notes *Saturday Review*'s Granville Hicks; "one hears in it a new voice. West is capable of feeling what Stephen Muir, the hero of [some of these] stories, feels—exaltation in the experience of natural beauty." Contributing to the quality of West's prose, Hicks explains, is "a great gift of language [which] seems like a kind of magic, and indeed it is. Mr. West's use of words is not merely wonderfully fresh; it is wonderfully exact. He is obviously a writer with a mind," the critic continues, "and, boldly as he thrusts out towards the very limits of what language can do, his control rarely falters. His material is the emotions, and the skill with which he can render them is matched by the subtlety with which he understands them."

West applies several themes from his stories to *The Ferret Fancier,* a novel about an Irish adolescent living in a predominantly Protestant community. "Like the boys in West's earlier stories, Simon is uncommonly responsive to nature in all its aspects, and, in this rigidly Protestant society, he becomes a kind of pantheist," Hicks summarizes. Anne O'Neill-Barna similarly describes Simon in the *New York Times Book Review* as "sensuous to the point where smells become vivid as tastes, immediately responsive to the feelings of others, attuned to nature, gullible, deceptive, honest, self-sufficient, chivalrous and, above all, kind. His story is his struggle to find himself," the critic states; *Los Angeles Times Book Review* contributor Vickie Putnam likewise terms the novel "an excellent portrayal of the purgatory of puberty." Despite Simon's awareness of his natural surroundings, which leads him to adopt a ferret, "one must not attribute to [him] a kind of Wordsworthian innocence," notes Hicks, "for one of the major themes of the book is his sexual awakening. . . . The changes in his own body offer him excitements and perplexities that stimulate and frighten him."

Part of the success of *The Ferret Fancier* is due to West's portrayal of Simon's conflicting emotions; "In describing Simon's physiological and psychological states, West uses the words Simon might have used, and uses them to good effect," Hicks remarks. O'Neill-Barna similarly observes that "the other characters, seen through Simon's eyes, are . . . both perfectly rendered and perfectly understood." Because of this, the critic adds, West's novel "is more than merely authentic as a social document and as behavior of the adolescent human male. Its uniqueness lies in its power of telling the truth. Truth is many-sided," the critic explains; "Simon's consciousness is complex." "Few writers have explored more authoritatively the mind of a boy or shown more aspects of boyhood experience," concludes Hicks. Simon "is passing through a period of intense adventure and great peril, and West has the power to make us live through it with him."

In *As Towns with Fire,* a novel following sometime-poet and pilot Christopher McMannan through war and peace during the 1930s and 1940s, West likewise exhibits "a natural gift for drawing together endless bits and pieces of setting, the complex details of characters interacting, to create a belief in the whole environment or the human group," details Webster Schott in the *New York Times Book Review.* While the critic faults West for an excess of detail, he admits that *As Towns with Fire* "does reach a compromised success. . . . Piling event upon event, pumping ever more words into the inflated body of his narrative, introducing still more characters, probing the same emotional struggles over and over again, West ultimately touches us. He sends us into another life." *New York Times* writer Thomas Lask echoes these criticisms, but comments that "the writing that deals with the outdoors is on the highest level: A Lawrentian appreciation of the natural world that is one of the most enduring traits of English fiction." It is this sensitivity towards natural settings that distinguishes West's writing, suggests Bittner: "West has been compared with [James] Joyce and [Samuel] Beckett, and if one does not seek word play or the broadly comic, it is possible to see the comparison," the critic explains. "But in his feeling for nature, for the persons and places of the Irish countryside, [West] adds another ingredient. For all their accomplishments this century, Irish writers have tended to be parochially Irish, or write mainly of urban settings or rural settings, but rarely both," the critic concludes. "West has broken through the barrier."

AVOCATIONAL INTERESTS: Philosophy, Christology, Celtic Christianity, Hibernian and Cymric mythology and archeology.

BIOGRAPHICAL/CRITICAL SOURCES:

BOOKS

Contemporary Novelists, St. James Press, 1986.
Foster, John Wilson, *Forces and Themes in Ulster Fiction,* Gill & Macmillan (Dublin), 1974.

PERIODICALS

Los Angeles Times Book Review, March 31, 1985.
New York Times, April 4, 1970.
New York Times Book Review, June 29, 1958, March 21, 1965, April 5, 1970.
Saturday Review, July 5, 1958, December 12, 1959, March 27, 1965.

—*Sketch by Diane Telgen*

*   *   *

WESTON, Allen
   See NORTON, Andre

*   *   *

WHEELER, Cindy   1955-

PERSONAL: Born May 17, 1955, in Montgomery, Ala.; daughter of Kenneth Bradford (a school supervisor) and Joanne (a teacher; maiden name Dingus) Wheeler; married Robert Patrick Lee (in publishing), July 26, 1980; children: Sally Virginia. *Education:* Auburn University, B.F.A., 1977; graduate study at School of Visual Arts, New York City, 1980. *Religion:* Episcopalian.

ADDRESSES: Home—60 Haywood St., Apt. 2-A, Asheville, N.C. 28801. *Office*—18 Wall St., Asheville, N.C. 28801.

CAREER: Zibart's Bookstore, Nashville, Tenn., children's book buyer and sales clerk, 1977-78; Alfred A. Knopf (publishers), New York, N.Y., editorial secretary in juvenile department, 1977-80; free-lance illustrator and author, 1980—. Assistant to the art director, Lothrop, Lee & Shepherd, New York, 1984-85. Co-owner, The Bookstore on Wall Street, Asheville, N.C.

AWARDS, HONORS: Rose included in Bologna International Children's Book Fair, 1985; Alabama Author's Award, Alabama Library Association, 1985, for *Marmalade's Christmas Present.*

WRITINGS:

SELF ILLUSTRATED

A Good Day, a Good Night (Junior Literary Guild selection), Lippincott, 1980.
Rose, Knopf, 1985.
Spring Is Here! (coloring book), Happy House, 1986.
A Day on the Farm (coloring book), Happy House, 1987.
Sally Wants to Help, Random House, 1988.

"MARMALADE" SERIES

Marmalade's Snowy Day, Knopf, 1982.
Marmalade's Yellow Leaf, Knopf, 1982.
Marmalade's Nap, Knopf, 1983.
Marmalade's Picnic, Knopf, 1983.
Marmalade's Christmas Present (Junior Literary Guild selection), Knopf, 1984.

ILLUSTRATOR

Charlotte Zolotow, *One Step, Two,* Lothrop, revised edition (Wheeler not associated with first edition), 1981.
The Scaredy Cats and the Haunted House, Random House, 1982.
Alice Schertle, *That Olive!,* Lothrop, Lee & Shepherd, 1984.
Ruth Horowitz, *Mommy's Lap,* Lothrop, Lee & Shepherd, in press.

OTHER

Merry Christmas, Little Mouse (coloring book), illustrated by Jan Brett, Happy House, 1986.
A New House for Little Mouse (picture book), illustrated by Stella Ormai, Happy House, 1987.

SIDELIGHTS: Cindy Wheeler told *CA:* "Writing and illustrating books for children gives me a chance to stay in touch with some of the first emotions I experienced as a child. With each of my books I try to share, simply and clearly, those feelings the way I remember them—uncomplicated, unsuspicious, happiness in its purest and most all-encompassing form."

*   *   *

WHEELER, Helen Rippier

PERSONAL: Education: Junior College of the Packer Collegiate Institute, A.A., 1946; Barnard College, B.A., 1950; Columbia University, M.S., 1951, Ed.D., 1964; University of Chicago, M.A., 1954.

ADDRESSES: Home—2701 Durant Ave., No. 14, Berkeley, Calif. 94704-1733.

CAREER: Hicksville Public Library, Hicksville, N.Y., library director, 1951-53; University of Chicago, Chicago, Ill., staff member of Laboratory School and part-time foreign student adviser, International House, 1953-55; teacher-librarian in a Chicago high school, 1955-56; Columbia University, Teachers College, New York, N.Y., staff member of Agnes Russell Center, 1956-58; City Colleges of Chicago, Chicago, library director and audio-visual coordinator, 1958-62; Columbia University, Latin American coordinator, 1962-64; Drexel Institute of Technology (now Drexel University), Philadelphia, Pa., adjunct assistant professor, 1964-65; University of Hawaii, Honolulu, associate professor and community colleges system consultant, 1965-66; Indiana State University, Terre Haute, associate professor, 1966-68; St. John's University, Jamaica, N.Y., associate professor, 1968-69; consultant and writer, 1969-71; Louisiana State

University, Baton Rouge, associate professor, 1971-73; consultant and writer, 1973—; sole proprietor of Womanhood Media Consulting. Provider of Getting Published professional development training; visiting scholar to Japan, 1984. Founding member, National Women's Studies Association Aging and Ageism Caucus.

MEMBER: International House Association, American Library Association, Association of College and Research Libraries, American Association of Community and Junior Colleges, American Association of University Professors, American Association for Affirmative Action, Association of Feminist Consultants, National Women's Studies Association, Women's Institute for the Freedom of the Press, National Organization for Women, American Association of University Women, Women Library Workers, Women Educators, California Society of Librarians, California Clearinghouse on Library Instruction, Social Responsibilities Round Table.

WRITINGS:

(Contributor) Charles Trinkner, *Better Libraries Make Better Schools,* Shoe String, 1962.
(Contributor) Florence Lee, *Principles and Practices of Teaching in Secondary Schools,* McKay, 1964.
The Community College Library: A Plan for Action, Shoe String, 1965.
A Basic Book Collection for the Community College Library, Shoe String, 1968.
Womanhood Media, Scarecrow, 1972, supplement, 1975.
Learning the Library: A Skills and Concepts Series (multimedia kit), Educational Activities, 1975.
Library Reference Information: How to Locate and Use It (multimedia kit), Educational Activities, 1979.
(Contributor) Dana Densmore, editor *Syllabus Sourcebook on Media and Women,* Women's Institute for Freedom of the Press, 1980.
(Contributor) James Danky and Sanford Berman, editors, *Alternative Library Literature, 1982-1983: A Biennial Anthology,* Oryx, 1984.
(Contributor) *The Women's Annual, 1983: The Year in Review,* G. K. Hall, 1984.
The Bibliographic Instruction-Course Handbook, Scarecrow, 1988.
Getting Published in Women's Studies, McFarland & Co., 1989.

Also author of video program, *Learning the Library,* 1987. Contributor to periodicals, including *Journal of Library History, Women Studies Abstracts, Library Journal, Choice, California Women, Mensa Bulletin,* and *Journal of Educational Equity.*

WORK IN PROGRESS: Aging Womanhood: A Handbook for Researching and Knowing about Women and Gerontology; Audiovisuals for Aging and Gender: 500 Nonprint Media.

SIDELIGHTS: Helen Rippier Wheeler is proficient in Spanish and has travelled extensively.

*   *   *

WHITE, John Wesley   1928-

PERSONAL: Born September 15, 1928, in Saskatchewan, Canada. *Education:* Moody Bible Institute, graduate, 1950; Wheaton College, Wheaton, Ill., B.A., 1952; Oxford University, D.Phil., 1963.

ADDRESSES: Office—Richmond College, Milliken, Ontario, Canada.

CAREER: Associate evangelist with Billy Graham, traveling to 100 countries, 1964—; Richmond College, Milliken, Ontario, chancellor, 1967—.

WRITINGS:

Re-entry: Striking Parallels between Today's News Events and Christ's Second Coming, Zondervan, 1970.
Mission Control, Zondervan, 1971.
Re-entry II, Zondervan, 1971, reprinted, Baker Books, 1986.
Future Hope, Creation House, 1974.
The Runaway, Crescendo, 1976.
The Land Columbus Loved, Gordon Press, 1976.
What Does It Mean to Be Born Again?, foreword by Billy Graham, Bethany Fellowship (Minneapolis), 1977.
The Man from Krypton: The Gospel According to Superman, foreword by Graham, Bethany Fellowship, 1978.
The Coming World Dictator, foreword by Graham, Bethany Fellowship, 1981.
Arming for Armageddon, Mott Media, 1983.
The Survivors, Harvest House, 1983.
The Christmas Mice (juvenile), Still Point, 1984.

Also author of *Everywhere Preaching the Gospel,* 1969.

WORK IN PROGRESS: Recovery, for Zondervan.

BIOGRAPHICAL/CRITICAL SOURCES:

PERIODICALS

New York Times Book Review, February 13, 1972.*

*   *   *

WHITE, Lawrence J.   1943-

PERSONAL: Born June 1, 1943, in New York, N.Y. *Education:* Harvard University, A.B. (summa cum laude), 1964, Ph.D., 1969; London School of Economics, M.Sc., 1965.

ADDRESSES: Home—110 Bleecker St., Apt. 21-B, New York, N.Y. 10012. *Office*—Stern School of Business, New York University, 90 Trinity Pl., New York, N.Y. 10006.

CAREER: Harvard University, Development Advisory Service, Cambridge, Mass., development adviser to governments of Pakistan and Indonesia, 1969-70; Princeton University, Princeton, N.J., assistant professor of economics, 1970-76; New York University, Graduate School of Business Administration, New York, N.Y., associate professor of economics, 1976-78; U.S. Council of Economic Advisers, Washington, D.C., senior staff economist, 1978-79; New York University, Graduate School of Business Administration, professor of economics, 1979—; U.S. Department of Justice, Antitrust Division, Washington, D.C., chief economist, 1982-83. Member of board of Federal Home Loan Bank, 1986-89.

MEMBER: American Economic Association.

WRITINGS:

THe Automobile Industry since 1945, Harvard University Press, 1971.
Industrial Concentration and Economic Power in Pakistan, Princeton University Press, 1974.
(Editor with L. G. Goldberg) *The Deregulation of the Banking and Securities Industries,* Lexington Books, 1979.
Reforming Regulation: Processes and Problems, Prentice-Hall, 1981.
(Editor with M. Keenan, and contributor) *Mergers and Acquisitions: Current Problems in Perspective,* Lexington Books, 1982.

The Regulation of Air Pollutant Emissions from Motor Vehicles, American Enterprise Institute for Public Policy Research, 1982.

The Public Library in the 1980s: The Problems of Choice, Lexington Books, 1983.

(Editor with A. Saunders) *Technology and the Regulation of Financial Markets: Securities, Futures, and Banking,* Lexington Books, 1986.

International Trade in Ocean Shipping: The U.S. and the World, Ballinger, 1988.

(Editor and contributor) *Private Antitrust Litigation: New Evidence, New Learning,* M.I.T. Press, 1988.

(Editor with J. E. Kwoka, Jr., and contributor) *The Antitrust Revolution,* Scott, Foresman, 1989.

CONTRIBUTOR

(With E. E. Bailey) W. G. Shepherd and T. G. Gies, editors, *Regulation in Further Perspective,* Ballinger, 1974.

R. E. Canes and M. J. Roberts, editors, *Regulating the Product,* Ballinger, 1975.

S. M. Goldfeld and R. E. Quandt, editors, *Studies in Non-Linear Estimation,* Ballinger, 1976.

W. Adams, editor, *The Structure of American Industry,* 5th edition, Macmillan, 1977, 6th edition, 1982.

(With E. S. Mills) A. F. Friedlaender, editor, *Approaches to Controlling Air Pollution,* M.I.T. Press, 1978.

D. H. Ginsburg and W. J. Abernathy, editors, *Government, Technology, and the Future of the Automobile,* McGraw, 1980.

R. R. Nelson, editor, *Government and Technical Progress: A Cross-Industry Analysis,* Pergamon, 1982.

P. B. Downing and K. Hauf, editors, *International Comparisons in Implementing Pollution Laws,* Kluwer-Nijhoff, 1983.

(With T. Pugel) I. Walter, editor, *Deregulating Wall Street,* Wiley, 1985.

E. Noam, editor, *Video Media Competition: Regulation, Economics, and Technology,* Columbia University Press, 1985.

(With D. Krupka) M. H. Peston and R. H. Quandt, editors, *Prices, Competition, and Equilibrium,* Philip Alan, 1986.

H. Mutoh, editor, *Industrial Policies for Pacific Economic Growth,* Allen & Unwin, 1986.

L. Weiss and M. Klass, editors, *Regulatory Reform: What Actually Happened,* Little, Brown, 1986.

(With D. Golbe) A. Auerbach, editor, *Mergers and Acquisitions,* University of Chicago Press, 1988.

(With Golbe) Auerbach, editor, *The Economic Effects of Mergers and Acquisitions,* University of Chicago Press, 1988.

R. J. Larner and J. W. Meehan, Jr., editors, *Economics and Antitrust Policy,* Quorum Books, 1989.

OTHER

North American editor, *Journal of Industrial Economics,* 1984-87.

WORK IN PROGRESS: Research on antitrust policy, financial regulation, and the "savings and loan financial debacle of the 1980s."

*   *   *

WHITE, William, Jr. 1934-
(Spinossimus)

PERSONAL: Born June 8, 1934, in Philadelphia, Pa.; adopted son of William (an accountant and auditor) and Ruth (McCaughan) White; married Sara Jane Shute (a nurse), September 8, 1956; children: Rebecca, Sara, William III, James M., Elizabeth, Margaret. *Education:* Haverford College, B.S., 1956; Westminster Theological Seminary, B.D., 1961, Th.M., 1963; Dropsie College for Hebrew and Cognate Learning (now Dropsie University), Ph.D., 1968. *Politics:* Christian-Social Democrat. *Religion:* Presbyterian (Reformed).

ADDRESSES: Home—2272 Patty Ln., Warrington, Pa. 18976. *Office*—Box 638, Warrington, Pa. 18976.

CAREER: Employed during his early career as mailman, hospital orderly, gas pumper, and mill hand; affiliated with U.S. Civil Service, Glenside, Pa., 1956-63; Temple University, Philadelphia, Pa., instructor in ancient history, 1964-68; Ellen Cushing Junior College, Bryn Mawr, Pa., assistant professor of biology and physics, 1966-68; East Carolina University, Greenville, N.C., assistant professor of history, 1968-70; Philadelphia College of Textiles and Science, Philadelphia, professor of history, 1970-71; North American Publishing Co., Philadelphia, editorial director, 1971-73; Old Testament editor, Thomas Nelson, Inc., 1976—; publisher, Franklin Institute Press, 1976-81; state publisher, Commonwealth of Pennsylvania, 1982-85; president, Nitech Research Corp., 1985—; Temple University, member of history department, 1988—. Emergency Care Research Institute, senior medical writer, 1972-74, managing editor, 1972-75. Publisher of *International Bulletin of Magnetic Resonance, Cancer Therapy Abstracts, Carcinogenesis Abstracts,* and *Nutrition and Cancer.* Consultant to numerous private and government organizations, including Auerbach Corp. and Data Communications.

MEMBER: American Association for the Advancement of Science, American Historical Association, Mensa, Intertel, Tyndale House (Oxford, England).

AWARDS, HONORS: National Endowment for the Humanities grant for study in Israel, 1968; International Committee for Chemical Research (Japan) fellow, 1969-70; Christian Booksellers Award, 1982.

WRITINGS:

(Editor and translator) *A Babylonian Anthology,* Morris Press, 1966.

(Contributor) Stephen Benko and John J. O'Rourke, *The Catacombs and the Colosseum,* Judson, 1970.

(Editor and contributor) *The North American Reference Encyclopedia of Women's Liberation,* North American Publishing, 1972.

(Editor with F. Little) *The North American Reference Encyclopedia of Ecology and Pollution,* North American Publishing, 1972.

(Contributor) *The Law and the Prophets,* Presbyterian & Reformed, 1973.

(Editor with R. Albano) *North American Symposium on Drugs and Drug Abuse,* North American Publishing, 1974.

(Contributor) *The New Zondervan Pictorial Bible Encyclopedia,* five volumes, Zondervan, 1975.

(With D. Estrada) *The First New Testament,* Thomas Nelson, 1978.

Van Til: Defender of the Faith (biography), Thomas Nelson, 1979.

(Co-editor) *The New King James Bible,* Thomas Nelson, 1979.

(Editor with J. I. Packer and M. C. Tenney) *The Bible Almanac,* Thomas Nelson, 1980.

(Contributor) *Theological Wordbook of the Old Testament,* two volumes, Moody, 1980.

(Contributor) *The New International Dictionary of Biblical Archaeology,* Zondervan, 1983.

Laser Printing: The Fundamentals, Carnegie Press, 1983.

Theological and Grammatical Phrasebook of the Bible, Moody, 1984.

(Co-editor) *Nelson's Expository Dictionary of Biblical Words,* Thomas Nelson, 1984.

Close-up Photography, Eastman Kodak, 1984.

(Editor) *Photomacrography,* Focal Press, 1987.

Subminiature Photography, Focal Press, 1990.

Commercial Electronic Printing, COPI, 1990.

Image Storage Technology, Academic, in press.

SELF-ILLUSTRATED JUVENILES; PUBLISHED BY STERLING

A Frog Is Born, 1972.
A Turtle Is Born, 1973.
The Guppy: Its Life Cycle, 1974.
The Siamese Fighting Fish: Its Life Cycle, 1975.
An Earthworm Is Born, 1975.
The Angelfish: Its Life Cycle, 1975.
(With wife, Sara Jane White) *A Terrarium in Your Home,* 1976.
The Edge of the Pond, 1976.
Forest and Garden, 1976.
The Cycle of the Seasons, 1977.
The American Chameleon, 1977.
Edge of the Ocean, 1977.
A Mosquito Is Born, 1981.

OTHER

Also author, with S. J. White, of *The Housefly,* 1981. Writer for radio and television. Contributor of over one thousand articles to numerous periodicals, including *International Journal of Intelligence and Counter Intelligence, Christian Scholar's Review, Westminster Theological Journal, Industrial Research, Photographic Applications in Science and Medicine, Government Data Systems,* and *Journey.* Editor, *Engineering* and *Science and Technology News;* associate editor, *Data Processing Magazine;* managing editor, *Health Devices;* contributing editor, *American Printer* and *Shutterbug;* technology and trends editor, *Electronic Publishing and Printing.*

WORK IN PROGRESS: A Grammatical and Exegetical Bible Sentence Book; Military Photography; Jesus Christ: His Life and Times; Studies of Mediaeval Oriental Versions of the Hebrew Bible.

SIDELIGHTS: William White, Jr., told *CA:* "As an author with a radical-Christian philosophy of science, I have tried to innovate the use of the latest tools and methods in the biomedical field for use in juvenile books on science. I have utilized the light microscope, micromanipulation, photomacroscopy, and scanning electron microscopy in illustrating explanations of growth-edge scientific ideas for young readers. This is done by using familiar life forms—turtles, lizards, exotic fishes—as the vehicle for demonstrating basic ideas in physiology, biochemistry, ethology, biophysics, and ecology."

White adds that he has recently advanced his "efforts into biological and non-biological systems. Of special interest has been the problem of coding of parallel relational information from language to language and from biotic system to biotic system. Recent work has centered on Computer Graphics (CG), Iconic Database Management Systems (DBMS), and investigating problems in AI applications to image processing."

AVOCATIONAL INTERESTS: Literature (particularly Japanese, Chinese, and Russian), microbiology, biotechnology, ichthyology, herpetology.

*   *   *

WHITMAN, Ruth (Bashein) 1922-

PERSONAL: Born May 28, 1922, in New York, N.Y.; daughter of Meyer D. (a lawyer) and Martha (Sherman) Bashein; married Cedric Whitman, October 13, 1941 (divorced, 1958); married Firman Houghton, July 23, 1959 (divorced, 1964); married Morton Sacks (a painter), October 6, 1966; children: (first marriage) Rachel Whitman, Leda Whitman; (second marriage) David. *Education:* Radcliffe College, B.A. (magna cum laude), 1944; Harvard University, M.A., 1947. *Politics:* Liberal. *Religion:* "Secular Jewish."

ADDRESSES: Home—40 Tuckerman Ave., Middletown, R.I. 02840. *Office*—1559 Beacon St., Brookline, Mass. 02146.

CAREER: Poet and translator. Houghton Mifflin Co., Boston, Mass., editorial assistant, 1941-42, educational editor, 1944-45; Harvard University Press, Cambridge, Mass., free-lance editor, 1945-60; *Audience* (magazine), Cambridge, poetry editor, 1958-63; Cambridge Center for Adult Education, Cambridge, teacher of poetry workshop, 1965-68; Radcliffe College, Cambridge, lecturer in poetry, 1970—. Lecturer in poetry, Harvard University, 1979-84. Poet-in-residence, Hamden-Sydney College, 1974, Mishkenot Sha'ananim, 1977, 1979, 1981, Holy Cross College, 1978, Centre College of Kentucky, 1980, 1987, and Kentucky Arts Commission, 1981. Visiting lecturer at Trinity College, Hartford, 1975, University of Denver, 1976, Massachusetts Institute of Technology, 1979, 1989, and University of Massachusetts—Boston, 1980. Director of Poetry in the Schools Program, Massachusetts Council on the Arts, 1970-73. Has read her own poetry on television and at numerous universities and cultural centers, including Harvard University, Tufts University, Brown University, Massachusetts Institute of Technology, Brandeis University, Wheaton College, Northwestern University, Folger Shakespeare Library, Tel Aviv University, and New School for Social Research.

MEMBER: P.E.N., Authors Guild, Authors League of America, Poetry Society of America (member of executive board, 1962—; regional vice-president, 1978—), New England Poetry Club, Phi Beta Kappa, Signet Club (Harvard).

AWARDS, HONORS: Reynolds Lyric Award, 1962, and Alice Fay de Castagnola Award, 1968, both for manuscript of *The Marriage Wig, and Other Poems,* William Marion Reedy Award, 1974, Consuelo Ford Award, 1975, and John Masefield Award, 1976, all from Poetry Society of America; fellowships from MacDowell Colony, 1962, 1964, 1972-74, 1979, and 1982, Radcliffe Institute for Independent Study, 1968-70, and senior Fulbright writer-in-residence program, Jerusalem, 1984-85; Jennie Tane Award, *Massachusetts Review,* 1962; grants from National Foundation for Jewish Culture, 1968, National Endowment for the Arts, 1974-75, Martin Tananbaum Foundation, 1979, 1980, Rhode Island State Council on the Arts, 1981, and Brookline Arts Council, 1988; Kovner Award, Jewish Book Council of America, 1969; Chanin Foundation Award, 1972, for translation; Guiness International Poetry Award, 1973; finalist in Virginia Commonwealth University manuscript competition, 1977; Urbanarts Award, 1987.

WRITINGS:

Blood and Milk Poems, Clarke & Way, 1963.

(Translator with Samuel Beckett and others) Alain Bosquet, *Selected Poems,* New Directions, 1963.

(Co-translator) Isaac Bashevis Singer, *Short Friday,* Farrar, Straus, 1966.

(Editor and translator) *An Anthology of Modern Yiddish Poetry,* bilingual edition, October House, 1966, 2nd edition, Workmen's Circle Education Department, 1979.

(Translator with others) Singer, *The Seance,* Farrar, Straus, 1968.

The Marriage Wig, and Other Poems, Harcourt, 1968.

(Editor and translator) *The Selected Poems of Jacob Glatstein,* October House, 1972.

The Passion of Lizzy Borden: New and Selected Poems, October House, 1973.

(Editor) *Poemmaking: Poets in Classrooms,* Massachusetts Council of Teachers of English, 1975.

Tamsen Donner: A Woman's Journey, Alice James Books, 1975.

Permanent Address: New Poems, 1973-1980, Alice James Books, 1980.

(Contributor) Hedges and Wendt, editors, *In Her Own Image: Women Working in the Arts,* Feminist Press, 1980.

Becoming a Poet: Source, Process, and Practice, Writer, Inc., 1982.

The Testing of Hanna Senesh, Wayne State University Press, 1986.

Laughing Gas, Wayne State University Press, 1989.

The Fiddle Rose: Selected Poems of Abraham Sutzkever, Wayne State University Press, 1989.

CONTRIBUTOR TO ANTHOLOGIES

The "New Yorker" Anthology, Viking, 1969.
The "New York Times" Anthology, Macmillan, 1970.
The Berkshire Anthology, Bookstore Press, 1972.
X. J. Kennedy, editor, *Messages,* Little, Brown, 1972.
Rising Tides, Washington Square Press, 1973.
Search the Silence: Poems of Self-Discovery, Scholastic Book Services, 1974.
To See the World Afresh, Athenaeum, 1974.
Another Way Out, Holt, 1974.
Images of Women in Literature, Houghton, 1977.

OTHER

Also translator of modern French and Greek poetry. Author and narrator of television documentary "Sachuest Point," 1977. Contributor to periodicals, including *Writer, Radcliffe Quarterly, Massachusetts Review, Jewish Quarterly, American Poetry Review, Antioch Review,* and *Boston Public Library Quarterly.*

WORK IN PROGRESS: A book-length novella in prose and poetry, *Hatshepsut, Speak to Me.*

SIDELIGHTS: By 1985, Ruth Whitman's *Tamsen Donner: A Woman's Journey* had sold the most copies (at 4,000) of any Alice James Books offering. She recorded her work for the Library of Congress in 1974 and 1981.

BIOGRAPHICAL/CRITICAL SOURCES:

PERIODICALS

Bennington Review, September, 1979.
Croton Review, number 6, 1983.
New York Times, November 10, 1985.
Poetry, May, 1964, March, 1970.
Radcliffe Quarterly, June, 1984.

WICK, Carter
See WILCOX, Collin

*   *   *

WIENER, Joel H. 1937-

PERSONAL: Born August 23, 1937, in New York, N.Y.; son of Philip Wiener; married Suzanne Wolff (a reading teacher), September 4, 1961; children: Paul, Deborah, Jane. Education: New York University, B.A., 1959; graduate study at University of Glasgow, 1961-63; Cornell University, Ph.D., 1965.

ADDRESSES: Home—267 Glen Court, Teaneck, N.J. 07666. Office—Department of History, City College of the City University of New York, Convent Ave. and 138th St., New York, N.Y. 10031.

CAREER: Skidmore College, Saratoga Springs, N.Y., assistant professor of history, 1964-67; City College of the City University of New York, New York City, associate professor, 1967-76, professor of history, 1977—, chairman of department, 1981-85. Visiting lecturer, University of York, 1971-73; member of conference on British Studies.

MEMBER: Royal History Society (fellow), Research Society for Victorian Periodicals (president, 1983-85), American Historical Association.

WRITINGS:

The War of the Unstamped, Cornell University Press, 1969.
A Descriptive Finding List of Unstamped British Periodicals: 1830-1836, Oxford University Press, 1970.
(Editor) *Great Britain: Foreign Policy and the Span of Empire, 1689-1970,* four volumes, McGraw, 1972.
Great Britain: The Lion at Home, four volumes, Bowker, 1974.
(Contributor) J. Don Vann and Rosemary T. VanArsdel, editors, *Victorian Periodicals: A Guide to Research,* Modern Library Association of America, 1978.
Radicalism and Freethought in Nineteenth-Century Britain, Greenwood Press, 1983.
(Editor) *Innovators and Preachers: The Role of the Editor in Victorian Britain,* Greenwood Press, 1985.
(Contributor) Ian Dyck, editor, *Citizen of the World,* St. Martin's, 1988.
(Editor) *Papers for the Millions: The New Journalism in Britain, 1850s to 1914,* Greenwood Press, 1988.
William Lovett, Manchester University Press, 1989.
(Contributor) Vann and VanArsdel, editors, *Victorian Periodicals: A Guide to Research,* Volume 2, Modern Library Association of America, 1989.

WORK IN PROGRESS: A history of the British press, 1830-1914.

AVOCATIONAL INTERESTS: Films, theatre, opera.

BIOGRAPHICAL/CRITICAL SOURCES:

PERIODICALS

Times Literary Supplement, November 9, 1984, June 20, 1986.

*   *   *

WILCOX, Collin 1924-
(Carter Wick)

PERSONAL: Born September 21, 1924, in Detroit, Mich.; son of Harlan C. and Lucille (Spangler) Wilcox; married Beverly

Buchman, December 23, 1954 (divorced, 1964); children: Christopher, Jeffrey. *Education:* Antioch College, A.B., 1948. *Politics:* Democrat. *Religion:* None.

ADDRESSES: Home—4174 26th St., San Francisco, Calif. 94131. *Agent*—Dominick Abel, 146 West 82nd St., New York. N.Y. 10024.

CAREER: Writer. Advertising copywriter in San Francisco, Calif., 1948-50; Town School, San Francisco, teacher of art, 1950-53; Amthor & Co. (furniture store), San Francisco, partner, 1953-55; owner of lamp firm, San Francisco, 1955-71, designing and manufacturing lamps and other decorative items for the home. *Military service:* U.S. Army, 1943.

MEMBER: Mystery Writers of America, Sierra Club, Aircraft Owners and Pilots Association.

WRITINGS:

The Black Door, Dodd, 1967.
The Third Figure, Dodd, 1968.
The Lonely Hunter, Random House, 1969.
The Disappearance, Random House, 1970.
Dead Aim, Random House, 1971.
Hiding Place, Random House, 1972.
Long Way Down, Random House, 1973.
Aftershock, Random House, 1975.
(Under pseudonym Carter Wick) *The Faceless Man,* Saturday Review Press, 1975.
The Third Victim, Dell, 1976.
Doctor, Lawyer, Random House, 1977.
(With Bill Pronzini) *Twospot,* Putnam, 1978.
The Watcher, Random House, 1978.
Power Plays, Random House, 1979.
Mankiller, Random House, 1980.
Spellbinder, Fawcett, 1981.
(Under pseudonym Carter Wick) *Dark House, Dark Road,* Raven House, 1982.
Stalking Horse, Random House, 1982.
Victims, Mysterious Press, 1984.
Night Games, Mysterious Press, 1985
The Pariah, Mysterious Press, 1987.
Bernhardt's Edge, Tor Books, 1988.
Silent Witness, Tor Books, 1990.
A Death before Dying, Henry Holt, 1990.

Also author of *The Judgment,* Henry Holt, and *Searching,* Tor Books.

WORK IN PROGRESS: Two books, *Swallow's Fall* and *The Magdalena Decision.*

BIOGRAPHICAL/CRITICAL SOURCES:

PERIODICALS

Washington Post Book World, October 19, 1986.

*   *   *

WILDE, Alan 1929-

PERSONAL: Born May 26, 1929, New York, N.Y.; son of Joseph and Dora (Cohen) Wilde. *Education:* New York University, B.A., 1950, M.A., 1951; attended University of Paris, 1952-53; Harvard University, Ph.D., 1958.

ADDRESSES: Home—410 Clarksville Rd., Princeton Junction, N.J. 08550. *Office*—Department of English, Temple University, Philadelphia, Pa. 19122.

CAREER: Williams College, Williamstown, Mass., instructor, 1958-61, assistant professor of English, 1961-64; Temple University, Philadelphia, Pa., associate professor, 1964-67, professor of English, 1967—, graduate chairman, 1975-85. Evaluator of manuscripts for nine university presses; evaluator of essays for ten literary journals. Consultant on fellowships and grants for Bunting Institute and National Endowment of the Humanities; consultant on matters of tenure and promotion at fourteen universities.

MEMBER: American Association of University Professors, Modern Language Association of America, Phi Beta Kappa.

AWARDS, HONORS: Fulbright fellowship, 1952-53; Charles Dexter travelling fellowship, 1958; research awards from Williams College, 1963, and Temple University, 1965, 1967, and 1971; Lindback Foundation Distinguished Teaching Award, 1975; *Arizona Quarterly* Annual Award for best essay of the year, 1984, for "Acts of Definition, or Who Is Thomas Berger?"; Guggenheim fellowship, 1986-87.

WRITINGS:

Art and Order: A Study of E. M. Forster, New York University Press, 1964.
(Contributor) John Hamilton McCallum, *Prose and Criticism,* Harcourt, 1966.
Christopher Isherwood, Twayne, 1971.
(Contributor) G. K. Das and John Beer, editors, *E. M. Forster: A Human Exploration, Centenary Essays,* New York University Press, 1979.
Horizons of Assent: Modernism, Postmodernism, and the Ironic Imagination, Johns Hopkins University Press, 1981, published with new preface, University of Pennsylvania Press, 1987.
(Contributor) William E. Cain, editor, *Philosophical Approaches to Literature: New Essays on Nineteenth- and Twentieth-Century Texts,* Bucknell University Press, 1984.
Critical Essays on E. M. Forster, G. K. Hall, 1985.
Middle Grounds: Essays in Contemporary American Fiction, University of Pennsylvania Press, 1987.
(Contributor) Jay Clayton and Betsy Draine, editors, *Contemporary Literature and Contemporary Theory,* University of Wisconsin Press, 1989.

Contributor to literary journals, including *Contemporary Literature, Modern Fiction Studies, Prose Studies,* and *Novel.* Associate of *Journal of Modern Literature,* 1970—. Member of editorial board, Contemporary Critical Literature Series, Sun and Moon Press, 1975-77, and Penn Studies in Contemporary American Fiction, University of Pennsylvania Press, 1987—. Member of board of review, Temple University Press, 1972-75, and of board of consultants, *Contemporary Literature,* 1981—.

WORK IN PROGRESS: The Literature of Experience: Fiction in an Age of Extremity; articles for literary journals.

BIOGRAPHICAL/CRITICAL SOURCES:

PERIODICALS

Times Literary Supplement, November 6, 1981.

*   *   *

WILKERSON, Cynthia
See LEVINSON, Leonard

WILLIAMS, Guy R(ichard) 1920-

PERSONAL: Born August 23, 1920, in Mold, Clwyd, North Wales; son of Owen Elias (a physician) and Beatrice Maud (a nurse; maiden name, Chadwick) Williams. *Education:* Attended St. Edward's School, Oxford, 1934-37; Hornsey School of Art, art teacher's diploma, 1950. *Religion:* Church of England.

ADDRESSES: Home—1A Earl Rd., East Sheen, London SW14 7JH, England.

CAREER: Parmiter's School, London, England, master in charge of drama, art, and careers, 1950-81. Artist and illustrator. Has had work exhibited at Royal Academy, London, and at many galleries.

MEMBER: Savile Club (London).

AWARDS, HONORS: Saxon Barton Prize, Royal Cambrian Academy, for an oil painting.

WRITINGS:

Woodworking, Museum Press, 1962.
Drawing and Sketching, Museum Press, 1962.
Sketching in Pencil, Pitman, 1963.
Tackle Leatherwork This Way, Stanley Paul, 1963.
(Editor) *Enjoy Painting in Oils,* Gollancz, 1963.
Instructions in Handicrafts, Museum Press, 1964.
Making a Miniature House, Oxford University Press, 1964.
Teach Your Child to be Handy, Pearson, 1964.
Tackle Drawing and Painting This Way, Stanley Paul, 1965.
Instruction for Home Handymen, Museum Press, 1966.
(With A. V. Gibson) *Your Book of Woodwork,* Faber, 1967.
Making a Miniature Theatre, Faber, 1967.
Working with Leather, Emerson Books, 1967.
Design Guide to Home Decorating, Transworld, 1967.
Collecting Pictures, Arco, 1967, Praeger, 1968.
A Career Abroad?, MacGibbon & Kee, 1968.
Collecting Cheap China and Glass, Corgi, 1969.
Making a Miniature Village, Faber, 1970, Puffin Books, 1977.
The World of Model Trains, Putnam/Deutsch/Rainbird, 1970.
Taking Up Drawing and Painting, Taplinger, 1971.
The World of Model Ships and Boats, Putnam, 1971.
(And illustrator) *Collecting Silver and Plate,* Corgi, 1971.
The Hidden World of Scotland Yard, Hutchinson, 1972.
The World of Model Aircraft, Putnam, 1973.
The Black Treasures of Scotland Yard, photographs by Beverly Lebarrow, Hamish Hamilton, 1973.
London in the Country: The Growth of London's Suburbs, Hamish Hamilton, 1975.
The Age of Agony: The Art of Healing, c. 1700-1800, Constable, 1975, Academy Chicago, 1986.
The World of Model Cars, Putnam, 1976.
The Royal Parks of London, Constable, 1978.
London Walks, Constable, 1981.
The Age of Miracles: Medicine and Surgery in the Nineteenth Century, Constable, 1981, Academy Chicago, 1988.
Guide to the Magical Places of England, Wales, and Scotland, Constable, 1987.
Augustus Pugin versus Decimus Burton: A Victorian Architectural Duel, Cassell, 1990.

JUVENILE

Use Your Hands!, Chapman & Hall, 1956.
Use Your Eyes!, Chapman & Hall, 1957.
Use Your Leisure!, Chapman & Hall, 1958.
Use Your Head!, Chapman & Hall, 1959.
Instructions to Young Collectors, Museum Press, 1959.

Use Your Spare Time!, Chapman & Hall, 1960.
Instructions to Young Model-Makers, Museum Press, 1960.
Use Your Legs!, Chapman & Hall, 1961.
Use Your Playtime!, Chapman & Hall, 1962.
Use Your Ears!, Chapman & Hall, 1963.
Let's Look at Wales, Museum Press, 1965.
Let's Look at London, Museum Press, 1965.
Indoor Hobbies, illustrated by Roy Chambers, Studio Vista, 1966.
Outdoor Hobbies, Studio Books, 1967.
Chester and the Northern Marches (history), illustrated by Graham Humphreys, Longmans, Green, 1968.
Making Mobiles, Emerson Books, 1969.
(Adaptor) Charles Dickens, *David Copperfield: The First Part of the Novel by Charles Dickens* (play), Macmillan (London), 1971.
(Adaptor) Dickens, *Pip and the Convict: From "Great Expectations" by Charles Dickens* (play), Macmillan, 1971.
(Adaptor) Dickens, *Nicholas Nickelby: From the Novel by Charles Dickens* (play), St. Martin's, 1972.
(Adaptor) Dickens, *A Christmas Carol, by Charles Dickens* (play), Macmillan, 1973.
(With others) *The Burning Fiery Furnace; David and Goliath: Two Plays for Young People,* Macmillan, 1975.

OTHER

Advisory editor, "Dramascript Classics" series, Macmillan, 1968-88; editor, "Enjoying Home and Leisure" series, Gollancz.

SIDELIGHTS: Guy R. Williams told *CA* that he is "deeply interested in young people's drama, and in producing and directing plays with them." He has also directed several Shakespearean productions, editing the texts and designing settings.

AVOCATIONAL INTERESTS: Gardening, local history.

BIOGRAPHICAL/CRITICAL SOURCES:

PERIODICALS

Washington Post Book World, January 10, 1988.

* * *

WILLIAMS, Tennessee 1911-1983

PERSONAL: Name originally Thomas Lanier Williams; born March 26, 1911, in Columbus, Miss.; choked to death February 24, 1983, in his suite at Hotel Elysee, New York, N.Y.; buried in St. Louis, Mo.; son of Cornelius Coffin (a traveling salesman) and Edwina (Dakin) Williams. *Education:* Attended University of Missouri, 1931-33, and Washington University, St. Louis, Mo., 1936-37; University of Iowa, A.B., 1938. *Religion:* Originally Episcopalian; converted to Roman Catholicism, 1969.

ADDRESSES: Home—1431 Duncan St., Key West, Fla.; also maintained residences in New York, N.Y., and New Orleans, La. *Agent*—Mitch Douglas, ICM, 40 West 57th St., New York, N.Y. 10019.

CAREER: Playwright, novelist, short story writer, and poet; full-time writer, 1944-1983; first published in 1927, winning third prize in an essay contest sponsored by *Smart Set* magazine; first published story in *Weird Tales,* August, 1928; first published under name Tennessee Williams in *Story,* summer, 1939. International Shoe Co., St. Louis, Mo., clerical worker and manual laborer, 1934-36; worked various jobs, including waiter and hotel elevator operator, New Orleans, La., 1939; worked as teletype operator, Jacksonville, Fla., 1940; worked various jobs, including waiter and theater usher, New York, N.Y., 1942; worked as screenwriter for M-G-M, 1943.

MEMBER: Dramatists Guild, National Institute of Arts and Letters, American Society of Composers, Authors, and Publishers (ASCAP), American Automatic Control Council (president, 1965-67), Alpha Tau Omega.

AWARDS, HONORS: Group Theatre Award, 1939, for *American Blues;* Rockefeller Foundation fellowship, 1940; grant, American Academy and National Institute of Arts and Letters, 1943; New York Drama Critics Circle Award, Donaldson Award, and Sidney Howard Memorial Award, 1945, all for *The Glass Menagerie;* New York Drama Critics Circle Award, Pulitzer Prize, and Donaldson Award, 1948, all for *A Streetcar Named Desire;* elected to National Institute of Arts and Letters, 1952; New York Drama Critics Circle Award and Pulitzer Prize, 1955, both for *Cat on a Hot Tin Roof; London Evening Standard* Award, 1958, for *Cat on a Hot Tin Roof;* New York Drama Critics Circle Award, 1962, for *The Night of the Iguana;* first place for best new foreign play, London Critics' Poll, 1964-65, for *The Night of the Iguana;* creative arts medal, Brandeis University, 1964-65; National Institute of Arts and Letters Gold Medal, 1969; received first centennial medal of Cathedral of St. John the Divine, 1973; elected to Theatre Hall of Fame, 1979; Kennedy Honors Award, 1979; Common Wealth Award for Distinguished Service in Dramatic Arts, 1981.

WRITINGS:

PLAYS

(Under original name, Thomas Lanier Williams) "Cairo, Shanghai, Bombay!" (comedy), produced in Memphis, Tenn., by Memphis Garden Players, July 12, 1935.

(Under original name) "Headlines," produced in St. Louis, Mo., at Wednesday Club Auditorium, November 11, 1936.

(Under original name) "Candles to the Sun," produced in St. Louis at Wednesday Club Auditorium, 1936.

(Under original name) "The Magic Tower," produced in St. Louis, 1936.

(Under original name) "The Fugitive Kind" (also see below), produced in St. Louis at Wednesday Club Auditorium, 1937.

(Under original name) "Spring Song," produced in Iowa City, Iowa, at the University of Iowa, 1938.

"The Long Goodbye" (also see below), produced in New York City at New School for Social Research, February 9, 1940 (closed after two performances).

(Contributor) Margaret Mayorga, editor, *The Best One-Act Plays of 1940* (contains "Moony's Kids Don't Cry"), Dodd, 1940.

Battle of Angels (also see below; produced in Boston, Mass., at Wilbur Theatre, December 20, 1940, withdrawn, January 1, 1941), New Directions, 1945.

"Stairs to the Roof," produced in Pasadena, Calif., at Playbox, 1944.

The Glass Menagerie (also see below; first produced in Chicago, Ill., at Civic Theatre, December 26, 1944; produced on Broadway at Playhouse, March 31, 1945), Random House, 1945, published as *The Glass Menagerie: Play in Two Acts,* Dramatists Play Service, 1948.

(With Donald Windham) *You Touched Me!: A Romantic Comedy in Three Acts* (produced on Broadway at Booth Theatre, September 25, 1945), Samuel French, 1947.

(Contributor) *The Best One-Act Plays of 1944* (contains "27 Wagons Full of Cotton"; also see below), Dodd, 1945.

"This Property Is Condemned" (also see below), produced Off-Broadway at Hudson Park Theatre, March, 1946.

"Moony's Kids Don't Cry" (also see below), produced in Los Angeles, Calif., at Actor's Laboratory Theatre, 1946.

"Portrait of a Madonna" (also see below), produced in Los Angeles at Actor's Laboratory Theatre, 1946, produced in New York City as part of "Triple Play," April 15, 1959.

"The Last of My Solid Gold Watches" (also see below), produced in Los Angeles at Actor's Laboratory Theatre, 1946.

27 Wagons Full of Cotton, and Other One-Act Plays by Tennessee Williams (includes "The Long Goodbye," "This Property Is Condemned," "Portrait of a Madonna," "The Last of My Solid Gold Watches," "Auto-da-Fe," "The Lady of Larkspur Lotion," "The Purification," "Hello from Bertha," "The Strangest Kind of Romance," and "Lord Byron's Love Letter" [also see below]), New Directions, 1946, 3rd edition with preface by Williams (contains two new plays, "Talk to Me Like the Rain and Let Me Listen" and "Something Unspoken" [also see below]), 1953.

"Lord Byron's Love Letter" (also see below), produced in New York City, 1947, revised version produced in London, England, 1964.

"Auto-da-Fe," produced in New York City, 1947, produced in Bromley, Kent, England, 1961.

"The Lady of Larkspur Lotion," produced in New York City, 1947, produced in London, 1968.

Summer and Smoke (first produced in Dallas, Tex., at Theatre '47, July 11, 1947; produced on Broadway at Music Box, October 6, 1948; revised as "Eccentricities of a Nightingale," produced in Washington, D.C., April 20, 1966, at Washington Theater Club), New Directions, 1948, published as *Summer and Smoke: Play in Two Acts,* Dramatists Play Service, 1950, published as *The Eccentricities of a Nightingale, and Summer and Smoke: Two Plays,* New Directions, 1964.

A Streetcar Named Desire (also see below; first produced on Broadway at Ethel Barrymore Theatre, December 3, 1947), New Directions, 1947, edition with preface by Williams, 1951, revised edition published as *A Streetcar Named Desire: A Play in Three Acts,* Dramatists Play Service, 1953, edition with foreword by Jessica Tandy and introduction by Williams, Limited Editions Club, 1982, edition with introduction by Williams, New American Library, 1984.

American Blues: Five Short Plays (contains "Moony's Kids Don't Cry," "The Dark Room," "The Case of the Crushed Petunias," "The Long Stay Cut Short; or, the Unsatisfactory Supper," and "Ten Blocks on the Camino Real"; also see below), Dramatists Play Service, 1948, reprinted, 1976.

Camino Real: A Play (also see below; expanded version of "Ten Blocks on the Camino Real"; produced in New York City at National Theatre, March 9, 1953), edition with foreword and afterword by Williams, New Directions, 1953.

The Rose Tattoo (also see below; produced in New York City at Martin Beck Theatre, February 3, 1951), edition with preface by Williams, New Directions, 1951.

Cat on a Hot Tin Roof (also see below; first produced on Broadway at Morosco Theatre, March 24, 1955), edition with preface by Williams, New Directions, 1955, published as *Cat on a Hot Tin Roof: A Play in Three Acts,* Dramatists Play Service, 1958.

"27 Wagons Full of Cotton" (also see below; part of triple bill entitled "All in One"), produced on Broadway at Playhouse, April 19, 1955.

Three Players of a Summer Game (first produced in Westport, Conn., at White Barn Theatre, July 19, 1955), Secker & Warburg, 1960.

(Librettist) Raffaello de Banfield, *Lord Byron's Love Letter: Opera in One Act,* Ricordi, 1955.

"The Case of the Crushed Petunias," produced in Cleveland, Ohio, 1957, produced in New York City, 1958.

Orpheus Descending: A Play in Three Acts (also see below; revision of *Battle of Angels;* produced in New York City at Martin Beck Theatre, March 21, 1957; produced Off-Broadway, 1959), New Directions, 1959.

Orpheus Descending, with Battle of Angels: Two Plays, with preface by Williams, New Directions, 1958.

A Perfect Analysis Given by a Parrot: A Comedy in One Act (also see below), Dramatists Play Service, 1958.

The Rose Tattoo, and, Camino Real, introduced and edited by E. Martin Browne, Penguin, 1958.

Garden District: Two Plays; Something Unspoken and Suddenly Last Summer (also see below; produced Off-Broadway at York Playhouse, January 7, 1958), Secker & Warburg, 1959.

Suddenly Last Summer, New Directions, 1958.

"Talk to Me Like the Rain and Let Me Listen," first produced in Westport, Conn., at White Barn Theatre, July 26, 1958, produced in New York City at West Side Actors Workshop, 1967.

I Rise in Flame, Cried the Phoenix: A Play about D. H. Lawrence (first produced Off-Broadway, 1958-59, produced Off-Broadway at Theatre de Lys, April 14, 1959), with a note by Frieda Lawrence, New Directions, 1951.

A Streetcar Named Desire, and, The Glass Menagerie, edited and introduced by E. Martin Browne, Penguin, 1959.

Sweet Bird of Youth (first produced at Martin Beck Theatre, March 10, 1959), edition with foreword by Williams, New Directions, 1959, revised edition, Dramatists Play Service, 1962.

Period of Adjustment; High Point Over a Cavern: A Serious Comedy (first produced in Miami, Fla., at Coconut Grove Playhouse, 1959 [co-directed by Williams], produced on Broadway at Helen Hayes Theatre, November 10, 1960, simultaneously published in *Esquire*), New Directions, 1960, reprinted as *Period of Adjustment; or, High Point is Built on a Cavern: A Serious Comedy,* Dramatists Play Service, 1961.

The Night of the Iguana (also see below; from Williams's short story of the same title; short version first produced in Spoleto, Italy, 1960, expanded version produced on Broadway at Royale Theatre, December 28, 1961), New Directions, 1961.

"The Purification," produced Off-Broadway at Theatre de Lys, December 8, 1959.

"Hello from Bertha," produced in Bromley, Kent, England, 1961.

"To Heaven in a Golden Coach," produced in Bromley, 1961.

The Milk Train Doesn't Stop Here Anymore (also see below; produced as one-act in Spoleto at Festival of Two Worlds, June, 1962, expanded version produced on Broadway at Morosco Theatre, January 16, 1963, revision produced on Broadway at Brooks Atkinson Theatre, January 1, 1964), New Directions, 1964.

"Slapstick Tragedy" (contains "The Mutilated" and "The Gnaediges Fraulein"; also see below), first produced on Broadway at Longacre Theatre, February 22, 1966 (closed after seven performances).

"The Dark Room," produced in London, 1966.

The Mutilated: A Play in One Act, Dramatists Play Service, 1967.

The Gnaediges Fraulein: A Play in One Act, Dramatists Play Service, 1967, revised as "The Latter Days of a Celebrated Soubrette," produced in New York City at Central Arts Theatre, May 16, 1974.

Kingdom of Earth: The Seven Descents of Myrtle (first published in *Esquire* as one-act "Kingdom of Earth," February, 1967, expanded as "The Seven Descents of Myrtle," produced on Broadway at Ethel Barrymore Theatre, March 27, 1968, revised as "Kingdom of Earth," produced in Princeton, N.J., at McCarter Theatre, March 6, 1975), New Directions, 1968, published as *The Kingdom of Earth (The Seven Descents of Myrtle): A Play in Seven Scenes,* Dramatists Play Service, 1969.

The Two-Character Play (first produced in London, at Hampstead Theatre Club, December, 1967), revised as *Out Cry* (produced in Chicago at Ivanhoe Theatre, July 8, 1971, produced on Broadway at Lyceum Theatre, March 1, 1973), New Directions, 1969.

In the Bar of a Tokyo Hotel (first produced Off-Broadway at Eastside Playhouse, May 11, 1969), Dramatists Play Service, 1969.

"The Strangest Kind of Romance," produced in London, 1969.

(Contributor) "Oh! Calcutta!," produced Off-Broadway at Eden Theatre, June 17, 1969.

"The Frosted Glass Coffin" [and] "A Perfect Analysis Given by a Parrot," produced in Key West, Fla., at Waterfront Playhouse, May 1, 1970.

"The Long Stay Cut Short; or, The Unsatisfactory Supper" (also see below), produced in London, 1971.

"I Can't Imagine Tomorrow" [and] "Confessional," produced in Bar Harbor, Me., at Maine Theatre Arts Festival, August 19, 1971.

Small Craft Warnings (produced Off-Broadway at Truck and Warehouse Theatre, April 2, 1972), New Directions, 1972.

The Red Devil Battery Sign (produced in Boston, June 18, 1975, revised version produced in Vienna, Austria, at English Theatre, January 17, 1976), New Directions, 1988.

"Demolition Downtown: Count Ten in Arabic," produced in London, 1976.

"This Is (An Entertainment)," produced in San Francisco at American Conservatory Theatre, January 20, 1976.

Vieux Carre (produced on Broadway at St. James Theatre, May 11, 1977), New Directions, 1979.

A Lovely Sunday for Creve Coeur (first produced under title "Creve Coeur" in Charleston, S.C., at Spoleto Festival, May, 1978, produced Off-Broadway at Hudson Guild Theatre, January 21, 1979), New Directions, 1980.

Clothes for a Summer Hotel: A Ghost Play (produced on Broadway at Cort Theatre, March 26, 1980), Dramatists Play Service, 1981.

Steps Must Be Gentle: A Dramatic Reading for Two Performers, Targ Editions, 1980.

"Something Cloudy, Something Clear," first produced Off-Off-Broadway at Bouwerie Lane Theater, September, 1981.

It Happened the Day the Sun Rose, Sylvester & Orphanos, 1981.

The Remarkable Rooming-House of Mme. Le Monde: A Play, Albondocani Press, 1984.

Also author of "Me, Vashya," "Not about Nightingales," "Kirche, Kutchen und Kinder," "Life Boat Drill," "Will Mr. Merriwether Return from Memphis?," "Of Masks Outrageous and Austere," and "A House Not Meant to Stand." Also author of television play, "I Can't Imagine Tomorrow." Contributor to anthologies. Contributor to periodicals, including *Esquire.*

Williams's plays appear in numerous foreign languages.

COLLECTIONS

Four Plays (contains "The Glass Menagerie," "A Streetcar Named Desire," "Summer and Smoke," and "Camino Real"), Secker & Warburg, 1956.

Five Plays (contains "Cat on a Hot Tin Roof," "The Rose Tattoo," "Something Unspoken," "Suddenly Last Summer," and "Orpheus Descending"), Secker & Warburg, 1962.

Three Plays: The Rose Tattoo, Camino Real, Sweet Bird of Youth, New Directions, 1964.

Baby Doll: The Script for the Film [and] *Something Unspoken* [and] *Suddenly Last Summer,* Penguin, 1968.

The Night of the Iguana [and] *Orpheus Descending,* Penguin, 1968.

The Milk Train Doesn't Stop Here Anymore [and] *Cat on a Hot Tin Roof,* Penguin, 1969.

Dragon Country: A Book of Plays, New Directions, 1970.

Battle of Angels [and] *The Glass Menagerie* [and] *A Streetcar Named Desire,* New Directions, 1971.

Cat on a Hot Tin Roof [and] *Orpheus Descending* [and] *Suddenly Last Summer,* New Directions, 1971.

The Eccentricities of a Nightingale [and] *Summer and Smoke* [and] *The Rose Tattoo* [and] *Camino Real,* New Directions, 1971.

The Theatre of Tennessee Williams, New Directions, Volume 1, 1971, Volume 2, 1971, Volume 3, 1971, Volume 4, 1972, Volume 5, 1976, Volume 6, 1981, Volume 7, 1981.

Three by Tennessee Williams, New American Library, 1976.

Cat on a Hot Tin Roof [and] *The Milk Train Doesn't Stop Here Anymore* [and] *The Night of the Iguana,* Penguin, 1976.

Selected Plays, illustrations by Jerry Pinkney, Franklin Library, 1977.

Tennessee Williams: Eight Plays, introduction by Harold Clurman, Doubleday, 1979.

Selected Plays, illustrations by Herbert Tauss, Franklin Library, 1980.

"Ten by Tennessee" (one-act plays), produced in New York City at Lucille Lortel Theater, May, 1986.

SCREENPLAYS

(With Gore Vidal) "Senso," Luchino Visconti, c. 1949.

(With Oscar Saul) "The Glass Menagerie," Warner Bros., 1950.

"A Streetcar Named Desire," 20th Century-Fox, 1951.

(With Hal Kanter) "The Rose Tattoo," Paramount, 1955.

"Baby Doll," Warner Bros., 1956, published as *Baby Doll: The Script for the Film,* New American Library, 1956, published as *Baby Doll; the Script for the Film, Incorporating the Two One-Act Plays which Suggested It: 27 Wagons Full of Cotton* [and] *The Long Stay Cut Short; or, The Unsatisfactory Supper,* New Directions, 1956.

(With Vidal) "Suddenly Last Summer," Columbia, 1959.

(With Meade Roberts) "The Fugitive Kind" (based on "Orpheus Descending"), United Artists, 1959, published as *The Fugitive Kind,* Signet, 1960.

"Boom" (based on "The Milkman Doesn't Stop Here Anymore"), Universal, 1968.

Stopped Rocking and Other Screenplays (contains "All Gaul Is Divided," "The Loss of a Teardrop Diamond," "One Arm," and "Stopped Rocking"), introduced by Richard Gilman, New Directions, 1984.

Also author, with Paul Bowles, of "The Wanton Countess" (English-language version), filmed in 1954.

NOVELS

The Roman Spring of Mrs. Stone (novel), New Directions, 1950.

Moise and the World of Reason (novel), Simon & Schuster, 1975.

STORIES

One Arm, and Other Stories (includes "The Night of the Iguana"), New Directions, 1948.

Hard Candy: A Book of Stories, New Directions, 1954.

Man Brings This Up Road: A Short Story, Street & Smith, 1959.

Three Players of a Summer Game, and Other Stories, Secker & Warburg, 1960, reprinted, Dent, 1984.

Grand, House of Books, 1964.

The Knightly Quest: A Novella and Four Short Stories, New Directions, 1967.

Eight Mortal Ladies Possessed: A Book of Stories, New Directions, 1974.

Collected Stories, introduction by Gore Vidal, New Directions, 1985.

Contributor of short stories to *Esquire.*

POETRY

(Contributor) James Laughlin, editor, *Five Young American Poets,* New Directions, 1944.

In the Winter of Cities: Poems, New Directions, 1956.

Androgyne, Mon Amour: Poems, New Directions, 1977.

OTHER

(Author of introduction) Carson McCullers, *Reflections in a Golden Eye,* Bantam, 1961.

Memoirs, Doubleday, 1975.

Tennessee Williams' Letters to Donald Windham, 1940-65, edited with commentary by Windham, [Verona], 1976, Holt, 1977.

Where I Live: Selected Essays, edited by Christine R. Day and Bob Woods, introduction by Day, New Directions, 1978.

Conversations with Tennessee Williams, edited by Albert J. Devlin, University Press of Mississippi, 1986.

A collection of Williams's manuscripts and letters is located at the Humanities Research Center of the University of Texas at Austin.

SIDELIGHTS: The production of his first two Broadway plays, *The Glass Menagerie* (1945) and *A Streetcar Named Desire* (1947), secured Tennessee Williams's place, with Eugene O'Neill and Arthur Miller, as one of America's major playwrights of the twentieth century. Critics, playgoers, and fellow dramatists recognized in him a poetic innovator who, refusing to be confined in what Stark Young in the *New Republic* called "the usual sterilities of our playwriting patterns," pushed drama into new fields, stretched the limits of the individual play, and became one of the founders of the so-called "New Drama." Praising *The Glass Menagerie* "as a revelation of what superb theater could be," Brooks Atkinson in *Broadway* asserted that "Williams's remembrance of things past gave the theater distinction as a literary medium." Twenty years later, Joanne Stang wrote in the *New York Times* that "the American theater, indeed theater everywhere, has never been the same" since the premier of *The Glass Menagerie.* Four decades after that first play, C. W. E. Bigsby in *A Critical Introduction to Twentieth-Century American Drama* termed it "one of the best works to have come out of the American theater." *A Streetcar Named Desire* became only the second play in history to win both the Pulitzer Prize and the New York Drama Critics Circle Award. Eric Bentley, in *What Is Theatre?,* called it the "master-drama of the generation." "The inevitability of a great work of art," T. E. Kalem stated in Albert J. Devlin's *Conversations with Tennessee Williams,* "is that you cannot imagine the time when it didn't exist. You can't imagine a time when *Streetcar* didn't exist."

More clearly than with most authors, the facts of Williams's life reveal the origins of the material he crafted into his best works. The Mississippi in which Thomas Lanier Williams was born March 26, 1911, was in many ways a world that no longer exists, "a dark, wide, open world that you can breathe in," as Williams nostalgically described it in Harry Rasky's *Tennessee Williams: A Portrait in Laughter and Lamentation.* The predominantly rural state was dotted with towns such as Columbus, Canton, and Clarksdale, in which he spent his first seven years with his mother, his sister Rose, and his maternal grandmother and grandfather, an Episcopal rector. A sickly child, Tom was pampered by doting elders. In 1918, his father, a traveling salesman who had been often absent—perhaps, like his stage counterpart in *The Glass Menagerie,* "in love with long distances"—moved the family to St. Louis. Something of the trauma they experienced is dramatized in the 1945 play. The contrast between leisurely small-town past and northern big-city present, between protective grandparents and the hard-drinking, gambling father with little patience for the sensitive son he saw as a "sissy," seriously affected both children. While Rose retreated into her own mind until finally beyond the reach even of her loving brother, Tom made use of that adversity. St. Louis remained for him "a city I loathe," but the South, despite his portrayal of its grotesque aspects, proved a rich source to which he returned literally and imaginatively for comfort and inspiration. That background, his homosexuality, and his relationships, painful and joyous, with members of his family were the strongest personal factors shaping Williams's dramas.

During the St. Louis years, Williams found an imaginative release from unpleasant reality in writing essays, stories, poems, and plays. After attending the University of Missouri, Washington University from which he earned a B.A. degree in 1938, and the University of Iowa, he returned to the South, specifically to New Orleans, one of two places where he was for the rest of his life to feel at home. Yet a recurrent motif in his plays involves flight and the fugitive, who, Lord Byron insists in *Camino Real: A Play,* must keep moving, and the flight from St. Louis initiated a nomadic life of brief stays in a variety of places. Williams fled not only uncongenial atmospheres but a turbulent family situation that had culminated in a decision for Rose to have a prefrontal lobotomy in an effort to alleviate her increasing psychological problems. (Williams's works often include absentee fathers, enduring—if aggravating—mothers, and dependent relatives; and the memory of Rose appears in some character, situation, symbol or motif in almost every work after 1938.) He fled as well some part of himself, for he had created a new persona, Tennessee Williams the playwright, who shared the same body as the proper young gentleman named Thomas with whom Tennessee would always be to some degree at odds.

In 1940 Williams's *Battle of Angels* was staged by the Theater Guild in an ill-fated production marred as much by faulty smudge pots in the lynching scene as by Boston censorship. Despite the abrupt out-of-town closing of the play, Williams was now known and admired by powerful theater people. During the next two decades, his most productive period, one play succeeded another, each of them permanent entries in the history of modern theater: *The Glass Menagerie, A Streetcar Named Desire, Summer and Smoke, The Rose Tattoo, Camino Real, Cat on a Hot Tin Roof, Orpheus Descending, Suddenly Last Summer, Sweet Bird of Youth,* and *Night of the Iguana.* Despite increasingly adverse criticism, Williams continued his work for the theater for two more decades, during which he wrote more than a

dozen additional plays containing evidence of his virtues as a poetic realist. In the course of his long career he also produced three volumes of short stories, many of them as studies for subsequent dramas; two novels, *The Roman Spring of Mrs. Stone* and *Moise and the World of Reason;* two volumes of poetry; his memoirs; and essays on his life and craft. His dramas made that rare transition from legitimate stage to movies and television, from intellectual acceptance to popular acceptance. Before his death in 1983, he had become the best-known living dramatist; his plays had been translated and performed in many foreign countries, and his name and work had become known even to people who had never seen a production of any of his plays. The persona named Tennessee Williams had achieved the status of a myth.

Plays, stories, poems, and personal essays were all drawn from the experiences of his persona. Williams saw himself as a shy, sensitive, gifted man trapped in a world where "mendacity" replaced communication, brute violence replaced love, and loneliness was, all too often, the standard human condition. These tensions "at the core of his creation" were identified by Harold Clurman in his introduction to *Tennessee Williams: Eight Plays* as a terror at what Williams saw in himself and in America, a terror that he must "exorcise" with "his poetic vision." In the preface to *The Rose Tattoo,* the playwright declared that "Snatching the eternal out of the desperately fleeting" was "the great magic trick of human existence." In an interview collected in *Conversations with Tennessee Williams,* Williams identified his main theme as a defense of the Old South attitude—"elegance, a love of the beautiful, a romantic attitude toward life"—and "a violent protest against those things that defeat it." An idealist aware of what he called in a *Conversations* interview "the merciless harshness of America's success-oriented society," he was ironically, naturalistic as well, conscious of the inaccessibility of that for which he yearned. He early developed, according to John Gassner in *Theatre at the Crossroads: Plays and Playwrights of the Mid-Century American Stage,* "a precise naturalism" and continued to work toward a "fusion of naturalistic detail with symbolism and poetic sensibility rare in American playwriting." The result was a unique romanticism, as Kenneth Tynan observed in *Curtains,* "which is not pale or scented but earthy and robust, the product of a mind vitally infected with the rhythms of human speech."

Williams's characters, then, endeavor to embrace the ideal, to advance and not "hold back with the brutes," a struggle no less valiant for being vain. In *A Streetcar Named Desire* Blanche's idealization of life at Belle Reve, the DuBois plantation, cannot protect her once, in the words of the brutish Stanley Kowalski, she has come "down off them columns" into the "broken world," the world of sexual desire. Since every human, as Val Xavier observes in *Orpheus Descending,* is sentenced "to solitary confinement inside our own lonely skins for as long as we live on earth," the only hope is to try to communicate, to love, and to live—even beyond despair, as *The Night of the Iguana* teaches. The attempt to communicate often takes the form of sex (and Williams has been accused of obsession with that aspect of human existence), but at other times it becomes a willingness to show compassion, as when in *The Night of the Iguana* Hannah Jelkes accepts the neuroses of her fellow creatures and when in *Cat on a Hot Tin Roof* Big Daddy understands, as his son Brick cannot, the attachment between Brick and Skipper. In his preface to *Cat on a Hot Tin Roof* Williams might have been describing his characters' condition when he spoke of "the outcry of prisoner to prisoner from the cell in solitary where each is confined for the duration of his life." "The marvel is," as Tynan stated, that Williams's "abnormal" view of life, "heightened and spotlighted and slashed with bogey shadows," can be made to touch his audience's more normal views, thus achieving that "miracle of communication" Williams believed to be almost impossible.

Some of his contemporaries—Arthur Miller notably—responded to the modern condition with social protest, but Williams, after a few early attempts at that genre, chose another approach. It is generally characteristic of Southern authors not to comment overtly on social problems because of these writers' Calvinistic distrust of programs and schemes for the perfectibility of man. Thus Williams insisted in a *Conversations* interview that he wrote about the South not as a sociologist: "What I am writing about is human nature." Moreover, as a romantic, Williams sought an ideal unobtainable through social action; recognizing, as he stated in *Conversations,* that "human relations are terrifyingly ambiguous," Williams chose to present characters full of uncertainties, mysteries, and doubts. Yet Arthur Miller himself wrote in *The Theatre Essays of Tennessee Williams* that although Williams might not portray social reality, "the intensity with which he feels whatever he does feel is so deep, is so great" that his audiences glimpse another kind of reality, "the reality in the spirit." Clurman likewise argued that though Williams was no "propagandist," social commentary is "inherent in his portraiture." The inner torment and disintegration of a character like Blanche in *A Streetcar Named Desire* thus symbolize the lost South from which she comes and with which she is inseparably entwined. It was to that lost world and the unpleasant one which succeeded it that Williams turned for the majority of his settings and material.

Like most Southern writers, Williams's work exhibits an abiding concern with time and place and how they affect men and women. "The play is memory," Tom proclaims in *The Glass Menagerie;* and Williams's characters are haunted by a past that they have difficulty accepting or that they valiantly endeavor to transform into myth. Interested in yesterday or tomorrow rather than in today, painfully conscious of the physical and emotional scars the years inflict, they have a static, dream-like quality, and the result, Tynan observed, is "the drama of mood." The Mississippi towns of his childhood continued to haunt Williams's imagination throughout his career, but New Orleans offered him, he told Robert Rice in the 1958 *New York Post* interviews, a new freedom: "the shock of it against the Puritanism of my nature has given me a subject, a theme, which I have never ceased exploiting." (That shabby but charming city became the setting for several stories and one-act plays, and *A Streetcar Named Desire* derives much of its distinction from French Quarter ambience and attitudes; as Stella informs Blanche, "New Orleans isn't like other cities," a view reinforced by Williams's 1977 portrait of the place in *Vieux Carre.*) Atkinson observed, "Only a writer who had survived in the lower depths of a sultry Southern city could know the characters as intimately as Williams did and be so thoroughly steeped in the aimless sprawl of the neighborhood life."

Williams's South provided not only settings but other characteristics of his work: the romanticism that tinges almost every play; a myth of an Arcadian existence now disappeared; a distinctive way of looking at life, including both an inbred Calvinistic belief in the reality of evil eternally at war with good and what Bentley called a "peculiar combination of the comic and the pathetic." The South also inspired Williams's fascination with violence, his drawing upon regional character types, and his skill in recording Southern language—eloquent, flowery, sometimes bombastic. Moreover, Southern history, particularly the lost cause of the Civil War and the devastating Reconstruction period, imprinted on Williams, as on such major Southern fiction writers as Wil-

liam Faulkner, Flannery O'Conner, and Walker Percy, a profound sense of separation and alienation. Williams, as Thomas E. Porter declared in *Myth and Modern American Drama,* explored "the mind of the Southerner caught between an idyllic past and an undesirable present," commemorating the death of a myth even as he continued to examine it. "His broken figures appeal," Bigsby asserted, "because they are victims of history—the lies of the old South no longer being able to sustain the individual in a world whose pragmatics have no place for the fragile spirit." In a *Conversations* interview the playwright commented that "the South once had a way of life that I am just old enough to remember—a culture that had grace, elegance. . . . I write out of regret for that."

Williams's plays are peopled with a large cast that J. L. Styan termed, in *Modern Drama in Theory and Practice,* "Garrulous Grotesques"; these figures include "untouchables whom he touches with frankness and mercy," according to Tynan. They bear the stamp of their place of origin and speak a "humorous, colorful, graphic" language, which Williams in a *Conversations* interview called the "mad music of my characters." "Have you ever known a Southerner who wasn't long-winded?" he asked; "I mean, a Southerner not afflicted with terminal asthma." Among that cast are the romantics who, however suspect their own virtues may be, act out of belief in and commitment to what Faulkner called the "old verities and truths of the heart." They include fallen aristocrats hounded, Gerald Weales observed in *American Drama since World War II,* "by poverty, by age, by frustration," or as Bigsby called them in his 1985 study "martyrs for a world which has already slipped away unmourned"; fading Southern belles such as Amanda Wingate and Blanche DuBois; slightly deranged women, such as Aunt Rose Comfort in an early one-act play and in the film "Baby Doll"; dictatorial patriarchs such as Big Daddy; and the outcasts (or "fugitive kind," the playwright's term later employed as the title of a 1960 motion picture). Many of these characters tend to recreate the scene in which they find themselves—Laura with her glass animals shutting out the alley where cats are brutalized, Blanche trying to subdue the ugliness of the Kowalski apartment with a paper lantern; in their dialogue they frequently poeticize and melodramatize their situations, thereby surrounding themselves with protective illusion, which in later plays becomes "mendacity." For also inhabiting that dramatic world are more powerful individuals, amoral representatives of the new Southern order, Jabe Torrance in *Battle of Angels,* Gooper and Mae in *Cat on a Hot Tin Roof,* Boss Finley in *Sweet Bird of Youth,* enemies of the romantic impulse and as destructive and virtueless as Faulkner's Snopes clan. Southern though all these characters are, they are not mere regional portraits, for through Williams's dramatization of them and their dilemmas and through the audience's empathy, the characters become everyman and everywoman.

Although traumatic experiences plagued his life, Williams was able to press "the nettle of neurosis" to his heart and produce art, as Gassner observed. Williams's family problems, his alienation from the social norm resulting from his homosexuality, his sense of being a romantic in an unromantic, postwar world, and his sensitive reaction when a production proved less than successful all contributed significantly to his work. Through the years he suffered from a variety of ailments, some serious, some surely imaginary, and at certain periods he overindulged in alcohol and prescription drugs. Despite these circumstances, he continued to write with a determination that verged at times almost on desperation, even as his new plays elicited progressively more hostile reviews from critics.

An outgrowth of this suffering is the character type "the fugitive kind," the wanderer who lives outside the pale of society, excluded by his sensitivity, artistic bent, or sexual proclivity from the world of "normal" human beings. Like Faulkner, Williams was troubled by the exclusivity of any society that shuts out certain segments because they are different. First manifested in Val of *Battle of Angels* (later rewritten as *Orpheus Descending*) and then in the character of Tom, the struggling poet of *The Glass Menagerie* and his shy, withdrawn sister, the fugitive kind appears in varying guises in subsequent plays, including Blanche DuBois, Alma Winemiller (*Summer and Smoke*), Kilroy (*Camino Real*), and Hannah and Shannon (*The Night of the Iguana*). Each is unique but they share common characteristics, which Weales as physical or mental illness, a preoccupation with sex, and a "combination of sensitivity and imagination with corruption." Their abnormality suggests, the critic argued, that the dramatist views the norm of society as being faulty itself. Even characters within the "norm" (Stanley Kowalski for example) are often identified with strong sexual drives. Like D. H. Lawrence, Williams indulged in a kind of phallic romanticism, attributing sexual potency to members of the unintelligent lower classes and sterility to aristocrats. Despite his romanticism, however, Williams's view of humanity was too realistic for him to accept such pat categories. "If you write a character that isn't ambiguous," Williams said in a *Conversations* interview, "you are writing a false character, not a true one." Though he shared Lawrence's view that one should not suppress sexual impulses, Williams recognized that such impulses are at odds with the romantic desire to transcend and that they often lead to suffering like that endured by Blanche DuBois. Those fugitive characters who are destroyed, Bigsby remarked, often perish "because they offer love in a world characterized by impotence and sterility." Thus phallic potency may represent a positive force in a character such as Val or a destructive force in one like Stanley Kowalski; but even in *A Streetcar Named Desire* Williams acknowledges that the life force, represented by Stella's baby, is positive. There are, as Weales pointed out, two divisions in the sexual activity Williams dramatizes: "desperation sex," in which characters such as Val and Blanche "make contact with another only tentatively, momentarily" in order to communicate; and the "consolation and comfort" sex that briefly fulfills Lady in *Orpheus Descending* and saves Serafina in *The Rose Tattoo*. There is, surely, a third kind, sex as a weapon, wielded by those like Stanley; this kind of sex is to be feared, for it is often associated with the violence prevalent in Williams's dramas.

Beginning with *Battle of Angels*, two opposing camps have existed among Williams's critics, and his detractors sometimes have objected most strenuously to the innovations his supporters deemed virtues. His strongest advocates among established drama critics, notably Stark Young, Brooks Atkinson, John Gassner, and Walter Kerr, praised him for realistic clarity; compassion and a strong moral sense; unforgettable characters, especially women, based on his keen perception of human nature; dialogue at once credible and poetic; and a pervasive sense of humor that distinguished him from O'Neill and Miller. Young commended his revolt against archaic dramatic conventions and his "true realism" with all its "variety, suddenness, passion and freedom"; he applauded Williams's relation to a tradition and his "free and true" language and motifs. In 1968, Bentley, commenting on Williams's influence on American drama, suggested that he "bids fair to become, theatrically speaking, the father of his country: the new playwrights derive from him, not from O'Neill, [Clifford] Odets, [Thorton] Wilder or Miller, . . . his only conceivable rivals." Crediting Williams with overcoming "resistance to emotional improvisations that dispensed with the conven-

tional dramatic forms," Atkinson termed Williams and Miller "two natural theater men" who resuscitated a failing art and dominated it in the years after World War II. In them, Frederick Lumley stated in *New Trends in Twentieth Century Drama: A Survey since Ibsen and Shaw,* "the immigrant strain is less conscious," because they learned from the European masters without becoming mere disciples. Miller identified Williams's "greatest value" as "his aesthetic valor," that is, "his very evident determination to unveil and engage the widest range of causation conceivable to him." Even in 1979, when Williams's career, near its end, had survived years of failed productions and bad reviews, Kerr would pronounce him "our finest living playwright," and Kalem would go further to insist that this "laureate of the violated heart" was "the world's greatest playwright."

Not surprisingly, it was from the conservative establishment that most of the adverse criticism came. Obviously appalled by this "upstart crow," George Jean Nathan, dean of theater commentators when Williams made his revolutionary entrance onto the scene, sounded notes often to be repeated. In *The Theatre Book of the Year, 1947-1948,* he faulted Williams's early triumphs for "mistiness of ideology," "questionable symbolism" "debatable character drawing," "adolescent point of view," "theatrical fabrication," and obsession with sex, fallen women, and "the deranged Dixie damsel." In short, Nathan saw Williams as a melodramatist whose attempts at tragedy were as ludicrous as "a threnody on a zither." Subsequent detractors—notably Richard Gilman, Robert Brustein, Clive Barnes, and John Simon—taxed the playwright for theatricality, repetition, lack of judgment and control, excessive moralizing and philosophizing, and conformity to the demands of the ticket-buying public. His plays, they variously argued, lacked unity of effect, clarity of intention, social content, and variety; these critics saw the plays as burdened with excessive symbolism, violence, sexuality, and attention to the sordid, grotesque elements of life. Additionally, certain commentators charged that Elia Kazan, the director of the early masterpieces, virtually rewrote *A Streetcar Named Desire* and *Cat on a Hot Tin Roof.* A particular kind of negative criticism, often intensely emotional seemed to dominate evaluations of the plays produced in the last twenty years of Williams's life.

Most critics, even his detractors, have praised the dramatist's skillful creation of dialogue. "What we need in the theater is a sense of language, a sense of texture in speech," Young wrote of *The Glass Menagerie,* in which he heard "the echo of great literature, or at least a respect for it." Twenty years later Bentley asserted that "no one in the English-speaking theater" created better dialogue, that Williams's plays were really "*written*—that is to say, set down in living language." Ruby Cohn stated in *Dialogue in American Drama* that Williams gave to American theater "a new vocabulary and rhythm" by expanding dialogue in range and content to embrace "nostalgia, frustration, sadness, gaiety, cruelty, and compassion." Praising Williams's "uncanny ear" for dialogue that was "effortlessly euphonious, rich in subtle gradations of the vernacular," Clurman concluded, "No one in the theater has written more melodiously. Without the least artificial flourish, his writing takes flight from the naturalistic to the poetic." Even Mary McCarthy, no ardent fan, stated in *Theatre Chronicles: 1937-1962* that Williams was the only American realist other than Paddy Chayevsky with an ear for dialogue and that although he sometimes abandoned real speech for "his special poetic long-play prose," he knew speech patterns and really heard his characters. There were, of course, objections to Williams's lyrical dialogue, different as it is from the dialogue of O'Neill, Miller, or any other major American playwright. Bentley admitted to finding his "fake poeticizing" troublesome at times, while Bigsby insisted that Williams was at his best only when he restrained "over-poetic language" and symbolism with "an imagination which if melodramatic is also capable of fine control." However, those long poetic speeches or "arias" in plays of the first twenty-five years of his career, became a hallmark of the dramatist's work.

Another major area of contention among commentators has been Williams's use of symbols, which he called in a *Conversations* interview "the natural language of drama." Laura's glass animals, the paper lantern and cathedral bells in *A Streetcar Named Desire,* the legless birds of *Orpheus Descending,* and the iguana in *The Night of the Iguana,* to name only a few, are integral to the plays in which they appear. Cohn commented on Williams's extensive use of animal images in *Cat on a Hot Tin Roof* to symbolize the fact that all the Pollitts, "grasping, screeching, devouring," are "greedily alive." In that play, Big Daddy's malignancy effectively represents the corruption in the family and in the larger society to which the characters belong. However, Weales objected that Williams, like *The Glass Menagerie*'s Tom, had "a poet's weakness for symbols," which can get out of hand; he argued that in *Suddenly Last Summer,* Violet Venable's garden does not grow out of the situation and enrich the play. Sometimes, Cohn observed, a certain weakness of symbolism "is built into the fabric of the drama."

Critics favorable to Williams have agreed that one of his virtues lay in his characterization. Those "superbly actable parts," Atkinson stated, derived from his ability to find "extraordinary spiritual significance in ordinary people." Cohn admired Williams's "Southern grotesques" and his knack for giving them "dignity," although some critics have been put off by the excessive number of such grotesques, which contributed, they argued, to a distorted view of reality. Commentators generally concurred in their praise of Williams's talent in creating credible female roles. "No one in American drama has written more intuitively of women," Clurman asserted; Gassner spoke of Williams's "uncanny familiarity with the flutterings of the female heart." Walter Kerr in *The Theatre in Spite of Itself* expressed wonder at such roles as that of Hannah in *Night of the Iguana,* "a portrait which owes nothing to calipers, or to any kind of tooling; it is all surprise and presence, anticipated intimacy. It is found gold, not a borrowing against known reserves." Surveying the "steamy zoo" of Williams's characters with their violence, despair, and aberrations, Stang commended him for the "poetry and compassion that comprise his great gift." *Compassion* is the key word in all tributes to Williams's characterization. It is an acknowledgment of the playwright's uncanny talent for making audiences and readers empathize with his people, however grotesque, bizarre, or even sordid they may seem on the surface.

Although they granted him compassion, some of his detractors felt Williams did not exhibit a clear philosophy of life, and they found unacceptable the ambiguity in judging human flaws and frailties that was one of his most distinctive qualities. Bentley chided Williams for his "besetting sin" of "fake philosophizing, a straining after big statements." Noting that Williams had "said that he only feels and does not think," the critic stated that perhaps "he only thinks he feels," since the "Serenity and Truth, of which he *speaks* and *thinks,* tend to remain in the head too— mere abstractions." On the other hand, Arthur Ganz in *Realms of the Self: Variations on a Theme in Modern Drama,* insisted that Williams's best work "derives its force from the strength of his moral temper, which leads him to censure even what he most wishes to exalt." One difficulty, for those concerned about his seeming lack of judgments on characters and their actions, stemmed from the playwright's recognition of and insistence on

portraying the ambiguity of human activities and relationships. Moral, even puritanical, though he might be, Williams never seemed ready to condemn any action other than "deliberate cruelty," and even that was sometimes portrayed as resulting from extenuating circumstances.

In terms of dramatic technique, those who acknowledged his genius disagreed as to where it was best expressed. For Jerold Phillips, writing in *Dictionary of Literary Biography Documentary Series,* Williams's major contribution lay in turning from the Ibsenesque social problem plays to "Strindberg-like explorations of what goes on underneath the skin," thereby freeing American theater from "the hold of the so-called well-made play." For Allan Lewis in *American Plays and Playwrights of the Contemporary Theatre* he was a "brilliant inventor of emotionally intense scenes" whose "greatest gift [lay] in suggesting ideas through emotional relations." His preeminence among dramatists in the United States, Jean Gould wrote in *Modern American Playwrights,* resulted from a combination of poetic sensitivity, theatricality, and "the dedication of the artist." If, from the beginning of his career, there were detractors who charged Williams with overuse of melodramatic, grotesque, and violent elements that produced a distorted view of reality, Kerr, in *The Theatre in Spite of Itself,* termed him "a man unafraid of melodrama, and a man who handles it with extraordinary candor and deftness." Agreeing that Williams's endings were melodramatic, Lewis compared them to Jacobean drama, powerful in that "they reach beyond the immediate locale to wherever brutality and ugliness suppress the cry for beauty." Robert Heilman believed, however, that like O'Neill, Williams himself despaired and thus did not develop "the authentic note of tragic completeness."

Other commentators have been offended by what Bentley termed Williams's "exploitation of the obscene": his choice of characters—outcasts, alcoholics, the violent and deranged and sexually abnormal—and of subject matter—incest, castration, and cannibalism. Robert Brustein, in *Seasons of Discontent: Dramatic Opinions, 1959-1965,* condemned his "Strindbergian identification of the human body with excrement and defilement" and the "obsessively sexual determinism of every character." Williams justified the "sordid" elements of his work in a *Conversations* interview when he asserted that "we must depict the awfulness of the world we live in, but we must do it with a kind of aesthetic" to avoid producing mere horror. Clearly he viewed himself as a realist, even a naturalist in the tradition of Emile Zola, who argued that the artist had a commitment to examine the unpleasant, grotesque elements of life.

Another negative aspect of Williams's art, some critics argued, was his theatricality. Gassner asserted in *Directions in Modern Theatre and Drama* that Kazan, the director, avoided flashy stage effects called for in Williams's text of *The Glass Menagerie,* but that in some plays Kazan collaborated with the playwright to exaggerate these effects, especially in the expressionistic and allegorical drama *Camino Real.* In a *Conversations* interview, Williams addressed this charge, particularly as it involved Kazan, by asserting, "My cornpone melodrama is all my own. I want excitement in the theater. . . . I have a tendency toward romanticism and a taste for the theatrical."

Depending on which critic one happened to be reading, Kazan appeared to be saint or sinner, the greatest blessing to come to Tennessee Williams's career or its greatest liability. No playwright was ever more cognizant than Williams of the fact that the script represented an incomplete play, that until it was mounted by a director, with the contribution of actors, set designers, lighting technicians, and costumers, it was in a sense merely an outline. Repeatedly he paid tribute to all those who managed to materialize the dreams that issued from his imagination. Kazan was a brilliantly innovative but controversial director whose staging of works by both Williams and Miller raised a number of questions as to the extent of his contribution: Did he merely enhance masterpieces, or was he significantly reworking the playwrights' material? Williams was so sensitive to this criticism that there came a point in his career when he saw fit to sever his ties with the director. Atkinson had nothing but praise for Kazan's "sensitive and scrupulous" direction, and Rasky attributed to the collaboration a theatrical revolution and argued that both were "diminished by Kazan's leaving." On the other hand, Bentley complained that through Kazan's insistence on changes in the final act of *Cat on a Hot Tin Roof,* "the professional pessimism" of "an avant-garde writer, is converted into its opposite." The relationship between Williams and Kazan seems destined to remain a part of any serious analysis of the plays with which both were involved.

Late in his career, Williams was increasingly subject to charges that he had outlived his talent. Beginning with *Period of Adjustment,* a comedy generally disliked by critics, there were years of rejection of play after play: *The Milk Train Doesn't Stop Here Any More, Kingdom of Earth, Small Craft Warnings, Out Cry, Vieux Carre, Clothes for a Summer Hotel, The Red Devil Battery Sign.* By the late 1960s, even the longtime advocate Brooks Atkinson observed that in "a melancholy resolution of an illustrious career" the dramatist was producing plays "with a kind of desperation" in which he lost control of content and style. Lewis, accusing Williams of repeating motifs, themes, and characters in play after play, asserted that in failing "to expand and enrich" his theme, he had "dissipated a rare talent." Berating him for "heavy-handed gongorism," John Simon said that Williams's style was becoming as "baroque" as his subject matter; Richard Gilman, in a particularly vituperative review entitled "Mr. Williams, He Dead," included in his *Common and Uncommon Masks: Writings on Theatre, 1961-1970,* charged that the "moralist," subtly present in earlier plays, was "increasingly on stage." Citing the dramatist's growing concern with his own unconscious, Brustein accused him of hypocritically pandering to "the very groups he assaults." Even if one granted a diminution of creative powers, however, the decline in Williams's popularity and position as major playwright in the 1960s and 1970s can be attributed in large part to a marked change in the theater itself. Audiences constantly demanded variety, and although the early creations of the playwright remained popular, theatregoers wanted something different, strange, exotic. One problem, Kerr pointed out, was that Williams was so good, people expected him to continue to get better; judging each play against those which had gone before denied a fair hearing to the new creations. Sadly, the playwright's accidental death came when his career, after almost two decades of bad reviews and of dismissals of his "dwindling talents," was at its lowest ebb since the abortive 1940 production of *Battle of Angels.* Since his death, however, an inevitable reevaluation has begun. Bigsby, for example, has found in a reanalysis of the late plays more than mere vestiges of the strengths of earlier years, especially in *Out Cry,* an experimental drama toward which Williams felt a particular affection.

Whatever the final judgment of literary historians on the works of Tennessee Williams, certain facts are clear. He was, without question, the most controversial American playwright, a situation unlikely to change as the debate over his significant and the relative merits of individual plays continues. Critics, scholars, and theatergoers do not remain neutral in regard to the man or his work. He is also the most quotable of American playwrights,

and even those who disparage the highly poetic dialogue admit the uniqueness of the language he brought to modern theater. In addition, he has added to dramatic literature a cast of remarkable, memorable characters and has turned his attention and sympathy toward people and subjects that, before his time, had been considered beneath the concern of serious authors. Amanda, Blanche, Stanley, Big Daddy, Brick, and Maggie—all are established as enduring members of the pantheon of great dramatic creations. With "distinctive dramatic feeling," Gassner said in *Theatre at the Crossroads,* Williams "made pulsating plays out of his visions of a world of terror, confusion, and perverse beauty." As a result, Gassner concluded, Williams "makes indifference to the theater virtually impossible." Following his death, some of those who had been during his last years his severest critics acknowledged the greatness of his achievement. Even John Simon, who had dismissed play after play as valueless repetitions created by an author who had outlived his talent, acknowledged in a 1983 *New York* essay that he had underestimated the playwright's genius and significance. Tennessee Williams was, finally, a rebel who broke with the rigid conventions of drama that had preceded him, explored new territory in his quest for a distinctive form and style, created characters as unforgettable as those of Charles Dickens, Nathaniel Hawthorne, or William Faulkner, and lifted the language of the modern stage to a poetic level unmatched in his time.

MEDIA ADAPTATIONS: "The Roman Spring of Mrs. Stone" was filmed by Warner Bros. in 1961; "Sweet Bird of Youth" was filmed in 1962; "Period of Adjustment" was filmed in 1962; "This Property Is Condemned" was filmed by Paramount in 1966; "I Can't Imagine Tomorrow" and "Talk to Me Like the Rain and Let Me Listen" were televised together under the title "Dragon Country," December 3, 1970, by New York Television Theatre; an adaptation of "The Seven Descents of Myrtle" was filmed by Warner Bros. in 1970 under the title, "The Last of the Mobile Hot-Shots"; *Summer and Smoke: Opera in Two Acts,* Belwin-Mills, 1972, was adapted from Williams's play, with music by Lee Hoiby and libretto by Lanford Wilson; "The Glass Menagerie" was filmed by Burt Harris for Cineplex Odeon in 1987; "A Streetcar Named Desire" was filmed for television in 1984 and broadcast on ABC-TV; "Cat on a Hot Tin Roof " was filmed for television in 1984 by International TV Group; "Summer and Smoke" was filmed for television in 1989 and broadcast on NBC-TV.

BIOGRAPHICAL/CRITICAL SOURCES:

BOOKS

Atkinson, Brooks, *Broadway,* revised edition, Macmillan, 1974.
Authors in the News, Gale, Volume 1, 1976, Volume 2, 1976.
Bentley, Eric, *What Is Theatre?,* Atheneum, 1968.
Bernstein, Samuel J., *The Strands Entwined: A New Direction in American Drama,* Northeastern University Press, 1980.
Bigsby, C. W. E., *Confrontation and Commitment: A Study of Contemporary American Drama 1959-66,* University of Missouri Press, 1968.
Bigsby, C. W. E., *A Critical Introduction to Twentieth-Century American Drama,* three volumes, Cambridge University Press, 1985.
Broussard, Louis, *American Drama: Contemporary Allegory from Eugene O'Neill to Tennessee Williams,* University of Oklahoma Press, 1962.
Brustein, Robert, *Seasons of Discontent: Dramatic Opinions 1959-1965,* Simon & Schuster, 1965.
Brustein, Robert, *Critical Moments: Reflections on Theatre and Society, 1973 1979,* Random House, 1980.

Cohn, Ruby, *Dialogue in American Drama,* Indiana University Press, 1971.

Concise Dictionary of American Literary Biography, 1941-1968, Gale,

Contemporary Literary Criticism, Gale, Volume 1, 1973, Volume 2, 1974, Volume 5, 1976, Volume 7, 1977, Volume 8, 1978, Volume 11, 1979, Volume 15, 1980, Volume 19, 1981, Volume 30, 1984, Volume 39, 1986, Volume 45, 1987.

Devlin, Albert J., editor, *Conversations with Tennessee Williams,* University Press of Mississippi, 1986.

Dickinson, Hugh, *Myth on the Modern Stage,* University of Illinois Press, 1969.

Dictionary of Literary Biography, Volume 7: *Twentieth-Century American Dramatists,* Gale, 1981.

Dictionary of Literary Biography Documentary Series, Volume 4, Gale, 1984.

Dictionary of Literary Biography Yearbook: 1983, Gale, 1984.

Donahue, Francis, *The Dramatic World of Tennessee Williams,* Ungar, 1964.

Downer, Alan S., *Fifty Years of American Drama 1900-1950,* Regnery, 1951.

Falk, Signi, *Tennessee Williams,* 2nd edition, Twayne, 1978.

Ganz, Arthur, *Realms of the Self: Variations on a Theme in Modern Drama,* New York University Press, 1980.

Gassner, John, *Theatre at the Crossroads: Plays and Playwrights of the Mid-Century American Stage,* Holt, 1960.

Gassner, John, *Directions in Modern Theatre and Drama,* Holt, 1966.

Gilman, Richard, *Common and Uncommon Masks: Writings on Theatre, 1961-1970,* Random House, 1971.

Gould, Jean, *Modern American Playwrights,* Dodd, 1966.

Gunn, Drewey Wayne, *Tennessee Williams: A Bibliography,* Scarecrow, 1980.

Heilman, Robert Bechtold, *Tragedy and Melodrama: Versions of Experience,* University of Washington Press, 1968.

Herron, Ima Honaker, *The Small Town in American Drama,* Southern Methodist University Press, 1969.

Kerr, Walter, *The Theatre in Spite of Itself,* Simon & Schuster, 1963.

Kerr, Walter, *Journey to the Center of Theatre,* Knopf, 1979.

Langer, Lawrence, *The Magic Curtain,* Dutton, 1951.

Laughlin, James, editor, *Five Young American Poets,* New Directions, 1944.

Leavitt, Richard F., editor, *The World of Tennessee Williams,* Putnam, 1978.

Lewis, Allan, *American Plays and Playwrights of the Contemporary Theatre,* Crown, 1965.

Little, Stuart W. and Arthur Cantor, *The Playmakers,* Norton, 1970.

Logan, Joshua, *Josh: My Up and Down, In and Out Life,* Delacorte, 1976.

Londre, Felicia Hardison, *Tennessee Williams,* Ungar, 1979.

Lumley, Frederick, *New Trends in Twentieth Century Drama: A Survey since Ibsen and Shaw,* Oxford University Press, 1967.

Maxwell, Gilbert, *Tennessee Williams and Friends: An Informal Biography,* World, 1965.

McCann, John S., *The Critical Reputation of Tennessee Williams: A Reference Guide,* G. K. Hall, 1983.

McCarthy, Mary, *Theatre Chronicles: 1937-1962,* Farrar, Straus, 1963.

Miller, Arthur, *The Theatre Essays of Tennessee Williams,* edited by Robert A. Martin, Penguin, 1978.

Nathan, George Jean, *The Theatre Book of the Year,* Knopf, *1947-1948,* 1948, *1948-1949,* Knopf, 1949.

Phillips, Gene D., *The Films of Tennessee Williams,* Art Alliance Press, 1980.

Porter, Thomas E., *Myth and Modern American Drama,* Wayne State University Press, 1969.

Rabkin, Gerald, *Drama and Commitment: Politics in the American Theatre of the Thirties,* Indiana University Press, 1964.

Rasky, Harry, *Tennessee Williams: A Portrait in Laughter and Lamentation,* Dodd, 1986.

Simon, John, *Acid Test,* Stein & Day, 1963.

Spoto, Donald, *The Kindness of Strangers: The Life of Tennessee Williams,* Little, Brown, 1985.

Steen, Mike, *A Look at Tennessee Williams,* Hawthorne, 1969.

Styan, J. L., *Modern Drama in Theory and Practice,* Volume 1, Cambridge University Press, 1981.

Tharpe, Jac, editor, *Tennessee Williams: A Tribute,* University Press of Mississippi, 1977.

Tischler, Nancy M., *Tennessee Williams: Rebellious Puritan,* Citadel, 1961.

Tynan, Kenneth, *Curtains,* Atheneum, 1961.

Weales, Gerald, *American Drama since World War II,* Harcourt, 1962.

Williams, Dakin, and Shepherd Mead, *Tennessee Williams: An Intimate Biography,* Arbor, 1983.

Williams, Edwina Dakin, as told to Lucy Freeman, *Remember Me to Tom,* Putnam, 1963.

Williams, Tennessee, *The Glass Menagerie,* Random House, 1945, published as *The Glass Menagerie: Play in Two Acts,* Dramatists Play Service, 1948.

Williams, Tennessee, *The Roman Spring of Mrs. Stone,* New Directions, 1950.

Williams, Tennessee, *Camino Real: A Play,* edition with foreword and afterword by Williams, New Directions, 1953.

Williams, Tennessee, *Cat on a Hot Tin Roof,* edition with preface by Williams, New Directions, 1955, published as *Cat on a Hot Tin Roof: A Play in Three Acts,* Dramatists Play Service, 1958.

Williams, Tennessee, *In the Winter of Cities,* New Directions, 1956.

Williams, Tennessee, *Orpheus Descending: A Play in Three Acts,* New Directions, 1959.

Williams, Tennessee, *The Theatre of Tennessee Williams,* New Directions, Volume 1, 1971, Volume 2, 1971, Volume 3, 1971, Volume 4, 1972, Volume 5, 1976, Volume 6, 1981, Volume 7, 1981.

Williams, Tennessee, *Memoirs,* Doubleday, 1975.

Williams, Tennessee, *Moise and the World of Reason,* Simon & Schuster, 1975.

Williams, Tennessee, *Androgyne, Mon Amour: Poems by Tennessee Williams,* New Directions, 1977.

Williams, Tennessee, *Tennessee Williams' Letters to Donald Windham: 1940-1965,* edited by Windham, Holt, 1977.

Williams, Tennessee, *Where I Live: Selected Essays,* edited by C. Day and B. Wood, New Directions, 1978.

Williams, Tennessee, *Tennessee Williams: Eight Plays,* introduction by Harold Clurman, Doubleday, 1979.

Williams, Tennessee, *Stopped Rocking and Other Screenplays,* New Directions, 1984.

Williams, Tennessee, *Collected Stories,* New Directions, 1985.

Windham, Donald, *Lost Friendships: A Memoir of Truman Capote, Tennessee Williams, and Others,* Morrow, 1987.

Yacowar, Maurice, *Tennessee Williams and Film,* Ungar, 1977.

PERIODICALS

After Dark, August, 1971.

Atlantic, November, 1970.

Esquire, November, 1969, September, 1971.
Modern Drama, Volume 2, 1959, Volume 15, 1972.
Nation, Volume 165, 1947.
New Republic, Volume 112, 1945.
New York, March 14, 1983.
New York Post (interviews), April 21-May 4, 1958.
New York Times, May 1, 1960, March 28, 1965, November 3, 1975.
Playboy, April, 1973.
Quarterly Journal of Speech, Volume 61, 1975.
Renascence, Volume 28, 1976.
Reporter, Volume 12, 1955.
Southern Review, summer, 1979.
Tennessee Studies in Literature, Volume 10, 1965.
Theatre Arts, January, 1962.
Washington Post, April 4, 1979.
Western Humanities Review, Volume 18, 1964.

OBITUARIES:

PERIODICALS

Chicago Tribune, February 26, 1983, February 27, 1983.
Los Angeles Times, February 26, 1983.
Newsweek, March 7, 1983.
New York Times, February 26, 1983.
Time, March 7, 1983.
Times (London), February 26, 1983.
Washington Post, February 26, 1983.*

—Sidelights by W. Kenneth Holditch

*   *   *

WILLIE, Charles V(ert) 1927-

PERSONAL: Born October 8, 1927, in Dallas, Tex.; son of Louis (a former Pullman porter and real estate broker) and Carrie (Sykes) Willie; married Mary Sue Conklin (an organist, singing teacher, and choir director), March 31, 1962; children: Sarah Susannah, Martin Charles, James Theodore. *Education:* Morehouse College, B.A., 1948; Atlanta University, M.A., 1949; Syracuse University, Ph.D., 1957; Harvard University, M.A., 1974. *Religion:* Episcopalian.

ADDRESSES: Office—457 Gutman Library, Graduate School of Education, Harvard University, Cambridge, Mass. 02138.

CAREER: Syracuse University, Syracuse, N.Y., instructor, 1952-60, assistant professor, 1960-64, associate professor, 1964-68, professor of sociology, 1968-74, chairman of department, 1967-71, vice-president of student affairs, 1972-74; Harvard University, Cambridge, Mass., currently professor of education and urban studies. Research sociologist, New York State Mental Health Commission, 1951-52; instructor in sociology at State University of New York Upstate Medical Center, 1955-60; research director of Washington, D.C., project, President's Committee on Juvenile Delinquency and Youth Crime, 1962-64; lecturer in sociology at the Medical School, Harvard University, 1966-67. Vice-president of House of Deputies, Episcopal Church General Convention, 1970-73.

MEMBER: Social Science Research Council (member of board of directors, 1969-74), American Sociological Society (fellow), Society for the Study of Social Problems, Eastern Sociological Society (president, 1974-75), Phi Beta Kappa.

AWARDS, HONORS: Faculty service award, National University Extension Association, 1967; D.H.L., Berkeley Divinity School at Yale University, 1972, Morehouse College, 1983, and

Rhode Island College; D.D., General Seminary, 1974; Distinguished Alumnus Award, Maxwell Graduate School of Citizenship and Public Affairs, Syracuse University, 1974; Male Hero Award, *Ms.* magazine, 1982; Society for the Study of Social Problems, Lee-Founders Award, and Distinguished Family Scholar Award, 1986.

WRITINGS:

Church Action in the World, Morehouse, 1969.
(Editor) *The Family Life of Black People,* C. E. Merrill, 1970.
(With Arline McCord) *Black Students at White Colleges,* Praeger, 1972.
(With Jerome Beker) *Race Mixing in the Public Schools,* Praeger, 1973.
(Editor with Bernard Kramer and Betram Brown) *Racism and Mental Health,* University of Pittsburgh Press, 1973.
Oreo: A Perspective on Race and Marginal Men and Women, Parameter Press, 1975.
A New Look at Black Families, General Hall, 1976, 2nd edition, 1981.
(Editor) *Black-Brown-White Relations: Race Relations in the 1970s,* Transaction Books, 1977.
(Editor with Ronald R. Edmonds) *Black Colleges in America,* Teachers College Press, 1978.
The Sociology of Urban Education: Desegregation and Integration, Lexington Books, 1978.
The Caste and Class Controversy, General Hall, 1978, 2nd edition, 1989.
The Ivory and Ebony Towers, Lexington Books, 1981.
(With Susan Greenblatt) *Community Politics and Educational Change,* Longman, 1981.
Race, Ethnicity and Socioeconomic Status, General Hall, 1983.
School Desegregation Plans That Work, Greenwood Press, 1984.
Five Black Scholars, University Press of America, 1985.
(With Michael Grady) *Metropolitan School Desegregation,* Wyndham Hall, 1986.
Effective Education, Greenwood Press, 1987.
(Editor with Inabeth Miller) *Social Goals and Educational Reform,* Greenwood Press, 1988.

*   *   *

WILSON, Margo 1942-

PERSONAL: Born October 1, 1942, in Winnipeg, Manitoba, Canada. *Education:* University of London, Ph.D., 1972; University of Toronto, M.S.L., 1987.

ADDRESSES: Office—Department of Psychology, McMaster University, 1280 Main St. W., Hamilton, Ontario, Canada L8S 4K1.

CAREER: McMaster University, Hamilton, Ontario, currently member of psychology department.

WRITINGS:

Sex, Evolution, and Behavior, Duxbury, 1978, revised edition, Willard Grant, 1983.
(Contributor with M. Daly) G. Hausfater and S. B. Hrdy, editors, *Infanticide: Comparative and Evolutionary Perspectives,* Aldine, 1984.
(Contributor with Daly) C. Crawford, M. Smith, and D. Krebs, editors, *Sociobiology and Psychology,* Lawrence Erlbaum, 1987.
(Contributor with Daly) R. Gelles and J. Lancaster, editors, *Child Abuse and Neglect: Biosocial Dimensions,* Aldine, 1987.
(With Daly) *Homicide,* Aldine, 1988.

(Contributor with Daly) D. Leger, editor, *Nebraska Symposium on Motivation,* Volume XXXV, University of Nebraska Press, 1988.

(Contributor) R. Bell, editor, *Texas Tech University Symposia on Interfaces in Psychology,* Volume VII, Texas Tech Press, in press.

*   *   *

WIRT, Frederick Marshall 1924-

PERSONAL: Born July 27, 1924, in Radford, Va.; son of Harry Johnson, Sr., and Goldie (Turpin) Wirt; married Elizabeth Cook, September 5, 1947; children: Leslie Lee, Sandra Sue, Wendy Ann. *Education:* DePauw University, B.A., 1948; Ohio State University, M.A., 1949, Ph.D., 1956.

ADDRESSES: Home—2018 Zuppke Cir., Urbana, Ill. 61801. *Office*—Department of Political Science, 375 Lincoln Hall, University of Illinois, Urbana, Ill. 61801.

CAREER: Denison University, Granville, Ohio, instructor, 1952-55, assistant professor, 1955-58, associate professor, 1958-62, professor of political science, 1962-66; University of California, Berkeley, visiting professor of political science, 1966-68, research political scientist at Institute for Government Studies, 1969-72, director of Institute for Desegregation Problems, 1970-72; University of Maryland, Baltimore County, Catonsville, professor of political science and director of policy sciences graduate program, 1972-75; University of Illinois, Urbana, professor of political science, 1975—. Visiting professor at University of Rochester and Nova University. Member of Granville City Charter Commission, 1964. Consultant to RAND Corp. and Stanford Research Institute (now SRI International). *Military service:* U.S. Army, 1942-45; became sergeant.

MEMBER: American Political Science Association (member of national council), American Educational Research Association, Policy Studies Organization, Midwestern Political Science Association.

AWARDS, HONORS: Grants from American Philosophical Society, 1965-67, 1973, 1981; grant from Ford Foundation, 1978-79; grant from National Endowment for the Humanities, 1978-80; grant from U.S. Department of Education, 1978-83; grant from Spencer Foundation, 1979.

WRITINGS:

Politics of Southern Equality: Law and Social Change in a Mississippi County, Aldine, 1970.
(WIth Roy D. Morey and Louis F. Brakeman) *Introductory Problems in Political Research,* Prentice-Hall, 1970.
(With B. Walter, F.F. Rabinovitz, and D.R. Hensler) *On the City's Rim: Politics and Policy in Suburbia,* Heath, 1972.
(With Michael W. Kirst) *The Political Web of American Schools,* Little, Brown, 1972, revised edition published as *Political and Social Foundations of Education,* McCutchan, 1975.
Power in the City: Decision-Making in San Francisco, University of California Press, 1974.
(With Kirst) *Schools in Conflict: The Politics of Education,* McCutchan, 1982, 2nd edition, 1989.
(With Douglas Mitchell and Catherine Marshall) *Culture and Education Policy in the American States,* Falmer Press, 1989.
Law, Attitudes, and Social Change: Civil Rights in the South, Duke University Press, in press.

EDITOR

(With Thomas Bentley Edwards) *School Desegregation in the North: The Challenge and the Experience,* Chandler Publishing, 1967.
(With Willis D. Hawley) *The Search for Community Power,* Prentice-Hall, 1968.
(With Hawley) *New Dimensions of Freedom in America,* Chandler Publishing, 1969.
Future Directions in Community Power Research: A Colloquium, Institute of Governmental Studies, University of California, Berkeley, 1971.
The Policy of the School: New Research in Educational Politics, Lexington Books, 1975.
(With Samuel Gove) *Critical Issues in Educational Policy,* Policy Studies, 1976.
(With Gove) *Political Science and School Politics: The Princes and Pundits,* Policy Studies, 1976.
(With Grant Harman) *Education, Recession, and the World Village,* Falmer Press, 1986.

OTHER

Editor of 25-volume series on politics of education, for Lexington Books. Contributor to education journals.

SIDELIGHTS: Frederick Marshall Wirt told *CA:* "My scholarly work is often stimulated by curiosity over anomalies, events not expected to exist. My special interests are American government, the politics of education, and urban politics. My field work includes sites as different as a Delta county in Mississippi and San Francisco.

"My politics of education work arose from work with scholars at Berkeley, and it has led to my editing a twenty-five-volume series on the subject for Lexington Books, to consulting and research on the efforts of citizens to control their schools, and studies in English-speaking nations."

*   *   *

WOOD, Sydney (Herbert) 1935-

PERSONAL: Born June 8, 1935, in Southport, England; son of Sydney (in sales) and Hilda (Denton) Marks; married Patricia Smedley, August 3, 1962; children: Simon, Catherine. *Education:* Trinity College, Oxford, B.A. (with honors), 1956; Victoria University of Manchester, Graduate Certificate in Education, 1957.

ADDRESSES: Office—Department of History, Northern College of Education, Aberdeen, Scotland. *Agent*—Frances Kelly Agency, 629 Fulham Rd., London S.W. 6, England.

CAREER: Assistant history teacher at coeducational grammar school in Nottingham, England, 1957-61; head of history department at boys' grammar school in King's Lynn, England, 1961-68; Northern College of Education, Aberdeen, Scotland, lecturer, 1968-74, senior lecturer in history, 1974—. Fellow at Magdalene College, Cambridge, 1965.

MEMBER: Scottish Records Association.

WRITINGS:

World Affairs: 1900 to the Present Day, Oliver & Boyd, 1970.
Britain's Inter-War Years, Blackie & Son, 1975.
The Vikings, Oliver & Boyd, 1977.
(With John Thwaites) *The American Revolution,* Heinemann, 1979.
The Edwardians, Oliver & Boyd, 1981.
The Railway Revolution, Macmillan, 1981.

The British Welfare State, 1900-1950, Cambridge University Press, 1982.

The World About Us, Macmillan, 1982.

(With John Patrick) *History in the Grampian Landscape,* R. Callander, 1982.

Victorian Life, J. Murray, 1984.

The Thirties, Oliver & Boyd, 1984.

The Shaping of Nineteen Century Aberdeenshire, Spa Books, 1985.

Life in Scotland, Basil Blackwell, 1989.

India: From Raj to Independence, Macmillan, 1989.

Contributor to history journals.

WORK IN PROGRESS: Research on a book of source materials on Scottish life since 1750; work on the development of childrens conceptual understanding in history; work on a textbook for the new standard grade course.

SIDELIGHTS: Sydney Wood wrote *CA:* "I am especially interested in local history, social history, and the relationship between the theory of history and its practice in schools and institutions of higher education.

"Scotland is a sufficiently small and centrally controlled educational unit to make curriculum reform feasible. As curriculum development officer to the groups involved in wholly overhauling history's contribution to the education of all fifteen- and sixteen-year-olds and more able pupils of seventeen and eighteen. I am fascinated by the possibilities as well as deeply concerned about the problem of resources.

"I am determined to do what I can to retain and improve history's place in the curriculum. This has not been, and is not easy, yet it seems to me that history provides a vital dimension to education."

*   *   *

WOODWARD, Bob
See WOODWARD, Robert Upshur

*   *   *

WOODWARD, Robert Upshur 1943-
(Bob Woodward)

PERSONAL: Born March 26, 1943, in Geneva, Ill.; son of Alfred E. Woodward (a judge) and Jane (Upshur) Woodward Barnes; married, November 29, 1974 (divorced); children: Mary Taliesin. *Education:* Yale University, B.A., 1965.

ADDRESSES: Home—3027 Q St. N.W., Washington, D.C. 20007. *Office—Washington Post,* Washington, D.C. 20007.

CAREER: Montgomery County Sentinel, Rockville, Md., reporter, 1970-71; *Washington Post,* Washington, D.C., reporter, 1971—. *Military service:* U.S. Navy, active duty, 1965-70; became lieutenant.

AWARDS, HONORS: Pulitzer Prize to the *Washington Post,* Drew Pearson Foundation award, Heywood Brun award, George Polk Memorial Award, Sidney Hillman Foundation award, Worth Bingham prize, and Sigma Delta Chi award, all 1973, all for investigative reporting of Watergate scandal; Worth Bingham Prize, 1986.

WRITINGS:

UNDER NAME BOB WOODWARD

(With Carl Bernstein) *All the President's Men,* Simon & Schuster, 1974.

(Contributor) Staff of the Washington Post, *The Fall of a President,* Dell, 1974.

(With Bernstein) *The Final Days,* Simon & Schuster, 1976.

(With Scott Armstrong) *The Brethren: Inside the Supreme Court,* Simon & Schuster, 1979.

Wired: The Short Life and Fast Times of John Belushi, Simon & Schuster, 1984.

Veil: The Secret Wars of the CIA, 1981-1987, Simon & Schuster, 1987.

Also co-writer, with Christopher Williams, of "The Nightmare Years," a screenplay for television based on William Shirer's memoir of the same name, in 1986; co-writer of "Under Seige," a movie made for television by National Broadcasting Corporation in 1986.

WORK IN PROGRESS: Newspaper work.

SIDELIGHTS: Bob Woodward had been with the *Washington Post* nine months on the night police beat when he was called upon to cover the arraignment of five men who had been arrested for breaking into the Democratic National Committee's offices in the Watergate complex. The astonished young reporter learned the burglars had CIA connections and that one of them, James McCord, was an employee of the Committee to Reelect the President. Woodward, teamed with Carl Bernstein, followed the story from a Washington courtroom through a complicated tangle of clandestine political activity into the highest offices of the White House. The affair eventually led, in part due to Woodward and Bernstein's persistent efforts, to the resignation of numerous government officials in the executive branch, including that of President Richard Nixon.

The reporter's first book, *All the President's Men,* was originally planned to be the culmination of their investigative work for their *Washington Post* stories. At the time—October, 1972—Woodward and Bernstein were the only reporters pursuing the story. The result of the scant attention from the rest of the press was a pile of information which they intended to use in a book about the secret activities of White House aides. Two chapters of this never-finished book were already written when Judge Sirica released to the press a letter he had received from James McCord. In the letter, McCord revealed the involvement of higher-ups in the burglary and the perjury and political pressure that had occurred during his trial. Realizing that by the time their book could be finished it would appear merely to be rehashing well-reported events, Woodward then suggested that their book should tell the story of how they reported the Watergate cover-up.

The story was told in a third person narrative style. The authors worried that a different style or more personal point of view might appear to be an "ego trip" when dealing with their successes, or worse, might become a defense or justification when dealing with their failures. The reporters openly acknowledged their mistakes: they approached grand jury members for information; they revealed a confidential source; and they overstepped some guidelines in certain rights to privacy. As reporters and authors, they wanted to be objective and honest. The third person narrative with its advantage of impartiality, it was decided, allowed them the best opportunity to do this. In addition, said Doris Kearns in the *New York Times Book Review,* "it turns Watergate into a fast moving mystery, a whodunit written with ease if not elegance." Critics praised the book wholeheartedly for its ability to sustain reader interest, for its behind-the-scenes explanation of the workings of a large metropolitan newspaper, and for its indispensible historical value. Reviewers commended the co-authors for their frankness and their fascinating, personal portraits of the men surrounding the president.

After the completion of *All the President's Men,* the reporters turned their attention back to the final ranklings of Watergate. They planned to follow six senators around for background for a book about the apparent upcoming impeachment trial of Richard Nixon, a project they dropped when it became obvious that the president was going to resign. They decided their next book would be based on the significant news in the day-to-day operation of the White House that was being overlooked by much of the rest of the press. The authors explained in the foreword to *The Final Days:* "Some of our most reliable sources said that the real story of those final days of the Nixon presidency had not been adequately told; to report that story and sort through the contradictions would require a concentrated effort of perhaps a year or more."

The authors, taking a leave of absence from the *Post,* hired two assistants and quickly fanned out a few days after Nixon's resignation to interview everyone associated with the White House who agreed to talk with them. Many sources demanded they not be identified before they consented to be interviewed, and some suggested that they would publicly deny any cooperation after the book appeared. Three hundred and ninety-four people were interviewed in six months. Many of them gave the authors access to their notes, memos, diaries, and logs.

In allowing the sources complete anonymity, Woodward and Bernstein knew they would have to accept responsibility for the accuracy of every statement made in *The Final Days.* In the foreword, the authors explained: "If we obtained two versions, we resolved disagreements through re-interviewing. If this proved impossible, we left out any material we could not confirm." Woodward added: "Anything in the book has been checked and rechecked. The more sensitive the material, the higher the standard we applied. There are several things being disputed now that we have as many as six sources for." The cross-checking and confirmation of all statements in the book was an enormous task of which the authors were quite proud.

The publication of *The Final Days* developed into a media event. Highlights of the book had been syndicated by *Newsweek* in a two-part, thirty thousand-word excerpt containing many of the most controversial passages. The issue that included the second part was the fastest selling issue in *Newsweek*'s history. Like *All the President's Men, The Final Days* was a sure bet for commercial success. Upon release in 1976, it sold one-half million copies in the first month. Another record was set in the book industry when paperback rights were sold at one and one half million dollars.

The people written about in *The Final Days* were reported to believe the account to be "basically accurate" and without "factual error"; yet most complained that the book's total effect was an exaggeration, an overdramatization, and a distortion. These people and a few critics blamed the book's style. *The Final Days* was a narrative written from the omniscient point of view. In a *Christian Science Monitor* review, John Hughes commented: "Woodward and Bernstein were not inside the heads of the participants at the moment crucial events took place, and yet the book unceasingly gives that impression." On the other hand, *New York Review of Books* contributor Nicholas von Hoffman defended the point of view. "Assuming they have a good base for believing that so-and-so did say or think something close to that at the time, there's no reason to object. Using such devices as 'he thought,' 'it seemed to her,' etc., may make the narrative flow more easily and there's no need to think history has to be dull

to be good." In fact, the self-imposed journalistic restraints limit the accuracy of the book, feels Von Hoffman, who concludes that, regarding Nixon's fall from power, *"The Final Days* isn't the last word."

John K. Galbraith, writing in the *Washington Post Book World,* felt that the authors of *The Final Days* could have analyzed flaws in the American political system instead of prolonging the public scrutiny of Nixon's demise. In Woodward's next book—*The Brethren: Inside the Supreme Court*—Woodward and co-author Scott Armstrong also decline to analyze what they uncover about the inner workings of the American government. Reviewers again question the reliability of the reporter's sources, and complain that some of the revelations in the best seller are of a personal nature and made in poor taste. That *The Brethren* has sold so well despite these concerns reflects Woodward's ability to satisfy public curiosity in the United States, a country in which, says Galbraith, "politics . . . has become a major spectator sport."

After John Belushi died of a drug overdose in 1982, his widow asked Woodward to write about the popular actor's death. With characteristic diligence, Woodward interviewed hundreds of people "and conducted a marathon paper chase" for supporting evidence, Matt Beer relates in the *Detroit News.* In Beer's opinion, the scene in which "a friend finds Belushi's bloated body amid the trash of a weeklong binge in a Hollywood hotel" presents, in Beer's words, "the gonzo lifestyle of the 1970s in its harshest, most revealing light ever." Many reviewers found the amount of detail in the book overwhelming and sometimes irrelevant. "John Belushi died of excess. And it is excess that deals a near-fatal blow to investigative reporter Bob Woodward's encyclopedic, intermittently tedious account of the comedian's death," notes Beer. People who had known Belushi also complained "that Woodward concentrated on the dark side of Belushi's life, providing exact details of the drugs, alcohol and tantrums that characterized his final days in Hollywood," reports Eleanor Randolph in the *Washington Post.*

Most notably dissatisfied with Woodward's portrayal of Belushi was his widow Judy Jacklin Belushi, who had hoped that his story might "communicate how 'drugs can ruin your life,' " as Randolph reports in the *Chicago Tribune.* Belushi said that although *Wired* succeeds on this level, it minimizes the positive aspects of her late husband's personality. She tried to block the distribution of the book on the grounds that it contained family pictures she had not authorized for use; however, the real reason, she told the *Chicago Tribune,* was that she wanted the public to know she did not approve of the book as a whole. Randolph records Woodward's response to these and other negative comments: "Read the book. It goes on and on about his talent, going into skit after skit. I think they are reacting to a strong and reasonable wish that it had been different, that it hadn't happened, and I understand they don't want to remember him this way. . . . I believe their distress is directed at what happened to John and not my reporting."

Woodward's next "rhubarb . . . on the ethics (if any) of investigative journalism and the relationship (if any) between its findings and 'history' " is *Veil: The Secret Wars of the CIA, 1981-1987,* notes Edwin M. Yoder, Jr., in the *Los Angeles Times.* Much of the information in *Veil* came from the late William Casey, formerly the director of the Central Intelligence Agency. The result is what has been called a largely sympathetic portrait of the director, who saw the CIA as an active branch of the Reagan administration; it was up to the CIA to make its own foreign policy using covert means when necessary, Casey felt. In *Veil,* "the mumbling, almost comic Casey familiar from TV emerges as a passionate anti-communist and wily strategic thinker, albeit with the cloak-and-dagger mind-set he developed as spymaster for the OSS [Office of Strategic Services] during World War II," relates David M. Alpern in *Newsweek.* Clarence Petersen remarks in the *Chicago Tribune* that "it would be hard to choose a more fascinating central character."

Angered by various parts of the book were Casey's widow, Ronald and Nancy Reagan, other journalists, and critics who felt that the book contained either too much or too little truth. Other reporters questioned Woodward's claim that the usually reticent Casey had granted him dozens of private interviews. Speaking to a "Today" show audience, Woodward said he supposes—as do many of the book's reviewers—that Casey cooperated in order to have some control over what would be said about the CIA. Woodward also felt Casey gave him unprecedented frequent access "as a defensive measure, to learn exactly how much [Woodward] knew about CIA operations," *Time* magazine reports. Yoder maintains that the key to the unusual relationship is the role of secrecy in contemporary political affairs: "The fact is that secrecy, a necessary feature of government, has suffered, in the postwar world of the national-security state, from a terrible elephantiasis: A whole structure of self-importance and self-deception has rooted itself in the culture of secrecy. Unless you understand this addiction, the games that reporters and officials play cannot be understood."

Some readers expressed disappointment that *Veil* revealed so little new information about the diversion of profits from Iran arms sales to the Contras in Central America. At the end of the book, Woodward records a conversation that took place in a hospital room shortly after Casey had undergone brain surgery. When asked if he knew of the diversion, Casey nodded his head to indicate yes; when asked for an explanation, he reportedly replied, "I believed." In the opinion of several reviewers, disputes about whether or not this exchange actually took place sidestep more important issues raised in the book. Writing in the *Chicago Tribune,* Roger Simon contends, "Nobody in this business has greater credibility than Bob Woodward. His devotion to careful fact-checking is not only legendary but also is supposed to border on mania. . . . If he was going to make it up, he could have made up better stuff than a head nod and two words."

More important, the reviewers suggest, are the other CIA activities disclosed in the book, such as a failed assassination attempt in Beirut that left 80 dead and hundreds injured. Woodward apparently agrees. The book's subject, he told *Los Angeles Times* writer Betty Cuniberti, is "Casey and the CIA, six years and one day, how essentially they went unmonitored, where he had in a certain sense a blank check within the executive branch to do what he wanted and that he was able to roll, or frustrate Congress. To a certain extent we all kind of have to face what happened. And it's not a very encouraging story."

Cuniberti reports that "There is a common thread in the criticisms leveled against all the books Woodward has written or co-authored. . . . And that thread, Woodward believes, is not inaccuracy. 'It's contested ground,' said Woodward, 'and it's essentially people living their lives and conducting their business a certain way and projecting a way that is untruthful.' "

MEDIA ADAPTATIONS: All the President's Men was made into a Warner Bros. film starring Dustin Hoffman and Robert Redford in 1976; a film version of *Wired* was produced by Edward S. Feldman for release in 1989.

BIOGRAPHICAL/CRITICAL SOURCES:

BOOKS

Woodward, Bob and Carl Bernstein, *All the President's Men,* Simon & Schuster, 1974.
Woodward, Bob and Carl Bernstein, *The Final Days,* Simon & Schuster, 1976.

PERIODICALS

Atlantic, June, 1976.
Chicago Tribune, December 2, 1979, December 16, 1979, May 27, 1984, June 3, 1984, September 9, 1987, September 30, 1987, October 4, 1987, October 5, 1987, October 9, 1987, October 12, 1987.
Christian Science Monitor, May 19, 1976.
Detroit News, July 1, 1984.
Encounter, October, 1980.
Esquire, December, 1983.
Globe and Mail (Toronto), October 17, 1987.
Harpers, April, 1980.
Los Angeles Times, June 17, 1984, September 27, 1987, September 28, 1987, September 30, 1987, October 1, 1987, October 2, 1987, October 6, 1987.
Los Angeles Times Book Review, June 17, 1984.
Miami Herald, July 17, 1974.
National Review, February 8, 1980, August 6, 1984.
New Republic, April 24, 1976, February 23, 1980.
New Statesman, May 21, 1976.
Newsweek, April 12, 1976, May 3, 1976, October 5, 1987, October 12, 1987.
New York Review of Books, June 10, 1976, February 7, 1980, November 19, 1987.
New York Times, April 7, 1976, December 3, 1977, June 2, 1984, September 19, 1984, January 12, 1986, September 30, 1987, October 3, 1987, April 15, 1989.
New York Times Book Review, June 9, 1974, April 18, 1976, December 16, 1979, January 13, 1980, December 21, 1980, June 10, 1984, September 6, 1987, October 18, 1987, September 4, 1988.
People, October 12, 1987, November 9, 1987.
Philadelphia Bulletin, July 10, 1974.
Publishers Weekly, April 26, 1976, October 14, 1983.
Saturday Review, May 3, 1976, May 29, 1976, March 1, 1980.
Time, April 22, 1974, December 30, 1974, April 12, 1976, May 3, 1976, March 10, 1980, June 11, 1984, October 12, 1987.
Times (London), April 18, 1985.
Times Literary Supplement, April 11, 1980, March 8, 1985, January 22, 1988.
Tribune Books, September 11, 1988.
Washington Post, December 2, 1979, May 30, 1984, May 31, 1984, June 1, 1984, June 4, 1984, June 5, 1984, September 27, 1987, October 4, 1987, October 15, 1987, May 10, 1988.
Washington Post Book World, April 11, 1976, December 16, 1979, September 27, 1987, August 28, 1988.

—*Sketch by Marilyn K. Basel*

* * *

WRIGHT, Judith (Arandell) 1915-

PERSONAL: Born May 31, 1915, in Armidale, New South Wales, Australia; daughter of Phillip Arundell and Ethel Mabel (Bigg) Wright; married Jack Philip McKinney (a philosophical writer; died, 1966); children: Meredith Anne. *Education:* Attended New South Wales Correspondence School, New England Girls' School, and University of Sydney. *Politics:* "Swing voter."

ADDRESSES: P.O. Box 93, Braidwood, New South Wales 2622, Australia.

CAREER: J. Walter Thompson (advertising agency), Sydney, Australia, secretary, 1938-39; University of Sydney, Sydney, Australia, secretary, 1940-42; Australian Universities Commission, Brisbane, Australia, clerk, 1943-46; University of Queensland, Brisbane, statistician, 1946-49. Part-time lecturer in Australian literature at various Australian universities. President, Wildlife Preservation Society of Queensland, 1962-74; member, Committee of Inquiry into the National Estate, Australia, 1973-74; member, Aboriginal Treaty Committee, 1978-83.

MEMBER: Society of Authors (Australia; council member), Australian Academy of the Humanities (fellow).

AWARDS, HONORS: Grace Leven Prize, 1953; D.Litt., University of New England, Armidale, Australia, 1963, Monash University, 1977, University of Sydney, 1977, Australian National University, 1980, University of New South Wales, 1985, Griffith University, 1988, University of Melbourne, 1988; *Encyclopedia Britannica* Award, 1964; Robert Frost Medallion, Fellowship of Australian Writers, 1975; Asan World Prize, Asan Memorial Association, 1984.

WRITINGS:

Kings of the Dingoes (juvenile), illustrated by Barbara Albiston, Oxford University Press, 1958.
The Generations of Men, illustrated by Alison Forbes, Oxford University Press, 1959, reprinted, 1975.
The Day the Mountains Played (juvenile), Jacaranda, 1960, Boolarong, 1988.
Range the Mountains High (juvenile), Lansdowne Press, 1962, 3rd edition, 1971.
Charles Harpur (biography and criticism), Lansdowne Press, 1963.
Country Towns (juvenile), Oxford University Press, 1963.
Preoccupations in Australian Poetry (history and criticism), Oxford University Press, 1965, new edition, 1966.
The Nature of Love (short stories), Sun Books (Melbourne, Australia), 1966.
The River and the Road (juvenile), Lansdowne Press, 1966, revised edition, 1971.
Henry Lawson, Oxford University Press, 1967.
Because I Was Invited, Oxford University Press, 1975.
The Coral Battleground (documentary), Thomas Nelson (Australia), 1977.
The Cry for the Dead, Oxford University Press, 1981.
We Call for a Treaty, William Collins/John M. Fontana, 1985.

POETRY

The Moving Image, Meanjin, 1946, revised edition, 1953.
Woman to Man, Angus & Robertson, 1949, 2nd edition, 1955.
The Gateway, Angus & Robertson, 1953.
The Two Fires, Angus & Robertson, 1955.
Birds, Angus & Robertson, 1962, 3rd edition, 1978.
Five Senses: Selected Poems, Angus & Robertson, 1963, revised edition, 1972.
City Sunrise, limited edition, Shapcott Press, 1964.
The Other Half, Angus & Robertson, 1966.
Collected Poems, Angus & Robertson, 1971, 2nd edition, 1975.
Alive: Poems 1971-1972, Angus & Robertson, 1973.
Fourth Quarter, and Other Poems, Angus & Robertson, 1976.
The Double Tree: Selected Poems, Houghton, 1978.

(Contributor) Fay Zwicky, editor, *Journeys: Poems,* Sisters (Carleton South, Australia), 1982.
Phantom Dwelling, Angus & Robertson, 1985.

EDITOR

Australian Poetry, Angus & Robertson, 1948.
(And author of introduction) *A Book of Australian Verse,* Oxford University Press, 1956, 2nd revised edition, 1968.
(And author of introduction) *New Land, New Language: An Anthology of Australian Verse,* Oxford University Press, 1957.
Judith Wright (selected poetry), Angus & Robertson, 1963.
Shaw Neilson (biography and selected poetry), Angus & Robertson, 1963.
(With Andrew Thomson) *The Poet's Pen,* Jacaranda, 1965.
John Shaw Neilson, *Witnesses of Spring: Unpublished Poems of Shaw Neilson,* Angus & Robertson, 1970.

SIDELIGHTS: A well-known author and poet in Australia, Judith Wright has been "outrageously neglected" outside of her native land, according to *London Magazine* critic D. M. Thomas. After years of publishing her verses in Australian periodicals, as well as in books in her homeland and abroad, Wright has accumulated much critical attention in Australia for her distinctly endemic poetry. One Australian reviewer, *Meanjin* contributor Elizabeth Vassilieff, considers Wright to be "the most interesting of Australian poets, with no exceptions." "Her poetry has the touch and feel of [Australia]," notes another *Meanjin* reviewer, S. Musgrove, "for she knows that man . . . must not lose that immediate contact" with the land. But although her poetry has gained her the most attention, Ken Goodwin writes in his *A History of Australian Literature,* "Judith Wright, in both poetry and prose, presents a wide panorama of the interests of the socially conscious present-day Australian."

Wright's prose writing includes children's stories, which she originally composed for her daughter, criticism, a biographical novel, *The Generations of Men,* and a historical work, *The Cry for the Dead.* The latter two books concern the author's own ancestors; Wright's grandfather, Albert Wright, figures prominently in both books, and the author takes much of her material for these books from her grandfather's diary. Next to other comparable novels, critics have viewed these retrospects on life in nineteenth-century Australia favorably. One "never has the feeling . . . that he is watching an artificial period-piece or costume melodrama," remarks *Meanjin* contributor Russel Ward. *New Statesman* critic V. S. Pritchett observes, too, that in *The Generations of Men* Wright "is also free of that family complacency which affects so many writers when they are describing their pioneer forebears." In another review of this book, Leonie Kramer writes in *Southerly:* "Judith Wright has shown herself to be a biographer of rare sensitivity." Kramer later concludes that the author's "prose transmits particularly well the atmosphere of the times, and the arid beauty of the country."

Both books not only tell the story of the author's family, but also that of the land itself. Albert Wright's diary becomes a helpful source in this regard, for, as Goodwin describes, "his book tells less of the official story than of the disastrous neglect of proper land-management procedures and the story of the brutal extermination of Aborigines." The tragic waste which these practices have brought to Australia is a concern in much of Wright's poetry as well. As a result, several of the author's poems are meditations "on the problem of how to give meaning to, or discover meaning in, this 'flowing and furious world,' " says *Australian Quarterly* critic R. F. Brissenden, quoting a poem from Wright's *Five Senses: Selected Poems.*

Maintaining a respect for the timelessness of the land throughout her work, Wright expresses in such poetry collections as *Alive: Poems 1971-1972* and *Fourth Quarter, and Other Poems* a horror "at the efficiency with which her fellow countrymen are raping their country," writes Peter Porter in the *London Observer.* Having been raised on a "station," or ranch, as a child, and being active as an adult in the conservation movement in Australia, Wright maintains a strong bond with her surroundings, which is evident in her poetry. She has, asserts Arthur Murphy in *Southerly,* an ability "to merge herself with all natural forces, delving deep into the almost inexpressible in verse of highly wrought formation and full content." But although several critics, such as one *Times Literary Supplement* reviewer, feel that her poems "about people, landscapes, and animals are good when she describes her subjects directly," Val Vallis remarks in the *Times Literary Supplement* that "the most commonly heard objection to her poetry as it progressed was that its author 'had gone too philosophical.' " *Carleton Miscellany* critic Keith Harrison, however, notes that even though one might see some "occasional vagueness" in her sometimes metaphysical poems, "the strengths of her work far outweigh the faults."

Some of these strengths, declares Elyne Mitchell in *Southerly,* include "vivid imagery, lovely songs of creation and of a creator, poems of philosophic journey, of the integration of dark and light, [and] of rebirth." Wright is a poet, who, as S. E. Lee characterizes her in *Southerly,* is "a rare combination of metaphysical thinker . . . and down-to-earth realist." Her "best poems then," concludes Lee, "integrate the intellect, passion, imagination and common sense of the thinker-mystic-poet-country wife." What is evident in both Wright's prose and poetry is "her bond to her native land and its once pastoral wilderness," asserts Margaret Gibson in the *Library Journal.* Goodwin summarizes the author's career this way: "Her lifelong quest [has been] to define Australia as a land, a nation and a metaphysical entity, in language that [shows] awareness of contemporary overseas writing in English but also [recognizes] the unique environment and society of Australia."

AVOCATIONAL INTERESTS: Gardening.

BIOGRAPHICAL/CRITICAL SOURCES:

BOOKS

Contemporary Literary Criticism, Gale, Volume 11, 1979, Volume 53, 1989.
Goodwin, Ken, *A History of Australian Literature,* St. Martin's, 1986.
Hope, A. D., *Judith Wright,* Oxford University Press (Melbourne), 1975.
Kramer, L., editor, *The Oxford History of Australian Literature,* Oxford University Press, 1982.
Walker, Shirley, *The Poetry of Judith Wright,* Edward Arnold, 1980.
Walker, Shirley, *Judith Wright,* Oxford University Press, 1981.

PERIODICALS

American Poetry Review, September/October, 1980.
Australian Quarterly, March, 1964.
Carleton Miscellany, summer, 1980.
Library Journal, June 15, 1978.
London Magazine, May, 1967.
London Observer, May 7, 1978.
Meanjin, September, 1946, March, 1950, June, 1960, December, 1962.
New Statesman, September 5, 1959.

Southerly, Volume 11, number 3, 1950, Volume 16, number 1, 1955, Volume 17, number 2, 1956, Volume 20, number 9, 1959, Volume 23, number 2, 1963, Volume 27, number 1, 1967.
Times Literary Supplement, September 10, 1964, April 9, 1976, October 15, 1982, November 27, 1987.

—*Sketch by Kevin S. Hile*

*   *   *

WYNAR, Lubomyr R(oman) 1932-

PERSONAL: Born January 2, 1932, in Lvov, U.S.S.R.; came to the United States in 1955, naturalized citizen, 1960; son of Ivan (a professor) and Eufrosina (a teacher; maiden name, Doryk) Wynar; married Anna T. Kuzmych (a sociologist), July 15, 1962; children: Natalia. *Education:* Attended University of Munich, 1949-51; Ukrainian Free University, M.A., 1955, Ph.D., 1957; Western Reserve University (now Case Western Reserve University), M.S.L.S., 1959.

ADDRESSES: Home—4984 Pheasant Ave., Ravenna, Ohio 44266. *Office*—School of Library Science, Kent State University, Kent, Ohio 44242.

CAREER: Case Institute of Technology (now Case Western Reserve University), Cleveland, Ohio, instructor in bibliography and periodicals librarian, 1959-62; University of Colorado, Boulder, assistant professor and director of Bibliographic Research Center, 1966-68, associate professor and director of library administration and assistant director of libraries, 1968-69; Kent State University, Kent, Ohio, professor of library science and ethnic studies, 1969—, director of Center for the Study of Ethnic Publication, 1971—. Faculty member at University of Denver, summers, 1961, 1963-65. Research associate at John Carroll University, 1962-76, and University of Illinois, 1986—. President of Intercollegiate Council on Ethnic Studies in Ohio, 1978-83.

MEMBER: American Historical Association, American Library Association (chairman of Slavic and East European section, 1971-73, 1980-81), American Association for the Advancement of Slavic Studies, Association for the Study of Nationalities (vice-president, 1977-79), Association of Ukrainian-American University Professors (president, 1982-84), Ukrainian Free Academy of Arts and Sciences in the United States (chairman of Commission on Immigration, 1969—), Ukrainian Historical Association (president, 1982-89), Shevchenko Scientific Society (vice-president of Historical and Philosophical Division, 1973-80), Ohio Library Association, Colorado Library Association.

AWARDS, HONORS: Best reference book award from American Library Association, 1972, for *Encyclopedia Directory of Ethnic Newspapers and Periodicals;* grant from U.S. Office of Education, 1977-78.

WRITINGS:

Andrew Voynarovsky: A Historical Study, Verlag Logos, 1961.
A History of Early Ukrainian Printing, 1491-1600, Graduate School of Library Science, University of Denver, 1962.
S. Harrison Thomson: A Bio-Bibliography, Library, University of Colorado, 1963.
History: A Bibliographical Guide, Library, University of Colorado, 1963.
Prince Dmytro Vshnevetskyi, Ukrainian Academy of Arts and Sciences, 1965.

Ukrainian Kozaks and the Vatican in 1594, Ukrainian Historical Association, 1965.

Guide to Reference Materials in Political Science, Colorado Bibliographical Institute, Volume 1, 1966, Volume 2, 1968.

The Early Years of Michael Hrushevsky, 1866-1894, Ukrainian Historical Association, 1967.

American Political Parties, Libraries Unlimited, 1969.

Michael Hrushevsky and the Schevchenko Scientific Society, 1895-1930, Ukrainian Historical Association, 1971.

Ethnic Groups in Ohio, Ethnic Heritage Program, Cleveland State University, 1975.

(Editor) *Habsburgs and Zaporozhian Cossacks,* Ukrainian Academic Press, 1975.

Encyclopedia Directory of Ethnic Organizations in the United States, Libraries Unlimited, 1975.

(With wife Ana Wynar) *Encyclopedia Directory of Ethnic Newspapers and Periodicals,* Libraries Unlimited, 1976.

(With Lois Butlar) *Building Ethnic Collections,* Libraries Unlimited, 1977.

(With Marjorie Murfin) *Reference Services,* Libraries Unlimited, 1977.

Guide to Ethnic Museums, Archives, and Libraries in the United States, Center for Ethnic Studies, Kent State University, 1978.

Ethnic Films and Filmstrip Guide for Libraries and Media Centers: A Selective Filmography, Libraries Unlimited, 1980.

Slavic Ethnic Libraries, Museums and Archives in the United States, American Library Association, 1980.

(Editor) *Atlas Istorii Ukrainy* (title means "Historical Atlas of Ukraine"), Ukrainian Historical Association, 1981.

Michael Hrushevsky's Autobiography of 1926, Ukrainian Historical Association, 1982.

Dmytro Doroshenko: 1882-1951, Ukrainian Historical Association, 1983.

Mykhailo Hrushevskyi: Bibliographic Sources, Ukrainian Historical Association, 1986.

Guide to the American Ethnic Press, Kent State University, 1986.

M. Hrushevsky: Ukrainian Russian Confrontation in Historiography, Toronto, 1988.

Managing editor of "Bio-Bibliographical Series" and editor of "Social Science Reference Series" for University of Colorado Library, 1963-65 and 1988—. Contributor of more than two hundred articles and reviews to academic journals. Editor of *Ukrainian Historian,* 1964—; founder and editor of *Ethnic Forum,* 1980—; editor, *Hrushevsky Studies,* 1980—. Section editor of ethnic studies in *American Reference Books Annual,* 1974—.

WORK IN PROGRESS: Bookculture in Medieval Kiev.

SIDELIGHTS: Lubomyr R. Wynar writes that his main interests are history, library science, ethnic studies, and bibliography. "I was initially trained as a historian in the area of East European history, with an emphasis on Ukrainian political, cultural, and social history of the sixteenth through the eighteenth centuries. Later, when I completed my studies in library science, I continued to be actively involved in both, researching various topics in Ukrainian historiography, primarily because this area of East European history has been rather neglected by American historians.

"As a librarian and library science educator, I have always recognized the important role that the library can play in providing services to American ethnic communities. In this respect librarians and information specialists should not only be able to recognize the special needs of the various ethnic groups within their communities, but must also be aware of voluminous amounts of ethnic materials published by such groups within this country. This literature, ranging from periodicals to newspapers, greatly impacts the American ethnic readership, and as such cannot be ignored by institutions whose primary role lies in information dissemination to all elements within society. The journal *Ethnic Forum,* which I initiated and am presently editing, is just one attempt to bring together ethnicity and librarianship.

"I believe very strongly that my research on Michael Hrushevsky (1866-1934), the leading Ukrainian historian and outstanding organizer of scholarly and cultural life in Eastern Europe, fills an essential gap in historiographical and bibliographical literature. Hrushevsky's rational schema of East European history as well as his historical studies deserve further analysis and elucidation by American and European historians. A major part of my research is devoted to the study of his life and his scholarly contributions." Many of Wynar's studies are published in English, Ukrainian, and German.

Y

YOUNG, Percy M(arshall) 1912-
(Percy Marshall)

PERSONAL: Born May 17, 1912, in Northwich, Cheshire, England; son of William Joseph (a clerk) and Annie (a nurse; maiden name, Marshall) Young; married Anna Letitia Carson, August 7, 1937 (deceased); married Renee Morris, February 10, 1969. *Education:* Selwyn College, Cambridge, B.A. and Mus.B., 1933, M.A., 1937; Trinity College, Dublin, Mus.D., 1937. *Religion:* Church of England.

ADDRESSES: Home—72 Clark Rd., Wolverhampton WV3 9PA, England. *Agent*—A. R. Watt, Ltd., 20 John St., London WC1N 2DL, England.

CAREER: Stranmillis Teacher's Training College, Belfast, Northern Ireland, director of music, 1934-37; musical adviser to city schools, Stoke-on-Trent, England, 1937-44; College of Technology, Wolverhampton, Staffordshire, England, director of music, 1944-65; lecturer, conductor, and composer, 1966—. Visiting scholar, University Center, Georgia, 1971; visiting lecturer, Bucknell University, 1972. Examiner at universities in Wales, London, and Birmingham, England.

MEMBER: International Kodaly Society (honorary member), Royal Musical Association, Royal College of Organists, Royal Commonwealth Society, British-Caribbean Association, Dolmetsch Foundation, Incorporated Society of Musicians, Performing Rights Society, Gesellschaft fuer Musikforschung, Society of Authors, National Book League, Hungarian Friendship Society, Hallische Haendel-Gesellschaft, Goettinger Haendel-Gesellschaft, Ernst Thaelmann Brigade (honorary member), Selwyn College Association, Grand Theatre Club, Old Blues, Wolverhampton Cricket Club, Wine Society.

AWARDS, HONORS: Handel Prize, Halle, East Germany, 1961; D.Mus., University of Birmingham, 1986; Barclay Squire Prize for Musical Palaeography, Cambridge University; diploma from the Hungarian government for research on Zoltan Kodaly.

WRITINGS:

Introduction to the Music of Mendelssohn, Dobson, 1949.
The Oratorios of Handel, Dobson, 1949, Roy, 1950, reprinted, State Mutual Book, 1981.
Messiah: Study in Interpretation, Dobson, 1951.
Vaughan Williams, Dobson, 1953.

A Handbook of Choral Technique, Dobson, 1953.
Biographical Dictionary of Composers, with Classified List of Music for Performance and Study, Crowell, 1954, reprinted as *A Critical Dictionary of Composers and Their Music,* Hyperion Press, 1982.
Elgar, O.M.: A Study of a Musician, Collins, 1955, 2nd revised edition, Greenwood Press, 1980.
(Editor and annotator) Edward Elgar, *Letters and Other Writings,* Bles, 1956, reprinted, Hyperion Press, 1985.
Tragic Muse: The Life and Works of Robert Schumann, Hutchinson, 1957, enlarged edition, Dobson, 1961.
Symphony, Phoenix House, 1957, Crescendo, 1968.
Music and the Young Child, McDougall's Educational Co., 1957.
Concerto, Phoenix House, 1957.
Johann Sebastian Bach: The Story of His Life and Work, Boosey & Hawkes, 1960.
Musical Composition for Pleasure, Hutchinson, 1961.
The Choral Tradition: An Historical and Analytical Survey from the Sixteenth Century to the Present Day, Norton, 1962.
The Concert Tradition, Norton, 1962, reprinted, 1981.
Zoltan Kodaly: A Hungarian Musician, Benn, 1964, Greenwood Press, 1976.
Letters to Nimrod: Edward Elgar to August Jaeger, 1897-1908, Dobson, 1965, reprinted, State Mutual Book, 1981.
World Conductors, Abelard-Schuman, 1966.
A History of British Music, Norton, 1967.
Great Ideas in Music, edited by Patrick Pringle, Maxwell, 1967, David White, 1968.
(Editor) Elgar, *A Future for English Music,* Dobson, 1968, reprinted as *Future for English Music: Lectures of Sir Edward Elgar,* State Mutual Book, 1981.
The Enjoyment of Music, E.M.I. Records (London), 1968.
Choral Music of the World, Abelard-Schuman, 1969.
The Bachs, 1500-1850, Crowell, 1970.
Sir Arthur Sullivan, Dent, 1971, Norton, 1972.
(Translator) Santeri Levas, *Sibelius: A Personal Portrait,* Bucknell University Press, 1973.
Alice Elgar: Enigma of a Victorian Lady, Dobson, 1976.
George Grove, 1820-1900: A Biography, Macmillan, 1980.
(Editor) Piotr I. Tchaikovsky, *Letters to His Family: An Autobiography,* translation by Galina Von Meck, Scarborough House, 1982.

FOR CHILDREN

Music Is for You: A Guide to Music for Young People, Lutterworth, 1948.

Music Makers, Dobson, 1951, Roy, 1953.

(Compiler) *Carols for the Twelve Days of Christmas,* Dobson, 1952, Roy, 1954.

More Music Makers, Roy, 1955.

Instrumental Music, Methuen, 1955, Roy, 1958.

The Story of Song, Methuen, 1956, Roy, 1958.

In Search of Music, Lutterworth, 1956.

(With Edward Ardizzone) *Ding Dong Bell,* Dobson, 1957, Dover, 1969.

Read and Sing, two volumes, Allen & Unwin, 1958.

Music Makers of Today, illustrated by Milein Cosman, Roy, 1958, 2nd edition, 1966.

Music and Its Story, Lutterworth, 1960, Roy, 1962, revised edition, 1970.

The Young Musician, Ted Nelson, 1961.

Handel, Dutton, 1961, revised edition, Dent, 1975.

(Under name Percy Marshall) *Masters of the English Novel,* Dobson, 1962.

Music, Ted Nelson, 1963.

Mozart, Benn, 1965, David White, 1966, reprinted edition edited by Janet Caulkins, Bookwright Press, 1987.

World Composers, Abelard-Schuman, 1966.

Beethoven, David White, 1966.

(Under name Percy Marshall) *Masters of English Poetry,* Dobson, 1966.

Britten, illustrated by Richard Shirley-Smith, David White, 1966.

Keyboard Musicians of the World, Abelard-Schuman, 1967.

Debussy, illustrated by Shirley-Smith, David White, 1968.

Tchaikovsky, illustrated by Shirley-Smith, David White, 1968.

Haydn, David White, 1969.

Stravinsky, illustrated by Shirley-Smith, David White, 1969.

Dvorak, illustrated by Paul Newland, David White, 1970.

Schubert, illustrated by Newland, David White, 1970.

A Concise History of Music, David White, 1974.

The English Glee, Oxford University Press, 1990.

The Spanish Lady (a critical and performing edition of Edward Elgar's opera), Novello, 1990.

SPORTS BOOKS FOR ADULTS

The Wolves: The First Eighty Years, Stanley Paul, 1959.

Manchester United, Heinemann, 1960.

Bolton Wanderers, Stanley Paul, 1961.

Football in Sheffield, Stanley Paul, 1962.

Football on Merseyside, Stanley Paul, 1963.

A History of British Football, Stanley Paul, 1968.

(With Derek Dougan) *On the Spot: Football as a Profession,* Stanley Paul, 1974.

Centenary Wolves, Wolverhampton Wanderers Football Club, 1976.

SPORTS BOOKS FOR CHILDREN

Football: Facts and Fancies; or, The Art of Spectatorship, Dobson, 1950.

Appreciation of Football, Dobson, 1951.

Football Year, Phoenix House, 1956.

Football through the Ages, Methuen, 1957.

OTHER

Editor and arranger of *Samuel Pepys Music Book,* 1942. Composer of numerous musical pieces, including "On Easter Knoll," "The Stolen Child," "Fugal Concerto," "Au Moyen-age," several suites based on themes from the seventeenth century, and church music. Editor, "Student Music Library" series, Dobson, 1951—. Contributor to *Grove's Dictionary of Music and Musicians, Book of Association Football, Football Yearbook, Encyclopedia Britannica, Collier's Encyclopedia, World Book Encyclopedia, Children's Encyclopedia,* and other publications in Germany and the United States.

WORK IN PROGRESS: "Joint general editor for a definitive edition of Gilbert and Sullivan operas"; editing collections, *The Madrigal in the Romantic Era, Music of the Great Churches,* and *Music for the Country Choir,* for Broude.

AVOCATIONAL INTERESTS: Traveling (Young has been to the United States, Germany, Switzerland, Japan, Hungary, and Africa), gardening, sports.

BIOGRAPHICAL/CRITICAL SOURCES:

PERIODICALS

New York Times Book Review, May 4, 1969.

Saturday Review, July 24, 1971.

Times Literary Supplement, April 22, 1965, November 24, 1966, February 15, 1968, March 14, 1968, March 28, 1968, August 7, 1969, July 2, 1970, September 11, 1970, April 2, 1971, December 3, 1971, July 5, 1974, November 23, 1979, May 16, 1980.

*   *   *

YOUNG, Robert
See PAYNE, (Pierre Stephen) Robert

Z

ZINDEL, Bonnie 1943-

PERSONAL: Born May 3, 1943, in New York, N.Y.; daughter of Jack C. (a certified public accountant) and Claire (Bromberg) Hildebrand; married Paul Zindel (a writer), October 25, 1973; children: David Jack, Lizabeth Claire. *Education:* Hofstra University, B.A., 1964.

ADDRESSES: Home—New York, N.Y. *Agent*—Curtis Brown, Ltd., Ten Astor Pl., New York, N.Y. 10003.

CAREER: Clairol, New York City, in public relations, 1964; Cleveland Playhouse, Cleveland, Ohio, director of public relations and audience development, 1969-71; WCLV-Radio, Cleveland, producer and interviewer for intermission feature of Boston Symphony programs, 1970-72; Henry Street Settlement Urban Life Center, New York City, in public relations, 1971-72; full-time writer, 1972—.

MEMBER: Playwrights Unit-Actors Studio, Women in Film.

WRITINGS:

"I Am a Zoo" (two-act play), first produced in New York City at Jewish Repertory Theatre, 1978.
(With husband, Paul Zindel) *A Star for the Latecomer* (young adult; also see below), Harper, 1980.
"Lemons in the Morning," first produced by A.M. Back Alley Theatre, 1983.
Hollywood Dream Machine, Viking, 1984.
"The Latecomer" (play; adapted from *A Star for the Latecomer*), first produced in New York City at Actors Studio Playwrights Unit, 1985.
Dr. Adriana Earthlight, Student Shrink (young adult), Viking, 1988.

WORK IN PROGRESS: Lifelines, a novel.

SIDELIGHTS: In their novel *A Star for the Latecomer,* Bonnie Zindel and co-author Paul Zindel "have addressed themselves to an important aspect of life with a less than heavy hand and a brisk, readable and unsentimental style," notes Jennifer Moody in the *Times Literary Supplement. A Star for the Latecomer* follows sixteen-year-old Brooke Hillary, a young dance student torn between following her own wishes to marry and settle down and satisfying her dying mother's hope that Brooke should enjoy the theatrical success that she never had. While *New York Times Book Review* contributor Cyrisse Jaffee faults the Zindels for

tending "toward preachiness," she also notes that "the reader becomes involved enough so that the final scenes between mother and daughter are heartfelt." V. K. Burg similarly comments in the *Christian Science Monitor* that while the mother-daughter bond is strongly drawn, "it seems that so much energy has gone into the creation of the central relationship that the authors had no spirit left for the others involved." Nevertheless, the portrayal of Brooke and her mother is "what makes this story so unusual," claims Jack Forman in the *School Library Journal,* who also commends "the involving, heartrending scenes of Brooke seeing her mother waste away physically while fighting valiantly . . . to maintain her dignity and strong support for Brooke." Concludes a *Publishers Weekly* reviewer: "Both Zindels deserve honors for creating a touching, compassionate and illuminating story of two loving people in conflict."

Zindel has garnered similar reviews for her two solo novels; Hope Bridgewater, for example, observes in her *School Library Journal* assessment of *Hollywood Dream Machine* that "the descriptions of California life style, [and] of the close friendship between two teenage girls," among other aspects, "are believable, yet the theme dominates at the expense of characterization." A *Times Literary Supplement* critic, however, calls this story of a young teen's complicated first romance "a thought-provoking novel, dealing with the problems of first love, parental love and self-love, and offering much common-sense advice." *Dr. Adriana Earthlight, Student Shrink* similarly demonstrates the complexities of adolescent life in the character of Adriana, who counsels all her friends on their problems while avoiding her own. "Adriana is a fascinating protagonist," remarks a *Publishers Weekly* reviewer, "and the complexity of her character is powerfully conveyed through natural-sounding dialogue and fluid narration."

Zindel once told *CA:* "There's a little voice inside each of us that tells the truth. One has to just learn how to listen to it, interpret it. It's a kind of wonderful language hidden in our nerves, in our heartbeat, in our emotions. It tells us who we are. I try to interpret mine and write about it."

BIOGRAPHICAL/CRITICAL SOURCES:

PERIODICALS

Christian Science Monitor, May 12, 1980.
New York Times Book Review, July 20, 1980.
Publishers Weekly, April 18, 1980, October 14, 1988.

School Library Journal, April, 1980, March, 1985.
Times Literary Supplement, July 18, 1980, August 16, 1985.

*   *   *

ZINDEL, Paul 1936-

PERSONAL: Born May 15, 1936, in Staten Island, N.Y.; son of Paul (a policeman) and Betty Beatrice Mary (a practical nurse; maiden name, Frank) Zindel; married Bonnie Hildebrand (a writer), October 25, 1973; children: David Jack, Lizabeth Claire. *Education:* Wagner College, B.S., 1958, M.Sc., 1959.

ADDRESSES: Home—New York, N.Y. *Agent*—Curtis Brown, Ltd., Ten Astor Pl., New York, N.Y. 10003.

CAREER: Tottenville High School, Staten Island, N.Y., chemistry teacher, 1959-69; playwright and author of children's books, 1969—. Playwright in residence, Alley Theatre, Houston, Tex., 1967.

MEMBER: Dramatists Guild, Writers Guild of America West, Authors Guild, Actors Studio.

AWARDS, HONORS: Ford Foundation grant, 1967; *New York Times Book Review* Outstanding Books of the Year selection, 1969, for *My Darling, My Hamburger;* Obie Award for best new American play, *Village Voice,* 1970, New York Drama Critics Circle Award for best American play, 1970, *Variety* award for most promising playwright, 1970, Pulitzer Prize in drama, 1971, New York Critics Award, 1971, and Vernon Rice Drama Desk Award for most promising playwright, 1971, all for "The Effect of Gamma Rays on Man-in-the-Moon Marigolds"; American Library Association (ALA) Notable Book selection and Best Books for Young Adults selection, both 1971, both for *The Effect of Gamma Rays on Man-in-the-Moon Marigolds;* D.H.L., Wagner College, 1971; ALA Best Books for Young Adults selection, 1981, for *The Pigman's Legacy;* Los Angeles Drama Critics Award for best American play, for "And Miss Reardon Drinks a Little."

WRITINGS:

NOVELS; FOR YOUNG ADULTS

The Pigman, Harper, 1968, reprinted, Bantam, 1983.
My Darling, My Hamburger, Harper, 1969.
I Never Loved Your Mind, Harper, 1970.
Pardon Me, You're Stepping on My Eyeball, Harper, 1976.
Confessions of a Teenage Baboon (also see below), Harper, 1977.
The Undertaker's Gone Bananas, Harper, 1978.
(With wife, Bonnie Zindel) *A Star for the Latecomer,* Harper, 1980.
The Pigman's Legacy, Harper, 1980.
The Girl Who Wanted a Boy, Harper, 1981.
(With Crescent Dragonwagon) *To Take a Dare,* Harper, 1982.
Harry and Hortense at Hormone High, Harper, 1984.
The Amazing and Death-Defying Diary of Eugene Dingman, Harper, 1987.
A Begonia for Miss Applebaum, Harper, 1989.

PLAYS

"Dimensions of Peacocks," first produced in New York, 1959.
"Euthanasia and the Endless Hearts," first produced in New York City at Take 3, 1960.
"A Dream of Swallows," first produced Off-Broadway at Jan Hus House, April 14, 1964.
The Effects of Gamma Rays on Man-in-the-Moon Marigolds (also see below; first produced in Houston at Alley Theatre,

May 12, 1965; produced Off-Broadway at Mercer-O'Casey Theatre, April 7, 1970; produced on Broadway at the New Theatre, August 11, 1970), Harper, 1971.
And Miss Reardon Drinks a Little (first produced in Los Angeles, Calif., at Mark Taper Forum, 1967; revised version produced on Broadway at Morosco Theatre, February 25, 1971), Dramatists Play Service, 1971.
The Secret Affairs of Mildred Wild, (first produced on Broadway at Ambassador Theatre, November 14, 1972), Dramatists Play Service, 1973.
Let Me Hear You Whisper [and] *The Ladies Should Be in Bed* ([the former based on his screenplay of the same title; also see below]; both plays produced Off-Off Broadway at the Nat Horne Musical Theatre as "Zindel X 2," April 29, 1982), Dramatists Play Service, 1973.
Ladies at the Alamo (first produced Off-Off Broadway at Actors Studio, May 29, 1975; produced on Broadway at the Martin Beck Theater, April 7, 1977), Dramatists Play Service, 1977.
"A Destiny with Half Moon Street," first produced in Coconut Grove, Fla., at Players State Theater, March 4, 1983.
"Amulets against the Dragon Forces" (based in part on his novel *Confessions of a Teenage Baboon*), first produced in New York City at the Circle Repertory Theatre, April 5, 1989.

SCREENPLAYS AND TELEPLAYS

"The Effect of Gamma Rays on Man-in-the-Moon Marigolds" (adapted from his play), National Educational Television (NET), 1966.
Let Me Hear You Whisper (produced by NET, 1966), Harper, 1974.
"Up the Sandbox" (adapted from Anne Roiphe's novel), National General, 1972.
"Mame" (adapted from Patrick Dennis's *Auntie Mame*), Warner Brothers, 1973.
(With Gerard Brach, Andrei Konchalovsky, and Marjorie David) "Maria's Lovers," Cannon, 1985.
"Alice in Wonderland" (adapted from Lewis Carroll's *Alice's Adventures in Wonderland* and *Through the Looking Glass*), Columbia Broadcasting Service (CBS-TV), 1985.
(With Djordje Milicevic and Edward Bunker) "Runaway Train," Cannon, 1986.
"Babes in Toyland" (adapted from the Victor Herbert operetta), National Broadcasting Company (NBC-TV), 1986.
"A Connecticut Yankee in King Arthur's Court" (based on Mark Twain's novel), NBC-TV, 1989.

OTHER

I Love My Mother (for children), Harper, 1975.
When a Darkness Falls (adult novel), Bantam, 1984.

Contributor of articles to newspapers and periodicals.

SIDELIGHTS: Paul Zindel was still teaching high school chemistry when he burst onto the literary scene with two powerful works in two different media: "The Effect of Gamma Rays on Man-in-the-Moon Marigolds," which became a Broadway hit and garnered Zindel an Obie Award and a Pulitzer Prize; and *The Pigman,* a novel for young adults which "critics of adolescent literature generally cite . . . as helping this subgenre break its ties with its past romanticism and move dramatically into a much more realistic mode," as Theodore W. Hipple describes it in a *Dictionary of Literary Biography* essay. While they are targeted at different audiences, both Zindel's drama and fiction contain elements in common, such as a strong ear for dialogue, characters that are generally misfits or outsiders, and an honest, realistic approach to life's often overwhelming problems. Frequently based on his own experiences, as Ruth L. Strickland notes in another *Dictionary of Literary Biography* piece, "Zindel's art is one which realistically combines humor and pathos, poetry and terror."

Although Zindel had seen some productions of his work prior to the New York premiere of "Marigolds" in 1970, he was still largely unknown to drama devotees. But when the play opened to rave reviews, "everyone was suddenly aware of 'Marigolds,' a relentless, powerfully drawn portrait of a bitter, frequently brutal mother and her two anguished daughters," relates Guy Flatley in the *New York Times*. The play presents the frequently hostile relationship between sarcastic Beatrice, who supports her family by boarding a semi-comatose old woman, and her two daughters. Ruth, the elder, is mentally unbalanced and becoming as resentful and emotionally crippled as her mother; her sister Tillie, however, is optimistic and interested in life and especially her science project, where gamma radiation has produced marigold blossoms both withered and vigorous. "Zindel, who writes alarmingly well, contrasts the fate of the poor marigolds with the fate of this tortured family," observes *New York Times* drama critic Clive Barnes. "We are all the product of our environment, all the product of our particular 'gamma-rays,' but some survive and some are destroyed." *Christian Science Monitor* contributor Alan Bunce also sees this parallel, and remarks that the flowers' "symbolism for this family is strong enough for meaning without weighting down the play's rampant activity."

While many critics believe the symbolism of "Marigolds" is effective, they particularly praise Zindel's forthright approach to depicting his characters' lives. As Harold Clurman of the *Nation* reports, "The play is 'old-fashioned,' harking back to a slice-of-life realism rarely practiced any more, [and] the clarity of its writing, the health of its spirit, and the touching courage of its basic statement are most sympathetic." The critic adds that "Marigolds" "faces life far more honestly than the muddy stream of playlets which speak gleefully about the world going to hell." Barnes similarly commends Zindel's realistic strategy: "This is the kind of true-life melodrama that fascinates Arthur Miller, and rather like Mr. Miller it is extremely successful. My heart was held by it," he continues. "And, unlike most of its genre, the ending is unusually satisfying."

Another satisfying aspect of "Marigolds" is the author's ability to create rounded characters; Barnes finds interesting "Zindel's taut regard for the things people say, and his skill at making insights from these things." Contributing to this skill is the dramatist's "sizable talent for writing penetrating dialogue, for probing the intensity of mental anguish, and for supplying strong dramatic moments in lieu of a strong plot," *Cue*'s Marilyn Stasio writes. *Village Voice* contributor John Lahr likewise observes that "there is so much good writing within the melodramatic machinery, so much insight into Beatrice and Tillie . . . that the play gives us intimations of our mortality." While *New York* reviewer John Simon believes that the plot of "Marigolds" is neither very original nor carefully crafted, he acknowledges that the play is "engaging," and notes that "its first strength lies in the sympathy and humor with which Paul Zindel views all its characters." The critic also says that "there are other virtues: an unassuming, leisurely sense of humor, and a pathos under strict surveillance lest it jerk obscuring tears. . . . Best of all, there is the ability to make the barest utterance grow into the stature of poetry." "It is difficult to know where praise of *Marigolds* should begin or end, and how to contain it," concludes T. E. Kalem of *Time*. The critic proposes, however, that "the ultimate accolade must go to Paul Zindel for creating a psychologically perceptive

ambience. . . . [It is] one of the honest and intelligent values of this splendid and tormented play."

"Bitterly funny and wrenchingly sad," Zindel's next production, "And Miss Reardon Drinks a Little," "presents a half-dozen shrewdly observed and eminently actable characters," states Richard L. Coe in the *Washington Post*. Chief among these characters are the three teaching Reardon sisters, the two eldest of which, Ceil and Catherine, are gathered to deal with the increasing insanity of the youngest, Anna. *Boston Globe* reviewer Kevin Kelly, who calls the play "funny and fierce and, well, absolutely extraordinary," declares that "within this simple format, with the three sisters stamped as stereotypes almost before we know them, Zindel draws together his drama and then, insight for insight, turns the stereotypes inside out and reveals the complexities of his characters." These characters, comments a *Variety* critic, "pulsate with pain and, in most cases, express themselves in convulsively comic terms. As with real people, they react to each other," the reviewer continues, "hurt and wound each other, and change during the course of an evening of unintentional, inescapable, pointless violence." It is with this violence that "Zindel is stating some hard facts about our increasingly uncomfortable world," Coe points out, adding that "there will be those who will loathe this play, some for its language, some for its ruthlessness."

Some critics were dissatisfied with "Miss Reardon," faulting the playwright for describing instead of developing its situation. Kalem, for example, notes that while Zindel's "wacky humor is present, along with his abrupt pathos, . . . and his frequently well-honed dialogue, . . . under it all, the plot, point, and purpose and direction of the play seem to have been lost." As Stasio explains, Zindel's "talent" for dialogue and character "is insufficient for sustaining the play. The sisters' conflict is a static situation, lacking dramatic action to develop it and a central crisis to resolve it." Nevertheless, as Barnes remarks, "far from all is lost. Zindel . . . is an accomplished writer. A few of his jokes are witty, and better still, some of them are relevant and locked into the character of the play." *Newsweek*'s Jack Kroll, however, finds "Miss Reardon" a "deceptively simple but sharply observed play," and asserts that Zindel is "that rarity—a playwright who can write intelligent, sensitive, entertaining plays for a wide public." " 'And Miss Reardon Drinks a Little' will probably and deservedly turn out to be the best American play of the season," concludes Kelly; the critic maintains that "with it, Paul Zindel more than confirms his early reputation."

Such critical opinion notwithstanding, Zindel did not have another acclaimed play until the success, almost twenty years later, of "Amulets against the Dragon Forces," a play that "illuminates the miracle by which . . . [a child] finds the courage to hold on to his own sweetness and his ability to love," as Laurie Winer describes it in the *Wall Street Journal*. "And in this impassioned new work," the critic continues, "Mr. Zindel gives us a teen-age protagonist who is as original, believable and decent as [J. D.] Salinger's Holden Caulfield." The child in question is Chris Boyd, who follows his mother from job to job as a home nurse; in their current circumstances, Chris is harassed by the patient's son, an alcoholic with a penchant for corrupting young men. "Though they have not all been created with equal depth by Mr. Zindel," Frank Rich remarks in the *New York Times*, "the characters are invariably fascinating—even the ravaged, nearly comatose patient who bites anyone who comes near her." Simon similarly observes that "Zindel writes juicy dialogue" for these characters, "simple yet idiosyncratic." While both Simon and Rich fault the author for overloading his drama with spectacular and strange events and people, they both find "Amulets" effective as a whole. "[When] we see the child at center stage trying to ward off the horrors," Rich concludes, "the child too genuine to dismiss as fiction, . . . 'Amulets' becomes gripping and disturbing despite its Gothic overkill."

While Zindel's stature in the theater community began fading after "Miss Reardon," his prominence as a writer of young adult novels was rapidly gaining tremendous proportions, due to the success of *The Pigman.* The novel is told alternately by two high school outsiders, John and Lorraine, who narrate their "epic" relationship with a lonely old man, Mr. Pignati. The two youths befriend the "Pigman," and after taking advantage of the friendship inadvertently contribute to his death. "Their 'epic' makes a very funny book at one level because Mr. Zindel catches the bright, hyperbolic sheen of teen-age language accurately and with humor," John Weston comments in the *New York Times Book Review,* adding that due to its subject, *The Pigman* is also "a serious book." "It is a somber and chastening story that gets better and better as it goes on," states David Rees in *The Marble in the Water: Essays on Contemporary Writers of Fiction for Children and Young Adults.* The critic explains that *The Pigman* "has coherent shape and direction, and its climax is particularly good: a chilling, sobering, morality-tale conclusion." While the novel may present a moral, Zena Sutherland of the *Bulletin of the Center for Children's Books* notes that "the story is effective because of its candor, its humor, and its skilful construction"; further, the writing "has the casual flavor of adolescence." As Diane Farrell concludes in the *Horn Book Magazine,* Zindel's novel is exceptional because "few books that have been written for young people are as cruelly truthful about the human condition."

Zindel's follow-up novel, *My Darling, My Hamburger,* also presents an honest treatment of a controversial issue. The title refers to a sex education teacher's suggestion that a girl propose going out for a burger when her boyfriend gets too eager, and the novel details the romances of two couples, one of which ends in pregnancy. "Second books are disappointments almost by definition, but 'My Darling, My Hamburger'. . . seems to me to be a better novel than 'The Pigman,' " asserts John Rowe Townsend in the *New York Times Book Review.* The critic describes the book as "concerned single-mindedly with sex and growing up; more precisely, it's about the predicament—funny, bitter and nervewracking—of men and women who are also children." Zindel once again presents a moral issue for his readers to consider, but does so in an entertaining manner, as *Children's Book Review* contributor Valerie Anderson explains: "The author's development of his theme is wholly sympathetic, engaging the good will of the reader throughout, and yet, so honest is his treatment that no surer way could have been found for underlining the moral issues." In addition, "in the main the reader is left to form his own judgments," as a *Times Literary Supplement* reviewer observes. "[This story] is told with such compassionate and loving awareness that the reader is swept immediately into the illusion that no outsider is recording their story: they are talking it out loud themselves," remarks Lavinia Russ in *Publishers Weekly.* "And that, my friends, is *writing.*"

It is Zindel's ability to recreate adolescent life that distinguishes his novels, as many critics observe; *Times Literary Supplement* writer Isabel Quigly, for example, states that "Zindel's people seem to take over his book entirely and live so vividly you forget there's a narrator at all. . . . The quality of [his work] lies its understanding of the incoherence as well as the precocious intelligence of its young, and its wry reaction to those damaging comics, their elders." Quigly adds in a later review that while Zindel's subjects "[are] not the stuff that teenage novels used to deal with . . . the stuff of teenage life is not what it used to be either, and what counts is the way Paul Zindel handles it, with a delicacy at once funny and heartfelt, outspoken and sensitive." Likewise, Zindel's themes of adolescent loneliness and youthful questioning "are universal and most of them classic," as Beverly A. Haley and Kenneth L. Donelson maintain in *Elementary English,* and the author "makes these primordial themes believable and relevant and significant to young people." The critics elaborate on one of Zindel's prominent themes, that "the protagonists are basically lonely because they are unable to establish communication with their parents. Ironically, the adolescents themselves seem to understand *why* the parents behave as they do and to forgive them," while their parents cannot do either. The result, write Haley and Donelson, is that "the instinctive wisdom of youth seems superior to the learned wisdom of adults."

This message, that adults are distant and even antagonistic, is one Zindel emphasizes throughout his fiction. "Teenagers *have* to rebel," the author told *Publishers Weekly* interviewer Jean F. Mercier. "It's part of the growing process. In effect, I try to show them they aren't alone in condemning parents and teachers as enemies or ciphers. I believe I must convince my readers that I am on their side," the author continued, which explains why "I write always from their own point of view." Zindel also noted to Paul Janeczko in *English Journal* that this sympathy for his teenage readers serves two functions in his work: "Through pathos I can see the world as one of the most hilarious and comic places that there can be to live. Then, by use of pathos again, I can look at another element and see the world as quite ghastly, see it through very morbid eyes and find everything threatening and dangerous."

This seemingly contrary viewpoint is crucial to Zindel's work, as Stanley Hoffman suggests in the *Lion and the Unicorn:* "If there is any one 'message' that runs through Zindel's works, it has to be this: if reality is ugly, in facing it we can prepare ourselves to see beyond the ugliness to something hopeful." In addition, this mix of hope and hostility contributes to the "black comedy" that "[perhaps] is the key to Zindel's adolescent novels," as Judith N. Mitchell proposes in *Voice of Youth Advocates.* It would be "a mistake to chide him for fantastic plot shifts, or a gallery of grotesqueries masquerading as normal people," the critic relates. "His exaggerations pinpoint the absurdities of normalcy, and his novels carry the theme of loving and being loved like contraband with a homing device." "Clearly the body of Zindel's work and its individual parts place him in the forefront of adolescent novelists," notes Hipple, for "few other writers match his awareness of teenagers' problems and attitudes. He even compensates for their dislike of reading by including in his books all manner of graphics," a technique which accommodates the audience Zindel has said he wishes to reach. Hipple concludes that "it is not at all surprising—indeed, it is gratifying—that he is among their most esteemed novelists."

MEDIA ADAPTATIONS: "The Effect of Gamma Rays on Man-in-the-Moon Marigolds" was made into a film by Twentieth Century-Fox in 1973; the rights to *My Darling, My Hamburger* have been sold to Qualis Productions, while producer Jerome Hellman has purchased the rights to *I Never Loved Your Mind; The Pigman* has been adapted for the stage.

BIOGRAPHICAL/CRITICAL SOURCES:

BOOKS

Children's Literature Review, Volume 3, Gale, 1978.
Contemporary Literary Criticism, Gale, Volume 6, 1976, Volume 26, 1983.

Dictionary of Literary Biography, Gale, Volume 7: *Twentieth-Century American Dramatists,* 1981, Volume 52: *American Writers for Children since 1960: Fiction,* 1986.

Rees, David, *The Marble in the Water: Essays on Contemporary Writers of Fiction for Children and Young Adults,* Horn Book, 1980.

PERIODICALS

Boston Globe, February 9, 1971, February 14, 1971.
Bulletin of the Center for Children's Books, April, 1969.
Children's Book Review, February, 1971.
Christian Science Monitor, May 2, 1970, March 1, 1971.
Cue, April 18, 1970, March 6, 1971.
Elementary English, October, 1974.
English Journal, October, 1977.
Horn Book Magazine, February, 1969.
Lion and the Unicorn, fall, 1978.
Nation, April 20, 1970, March 15, 1971.
Newsweek, April 27, 1970, March 8, 1971.
New York, May 4, 1970, March 15, 1971, April 17, 1989.
New Yorker, April 18, 1970.
New York Times, April 8, 1970, April 19, 1970, July 26, 1970, November 22, 1970, February 26, 1971, March 2, 1971, March 7, 1971, April 9, 1971, April 2, 1989, April 6, 1989.
New York Times Book Review, November 3, 1968, November 9, 1969.
Publishers Weekly, September 22, 1969, December 5, 1977.
Saturday Review, May 2, 1970, March 20, 1971.
Time, April 20, 1970, March 8, 1971, May 17, 1971.
Times Literary Supplement, April 16, 1970, December 10, 1976, April 7, 1978.
Variety, March 3, 1971.
Village Voice, April 16, 1970.
Voice of Youth Advocates, October, 1981.
Wall Street Journal, April 12, 1989.
Washington Post, January 27, 1971.

—*Sketch by Diane Telgen*

*   *   *

ZINSSER, William (Knowlton) 1922-

PERSONAL: Surname is pronounced *Zin*-zer; born October 7, 1922, in New York, N.Y.; son of William H. and Joyce (Knowlton) Zinsser; married Caroline Fraser, October 10, 1954; children: Amy, John William. *Education:* Princeton University, A.B., 1944. *Politics:* Democrat. *Religion:* Presbyterian.

ADDRESSES: Home—45 East 62nd St., New York, N.Y. 10021. *Office*—128 East 56th St., New York, N.Y. 10022.

CAREER: New York Herald Tribune, New York City, feature writer, 1946-49, drama editor, 1949-54, film critic, 1955-58, editorial writer, 1958-59; free-lance writer, 1959—; Yale University, New Haven, Conn., member of English faculty, 1970-79, master of Branford College, 1973-79; Book-of-the-Month Club, New York City, executive editor, 1979-87. Entertainment critic for television program "Sunday," NBC-TV, 1963-64. Member of board of governors, Brooklyn Museum, 1965-72. *Military service:* U.S. Army, 1943-45; served in North Africa and Italy; became sergeant.

MEMBER: Century Association (New York), Coffee House (New York).

AWARDS, HONORS: Honorary degrees from Rollins College, University of Southern Indiana, and Wesleyan University.

WRITINGS:

Any Old Place with You, Simon & Schuster, 1957.
Seen Any Good Movies Lately?, Doubleday, 1958.
Search and Research, New York Public Library, 1961.
The City Dwellers, Harper, 1962.
(With Howard Lindsay, Harry Golden, Walt Kelly, and John Updike) *Five Boyhoods,* Doubleday, 1962.
Weekend Guests, Harper, 1963.
The Haircurl Papers, Harper, 1964.
Pop Goes America, Harper, 1966.
The Paradise Bit (novel), Little, Brown, 1967.
The Lunacy Boom, Harper, 1970.
On Writing Well: An Informal Guide to Writing Nonfiction, Harper, 1976, 3rd edition, 1986.
Writing with a Word Processor, Harper, 1983.
Willie and Dwike: An American Profile, Harper, 1984.
(Editor) *Extraordinary Lives: The Art and Craft of American Biography,* American Heritage Publishing, 1986.
(Editor) *Inventing the Truth: The Art and Craft of Memoir,* Houghton, 1987.
Writing to Learn, Harper, 1988.
(Editor) *Spiritual Quests: The Art and Craft of Religious Writing,* Houghton, 1988.
Spring Training, Harper, 1989.
(Editor) *Paths of Resistance: The Art and Craft of the Political Novel,* Houghton, 1989.
(Editor) *Worlds of Childhood: The Art and Craft of Writing for Children,* Houghton, 1990.

Columnist for *Look,* 1967, *Life,* 1968-72, and the *New York Times,* 1977. Contributor to magazines, including *New Yorker.*

SIDELIGHTS: "I don't think writing is an art," William Zinsser told *Publishers Weekly* interviewer Sybil Steinberg. "I think sometimes it's raised to an art, but basically it's a craft, like cabinet-making or carpentry." A seasoned author and journalist, Zinsser recommends a workmanlike approach to writing in *On Writing Well: An Informal Guide to Writing Nonfiction;* he claims that "the only way to learn to write is to force yourself to produce a certain number of words on a regular basis." *On Writing Well* had its genesis in a writing course that the author taught at Yale University in the 1970s; the class proved so popular that Zinsser decided to expand it into a book. Now in its third edition, *On Writing Well* has sold over half a million copies and is in use in classrooms throughout the United States. "Zinsser is a veteran journalist, and *On Writing Well* exhibits his savvy," notes *Washington Post Book World* contributor Dennis Drabelle. "Like Strunk and White's *The Elements of Style,* to which it pays homage, Zinsser's book is crisp and bossy." Sherwin D. Smith similarly praises Zinsser's guide, observing in the *New York Times Book Review* that the author's "message can be absorbed with profit by any writer, no matter what his experience or his field."

Part of Zinsser's success is due to his attempts to personalize his guide and make himself "very accessible to the reader," as he described to Steinberg. "I think that *On Writing Well* has been successful because readers know they're not learning from a professor of rhetoric, but from someone who actually has struggled with the craft of writing," the author explained. He likewise opens himself up in *Writing with a Word Processor,* where, he related, "I wanted the reader to become involved with me and my own anxieties and apprehensions and phobias in writing with a new technology. If I make myself vulnerable," Zinsser added, "and if readers identify with me, they will learn as I do." In a third volume, *Writing to Learn,* the author addresses the anxiety that writing itself can inspire. "Zinsser wants to relieve our fear of writing," summarizes Chicago *Tribune Books* critic John Blades, "which, he says, is not the intimidating task that English teachers so often make it seem." By giving examples of clear, organized, comprehensible writing by men and women from many disciplines, Zinsser demonstrates that by "writing to learn" about any subject, an untrained author can write well. "Happily," Blades continues, "Zinsser did not confine himself to reprinting excerpts from other writers' work. . . . He provides many of his own best examples of lucid prose, describing [his own] 'writing-to-learn' assignments." The critic concludes that in *Writing to Learn,* "Zinsser writes so well himself that he makes us forget, if only temporarily, how frightening it can be."

One of Zinsser's own "writing to learn" exercises came during the preparation of the biography *Willie and Dwike: An American Profile;* working in a new genre, Zinsser needed to find a new approach to writing. As he told Steinberg, "in this book I tried to stay out of it as an explainer. I saw it as my job to gather the material and arrange it, to put a shape to it. That's something new I learned at this late stage of my career." Zinsser collected his material on pianist Dwike Mitchell and bass and French horn player Willie Ruff by accompanying them on concerts in the United States; he also went with them on a precedent-setting trip to China, where the duo became the first American jazz musicians to perform. Although noted for their jazz playing, the two men, who are black, have also been classically trained and frequently explain the history of their music during appearances. "They are on almost all counts remarkable men, and in 'Willie and Dwike' William Zinsser pays them precisely their due," comments the *Washington Post*'s Jonathan Yardley; "he writes about them with undisguised admiration and affection, and he conveys a real sense of what has made them successful as musicians and as men."

Zinsser, who has known the duo since the early 1970s, uses an informal method to relate their story, and "it is a good measure of his own considerable skills that 'Willie and Dwike' comes to us seemingly straight from Ruff and Mitchell," a *New Yorker* critic asserts. Richard P. Brickner similarly commends this method in the *New York Times Book Review:* "Through Mr. Zinsser's elegant use of anecdote, interview and personal observations, the reader learns a lot, all of it engrossing, about a black musician's life on the Midwestern road, past and present." "It has always been a pleasure to listen to [the Mitchell-Ruff Duo]," concludes Yardley; "now, thanks to William Zinsser's lovely little book, it is an equal pleasure to make their acquaintance."

"Like *Willie and Dwike,*" Zinsser told *CA, Spring Training* is "very much a book about America, which I consider one of my subjects, and about teaching and learning, which is my main subject." For *Spring Training* Zinsser attended the Pittsburgh Pirates' camp in Bradenton, Florida, associating with management, coaching staff, players, and umpires. The result is what the author calls a combination of "my lifelong vocation (writing) with my lifelong addiction (baseball)." "Zinsser is at heart a teacher," notes *New York Times Book Review* contributor Lawrence S. Ritter, and "to judge by this book, he is a very good one indeed. Virtually everyone he talked to manages to be instructive," the critic elaborates, "clearly explaining in entertaining fashion what he does and how he does it. This is no doubt the result" of Zinsser's skill at framing his questions and answers, Ritter adds, concluding that *Spring Training* is "amusing as well as informative."

AVOCATIONAL INTERESTS: Playing jazz piano.

BIOGRAPHICAL/CRITICAL SOURCES:

BOOKS

Zinsser, William, *On Writing Well: An Informal Guide to Writing Nonfiction,* Harper, 1976, 3rd edition, 1986.

PERIODICALS

Chicago Tribune, November 8, 1988.
Los Angeles Times Book Review, July 22, 1984.
New Yorker, September 3, 1984.
New York Times, January 28, 1976, March 31, 1983.
New York Times Book Review, February 29, 1976, July 15, 1984, April 23, 1989.
Publishers Weekly, June 29, 1984.
Tribune Books (Chicago), April 17, 1988, April 2, 1989.
Washington Post, June 20, 1984, July 15, 1986, November 17, 1987.
Washington Post Book World, February 24, 1980.

—*Sketch by Diane Telgen*